ROMAN AND MEDIEVAL OCCUPATION IN CAUSEWAY LANE, LEICESTER

Roman and Medieval Occupation in Causeway Lane, Leicester

Excavations 1980 and 1991

by
Aileen Connor and Richard Buckley

with contributions from:

Peter Boyer, Richard Clark, Nicholas J. Cooper, Paul Courtney, G.B. Dannell, Siân Davies, John Davies, Jon Dawes, Brenda Dickinson, Richard Evershed, Louisa Gidney, Tony Gnanaratnam, Anne Graf, James Greig, Kay Hartley, David Higgins, Scott Martin, Angela Monckton, G.C.Morgan, Rebecca Nicholson, Alan Peacey, Richard Pollard, Susan Ripper, Deborah Sawday, Peter Skidmore, J.Wakely and D.F.Williams

Leicester Archaeology Monographs No. 5

1999

University of Leicester Archaeological Services,
School of Archaeological Studies, University of Leicester
and Leicester City Museum Service for the Inland Revenue

ISBN 0 951 0377 81

Published by
University of Leicester Archaeological Services,
School of Archaeological Studies,
University of Leicester

Front Cover: Area 3 during excavation, view south towards Area 2.
Rear Cover: Plate brooch, second century AD (Cat. no 28, Sf2391).

Designed and produced by
The TypeFoundry, Northampton

Contents

INTRODUCTION AND BACKGROUND *RB & AC*

THE ROMAN PHASES *AC & RB*

DISCUSSION OF THE ROMAN RESEARCH THEMES *AC &RB*

THE POST-ROMAN PHASES *AC with RB*

DISCUSSION OF THE POST-ROMAN RESEARCH THEMES *AC & RB*

HISTORICAL BACKGROUND *Paul Courtney*

THE ENVIRONMENTAL EVIDENCE edited by *Angela Monckton*

Figures

ROMAN PAINTED WALL PLASTER

THE BUILDING MATERIALS

THE ENVIRONMENTAL EVIDENCE

THE ANIMAL BONES

THE EGGSHELL

FISH REMAINS

OYSTERS

Plates

Tables

THE SMALL FINDS

THE ROMAN GLASS

THE BUILDING MATERIALS AND INDUSTRIAL RESIDUES

THE ENVIRONMENTAL EVIDENCE

ENVIRONMENTAL SAMPLING

ANIMAL BONE

THE EGGSHELL

FISH REMAINS

OYSTERS

THE MINERALISED FLIES

THE MINERALISED WOODLICE

THE PLANT REMAINS

THE POLLEN

CHARCOAL

HUMAN BONE

Plate 1: *The excavation team*

Acknowledgements

A project of this size depends on the contributions of many individuals and organisations to whom we are grateful, but we should like to mention the following for their particular assistance.

The project was financed by the Inland Revenue, and particular thanks are due to David Smith, Mike Ward and Philip Cross for their co-operation and the unenviable task of securing the necessary funding. The project was monitored by English Heritage, and we should like to thank John Hinchcliffe, Tony Wilmott, Tim Williams and Tony Fleming for their support and advice during all stages of the work. Our colleagues at Leicestershire Archaeological Unit, in particular John Lucas, Jean Mellor, Terry Pearce, Deborah Sawday, Patrick Clay and Richard Pollard provided considerable help and encouragement and Julie Wigmore oversaw the arrangements for an on-site display of results and finds together with the public viewing platform. The contributions of staff of Leicestershire Museums, Arts and Records Service is also gratefully acknowledged, in particular Anne Graf for planning matters, Anthony Read for the conservation of the finds, Fiona Marshall for her support in creating a computerised site database, John Martin for identification of stone samples, Steve Thursfield for overhead photographs, John Mathias and Derek Lott for laboratory facilities and Glenice Beck and Jane Betts for assistance with financial management. Thanks to George McTurk, Leicester University, for electron microscopy. We are grateful to Neil Christie in particular for his assistance with editing of the excavation section and also to Roger Ling, James Greig, Richard Pollard, John Lucas, Graham Morgan, Graeme Barker, Annie Grant, David Mattingly, Hilary Cool and Alan McWhirr for reading and commenting on the draft specialist reports. The draft report was refereed by Steve Roskams and David Mattingly who provided many helpful comments for improvements to the text. Thanks also to Angela Monckton for reading and commenting on the text during its preparation, and to Tony Baker, Josephine Buckley, Adrian Butler, Matt Beamish and Dawn Harvey for helping to tie up loose ends. The report as a whole was edited by Richard Buckley, with whom the final responsibility must lie for any errors or omissions.

Last, but not least, we should like to thank the excavation staff, many of whom appear on the accompanying photograph. *Supervisors:* Josephine Sharman and Julian Hagar; A*ssistant Supervisors:* Peter Boyer, David Mackie, Toby Catchpole and Reuben Thorpe; *Finds Supervisor:* Ruth Prior; *Conservator:* Anthony Read; *Assistant Conservator:* Katherine Hall; *Roman Pottery Specialist:* Richard Clark; *Post Roman Pottery Specialist:* Siân Davies; *Environmentalist:* Angela Monckton; *Finance Assistant:* Joyce Lock; *Publicity:* Julie Wigmore; *Site Assistants:* Paul Atkins, Katherine Atherton, Bill Barkle, Josie Barnacle, Jackie Bates, Adam Bennison, Bob Burrows, Adrian Chadwick, Lynden Cooper, Trevor Dingle, Gary Evans, Neil Finn, Luke Fagan, Tony Gnanaratnam, Stefan Gula, Kate Hibbins, Tim Higgins, Lucy Hind, Lou Huscroft, Emma Jones, Wain Lancaster, Dominic Latham, Gerry Martin, John Minkin, Dominic Pullen, Sarah Reilly, Susan Ripper, Charlotte Rowley, Nicholas Sambrook, Martin Shore, Rebecca Stancer, John Taylor, Adrian Ward, Sally Warren, Jeannette Wells; Lucy Wheeler, Suzanne Whitehead; *Trainees:* David Hopkins, Paul Saunders; *Volunteers:* John Barker, Tim Barnacle, Dillon Bickerstaff, Richard Cuttler, Nicola Conn, Carole Fletcher, Alison Gee, Karl Hurst, Christine Leshko, Lynn Millward, Sarah McRann, Anna Morris, William Newnham, Vivien Pallant, Suzanne Parrot, Alice Robinson, Suzanne Rose, Judy Sault, Peter Seary, Cassie Thompson, Charlie Tucker, Joyce Tucker, Jenny Wakely, Elizabeth York and twenty students from the School of Archaeological Studies, Leicester University.

INTRODUCTION AND BACKGROUND
Richard Buckley and Aileen Connor

Circumstances of the project   *RB*

Proposals for the redevelopment of a site on Causeway Lane, within the historic core of Roman and medieval Leicester, led to a small-scale excavation in 1980, followed by evaluation and subsequently full excavation of most of the site in 1991 by Leicestershire Archaeological Unit (LAU). The fieldwork and post-excavation analysis was funded by the Inland Revenue. Richard Buckley directed the 1980 excavation and managed the 1991 project. The evaluation and excavation of 1991 were directed respectively by Gerry Martin and Aileen Connor. The latter also directed the post-excavation assessment and analysis. Towards the end of the post-excavation analysis, LAU was closed down by Leicestershire County Council and the remaining work leading to publication of this volume was completed by the newly-established University of Leicester Archaeological Services (ULAS). All archive records and materials are held by the Jewry Wall Museum, St. Nicholas Circle, Leicester (Accession Codes A475.1979 and A1.1991). This report presents the detailed results of the fieldwork.

Site location, geology and topography   *AC*

The site, occupying an area of 1,875m², lies within the town walls of Roman and medieval Leicester, on the north side of Causeway Lane, adjacent to its corner with East Bond Street (NGR SK 5846 0481), in an area commonly known as the north-east quarter (fig. 1).

The geology comprises alluvial sands and gravels above Mercia mudstone (formerly known as keuper marl, Pye 1972, 22-3), typical of this part of Leicester. Topographic survey of the natural ground level (Lucas 1980-81) shows that the site lies at the top of an escarpment overlooking the river Soar to the west. The top of the natural sand and gravel occurs between 57.5m and 59m above OD, some 1m – 2.5m below the present ground surface (fig.2).

Planning background   *RB with Anne Graf*

Initial development proposal

Following demolition of the Bond Street Maternity Hospital in 1974, the land was purchased by the Property Services Agency (PSA) for redevelopment. This was to be carried out in two stages: firstly the

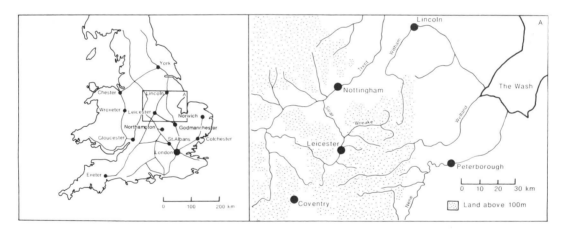

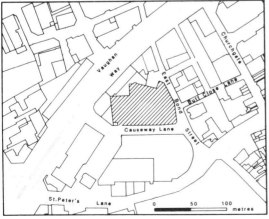

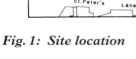

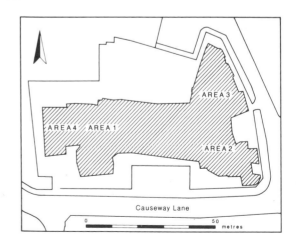

Fig. 1: Site location

construction of temporary accommodation with car parking in 1978-79, to be replaced by a permanent Crown building scheduled for 1980-81. In view of the high archaeological potential of this part of the city, approaches were made to the PSA in 1979 by Jean Mellor of the (then) Leicestershire Museums Archaeological Field Unit (LMAFU) for permission to undertake excavation of the site prior to redevelopment.

Cellar survey

Initial research, by John Lucas (of LAU), to assess the potential survival of archaeological deposits involved a survey of cellars which were suspected to exist on the site. From 1849 onwards, planning regulations required the deposition of plans with the borough authorities prior to consent being given for new buildings or major alterations. The Leicester Sanitary Authority plans 1849-1934 are deposited in the Leicestershire Records Office where they are catalogued by street. These plans provide information on the depths of cellars beneath ground level, enabling comparison with contour plans allowing the likely depth of made ground above natural geology in the city to be calculated (Lucas 1981-82, 1-9). Uncellared areas were identified at the west end of the site, and to the north beneath the temporary Unemployment Benefit Office building, and were therefore regarded as being of high archaeological potential. For the remainder of the site archaeological deposits were considered to be potentially extant beneath cellar floors and between cellars.

Evaluation/excavation 1980

It was subsequently proposed to carry out an evaluative excavation at the west end of the site, to assess the survival of archaeological levels, with further excavation dependent on the results. The evaluation took place between March and May 1980 with £5,000 of grant aid from the Department of the Environment and a team of excavators on a government 'Special Temporary Employment Programme' (STEP). Overburden was stripped by a Drott 100B excavator and stockpiled within the small area at the west end of the site . It was immediately apparent that all traces of horizontal stratification above the natural sand and gravel had been destroyed by medieval and post-medieval cultivation, leaving only earthfast features – mainly Roman and medieval pits. The cultivation episodes had resulted in the build-up of some 2.0-3.5m of so-called 'garden soil' (Buckley 1979-80).

The development proposed for 1980-81 was subsequently postponed, and the site remained a car park for the next eleven years. In view of the small amount of rescue archaeology funding available and the fact that the threat had receded, no further areas were excavated at that time.

Final development proposal

In 1989, Leicester City Council learnt that the site was to be redeveloped by the Property Services Agency (PSA) for the Inland Revenue and sought comments from their archaeological planning adviser, Leicestershire

Museums, on the archaeological implications. The PSA had consulted the local authority for any observations and conditions following the normal planning clearance procedure on Crown Developments under DoE Circular 18/84. At this stage the building had, however, already been designed. Planning Policy Guidance Note 16 'Archaeology and Planning' was still in a draft form at the time (published only in November 1990), but its principles had been embodied in the Leicester City Council supplementary planning guidance document 'A Policy for Archaeology and Planning' (1988), which had been drawn up in consultation with Leicestershire Museums, and these principles were followed in the subsequent negotiations regarding archaeological provision on the Causeway Lane site. This was possibly the first site on which a government department accepted the archaeological implications of PPG16 and the funding of the excavations by the Inland Revenue may have been an important precedent in national terms for government development. (DOE information note 16/93 on 'Archaeology and Crown Development' followed in July 1993, confirming the precedent).

Although the 1980 excavation had revealed comparatively little likelihood of deep stratification, it was considered, in view of the large area (over 1800m2) and the unpredictable survival of archaeological deposits in an urban context, that further archaeological field evaluation (AFE) should take place. Potential damage to surviving archaeological deposits from the piles for the new structure had been estimated at about 10%. Redesign of the building to protect archaeological levels was no longer an option and hence at the late design stage at which consultation took place, the Director of Leicestershire Museums advised the Planning Authority that planning clearance should be conditional on provision for archaeological evaluation and any subsequent necessary programme of archaeological work.

Evaluation 1991

Evaluation took place over a period of three weeks in January 1991 and sought to employ as non-destructive a strategy as possible through emptying backfilled cellars and removing their walls to provide a view of parts of the site in section. Cellars for evaluation were selected from the survey already carried out. In the north-east corner of the site (Area 3), the cellar section indicated that deep stratification and structural remains were likely, but also hinted at the presence of large post-medieval quarries. The trench in the centre of the site (Area 1) indicated the potential for about 1.0m of stratification above the natural sand and gravel, with probable evidence for early Roman timber buildings and medieval activity.

A project design with costings was subsequently produced by RB for full excavation of the footprint of the proposed building. This was approved by English Heritage and the Inland Revenue in mid-March 1991. Although construction of the new building was scheduled for July 1991, agreement was reached to delay the redevelopment until late September 1991 to allow time for the excavation.

Excavation and analysis   *AC*

Strategy

Excavation began on March 29th 1991 and continued until September 13th 1991. A total of fifty staff were employed on the excavation and a further fifty unpaid volunteers helped for short periods of time throughout the excavation

The site was excavated in three areas: Area 1 comprised the western end of the site, Area 2 the south-east end, and Area 3 the north-east end (fig.1). The results from the area excavated in 1980, to the west of Area 1, are included in this volume as Area 4. Areas 1 and 2 were opened at the same time, but Area 2 was completely recorded and excavated by mid-July whereas Area 1 was not completed until the end of the excavation, reflecting their widely differing levels of preservation. Area 2 had largely been truncated by 16th-century garden soil horizons down to the natural gravel, whereas archaeological layers in Area 1 had been formed in a hollow and therefore protected from truncation. Fortunately, the 19th and 20th century cellarage was found to be far less extensive than initial estimates based on documentation and evaluation had suggested, and those areas unaffected by gravel quarrying remained essentially undisturbed. Area 3 was examined on completion of Area 2, after the demolition of the Unemployment Benefit Office, but was not totally excavated: surviving horizontal stratigraphy was fully investigated, whilst Roman gravel extraction pits were sampled to provide information on relationships, depth, dimensions, and finds retrieval (including environmental samples).

As the entire development area was to be excavated with the exception of the area of the 1980 site (Area 4; to be reserved for site accommodation), all spoil had to be taken off site. Overburden was 1m – 2.5m thick, resulting in *c.*3,600-4,500m^3 of spoil. This was removed by two 'Poclain' 360° tracked excavators and one 'Caterpillar' bulldozer and carried away by a fleet of six ten-ton lorries. The overburden – consisting mainly of 'garden soil' – was removed in spits to within 0.5m of the uppermost archaeological deposits and then carefully peeled back by the two Poclains using ditching blades to produce a smooth surface.

This garden soil is a deposit common to the northeast quarter of Leicester, and is presumed to derive from late medieval and early post-medieval manuring and cultivation. The soil's removal exposed an interesting topography, demonstrating the true extent of truncation (fig. 2). A large central area disturbed by 18th-century quarrying for sand and gravel effectively divided the site into the three noted areas, with no stratigraphic connections. Stratigraphic survival thus differed widely over the site: in Area 1 a depth of over 1.0m was common; in Area 2 up to 30cm survived around the edge, but much had been truncated to the top of natural gravel only leaving cut features undisturbed; in Area 3, extensive Roman quarrying had removed much of the natural gravel deposits and it was therefore difficult to determine what depth of horizontal stratigraphy had survived, although above the uppermost fill of the quarry pits about 1.0m of stratified deposits existed.

All the surviving archaeological deposits were either of Roman or medieval date, with no stratified deposits dating to the intervening centuries, although some artefacts found in later contexts could be dated to this period.

Excavation methodology

It was considered a high priority to excavate all Roman stratified layers by context and to empty fills from any cut features, particularly pits. Whilst this was achieved in Area 2, Area 3 was only available for excavation for six weeks prior to the excavation deadline. Truncation along the southern edge of the latter indicated that deposits survived to a depth in excess of 2.5m. Accordingly, in order to gain as much information as possible, identifiable pits were half sectioned by hand, the remaining layers excavated by machine and the resulting spoil checked for finds. In Area 1 an extensive homogeneous Roman deposit was encountered which was excavated in a series of 100mm spits in 5m squares until properly differentiated layers were revealed. After the removal of all the stratified layers, a series of pits was encountered which were half sectioned. Some were excavated only as far as was safe and practicable given their great depth; one phase 5 pit had the added complication of an early 20th-century concrete pile driven into one edge, removal of which caused additional damage.

Whilst truncation by later activity, particularly quarrying in the 18th century and Victorian buildings, had caused some damage to many Roman deposits, the level of disturbance was clearly much greater for the post-Roman and medieval contexts. Hence although the 1991 site evaluation had identified certain potential areas of investigation, it had also suggested that the survival of post-Roman levels was likely to be limited to pits. Since previous excavations in Leicester had undertaken full excavation and recording of medieval pits and detailed recording of sample areas of post-Roman garden soils, this strategy was considered to be of lower priority at Causeway Lane: thus all pits were half sectioned, but only a sample was fully excavated and a sample augered. The only exceptions to this policy were on Area 3, where the late commencement of excavation and the unexpected depth of Roman stratigraphy led to the more rapid removal of the medieval and post-medieval deposits. This resulted in separate pit fills remaining unrecorded, pits not being fully excavated, and profiles only recorded rather than full sections.

Recording

An Electronic Distance Measurer (EDM) was used to install a grid across the site to within 1 degree west of Ordnance Survey Grid North; this had to be reinstated periodically to allow for lowering of stratification. The grid was kept at 5.0m intervals where possible, but modern intrusions, particularly concrete piles and steel

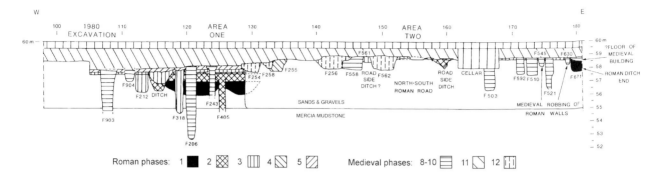

Fig. 2: *Composite section west-east across the site, showing features of all periods.*
Horizontal interval in metres; vertical interval in metres above Ordnance Datum.

reinforcing in walls, meant that this was not always practicable. All heights were calculated to above Ordnance Datum. All stratigraphic units were given a unique context number, and where contexts filled a cut such as a pit or ditch, a feature number was allocated. Contexts and features were recorded on LAU pro-forma feature and context sheets. All plans were drawn in pencil on pre-printed A2 sheets of drafting film at a scale of 1:20; obvious cuts were usually drawn before and after excavation, whilst individual contexts within those cuts were not normally drawn in plan. Where cuts could not be positively identified at the pre-excavation stage, each layer was drawn separately. Single context planning was used where appropriate. Sections were normally drawn at a scale of 1:10; those through deep features were drawn as composite (or running) sections and some loss (up to 100 mm) was noted at the interface.

Post-excavation analysis

Four levels were used to aid in the analysis of the evidence from Causeway Lane:

1. Those individual contexts (000) recorded on site that could be demonstrably shown to be stratigraphically and interpretatively linked were placed into subgroups (000/0).
2. Such subgroups were amalgamated into groups (G): these could either be linked stratigraphically or be interpreted as being similar or associated.
3. Groups were amalgamated to form subphases (sub 0.0): this relied upon site information and data from finds specialists to contribute towards dating and interpretation of the site record.
4. Groups of subphases were placed into a phase (phase): this relied upon interpretation and dating drawn from all sources of evidence, and was the only level that attempted to achieve correspondence across all areas of the site.

As noted above, little stratigraphic evidence from the post-Roman period was available for examination. Accordingly, the relevant evidence was examined in two ways. The first sought to identify stratigraphic changes and similarities within and between discrete features (usually pits). So all pit fills were initially grouped on the basis of their position within the pit and primary,

secondary and tertiary deposits were identified where possible. The second approach analysed the spatial distribution and postulated a series of building 'plots', which were then tested for similarities and differences across the site. The first method had limited success since much of the pottery was broadly dated to between the mid-11th and the mid-13th century (Davies and Sawday, below), although the relationships between the upper, slumped fills and the overlying garden soil truncation were made more evident. The second approach proved more successful, particularly in Area 1 where the pits fell into neat north-south running lines, whereas in Areas 2 and 3 truncation, intercutting and other features confused the evidence.

Archaeological background   *RB*

This section is intended to provide a broad chronological framework for the development of the town in the Roman and post Roman periods to provide a context for the results of the project.

Introduction

The Causeway Lane site lies in a part of Roman and medieval Leicester where comparatively little fieldwork has been undertaken. The majority of large scale excavations undertaken before 1980 were located in the western part of the town, with results biased towards public and high status buildings of both the Roman and medieval periods, with little evidence for occupation which might be considered 'low status'. The location of the site – at the intersection of two Roman streets and on the corner of two medieval streets – meant that its archaeological potential was never in doubt. Before the 1991 excavation, the only field projects in this quarter of the town comprised sections across the town defences at Elbow Lane, Butt Close Lane, Sanvey Gate, Churchgate and St. Peter's Lane (Buckley and Lucas 1987); an excavation in Elbow Lane (Lucas 1989), the small excavation at Causeway Lane in 1980 (Buckley 1979-80) and two large excavations at St. Peter's Lane and Little Lane in advance of the Shires shopping centre development in 1988-9 (Lucas and Buckley 1989, 105-6).

Of published excavations within the walls, most are concerned with Roman activity and comprise the Jewry wall site (Kenyon 1948), Elbow Lane (Lucas 1989) and groups of small sites in the Bath Lane (Clay and Mellor 1985) and West Bridge areas (Clay and Pollard 1994) along with a series of sections across the town defences (Buckley and Lucas 1987).

Comparatively little large scale excavation of medieval sites in Leicester has been undertaken so far, and only the examination of the extra-mural Augustinian Friary in 1973-78 has been published in detail (Mellor and Pearce 1981). Whilst the latter clearly represents a milestone for Leicester's medieval archaeology, with its detailed analysis of the site sequence, finds and environmental assemblages, the results cannot, perhaps, be regarded as typical of domestic occupation in the town as a whole. Although excavation of medieval structural sequences has been carried out in St. Nicholas Circle (Mellor and Pearce forthcoming), High Street (Cooper 1993), Bonners Lane (Finn 1994) and in a minor way elsewhere, most of the evidence we have so far relates to back-yard activity – mainly rubbish pits, cess pits and wells. Modern road widening has meant that access to medieval street frontages is rarely possible and when it is, there is often considerable destruction from 19th century cellars.

The Roman period

Summary of chronology

Initial urban occupation in Leicester is dated to the late first century BC and consisted of Iron Age settlement occupying an area of *c.*10ha on the west bank of the river Soar. After the Conquest, there is limited evidence to suggest that a small fortlet was established to control the crossing point of the river near the present West Bridge (Clay and Pollard 1994, 46). Evidence for timber buildings of the pre-Flavian period has been encountered, with the suggestion, on the basis of uniformity of alignment, that they have more in common with buildings within a fort than with a native settlement or vicus. Timber buildings later in the first century are on a different alignment, and are considered to represent

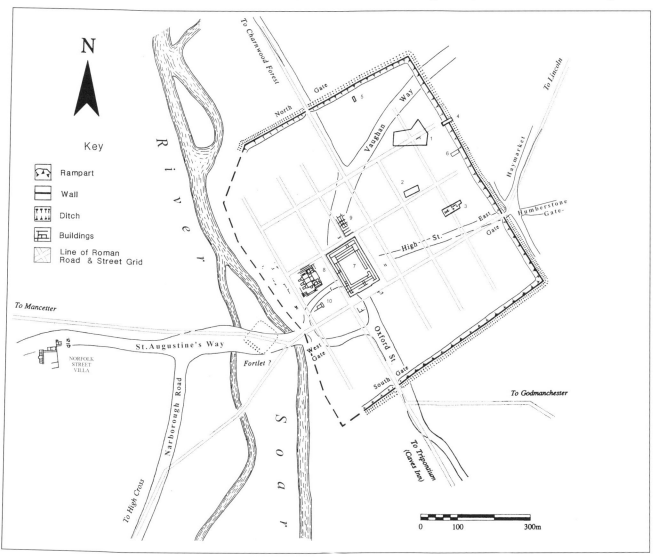

Fig. 3: *Roman Leicester.* *Excavations referred to in the text: 1. Causeway Lane; 2. St. Peters Lane and 3. Little Lane (Shires, 1988-89; Lucas and Buckley 1989); 4. Butt Close Lane (Buckley and Lucas 1987, Site 4); 5. Elbow Lane (Lucas 1989); 6. St Peters Lane (Buckley and Lucas 1987, Site 3); 7. The forum; 8. Jewry Wall (baths) site; 9. Blue Boar Lane, town house and macellum; 10. St. Nicholas Circle, Mithraeum.*

the first Roman town, expanding to the east from the river, with the presence of wall plaster and *opus signinum* suggesting the gradual adoption of Roman tastes (*ibid.,* 46). Ditches from the Little Lane excavation (Lucas and Buckley forthcoming) perhaps point to field systems beyond the settled area.

In the early second century, the street grid appears to have been formalised, if not entirely laid out, and at the same time, Ratae was probably established as a civitas capital. Timber buildings of this period are aligned on the street grid, and have been found beneath the northern and eastern defences, pointing to the rapid expansion of settlement (Buckley and Lucas 1987). In the middle and later years of the second century, a major programme of public and private building was undertaken. This included the construction of the forum and basilica complex, the Jewry Wall public baths, at least one temple and a variety of domestic, commercial and industrial premises (Clay and Mellor 1985; Clay and Pollard 1994). On most Roman sites in the town, masonry buildings begin to appear in this period, some perhaps commercial and domestic properties whilst others might be described as palatial town houses.

In the late second or early third century, the town was defended with a rampart and ditch, a wall perhaps being added later in the third century (Buckley and Lucas 1987). There is some evidence for suburban occupation outside the walls, to the north (Northgates: Buckley 1987, 92; Sanvey Gate: Finn 1993) and south (Bonners Lane: Finn 1994), comprising both timber and, possibly, substantial masonry buildings. To the west, across the river, excavations at Great Holme Street have suggested the existence of an industrial suburb, with evidence of pottery kilns and an abattoir (Lucas forthcoming a). Cemeteries surrounded the town, although few have been subjected to controlled excavation, that at Newarke Street being one of the most extensive (Cooper 1996).

Evidence from the fourth century still remains elusive. This may be due to truncation from medieval activity, although a decline in urban occupation is possible in view of the evidence for street metalling having been dug into (Redcross Street: Clay and Pollard 1994, 48) together with evidence for the illegal extraction of silver from coinage within the ruins of the macellum (Wacher 1974, 353).

The north-east quarter
Previous fieldwork has left a considerable gap in our knowledge of Roman urban topography in the north-east quarter of the town, the evidence coming mainly from small trenches across the defences and from excavations in advance of the Shires development. The boundaries of this notional 'quarter' are the defences to the east and north, the main east-west street carrying the Fosse Way to the south, and the street leading to the north gate, possibly a minor route, to the west. The Leicestershire Sites and Monuments Record (50 SE.PH, Abbey ward) lists a number of chance finds in the vicinity including two mosaic pavements and a late Roman coin hoard from the corner of Causeway Lane

and East Bond Street (J. Davies, below). In addition, an approximate idea of the street pattern may be gained by projecting the grid from known alignments. The earliest clear evidence of Roman activity was found on the Little Lane excavation (Shires; 1988-9), and comprised probable field ditches dating to the first century AD, suggesting that this quarter was perhaps still in agricultural use at that time. The same site produced evidence from the late first – early second century for a north-south street (that which passes through the Causeway Lane site), fronted on both sides by timber buildings including one with a timber-lined cellar. Timber buildings of the same period were found sealed beneath the late second century rampart at Butt Close Lane and Elbow Lane (Buckley and Lucas 1987, 49-50). On the basis of alignment, this activity all seems to post-date the street grid (*c*.100AD) and possibly the establishment of the town as a civitas capital. It is clear that the town expanded rapidly in the late first - early second century from the original focus of settlement on the east bank of the Soar, to the line of the late second century defences on the north and east sides, and possibly beyond. Later occupation in this quarter is only known from the Little Lane site, comprising the remains of substantial masonry buildings of the late second to third centuries again fronting the north-south street. On the St. Peter's Lane excavation (Shires, 1988-9), almost all Roman activity had been obliterated by post-Roman cultivation, save for a north-south ditch and a possible robbed stone cellar (Lucas and Buckley 1989, 105-6). In the fourth century, the evidence for occupation is based almost entirely on artefacts. On most sites in this quarter, little evidence of floors or the superstructure of walls has survived post-Roman cultivation or robbing respectively.

It is difficult at present to characterise the status of occupation in this quarter. One might speculate – on the slenderest of evidence – that the location of wealthier districts of Roman Leicester was influenced by factors including the proximity of major public buildings (the forum and the baths), the major east-west route through the town (the Fosse Way) and perhaps even a good view across the river. Certainly the densest concentration of mosaic pavements, some of which are of exceptionally high quality, is in the western half of the town (Johnson 1980, 1). There are only a few in the north-east quarter, perhaps supporting the idea that this was rather a backwater, albeit one which must have contained buildings of some architectural pretension.

The Post Roman Period

The topography of Saxon and medieval Leicester
The nature of occupation in Leicester after the end of Roman Britain remains difficult to define due to the comparative dearth of archaeological evidence. Recent excavations some 250m to the south of the town, adjacent to the Roman road to Tripontium (Caves Inn) revealed the truncated remains of two sunken featured buildings associated with finds of the fifth-sixth centuries (Finn 1994, 167; Gossip 1998,

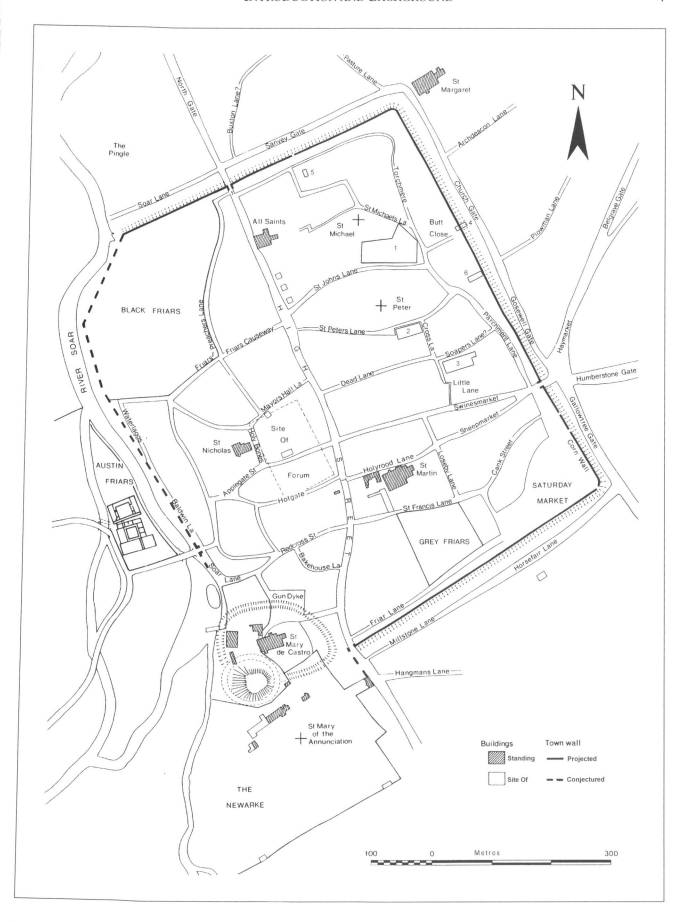

Fig. 4: *Medieval Leicester. Excavations referred to in the text: 1. Causeway Lane; 2. St. Peter's Lane and 3. Little Lane (Shires 1988-9; Lucas and Buckley 1989); 4. Butt Close Lane (Buckley and Lucas 1987, Site 4); 5. Elbow Lane (Lucas 1989); 6. St. Peters Lane (Buckley and Lucas 1987, Site 3).*

159-60). These represent the first Anglo-Saxon structures to be located in or near the Roman town, but may indicate no more than a small suburban settlement and the evidence cannot be taken at present to suggest the continuation of urban life (P. Courtney pers. comm.). Within the walls, no structures of this period have been identified as yet, although pottery and other finds have been made in the north-east quarter at St Peter's Lane (Shires), Causeway Lane and elsewhere, but always residual in later contexts.

Leicester became a Mercian bishopric soon after 670, one of the five Boroughs of the Danelaw in 877 and – based on the Domesday Survey – was apparently a flourishing town at the time of the Norman Conquest, with 322 houses, 65 burgesses and six churches (Ellis 1976, 38-9). There is little archaeological evidence so far, however, for late Saxon occupation, and only the church of St. Nicholas has fabric of this period. Courtney argues that it cannot be assumed that the town had an urban character by the tenth century despite its strategic military importance (1998, 114). Instead, he suggests (below p.91) on the basis of the distribution of finds, that the main street of Leicester in the Saxo-Norman period was the north-south running axial road, the medieval 'High Street' (later renamed Highcross and Southgate Streets). This takes the shortest route between the north and south gates, and apparently respects the Roman forum (Buckley and Lucas 1987, 56). As the town's widest street, it would initially have served as the chief market and was, perhaps, the focus of pre-Conquest occupation.

After the Conquest, a motte and bailey castle was constructed in c.1068 at the south-west angle of the Roman defences in a position where it would dominate the town. In the early 12th century, the timber elements of the castle began to be replaced in stone and St Mary de Castro was endowed as a collegiate church. Other churches were clearly rebuilt at this time, as shown by surviving Romanesque fabric, and work commenced on the great abbey of St. Mary de Pratis outside the north suburb after 1143. Of domestic occupation in this period, archaeology has furnished little evidence. The stone undercroft on Guildhall Lane may relate to a high status merchant's house (Hagar and Buckley 1990), whilst at Causeway Lane and Sanvey Gate (Finn 1993) intensive backyard activity in the 12th century suggests a growth in population. The archaeological record also attests robbing of Roman walls on a large scale at this time, which it is tempting to associate with a building boom in major secular and religious structures.

By the 13th century, the topography of medieval Leicester comprised the core of settlement contained within the Roman walls, with suburbs outside each of the gates. The intra-mural area was dominated by the castle, the friaries of the Dominicans and Franciscans, which were established in the 13th century, the Saturday Market and six churches. Another friary, that of the Augustinians, was established outside the west gate in the mid 13th century (excavated 1973-8; Mellor and Pearce 1981, 1). The street pattern was perhaps largely in place by this time, and remained relatively intact until the late 19th -20th century.

The north-east quarter
Causeway Lane lies in a part of the north-east quarter of the medieval town known as 'The Lanes'. It was called St. John's Lane from at least the 15th until the 19th century, although alternative names of Jailhall Lane and Bridewell Lane were also used, and became Causeway Lane in 1806 (see below p.92). The lane ran east to join Torchmere, now East Bond Street, which, it has been suggested, could be a pre-Conquest intra-mural street (Buckley and Lucas 1987, 57). There were three parochial churches in the north-east quarter, comprising All Saints, St Peters and St Michaels. Although all three are first documented in 1220 (see below p.91), surviving fabric in All Saints and fragments from the now demolished St. Peter's suggest a 12th century or earlier origin. The site lay in St. Peters parish and the church was probably opposite the excavation area, on the south side of Causeway Lane (see below p.91).

The excavations on Causeway Lane have demonstrated intensive 12th century urban back yard activity in, what was apparently, a series of narrow plots whilst the St. Peters Lane (Shires) site to the south has shown organised gravel quarrying in the same period. However, there appears to have been a sudden population decline in the late 12th to early 13th centuries from which the area did not recover until the 19th century. In the archaeological record, particularly on the Causeway Lane and St Peters Lane (Shires) sites, this hiatus has manifested itself by a lack of pits or other features after the 12th century, and the considerable build up of so-called 'garden soil'. This is a substantial deposit of dark brown loam, up to 3.5 metres in thickness, which has been taken to represent manuring and cultivation. The churches of St. Michael and St. Peter had been abandoned by the end of the 16th century and their parishes were absorbed by All Saint's. Maps of the 17th and 18th centuries indicate that much of the north-east quarter by this time was occupied by gardens and orchards.

The decline is difficult to explain. In the early 18th century Samuel Carte suggested it was due to the sack of Leicester in 1173 by the forces of Henry II, although Courtney believes towns generally recovered rapidly from such short-term crises unless other factors were at work. Instead, he proposes the rise in importance of the medieval Swinesmarket (modern High Street), and the appearance of continually built-up frontages in the borough for the first time, creating higher population densities along the main commercial streets, whilst prompting contraction in less favourable areas (see below p.91).

Summary of the main results of the project
AC & RB

The Causeway Lane site in the Roman period

Excavation and post-excavation studies clearly highlighted the differing character of Roman deposits within each of the four excavated areas. Area 1 (*insula* XI) showed most potential for the early Roman period, a deep stratified sequence being available for the early first through to mid-second century. This sequence mainly comprised cultivation layers, make-up and metalling, with well stratified deep cut features (pits and wells). Some late second/early third-century features were also evident but these were few, and in the case of the possible timber structure, difficult to stratify accurately. Area 2 (*insula* XIX) also showed evidence for early Roman cultivation, as well as ditches of east-west and north-south orientation suggestive of plot boundaries, but overall the stratigraphy was restricted here. The ditches pre-dated a largely robbed mid-second century stone structure, which may have continued in occupation into the third century, when an annexe or second building was erected. Possibly contemporary with the building(s) were a number of third-century pits and yard surfaces. Large pits in Area 3 (*insula* XII) indicated gravel extraction, with the backfills containing a very large assemblage of late third and early fourth century pottery, as well as painted wall plaster and coins (extending to AD 380). Subsequently, consolidated levelling combined with post and stake holes suggests the presence of flimsy timber structures. Little evidence for Roman occupation had survived on Area 4 (*insula* XI), although there was a large number of Roman finds found in medieval pits in this area.

The evidence overall suggested the possibility that a cross-roads had existed on the site in Roman times and that Areas 1 and 4 lay to the north-west, Area 2 to the south-east and Area 3 to the north-east of this junction.

The Causeway Lane site has provided a rare opportunity to examine changing land-use for parts of three *insulae* in an area of the town which has seen comparatively little archaeological excavation. In addition, the results have provided important information for an area which is perhaps more typical of the town as a whole – away from its hub with its wealthy town houses, public buildings and market. The evidence is admittedly fragmentary: pitting of the medieval period, together with 18th century gravel quarrying, Victorian foundations and cellars had destroyed the physical association of streets and plots. In addition, there was considerable variation in the quality of stratification between the different areas due to truncation by medieval and post-medieval cultivation. The impact of depositional processes – including residuality, slumping, truncation and re-deposition – on the interpretation of the site sequence is discussed in more detail below (p.17).

Apart from some small scale gravel quarrying and possible cultivation in the late first century, all Roman occupation on the site appears to relate to the planned town. One of the major issues addressed is the date at which town planning in the form of regular *insulae* was imposed. The results have suggested that the process was probably more complex than previously supposed, with *insulae* appearing perhaps as early as the late first century, but division into plots, occupation and street metalling following later. The latter was clearly main-

Table 1: *Summary of the site phasing with approximate dates and subphases within the excavated zones.*

Phase	Subphases			Approximate Dates AD
	Areas 1 & 4	Area 2	Area 3	
1	1A			Mid-late 1st century
	1B			Late 1st century
	1C			Mid 1st-mid 2nd century
2	2C			Late 1st century
	2A, 2I			Late 1st-early 2nd century
	2B, 2D, 2E, 2J,		2L	Early 2nd century
				Early 2nd century
	2F, 2G, 2H			Early – mid-2nd century
		2K		Late 1st- mid-2nd century
3		3E		Late 1st century
	3A, 3C			Early-mid 2nd century
	3B	3F		Mid 2nd -Early 3rd C.
	3D			Late 2nd-mid 3rd C.
		3G		Mid 3rd-4th century
4	4A			Mid-late 3rd century
5	5A, 5B			?Early-mid 3rd century
	5C			Mid-late 3rd century
	5D			Late 3rd-early 4th century
			5E, 5F	Early 4th century
			5G, 5H	Early-mid 4th century
6			6A,	Early-mid 4th century
			6B	Mid-late 4th century
7				?Early post-Roman
8				11th-12th century
9		9.1, 9.2, 9.3, 9.4, 9.5, 9.6		Early 12th-mid 13th C.
10				Mid 13th-early 14th C.
11				16-17th century
12				18th-20th century

tained throughout the Roman period, but was possibly encroached upon in places (below p.52).

The occupation on the site is apparently residential in character (below p.52) and in general conforms to the classic sequence observed on other Leicester sites: timber buildings of the late first to early second century, followed by more substantial stone buildings from the mid second century with a comparative lack of occupation in the third and fourth centuries. Evidence suggests that formal plot boundaries were probably established in the late first-early second century and that these continued to exert influence for some time on topographic development. In Area 1, the landuse exhibits continuity over a long period of time, with successive timber buildings and gravel yards occupying the same spot (below p.52). Of particular interest is the change from essentially domestic occupation in Area 3 in the late third century to gravel quarrying on an organised scale, but still respecting the street grid and possibly plot boundaries (below p.52).

Most of the structures of the Roman period identified on the site were of timber, exhibiting a variety of constructional techniques and differing status, including strip buildings, sheds and outbuildings (below p.53). Construction in timber continues through to the third century in Area 1, whilst Area 3 shows some evidence for a possible timber structure of the fourth century. The stone structure of Area 2 is a classic urban strip building, perhaps with a corridor (below p.54). The finds assemblage has provided considerable information on the range and variety of building materials including tile, slate, painted wall plaster, tesserae, window glass and fragments of burnt daub (below p.55). Whilst some of these derive from buildings on the site or in the immediate vicinity, others – in particular the large assemblage of painted wall plaster in Area 3 – were almost certainly tipped on the site following demolition of a substantial building elsewhere.

From the outset, analysis of environmental samples to recover plant and animal remains was considered to be a high priority in order to characterise the diet, health and living conditions of the inhabitants of the site in the past. The results have provided a wealth of information to complement that from the excavations at the Shires (Little Lane and St. Peter's Lane) in 1988-9 (Monckton forthcoming). Analysis of the plant remains and mineralised seeds has shown the range of foodstuffs which was being brought in for human and animal consumption, including cereals, hay, pulses, nuts, coriander, peas and fruit (below p.55-6). In addition, light has been shed on agricultural practices by the identification of hay meadow species of plants (p.57). Analysis of the fly puparia and parasites has given further insights into public health and the disposal of faecal waste, including the identification of possible manuring (p.56). The animal bone analysis has provided detailed information on the management and exploitation of domestic species as draft stock, for dairy and meat produce. It has also demonstrated

the changing preference in meat consumption from sheep to cattle as the town became increasingly Romanised, supplemented by fowl – for meat and eggs – and to a limited extent, wild species (below p.55-6). The fish remains constituted the largest assemblage so far from Roman Leicester and have indicated the reliance on freshwater species, although the presence of marine fish and oysters has confirmed long-distance trade to one of the most landlocked towns of Britain.

From the earliest Roman phases, the finds and environmental assemblage attests local trade in food products, fuel and building materials from the hinterland of the town, whilst the pottery assemblage indicates the range of imported wares which were coming into Leicester from elsewhere in Britain and beyond (Clark, below). Although the site appears to have been primarily residential for much of the period, there is some evidence of industry, comprising horners' and probably skinners' or tanners' waste, offcuts from bone working and small scale bronze or brass casting and possibly glass making (below p.305).

One of the most contentious areas of study in relation to Roman towns is the nature of occupation in the late third and fourth centuries. At Causeway Lane, the truncation of later Roman levels by cultivation – including the destruction of street metalling, masonry and floors – is not in doubt, particularly in Area 2. Elsewhere on the site, timber buildings continue into the late third century, whilst fourth century activity is represented by quarrying and a possible timber structure (pp.59-60).

The Causeway Lane site in the post-Roman period

Anglo Saxon

The excavation produced possible evidence for early Anglo-Saxon occupation in the vicinity. A few sherds of residual pottery and a brooch fragment attest activity in the fifth-sixth century in common with the St. Peters Lane and Little Lane (Shires) sites to the south (below p.83). An insubstantial timber structure cutting late Roman deposits in Area 3 could be early Anglo-Saxon rather than Roman, and if so represents the first structural feature from this period within the town walls. Evidence from the site has also shown that Roman fabric persisted into the medieval period, with street metalling and parts of the superstructure of stone buildings surviving into at least the 12th century.

Medieval

The only horizontal stratification of the medieval period which had escaped truncation occurred on the eastern edge of Area 2 and presumably continued beneath East Bond Street. The layers here seemed to indicate the presence of several phases of a 12th to 13th century timber structure with associated pits nearby containing fills of a similar date. Elsewhere the cut features were almost all moderate or deep pits, many with timber or clay lining, with fills dated to the 12th to early 14th century. These pits fell into lines and it is likely that they represent evidence of individual properties.

Hence, with the exception of part of Area 2, most of the archaeological evidence from the medieval period at Causeway Lane represents back-yard activity. The finds and environmental assemblages have presented a wealth of material data for archaeological study providing a clear picture of the nature and status of domestic occupation, trade and industry, diet and health in this part of medieval Leicester.

The linear distribution of pits on the site has attested intensive 12th century occupation in narrow plots for the first time in this part of the town. Analysis of the finds assemblages from the different plots suggests essentially domestic occupation with simple household 'industry', but with perhaps more commercial production at the eastern end of the site (below pp.85-86). In Area 2, some horizontal stratification survived and one

plot produced evidence for a timber structure which re-used the partly demolished walls of a Roman stone building (p.86ff). The dating evidence suggests that this intensive occupation was relatively short-lived and had declined considerably by the mid-13th century, to disappear finally by the early 14th, to be replaced by dark, humic garden soils.

By far the greatest contribution the Causeway Lane excavation has made to our knowledge of the medieval town comes from the study of the contents of the many pits found on the site. Analysis has indicated the presence of industry, in the form of tanning and soap-making (below p.87), cupellation and ironworking (p.88). In addition, a tanner or tawyer (oil-tanner) may have been operating on the site and trade in skins and furs from small animals is suggested (p.88). The finds assemblage suggests that goods were for the most part traded relatively locally, although fish was coming from the east coast (p.89) and grapes and figs from further

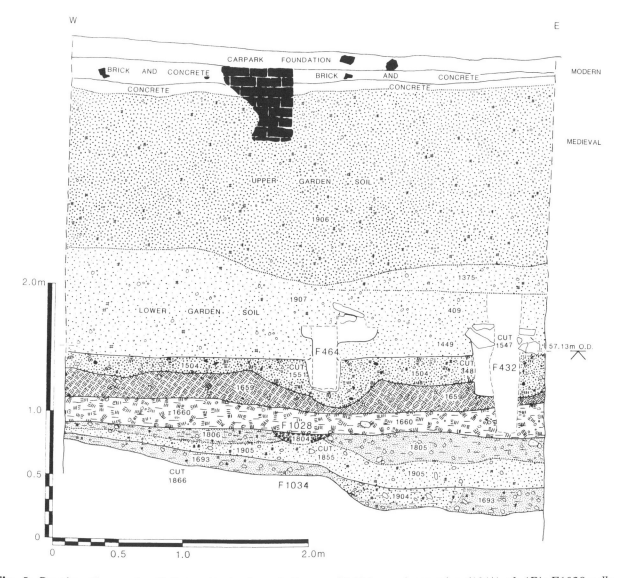

Fig. 5: *Section through all deposits in Area 1.* *Roman: F1034 gravel extraction (131/1, ph.1B); F1028 gully (structure B, ph.2A); F464 and F432 post holes (structure H, ph.5A). Medieval: lower and upper garden soils.*

afield (p.89). There is little evidence for high status imported luxury goods, and the pottery for the most part comes from the midland and eastern counties (p.89).

The faunal and environmental assemblages indicate the consumption of a relatively wide range of food stuffs (p.89), including fish, meat, poultry and game, eggs, cereals, vegetables and fruit. Wild food resources were only slightly represented, as were exotic imports of fruit; fish bones were from those fish at the cheaper end of the market (below p.337). Residues from pottery sherds suggest an apparent preference for pig or boar fat for cooking (below p.197).

Many of the pits were timber or clay lined and provided evidence for the disposal of latrine waste, animal dung and general domestic rubbish in much greater quantities than in the Roman period. It is clear that lime was dumped into the pits to seal such deposits and counteract the nuisance from flies. There is also evidence (from flies which breed in the dark) that pits were covered in some way. Other aspects of daily life are represented by pottery lamps containing fat residues

from cattle or sheep (below p.337) whilst the plant remains include rushes presumably for floors or bedding.

Post-medieval and modern occupation

Other than a very few pits which were backfilled during the 16th and 17th centuries, the site seems to have been open ground or orchards from the 14th until the 18th century. Gravel extraction then destroyed much of the central area of the site and any direct links between the three excavated areas. An interesting group of clay pipes and a large part of a kiln was dumped on the site in the early 19th century, found sealed beneath a mid-19th-century cellar. The second half of the century witnessed considerable development on the site beginning with a row of terraced houses along Causeway Lane and continuing with a variety of factories, a tram depot, housing, a new street and, most recently, hospitals, the latter demolished only in 1974 when the site became a car park and the site of the Unemployment Benefit Offices (see Courtney, below).

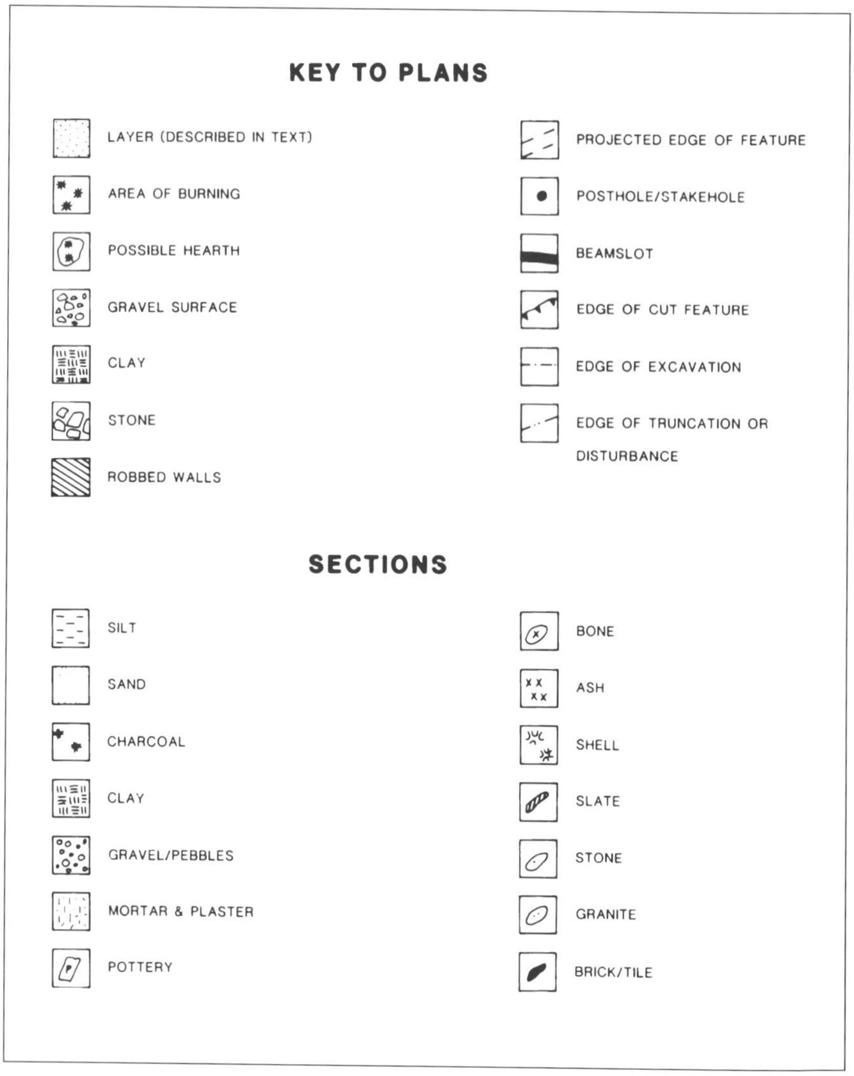

KEY TO PLANS

	LAYER (DESCRIBED IN TEXT)		PROJECTED EDGE OF FEATURE
	AREA OF BURNING		POSTHOLE/STAKEHOLE
	POSSIBLE HEARTH		BEAMSLOT
	GRAVEL SURFACE		EDGE OF CUT FEATURE
	CLAY		EDGE OF EXCAVATION
	STONE		EDGE OF TRUNCATION OR DISTURBANCE
	ROBBED WALLS		

SECTIONS

	SILT		BONE
	SAND		ASH
	CHARCOAL		SHELL
	CLAY		SLATE
	GRAVEL/PEBBLES		STONE
	MORTAR & PLASTER		GRANITE
	POTTERY		BRICK/TILE

Key to plans and sections, figs. 7-52

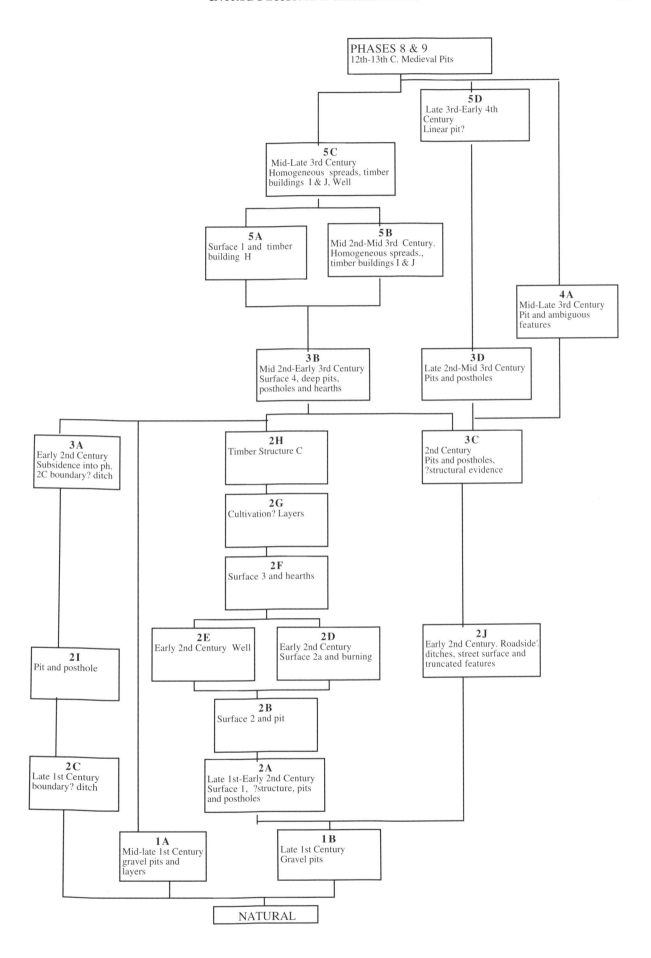

Fig. 6: Insula *XI* (Area 1) Subphase matrix for Roman deposits

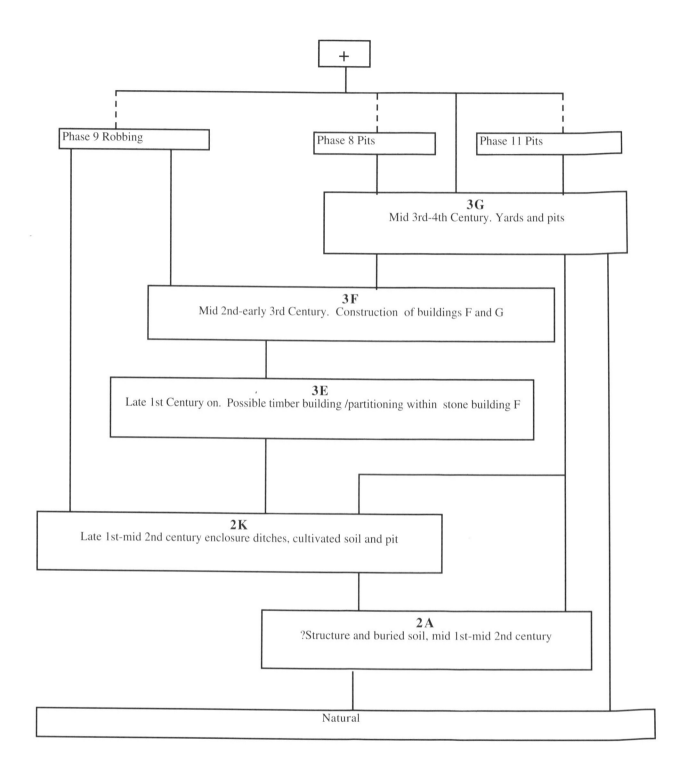

Fig. 7: Insula *XIX (Area 2) subphase matrix for Roman deposits*

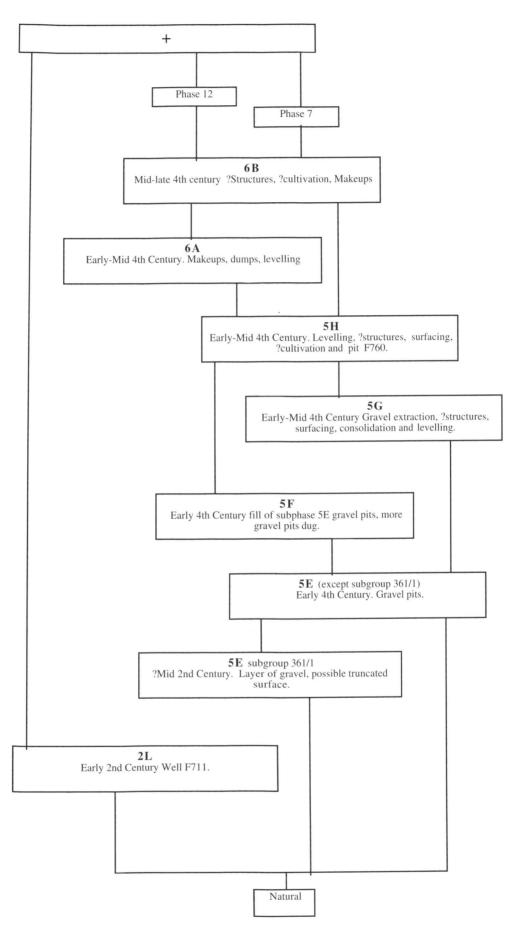

Fig. 8: Insula *XII (Area 3) subphase matrix for Roman deposits*

THE ROMAN PHASES

Aileen Connor and Richard Buckley

INTRODUCTION

Quality of the evidence

Survival of the Roman levels was extremely variable as a result of horizontal truncation from medieval and post medieval cultivation episodes together with disturbance from medieval pitting, 19th – 20th century buildings and 18th century gravel quarries. The former had caused destruction of most horizontal stratification in Areas 2 and 4 leaving mainly features cutting the natural sand and gravel. Fortuitously, a slight natural hollow in Area 1 meant that a particularly good Roman stratified sequence had survived, as reflected by the large number of subphases allocated to the deposits in this area. The 18th century quarries had destroyed stratigraphic relationships between the three areas examined, whilst 19th – 20th century foundations had caused more localised damage. The northern part of Area 1 was somewhat isolated from the rest due to the presence of early 20th century basement foundations. Although these were removed during machining, the reinforced concrete baseplates had to be left in place to avoid the risk of damaging the soft archaeological layers. During the course of the excavation it was subsequently possible to remove some of these baseplates manually. Such disturbances created difficulties in relating deposits from the southern area with those on the larger northern area. Accordingly, the former have been phased separately and are placed in phase 2 on the grounds that their pottery had a broadly similar date range to this phase.

Depositional processes

As part of the analysis, it was considered important to investigate depositional processes in order to make a qualitative assessment of the stratigraphic evidence, and gain a better understanding of the nature of site formation. This involved consideration of the physical characteristics of soils and features together with the wear, abrasion and fragment sizes of different material types. Pottery was found to be a particularly useful indicator, but animal bone, glass, and building materials also made a contribution.

Residuality appeared to be low in most of the deposits, with the notable exception of make-up layers in Area 1 and the backfills of the quarry pits in Area 3. The latter showed evidence for particularly high residuality, to the extent that some deposits such as G360/1 (phase 5E) were made up from entirely residual material. Other backfills in the quarry pits contained mainly third century residual pottery, although G359/4 (phase 5C) also contained a large quantity of unabraded wall plaster thought to be fourth century in date on typological grounds (Ripper, below) and therefore contemporary with the final deposition date. These tightly dated residual assemblages deposited at a later date may suggest that the material derived from different sources. High residuality was, therefore, almost entirely to be found in make-up layers derived from a source outside the site.

Particular difficulties were encountered in establishing the relationships between post holes and surrounding deposits in Area 1, leading to the necessity to make deductions about features which were not necessarily firmly based in their stratigraphic relationships. For example, Structures I and J appeared to be stratigraphically placed in two subphases, 5B and 5C, separated by homogeneous brown loams (G164), yet common sense suggested that the post holes were part of one and the same building. One possible explanation for this may have been the piecemeal nature of decay and abandonment of the structures, with the stratification perhaps reflecting phases of destruction rather than construction. Similar problems were encountered on the Little Lane (Shires) site where the granite packing of post holes protruded through layers of a later phase, suggesting the reworking or cultivation of deposits through which they had been cut (J. Lucas pers. comm.). High average sherd weight of pottery has been taken to indicate contexts with minimal reworking or redeposition. Where there are no links or joins with earlier strata in such assemblages, despite obvious residuality, this has been interpreted as an indication of deposits deliberately brought onto the site from elsewhere.

Several deep features in all periods had been deliberately backfilled and overlying deposits had clearly slumped into them, after which levelling sometimes took place. Voids were a clear indicator of organic materials in pits, and must have been a major contributory factor to slumping. An example of this process of slumping and levelling may be seen for ditch G140 in phases 2C, 3A and 3B.

Reporting conventions and abbreviations

During analysis, an attempt was made to create a concordant phasing system across all areas of the site. Although this has worked reasonably well, there are some anomalies in dating due to the receipt of additional information from specialists after the site had been phased. The phases are presented in presumed chronological sequence with subphases grouping together evidence reflecting activity of a similar date and character in each area. It should be noted that the stratigraphic relationship between any two subphases can be identified through the site matrices (figs.6-8). Where subgroups encompass a number of discrete features, the relevant feature numbers are quoted when necessary for ease of reference to the plans. Dating and details of the small finds present are given for each subphase. Small finds are referred to by catalogue number, small find number and group and include coins.

PHASE 1 Late first century AD

Cultivation, gravel extraction and a possible timber structure

Phase 1A (fig. 9)

Group 180 *Area 1: Buried soil remnants or possible cultivation (180/1)*

Group 177 *Area 1: Gravel pits and post hole (177/1)*

All of the deposits and features of this phase were severely truncated.

G180 – Overlying the natural sands and gravels were the truncated remains of layers of discoloured sand containing small amounts of Roman pottery, tile and a fragment of glass (180/1).

G177 – The layers had been cut by three sub-circular pits and a post hole, 177/1. Although stratigraphically later, these have been assigned to this sub phase on the basis of the dating evidence. The pits were all less than 0.5m in depth, probably due to truncation from above, and c.1.5m in diameter; filled with a mixture of re-deposited sandy gravel, crushed and decayed limestone, and frequent rounded stones/cobbles. The post hole, (0.3m diameter by 0.3m deep) contained a greyish

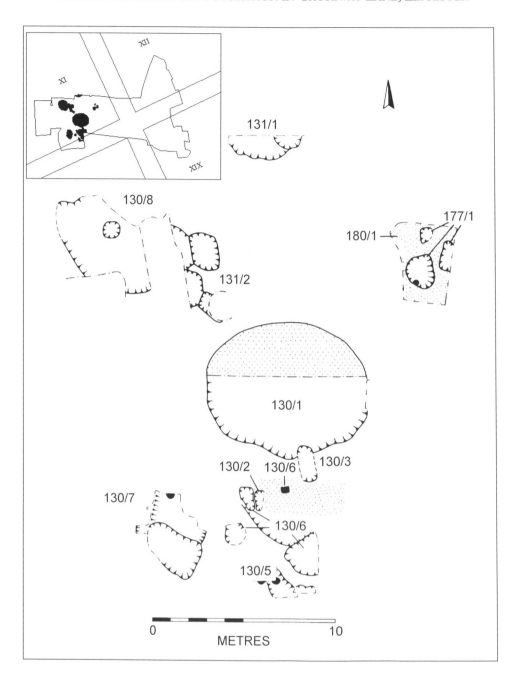

Fig. 9: *Plan of phases 1A and 1B*

brown sandy loam and cut through a corner of one pit. The latter was contaminated with a small quantity of medieval pottery.

Small finds: none:

Ceramic dating: *c. AD 75-100.*

Phase 1B (fig. 9)

Group 130   *Area 1: Gravel extraction pits and post holes (130/1-8)*

Group 131   *Area 1: Gravel extraction pits (131/1-2)*

G130 – A number of sub-circular pits and possible post holes cut into the natural sand and gravel. The pits varied enormously in size from the largest, at 8.5m in diameter by 1.5m deep, to the smallest, at 0.4m diameter by 0.15m deep. The former lay in the centre of Area 1 and overlying layers had

slumped into it. All of the pits were irregular and filled by a mixture of sands, gravels, leached silts and were characterised by iron panning. Some of the pits in this group contained post holes of uncertain function, but which appeared to be associated.

G131 – Other possible gravel pits were identified, all shallow and ambiguous in plan and section.

Small Finds: *Flint* 217 – sf7002, 130/5

Ceramic dating: *c. AD 70-85*

Phase 1C (fig. 10)

Group 200   *Area 2: ?Cultivation deposits (200/1-2)*

Group 208   *Area 2: ?Timber structure,* **Structure A:** *beamslot (208/1), pit (208/2) and post holes (208/3)*

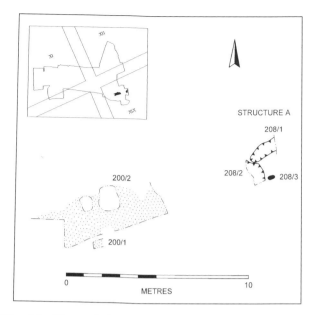

Fig. 10: *Plan of phase 1C*

G200 – Overlying the natural sands and gravels were two patches of leached light brown silt and sandy clay: 200/2 was *c.* 6.0 by 2.0m, whilst 200/1 was just 0.35 by 0.18m but slightly thicker at 0.12m; both were truncated by features attributed to phase 2K. Both possibly form remnants of an early Roman buried soil and are probably contemporary with those in area 1, phase 1A, but assigned to this subphase on the grounds because they are in a different area.

G208 – Structure A – Spatially unrelated to the cultivation layers were three features interpreted as a possible timber structure, G208, which was stratigraphically earlier than stone building G210 (phase 3F). G208/1 (plate 2) was an E-W orientated possible beam slot of curvilinear form which continued beyond the edge of the excavation; it was 0.66m wide by 0.72m deep with near vertical sides and a flat base. It was filled with interleaving dark greyish brown ashy sandy silt and much lighter yellowish brown silt sand and gravel layers. Finds included pottery, animal bone (including a wild species), eggshell and iron objects. G208/2 was a pit measuring 1.5 by 0.8m and 0.33m in depth and 208/3 a post hole measuring 0.34 by 0.19m of 0.16m depth.

Small Finds: Hone 192 – sf4573, 208/1.

Ceramic dating: AD 70-100, but group 208/2, AD 120-150.

Discussion of phase 1

The earliest phase of activity on Area 1 consisted of a series of shallow pits of irregular form dug into the natural ground which may have been associated with small scale quarrying for sand and gravel. The pits were of a different character to those in area 3, phase 5, which appear to represent comparatively large scale organised quarrying.

The pits probably lay open for some time since iron panning was present and their fills of clean sands and gravels contained few finds. The sand and gravel fills either represent soil-contaminated aggregate thrown back in, or weathering of the natural sand and gravel. Their upper fills were very similar, suggesting that final

deliberate backfilling occurred quickly, with possible importation of materials, such as crushed and decayed limestone. On the basis of the ceramic evidence, this backfilling took place in the late first to early second century AD, and was possibly designed to create level ground in preparation for phase 2 occupation.

A buried soil containing possible evidence of manure including animal dung and fish bones, suggests that parts of Area 2 were under cultivation in the mid to late first century AD; the same may also have been true of Area 1. On the nearby Little Lane site, evidence for field ditches in the first century also suggested cultivation and indicated that occupation had not yet spread this far east from the focus of early post-Conquest activity adjacent to the Iron Age settlement on the east bank of the Soar (Lucas and Buckley forthcoming).

Contemporary with, or slightly later than, the cultivated ground was a possible timber building, Structure A, whose alignment roughly matched the street grid, believed to have been established in the first quarter of the second century (Clay and Pollard 1994, 47). The ceramic evidence indicated a likely abandonment already in the first half of the second century, and for this reason it has been phased prior to the elements of street grid in phase 2. Town planning and its influence on alignments is discussed in more detail below (p.51). It seems possible that the building was demolished to make way for the stone building of phase 3. Besides this putative building, the Causeway Lane site

Plate 2: *Beam slot 208/1, phase 1C*

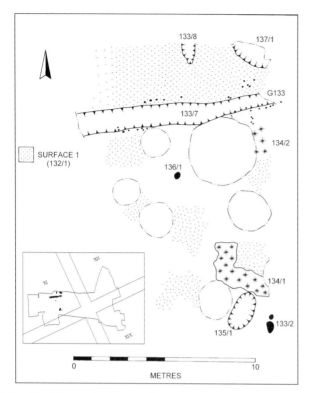

Fig. 11: *Plan of phase 2A*

appears undeveloped at this time, in contrast with the Shires Little Lane site to the south (fig. 37), and the defences sites of St. Peter's Lane to the south-east, and Butt Close Lane to the north-east, each with late first – early second century timber buildings (Lucas and Buckley, forthcoming; Buckley and Lucas 1987, sites 3 and 4).

In Area 3, no phase 1 deposits were identified, due chiefly to severe truncation from Phase 5. This should not be taken as evidence of no occupation, since residual first century material occurred which may represent disturbed occupation contexts or, alternatively, may denote imported rubbish.

PHASE 2 late first to mid second century AD

Establishment of insulae and boundary ditches, appearance of timber buildings, gravel surfaces, hearths, pits and wells.

Phase 2A (fig. 11)

Group 132	*Area 1: gravel surface,* **Surface 1***: (132/1)*
Group 133	*Area 1:Possible timber structure,* **Structure** **B***: gullies (133/7-8), stake holes (133/1 & 133/3-6) and post holes (133/2)*
Group134	*Area 1: hearth rakings (134/1)*
Groups 135-137	*Area 1: post holes and pit (135/1, 136/1 & 137/1)*

G132 – Surface 1 – Interleaving layers of compacted gravel and yellowish brown sandy loam formed surface 1, G132, which overlay and slumped into the phase 1B gravel pits. These layers were more compacted to the north of Area 1 and patchy to the south of gully 133/7.

G133 – Structure B – Thirty-nine small circular stake holes (133/1, 133/3-6) cut surface 1 and lay in four roughly

linear groups, two each side of, and parallel with shallow gully 133/7 on an E-W orientation. Fourteen of the stake holes (133/1, 133/6) appeared as voids whilst the others contained brown sandy silts derived from the immediately surrounding soils. Gully 133/7 measured 6.2m by 1.56m and 0.27m deep, and was filled with sandy loam layers containing large quantities of pebbles, possibly derived from surface 1. The uppermost fill held a charcoal rich layer which spread beyond the edges of the cut and merged into the layers beyond. There was no evidence to suggest that the gully continued west beyond ditch G140 (phase 2C). The southern end of a second gully, 133/8, lay at right angles to and north of 133/7 and measured 1.4m long, 0.38m wide and 0.06m deep. Ten metres to the south of gully 133/7 were two post holes, 133/2, which lay close to pit 135/1. All of these features were cut through surface 1.

G133 has been taken as a coherent group, with the gullies and stake holes perhaps representing the sides of a timber building, structure B. The parallel rows of stake holes imply wattle shuttering between which clay, daub or mud brick could be placed. An alternative interpretation is that G133 represents a plank lined drain (see below p.28).

G134. Immediately to the north of pit 135/1 was an L-shaped area of burnt sand layers and ashy deposits, 134/1. This had been truncated to the east by a well G166 (phase 5C). A second ashy deposit, 134/2, lay to the north and may represent hearth rakings.

G135-7. Other features cut through surface 1: pit 136/1 (not on plan), 1.08m deep but truncated by G147 (phase 2E), was perhaps originally circular in plan of *c.* 1.4m diameter; it was filled with brown loams and sandy silts. Post hole 136/1 was 0.34m in diameter and 0.32m deep; it perhaps belongs with post holes identified in phase 3B. Pit 137/1 was severely truncated. G135/1 was a shallow oval pit which measured 1.5m long by 0.7m wide and 0.3m deep and was filled with a yellowish brown sandy loam.

Small Finds: Bead 72 – sf3021, 134/1; *Coin?-* sf2418, 134/1.

Ceramic dating: AD 70-100

Stratigraphic dating: late first century+

Phase 2B (fig. 12)

Group 138	*Area 1: Make ups and gravel surface,* **Surface 2***:* *(138/1-3)*
Group 139	*Area 1: pit (139/1)*

G138 – Surface 2 – Sealing the features of phase 2A was a series of widely disparate layers ranging from 138/1, a finds rich organic layer, to 138/2, layers of loam and re-deposited sands, gravels and clay. These were probably make-up layers for surface 2: G138/3 and contained most of the pottery, tile and bone for this subphase. Alternatively, they could represent usage and perhaps patching of surface G132 of phase 2A. The overlying 138/3, a more homogeneous group of layers consisting mainly of compacted gravels in a matrix of sandy loams, covered an area of roughly 15 by 15m and probably represents a later surface.

G139 – At the furthest eastern extent of surface 138/3, no function could be ascribed to pit 139/1 which measured 1.8m by 1.4m, and was 0.66m deep. It had cut surface G132 (phase 2A) and was sealed beneath surface G143 (phase 2D).

Small Finds: Bead 62 – sf3011, 138/2.

Ceramic dating: AD 70-100

Stratigraphic dating: late first century+

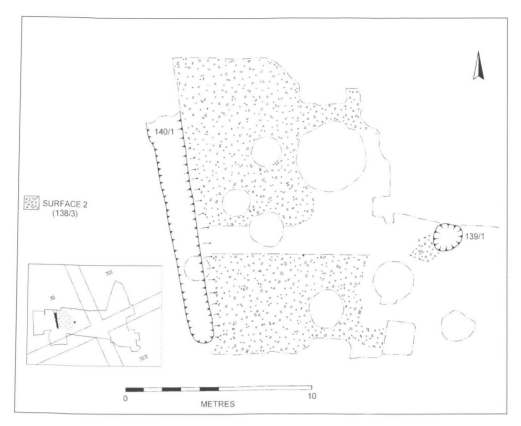

Fig. 12: *Plan of phases 2B-2C*

Plate 3: *Boundary ditch 140/1, phase 2C, view south-east*

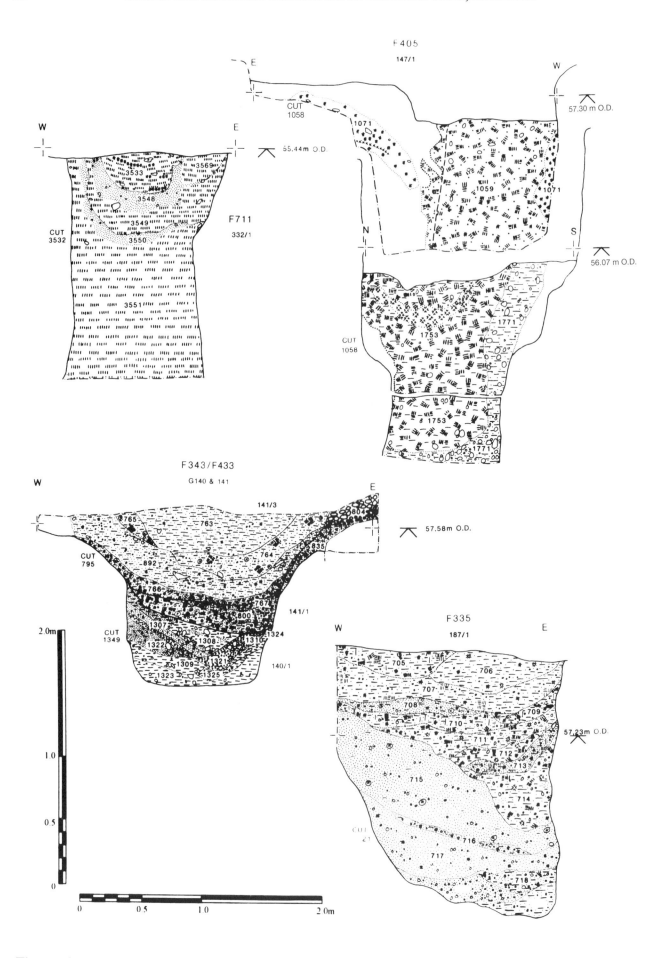

Fig. 13: *Sections, phases 2C, 2E*

Phase 2C (figs. 12 & 13)

Group 140 *Area 1: boundary ditch (140/1)*

G140 – Close to the western edge of Area 1, ditch 140/1 was traced for 12.4m, with an upper width of 2.2m and base width of 0.9m. Due to slumping, and the successive build up of adjacent surfaces to the east, estimates of its original depth are problematic, although the level of natural to the west of the ditch implies a minimum depth of 1.5m, though with a higher east side to the base. The base was reasonably flat with an intermittent V-shaped trench which meandered from side to side. The original cut may have been flat based and steep sided, the sand and gravel edges becoming rapidly degraded soon after construction. The ditch was re-cut following the same alignment but slightly shallower. The north end of the ditch was truncated by a large pit 152/1 (phase 3B), but it most probably continued. Finds from the earliest fills suggested a similar date to phase 2B, and its re-cut contemporary with surface 3 (phase 2F). The fact that the ditch appears to respect the line of the roadside ditches G172 of phase 2I indicates that it is perhaps broadly contemporary.

Small finds: none

Ceramic dating: *late first century AD.*

Phase 2D (fig. 14)

Group 143 *Area 1: surface,* **Surface 2a** *(143/1)*
Group 144 *Area 1: ?hearth rakings (144/1)*

G143 – Surface 2a – Overlying surface 2 (G138, phase 2B) was a series of silty sand and loamy sand layers ranging in colour from yellowish to greyish brown. Many of the layers contained few or no pebbles, although occasional more densely pebbled areas existed. In view of this, the group is interpreted as resurfacing of G138. Some layers had been funnelled into a cut for a Victorian cellar, which may have caused some contamination.

G144 – Also overlying surface 2 (phase 2B), but physically unconnected to surface 2a, were interleaving layers of silt sands and loams, all displaying evidence of burning, heating or

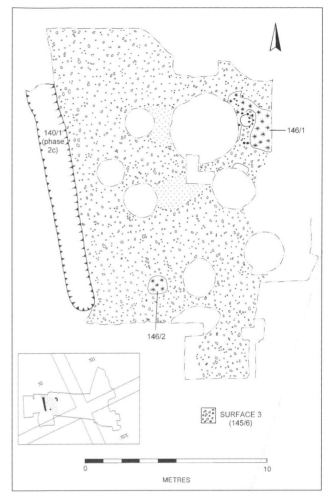

Fig. 15: *Plan of phase 2F*

containing ash or charcoal. These layers may represent rakings from a hearth.

Small Finds: *Brooches* 4 – sf2357, 143/1& 24 – sf2337 (1552), 144/1; *Beads* 63 – sf3008, 144/1 & 74 – sf3010, 144/1; *Metal Hairpin* 56 – sf2356,144/1; *Spindle-whorl* 134 – sf4506, 143/2 ; *Spoon* 135 – sf91, 144/1; *Gaming Counters* 159 – sf89 144/1 & 160 – sf90, 144/1; *Coin* – sf2343, 144/1 (AD 69-79).

Ceramic dating: *AD 70-100*

Stratigraphic dating: *late first – early second century AD+*

Phase 2E (figs. 13 & 14)

Group 147 *Area 1: well (147/1)*

G147 – Well 147/1 was not completely excavated, but augering showed it to be approximately 2.7m deep. It was circular in plan, of surface diameter 1.7m narrowing to 0.95m. Three distinct fills were excavated: the upper backfill resembled surface G145 (phase 2F) which had sealed and slumped into it; the central fill was rich in organic material and included oyster shells, fly puparia and parasites indicating the presence of sewage, and the re-use of the well as a rubbish or cess-pit. The puparia showed evidence of having been deliberately killed during the summer months, indicating that the pit had been open and accumulating rubbish during this season. The well also showed evidence of timber-lining which, although decayed, had left a vertical interface between the central fills of the pit and a narrow vertical deposit (context 1071) around its edges, which may have accumulated whilst the timber lining existed. The well either cut through or was respected by surfaces 2 (phase 2B) and 2a (phase

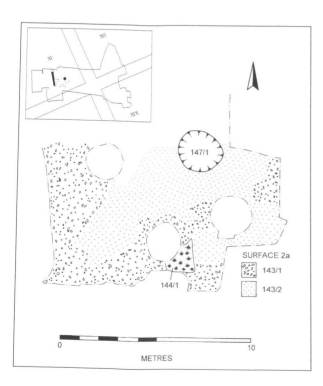

Fig. 14: *Plan of phases 2D and 2E*

Plate 4: *Hearth lined with fragments of amphora, phase 2F*

2D); finds in its fill were contemporary with the latter. The well was sealed by surface 3 (phase 2F).

Small Finds: *Brooch 17 – sf2147, 147/1.*

Ceramic dating: *AD 100-130*

Phase 2F (fig. 15)

Group 145   *Area 1: surface,* **Surface 3** *(145/6), and make-ups (145/1-5)*

Group 146   *Area 1: hearths (146/1-2)*

G145 – Surface 3 – A series of sandy silt and clay make-up layers interspersed by thin lenses of organic and charcoal rich loams (145/1-5; not shown on plan) sealed and slumped into well 147/1 (phase 2E) and gully 133/7 (phase 2A), and patchily covered much of Area 1, yet respected ditch 140/1 (phase 2C) to the west. Make-up layers 145/1 were associated with surface 3, and 145/2-4 are likely to be associated since they were similar in type and level to 145/1. Overlying 145/1 was a compacted gravel layer 145/6 which formed surface 3 and replaced surface 2a (phase 2D). Surface 3 was approximately 0.05-0.1m thick and covered an area 13 by 8m east of ditch 140/1 (phase 2C).

    G146 – Two hearths lay on surface 3. G146/1 occupied a substantial hollow, lined with large fragments of broken amphorae, and surrounded by 16 stake holes (plate 4). Two cuts were identified, suggesting that the hearth had been re-laid at least once. The reddened layers 145/5 beneath the hearth had probably been discoloured by heat from it. Hearth bottom slag and vitrified clay were recovered from both surface 3 and its make-ups 145/6 and 145/3, deriving from either hearth 146/1 or a second, less substantial area of burning, 146/2, whose charcoal unusually contained only a small amount of oak. A little medieval pottery contaminated this subphase.

Small Finds: *Brooch 10 – sf2323, 145/1.*

Ceramic dating: *AD 80-120*

Stratigraphic dating: *early second century AD or later.*

Phase 2G (fig. 16)

Group 148   *Area 1: cultivation or abandonment (148/1-2)*

G148 – Covering much of Area 1 and sealing most of the earlier phases was a group of homogeneous dark yellowish brown and dark greyish brown fine silty clays and sandy silts with few pebbles. These deposits formed a 0.1-0.2m thick layer east of and apparently respecting ditch G140 (phase 2C). The ceramics suggested a date similar to the slumped backfills within the ditch (141/1, phase 3A). Numerous finds were recovered from this subphase, including bloom or billet from nearby iron-working.

Small Finds: *Brooch 21 – sf2263, 148/2; Bead 68 – sf3009, 148/2.*

Ceramic dating: *AD 100-125.*

Stratigraphic dating: *early second century AD or later.*

Phase 2H (fig. 16)

Group 149   *Area 1: timber structure,* **Structure C:** *post pits and post holes (149/3, 149/5), ?wall trenches (149/4), wall or hearth surround (149/1), clay deposits (149/2)*

G149 – Structure C – Several features cut phase 2G layers on the northern edge of Area 1 and may relate to the remains of a timber building. The features included three post pits and a post hole, 149/3. The post pits were 0.7-0.8m in diameter, one of depth 0.4m, the others simply depressions 0.05 and 0.15m deep; the post hole was 0.08m in diameter by 0.06m deep. The shallow depth of some of these features may have resulted from truncation by surface 4 (phase 3A) which was above. West and south of these post pits lay red clay layers,

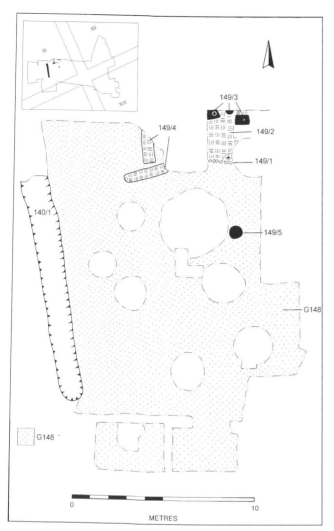

Fig. 16: *Plan of phases 2G and 2H*

Phase 2I (fig. 17)

Group 142 *Area 1: pit (142/1) and post hole (142/1)*

G142 – A pit and a post hole cut through the lower backfills of ditch G140 (140/1, phase 2C). Pit 142/1, towards the southern end of the ditch, was 1.1m by 0.54m and 0.9m deep, backfilled with dark brown clay loam and sandy loam and truncated by a later feature. Post hole 142/1 was 0.37m by 0.35m, but only 0.03m in depth. The location of these features within the ditch is almost certainly coincidental and it is likely that they both post-date its disuse. Slumping of the upper ditch fills, together with later levelling up (141/1, phase 3A), probably destroyed all evidence for the original cut lines.

Small finds: *none*

Ceramic dating: *inconclusive.*

Stratigraphic dating: *late first century AD or later.*

Phase 2J (fig. 18)

Group 172   *Area 1: roadside ditches (172/1-3)*
Groups 178 and 9   *Area 1:Street metalling (178/1, 179/1)*
Groups 173-7, 181-4, 186 *Area 1:Ambiguous features*

The majority of the features (G173-177, 181-4, 186) were ambiguous in shape and function due to the extremely truncated nature of the area, but included possible pits and post holes. Only features G172, 178 & 179 merit comment:

G172 – Possible ditches 172/2 and 172/3 followed similar ENE/WSW orientations and were *c.* 2.0m wide by 0.33m deep, and with a longest uninterrupted run of about 4m. The excavated depth does not reflect the original cut since truncation was so severe in this area. The backfills within the ditches derived mainly from the sands and gravels through which they had been cut, and finds were sparse. At right angles to this ditch was the suggestion of another ditch 172/1, even more severely truncated. Ditch 172/1 was 1.0m deep in places and less than 1.5m wide. Evidence for a continuation of the latter to the NW had been destroyed by intense medieval pitting. Given their similar alignments to ditches in Area 2,

149/4 which could be interpreted as the base of wall trenches. One was N-S orientated, very shallow and measured 3.0 by 1.0m, lying at right angles to the other, which was made up from several layers of clay covering 2.0 by 1.5m. Both features continued beyond the edges of the excavation. To the east and north of these possible wall bases was 149/2, interleaving layers of yellowish brown sand and reddish brown marl over an area at least 2.0 by 1.5m. These layers continued beyond the north edge of the excavation and were truncated to the east and west. Their southern extent was roughly defined by 149/1, a row of loose, rough hewn granite blocks in a layer of compact mixed clay. These were aligned E-W and formed an approximate alignment with the possible E-W wall base to the west (149/1). These granite blocks perhaps formed a surround to a possible hearth situated towards their eastern end; alternatively they derive from a wall. Post pit 149/5 to the south may relate to the same structure. This possible timber building was on a similar alignment to its predecessor, structure B (G133, phase 2A).

Small Finds: *Spur 184 – sf2362, 149/3.*

Ceramic dating: *AD 125-150.*

Stratigraphic dating: *early second century AD or later.*

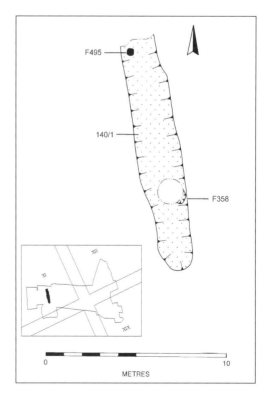

Fig. 17: *Plan of phase 2I*

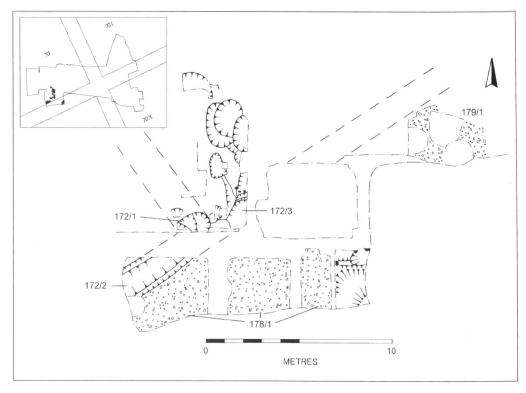

Fig. 18: *Plan of phase 2J*

172/2 and 3 may have served as a roadside ditches, whilst 172/1 may have served a boundary or drainage function.

G178-9 – Two patches of compacted gravel, 178/1 and 179/1 may be remnants of a street surface associated with the above ditches, unless they form a continuation of surfaces 1, 2 or 3 (phases 2A, 2B, & 2F respectively).

Small Finds: *Bead 64 – sf3002 182/1.*

Ceramic dating: *early second century AD.*

Phase 2K (fig. 19)

Group 201	Area 2: cultivation or abandonment
Groups 202 & 204	Area 2: E-W roadside ditches (202/1-4; 204/1-2)
Groups 203 & 212	Area 2: N-S roadside ditches (203/1-2; 212/1-2), post hole (212/3)
Group 205	Area 2: pit (205/1)

G201 – The earliest layers in this phase are grouped together in G201 and covered an isolated triangular area measuring 2.0m by 2.0m and 0.95m thick. Unfortunately this was severely truncated by both a later Roman ditch (G202) and by modern intrusions. The layers were generally thin, and consisted of light to dark yellowish brown sandy silts with occasional lenses of ash and burnt bone. The horizontal nature of the layers suggested that they were a buried/cultivated soil, as supported by the presence in one context of parasite ova from animal dung presumably derived from manuring. The desposits could alternatively point to desertion of this part of the site.

G202 & G204 – Group 201 was truncated to the south by G202, interpreted as the southern ditch of an E-W street. The earliest cut 202/1 was 2.6m wide by 1.2m deep (base OD 57.67m), at least 11.5m long, and filled with light brown silt. Recut 202/3 was 0.6m deep by 2.4m wide. Both cuts featured very degraded sloping sides. Severe truncation, by modern

intrusions and by the foundations of stone structure G210 (phase 3F), obscured the plan of the ditch, although fine brown silty clay layers (G204) formed the remnants of the lower fills continuing east. Alternatively, in common with G201, these layers may represent the base of a buried soil lying in a hollow created either by deliberate terracing or by gravel extraction. The area to the N of G202, where one would expect evidence of street metalling, had been destroyed by 18th century gravel extraction and cellars, and the continuation of the ditch to the west had also been destroyed by cellars.

G203 & G212 – To the west of G202, and isolated from it by later intrusions, were G203 and G212, probable roadside ditches associated with a N-S street. Enough survived of G203 to determine that its approximately N-S orientation was at right angles to ditch G202; pottery suggested an infilling date of mid-late first century AD, thus earlier than the early-mid second century date for G202. Two cuts were identified for this ditch: 203/1 was 2.25m wide, 0.7m deep and filled by layers of yellowish brown sand and loamy sand; the later recut 203/2 east of the original cut was 0.93m wide by 0.47m deep, with steeply sloping sides, and a flat base. Just over 9m to the west was a 2.0m length of very truncated N-S ditch G212. This was over 1.0m deep with gradually sloping sides; its lower fill was a layer of gravel slumped from the sides; subsequent fills were silty with some charcoal. Post hole 212/3 had been cut through its upper fills, but was truncated by subsequent re-cutting of the ditch. Ditch recut 212/2 was just 0.45m deep and filled with a dark yellowish brown silty sand.

G205 – Pit G205, of dimensions 2.2m by 2.02m and 1.37m deep, cut the south end of G203; this had very steep sides breaking to a concave base and was filled with lenses of dark grey loam and yellowish brown silt sands. This pit was badly truncated by F553 (a medieval robber trench) and F538 (an early post-medieval pit).

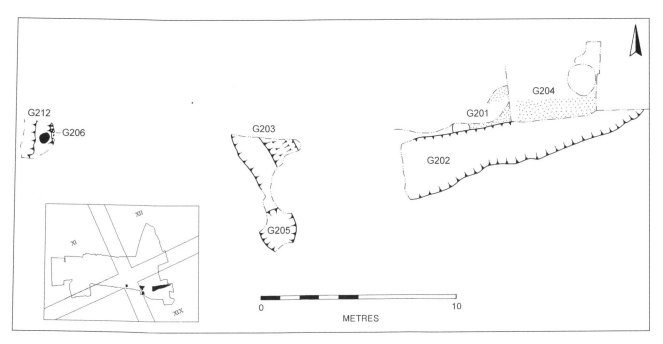

Fig. 19: *Plan of phase 2K*

Small Finds: *Brooches* 3 – sf2003, 201/2, 18 – sf1526, 203/1 & 20 – sf6112, 201/2; *Beads* 65 – sf3004, 201/2 & 66 – sf3005, 201/2; *Spoon* 136 – sf2208, 201/2; *Coins* – sf2002, 201/2 (AD 69-79) & sf2205 (AD 66).

Ceramic dating: G203: *AD 70-100;* G201/G202/204/205: *mid to late second century AD.*

Phase 2L (fig. 13 – section)

Group 332   *Area 3: well (332/1)*

G332 – A circular, vertically sided well was the only Area 3 feature assignable to phase 2. This was 1.25m in diameter and excavated to a depth of 1.8m, although augering indicated a minimum depth of 3.84m (51.6m at its base). Its original depth may have been more than 6m since up to 2.5m of the upper part of the feature had been truncated by 18th century gravel extraction. The well was backfilled with interleaving layers of clean sand and dark greyish green sandy loam; the clay may indicate lining of the well. A tightly dated pottery assemblage together with the homogeneity of the fills suggests the well was backfilled relatively quickly.

Small Finds: *Toilet Spoon* 117 – sf74, 332/1; *Tool Handle Pommel* 188 – sf2282, 332/1.

Ceramic dating: *AD 80-120.*

Discussion of phase 2

Establishment of insulae and plots

Phase 2 sees the first evidence of town planning with the establishment of the orthogonal street grid creating regular *insulae*. Although the site lies at the intersection of two streets, based on projected alignments, evidence for these was particularly fragmentary due to extensive 18th century gravel quarrying. The roadside ditches have been grouped together in phases 2J and 2K, whilst the metalling has been assigned to phase 3G as it is stratigraphically later. The dating evidence would suggest that ditches creating the *insulae* were perhaps laid out in the late first century, and that the metalling followed later, perhaps as the plots were developed.

The evidence for the north-south street line is the most certain, the alignment of the east ditch G203 coinciding with projections of the ditch found on the Little Lane (Shires) site (Lucas and Buckley 1989; Lucas 1990). The dating of the fill is mid to late first century, and the recut may be contemporary with the earliest street metalling G206 of phase 3G. The projected alignment of the east west ditch is rather more problematic as fragments of metalling have only been recorded two *insulae* away to the west, north of the Macellum (LM archive) and to the east at Butt Close Lane (Buckley and Lucas 1987, 36). The latter comprised a sequence of metallings with a *TPQ* of the late third century, post dating the rampart. Although these could represent successive yard surfaces, they do fall within the projected line of the east west street (fig.3). At Causeway Lane, two ditches, G172 (phase 2J) and G202/G204 (phase 2K), may represent the north and south ditches of this street respectively, although this interpretation is questionable on the grounds that the projected width at over 25m is unusual for Leicester and the alignment is not at right angles to the north-south street. A partial explanation may be provided by the fact that the ditches are not contemporary: G172 is of a similar date to the north-south ditch G203, whilst G202/G204 would seem to be rather later in the mid second century. This could suggest that G172 relates to the initial establishment of *insulae*, its pair to the south having been destroyed by later activity. G202/G204 was then perhaps cut when the first metallings were laid, or represents a later element in the street grid to the east of the north-south street. Alternatively, G202/G204 could instead represent a boundary ditch creating a plot division in *insula* XIX. Ditch G140 in *insula* XI almost certainly represents such a boundary: it terminates before reaching the line of the east-west ditch G172, and the phase 2 activity appears to respect it.

In summary, the earliest phase 2 activity probably comprised the laying out of the *insulae* with ditches, followed by the development of plots including subdivision with one or more boundary ditches.

Insula XI (Area 1)

The earliest development of *insula* XI (Area 1) in the late first to early second century comprised a gravel yard surface, surface 1, possibly associated with an insubstantial timber building, structure B (G133) perhaps with mud walls. The north-south boundary ditch G140, of substantial dimensions, was apparently respected by the timber structure reinforcing the idea that it represents an early plot boundary. An alternative interpretation of G133 is that it is a timber drain, the sides formed by planks laid on edge, and supported by stakes. Structures of this type are known from London and elsewhere (Wilmott 1991, 30). If this theory is correct, G133 could perhaps have drained into the boundary ditch G140. The latter was aligned to the south with a severely truncated ditch on the St. Peter's Lane (Shires) excavation (F95; archive). This was possibly backfilled as early as the first century AD. The alignments are perhaps most likely to be coincidental, but if not, would seem to suggest that the ditch was a significant boundary within the townscape.

Surface 1 was repaired on a number of occasions before the yard was completely resurfaced, surface 2, respecting the boundary ditch but sealing the early timber building, suggesting that the latter was comparatively short-lived. The large quantities of unabraded pottery and other finds within the make-ups for surface 2 suggest that the soil was a mixture of rubbish and land clearance imported onto the site. Isolated patches of burning (G143) including a vitrified brick or tile possibly from a furnace (Morgan, below p.307), and a deep timber-lined well G147 (phase 2E), subsequently re-used as a cess pit, were associated with surface 2. The well perhaps indicates backyard activity relating to a structure lying to the north, beyond the limits of the excavation and was one of only two found to have been backfilled during this phase, the second being in *insula* XII (Area 3, phase 2L). The relatively large quantity of metal slag associated with partial resurfacing of the yard (surface 2a) implies nearby metal working and may even be linked to the presence of burnt areas on the yard surface. No hearths or other features could be directly linked to metal working, however, and the slag may have been imported by chance.

Final resurfacing, surface 3, sealed the backfilled well G147 and may have been contemporary with a recut of the north-south boundary ditch. Two hearths were associated with this surface, one of which was lined with fragments of amphora (plate 4).

There then appears to have been a hiatus with the last yard surface being sealed by substantial deposits of fine silty clays and sandy silts probably imported as another make-up deposit, as garden soil, or perhaps as a general rubbish dump which was subsequently levelled. This deposit was associated with another timber structure, structure C (G149, phase 2H), in a similar position to structure B (G133) and on a similar alignment, suggesting that the divison of the plot into backyard areas and building areas persisted. Both the timber building and possible make-up or cultivation deposits are dated no later than the early second century by the finds. This would suggest a period of extremely rapid change and intense activity, since well G147 and surface 2a also went out of use in the early second century.

Subsequently, the ditch seems to have been backfilled with soft, possibly organic materials since several episodes of slumping and attempts to consolidate and resurface the ditch were identified in phases 2 and 3.

The overwhelming impression in this *insula* is of quite intensive backyard activity in a plot defined by a major boundary ditch. Although little structural evidence was found, the presence of quantities of tile may suggest more substantial structures to the north, beyond the limits of excavation.

Insula XII (Area 3)

Evidence of domestic activity within this *insula* was provided by a clay-lined well G332 of at least 6.0m depth, with finds signifying that backfilling probably occurred as a single phase in the early to mid second century. Unfortunately late third century truncation had destroyed all other earlier deposits, thus obscuring the significance of this activity although much residual second – and third century material occurred in phases 5 and 6 which is suggestive either of continued occupation or of imported rubbish deposits.

Insula XIX (Area 2)

As discussed above, G202/G204 either represent a roadside ditch or a boundary division in this *insula*. If the latter, it would create rather a narrow plot on the basis of the projected alignment of the east-west street. This need not be too much of a problem as some strip buildings at Silchester were as little as 6m wide, although more often 9m (Rivet 1964, 87; fig.6).

Other activity in this *insula* in this period is lacking, although a review of the evidence since the site was phased suggests that timber structure A (G208, phase 1C) is perhaps more likely to be contemporary with the establishment of *insulae* and should be assigned to this period.

PHASE 3 mid second to early third century AD

In Area 1, disuse of ditch G140 and further yard surfaces associated with deep pits and hearths. Buildings in timber and stone in Area 2. No evidence of activity in Area 3.

Phase 3A (figs. 13 & 20)

Group 141   *Area 1: backfill of phase 2C ditch G140 (141/1)*
Group 142   *Area 1: pit (142/2) and post hole (142/3)*

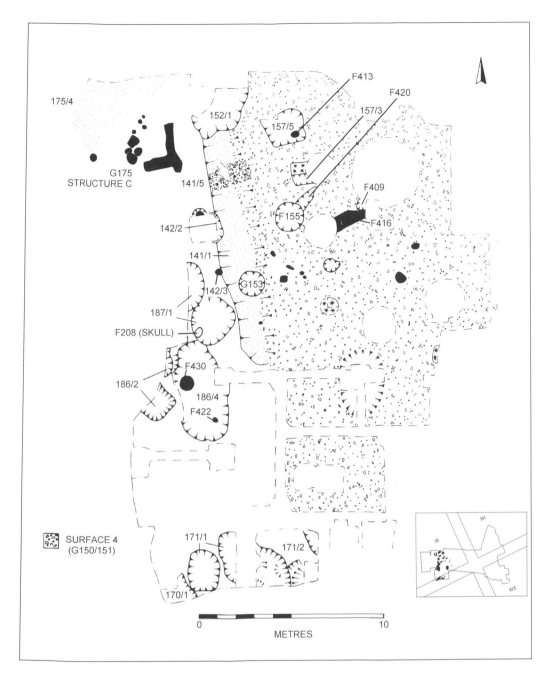

Fig. 20: *Plan of phases 3A, 3B, 3C, 3D*

G141/1 – The phase 2C ditch G140 was backfilled and levelled with mid to dark brown sandy loams, 141/1 (not on plan). Significant quantities of horn cores were found within the backfills, and subsequently in phase 3B, suggesting a nearby tannery.

G142 – Cutting these backfills were a pit and post hole. Pit 142/2 was sub-circular, 1.0m in diameter and at least 0.8m deep; finds included numerous pottery sherds and animal bones. Post hole 142/3 was 0.22m in diameter by 0.22m deep and filled with a mixed yellowish brown sandy silt. Subsequent slumping of the ditch fills caused severe truncation of both these features.

Small Finds: *Brooch* 7 – sf2118, 141/1; *Armlet* 95 – sf2194, 141/1; *Finger Ring* 101 – sf2221, 141/1; *Bead* 84 – sf2198, 141/1.

Ceramic dating: *AD 125-150.*

Phase 3B (figs. 13, 20 & 21)

Groups 150-1	*Area 1: surface,* **surface 4** *(150/1; 151/1)*
Group 141	*Area 1: consolidation of ditch G140 and construction of causeway (141/2-5)*
Groups 152-3 & 155	*Area 1: Pits and wells (152/1;153;155)*
Groups 154&156	*Area 1: ambiguous features associated with G150-1: ?occupation (G154); post holes (G156: F413); pit (G156: F409); linear feature (G156: F416);*
Group 157	*Area 1: post holes (G157); ?hearths (157/3); pit (157/5)*
Group 170	*Area 1: pit (F393)*

***G150-1* – Surface 4** – A thick deposit of mixed loam and clay formed the make-up for a very compacted gravel surface G150 & 151, dressed with fine compacted gravel of thickness

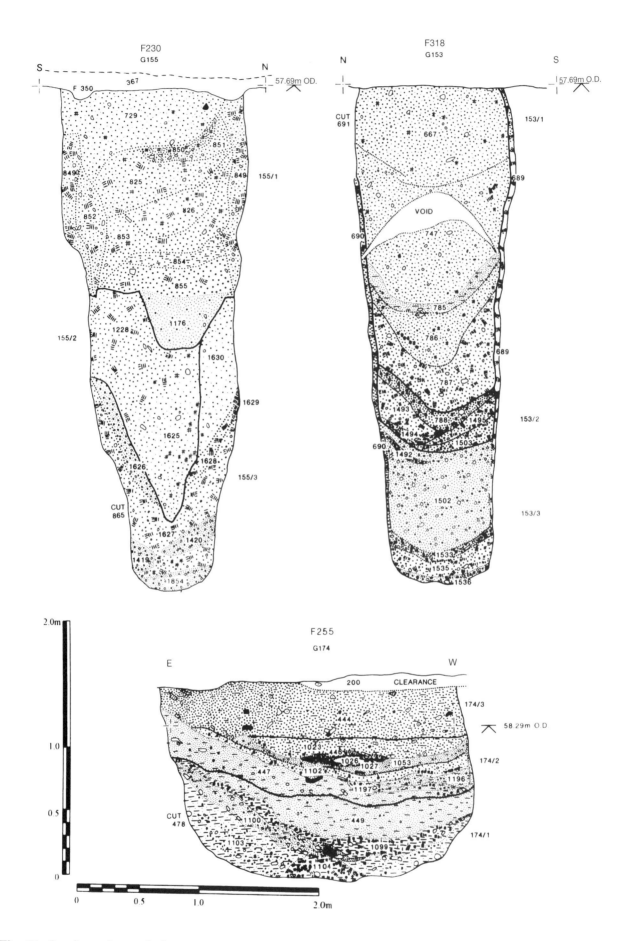

Fig. 21: *Sections through G153 (phase 3B), G155 (phase 3B) and G174 (phase 4A)*

0.15m-0.25m. Gravel patches in the surface may represent repairs.

G141/2 – The gravel 141/2 covering the soft ground of the phase 2C ditch (G140; & backfills 141/1of phase 3A) had slumped into it, with subsequent levelling by layers of sandy silts, 141/3. The deeper hollows were consolidated by 141/4, layers of sandy loam containing numerous pebbles, which created level ground merging with surface 4. Additional slumping towards the north end of the ditch created a hollow of 1.5m, which was filled with frequent pebbles held in a clay bed. This compacted surface may have formed a solid causeway over soft ground.

G152-3 – Cutting through the fills of ditch G140 at its northern end was a large 3.0m diameter sub-circular pit 152/1 of at least 2.0m depth (not fully excavated), with sloping sides towards the top, but almost vertical from 1.0m depth. The pit was lined with clay derived from the natural Mercia mudstone. It was backfilled with very loose sandy loam, some of which was olive green in colour and 'cessy' in nature; indeed, fly puparia from one of the lower excavated fills was consistent with the disposal of sewage. A second circular well G153, 1.34m in diameter and 3.96m deep, showed signs of timber lining where it cut through sands and gravels; the lower Mercia mudstone is more stable and needs little support. The upper fills, 153/1, were homogeneous yellowish brown silty sands and sandy loams suggestive of slumped layers or levelling rather than rubbish deposits. The underlying 153/2 comprised a sequence of organic layers interleaved with relatively clean red brown clays, perhaps suggesting disposal of rubbish deposits capped off by clean soil. The lower fills, 153/3, may be primary well deposits: these were not waterlogged but were intermingled with slumped sands and gravels and evidence of collapsed timber lining. This suggests that the well had been abandoned for some time before it was used as a convenient rubbish dump. The well was cut through the levelling fills of ditch G140 and must therefore post date these.

G155 – A third circular well was 4.0m deep, of diameter 1.46m, narrowing to just 0.7m at its base; traces of timber lining were also evident here. The uppermost layers, 155/1, appeared to be slump and levelling layers; these covered a thick deposit (155/2) containing evidence of sewage and suggesting the well formed a cess-pit as a secondary function. Slumped sands and gravels mixed with a clean brown clay formed the primary fills 155/3, although fly puparia in context 1627 reveal that sewage leached down from above.

G170 – The fourth pit to be associated with surface 4 was G170 (not shown on plan). It is placed in this category by virtue of the fact that a fragment of glass from the pit joined with one from G153. The pit had a maximum diameter of 2m, but severe truncation from above left only 0.4m of its depth remaining. It was backfilled with layers of sandy silt, some of which appeared to have been contaminated by sewage. Pottery was concentrated in the uppermost slumped contexts of these wells and may represent deliberate filling or masking of lower sewage deposits.

G156 – Other ambiguous features cutting surface 4 comprised a shallow pit, F409, post hole F413, and a NE-SW oriented linear feature, F416. All had suffered some truncation, and finds helped little in clarifying their original function. They may be related to surface 4, since they cut it and were overlain by 154/2 layers thought to represent a repair to the surface.

G154 – Overlying and infilling hollows within surface 4 were spreads, layers and deposits often showing signs of burning, G154 (not on plan). These are likely to be deposits caused by human activity on surface 4. The burnt patches, whilst not true hearths, could represent areas where a single fire had been lit; some patches appeared somewhat inorganic and could denote repairs to the surface.

G157 – In the centre and towards the northern part of the area and cutting through G154 was a group of small features, mainly post holes, which appeared to rest on or in surface 4. A small area of burning, F357, lay c. 5.0m north of post holes G157 and adjacent to a shallow linear cut 157/3; a shallow square pit, 157/5, of 2.2 by 1.5m by 0.3m deep was located further north. No clear structural purpose could be ascertained for these elements.

Small Finds: *Brooches* 5 – sf2201, 151/1; 8 – sf2099, 153/1; 13 – sf2148, 154/1; 15 – sf2116, 141/3; 29 – sf2169, 154/1; *Hairpins* 41 – sf58, 152/1; 51 – sf46 & 69- 141/4; 59 – sf 2162, 155/1; *Beads* 61 – sf3012, 151/1 & 76 – sf3017, 153/1; *Armlet* 94 – sf2199, 152/1; *Intaglio* 105 – sf3003, 150/1; *Toilet Implements* 110 – sf2207, 141/3, 112 – sf1792, 153/2; *Spoon Probe* 120 – sf2152, 141/4; 122 – sf2176, 157/5 ; *Spoon* 138 – sf2188, 151/1; *Candleholder* 146 – sf2200, 156/1; Box Fittings 153 – sf2209, 141/5; *Gaming Counters* 158 – sf56, 150/1; 176 – sf4511, 154/1; Hone 191 – sf4566, 141/4; *Loop Headed Pin* 194 – sf2192, 154/1; *Coins:* sf2325, 153/3, 1717- 1724, sf2187, 154/1 (AD 98-117), sf 2101, 154/3 (1st C – AD 235), sf2170, 157/5 (AD 98-117).

Ceramic dating: *mid second to early third century AD.*

Phase 3C (fig. 20)

Groups 171 & 186   Area 1: Poorly stratified pits and post holes (171/1-2; 186/2; 186/4)

Group 175   Area 1: ?timber structure, **structure D**: gully (175/1); post holes (175/2-3); make-up (175/4)

G171 & 186 – Various other features, generally poorly stratified, are assigned to Phase 3 on the basis of pottery dating, although certain features, particularly within G171, were stratigraphically earlier than features in G170 (phase 3B). The latter consisted of cut features in the south-west corner of Area 1 of varied form, but each with backfills of slumped gravel derived from the surrounding natural. Approximately 5m to the north of this group of pits was a second group of intercutting features 186/2, 186/4; these were shallow, rectilinear and slightly irregular, likewise with backfill layers of naturally derived sands and gravels. Both groups of pits were effectively isolated from other areas of the site by severe truncation.

G175 – Structure D – Other poorly stratified features assigned to this subphase by their pottery include a group possibly relating to a timber structure located in the north west of Area 1. These features were physically close to one another and included an L-shaped gully, 175/1, approximately 2.0m long E-W by 2.5m N-S by 0.55m wide and 0.15m deep. The post holes 175/2-3 lay directly west of this gully on a N-S line. To the west was a badly preserved irregular, c. 3.0m by 3.0m area of dark to yellowish brown spreads, 175/4, which may have been make-ups for a surface. Since levels are consistent, these layers potentially represent an extension to make-ups on the east side of the phase 2C ditch G140 for surface 2 of phase 3B.

Small Finds: *Brooch* 1 – sf2273, 175/4; *Toilet Spoon* 116 – sf2300, 186/4; *Needle* 125 – sf45, 186/2; *Box Fitting* 154) Sf2340 186/4; *Gaming Counter* 166 – sf57 186/4; Spur 186 – sf1488, 186/2.

Ceramic dating: *mid to late second century AD.*

Phase 3D (fig. 20)

Groups 183 & 187   *Area 1: Post holes and pits (183/3:F422 &*
F430; 187/1)

G183 & 187 – Stratigraphically later than phases 3B and 3C, these features were dated by their Roman pottery assemblage, although a small amount of medieval pottery contaminated some of the upper layers. They comprised two large pits, 187/1 which had been partly excavated in 1980 (causing some difficulties in correlating the fills) and two post holes, F422 and F430. The pits had a similar range of backfills, comprising varied silty sands with some charcoal, and both were deep and broad (2.5m in diameter – larger than other phase 3 pits). The pits largely cut through natural sands and gravels and not the loose backfill of other features. Part of a human skull (Wakely, below, p.00) came from the top fill of the northernmost pit; this was damaged, suggesting re-deposition from elsewhere.

Small Finds: *Brooch* 16 – sf1461, 187/1; *Hairpins* 38 – sf9, 187/1; 39 – sf10, 187/1 & 55 – sf 2016, 187/1; *Gaming Counters* 168 – sf117, 187/1 & 177 – 187/1; *Hone* 190 – sf4556, 187/1; *Coin* sf2100, 187/1 (AD 193-211).

Ceramic dating: *mid to late second century AD.*

Phase 3E (fig. 22)

Groups 209 & 220   *Area 2: timber structure, **structure E:***
beam slots (209/4-6); post holes
(209/3); stake holes (220/1); pits (209/1-2)

G209 – Structure E – Cutting through the upper fills of E-W roadside ditch G202 of phase 2K were a possible beam slot 209/4 of 1.4m length and three post holes, 209/3. Slot 209/6, 5m long, lay 2m south of and parallel with 209/4; a further slot 209/5 of just 0.4m length lay south of 209/6 and at right angles to it. The beam slots were all 0.2m wide by 0.09m, 0.2m and 0.23m deep respectively, all with steep sides, sharp edges and flat bases; their fills were silty sand ranging in colour from dark to yellowish brown, probably derived from the layers through which they were cut. Three stake holes, 220/1, lay close to the

north wall of stone structure G210 of phase 3F, forming a slight curve but aligned with 209/4. In addition, two small pits, 209/1 and 209/2 (not on plan), may be associated with these structural features. Overall, these features probably represent a timber structure, certain elements of which stratigraphically predate stone structure G210 (phase 3F); although they could alternatively represent internal partitions within it. Finds from the fills of ditch G202 (phase 2K) provide a *TPQ* of the early – mid second century for structure E. The few finds from the structural features themselves are of a late first century date, offering no clarification of the dating.

Small finds: *none*

Ceramic dating: *undiagnostic late first century AD assemblage.*

Stratigraphic dating: *early – mid second century AD or later.*

Phase 3F (fig. 22)

Group 210   *Area 2: Stone structure, **structure F**: external*
walls (210/1) internal walls (210/2-3)
Group 211   *Area 2: Stone structure, **structure G**: wall*
(211/1: F660); gravel surface: (211/2)

G210 – Structure F – On the same alignment as the phase 3E beam slots were two groups of foundation trenches for stone walls, almost entirely robbed out, probably in the 12th century (Phase 9). A north external wall, two further possible external walls to the west and south, 210/1, and three probable internal walls, 210/2, form structure G210. The north wall was 14m long, 1.0m deep and 0.8m wide, making it the largest of the foundation trenches. Up to three courses of Dane Hills sandstone rubble and large granite blocks in a matrix of yellow sandy gravel survived as footings in the trench base (Plate 14). The western end of the wall was truncated by a Victorian cellar, but an area of robbing west of the cellar indicated that the wall continued for a further 7m west before returning south, the latter represented solely by a 2m length of robbing. The south wall was completely robbed and severely truncated. Accepting these three walls as external, the dimensions of the E-W orientated building

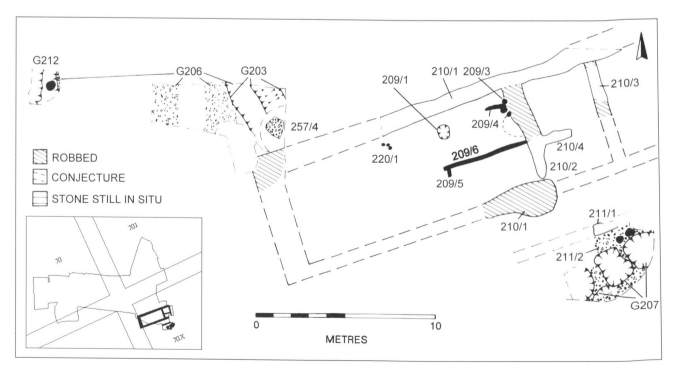

Fig. 22: *Plan of phases 3E, 3F and 3G*

Plate 5: *Section showing the foundations of structure F (G210), phase 3F*

would have been 5m wide by at least 20m long, with clear indications that the north wall continued further east, beyond the limits of excavation. Internal divisions creating rooms of 5m by 13m, 3m square and 3m by 2m can be reconstructed: partitions 210/2-3 had been partially robbed, but both preserved sections of stone footings. An earliest construction date in the mid second century can be offered, since the north wall cut ditch fills containing pottery of this date.

G211 – Structure G – The extant section of the stone footings of wall 211/1 2.0m long and 0.55m wide, located parallel with and 8.0m south of 210/1 (north wall) may denote a corridor to structure F or part of a second building. Immediately south of 211/1 was a fragment of compacted gravel surface (or make-up) 211/2; it was impossible to determine whether this was an internal or external surface, although the presence of pits cutting through the surface in phase 3G suggest it was external. The ceramic assemblage from the foundation trench implies construction no earlier than the late second or early third century AD, and thus contemporary with or slightly later than structure F.

Small finds: none

Ceramic dating: mid to late second century AD

Stratigraphic dating: mid second century AD or later

Phase 3G (fig. 22)

Group 206   *Area 2: street metalling (206/1-3)*
Group 207   *Area 2: metalling (207/5-6) and pits: (207/1-4)*

G206 – There was fragmentary evidence to the west of G203 (phase 2K) of street metalling comprising a layer less than 0.1m thick of compacted cobbles in a matrix of yellowish brown sand. The layers had been severely truncated from above and on all sides. The natural gravels on which these deposits lay showed a distinct convex curve reminiscent of the *agger* of a Roman road. Additionally, a large fragment of consolidated metalling 257/4 (phase 9) found in a medieval

pit cutting through G206 indicates several remetallings of the street, for which all *in situ* evidence had been destroyed by later activity. The fragments of metalling 206/1-2 partially overlay the initial cut, 203/1 of north-south ditch G203 and are perhaps contemporary with the recut, 203/2 just to the east.

G207 – Immediately south of structure G (phase 3F), and cutting gravel surface 211/2, was a sub-rectangular pit 207/1, measuring 2.06m by 1.6m, and 1.1m deep. Sealing the pit and spreading over the earlier gravel surface were layers of metalling, 207/5, cut by three further sub-rectangular pits, 207/2-4. The latter contained a mid third to fourth century pottery assemblage, suggesting that structures F/G continued in use at least until this date. The pits were similar in shape to 207/1 but slightly smaller. All had similar fills, appearing to have been rapidly backfilled with a variety of rubbish including quantities of building materials and animal bone. The pits were sealed by 207/6, another layer of metalling, containing fourth century ceramics, which lay directly below medieval garden soil; accordingly any later layers may have been truncated.

Small Finds: Flint 218 – sf7022, 207/5.

Ceramic dating: mid second century, but resurfacing of yard – early fourth century AD.

Discussion of phase 3

Streets

Fragmentary evidence of the earliest metalling of the north-south street, comprising compacted gravel on a slightly convex surface, survived in Area 2 and sealed the backfill of the earliest roadside ditch G203, phase 2K.

This adds weight to the idea that the streets were not themselves metalled until development of the *insulae* themselves was in progress. The recut of the roadside ditch is perhaps contemporary with the first street metalling. That there were several resurfacings of this street is shown by a substantial chunk of consolidated gravel metalling 0.5m thick which had fallen into a medieval pit (phase 9). All but the earliest *in situ* metalling had been destroyed by later truncation.

Insula XI (area 1)

In this area, activity remained of a similar character to that in the previous phase with the yard continuing in use and being resurfaced once again (surface 4), but no longer respecting the possible phase 2C plot boundary ditch G140. The latter had probably been backfilled by the time surface 4 was laid, but was clearly unconsolidated and may have contained a lot of organic matter since it suffered from at least three major slumping episodes whilst yard surface 4 was in use. The construction of the yard surface over the ditch, together with the possible disposal of waste from a nearby tannery, probably contributed to this settling and compaction. Several pits were cut through the presumed metalling, G178-9 of phase 2J on the line of the east-west street. As discussed above, this could either represent a yard surface or street metalling. If the latter, it may suggest a level of encroachment in this phase, but could alternatively be much later.

In use at the same time as surface 4, although cutting it, were pits and wells suggesting reasonably intensive backyard activity perhaps associated with buildings lying beyond the excavation to the north. Pits G153 and G155 (phase 3B) were particularly deep and regular, as well as lined, and perhaps served as wells, later as convenient rubbish and sewage dumps. As deeper pits have been found elsewhere in Leicester (Lucas and Buckley, forthcoming), the Causeway Lane pits may have been groundwater- rather than watertable-wells, unless the watertable was somewhat higher in this area at this time. Whilst no waterlogged material was recovered from these pits, this could be due to later changes in the water table rather than reflecting the contemporary environment. The pits dug and backfilled in phase 3D contained pottery in the late second to mid-third century date range implying their disuse and that of surface 4 in phase 5.

Finally, limited structural evidence was found in this phase, comprising post holes, an L-shaped gully (structure C), hearths and areas of burning associated with surface 4, suggesting continuing backyard activity such as fences, flimsy sheds and external fires.

Insula XIX (area 2)

In contrast to the backyard activity in Area 1, Area 2 offered evidence for street frontage buildings. A timber building, structure E, may have been constructed following the backfilling of the earlier plot boundary ditch in the early to mid second century. Together with a group of possibly associated rubbish pits, it appears to be stratigraphically earlier than the stone building, structure F (phase 3F) matching typical sequences elsewhere in Leicester. However, given the fragmentary nature of the evidence, the similarity in alignment with the stone building on the same site, and the possibility that the rubbish pits are not associated, the timber structures could alternatively represent internal partitions in the stone building.

The stone building, structure F, was constructed at the north-west corner of *insula* XIX after the east-west ditch G202 had been backfilled. That the builders were aware of the soft fill of the ditch is shown by the deeper foundation trench for the north wall. The building was largely robbed out by 12th century quarrying, but an imprint remained to show a long, narrow east-west oriented form with some stone divisions and – depending on the interpretation of structure E – possible internal timber partitions. It is worth noting that a short length of beam slot, with evidence for subrectangular posts in its base, was excavated 0.60m to the north of structure F, but on a slightly different alignment. In view of the presence of some medieval pottery in its fills, this has been assigned to the medieval period (phase 9, 263/1) although the material could be intrusive. If so, it is conceivable that it instead represents evidence for a timber verandah on the long side of structure F, fronting the east-west street. It is debatable whether structure G formed a southern extension or corridor to structure F or a separate building. Its construction can be set to the early third century, and as structure F must have been built after the first half of the second century, the two may have been contemporary.

A succession of pits just south of structure G and cutting through the gravel surface show this as an external yard surface. The pits were backfilled in the mid-third to fourth century, suggesting that the stone building was occupied during this period. There were few environmental indicators of general rubbish deposition, and none to indicate sewage. Resurfacing over the backfilled pits suggests that they were not open for any great length of time. Unfortunately few rubbish deposits and no wells or cesspits were found directly associated with the stone building, although phase 3, 4 and 5 deposits in Area 1 were probably contemporary with it.

Insula XII (area 3)

Although no deposits were specifically allocated to phase 3, the phase 5E layers 361/1 may in fact belong to this time, since these layers had been cut by phase 5 gravel extraction pits, and pottery from this group may be as early as the mid second century. This date better fits the phase 3 deposits and would suggest phase 2 occupation continued in this part of the *insula* at least until the middle of the second century and possibly later. This also raises the possibility that the gravel extraction of phase 5 commenced in this area from the late second or third centuries. Since the quarry pits can only be dated by their backfilling – to the early fourth century – they are discussed under phase 5 (below pp.44-6).

PHASE 4 early to mid third century AD

The Phase 4 features were, with one exception, severely truncated and undiagnostic; they continue the general trend of 'backyard' activity for Area 1.

Phase 4A (figs. 21 & 23)

Group 174   *Area 1: pits:* (G174: F255)
Group 183   *Area 1: ambiguous features:* (183/1: F239, F260, F311, F331, F336, F378, F399)

G174 – Rubbish pit F255 was of oval form, *c.* 4.0m by 2.5m, of depth 1.5m. Three stages of backfilling were identified, the earliest 174/1 a mix of dark brown sandy loams and re-deposited gravel derived from the surrounding natural. Few finds were recovered from this subgroup, although charcoal and some mortar were present. The second stage backfill layers, 174/2, consisted of more silty and sandy loams with occasional lenses of re-deposited natural; these contained much charcoal, mortar, oyster shell and charred plant remains. Some burning was also evident on the pottery. This evidence suggested that rubbish was burnt either in the pit or nearby and then deposited into the pit. The latest fills, 174/3, were cleaner dark brown sandy loams with little evidence for burning, but contained an unusually large amount of mortar for this area of the site.

G183 – Features in this group were assigned to Phase 4 on pottery content and because they were stratigraphically later than phase 3C. They were located in the south-west corner of the site, cutting through the possible E-W street metalling of phase 2J. Only F239 and F331 were not truncated by modern intrusions: these were small circular shallow features 0.4m and 0.6m in diameter and less than 0.2m deep. F311, however, had a depth of 1.08m and was probably sub-rectangular in plan; it was backfilled with many thin layers and lenses of yellowish brown sandy loam, and a darker grey silt of more organic content. Remaining features in the group were all under 0.2m deep.

Small Finds: Bone Hairpins 31 – sf44, 174/2; 32 – sf 62, 174/3; 50 – sf 40, 174/3; *Beads* 77 – sf3006, 174/2; 83 – sf5040, 174/2; *Armlet* 88 – sf5019, 174/2; *Candleholder* 148 – sf2181,

183/1; *Bone Gaming Counter or Inlay* 167 – sf64, 174/2; *Spur* 187 – sf6314, 174/2; *Figurine* 211 – sf4502, 174/2; *Coin* sf2143, 174/2 (AD 140-144).

Ceramic dating: early to mid third century AD.

PHASE 5
late second to mid/late fourth century AD

A timber structure, well and resurfacing of yard in Area 1. Gravel extraction in Area 3 commencing between the mid- and late third century.

Phase 5A (figs. 5 & 24; plate 6)

Group 158   *Area 1: surface,* **surface 5** (158/1-4)
Groups 160-1   *Area 1: timber building,* **structure H**: post holes (159/1: F383, F385; 160/1: F432, F464, F468, F480; 160/2: F496; 160/4: F294, F295); post-pad (160/5: F301); ?walls (160/2: F439-40); ?drain (160/3: F460; 160/4: F463, F470).
Group 161   *Area 1: layers* (161/1-3)

G158 – Surface 5 – The make-up 158/1-4 for surface 5 was 0.35m thick and consisted of small cobbles in a brown clay loam matrix, interleaved with a compact pinkish clay. This was surfaced with cobbles (158/5) of size 0.02-0.04m. Mixed with these was a soft brown loam and some tile and limestone fragments. This latest gravel surface was the most highly compacted and best made of any the surfaces encountered on the site. Its full extent is unknown as it continued beyond the excavation to the north.

G160-1 – Structure H – A number of features were associated with surface G158 which may be evidence for fencing or possibly for a timber building: post holes in groups 159/1 and 160/1-2; post pad F301; walls? F439 and F440; drain? F460, F463 and F470; and layers 161/1-3. The post holes all cut surface 1. F432 and F464 had post pipes at 0.3m diameter by 0.57m deep and 0.25m diameter by 0.64m deep respectively; around the top of both post pipes was a 0.7m

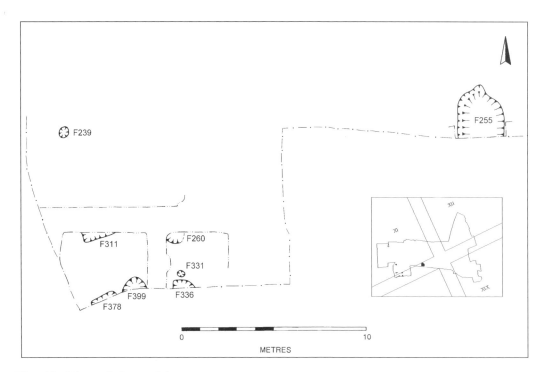

Fig. 23: *Plan of phase 4A*

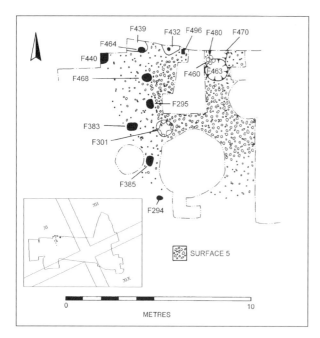

Fig. 24: *Plan of phase 5A*

diameter by 0.3m deep cut packed with undressed angular fragments of granite. Both post pipes had vertical sides and a flat base. F468 and F480 were shallower, perhaps from truncation; F468 had much charcoal suggesting remnants of a burnt post, whereas F480 was packed with stone, suggesting a solid base for a post. F496 was smaller at 0.19m in diameter by 0.16m deep, but was also packed with small stones. F294 and F295 were less than 0.13m deep with diameters of 0.35m and 0.5m. A circular setting of stone, F301, almost 1.0m in diameter, acted either as a post pad or as a hearth (although no

signs of heat were identified). Two areas of random rubble mixed with decayed mortar, F439, F440, were possibly wall footings or demolished walls: both were very shallow at 0.05m and 0.15m. A N-S alignment is suggested for this structure (see F464, F468, F294, F295, F385) in conjunction with an E-W alignment (F440, F439, F464, F432, F496).

F463 was a circular pit 1.2m diameter by 0.5m deep, whose sandy silt fills contained animal bone, abundant faecal material and some building materials. It was closely associated with F470, a gully 1.1m wide by 0.4m deep apparently leading into the pit. The fills closely resembled those in the pit (although the gully contained more building debris) and appeared to have been deposited at the same time. As the gully base sloped down towards the pit it perhaps functioned as a drain, with the pit as a sump. Lying over the edge of both gully and pit was F460, a group of four un-perforated slates laid flat in a square 0.66m by 0.61m, perhaps a drain cover. This possible drain may be associated with structure G160.

G161- Several layers of soft mixed sandy loams and sandy silts patchily covered surface G158. None had a relationship with the structural elements of structure G160 although 161/3 predated post hole 160/4.

Small Finds: *Brooch* 2 – sf2119, 158/5; *Bone Hairpin* 33 – sf84, 161/1; *Shale Bowl fragments* 142 – sf5010, 161/1; 143 – sf5011, 161/1; 145 – sf5032, 161/3; *Gaming Counters* 156 – sf3014, 160/4; 164 – sf20, 161/1; *Scabbard Fitting* 210 – sf2341, 161/1; *Coins* sf2327, 160/4; sf 2105, 160/5 (AD 98-117).

Ceramic dating: *late second to early third century AD.*

Phase 5B (fig. 25)

Group 162   *Area 1: spreads*
Group 163   *Area 1: timber building,* **structure I***: post holes (163/1-5: F282, F287, F289, F293, F296, F300, F308-9, F312, F314, F317, F332, F344, F350)*

Plate 6: *Structure H post hole showing packing, phase 5A*

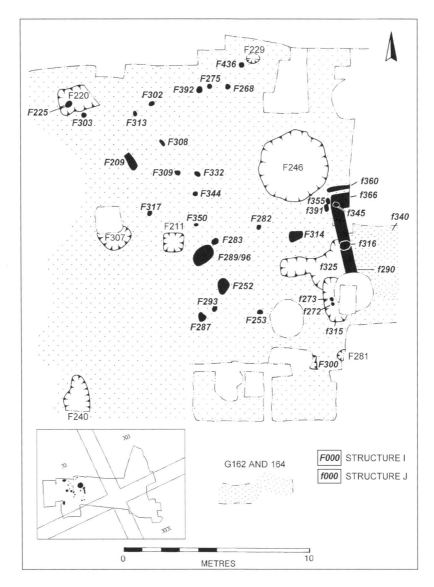

Fig. 25: *Plan of phases 5B, 5C and 5D*

Group 167 *Area 1: pits associated with G163:* (167/1: F307; 167/2: F211)

Group 165 *Area 1: structure J:* (165/1-2: F315, F325)

G162 – Sealing layers and features in phase 3B, but stratigraphically and physically unrelated to phase 5A, was a group of largely homogeneous mid brown sandy loam layers (not on plan). These were *c.* 0.2m thick with some pebbles and patches of pinkish clay scattered throughout, and yielding large amounts of pottery. The pottery showed little abrasion and residuality was also high suggesting that the layers may have been imported as make-up for the timber building G163. Pottery links with the make-up for surface G145 of phase 2F indicates that the soil for made ground was derived from the same source. Two near complete pots were recovered from these layers, including a re-used late second century jar which contained a cremation. The layers sealed surface G150-1 (phase 3B) and may also post-date surface G158, phase 5A, whilst not physically overlying it.

G163 – Structure I – Cutting through these make-ups were fourteen post holes (163/1-5), all truncated from above, and none deeper than 0.13m, and most of 0.15-0.4m diameter. Whilst F350 had been packed with a large granite stone, the others contained only pebbles in their backfills, although

several post holes also held quantities of charcoal. Many of the post holes formed a rough NW-SE orientation over a distance of 10m: although irregularly spaced, these posts were never more than 2.0m apart. They may have performed a structural function with post holes in phase 5C.

G167 – Two pits were located east of Structure G163, F307 was sub-rectangular, 1.33m by 1.0m by 1.2m deep, backfilled with yellowish brown sandy loams, and truncated by a concrete pile; pit F211 lay closer to the structure, was square in plan (1.18m by 1.08m) but just 0.15m deep, and contained a dark brown sandy loam, a reddish brown clay and few finds.

G165 – Structure J - At the eastern edge of Area 1 and suffering severe truncation were F315 and F325. F315 was a sub-rectangular cut 2.4m by 0.8m by 0.41m deep filled with a yellowish brown sandy loam containing moderate amounts of charcoal and ash. The cut was approximately N-S oriented and at the north merged into F325, an E-W linear feature, which bulged out and became more ambiguous at its east end; this was 2.93m by 1.0m by 0.19m deep. Together, the two features appear to form a corner. Located in the top of F325 a group of stones and broken tiles formed a linear curve, probably partially truncated. These features may be associated with G165, phase 5C.

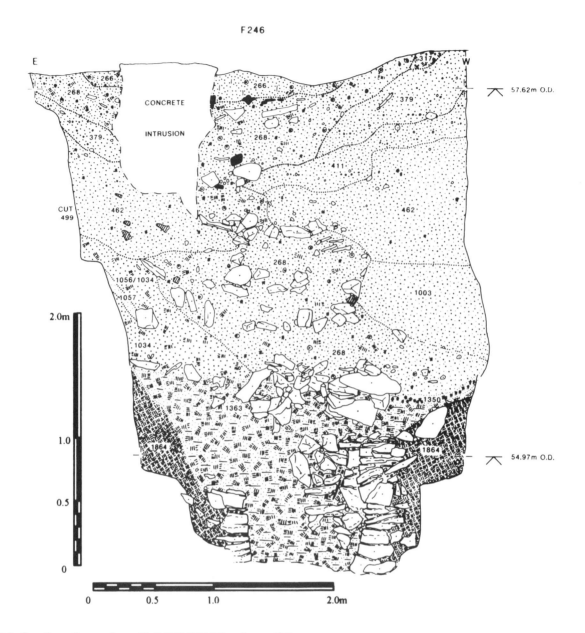

F 246

2.0m

1.0

0.5

0

0 0.5 1.0 2.0m

Fig. 26: *Section through well G166 (F246), phase 5C*

Small Finds: *Brooches* 11 – sf2164, 162/5; 14 – sf2080, 163/1; 26 – sf2165, 162/5; *Beads* 60 – sf3015, 167/1; 67 – sf3013, 165/1; 75 – sf3016, 167/1; *Toilet Spoons* 115 – sf2079, 163/1; 118 – sf2083, 162/5; *Needle* 128 – sf2074, 163/1; *Candleholder* 147 – sf2131, 162/5; *Gaming Counters* 157 – sf30, 162/5; 163 – sf19, 163/1; *Lock Bolt* 206 – sf4011, 162/5; *Coin* sf2180, 162/1 (AD81-96).

Ceramic dating: late second to early third century AD.

Phase 5C (figs. 25 & 26; plate 7)

Group 164 *Area 1: spreads* (164/1-2)

Group 163 *Area 1: timber building, structure I:* post holes and beam slot (163/6: F302-3, F313; 163/7: F209, F225, F253, F268; 163/8: F275, F392; 163/9: F252; 163/10: F436)

Group 165 *Area 1: timber building, structure J:* post holes, ?robber trench and ?floor make-up (165/3: F272-3; 165/4: F360, F391; 165/5: F345, F355, F366; 165/6: F290, F316, F340) ;

Group 166 *Area 1: well:* (G166: F246)

Group 169 *Area 1: other structural features* (169/1: F281; 169/2: F220; 169/3: F229)

G164 – A fairly thick layer of homogeneous brown sandy loams, 164/1-2 appeared to seal the features of phases 5A and 5B. As clear interfaces were not visible between the layers, they were excavated in spits. The nature of this group of layers was such that it was likely to obscure features, and cannot therefore be taken as an accurate boundary between phases 5A and 5B.

G163 – Structure I – Cutting through these spreads were several post holes and a possible beam slot. The post holes were all less than 0.2m deep, their sides were gently sloping and degraded indicating post-depositional disturbance. F302, F303 and F313 were packed with granite and/or slate. Post holes F436, F225, F268, F275, F392, F302, F313, F303 were roughly WSW-ENE aligned and at 90° to the NNW-SSE alignment formed by phase 5B post holes. F253, F252 and F283 fitted the latter alignment, but this last feature contained a sherd of medieval pottery, possibly intrusive. A likely beam slot,

F209, 1.64m by 0.45m by 0.36m deep, lay parallel with, and to the west of the NNW-SSE aligned post holes, and may belong with the structure. If F209 belongs with Structure G163, a coin of AD 268-270 found in its backfills would suggest a late third century date at earliest for the structure's abandonment.

G165 – Structure J – This comprises a group of features which may relate to a structure and may be associated with Structure G165 of phase 5B (those features which occurred above G164 are described here, those below G164 are under phase 5B – although this division may be somewhat arbitrary). The group includes post holes, a possible robber trench and make-up for a floor. Post holes F272, F273, F345, F355 and F316 clustered near Structure G165 but formed no particular pattern. A possible N-S oriented robber trench F290 may be associated with post hole F316, suggesting a post-and-trench constructed wall. To the north, F366 may be a continuation of F290, forming a corner to the structure, with a shallow linear feature, F360, perhaps serving as an eaves-drip gully. Adjacent and to the east of F290 was F340, a 0.3m thick spread of compacted yellowish sandy silt perhaps representing the make-up for a floor, but which was truncated on all but its west side, leaving an area only 2.2m by 3.1m intact.

G166 – Well F246 was 3.5m in diameter at the top where it was cut through sands and gravels and 0.5m of Roman make-ups and surfaces, narrowing to 2.4m as it reached Mercia mudstone. It was at least 3.78m deep, but could not be excavated further for safety reasons, nor was augering possible due to extensive building rubble in its backfills, presumably collapsed from the lining. This lining was of stone, tile and slate; the lowest excavated levels had not suffered collapse, and 166/8 was thus *in situ*. Lying above the lining was rubble and clay collapse from the upper levels of the well (166/4-7). These collapse layers were surrounded and sealed by 166/3, silt deposits. The final upper fill 166/1 was a yellowish brown sandy loam containing much mortar, slate, and other building materials along with animal bone and general rubbish deposits.

G169 – This group comprises a ?pit, F220, and two post holes, F281 and 229 which may be related to structures I/J, although this remains uncertain.

Small Finds: *Brooch* 23 – sf2086, 164/1; *Hairpin* 54 – sf2025, 164/1; *Armlets* 86 – sf4557, 169/2; 98 – sf2231, 166/4?; *Toilet Spoon* 114 – sf2026, 164/1; *Spindle-whorl* 133 – sf4529, 166/3; *Shale Bowl* 141 – sf5024, 166/4; *Gaming Counter* 178, 164/1; *Coins*: sf2013, 163/7 (AD 268-270); sf2063, 164/1; sf5004, 166/4 (AD 69-79); sf5003, 166/4 (AD140-143).

Ceramic dating: *late second to early third century AD.*

Phase 5D (fig. 25)

Group 186   *Area 1: pit (186/1: F240)*

G186 – F240 was an elongated pit of 3.5m by 1.2m and 0.45m in depth. It contained several layers of sandy gravel derived from the natural, but also layers of silty loam containing animal bone, building materials and a late third century assemblage of pottery. Two medieval sherds in its upper fill are probably intrusive.

Small Finds: *Bead* 81 – sf134, 186/1; *Spoon* sf2027, 186/1; *Coin*: sf2047, 186/1 (AD 69-71).

Ceramic dating: *mid third – mid fourth century AD.*

Phase 5E (figs. 27, 28 & 29; plate 8)

Groups 339, 360-1   *Area 3: gravel extraction pits (339/1-5; 360/1; 361/1)*

G339, 360-1 These are the earliest Phase 5 features and layers in Area 3. Layer 361/1 consisted of a single layer of yellowish brown silty sand which was probably derived from the local sands and gravels. It was severely truncated by 360/1, a group of six pits on its western edge, and was obscured by the edges of the excavation everywhere else. Pits 360/1 were stratigraphically-linked, all sub-rectangular or square in plan, generally 2.0m by 2.0m, with flat bases and vertical sides;

Plate 7: *Roman stone-lined well G166, phase 5C*

Plate 8: *Gravel extraction pits, phases 5E-F, view north*

commonly, a very low ridge of gravel was found between each pit. The primary fills within 339/2-5 were derived from the natural subsoil through which they were cut, being yellowish brown to brown, compacted silty sands with few inclusions other than charcoal and rounded pebbles. 339/1, however, contained a reddish clay, presumably derived from the natural Mercia mudstone. Potentially, a deeper pit was excavated as a sample to test the depth of sands and gravels during/before quarrying. The only identifiable primary fill in the 360/1 pits was a slightly organic olive brown silty loam, from which derived pottery, bone, and a lump of lead ore (crucible fragment) which may have been used for glazing pottery or making enamels. This fill, unlike the others, was more rubbish-like in appearance and apparently not derived from the sand and gravel.

Small Finds: *Bone Hairpins 37 – sf135, 360/1, 52 – sf114, 339/4; Armlet 91 – sf2409, 360/1; Gaming Counter 172 – sf4591, 360/1; Bone Working offcut 213 – sf126, 339/4; Coin: sf5046, 360/1.*

Ceramic dating: *late third to early fourth century (except 361/1 – mid second century).*

Phase 5F (figs. 27, 28 & 29)

Group 339/9   *Area 3: backfill of phase 5E pits: (339/9)*
Group 339/6-8   *Area 3: gravel extraction pits ((339/6-8)*
Group 364   *Area 3: machine-excavated deposits (364/1: F796, F776, F797 F768, F788, F764)*

G339/9 – Three pits in groups 339/1-5 of phase 5E were partially backfilled with naturally derived layers of yellowish brown sandy silt intermingled with layers of loam (339/9) containing general rubbish including charcoal, mortar, plaster and much oyster shell.

  G339/6-8 – Directly south of, and later than G339/9, were pits 339/6, 339/7 and 339/8, whose primary fills were yellowish brown to olive brown sandy silts; 339/8 also contained a large

number of oyster shells and lumps of limestone. 362/1 and 362/2 (not on plan) were sub-rectangular pits cutting through natural sands and gravels with primary fills derived from these, and secondary rubbish fills 362/3 which included large

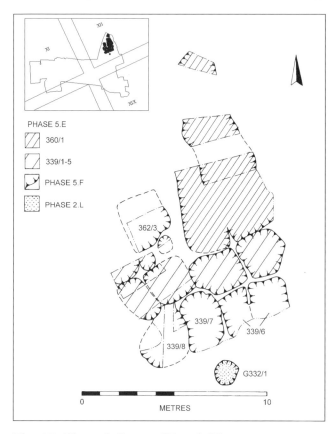

Fig. 27: *Plan of phases 5E and 5F*

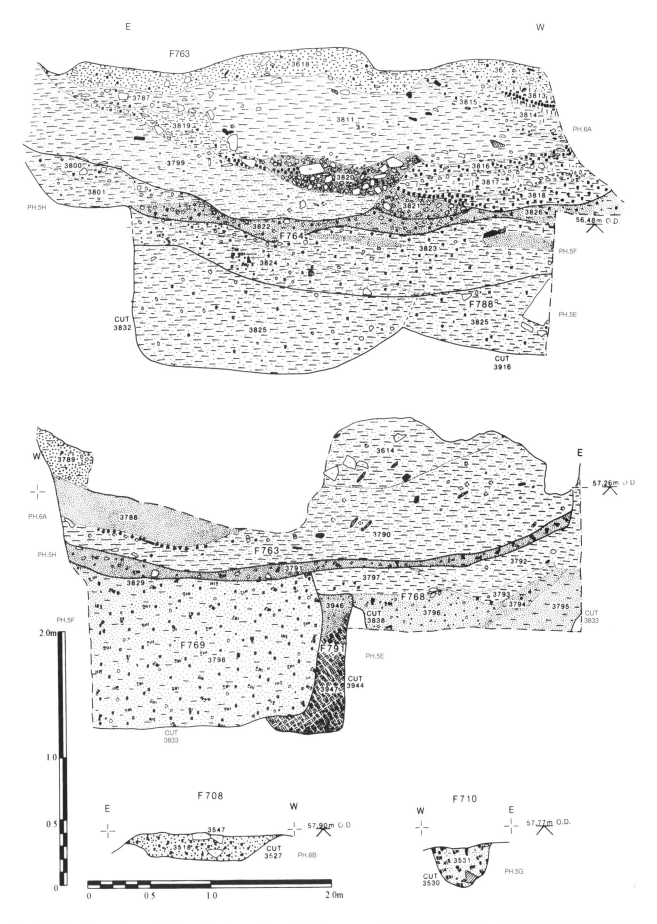

Fig. 28: *Sections through Area 3, phases 5 and 6, features: G339 (F769, F791), ph.5E; G364 (F764, 768, 788), ph. 5F; G356 (F710), ph.5G; G338 (F763), ph.5H; G363 (F708), ph.6B*

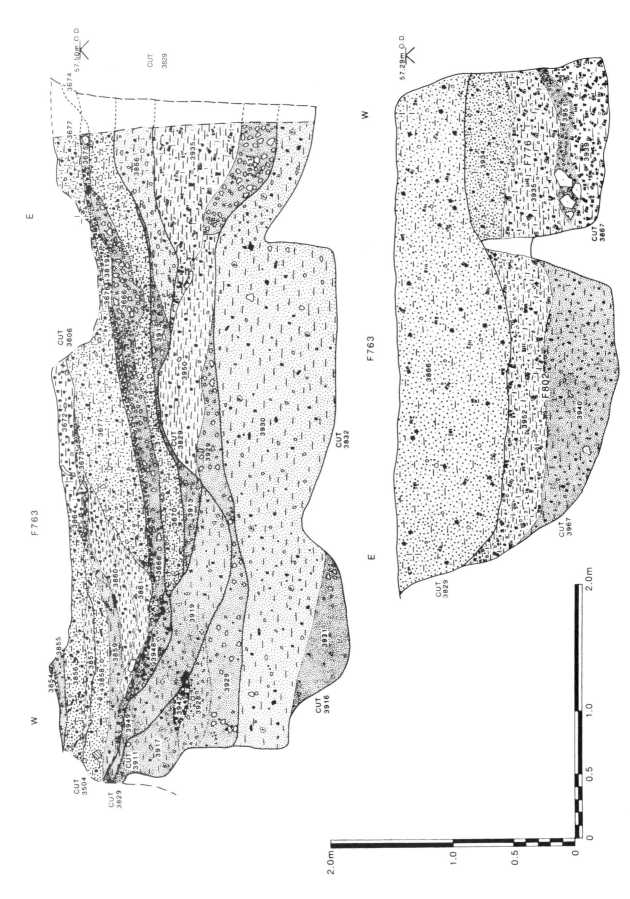

Fig. 29: Section through Area 3, phases 5 and 6 features: G339 (F802), ph.5E; G364 (F776), ph.5F; G338 (F763), ph.5H

Plate 9: *Structure K stake holes (F356-7), phase 5G*

amounts of Roman tile and pottery, animal bone and sundry materials.

G364 – As with phase 5E, time constraints prevented total hand excavation: 364/1 identifies those deposits which were excavated by machine and picked over by hand to recover finds. These were dark yellowish brown sandy silts with frequent charcoal and pebbles, representing the upper fills of pits in groups 339/1-5 of phase 5E, the lower 0.6m of which were hand-excavated.

Small Finds: Toilet Implement: 124 – sf2408, 339/7; *Needle* 126 – sf116, 339/7; *Bone Working offcut* 212 – sf122, 362/3; *Coins:* sf2382, 339/7 (AD 202-210); sf2363, 339/9 (AD 201); sf2400, 339/9 (AD 162-163).

Ceramic dating: first quarter of fourth century AD.

Phase 5G (figs. 28 & 30; plate 9)

Group 359	*Area 3: Consolidation and levelling of gravel extraction pits (359/1-4) (not on plan) -*
Group 356-7	*Area 3: Possible structural features, **structure K**: stake holes (356/1, 357/1-4)*
Groups 334, 337	*Area 3: pits (334/1-2, 337/1-3)*
Group 355	*Area 3: pit (355/1)*
Group 333	*Area 3: pit (333/1)*
Group 358	*Area 3: gravel surface (358/1)*

G359/4 filled and consolidated those pits dug in phases 5E and 5F. 359/4 layers contained enormous quantities of building debris, including over 51 kg of slate, 172 kg of tile, 7 kg of mortar, and 639 kg of wall plaster, nearly 250 kg of which were deposited in context 3879. There were also 16 kg of animal bone and 7 kg of oyster shell, but no environmental materials were recovered in significant quantities. The layers were interleaving yellow brown and strong brown silty sands and sandy silts, except for context 3943, the earliest of this group of backfills, which was a red compacted gravel layer, containing

relatively few building materials. 359/3, a moderately compacted dark brown sandy clay silt, sealed these layers of demolition materials, but was almost devoid of finds. Consolidation and levelling of the pits was completed by 359/2, a layer of brown silty sand containing over 7 kg of wall plaster, and 359/1, a thin layer of loosely compacted grey silty sand, which contained abundant charcoal fragments.

G356-7 – Structure K – Towards the southern edge of the backfilled quarries, four stake holes G357 cut through quarry

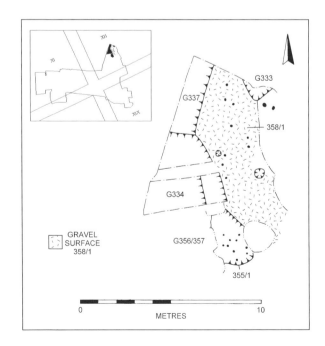

Fig. 30: *Plan of phase 5G*

fills 359/4. These stake holes were 0.05m deep, but were truncated by pit 355/1, and so could have been deeper. They were possibly sealed by gravel surface 358/1, unless cut through the surface along with G356. The latter consisted of 18 stake holes and two post holes, which combine to suggest fences or flimsy buildings set over the backfilled quarry area.

G333 – Pit 333/1 was 1.28m by 1.24m and 0.45m deep, filled with dark greyish brown sandy silts with evidence of burning and large amounts of charcoal and slag.

G355 – Pit 355/1 was 0.3m deep, flat based, and irregular filled with over 8 kilos of crushed slates in a dark greyish brown sandy silt.

G334, 337 – Cutting through the western edge of make-up layers G359 and gravel surface G358 were G337 and G334, a series of rectangular pits very similar to the earlier quarry pits (phases 5E & 5F).

G358/1 – A compacted gravel surface, 0.05-0.08m in thickness, bonded in a mixture of strong brown silty sand and mortar appeared to seal the G357 stake holes and spread over most of the quarry area.

Small Finds: Bone Hairpins 35 – sf121, 334/1; 48 – sf81, 334/2; *Brooch* 25 – sf2404, 359/4; *Bead* 80 – sf5044, 334/2; *Bone Furniture Handle* or *Box Hinge* 151 – sf97, 333/1; *Gaming Counter* 171 – sf4582, 359/4; *Knife* 189 – sf6128, 359/4; *Bone-working Offcut* 214 – sf124, 359/4; *Antler Offcut* 216 – sf112, 359/4; *Coin:* sf2302, 334/2 (AD 388-395).

Ceramic dating: third quarter of fourth century AD.

Phase 5H (figs. 28, 29 & 31)

Group 338	Area 3: subsidence and levelling (338/1: F761; 338/2: F763)
Group 354	Area 3: pit (354/1: F760)
Group 353	Area 3: cultivation (353/1)
Groups 343, 351-2	Area 3: resurfacing (343/2; 351/1; 352/1) not on plan.

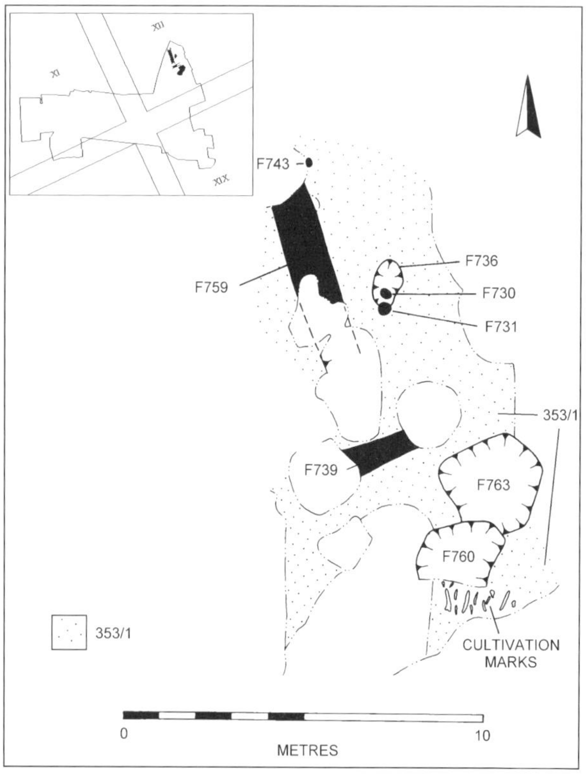

Fig. 31: *Plan of phase 5H*

| Groups 345 & 349 | Area 3: ?structural features, structure L: gullies (345/1: F759; 349/1: F739); post holes (346/1:F743; 347/1: F730, F731), Pit (350/1: F736) |

G338 – F761 and F763 were subsidence hollows in gravel surface 358/1. Interleaving layers of yellowish brown sandy gravels, infrequently interspersed with dark grey to black sandy silts, levelled the ground within these hollows.

G354 – These levelling layers were cut by a 0.6m deep, sub-circular pit 354/1 (F760) of 2.2m by 1.5m, backfilled with dark greyish brown silt sand loam and containing crucible fragments.

G353 – Sealing F760, and spreading over large parts of the area was 353/1, light to dark yellowish brown mixed sandy silts containing some fragmented building materials and a crucible fragment, possibly churned up from the layers below, which may have been the remnants of a leached cultivation soil. Several narrow, shallow linear cuts were identified cutting through 353/1 at the southern end of Area 3 where they had been truncated. These cuts were all oriented N-S and may have been cultivation marks.

G343, 351-2 – Completely sealing these marks, and covering the south of Area 3 was G351 (not shown on plan), a moderately compacted yellow brown gravel and sand, which merged into 343/2, a layer of yellow silty sand extending over most of the northern part of Area 3.

G345 & 349 – Structure L – Cutting through 351/1 and 343/2 were several possible structural features. Gullies 345/1 (F759) and 349/1 (F739) were at right angles to one another. F759 was 1.1m wide by 0.25m deep by 5m N-S, but truncated at both north and south ends. F759 was backfilled with building debris, in a dark greyish brown silty loam. F739 lay approximately 3.0m to the south, was 0.8m wide by 0.12m deep and 2m long E-W, with an irregular degraded profile; it was truncated at both east and west ends. It was backfilled with a dark brown sandy silt containing a small quantity of pot, mortar, plaster and tesserae. Post hole 346/1 (F743) was at the north-east edge of F759. F743 was 0.26m in diameter by 0.13m deep and filled with a dark brown sandy loam with much charcoal, possibly caused by *in situ* burning of a post. Some 4.0m to the south lay G347 (F730, F731), a pair of post holes, 0.45m and 0.25m in diameter by 0.2m and 0.3m deep. They both contained compact dark grey silty sand, with a small amount of charcoal and pebbles. The post holes were cut through, and were possibly associated with, G350 (F736); this contained some slag which may have derived from a hearth or furnace lining.

Small Finds: Brooch 28 – sf2391, 354/1; *Toilet Implement* 123 – sf2387, 338/2; *Coins:* sf2385, 338/2 (AD 235-236); sf2330, 350/1 (AD 354-364).

Ceramic dating: early to mid fourth century.

Discussion of phases 4 and 5

Insula XI (Area 1)

The small group of features allocated to Phase 4 were probably backfilled in the second half of the third century and therefore at the same time as Phase 5. The backfill of F255, G174, indicated a use as a repository for burnt material (including plant remains) from close by, rather than as a fire pit, with various potsherds featuring sooting and burnt residues, probably largely from post-depositional burning. The pottery assemblage perhaps derived from a wealthier domestic household than has been seen elsewhere on the site, as supported by the presence in the pit of a number of interesting small finds, notably the Venus figurine, the sole item of religious significance to be found on this site, items of personal adornment and a likely gaming counter. Significant also were the possible hay deposits suggesting the presence of a nearby stable. The pit demonstrates the continuing use of Area 1 as a yard, although it may also be associated with the phase 5 timber structures.

Phase 5 deposits were stratigraphically later than phase 3 and dated by the pottery to the mid second to late third century, except for phase 5D which was thought to belong the late third to fourth century AD. Additional dating evidence was provided by a coin (SF2013) dated to AD 268-270 found in slot F209, possibly associated with timber Structure C.

Only partial resurfacing (surface 5) of the yard was recognised. Structure G, either fencing or a small building, was erected on this surface, probably aligned on the street grid. Much of the yard area was then covered in successive deposits of homogeneous loams, which both appeared to seal and be cut by post holes from Structures I and J, possibly indicating resetting of posts over a period of time. However, interpretation was problematic, notably in relating the post-built Structures I and J to the horizontal stratigraphy, since the two structures appeared to be split into two subphases, 5B and 5C. It is possible that the phase 5B post holes were simply not recognised at the same time as the phase 5C post holes and so in reality they all belong with the later subphase. Alternatively the problem may have been caused during deposition: both structures may already have become derelict by phase 5C, with phase 5B posts already removed and phase 5C posts simply continuing to stand. This would give the impression of posts inserted through phase 5C deposits when they had in fact simply been standing as deposits accumulated around them. Similar problems of excavation and interpretation of post holes associated with homogeneous deposits of loam occurred on the Little Lane (Shires) excavation (J. Lucas pers. comm.)

Structures I and J may also be interpreted as either buildings or fences, again possibly aligned on the street grid. The soil deposits may have been imported as make-ups for the structures, or as garden soil onto which fences were built.

A stone, tile and slate-lined well, F246, was also cut in this phase; its large upper diameter was probably caused by slumping and collapse of the sides, since where it cut through the more solid Mercia mudstone it was only slightly larger in diameter than other wells. The well and post holes of Structures I and J all cut through make-up layers attributed a late second to early third century date. The well was probably backfilled after the later third century and may therefore have been in use for much of the third century. Structures I and J and well F246 were probably associated elements (see fig. 25) with the well pit effectively enclosed on at least three sides by the post hole alignments of I/J.

Insula XIX (Area 2)

No layers were allocated to this phase here, although the stone building(s) of phase 3F probably continued in occupation into the fourth century since backfilled pits and yard surfaces in phase 3G were dated as late as the fourth century on ceramic evidence. It is conceivable that the large quantities of wall plaster and building materials dumped in Area 3 in the fourth century derive from the destruction or perhaps refurbishment of this building. However, the walls appear to have survived, at least in part, into the medieval period and the wall plaster designs do seem to be rather sophisticated for a simple strip building, and are perhaps more likely to have been brought to the site from elsewhere.

Insula XII (Area 3)

For Area 3, the earliest of the phase 5 deposits only occur at the end of the third century or even early fourth, with deposition subsequently apparently continuing right through the fourth century (see phase 6, below). Occupation over Area 3 may well have been of a similar nature to that in Area 1 in this period, namely domestic housing or backyard areas, though the evidence is scarce.

The north-east area of the site was almost entirely quarried for sand and gravel some time between the mid second and late third century. Presumably these materials were employed for building work throughout the town. The earliest backfilling of these quarry pits was dated by pottery and coins to the late third to early fourth century. Later, probably from the first half of the fourth century (although two coins of the second half of the century were recovered), there was more deliberate backfilling and consolidation of the quarried areas. These quarries were regular, sub-rectangular pits, approximately aligned with the street grid; most were cut to the base of the gravel, although one pit was deeper suggesting some quarrying of the underlying Mercia mudstone. The southern edge of the Roman quarries coincides with the northern edge of 18th century quarries, signifying that, since the same resource was sought by both, the quarry men of the 18th century stopped when it became obvious that gravels here had been already removed.

Backfilling with general rubbish, both domestic and structural, may have begun soon after the pits were dug and thus while the area was still being quarried. Large quantities of oyster shells, animal bone, pottery, and building rubble were present, much of which may be residual since a large proportion of the pottery was of second century date. Some backfills contained layers of wall plaster and rubble which formed a firm area of hardstanding adjacent to further quarry pits. The dumped material included layers which were almost entirely made up of wall plaster or a mixture of wall plaster, slate and tile. These layers contained similar amounts of wall plaster, suggestive of isolated dumps, possibly from different sources, one of which may have been a nearby building (see *insula* XIX above). A number of features had cut through and lay above this surface, including possible timber structures or fencing (Structures K and L), a hearth and a dump of roof slate which may have been left as a by product of slate trimming.

The later quarries were completely filled in and the surface consolidated, levelled and covered by a soil which may have been cultivated, although it is perhaps more likely to have been imported as make-up for surfacing through which a small number of structural features, possibly representing fences, had been cut.

PHASE 6 mid to late fourth century

Area 3 make-ups, levelling layers and traces of flimsy timber structures, similar in character to the later subphases of Phase 5. Some contamination from medieval deposits was recognised.

Phase 6A (figs. 28 & 32)

Groups 333, 348, 336 & 338
    Area 3: Dumps, spreads and levelling layers (343/1; 336/1; 348/1; 338/1)
Groups 341-2, 344 *Area 3: pits (341/1, 342/1, 344/1)*
Group 367 *Area 3: Make-ups? with iron-working debris (367/1)*

G333, 348, 336 & 338   Layers 348/1, 343/1, 338/3, and 336/1 (not on plan) overlay and sealed phase 5H features. These layers were yellowish brown to dark brown silts and sandy silts, some containing occasional charcoal. Finds were in excess of 20 kg bone, 113 kg tile, 4 kg mortar, 1 kg opus signinum, 8 kg oyster shell, 4 kg slate, and 5 kg wall plaster. Contamination was indicated by the presence of 20 sherds of medieval pottery. A number of features were identified as cutting through these make-up layers.

G341-2, 344 – Cutting through 348/1 was 344/1 (F728), a 0.32m deep pit, backfilled with a dark brown silt loam containing building material, particularly tile. The pit had been severely truncated. Cutting through layers 338/3, were two irregular, shallow and very truncated pits, 341/1, backfilled with a dark yellowish brown sandy silt also containing building material. Pits 342/1-2 were both very shallow, and *c.* 1m in diameter, although 342/1 was truncated. Both were backfilled with brown silty loam.

G367 – Make-up layers 367/1 were brown sandy silt loams containing much pot, tile, and animal bone. A fragment from a possible glass furnace, fragments of vitrified clay including hearth lining from iron working and iron concretions were also recovered from these deposits as well as a wide range of small finds, including iron objects such as nails, blades, a key, a staple, and a chisel. Such relatively large quantities of iron objects signify the derivation of these make-up layers from an area of iron working.

Small Finds: *Bone Hairpins* 42 – sf82, 338/3; 45 – sf77, 338/3; 49 – sf107, 338/3; *Bone Inlay* 149 – sf88, 338/3; *Gaming Counter* 161 – sf95, 367/1; *Smoothing Implement* 193 – sf4512, 338/3. *Coins* : sf2334, 336/1 (AD 138-161); sf2342, 338/3 (32-31 BC); sf2336, 338/3 (1st C- AD 235); sf2332, 341/1 (AD 138-161); sf2344 , 348/1 (AD 228-231).

Ceramic dating : *c.* AD 350-400.

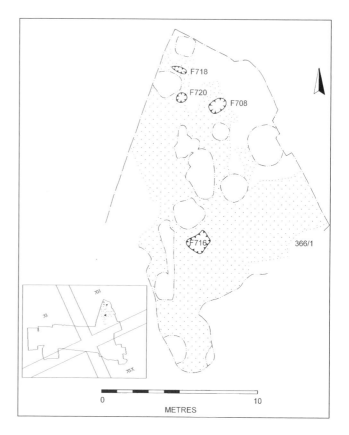

Fig. 32: *Plan of phase 6A*   **Fig. 33:** *Plan of phase 6B*

Plate 10: *Structure M (335/1), phase 6B*

Phase 6B (figs. 28 & 33; plate 10)

Groups 335 & 363   *Area 3: structural features,* **Structure M:** pits (363/1: F708; 335/1: F716); post holes (363/1:F718, F720)

Group 365   *Area 3: demolition dump (365/1),* not on plan.

Group 366   *Area 3: ?Cultivation (340/1) Make-ups and ?resurfacing (366/1)*

G335 & 363 – Structure M – Two post holes and a pit (363/1) cut through make-ups 367/1 (phase 6A). Post holes F718 and F720 were just over 1.0m apart on a N-S alignment; they both contained several 0.2m square undressed granite stones, which may have been post-packing. Pit F708 contained undressed granite and large quantities of charcoal within its dark brown loam fill; this may have been a small fire or hearth or, alternatively, merely a large post hole. Cutting through dumps 336/1 (phase 6A) and 8.0m to the south of F718 and F720, was 335/1 (F716), a shallow, 1.2m by 1.2m pit, of 0.2m depth. The pit contained a large slab of well consolidated mortar and granite fragments, suggestive of a foundation for a pillar. No similar features were found, although F716 lay so close to the edge of truncation by 18th century quarries that this is perhaps unsurprising.

G365 – Dumps of demolition material, 365/1, covered much of Area 3. It comprised an organic, grey soil containing large amounts of building material, including some sizeable fragments.

G340 – Merging into 365/1 were layers of dark greyish brown loam 340/1 containing fragmented building materials, and interpreted as possible cultivation.

G366 – Sealing 340/1 was the latest Roman deposit in Area 3, an extensive layer of compacted sandy mortar and wall plaster (366/1), which formed a coherent and extensive make-up. A tiny amount of medieval pottery was found within this layer, suggesting some contamination. The make-up was beneath, and truncated by, medieval and post-medieval garden soil. Some structural features were found cutting through this surface and may be contemporary with it but are described in Phase 7 as relating to possible sub-Roman activity.

Small Finds: Armlet 87 – sf5026, 340/1; *Coins:* sf2298, 340/1 (AD 337-340); sf2295, 340/1 (AD 287-293); sf2305, 340/1 (AD 260-268); sf2294, 340/1 (AD 270-284); sf2307, 340/1 (AD 270-274); sf2306, 340/1 (AD 260-268); sf2293, 340/1 (AD 270-284); sf2339, 363/1 (AD 375-378).

Ceramic dating: c. AD 375-400.

Discussion of phase 6

Insulae XI and XIX (Areas 1 and 2)

No features or deposits were thought to belong to phase 6 on Areas 1 and 2. The buildings identified in phases 5 and 3 respectively perhaps continued in use at this time, but there is nothing to suggest occupation any later than the early fourth century here, although this could be a result of later truncation.

Insula XII (Area 3)

Accordingly, it is possible that the fourth century occupation on Area 3 may have been in isolation. After the gravel extraction episode in the previous phase, a concerted effort seems to have been made here in phase 6 to level the area and make it suitable for domestic use or cultivation.

However, the quantities of material recovered from phase 6A perhaps suggests that Area 3 had by this time become a general rubbish tip or dumping ground for more occupied areas of the town. A broad range of material was recovered: in addition to pottery, coins spanned the first century BC to the late fourth century AD (Davies, below p.235), whilst the best preserved oysters from the site also came from these deposits (see Monckton, p.338). Many layers within this phase also showed signs of contamination by medieval deposits, probably because they were physically truncated by medieval garden soil.

Nonetheless, there was evidence for a number of possible structural features (structure M) as well as the deposition of layers which appeared to constitute make-ups for a surface (G365) or evidence for cultivation (G340). The latest layers of crushed wall plaster were almost certainly laid as a make-up for a surface which was removed or reworked by later activity. Whilst it is possible that features identified as early post-Roman Phase 7 may have been associated with the truncated wall plaster surface, all the datable materials are Roman (apart from a few contaminant medieval potsherds).

There was a general clustering of coins dated to the late third century in phase 6B, yet with two fourth century issues present. Since one of the latter was sealed by a layer of wall plaster (363/1) it would seem unlikely that the coin was a contaminant, although a small number of medieval potsherds were found in the same context. As noted, the bulk of the pottery from the phase offers an earlier date range, but with some fourth century material proposed. This discrepancy between the dating for the majority of the pottery and coins and occasional pottery fragments, suggests that residuality was very high. Other finds seem to support this, such as the noted oyster shells which compared well with shells found in late second century deposits on the Shires site. The good preservation of the shells perhaps indicates that they were transported to their final place of deposition as a coherent rubbish group.

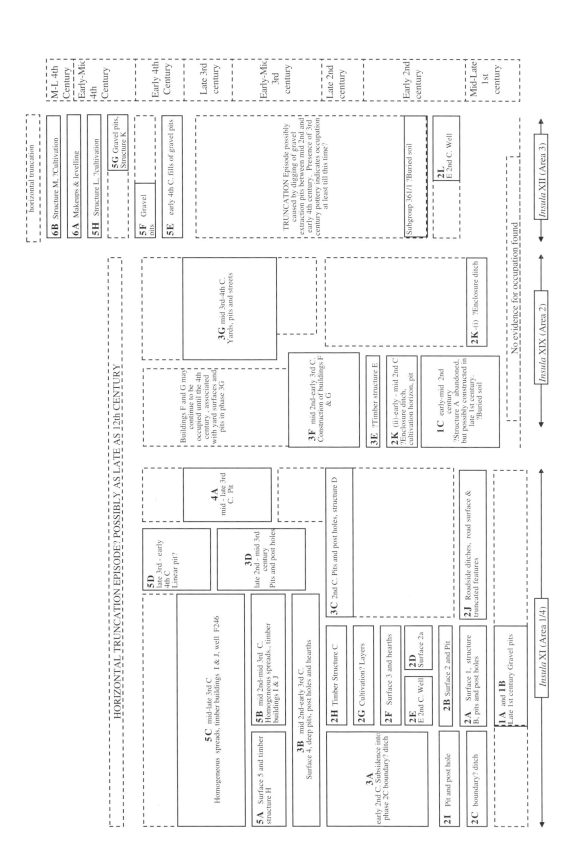

Fig. 34: *Land-use diagram showing all areas of the site during the Roman period*

DISCUSSION OF THE ROMAN RESEARCH THEMES

Aileen Connor and Richard Buckley

Land-use, town planning and settlement patterns

Early activity

Evidence from Causeway Lane suggests that the site remained virgin ground until the end of the first century AD, with occasional finds of flint tools in Roman contexts probably indicating no more than chance losses. During the earliest phases, in the later first and early second century, cultivation is tentatively identified as the main activity, with parasite ova (Boyer, below) and a few abraded finds possibly indicative of manuring. In addition, it is possible to recognise some early small-scale gravel extraction in *insula* XI (Area 1). The presence of crushed limestone in the quarry pit fills is unusual in Leicester. The nearest sources of limestone are Crown Hills, Evington, two miles to the east, Barrow upon Soar eight miles to the north and Kilby Bridge six miles to the south, and it does not normally (with the notable exception of the south wing of the forum; Clay and Mellor 1985, 32) feature as a building stone in the Roman or medieval periods. Instead, the material may attest small scale lime burning in the vicinity, presumably for producing mortar and plaster using sand and gravel aggregate. Evidence for a first century lime kiln was present on a site in Bath Lane and was taken to relate to mortars and renders for timber buildings since construction in stone does not become common in Leicester until the mid second century (Clay and Mellor 1985, 32-34). Other sites in the vicinity of Causeway Lane, particularly Little Lane (Shires; Lucas and Buckley 1989) show a similar lack of occupation before the end of the first century, confirming existing models for the development of the Roman town, with a gradual spread eastwards, presumably into areas previously occupied by the fields of the Iron Age and early Roman settlements.

Town planning

The first tangible pattern in the landuse of the site, and indeed probably for this part of the town as a whole, comes in the very early second century when town planning becomes formalised with the establishment of the street grid on an alignment approximately 26° – 28° west of Ordnance Survey grid north. In common with Causeway Lane, excavations nearby at St. Peters Lane and Butt Close Lane (Buckley and Lucas 1987, sites 3 and 4) and Little Lane (Shires) have produced no evidence of structural activity which is demonstrably earlier than the street grid on the basis of alignment. This is rather a different picture from that in the western part of the town, where post-grid structures are preceded by three phases of first century buildings on significantly different alignments (Clay and Pollard 1994, 46). Also in this area, the grid is dated by finds 'no

later than 120' beneath the street metalling, whilst finds from metalling and associated roadside ditches taken together suggested use from the first quarter of the second century (Clay and Pollard 1994, 47). At Causeway Lane, the reconstructed position of two streets on approximately north-south and east-west alignments, forming a cross roads, is based on direct, if slight, physical evidence, but is reinforced by details such as the position and orientation of buildings and by excavated data from other sites close by where streets have been identified (Little Lane and Butt Close Lane). Physical evidence for the north-south street was a short, intermittent and truncated section of metalling in *insula* XIX (Area 2), lying on a slightly convex surface with two parallel side ditches approximately 10m apart. By projecting this street southwards, it could be inferred that it was the same as that found on the Little Lane (Shires) site in 1988 (fig. 3). One of the medieval pits cutting through the street surface contained a chunk of fallen consolidated gravel, indicating an original road thickness of at least 0.5m. This, in common with the adjacent stone structure, clearly survived until the later medieval period when it was truncated by possible cultivation episodes. The north-south street at Little Lane (Shires) was rather better preserved, with evidence for five remetallings (Lucas and Buckley 1989, 106). The east-west street at Causeway Lane was represented by fragments of roadside ditches, together with areas of compacted gravel, suggestive of very truncated metalling.

Stratigraphic evidence of the north-south street shows that the first roadside ditch had already been filled and recut before the first street metalling was laid. The ditch fill contained pottery of mid to late first century date. The east-west roadside ditch west of this line (between *insulae* XI and XVIII) appears to be broadly contemporary, whilst that to the east (between *insulae* XII and XIX) is apparently later, in the early to mid second century. At Butt Close Lane, metalling which could be associated with the latter seals rampart wash dated by the pottery to the late third-fourth century (Buckley and Lucas 1987, 36-38). The phasing of the individual elements of street grid is discussed in more detail above (pp.27-8), but the results do seem to suggest that the creation of *insulae* and the metalling of streets, at least in this part of the town, was undertaken in a rather piecemeal fashion.

It would now seem more likely that ditches were initially dug to define the *insulae* and possibly individual plots, perhaps as early as the late first century, with street metalling following later, as development proceeded. This may be supported by evidence that an area was set aside for the forum in the late first century but was not developed until the mid second century (Wacher 1983,

336). Excavation in other towns, such as Verulamium, has shown that areas along the main streets were first to be built up, with the land behind being infilled over time. The imposition of town planning clearly has a very major and detectable influence on the subsequent development and redevelopment of plots in terms of the comparatively rigid alignment of structures and other features. Whilst some variation is apparent at Causeway Lane, it is suspected that this is not enough to be significant. Some encroachment on to road lines is also detectable (phase 4), but may not be particularly unusual as it also occurs at Little Lane (Shires; J. Lucas, pers. comm.) and the extra-mural site at Bonners Lane (N. Finn, pers. comm.). Another major effect of urbanisation was almost certainly the creation of a complex pattern of property holding. The development of *insulae* and plots presumably involved a considerable number of commercial transactions as land was bought, sold and leased. The nature of landholding in the Iron Age, and how this changed with the Roman Conquest is currently a matter for speculation. In a territory such as that of the Corieltauvi, where there is little evidence to suggest fierce resistance to Roman rule, it would seem likely that the majority of land remained in the ownership of the ruling elite, perhaps in their new role as decurions. Certainly the main qualification for membership of the ordo was wealth, much of which must have derived from estates. That the landowners were not all necessarily resident in Britain has been shown by Johnson (1980, 14) who cites the case of Melania the younger who held property throughout the empire, including some in Britain. In the three *insulae* represented in part at Causeway Lane, the likelihood is, therefore, that the land was either owned, leased or rented by a number of individuals, perhaps of differing wealth or social status. The question of whether this is reflected by variability in landuse and by the nature of the structural and finds evidence is discussed in the following sections.

Land use patterns

Land use in *insula* XI (area 1), after initial cultivation and possible gravel extraction, is characterised by intensive domestic occupation in the second century consisting of successive timber buildings with an associated metalled yard which was resurfaced on a number of occasions. To the west of this, is a possible north-south boundary ditch, perhaps defining the plot, and probably contemporary with the establishment of the street grid. Although there is a brief hiatus in the second century, with possible abandonment or cultivation, further timber buildings and yard surfaces appear later in the century, and seem to continue into the next. There is no clear evidence for activity continuing beyond the close of the third century, although the area was truncated by medieval cultivation episodes. The insubstantial nature of the timber buildings, together with the yard, hearths, wells and possible small scale craft working and industry, leads to the most obvious conclusion that back yard or garden

activity associated with a more substantial structure elsewhere is represented here. This might be supported by the fact that this area produced the largest quantities of window glass on the site, introduced in make-up deposits, unless one or more of the timber structures had glazed windows. An alternative interpretation might be that the evidence instead indicates low status occupation of a single plot, with little change in the fortunes of successive occupiers throughout the period. One of the phase 2 structures could be viewed as a possible byre or pen, indicating stock holding or rearing. Similar activity might be suggested by the structures of phase 5, where one at least (Structure J) has the appearance of a narrow building of sill beam construction with a small enclosed back yard or pen defined by post holes. Of particular interest is the apparent continuity of land use over a long period, with the timber structures occupying more or less the same spot and respecting the line of the plot boundary ditch after it had filled.

In *insula* XIX (area 2), some land was perhaps still under cultivation at the same time as the timber buildings were standing in *insula* XI, signifying a slightly later start to urban development. This might be supported by the suggestion that the eastern arm of the east-west street is a later element in the grid (see above pp.27-8). Land use thereafter follows the more classic pattern encountered elsewhere in Leicester, with two timber buildings, perhaps of the late first – early second century, followed by a stone structure in the mid second century. The latter could represent a shop with living accommodation to the rear, although there is no clear evidence for this (see below pp.54-5). The entire area was severely truncated, and only earthfast features survived, with no evidence for later activity. In contrast with *insula* XI (area 1), evidence of only a small amount of rubbish disposal was found, although this should not be unexpected adjacent to the street frontage.

Minimal evidence for second century activity in *insula* XII survived due to the later quarrying, although one deep well, containing a typical rubbish assemblage, is suggestive of domestic occupation in this period. Possibly in the late third century, land use in this part of the *insula* shows a profound difference to that encountered elsewhere on the site, with comparatively large scale quarrying, presumably for sand and gravel. That the street grid, and perhaps plot boundaries, still exerted an influence on activity is shown by the neatly aligned quarry pits. The exploitation of the land in this way is of considerable interest, and is open to a number of different interpretations depending on whether it is seen as reflective of the fortunes of individuals or the town as a whole. If the former, it might imply that the monetary value of the plot was low, perhaps because the demand for building land in the town was not particularly great, and that quarrying was simply the most cost-effective way of achieving short term financial gain. Alternatively, and more controversially, it could support the view that urban decline had set in by the late third century.

The quarry pits were later backfilled with significant quantities of building materials, presumably indicating demolition of a substantial building nearby. Land use after this is of a much less tangible nature, with limited evidence for surfaces and possibly insubstantial timber buildings of the fourth century.

Structures

Timber

Whilst the evidence for some timber structures at Causeway Lane was limited to little more than an occasional post hole, for others the data were more substantial and it was possible to identify the orientation, and even the ground plan, of some of these. In all, eleven, possibly twelve timber structures were discerned, covering every Roman phase except phase 4. These comprise:

Insula XI

Structure B (G133 Phase 2A). A shallow gully with a line of stake holes on each side, perhaps indicating wattle shuttering between which clay, daub or mud brick could be placed. An alternative interpretation is that it represents a plank lined drain (see above p.00). Late first – early second century.

Structure C (G149, Phase 2H). Post pits and post holes, with remnants of a possible wall trench and a hearth. Mid first – mid second century.

Structure D (G175 Phase 3C). An L-shaped gully or beamslot associated with a post hole alignment. Second century.

Structure H (G160-1 Phase 5A). Post hole alignments, and possible truncated wall footings. Late second century.

Structure I (G163 Phase 5B). Alignments of post holes and a possible fragment of beam slot. Mid second – mid third century.

Structure J (G165 Phase 5C). Possible beam slot with post holes, forming the corner of a building and perhaps associated with a enclosed back yard. Mid second – mid third century.

Other possible structural features in this area include G137 (phase 2A) and G157 (phase 3B): post holes associated with a shallow linear cut. Dating: mid second – early third century.

Insula XII

Structure K (G356-7 Phase 5G). Stakeholes, perhaps forming flimsy structure. Early – mid fourth century.

Structure L (G345 – 50 Phase 5H). Possible beamslots or wall trenches and post holes. Late fourth century.

Structure M (G335 and 363 Phase 6B). Post holes and possible post pad associated with hearth. Late fourth century.

Insula XIX

Structure A (G208 Phase 1C). Possible beamslot. Late first – mid second century.

Structure E (G209, G220 Phase 3E). Beamslots forming two parallel wall lines and post holes. Mid second century.

Three structures could be assigned construction dates as early as the late first century AD. Possible structure G137/G157 (insula XI) was the most securely dated, being sealed by an early second century surface (surface 1) and perhaps cut by a late first – mid second century ditch (G140). The other two structures thought to date

to this period were less secure: Structure A, on the eastern edge of the excavation, was abandoned after the mid second century, but its occupation date was undetermined. Structure E likewise terminated in the mid second century when it was succeeded by a stone building. The alignment of these structures, in common with that of the possible plot boundary ditch G140, is some 16° closer to OS north than that of the street grid. Whilst it is tempting to interpret this as possible evidence of structures pre-dating the latter, it is suggested that such comparatively minor variation is perhaps to be expected. Indeed, stone structure F is some 7° closer to grid north, and there is little doubt that this post dates the grid. Alignment of Flavian timber buildings in the western part of the town differed from the later street grid by 30° or more (Clay and Pollard 1994, fig.42), suggesting that this is the level of variation which should be taken as significant (see also above p.52).

In the second half of the second century, the timber buildings in insula XIX (Area 2) were replaced in stone. In insulae XI and XII, however, the timber building tradition appears to have continued at least into the late third and possibly into the fourth century, and there are no stone successors. One possible explanation may be these areas were backyards and gardens, and the timber structures represent outbuildings rather than houses or shops. Alternatively, as discussed above, they may simply suggest that the occupants were never wealthy enough to be able to afford to rebuild in stone. Structure I/J in insula XI, for example, may represent a timber strip building with its own enclosed back yard and well rather than an ancillary building.

This persistence in building in timber is well attested elsewhere, as at Verulamium where the early buildings were largely replaced in stone only when a fire in the mid second century prompted redevelopment (Wacher 1974, 209-10; Niblett 1990). Leicester suffered no such mid-imperial conflagration to prompt the need for a second-third century transition into stone, although the centre of the town appears to have been devastated by fire during the latter half of the fourth century (Wacher 1974, 357). Fieldwork is now beginning to provide more of an insight into the diversity of buildings of differing status within the town.

Despite the lack of stone buildings in insula XI, a comparatively large amount of window glass was recovered mainly from late second – mid third century deposits in this area. The glass may have travelled no great distance, since it showed little post-depositional wear, perhaps deriving from a building in the immediate vicinity, although it would seem unlikely to have originated from the insubstantial phase 1 or 2 timber structures here. A further possibility is that the glass arrived by chance, brought in amongst make-ups.

Other building materials were recovered from insula XI, including approximately ten times the quantity of tile from insula XIX (Area 2), even though there was little evidence for timber buildings substantial enough for

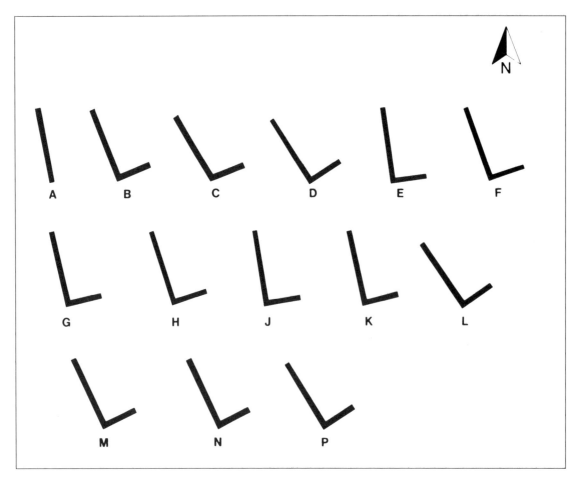

Fig. 35: *Orientation of key Roman features*

Key

A = Ditch G140, phase 2C
B = Phase 2K possible roadside ditches
C = Phase 2J possible roadside ditches
D = Structure B phase 2A
E = Structure A phase 2A

F = Stone building, structure F, phase 3F
G = Structure D, phase 3C
H = Structure H phase 5A
J = Structure I/J phase 5B/C
K = Structure J phase 5B/C

L = Possible area 3 structure phase 5
M = Bonners Lane Roman Building (Finn 1994)
N = Little Lane Roman Building (Lucas & Buckley 1989)
P = Roman Street Grid

bearing tile roofs, save perhaps Structure I/J. Such tile fragments were distributed throughout a number of features as generally fairly small, abraded pieces, contrasting somewhat with the evidence from the pottery assemblage. The largest quantities came from two features (Martin, below p.303): F246, the well associated with Structure I/J, and the upper backfills of ditch G140. In the first case, the tile was apparently used with stone and slate as a lining whilst in the second, it was probably deliberately dumped in an attempt to level the ditch. Fragments of wall plaster, tesserae, and *opus signinum* were also present in small quantities, and two fragments of worked stone were found re-deposited in medieval pits (Gnanaratnam, below p.306). Unfortunately, none of the building materials could be related to the timber buildings.

Stone buildings

In *insula* XIX (Area 2) there was evidence for a stone strip building (Structure F) constructed with stone foundations and dated to the mid second century AD or later. It was located at the junction of the east-west and

north-south streets, presenting its narrow facade to the latter. In orientation, it is slightly askew to the street grid. Although heavily robbed and truncated by later activity, an almost complete plan survived, indicating a building at least 20m long and 5m wide divided internally by stone foundations to create a front room 5m by 13m with two smaller rooms to the rear, measuring about 3m square and 3m by 2m. A stone wall to the south (Structure G), parallel with the long side, either represents a corridor or possibly another strip building. Whilst it is possible that timber beamslots within, and to the north of Structure F are associated, it would seem more likely that they represent an earlier timber building (see above p.32).

The foundations of Structure F were generally shallow although this cannot be taken to mean that it was an insubstantial building since in this part of the site, up to 1m depth of horizontal stratification may have been lost through later truncation. The north wall foundation survived to a depth of 0.5m, but had perhaps been cut deeper to compensate for the soft fills of the ditch which it cut. Buildings of a similar period and construction, fronting the same north-south street, have been found at the Little Lane (Shires) site. Here truncation was less severe and the foundations were up to 1.2m deep in places, leading to the suggestion that the building was perhaps of more than one storey (J. Lucas pers. comm.). No clear evidence has yet come to light in Leicester for the superstructure of such buildings. Some may have had stone-walled ground floors with timber framed upper storeys, whilst others perhaps had low stone plinths supporting timber framing. Of note is the fortuitous survival of a fragment of the superstructure of Structure F, constructed of mortared Dane Hills sandstone. This had fallen into a medieval pit, thus providing evidence that the plinth of the building at least survived in some form into the medieval period.

Earlier stone buildings have been recorded in the western part of Leicester (Clay and Mellor 1985, 35), but the dating of Structure F is consistent with that of the stone building phases from Little Lane and coincides with the period of known urban expansion and prosperity.

Indirect evidence of structural details

Whilst the study of building materials from the site is not without interest, none of the assemblages appear to relate to destruction deposits which may be associated with identifiable structures. *Insula* XI produced tile in small quantities from the earliest phases, with more abundant finds from the filling of the plot boundary ditch and make-ups for the many surfaces in this area in the second to third centuries. Minute amounts of wall plaster and tesserae appear from the early second century, with deposition of roofing slate and *opus signinum* from the mid second to early third centuries. As mentioned above, most of the window glass (representing about 0.33 sq.m.) came from *insula* XI, with only nine fragments recovered from *insula* XIX. None of it could definitely be associated with structures, and it seems more likely that it derived from elsewhere.

Insula XIX produced only small quantities of building materials, despite the presence of a masonry structure, reflecting the considerable truncation of stratification in this area. By contrast, large assemblages of tile, painted wall plaster, and roofing slate were recovered from the fourth century gravel quarries of *insula* XII (Area 3) and probably derive from the demolition of a single masonry building. This interpretation is supported by the painted wall plaster, which survived in large fragments and was apparently from a few discrete decorative schemes (see Ripper, below). Such dumping of plaster is paralleled at the Norfolk Street Roman villa, just outside Leicester, where a disused water tank was filled with large quantities of material deriving entirely from three second century designs (Buckley forthcoming). Interestingly, this material could only be linked with the nearby building from which it came by one or two fragments, indicating a very conscientious clearing-up operation. At Causeway Lane, attempts were made to find links between the material dumped in the quarries and structure F in *insula* XIX, but the results proved inconclusive. Instead, it is perhaps more likely that the plaster (and by association the tile) derives from a higher status building, as shown by the sophisticated decorative schemes, with marbled panels and illusionistic architectural perspectives. On the basis of style, particularly in the form of marbling, the plaster is conventionally dated to the fourth century, although at Norfolk Street, similar designs are thought to be as early as the mid second century (Buckley forthcoming). Incidental structural details from the dumps of building material included evidence for plaster architraves together with fragments of probable ceiling plaster, on the basis of lath impressions and a repeating floral design. A fragment of wall superstructure also survived (F374) and was made up of seven mortared blocks of roughly squared Dane Hills sandstone with plain white external plaster, indicating a need to whitewash or render the rather rough stonework.

Evolving social conditions in Roman Leicester

The diet, health and wealth of any population or group of people is difficult to ascertain accurately from the archaeological record, although recovered food and environmental data provide important clues. This provides complementary data to that from skeletal remains which of course form the best and most direct guide for the general health of a population. Although such remains were present only as occasional fragmentary and disturbed finds at Causeway Lane, recent excavations of part of a cemetery in Newarke Street (Cooper 1996), have shed more light on these questions.

Food and drink

The Causeway Lane food remains comprised animal bones, fish remains, charred cereal grains and seeds, pollen, oyster and eggshell. Supplementary information could be derived from certain pottery types, and by inference from other Roman period sites examined in Leicester (particularly the Shires).

The principal evidence is for animals, particularly cattle, sheep and pig, typical of most Romano-British urban contexts (cf. King 1978, 1984). Deposition of animal bone occurs mainly from phase 2 onwards, suggesting that the site had not achieved urban domestic consumption prior to this. It has been shown that Roman *civitas* centres had a distinct preference for cattle products (beef in particular), in contrast with the earlier unromanised civilian sites where higher proportions of sheep/goat appear in the faunal assemblages (King 1978; 1984). By the later Roman period the consumption of sheep, cattle and pig had become much more homogenised, and this pattern seems to be followed by the animal bones found at Causeway Lane (see Gidney, below). Beef seems to have been the preferred meat throughout the Roman period although mutton was also popular in the earlier phases, suggesting that the diet of the local population became more

Romanised over time. As Gidney suggests, however, the apparent preference for beef may have more to do with the supplier, since most of the cattle had reached maturity before being killed and were therefore not the best age for meat. Pig was less frequent except in the fourth century deposits, which may reflect the countrywide trend noted above, although residuality was such in this phase that it is by no means certain that the pig bones were contemporary with the latest material.

Domestic fowl and their eggs were also well represented throughout the Roman phases, particularly in the fourth century (although residuality may again be a factor here – Boyer, below). Occasional wild bird species must have added some variety but are present on a very small scale. Small freshwater fish and eels are also attested throughout the Roman period, even occurring as early as Phase 1 in the late first century (Nicholson, below). The variety of birds and fish apparently consumed by the local population were, however, limited when compared with lists of birds and fish found elsewhere (Allason-Jones 1989, 103). Indirect evidence from amphorae found on the site suggests that the fish sauce, *garum* or *liquamen*, which was used as a condiment, was available, probably imported from southern Spain or Italy, or even London where a garum factory was active throughout the Roman period (*ibid.*, 104). Whilst shellfish, such as mussels and whelks, were recovered in small quantities, oysters were more plentiful (Monckton, below). The best preserved group came from phase 6, yet probably derived from an earlier context along with much of the associated pottery.

The pigs and domestic fowl may have been kept within the town for home consumption. The mature age of death of the cattle might suggest that milk and dairy products were also an important part of the diet. Milk was regarded as a poor substitute for beer or wine and was thought suitable only for children and invalids; cheese was popular, however, and may have been the main produce (Allason-Jones 1989, 106).

There was also direct evidence of cereals, fruits, nuts, pulses and vegetables. Herbs and seasonings included poppy seeds and coriander, although there must have been many other plants which have not survived. There must also have been wine, olive oil, and possibly dates, since vessels carrying these products were all found within the rubbish deposits. The majority of the vessels which would have carried the olive-oil were from Baetica in southern Spain, which was also the major olive-oil source for London and Verulamium (Milne 1985, 106-112). A small amount had also been imported from North Africa. The amphorae suggest that Italian, Gaulish and Rhodian wine was drunk by the locals (Allason-Jones 1989, 107). Beer may also have been drunk, although barley has many uses, and if beer was imported to the site it has left no trace.

Overall, the range of food stuffs recovered from the site is limited. This may simply be due to a bias in preservation, or in sample size, although scanning of samples not selected for detailed analysis only produced two additional species (A. Monckton, pers. comm.). An alternative explanation is perhaps that it reflects access to basic foodstuffs and a few occasional luxuries by the local population, but that their diet did not extend to the range found in larger towns such as London, which had more direct access to imports.

Living and cooking are closely dependent on water supply. In all, six wells were identified, five in *insula* XI (Area 1), the other in *insula* XII (Area 3), with at least one active in each of Phases 2-5; best constructed was a large stone and slate-lined well which was backfilled in the second half of the third century (phase 5). The apparent lack of wells in *insula* XIX (Area 2) might suggest reliance on another water source, although there is little evidence from Leicester so far for a municipal supply of piped water. There is fragmentary evidence for a possible public fountain at the intersection of two streets to the east of the forum on Guildhall Lane (Hagar and Buckley 1990, 99-100) but this may have been atypical of the town as a whole. Leicester's Raw Dykes have been proposed as a possible aqueduct, but this interpretation is thought to be questionable (Clay and Mellor 1985, 29). Although aqueducts are known at Lincoln and Dorchester, and sluices at Wroxeter (see Forbes 1979, 671), not all inhabited zones of towns may have been so served and instead depended on water drawn either from the river or from wells.

Health

All of the wells had been backfilled with rubbish including latrine waste, suggesting secondary functions as cess-pits. Seven excavated pits in *insula* XI (Area 1) contained parasite ova indicative of the disposal of latrine waste (Boyer, below) which seems to be consistent with the area being a backyard or garden. One of these pits had initially acted as a well, but the remainder were probably dug for deliberate waste disposal. Skidmore also (below) identifies likely cess deposits from the presence of certain types of fly puparia in particular pits and notes efforts to kill the flies and mask the smell in both the Roman and more obviously in the medieval periods through the scattering of lime.

Boyer's study of the parasite ova has shown that local inhabitants would have suffered from parasites of the gut, although the evidence indicates that these were more commonplace in the medieval period, perhaps pointing to a better standard of hygiene, or simply differences in preservation. These parasites would have caused little distress to a healthy adult, but young children, the old and the sick may have suffered more severely. Evidence of the sheep liver fluke was also found and Boyer considers this an indicator of contaminated meat. Interestingly the evidence for sewage disposal from the parasite ova was almost entirely confined to phase 2 in *insula* XI (Area 1), suggesting either that the health of the local population improved over time or, perhaps more likely, that latrine waste was being disposed of elsewhere.

Wealth and social status

It would seem likely that in the Roman period some areas of the town were at a premium over others, and that location was the prime factor governing land values just as it does today. Hence, structures on the west side of the town, overlooking the river, appear to be higher status on the basis of plan, the presence of tessellated floors and richly painted walls. The distribution of tessellated pavements from Roman Leicester shows rather a blank spot in the vicinity of Causeway Lane and in the north-east quarter of the town generally, suggesting that occupation in this area was perhaps more typical of the population at large than the relatively richer *insulae* to the west. Johnson (1980, 11) has suggested that any city might go through phases of redevelopment, prosperity or decline, and each block within the walled area needs assessment to distinguish periods of construction and careful use or squalid occupation and decay. One of the research aims of the Causeway Lane project was to determine whether the finds assemblage, structural evidence and land use patterns might assist in characterising wealth and status and how this changed over time.

The question of whether food debris and in particular animal bones can be used to distinguish social differentiation has been discussed by Ijzereef (1989, 41-54), who scrutinised 17th and 18th century deposits from properties in Amsterdam, and identified differences between Jewish and non-Jewish households and between rich and poor households. Extrapolating from 18th century Amsterdam to Roman Leicester is somewhat tenuous, but Ijzereef noted significant factors which could be relevant to any period. In particular the poorest households generated waste from animal bones, especially cattle, which was regarded as coming from the parts of the carcass which would not normally be eaten, and which perhaps came through the charity of the butcher. By contrast the richest households showed less reliance on beef, and only on the best cuts, combined with a much wider variety of meat was eaten. At Causeway Lane, the animal bone assemblage was only moderately varied: a relatively varied range of meats utilising all parts of the carcass seems to suggest that the diners were of moderate wealth and status, able to afford the better cuts of meat, but not averse to eating cheaper cuts. The butchery marks on the animal bone, although made by an unsophisticated technique (Gidney, below) are considered typically urban (Maltby 1989, 91).

In relation to status, analysis of the pottery and small finds offers no clear pointers, with comparatively little which might be considered atypical for a Leicester urban assemblage. Amongst the pottery are notable groups of fine and specialist traded wares, including high quality imported and traded colour coats from the Lezoux kilns of Central Gaul and Colchester in the earlier subphases of phase 2 (Clark, below p.120). Although it is tempting to take this as indicative of a higher status assemblage, it may instead simply reflect the increasing supply and availability of fine wares in this period (N. Cooper pers. comm.). Perhaps more reliable is evidence from a pit (F255) in phase 4, which was unusual in its varied assemblage of food remains, the presence of late samian and imported colour coats and other atypical finds, including a Venus figurine. The presence of a horseshoe and evidence for hay points to stabling, and perhaps supports the view that the rubbish derives from a comparatively wealthy household, although not necessarily on this site. For the most part the fairly wide range of small finds suggest a typically Romanised domestic assemblage, very similar to that from the Shires except for the lack of any materials associated with writing or market activities (see Cooper, below). The latter may suggest the absence of nearby commercial and administrative activity, but need not have any bearing on the status of the local population. Of note, but difficult to explain in view of the lack of occupation on the site in this period, is the high proportion of early brooches outside the focus of Iron Age and early Roman settlement in the western part of the later town (Cooper, below).

The nature of the structural evidence on the site has been discussed in more detail above, but it is likely that all of the buildings examined were of modest construction and of lower status than the well appointed town houses known from elsewhere in Leicester (Clay and Mellor 1985; Clay and Pollard 1994). Those in *insula* XI were all of timber, and perhaps comparatively short-lived judging by the evidence for successive rebuilding on more or less the same spot. They may represent low-status occupation in a single plot, although it is also possible that they were subsidiary to a more substantial building outside the confines of the site, suggested by quantities of window glass. The stone structures of *insula* XIX (Area 2) seem to be modest strip buildings, and despite the large quantities of building materials found, it is unknown whether they had tessellated floors, painted walls or even tile or slate roofs. Finally, the sizeable quantities of dumped painted wall plaster in the quarries of *insula* XII (Area 3), even if not deriving from the immediate site, at least reinforce the picture of domestic structural ornamentation in Leicester between the second and fourth centuries AD provided by other sites such as Blue Boar Lane and Norfolk Street villa.

Trade and industry

Raw materials

Some exploitation of the natural resources of the site took place in the Roman period, with evidence for the quarrying of sand and gravel, and to a lesser extent, the underlying Mercia mudstone. The former was presumably used for yard and street metalling and as an aggregate in mortar and plaster. In view of the clayey consistency of the latter, it may have been used as a bonding material. The sand and gravel quarrying of the first century in *insula* XI (area 1) seems to have been of a minor nature, whilst that in *insula* XII, between the mid second and late third centuries, was apparently on an organised scale and could represent a commercial operation. The significance of this in relation to land use on the site is discussed in more detail above (pp.52-3).

In general, raw materials for building were brought into the site, with slate from Charnwood, sandstone from Dane Hills (just to the west of the town) and limestones imported from Leicestershire and Derbyshire among the range of building materials employed in the Roman period structures, attesting local and regional trade.

Charred remains of hay, possibly from a stable, was found in a Phase 4 pit in *insula* XI (area 1) whilst straw, rushes and sedges were all probably locally grown and brought into the town for a variety of purposes, such as flooring, animal bedding and possibly roofing. Charcoal may also have been produced locally, with some evidence from the site to suggest the deliberate selection of oak (Morgan, below p.365).

Crafts

The presence of particular crafts and industries are suggested by finds from Causeway Lane, but this cannot be taken as incontroverible evidence for such activities taking place on the site itself. Some of the material may well have been imported as rubbish from elsewhere, particularly the backfills of the phase 5 quarry pits in *insula* XII. Elsewhere in Leicester, evidence for several crafts and industries in the Roman period has been noted, including a glass-maker in the macellum in the fourth century, who also engaged in the illegal activity of melting down the base silver coinage to recover the silver (Wacher 1974, 65). Rubbish deposited at Causeway Lane also contained possible evidence for this practice, although residual in a medieval context. A late second/third century horners' factory occupied the abandoned courtyard house in Blue Boar Lane (Wacher 1974, 348), and a large assemblage of horn cores in phase 3 deposits on the Causeway Lane site indicate nearby horn working or tanning in the early second to early third century.

Nearby crafts are reflected in imported rubbish containing evidence of bronze- or brass-casting, and possibly glass-making, and in the discovery of bone-working offcuts in make-ups in the yard area of *insula* XI (Area 1). The constant yard resurfacing and numerous hearths here, including evidence for iron working, indicates that domestic craft working may even have been taking place on the site. Evidence for small-scale metalworking has also been found on other nearby sites, such as Butt Close Lane just to the east (Buckley and Lucas 1989, 49).

Commerce

Buildings that may have served as shops are suggested for sites in the western part of the town (Clay and Pollard 1994, 46), and a cellar/store room on the Little Lane (Shires) site which contained amphorae is perhaps indicative of commercial premises (Lucas and Buckley

forthcoming). The size, plan and street front location of the building in Area 2 at Causeway Lane plausibly recommends a shop function, perhaps with residential accommodation to the rear, although finds provide little support for this claim.

Trading links   *Nicholas J. Cooper*

With the exception of the local raw materials and imported foodstuffs discussed above, evidence for trade links is confined to the recognised sources of pottery supplied to the town. A number of studies of pottery supply to urban centres such as London (Marsh 1981), Chelmsford (Going 1987) and Cirencester (Cooper 1998) have started to establish a consistent pattern of consumption across the province which mirrors what is known of changes in both the location of production within Britannia and the declining level of commercial links with the Continent (cf. Fulford 1977; Going 1992). The evidence from Causeway Lane would tend to corroborate this pattern with shifts in the relative levels of local, non-local British, and continental suppliers of pottery over time. The following section draws information from the report on Roman pottery (Clark, below) in order to summarise the situation in broad terms. Percentage supply figures are quantified by EVEs (estimated vessel equivalents) unless otherwise stated.

During the mid-late first century (phase 1 Clark, table 9) supply is split between local sources for utilitarian grey and calcite-gritted wares (80%) and continental sources for finewares which are confined to samian from Southern Gaul (18%). Specialist wares contribute less than 1% even by weight and include imported amphorae containing olive oil from Southern Spain, with mortaria from the Verulamium region representing the only non-local British contributions at this time (if it assumed that the Dorset Black Burnished ware is intrusive). The pattern of supply is very similar to Ceramic phase 2 at both Cirencester (Cooper 1998, 327) and Chelmsford (Going 1987, 108).

The late first to mid-second century (phase 2, table. 12) sees a broadening of both the non-local British and continental sources of supply, although the contribution from local suppliers still amounts to over 70%. Samian ware contributes nearly 16% and though initially still from Southern Gaul, this source is quickly eclipsed by products from Central Gaul, an area which also supplied colourcoated and lead glazed wares. Although still only contributing less than 1% (8% by sherd count), amphorae testify to links with the Eastern Mediterranean, Italy and Spain. Mortaria continue to be supplied from Verulamium but from the early second century also come from Mancetter-Hartshill in Warwickshire. The presence of Black Burnished Ware 1(BB1) from Dorset (2%) from the late first century onwards, prior to its expansion in the mid-second century probably indicates the importance of the Fosse Way as a channel of trade from the south.

During the second half of the second century and into the early third (phase 3, table 15), continental fineware importation maintains a level of around 18%, although this is almost all Gaulish Samian ware, before starting a steady decline during phases 4 and 5, prolonged by the curation of vessels and the high residual content of the groups. The most important changes to supply concern the rise of non-local British sources of both coarsewares (BB1 rising to 8%) and finewares (e.g. limited amounts of colourcoats from the Lower Nene Valley around modern Peterborough). Mortaria continue to come predominantly from Mancetter-Hartshill and this tends to reinforce the impression that channels of trade are funnelled through the Fosse Way / Watling St. junction to the south and south west rather than from the north or east at this time.

In phase 4 (mid-late third century, table 22), the non-local component dominated by BB1 at 26%, begins to make a major contribution, complemented by a wider range of colourcoated vessels (7%) from the Lower Nene Valley. The levels of BB1 are comparable to those much closer to the source such as Cirencester (Cooper 1998, Ceramic Phase 5, 333, table 23), and Alcester (Evans 1995, fig.66), and a greater proportion of the otherwise locally produced greywares are coming from non-local sources such as the Lower Nene Valley. However, the latest continental imports still figure and include Samian ware from Eastern Gaul and 'Rhenish ware' colourcoats from both Lezoux in Central Gaul and Trier in Eastern Gaul.

The later third and fourth century (phase 5, table 22 and phase 6, table 28), sees a continued broadening of the non-local British element to include limited amounts of the fine ware products of Oxfordshire and Much Hadham, Herts., with imports of colourcoats continuing from Trier. Non-local coarsewares such as BB1 maintain a level of nearly 20% initially and rising to nearly 30% during the fourth century. This period sees the growth of two major rural-nucleated industries in the south of Britain; Oxfordshire based in the Thames Valley, and the Lower Nene Valley around modern Peterborough. Leicester appears to lie on the watershed between the seemingly complementary distribution networks of the two industries and supply is dominated by neither. This is most clearly demonstrated by the supply of mortaria which come from both industries as well as the traditional source of Mancetter-Hartshill. As the fourth century progresses, the tendency to promote links to areas to the south and south east is more apparent, the most significant new addition being the appearance of calcite-gritted wares from Harrold in Bedfordshire.

In summary, if pottery can be safely used as an index of trade in other goods which do not survive, then it would appear that although centrally placed within the road network, Leicester drew products predominantly from the south and south east of this network. It must be borne in mind that the major centres of production of ceramics, as well as the 'down the line' trade route for imports (through London) lay in this direction, and so for manufactured goods and certain agricultural products this may well hold true. However, it may be the case that a volume of products of a more primary nature (agricultural, mineral) which did not use pottery in their transport could well have come from directions north, particularly given access along the Fosse Way and the River Trent.

The fourth century and later

The evidence for the fourth century in Leicester is remarkably sparse, deriving mainly from the presence of finds – particularly pottery and coins – as deposits of this period have only been encountered comparatively rarely on excavations. The traditional view is that Romanised town life continued in Ratae until late in the fourth century (Mellor 1976, 21), with continuing mainten-ance and refurbishment of buildings attested by tessellated pavements of the period, both within the town (Clay and Mellor 1985; Clay and Pollard 1994) and at the extra-mural villa at Norfolk Street (Lucas forthcoming). At Butt Close Lane, a building was constructed adjacent to the rampart no earlier than AD321-2 (Buckley and Lucas 1987, 36) whilst at Little Lane (Shires), the stone structures and associated gardens are believed to have continued in use into the fourth century (J. Lucas pers. comm.). The evidence cited above is admittedly limited, but it is clear that fourth century levels on most sites have suffered significant truncation by medieval cultivation, pits and later activity. This argument, however, has been questioned (Faulkner, unpub.) on the grounds that mortar floors would be resistant to truncation through cultivation and that we should also expect to find evidence for the walls of fourth century buildings where they cut deep into underlying deposits. Against this view is the fact that no floor levels for second century masonry buildings survived either at Little Lane (Shires) or Causeway Lane. In addition, the tough concreted street metallings at Causeway Lane – attested by a large fragment which had fallen into a medieval pit – had been largely destroyed, together with most horizontal stratification in Areas 2 and 4. At nearby St. Peter's Lane (Shires), severe truncation resulted in medieval garden soils resting directly on the natural sand and gravel, leaving only earthfast features, including a possible robbed Roman cellar. The apparent lack of fourth century wall foundations may simply be explained by the longevity of second century masonry buildings and the clear evidence for refurbishment with new floors and wall paintings (e.g. Site 1, Clay and Mellor 1985; Norfolk Street villa). Caution must also be observed in the phasing of robbed buildings; these are generally dated by underlying make-up deposits, but the association cannot be proved as truncation may have occurred after robbing, and they could instead be much later.

Some evidence, if taken at face value, could support an argument for much earlier urban decline. Features cutting street metalling on a site at Redcross Street included a channel on a different alignment to the grid and containing third to fourth century finds (Clay and

Pollard 1994, 36, 38). Whilst this could be suggestive of the decline in civic control, such encroachment on to street lines may not be unusual (see above p.52) and, as the authors noted, the finds could well be residual and instead attest sub-Roman activity. Whilst it has been argued that signs of commerce and 'illegal activities' in the fourth century forum are indicative of decline (Wacher 1974, 353), Carver instead considers this same evidence as a sign of the continued importance of the forum to the life of town (1987, 27), and therefore a sign of both change and renewed vigour. For other towns, instances of late intramural burials are seen as representing a breakdown in civic authority (Ottaway 1992, 112 for Canterbury); as yet such evidence is absent from Leicester, and where burials do occur these tend to be early, and possibly Iron Age in date, although two second century cremations within the town walls are known, one on this site and one found at Castle Yard. Otherwise the extramural Roman cemetery to the south east of the city continues into the later fourth century (Cooper 1996).

At Causeway Lane, the only clear evidence for activity in the fourth century comes from *insula* XI (Area 3) where the quarry pits were certainly backfilled in this period with building debris. It has been argued that this material may have derived from nearby buildings, perhaps even the masonry structures in *insula* XIX (Area 2), although it is equally possible that it came from elsewhere. Interpretation of this deposit is problematic: does it simply reflect demolition or refurbishment of a nearby building, or is it representative of more widespread demolition of parts of a town in decay? Finds of 'paint pots' amongst the wall plaster in the quarry pits could support the theory of a phase of refurbishment, comprising the removal of existing frescoes, followed by replastering and painting. Alternatively, they may be residual. Another question might be whether the use of this plot for quarrying and later dumping of hard core is suggestive of a decline in land values. Even if this were true, it would be dangerous to assume that the fortunes of a single plot are reflective of those of the town as a whole (see above p.52). Since the area was reused by timber structures after final backfilling in the second half of the fourth century (on coin evidence), we can at least identify some form of continued occupation although it does not provide any indication of the status and character of that occupation. It can also be argued (see below) that occupation continued into the early post-Roman period (phase 7), although the evidence for this is fragile, and not as secure as the tentative fifth and sixth century occupation suggested at Canterbury where a coin of AD 480 was recovered (Ottaway 1992, 112), and at Wroxeter with its much-discussed timber building complex on the site of the baths *insula* (Dixon 1992, 147).

THE POST-ROMAN PHASES

Aileen Connor with Richard Buckley

INTRODUCTION

Six phases of depositional evidence were identified for the post-Roman period (phases 7-12). The majority of the evidence was confined to phases 8 and 9 (mid-11th to late 12th century). Where features were stratigraphically intercutting, the earlier feature was allocated to phase 8 and all features in Area 2 which were either stratigraphically or interpretatively identified as earlier than robbing, were included under phase 8. Phase 10 includes only three features which were demonstrated by pottery to have been backfilled during the later 12th – mid-13th century. Phase 11 includes those features which were probably backfilled sometime between the early 16th and the late 17th century. Phase 12 includes all features and deposits of 18th-century date and later.

PHASE 7 (fig. 36)
? Anglo-Saxon, fifth – sixth century AD

A number of groups of contexts on the site certainly post-dated the latest Roman deposits and were apparently earlier than the earliest medieval contexts. These comprised post hole F929 (128/4) on Area 1, four post holes with two possible beam slots F713, F717, F721, F722, F723, F725 (G304), and a group of three shallow, sub-circular pits, and two shallow sub-square pits F705, F706, F707, F709, F724 (G305) from Area 3 (fig.36). The only dateable finds derived from G305, notably two sherds of early Saxon pottery from the largest of the sub-circular pits (305/3). This pit also contained a large quantity of building stone, some faced. A single fragment of possibly intrusive

medieval pottery was recovered from 305/4, a roughly square pit which was remarkable for the large amount of fragmented slate contained in its backfill – since the site policy was to discard all except obviously shaped slates, it is not possible to say whether slate working was being carried out, or whether the slate had been collected here for some other purpose.

The area 3 features all cut through the latest phase of surfacing, assigned to the Roman period (phase 6) on the basis of finds. The possibility remains, however, that the surface and the features are in fact contemporary. It is also perhaps worth noting that other phase 6 features could conceivably be of the 5th – 6th century. Indeed, two sherds of Saxon pottery were recovered from phase 6A, although they may be intrusive.

Apart from the four sherds of pottery referred to above, a number of other finds could be dated to the early Anglo Saxon period, although they were residual in medieval and later contexts. These comprised a fragment of a silver-gilt brooch dated to the 5th century (cat. 30, sf2010, phase 12), a bone pin-beater, possibly Saxon (cat. 131, sf9010 phase 11) and 24 further sherds of pottery.

Discussion of phase 7

Although little definite evidence emerged for Saxon occupation on the site, finds of pottery of this period do at least suggest some presence or activity – indeed, at least one sherd of Saxon pottery was found on every excavation area. It is difficult, however, to be chronologically exact about such possible activity. The few ceramic finds (Blinkhorn, below p.165), combined with possible Saxon small finds (brooch fragment, see Liddle, below p.253, and pin-beater, see Cooper, below p.267) are all of the early Saxon period (fifth-sixth centuries AD), with no material which could be ascribed to the middle or late Saxon periods when Leicester is known to have been settled (see above p.8). In keeping with other excavations in Leicester, there are few features to attribute with any certainty to this phase. Area 3 produced tentative evidence of structural activity of uncertain form, together with pits backfilled with much slate, perhaps suggesting small-scale on-site (re)working of robbed Roman slate. Reuse of Roman materials in Saxon contexts has been recognised elsewhere, for example reuse of tile at Shorts Gardens, London (reused in ninth-century hearths – Connor, unpublished archive), and St. Peter's Street, Northampton (Williams 1979, 322).

For the missing mid- and late Saxon periods a number of pottery fabrics found to be residual in medieval contexts (Davies and Sawday, below) may be relevant and at least hint at a renewed presence from the ninth or tenth century.

PHASE 8 (figs. 37 & 38)
mid-11th to late 12th century

In Area 1 a small number of features, mostly pits, were stratigraphically earlier than features in Phase 9 (as noted above, the majority of the medieval features were placed in phase 9, based on the pottery dating), although finds from

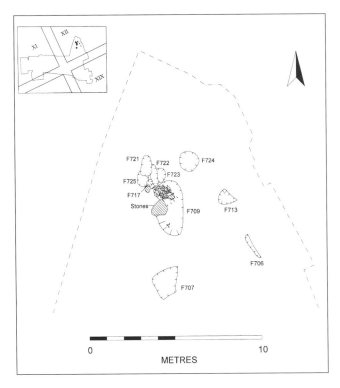

Fig. 36: *Plan of phase 7*

Fig. 37: *Plan of phases 8, 9, 10 and 11*

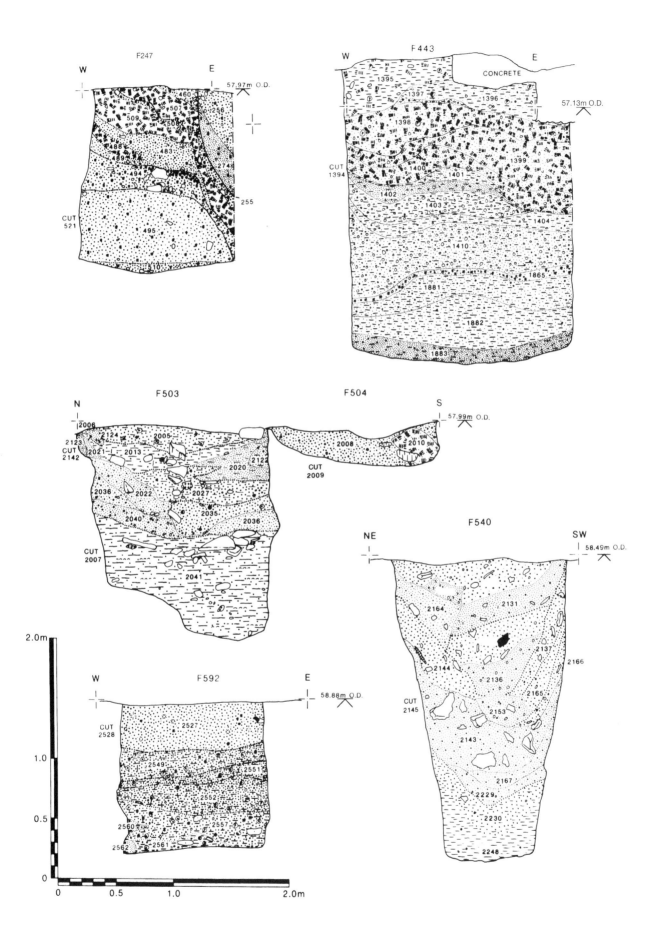

Fig. 38: *Sections through medieval features: phase 8, F247, F443, F504, F540, F592; phase 9, F503*

these features were not demonstrably earlier. Most of the features were heavily truncated. The pottery collected shows that nearly twice as much Roman as medieval pottery (by weight) was deposited within the pits of this phase in Area 1, contrasting with phase 9 and with Area 2, phase 8, which had over twice as much (by weight) medieval to Roman pottery. The figures for Area 1 change somewhat, however, when the material excavated in 1980 (Area 4) is removed from the calculations, since the ratio of medieval to Roman pottery then becomes roughly equal. In fact out of 3,533g of pottery recovered from the Phase 8 features, only 230g were medieval.

Area 2 had suffered from the same horizontal truncation observed elsewhere on this site and on other sites in north-east Leicester. The general level of truncation was to *c.* 59m OD. There was also truncation by Victorian cellars and an enormous 18th-century gravel pit, leaving remnants only of the very deepest pits. Phase 8 here consisted of six rectangular pits, two sub-circular pits, one post hole, and two circular wells. These features all appear to pre-date the phase 9 robber trenches, either stratigraphically or on the grounds that their fills included building rubble suggestive of backfilling during robbing of the Roman building, and contained finds earlier than the robbing phase; in a few cases they appear to have been dug whilst the Roman building was still partially standing (F510, F521, F579).

Small Finds: *med. coin* – sf5009, date: 1189-1199; *beads 78* – sf3018, 247/2 & 71 – sf3019, 247/2, *buckle* 107 – sf2117, 247/2.

Dating: *c.* 11th -12th century

Phase 8 pits

Twenty-five pits were backfilled on the site during phase 8, eleven of which were circular, thirteen were rectangular and one could not be assigned to a category. As noted, those in Area 1 were cut from between 58m and 58.26m OD; for Area 2 the estimate is 59m OD. However, some horizontal truncation may also have occurred and so the original level of cut may be from even higher. Various types of pit were recognised:

Deep pits (wells?)

Deep pits are defined as those whose base was below 56m OD which was the approximate level of interface between the natural free-draining sands and gravels and underlying impervious clay (Mercia mudstone). The deeper pits were often the most difficult from which to retrieve primary fills since in several cases they were not excavated fully or they were only augered to ascertain depth and retrieve samples. Seven pits belong to this category, three of which were circular, the remainder being rectangular:

(i) Circular Pits. Area 1: F443 (113/6, 119/7, 119/8); Area 2: F540 (246/1, 247/1), F568 (246/2, 247/2) – Three very deep, circular pits which may originally have functioned as wells were allocated to phase 8. F540 (fig.40) was 1.4m in diameter by 2.5m deep (55.10m OD at its base), with steep sides, but truncated by a Victorian cellar; it may later have been used for the disposal of latrine waste and general domestic rubbish, since its fills were particularly rich in animal bone (including chewed fish bones – Nicholson, below) and contained fly puparia indicative of putrid conditions (Skidmore, below). The truncated upper fills of the pit (247/1) contained large quantities of Roman building materials, suggesting the pit was deliberately

Plate 11: *General view of Area 1, looking north, after excavation of many of the medieval pits.*

backfilled when robbing of the adjacent Roman building took place. F568, severely truncated by 18th-century pitting, was 1.8m in diameter and over 2.0m deep (54.87m OD at its base). A dark humic stain around its sides indicate a likely wood lining; dark and greyish brown sandy loam layers interspersed with re-deposited gravel fills may denote layers of domestic rubbish covered with clean gravel and the find of a complete pot towards the base may indicate soft or liquid fills (i.e. the pit served as a cesspit). There were also possible remnants of an ashy or lime deposit within the fills, perhaps representing lime poured into the pit to cover the smells of its contents; whilst fly puparia from here certainly imply cess deposits (Skidmore, below). A medieval belt buckle (sf2117), of a type dated in London to late 12th to late 14th century was also recovered from the backfills of this pit (Cooper, below). The only Area 1 Phase 8 pit in this category was F443 (fig. 40), which was deep, with steep sides, but otherwise undistinguished.

(ii) Square/Rectangular Pits. Area 2: F521 (249/3), F579 (248/2, 249/2), F604 (247/3), F609 (250/1, 251/1), F620 (251/2) – Four pits belong to this category. F521 and F579 were intercutting rectangular pits (F579 was the earlier) dug on the east side of a Roman wall which presumably still stood when the pit was dug (a chunk of fallen mortared Roman masonry, 0.90 by 0.42 by 0.30m, came from backfill 249/3 of F521). Pit F579 was 1.60 by 1.30m in plan and 2.01m deep, backfilled with layers of dark brown sandy loam and yellow re-deposited gravel, with occasional fragments of Roman building materials in addition to the usual range of general rubbish deposits (yet with an unusually small assemblage of pottery considering its size); it was truncated by a Victorian cellar wall on its east side and by F521 on its north-west side. F521 was excavated to 2.12m deep (not its full depth); its upper plan dimensions were 2.30 by 2.50m, where its edges were very degraded. Its fill contained quantities of Roman building materials and soft sandy loams interspersed with re-deposited sandy gravels in a similar manner to F568, thought to be a well. The presence of fly puparia implies its use as a cesspit. F609 had also been severely truncated by 18th-century gravel pitting, surviving to a depth of just 1.0m (base at 55.45m OD): it was backfilled with dark greyish brown sandy loams and yellowish brown silts, and contained the same range of Roman building materials as other pits in this area. Similar was F620, which also contained many chewed fish bones (Nicholson, below) in its lower backfills (251/2); the pit was rectangular in shape and severely truncated from above (base at 55.20m OD). Likewise F604 (base at 55.20m OD), which merely contained the usual assemblage of building debris.

Moderately deep pits

A moderately deep pit is defined as one whose base is below 57m OD (58m OD for Area 2), i.e. deeper than 1.0m, but whose base did not cut through the lower level of the natural gravel into the mudstone below, i.e. not as deep as 56m OD. Thirteen pits belong within this category:

(i) Circular Pits. Area 4: F907 (111/5, 124/4); Area 1: F245 (111/2, 117/2, 124/2), F363 (111/4, 117/3, 124/3); Area 2: F657 (244/2) – Four pits fall into this category. Pit F907 fell between 'plots' A and B and had slumped sand and gravel in its base (111/5), whilst the remainder of its fills (124/4) were loam and sandy gravel, which may well have been almost entirely slumped from the edges of the pit and layers above. The pit was very truncated by F903 (phase 9). F245 had a circular cut *c.* 1.30m in diameter and at least 1.20m deep (it was not fully excavated); its vertical sides suggested that it had either been lined or that any evidence of collapse had been removed by truncation from above; the backfills comprised

alternating (perhaps slumped) layers of yellowish brown sandy gravel and an organic loam (117/2), but featured few finds. More productive were the uppermost deposits, though these dark brown silty loam layers (124/2) were more likely to have slumped into the pit from the garden soil above. Finds included building materials in particular, such as fragments of undressed stone and slate offcuts. F363 was 1.0m deep and 0.86m in diameter, and was filled with dark brown 'cessy' loam and dirty gravel, possibly to cover the 'cessy' layers. Pit F657 in Area 2 had a diameter of over 2.5m but was just over 1.0m deep with gently sloping sides and a rounded base. The overall lack of shallow and moderately deep pits on Area 2 may result from the severe truncation by the cutting of gravel quarries in the 18th century.

(ii) Square/Rectangular Pits. Area 1: F269 (112/1, 125/1), F247 (112/5, 118/3), F482 (114/3, 120/4, 127/3); Area 2: F606 (250/3), F542 (251/4), F592 (265/1), F539 (251/5), F569 (250/2) – Eight pits fall into this category. F269 on plot B was heavily truncated; it was excavated to 1.23m (56.94m OD) depth, revealing vertical cut (112/1). F247 (fig. 40) was approximately 1.50m square by 1.50m deep (56.44m OD at its base), and was backfilled with dark brown sandy loam with lenses of re-deposited marl becoming more frequent towards the top of the feature, perhaps used to level and consolidate the fills. F482 (2.10m square by 1.90m deep), much truncated on plot F, contained fills which when sampled indicated a likely use as a cess-pit. F606 was 1.55m square by 1.31m deep, backfilled with many very sandy layers with occasional thin layers of greenish loam, possibly 'cess' deposits; Roman building materials were again in evidence. The pit was probably lined with wood, since a dark stain was noted around its sides. F539 was of similar size to F606, but of depth 1.39m; it was backfilled with dark brown silty loam (251/5) and frequent Roman building materials; it was also very truncated and contained many patches of weathered Mercia mudstone which may have been re-deposited from the natural or may have been used to line the pit. F542 was a large, moderately deep (1.05m) rectangular pit, with evidence of wattle and daub lining. F592 was rectangular, 1.25m deep (57.58m at its base), containing discarded building materials in its backfills. F569 was also severely truncated by quarrying but contained an almost complete dog skeleton (Gidney, below).

Shallow pits

Only four pits in phase 8 fell into this category; this may be a product of truncation, the shallower pits being the ones which had suffered complete destruction. The extant examples were all circular or sub-circular in plan and less than 1.0m in depth. They were distributed as follows: Area 4: F914 (109/5, 115/5), F915 (109/3, 115/3); Area 1: F248 (109/1, 115/1); Area 2: F504 (244/1). The latter, F504, may belong with plot H-J. Of the others, F914 was identified as being stratigraphically earlier than the main body of pits in plot A; it had a shallow circular cut (109/5) (max. diameter of 1.50m by 0.60m deep), and was backfilled (115/5) with a dark brown sandy silt loam. It had been heavily truncated by F911, Phase 9 plot A. F915 lacked diagnostic finds. F248 was 0.64m deep, but may have been as much as 1.72m in diameter; it was filled with mixed clay silt sands which were olive in colour and perhaps indicative of the deposition of excreta.

Ambiguous shaped pits.

Only one pit, F442 (121/2) in Area 1, could not be assigned to a particular category in this phase, due to severe truncation by a Victorian cellar.

PHASE 9 (figs. 38 & 41)
mid-11th to late 12th century

As noted above, the majority of the medieval features were allocated to phase 9: twenty seven pits, either square or circular in shape and of varying depths, were located within Area 1 (all allocated to plots A-G); twenty pits were located in Area 2; and seven in Area 3. Area 2 additionally had evidence for one and perhaps two timber buildings (possibly associated with pits within plot J), as well as evidence for the robbing of stone from Roman buildings, and even the robbing of Roman street metalling. Six of the Area 2 pits also exhibited an unusual greenish white powdery fill which is likely to be the residue from an industrial process.

Small Finds: *Buckle* 106 – sf2034, 118/2, *box* 155 – sf2017, 126/3, *box fitting* 152 – sf2241, 120/5, *armlets* 90 – sf5031, 307/2; 97 – sf2316, 307/2, *brooches* 19 – sf9037, 119/10; 22 – sf2136, 129/1; *bead* 79 – sf4570, 253/3, *med. coin* – sf5023, date: 1205-1210; *gaming counters* 174 – sf4558, 114/5; 175 – sf4562, 254/9; *harness fitting* 183 – sf1714, 120/8; *bone inlay* 150 – sf7, 120/2; *ca nail* 196 – sf9049, 116/3; *bone pins* 43 – sf9046, 120/9; 47 – sf26, 254/10; 53 – sf9027, 122/1; *ca pins* 58 – sf2345, 315/3, *ca finger rings* 102 – sf2389, 315/3; 104 – sf2028, 252/6; *spoon* 139 – sf9030, 124/5, *toilet spoon* 119 – sf2144, 254/9; *sheet fitting* 203 – sf2048, 260/3; 205 – sf5014, 261/7; *spur* 185 – sf1028, 120/3; *spindle whorl* 132 – sf5007, 120/5; *stud* 199 – sf2171, 253/1.

Ceramic dating: *early 12th – mid 13th century*

Phase 9 pits

Fifty-four pits were backfilled on the site during phase 9, thirty-one of which were circular, twenty square or rectangular, and three of ambiguous shape. Definitions for 'deep' and 'moderately deep' pits are provided above (phase 8).

Deep pits (wells?)

Twenty-four pits fell into this category: thirteen were circular, nine square/rectangular, and two were of ambiguous form:

(i) Circular Pits. Area 1: F217 *(113/7, 119/6, 126/3),* F243 *(111/3, 117/4),* F257 *(113/4, 119/5, 126/6),* F389 *(113/5, 126/5),* F491 *(111/1, 117/1, 124/1); Area 2:* F605 *(261/2),* F613 *(261/3),* F614 *(261/4),* F616 *(251/3, 261/6); Area 3:* F727 *(306/2, 307/2, 308/2),* F732 *(306/3, 308/3),* F908 *(113/8, 119/9, 126/4),* F911 *(113/9, 119/10, 126/7)* – Thirteen large, deep, circular pits were backfilled during phase 9, with the majority distributed across Areas 1 and 2. One Area 2 pit, F605, was excavated to its full depth (55.76m OD) as were the two Area 3 pits (54.76m and 55.5m respectively); remaining pits were excavated to 1.6-2.0m depth, and pit F217 was augered to 55.64m OD. The pits were all similar in profile, having steep, almost vertical sides, and, where cleared, a tapering, slightly concave base. Diameters varied: where measurements were possible (i.e. with limited truncation) eight pits were between 2.2-3.0m (F217, F243, F616, F908, F911); seven between 1.0-1.8m (F257, F491, F613, F614, F727, F732). Only three pits (F243, F257, F491) showed signs of lining in the form of red clay adhering to their sides, probably derived from the Mercia mudstone through which the pits had been cut. F243 had a particularly thick band of clay (200mm) around its sides, and F257 additionally had slates intermittently pushed into the clay around its edges. Two phases of backfilling were observed in many of the pits; others had either been too truncated or were cleared extremely rapidly towards the end of the excavation (e.g. F732). These fills basically consisted of secondary rubbish deposits, above which were fills which closely resembled the overlying garden soils. Links between finds from the upper fills of the pits and the garden soils attest slumping as the rubbish deposits settled. The latter generally comprised slight variations of dark greyish brown sandy silts interleaved with sands and gravels. F908, however, contained a white powder

Plate 12: *Medieval pit F207, phase 9*

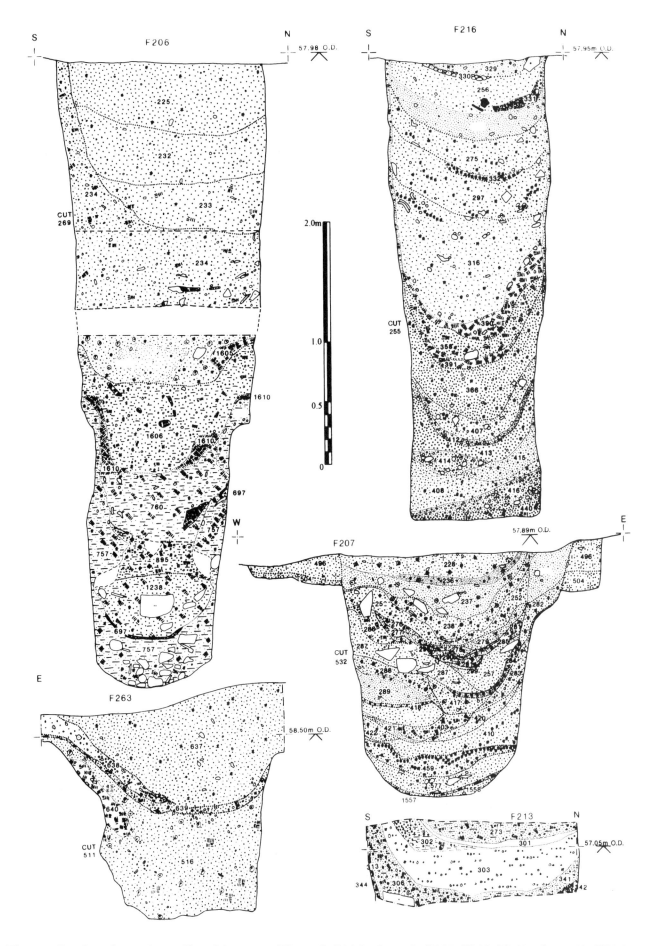

Fig. 39: *Section through medieval features. Phase 8: F216; phase 9: F207, F213, F263; phase 10: F206.*

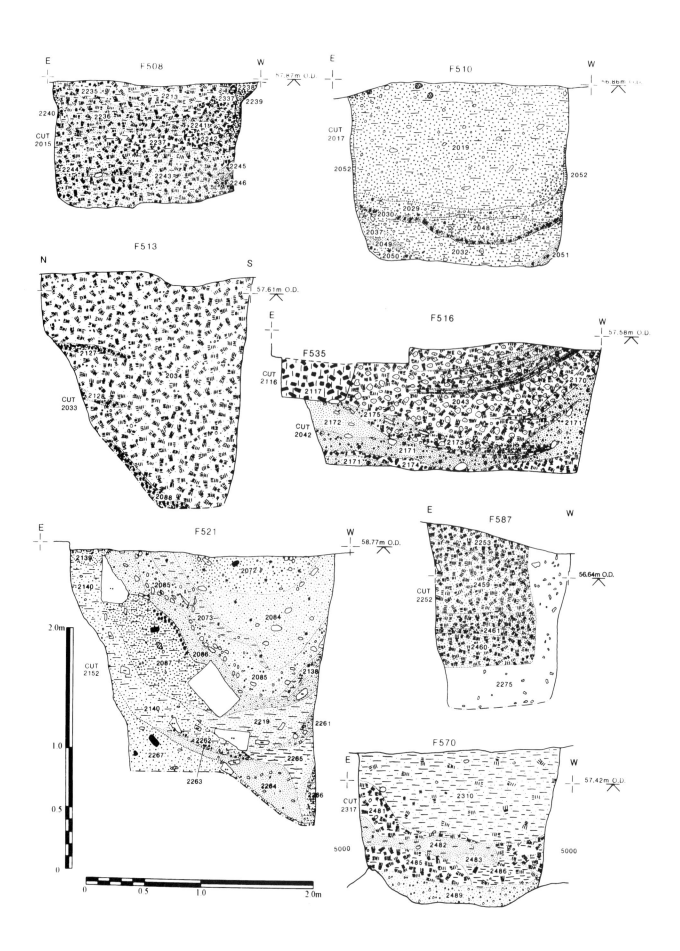

Fig. 40: *Section through medieval features. Phase 8: F521; phase 9: F508, F510, F513, F516, F570, F587*

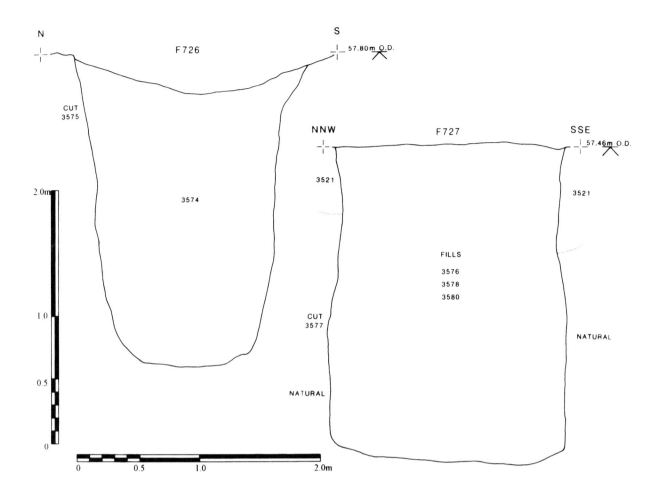

Fig. 41: *Profiles of phase 8 pits F726 and F727*

(in 119/10) which was very similar to the lime deposits found in some pits on Area 2 to the east, including F507. The pits in Area 3 contained much larger quantities of residual Roman material than those in the west end; F727, in particular, contained only small quantities of medieval pottery compared to large amounts of Roman pottery, wall plaster, tile and slate.

(ii) Square. Area 1: F203/F238 (114/2, 120/1, 127/1); F204/F228 (114/5, 120/6, 127/5); F207 (114/4, 120/7, 120/8, 127/4); F216 (114/1, 120/2, 120/3, 127/2); F263/F264 (114/7, 120/5, 127/7); Area 3: F714 (313/3, 315/3); F719 (313/2, 314/2, 315/2); F726 (309/1, 310/1); Area 4: F903 (114/6, 120/9, 127/6) – Nine deep square pits were backfilled during phase 9, all except three (F714, F719, F726) being located in Area 1. Three pits were excavated completely (F204/228, F207, F216), the others were either augered or excavated to below 56m OD. F216 (on plot D) was the deepest of the fully excavated pits at 54.02m OD at its base, nearing 4.0m in depth from the top. F903 may have been of like depth since augering showed it continued below the excavated depth of 54.75m OD. Pits F216, F263/4 (plot G) and F903 (plot A) showed evidence of lining, with a dark wood stain around the sides of F216 and F903, whilst F216 and F263/4 also had fragments of clay adhering to the sides (above the level of the cut natural clay) suggesting wattle and daub. Interestingly the decay and collapse of this lining was shown to have occurred after the pit was partly backfilled. Pit dimensions varied from a neat 1.44m square (F216) to a

rectangular 1.05m by 2.0m (F903). Except where slumping had seriously damaged the original shape of the pit (F204/228) they all had vertical sides, and (where excavated) flat bases. Two pits F216 (plot D) and F207 (plot C) were particularly interesting. Four phases of filling were identified within F216, the earliest (114/1) comprising mainly re-deposited natural and containing only a small quantity of animal bone, pottery and tile; the next two fills (120/2 and 120/3) contained much animal bone, by far the largest recovered from any pit of this period on the site, and these included a large number of young cat, possibly indicating a trade in cat furs in the vicinity (Gidney, below); fish remains and eggshell were also recovered from these fills, but insufficient to denote that cesspit waste was deposited here, and suggesting instead that the pit served mainly for disposal of waste from trade, with perhaps some household rubbish mixed in. The depth of this pit, however, suggests a former purpose as a well. The pit's uppermost fills (127/2) contained a reasonably large quantity of building materials, including stone, tile and even a few tesserae, but since there was no evidence for a Roman building on this part of the site, the materials were probably waste from reused Roman materials taken from elsewhere. F207 was unusual in its large dimensions in plan (3.06 by 2.58m): this size was partly due to the remnants of a foundation trench (114/4) on the surface surrounding the pit, which may once have held a surrounding wall (some stone remained in the backfill of this trench but had

Plate 13: *Medieval pit, F537, showing Roman street metalling which had slumped into it. Phase 9*

mostly been removed). Although cut below the level of the underlying Mercia mudstone, the pit was not deep enough to suggest a use as a well. The lower fills of the pit and the fills of the surrounding trench contained building materials such as slate, wall plaster and granite, which may have come from a stone housing around the pit. The function of the pit is debatable, but the stone housing may have functioned as a screen, suggestive of a cesspit or latrine. The pit also contained an unusual quantity of burnt wood and ash (120/7, 120/8), as well as eggshell and chicken bones.

(iii) Ambiguous shaped pits. Area 2: F587 (260/3); F513 (260/4) – Two deep and severely truncated pits were excavated which could not be assigned to either a rectangular or circular category. F587 was 55.66m OD at its base and may have been used for the disposal of cess since insect remains came from its fills (Monckton, below). F513 was even deeper at 55.21m OD at its base, and environmental evidence supported the interpretation of 'cess'-like fills.

Moderately deep pits

Twenty-one pits fell into this category. Six of these contained an unusual deposit which was possibly residue from an industrial process. Fourteen pits were circular in form, seven square/rectangular, and one ambiguous in shape.

(i) Circular Pits. Area 2: F503 (260/1), F507 (256/6), F508 (256/3), F509 (256/4, 257/1, 257/2), F511 (261/1), F516 (256/2), F537 (256/5, 257/3-5), F550 (260/2), F558 (261/7), F570 (256/1), F627 (290/2), F632 (261/5); Area 3: F712 (311/1, 312/1); Area 4: F909 (111/6, 117/5, 124/5) – Most of these pits lay in Areas 2 and 3. Ten were excavated to their base, six of which had been cut to a depth of between 56.3 and 56.7m OD (F503, F516, F570, F627, F632, F712); and three

to between 57.4m OD and 58m OD. In common with the deep circular pits, the profiles of all these pits was very similar, with steep sides and slightly concave bases. The diameters varied, the smallest being 1.5m (F570), and the largest 2.65m (F616). Four pits (F507, F511, F537, F550) were not fully excavated at between 56.5 and 57m OD. Only F509 and F537 appeared to have more than one phase of backfilling. Most fills were normal rubbish deposits, except that F537 also contained a 0.5m square and 0.5m thick chunk of concreted gravel metalling in its upper fills, clearly deriving from the adjacent Roman street. In addition to these deposits, F509 and F537 contained a pale olive coloured fill (256/4, 256/5) in common with a number of other pits of similar dimensions in Area 2 (F507, F508, F516 and F570 – though these were filled only with this material). This fill contained lime concretions, wood ash, and in some cases bone ash and also hearth residues, which can be linked with likely industrial activity (Morgan, below p.307). A pottery link between F570 and F614 (a deep circular pit) suggests that their filling was contemporary.

(ii) Square/Rectangular Pits. Area 1: F213 (112/3, 118/1), F214/F231 (112/4, 118/2), F242 (112/2, 125/2), F438 (118/4, 112/6); Area 2: F510 (248/1, 249/1), F549 (253/9); Area 3: F704 (313/1, 314/1, 315/1) – Seven square/rectangular pits were located on the site. The four pits (F213, F214, F242, F438) in Area 1 and F704 in Area 3 were all cut to approximately 56.5m OD; pits F510 and F549 in Area 2 were 57.26m OD and 57.73m OD respectively. Pits F214, F242, F438 and F704 were square (1.50m, 0.80m, 1.10m and 1.50m square respectively), the remainder rectangular, ranging from 1.7-1.9m long by 1.3-1.8m wide. All had steep or vertical sides and flat bases. Only pit F510 showed evidence of lining, comprising a dark stain around its sides, and a narrow

projecting ledge approximately 0.3m from its base, perhaps suggestive of wattle. F510 notably was located adjacent to the west side of Roman wall footings (the only section of the wall that had not been completely robbed was that which lay directly between F510 and F521 and F579 – phase 8 on the east side of the same wall); F510 was much more regular in shape than F521 and F579 and appeared not to have suffered from degradation of its sides, even at the top. Throughout, the pit fills were uninformative, although that of F213 contained parasites indicative of faeces (Boyer, Archive).

(iii) Ambiguous Shaped Pits. Area 1: F349 (121/4) – Only one pit of moderate depth was too truncated to assess its shape; indeed, truncation had removed much of its fills.

Shallow pits
Eight pits fell into this category.

(i) Circular Pits. Area 1: F262 (121/12), F492 (109/2, 115/2); Area 4: F910/12 (109/4, 115/4, 122/1), F925 (109/6, 122/2) – Four very shallow circular pits were observed, all between 0.20m and 0.80m deep, located at the west end of Area 1. The pits varied in diameter between 1.9m and 0.8m, and were filled with very dark brown silty loams.

(ii) Square Pits. Area 1: F235 (110/1, 116/1), F265 (110/2, 116/2, 123/1), F276 (110/3, 123/2); Area 4: F916 (110/4, 116/3) – These four pits were between 0.48m and 0.8m deep, and varied in size from 0.5m to 2.0m long; F235 was of particular interest as it contained hammerscale suggesting possible ironworking in the vicinity.

Phase 9 timber buildings

Related Contexts and Features: 253/1 (2912, 2722, 2721, F647, F648, F689); 253/2 (F626); 253/3 (2160, 2377, 2468); 253/4 (2363, 2650, 2651); 253/5 (F588, F611, F687); 253/6 (2325, 2362); 253/7 (F573); 253/8 (F583); 253/9 (F549); 254/1 (F653); 254/2 (F653); 254/3 (F653); 254/4 (2363, 2650, 2651); 254/5 (F665); 254/6 (F662); 254/7 (F670); 254/8 (F653); 254/9 (F615); 254/10 (F615); 254/11 (F670); 255/1 (F615); 255/2 (F688); 258/1 (F522/5) 258/2 (F526-32) 262/1 (F639-41); 263/1 (F594-99); 290/1.

Lying against the east edge of the excavation (Area 2) and continuing beyond this and possibly beneath East Bond Street were several layers and features forming the evidence for a timber structure or structures (fig. 43). Given its location and fragmented character, it was not possible to be certain whether it represents one building with two rooms or two separate structures. The orientation and location of the deposits and cuts suggests that the alignment of the former Roman stone building F/G on the site was respected, and earlier elements of the structure (G253) may even have utilised parts of that building in their construction, specifically the north wall. Six phases were identified within the timber building, five of construction (subphases 9.1-9.5) and one of demolition (9.6).

Subphase 9.1 (fig. 42)

Floor? 253/1; Post holes: F674, F647, F648 – The earliest stratigraphic evidence for a medieval timber building in Area 2 was a compact yellowish brown sandy clay (253/1), possibly the base of a floor lying in a shallow cut (F689). This was approximately 0.10m deep, a minimum of 2.40m wide (north-

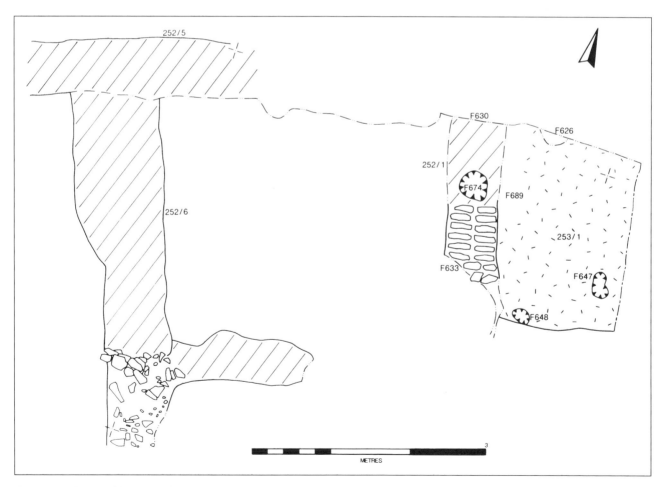

Fig. 42: *Plan of Phase 9.1 medieval timber building*

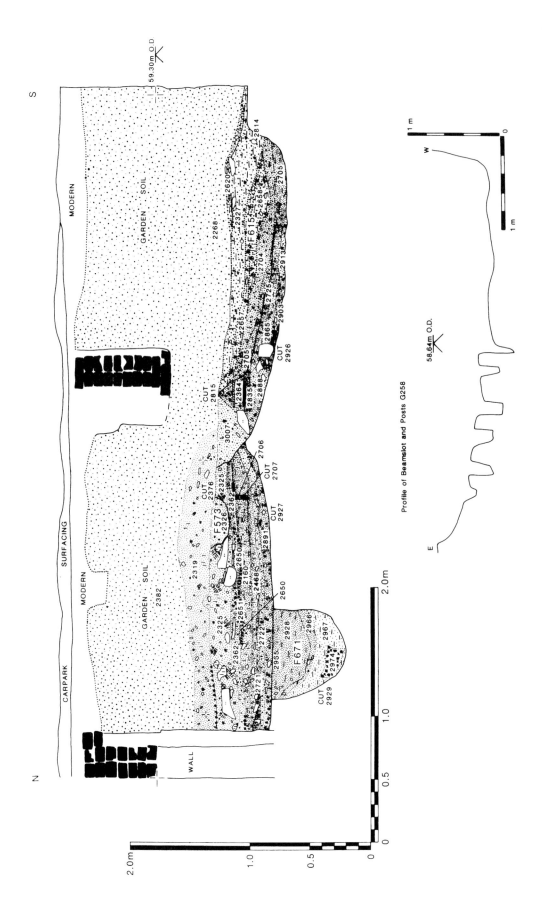

Fig. 43: *Section through floor of medieval timber building (east baulk on figs 45–49), and profile of G258*

Plate 14: *Slot and post holes associated with the phase 9 timber building*

south), truncated at its north end by a Victorian cellar wall and a minimum of 1.70m east-west, its eastern edge obscured beyond the edge of excavation. This layer abutted the edge of the remains of a Roman wall (F633, phase 3F). This Roman wall was partially robbed out at its north end (F630) and what appeared to be the remains of a post hole was located here (F674). The relationship of this robbing to the floor levels is unfortunately impossible to determine. The presence of the post hole may suggest that the wall was partially robbed out to provide a doorway, the post hole possibly representing the remains of that doorway. Two shallow (less than 0.10m deep) post holes (F647, F648) cut through this compacted floor layer, of diameter 0.35 and 0.25m respectively. At this early stage of its existence, this building may have utilised more than one earlier Roman wall as its fabric.

Subphase 9.2 (fig.44)

Floor? (2721); Post holes: F647, F648, F626 – The earlier floor layers were sealed by thin bands of dirty yellow sand above which was a layer of very compacted sand mixed with crushed wall plaster which formed either a floor make-up or an actual floor. The upper compacted layer (2721) spread over Roman wall F633 and the robbed portion of the wall (F630), suggesting that the wall had by this time been completely demolished and that the structure had either extended westwards (away from the street frontage), or that internal

changes were being undertaken. Post holes F647 and F648 remained visible but this may be a result of later truncation/excavation, as the layers were all extremely thin, and could have been damaged very easily. A third post hole (F626) was visible at this level cutting through 2721. It is uncertain if any of the remaining Roman walls still continued in use.

Subphase 9.3 (fig. 45)

Floor? Layers: 253/3 (2160, 2377, 2468); Hearth?: 253/4; Post holes: F648, 253/5 (F611, F687, F588), Pit: 253/9 (F549) – Further layers (253/3) were deposited which clearly spread across the demolished and robbed wall F630/F633 and continued briefly further west. F648 continued to be visible, but F626 and F647 were obscured, suggesting that the posts from these had been removed and a new floor laid; however, four stake holes (F611) and one slightly larger post hole (F687) clustered around the redundant F647 implying a survival of function but with changed format. The somewhat larger post hole F588 also cut through the floor layers at this level. The post holes overall make no discernible pattern, but lie close to an area of burning and ash (253/4 – a hearth?), and so may have supported an associated hearth structure. A small sub-rectangular pit (F549), of less than 1.0m depth, cut this floor at the west end. It may have been lined with an organic material which left a vertical coating of sand around its edges. This may

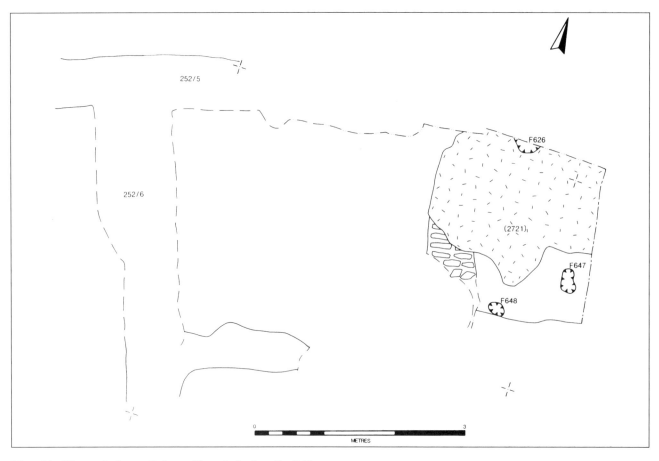

Fig. 44: *Plan of phase 9.2 medieval timber building.*

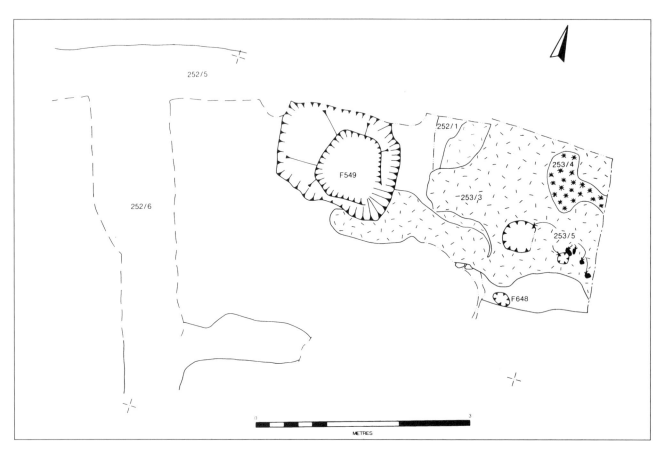

Fig. 45: *Plan of phase 9.3 medieval timber building*

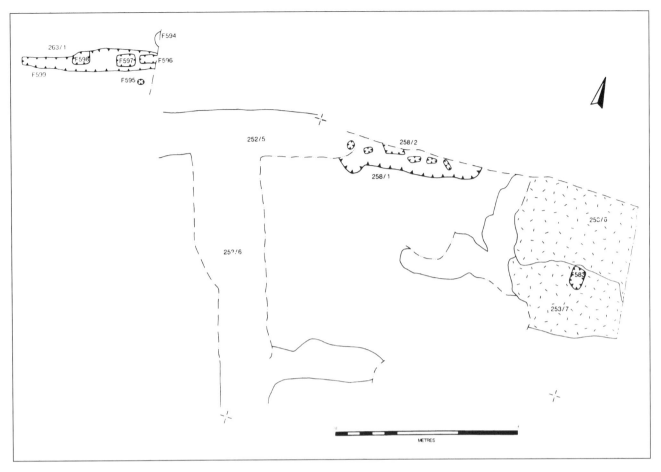

Fig. 46: *Plan of phase 9.4 medieval timber building*

have been a storage pit, although its location could be structural if the Roman walls to the north and west were beginning to crumble. Alternatively, the presence of dense fayalite and charcoal (deriving from a hearth bottom or possibly tap slag?) in the floor layers around and in the backfill of F549 may denote an industrial function linked into nearby iron working.

Subphase 9.4 (fig. 46)

Floor? layers 253/6 (2325, 2362), 253/7; **Post hole** 253/8 (F583); **Beam slot** 258/1 **and posts** 258/2 (F526-32); **Slot and posts** 263/1 (F594-99) – More floor layers (253/6-7) were deposited, apparently keeping close to the original line of wall F633, although potentially these layers had spread accidentally when wall F633 was demolished and removed. The edge of these deposits may also have been caused by truncation: the area had been excavated in two phases, first by machine and later by hand, and so the earlier machine dug layers may have been overcut, thus giving a false edge here. A single post hole (F583) cut through these layers, again positioned very close to a former post hole (F588); it seems unlikely that this is coincidence, and the location probably rather reflects the crucial nature of the function which it performed. Demolition and removal (252/5) of all but the footings of the north Roman wall must have taken place by this time, since a short length of slot containing post holes (258/1-2) had replaced the eastern part of this wall. Pit F549 may also have been backfilled by then since the beam slot appeared to truncate F549's north edge (though both features contained material suggesting a similar backfilling date in the 13th century). Truncation to the east by the walls of a Victorian cellar and to the west by a later pit meant little survived of the beam slot, but voids

representing post holes appeared closely spaced along its length: these may be remnants of impressions left by a sill beam. The remaining Roman walls associated with the medieval timber building had probably been robbed out by this time since, stratigraphically, robber trench 252/5 was later than both robber trenches 252/6 and 252/3. Pit F549 also contained Roman building materials such as tile, slate, mortar and wall plaster in its backfills, as well as likely intrusive medieval period slag. To the west lay a second length of beam slot (263/1) with larger but shallower posts (or spade marks?) which contained two small sherds of medieval pottery. Whilst it followed a similar (but not identical) alignment to 258/1-2, it was almost parallel with the north wall of the Roman building and may have been contemporary or even earlier than it, the medieval pot simply being contaminant from overlying soil.

Subphase 9.5 (fig. 47)

Floor? 254/1-3; Hearth rake-out? 254/4; Post holes 254/5-7, 254/11, 262/1 – In this phase all the floor layers were still visible as were the slot and post features G258 and G263. However, the floor may now have extended to the south for a minimum of 3.0m (254/1-3), at which point it was truncated by a Victorian cellar. Layers of ash and slag (254/4) formed a narrow arcing band over the floor and a number of post holes (254/5-7, 11) cut through the floor. The relationship between these floor layers and those of subphase 9.4 is extremely tenuous, based entirely on a narrow interface seen in section. The floor layers appeared to extend over robber trench 252/3. Some 5.0m to the south a small group of post and stake holes (262/1, not illustrated) was excavated which formed a line with 254/5-7 and 254/11; these lacked finds and, since they cut

Fig. 47: *Plan of phase 9.5 medieval timber building*

through Roman deposits and were sealed by medieval garden soil, could not be securely phased, although a medieval date seems most likely. Three were approximately 0.3m in diameter at the base; the remaining four were little more than stake holes some 50mm in diameter, and less than 50mm deep. if these posts relate to the timber building, then this may have been at least 5.0m longer on its north-south axis.

Subphase 9.6 (fig. 48)

Floor?/Demolition? *254/8-10;* ***Garden Soil*** *255/1, 255/2, 290/1* – The southern part of the floor may have been resurfaced (254/8-9), since the ash and slag (254/4) was covered. Some layers in this final timber building phase appeared to be remnants of demolition (254/10) and it is possible that 254/8-9 also represent demolition rather than re-flooring. Subsequently the area of the building may have suffered from truncation or reworking from the deposition of overlying garden soils (255/1, 290/1), possibly in the late 13th/early 14th century on ceramic evidence, implying the building's abandonment before the early 14th century.

Phase 9 robbing of Roman building

Related contexts and features: F630, F674 (252/1) F553 (252/2) F556, F603 (252/3) F659 (252/4) F536/F646 (252/5) F545 (252/6).

Evidence for the robbing of Roman stone building G252 (Area 2, phase 3F, structures F and G) chiefly consisted of regular trenches which closely followed the original Roman foundation cuts, backfilled with unwanted waste stone from the robbing; this robbing was probably periodic (fig. 50).

Six robber trenches were identified amidst the Roman stone buildings in Area 2. Four of these trenches (252/1/3/5/6) had a close relationship with the medieval timber building described above (pp.00), the clearest being F630. F630 was a 2.04m by 0.74m trench, 0.32m deep, and represents the partial robbing of wall F633, the most easterly of the north-south oriented Roman walls; robbing certainly occurred before or during the earliest phases of construction of the medieval building. How quickly robbing of the remaining nearby stone walls occurred is unclear: the stratigraphy suggests that the most southerly east-west oriented wall was robbed first (252/3), followed by the adjacent north-south wall (252/6), and finally the most northerly of the east-west walls (252/5). The latter certainly occurred before the trench and post wall G258 was erected, and probably took place almost immediately prior to this event, allowing the medieval timber building to continue in use relatively uninterrupted. Two other robber trenches (252/2, 252/4) had removed Roman stone walls: 252/2, 2.0m by 2.06m and 0.96m deep, removed the north-west corner of structure F; 252/4, of 1.96 by 0.67 and 0.5m depth, removed part of a wall probably belonging to structure G. Other indications of robbing came from the backfills of pits F579 and F537, both of which contained large chunks of Roman robbed materials, notably mortared masonry and a 0.50m square block of consolidated street gravel respectively. Since many other medieval pits in Area 2 contained Roman building materials, the possibility is strong that many such materials were still available at this time, including a Roman street – potentially the latter was being exploited as a convenient quarry for gravel (see pp.00 below for full discussion).

It is difficult to assign an accurate date to any of the robber trenches from their backfills alone, since they all contained little, if any, dateable material. Similarly the quantities of dateable items from the timber structure were minimal. From 252/2 and 252/5 pottery suggested very tentative dates of the 12th and 13th centuries respectively. These could at least provide a broad chronology for the robbing and indicate that the medieval timber building continued in use into the 13th century, a date supported by the small quantity of pottery from 253/7, a repair to the earliest floor identified belonging with the timber building. The overlying garden soil produced pottery in the 11th- to early 14th-century date range suggesting a deposition date in the early 14th century or later and therefore a possible abandonment of the building at this time.

PHASE 10 (figs. 37 & 39) 13th-14th centuries AD

Small Finds: buckle plate 108 – sf2146, 119/3; 109 – sf2172, 119/3; *shale bowl* 144 – sf5001, 126/2, *bone die* 181 – sf37, 126/2.

Ceramic dating: 13th-14th centuries AD

Phase 10 pits

Deep circular pits (wells?) F205 (113/1, 119/1, 126/2), F206 (113/2, 119/2, 119/3, 126/1), F218 (113/3, 119/4) – The backfilling of three deep circular pits in Area 1 was assigned to this phase. Stratigraphically there was nothing to indicate that these pits were any later than the phase 9 features, but the

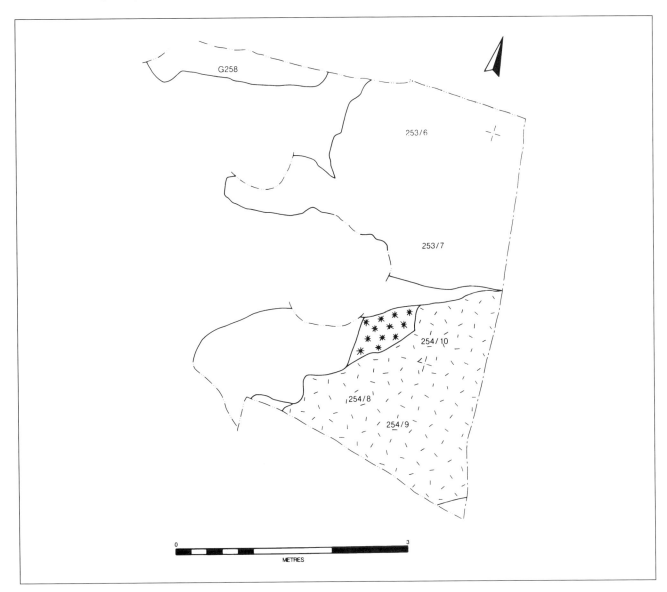

Fig. 48: P*lan of phase 9.6 medieval timber building*

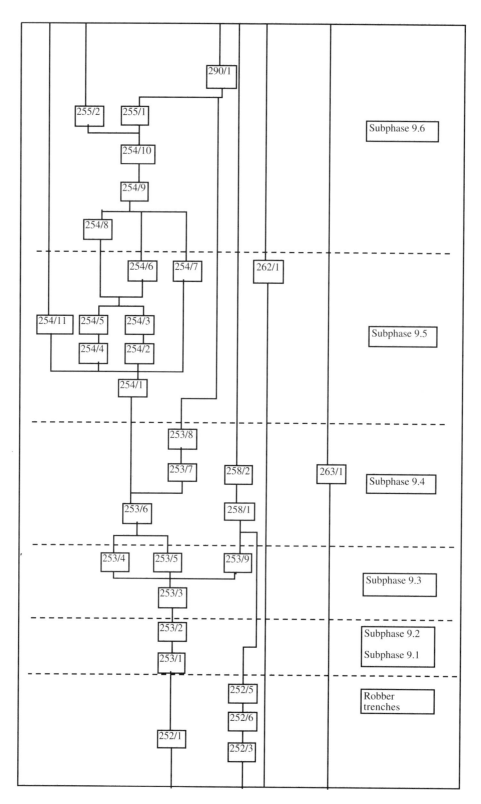

Fig. 49: *Subgroup matrix showing medieval timber building and robber trenches*

pottery assemblage from their backfills indicated a late 13th-century date. F205 and F206 were adjacent to one another (plot D), F218 lay some metres to the south-east (in plot E). No other contemporary features were found elsewhere, and the range of dating evidence from the site as a whole suggests minimal activity during this period and indeed until the 18th-century gravel quarrying. F205 was not fully excavated but was augered to a depth of 52.95m OD; the fully-excavated

F206 reached 52.71m OD; and F218 was slightly deeper, augered to a depth of 52.52m OD; thus all three pits had a depth of over 5.0m, by far the deepest medieval pits encountered. The three pits were similar in diameter, from 1.6m (F218) to 1.78m (F206), and had similar profiles with very steep almost vertical sides at the top narrowing as they descended (F206 narrowed to 1.0m at its base). Traces of lining were noted around their tops where the pits were cut through gravel, but this did not continue below the interface with the underlying Mercia mudstone; dark staining mixed with clay derived from the natural, adhering to their sides, suggested wattle and daub lining. That around F206 appeared to have collapsed into the partly backfilled pit, but may then have been relined and continued in use, as evidence of collapsed lining was also found at a higher level. Pit F206 indeed had three distinct phases of infilling, the earliest fills contained fragments of collapsed lining (119/2) including mineralised wood fragments, and patches of clay and small stones; the upper layers of the secondary phase of rubbish deposits (119/3) also contained fragments of decayed wood and clay lining in addition to a large assemblage of rubbish deposits including pottery and animal bone; by contrast, the uppermost fills had more in common with the overlying garden soils that had been machined away. A rapid phase of rubbish deposits filled the lowest excavated portion (down to 55.39m OD) of F218, with the fills above being very reminiscent of the overlying garden soils and possibly slumped into the settling rubbish fills below.

DISCUSSION OF PHASES 8-10

Nature of activity

The archaeological evidence for medieval occupation in phases 8-10 at Causeway Lane was characterised by a large number of pits. These were nearly all cut 1.0m or more below the probably truncated surface of archaeological deposits. The two main shapes in plan were circular and rectangular, although variations did occur. The pits were almost entirely discrete, with only a few examples intercutting, and then usually only once. The majority appear to have been cut either for water collection or for the disposal of rubbish and/or as cesspits; none seemed cut specifically for gravel extraction. Several pits at Causeway Lane showed evidence of having been lined, either by a wattle framework or by timber planking, and occasionally with clay; only two displayed evidence for stone lining, but in both cases these had been largely robbed of their stone, leaving only a small quantity in the backfill of the surrounding foundation trenches. Special attention was given to the frequency of pits (particularly in Area 1) which formed linear clusters on north-south alignments and a series of possible building plots, A-H-J, was assigned to provide a framework for post-excavation analysis (see below). The pitting at Causeway Lane contrasts strongly with that recorded on the nearby St. Peter's Lane (Shires;1988-9) site, where the medieval pits appeared largely designed for gravel extraction, were generally much larger and less regular in plan, and were intercut to an extent that was almost impossible to disentangle (Lucas and Buckley, forthcoming).

Three other categories of evidence were also present and comprised robber trenches, structural features, and thick, almost black, loam deposits covering much of the site. The latter have been found elsewhere in Leicester, particularly in the north-east quarter, and are locally known as 'garden soil'. The robber trenches were all located in Area 2 where they had removed most of the stone from Roman buildings. Evidence for medieval timber structures likewise was located in Area 2, probably

fronting onto East Bond Street, formerly known as Torchmere (Courtney, below); this is discussed in more detail below (p.86). The 'garden soil' was largely machined away leaving only samples in Areas 1 and 2 to be hand excavated – a decision made because hand clearance of larger areas of 'garden soil' on the Shires excavations had proved to be unproductive (Lucas and Buckley forthcoming), and because inadequate time was available to hand excavate such huge quantities of apparently homogeneous soils.

Pits and plots

Given the lack of cartographic and documentary evidence (Courtney below) for the north-east quarter of Leicester during the Middle Ages, minimal possibility existed of linking the Causeway Lane medieval pits to individual properties. Hence the emphasis here is very much on the site archaeology alone and on comparison with other sites in Leicester and elsewhere, notably Southampton and Northampton.

Because of the documentary lacunae, certain assumptions were made for the Causeway Lane site. A sharp break in the level of the underlying natural gravel was recorded during the 1980 excavation of the west end of the site (Area 4). This followed a north-south alignment, in common with medieval pit alignments (see below), and it seems reasonable to suggest that this distinct change in the land represented a boundary, possibly between properties. All the 'plots' on the site began at this line. Using this as a starting point, three main avenues have been explored:

1. Pits grouped into 'plots' on the grounds of alignment.
2. Pits which link in with 19th-century property boundaries.
3. Pits connected with the putative 'two pole' property measurement.

Pits and plot alignment

This was possible for Areas 1 and 4 where the largely discrete pits showed a distinct north-south linear distribution, at right angles to Causeway Lane. By imposing lines between the pit alignments, a pattern emerged of properties averaging 3.35m; this was valid for all properties with the exception of plots A and B at the west end of the site, both of which were somewhat wider. Further east, however, this hypothesis became less convincing, probably due to the lack of evidence (much of the central portion of the site had been destroyed by 18th-century quarrying), and the addition of a second street (Torchmere, now East Bond street), which perhaps induced properties to take a more east-west alignment at the east end of the site.

Pits and 19th-century properties

Although the earliest map to show the existence of properties is of 1828, its scale is not usable. The earliest map to show good evidence for properties along Causeway Lane is the 1887 first edition Ordnance Survey at a scale of 1:500 (fig. 54). Unfortunately, however, by 1887 the site was already being redeveloped, with a Dispensary replacing the cottages to the east and changes to the west end making comparison of properties somewhat difficult. Thus only a short central zone could be usefully compared to the medieval pit distribution. At first glance there appeared to be little correlation between the excavated and map data, but two areas of coincidence did emerge: firstly, the 19th-century properties followed a very similar alignment to that of the medieval pits (north-south and perpendicular to Causeway Lane); and secondly, the most westerly of the 19th-century properties contained medieval pits entirely within its boundaries. Whilst the former is perhaps unsurprising since the eastern end of Causeway Lane seems to have changed little since it was first mapped in the early 17th century, the latter, although a small sample, may be significant.

Pits and poles

The pole (5$^{1}/_{2}$ yds, 5.03m) or, more accurately, two poles (11 yds, 10.06m), seems to have been a basic unit for property measurements elsewhere in Leicester (J. Hagar pers.comm.). Commencing from the western end of the site, the artificial imposition of plots of two poles width revealed that:

1. The most westerly of the Victorian property boundaries (alignment A) was two poles east of the change in natural, i.e. our original starting point; further east another two properties (alignment B) coincide with the two pole measurement.
2. The medieval pits fall neatly into the imposed plots with only minor infringement.
3. The two pole measurement coincides with the properties defined at A above, so that alignments A and B join to become a property two poles wide, C, D and E join to become a second property of like width, and F, G and H become a third such property (see fig.54). This putative reconstruction breaks down further east, again due to late destruction. It should be noted that in order to test the above theory of property division, specialists were asked to analyse finds by plot; their results are discussed in detail below.

Eight pit alignments or 'plots' were thus identified on Area 1 (A-G), a ninth on Areas 2/3 (H), and a tentative plot (J) possibly associated with medieval structures on Area 2. Plots A-G were all north-south oriented, suggesting frontages on Causeway Lane; whilst plot H was also north-south, analysis of finds, particularly the post-Roman pottery, suggested that this plot was in fact a combination of several on an east-west alignment (fronting onto East Bond Street); plot J follows an east-west alignment. All the pits on plots A-H were likely to have originally been cut from 58m OD or above (this is taken as the starting point when suggesting the category of depth into which each pit falls). Those pits falling within Area 2 may originally have been cut from approximately 59m OD; certainly those features in the south-east corner, which showed least depth of truncation were cut from this level.

PHASE 11 (fig. 37)

late medieval – post-medieval

Certainly by the early 17th century, this part of Leicester appears to have been given over to gardens and orchards (Courtney, below). This would account for the relative scarcity of features dating to this period on the site, with excavated features being confined almost entirely to a few pits and garden soil.

Small Finds: Pin-beater 131 – sf9010, 126/2; *ca armlet* 93 – sf2045, 259/3; *bone pin* 46 – sf9011, 108/1.

Ceramic dating: Late to post-medieval

Phase 11 pits

Nineteen pits were backfilled in this phase: most (fifteen) were too truncated to categorise; the remaining four were all circular.

Truncated pits F512 (259/3), F520 (259/2), F544 (259/5), F551 (259/1), F552 (259/4), F586 (259/6), F538 (291/1), F563 (291/2), F564 (291/3), F560 (291/4), F612 (291/5), F506 (291/6), F652 (291/7), F505 (292/1), F631 (292/2) – Fifteen pits, all in Area 2, were backfilled during phase 11. As all were severely truncated by 18th-century quarrying and many had only the base surviving, it was not possible to reconstruct either original plans or profiles; some appeared circular, and some were of shallow or moderate depth. Their fills generally resembled the surrounding post-medieval garden soils, a dark greyish brown to black sandy loam. The pits formed no clear spatially related group.

Deep pits F703 (306/1, 307/1, 308/1), F564 (264/1), F576 (291/8) – Three pits fell into this category. One deep circular pit (F703), of diameter 1.8m, located in Area 3 was backfilled during phase 11: it had steep, almost vertical sides and it was not fully excavated at 56.10m OD; its backfill comprised layers of greyish and occasionally yellowish brown sandy silts and clay silts interleaved with occasional lenses of ash and containing large quantities of domestic rubbish such as animal bone, pottery, slates and tiles. Its animal bone assemblage ratios reflected those seen elsewhere at Causeway Lane and at the Shires (Gidney, below). The upper fills (308/1), which probably include slumping from the overlying layers of garden soil, varied from dark greyish brown silty clay to dark yellowish brown sand and gravel. Pit F564 in Area 2 was not fully excavated at 57.65m OD (having been cut from 58.80m OD) and as it lay on the edge of the excavation its full plan was not exposed; it was, however, at least 1.3m in diameter. Pottery finds suggested a mid 16th century date for its backfilling, although an extremely wide date range of pottery was present, including some Saxon material, and much building debris including stone, slate, and tile appeared to have been deposited to fill the pit; this evidence may indicate that it had served as a well. The same may be true for Pit F576, also circular of 1.90m diameter, excavated to 57.85 (a depth of 1.4m below its top), though with an augered depth at 55.3m OD. Although near vertical, the pit's sides were much more irregular than any others excavated on the site, with the irregularity perhaps caused by the collapse of a wattle and daub lining, still evident in some parts. Pit F576's backfills, however, were similar to those in other pits of this date.

Moderately deep pit F591 (264/2) – Only pit F591 fell into this category: this cut through F564 from approximately 58.3m OD (or higher originally since the upper portion had been destroyed during reworking of garden soils). It was fully excavated at 57.2m OD, was circular in shape, but unlike the deep pits had gentler, more degraded edges; its base diameter was only 0.6m compared to just over 2m at the top.

Garden soil 108/1 (291/10) (not shown on plan) – Layers of overlying garden soil were hand-excavated in Area 1 in 1980, and pottery from these layers suggested a late medieval or early post-medieval date. Of particular interest were a number of sherds in these layers which were found to link with pottery from the upper fills of features below. This dark sandy loam occurred elsewhere on the site, but was largely machined away. On those parts of the site where a portion was available for excavation this was found to have different dates, suggesting that the apparently homogeneous soils were in fact the product of different phases of deposition.

Ditch/gullies F574 (291/9), F559 (291/11), F905 – Two features on the south-east area of the site may relate to severely truncated ditches or gullies. A further gully was excavated in Area 4 but could not be securely phased.

PHASE 12 (fig. 50) **Post-medieval**

It is important to note that only a sample of the latest deposits were excavated by hand: the majority of the deposits were either removed by machine, or excavated very rapidly. A full description of these deposits is retained in archive and only a short summary, with details of key deposits, is published here.

Small Finds: stone ball 180 – sf4559 296/1; *bead* 73 – sf3007 302/1; 82 – sf4578, 207/5; *armlets* 85 – sf4571, 301/1; 89 – sf5022, 302/2; 92 – sf2261, 301/1; 96 – sf2254, 301/1; *brooches* 9 – sf2053, 100/1; 12 – sf2095, 104/1; 27 – sf2008, 100/1; 30 – 2010, 100/1); *counters* 170 -sf4572, 301/1; *spatula* 121 – sf2037, 100/1, *ca nail* 197 – sf9007, 100/1, *needles* 129 – sf2317, 301/1; *bone object* 224 – sf73, 301/1, *bone pins* 40 – sf11, 100/1; 44 – sf59, 301/1; *finger rings* 100 – sf2251, 100/1; 103 – sf2247, 301/1), *spoon* 140 – sf2277, 302/1).

Dating: Post-medieval

Subphase 12.1

18th century quarry pits F234, F256, F404, F441 (102/1), F500 (293/1), F582 (293/2), F593 (293/3), F518 (293/5), F567 (293/4), F584 (293/6), F517, F523 (293/7), F701 (302/1), F702 (302/2) – An area of approximately 600m² in the centre of the site consisted of large quarry pits, presumably for gravel, cut during the 18th century. Since this quarrying affected all three areas of the site to a greater or lesser extent, as noted only a sample of these were excavated by hand, the remaining fills being removed by machine. The sample showed that these backfills could be dated to the 18th century, whilst a large number of earlier finds, particularly Roman, was present, showing that residuality was very high. The quarried pits were probably backfilled rapidly, since clear dump layers could be discerned in the sections, including layers of re-deposited garden soil, low grade gravel and some bands of much paler brown soil which were probably re-deposited from disturbed Roman layers. F500 was the largest of these pits, covering much of Area 2, although F701 and F702 in Area 3 were almost as extensive. The Area 3 quarry pits are of interest since they appear to have been dug to follow a seam of gravel, but on finding the area to have been previously heavily quarried (see phase 5), pit cutting abruptly terminates. The pit diggers presumably must also have encountered the Roman layers in Area 1 and halted quarrying in this direction too

Subphase 12.2

Post-18th century quarry activity F566 (294/1), F554 (294/2), F581 (294/3), F562 (294/4), F548, F621 (294/5), F675 (294/6), F589 (294/7), F590 (294/8), G103, G106 – Eight pits

were (rapidly and not fully) excavated which certainly post-dated the backfilled 18th-century quarries. All were located in Area 2, were either circular or sub-circular in form, and dug to between 57.3m and 58m OD. The exception was F554 which was a circular (1.3m diameter) brick-lined well, excavated to 56.62m OD: its bricks were specially made, unfrogged, and curved to fit the sides of the well and very loosely mortared. F581 was sealed beneath a 19th-century cellar and cut into the fills of the 18th-century quarry pits described above (subphase 12.1); usefully, its backfill contained waste from a clay pipe kiln (Higgins, below). Additional pits (G103) were excavated in Area 1 which probably post-date the quarrying but pre-date the subphase 12.3 cellars. Finally, several features (G106) observed only in section cut through the quarry backfills but were sealed beneath cellars; their nature was thus uncertain.

Subphase 12.3

Victorian and later activity F501, F502, F541, F535, F580, F524, G101, G105, F700 (300/1) – Development of the excavated zone in the 19th century caused some substantial intrusions, the earliest of which consisted of brick-built cellars belonging to terraced properties fronting onto East Bond Street, the eastern end of Causeway Lane and to the south of Countess Street (Courtney, below). Fortunately these cellars had generally caused little damage to earlier deposits, since they had only cut through the 2.0m deep garden soils. However, the cellars along Causeway Lane were later extended and deepened when the Dispensary was built and the houses were converted for use with the East Bond Street maternity hospital. Those cellars fronting onto Countess Street, meanwhile, were somewhat deeper, but inflicted little stratigraphic damage since the area below had already been destroyed by the subphase 12.1 gravel quarries. One of these cellars sealed the noted early 19th-century clay tobacco pipe and kiln dump F581. The East Bond Street maternity hospital was extended in the early 20th century and deep cellars were inserted. Their foundations were still evident in Area 1 fronting onto Causeway Lane, built from steel reinforced concrete. To the north of these foundations were the concrete piles for the former, late 19th-century horsedrawn tram depot which was accessed from Countess Street. A number of post holes (G105) were found associated with the cellars and have been interpreted as scaffolding supports, used in construction. Countess Street itself (F700) was discovered during machining of Area 3, less than 0.30m below the modern surface: it comprised granite setts and cobbling, with most of the larger setts removed when the street had been decommissioned, although some kerb stones remained *in situ*. Finally, the most recent function of the site before excavation had been as a car park and Unemployment Benefit Office, neither of which left deep foundations and were totally removed by machine in initial clearance work.

UNPHASED STRUCTURAL FEATURES

Post holes and gully F278 (128/1), F283 (128/2), F284 (128/3) – Two groups of possible structural features (post holes and a gully) were unphased. Of these, F283 contained one sherd of medieval pot which may be intrusive, and as a feature it would fit well with the post hole structure described as part of phase 5. Two post holes and a gully located in Area 1 and eight post holes in Area 2 may have been backfilled during this phase. The Area 1 features were closely set, but formed no coherent pattern.

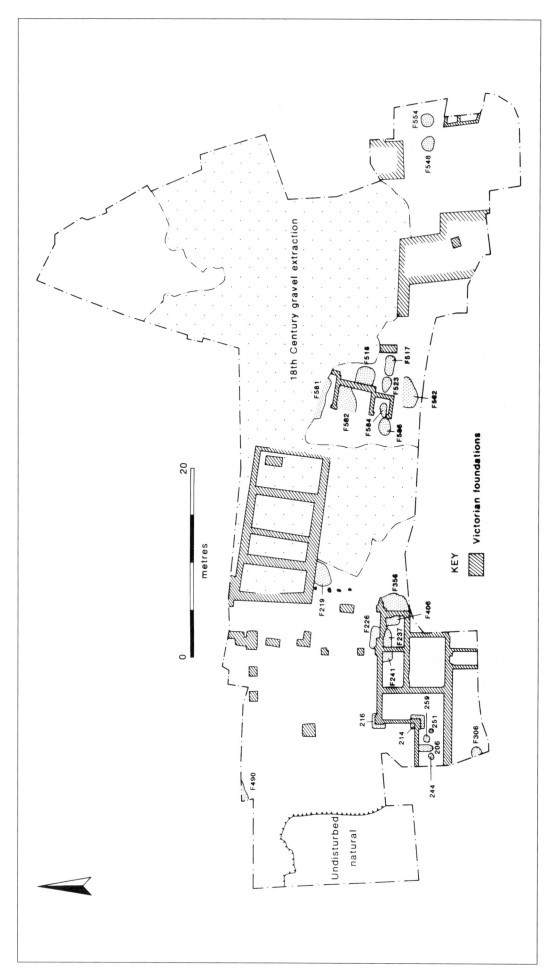

Fig. 50: *Plan of post-medieval features*

DISCUSSION OF THE POST-ROMAN RESEARCH THEMES

Aileen Connor with Richard Buckley

This section expands upon the interpretation offered above in the detailed discussion of the excavated sequence. The aims here are to analyse how far the distribution of identified pits correlate with proposed 'plot' units within this zone of north-east medieval Leicester, to assess the structural evidence for medieval settlement, and to comment on the contribution such reconstructions can offer for enhancing current understanding of the town between the Roman and modern eras.

THE ANGLO SAXON PERIOD

In common with other excavated sites in Leicester, there is a hiatus at Causeway Lane between the latest Roman activity and the intense occupation of the 11th – 12th centuries. However, quantities of pottery and two small finds of the Anglo Saxon period were recovered from the site and a few features, some perhaps structural, have been tentatively identified as evidence of activity in this period, although all are severely truncated and of no definite form. In addition, some doubt must remain over the dating of the latest Roman activity in Area 3, currently assigned to phases 6A and 6B. There are clearly inherent difficulties in dating structural features – such as post holes and beam slots – which cut the latest Roman deposits, given that such features rarely produce many finds and assemblages will therefore be dominated by residual material. Indeed, excavation in 1996 of a major Anglo Saxon rural settlement at Eye Kettleby in Leicestershire produced only a handful of finds from twenty halls, the majority of the assemblage deriving from sunken-featured buildings and pits (N. Finn pers. comm.). In the latter instance, the post-built halls can only be dated by their form, and by association with the sunken featured buildings. Similarly, highly truncated evidence of a structure associated with a few sherds of fifth-sixth century pottery from Oxford Street, Leicester in 1997 (Gossip 1998, 159-60) can only be confidently assigned to the Anglo Saxon period in view of the presence of a definite sunken featured building from just across the road on Bonners Lane (Finn 1994, 165-70; F.Gossip pers. comm.).

Other sites in this part of Leicester have produced finds of the fifth-sixth century, in particular St. Peters Lane (Shires 1988), with 55 sherds of pottery and a composite bone comb, and Little Lane (Shires 1988) with 29 sherds of pottery. In addition, a pit excavated on Butt Close Lane in the 19th century produced finds of the period, and there are indications of a small cemetery outside the East Gate (P.Liddle pers. comm.). Although the quantities of material are comparatively small, the sherd densities compare favourably with those recovered from fieldwalking and excavation of the Eye Kettleby site referred to above. Here, about 141 sherds were recovered by fieldwalking from 13 ha, or 10.8 sherds per ha. Subsequent excavation of 4.5 ha revealed 20 halls and 25 sunken featured buildings and about 3000 sherds of pottery, or 666.6 sherds per ha. At Causeway Lane and the Shires, 112 sherds were recovered from 0.272ha, or about 411 sherds per ha. Whilst it is true that such comparisons are perhaps of doubtful validity, the quantities of material must surely attest a reasonably high level of activity in this area in the fifth–sixth centuries, perhaps of a similar character to a dispersed rural Anglo Saxon settlement, but located within the walls of the Roman town.

THE MEDIEVAL PERIOD

(Late 11th-Early 14th Century)

Both the Causeway Lane and St. Peter's Lane (Shires, 1988-9) excavations (fig. 4) suggest that the north-east quarter of the town was occupied from the early 12th until the mid-13th century, tailing off in the early 14th century (cf. sequence in Elbow Lane – Lucas *et al.*, 1989, 24), with both domestic and probable industrial activity evident. The nature of this settlement is discussed below. At each a definite hiatus in occupation can be recognised: at St. Peter's Lane activity is renewed in the late 15th /early 16th century; at Causeway Lane, by contrast, inactivity persists until the 19th century (bar some minor pitting in the 16th/17th century).

In terms of site functions, we may argue for initial domestic settlement with simple household 'industry' at Causeway Lane, with perhaps more commercial production in the eastern zone. This had largely disappeared by the mid-13th century and was fully gone by the early 14th, to be replaced by dark, humic garden soils, most probably representing gardens or orchards. Whilst some other towns seem to show this tendency for areas of abandonment in the fourteenth century, as revealed at St. Peter's Street in Northampton (although there development recommenced in the early 15th century – Williams 1979, 145), elsewhere we see a rapid expansion, infilling of backyard areas and subdivision of properties, as witnessed at Canterbury, Winchester and York (Ottaway 1992, 173). For Causeway Lane the 12th- and 13th-century activities were perhaps not conducive to denser population, either as a result of wetter ground, or else because the settlement focus shifted, with greater emphasis given to filling out the main market streets, notably Highcross and High Street (see discussion by Courtney, below).

The location and evolution of properties
(fig. 51)

Many pits in Areas 1 and 4 in particular fell into linear alignments on a north-south orientation (plots A-G) and, since no property frontages were excavated in these areas, it is argued that each alignment belonged to one property (with its frontage on Causeway Lane, medieval St. John's Lane). Certainly the ordered nature of the pitting suggests that the pit diggers were confined to long narrow plots, contrasting with the pits on the St. Peter's Lane site (Lucas and Buckley forthcoming), which showed no order, either spatially or in their individual shapes. Towards the east, the excavated pits became less ordered, partly as a result of disturbance from later activity, particularly 18th-century gravel pitting, and partly because of the presence of East Bond Street (Torchmere) which will have affected such orientation: hence plot H was slightly skewed to that followed by plots A-G yet was more closely aligned to East Bond Street; potentially pits in this group could also relate to the rubbish from one household. However, if the pits did all belong to one plot, it would be extremely long; indeed, two of the pits were slightly out of alignment. Hence it was perhaps not surprising to find that pottery from the pits was diverse and did not support the theory that the pits may have been dug and used by one household. Alternatively. these pits were

totally unconnected and the alignment noted was coincidental or due to their location towards the rear of these properties (this may also explain the apparent alignment of F503 and F504, both located towards the rear of plot J, a property possibly associated with a timber building and fronting onto East Bond Street – see below).

The table below summarises the presumed plots and their pits across phases 8 to 10.

This phasing was based on a combination of stratigraphic and ceramic information. Initial stratigraphic phasing (with the aid of spot dates) suggested that phases 8 and 9 in all the plots were very similar in date, and that Phase 10 was slightly later. The date of the backfilling of the pits relies heavily on the ceramic assemblages found within them, as few other dateable objects were found. Two decorated buckle plates were found in F206 (phase 10, plot D) one of which may date to AD 1200-1350 (Cooper, below, p.263) – in keeping with the date range of the ceramic assemblage recovered. Closer examination of the ceramic assemblage (Davies and Sawday, below) has shown that phase 10 and phases 8 and 9 in plots E, F and G all have a similar late 13th-early 14th century termination date. Plot B is slightly earlier with a mid-to late 13th century terminus; plots A, C and D (phase 9) have an earlier termination date of late 12th – early/mid-13th century; whilst plot D phase

Table 4: *Phase 8, presumed plots and pits*

Plot	A	AB	B	C	D	E	F	G	H
Phase 8	F914	F907	F245 F269 F915	F363	F247 F248		F442 F443 F482		F604 F609
Phase 9	F491 F903 F908 F911 F925		F203/38 F204/28 F217 F235 F262 F292? F349 F384? F492 F909 F910/12 F913?	F207 F276 F444?	F214/31 F216 F242 F244?	F279	F213 F243 F297? F298? F389	F257 F263/4 F265 F438	F513 F587 F714 F726 F727
Phase 10					F205 F206	F218			

The suggested dates for these plots are as follows:

Plot A –	Phases 8 & 9	Late 12th – Early/mid 13th century
Plot B –	Phases 8 & 9	Mid – Late 13th century
Plot C –	Phase 9	Late 12th – Early 13th century
Plot D –	Phase 8	Late 11th – Mid/late 12th century
	Phase 9	13th century
	Phase 10	Late 13th – Early 14th century
Plot E –	Phase 9 & 10	Late 13th – Early 14th century
Plot F –	Phases 8 & 9	Late 13th – Early 14th century
Plot G –	Phase 9	Late 13th – Early 14th century
Plot H –	Phases 8 & 9	Early/mid-12th – Mid/late 13th century

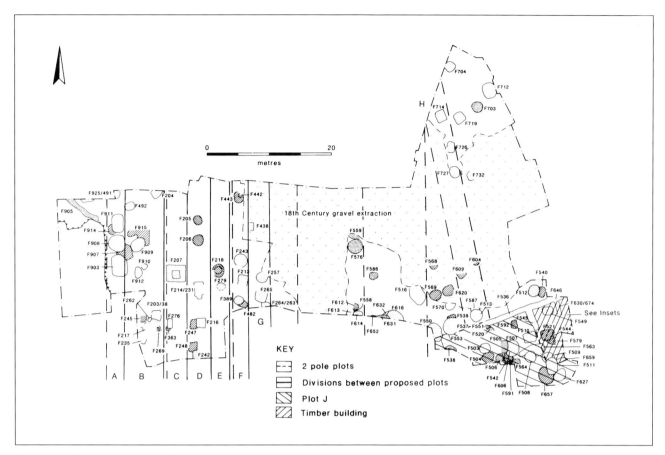

Fig. 51: *Plan of the site showing proposed location of medieval plots*

8, dated to late 11th-mid/late 12th century, has the earliest occupation in these plots.

From these dates one may observe certain changes in the plots, perhaps representing boundary movements. The earliest backfilling occurred in two phase 8 pits towards the south (the front of plot D); no other pit in plots A-G had a comparable early backfill date, although some features in Area 2, notably the phase 8 pits associated with the timber building and some of the robber episodes, were of 12th-century date. Pit digging continued further north, or away from the frontage on plot D (phase 9), and their backfills belonged to the late 12th – early/mid-13th century. Pits on neighbouring plots A and C were also backfilled during this period, and on plot B slightly later in the 13th century. By the end of the 13th century, however, all of the pits on plots A, B, C and at the front of plot D had been backfilled. Pits at the rear of plot D (phase 10) and on E, F and G, on the other hand, remained open until the late 13th-early 14th century.

However, given that Saxo-Norman wares were certainly present in pits on all the plots (Davies and Sawday, below), one might argue that some pits were simply in use for longer than others; in contrast, the pit diggers on plot D may have had a preference for digging new pits, rather than reusing old ones. A reason for the latter could be viewed in the fact that one phase 9 pit contained waste from cat-skinning,

which would have been extremely noxious (see below p.327).

Generally the rubbish from plots A-G phases 8-10 was of a domestic nature. Plots B, C, D and F all showed evidence of the disposal of latrine waste in at least one pit (F206, F207, F213, F235, F482 – nb. however, that environmental samples were not available for study from plot A since those features were excavated in 1980: A475-1979). The presence of a well on each of the plots may suggest that the plots served individual households, whereas the lack of evidence for a cess-pit on either plot E or G could be taken to indicate a combination of plots serving one household in the later 13th-early 14th century. The ceramic evidence further suggests that plots D and E may have been under one ownership at this date (Davies and Sawday, below, p.182-3).

Adjacent plots C and D showed marked differences from each other in a number of ways, with more pits present on plot D (perhaps showing a longer usage of D, since C had a 12th -13th-century date for backfilling, whereas pits on D began to be backfilled in the late 11th – early 12th century and continued into the 14th century) and a wider range of finds existing in D (including in F216 a large quantity of cat skeletons, perhaps waste from cat skins, and, as in the adjacent phase 8 pit F247, bones from young sheep, goat, dog and a foetal calf, all probably killed for their skin (Gidney, below, p.327), although from phase 10 finds were of a more normal 'domestic' rubbish character. Interestingly, the waste in the phase 10 pits on plots D and E may be suggestive of rubbish deposited from an inn (Davies and Sawday, and Nicholson, below), such as the presence of herring and eel. Also of note is the rubbish disposed in plot C in F207, a deep square pit, which may have been used as a cess-pit or a latrine. This also yielded eel and herring as well as young chicken bones and egg-shell, and frog and toad bone, possibly indicating that the pit had been backfilled during the spring (Gidney, below p.328 and Boyer, below pp.329-33) and possibly also an indication of chicken rearing and breeding (Coy 1989, 32). The range of plants, particularly fruit, from this pit was also rather greater than elsewhere (Monckton, below p.355), either because of better preservation or perhaps because they derived from a wealthier household. The latter contention is not, however, supported by a more abundant pottery assemblage.

The timber building(s) and associated features, plot J

As noted in the phasing descriptions above, convincing evidence emerged for one or two medieval timber structures in Plot J, although damage from post-medieval truncation and a 19th-century cellar meant that complete plans could not be recovered. Associated finds were sparse and so limited the analysis of the layers directly associated with the building(s), hence the need to integrate with these the tentative discussion regarding pits and plot arrangements. However, it should be stressed that even such fragile remains are important, given the rarity of excavated structures of like date in Leicester. Dating was accordingly problematic: the limited ceramic evidence offered a date range for the timber building of between the 12th and 14th century. Its end date is provided by layers of 'garden soil' sealing the structural deposits, and the earliest of these (G290) contained 13th- to 14th-century pottery. As noted, whilst the building reused Roman walls, there is no dating evidence for the first robbing out of these elements; however, a late 13th-century ceramic date emerged for robbing F536 in the later phases (figs. 46 & 47) of the building, whilst two internal pits (F521, F579) with 12th-century backfills provide clearer guides to the period of usage.

Plan and orientation

The building(s) was undoubtedly located (partly or completely) within the walls of a Roman building, but it is questionable how many of these walls were still standing and re-utilised given that the stratigraphic evidence relating the Roman wall (F633) to the earliest floor layers within the medieval building was uncertain. Wall robbing clearly did not take place in one moment, with the earliest robbing episodes being F630, F556/603 and F545, and the latest F536/646: the earliest lacked finds, the latest contained a small ceramic assemblage suggesting a late 13th-century date. Certainly there was no evidence to suggest that any of these walls had been demolished prior to a structure being erected in the

medieval period; rather we should envisage that certain of the Roman walls were allowed to stand as useful elements to the timber structure, whilst others were demolished, until, possibly, all the stone walls were removed, leaving only a timber framed building in its place. The robbed stone may have been used elsewhere on the site, or, more probably, in the absence of dressed stone from the excavation, was carted elsewhere, perhaps sold by the timber house owners.

The full plan of the medieval building is difficult to determine. The best evidence was for the north wall which had utilised the Roman building in its earlier phases, later replacing the stone wall with a post and slot construction on the same alignment. The west wall may also have utilised the Roman building in its earliest phases, followed by a robbing episode (F546) after which the west side of the building may have remained open; alternatively the location of the wall changed, either extending further westwards (although no floor layers had survived to the west) or contracting towards the east, perhaps reflected in a number of post holes lying roughly parallel with the Roman wall F633. The south wall may likewise have used Roman walls in its construction. The surviving floor layers in the later phases of the building suggest the internal north-south dimension of the building was at least 5.0m. The east wall lay beyond the edges of the excavation, probably adjacent to medieval Torchmere and close to the edges of modern East Bond Street. Overall dimensions could thus be estimated at c. 8.0 x 5.0m. Given the apparent re-use of walls of the Roman building, it should have followed a similar if not identical orientation, ENE-WSW.

Using the cartographic evidence (see Courtney, below), there are two possible streets on which the house frontage lay. The modern streets of Causeway Lane and East Bond Street seem to have existed from at least the late 13th century, appearing in 1610 as St. John's Lane and Torchmere respectively, and largely follow the medieval orientations. Since these streets do not form a right-angle at their junction, the excavated building can be seen to align more readily with Torchmere. In addition, the distance from modern Causeway Lane to the north wall (or rear wall if Causeway Lane is taken as the frontage) is approximately 16m, which may be considered to be too deep for a single building; in contrast the distance from East Bond Street to the presumed west wall is 8.0-10.0m, a more usual depth for a medieval building.

Internal features and building function

Phase 8 pits F521 and F579 both appeared set within the medieval timber structure and respected the Roman wall (robbing episode F545) thought to have been used initially as the external west wall. The latter must have become unstable soon after, as a fragment of superstructure had fallen into F579. The pits also cut through the floor of the medieval structure, although the ceramic assemblage suggests backfilling in the 12th century which is at odds with the 13th century date for phases of re-flooring within the building. However, it would seem possible that the pits were dug whilst the building was in use, as at the 12th century undercroft in Guildhall Lane, Leicester (Hagar and Buckley 1990, 99-101). Here, several cess pits cut the earliest floor levels and have been taken to indicate a decline in the status of the structure over time.

Several of the fills within pits F521 and F579 contained layers with evidence of putrid deposits, possibly 'cess' (Skidmore, below), sandwiched between clean layers of re-deposited sand and gravel, indicative of a use as cess pits or latrines. Evidence from the study of flies may suggest that these pits were covered. The analysis of woodlice has suggested the presence of animal dung, perhaps suggesting stable manure (see Dawes, below). Although there is a possibility that similar deposits could result from industrial activities, such as tanning (see below), such 'industrial' debris is nonetheless fairly limited and insufficient to point to anything other than a domestic function for the building.

Associated property and plot? features

Given that the locations of the external walls of the medieval building are somewhat tenuous and that finds were few, so the location of associated features or even a plot can only be regarded as extremely speculative. Nonetheless, certain features and areas of ground are more likely to be associated with the medieval building than others: the first area includes the plot of land immediately to the rear (west) of the structure; the second includes all the area to the south, assuming that the building was so close to the corner of St. John's Lane and Torchmere that it may have occupied a corner plot. Within this area only those pits with a backfilling date similar to that of the building were likely to have been associated with it. Only F503, F504, F510 and F592 were located immediately behind the timber building; of these F504 and F592 were both placed in phase 8 and with 12th-century backfills; F510 by contrast revealed a 13th-century assemblage. For the hypothetical corner plot, pits F507, F606, F591, F564, F508, F509, F511, F657 could be associated with the building, all bar F606 and F657 belonging to phase 9.

Industries

Phase 9 pits F507-509, F516, F537 and F570 in Area 2, featured varying amounts of a pale olive coloured deposit within their fills (allocated a single group number (256) in post-excavation analysis to identify them easily). This deposit contained varied amounts of lime, calcareous concretions, fuel ash slag, kiln residues and some bone ash (Morgan, below p.307), in some pits to the exclusion of other fills (e.g. F516), whereas others contained other rubbish deposits allocated to a separate group (257). Pottery from these deposits (of largely 13th-century date) revealed very little lime residue except in pits F508-510; links were noted between nearby F507 and F508 and also F605, although the latter lacked noticeable amounts of lime (Davies and Sawday, below p.189). All six pits were

circular or sub-circular in plan, of moderate depth (1.5-2.5m).

The fills within these pits contrasted with most others on the site, although samples from a number of other pits (F204, F207, F513, F568) contained some of the same materials, in particular the calcareous concretions, which may denote a deposit to counteract odours (see below). The majority of the pits were situated on Area 2, with, as noted above, three of the pits located within Plot J, and thus in proximity to the timber building. If the theory that the whole site had been divided into individual properties or 'plots' is correct, then these pits were apparently scattered through different though adjacent plots.

That these fills represent an industrial rather than domestic function is indicated by various factors: firstly, the finds assemblages from these pits was rather limited, and whilst the pottery forms present suited a domestic assemblage some sherds, particularly from F508 and F509, were covered with a lime deposit heavier than would normally be expected in a domestic context; secondly, the general lack of finds also suggests a purpose other than the disposal of domestic waste – indeed, few animal bones were recovered, and only F537 showed any evidence for the possible disposal of 'cess', and that was in a more normal rubbish deposit found within that pit. The use of lime has been suggested in keeping cess and domestic rubbish pits relatively free of smells and flies in high summer (Skidmore, below p.342), but in the case of these six pits, flies associated with 'cess' were not present in the possible industrial deposits.

The nature of the industrial process

The main elements present within the lime-rich matrix of these fills comprised calcareous concretions, fuel ash (probably derived from wood), some hearth or kiln residues, and occasional bone ash. Morgan (below p.307) argues that these elements may result from lime burning, although he notes also that the bone ash may have been used in cupellation. Lime is, however, an important part of a number of other industrial processes: (1) in the pre-tanning process, lime is employed to facilitate the removal of hair and to 'plump' the skin (Waterer 1979, 152; wood ash could also be used or combined with the lime – Shaw 1987, 46); (2) lime was also a major component in the preparation of young goat or calf skins for making parchment (Saxl 1979, 189); (3) soap-making also requires lime, particularly for soft-soap which was commonplace from as early as the 12th century in the cleaning of textiles: this soap was made from caustic potash lye created by running water through layers of wood ash and lime, then mixing with animal fats (Taylor and Singer 1979, 355-6); (4) lime greatly served the building trade in producing plaster, mortar, cement and attractum (for infilling thick walls) (ibid., 355); (5) finally, lime was also required in glass manufacture. The most likely industries represented here are tanning and soap-making, which could take place near to one another since they both rely on animal products; both, however, produce extremely unpleasant smells.

Trade in skins and furs

Closely related to the tanning industry was the trade in skins and furs from small animals, such as appears to be represented in the phase 8 and 9 plot D pits. The main trade seems to have been cats, although lambs, dogs, and young calves may also have been used (Gidney, below). Dates for the pits suggest that the trade may have ceased by the middle of the 12th century. The location of the trade waste is interesting, however, considering its close proximity to a possible tanning workshop (on Area 2). The scale of the operation was probably quite small, but diverse: the range of skins may represent waste from a fell monger acting as a middle man in the buying and selling of skins, with the calf and goat skins perhaps sold on to a parchment maker (Parchment Lane is only a short distance away), the cat and lamb skins probably used for their fur, and the dog and goat skin perhaps for gloves (Serjeantson 1989, 129). Alternatively the householder may have been a tawyer, or oil-tanner, with the skins and furs prepared by smoking and removal of the fat and flesh, and the skins then placed in barrels or troughs, soaked in oil and trodden or beaten. House 10 at St. Peter's Street, Northampton, has been interpreted as a possible skin dressing workshop in the 16th/17th century (Williams 1979, 147). Evidence of waste from a fell monger or related trade was also found in the phase 10-12 (AD 1100-1550) deposits at St. Peter's Lane, Leicester (Lucas and Buckley 1989), where the range of skins included horse and dog with less emphasis on cat. Other crafts were represented here including horn working (Gidney *in* Lucas and Buckley forthcoming), and the deposits overall were interpreted as being a municipal dump, rather than purely domestic rubbish.

Water source

A significant problem for any such industry in this part of Leicester may have been water supply, especially vital to many of the stages in leather, fur and soap production. A large water course such as the River Soar would not have been essential, since smaller streams and tributaries would have been equally appropriate (cf. Norwich – Ayers 1994, 67). Although modern Leicester has few natural streams, this could be due to changes in the water table, caused particularly during last century when large areas of Leicester were deliberately drained in an attempt to stop the spread of disease . The name of the excavation site also indicated that there might once have been rather more water, with the road having to be raised up to avoid wet ground (Courtney, below p.92). Martin (1990, 23) has argued that medieval Torchmere may have been named because it followed a watercourse or at least marshy area, and Courtney mentions a case of flooding because of a blocked watercourse near Causeway Lane. 17th and 18th-century documentary references indeed suggest that water ran in the north and east ditches of the town defences, and that these acted as

drainage for other watercourses (Lucas and Buckley 1987, 63). During excavation it was apparent that even the deepest pits on the site contained little waterlogged material and, on the assumption that they served as wells, this would seem to suggest a much higher water table in the medieval period.

A list of the equipment needed for the working of a tannery includes 'at least three lime pits for the initial immersion of hides before fleshing and un-hairing' and 'two or three mastering pits containing a mixture of hen or pigeon manure or dog dung and water for treating calf skins' (Jenkins 1978, 10). The first of these requirements was fulfilled if the six pits containing lime and wood ash are taken to be directly involved. The pits for the latter requirement are not so easily identified, however, although chicken manure could have been in plentiful supply given the quantities of domestic fowl bones found, and dog dung likewise (Gidney, below). The dogs may have had another important role in these pre-tanning stages of preparing skins in that they have been documented at Welsh tanneries for the purpose of gnawing off the fat and flesh from skins before they were soaked in lime, and for killing rats (Jenkins 1978, 206) – though at Causeway Lane there was surprisingly little evidence for the presence of rats or other small vermin.

Soap making may also be the industry represented, bearing in mind that Soapers Lane lay close by. It is likely that both these processes co-existed in close proximity, since both used the same raw materials (fats for soap making, skins for tanning). Another related activity could have been horn working, waste from which has been found in deposits of like date at St. Peter's Lane.

Other industries

Slight evidence for small-scale cupellation existed in plot B, with possible waste from this found in adjacent plot C. This may just be a chance find, unless it denotes occasional trade carried out by an opportunistic householder. Hammerscale was found in another of the pits in plot B (F235), suggesting possible small-scale ironworking.

Trade and economy

Billson (1920) lists fifty trades from the first roll of the guild merchant of 1196, many associated with three main areas: 1. the procurement and preparation of food; 2. the preparation of skins and leather goods and 3. the preparation of wools and textiles. In addition to these, excavations, both here and elsewhere in Leicester, show a number of other trades and industries to have been active: pottery is thought to have been made in the vicinity of South Bond Street or Freeschool Lane (Davies and Sawday, below); as noted above, some small-scale metalworking is attested at Causeway Lane; and hornworking was carried out in the vicinity of St. Peter's Lane (Shires;1988-9). Wool and textiles cannot be easily traced in the archaeological record and it is not easy to gauge levels of trade in these; likewise for metalwork where we can assume a high level of recycling of metals.

The recovered food remains allow for some consideration of local and regional trade contacts: fish were either caught locally or brought from the east coast, and the predominance of traded pottery from the more eastern counties may not be coincidental; pigs, goats and domestic birds are likely to have been reared in the town itself, and cattle too may have been reared chiefly in pastures adjacent to Leicester. Wider contacts are, however, revealed in references to long distance movements of both cattle and sheep including one in May 1323 by John le Barber who moved 33 cattle and 1500 sheep from the Fens to Tadcaster in North Yorkshire (O'Connor 1989, 14).

Given problems of freshness, most fruits, vegetables and cereals are likely to have been grown and sold locally, although undoubtedly preserved or dried fruits could have been imported, such as is suggested by the presence of fig seeds and a grape pip (Monckton, below).

Pottery offers a more tangible guide to trading links: contact with Lincolnshire, Nottinghamshire, Northamptonshire, Warwickshire, Oxfordshire and possibly Bedfordshire are all implied by the range of wares recovered at Causeway Lane and reflect a similar pattern to that seen elsewhere in Leicester. These are discussed in more detail below by Davies and Sawday. Presumably, unless the ceramic vessels were used to carry foodstuffs, many of the traded wares from further afield were traded as commodities in their own right.

In summary, the general pattern from the archaeological record suggests that goods were for the most part traded relatively locally, and that luxury goods from further afield did not reach the average town dweller, or at least the town dweller of the north-east quarter.

Society and environment

Ever greater emphasis is now being placed on the analysis of environmental materials to provide data regarding society in terms of health, diet, living conditions, and even status across all periods. At Causeway Lane careful sampling strategies allowed for a wide variety of remains to be recovered, including animal and fish bones, eggshell and plant remains, as well as parasites and insects such as flies and woodlice (see individual reports below), which all contribute to assessing the medieval population here. Pottery too provides additional support, with the analysis of residues yielding evidence on diet and also the types of lighting and fuel used. These different strands of evidence are discussed below.

Living conditions

The presence of mineralised fly puparia, fruit stones and parasite eggs together with 'cessy' and mineralised residues on a number of sherds from different features is strongly suggestive of latrine waste and other organic decaying rubbish. There is evidence to suggest that lime was dumped into the pits to counteract smells and the nuisance from flies. That some pits were covered is suggested by the presence of flies which breed in the dark (Skidmore, below). Much of this organic waste may have derived from normal human waste, coupled with waste from pigs and chickens kept by the householders. In addition the noted industrial activities utilising animal skins will have also produced noxious odours, likewise requiring heavy use of lime. Significantly such 'liming' is also evident in some of the Roman pits of the site, indicating this as a centuries-old method. For other aspects of daily life, several pottery lamps were found with residues pointing to the use of fats from cattle or sheep for the purpose of lighting. Environmental remains included a little evidence of rushes which may have been used for such purposes as flooring (or even bedding).

Diet

A relatively wide range of food types suggests a reasonable diet in medieval Causeway Lane: fish (particularly herring and eel), meat (especially from cattle and sheep/goat, and to a much lesser degree pig and veal), birds, especially domestic fowl, and eggs were all consumed along with cereals (bread wheat, rivet wheat, barley, rye, and oats,) vegetables (broad bean, pea, leek), possible leafy plants (cornsalad) and fruit (sloe, bullace, damson, hazelnut, elder, apples, blackberry, fig and grape). Wild food resources were only slightly represented, with only herring and eel in any quantity; this pattern is not uncommon for medieval towns (e.g. York – O'Connor 1989, 19). The pig, domestic fowl, and goats, may all have been reared in the backyards of houses in Leicester, as occurs at medieval York and Lincoln, although in York evidence for pig rearing diminishes after the thirteenth century (*ibid.*, 17). Finally, residues from sherds from various pottery vessels (Evershed, below p.197) have identified an apparent preference for pig or boar fat for cooking.

Health

Waldron (1989) offers useful discussion of the impact of urban living on human health through the evidence of skeletal remains, arguing primarily that living in a medieval urban context will have meant greater susceptibility to disease. He notes evidence for both rickets and scurvy, with scurvy endemic during northern European winters when fresh fruit and vegetables were unobtainable. We lack skeletal evidence from Causeway Lane, however, to contribute to this discussion, although the presence of parasites is attested (see Boyer, below), and we can guess that contaminated meat was sometimes eaten and that occasional poisonous corncockle seeds were mixed in with the cereals by accident and caused stomach upsets. Despite this, the range of food remains recovered do at least testify to the availability of a reasonably healthy diet to some, if not all, the population.

Social Status

This can only be inferred, if the diet, health and living conditions are all considered along with the range and diversity of other objects, particularly metal objects and pottery. In post-medieval Amsterdam work by Ijzereef

(1989) to assess the relative wealth of neighbouring properties found that the wealthiest properties had a low percentage of cattle bones in their cess-pits, whilst the poorest households appeared to have little good meat, with most of the bones being leftovers of carcasses, perhaps butchers' scraps. The range of wild animals consumed, however, was limited, implying insufficient resources to purchase more unusual food stuffs (O'Connor 1989, 22). Broadly, the medieval deposits at Causeway Lane would suggest consumers able to obtain unusual food stuffs only extremely infrequently – in keeping with many other towns of this date (*ibid.*, 19-21). In fact, other foods support this conclusion: fish bones were from those fish at the cheaper end of the market (Nicholson, below p.337); contaminated meat may sometimes have been eaten; and pottage was probably a staple food. Non-perishable items reveal a basic range of equipment, but with little evidence for luxury or leisure goods, bar two belt buckles, a die and some gaming counters (all deriving from plot D phase 10, but perhaps linked to an inn or tavern – see above).

Late and post-medieval inactivity

As noted, a hiatus exists in the archaeological record between the early 14th and 16th centuries for several Leicester sites. It is debatable whether this gap is caused by a lack of occupation in many areas at this time, whether it results from a change in the practices of the townspeople, or is a case of later reworking destroying the evidence for earlier occupation. Such changes may have involved a move away from traditional pit digging, with rubbish instead being carted away from the town rather than being dumped within it. This is attested elsewhere, and in part was a response to the threat of plague and disease (outbreaks of plague affected England at least 30 times between 1348 and 1485: Platt 1976, 101) which was believed to be spread by smell. However, even with this as a possibility, some residual evidence of occupation would be expected from later pottery, though such was lacking. Instead, both here and elsewhere in north-east Leicester, there is a deep build up of dark, loamy soils, similar to the dark earths of much earlier date seen in other towns such as Worcester and London, and locally known as 'garden soils'.

Although there is a lack of evidence for occupation, this may be explained by truncation or reworking to form these garden soils. Pottery from the small sample of garden soil excavated suggests three likely episodes of truncation or reworking: one in the 13th century, probably at the end of phase 9; a second, perhaps long process in the 16th/17th century before it came under cultivation in Phase 11; and a third in the 18th century, with gravel extraction on the site. The presence of these thick garden deposits and their rather minimal finds content certainly combine to suggest to a genuine lack of occupation. As Courtney argues below, this lack need not be linked to military events such as the sack of Leicester in 1173 or its ravaging by the king's men in 1329, although the latter date does fit neatly with the end of occupation on Causeway Lane and elsewhere in the north-east quarter.

On a national level, recurring visitations of plague throughout the 14th century reduced many urban populations, although it appears that these losses were relatively short-term. Potentially, however, north-east Leicester may not have appealed for swift resettlement, with its (still obvious?) debris from tanning, skinning, soap-making, or other such industries; fear of disease may conceivably have prevented the area from being reoccupied until the 19th century, even if these unpleasant trades had long since been encouraged to move to the outskirts of the town (the area outside the town to the north had the highest number of tanners in the early 17th century – Allin 1981, 3).

Yet whilst the Black Death undoubtedly had some impact (cf. Gloucester – Holt 1990, 142), economic and thus social conditions were already at a low ebb in the early 14th century, as in the Great Famine of 1315-17 (Harvey 1991, 20-21), followed by the severe cattle plague of the early 1320s (Dyer 1989, 267); furthermore, Bailey (1991) has argued that climatic factors had a strong influence on economic decline at the end of the 13th and beginning of the 14th century.

A final explanation relates to the decline in the wool trade, in which Leicester, in common with many other Midland towns, had prospered in the 13th century, being listed as one of the most important centres of cloth manufacture at that time (Reynolds 1977, 61). The age of death of sheep brought into the town show that their main economic importance was in the production of wool rather than meat, and that the townsfolk had to put up with meat from animals that had lived beyond their prime meat producing years (Gidney, below). The wool trade, however, suffered in the late 13th century, primarily due to the growing competition from the Flemish wool trade partly brought about by Edward I levying taxes on the internal wool market and licensing foreign merchants to trade in England as a way of raising revenues for his Scottish wars (Harding 1993, 146). We cannot of course specifically link these events into the decline of Causeway Lane site.

Whatever the causes, however, it seems indisputable that many peripheral areas of Leicester were abandoned during this period, with re-population or development in some quarters delayed until as late as the 19th century. This reflects the claim that nationally the urban population levels of the early 14th century were not matched until the 18th century (Schofield and Vince 1994, 18).

HISTORICAL BACKGROUND

Paul Courtney

This section outlines the topographic history of the Causeway Lane site and its surroundings. Reduced attention is given to the medieval period since the topography of St. Michael's parish has been recently discussed by Janet Martin (1990); in addition, the forthcoming volume of the Shires excavation will analyse the area immediately to the south around St. Peter's and Freeschool Lanes (Courtney, forthcoming).

Causeway Lane and the topographic development of Leicester

Analysis of the town plan of Leicester leaves little doubt that the main street in the Saxo-Norman period was the north-south running axial road, the medieval 'High Street' which, after declining in importance, was re-named in the post-medieval period as Highcross and Southgate Streets. This was the town's widest street before the 19th century (fig. 4) and would initially have served as the chief market for the town (the market square in the south-east of the walled town is unlikely to date to before the 12th century on evidence from other towns – see Courtney 1994, 123-6 and 1996). It is unclear to what extent the town extended beyond the primary north-south street before the Conquest, but certainly by the 12th century expansion is evident – reflective of a rising national population – with settlement attested for the first time in Sanvey Gate, outside the north wall, and on the Causeway Lane site.

The apparent contraction of settlement on the Causeway Lane site by the ?mid-13th century is more difficult to explain. Whilst the sack of Leicester in 1173 seems a ready explanation, archaeological proof is absent; in any case towns generally recovered rapidly from such short-term crises unless other factors were at work. An alternative explanation arises from recent excavations in the modern High Street, the medieval Swinesmarket, which replaced Highcross Street as the main commercial location by the 16th century: here, excavation on the Cameo cinema site suggests that narrow burgage plots first appeared in the 13th century, presumably replacing much larger earlier plots or *hagae* (Cooper 1993); such subdivisioning may have allowed continually built-up frontages for the first time in the borough and created higher population densities along the main commercial streets, whilst prompting contraction in less favourable areas.

Medieval parishes

Three medieval parochial churches lay in the north-east quadrant of the walled town. All three are first documented in a list of 1220 (Rot. Hugh, 1, 238). The most important of these was All Saint's, located on the east side of Highcross Street, as noted, once the main thoroughfare of the town; this suggests that it was the oldest church, possibly of pre-Conquest origin. St.

Michael's and St. Peter's, by contrast, were relatively poorly endowed but were of parochial status and possessed cemeteries. Both churches lay in the back lanes but had been abandoned by the end of the 16th century and their parishes were swallowed up by All Saint's, thus making their exact extent uncertain. However, deeds in the Wygston's Hospital collection indicate that the boundary between St. Peter's and St. Michael's parishes ran for at least part of its length between St. John's Lane and St. Michael's Lane, probably Grape Street (Thompson 1933, nos 628, 641, 667, etc.). The actual sites of these churches are also disputed themselves: Janet Martin (1990, 24-5) has recently made a convincing case for locating St Michael's in the vicinity of All Saint's church, in contrast to the more south-easterly position recommended by Billson (1920, pl. opp. xii). It may have been associated with the North Gate as many dedications to St. Michael have associations with town gateways. St. Michael's decline and disappearance are far from clear but the parish seems dependant upon St. Peter's by 1477, if not yet absorbed into it (Martin 1990, 24). After the Dissolution, St. Peter's came into the possession of the duchy of Lancaster but was demolished about 1573 (PRO DL44/211 & RBL, 3, xlv, 139-40 and 151). In 1634 archdeacon Laud described its churchyard in his visitation as a cabbage ground (Percival More 1907-8, 518). The parish of St. Peter's, and thus also that of St. Michael's, was not formally incorporated into All Saint's until 1591 (RBL, 3, 271). Mrs Fielding Johnson (1891, 43) noted how great numbers of human bones and fragments of ecclesiastical sculpture were found while digging the foundations of a warehouse near the angle of St. Peter's Lane and West Bond Street in 1839; no traces were found, however, in recent excavations on this corner (Lucas and Buckley, forthcoming). Furthermore, a deed of 1725 locates the churchyard on the south side of a property fronting onto St. John's Lane (LRO 1D63/23), suggesting that the church and churchyard lay on the north side of St. Peter's Lane, probably under the present multi-storey car park (Courtney, forthcoming).

The Lanes

The north-east quarter between the walls and the frontages of Highcross Street and High Street (the medieval Swinesmarket) was known as the 'backlanes'. Until the 19th century these were occupied primarily by gardens. In the early 18th century Rev. Samuel Carte suggested that this area had been deserted after the town's sack in 1173 (BL Add Ms 5822 f.182v).. Some deeds survive for this quarter of the town from the end of the 13th century, revealing that St. John's Lane, the modern Causeway Lane, ran east to join a lane known as

'Torchmere' which approximately followed the town wall; another medieval lane ran from Torchmere towards St. Michael's church, known as St. Michael's Lane – this can probably be identified with Grape Street (Martin 1990; Courtney, forthcoming). St. John's Lane is first recorded in 1484 and it presumably drew its name from the St. John's Hospital on Highcross Street (RBL, 2, 307); indeed, it was still called St. John's Lane as late as the 1828 Leicester town plan. However, deeds in the Wygston's Hospital collection of 1454 to 1517 refer to it by the alternative name of Jailhall Lane, after the gaol at its western end (Thompson 1933, nos. 624, 702). In 1725 it was also referred to as Bridewell Lane (LRIO D63/23). The same thoroughfare was first termed Causeway Lane in a deed of 1806 (LRO 14D57/88/49), a name implying that the road was raised up; in fact in 1744 the nearby Churchgate was provided with a 'Midle causey' 12 foot wide with gutters on either side (RBL, 5, 153-4). A Quarter Sessions case of 1764 refers to a watercourse by 'Churchway' in Causeway Lane which had been blocked and was causing flooding (LBR 7, 117).

Medieval and early modern topography

Part of the development site which lay to the west of Countess Street belonged to Wygston's hospital in 1865 (see below). This can tentatively be identified with two adjoining gardens held by the charity which were described as running between St. John's Lane and St. Michael's Lane; the northernmost garden lay in St. Michael's parish and the southernmost in St. Peter's. The gardens can be traced in deeds from 1459 to 1517 which identify the owners of these as well as the adjoining properties (Thompson 1933, nos. 628, 641, 702 etc.). The gardens were presumably granted to the hospital in the 16th century.

As far as can be ascertained from the surviving deeds,

medieval occupation in the 'backlanes' was limited to Dead Lane (now Freeschool Lane) and Parchment Lane (now New Bond Street) (Courtney, forthcoming). In addition, at least one tenement lay east of St. Peter's church (Bodl. Laud Misc 625, fos. 97v, 178v and 189v). As Martin (1990) has indicated, the surviving deeds of the early 14th century onwards from St. Michael's parish mention only gardens, although the parish probably once included some properties in Highcross Street as well as in some of those which encroached upon the town ditch in the late medieval period (Lucas 1978-79). Such limited (and still contracting?) settlement probably accelerated the abandonment of the two churches in this area, although the evidence from Lincoln has indicated that some urban parishes comprised merely a few households (Hill 1965, 147).

Comparison of the Speed map of c.1610, the Stukeley map of 1722, and the 1741 Robert's map suggests little or no outward expansion of the town despite considerable population growth. Figures for All Saint's parish given below are based on estimates derived from family listings, using a multiplier of x5, and the more exact figures of the 1801 census (Nichols 1795, 534; VCH, 3, 179-80). The increase before the 19th century was presumably accommodated by the re-use of abandoned property and by property sub-division.

All Saints Parish Population (* estimate)

Year	1564*	1712*	1792*	1801	1831	1841	1851	1881
Pop	c.465	c.1100	c.2505	2838	3284	4608	5131	6371

Stukeley indicates no housing in Dead Lane or St. Peter's Lane. This may present a fairly accurate picture since his positive evidence of housing in Parchment Lane and Goldsmiths' Grove is well attested by deed evidence. The last dwelling to be firmly documented in Dead Lane was a cottage in 1511 which had become a stable by 1517-18 (Courtney, forthcoming). Robert's 1741 map (fig. 52) offers a similar picture to Stukeley

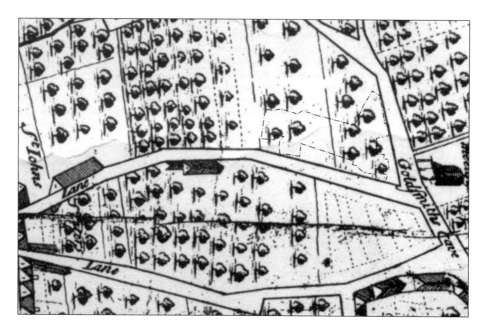

Fig. 52: *Robert's map of Leicester, 1741; enlarged extract showing location of site*

except that the block now formed by South, West and North Bond streets is shown as built up. Roberts also illustrates a single property on the south side of St. John's Lane (Causeway Lane). This may be the house of John Crooke, mentioned in a deed of 1725 (LRO 1D63/23). A bastardy case of 1758 refers to the house of John Adams, a framework knitter in Causeway Lane (RBL, 7, 104), whilst in 1791 an application was made for a certificate for a Roman Catholic meeting house to be held at the dwelling of the widow Elizabeth Wilkin, also in Causeway Lane (*ibid.*, 180); finally, there are also scattered references to properties in the lane from the early 19th century, some possibly newly built, but none of these have been securely located (e.g. LBR, 6, 332 and LRO 14D57/88/49).

Nineteenth-century developments

An 1804 map of Leicester indicates that the backlanes were still undeveloped in the early 19th century; however, the 1828 map (fig. 53) depicts piecemeal development as already underway, an impression confirmed by the 1828 Pigot's Directory, whilst maps of 1840 and 1844 indicate that development was still expanding but by no means complete. The maps of 1828, 1840 and 1844 indeed show the excavation site as still undeveloped apart from a row of buildings along the Causeway Lane frontage. These can be identified as numbers 1, 3, 5, 7 and 9 in the 1851 and 1861 censuses (LRO microfilm 27 & 101). They appear to have been houses occupied by artisans, including a wheelwright, hosier, blacksmith and dressmaker in 1861 (LRO microfilm 101). There is no indication of the building presumably associated with the early 19th-century cellar (F581 – phase 12) on the south side of what was later Countess Street; this may thus have been an outbuilding of one of the houses fronting Causeway Lane. Later town plans are insufficiently detailed to shed any light on

the site's development until the 1887 25ins to the mile Ordnance Survey map (XXXI.10) (fig. 54) by which time the whole property block had been radically redeveloped.

The title deeds (held by Property Holdings (PH) department of the D.O.E.) for the property developed for the Inland Revenue building fill out this picture, indicating two distinct blocks of property in the 19th century. The land immediately north and south of Countess Street belonged before 1865 to the countess of Devonshire's charity, a local charity associated with a hospital, probably founded in the early 17th century, which had formerly stood near Leicester Abbey before being demolished around 1796 (Wrights Directories of 1863, 202 and 1874, 329). The trustees were advised by the charity commission to sell all their property for building plots (VCH 4, 410 & 412) and they subsequently put up their land in Causeway Lane for sale in six blocks, some of which fronted a proposed new street (Countess Street). Unlike surrounding streets, this land appears undeveloped, since no structures are described on the property. Accordingly it seems likely that the buildings recorded on the 1828 and 1844 maps along Causeway Lane were demolished and that the subsequent houses along this frontage were newly erected shortly after the 1865 sale with no continuity of occupiers. For the latter buildings, the PH deeds and planning applications indicate rapid development, mostly with artisan terraced housing (LCSAP nos. 216, 408, 591, 758, etc.), whilst census and directory evidence reveal that the houses were largely inherited by hosiery workers and craftsmen. In addition a boot and shoe factory and warehouse were constructed on the south side of Countess Street. In 1871 its owner lived adjacent to his works, but this was no longer the case by 1881 (LRO microfilm 80 and 129). A block of property on the corner of Causeway Lane and East Bond Street

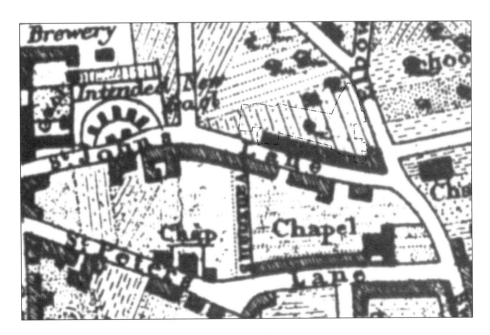

Fig. 53: *1828 map of Leicester; enlarged extract showing location of site*

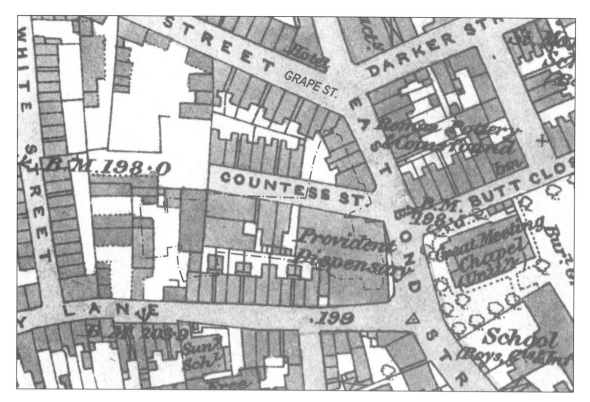

Fig. 54: *1887 25 ins to the mile Ordnance Survey map.*
Extract, not to scale, showing site location

was also purchased in 1865 by the trustees of the Leicester Provident Dispensary. Harrod's Directory of 1870 describes its function as 'to place medical assistance within the reach of the working classes by means of their own small weekly payments'. The dispensary soon expanded and purchases of adjacent property by its trustees included in 1902 the adjacent shoe factory.

Less is known about the second block of property which lay to the west of Countess Street stretching from Grape Street to Causeway Lane. The Devonshire charity deeds state that it was owned by another charity associated with Wygston's Hospital in 1865. The first deed to survive, along with a site plan, dates to 1901, by which date it was entirely occupied by a stabling yard with accommodation for horses belonging to the Leicester Tram company, operative from 1894 (Waddington 1931, 35-38; LCSAP no. 1652). The history of the site before this date is more obscure. The 1887 OS map (fig. 54) shows a series of industrial or commercial buildings arranged around yards; directory evidence suggests that the southern part at least was occupied by a brass foundry from 1870-75 onwards but it is uncertain if the foundry extended to the Grape Street frontage; a stable for which a planning application was made in 1881 (LCSAP no. 14443: plan missing) perhaps lay at the north end. At the end of 1901 the Leicester Tramways property was purchased

by the local authority as part of its take-over of the company with the aim of introducing electric tramlines. The property continued to be owned by the corporation but was subdivided and redeveloped: the southern part was used for the short-lived Star Works, a hosiery machine factory, built *c.*1909-11; in 1926 the former factory site was leased by Leicester Corporation to the hospital (PH deeds).

The maternity hospital adjacent to the dispensary was opened in 1905 (LRO DE3479/1). The dispensary (later the Leicester Royal Infirmary) and the hospital had expanded to take over nearly all of the former Devonshire charity lands by 1923, the only exception being a block of land (excavation Area 3) on the corner of East Bond Street and Countess Street which continued to be occupied by private housing. In the 1960s the street network of the surrounding area was drastically remodelled by the building of Vaughan Way. This was accompanied by extensive (and unattractive) commercial-style development in concrete as well as the rapid disappearance of domestic housing from this part of Leicester. In 1974, following its closure, the site of the maternity hospital and infirmary, as well as the adjacent properties on Grape Street, were purchased by the Crown for intended redevelopment and later demolished. At the time of the 1980 excavation, the site was occupied by a temporary timber office building and a car park.

THE ROMAN POTTERY

Richard Clark

with contributions by *G. B. Dannell, Brenda Dickinson, Kay Hartley, R. Pollard and D. F. Williams*

INTRODUCTION
Richard Clark

Methodology

Quantification.

A total of 55,014 sherds, weighing 987.6 kg., was recovered during the Causeway Lane excavations. The assemblage represents one of the largest recovered from within the city of Leicester.

The pottery assemblage has been quantified using sherd count and weight (g.). In addition, selected groups have been quantified by Estimated Vessel Equivalents (EVEs), using rims alone (Orton 1975). This final method provides an objective quantification of the pottery in terms of the proportion of each rim type represented, a complete vessel rim is equal to 1.00 EVE. As Monaghan comments (1993, 681), EVEs. utilise rim sherds which are the most diagnostic of date, form and origin. It is hoped the range of methods utilised will permit comparison with existing and future assemblages from both Leicester, and sites outside the city. Amphorae, mortaria and samian have been included in the quantification, however no attempt has been made to filter out residual pottery, as the dating of the principal wares are insufficiently well established at the time of writing. It should be noted that in some contexts, notably among the Period 5 phases from Areas 3, virtually all the pottery might be residual.

Two further measures Brokenness (BRK) and Average Sherd Weight (ASW) have calculated from the recorded data and provide information on the condition of the assemblage. The brokenness value provides an estimate of the integrity of the ceramic assemblage, the lower the value the less disturbed the assemblage (Orton 1985, 114-120). Average Sherd Weight (ASW) and brokenness have been calculated solely on the basis of the Grey Wares (GW) present in any given assemblage; the fabric comprises, with few exceptions, the major proportion of all Flavian and later ceramic assemblages. The wide range of GW forms produced throughout the Roman period limits the bias inherent in fabrics dominated by storage vessels and fine table wares.

Fabric and form analysis.

The subdivision of fabrics and forms has been discussed elsewhere (Pollard 1994). Analysis of the fabrics was based upon the Leicester and Leicestershire Pottery Fabric Reference Collection, using a combination of macroscopic and microscopic examination, the latter utilising a binocular microscope (x20). A brief summary of the fabrics identified has been included below; this is followed by a more detailed record of the fabrics recognised at Causeway Lane. Munsell codes and colour names have been used for the detailed fabric descriptions.

The Form Type Series is designed as a hierarchical scheme defining vessel class, from closed to open, subdivided by type (e.g. a jar with an everted rim [3H], and identifying specific forms within that [3H2]). The analysis of the Causeway Lane assemblage utilised the system established for the study of Roman pottery from the Shires excavations (Pollard forthcoming e).

Abbreviations

Fabric abbreviations.

Frequency. (% Of field covered by type of inclusion).

Ra.	Rare	<1%
Sp.	Sparse	1 – 9%
Mo.	Moderate	10 – 19%
Fr.	Frequent	20 – 49%
Ab.	Abundant	50%+

(Field = area of fracture examined).

Size of inclusion.

VF	Very fine	Up to 0.1mm
F	Fine	0.1 – 0.25mm
M	Medium	0.25 – 0.5mm
C	Coarse	0.5 – 1.0mm
VC	Very coarse	>1.0mm, quoting the maximum size.

Shape of inclusion (as Orton 1977a).

R	Rounded
SA	Sub-angular
A	Angular

Sorting of inclusion size (ibid.).

i/s	ill-sorted
w/s	well sorted

Wares and fabric groups.

AM	Amphora fabrics.
BB	Black-burnished ware.
C	Colour-coated ware.
CG	Calcite gritted ware.
GT	Grog tempered ware.
GW	Grey wares.
LG	Lead Glazed ware.
MC	Miscellaneous Coarse wares.
MD	Micaceous ware.
MG	Mixed gritted ware.
MO	Mortarium fabrics.
OW	Oxidised ware.
PR	Pompeian Red wares (Peacock 1977a).
SW	Sandy ware.
TN	Terra Nigra.
WS	White sipped ware.
WW	White wares.

Form abbreviations.

1:	Flagon and jug.
2:	Flask.
3:	Jar and Storage Jar.
4:	Bowl-Jar.
5:	Bowl.
6:	Dish.
7:	Platter.
8:	Cup.
9:	Beaker.
10:	Lid.
11:	Miscellaneous.

Additions to the Pottery Fabric Type Series.

Mortarium fabrics.

MO31 [A1-1991.15604; Context: 3828]. A hard, smooth fabric with a finely irregular fracture. Pinkish white (7.5YR 8/2) to very pale brown (10YR 8/3) surfaces and white to pinkish white (5YR 8/1-2) margins. Wheel thrown and the exterior possibly wiped. Inclusions: moderate to frequent well-sorted VF-F SA quartz, with sparse well-sorted F SA calcite and red ironstone and rare ill-sorted VC calcite and red ironstone. The trituration grit has been lost, however it probably included VC (<8mm) A-SA red ironstone and possibly quartz. Source: unknown, possibly Midlands (K. Hartley, pers. comm.) cf. also MO21.

MO34 [A1-1991.17796, 17797, 17808; Context: 1072, 1052, 3908]. A hard, smooth fabric with a finely irregular fracture. White (5YR 8/1) to reddish yellow (5YR 7/6) surfaces and white to pinkish white (5YR 8/1-2) margins. Wheel thrown and the exterior wiped. Inclusions: frequent well sorted sub-visible to VF SA quartz, sparse ill-sorted VF-VC (<2.0mm) A-SA red and black ironstone and sparse well-sorted VF 'white' mica. Trituration grit include C-VC (<2mm) A red ironstone and unidentified C-VC (2mm) R grey rock fragments. Source: possibly Lincoln or the Lincolnshire area (K. Hartley, pers. comm.) cf. also A39-1988.8759, 8760; Context: 2, 992.

Amphora Fabrics.

AM35 [A1-1991.17911, 17961; Context: 3836, 268]. A hard, sandy fabric with a hackly fracture. Reddish yellow (5YR 6/6) well fired core and margins, with a very pale brown (10YR 8/3) slipped exterior surface. Wheel thrown. Inclusions: moderate ill-sorted F-C (<1.0mm) A quartz, sparse to moderate ill-sorted F-C R calcite, rare to sparse ill-sorted F-C SA red and black ironstone, rare ill-sorted F-C rock fragments and rare well-sorted F white and gold mica. Form: A straight body sherd from a ribbed, possibly cylindrical vessel. Source: Uncertain. Williams (below) suggests an East Mediterranean origin.

AM36 [A1-1991.15082, 15309, 15342, 15415, 18733, 18734; Context: 3518, 3593, 3602, 3619, 3505, 3501]. A hard fabric with a smooth slightly soapy texture and a fine fracture. Well fired reddish yellow (5YR 6-7/6) interior and exterior surfaces and slightly darker reddish yellow (5YR 6/8) core. Wheel thrown and the exterior possibly wiped. Inclusions: sparse well-sorted VF-M (<0.5mm) SA quartz, sparse well sorted F (<0.25mm) R inert white inclusions, sparse well-sorted VF-M (<0.5mm) SA red ironstone and sparse well-sorted VF 'white' mica. Form: All bar one sherd (15415) were from the lower body and/or shoulder of a ribbed vessel, the final piece may suggest a cylindrical form. The ribbing is most pronounced on the shoulder and appears to end short of the base, which may take the form of a spike. Source: Uncertain. Williams (below) suggests an East Mediterranean origin.

Coarse Wares.

WW13 [A1-1991.18898; Context: 1176]. A very hard, rough fabric with a hackly fracture. Light grey (10YR 7/1) to white (10YR 8/2) exterior surface, very pale brown to yellow (10YR 8/4-6) interior surface, and a light grey (10YR 7/1) to yellow (10YR 8/6) section. Wheel thrown with no apparent surface treatment. Inclusions: moderate ill-sorted F-C A-SA quartz, sparse ill-sorted F-VC (<8mm) A red ironstone, rare well-sorted F SA grey rock fragments, and rare ill-sorted F-M A-SA possible fine quartz sandstone. Source: Derbyshire (T. Martin, pers. comm.).

W10 [A1-1991.18325.01; Context: 3879]. A hard, smooth, well fired fabric with a fine fracture. Reddish yellow

(5YR 6/6-8) surfaces, with light red (2.5YR 6/6) margins and a thin light reddish brown (2.5YR 6/4) core. The type sherd is wheel thrown with a burnished and decorated exterior surface (fig. 75, 250, 250a). Inclusions: sparse ill-sorted VF-M SA quartz, rare ill-sorted F-C A-SA red and black ironstone and rare wheel-sorted VF 'white' and 'gold' mica, most clearly visible on the burnished surfaces. Source: York, Eboracum ware (Perrin 1981, 58; Monaghan 1993, 705-710).

THE SAMIAN WARE Edited by *Richard Pollard*

Introduction

The following reports are abridged from more extensive documents held in the Site Archive. The samian from Area 4 was catalogued by Brenda Dickinson and Brian Hartley, c. 1984. Geoff Dannell identified the material from the 1991 excavations, and wrote detailed reports on over 200 decorated pieces; a selection of the most important, from the specialist's point of view, is published here. Brenda Dickinson reported on all of the stamps from 1991; full publication of those from Roman strata, with a handful of others of intrinsic interest, is presented. The third element of the samian report is the section on unusual forms of samian, selected by Geoff Dannell and Richard Clark. The graffiti recognised on twelve samian vessels or fragments are reported below (G1-7, G18-22 **pp 00**).

Decorated samian (figs 55 – 58) *G.B. Dannell*

PHASE 1

Phase 1B

1. Context: 1740 (Extension No. .17949.01) subgroup: 130/4 + phase 2B, context: 1616 (Extension No. .14860.01) subgroup 138/1. Form: Drag. 29. Description: The upper zone can be seen on a Drag. 29 from York, cf. Dickinson and Hartley 1993, fig. 278. 2642, with perhaps the same striated rods from the lower zone; same general comments as no. 2 below. Date: *c.* AD 55-70. Kiln: S.G.

PHASE 2

Phase 2B

2. 1616 (.14860.03) sg 138/1. Drag. 29. The goat is O. 1828. It occurs at La Graufesenque on bowls that have a strong connection to a decorator who appears to have worked for Mommo, Passienvs and Peregrinvs among others. This occurrence is on sherd H 1259 in the temporary catalogue of the reappraisal of the Hermet/Rey collection being undertaken there; it is intended that a full concordance will be published when the work is finished. The group has been assigned temporarily the soubriquet of T-12, following the precedents of Central Gaul. *c.* AD 55-70. S.G.

3. 1632 (.14893.02) sg 138/2 + phase 2D, 1511 (.14612.01) sg 144/1 + Phase 2G, 1660 (.14947.02) sg 148/2 and probably from same vessel 1218 (.13937.01) sg 148/2. Drag. 30. This ovolo is associated with the mould-stamps of Ivstvs. The range of accompanying decoration is very extensive. The bird charmer is not catalogued; the goose is a version of O. 2320; the monkey is O. 2147 and the putto is probably a version of O. 436. *c.* AD 70-85. S.G.

Phase 2G

4. 1218. (.13937.03) sg 148/2. Drag. 30. Small double-bordered ovolo with plain tongue; this is an interesting ovolo

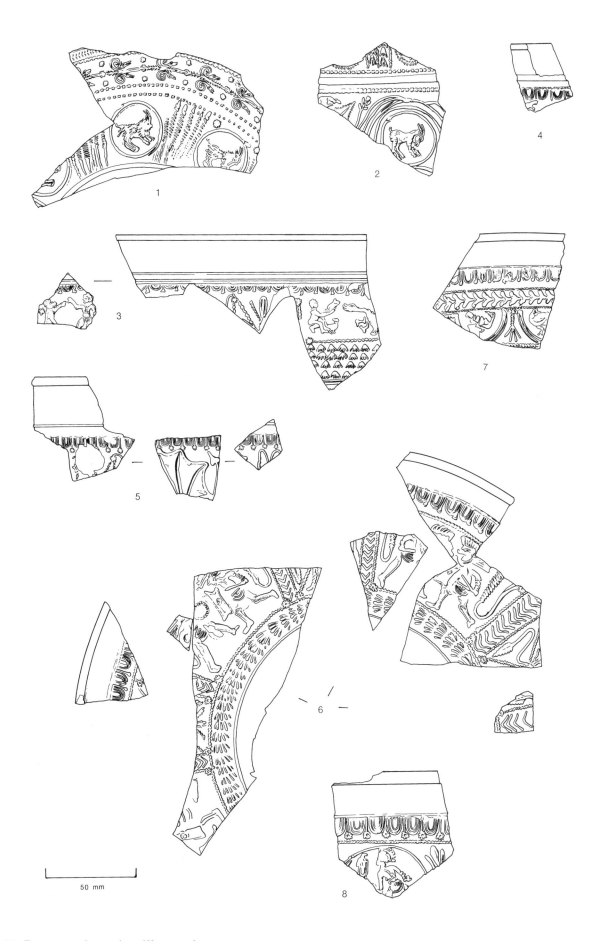

Fig. 55: *Decorated samian illustrations*

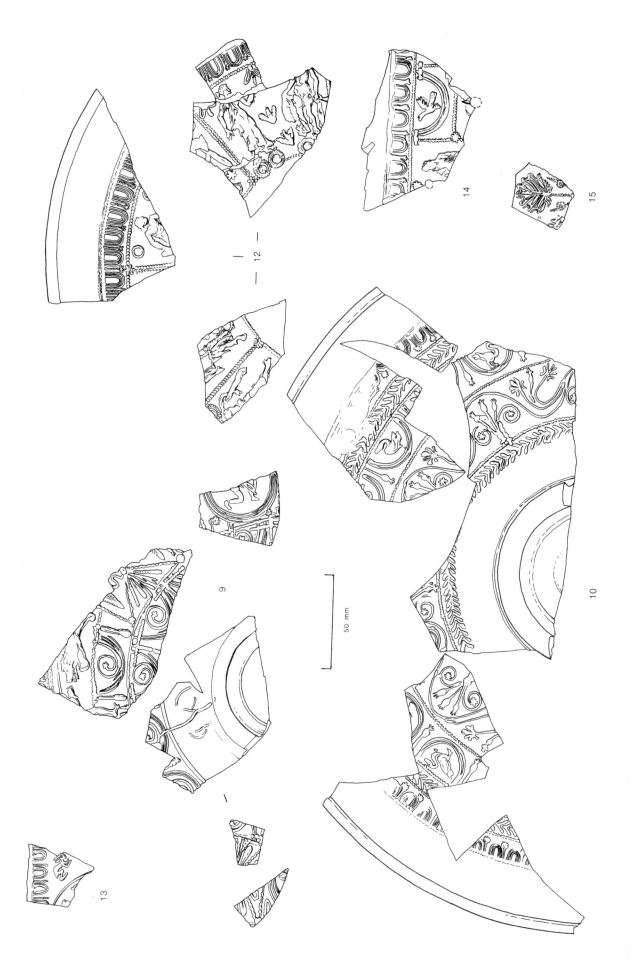

Fig. 56: *Decorated samian illustrations*

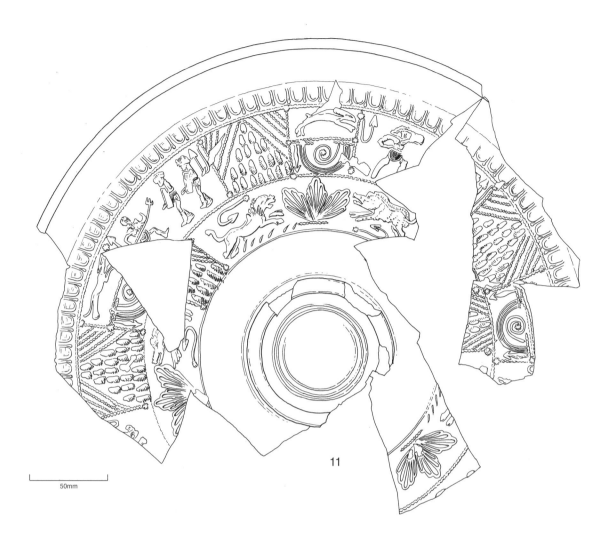

11

50mm

Fig. 57: *Decorated samian illustration*

from two points of view. First, it appears to be the ovolo used by Masclvs with a seven-pointed, hollow-centred rosette tip (signed in the mould, also from Leicester: Dannell 1985, fig. 36.5); secondly, it appears on a small Drag. 37 'with big clumsy strap-handle' (verb. pers., Brenda Dickinson) from Cirencester (1980/137 (40)). This may represent one of the earliest Drag. 37s created, or is a sport. *c.* AD 50-70. S.G.

5. 1218 (.13937.02) sg 148/2. Drag. 30. This ovolo has recently been found on a Drag. 37 with a signature of Pontvs below the decoration (verb. pers. Brenda Dickinson (Alcester, 1991, B 5280)). His early stamps appear on Ritt. 8, which went out of fashion in the mid-60s AD and his decorated Drag. 29s suggest a date spanning, *c.* AD 65-80, cf. Knorr 1952, Taf. 50A; Hartley (1972), fig. 88.67. The Alcester 37, is in the 'transitional' style so well represented at Pompeii, cf. Atkinson 1914, Pl. VIII.46, for a similar layout. *c.* AD 65-80. S.G.

6. 1218 (.13937.14-15) sg 148/2. Drag. 37. The ovolo is associated with signatures of Memor, cf. Atkinson 1914, Pl. XlV.73/74, Mommo & Trim... The gladiators are O. 1007 & 1008, who are on a Drag. 37 with the same ovolo from London (Museum of London, Box 52). The V-shaped wreath is a common association and the basal wreath is on a Drag. 37. in the style from London (Museum of London, 4785G). Partly burnt. *c.* AD 70-85. S.G.

Phase 2J

7. 553 (.11126.01) sg 184/1. Drag. 37. This ovolo is already known from Leicester (Blue Boar Lane, 1958 B XVI (39); St. Nicholas Circle, A164.1969.3001, archive illustration 117) also Dorchester (Site 45 190 (61)), Verulamium (M8 (2)), and Richborough (78305586). It is the same as that on the Fishbourne Drag. 37, cf., Dannell 1971, fig. 135.93, and Richborough Drag. 37, cf. Simpson 1968, Pl. 80. 15, where the tongue can be seen to end in a small circle. It has remained obstinately anonymous hitherto.

The current sherd adds two birds which, when taken together with the four-lobed frond suggest that this may be the work of Sabinvs iii, cf. Knorr 1919, Taf. 69.17 & 18, and Stanfield 1937, fig. 11. 40 & 52. The astragalus suspending the demi-medallions may be his 56. The internal stamp of Sabinvs iii on Drag. 29 with similar demi-medallions and birds comes from Narbonne, cf. Fiches *et al.* 1978, fig. 3.9. The bifid making the lower straight wreath on the Fishbourne bowl is very similar to that on a signed Sabinvs iii Drag. 30 from Narbonne, cf. Fiches *et al.* 1978, fig. 14.5. The frond can be seen again there on 2, and on fig 15. 1, 2, 3 & 5. The nose of the boar, *ibid.* fig. 15.1 & 16.3 can just be seen on the Fishbourne sherd. *c.* AD 70-85. S.G.

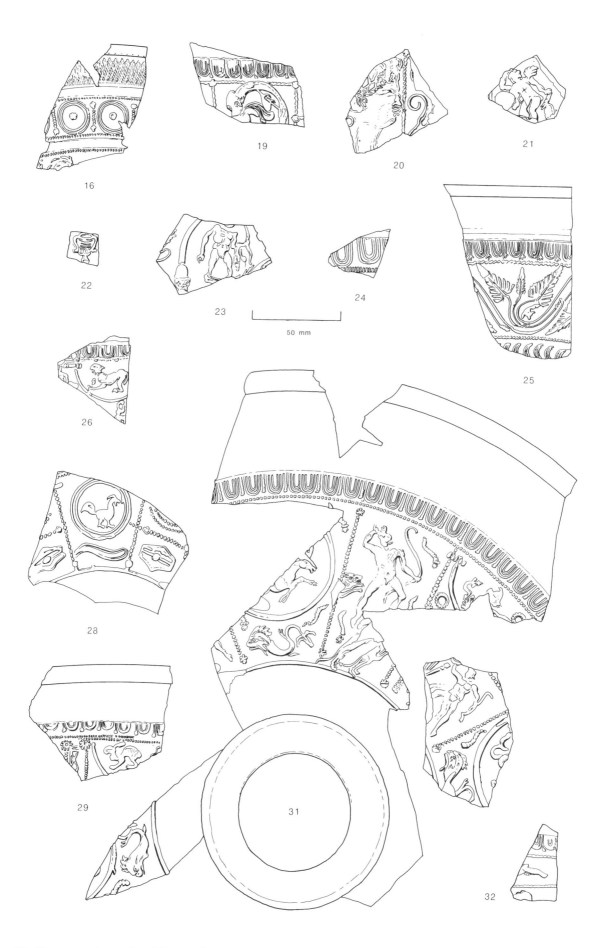

50 mm

Fig. 58: *Decorated samian illustrations*

Phase 2K

8. 2942 (.12216.01) sg 201/1. Drag. 37. This is the Frontinvs ovolo, with an attached rosette tip, cf. Hermet 1934, pl. 85.2, placed to the right of the tongue. The gladiators are not known to me from his work. *c.* AD 70-90. S.G.

Phase 2L

9. 3533, 3549, 3551 (.15141.01, 15182.01, 15190.01) sg 332/1. Drag. 37. The style is similar to that of the final group of potters making both Drag. 29 and 37, cf. Knorr 1919, Taf. 23. The decoration is scant: there are the remains of a bestiarius and a boar; and an archer, O. 268 type, but the rest is fairly ordinary. The upper limit of the vessel appears to have a vestigial central moulding, but it is difficult to distinguish whether this is a memento of Drag. 29 on a 37. There are three letters of a signature present, the style of which is fairly similar to those on two vessels from Verulamium, cf. Hartley 1972, D75 & 76, (stamp report, no. 29). The ovolo appears to have a tongue ending in a trident bent to right. The blurred pendant is very similar to that on D75 and note that the bar from which the festoons hang is in fact a repeated astragalus, as D76, which also has the archer. The pinnate leaf can be seen on D78, ibid. The grass-tuft is known from a bowl that also has the characteristic four-pronged pendant seen on D76. The inverted bush or grass tuft in the St. Andrew's cross is on a Drag. 37 from Verulamium (1956 u/s). *c.* AD 75-90. S.G.

PHASE 3

Phase 3A

10. 832, 903 (.12683.02, 12931.01) sg 141/1 + phase 3B: 762, 763, 765 (.12454.02, 12490.01, 12501.01) sg 141/3; 747, 785, 787 (.11976.01, 12537.01, 12544.01) sg 153/1; 788, 1494, 1495 (.12550.01, 14507.01, 14512.01) sg 153/2 + phase 9: 253 (.10213.01) sg 120/7. Drag. 37. The Calvvs ovolo with large rosette tip (cf. Dannell 1971, fig. 130, a bowl from the same mould of which has turned up at La Graufesenque with a mould signature of CALVOS, and a plain-ware stamp of PATRICIVS on a handle). All of the decorative details are known from bowls with this ovolo. *c.* AD 70-85. S.G.

11. 833, 872, 873 (.12695.04, 12838.01, 12844.01) sg 141/1 + Phase 3B: 1052, 1055 (.18223.01, 13546.02) sg 141/4 + 749 (.11989.01) sg 157/2. Drag. 37. The ovolo used by M. Crestio, Patricivs & C. Val[erivs] Alb[anvs], cf. Hull 1958, fig. 48.3. The Patricivs Drag. 37, stamped in the mould, also comes from Verulamium (VER 1932, Ins. IV, Building 8). Much of the decoration is known from bowls with this ovolo from London (Museum of London): the fan is common (3805G, 3750G, 6545L); the festoon and swag on 5817G and 6545G. The lion is on 4680G. See also the Drag. 29 from Asciburgium, with the internal stamp of Ivcvndvs (Vanderhoeven 1976, 496), which has very similar features. The gladiators are O. 1041 & 1042, and a version of 1020 (which is a stamped M. CRESTIO type, cf. Knorr 1952, Taf. 19D). A related bowl with the more usual M. CRESTIO ovolo can be seen from Salzburg (Karnitsch 1970, Taf. 16.1). *c.* AD 75-90. S.G.

Phase 3B

12 1017 (.18185.01) sg 141/2, + 969, 979, 1016, 1162 (.13155.07, 13189.01, 13349.01, 13794.01) sg 141/4. Drag. 37. The ovolo is Rogers B18. The figures are a seated man, D. 472 type; a Mercury, D. 290 type, a woman in a tunic, O. 363, and what appears to be a greaved male figure, with a shield resting on the ground in his right hand, and a club in the left. The motifs include beaded circles, Rogers C292, seven-beaded rosettes, Rogers C280 and two trifid motifs, Rogers G154? & G27?.

Several parallels occur in the work of Drvsvs ii; the ovolo is on a mould from Lezoux, which also has the signature Caleni, inscribed before firing (at Taurin, Lezoux; 1970, C5 +). The

seated figure, woman in a tunic and beaded circle, are on bowls from Wroxeter (Atkinson 1942, pl. 41, H60), Wilderspool and Segontium (Wheeler 1924, fig. 74.55), respectively. However the use of beads below the decoration, and the style in general do not suggest that the mould was made by or for him.

The following features appear on bowls in the style of one of his contemporaries, Secvndinvs ii (Rogers' Secvndinvs I): the use of beads below the decoration (almost always), the beaded circle (London, ex. Guildhall Museum, 1932.196), and the figure in a tunic (Great Chesterford). The rosette is on a Drag. 37 from Brecon, perhaps with the second of the trifid motifs, cf. Wheeler 1926, fig. 83. S169. The latter is also on a Drag. 37 in his style from Chester. He perhaps also used the ovolo (on a bowl from London, ex. London Museum, A16459).

It is impossible to be certain of the style of Secvndinvs ii because, unfortunately, so few of his stamped bowls are known. The overall impression from the bowls assigned to him by Rogers is that he did not make great use of figures, and this would mitigate against him as the maker of the current vessel. There is an anonymous Hadrianic potter, whose bowls often lack ovolos, who used the Mercury, ring and rosette on a bowl from Holt, cf. Grimes 1930, fig. 45.115. Although the current piece cannot be assigned to a particular potter, there is no doubt that the date is Hadrianic, or early-Antonine. *c.* AD 125-140. C.G.

This report has been taken from notes entirely provided by Brenda Dickinson, to whom many thanks are due for the arduous task of chasing up the parallels for a difficult piece.

13. 1072 (.13622.01) sg 151/1. Drag. 37. This is a very rare ovolo, known to me only from London (Museum of London, 5879G & 5950G), on two other Drag. 37s. The first has a scroll composed of the upper zone bud, and the lower zone tendril binding to be seen on a Drag. 29 from Vindonissa, stamped by Primvs, cf. Knorr 1952, Taf. 51 B. The latter has a copy (?) of the frond which appears on bowls stamped by Stabilio, cf. Knorr 1919, Taf. 79.6. There is a suggestion that the tongue of the ovolo is beaded. *c.* AD 65-80? S.G.

14. 1020 (.13368.01) sg 152/1. Drag. 37. The ovolo is Rogers B234 but the bird is uncatalogued. The use of a rosette as border binding suggests an early Antonine date. Rivet hole present. *c.* AD 140-160. C.G.

15. 1139 (.13757.01) sg 154/2. Drag. 29 or 37. I don't know this beautiful leaf at all. *c.* AD 65-80? S.G.

16. 791 (.12559.01) sg 154/2. Drag. 29. This form was made at Les Martres de Veyre, and this one is in the style of Potter X - 13, cf. S & S ii, Pl. 46.531. The dolphin is the one on Pl. 43.491, there. *c.* AD 100-120. MdV.

PHASE 4

Phase 4A

17. 449 (.18542.01) sg 174/1. Drag. 37. Stamped in the mould by Cinnamvs ii (stamp report no. 68); the figure is D. 523. *c.* AD 150-170. CG. Not illustrated.

PHASE 5

Phase 5A

18. 1504 (.14534.02) sg 158/1 + (unphased), 821 (.17564.01) sg 129/1 + phase 12, 880 (.17990.02) sg 101/1. Drag. 37. Stamped within the decoration by Cinnamvs ii (stamp report no. 75); in the same vertical panel, his trifid serrated leaf, Rogers H109, the base of which is superimposed on the horn of the pan mask, D. 675. The foot stand of a vulcan, cf. D. 39, lies above the leaf. The panel to left has Perseus, D. 146, flanked on either side by the candelabrum, Rogers

Q27, with the lozenge, Rogers U33, above. *c.* AD 150-170 on decoration; *c.* AD 150-180 on stamp. Lezoux. Not illustrated.

19. 1581 (.14758.01) sg 158/1. Drag. 37 This is a rather worn example of a rare ovolo. Pieces from London and Richborough (Museum of London, G5940G & 78305053) both have trifid wreaths below the ovolo which suggest Calvvs. Another fragment from Leicester (St. Nicholas Circle, A164.1969.2007, archive illustration 113) is more in the style of the free-style Germanvs moulds. This piece associates the ovolo with the figure H. 58. The style of the panels suggests a later Flavian date for this piece. *c.* AD 80-95? S.G.

20. 588 (.11155.01) sg 161/1. Drag. 37 Large bust, not known from elsewhere. Hadrianic – Antonine? C.G.

Phase 5C
21. 1375 (.14264.01) sg 164/1. Drag. 37. Putto, apparently dragging a large *olla*. It is not O. 443 or one of its variations, because the figure is clearly standing, and not seated, and the curvature of the *olla* is clear. Flavian. S.G.

22. 514 (.11073.03) sg 166/3. Drag. 37. Cantharus not catalogued by Rogers. Antonine? C.G.

23. 1350 (.14224.02) sg 166/5. Drag. 37. Hercules, D. 443, the hand is clearly visible, but the club missing, so it must be a separate *poinçon*. The heavy arcade is similar to that used by Cinnamvs ii, cf. S & S i, Pl. 161.47. *c.* AD 150-170? C.G.

Phase 5E
24. 3954 (.18537.01) sg 360/1. Drag. 37. The ovolo is 55c (Ricken-Fischer 1963), used by Reginvs i, cf. Ricken-Ludowici 1948, Taf. 16.12F for the roped border. Antonine. Rheinzabern.

Phase 5F
25. 3960 (.15912.01) sg 339/6 + 3675 (.15506.01) sg 338/3. Drag. 37. The ovolo used by M. Crestio (Museum of London, 3462M, stamped in the mould). Neither of the leaves have been noted before with it. *c.* AD 75-90. S.G.

26. 3795 (.15569.02) sg 362/3. Drag. 37. The ovolo is Rogers B176, used by Casvrivs, which is the style for this vessel. The panther is not catalogued. *c.* AD 160-195. C.G.

Phase 5G
27. 3953 (.15890.01) sg 334/1. Drag. 37. Two sherds from a bowl stamped in the mould by Laxtvcissa (stamp report no. 110). The ovolo is the usual hammer-head, Rogers B206; in a free-style scheme, the goat is O. 1842; the lion to right, O. 1510. The small leaf tip is Rogers K37. 130-160 on decoration; *c.* AD 145-175 on stamp. Lezoux. Not illustrated.

28. 3608 (.15361.01) sg 337/2. Drag. 37. The details offer conflicting evidence: the shield is Rogers U210, used by Cinnamvs ii, Doeccvs, and Servvs iii; the cock is O. 2344A, and the gadroon, Rogers U148, attributed to Atilianvs and Servvs ii. The fabric is pale, and the slip dark, and not unlike that of Montans. It was used by the late workshops of Paternvs ii. *c.* AD 165-200? C.G.

29. 3879 (.15748.01) sg 359/4. Drag. 37. The ovolo is similar to that used by Ianvaris ii and Paternvs ii, cf. S & S i, p.212, not easily recognisable as Rogers B114; the hare O. 2116; the rosette like Rogers C213?, and the column P3. The rosette, and the use of the finely beaded bar to form the border are similar to Ianvaris's work, cf. S & S i, Pl.119.11. *c.* AD 145-175. C.G.

30. 3879 (.17648.01) sg 359/4. Drag 30. Stamped in the mould by Divixtvs i (stamp report no. 116). Satyr, O. 591, in same panel as stamp; fragment of caryatid in panel to left, O. 1207a? This may be from the same mould as S & S i, Pl. 115.1. The ovolo has been truncated by the moulding

of the rim zone; it appears to be *ibid.* fig. 33.2, drawn from the same vessel; however Rogers B52, identified with the latter, is slightly smaller than the ovolo here, which matches the size of his B11, but is smaller than S & S i, fig. 33.1 (report on the decoration by Richard Pollard). *c.* AD 150-180 on the stamp. Lezoux.

POST-ROMAN AND UNPHASED
31. Phase 12, 200 (.10006.01) sg 100/1. Drag. 37. The ovolo is Rogers B160, used by Doeccvs. The figures are from the left: sea-stag D. 37; dolphin, D. 1052; dog head, O. 1917(?); satyr, D. 384, rigged out as a hunter (cf. S&Si Pl. 149.31 for an erroneous restoration); perhaps the same dog, and dolphin, 2318A (type). In the background are the cornucopia, Rogers U245, and wreathed circle E58. The astragalus is R18, and the bold borders, double medallions and festoons are well illustrated in S & S i, Pls. 147-151. *c.* AD 165-200. C.G.

32. Unphased 8039 (Area 4, .1640) Drag. 37. The ovolo has a tongue apparently turning to the right, and the zones of decoration are separated by a cable border so blurred as almost to appear as a straight line. The upper zone includes a hare to the left. The bowl is not closely datable, but is unlikely to be earlier than the beginning of the 2nd century. Banassac ware is not particularly common in Britain; a piece from Magazine Walk, Leicester has been published (Dickinson and Hartley 1987, fig. 34.1), and another comes from Causeway Lane, belonging to the ?Natalis group (Dannell 1994, no. 166, dated *c.* 90-115; cf. Knorr 1905, Taf. XV.5, and Knorr 1912, Taf. XXIV).

Unusual samian forms (fig. 59)

The identifications are by Geoff Dannell.

PHASE 3
S1. Drag. 16, SG, pre-Flavian. (.14040.04) context 1259, subgroup 141/1: phase 3A

S2. Drag. 18 or 18/31, SG. Dannell comments that this appears to be a late SG piece, which would place it at the very end of the 1st century or the very early 2nd: Trajanic? (.12683.01, 12695.03, 12524.01, 18196.01, 10179.01) 832, 833, 141/1: 3A; 773, 969, 141/4: 3B; + Phase 5, 235, 164/1: 5C

PHASE 5
S3. Ribbed beaker, Stanfield 1929, fig. 6.29-34 (Cam 404); CG, 2nd century. (.15361.01) 3608, 334/2: 5G

S4. Probably a lid, if so, illustrated inverted here. Rheinzabern, late 2nd to 3rd century. Slight step at outer edge of wall int. (.18540.01) 3879, 359/4: 5G

Post-Roman, PHASE 12
S5. Drag. 30R, cf. Oswald & Pryce 1920 Pl. LXXVI.3; Dannell refers to the decoration as 'cut glass', but rouletting is the usual means by which the incised decoration on Drag 30 was achieved. CG (?); Drag 30R is generally dated to the 2nd, and perhaps into the 3rd century (Webster 1993a, 41). (.18788.01) 2269, 293/1: 12

Samian potters' stamps   *Brenda Dickinson*

Comments on the stamps for the Shires and Causeway Lane.

The Shires excavations produced 124 stamped or signed samian vessels, and Causeway Lane produced 147. They divide into fabrics thus.

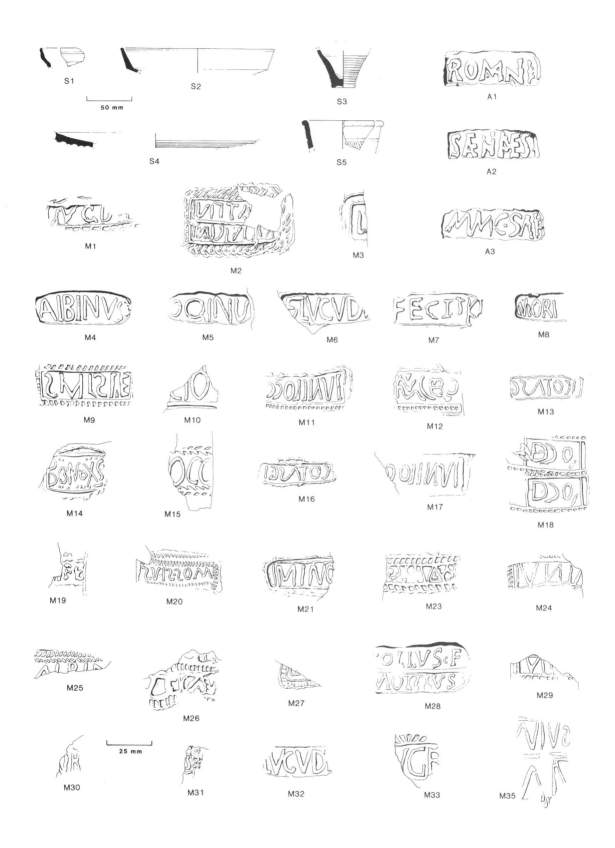

Fig. 59: *Unusual samian forms; amphorae stamps; mortaria stamps*

	The Shires	Causeway Lane
South Gaul	34%	37%
Les Martres-de-Veyre	8%	11%
Lezoux	55%	45%
East Gaul	3%	7%

The accumulations of South Gaulish ware were much the same on both sites. Both produced proportionally little Central Gaulish ware from Les Martres-de-Veyre, but that is normal for Leicester as a whole, and probably means that it was unable to obtain supplies on the same scale as from the South Gaulish factories at La Graufesenque. The proportion of Les Martres ware from Causeway Lane is about average for Britain, but it must be noted that some of the material is Hadrianic or early-Antonine, and that the 'Trajanic gap' is much the same on both sites.

The biggest difference between the two sites lies in the proportions of Lezoux ware. Just over half the stamped vessels from the Shires came from there, but at Causeway Lane the proportion was 10% less.

Most or all, of the Causeway Lane East Gaulish stamped vessels are Rheinzabern ware; at the Shires two came from Rheinzabern, one from La Madeleine and one perhaps from the Argonne. Causeway Lane produced over twice as much East Gaulish ware as the Shires, but the proportions from both sites are lower than normal for Britain as a whole. A similar scarcity of East Gaulish products is observable at other sites in Leicester, probably because of its remoteness from the points of entry.

Both sites produced some substantially complete vessels, but while the total from Causeway Lane is unremarkable, there is an unusually large number from the Shires. It is difficult to assess the significance of this, as both first and second century vessels are involved. The most interesting context is F186, where 10 of the 29 vessels were half, or more than half, complete. All had footrings which showed some wear, however, so they cannot have been a group of new pots damaged in a shop or in transit. On the whole, an early Antonine date would fit the stamped material from this context, with the exception of the decorated East Gaulish bowl of Cobnertus, though sherds from this were found in other contexts, too.

The general impression from the stamp evidence, then, is of two sites with extensive first century activity, from Nero onwards, both receiving much less Trajanic samian, though almost certainly not as a result of diminishing occupation. Causeway Lane seems to have had its most intensive occupation in the later Hadrianic to mid-Antonine period; the accumulation from the Shires seems to have been proportionally rather less in the Hadrianic period than at the neighbouring site. Both collections of stamps suggest that the quantities of discarded samian began to decline in the later second century and continued into the first half of the third century.

Finally, while there are some similarities between the two assemblages, they do not have many potters in common, and even fewer dies, and it would be unwise to draw any firm conclusions from the stamps alone.

Catalogue of samian potters' stamps

Each entry gives: context, museum extension/part number, subgroup, potter (i, ii, etc., where homonyms are involved), die number, form (in Dragendorff/Dechelette/Knorr/Walters series unless otherwise stated), reading of the stamp, published example, pottery of origin, date.

(a), (b) and (c) indicate:

(a)	Stamp attested at the pottery in question.
(b)	Potter, but not the particular stamp, attested at the pottery in question.
(c)	Assigned to the pottery on the evidence of fabric, distribution and, or, form.

Ligatured letters are underlined.

PHASE 1

Area 1

Phase 1B

1(60) 1282 (.17616.01) 130/6 Pass(i)enus 33a" 15/17 or 18 [P]ASSEN La Graufesenque (a). *c.* AD 70-85.

PHASE 2

Area 1

Phase 2B

2(35) 1616 (.17665.01) sg 138/1 Inventus 1a 29 INVENTI (Rebuffat & Marion 1977, p.46, 427) La Graufesenque (a). *c.* AD 55-75.

3(59) 1632 (.17666.01) sg 138/2 Pass(i)enus 33a, 33a' or 33a" etc. 15/17 or 18 PA·S[SEN] La Graufesenque (a). *c.* AD 60-85.

4(112) 1632 (.17667.01) sg 138/2 OF[(?) on Drag 27g, South Gaulish. Neronian or early-Flavian.

5(61) 1646 (.17669.01) sg 138/2 Pass(i)enus 63a 27g PASSIE La Graufesenque (b). *c.* AD 50-65.

Phase 2D

6(5) 1264 (.17828.01) sg 143/2 Albus i 9a 27g ALBVS.FE La Graufesenque (a). With graffito (G18) inscribed under the base, after firing. *c.* AD 50-65.

7(91) 1264 (.17829.01) sg 143/2 Senicio 6d 27g SENIC(I)O La Graufesenque (a). *c.* AD 40-65.

8(111) 1511 (.17628.01) sg 144/1 edge of stamp, on Drag. 27g, South Gaulish. Neronian or early-Flavian.

Phase 2E

9(58) 1058 (.17580.01) sg 147/1 Pass(i)enus 33a' 15/17 or 18 PASSEN La Graufesenque (a). *c.* AD 60-70. From a die made from 33a, by *surmoulage*.

10(27) 1059 (.17581.01) sg 147/1 Dontio 6a 27g DONTIOII(IC)I (Dickinson 1984, S12). La Graufesenque (a) *c.* AD 65-95.

11(67) 1753 (.17673.01) sg 147/1 Pontus 8g 27 OFRONTI La Graufesenque (a). Complete, in two pieces, with heavily worn footring and some of the internal glaze ground away. *c.* AD 70-90.

12(26) 1753 (.17674.01) sg 147/1 Dometos 1a 33 [DOMETO] SLT Les Martres-de-Veyre (b). *c.* AD 100-130.

Phase 2F

13(48) 1470 (.17623.01) sg145/1 Martialis i 12b 29 MAR[TIALIS] (Laubenheimer 1979, no.115) La Graufesenque (a). *c.* AD 50-65.

14(101) 1506 (.17627.01) sg 146/1 + Phase 2G, 1218 (.17595.01) sg 148/2 Virtus i 6a 27g FV[IRT] retr. La Graufesenque (a). Part of lower half of vessel, condition as no. 11. *c.* AD 60-80.

Phase 2G

15(21) 1218 (.17597.01) sg 148/2 Cotto ii 3a 29 OFCOTOI retr. (Hermet 1934, no.39) La Graufesenque (a). *c.* AD 70-85.

16(22) 1218 (.17598.01) sg 148/2 Crispus ii 12a 29 CRISPVX (Hermet 1934, no.45, but with X at the end) La Graufesenque (a). *c.* AD 60-80.

17(57) 1218 (.17599.01) sg 148/2 Pass(i)enus 5a 29 [OFPASS]ENI (Durand-Lefebvre 1963, no.547) La Graufesenque (a). *c.* AD 65-80.

18(68) 1218 (.17603.01) sg 148/2 Pontus 8h cup OFPONTI La Graufesenque (a). *c.* AD 65-90.

19(77) 1218 (.17600.01) sg 148/2 Rufinus iii 2a 29 [OF.RVF]INI La Graufesenque (a). *c.* AD 70-85.

20(78) 1218 (.17596.01) sg 148/2 Rufinus iii 4c or 4c' 27g

OFRVFIN or OFRVFI (Durand-Lefebvre 1963, no.634) La Graufesenque (a). Half of vessel. *c.* AD 65-90.

21(79) 1218 (.17604.01) sg 148/2 Rufinus iii 15a 15/17 or 18 [RV]FINI.MA La Graufesenque (b). *c.* AD 70-90.

22(105) 1218 (.17593.01) sg 148/2 C[or S[on Drag 15/17 or 18, South Gaulish. Neronian.

23(161) 1218 (.17602.01) sg 148/2 Drag 37, South Gaulish. Flavian. The base would not have been stamped, but the type of ring which surrounds most plainware stamps has been incised in the centre.

Phase 2H

24(113) 1719 (.17670.01) sg 149/1 M[on Drag 27g South Gaulish. Neronian or early-Flavian.

Area 2
Phase 2K

25(117) 2948 (.17556.01) sg 201/2 SA [or] S on Drag 27g, South Gaulish. Flavian.

26(84) 2914 (.17553.01) + 2933 (.17555.01): sg 202/3 Sacirotus 1a 18/31 SACIR°+.MAS Les Martres-de-Veyre (a). *c.* AD 100-120

27(124) 2914 (.17554.01) sg 202/3 CO[on Drag 18/31, Central Gaulish. Hadrian*c.*

28(50) 2914 (.17551.01) sg 202/3 + Phase 3, Phase 5B, 755 (.17529.01) sg 162/5 Maximus ii 4a 33 MAXIMI (Hartley 1972, S145) Lezoux (a). *c.* AD 150-180.

Area 3
Phase 2L

29(3A) 3533, 3549, 3551 (.15141.01, .15182.01, 15190.01) sg 332/1 Drag 37, South Gaulish, with part of a cursive mould-signature below the decoration (decorated samian report no. 9, fig. 56). The reading is]SA, retr, followed by either R or less probably, P. A rather more complete signature of the same potter appears on a bowl from Verulamium (Hartley 1972, D76). A reappraisal of this suggests that it reads]SSA retr, or possibly]ASSA retr, followed by the same letter as on the Leicester bowl. Unfortunately, this does not match the name of any known South Gaulish potter, so the signature cannot be completed. *c.* AD 75-90.

30(95) 3549 (.17631.01) + 3551 (.17632.01) sg 332/1 C. Silvius Patricius 12b 15/17R or 18R C·SILVIP La Graufesenque (b). *c.* AD 70-90.

PHASE 3
Area 1
Phase 3A

31(6) 1194 (.17588.01) sg 141/1 Atica 1a 27g AT-ICAE La Graufesenque (c). *c.* AD 70-100.

32(109) 1240 (.17610.01) sg 141/1 CALL[or GALL[? on Drag 15/17 or 18, South Gaulish. Neronian or early-Flavian.

33(64) 1240 (.17609.01) sg 141/1 Patricius i (probably) 17g 15/17 or 18 PAT[RIC] La Graufesenque (b). *c.* AD 70-90.

34(115) 1259 (.17612.01) sg 141/1]II on Drag 15/17 or 18, South Gaulish. Flavian.

Phase 3B

35(47) 801 (.17562.01) sg 141/4 Marcellinus i 1c 27 MARC·II[LLINI] Les Martres-de-Veyre (c). *c.* AD 115-135.

36(108) 979 (.17573.01) sg 141/4]RE[? on Drag 15/17 or 18, South Gaulish. Neronian-Flavian.

37(123) 1211 (.17592.01) sg150/1]SF on Drag 27, Les Martres-de-Veyre. Trajanic.

38(28) 1219 (.17606.01) sg 150/1 Felix i 4d 27g °FFEIC(I) La Graufesenque (a). *c.* AD 45-70.

39(100) 1221 (.17608.01) sg 150/1 Virtus i 1a 29 OFVIRTVTIS (Knorr 1907, Taf.XXXII, 292) La Graufesenque (b). *c.* AD 70-85.

40(12) 1263 (.17614.01) sg 150/2 Calvus i 5tt 15/17 or 18 OF.CALVI La Graufesenque (a). *c.* AD 65-85.

41(98) 1072 (.17583.01) sg 151/1 Surdillus 5a 18/31-31 SVRDI[LLVSF]. The potter is known to have worked at Les Martres-de-Veyre, but this is almost certainly in Lezoux fabric. Hadrianic.

42(10) 1072 (.17582.01) sg 151/1 Borillus i 4a 31 [BORILL]I.OFF Lezoux (a). *c.* AD 150-180.

43(83) 982 (.17575.01) sg 152/1 Sacrapus 2a 38 or 44 SAC[RAPVS] (Durand-Lefebvre 1963, no.646) Les Martres-de-Veyres (b). *c.* AD 100-125.

44(76) 982 (.17574.01) + 984 (.17576.01) sg 152/1 Regulus i 9b 33 RIIGVLVSI Lezoux (a). *c.* AD 150-180.

45(4) 984 (.17539.01) sg 152/1 Albucius ii 6a 33 ALBVCI Lezoux (a). *c.* AD 150-180.

46(178) 984 (.17577.01) sg 152/1]SF on Drag 33, Central Gaulish. Antonine.

47(15) 1198 (.17590.01) sg 152/1 Catullinus i 1a concave dish [CATVL]LINVS Les Martres-de-Veyre (c). *c.* AD 100-120.

48(81) 667 (.17533.01) sg 153/1 Rufus iv 1a 18/31R RVFV[S·F·] Lezoux (c). *c.* AD 150-180.

49(86) 1041 (.17578.01) sg154/1 Sacroticus 1a 18/31R SACR[OTICIM] Lezoux (c). *c.* AD 125-150.

50(20) 1052 (.17579.01) sg 154/1 Cotto ii 1c 15/17 or 18 OFCOTTO La Graufesenque (b). *c.* AD 70-95.

51(36) 791 (.17560.01) sg 154/2 Iullinus i 7a 15/17 or 18 [IV]LLIN La Graufesenque (a). *c.* AD 80-100.

52(122) 791 (17559.01) sg 154/2 I[or]I on Drag 27, Les Martres-de-Veyre. Trajanic.

53(13) 754 (.17547.01) sg 154/3 Carillus iii 4a 29 [CAR]ILLFE La Graufesenque (a). *c.* AD 70-85.

54(52) 754 (.17546.01) sg 154/3 Moxius ii 2a 31 MOX[IVS·F]. Graffito (G19). The stamp is known from Lezoux, but many examples, including this one, seem to be in the fabrics of Les Martres-de-Veyre. *c.* AD 130-160.

55(134) 754 (.17548.01) sg 154/3 M[on Drag 33, Central Gaulish. Antonine. Footring heavily worn.

56(56) 1176 (.17587.01) sg 155/1 Ovidius 1a 33a OVIDIM Les Martres-de-Veyre (a). *c.* AD 100-120.

57(8) 814 (17563.01) sg 157/3 Banoluccus 1a 31 BAN[OLVCCI] Lezoux (c). *c.* AD 140-170.

58(125) 694 (.17534.01) sg 157/5]I.M on Drag 18/31 or 31, Central Gaulish. Hadrianic or early-Antonine. Glaze ground off under the base.
See also no. 87 below.

Phase 3C

59(106) 1153 (.17586.01) sg 186/4]C·IS on Drag 27g, South Gaulish. Neronian.

Phase 3D

60(107) 261 (.17507.01) sg 187/1 A[on Drag 15/17 or 18, South Gaulish. Neronian or early-Flavian.

61(2B) 270 (.18113.01) sg 187/1]M? on Drag 18/31, Central Gaulish. Trajanic or Hadrianic.

62(43) 300 (17509.01) sg 187/1 Lollius ii 2a 18/31R [L]OLLI·M (Walke 1965, no.196) Lezoux (a). *c.* AD 140-160.

63(23) 304 (.17510.01) sg 187/1 Divicatus 1a (possibly) 33 DIV(IC)[ATIM] Lezoux (a). *c.* AD 140-170.

64(51)   674 (.17676.01) sg 187/1 Mercator ii 2c 18/31 or 31 ME[RC]AF (Knorr 1921, Taf. X, 140) Lezoux (b). *c.* AD 125-150.

Area 2

Phase 3F

65(39)   2150 (.17535.01) sg 210/1 Latinus i 2a 33a LATINVSF Les Martres-de-Veyre (a). *c.* AD 100-120.

Phase 3G

66(136)   2911 (.17550.01) sg 207/4]-M on Drag 33, Central Gaulish. Antonine. Footring heavily worn. Graffito (G20).

67(135)   2758 (.17545.01) sg 207/6]NI on Drag 33, slightly burnt, Central Gaulish. Antonine. Footring worn.

PHASE 4

Area 1

Phase 4A

*68*449 (.18542.01) sg 174/1 Cinnamus ii CIN[...] retr., in decoration (decorated samian report no. 17) Lezoux. AD 150-170 on decoration (not examined by Dickinson).

69(62)   446 (.17541.01) sg 174/2 Pateratus 1a 31 [·PATER]ATIOF (Walke 1965, nos. 227 and 229) Lezoux (a). *c.* AD 135-155.

70(29)   446 (.17542.01) sg 174/2 Flo- Albinus 4b 31 [F·AL]BINIO[F] Lezoux (b). *c.* AD 150-180.

71(143)   447 (.17584.01) sg 174/2 M[on Walters 80, Central Gaulish. Mid- to late Antonine. Footring heavily worn.

72(72)   444 (.17540.01) sg 174/3 Quintus v 5a 33 QVINTIM Lezoux (a). *c.* AD 160-200.

PHASE 5

Area 1

Phase 5A

73(73)   1501 (.17625.01) sg 158/1 Reburrus ii 11a 31 REBV[RRIM] Lezoux (a). *c.* AD 140-170.

74(74)   1501 (.17624.01) sg 158/1 + Phase 5C 1336 (.14205.01) sg 164/1 Regalis ii 1a 31R REGALISFE (Ludowici 1927, 277, b) Rheinzabern (a). Complete, in two pieces. The footring is heavily worn and some of the internal glaze has been ground away. Late C2 or first half of C3.

75(17)   1504 (.14534.02) sg 158/1 + phase 12, 880 (.17990.01) sg 101/1 + (unphased), 821 (.17564.01) sg 129/1 (decorated samian report no. 18) Cinnamus ii 5b 37 CI[NNAMI] retr. (Walke 1965, Taf. 39, 11) Lezoux (a). *c.* AD 150-180.

76(132)   1504 (.17626.01) sg 158/1 POT[or ROT[on Drag 18/31R or 31R, Central Gaulish. Antonine, probably after *c.* AD 160.

77(71)   951 (.17570.01) sg 158/4 Quintilianus i 1b cup [QVI]NTIL(IA)NIM Lezoux (a). *c.* AD 125-150.

78(121)   1550 (.17679.01) sg 160/1]\ IC? on a cup, South Gaulish. First-century.

Phase 5B

79(87)   792 (.17561.01) sg 162/3 Sarrutus 1a 15/17 [OF.SA]RRVT (Walke 1965, no.336) La Graufesenque (a). *c.* AD 70-90.

80(177)   848 (.17568.01) sg 162/3]CIR[? on Drag 31, Central Gaulish. Antonine.

81(14)   629 (.17531.01) sg 162/5 Castus i 10a 15/17 or 18 CA[STVS.FE] (Ulbert 1959, Taf. 44, 66) La Graufesenque (a). *c.* AD 50-70.

82(120)   651 (.17532.01) sg 167/1]ANI? on Drag 27, South Gaulish. Flavian-Trajanic. The central boss on the base has been pushed down with finger and thumb, leaving prints.

Phase 5C

83(46)   473 (.17524.01) sg 163/7 Mansuetus ii 2a' 33 MA.SV.ETIc (originally ... ETo) Lezoux (a). *c.* AD 150-180.

84(130)   498 (.17511.01) sg 164/1 IA[on Drag 18/31R-31R, Central Gaulish. Mid-Antonine.

85(133)   498 (.17525.01) sg 164/1]A on Drag 31, Central Gaulish. Antonine. Footring worn; graffito (G21).

86(3)   522 (.17512.01) sg 164/1 Albucius ii 6a 33(?) ALBVCI Lezoux (a). *c.* AD 150-180.

87(1B)   889 (.18136.01) sg 164/1 + phase 3B: 1219 (.18205.01) sg 150/1 Atepomarus ii 10b 24 [ATEPO]MAR Lezoux (b). *c.* AD 50-65.

88(7)   1336 (.17619.01) sg 164/1 Attius ii 6a' 33 [AT]TIVS<EF> Lezoux (b). *c.* AD 135-160/165.

89(126)   1375 (.17620.01) sg 164/1 OF[retr. on Drag 18/31 or 31, Central Gaulish. Hadrianic or early-Antonine.

90(110)   843 (.17567.01) sg 165/4 M...? on Drag 27g South Gaulish. Neronian or early-Flavian.

91(9)   514 (.17526.01) sg 166/3 Banvillus 2a 42(?) [BANVI]LLIM (Miller 1922, pl. XXXVII, 2) Les Martres-de-Veyre (a). *c.* AD 130-150.

92(114)   462 (.17543.01) sg 166/4]IC[on Drag 29, South Gaulish. Neronian or early-Flavian.

93(140)   462 (.17530.01) sg 166/4 POTTA[? or ROTTA[? on Drag 31, Central Gaulish. Mid- to late-Antonine.

94(119)   268 (.17558.01) sg 166/5]I\I\/ on form 27, South Gaulish. Flavian-Trajanic.

Area 3

Phase 5E

95(45)   3939 (.17659.01) sg339/4 Macer i 2a 15/17 or 18 MAC.RI.MA[N] or MAC.RI.MA (Hartley 1972, S140) La Graufesenque (a). *c.* AD 50-65.

96(97)   3954 (.17769.01) sg 360/1 Sollemnis i 5a 18/31 or 31 SO[LIIMNI] Lezoux (b). *c.* AD 125-150.

97(53)   3954 (.17660.01) sg 360/1 Moxius v 1a 38 or 44 [M]OXIMA Lezoux (a). *c.* AD 160-190.

98(89)   3954 (.17661.02) sg 360/1 Secundinus vi 3a 33 SIICVNDINIM (Dickinson 1986, no.3.189-90) Lezoux (a). *c.* AD 160-190.

99(145)   3954 (.17663.01) sg 360/1]DVS? on Drag 31, East Gaulish (Rheinzabern). Late C2 or first half of C3.

100(94)   3954 (.17662.03) sg 360/1 Severianus ii 4b 32 etc. SEVERIANVS (Ludowici 1927, 229, e) Rheinzabern (a). *c.* AD 200-260.

Phase 5F

101(82)   3961 (.17664.01) sg 339/6 Sacer-Vasil- 1a' (by *surmoulage*) 18/31 SACER.VASILF Les Martres-de-Veyre (a). *c.* AD 100-120.

102(32)   3936 (.17658.01) sg 339/7 Habilis 5d 38 or 44 HABILIS.F Lezoux (b). *c.* AD 150-180.

103(55)   3792 (.17643.01) sg 362/3 Niger ii 5c' 27g [FN]GII (originally OFNGR) La Graufesenque (a). Graffito (G22). *c.* AD 50-70.

104(103)3792 (.17642.01) sg 362/3 Vitalis iii 2a 18/31 [V]+ALISMSF; (Hartley 1972, S58) Les Martres-de-Veyre (a). *c.* AD 100-120.

105(16)   3792 (.17644.01) sg 362/3 Cinnamus ii 4a 33 CINNAMI.M (with NN and AM ligatured) Lezoux (b). *c.* AD 135-160.

106(31) 3792 (.17645.01) sg 362/3 Habilis 1a 38 HABILISM Lezoux (a). *c.* AD 150-180.

107(139)3795 (.17768.01) sg 362/3]VS or SA[on Drag 46, Central Gaulish. Antonine.

Phase 5G

108(1) 3668 (.17640.01) sg 334/1 Advocisus 1b 33 [ADVOCIS]I-O (usually registering as ...I-OF) Lezoux (b). *c.* AD 160-190.

109(2A) 3953 (.15890.02) sg 334/1 SI[or]IS on Drag 27, Central Gaulish. Hadrianic or early-Antonine.

110(1A) 3953 (.15890.01) sg 334/1 Laxtucissa 5a 37 (decorated samian report no. 27) [LAXTV]CISF retr. in the decoration (Karnitsch 1959, Taf. 41, 1) Lezoux (a). *c.* AD 145-175.

111(25) 3608 (.17636.01) sg 334/2 Doccius ii 4d 31 [DOCC.I.V].SF Lezoux (b). *c.*AD 155-175.

112(34) 3872 (.17647.01) sg 357/2 Illixo 8a 31 [.I]LLIXO. Lezoux (a). *c.* AD 150-180.

113(80) 3879 (.17652.01) sg 359/4 Rufus iii 3g 27g °FRVFI retr. (Simon 1978, C777) La Graufesenque (a). *c.* AD 65-95.

*114(*118)3879 (.17650.01) sg 359/4 IIII on Drag. 27g, South Gaulish. Flavian-Trajanic.

115(104) 3879 (.17651.01) sg 359/4 Vitalis iii 2a 18/31 [V+ALIS]MSF (Hartley 1972, S58) Les Martres-de-Veyre (a). *c.* AD 100-120.

116(24) 3879 (.17648.01) sg 359/4 Divixtus i 9d 30 (decorated samian report no. 30) DIVIX.F (Miller 1922, pl XXXVII, 12) Lezoux (a). *c.* AD 150-180.

117(85) 3879 (.17654.01) sg 359/4 Sacrillus 3a 31R SAC[RILL·I·]M (Dickinson 1986, no.3.180) Lezoux (a). *c.* AD 160-200.

118A(69)3879 (.17649.01) sg 359/4 Quartinus 31 QVAR[TINVsF] (Ludowici 1927, 227, a) Rheinzabern (a). Late C2 or first half of C3.

118B(70)Unphased: 3910 (.17657.01) sg 332/2 31 or 31R. A second example of this stamp.

PHASE 6

Area 3

Phase 6A

119(33) 3640 (.17638.01) sg 338/3 Ianuarius vi 3a 31R IANVARIVSF Rheinzabern (b). Late C2 or first half of C3.

120(2) 3666 (.17639.01) sg 338/3 Advocisus 2a' 79 or 80, or Ludowici Tg or Tx [A]DVOCISI-O Lezoux (a). On the later version of the stamp, as here, the C has almost closed up. Burnt. *c.* AD 160-190.

121(144)3673 (.17641.01) sg 338/3]/SF? on Drag 31, East Gaulish (Rheinzabern). Late C2 or first half of C3.

122(142)3610 (.17637.01) sg 341/1]IM on Drag 38 or 44, Central Gaulish. Mid- to late-Antonine. Internal glaze ground away.

123(54) 3836 (.17646.01) sg 367/1 Namilianus 1a 33 NAMILIANI Lezoux (a). *c.* AD 160-200.

124(11) 3890 (.17656.01) sg 367/1 Calava 2b 33 [CAL]AVA·F (Simpson 1987, no.41b) Lezoux (a). *c.* AD 125-150.

125(137)3890 (.17655.01) sg 367/1 A..B..CI? on Drag 33, Central Gaulish. Antonine. Perhaps a stamp of Albucius ii, but too blurred for precise identification.

Phase 6B

126(141)3560 (.17634.01) sg 363/1]RIM on Drag 31R, Central Gaulish. Mid- to late-Antonine.

An additional 30 stamps were recovered from post-Roman and unphased contexts on Areas 1-3, and 10 from Area 4. These include 10 unidentified pieces – 2 SG, 5 CG on plain vessels and 1 on a Drag 37 (below), and 2 EG (below); 4 La Graufesenque on plain vessels (earliest, *c.* AD 50-65) plus 2 on Drag 29 bases (below); 2 Les Martres-de-Veyre (1 below); 18 Lezoux on plain vessels (latest *c.* AD 160-200) plus 2 on Drag 37 (below); and 2 Rheinzabern (below). Amongst these are the following, selected by Pollard on grounds of uncommon source and/or date, or other details. Reports on the remainder are held in the site archive. Area 4 identifications (including nos. 132, 134) are by Dickinson and Hartley, *c.* 1984.

127(41) Phase 8, 861 (.17569.01) sg 117/3 F343 Licinus 7b 29? LICINI[ANAO] (Fiches 1978, no.61) La Graufesenque (a). *c.* AD 40-60.

128(66) Unphased, from evaluation: 50 (.17500) Pontus 8a 29 [OF.]PONTI La Graufesenque (a). *c.* AD 70-85.

129(75) Phase 12, 204 (.17506.01) sg 101/1 Reginus ii 1a 31 REGIN[I.M] (Steer 1961, 107, 7) Les Martres-de-Veyre (c). *c.* AD 130-150.

130(30) Phase 12, 200 (.17502.01) sg 100/1 Flo-Albinus 4c 37 rim F.ALBINIOF (Karnitsch 1959, Taf. 41, 4) Lezoux (b). *c.* AD 150-180.

131(138)Phase 12, 200 (.17505.01) sg 100/1 /[or]/ on Drag. 37 rim, Central Gaulish. Antonine.

132 Phase 9, 8032 (Area 4) (.1635) sg 116/3 Cenaboca Drag. 33 CENABOCA retr. Lezoux (c). Mid to late Antonine. Graffito (G6).

133(65) Phase 12, 2000 (17513.01) sg 296/1 Pompeius iii Uncertain 1 31R PON[Rheinzabern (c). Late C2 or first half of C3.

134 Phase 9, 8019 (Area 4) (.1625) sg 122/1 Potentinus ii 1b 31 (Ludowici Sa) POTIINTINVS Rheinzabern (a). Late C2 or early C3. This potter is dated only by his forms. Those with die 1b include Drag 32 and its derivatives and Drag 40.

135(146)Phase 8, 2575 (.17537.01) sg 247/2]/ on Drag. 31R, East Gaulish. Late C2 or first half of C3.

134(147)Phase 9, 2268 (.17520.01) sg 290/1] VSFE on a concave dish, East Gaulish. Late C2 or first half of C3.

A further 33 fragments from Areas 1-3 have parts of single letters or merely show the beginning or end of the frame. These comprise 19 South Gaulish (the earliest a Claudian-Neronian Drag 24), 1 from Les Martres-de-Veyre, 12 Central Gaulish, and one East Gaulish (a late C2 or 1st half C3 Drag 31).

THE AMPHORAE
D.F.Williams

Editorial note: the following is an abridged version of the report submitted by the author; the full report is held in the Site Archive.

Introduction

Some 1700 amphora sherds were recovered from the 1991 excavations at Causeway Lane, Leicester. These consist predominantly of body sherds, but also included in this total are a few rims, handles and bases. The classification of this material has been based on a study of the forms and fabrics, and the identifications are set out below in a series of tables showing the frequency of each type. The use of form names is based upon the work of Dressel (1899), Laubenheimer (1985), the Haltern, Camulodunum and Fishbourne series (Loeschcke, 1909; Hawkes and Hull, 1947; Cunliffe, 1971), Beltran (1970) and those terms in common usage (Peacock and Williams, 1986).

Table 5: *Total amphorae from all three areas* *% Total of Each Type*

	% By Weight-		% By Count-	
Dressel 20	123,918g	90.1%	1,458	83.9%
Gauloise 4	6,928g	5.1%	177	10.2%
Haltern 70	49g	<0.1%	1	<0.1%
Camulodunum 186C	423g	0.3%	2	0.1%
Camulodunum 186sp	1,242g	0.9%	15	1.0%
Rhodian	1,920g	1.4%	36	2.1%
Dressel 2-4	1,760g	1.3%	7	0.4%
Carrot	438g	0.4%	16	0.9%
Fishbourne 148.3	47g	<0.1%	2	0.1%
North African	83g	<0.1%	2	0.1%
?Eastern Mediterranean	139g	0.1%	12	0.7%
Verulamium Fabric	298g	0.2%	2	0.1%
Unassigned	264g	0.2%	8	0.5%
Totals	137,509g	100.0%	1,738	100.0%

Overall Comments

Sherds of amphorae that once carried Spanish olive oil from Baetica (Dressel 20) and southern French wine (Gauloise 4) comprise some 94-95% of the overall count and weight of amphorae from the site. Dressel 20 alone accounts for 84-90% of the count and weight of the sherds. Indeed, this figure would be even higher if slightly less than half a complete Dressel 20 amphora had not been left out of the totals from Area 1 (see below). The proportion of Dressel 20 vessels present is likely to be distorted to some extent by the large size of this thick-walled amphora with its ability, once broken, to shatter into many pieces. However, taking into account the detailed information we have on the relative proportions of amphorae sherds from other sites, there can be little doubt that Dressel 20 is the most commonly found amphora form in Roman Britain (Williams and Peacock, 1983). With the later form Dressel 23, it testifies to the large amount of Baetican olive oil that entered the province up to the end of the third century AD and possibly beyond (Carreras and Williams, 1995). By the early second century AD Gauloise 4 had become the commonest wine amphora reaching Britain, and it continued to be imported until around the late third century AD.

Somewhat lesser quantities occur of the wine amphorae Dressel 2-4 and Rhodian, the carrot form and the fish sauce varieties Camulodunum 186C/sp. The few remaining sherds suggest that a variety of other types are present only in small amounts: Haltern 70, Fishbourne 148.3, North African, ?Eastern Mediterranean and Verulamium region fabric.

The analysis of the assemblage by area

Areas 1 and 4

Table 6: *Amphorae from Area 1 and 4* *% Total of Each Type*

	% By Weight-		% By Count-	
*Dressel 20	94,840g	93.5%	1,235	89.5%
Gauloise 4	2,616g	2.7%	79	5.8%
Haltern 70	49g	<0.1%	1	<0.1%
Camulodunum 186sp	772g	0.8%	6	0.4%
Rhodian	1,920g	1.9%	36	2.7%
Dressel 2-4	439g	0.4%	4	0.3%
Carrot	239g	0.2%	10	0.8%
North African	59g	<0.1%	1	<0.1%
?Eastern Mediterranean	14g	<0.1%	1	<0.1%
Verulamium Fabric	298g	0.3%	2	0.1%
Unassigned	230g	0.2%	6	0.4%
Totals	101,476g	100.0%	1,381	100.0%

* Does not include just under half of a Dressel 20 vessel, missing its rim and base but with neck and handles complete and with the majority of the girth remaining. The shape of the handles suggest a second century AD date. Approximately 12,800kg in weight (fig. 59.118).

Dressel 20 stamped handles (fig.59; all fabric AM9A)

A1. ROMANI(with palm). Made at the kilns at La Delicias on the banks of the River Genil and probably dated to the Flavian period (Callender, 1965, no. 1541; Remesal, 1986, no. 224). (17713.01) context 832, sub-group 141/1: Phase 3A.

A2. SAENIANES. Dating between the second half of the first century AD and the first half of the second century AD (Callender, 1965, no. 1559a; Remesal, 1986, no. 239). (13970.01) 1221, sg 150/1: Phase 3B.

A3. MMCSAE. Associated with the kilns at El Tejarillo on the north bank of the River Guadalquivir near Arva and dated to the second half of the second century AD (Callender, 1965, no. 1049; Remesal, 1986, no. 71). (17710.01) 758, sg 157/5: Phase 3B (profile, fig. 68.137).

Comments

The Rhodian amphorae material, some 36 sherds, only occurs in Area 1 and belongs predominantly to Peacock's Fabric Group 2 (1977). This fabric most probably comes from the Rhodian Peraea, where kiln sites associated with this form have recently been discovered (Empereur and Tuna, 1989). Although the Rhodian style amphora appears to have continued to have been made into the early second century AD, in Britain this type is commonly recovered from early Roman military sites (Peacock, 1977). The form mostly carried wine.

One rim and a number of rilled body sherds occur of the small carrot amphora with its characteristicly tapered body (Peacock and Williams, 1986, Class 12). A recent view suggests that this form may have originated in Egypt and carried dates (Tomlin, 1992). Carrot amphorae are again often associated with early military sites in Britain (and Germany).

One rim of the first century AD Haltern 70 amphora from Baetica is present. However, as it occurs in a somewhat similar fabric to Dressel 20, it is possible that a few of the plain body sherds included with the latter material may in reality be Haltern 70 (Peacock and Williams, 1986, Class 15).

A consideration of the fabric of the likely four Dressel 2-4 body sherds suggest that three may have an Italian origin. The majority of the Dressel 2-4 finds in Roman Britain probably arrived during the first century AD, though the form continued to be made on a smaller scale into the third century AD (Freed, 1989).

One plain body sherd can be identified by its fabric as North African, though as the actual amphora form involved is unknown, dating is difficult. North African cylindrical forms reached Britain as early as the middle of the second century AD (Tyers, 1984), though the majority of vessels seem to have arrived later than this, during the third, fourth and to some extent fifth centuries AD (Peacock, 1977; Williams and Carreras, 1995). The main content carried was probably olive oil.

Two thick and rather granular plain body sherds may come from the Verulamium region. Certainly the size and texture of the frequent quartz grains present are similar in thin section to sandy pottery analyzed by the writer from this area. These two sherds may in fact be from a flagon, though a flat-bottomed amphora form seemingly based on the French Gauloise 4 was also made in the region (a number of the latter vessels have recently been identified from London. Information from Dr. Roberta Tomber).

The Camulodunum 186sp sherds belong to southern Spanish fish-produce amphorae and probably date to the first two centuries AD.

Also in this group is a body sherd which may possibly have originated from the eastern Mediterranean region.

Area 2

Table 7: *Amphorae from Area 2* % *Total of Each Type*

	% By Weight-		% By Count-	
Dressel 20	2,733g	55.3%	42	70.0%
Gauloise 4	549g	11.1%	14	23.4%
Camulodunum 186C	423g	8.5%	2	3.3%
Dressel 2-4	1,241g	25.1%	2	3.3%
Totals	4,946g	100.0%	60	100.0%

Comments

Only 60 amphorae sherds were recovered from Area 2 and these consisted mostly of Dressel 20 and Gauloise 4, all body sherds. Also present in this group were a rim and body sherd of the southern Spanish form Camulodunum 186C/Beltran IIA which carried *garum* or *liquamen* fish sauces, sometimes also salted fish, up to the early second century AD (Peacock and Williams, 1986, Class 18). Together with an Italian Dressel 2-4 rim.

Area 3

Table 8: *Amphorae from Area 3* % *Total of Each Type*

	% By Weight-		% By Count-	
Dressel 20	26,345g	84.7%	181	60.7%
Gauloise 4	3,763g	12.1%	84	28.2%
Camulodunum 186sp	470g	1.5%	10	3.4%
Dressel 2-4	80g	0.3%	1	0.3%
Carrot	199g	0.6%	6	2.0%
Fishbourne 148.3	47g	0.2%	2	0.7%
North African	24g	0.1%	1	0.3%
?Eastern Mediterranean	125g	0.4%	11	3.7%
Unassigned	34g	0.1%	2	0.7%
Totals	31,087g	100.0%	298	100.0%

Comments

Area 3 also has high percentages of Dressel 20 and Gauloise 4. It lacks any of the early Rhodian material, although it does include a large fragment of carrot amphora with some smaller body sherds. One North African sherd and eleven potential eastern Mediterranean sherds are present, some of which at least may be late in date. In addition, two sherds are recorded of a sandy fabric likely to belong to the type known as Fishbourne 148.3, as yet undesignated, but previously found in small numbers in Leicester. The single Dressel 2-4 body sherd is in the 'black sand' fabric characteristic of the Bay of Naples region of Campania (Peacock and Williams, 1986, Class 10).

THE MORTARIUM STAMPS *Kay Hartley*
(fig. 59)

Editorial note: M1-M31 were reported on in June 1993, as part of a study of selected mortaria from A1.1991 (Areas 1-3) (Hartley 1993). M32-M35, along with the Gillam 272 (fig. 80.337), and stamps from 'Defences' sites (Hartley 1987) were reported in January 1986 (*ibid.*, 1986).

PHASE 2

M1. Fabric: MO7. Source: Verulamium region (profile, fig. 63.47). Description: burnt throughout. LVGD[\fec, counterstamp of Albinus. Date: AD 60-90. (Extension No. .17721.01) context 1481, sub-group 145/3: phase 2F.

M28. (unstamped sherd from 1315, sg 145/1: phase 2F); see below.

M2. MO12. Mancetter-Hartshill (fig. 64.78). Burnt. Retrograde stamp of G. Attius Marinus. AD 100-130. (.17705.01, .17708.01, .17256.01) 2150, sg 210/1: phase 3F (stamp); 2914, 2933, sg 202/3: phase 2K.

M3. MO4. Mancetter-Hartshill (fig. 64.79). Fragmentary stamp, not identified, probably either initial D or retrograde CI. AD 140-175. (.17707.01) 2807, sg 202/3: phase 2K.

M4. MO7. Verulamium region (fig. 65.89). Albinus. AD 60-90. (.17709.01) 2987, sg 204/2: phase 2K.

M5. MO7. Verulamium region (fig. 65.91). Doinus. AD 70-110. (.17722.01) 3549, sg 332/1: phase 2L.

PHASE 3

M6. MO7. Verulamium region (fig. 66.103). F.LVGVDV, counterstamp of Albinus (Hartley 1972, 1984). AD 60-90. (.17719.01) 1259, sg 141/1: phase 3A.

M7. MO7. Verulamium region (fig. 66.104). Heavily worn and burnt. FECIT counterstamp of Marinus (Hartley 1994, fig. 48.8). Optimum date AD 70-110. (.17715.01) 1051, sg 141/1: phase 3A.

M8. MO7. Verulamium region (fig. 66.117). Burnt. MORI[, for Moricamulus. Optimum date AD 80-110. (.17714.01) 936, sg 142/1: phase 3A.

M9. MO18. Mancetter-Hartshill (fig. 66.120). Burnt. Contracted stamp of Similis ii. He may be the same potter as Similis i, but if so this is his later work. Optimum date AD 150-170. (.17711.01) 801, sg 141/4: phase 3B.

M10. MO4/18, though MO18 likely in view of the potter's other work. Mancetter-Hartshill (fig. 66.121). Parts of]CTO[surviving, of Victor. Optimum date AD 100-130. (.17712.01) 801, sg 141/4: phase 3B.

M11. MO4. Mancetter-Hartshill (fig. 67.125). Worn. IVNILOCC, retrograde, for Iunius Loccius. AD 145-175. (.17718.01) 1198, sg 152/1: phase 3B.

M12. MO4. Mancetter-Hartshill (fig. 68.140). Worn, upper surface pitted and damaged. Incomplete stamp, almost certainly retrograde, from a die of Loccius Vibo, where the lettering is corrupt; the 8-like letter is the B. Optimum date AD 135-165. (.17716.01) 1088, sg 186/2: phase 3C.

M13. MO12. Mancetter-Hartshill (fig. 68.145; possible graffito, fig. 60.G8). Two impressions, retrograde, reading ICOTASG from right to left, for Icotasgus. AD 130-160. (.17702.01) 304, sg 187/1: phase 3D.

PHASE 5

M14. MO4? Mancetter-Hartshill (fig. 71.187). A badly impressed stamp; when normal this would read BONOXS for Bonoxus. This example could be from a new die from which the N has been expunged; as the borders are complete, it is difficult to see how it could be a mis-impression or bis impression (i.e. twice impressed, one over the other). Bonoxus was a relatively minor potter. Optimum date AD 130-155. (.17704.01) 522, sg 164/1: phase 5C.

M15. MO4? Mancetter-Hartshill (fig. 71.188).]OCC[, retrograde. Loccius Proc(...), for some such name as Loccius Probus or Proculus. Optimum date AD 135-165. (.17703.01) 498, sg 164/1: phase 5C.

M16. MO12. Mancetter-Hartshill (fig. 72.204). Icotasgus, same die as M13. AD 130-160. (.17729.01) 3930, sg 339/4: phase 5E.

M17. MO4. Mancetter-Hartshill (fig. 72.213). IVNILOCCI retrograde, for Iunius Loccius. AD 145-175. (.17730.01) 3954, sg 360/1: phase 5E.

M18. MO19. Mancetter-Hartshill (fig. 73.224). LOCCIVIBO retrograde, Lambda L; for Loccius Vibo. Optimum date AD 135-165. (.17727.01) 3908, sg 339/7: phase 5F.

M19. MO19. Mancetter-Hartshill (fig. 73.225). Fragmentary stamp, probably reading]FE. Probably a stamp which reads CICVRFE when complete. Optimum date AD 150-175. (.17807.2) 3908, sg 339/7: phase 5F.

M20. MO4. Mancetter-Hartshill (fig. 73.226). Retrograde stamp of Mossius. AD 135-165. (.17728.01) 3908, sg 339/7: phase 5F.

M21. MO19. Mancetter-Hartshill (fig. 73.236). Minomelus. AD 130-165. (.17724.01) 3792, sg 362/3: phase 5F.

M22. MO4. Mancetter-Hartshill. Border of stamp only; too little for identification but probably someone like Icotasgus. AD 130-160. Not illustrated (.17723.01) 3792, sg 362/3: phase 5F.

M23. MO12. Mancetter-Hartshill (fig. 74.247). Semi-literate stamp. Optimum date AD 110-130. (.17725.01) 3879, sg 359/4: phase 5G.

M24. MO12/19, but MO19 certain from potter's other work. Mancetter-Hartshill (fig. 74.248). Burnt. Iunius, with N retrograde. Optimum date AD 150-175. (.17726.01) 3879, sg 359/4: phase 5G.

POST-ROMAN PHASES

M25. MO10. Verulamium region (fig. 78.308). Slightly burnt. ALBIN[for Albinus (die as Hartley 1972, fig. 145.2). AD 60-90. (.17720.01) 1459, sg 100/1: 3, Phase 12.

M26. MO12. Mancetter-Hartshill (fig. 78.309). VITA[, left to right; stamp of Vitalis iv. AD 115-145. (.17700.01) 200, sg 100/1: 3, Phase 12.

M27. MO18. Mancetter-Hartshill (fig. 78.310). Similis i, stamp retrograde, with parts of the final]IS. Optimum date AD 130-160. (.17701.01) 200, sg 100/1: 3, Phase 12.

M28. MO15. Gallia Belgica (fig. 78.311). When complete, the stamp reads MOTTIVS BOLLVS.F from the bottom left (Hartley 1977, 7, Group II potter). AD 50-85. (.17717.01, .14162.01, .13508.01) 1101, sg 102/1: 3, Phase 12 (stamp); 1315, sg 145/1: phase 2F; 1047, sg 162/7: Phase 5B.

M29. MO19? Mancetter-Hartshill (fig. 78.315). IV[and the first stroke of N from a die of Iunius. Optimum date AD 150-175. (.17706.01) 2133, sg 252/5: Phase 9.

M30. MO4? Mancetter-Hartshill (fig. 79.323). Fragmentary, almost certainly]VR[from a stamp of Maurius. This would never have the grit that goes with MO12. Optimum date AD 150-175. (.17842.01) 3568, sg 314/2: Phase 9.

M31. MO19. Mancetter-Hartshill (fig. 79.324). Sennius, stamp reads left to right; probably final S surviving. AD 150-175. (.15293.01) 3583, sg 301/1, Phase 12.

M32. MO7. Verulamium region (fig. 79.332). Well worn. FLVGVDV counterstamp of Albinus; probably the same die as Hartley 1972, fig. 145.6, used with ibid. fig. 145.5. AD 60-90. (Area 4, .1516) 8021, sg 119/10: Phase 9.

M33. MO7. Brockley Hill (fig. 79.333). One of six dies of Matugenus; two of his name-dies record him as the son of Albinus; his earliest mortaria have much in common with those of his father. Active within the period AD 80-125. (Area 4, .1604) 8004, sg 108/1: Phase 11.

M34. MO12. Mancetter-Hartshill (fig. 79.334). Very badly battered (stamp not illustrated). Retrograde stamp of Candidus ii, die as Hartley 1987, fig. 34.61A, with CAN ligatured and cursive Ds. The rims and stamps differ considerably from those of Candidus i who worked in the Verulamium region, so that they are best considered separately though from the point of view of date they could well be the work of the same man. The rim profiles of Candidus ii point to a date within the period AD 100-140. (Area 4, .1281) 8014, unphased.

M35. MO19. Mancetter-Hartshill (fig. 79.335). Stamped twice close together with die 2 of Iunius, with S reversed.

Dating evidence available in 1985 suggested *c.* AD 155-185, but cf. M29 above. (Area 4, .1289) 8014, unphased.

THE GRAFFITI (fig. 60)

identified by *Mark Hassall*

The majority of the graffiti were submitted to Mark Hassall, and published in *Britannia* (Hassall and Tomlin 1982, 1994). The identifications are reproduced here for completeness, along with a few others. All were incised after firing, except G8. Samian ware identifications are by Brenda Dickinson (stamps) and Geoff Dannell, the mortarium by Kay Hartley, and the others by Richard Clark.

G1. Samian, CG, Drag. 33, Antonine. Upper body ext.: IIC, perhaps 'ninety-eight' (Hassall and Tomlin 1994, item 25). (.18252.01) context 631, sub-group 162.5: phase 5B.

G2. Samian, CG, Drag. 18/31, Hadrianic-Antonine. Underside of base.: N or more probably IV, 'four' (*ibid.*, item 20). (.18246.01) 3792, sg 362/3: phase 5F.

G3. Samian, CG, Drag. 31, late 2nd century. Upper body ext.: X, 'ten', or mark of ownership. A second diagonal scored line, running from top right to bottom left, parallel to the second stroke of 'X', perhaps represents a blundered first attempt, abandoned as being cut too near the rim (*ibid.*, item 21). (.18244.01) 3879, sg 359/4: phase 5G.

G4. Samian, EG, Drag. 33, late Antonine. Under the footring: LX, 'sixty' (*ibid.*, item 24). (.18245.01) 3866, sg 338/2: phase 5H.

G5. Samian, CG, Drag. 33, Antonine. Base, showing considerable wear, and possibly trimmed to form a lid or disc/counter. Underside: one or possibly two graffiti. A fainter, primary text (a), and inverted to it, a secondary text (b) more boldly scored and blundered. (a) XXI, 'twenty-one'. (b) I or C (*ibid.*, item 23). (.15419.01) 3640, sg 338/3: phase 6A.

G6. Samian, CG, Drag. 33, mid to late Antonine (stamped, report no. 132). Inside the footring: three strokes, joining. (Area 4, .1635) 8032, sg 116/3: Phase 9.

G7. Samian, Rheinzabern, Drag. 37, late 2nd-mid 3rd century; rim with fragment of ovolo. Below the rim ext. and inverted with respect to the rim: XXI, 'twenty-one' (*ibid.*, item 22). (.18247.01) 3535, sg 340/1: phase 6B.

G8. MO12, Mancetter-Hartshill, stamps of Icotasgus, AD 130-160 (stamps, report no. M13, form fig. 68.145). Cut before firing on the interior below the rim: MID [...], or just conceivably, if inverted, [...] CIIV . (*ibid.*, item 26). R. Pollard comments: This mark is at the point where the flange flares out from the body, and could conceivably have arisen from stretching of the clay during drying as the heavy flange began to tear away from the body, rather than being a deliberate graffito. (.17702.01) 304, sg 187/1: phase 3D.

G9. OW3, jar (fig. 67.127). Underside of base: X, 'ten', or a mark of ownership (*ibid.*, item 28). (.18248.01) 1202, sg 152/1: phase 3B.

G10. GW, jar (fig. 66.109). Underside of base: asterisk. (.12840.01) 872, sg 141/1: phase 3A.

G11. GW, bowl (fig. 74.243). Flange: X (cf. G9; *ibid.*, item 30). (.15367.09) 3608, sg 334/2: phase 5G.

G12. GW1, dish (fig. 77.286). Underside of base: X (cf. G9; *ibid.*, item 32: not, as given there, BB1). (.15637.09) 3836, sg 367/1: phase 6A.

G13. BB1, dish, mid 4th century? (fig. 72.219). Body ext.: X (cf. G9; *ibid.*, item 29). (.18272.01) 3954, sg 360/1: phase 5E.

G14. BB1, dish, late 3rd to mid-4th century? (fig. 76.260).

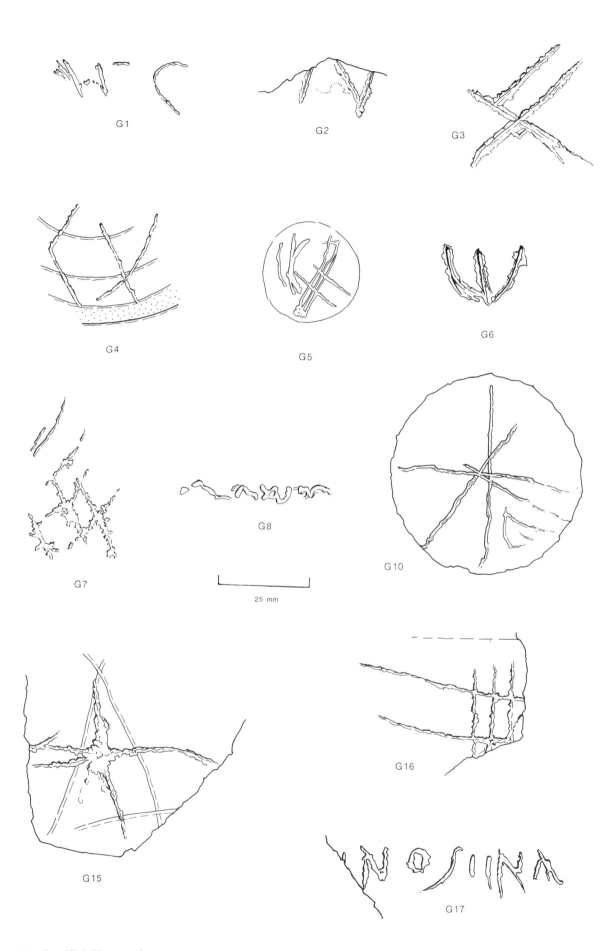

Fig. 60: *Graffiti illustrations*

Body int.: two diagonal strokes at edge of sherd; part of X? (cf. G9). (.15668.08) 3866, sg 338/2: phase 5H.

G15. BB1, dish, mid-3rd century? (fig. 76.263). Body ext.: X (cf. G9; *ibid.*, item 31). (.15625.06) 3827, sg 354/1: phase 5H.

G16. BB1, jar. Shoulder ext.: two horizontal lines, cut by three shorter, vertical lines, perhaps representing a numeral between guide-lines, III, 'three' (*ibid.*, item 27). R. Pollard comments: this post-firing graffito recalls marks on the shoulders of GW jars made at Rowlands Castle in the 2nd-3rd century (type Fishbourne 313: Cunliffe 1971), and CG jars from south Essex in the 1st century (Jones 1972), which seem to have been cut during production, perhaps as tally/batch-marks. (.15638.02) 3836, sg 367/1: phase 6A.

G17. BB1, deep bowl-dish, 3rd century (fig. 81.354). Body ext.:]\NOSIINA, ']inosena'? (Hassall &Tomlin 1982, item 53; the top of an extra vertical stroke, not recorded there, is visible before the N at the edge of the sherd). (A475.1979.1336) 8009, sg 128/5: Phase 11.

G18-22. Samian, stamped vessels reported on by Brenda Dickinson (above). Graffiti described by Richard Pollard. Not illustrated.

G18. La Graufesenque, Drag. 27g, *c.* AD 50-65 (stamp no. 6). Underside of base: X (cf. G9). (.17828.01) 1264, sg 143/2: phase 2D.

G19. Les Martres-de-Veyre, Drag. 31, *c.* AD 130-160 (stamp no. 54). Group of three notches cut into bottom edge of footring. (.17546.01) 754, sg 154/3: phase 3B.

G20. CG, Drag. 33, Antonine (stamp no. 66). Underside of base: part of ?asterisk. (.17550.01) 2911, sg 207/4: phase 3G.

G21. CG, Drag. 31, Antonine (stamp no. 85). Underside of base: M. (.17525.01) 498, sg 164/1: phase 5C.

G22. La Graufesenque, Drag. 27g, *c.* AD 50-70 (stamp no. 103). Underside of base: at least six lines, roughly radial, possibly an asterisk. (.17643.01) 3792, sg 362/3: phase 5F.

THE ROMAN POTTERY BY PHASE

Richard Clark

PHASE 1

Area 1

Phase 1A (Sub-groups: 177/1, 180/1).

Assemblage: 95 sherds, 1625g, 1.01 EVEs, Average Sherd Weight (ASW): 12.7 g.

A small assemblage derived from two sub-groups (177/1, 180/1), the former incorporating a range of pits and post holes; both groups are highly truncated. The overall impression is of a mid to late 1st century assemblage, dominated by cooking and storage jars (42.6%) in grey and shell-tempered fabrics, with South Gaulish samian platters (Drag 18), bowls (Drag 29 & 37) and a cup (Drag 27), accompanied by table vessels in 'Romanized' and 'native' coarse wares. The balance of the pottery argues for an early date, with perhaps the latest element an everted rimmed jar (GW10, fig.61.1) of Flavian to Trajanic date. The vessel is probably a product of the Upper Nene or Northamptonshire potteries and is paralleled at Brixworth (Woods, 1972, fig. 24, 176-7).

With the exception of a single fragment of Central Gaulish samian, which can best be interpreted as intrusive, the samian supports a mid to late 1st cent. AD date of deposition. It is entirely pre- or early Flavian, with a single South Gaulish Drag.37 bowl representing the latest element.

The pottery assemblage suggests a *terminus post quem* (TPQ)

for the deposition of between AD 75 – 100. Links between the two sub-groups (177/1, 180/1) were identified, notably including the GW10 jar.

Illustrations: figs .61-81.

Phase 1B (Sub-groups: 130/1-7, 131/2).

Assemblage: 366 sherds, 7462g, 4.15 EVEs, ASW: 12.3g.

The pottery is drawn from a group of pits and cut features, tentatively interpreted as a result of early gravel extraction, sealed beneath Surface 1 or associated features. Joins between vessels in Phases 1B, 1C and 2B, incorporating the overlying surfaces, underline the disturbed nature of the assemblage, and may explain the presence of a single sherd of black-burnished ware (BB1).

The pottery continues the same themes as Phase 1A, a late 1st cent. AD assemblage with an element of earlier material. Phase 1B has Flavian and pre-Flavian samian, the former including a stamped platter (Dickinson, above no.1, AD 70-85) and a fragment of a Drag.37 bowl (Dannell, above no.1, AD 55-70). Shell-tempered (CG1) jars characteristic of the 1st cent. AD form the bulk, by weight (49.3%) of the assemblage, however, the proportion is distorted by the predominance of heavy storage jars (Brown 1994, fig.21, 8-12), the fabric representing only 10% by EVEs. Butt beakers in both MC3 and OW6 provide a rare glimpse of a Gallo-Belgic element in the assemblage. The presence of necked bowls and a platter (MC3, fig. 61.3), both forms that were to span the early Roman period, also support the impression of a continuation of the indigenous traditions.

The development of a 'Roman' assemblage is also evident, forms and fabrics that were to dominate the late 1st-early 2nd cent. AD, particularly grey ware everted rimmed jars (Pollard 1994a, fig.55, 104; LAU Forms 3/F/1-3), are already common (19.5% by EVEs). Much of a near complete waisted beaker (OW6, fig. 61.2) was recovered from sg130/1, it can be broadly paralleled at Colchester (Cam 85c, 397) and may date from as early as the Claudian period (Hawkes and Hull, 1947).

Excluding the probably intrusive BB1 sherd, the ceramic assemblage indicates an accumulation of material between AD 75-100. The presence of the stamped samian platter suggests a *TPQ c.* AD 70-85.

Illustrations: fig. 61.2-3.

Area 2

Phase 1C (Sub-groups: 200/1, 208/1-2).

Assemblage: 165 sherds, 5018g, 4.14 EVEs, ASW: 15.5g

The phase can be subdivided into two elements: sg200/1, described as 'layers', and sg208/1-2, respectively the fills of a possible beam slot (F671) and pit (F672).

The former contained a single jar base in GT5/6, a grog-tempered 'transitional' grey ware with crude vertical combing. The dating of these 'transitional' wares has been discussed by Pollard (1994, 75) and can be broadly assigned to the mid to later 1st cent. AD, although jars in GT5/6 may well have continued in use until the early 2nd cent. AD. Sherds of possibly the same vessel were recovered from F572 context 2344, (sg203/1).

Subgroup 208/1 incorporates the bulk of the material from the phase (143 sherds/4509 g); of which a substantially complete grooved butt beaker in SW2, represents the major element (fig. 61.8). The vessel although of unusually large size, can be compared to material from Verulamium (Stead & Rigby 1989, fig.61, 6R12), and probably dates to the mid-1st cent. AD. The associated material includes the remains of a necked storage jar (GW5, fig. 61.6), examples of which can again be

Table 9: EVE's by ware and vessel class for Phase 1

Fabric	Flagon	Flask	Jar	Bowl/Jar	Bowl	Dish	Platter	Cup	Beaker	Lid	Amphora	Mortarium	EVEs	SHD	WGT
SAMIAN					0.13		0.92	0.63					1.68	59	339
C													0.00	0	0
MFW													0.00	0	0
MO													0.00	1	10
AM													0.00	2	80
WW	0.50				0.08								0.58	17	287
WS													0.00	1	4
OW				0.06	0.05				0.54				0.65	43	518
GW			3.30		0.07		0.07		0.32				3.76	226	2989
BB1													0.00	6	50
RBCl			0.23										0.23	14	187
CG1			0.54										0.54	118	4357
GT1-4					0.13								0.13	13	234
Misc Ntv				0.10			0.15		1.22				1.47	68	3631
Misc Trn			0.10										0.10	58	1419
Grand Total:	0.50	0.00	4.17	0.16	0.46	0.00	1.14	0.63	2.08	0.00	0.00	0.00	9.14	626	14105
Percent. (EVEs):	5.47	0.00	45.62	1.75	5.03	0.00	12.47	6.89	22.76	0.00	0.00	0.00	100.00		

	EVEs(%)	SHD(%)	WGT(%)
SAM	18.38	9.42	2.40
C	0.00	0.00	0.00
MFW	0.00	0.00	0.00
MO	0.00	0.16	0.07
AM	0.00	0.32	0.57
WW	6.35	2.72	2.03
WS	0.00	0.16	0.03
OW	7.11	6.87	3.67
GW	41.14	36.10	21.19
BB1	0.00	0.96	0.35
RBCl	2.52	2.24	1.33
CG1	5.91	18.85	30.89
GT1-4	1.42	2.08	1.66
Misc Ntv	16.08	10.86	25.74
Misc Trn	1.09	9.27	10.06

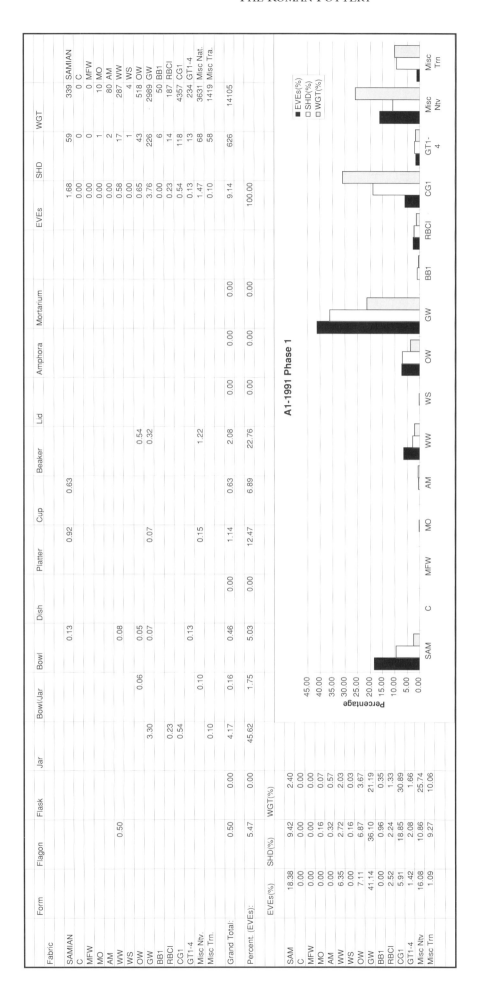

A1-1991 Phase 1

seen amongst the local Verulamium wares (*ibid.* fig.66, 5B1).

The Gallo-Belgic and 'transitional' element to the assemblage is complemented by 'Romanized' coarse wares (WW4, fig. 61.4) of the mid-1st cent. AD onward. The latter includes a necked jar (Kenyon 1948, Fig25, Type C.8/9; Pottery Form 3/L/2), a form originating in the late 1st and possibly lasting into the second quarter of the 2nd cent. AD (Pollard 1994 fig.54, 73).

A small quantity of undiagnostic BB1 was recovered from the beam slot (sg208/1). Conventionally the presence of this later fabric would suggest deposition of the assemblage during the early to mid-2nd cent. AD. However, as the later material was recovered from a single context within sg208/1 (2928), it is conceivable that the feature represents an early group disturbed or redeposited by later activity. Alternatively the material may simply be intrusive.

Subgroup 208/1 contains a number of vessels with links and joins between contexts. The majority of the butt beaker and the associated jar came from contexts 2967 and 2974. There are also joins with context 2928. It was not possible to identify links with the overlying stratigraphy.

A second cut feature F672, provided a small but datable group (10 sherds/109g), including sherds of an early Midlands, probably Mancetter/Hartshill, mortarium (MO12), a BB1 body sherd and Central Gaulish samian of mid-2nd cent. date. The size of the assemblage limits any interpretation, however, it appears the fills must date to the early to mid 2nd cent. AD. A grey ware storage jar provides the only identifiable coarse ware form.

The phase incorporates two distinct groups of material, first, sg200/1 and the bulk of sg208/1, with the exception of context 2928, and second, the latter context and sg208/2. The ceramic assemblage would suggest a *TPQ* for the former *c*. AD 70-100, the latter *c*. AD 120-150.

Illustrations: fig. 61.4-8.

DISCUSSION OF THE POTTERY FROM PHASE 1 (Phases: 1A, 1B, 1C), Table 9.

Assemblage: 626 sherds, 14.1kg., 9.14 EVEs.

A comparison of the Phase 1 material with the assemblages from the West Bridge area, suggests the Causeway Lane groups were deposited no later than the Flavian period. Pollard (1994, 77) argues that the last quarter of the 1st cent. AD witnessed a rapid change in the ceramic assemblage; notably the appearance in quantity of reduced wares at the expense of the preceding indigenous pottery and coupled to this the appearance of forms of a truly 'Roman' type. The Phase 1 assemblage can be seen in this light. The pre-Roman ceramic repertoire, remains well represented (25.7% by weight). The predominance of shell-tempered wares (CG1, 30.9% by weight) can be contrasted to the 8.1% recovered from later 1st and early 2nd cent. contexts at Leicester (*ibid.*, Table 7).

Table 10: *Phase 1. Percentage of selected ware groups (weight).*

Phase	MC2/3	TRANS	CG1	GW	BB1	BRK	ASW	SHD/WGT
1A	6.5	7.6	36.4	35.3	-.-	-.-	12.7	95/1625
1B	7.5	11.1	49.3	21.4	0.1	-.-	12.3	366/7462
1C	63.8	9.3	1.8	20.1	0.9	-.-	15.5	165/5018
Total (Ph.1)	25.7	10.6	30.9	21.2	0.4	60.1	13.2	626/14105

However, the appearance in quantity of grey ware fabrics (21.2%) and vessels characteristic of the Flavian period such as neckless jars with everted rims (Pollard 1994, fig.54, 65), often with rusticated decoration (8.1% of GW sherds), adds weight to the impression of a Flavian rather than pre-Flavian group. The rarity of forms and decorative motifs such as barbotine ring and dot schemes, more commonly found in late Flavian and

Trajanic groups, suggest a Vespasianic or early Flavian *TPQ* for the deposition of the assemblage (*ibid.*, 77). Pollard (1994, 77; table 10) drawing on a number of Leicester sites, suggests the introduction of the majority of barbotine motifs, can be dated to the early 2nd cent. AD.

The samian seems to support this conclusion. In each case the predominant element is pre- or early Flavian, with little that need date later than the third quarter of the 1st cent. AD. Indeed there is a considerable element of earlier material including a Claudio-Neronian Ritt.1 platter and several pre-Flavian decorated and undecorated vessels.

Table 11: *Percentage of samian EVEs by dated range.*

Phase	Pre-Flavian		Nero/Vespas.		Flavian		Hadr/Anton.		Total
	EVEs	%	EVEs	%	EVEs	%	EVEs	%	EVEs
1A:	0.03	10.3	0.26	89.7	0.00	-.-	0.00	-.-	0.29
1B:	0.13	11.9	0.54	49.5	0.42	38.5	0.00	-.-	1.09
1C:	0.00	-.-	0.19	63.3	0.02	6.7	0.09	30.0	0.30
Total:	0.16	10.0	0.99	62.3	0.44	27.7	0.09	5.4	1.68

A small quantity of the southern Spanish amphora fabric AM9a, probably a Dressel 20 vessel was recovered from Phases 1A and 1B. In conjunction with the South Gaulish samian this represents the only obvious continental element of the assemblage. Regional trade is attested by the presence of CG1, calcite-gritted pottery of the south-east midlands (Northants and Bedfordshire), and possibly BB1. The introduction of Dorset black-burnished ware is conventionally dated to the early 2nd century AD; therefore its presence within the phase 1 assemblage is likely to be intrusive. However, the appearance of early forms in both Areas 3 and 4 (see below **p.00**) may imply a rare, early introduction of the ware at Leicester.

PHASE 2

Area 1

Phase 2A (Sub-groups: 132/1, 133/1-2, 133/7-8, 134/1-2, 135/1, 136/1, 137/1).

Assemblage: 588 sherds, 11.7kg., 7.72 EVEs. ASW: 14.0g.

The largest groups of material were derived from the fill of the east-west gully (sg133/7), and surface 1 (sg132/1), with smaller groups recovered from an associated pit (sg135/1) and a possible hearth (sg134/1-2). Links and joins were identified between Surface 1 and the pit fills (sg135/1), and between the gully and hearth. Joins were also identified from the underlying quarry fills in Phase 1 (sg130/1, sg130/4; Phase 1B), in Surface 1 and a later post hole (F1022). The limited post-depositional disturbance and relative intactness of the assemblage is suggested by the low brokenness value (49.2).

The pottery closely parallels the Phase 1 assemblage. Surface 1 and its associated features can be dated to the late 1st cent. AD. Pre-Flavian and early Flavian samian is well represented, although a notable absentee is the Drag 37 bowl, present in quantity by the AD80's (Webster 1987, 32). The high percentage (53.1% by weight) of pre-Roman fabrics, dominated again by storage jars in CG1A and grog-tempered wares (fig. 61.11), is complemented by the presence of GW (22.2%) and 'transitional' wares (10.8%).

Cooking and storage jars in all fabrics are the most common vessel class forming nearly 42% of the assemblage. These are accompanied by a range of bowl forms (35.2%) including the long-lived necked and carinated bowls of Gallo-Belgic type (fig. 61.17), as well as typically 'Roman' flanged bowls (fig. 61.12, 16), the latter in colour-coated ware. A late 1st cent. A.D GW necked jar (Kenyon Type C.8/9; see Phase 1C above), and the lack of forms such as everted rim jars current during the 2nd cent. AD, suggests a similar *TPQ* to that for Phase 1. The absence of barbotine motifs is again apparent;

Table 12: EVE's by ware and vessel class for Phase 2

Fabric	Flagon	Flask	Jar	Bowl/Jar	Bowl	Dish	Platter	Cup	Beaker	Lid	Amphora	Mortarium	VTU	EVEs	SHD	WGT
SAMIAN					4.13	1.47	6.07	7.26	0.74					19.67	948	6999
C					0.20				0.31					0.51	26	186
MFW					0.09				0.29	0.11				0.49	21	105
MO												2.61		2.61	87	6615
AM											0.69			0.69	979	34678
WW	5.61		0.90	0.05	0.19								0.06	6.81	837	10217
WS	0.15													0.20	51	581
OW	1.68	0.12	1.64	0.49	0.10	0.26	0.27		2.61	0.05				7.22	450	4836
GW	0.20	1.28	39.71	0.95	9.59	0.71	2.85		6.58	1.36			0.17	63.40	4914	53880
BB1	0.30		1.10						0.41	1.02				2.83	92	1162
RBCI			1		0.52									1.58	60	1130
CG1			9.05											9.05	1664	43442
GT1-4														0.00	0	0
Misc Ntv			1.84	0.12	1.68		0.24		0.28	0.12				4.28	548	14981
Misc Trn			4.65	0.25	0.53		0.23		0.35					6.07	457	9526
Grand Total:	7.94	1.40	59.89	1.86	17.03	2.44	9.72	7.26	11.57	2.66	0.69	2.61	0.23	125.41	11134	188338
Percent. (EVEs):	6.33	1.12	47.76	1.48	13.58	1.95	7.75	5.79	9.23	2.12	0.55	2.08	0.18	100.00	100.00	

Fabric	EVEs(%)	SHD(%)	WGT(%)
SAM	15.68	8.51	3.72
C	0.41	0.23	0.10
MFW	0.39	0.19	0.06
MO	2.08	0.78	3.51
AM	0.55	8.79	18.41
WW	5.43	7.52	5.42
WS	0.16	0.46	0.31
OW	5.76	4.04	2.57
GW	50.55	44.14	28.61
BB1	2.26	0.83	0.62
RBCI	1.26	0.54	0.60
CG1	7.22	14.95	23.07
GT1-4	0.00	0.00	0.00
Misc Ntv	3.41	4.92	7.95
Misc Trn	4.84	4.10	5.06

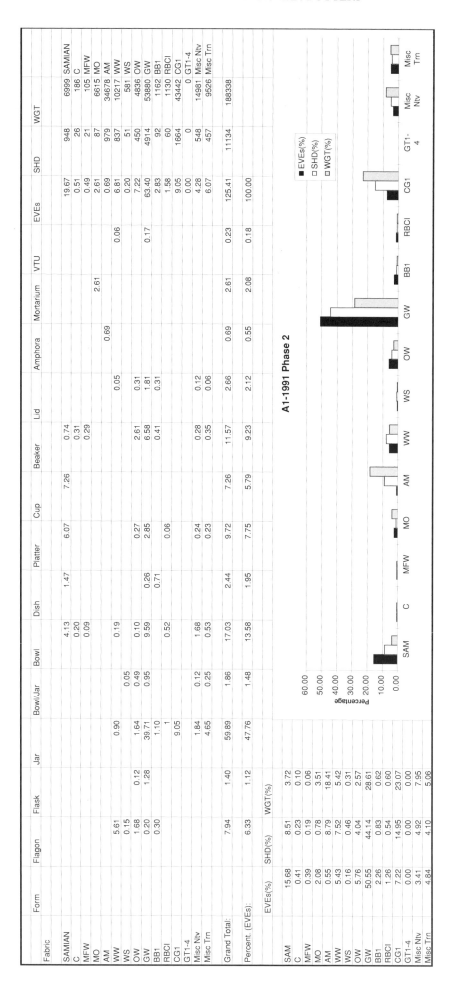

A1-1991 Phase 2

Legend: ■ EVEs(%) □ SHD(%) □ WGT(%)

approximately 9.3% of the GW pottery carrying rusticated decoration. Platters (13.2%) in both samian and coarse wares (fig. 61.10), beakers (6%) and samian cups (2.5%), comprise the rest of the assemblage.

Regional and continental traded wares make-up 8.2% by weight of the phase assemblage. The former includes a GW10 wide-mouthed bowl (fig. 61.14), paralleled amongst the Brixworth material (Woods 1972, fig.12, 62). A similar vessel from the West Bridge area of Leicester (Pollard 1994, fig.54, 85) has been dated to the late 1st to early 2nd cent. AD. White wares from the Verulamium region make their first appearance, and include a mortarium body sherd (MO7). The south Spanish fabric (AM9A), probably from a Dressel 20 olive oil amphora, and Rhodian (AM8) amphorae complete the traded wares.

Overall the phase assemblage indicates a *TPQ c.*AD 70–100.

Illustrations: figs. 61.9-16; 62.17-19.

Phase 2B (Sub-groups: 138/1-3, 139/1).

Assemblage: 1382 sherds, 22.6 kg., 18.32 EVEs. ASW: 10.0g.

A large and rich assemblage came from the make-up layers for Surface 2 (sg138/1-2), with the surface itself producing a small but datable group. Joins were recorded between the make-up and underlying quarry fills (sg130/4, Phase 1B), with fragments of a carrot amphora (Cam 189; Peacock & Williams, Class 12) also found on Surface 2a (sg143/2, Phase 2D). The overall impression is once again of a late 1st cent. assemblage. In contrast to the earlier phases the grey ware ASW is relatively low, however, the GW brokenness (58.7) suggests again an undisturbed assemblage and is comparable with the Phase 2A values.

An early samian assemblage incorporates stamped and decorated vessels in conjunction with predominantly pre- or early Flavian forms (68.1% by EVEs). The latter include a second Ritt 1 platter, Drag 22/3 dish and Drag 24/5, Ritt 9 cup forms. The Drag 37 bowl is again absent suggesting a deposition during the early Flavian period. Sherds from two colour-coat (C3) vessels, probably beakers, can be attributed to kilns from Central Gaul (Lezoux) and Colchester. The matt 'chestnut-brown' surface of the former may suggest a pre-Flavian date (Greene 1979, 43), whilst the latter carries a patchy quartz roughcast and wiped surface (Greene 1978, 26). A close parallel from the southern range of the Leicester forum (A302.1971) has been identified as a product of the pre-Flavian kilns at Colchester (R. Symonds pers. comm.).

A range of shell-tempered jars again dominates the coarse wares. The proportion of CG1 within the phase assemblage (37.9% by weight), is however, distorted by the massive size of the storage jars; in contrast the ware forms just 19.8% of the sherd total. GW jars were the most common class recovered (28% EVEs), with the presence of the later everted rim jar, possibly indicating activity into the 2nd cent. AD. However, the absence of barbotine decorated vessels and the common occurrence of rusticated decoration, 16.2% of GW sherds (79 sherds), appears to argue for a *TPQ* of c.AD70-100 for the deposition of the assemblage. Early ring-necked WW and OW flagons (fig. 62.20, 25), and platters (fig. 62.23, 29) complete the impression of a typical late 1st cent. domestic assemblage.

The traded wares include an unusually wide range of amphorae, Rhodian (AM8), Baetican (AM9A), Gaulish (AM12/3) and the Eastern Mediterranean/ Egyptian (AM18) fabrics area all well represented. Sherds of a probable Italian amphora (AM25) in a variant of the `black sand' fabric (Peacock & Williams, 1986), and from a south Spanish vessel (AM7) complete the range. Trade in fine wares (see above) is also complemented by the presence of a Verulamium region mortarium (Gillam Type 240).

Illustrations: fig. 62.20-30.

Phase 2C (Sub-group:140/1).

Assemblage: 64 sherds, 869g, 1.17 EVEs. ASW: 12.1g.

A small assemblage was recovered from the primary fills of the north-south ditch F433. The assemblage was too small to provide useful estimates of brokenness or ASW. No joins were identified with the surrounding stratigraphy.

A small collection of South Gaulish samian was recovered and included two Drag 37 bowls, ascribed a late 1st cent. AD date. Grey wares predominate (39% by weight), represented by a range of jars, platters and beakers. A poorly rusticated, everted rim jar in a native reduced fabric (MC1, fig. 62.33), perhaps indicates a local potter's attempt to cater to the market for 'Romanized' ceramic types. A second Verulamium region mortarium (Gillam Type 240) and a collared flagon (fig. 62.31), possibly a finer (WW4) product of the same industry, are the only obvious traded wares. Overall this small group can be assign a tentative *TPQ* of the late 1st century AD.

Illustrations: fig. 62.31-33.

Phase 2D (Sub-groups: 143/1-2, 144/1).

Assemblage: 1513 sherds, 19.9kg., N/A EVEs. ASW: 8.7g.

The assemblage derives from the use and repair of Surface 2 and 2a. The majority of links were identified between and within the various phase elements, especially the burnt layers (sg144/1). However, links with the underlying make-up (sg138/2, Phase 2B) and the make-up and compacted gravel of Surface 3 (sg145/1 and 6) have also been noted. The low ASW (8.7g) is consistent with the interpretation of the phase as a surface.

The phase produced only South Gaulish samian, with once again the Drag 37 bowl absent. Pre- and early Flavian material is well represented, and includes three stamped vessels. However, in contrast to the Period 1 phases, the major element (44.5% by EVEs) is of Flavian date. The absence of later Flavian and Trajanic samian need not suggest the replacement of the surface before the early 2nd cent. AD, as this period coincides with the nadir of samian importation to Britain (Marsh 1981).

Continental fine wares include a barbotine decorated cup, or beaker, in Central Gaulish lead glazed ware (LG2, MacRobert 1987, 66; Greene 1979, 90, Fabric B), and a roughcast Lyon ware beaker (C14, *ibid.*, 24, fig.8, Type 20). Greene (*ibid.*, 99) notes that the two fabrics are frequently found in conjunction. Possible Lower Rhineland products are also represented in the form of a barbotine scale decorated cup (fig.66, 122) and a body sherd of a roughcast beaker. A Colchester (C3) colour-coat beaker completes the suite of pre-Flavian fine wares. Both the Phase 2B and 2D assemblages include exceptionally rich and diverse fine ware assemblages, perhaps indicative of a high status source for the pottery.

As in Phase 2C GW vessels, predominantly jars, are the most common form/fabric combination, with rusticated decoration again common. The absence of barbotine motifs and tall everted rim jars (Pollard 1994, fig.55, 105), and the relatively high levels of CG1/1A (32.3% by weight) continue to again suggest a *TPQ* of c.AD 70-100 for the assemblage. 'Gallo-Belgic' and 'transitional' fabrics, possibly residual, are represented (respectively 7.5% and 5.5% by weight), the latter includes both vessels of indigenous (fig. 62.36) and Romano-British form (fig. 62.35).

The presence of the Midland mortarium fabric (MO12) dated broadly to the late 1st to mid-2nd cent. AD, could represent early production at the Mancetter-Hartshill kilns. The more usual quartz rich Verulamium fabrics (MO7 and MO10) are also represented and comprise the bulk of the mortaria present. A rare import from the Central Gaulish potteries (MO8), was also recovered, and can be attributed a date of between AD50-85 (Hartley in archive).

The range of amphorae types mirrors the Phase 2B assemblage. Their variety adds substance to the impression of an increasingly sophisticated community with a taste for the oil, wine and fruit of the Mediterranean. The normally ubiquitous Spanish AM9A fabric does not as yet dominate the amphorae assemblage, while both the Rhodian (AM8, AM10) and the carrot amphorae (Cam 189, AM18) both characteristic of 1st century assemblages are well represented.

Illustrations: fig. 62.34-36, fig. 66.122.

Phase 2E (Sub-group: 147/1).

Assemblage: 136 sherds, 2939g, 1.26 EVEs. ASW: 17.5g..

Although a small assemblage the pottery recovered from the fill of the well (sg147/1) reveals a very different ceramic composition than previous groups. Non-joining fragments of an oxidised jar were noted linking contexts within the fill. The high ASW is consistent with a low level of post-depositional disturbance; this is supported by a low brokenness value (65.3) and might suggest the fill represents a secondary refuse deposit.

The high proportion of pre- and early Flavian samian recovered from previous phases is reversed in Phase 2E. The worn South Gaulish material, including a complete stamped Drag 27 (Dickinson above, no.11), and a stamped Drag 33a from Les Martres-de-Veyres potter (Dickinson above, no.12), demonstrates deposition during the early second century (AD 100-130).

The presence of an early example of BB1 coupled with the increased dominance of GW (29.78% by weight) at the expense of both CG1 and the 'native' (MC2/3) fabrics, can be paralleled in both at Causeway Lane (Area: 3, Phase 2L), and at sites throughout Leicester (Pollard 1994, 76; Marsden, forthcoming). The pit produced the first example of a 'ring and dot' barbotine motif; the latter appears to be introduced by the end of the 1st cent. AD (Pollard 1994, table: 10). The ceramic assemblage supports a *TPQ* of the early 2nd century AD for the filling of the feature.

Illustrations: fig. 62.37

Phase 2F (Sub-groups: 145/1-6, 146/1-2).

Assemblage: 1762 sherds, 38.8kg., N/A EVEs. ASW: 9.9g..

The construction and use of Surface 3 produced a reasonably large assemblage dominated by the shattered remains of what appears to be a single Dressel 20 olive oil amphora (sg146/1: 744 sherds/23.1kg.). Once again the relatively low ASW (9.4g) from the make-up and gravel surface (sg145/1-6) supports the functional interpretation. It is notable that the ASW for the hearths (sg146/1-2) produces a much higher figure (15.8g). In addition to joins between the various make-up and gravel layers, a stamped mortarium (MO15) had joins with sg162/7 (Phase 5B) and sg103/1 (unphased). Links and joins with the overlying silts (Phase 2G) were also noted, derived from both Surface 3 and the amphora hearth. Finally, joins with the underlying stratigraphy suggest the presence of residual material within the phase assemblage.

The samian is typical of the late 1st to early 2nd cent. AD, predominantly Flavian in character, but with a high proportion (42.0% by EVEs) of earlier material. Once again the absence of Trajanic and late Flavian South Gaulish material does not preclude use of the surface into the early 2nd century.

The phase assemblage remains dominated by grey ware jars, bowls, platters, and beakers, with the everted rimmed jar a particularly common form. Rustication of various types remains the most common applied decoration (6.25% of the GW sherds), with barbotine schemes rare (0.6%).

Fine wares include roughcast beakers imported from the Central Gaulish kilns, and two Colchester products. The sand roughcasting and patchy finish of one clearly emulates a 1st cent. AD Lyon ware beaker (Greene 1979, 25, Type 20). The rilled decoration of the second (fig. 62.43) also appears on a residual beaker in Phase 5C (586, sg164/1).

Regionally traded wares include a GW10 (Northants/Upper Nene Valley) sherd of indeterminate form, a large collared flagon (fig. 62.44) and a counter-stamped mortarium of the potter Albinus dated to the second half of the 1st cent. AD (fig. 63.47), both the latter two vessels were products of the Verulamium potteries. A mortarium (fig. 62.38) probably from south-west Britain, can be again dated to the later 1st cent. AD. The phase assemblage suggests a *TPQ* of c.AD 80-120.

The amphora hearth (Sub-group 146/1).

The hearth produced a small assemblage (144 sherds, 3898g, 1.86 EVEs) in addition to the shattered remains of the amphora. Peacock and Williams (1986, 52) have calculated the weight of a complete Dressel 20 amphora at c.28.4 kg. The fragmentary vessel recovered from sg146/1 appears to have had the majority of its upper body including neck, rim and handles removed, with the hearth incorporating the rest of the vessel.

Dating of the feature is problematic due to the limited size of the assemblage. The presence of a heavily scored CG1A storage jar (fig. 63.46), probably of 1st century date, alongside everted rim and barbotine decorated GW jars, suggests a *TPQ* of the late 1st to early 2nd cent. AD.

Illustrations: figs. 62.38-47.

Phase 2G (Sub-groups: 148/1-3).

Assemblage: 3525 sherds, 55.4kg., 57.32 EVEs. ASW: 12.2g.

The sandy silts (sg148/1-3) that comprise Phase 2G sealed Surface 3. These homogenous layers produced an assemblage that was examined as a single unit. A large number of links and joins were identified within the phase assemblage, while joins with the underlying stratigraphy, notably the preceding gravel Surfaces 2 and 3, indicate the presence of residual material. Links were also identified with the recut and slumping of F433 (Phase 3A, sg141/1) and the make-up for Surface 4 (Phase 3B, sg150/1).

The ASW is unexceptional (12.2g), however once again the low brokenness value (56.7) suggests the assemblage represents fairly intact material that saw limited post-depositional disturbance, as such this would argue against an interpretation of the layers as evidence for cultivation.

The samian assemblage, with the exception of single 1st cent. AD Lezoux and Montans products, is exclusively South Gaulish in origin, and predominantly Flavian in date (57.7% by EVEs). As mentioned above, the absence of Trajanic and low level of diagnostically late Flavian material does not rule out the possibility that the layers are of early 2nd century date. However, the low level of pre-Flavian samian (11.8% by EVEs) contrasts the Phase 2G assemblage with the preceding phases. The coarse wares are 'Romanized' in character, with 'Gallo-Belgic (5.0% by weight) and 'transitional' (3.5%) pottery again implying limited levels of residuality among the phase assemblage.

The predominance of GW's, especially everted rim jars (fig. 63.51, 54-5, 57-8) apparently at the expense of the equivalent calcite-gritted forms, contrasts strongly with the Phase 1 and early Phase 2 (2A, 2B) phases. Despite this the quantity, by weight, of CG1 remains high (25.7%), comparable to pre-Flavian assemblages from the West Bridge sites (Site 1, Phase 1: 24.5%; Site 2, Phase 2: 27.2%). However, the low Causeway Lane sherd and EVE percentages indicates a preponderance of large necked storage jars, a form that appears to have supplemented rather than competed with the GW vessel range. Body and rim sherds of a *serium*, a large storage vessel in a grog-tempered fabric (GT3a, fig. 63.64) were recovered from this assemblage. Three vessels of this type were identified at Little Lane (Pollard forthcoming e) and may have been set in the ground while in use (Richardson 1986, 106).

The presence in quantity of later 1st and 2nd cent. AD jar forms (fig. 63.55) and barbotine dot and rib decorative motifs, noted among the GW's (as Phases 2E-2F), suggests a late 1st to early 2nd cent. AD date. However, the absence of BB1 in such a large assemblage, or indeed any material that need date later than the early second cent. AD argues for a *terminus ante quem* (*TAQ*) during the first quarter of the 2nd cent. AD.

The range of fabrics and forms appears to suggest a storage and perhaps culinary function. A limited range of table wares occurs in both fine and coarse fabrics. With the exception of the samian assemblage, the only fine wares present include an imported Central Gaulish lead-glazed beaker (LG1, fig. 63.48; Greene 1979, fig.43, 7) of pre-Flavian date, and a flange-rimmed bowl in a mica-dusted fabric (MD3; Marsh 1978, Type 34). As with the samian assemblage vessels of these types may have had an extended life. Both the WW and WS are under-represented for an assemblage of this size (Pollard 1994, table 8).

Regional traded wares include a bowl and platter (GW10, fig. 63.60) from the Northants/Upper Nene valley kilns, and mortaria and flagons in various Verulamium fabrics. Amphorae attest to long distance trade of specialist produce, predominantly Spanish/Baetican olive oil vessels, but also include Gaulish, Rhodian and Italian wine amphorae.

Illustrations: fig. 63.48-68.

Phase 2H (Sub-groups: 149/1-5).

Assemblage: 220sherds, 2696g, 2.59EVEs. ASW: 8.1g.

A small assemblage with pottery derived mainly from the hearth and floor level (sg149/1), additional material came from the post holes (sg149/3) and floor (sg 149/4) of Structure C. Joins were noted between the hearth and the associated floor surface. Although the assemblage has a low average sherd weight, the brokenness value (67.3) is unremarkable. This may indicate existing refuse incorporated within the floor make-ups/surfaces.

The samian assemblage is once again wholly South Gaulish in origin and predominantly Flavian in date. A decorated Drag 37 bowl of the potter Severus (Dannell in archive, no. 103) provides the latest closely datable piece (AD 75-90). A small quantity of stamped and unstamped pre- and early Flavian samian coupled with fragments of two Drag 29 bowls, a form that had been superseded by the Drag 37 during the AD 80's, indicates the presence of residual material in the phase assemblage. However, the scarcity of later 1st and early 2nd cent. AD samian may suggest the curation and survival in use of earlier material. The relatively high proportion of 'transitional' pottery (18.4% by weight) appears to support the presence of a substantial residual element to the assemblage. However, Pollard (1994, 75) has suggested the grog-tempered storage jar (GT3 & 5/6), much like its calcite-gritted counterpart may have had an extended life, spanning the early years of the 2nd cent. AD.

The assemblage includes a high proportion of grey wares, predominantly of utilitarian everted and necked jar types. The body sherds of a possible *dolium/serium* may be from the Phase 2G vessel. The presence of BB1 sherds in a relatively small assemblage suggests a *TPQ* for the phase during the second quarter of the 2nd cent. AD.

The amphorae include two Rhodian fabrics, AM8 identified as Peacock's Fabric Group 2, probably from Peraea, and AM10 compared by Pollard (*ibid.*, 113) to Peacock's Fabric Group 1. Both are commonly regarded as wine containers and have been recovered on early Roman military sites (Williams, above p00).

Illustrations: n/a.

Phase 2I (Sub-groups: 142/1).

Assemblage: 8 sherds, 84g, n/a EVEs. ASW: 10.5g.

Drawn from the backfill of the north-south ditch (F343), this assemblage can at best be ascribed a general Roman date. It produced a small and undiagnostic assemblage, including necked and everted rim jars in grey and calcite-gritted wares.

Illustrations: n/a.

Phase 2J (Sub-groups: 172/1-3, 173/1-2, 176/1, 178/1, 179/1, 181/1, 182/1, 183/2, 183/4-5, 184/1, 186/3).

Assemblage: 356 sherds, 6644g, 3.43 EVEs. ASW: 10.8g.

The phase comprises a series of generally small, strati-graphically isolated features, with the ditch (sg172/3) and pit fills (sg184/1) producing the bulk of the phase assemblage. The disturbed nature of the phase is perhaps reflected by the highly broken nature of the pottery (Brokenness: 108.6). Links and joins were noted among the ditch fills of G172, with fragments of a GT1 storage jar linking F484, F485 and F486. A possible link was also noted with sg173/1.

The small samian assemblage (27 sherds/231g) is again of late 1st cent. date, with only South Gaulish material represented. The survival of pre- and early Flavian forms such as the Drag 22/4 and Drag 29 indicates the presence of residual material, however, the Drag 15/17 platter is a notable absentee.

The coarse pottery assemblage shares many of the themes described above, the predominance of GW over CG1 and the appearance of BB1 are characteristic of an early 2nd cent. assemblage. sg172, the possible roadside ditches, produced pottery from only one of its sub-groups (sg172/3). The material is of a different character to the remaining phase assemblage, with the broken remains of a single GT1 storage jar (fig. 64.69) comprising 87.3% (by weight) of the assemblage. The vessel form and decorative style can be paralleled widely (Pollard 1994, fig.51, 14; Marney 1989, fig.37, 82-3), and is clearly of 'Belgic' inspiration. However, the presence of grey ware sherds, suggests a date of deposition no earlier than the later 1st cent. AD.

A group of shallow pits (G184) yielded the largest and most varied assemblage, with the majority of the pottery from F388. Joins were identified between two of the pits (C1181, F418; C1033, F407). Both the ASW (13.4g) and brokenness (73.5) values suggest the sub-group was less disturbed than the remainder of the phase assemblage. An early Flavian Drag 37 (fig. 55.S7) provides the most closely datable pottery from the assemblage, with a mica-dusted beaker (Marsh 1978, fig.6.10, 22.2) supporting a late 1st cent. AD *TPQ*. A Verulamium mortarium and various grey ware vessels including, a triangular reed-rimmed bowl (Tyers & Marsh 1978, fig.240, IV.A.8) may date as late as the early 2nd cent. AD. However, the high proportion of 'native' wares CG1 and MC2/3 (19.9%, 36.7% by weight), and the lack of later forms and barbotine decorative motifs on the GW's, suggests G172 and G184 are substantially residual in content.

The presence of two sherds of BB1 among the remaining assemblage (G181, F249) suggests a *TPQ* for the phase during the early 2nd cent. AD.

Illustrations: fig.64.69; 63.70-71.

Area 2

Phase 2K (Sub-groups: 201/1-3, 202/1-4, 203/1-2, 204/1-2, 205/1).

Assemblage: 1262 sherds, 17.6kg, 21.55 EVEs. ASW: 9.6g.

Phase 2K provided the largest assemblage from Area 2, with G201 and G202 producing the bulk of the pottery. Useful groups were also recovered from G203 and sg204/2. Joins were noted within sg201/1 and between that and sg201/2. Fragments of a riveted Drag 37 bowl (Dannell in archive, 47) found in sg201/1 were also recovered from the overlying stratigraphy (sg293/3, sg294/7, sg296/1, Phase: 9 & 12), and indicate the post-Roman truncation of these deposits. Links and joins were also recorded between the sub-groups of G202, and a possible link between sg203/1 and sg200/1 (Phase 1). Brokenness and ASW values suggest the ditch fills of G202 (sg202/1 and sg202/3) are of a similar character, and can be contrasted with sg203/1 and perhaps G201.

Phase 2K contains two distinct groups, G203, and G201/G202/204/205. The former a late 1st cent. AD assemblage, Ph: 2K(i), with a strong Gallo-Belgic and 'transitional' element, the latter, early to mid-2nd cent. AD in date, Ph: 2K(ii). Phase 2K(i) can perhaps be further sub-divided, the samian especially suggesting a later date of deposition for the fills of the ditches G202.

Phase 2K(i)

Assemblage: 111 sherds, 2038g, 2.43EVEs. ASW: 7.1g.

Sub-groups 203/1 and 203/2, respectively the fills of the north south ditch (F572), and its recut (F669), cannot be separated in terms of their ceramic date. The pottery from both features includes 1st century samian, including a mid-1st cent. Drag.29 (Dannell in archive, 52).

Gallo-Belgic and 'transitional' fabrics dominate the coarse wares (table 13). These include substantial fragments of a GT5/6 jar (fig. 64.73) which can be paralleled with a pair of squat and robust cooking pots from Brixworth (Woods 1972, fig.26, 193-4), dated there to *c*.AD 70-120. The majority of the remaining vessels, early CG1a and MC3 ledge-rimmed jars and a possible butt beaker rim, underline the early nature of the ceramic content. Perhaps the latest element recovered was a GW small necked jar, however the vessel need date no later than the late 1st cent. AD (MacRobert 1987, fig.31, 13). A similar vessel has been recorded among the large 'Group 1' assemblage incorporated in construction make-up under the south range of the Leicester forum (Pollard forthcoming a, Group 1, 2). The pottery therefore indicates a *TPQ* *c*.AD 70-100.

Phase: 2K(ii).

Assemblage: 1151 sherds, 15.6kg, 19.12 EVEs. ASW: 9.7g.

The samian assemblage from Phase 2K(ii) dates from the early to mid-2nd cent. AD. Sub-group 202/3 forms the latest element, with a stamp of the Antonine potter Maximus (Dickinson above, no.28; AD150-180) and mid-2nd cent. plain vessels (Drag 18/31).

The coarse pottery supports the samian dating; the early ceramic material present in G203 is absent from the later ditch (G202). The prevalence of rusticated motifs noted among the Phase 1 and early Phase 2 phases, is replaced by barbotine schemes in Phase 2K(ii), and can be seen clearly in sg201/1-2. Pollard suggests the latter occur during the early 2nd cent. AD and is completed by the Hadrianic period (Pollard 1994, 77).

The pottery from the early fills of ditch G202 (sg202/1) suggests a *TPQ* of *c*.AD 120-160. Central Gaulish samian and a BB1 jar (Gillam Type 118) again provide the dating. A single

roughcast beaker may be an early product of the Lower Nene Valley industries, attributed an export date of the mid to later 2nd cent. AD (Howe *et al.* 1980, 7), however, the absence of GW1, grey ware copies of BB1 products, and the later Mancetter-Hartshill mortarium fabric (MO4), argue against a later date.

A mid to late 2nd century date for the ditch recut (sg202/3), dated by the presence of Antonine samian, is also demonstrated by the coarse pottery. BB1 although present in both G201 and G202, is more common and incorporates a wider range of forms in sg202/3, the latter includes jar (Gillam Type 125; fig. 64.87) and dish (Gillam Types 219, 220) types as well as lids and the less common pinch neck jug (Wallace and Webster 1989). OW roughcast beakers and the GW necked and cordoned jar (fig. 64.82), forms typical of the mid to late 2nd century, appear for the first time, as do stamped mortaria dated to the early and mid-2nd cent. AD (Hartley, above no. M2, M3; fig. 64.78 and 79).

Regional imports include a possible GW Alice Holt bead-rimmed jar of Lyne and Jefferies Class 4 (Lyne pers. comm. and Lyne & Jefferies 1979, fig.15, 4.11; fig. 64.83). A vessel in the pale grey fabric (GW4/7) of the Lower Nene valley, and the coarse gritted WW1 of the Northamptonshire area (MacRobert 1985, 105). All are current during the first half of the 2nd cent. AD.

Sub-group 204/2 contained a small group of pottery dominated by a stamped mortarium of the potter Albinus (Hartley, above, no.M4; fig. 65.89), dated to the late 1st cent. AD. However the presence of a BB1 jar rim pushes the date of deposition to the early/mid-2nd cent. AD.

The pottery from sg205/1 produced little diagnostic material, a CG Drag 18/31 and a single Central Gaulish 'Rhenish' ware sherd suggests a *TPQ* of the mid-2nd cent. AD for the overlying stone building, Structure F (Phase 3F).

Table 13: *Percentage weight of selected ware groups, BRK (GW) and ASW (GW).*

Ph:2K/i/ii	MC2/3	TRANS	CG1	GW	BB1	BRK	ASW	SHD/WGT
sg203/1	20.4	56.9	15.2	5.0	-.-	35.5	7.8	88/1738
sg201/1	0.8	0.3	37.7	35.8	3.8	73.6	6.8	406/3616
sg201/2	6.8	3.8	18.5	37.6	-.-	51.1	9.2	145/1680
sg202/1	-.-	-.-	8.2	31.2	3.5	42.6	13.1	59/1681
sg202/3	-.-	-.-	12.3	29.7	12.1	45.9	12.7	476/7292
sg204/2	-.-	-.-	14.5	5.8	1.2	100.0	5.0	75/1200

Illustrations: figs 64.72-88; 65.89-90

Area 3

Phase 2L (Sub-group: 332/1).

Assemblage: 302 sherds, 7940g, 6.58 EVEs. ASW: 18.9g.

The assemblage derives from the backfill of a well truncated by 18th. century quarrying. The sub-group contains three contexts of which 3551 produced the bulk of the ceramic assemblage. Cross context links were noted throughout the feature, especially between 3549 and 3551. Fragments of a South Gaulish samian Drag.37 bowl (Dannell above, no. 9) as well as a number of coarse ware vessels (fig. 65.95) were found in each context.

It is noticeable that 3533 has a lower ASW (9.3g) than the rest of the sub-group (19.9g), this is best explained by the small size of the assemblage, but may indicate post-depositional disturbance associated with the truncation of the feature.

The number of links, the homogeneity of the assemblage, and the high ASW of the bulk of the sub-group, including a substantially complete GW10 jar (fig. 65.99), imply the use of fresh material dumped possibly as a deliberate act and derived from the same source.

The range of fabrics and forms is typical of the late 1st-early 2nd cent. AD, with Gallo-Belgic and 'transitional' fabrics (MC3, CG1a, MG3 and GT5/6), rare after the late 1st cent. AD, giving way to the more dominant fabrics of the Romanized assemblage (Pollard 1994).

Table 14: *Comparison of Phase assemblages: Causeway Lane Phase 2L & West Leicester Site 1, Phase 7 & Site 2, Phase 2. Percentage weight of selected ware groups, BRK (GW) and ASW (GW).*

Site/Phase	MC2/3	TRANS	CG1	GW	BB1	BRK	ASW	SHD/WGT
CL/2L	1.9	0.7	4.7	32.3	0.6	-.-	18.9	302/7940
WL1/Ph7	2.5	-.-	6.6	59.1	0.9	-.-	14.7	532/7381
WL2/Ph2	4.4	0.7	9.3	34.3	1.1	-.-	12.8	1170/21194

The samian is entirely South Gaulish including fragments of a signed bowl (Dannell above, no. 9) and a single stamped vessel (Dickinson above, no. 30), both suggesting a Flavian date. This is further supported by a stamped mortarium of the Verulamium potter DOINUS (Hartley above, no. M5; fig. 65.91), one of probably three vessels from the same source. The Verulamium potteries represent the major exporter of mortaria to Leicester from AD 60-100, a position that is gradually eroded by the Mancetter kilns from the later 1st cent. onward. The presence of well stratified BB1 in both 3533 and 3551 might be argued to suggest a Hadrianic date of deposition. However, the unusual form of the dish (fig. 65.100) can be paralleled by flanged and reed-rimmed dishes at Exeter (Holbrook & Bidwell 1991, fig.32, 52.1-2) possibly dated to as early as the late 1st cent. AD (*ibid.*, 97). Consequently an early *TPQ* is suggested for Phase 2L, *c.*AD 80-120.

Illustrations: fig. 65.91-101.

DISCUSSION OF THE POTTERY FROM PHASE 2 (Phases: 2K, 2A-2I, 2J, 2L).

Assemblage: 11134 sherds, 188.3kg, 125.41 EVEs, ASW: 11.0g.

The ceramic composition of Phase 2 has much in common with both the Phase 1 and 3 assemblages, and appears to span a period between the late 1st and the mid 2nd century. The major factor in all three phase groups is the predominance of the locally produced grey ware component. It comprises well over a quarter of the Phase 2 assemblage and provides a clear indication of the development of a 'Romanized' suite of forms. The major products include jars of typical Flavian-Trajanic type, but also flanged bowls and globular beakers, all well attested from sites within Leicester (Clamp 1985, Pollard 1994).

The increase in the use of GW vessels, especially the wide variety of beaded and everted rim jar forms (fig. 61.13) appears to have caused a consequent decline in the demand for the ledge rim calcite-gritted jars. The latter can be compared with products from the Harrold kilns, and are dated to the late 1st century AD.

A series of ceramic divisions are visible within the Phase 2 assemblage. The stratigraphically early Surfaces 1 and 2, with their associated features are ceramically very similar to the Phase 1 assemblages. They can be dated by their samian component to the last quarter of the 1st cent. AD; pre-Flavian and early Flavian samian is well represented. However, the absence of the Drag 37 bowl, present in quantity by the AD 80's (Webster 1987, 32), indicates the yard surfaces must have seen considerable use, requiring repair, before the last quarter of the 1st century AD; a suggestion perhaps supported by the relatively low ASW of Phase 2B.

The early phases (Phases 2A-2B) are notable for their large and diverse assemblages, a feature also apparent in the subsequent repairs and resurfacing (Phase 2D). The range of fine and specialist traded wares indicates the wealth of the assemblage, incorporating high quality imported and traded colour-coats from the Lezoux kilns of Central Gaul and Colchester. The diversity of amphora fabrics also suggests the developing 'Romanized' tastes of the Leicester market. All the major suppliers are represented within the phase assemblage, including sources as diverse as the Eastern Mediterranean (AM18), Rhodes (AM8), Italy (AM25), Spain (AM7, 9a) and Gaul (AM12/3). They attest to the supply of continental wines, olive oil and possibly dates (Hird 1992, 61-2).

The primary fills of ditch F433 and the Surface 2a (2C-2D) produced an assemblage indicative of the late 1st century. The key addition to the earlier deposits is the appearance in quantity of the Drag 37 bowl, suggesting deposition during the last quarter of the century. However, the absence of barbotine decorated GW jars appears to indicate a closing date for the assemblage by the turn of the 1st cent. AD. The continued use of the yard surfaces is again indicated by the low ASW (8.7g.).

The Verulamium potteries provide the majority of mortaria recovered from 1st century contexts at Leicester; a position that is gradually eroded by the Mancetter-Hartshill kilns from the later 1st cent. AD. The presence of the Midland mortarium fabric (MO12) among the Phase 2D assemblage may represent early production of that industry. Hartley (1994, 66-7) has commented on the presence at Leicester of stamps attributed to the potter Erucanus; his work dates to perhaps as early as the 80's AD. The more usual quartz rich Verulamium fabrics (MO7 and MO10) are also represented and comprise the bulk of the mortaria present.

Surface 3 and the subsequent sealing layers (Phase 2F, 2G) can again be compared to the earlier deposits. However, the appearance of barbotine decorated GW jars suggests the final use of the surfaces occurred after the turn of the 1st century. Traded wares include a variety of regional fabrics; calcite-gritted wares (CG1a) and Northamptonshire grey wares (GW10), coupled with mortaria and table wares from the Verulamium potteries, all indicate the importance of Leicester's contacts with the south and south-east of the province.

The pit fills (2E) and features associated with Structure C (2H) incorporate material implying activity as late as the second quarter of the 2nd century AD. The presence of Trajanic samian in the pit fills of Phase 2E, coupled with an increased proportion of late Flavian forms points to the early 2nd century date of these and the subsequent layers. The coarse wares are also indicative of the early 2nd century. All incorporate small quantities of BB1 and barbotine decorated grey wares. The absence of significant quantities of Central Gaulish samian and BB1 provide crucial evidence for placing the closing date for Phase 2 in Areas 1 and 3 within the period AD 110-140. The occurrence of BB1 in Phase 2E and in the Area 3 well (Phase 2L) may be used to suggest that all subsequent phases should be confined within that time span.

The latest element of the Phase 2 deposits are represented by the backfill of the ditches in Area 2 (G202). The inclusion of Antonine samian of the mid-2nd century and coarse wares incorporating both BB1 and barbotine decorated grey wares clearly point to deposition as late as the middle of the century.

PHASE 3

Area 1

Phase 3A (Sub-groups: 141/1, 142/2-3).

Assemblage: 1562 sherds, 45.2kg, 23.75 EVEs. ASW: 14.50g.

The bulk of the phase assemblage was derived from the backfill of ditch F433 (sg141/1: 1334 sherds/29.8kg.). A smaller group (sg142/2-3: 228/15.4kg.) incorporates pottery from F377 and F371, both features cut the backfill of the ditch. The former

Table 15: EVE's by ware and vessel class for Phase 3

Fabric	Flagon	Flask	Jar	Bowl/Jar	Bowl	Dish	Platter	Cup	Beaker	Lid	Amphora	Mortarium	VTU	EVEs	SHD	WGT
SAMIAN			0.20		2.26	0.37	2.60	4.33					0.09	9.85	1472	13271
C					0.06				1.40					1.46	157	1196
MFW									1.29					1.29	40	231
MO												1.76		1.76	110	9453
AM											0.16			0.16	393	59581
WW	3.42		0.11		0.35				0.33					4.21	1230	16107
WS														0.00	89	1140
OW	1.00		0.30		0.76	0.08	0.20		1.45					3.79	676	8348
GW	0.11		10.94	1.21	4.35	0.69	0.81		4.04	1.94			0.09	24.18	4910	69757
BB1			2.35			2.17				0.22				4.74	784	11574
RBCI			0.29			0.07			0.47					0.83	53	469
CG1			3.60											3.60	1349	40419
GT1-4					0.10									0.10	92	2900
Misc Ntv			0.06											0.06	232	4413
Misc Trn			0.20											0.20	254	6691
Grand Total:	4.53	0.00	18.05	1.21	7.88	3.38	3.61	4.33	8.98	2.16	0.16	1.76	0.18	56.23	11841	245550
Percent (EVEs):	8.06	0.00	32.10	2.15	14.01	6.01	6.42	7.70	15.97	3.84	0.28	3.13	0.32	100.00		

	EVEs(%)	SHD(%)	WGT(%)
SAM	17.52	12.43	5.40
C	2.60	1.33	0.49
MFW	2.29	0.34	0.09
MO	3.13	0.93	3.85
AM	0.28	3.32	24.26
WW	7.49	10.39	6.56
WS	0.00	0.75	0.46
OW	6.74	5.71	3.40
GW	43.00	41.47	28.41
BB1	8.43	6.62	4.71
RBCI	1.48	0.45	0.19
CG1	6.40	11.39	16.46
GT1-4	0.18	0.78	1.18
Misc Ntv	0.11	1.96	1.80
Misc Trn	0.36	2.15	2.72

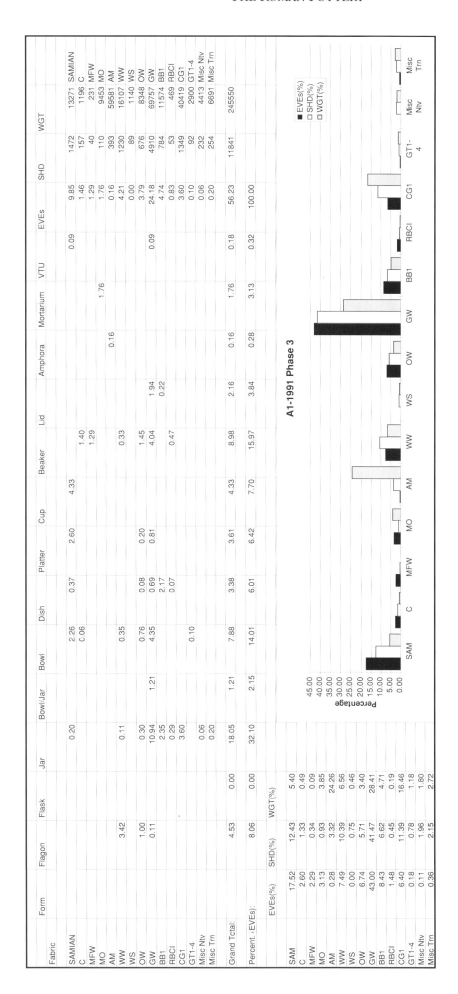

A1-1991 Phase 3

Legend: ■ EVEs(%) □ SHD(%) □ WGT(%)

includes a substantial fragment of a Dressel 20 amphora (AM9a, fig. 66.118). Links were noted with the underlying stratigraphy (Phase: 2G, sg148/1-3) indicating the presence of some residual material and with the fills of a later well cutting the backfill of F433 (Phase: 3B, sg153/1). Internal links and joins have also been identified throughout sg141/1, reinforcing their treatment as a homogeneous deposit. The ASW for sg141/1 is relatively high (15.3g) and with a similarly low breakage rate (54.2), this contrasts with sg142/2-3, which yielded both a lower ASW, and a significantly more fragmentary assemblage (BRK: 1225.0). The results suggest the ditch was rapidly backfilled possibly from a single source, with once again limited subsequent disturbance. The presence of an intact GW beaker from the deposit supports this hypothesis (GW3, fig. 66.109).

Table 16: *Percentage weight of selected ware groups, BRK (GW) and ASW (GW).*

Ph:3A	MC2/3	TRANS	CG1	GW	BB1	BRK	ASW	SHD/WGT
sg141/1	2.0	1.7	34.6	32.6	0.4	54.2	15.3	1334/29795
sg142/2	0.7	0.3	2.8	6.2	0.1	1225.0	9.7	227/15373
sg142/3	-.-	-.-	-.-	100.0	-.-	-.-	16.0	1/16
Total	1.3	1.2	23.7	23.6	0.3	61.9	14.5	1562/45184

Samian provides the vast majority of the fine ware assemblage, accompanied by mica-dusted ware (MD6, fig. 66.102), a single colour-coat (C2) and a sherd of lead-glazed (LG4a) pottery. Stamped and decorated South Gaulish samian suggest a *TPQ* for the backfill of F433 during the late 1st to early 2nd cent. AD. However, the limited supply of Trajanic samian (Marsh 1981), coupled with the presence of a single Les Martres-de-Veyres dish, an industry producing during the early 2nd cent. AD, may support a somewhat later date.

The coarse wares are predominantly 'Roman' in character, with grey ware the most common fabric type (sg141/1: 32.6% by weight) and calcite gritted wares (CG1 and CG1a) providing a secondary element (sg141/1: 34.6%). Jars and bowls comprise the bulk of the vessel classes recorded; notably the everted rim 'cooking jar' (LAU Type: 3F, 2.25 EVEs), large storage vessels (LAU Type: 3M, 1.60 EVEs) and grey ware flanged bowls (LAU Form: 5F4, 1.34 EVEs). However, the broad range of forms and fabrics underlines the diversity of the assemblage, and suggests a domestic origin for the material, with perhaps a secondary storage function. A body sherd from a *serium* (fig. 66.115; see Phase 2G-2H above) and the base of a similarly large WW4 flagon or amphora, probably a product of the Verulamium kilns (Castle 1978) may reflect this latter purpose.

A pit (sg142/2, F377/371) was found cutting the backfills of F433, its contents although otherwise unexceptional, contained approximately 50% of a discarded Dressel 20 amphora (AM9a, fig. 66.118). The vessel appeared to have been reused in some fashion, resulting in the deposition of a residue on the interior upper body and neck. The deposit was examined by Dr Karl Heron, and may be derived from plant matter, perhaps from the leaf waxes of vegetables (Heron pers. comm.).

The accompanying pottery can be broadly dated to the early 2nd cent. AD, with a stamped Verulamium mortarium (fig. 66.117) suggesting a *TPQ* for the deposition of the material during the late 1st cent. AD. The fragmentary nature of the deposit (see above) may suggest the material includes a high residual content.

The phase assemblage includes a number of regional imports, including Nene Valley grey ware (GW4/7), where production has been dated to the second quarter of the 2nd cent. AD. Both sub-groups contain a small amount of BB1, conventionally dated to the first quarter of the 2nd cent. AD at the earliest, a BB1 lid represents the only identifiable form. The fragmentary remains of at least one 'poppy-head' beaker

typologically datable to the late 1st to early 2nd cent. AD (fig. 66.114; Tyers 1978) and stamped Verulamium region mortaria (fig. 66.103, 104, 117; Hartley above, no. M6, M7, M8) stress the continued importance of the pottery industries of south-eastern England. A limited range of amphorae complete the imported pottery, these include the ubiquitous Spanish amphora fabric (AM9a) as well as AM7, again Spanish in origin, and Gaulish AM12/3.

Illustrations: fig. 66.102 – 118.

Phase 3B (Sub-groups: 141/2-5, 150/1-2, 151/1, 152/1, 153/1-3, 154/1-3, 154/5, 155/1-3, 156/1, 157/1-5).

Assemblage: 8182 sherds, 163.3kg, 26.30 EVEs, ASW: 14.3g.

Selected sub-groups were examined in detail from the phase 3B assemblage, these include two wells cutting Surface 4 (sg153/1-3, sg155/1-3), a group of post holes, a hearth (sg157/1-4) and an associated pit (sg157/5) possibly representing use of Surface 4. The ceramic assemblage as a whole would appear to suggest activity spanning the mid 2nd to early 3rd century AD, with the latest element formed by the backfills of features comprising sg157/5.

Construction and repair of Surface 4 (G141, 150-1).
Analysis of the samian derived from the make-up layers and surface suggests a *TPQ* of the third quarter of the 2nd cent. AD. Stamped samian provides dates for sg141/4 (Dickinson above, no. 35, AD115-135) and sg151/1 (Dickinson above, no. 42, AD150-180). The decorated material suggests similar dates for sg141/4 (Dannell in archive, no. 142, AD150-170), with Antonine samian in sgs150/1 and 151/1. However, the samian assemblage clearly contains a high proportion of residual material notably 141/2-4. The recovery of a mica-dusted cup (MD6, fig. 66.119) may also reflect the presence of residual material. Context 1032 (sg151/1) produced the shattered remains of a calcite-gritted storage jar (CG1a, fig. 67.124). A mortarium stamp of Similis (Hartley above, no. M9; fig. 66.120) (sg141/4) supports the mid-2nd cent. AD date for the construction of Surface 4, with perhaps a closing date for the use of the surface toward the last quarter of the century.

Sub-group 152/1 (F376) produced a samian assemblage that contrasts with Surface 4, suggesting a slightly later date of deposition. Although the stamped and decorated samian again indicates a *TPQ* of the third quarter of the 2nd century AD (Dickinson above, no. 42: 4, 76, AD150-180; Dannell in archive, no. 120: 120, AD: 160-190), the subgroup includes plain forms characteristic of the mid and later 2nd century (Drag 31 and 38) absent from the G141 and 150-1. A mortarium stamp of Iunius Loccius has been dated to the mid-2nd century (Hartley above, no. M11; fig. 67.125); the pit also produced a candlestick probably reworked from a tazza base (WS2, fig. 67.126).

As with sg152/1 the burnt layers and spreads overlying Surface 4 (G154) suggest deposition during the second half of the 2nd cent AD (Dickinson above, no. 54, AD130-160; Dannell in archive, no. 154, AD160-190). The plain vessels provide a contemporary range of forms.

Table 17: *Selected sub-groups and phase total: 3B*

Ph:3B	MC2/3	TRANS	CG1	GW	BB1	BRK	ASW	SHD/WGT
sg153/1	0.4*	0.3*	6.9*	10.0*	3.4*	44.9	12.8	327/16205*
sg155/1	4.0	1.8	16.7	26.2	12.9	79.9	9.6	576/7182
sg157/5	-.-	-.-	3.0	30.0	6.7	52.0	17.3	326/7527
Total	3.9	3.4	16.1	30.0	5.2	-.-	14.3	8182/163281

Figures include fragmentary amphorae: 40 sherds/11759g.

The circular well (G153), comprises three sub-groups of which sg153/1 produced the majority of the pottery assemblage (327 sherds/16.2kg). The feature cuts the backfill of ditch F433, and stratigraphically post-dates the subsequent slumping and levelling-up (sg141/2-4). The upper levels (sg153/1) have been interpreted as consolidation of the back-filled well. The deposit contained the shattered remains of a Dressel 20 amphora (40 sherds/11.8kg). The lower sub-groups, primary well deposits (sg153/3) and intermediate organic layers (sg153/2), produced a small assemblage (108 sherds/1977g).

Links and joins were chiefly confined to the consolidation of the well fills (sg153/1); a low breakage rate was also noted (44.9). Joins were recorded with the backfill of F433 (sg141/1) and the overlying stratigraphy (Phase 5C, sg164/1).

Two separate elements to the ceramic assemblage can be recognised, the primary silts and initial backfill, and the final phase of consolidation. The lower sub-groups (sg153/2-3) reflect the late 1st to early 2nd century ceramic assemblage, a predominance of GW and calcite-gritted forms, additionally they include very little BB1 (0.2% by weight). In contrast sg153/1 is dominated by grey wares including a range of everted rim jars (LAU Type: 3F, 3G) and incorporates a substantial proportion of BB1 including a dish (fig. 67.129) datable to the early to mid-2nd cent. AD. An Antonine samian stamp provides a *TPQ* for the assemblage (Dickinson above, no. 48, AD140-170).

The second well (G155) contains three sub-groups in much the same sequence; however, the intermediate fills (sg155/2) are more obviously cessy. As with G153 the bulk of the assemblage is derived from the final phase of consolidation and backfilling (sg155/3: 576 sherds/7182g). A single link was noted within sg155/1. ASW were low for the feature as a whole, while breakage rates suggest a fragmentary assemblage (sg155/1: 9.6g/79.9).

The ceramic content of the levelling/make-up layers (sg155/1) again contrasts with the early backfill (sg155/2-3). The samian evidence suggests the final phase of levelling took place during the mid-2nd cent. AD, with a range of decorated and plain vessels incorporating Hadrianic and Antonine forms (Drag 33, 38), a single Drag 79 dish, may indicate a mid to later 2nd cent. AD date. This is confirmed and advanced by the coarse wares both in terms of their composition and content. The ascendancy of grey ware forms during early to mid-2nd cent. AD is now clearly challenged by the arrival in quantity of BB1 (12.9% by weight). The chief jar form present is the everted rim BB1 vessel (fig. 67.131, Gillam Type 125: 1.04 EVEs). The assemblage also sees the appearance of the oxidised Antonine-Severan roughcast beaker (LAU Form 9D2-4), a form increasingly common throughout the later 2nd century.

The presence in context 729 (sg155/1) of a range of later Roman forms and fabrics, including samian (Dannell in archive, no. 150, 151), colour coats (C2, 3, 7, 11, 12CG, 13, 17) and a single 'Cam 306' bowl is problematic. The latter has been dated to the 3rd cent. AD. However, all are confined to a single context and appear to represent intrusive material caused perhaps by continued slumping.

Regional imports include a sherd of Derbyshire white ware (WW13, pers comm. T S Martin). It is noticeable that the slight but constant thread of regionally imported grey wares (GW4/7, GW10, GW11) is absent from G155. This may reflect the increasing competition caused by the appearance of BB1.

The group of features and an associated pit comprising G157 can be differentiated on the basis of their ceramic composition. The bulk of the group assemblage was derived from the pit (326 sherds/7527g); it yielded pottery with a high ASW and a relatively low breakage rate (17.3g/52.0). This can be contrasted with the associated features that produced a considerably more fragmentary assemblage (BRK: 262.5). In contrast the group of post holes (sg157/1-2) provided a small, and apparently residual assemblage. Links and joins were noted, between the putative structural sub-groups and the underlying stratigraphy (Phase 3A, sg141/1). GW and CG fabrics formed the major element of both sub-groups, with rusticated jar forms stressing the residual content. A substantial fragment of a 1st to 2nd century mica-dusted beaker (MD4, fig. 67.133) was recovered from F341. The possible hearth (sg157/3) and associated slot (sg157/4) produced a more diagnostic assemblage. A stamped samian Drag 31 (Dickinson above, no. 157, AD140-170), coupled with BB1 and an Antonine-Severan rouletted beaker suggests a *TPQ* for its backfill during the mid to later 2nd cent. AD. The assemblage is predominantly grey ware, with a possible link identified between the two sub-groups.

The shallow pit (sg157/5), located to the north of the above groups, produced a well-dated assemblage. With both fine and coarse ware forms indicating accumulation of the assemblage from the late 2nd cent. AD. The latest element of the assemblage appears to date to the early 3rd cent. AD, with a number of vessels, including an early hammer-head mortarium (MO4, fig. 68.135) and BB1 jar forms (Gillam 145), that must date to the first half of the 3rd century AD. The rim and stamped handle of a Dressel 20 amphora were recovered from various contexts within the feature (Williams above, no. A3; fig. 68.137). Williams dates the vessel morphologically to the late 2nd to early 3rd cent. AD and the stamp to the second half of the 2nd cent. AD.

The ASW (17.3g) and breakage rates (52.0) for the assemblage indicate the deposition of fairly fresh refuse, with little subsequent disturbance, although joins were recorded with Phase 5A (sg158/5 and 160/5). The wide range of utilitarian forms, including the mortarium and a variety of jar and bowl forms suggest a domestic function.

Illustrations: figs. 66.119-122; 67.123-133; 68.134-139.

Phase 3C (Sub-groups: 171/2, 175/1-4, 186/2, 186/4).

Assemblage: 916 sherds, 16.8kg, ASW: 12.5g.

The phase comprised a series of poorly stratified features, datable on the basis of their ceramic composition and content. Three sub-groups have been examined (sg171/2, 175/4, 186/4) together they form 79.4% (by weight) of the phase assemblage.

Table 18: *Selected sub-groups phase 3C*

Ph:3C	MC2/3	TRANS	CG1	GW	BB1	BRK	ASW	SHD/WGT
sg171/2	-.-	19.0	62.9	12.7	0.7	-.-	3.9	88/921
sg175/4	0.3	2.8	16.5	43.3	14.1	-.-	9.6	206/2157
sg186/4	1.1	1.6	8.7	23.0	4.9	-.-	17.3	372/10243
Total	1.4	2.6	12.9	24.9	6.6	-.-	14.3	916/16771

Sub-group 171/2 contains a high degree of residual material. The very low ASW (3.9g) and fragmentary nature of the pottery may suggest an assemblage repeatedly disturbed. The samian is predominantly Flavian (late 1st cent. AD) with a single Drag 33 cup of Central Gaulish manufacture. The assemblage composition, notably the dominance of the calcite-gritted wares (62.9% by weight), but also the high percentage of 'transitional' wares, confirms the impression of a substantial residual element. However, the presence of BB1 implies a *TPQ* for the assemblage deposition no earlier than the early to mid-2nd cent. AD.

In contrast sg186/4, similar features to the north of G171, provided a very different, tightly datable assemblage. The ASW (17.6g) is affected by the survival of a GW double-handled jar (fig. 68.142, 8 sherds/1040g). Joins were noted with sg187/1 (Phase 3D). A decorated Central Gaulish samian Drag 37 provides a late Antonine *TPQ* (Dannell in archive, no. 229, AD150-170), a date supported by the coarse wares. The late 1st to early 2nd cent. AD assemblage in G171 has been replaced by one predominant in GW, with BB1 a significant element A stamped Mancetter-Hartshill mortarium dated to the mid-2nd cent. AD (Hartley above, no. M12, fig. 68.140) was recovered from sg186/2. The vessel's condition, pitted and damaged, compares poorly with the rest of the subgroup assemblage perhaps suggesting it represents residual material.

The make-up layers sg175/4 produced a very similar assemblage to sg186/4; again the samian indicates an *TPQ* during the mid 2nd century, with GW the main coarse component of the assemblage. The phase would seem therefore to support a *TPQ* of the mid to late 2nd century AD.

Illustrations: fig. 68.140-143.

Phase 3D (Sub-groups: 183/3, 187/1).

Assemblage: 802 sherds, 14.6kg, ASW: 15.5g.

The phase comprises two sub-groups, sg183/3, 187/1, with the bulk of the assemblage derived from the latter (757 sherds/14219g). The ASW is relatively high (15.6g) suggesting an intact assemblage. The impression supported by the ceramic links observed, with joins noted throughout F334 (sg187/1); joins were also noted with sg186/4 (Phase 3C).

Table 19: *Selected sub-groups phase 3D*

Ph:3D	MC2I3	TRANS	CG1	GW	BB1	BRK	ASW	SHD/WGT
Sg187/1	0.2	0.6	4.0	33.8	7.8	-.-	15.6	757/14219
Total	0.2	0.6	4.1	33.9	8.3	-.-	15.5	802/14626

The dating of the samian clearly suggests the assemblage was accumulated over a relatively short period, and derived from predominantly fresh and contemporary material. Approximately 75% (by EVEs) of the samian assemblage can be dated to the mid to later 2nd cent. AD. Examination of the decorated Central Gaulish samian revealed a similar date range, with a *TPQ* of the mid/late-2nd cent. AD (Dannell in archive, no. 226, AD150-170). The apparently high proportion of colour-coats (3.5% by weight) can be explained by the survival of a substantially complete roughcast beaker (C2, fig. 68.144), the latter may well be a product of the Nene Valley kilns where production commences during the later 2nd cent. AD. A stamped mortarium of the potter Icotasgus (Hartley above, no. M13; fig. 68.145) further supports a late 2nd century date for the assemblage.

A wide range of coarse wares accompany the samian and fine wares, including two 'London ware' compass inscribed bowls (fig. 68.146). The type is believed to have been produced in the Lower Nene Valley where a date range *c*.AD 90-150 is ascribed; however, their presence in the subgroup assemblage may indicate their continued use into the second half of the 2nd cent. AD. The most striking feature of the assemblage is the dearth of calcite-gritted wares (CG1/CG1a: 4.0% by weight). A number of finely rilled body sherds may indicate the presence of forms datable to the later 2nd/3rd century (Brown 1994). The increased significance of BB1 characterises itself both in the rising percentage of the fabric present and in the growth of 'BB1-types' produced in the local GW's (GW and GW1). The standard range of BB1 forms is augmented by a handled beaker (fig. 68.147, Gillam Type 65).

The pit group can be compared with the Group II deposits from the Forum (Pollard forthcoming a). The assemblage comprises mainly Hadrianic to Antonine material, with nothing that need post-date the later 2nd cent. AD. The range of relatively intact fine and coarse table wares may suggest a domestic, non-culinary function.

Illustrations: fig. 68.144-147.

Area 2

Phase 3E (Sub-groups: 209/1, 209/3).

Assemblage: 4 sherds, 20g, n/a EVEs

An undiagnostic assemblage lacking closely datable pottery, a general date of the late 1st cent. AD onward can be suggested, based upon the presence of 'Romanized' grey wares.

Illustrations: n/a.

Phase 3F (Sub-groups: 210/1-3, 211/1).

Assemblage: 151 sherds, 1270g, 4.53 EVEs

The phase assemblage is mainly derived from the east/west foundation trench (sg210/1), and clearly incorporates residual material from the underlying ditch sequence (sg202/1&3) including fragments of a stamped mortarium mentioned in Phase 2K(ii) (Hartley above, no. M2; fig.64, 78). Links were also noted within the sub-group. Low average sherd weight and brokenness values can in part be explained by the absence of GW storage vessels.

The mortarium stamp recovered from the truncated ditch fills sg202/3 (Ph: 2K(ii), suggests a mid-2nd century *TPQ* for the construction of Structure F. However, Central Gaulish samian from the construction trench itself somewhat advances this date, with both plain and decorated forms (Drag 37, 18/31) datable to the middle to end of the century. The limited coarse wares correspond with the samian dating; the ratio of CG1/GW/BB1 is comparable with mid and later 2nd cent. AD assemblages at the 'Temple' (A164.1969) and 'Forum' (A302.1971 & A295.1973) (Pollard 1994, table 79). Indicators of the Flavian and Trajanic assemblages, such as rusticated grey wares are also on the wane, with the trend toward barbotine motifs, mentioned above, clouded only by the presence of some residual material. As a group the assemblage seems domestic in origin with the absence of storage jars and perhaps amphorae.

Sub-group 211/1 (3 sherds/32g) is too small to provide more than dating evidence. However, the presence of a BB1 grooved flat-rimmed dish (Gillam Type 227) suggests a date for the feature during the late 2nd to early 3rd cent. AD. Holbrook and Bidwell (1990, 98) suggest the introduction of the form should be dated to the last decades of the 2nd cent. AD with production continuing until the mid to later 3rd cent. AD.

Illustrations: n/a.

Phase 3G (Sub-groups: 206/2, 207/1-6, 212/1).

Assemblage: 223 sherds, 4418g, 3.75 EVEs, ASW: 12.4g.

The metalled surfaces (sg206/2) incorporated a small (6sh/37g) but broadly datable assemblage. GW jars indicate a 2nd cent. AD date of deposition, with BB1 and possibly a colour-coat (C2) vessel suggesting a *TPQ* of the mid to later 2nd cent. AD.

Group 207, the sequence of pits and metalling to the south of building 1A, produced clearly the latest material from Area 2, and can be compared to the Phase 5 assemblages from Areas 1 and 3. Links were noted between the pits and the associated make-up levels and surfaces. (sg207/1 and sg207/6). ASW and 'brokenness' values for the phase were unexceptional; however, sg207/1 had both the largest assemblage and the highest ASW (17.0), perhaps suggesting a deposit of relatively fresh refuse.

The samian assemblage reflects the late date, with Central Gaulish material, including two fragmentary stamps (Dickinson above, no. 66-67), a mortarium and plain forms (Drag 45, Drag 31/31R) identified. An East Gaulish W81 bowl completes a late group. However, it is the coarse pottery and their associated specialist wares that date the assemblage. Hammerhead mortaria dated by Hartley to the mid-3rd to 4th cent. AD, were recovered from sg207/1 and the later pit sg207/4, a date supported by the presence of obtuse latticed BB1.

A single CG1 necked jar (Brown 1994, fig.26, 94) was recovered from sg207/1, with a rilled body sherd in the same fabric, from sg207/4. Brown in his study of the Harrold pottery industry, describes jars with triangular, drooping rims *(ibid.,* 59), and dates their introduction to the second half of the 2nd cent. AD. Although he indicates the presence of fine rilling among these vessels throughout much of their period of production, the technique appears to have become more common on later vessels. Taken together the evidence would suggest a *TPQ* during the mid to late 3rd century,

The resurfacing (sg207/5) cannot be dated accurately, with the subsequent pits (sg207/2-3) providing small (20sh/186g) and chronologically undiagnostic ceramic groups. However, sg207/4, a pit cutting the re-metalled surface, produced a small but datable assemblage. As mentioned above the recovery of a mortarium of the Mancetter-Hartshill industry (MO4), calcite-gritted ware (CG1) and BB1 imply deposition post-dating the 3rd century. However, the presence of Much Hadham ware (OW9) suggests a considerably later date of deposition. As Marney (1989, 122) states, the Hadham potteries appear to export widely only during the 4th cent. AD, a date broadly supported by the Causeway Lane groups. The final resurfacing (sg207/6) further reinforces the late dating, with fragments of a flange-neck colour-coat flagon (C2), probably a Nene Valley product, and further Much Hadham ware. It would appear therefore that the ceramic assemblage is indicating continued use of Structure F and the accompanying surfaces into the 4th century.

Group 212, the probable roadside ditches, produced pottery from only one context (2281). A total of 12sh/200g were recorded amongst which the presence of a single sherd of BB1 provides the clearest indication of date. A *TPQ* for deposition of the assemblage during the second quarter of the 2nd century is suggested.

The phase assemblage incorporates a diversity of activities ranging between the silting of the roadside ditches, perhaps during the middle of the 2nd century AD, to the resurfacing of the yard surface associated with Structures F and G during the 4th century.

Illustrations: fig. 69.148-152.

DISCUSSION OF THE POTTERY FROM PHASE 3 (Phases: 3E-G, 3A, 3B, 3C-3D).

Assemblage: 11841 sherds, 245.6kg, 56.23 EVEs, ASW:14.21g.

Phase 3 witnesses extensive activity across the site, pottery dates for many of the features from Area 1 overlap, with activity apparently condensed into the mid to later 2nd cent. AD, but ranging as late as the early 3rd century (Phase 3B, sg157/5). The phase assemblage is again characterised by the pre-dominance of grey wares, the fabric comprises a wide range of utilitarian forms of which the everted rim jar is the most common. However, it is the arrival of BB1 (*c*.5% by weight) that marks out the phase assemblages. The narrow range of vessel forms, mainly jars, dishes and lids, appears to have made an immediate impact upon the suite of fabrics and forms current during Phase 2. The popularity of BB1 forms was clearly that of functional, cheap/well priced and readily available utensils able to compete with the locally produced pottery. The ware's success is reflected in the proliferation of copies both in form and design (Fig. 68. 138).

As with BB1, calcite-gritted wares (CG1a/CG1) encompass a limited range of forms, suggesting they are the product of a well controlled trade. The 'type' ware has been well documented by Brown in his study of the Harrold Kilns, Bedfordshire (Brown 1994). The predominant calcite-gritted

form during the 2nd century present at Causeway Lane remains the storage jar (LAU Form 3M2, fig.67.124), a vessel that sees little real change throughout the late 1st and 2nd cent. AD. The possible simplification of the decorative motifs employed on vessels of the 2nd century, scoring or rilling, may perhaps represent stream-lining of the production process and functional improvements.

The nature of the decline of calcite-gritted ware has already been described (Pollard 1994, 77). As the dominant fabric of the early to mid-1st cent. AD calcite-gritted wares were challenged during the latter half of the century by the local grey wares. Both fabrics were competing as producers of cooking vessels, a role increasingly usurped by the GW products of the Leicester kilns (e.g. Great Holme Street, Pollard forthcoming b). Pollard has noted the storage jar may have formed an increasing element of the CG1 repertoire during the 2nd cent. AD.

Given the non-local source of production and the continuity of form and supply, it seems likely that the ware can be reasonably interpreted as indicators of trade; in which case the decline of the fabric during the 2nd cent. AD may reflect the gradual eclipse not of the vessel type but of its contents. It is apparent that the form does not outlast the fabric, although there are a number of GW vessels that can be defined as storage jars, none are obvious successors to the CG1 vessel (Table 20).

Illustrations: figs. 66, 102-121; 67.123-133; 68.134-147; 69.148-152

Table 20: Ratio of the main coarse wares (*Phases 3A, 3B, 3C, 3D, 3F, 3G*).

	Ph:3A	*Ph:3B*	*Ph:3C*	*Ph:3D*	*Ph:3F*	*Ph:3G*
CG1a %*	50.2	31.4	29.0	8.9	14.1	31.3
CG:GW	1:1.0	1:1.9	1:1.9	1:8.3	1:3.4	1:1.6
CG:BB1	87.2:1	3.1:1	2.0:1	1:2.0	1:2.7	1.6:1
GW:BB1	85.6:1	5.7:1	3.8:1	4.1:1	1.3:1	2.5:1
Sh/Wt (kg)	1562/ 45.2	8182/163.3	916/ 16.8	802/ 14.6	151/ 1.3	223/ 4.4

* CG1a as a proportion (%) of the main coarse wares (CG1a, GW & BB1).

PHASE 4

Area 1

Phase 4A (Sub-groups:174/1-3, 183/1).

Assemblage: 1589 sherds, 26.1kg., 25.69EVEs, ASW:14.9g.

Table 21: *Selected subgroups phase 4A*

Phase:4	*MC2l3*	*TRANS*	*CG1*	*GW*	*BB1*	*BRK*	*ASW*	*SHDlWGT*
sg174/1	-.-	-.-	6.4	21.7	43.2	-.-	17.6	225/3314
sg174/2	0.1	0.7	5.9	24.9	27.2	-.-	13.7	704/10369
sg174/3	-.-	-.-	15.1	30.4	19.2	-.-	16.5	562/9519
sg183/1	1.3	0.5	11.0	22.5	-.-	-.-	15.0	98/2947
Total	0.2	0.3	7.7	29.0	23.1	61.0	14.9	1588/26179

The bulk of the phase assemblage was recovered from pit F255 (G174: 1491 sherds/23.2kg), a further seven truncated features (G183) yielded small and largely undiagnostic assemblages (98 sherds/2947g).

Three sub-groups comprise the backfill of pit F255, sg174/1 the smallest element (225 sherds/3314g) represents an initial phase of disuse; the subsequent recut and backfill (sg174/2-3) produced the bulk of the pottery recovered from the pit. Links and joins were noted between all three sub-groups and especially within sg174/2, perhaps suggesting the deposit represents a single event. ASW's are high for the primary backfill (sg174/1: 17.6g) and the final make-up layers (sg174/3: 16.5g). Coupled with several substantially complete vessels recovered from sg174/1, this may indicate the assemblage represents a primary or 'fresh' deposit.

The initial backfill of pit F255 produced a small but closely datable assemblage dominated by the remains of four vessels,

Table 22: EVE's by ware and vessel class for Phase 4

Fabric	Flagon	Flask	Jar	Bowl/Jar	Bowl	Dish	Platter	Cup	Beaker	Lid	Amphora	Mortarium	EVEs	SHD	WGT
SAMIAN					1.44	0.39	0.16	2.23					4.22	142	1694
C					0.14	0.08			1.56	0.11			1.89	205	1058
MFW	0.44												0.44	1	10
MO												1.53	1.53	30	3037
AM													0.00	25	1239
WW	0.17				0.32								0.49	84	721
WS													0.00	6	61
OW			1.00			0.14							1.14	54	1261
GW			4.53	1.21	0.35	0.53			1.72				8.34	509	7603
BB1			3.20			3.55							6.75	412	6056
RBCl			0.05										0.05	51	1193
CG1			0.84										0.84	61	2084
GT1-4													0.00	1	42
Misc Ntv.													0.00	1	37
Misc Trn.													0.00	6	83
Grand Total:	0.61	0.00	9.62	1.21	2.25	4.69	0.16	2.23	3.28	0.11	0.00	1.53	25.69	1588	26179
Percent. (EVEs):	2.37	0.00	37.45	4.71	8.76	18.26	0.62	8.68	12.77	0.43	0.00	5.96	100.00		

	EVEs(%)	SHD(%)	WGT(%)
SAM	16.43	8.94	6.47
C	7.36	12.91	4.04
MFW	1.71	0.06	0.04
MO	5.96	1.89	11.60
AM	0.00	1.57	4.73
WW	1.91	5.29	2.75
WS	0.00	0.38	0.23
OW	4.44	3.40	4.82
GW	32.46	32.05	29.04
BB1	26.27	25.94	23.13
RBCl	0.19	3.21	4.56
CG1	3.27	3.84	7.96
GT1-4	0.00	0.06	0.16
Misc Ntv	0.00	0.06	0.14
Misc Trn	0.00	0.38	0.32

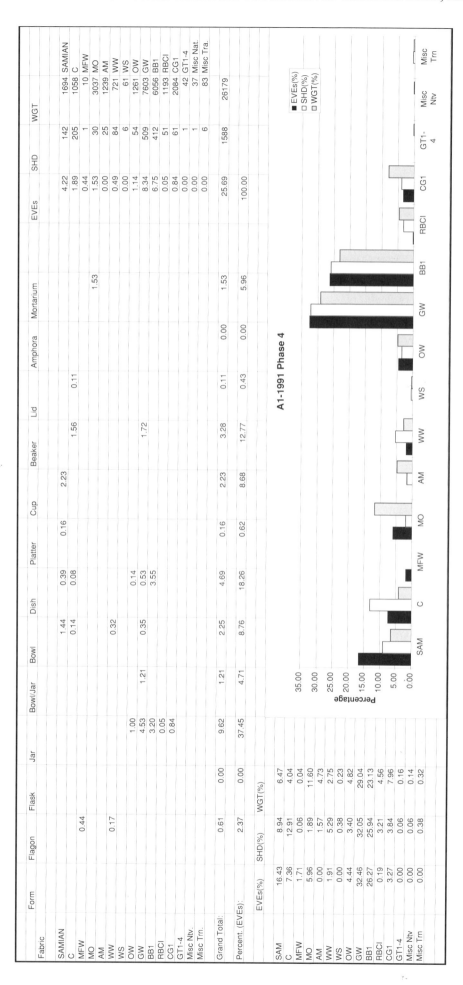

A1-1991 Phase 4

these were all recovered from a single context (1100); they comprise a colour-coat beaker (C2, fig. 69.153), a ring-necked flagon (WW3, fig. 69.154) and two BB1 jars (fig. 69.155, 156). The beaker, probably a product of the Nene Valley colour-coat industry, is decorated with a panel of phalli 'en barbotine'. Despite the absence of the rim, the vessel is datable to the late 2nd to 3rd cent. AD (Howe *et al* 1980, fig.3, 28-9, 34). Webster (1989, 9 & fig.2, 20-1) illustrates a number of close parallels including a cornice rim beaker from Lincoln and a plain rimmed vessel from Colchester (Hull 1963, fig.54, 2). The phallus motif occurs with some frequency and has been interpreted as a symbol of potency and good luck. The flagon (WW3, Arch 395) has the vestigial ring-neck and low girth typical of the mid to later 2nd cent. AD (Gillam Type 8, AD 140-180). However, it is the BB1 (fig. 69.155, 156) jars that provide the clearest indication of the date of deposition, both share the obtuse lattice typical of later BB1 jar forms (Gillam Types 145-6) indicating a *TPQ* for the subgroup of the mid 3rd century. Farrar (1981, 426-7) following an examination of the first Darfield hoard, has argued for an earlier inception of Gillam's Type 146, suggesting a date during the first half of the 3rd cent. AD. Such is consistent with the broader dating of the sub-group assemblage. The limited range of colour-coats, and predominance of the beaker forms, may support the dating of the deposit during the early to mid-3rd cent. AD. It is interesting to note the absence from sg174/1 of the utilitarian colour-coats, oxidised bowl (Cam 306) and imports generally ascribed to the later 3rd and 4th cent. AD.

The secondary fills of F255 (sg174/2), despite an obvious residual element, produced a closely datable assemblage. Joins noted between the sub-groups, including an almost complete BB1 dish (fig. 69.162) indicate the disturbance of the previous fills (sg174/1). The absence of a chamfered profile, burnished arc decoration and the flat rim of this vessel, suggests a hybrid conical dish form probably of the late 2nd or early 3rd cent. AD. The sub-group is, however, especially notable for the preponderance of ledge-rim jars (fig. 69.158, 159, 160), the form appears to be rare as a product of the local pottery industry prior to the 3rd cent. A.D, however, the type may be generally paralleled among the more pronounced ledge-rim CG1 jars of the later 2nd cent. AD (Brown 1994, fig.26, 106, 119-120), and perhaps more locally with the ledge-rim jars of the Derbyshire ware industry (Martin forthcoming).

Apparently the latest elements within the group assemblage include a single abraded colour-coat plain rim dish (C2, Howe *et al* 1980, fig.7, 87), recovered from context 450, the piece may be intrusive but could indicate deposition as late as the later 3rd cent. AD. This late date of deposition may be supported by the presence of a calcite-gritted jar of unusual form and fabric (CG3c, fig. 69.163). Unfortunately the rim was not present, however, the profile resembles the tall, high shouldered jars of the 4th cent. AD (Gillam Type 160). The sparse shell-tempering and brownish-grey surfaces are similar to vessels from late Roman groups at Lincoln (Darling 1977, 28), this may suggest the vessel was originally lid-seated.

The high proportion of carbonised plant remains recovered from sg174/2 suggests burning either within or nearby F255. This may be supported by the traces of sooting and occasional burnt residues identified on vessels from various contexts within the recut of pit F255 (C446, 447, 1026, 1027). Fire affected sherds occur in contexts 446, 1023 and 1027, the majority of the latter are samian sherds heavily sooted and/or partially reduced; the remainder are grey ware or BB1 forms showing signs of oxidation. Sooting on kitchen wares especially vessels such as the GW, BB1 and OW cooking jars can easily be explained as evidence of use rather than any *in situ* burning. However, the sooting and 're-firing' of vessel clearly in a fragmentary state, and of table wares (Samian, C2, WW, WS) unlikely to come into contact with fire during their use, tends to support the suggestion of a fire within the pit.

The final backfill of F255 (sg174/3) yielded an assemblage dominated by the local GW's and imported BB1. The former provides a range of utilitarian forms of which the necked jar (fig. 70.165) is the most common. BB1 provides the bulk of the cooking jars (Gillam Types 145/6) and dishes, the latter includes plain and groove rim forms (Gillam Types 329, 227) typical of the 3rd cent. AD. The range of BB1 vessels coupled with the absence of flat and flanged rimmed dishes, may suggests a *TPQ* for the date of deposition during the middle of the century, a date supported by the presence of a pair of Mancetter-Hartshill hammer-head mortaria (MO4).

The high percentage (15.1% by weight) of calcite-gritted ware is represented by a substantial portion of a single calcite-gritted necked jar (CG1b, fig. 70.166). A small quantity of probably residual material was identified including a flanged bowl (WW2, fig. 69.164), the latter appears to have been burnt and may be derived from the burnt material located in sg174/2.

Illustrations: figs. 69.153-164; 70.165-166

DISCUSSION OF THE POTTERY FROM PHASE 4. (Phase 4A).

Assemblage: 1589 sherds, 26.1kg., 25.69EVEs, ASW: 14.9g.

The phase sees a decline in the samian component of the fine ware assemblage. However, late 2nd Central Gaulish and early 3rd century East Gaulish samian indicate late supply. Several examples of late stamped and decorated samian vessels were recorded from pit F255 (G174). However, the proportion of fine table wares increases due to a marked rise in the colour-coats present. The latter are dominated by the products of the Lower Nene Valley and comprise a limited range of forms, including both cornice and plain rimmed beakers (Howe *et al* 1980, fig.3, 30, 34), flagons and 'Caistor-boxes'. The first apparently replaces the rouletted beaker in the ceramic repertoire, characteristic of the Antonine/Severan period. A single colour-coat dish (*ibid.*, fig.7, 87, late 3rd to 4th cent. AD) is perhaps the latest piece recovered from F255. The fine wares are completed by imported Trier and Central Gaulish (Lezoux) colour-coats (C12CG, C12T) of both beaker and cup form. The former are diagnostically 3rd cent. AD in date. The presence of late samian and imported colour-coats, 'Rhenish' wares representing among the finest examples of the latter, suggest a high status assemblage.

The composition of the Phase 4 coarse wares demonstrates a significant change from the earlier Phase assemblages. Most obviously, BB1 becomes significantly more common, rivalling even the local GW's. The ware represents approximately 25% (by weight) of the assemblage, with the obtuse latticed jar (Gillam Types 145/6), plain rim (Type Gillam 329) and groove rim dishes (Gillam Types 226/7), providing the bulk of the forms present (ratio jar/dish, 1:2). The composition of the assemblage and range of forms present appears to indicate the main coarse wares compliment one another, rather than directly competing. The necked jar (Kenyon 1948, fig.25, Type E.26) and wide-mouthed bowl (*ibid.* fig.24, F.17/8) dominate the GW repertoire, with a variety of cooking jars, including some everted rim 'BB1 types' produced, but noticeably less common than their BB1 equivalent. Both plain and flat/groove rimmed dishes are almost exclusively BB1, with very few produced in other fabrics.

The range of coarse wares includes a number of regional imports, Pink-grogged ware (GT3a, Booth and Greene 1989), Nene Valley GW's and a range of shelly wares including calcite-gritted wares (CG1b, fig. 70.166), possibly the product of the Harrold kilns, Northamptonshire (Brown

Table 23: EVE's by ware and vessel class for Phase 5

Fabric	Flagon	Flask	Jar	Bowl/Jar	Bowl	Dish	Platter	Cup	Beaker	Lid	Amphora	Mortarium	EVEs	SHD	WGT
SAMIAN					10.52	1.16	2.26	8.11	0.45			0.30	22.80	1542	19347
C	0.25				0.56			0.28	7.81	0.37			9.27	895	7023
MFW						0.06		0.17					0.23	13	187
MO												10.20	10.20	258	18684
AM											1.91		1.91	363	38409
WW	17.15				1.71				0.13	0.15			19.14	913	11629
WS	0.25				0.40								0.65	63	927
OW			1.16		1.61	0.16			8.50				11.43	621	7345
GW			38.43	0.22	8.57	4.43	0.35		5.56	2.36			59.92	4623	62971
BB1			14.65			20.38			0.37				35.40	1628	22912
RBCI	1.00		2.47		0.49								3.96	115	2405
CG1			5.77										5.77	781	22567
GT1-4			0.62										0.62	30	1871
Misc Ntv.					0.06								0.06	45	884
Misc Trn.			0.72						0.39				1.11	172	4634
Grand Total:	18.65	0.00	63.82	0.22	23.92	26.19	2.61	8.56	23.21	2.88	1.91	10.50	182.47	12062	221795
Percent. (EVEs):	10.22	0.00	34.98	0.12	13.11	14.35	1.43	4.69	12.72	1.58	1.05	5.75	100.00		

	EVEs(%)	SHD(%)	WGT(%)
SAM	12.50	12.78	8.72
C	5.08	7.42	3.17
MFW	0.13	0.11	0.08
MO	5.59	2.14	8.42
AM	1.05	3.01	17.32
WW	10.49	7.57	5.24
WS	0.36	0.52	0.42
OW	6.26	5.15	3.31
GW	32.84	38.33	28.39
BB1	19.40	13.50	10.33
RBCI	2.17	0.95	1.08
CG1	3.16	6.47	10.17
GT1-4	0.34	0.25	0.84
Misc Ntv	0.03	0.37	0.40
Misc Trn	0.61	1.43	2.09

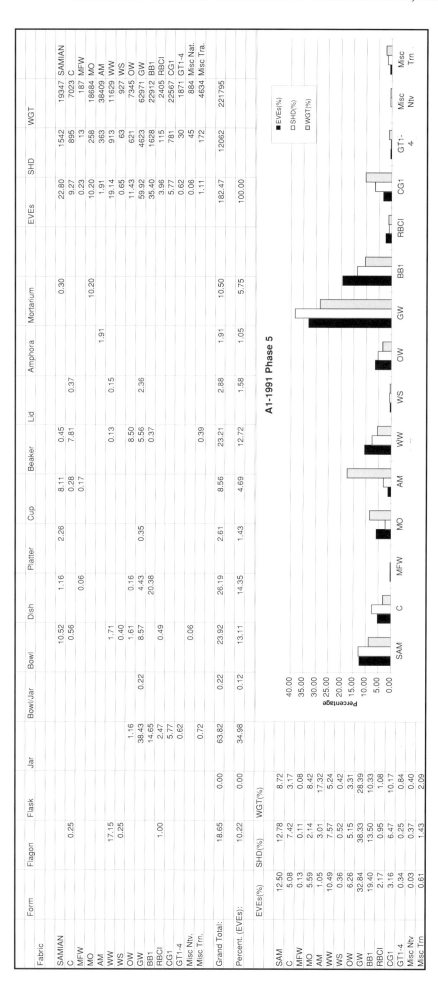

A1-1991 Phase 5

Legend: ■ EVEs(%), ☐ SHD(%), ☐ WGT(%)

1994), a Greetham/Bourne ware jar (CG3b) and a substantial part of a calcite-gritted jar (CG3c, fig. 69.163) possibly paralleled by vessels from Lincoln. Long distance supply is demonstrated by the presence of fragments of various amphorae among the phase assemblage. These include the Dressel 20 (AM9a/b) olive oil amphora, ubiquitous from the 1st cent. AD., and Gaulish and Spanish wine amphorae (AM12/3, AM7). As mentioned, 'Rhenish' wares and samian complete the imports.

The assemblage incorporates a wide range of fabrics and forms diagnostic of the mid to late 3rd cent. AD and suggestive of a domestic and perhaps high status origin. The composition of the ceramic assemblage derived from the backfill of pit G174 (F255), characterised by an unusually high proportion of BB1 (23.13% by weight), may suggest the fills are is derived from a single source. A *TPQ* for the phase of the mid 3rd century seems likely.

Illustrations: figs. 69.153-164; 70.165-166

PHASE 5

Area 1

Phase 5A (Sub-groups: 158/1-5, 159/1, 160/1, 160/4-6, 161/1-3).

Assemblage: 1170 sherds, 16.3kg., 18.61 EVEs, ASW: 11.0g.

Dating of the samian wares suggests formation of the make-up layers (sg158/1-4) of Surface 5 (sg158/5) during the later 2nd to early 3rd century. A near complete stamped East Gaulish Drag 31R bowl (Dickinson above, no. 74) was recovered from sg158/1 with joins in sg164/1 (Phase 5C); the compacted cobble surface (sg151/5) provides a similar date range. All the sub-groups contain a clear residual component. Structure H produced decorated Drag 37 bowls from sg160/1 (AD150-180) and sg161/1 (AD160-190) providing a date of construction during or after the later 2nd cent. AD.

Table 24: *Selected sub-groups phase 5A*

Subgroup	MC2/3	TRANS	CG1	GW	BB1	BRK	ASW	SHD/WGT
sg158/1	0.4	1.6	5.2	21.9	7.4	39.3	18.0	151/3890
sg158/5	–.–	–.–	7.5	26.4	4.2	152.2	12.9	91/1979
sg160/4	–.–	–.–	11.6	34.6	19.4	100.0	8.6	150/1463
sg161/1	–.–	0.3	6.1	43.5	8.3	68.2	10.5	416/4689
Total	0.1	0.6	6.7	32.6	8.7	–.–	–.–	808/12021

The largest assemblages were derived from the make-up layers below surface 5 (sg158/1: 151 sherds/ 3890g) and layers ascribed to Structure H (sg161/1: 417 sherds/ 4763g). ASW indicate clear taphonomic differences between the two elements with Structure H producing consistently lower sherd weights (ASW: 4.2-10.5g) compared to the make-up horizons (ASW: 12.9-18.0g). Additionally the lower breakage rate of the latter (39.3) indicates limited subsequent disturbance.

The dating suggested for sg158/1 by the samian wares is supported by the coarse ware assemblage. The presence of early fabrics (MC2/3, Trans) and forms such as the GW platter and Flavian-Trajanic jar types indicates the survival of residual material. As no links were observed with the underlying stratigraphy it may suggest the levelling layers were derived from outside the immediate area, or indeed beyond the limit of the site.

The distribution of fabric types, however, demonstrates the increased significance of BB1 (7.4% by weight), comparable with the latest elements of the Phase 3 assemblage (sg157/5, ph: 3B; sg186/4, ph: 3C; sg187/1, ph: 3D). The single most common form is however, the OW rouletted beaker (LAU Type 9D), a type characteristic of later 2nd and early 3rd cent. AD assemblages.

The gravel surface (sg158/5) yielded material with the lowest ASW (12.9g) and highest breakage rate (152.2) of the group, this appears consistent with its use as a yard. Little closely datable pottery was recovered from the gravel surface itself, however, the coarse wares again support a samian led late 2nd to early 3rd century *TPQ* for its construction.

The majority of the Structure H sub-groups yielded small and undiagnostic assemblages, the linking factor being their fragmentary condition. ASW's from the post holes comprising sg159/1 and 160/1, and from the post pad or hearth (the pottery shows no signs of burning) sg160/5 were all noticeably low (ASW < 10.5g). The small amount of pottery (6 sherds/95g) from sg160/6 precludes comparison. It is therefore not possible to further clarify the late 2nd century *TPQ* suggested for the construction of Structure H already provided by the samian.

A larger assemblage was recovered from the possible drain and sump (sg160/4). Again the ASW was low (8.6g), the high breakage rate (100.0) suggests a shattered and disturbed assemblage. No links were noted outside the sub-group, a BB1 jar was observed with joins between contexts 1515 and 1553. The composition of the sub-group indicates a low degree of residuality, although some material notably a lid-seated calcite-gritted jar (fig. 70.172) may represent material disturbed by the construction of Structure H. An obtuse latticed BB1 jar (fig. 70.171, Gillam Type 145) provides a *TPQ* for the final silting of the sump during the mid-3rd cent. AD, a date supported to some degree by the Nene Valley GW4/7 dish recovered from the same context (fig. 70.170; Howe *et al* 1980, fig.2, 17). The limited size of the assemblage precludes extensive discussion; however, it is interesting to note the most common jar is the everted rim type (cf. fig. 74.252), apparently derived from the typical BB1 jar. The form is frequently carries lattice burnishing aping the BB1 prototype.

The same trends can be witnessed among the sg161/1 pottery, links are again apparent within the sub-group. The assemblage is both larger and more intact (ASW: 10.5g, BRK: 68.2) than the 'structural' elements (G159, 160), perhaps suggesting less disturbance, or rapid accumulation of the layers. The sub-group contains little material pre-dating the mid-2nd cent. AD, 82.1% (by EVEs) of the samian is of Antonine or later date. The predominance of the everted rim jar is again clear, the form provides more than half (1.61 EVEs, 53.0%) of all the jars recovered from the sub-group, the bulk of which are BB1. The popularity of the BB1 jar is not matched by dishes in the same fabric, with the majority of 'BB1- type' forms produced in GW1.

The phase assemblage therefore indicates activity perhaps commencing with the formation of the make-up layers and construction of Structure H during or soon after the late 2nd century AD, with establishment of the metalled surfaces perhaps in the early 3rd century. Use of the structure if associated with the adjacent drain and sump might be postulated into the mid 3rd century.

Illustrations: fig. 70.167-173.

Phase 5B (Sub-groups: 162/1-7, 163/1+4-5, 165/1-2, 167/1-2).

Assemblage: 2474 sherds, 44.2kg., 35.12 EVEs, ASW: 13.0g.

Table 25: *Selected subgroups phase 5B*

Subgroup	MC2/3	TRANS	CG1	GW	BB1	BRK	ASW	SHD/WGT
sg162/5	1.5	1.8	29.2	21.9	7.4	39.3	18.0	151/3890
sg163/1	–.–	0.9	8.6	26.4	4.2	–.–	8.6	231/2654

The phase can be divided into four elements each comprising a single group; the 'cultivation' horizons sealing the earlier layers (G162), the post holes forming Structure I (G163), the features interpreted as Structure J (G165), and finally G167, an assemblage drawn from two pits (F307, F211); it is suggested the latter may be associated with or succeed Structure I. With the exception of G162 the bulk of each element is derived from a single sub-group (sg163/1, 165/1 and 167/1), each forming over 90.0% of their respective assemblages.

ASW's for the phase suggest similar depositional processes as exhibited in Phase 5A, with noticeably lower values for the two structures (Structure I: 8.7g, Structure J: 8.6g). The homogenous layers (G162) do not share these low ASW's, with sg162/3 remarkable for the preservation of two substantially complete vessels (fig. 70.176, 179/180) the latter containing the cremated remains of an adult. Links and joins were noted within the phase groups and with the underlying stratigraphy. The remains of a 1st cent. AD stamped mortarium (MO15, fig. 78.311) was identified, with joins among the make-up layers of Surface 3 (Ph:2F, sg145/1) and the post-Roman overburden.

A high degree of residuality characterises much of G162. This can best be illustrated by the relatively high percentage of CG1 present among the constituent sub-groups (>17.0% by weight), notably sg162/1, 162/3 and 162/5-7, and the presence of a number of 1st and early 2nd cent. AD coarse ware forms (fig. 70.177, 183). Sub-group 162/5 comprises the bulk of the group assemblage (853 sherds/15.3kg.), with a single context (893) comprising the bulk of the sub-groups residual material. The material is clearly drawn from earlier late 1st cent. AD deposits, incorporating a fragment of 'carrot' amphora (Cam 189, AM18), GW rusticated jars with the assemblage dominated by a variety of 1st cent. AD CG1 forms, notably the ledge rim jar (Brown 1994, fig.25, 47). The absence of BB1 from this assemblage and the exclusively 1st century samian, may suggest the wholesale dumping of residual material possibly as some form of make-up. Sub-group 162/7 can be compared to context 893, producing a rather smaller assemblage (138 sherds/3773g), very similar in composition, sharing the absence of BB1 and 2nd century samian.

The layers overlying Surface 4 (sg162/3), produced an unusually intact assemblage (ASW: 22.0g, BRK: 38.2) incorporating two near complete GW jars (fig. 70.176, 179/180). Both vessels were found in close association: the first, a necked jar, is of an unusual form but can be paralleled on a number of Leicester sites (Pollard forthcoming a, archive illus. 109; forthcoming d, archive illus. 245, 261-3) and is believed to date from the late 2nd century AD. A similar vessel was recovered from the Phase 3 deposits at Towcester, and is there dated to the late 3rd to 4th cent. AD (Woodfield 1983, fig.25, 121). The second, an everted rim vessel with its lid *in situ*, was found to contain the cremated remains of an adult, possibly female (Wakely below, p.365). The lid was pierced during manufacture perhaps to form a steam-hole.

G162 may represent limited cultivation of the area, however the intact nature of sg162/3 and the discrete survival of 'residual' material (sg162/7, context 893, sg162/5) suggests such activity was at best sporadic and succeeded by further dumping/levelling. The group can at best be ascribed a *TPQ* during the late 2nd cent. AD, with stamped CG samian of Antonine date recovered from the same context.

Cutting these layers the post holes of Structure I produced a single assemblage of any size (sg163/1, 231 sherds/2654g). The presence of Antonine-Severan OW's and BB1 including an 'incipient' flanged dish (Gillam Types 226/7) suggests a *TPQ* from the end of the 2nd cent. AD to the early 3rd century. Colour-coats, including a funnel-necked beaker (LAU Type 9F2; Howe *et al* 1980, fig.4, 37-39) are probably of Nene Valley manufacture and date to the late 2nd to 3rd cent. AD. Structure J also produced only one sub-group of any size

(sg165/1, 75 sherds/715g). Despite the small size of the assemblage the composition underlines the late 2nd to early 3rd cent. AD date of the deposition, with a low percentage of CG1 and BB1 now representing 10.0% (by weight) of the pottery. A single mortarium sherd of the Mancetter-Hartshill potteries was recovered from sg165/2 (Gillam Type 254, AD140-180).

The vast bulk (99.2% by weight) of the pottery from G167 was recovered from F307, indicating a very different derivation for the backfill material for the two features, and possibly suggesting a functional difference. A high degree of residuality is apparent within both pits, with the samian from F307 predominantly Flavian or Trajanic, a single undiagnostic Central Gaulish fragment represents the only piece potentially contemporary with the deposition. Once again the high percentage of CG1 (23.0% by weight), the presence of late 1st and 2nd cent. AD forms such as rusticated and barbotine GW jars and coarse ware platters, suggest the bulk of the assemblage dates to the early 2nd cent. AD. The mid-2nd century date of the BB1 component (5.2% by weight) and the absence of the ubiquitous Antonine-Severan OW beaker might suggests redeposition of the assemblage around the middle of the 2nd century. However, a single obtuse latticed BB1 body sherd is likely to imply a *TPQ* for the capping of F307 as much as a century later. The second pit (F211) provided very little pottery (8 sherds/80g) too small an assemblage to provide accurate information.

Functionally, the features may appear very different due to the preponderance of material from F307. However, as both features yielded primarily residual pottery their ceramic component appears incidental, perhaps indicating the source of the backfilling material differed between the use of each pit.

The phase assemblage shares a similar range of dates with Phase 5A. The make-up or cultivation horizons G162 appear to have accumulated during the late 2nd century AD, with construction of Structures I and J occurring at or after the turn of the 3rd century. Although the fills of F307 and F211 date almost exclusively to the mid 2nd century, it is suggested that the backfilling event is likely to have occurred during the mid 3rd century.

Illustrations: fig.70.174-183; 71.184-186

Phase 5C (Sub-groups: 163/6-10, 164/1, 165/4-6, 166/1-7, 168/1, 169/1-3).

Assemblage: 3088 sherds, 44.0kg., ASW: 11.5g.

Table 26: *Selected subgroups phase 5C*

Subgroup	MC2/3	TRANS	CG1	GW	BB1	BRK	ASW	SHD/WGT
sg163/6-10	–.–	–.–	6.5	33.7	10.6	–.–	8.0	126/1072
sg164/1	0.4	1.5	15.1	31.4	8.8	–.–	12.8	975/15728
sg165/4-6	0.7	1.8	8.7	41.7	3.1	–.–	10.4	177/1925
sg166/1-7	0.1	5.9	10.0	28.7	10.9	–.–	11.1	1631/23368
sg168/8	–.–	–.–	8.6	40.8	11.2	–.–	11.8	73/752

The homogeneous layers comprising G164 produced a sizeable ceramic assemblage (975 sherds/15.7kg.) dominated by range of utilitarian coarse wares (GW, BB1 and CG1). Again no cross group links or joins were noted within the assemblage, however, the ASW (12.8g) was noticeably higher than G163 and 165 (Structures I and J). The group appears to incorporate a high proportion of residual material, notably contexts 844, 889 and, 899, including a second stamped vessel of the 1st cent. AD Lezoux kilns (see sg163/6-10 above). Additionally, the absence of BB1 among the above-mentioned contexts suggests they derive from deposits of 1st or early 2nd century date. However, the presence of late second and third cent. AD samian (Drag 31R, 79/80 and East Gaulish Drag 37) among the G164 layers indicates a *TPQ* for their deposition. Both the stamped mortaria (fig. 71.187, 188) and the oxidised rilled beaker (fig.

71.190), combined with the high proportion of calcite-gritted wares (15.1% by weight) reinforce the impression of a sizeable residual component. The higher ASW and the clear residual element to the ceramic assemblage may suggest the deposits represent the formation of make-up layers.

The post holes and features interpreted as elements of Structure I (sg163/6-10) produced a series of small groups, the largest from F209 (sg163/7: 68 sherds/1787g). As with assemblages from the earlier structures the ASW was low (8.0g), no links or join were noted within the assemblage. The residual component of the sub-group is indicated by the presence of various 1st cent. AD samian forms including a rare Drag 24/5 cup from Lezoux. Fragments of two Central Gaulish Drag 33 cups, one stamped (Dickinson above, no. 83, AD150-180) and a bowl of 2nd cent. date, represent the latest samian from the group. The fine wares include a small range of colour-coats, all of probable Nene Valley production. Both plain and cornice rim beakers and a 'Caistor box' are represented, suggesting deposition during or after the 3rd cent. AD, a date supported by the fragmentary remains of a Mancetter-Hartshill hammer-head mortarium.

Subgroups 165/4-6 produced a small and fragmentary assemblage, with the bulk of the material derived from sg165/6 (104 sherds/1240g). The samian suggests a late Antonine date for construction/repair of Structure J (Drag 31R). However, as with G163 the high percentage of early samian indicates a significant residual element to the assemblage. The coarse wares are equally unhelpful, with no piece able to support a date later than the late 2nd cent. AD.

The backfill of the stone lined well F246 (sg166/1-5), formed the bulk of the phase assemblage (1631 sherds/23.4kg.). Unfortunately, all except a small amount of undiagnostic material was derived from the demolition and backfilling of the well, with much of the material associated with the collapsed clay lining (sg166/4). Links and joins were noted within the feature, notably between sg166/1 and 166/5. The ASW was relatively low (11.1g) suggesting the backfill comprised redeposited rather than fresh material.

The feature provides a very different and diagnostically later assemblage than Structures I and J. The collapsed clay and rubble lining (sg166/5) yielded colour-coat indented beakers and a hemispherical bowl, probably Nene Valley products, coarse wares including reduced and oxidised Cam 306-type bowls and BB1 datable to the mid-3rd to 4th cent. AD. A Cam 306 bowl (fig. 71.192, 195) was also recovered from sg166/2-4, suggesting it represented a popular addition to the late Roman ceramic assemblage. A dolium recovered from sg166/5 may represent residual material (fig. 71.196).

The latest BB1 forms, jars with the over-sailing rim (Gillam Types 147/8) and bead and flange dishes (Gillam Type 228) are noticeably absent from the F246 ceramic assemblage. However, the use of obtuse lattice motifs, the presence of groove rim dishes (Gillam Type 227) and the ubiquitous dog-dish all point to a *TPQ* for the backfilling of the well during the later 3rd cent. AD. The presence of hammer-head mortaria tends to support the dating. Probably the latest diagnostic piece, an everted and rilled calcite-gritted jar (fig. 71.191), was recovered from the upper fills of F246. The vessel may be dated to the early 4th cent. AD (Brown 1994, fig.34, 252). Regional imports include body sherds of oxidised Hadham ware (OW9) from a number of contexts, a groove rim dish probably from the Greetham-Bourne kilns (CG3b, fig. 71.193) and Derbyshire ware. A single sherd of the amphora fabric AM2b may indicate the appearance of this fabric during the later 3rd cent. AD.

The assemblage indicates the continued use of the area during the third century, best attested by the late assemblage contained within the backfill of F246, a *TPQ* for which may date as late as the early 4th century. However the absence of much in the way of contemporary pottery outside the well backfill may indicate the low intensity, or non-domestic activity represented on site. A broad *TPQ* for the construction repair of Structures I and J might be postulated during the early years of the 3rd century. The remaining assemblages (G168, 169) produced small and undiagnostic groups, all share *TPQ's* of the late 2nd century AD.

Illustrations: fig. 71.187-197.

Phase 5D (Sub-groups: 186/1).

Assemblage: 184 sherds, 5948g, 4.59 EVEs, ASW: 19.5g.

Phase 5D comprised a single sub-group (186/1) and feature (F240), stratigraphically isolated from Area 1. The phase assemblage yielded the latest closely datable material from Area 1, suggesting a *TPQ* for the date of deposition probably during the early 4th cent. AD. A number of fragmentary but near complete vessels were recovered, including a bead and flanged BB1 bowl and jar (figs.71. 202, & fig.72.203).

The high ASW is complemented by a low breakage rate (34.9). The assemblage most probably represents a relatively undisturbed refuse disposal, perhaps, given the intact nature of the pottery, from a source very close to its point of recovery. Joins were identified between the main contexts (348, 349 and 381). The small amount of residual material includes abraded Central Gaulish samian.

Given the relatively small size of the assemblage, the majority of later Roman fabrics are represented. BB1 comprises the main component (45% by weight), although clearly distorted by the bowl and jar forms mentioned above. The GW vessels (19.6%) include ledge rim and necked jars (cf. figs. 69.160; 71.201) as well as a wide-mouthed bowl (cf. fig. 77.279); all forms characteristic of Leicester's late Roman GW assemblage (Pollard forthcoming c). A less common form, the squat everted rim flask (LAU Form 2A2, fig.71, 200), was also identified. The form appears to have remained a constant if minor element of the Roman assemblage; a very similar vessel was recovered from the early 2nd cent. AD pit group from Area 3 (sg332/3, Phase 2L; fig. 65.95).

Other fabrics included an oxidised rim and lower half of two Cam 306 bowls (fig. 71.199), a single sherd of Much Hadham ware (OW9), and sherds from a finely rilled CG1B storage jar. Two mortaria, probably Mancetter-Hartshill products, can be typologically dated to the mid-3rd to mid-4th cent. AD (MO4, cf. Gillam Type 284).

Illustrations: fig. 71.198-202.

Area 3

Phase 5E (Sub-groups: 339/4-5, 360/1, 361/1).

Assemblage: 845 sherds, 17.4kg, 24.60 EVEs, ASW: 15.6.

The majority of the assemblage was recovered from two sub-groups (339/4, 360/1) together they comprise 91.2% (by weight) of the ceramic assemblage. Both form the backfill of Area 3 quarry pits, with sg360/1, a primary deposit, yielding the bulk of the pottery and possibly representing rubbish brought on to the site. It is notable that of the two pit groups, G339 and G360, the former produced pottery from only two of its five sub-groups, with just sg339/4-5 providing a usable assemblage. No links or joins were noted either within or between the various layers comprising G339 or G360.

Sub-group 361/1, stratigraphically the earliest element of the phase assemblage, produced a small assemblage, suggesting deposition perhaps as early as the mid-2nd cent. AD.

In contrast, subgroups 339/4 and 360/1 both include material indicating deposition during the first half of the 4th cent. AD. The fills of either sub-group differ markedly in their ceramic composition, with sg339/4 incorporating a much larger element of residual pottery, clearly suggesting varying sources and depositional processes. The impression that the fills of sg360/1 represent deliberate refuse disposal is supported by the quantity of material recovered, its relatively high ASW (16.9 g), and the tighter ceramic dating. Breakage rates for the two assemblages are similar perhaps indicating the shared function of the two deposits, and their limited subsequent disturbance. The sealing layers of the quarry pits (sg339/4) include a clearly residual element; the assemblage spans the Roman occupation of the site from the mid-1st to 4th cent. AD The assemblage may include material derived from the clearance of the overburden prior to the gravel extraction.

However, the presence of GW necked jars and wide-mouthed bowls, forms introduced during the late 2nd cent. AD, late BB1 vessels (Gillam Types 145, 329), and a sherd of Much Hadham ware (OW9) (see 3G above), suggests a *TPQ* for the date of deposition during the early 4th cent. AD. A substantial portion of a coarse oxidised necked jar with incised decoration around the girth (fig. 72.205) may also indicate the survival of contemporary material; the incised linear motif can be paralleled from a late 3rd cent. AD rubbish pit in Area 1 (Phase: 4A, sg174/2; fig. 69.158).

The smaller sg339/5 assemblage has a more chronologically diagnostic assemblage, despite a residual element apparent among both the samian and coarse wares (GW3, fig. 72.206). The sub-group includes hammer-head mortaria (MO4; Gillam Types 281, 282) dated by Hartley to the 3rd cent. AD (in archive) and colour-coat beakers in a variety of fabrics, probably products of the Nene Valley industry. The latter are supplemented by Much Hadham ware (OW9) in addition to the ubiquitous late BB1 jar. Together they again imply a date of deposition no earlier than the late 3rd century and probably as late as the early 4th cent. AD.

The bulk of the assemblage was derived from the pit group sg360/1. As noted above the assemblage is of a very different character to the preceding sub-groups, and appears to represent the redeposition of a single episode of refuse disposal, largely uncontaminated by residual material. Followed by the deposition of make-up or sealing layers derived from a 3rd century source.

The assemblage falls into two parts: a contemporary element providing a *TPQ* during the early 4th cent. AD, and including the fragmentary remains of two Much Hadham flagons (OW9, fig. 72.215-6), a diagnostically late BB1 jar (Gillam Type 148), and oxidised Cam 306 bowl (cf. Phase 5C, sg166/4-5; fig. 71.195). Notably absent is the late shell-tempered fabric CG1b, characteristic of the Area 1 later Causeway Lane phases. Second, a large tightly datable early to mid-3rd cent. AD group. The samian assemblage includes stamped (Dickinson above, no. 97-8) and decorated vessels (Dannell above, no. 24) of late Antonine date, products of the Central Gaulish industries, and two stamped plain wares of the Rheinzabern kilns, the latter including a Drag 32 dish of Severianus (Dickinson above, no. 100, AD 200-260). The wide range of regional and continental imports is also of note. These include colour-coats, grey wares and a possible mortarium from the Nene Valley industries (fig. 72.209, 211), an imitation Drag 33 cup, possibly an Oxfordshire product (C13, fig. 72.210), and 'Rhenish' beakers of both Central Gaulish and Trier manufacture. The latter industry in particular reached its *floruit* during the 3rd century (Symonds 1992, 46).

The main feature of the coarse wares is the predominance of BB1, 22.8% by weight, a marked contrast to sg339/4 (6.1%).

The forms are likewise of note, with the predominance of the flat groove rim dish (Holbrook & Bidwell Type 43; Gillam Type 227), obtuse-lattice jars (cf. Gillam Type 145) and plain rim dishes (fig. 72.219), suggesting a date during the early to mid-3rd cent. AD. Regional trade may be indicated by the presence of a GT3A storage jar (fig. 72.220), the fabric can be compared to Marney's Fabric 2 (1989, 174), the soft pink-grogged fabric of the south Midlands. Marney comments that at Milton Keynes the 3rd cent. AD saw the main period of production, with considerably lower quantities recovered from 4th cent. AD deposits (*ibid.*, 66)

The pottery therefore offers a *TPQ* for the earliest activity within Phase 5E from the mid 2nd century AD. Quarrying is likely to have begun during the late 3rd to 4th century, but the first ceramic indication remains the early 4th century backfills of G339 and G360.

Illustrations: fig. 72.203-220.

Phase 5F (Sub-groups: 339/6-9, 362/3, 364/1).

Assemblage: 1717 sherds, 37.7kg., 44.52 EVEs, ASW: 16.1.

The phase produced a large assemblage, in general of similar character to Phase 5E. Four sub-groups form the bulk of the assemblage, (sg339/7, 339/9, 362/3 and 364/1), with the largest assemblage from sg339/7 (46.6% by weight). The date of deposition appears again to fall within the early 4th cent. AD, however, the groups all include high levels of residual material, notably sg339/6, 339/8. The subsequent disturbance of these layers is indicated by links and joins with the overlying stratigraphy (Ph. 5G-6A). Links were also noted within sg339/7. ASW are abnormally high in sg339/6 (24.8g) and 362/3 (24.0g), the latter also sharing a remarkably low breakage rate (18.3). Values for the former sub-group may be explained solely by the small size of the assemblage (54sh/1159g). However, the latter indicates an intact group, suffering little subsequent disturbance. In contrast sgs339/7 and 339/9 (BRK: 53.7, 63.9) are considerably less intact.

The bulk of the samian assemblage is of Central Gaulish production, and includes two late Antonine Drag 37's (Dannell above, no. 26). A notable East Gaulish element (sgs339/9, 364/1) is also present, possibly dating as late as mid-3rd cent. AD.

The backfill of the quarry pits (sg339/6) produced a small and predominantly residual group, with a preponderance of GW's and a high percentage of BB1. The latter included forms ranging in date from the mid-2nd to late 3rd cent. AD. A very worn WS2 flange bowl (fig. 73.222) may indicate the extended life of some of the material, but it is certainly residual given the probable 4th cent. AD deposition. A 'Rhenish' beaker of Trier manufacture represents the latest datable piece (*c.*3rd cent. AD; Symonds 1992, 46).

The dating of sg339/7 is also somewhat problematic. Despite the large assemblage size, there are few closely datable pieces, consequently the date of deposition is indicated by a single bead and flange BB1 dish (Gillam Type 228), and substantial fragments of a late CG1B necked jar; together they suggest a late 3rd to 4th century date of deposition.

GW's dominate the sub-group assemblage (24.7% by weight), and includes both contemporary and residual material. Dating these wares remains difficult; the dominant GW forms of the later Roman period, necked jars and bowls became widespread from the late 2nd cent. AD. The sub-group includes a substantially intact wide-mouthed jar (fig. 73.232). BB1 forms a rather smaller proportion of the phase assemblage (Phase 5E: 18.6% by weight; 5F: 13.1%) and incorporates a range of forms dominated by 2nd cent. AD jar and dish forms, perhaps reflecting a different source of backfill. The high level of residual material is further indicated by the recovery of three mortaria stamps dating to the mid to later 2nd cent. AD (Hartley above, no. M18-20; fig. 73.224, 225, 226), and a roller-stamped beaker (fig. 73.227) of the same date.

Sub-groups 362/3 and 364/1, as with 339/7, include substantial quantities of residual material, probably the bulk of the assemblage. Again a small proportion of the assemblage suggests 4th cent. AD deposition. The small tankard (GW3, fig. 73.239) may be residual in sg362/3, and unparalleled in Leicester. Kenyon (1948, fig 46, 20), records a tankard of typical Severn Valley type from Level III at Jewry Wall, a form dated by Webster (1976, fig.7, 40) to the 2nd/early 3rd cent. AD.

Sub-group 339/9 represents further backfill of the phase 5E pits, and appears to comprise a combination of contemporary and residual, possibly deliberately derived refuse. The samian assemblage as mentioned includes a broad range of sources and dates, but significantly includes one of the few diagnostically late pieces (East Gaulish samian, Trier, Drag 32). Nene Valley products again dominate the colour-coats, with a range of cornice and plain rim beakers, the latter include funnel-mouthed vessels of the mid to late 3rd cent. AD (Howe et al 1980, fig.4, 38-9).

However, it is among the coarse wares that the date of the deposit is most evident. A variety of late fabrics and forms were recovered, including Much Hadham ware (OW9), an Oxfordshire mortarium (MO1), late BB1 vessels (Gillam Types 145, 228 and 329) and a late CG1B rilled jar (Brown 1994, fig.24, 245). Together these suggest a *TPQ* for the phase assemblage date during the first half of the 4th cent. AD.

Illustrations: fig. 73.221-240.

Phase 5G (Sub-groups: 333/1, 334/1-2, 337/1-3, 355/1, 356/18, 357/2-3, 358/1, 359/1-4).

Assemblage: 2036 sherds, 47.8kg, 53.49 EVEs, ASW: 18.8g.

The phase combines three related events, the further backfilling and consolidation of the Phase 5E-2 quarry pits (G359), followed by the levelling of the area and laying of a gravel surface (G356-8), the use of the surface and excavation of a series of pits (G333-4, 337, 355).

Links and joins between the pit sub-groups 334/1-2 and 337/1 were noted, and from the underlying make-up (G359) to pit sg333/1. Links and joins were also found within the main sub-groups. Breakage rates varied across the phase, with a clear difference between G333 and G334/337, the latter groups produced a considerably more intact assemblage (BRK: 65.5; 31.0 and 38.2) with a high ASW (13.8g; 25.9g and 22.6g). The surface and stake holes (G356-8) yielded the lowest ASW (12.9g), well below the phase average (18.8g). Both the consolidation and the pitting provided usable groups, with sg359/4 forming the largest element. Pits 334/1-2 and 337/1-3 also produced sizeable groups. The levelling and gravel surface itself produced very little material, suggesting the surface was kept fairly clean and/or was occupied for a relatively short time.

The bulk of the phase assemblage dates to the 3rd cent. AD with a limited proportion of earlier material. The key groups all produced later 2nd cent. AD stamped or decorated samian (Dickinson above, no. 108 & 117; Dannell above, no. 28 & 30), with sg359/4 including a single EG example, possibly dating as late as the early/mid 3rd cent. AD (Dickinson above, no. 118a). Chronologically the pottery sub-groups cannot be separated; the composition of the backfill (sg359/4) and pit (sg334/1), stratigraphically the earliest and latest elements, bear close comparison. In each case GW's form the major element (*c.*28% by weight), with BB1 (*c.*5-10%) the next most common coarse fabric. The exception is sg333/1 where BB1 comprises over 30% of the pottery. However, this may be the product of the small size of the assemblage, dominated by a single BB1 groove rim dish (fig. 74.241).

Coarse ware vessels from the quarry backfill (G359) indicate a *TPQ* for the deposition of the sub-group during the early-mid 4th Cent. AD. A single bead and flange BB1 dish (Gillam Type 228) was recovered from sg359/4, with a Cam 306 bowl and sherds from a Much Hadham vessel, probably a flagon. Three necked jars in the calcite-gritted fabric (CG1B, fig. 74.254) may foreshadow the increased importance of Late Roman calcite-gritted ware. The assemblage includes a considerable quantity of residual material, with much of the pottery clearly dating to the 3rd cent. AD. The mortaria provide a case in point, despite the ubiquitous late hammer-head form dominating the class, Hartley dates the latest examples to the 3rd cent. AD. (MO4, fig. 74.249) with stamped residual 2nd century forms completing the range (fig. 74.247, 248).

The group of stake holes sg357/2-3 cut the quarry backfill (sg357/4). Together with surface G358, they produced a small but broadly datable assemblage. Once again the pottery comprises mainly GW, with however BB1 providing the most datable piece, an everted rim jar (Gillam Type 147, AD290-370). A hammer-head mortarium dated by Hartley (in archive) from the mid-3rd to the early 4th cent. AD is the only other diagnostic vessel.

The latest phase elements, the pit groups G334 and 337 produced similar assemblages to the backfill G359. The recovery of a late 4th cent. AD coin from the backfill of pit sg334/2, points to the late date of deposition. The pottery assemblage can at best suggest a date of deposition during the 4th century AD. Furthermore the material argues against, although not precluding, deposition later than the mid-4th century. Late fabrics and forms are present, including examples of GW forms such as the flanged bowl (cf. fig. 74.243), bead and flange dish, necked jars and wide-mouthed bowl/jars; all are typical of, but not exclusive to the 3rd and 4th cent. AD grey wares of the East Midlands (Todd 1968, 194-5). Late BB1 forms and a second Cam 306 bowl further suggest a *TPQ* during the 4th cent. AD; however, the group is very different in ceramic composition to the later 4th cent. AD assemblage from Silver Street, Leicester (Pollard, forthcoming c). Notably absent are the utilitarian colour-coats, and Late Roman calcite-gritted wares, both key elements of the Silver Street assemblage. The presence of BB1, a ware that appears to have ceased volume trade in the last quarter of the 4th cent. AD, also suggests the sub-group dates at latest to the third quarter of the 4th century (table 23).

The phase assemblage incorporates a number of vessels covered with paint, pigment (red 10R 4/6) and lime wash residues (Morgan, below pp.299-300). These include the lower body of an indented colour-coat beaker (C2, fig. 74.245). A fragment of the indented zone was recovered from the same deposit without any trace of pigment or lime wash, suggesting the reuse of the lower portion of the vessel was contemporary and perhaps associated with the deposition of the material. Substantial fragments of a groove-rim BB1 dish were recovered from the hearth pit 333/1 with splashes. A fragmentary wide-mouthed bowl was recovered from sg338/1 (Ph: 5H) with a red paint (a mix of lime wash and pigment) thickly covering its interior surfaces.

Illustrations: 241, 242, 243, 244, 245, 246, 247, 248, 249, 250, 251, 252, 253, 254, 255.

Phase 5H (Sub-groups: 338/1-2, 343/2, 345/1, 347/2, 349/1, 350/1, 351/1, 353/1, 354/1).

Assemblage: 732 sherds, 12.1kg., 13.49 EVEs, ASW: 12.4g.

The phase produced a relatively small assemblage, derived mainly from the final backfill (sg338/1-2) and levelling of the

Phase 5E quarry pits. Reasonable collections were recovered from the subsequent pit (sg354/1), the probable cultivation layer and the make-up layers (sg351/1, 343/2). The remaining groups produced no diagnostic material.

Some disturbance of the underlying stratigraphy is suggested, with a number of links/joins between the make-up layers of Phase 5G (sg359/4) and sub-group 338/2. A single join was also noted between sg338/1 and sg367/1 (Phase 6A). Breakage rates and ASW clearly distinguish the larger phase groups. The pit (sg354/1) incorporates the most intact material, with both a high ASW (19.9g) and low BRK (32.5). Make-up layers (sg338/1-2 and 353/1 appear of similar character (BRK 51.5, 47.4). Sub-group 353/1 has both a low ASW (4.8g) and a high BRK (466.7). Together they provide strong support for the interpretation of the layers as a cultivation horizon.

As mentioned the make-up layers sg338/1-2) formed the largest element of the phase assemblage (285 sherds/6123g). GW and BB1 vessels comprise the bulk of the sub-group, including the paint stained wide-mouthed bowl (fig. 74.256) mentioned above (Phase 5G), and an unusual GW 'Caistor-box' (fig. 74.258). BB1 everted rim jars (cf. Gillam Type 146, fig. 74.259) and flange and bead dishes (Gillam Type 228, fig. 76.260, 261) suggest a *TPQ* for the group's deposition perhaps as late as the early 4th cent. AD.

The limited range of colour-coat vessels, with a beaded funnel mouthed beaker (C11, Howe *et al* 1980, fig.5, 52) perhaps the latest form, and the absence of late calcite-gritted wares suggests the formation of the assemblage was completed by the early to mid 4th cent. AD. The rims of five Mancetter/Hartshill mortaria were present among the backfill, Hartley (in archive) dates three (Gillam Type 284) from the mid-3rd to early 4th cent. AD, with the final pair of 3rd century date. The high percentage of samian wares (15.6% by weight) and the recovery of 1st and 2nd cent. AD coarse ware forms and fabrics (GT5/6, fig. 74.257) clearly indicate the residual content of some of the group.

A shallow, probably truncated, pit sg354/1 cuts into the levelling layers (sg338/1-2). The assemblage is of a similar character to the underlying material, and cannot be separated chronologically. The BB1 groove rim dish (Gillam Type 227, fig. 76.263) appears a late, near flanged example. Residual material is again present, including a fragment of South Gaulish samian.

The fragmentary collection recovered from the cultivation horizon (sg353/1) incorporates a broader range of colour-coats than the preceding phases, including a Drag 31 derived bowl (C2, Howe *et al* 1980, fig.7, 80) and a sherd of Oxfordshire (C13) colour-coat, provides a *TPQ* for their accumulation (early to mid-4th cent. AD).

Illustrations: figs. 74.256-259; 76.260-263

DISCUSSION OF THE POTTERY FROM PHASE 5. (Phases: 5A-5C, 5D, 5E-5H).

Assemblage: 12246 sherds, 225.5kg., 159.30EVEs.

The samian assemblage includes stamped and decorated vessels of late Antonine date, products of the Central Gaulish industries, as well as vessels of the Rheinzabern kilns, suggesting samian importation possibly as late as the mid-3rd century. A wide range of regional and continental fine ware includes colour-coats from the Nene Valley and Oxfordshire industries, complemented by probably residual 'Rhenish' vessels of both Central Gaulish and Trier manufacture. As with the preceding phase assemblage the proportion of 'fine' table wares increase specifically in the form of products of the Lower Nene Valley industries. However, the appearance of the colour-coat variant of the Drag 38 bowl, represents perhaps the latest element.

As with the fine wares the composition of the Phase 5 coarse ware assemblage can be closely compared to the preceding phase assemblage. The significant change from the earlier deposits include the introduction of a range of regional imported coarse wares all of which indicate a *TPQ* for deposition of the assemblage during the late 3rd or early 4th century.

BB1 and grey wares continue to dominate the coarse ware assemblage. BB1 forms *c.*18% of the coarse ware assemblage and in Phases 5E and 5H continuing to challenge the ubiquity of the local GW's. Dishes of all the main utilitarian forms are chiefly the products of the BB1 kilns (*c.*75% of the dish assemblage). The GW forms also demonstrate a stable repertoire, necked jars and wide-mouthed bowls dominate. Long-distance regional and provincial imports as exemplified in the ceramic record also shows evidence of continuity. The range of fabrics present replicates those referred to in the Phase 4 discussion.

Table 27: *Proportions of Roman pottery fabrics from selected phases (EVES)*

FABRICS	5E EVEs/ %	5F EVEs/ %	5G EVEs/ %	5H EVEs/ %
Samian	3.09/12.6	5.04/11.3	6.58/12.3	2.94/22.1
Fine Wares	1.50/ 6.1	1.04/ 2.3	3.76/ 7.1	1.44/10.8
Amphorae	– / –	0.51/ 1.1	0.93/ 1.7	0.24/ 1.8
Mortaria	1.84/ 7.5	2.50/ 5.6	3.93/ 7.4	0.44/ 3.3
Local CW	9.15/37.2	23.99/54.0	26.63/49.9	4.29/32.3
Import CW	9.04/36.7	11.37/25.6	11.50/21.6	3.95/29.7
TOTAL:	24.61/ %	44.45/ %	53.33/ %	13.30/ %

Illustrations: figs. 70.167-183; 71.184-202; 72.203-220; 73.221-240; 74.241-249, 251-259, 75.250, 76.260-263.

PHASE 6

Area 3

Phase 6A (Sub-groups: 336/1, 338/3, 342/1-2, 343/1, 344/1, 348/1, 367/1).

Assemblage: 2832 sherds, 56.13kg., 57.52 EVEs, ASW: 20.6g.

The phase comprises three elements; first, a sequence of layers forming a surface over the cultivation and occupation of Phase 5H (sgs336/1, 338/3, 343/1 and 348/1). Second, a number of pits cut into the surface (sgs.341/1, 342/1-2 and 344/1), however, none yielded much material possibly suggesting a non-refuse function, and finally a make-up layer (sg367/1) laid over the pitting.

Of the initial make-up layers sgs336/1 and 338/3 incorporated sizeable assemblages, while the remaining sub-groups produced only 58 sherds/681g. ASW's are high for the former sub-groups (34.3, 24.4g) with sg338/3 producing the more intact material (BRK: 32.2). The subsequent make-up (sg367/1) formed the bulk of the phase assemblage (1596 sherds/24102g), however, its ASW and brokenness (respectively 16.2g and 99.0) suggest a less intact, and probably more disturbed assemblage than the earlier elements (sg336/1 and 338/3). Links and joins were noted between sg338/3 and 339/6 (in Phase 5F), and within the phase between sg336/1 and 367/1.

The presence of residual material among the groups is indicated in part by the occurrence of samian wares among all the major sub-groups. Stamped vessels include the work of a number of East Gaulish potters (Dickinson above, no. 119 & 121) datable to as late as the early to mid-3rd cent. AD. However, earlier 1st and 2nd cent. AD material is present suggesting some disturbance of the earlier stratigraphy.

The GW and BB1 components together represent more than half of the ceramic assemblage of both sgs336/1 and 338/3. The former predominantly provides necked and wide-mouthed jars and bowl/jars (fig. 77.278, 279), the latter cooking jars and (Gillam Type 145/6) and dishes (fig. 77.283,

Table 28: EVE's by ware and vessel class for Phase 6

Fabric	Form	Flagon	Flask	Jar	Bowl/Jar	Bowl	Dish	Platter	Cup	Beaker	Lid	Amphora	Mortarium	EVEs	SHD	WGT
SAMIAN						3.37	0.55	0.09	2.17				0.20	6.38	205	4080
C		1.63	0.12	0.49		0.64	0.98			5.78	0.50			10.14	689	6180
MFW														0.00	1	16
MO													6.76	6.76	113	7060
AM												0.56		0.56	67	3817
WW		0.46		0.37		0.25								1.08	99	1004
WS						0.06								0.06	5	70
OW				0.06		0.17				0.67				0.90	47	729
GW		1.00	0.24	10.27	0.96	3.54	3.38			0.65				20.04	1035	20075
BB1				8.13			12.75							20.88	897	15065
RBCI				0.92	0.70		0.16							1.62	64	1115
CG1				2.46			0.13							2.59	173	6670
GT1-4														0.00	7	286
Misc Nat.														0.00	0	0
Misc Trn.														0.00	0	0
Grand Total:		3.09	0.36	22.70	1.66	8.03	17.95	0.09	2.17	7.10	0.50	0.56	6.96	71.01	3402	66167
Percent (EVEs):		4.35	0.51	31.97	2.34	11.31	25.28	0.13	3.06	10.00	0.70	0.79	9.80	100.00		

	EVEs(%)	SHD(%)	WGT(%)
SAM	8.98	6.03	6.17
C	14.28	20.25	9.34
MFW	0.00	0.03	0.02
MO	9.52	3.32	10.67
AM	0.79	1.97	5.77
WW	1.52	2.91	1.52
WS	0.08	0.15	0.11
OW	1.27	1.38	1.10
GW	28.22	30.42	30.34
BB1	29.40	26.37	22.77
RBCI	2.28	1.88	1.69
CG1	3.65	5.09	10.08
GT1-4	0.00	0.21	0.43
Misc Ntv	0.00	0.00	0.00
Misc Trn	0.00	0.00	0.00

A1-1991 Phase 6

Legend: ■ EVEs(%) □ SHD(%) □ WGT(%)

Y-axis — Percentage: 35.00, 30.00, 25.00, 20.00, 15.00, 10.00, 5.00, 0.00

X-axis categories: SAM, C, MFW, MO, AM, WW, WS, OW, GW, BB1, RBCI, CG1, GT1-4, Misc Ntv, Misc Trn

284, 285). The range of later BB1 forms suggests deposition during the 4th cent. AD, with a GW Cam 306 (fig. 77.281) and bowl of Swanpool type D13-23 (Webster and Booth 1947; fig. 77.280) supporting the date.

The noticeably high proportion of colour-coats (*c*.10% by weight) can be compared to the final element of Phase 5H. However, the Phase 6A assemblage includes a considerably broader range of utilitarian forms, such as the flanged and plain rim dishes (Howe *et al* 1980, fig.7, 79, 87), as well as table wares (fig. 76.265). Oxfordshire colour-coats are again present including the Young Type C81 bowl (*c*.AD 300-400). The occurrence of this ware provides external dating for the assemblage; the fabric is uncommon in Leicester prior to the 4th cent. AD, suggesting a *TPQ* for the assemblage deposition during the early to mid-4th cent. AD.

Regional imports include mortaria from the Mancetter-Hartshill kilns dated by Hartley from the mid-3rd to mid-4th cent. AD. A single Oxfordshire vessel (Young Type C97/9) and a collared flagon in Much Hadham ware (OW9, fig. 76.270). However, the single pink-grogged sherd (GT3a), Nene Valley grey wares (GW4/7, fig. 77.282) and Derbyshire ware (DS) represent industries or products on the wane during the 4th cent. AD. Martin (forthcoming) has suggested Derbyshire ware ceased volume production during the mid-4th cent. AD, citing its absence from a mid to late 4th century group from Carsington, Derbyshire.

The final make-up (sg367/1) shares many of the characteristics of the preceding sub-groups, the dominance of GW, BB1 and colour-coats and their range of forms. Many of the fabrics are common to both sub-groups, including an Oxfordshire colour-coat (C13) and Much Hadham ware (OW9). However, sg367/1 provides the first identifiable lower Nene Valley mortarium (MO6, fig. 76.273). Hartley suggests a broad date range, mid-3rd to the later 4th cent. AD.

However, the most distinctive contrast between the two make-up layers is the considerably greater proportion of calcite-gritted ware among the later (sg367/1) deposits (16.7% vs. 6.2%, sg338/3), including late Roman calcite-gritted forms. The latter suggests the continued accumulation of material well into the second half of the 4th cent. AD. BB1 is well represented including a range of late forms (Gillam Type 145/6, 228 and 329). The high percentage indicates the success of the ware, perhaps suggesting a rise in its use during the early to mid-4th cent. AD, perhaps at the expense of the local GW industry.

Continental imports are limited to Central Gaulish colour-coats (C12CG/T) and samian wares, all certainly residual by the 4th cent. AD. Amphorae represent the only indicators of contemporary late Roman trade. Phase 6A witnesses the appearance in Area 3 of AM2b, a single sherd was recovered from the backfill of the Area 1 stone lined well (F246, G166, Phase 5C); Williams (above) has suggested the form is probably of eastern Mediterranean origin. A single body sherd of AM20, tentatively identified as from the Chalk 6 type amphora (Peacock and Williams 1986, Class 50), supports deposition of the make-up layers (sg338/3) during the later 4th century AD.

Illustrations: figs. 76.264-277; 77.278-286.

Phase 6B (Sub-groups: 335/1, 340/1, 363/1, 365/1, 366/1).

Assemblage: 579 sherds, 10032g, 13.49 EVEs, ASW: 17.1g.

Only two sub-groups produced assemblages of any size, the hearth and post holes (sg363/1; 87sh/2273g), and the make-up layers (sg340/1 and 365/1; 476sh/7506g). A pit (sg335/1) and final surface (sg366/1) produced small, undiagnostic groups. The ASW is high for the hearth (23.3g) with a low breakage rate (46.3), this contrasts with the considerably lower ASW for

the make-up (sg340/1, 15.8g). The low breakage rate (49.9) of the latter suggest both the hearth and make-up layers saw little post-depositional reworking, with the hearth comprising a particularly intact assemblage. No links and joins were noted among the phase assemblage.

The two phase sub-groups are very different in composition; the high BB1 and GW proportions (27.2%:25.6% by weight) of the hearth assemblage, comparable to the preceding Phase 6A assemblage, give way to the dominant GW component of sub-groups 340/1 and 365/1 (12.3%:42.8% by weight). The coarse ware assemblage incorporates a number of late forms, including a small BB1 jar and dish (fig. 78.301, 302), the high bead of the latter appears distinctive of the latest BB1 forms from Causeway Lane. Much of the GW assemblage of sub-group 340/1, can be paralleled among the Swanpool repertoire and clearly duplicates the BB1 role (Webster & Booth 1947); notably the ubiquitous GW 'dog-dish' (Swanpool Type E2-7; Gillam Type 330), a form virtually monopolised by BB1 from its inception during the later 2nd century. Other GW forms include bead and flange dishes (fig. 78.300) and cooking jars (fig. 77.296). New forms include the double lid-seated jar typical of late assemblages at Lincoln (Darling 1977, fig. 77.296). The form is a rare feature of Leicester groups with examples known from Norfolk Street and the 'Temple', both late assemblages. The hearth (sg363/1) includes a second unusual GW form, a slack shouldered, necked jar with rouletted decoration (fig. 77.289). The vessel has not been paralleled among late assemblages outside Causeway Lane, with a single vessel from Phase 5G (fig. 74.251) providing a comparison.

The sub-groups share relatively high levels of calcite-gritted wares (7.0%:8.4% by weight), including characteristic late Roman calcite-gritted types such as the flanged dish (fig. 78.305; Brown 1994, fig.28, 134) and increasingly common, the everted rim jar. The decline in BB1 jars noted among the make-up layers is compensated for or by a corresponding increase in the proportion of CG1b vessels. The latter, with the characteristic drooping triangular rim, appears to represent the main jar form produced at Harrold during the later 4th century (*ibid.*, 105).

The colour-coats, again chiefly lower Nene Valley products, continue to diversify in range. Beakers remain the most common vessel class (Howe *et al* 1980, figs. 4-5, 42, 50, 55), with bowls in various samian derived forms (Drag 38, 31, 37). The appearance of jars and dishes among the Phase 6A assemblage continues and strengthens, the plain rim dish (*ibid.*, fig.7, 87) may in part be filling the gap left by the BB1 form in the latter part of the 4th cent. AD. A notable absentee among the late colour coats is Oxfordshire ware; a single white-slipped mortarium (fig. 77.292) represents the only apparent representative of this late industry. The absence of products of the Oxfordshire kilns among this late assemblage may perhaps indicate an association between the supply of that ware and BB1 to *Ratae*. Oxfordshire fabrics never form a particularly large element of the Leicester assemblage, and their appearance at all may relate to the industry's proximity to an already established ceramic route. The collapse of the BB1 trade during the late 4th century may make organised trade to *Ratae* no longer economically viable.

The specialist and traded wares include a range of late mortaria including an Oxfordshire vessel as mentioned above, and complimentary lower Nene valley and Mancetter products (figs.77.290-1, 293-4; 78.306). A small quantity of regionally traded wares are dominated by fragments of probably a single Much Hadham flagon (OW9), with pink-grogged ware also represented. Imports include 'Rhenish' wares, probably residual, although possible 4th century products of the Trier kilns have been noted among the post-Roman material (fig. 78.313). Small quantities of amphorae mainly Spanish (AM9a/b) and Gaulish fabrics (AM12/3) were also recovered.

The Phase 6B assemblage appears to represents the at least one strand of the late 4th century ceramic tradition at Leicester. The relatively small body of evidence cannot pretend to address all the questions to be asked of the material, and further evidence will highlight gaps in the current record. However, the pottery clearly demonstrates the late 4th century date of both subgroups and suggests a *TPQ* for the make-up layers of the last quarter of the century.

Illustrations: figs. 77.287-299; 78.300-307.

DISCUSSION OF THE POTTERY FROM PHASE 6 (Phases: 6A, 6B).

Assemblage: 3402 sherds, 66.2kg., 71.01EVEs, ASW: 19.4g.

High ASW's (19.4g) and low breakage rates (51.6) indicate limited post-deposition disturbance of the Phase 6 levels. Elements from the latest Area 1 (Phase 4A, 5D) and 2 (3G, sg207/1) phases also demonstrate good levels of preservation, and suggest relatively slight post-Roman disturbance of the surviving stratigraphy.

The dwindling proportion of samian ware present within the phase groups (6A: 6.27%; 6B: 5.58%) indicates a level of residuality, although curation of the samian assemblage cannot be discounted.

Phase 6 is dominated by coarse wares probably of local manufacture, incorporating a range of vessels broadly similar to those evident among the preceding Phase 4 and 5 assemblages. Many of the grey and oxidised wares can be paralleled by products of the industry typified by the Swanpool (Lincolnshire) kiln (Webster & Booth 1947); notably wide-mouthed bowls, plain and flanged and in-turned dishes. The presence of the double-lid seated jar (fig. 77.296) may suggest association with the ceramic traditions of Lincolnshire and the north-east (Todd 1968; Darling 1977). However, the occurrence of coarse ware forms not paralleled at Swanpool, including necked and slack shouldered jars (fig. 77.289) and the 'Cam 306' type bowls (fig. 77.281), suggest the Leicester assemblage embraces a wide range of influences. The jar form has not been paralleled outside Causeway Lane. However, the bowl is more widely known and includes both parallels among late assemblages at Leicester, and other sites from as far afield as Colchester, New Fresh Wharf, London (Richardson 1986) and Towcester (Woodfield 1983).

The diversity of sources is indicated by the importance of regionally traded coarse wares. The most significant of which are the late Roman calcite-gritted wares (CG1b), probably products of the Harrold kilns, Bedfordshire. The Causeway Lane assemblage appears to incorporate only a small proportion of the forms exported from Harrold, with the cooking jar the major element. The increasing proportion of CG1b jars present in the phase assemblages, comprising c.10% of the Phase 6A jars, and c.16% of 6B demonstrates the importance of this ware. The success of the Late Roman calcite-gritted wares may be indicated by the duplication of the classic drooping or undercut everted rim by vessels produced in other, probably local fabrics, notably the oxidised jar (fig. 77.295).

BB1 also remains a significant element of the phase assemblage, comprising approximately a quarter of the pottery. However, it is noticeable that Phase 6B see a distinct drop in the proportion of BB1 present with the fabric comprising only c.12.3% (by weight) of the final make-up (sg340/1). The diversity of other coarse wares (GW, CG1b and OW) may suggest the replacement of BB1 by other fabrics. This decline may correspond with the postulated downturn in the supply and production of BB1 datable to the second half of the 4th

century (Holbrook and Bidwell 1991, 94), and thus suggests the closing date for the Phase 6 assemblage dates to the latter half of the 4th cent. AD.

The importance of colour-coat vessels becomes increasingly apparent by Phase 6, representing c.9-10% (by weight) of the ceramic assemblage, a proportion perhaps underestimating the significance of the ware. An examination of the EVEs percentages, clearly shows the growing popularity of the colour-coated kitchen ware forms. The earlier Phase 4 and 5 assemblages had seen a range of 'table wares' produced in colour-coat fabrics, these include beakers, bowls and the occasional flagon. However, both Phases 6A and 6B see the introduction of dish and jar forms; the former provides both plain rim and flanged bowls, and comprises c.5.0% (by EVEs) of the dishes from both phases. The jar class consists of mainly wide-mouthed forms (Howe *et al* 1980, fig.7, 75-7), although body sherds suggest the presence of narrow-mouthed vessels. Jars form c.1.5% of the Phase 6A class assemblage, a figure that rises to c.5.0% by Phase 6B, an increase that suggests the rapid introduction of the class and its immediate popularity. Bowls of various forms, notably the 'Drag 38' vessel, also witness a rapid rise in the latter phase, forming 19.4% of the assemblage.

The absence of Oxfordshire colour-coats (C10, C13) from 6B is unexplained, the wares are known in both Phase 6A and from post-Roman deposits. It seem likely that although Oxfordshire products are known from late 3rd and 4th century deposits at Leicester, the city falls outside the industry's main markets.

The Mancetter-Hartshill industry, the major suppliers of mortaria to Leicester during proceeding phases, also appears to experience late competition from the Lower Nene Valley potteries. This may indicate either the waning of the former industry during the later 4th century, or the growing strength of the latter. Hartley (1973, 42) has indicated the Mancetter-Hartshill industry, dominant producers of mortaria from the early 2nd century, may have been in decline during the later 4th cent. AD. This is perhaps supported by the apparently limited importance of mortaria production to the lower Nene Valley potteries, despite which Phase 6B includes at least three separate vessels (figs.77.293-4; 78.306). In contrast to the lack of Oxfordshire colour-coats, mortaria are present in both phases suggesting the product had a wider distribution.

The less common regional traded wares are dominated by Much Hadham ware (OW9), a feature of both phases. The range of forms represented are limited with body sherds indicating closed forms, probably flagons. This would concur with earlier phase assemblages. It is interesting to note the absence of Derbyshire ware form the 6B assemblage, although present among the 6A and Phase 5 assemblages. Both Birss (1986, 10) and Martin (forthcoming) comment that the industry appears to have collapsed by the later 4th cent. AD.

The phase sees relatively low proportion of imported wares. Trier 'Rhenish' colour-coats provide the only possibly 'contemporary' material identified with the exception of amphorae. Although Phase 6A incorporates a wide range of fabrics the presence of residual material is problematic. The presence of late forms including body sherds from the Chalk Type 6 amphora (cf. fig. 79.326) and ribbed sherds in apparently late fabrics, such as the micaceous AM2b and AM35, attests to *Ratae's* continued access to the late Roman sources of supply, and to the local demand for those products. It is interesting to note the continued presence of Gaulish (AM12/3) amphorae among the Phase 6 assemblage. However, the small proportion of amphora in Phase 6B contrasts with the diversity of sources in 6A, and may reflect the final waning of those continental associations.

Illustrations: fig.76.264-277; 77.278-298; 78.299-307.

DISCUSSION OF THE LATE ROMAN ASSEMBLAGES.   *Richard Clark*

The late Roman coarse ware assemblage recovered at Causeway Lane embraces a wide range of differing influences reflecting the geographical situation of the city at the heart of the Roman province. The diversity of forms available to the pottery purchaser during the 1st and 2nd century AD (Phases 1-3) is reduced to a repertoire based upon functionality and versatility. BB1 cooking pots, bowls and dishes, the ubiquitous wide-mouthed jar, calcite-gritted ware jars and the occasional Lower Nene Valley indented beaker form the key elements of the later assemblage.

The predominant theme of the later ceramic phases (4-6) at Causeway Lane is formed by the growing importance of BB1, apparently at the expense of the local GW suppliers. However, initial competition appears to evolve into co-existence, the GW industry becoming increasingly complementary in terms of its repertoire of forms. The development of specialised forms can be paralleled throughout the Midlands, and has been discussed by Todd (1968). Comparison with pottery published from the Swanpool kiln provides clear parallels both in terms of form and technique. Wide-mouthed jar and bowl forms, often elaborately burnished and occasionally self-slipped, coupled with plain and flanged dish forms provide much of the assemblage. However, as Todd (1973, 124) has noted the Leicester assemblage incorporates wares and types peculiar to that locality. It is likely that the city and its hinterland used both fine and coarse pottery that had close affinities with contemporary ceramics to the south and south-east rather than material from north Lincolnshire. The presence of forms typologically similar to the products of the Lincolnshire and south Yorkshire appear to represent 'outliers' rather than deliberate supply or trade.

The marked contrast between the coarse ware assemblages of Leicester and Lincoln is exemplified by the near absence at Leicester of the typical 'double-lid seated' jars so prevalent in the late assemblage from The Park, Lincoln. Leicester is very much on the fringes of the region described by Darling (1977, 28) as characterised by its use of lid-seated jars. Although both a 'Dales ware' type (fig. 79.321) and the 'double lid seated jars' (fig. 77.296; Swanpool Type H) were recovered from Causeway Lane.

The presence of ledge-rim or lid-seated vessels among the Leicester ceramic repertoire (fig. 69.158-160) appears to represent a clear break with the Swanpool range. No clear inspiration for this form is apparent, although the variety of CG1 ledge-rim jars (Brown 1994, fig.27, 106) and the appearance of Derbyshire ware vessels may have led to some demand for the type. Clear parallels can be drawn with the Ravenstone kiln, in north-west Leicestershire, and suggest the majority of lid-seated vessels are probably of local manufacture.

A number of rim, body and base sherds from the 'Cam 306' type bowl, an open, plain or slightly bead rimmed bowls, with a narrow and slightly splayed base, were recovered from late groups at Causeway Lane (Phase 3G; Phases 5D, 5E & 5G; Phase 6, Phases: 6A-6B). The form seems primarily functional, with turning marks apparent on the interior, and the bases cut roughly from the wheel, leaving a characteristic 'cheese-wire' mark. The vessels are generally produced in an oxidised coarse sandy fabric (OW3, fig.69.150; 71.195; 199); however, a minority are reduced (GW5, fig. 72.192), although there seems no variation in fabric or finish.

The bowl has been recovered from a number of sites in Leicester, notably the Forum (A302 & 295, Group III, 138, 150, 151), Norfolk Street villa (A287.1975, Phase 4C, 177),

the 'Temple' well (A164.1969, 81) and most recently Little Lane (A39.1989, Phase 6.3). In all bar the last case the assemblages have been ascribed a late Roman date. At Norfolk Street the vessel is accompanied by BB1 forms including the Gillam Type 147 jar and a probable Nene Valley beaker unlikely to predate the 3rd cent. AD (Howe *et al* 1980 fig.5, 50). The 'Temple' group remains the largest (20.26 EVEs) well stratified 3rd cent. AD assemblage from Leicester. The limited apparent residuality adds to the significance of the group, with an overall date range covering the 3rd cent. AD. The range of BB1 forms (Gillam Type 146, 148, 227) and various utilitarian colour-coats (jars, bowls and jugs) suggest a date of deposition during the later 3rd cent. AD.

The earliest example was recovered from the Little Lane site, among the backfill of the cellar (F186). Pollard (forthcoming d) argues for a mid-2nd cent. AD date for the bulk of these deposits, with deposition c.AD180. However, the occurrence of some later material may indicate some intrusion or disturbance.

Beyond Leicester, the 'Cam 306', regarded by Hull (1958, 228) to date from c.AD 175, has been supported by the recovery of securely stratified examples from New Fresh Wharf, London, and there dated to the late 2nd to 3rd cent. AD (Richardson 1986, 128, 1.201). However, the form appears to have remained current in London throughout the 3rd cent. AD, and is apparently in production at Southwark during the later part of the century (Yule 1982). This extended life is further supported by Hammerson (1988, 212-213) who dates a deposit at the District Heating Scheme, Southwark, (containing 51 rims and 5 bases) to the end of the 3rd cent. AD.

It is interesting to note the occurrence of a similar bowl in the Rhineland (Fulford 1975, 177 and fig.1, 6-8), and there dated to the late 3rd to 4th cent. AD. Gose (1950, fig.47, 491-93) illustrates a number of these vessels, several of which are directly comparable, morphologically, to the Causeway Lane pieces.

The 4th century, or perhaps the late 3rd, shows the growing importance of a range of regional ceramic industries, and specialist suppliers. The arrival of small quantities of Oxfordshire colour-coats, to accompany mortaria of the same industry, the more typical products of the Lower Nene Valley and the occasional Much Hadham vessel, provide an example of these regional industries. Neither the Oxfordshire nor Hadham supplies represent a significant proportion of the late assemblage (respectively c.0.25%, and c.1.0% by weight), however, their presence reinforces the image of a healthy trade network linking Leicester to the south Midlands and south-east.

The importance of these regional trade connections is best exemplified among the coarse wares. By the late 4th century non-local coarse wares also indicate the southerly bias of the Leicester ceramic assemblage. It appears that the later 4th century saw the apogee of production at Harrold, Bedfordshire (Brown 1994, 105), with the rise in the proportion and variety of calcite-gritted wares among the Phase 5 and 6 assemblages at Causeway Lane probably directly attributable to the success of that industry. Other sources are possible, and indeed likely, some of the forms identified at Causeway Lane cannot be paralleled among Harrold products (fig. 70.166). However, the Harrold kilns appear to supply the major element of the late Roman calcite-gritted wares. The major form represented is the cooking/storage jars, with plain everted or undercut, triangular rims (Brown 1994, fig.34, 243; fig.37, 310). With flanged bowls appearing only in the final phase (6B).

The strength of the Lower Nene Valley industry is exemplified by its domination of the colour-coat trade, producing table and kitchen wares, as well as mortaria. The appearance of coarse ware forms in colour-coat fabrics is regarded as a characteristic feature of the late Roman ceramic repertoire, and their production has been dated from the late 3rd to 4th century (Perrin 1981, 447f). Although the Phase 6 assemblage at Causeway Lane witness an increase in the proportion of Nene Valley colour coats, with the fabric comprising *c.*10% of the final make-up layers from Area 3. The proportions do not reflect the levels expected during the last quarter of the 4th century. Colour-coats and other fine wares comprised over 20% of the assemblage at The Park, Lincoln (Late 4th cent. AD), *c.*25% of the assemblage at Carsington, Derbyshire (Birss 1986) and over 50% at Great Casterton (Perrin 1981, 449). The implication must be that the closing date for the ceramic composition of the Area 3 assemblage dates to not much later than the third quarter of the 4th century AD. Alternatively other sources of supply, probably greywares, are addressing the ceramic requirements of the population.

Specialist wares, notably the mortarium, also witness a diversification of sources. After *c.*AD 250 three potteries contribute mortaria to the Leicester assemblage, Mancetter-Hartshill, the Lower Nene Valley and the Oxfordshire kilns. Darling (1977, 23) speculates as to the dearth of mortaria among a late rubbish deposit at Lincoln, suggesting the use of 'Drag 38' type bowls to replace the mortaria. No such shortage is apparent at Causeway Lane, the class comprising *c.*10% by weight of the assemblage throughout.

Amphorae provide the main indicator of contemporary continental trade amongst the late Roman ceramic assemblage. Obviously, this remains dominated by the Baetican Dressel 20 (AM9a/b) olive oil amphora. However, significant quantities of Gaulish and Spanish wine amphorae (AM12/3, AM7) mark out the assemblage. The appearance of the micaceous AM2b among Phase 5 and 6 contexts, probably of eastern Mediterranean origin (Williams, above p.00), and AM20/35, tentatively identified as from the Chalk 6 type amphora (Peacock and Williams 1986, Class 50), attests to *Ratae's* continued access to the late Roman sources of supply, and to the local demand for those products. However, the small proportion of amphora in Phase 6B contrasts with the diversity of sources in 6A, and may reflect the final waning of those continental associations.

CATALOGUE OF ILLUSTRATIONS.

Editorial Notes

The catalogue is arranged by phase and area for the Roman phases, the post-Roman phases do not follow phase order.

Each catalogue entry description is followed by the stratigraphic information relating to it, and comprises the Leicester City Museums extension number, the context number, feature number (where applicable), and subgroup number, in addition, the post-Roman phases also show the phase number.

PHASE 1

Phase 1A fig. 61

1. GW10 Ledge rim jar (LAU Form: 3E1), opposed burnished lines defined by cordons, forming a herring-bone pattern. Cf. Woods 1972, fig.24, 176-7; Marney 1989, fig.31, 26, 28-9. 14421+14427, (1460)+(1461), sg180/1+177/1.

Phase 1B

2. OW6 Waisted beaker (LAU Form: 9B1), rouletted. Cf. Colchester (Cam 85c, 397), rouletted and roughcast examples have been recovered among kiln material (Hull 1963, fig. 57, 8). Hull suggested Cam 85c developed from the Gallo-Belgic girth-beaker, and may date to as early as the Claudian period (Hawkes and Hull, 1947). Vessels of similar form have also been identified on

the continent (Anderson, 1980, fig.8, 4) dated to the second cent. AD. Although both the Cam 397 and the continental examples share the globular, waisted profile of the Causeway Lane vessels, the beaded rim of the latter suggest the earlier, possibly Claudian, Cam 85c than the second cent. AD date attributed to the latter (Hull 1963, 105). 16054+16009, (1889)+(1786), sg130/1+132/1.

3. MC3 Platter (LAU Form: 7A3), burnished int. and ext. with a cordon at the interior basal angle. Reddish yellow (5YR6/6) surfaces with a dark grey (10YR4/1) core. Cf. Marsh & Tyers 1978, fig.242, V.A. 15955+18529, (1740)+(1756), sg130/4.

Phase 1C

4. WW4 Bead rimmed flagon (LAU Form: 1F2). 12071, (2928), sg208/1.

5. GW5 Neckless ledge rim jar (LAU Form: 3D1). 12173, (2928), sg208/1.

6. GW5 Necked jar (LAU Form: 3M2). 11997, (2964), sg208/1.

7. GW5 Necked jar (LAU Form: 3M1), burnished neck and body. 12173, (2928), sg208/1.

8. SW2 Grooved butt-beaker (LAU Form: 9A3), fine combed decoration defined by cordon above, and groove below zone. Burnished spiral on lower half of body. Black exterior and very dark grey interior surfaces. Comparable to vessels from the Verulamium King Harry Lane site (Stead & Rigby 1989, fig.61, 6R12), the plain rim suggests a mid-1st cent. AD date. Pollard 1994, fig.53, 47. 12061+18452+18450+18453, (2974)+(2967)+(2928), sg208/1.

PHASE 2

Area 1

Phase 2A

9. GW5 Carinated bowl (LAU Form: 5D2). 16010, (1786), sg132/1.

10. GW5 Platter (LAU Form: 7E1) Cam 32c. Everted rim with fine combed lines around interior. 15974+16217, (1752)+(1757), sg132/1+135/1.

11. GT1 Necked storage jar (LAU Form: 3M2), incised oblique linear motif around shoulder. Probably coil built. 15976, (1752), sg132/1.

12. WW2 Flanged rim bowl (LAU Form: 5F3), grooved at interior of flange. Marsh & Tyers 1978, fig.240, IV.A.1. 16042+16022, (1873)+(1853), sg133/1.

13. GW5 Ledge rim jar (LAU Form: 3E1). 16003, (1769), sg133/7.

14. GW10 Bowl (LAU Form: 5G3) with pronounced carination. Similar bowls have been recovered from the Brixworth kilns. Woods 1972, fig.12, 61-5; Pollard 1994, fig.54, 85. 15937, (1706), sg133/7.

15. WS2 Jar or bowl (LAU Type: 4B-), red paint at point of rim. 18630, (1688), sg134/1.

16. C21 Bowl (LAU Form: 5H2), cf. Ritt.12, a samian form unlikely to have been produced after *c.*AD 80 (Webster 1993a, 47). The fabric and distinctive range of forms have also been noted at Lincoln (Darling, 1984, 52). Drag.18 platter was identified at St. Nicholas Circle, Leicester (Pollard 1994, fig.50, 1). 18635, (1757), sg135/1.

17. GT1 Necked bowl (LAU Form: 5A2), burnish chevrons around shoulder, coil built. Pinkish grey (7.5YR6/2) to very dark grey surfaces. Parallels can be drawn from St. Nicholas Circle, Leicester (ibid. fig.52, 41, 42). The form appears to have had an extended life, with examples dated to the 2nd cent. AD at Towcester (Woodfield 1992, fig.8, 9). 16218, (1757), sg135/1.

18. GT6 Small ledge rim jar (LAU Form: 3D1). Fabric and form suggest 'native' precursor (Marney 1989, fig.35, 27). Marsh & Tyers (1978, fig.235, II.A.16) note ledge rims are typical feature of Essex region during 1st cent. AD. 18637, (1757), sg135/1.

19. MC2 Platter (LAU Form: 7D2), cf. Cam 28c. Reddish yellow (5YR6/8) to light brown (7.5YR6/4) surfaces. 16219, (1757), sg135/1.

Phase 2B

20. OW3 (LAU Form: 1C1) Ring-necked flagon, wide mouth and well defined moulding suggests early date (Marsh & Tyers 1978, fig.232, I.B.1). 14863, (1616), sg138/1.

21. GW2 Small necked jar (LAU Form: 3L1), cf. Kenyon 1948, Jewry Wall Necked jar Type C.9. 14864, (1616), sg138/1.

22. GW5 Bead rim jar (LAU Form: 3B3), incised horizontal lines below shoulder groove. 14864, (1616), sg138/1.

23. GW6 Platter (LAU Form: 7B2), cf. Cam 28a. Traces of radial decoration on interior. Exterior base wheel finished with groove at base/wall angle. 14864, (1616), sg138/1.

24. AM18 Rim and handle stub of rilled amphora, Cam 189 (Peacock & Williams 1986, Class 12). 17908+17914, (1632) + (1264), sg138/2 + 143/2.

25. OW3 Ring-necked flagon (LAU Form:1C1), cf. Kenyon 1948, Jewry Wall Ring-neck Jug Type A.1. 14899, (1632), sg138/2.

26. GW3 Ledge rim jar (LAU Form: 3D1). 14900+14619, (1632) +(1511), sg138/2+144/1.

27. GW3 Wide mouthed bowl (LAU Form: 5C1). Cf. Pollard 1994, fig.67, 291. 14925, (1646), sg138/2.

28. GW5 Ledge rim jar (LAU Form: 3D1) as 5. 14900, (1632), sg138/2.

29. GW5 Platter (LAU Form: 7A1), footring and moulding at base/wall angle suggest parallels with early Flavian Drag 18 (Webster 1993a, 31). 14900, (1632), sg138/2.

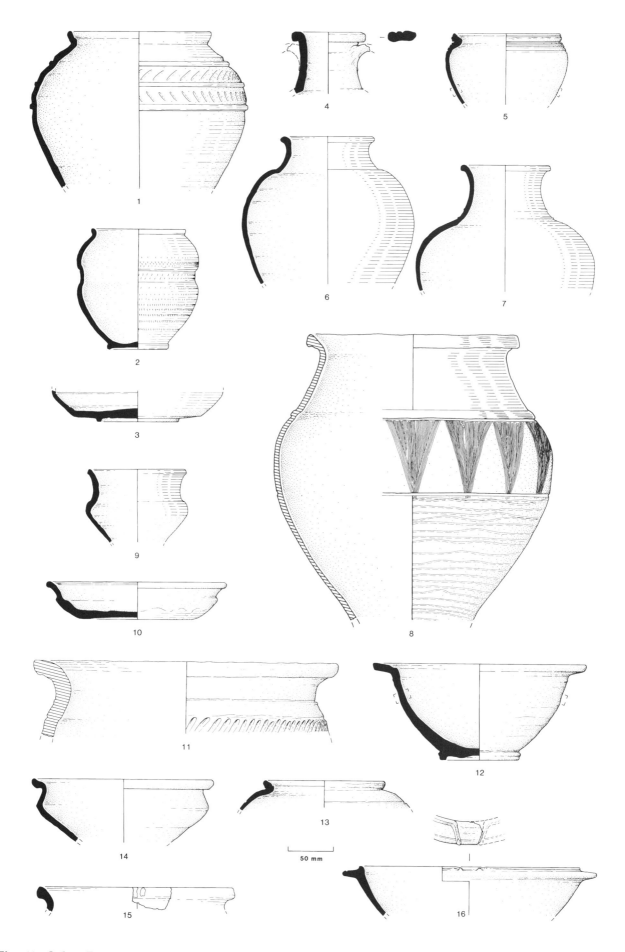

Fig. 61: *Other Roman pottery illustrations*

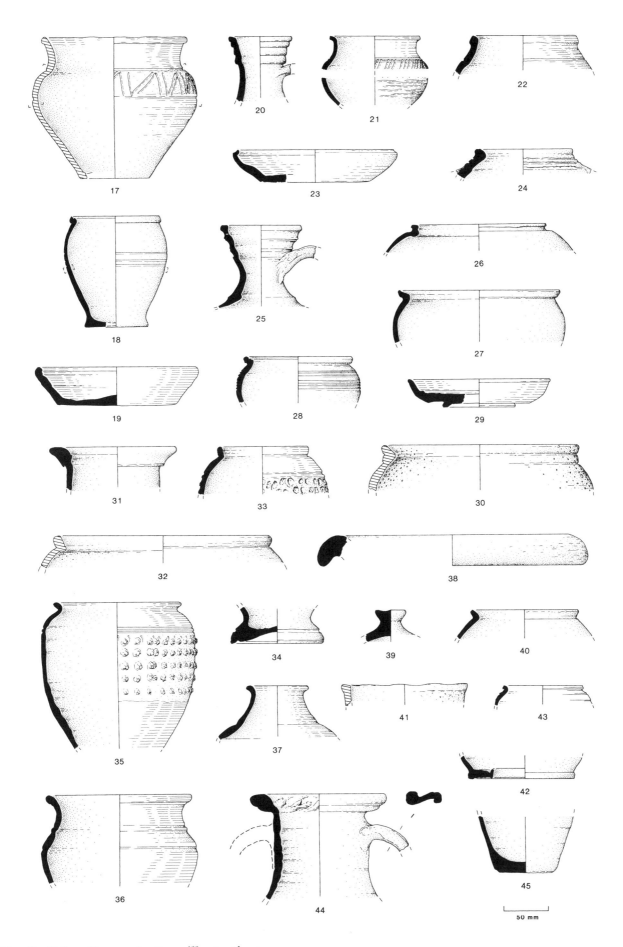

Fig. 62: *Other Roman pottery illustrations*

30. MG1 Bead rim jar (LAU Form: 3D2). Coil built and possibly wheel finished. Grey to dark grey surfaces. 14901, (1632), sg138/2.

Phase 2C

31. WW4 Collared flagon (LAU Form:1A3), probably a Verulamium product. 14149, (1309), sg140/1.

32. GT1 Ledge rim jar (LAU Form: 3E1), cf. Pollard 1994, fig 53, 52. Probably coil built. Reddish yellow (5YR6/6) to grey (5YR6/1) surfaces. 14191, (1324), sg140/1.

33. MC1 Everted rim jar (LAU Form: 3F1), pinched decoration, possibly attempting to copy rustication. Lower body burnished with vertical incised decoration below the pinched zone (body sherd not illustrated). 14199, (1330), sg140/1.

Phase 2D

34. GW3 Pedestal base (LAU Form: 3P1), an uncommon form in Leicester (Pollard 1994, fig.52, 45). 14772, (1587), sg144/1.

35. MG3 Everted rim jar (LAU Form: 3F2), large dot barbotine panel. 14699, (1552), sg144/1.

36. MG3 Necked bowl (LAU Form:5A2), as 17. 14623, (1511), sg144/1.

Phase 2E

37. GW3 Flask with everted rim (LAU Form: 2A2). 13580, (1059), sg147/1.

Phase 2F

38. MO17 Mortarium flange (Gillam Type 237, c.AD60-90), rilling or drag lines around top of flange. South-west England represents the most likely source, other examples are known from Leicester (Hartley 1993, in archive). 14436, (1470), sg145/1.

39. GW5 Lid handle (LAU Class: 10), burnished line around top of handle. 14400, (1454), sg145/1.

40. MG3 Bead rim jar (LAU Form: 3B2). 14452, (1470), sg145/1.

41. MC2 Plain rim jar (LAU Form: 3B1). Probably coil built, poorly fired and abraded. 14573, (1510), sg145/1.

42. WW4 An unusual jar base (LAU Class: 11), with what appears to be a central hole. The base, barring the effects of weathering and abrasion, seems well finished. A similar vessel was recorded at Usk by Webster (Webster 1993b, fig.135, 24), the latter has a narrow girth and has been described as a candlestick. 14432 + 14490, (1467), (1491), sg145/3.

43. C2 Globular bead rim beaker (LAU Form: 9B1) with finely rilled surface. Very pale brown (10YR8/3) fabric and patchy light reddish brown (5YR6/4) colour-coat suggest a Colchester provenance (Greene 1978, 26). The surface treatment may represent a fusion of 'native' and Roman traditions (Cam 93 and 84B); the technique also appears on a residual beaker in Phase 5C ((586), sg164/1). One of two possible Colchester products from the phase assemblage. The sand roughcasting and patchy dark greyish brown (10YR 4/2) colour-coat of the second vessel clearly emulates Lyon ware beaker forms (Greene 1979, 25, Type 20). 14171, (1316), sg145/6.

44. WW4 Flagon (LAU Form: 1G1), possibly two handled, a similar vessel was recovered from Flavian/Trajanic layers on the south range of the Forum, Leicester. 14238, (1355), sg146/1.

45. GW6 Jar base (LAU Class: 3). 14548, (1506), sg146/1.

46. CG1a Necked storage jar (LAU Form: 3M2). Fine horizontal combing around shoulder with coarse vertical scoring below, cf. Brown 1994, fig.22, 9. Coil built. 14062, (1273), sg146/1.

47. MO7 Burnt mortarium (Gillam Type 240) with the counterstamp of Albinus. (Stamp fig. 59.M1, Hartley above). 17721, (1481), sg148/3.

Phase 2G

48. LG1 Beaker (LAU Form: 9B2) with angular everted rim, edge of under glaze barbotine dot panel. Fine white paste and translucent glaze indicates Central Gaulish manufacture (Greene 1979, 90 & fig.42, 16). 11885, (1227), sg148/2.

49. AM8 Handle of Rhodian amphora, Cam 184 (Peacock & Williams 1986, Class 9). 17921, (1218), sg148/2.

50. OW Lid (LAU Form: 10A1), amphora stopper. 13942, (1218), sg148/2.

51. GW Everted rim jar (LAU Form: 3F1). 13943, (1218), sg148/2.

52. GW Necked jar (LAU Form: 3L1). 13943, (1218), sg148/2.

53. GW Necked bowl (LAU Form: 5C3). 14952, (1660), sg148/2.

54. GW3 Everted rim jar (LAU Form: 3F2). Burnished chevrons around shoulder with rusticated zone on upper body demarcated by grooves above and below zone. Variety of decorative motifs reminiscent of the products of the kiln at Great Holme street, Leicester. However, there is no evidence for production of rusticated vessels at Great Holme street (Pollard forthcoming b, 1). 13943, (1218), sg148/2.

55. GW3 Everted rim jar (LAU Form: 3F4), rusticated 'dashes' around body. 13943, (1218), sg148/2.

56. GW5 Small necked jar (LAU Form: 3L1), as 21 above. 13943, (1218), sg148/2.

57. GW5 Ledge rim jar (LAU Form: 3D1), combed decoration on shoulder. 13943, (1218), sg148/2.

58. GW9 Necked jar with lid seating (LAU Form: 3E1). 13943, (1218), sg148/2.

59. GW10 Bowl (LAU Form: 5E2), burnished vertical lines around waist.

Possibly derived from samian forms Drag 29 and 30. Kenyon 1948, fig.44, 24. 18783, (1227) + (1660), sg148/2.

60. GW10 Platter (LAU Form: 7A1). 18765, (1218), sg148/2.

61. CG1a Ledge rim jar (LAU Form: 3D1), cf. Brown 1994, fig.24, 35. 13944, (1218), sg148/2.

62. CG1a Ledge rim jar (LAU Form: 3D1), cf. Brown 1994, fig.24, 37. combed motif similar to calcite-gritted storage jars. 13944, (1218), sg148/2.

63. CG1a Ledge rim jar (LAU Form: 3D2), Brown 1994, fig.25, 44. 14953, (1660), sg148/2.

64. GT3a Seria rim (LAU Form: 3Q1), see 115, 196 below. 18782, (1218), sg148/2.

65. GT5/6 Everted rim jar (LAU Form: 3J1). 13945, (1218), sg148/2.

66. MC1 Everted rim jar (LAU Form: 3J1). 13946, (1218), sg148/2.

67. MG3 Everted rim jar (LAU Form:3G3). 14956, (1660), sg148/2.

68. MG3 Carinated beaker (LAU Form: 9J2). 14360, (1416), sg148/3.

Phase 2J

69. GT1 Necked storage jar (LAU Form: 3M2). 13978, (1223), sg172/3.

70. GT5/6 Platter (LAU Form: 7A1). 14322, (1408), sg178/1.

71. GT2 Bead rim jar (LAU Form: 3B4). 11133, (553), sg184/1.

Area 2

Phase 2K(i)

72. GT5/6 Everted rim jar with lid seating (LAU Form: 3E1). 18507, (2342), sg203/1.

73. GT5/6 Everted rim jar (LAU Form: 3E1). 18524, (2342), sg203/1.

Phase 2K(ii)

74. AM9a Rim sherd of Dressel 2-4 amphora (Peacock & Williams 1986, Class 10). 16182, (2932), sg201/1.

75. GW4/7 Everted rim jar (LAU Form: 3F3). 18467, (2942), sg201/1.

76. GW9 Flanged bowl (LAU Form: 5F4). 12220, (2942), sg201/1.

77. MG3 Flanged bowl (LAU Form: 5F4). 12249, (2978), sg201/2.

78. MO12 Mortarium (Gillam Type 242) stamped by G. Attius Marinus. (Stamp fig. 59.M2; Hartley above). 17708+17256+17705, (2914) + (2933) + (2150), sg202/3 + 210/1.

79. MO4 Mortarium (Gillam Type 254) with fragmentary stamp, potter unidentified. (Stamp fig. 59.M3; Hartley above). 17707, (2807), sg202/3.

80. AM7 Rim sherd of a Cam 186c amphora (Peacock & Williams 1986, Class 18). 12078, (2807), sg202/3.

81. OW2 Everted rim beaker (LAU Form:9B1). 12157, (2914), sg202/3.

82. GW3 Necked jar (LAU Form: 3M4). 12158, (2914), sg202/3.

83. GW6 Bead rim jar (LAU Form: 3B4), possibly a product of the early Alice Holt industry (M Lyne pers. com. 1992.). Cf. Lyne & Jefferies 1979, fig.15, Class 4.11. 12132, (2892), sg202/3.

84. GW6 Carinated and cordoned bowl (LAU Form: 5D2). 12158, (2914), sg202/3.

85. GW6 Bead rim dish (LAU Form: 6D1), cf. Gillam Type 307. 12158, (2914), sg202/3.

86. GW2 Lid (LAU Form: 10A5), an unusual form possibly a dish or platter. No sooting noted. 12082, (2807), sg202/3.

87. BB1 Everted rim jar (LAU Form: 3H1) cf. Gillam Type 125. 12160, (2914), sg202/3.

88. CG1a Ledge rim jar (LAU Form: 3E1) cf. Brown 1994, fig.24, 37. 12189, (2933), sg202/3.

89. MO7 Mortarium (Gillam Type 240) stamped by Albinus. (Stamp fig. 59.M4; Hartley above). 17709, (2987), sg204/2.

90. CG1a Bead rim jar (LAU Form: 3B3) cf. Brown 1994 fig.25, 47. 12267, (2997), sg204/2.

Area 3

Phase 2L

91. MO7 Mortarium (Gillam Type 240) stamped by Doinus. (Stamp fig. 59.M5; Hartley above). 17722, (3549), sg332/1.

92. MO7 Mortarium (Gillam Type 241). 15191, (3551), sg332/1.

93. WW2 Ring-necked flagon (LAU Form: 1C3). 15192, (3551), sg332/1.

94. OW2 Everted rim bowl/jar (LAU Form: 5A2). 15194, (3551), sg332/1.

95. GW3 Flask with everted rim (LAU Form: 2A2). 15189 + 18020, (3549) + (3551), sg332/1.

96. GW5 Jar (LAU Class: 3). 18021, (3551), sg332/1.

97. GW5 Carinated bowl (LAU Form: 5D1). 18021+18026, (3551) + (3549), sg332/1.

98. GW6 Ledge rim jar (LAU Form: 3E1). 15195, (3549), sg332/1.

99. GW10 Everted rim jar with lid seating (LAU Form: 3E1). 18019, (3551), sg332/1.

100. BB1 Flanged bowl (LAU Form: 6E2), grooved on upper surface of flange, cf. Holbrook & Bidwell 1991, fig.32, 52.1-2. 15198, (3551), sg332/1.

101. MG2 Jar (LAU Class: 3). 18024, (3551), sg332/1.

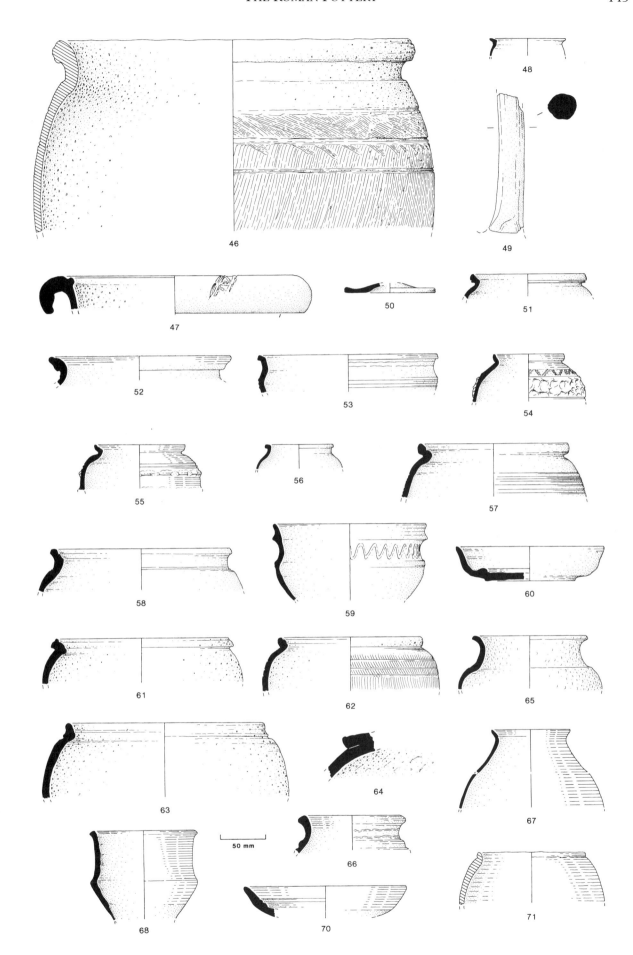

Fig. 63: *Other Roman pottery illustrations*

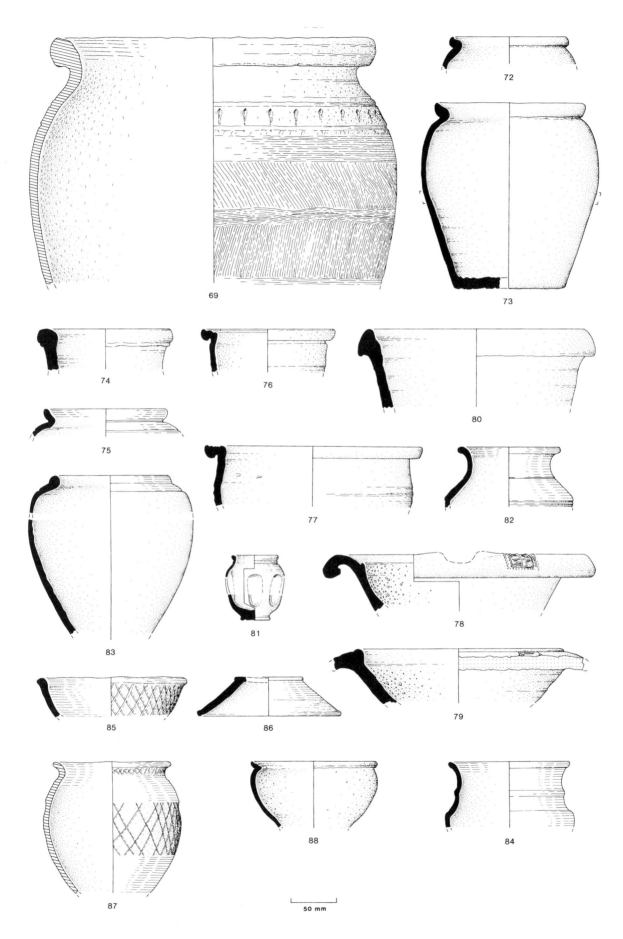

Fig. 64: *Other Roman pottery illustrations*

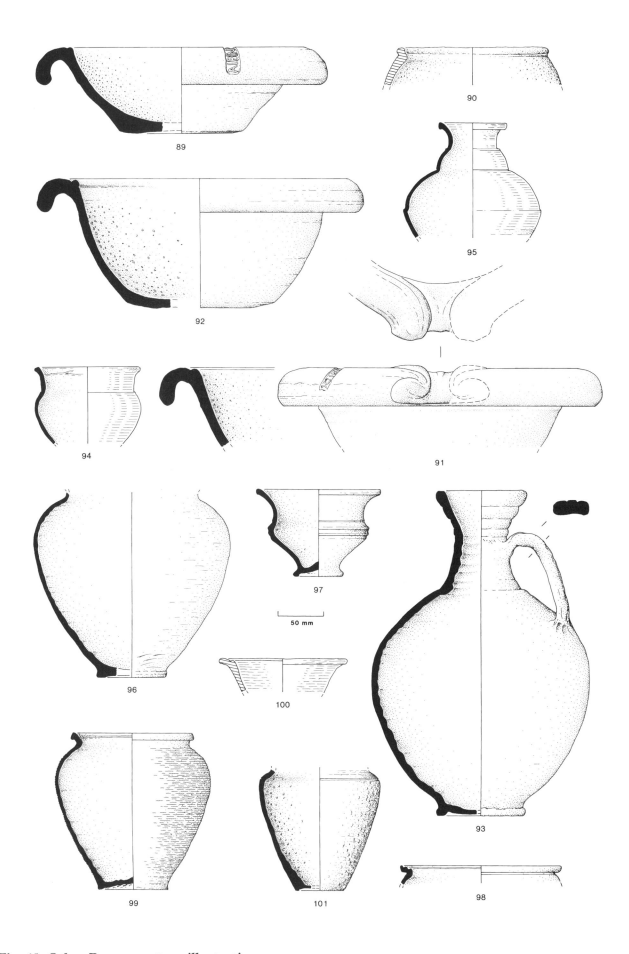

Fig. 65: *Other Roman pottery illustrations*

PHASE 3

Area 1

Phase 3A

102. MD6 Plain everted rim beaker (LAU Form: 9B2). 13859, (1194), sg141/1.

103. MO7 Mortarium (Gillam Type 243) flange with counterstamp of Albinus. (Stamp fig. 59.M6; Hartley above). 17719, (1259), sg141/1.

104. MO7 Mortarium (Gillam Type 243), as 102 above. (Stamp fig. 59.M7; Hartley above). 17715, (1051), sg141/1.

105. AM20 Handle of unidentified amphora. 18844, (906), sg141/1.

106. WW3 Flagon (LAU Form: 1E1) with flaring bead rim. 18842, (3954), sg360/1.

107. WW4 Base of large flagon/amphora, probably a Verulamium region product. 18849 + 18845 + 13934 + 18846, (1194) + (1240) + (1215) + (1259), sg141/1.

108. OW3 Collared flagon (LAU Form: 1A4). 13037, (936), sg141/1.

109. GW3 Everted rim beaker (LAU Form: 9B1), graffito (fig. 60.G10; report p00) on base. 12840, (872), sg141/1.

110. GW3 Platter (LAU Form: 7D1) Cam 16a. 13521, (1051), sg141/1.

111. GW5 Carinated bowl (LAU Form: 5D2). 14044, (259), sg141/1.

112. GW6 Jar (LAU Form: 3E2) with moulded and lid-seated rim, incised herring-bone pattern around girth. 13090 + 13093, (958 + (959), sg141/1.

113. CG1a Ledge rim jar (LAU Form: 3E2), fine horizontal rilling, cf. Brown 1994, fig.25, 43, 46. 18866, (935), sg141/1.

114. GW11 Poppy-head beaker (LAU Form: 9C4), typologically datable to the late 1st to early 2nd cent. AD (Tyers 1978), sg141/1.

115. GT3a Body cordon from seria/dolia (LAU Form: 3Q1), see 64, 196 (Hammerson 1988, fig.123, 1083). 18868, (1194), sg141/1.

116. GT5/6 Necked jar (LAU Form: 3M1), burnish vertical lines around neck, combed wavy band beneath. Girth shows signs of knife trimming. 12693 + 12701 + 11364, (832) + (833) + (667), sg141/1.

117. MO7 Mortarium (Gillam Type 240) flange with stamp of Moricamulus. (Stamp fig. 59.M8; Hartley above). 17714, (936), sg142/2.

118. AM9a Dressel 20 amphora (Peacock & Williams 1986, Class 25), rim and lower body removed. Residue around shoulder and neck. Vessel found in one piece. 18018, (936), sg142/2. Scale 1:8

Phase 3B

119. MD6 Campanulate cup (LAU Form: 8D4), beaded rim. Cf. Drag 27 (Marsh 1978, fig.6.8, 12.9). 12628, (820), sg141/4.

120. MO18 Stamped mortarium (Gillam Type 257) of Similis. (Stamp fig. 59.M9; Hartley above). 17711, (801), sg141/4.

121. MO18 Flange fragment from mortarium of Victor. (Stamp fig. 59.M10, Hartley above). 17712, (801), sg141/4.

Phase 2D

122. C2 Cup (LAU Form: 8D1) with applied/barbotine scales and roughcast interior. A continental import, various sources are possible with the Lower Rhineland perhaps the most likely (Greene 1979, fig.24, 4). 14116, (1264), sg143/2.

Phase 3B (continued)

123. AM8 Basal knob from Rhodian amphora Cam 184 (Peacock & Williams 1986, Class 9). 17926, (1210), sg150/1.

124. CG1a Necked storage jar (LAU Form: 3M2) approximately half the vessel was recovered, cf. Brown 1994, fig.22, 11. 13466, (1032), sg151/1.

125. MO4 Stamped mortarium Gillam Type 243) of Iunius Loccius AD145-175. (Stamp fig. 59.M11; Hartley above). 17718, (1198), sg152/1.

126. WS2 Candlestick (LAU Class: 11), reworked from the stand of a tazza or similar vessel. Sooting around mouth. 13525, (1030), sg152/1.

127. OW3 Jar base (LAU Class: 3). Graffito (fig. 60, G9) on ext. base. 18248, (1202), sg152/1.

128. C3 Cornice rim beaker (LAU Form:9D1). 11354, (667), sg153/1.

129. BB1 Flanged dish (LAU Form: 6D2) cf. Gillam Type 220. 11884, (747), sg153/1.

130. WW2 Ring-necked flagon (LAU Form: 1C4). 12551, (788), sg153/2.

131. BB1 Everted rim jar (LAU Form: 3H1) cf. Gillam Type 125. 13814, (1176), sg155/1.

132. GW2 Everted rim bowl/jar (LAU Form: 4B2). 14002, (1228), sg155/2.

133. MD4 Globular beaker with everted rim (LAU Form: 9B1). Bosses forming triangular group. Marsh dates the form to the late 1st-early 2nd cent. AD (Marsh 1978, 20.6) (Marsh 1978, fig.6.9, 20.6), (749), sg157/2.

134 C2 Bag-shaped beaker (LAU Form: 9F1) with groove beneath rim, perhaps vestigial cornice. 11400, (694), sg157/5.

135. C2 Segmental bowl (LAU Form: 5N2). 11400, (694), sg157/5.

136. MO4 Heavily ribbed hammer-head mortarium (Gillam Type 281). 12438, (694), sg157/5.

137. AM9B Rim and stamped handle (fig. 59.A3) from a Dressel 20 amphora (Peacock & Williams 1986, Class 25). 11402 + 12404 + 12609 + 17710, (694) + (746) + (818) + (758), sg157/5

138. GW6 Everted rim jar (LAU Form: 3H2). Wheel thrown imitation of BB1

jar (Gillam Type 116). 11405, (694), sg157/5.

139. BB2 Flange rim pie-dish (LAU Form: 6D1) Gillam Type 310. 18912, (758), sg157/5.

Phase 3C

140. MO4 Stamped mortarium of Loccius Vibo (Gillam Type 244). (Stamp fig. 59.M12; Hartley above). 17716, (1088), sg186/2.

141. WW2 Ring-necked flagon (LAU Form: 1C5). 13603, (1075), sg186/2.

142. GW5 Double-handled jar (LAU Form: 3N1). 13790, (1153), sg186/4.

143. GW5 Tripod bowl with plain flanged rim (LAU Form: 5F3), cf. Pollard 1994, fig.58, 139). 13790 + 10478, (1153) + (304), sg186/4+187/1.

Phase 3D

144. C2 Cornice rim beaker (LAU Form: 9D2), clay roughcast. 10473, (304), sg187/1.

145. MO12 Stamped mortarium of Icotasgus (Gillam Type 243). (Stamp fig. 59.M13; Hartley above) with possible graffito on the interior (fig. 60.G8). 17702, (304), sg187/1.

146/146a. GW12 Hemispherical bowl (LAU Form: 5N2), with combed, stamped (145a: two concentric rings, scale 1:1) and rouletted decoration, cf. Pollard 1994, fig.52, 32. 10478 + 16111, (304) + (674), sg187/1.

147. BB1 Handled beaker (LAU Form: 9Z2), cf. Gillam Type 65. Burnished motif on the exterior of the base. 16089, (670), sg187/1.

Phase 3G

148. WW3 Small bead rim beaker (LAU Form: 9D4), see 287. 12203, (2936), sg207/1.

149. GW3 Cauldron (LAU Form: 4C2). 11939 + 12204) (2758) + (2936), sg207/1+207/6.

150. OW3 Deep plain rim bowl (LAU Form: 5M1), cf. Cam 306. 11938, (2758), sg207/6.

151. CG3b Necked jar (LAU Form: 3M2). 11941, (2758), sg207/6.

152. OW2 Flanged hemispherical bowl (LAU Form: 5L1). 12149, (2911), sg207/4.

PHASE 4

Phase 4A

153. C2 Bag-shaped beaker (LAU Form: 9F1), probably a Nene Valley product decorated with phalli 'en barbotine'. The motif can be paralleled at Lincoln (Webster 1989, fig.2, 20-1). 13667, (1100), sg174/1.

154. WW3 Ring-necked flagon (LAU Form: 1C5). 13668, (1100), sg174/1.

155. BB1 Everted rim jar (LAU Form: 3H2), cf. Gillam Type 145, AD 230-300. 13671, (1100), sg174/1.

156. BB1 Everted rim jar (LAU Form: 3H2), cf. Gillam Type 146; Farrar 1981, 426-7, fig.24.1). 13671, (1100), sg174/1.

157. MD4 Flagon with everted rim (LAU Form: 1A4). 11739, (452), sg174/2.

158. OW3 Ledge rim jar (LAU Form: 3E2). Incised linear decoration, see 205. The form can be paralleled at the Ravenstone kiln site in north-west Leicestershire (Boyer 1989). 13400, (1023), sg174/2.

159. OW3 Ledge rim jar (LAU Form: 3E2). Incised linear decoration, as 158 above. 13435, (446), sg174/2.

160. GW6 Ledge rim jar (LAU Form: 3E2) cf. 158-9 above. 11710, (446), sg174/2.

161. BB1 Everted rim jar (LAU Form: 3H2) Gillam Type 145. 11720, (447), sg174/2.

162. BB1 Flanged dish (LAU Form: 6D2) Gillam Type 224. 13545, (1053), sg174/2.

163. CG3c Jar (Gillam Type 160), groove on shoulder. 13428, (1026), sg174/2.

164. WW2 Flanged segmental bowl (LAU Form: 5H3), Brown paint. 11689, (444), sg174/3.

165. GW5 Necked jar (LAU Form: 3M2). 11691, (444), sg174/3.

166. CG1b Necked jar (LAU Form: 3M2), with fine horizontal rilling on the body. The form cannot be closely paralleled at Harrold. 11699, (445), sg174/3.

PHASE 5

Phase 5A

167. CG1 Neckless ledge rim jar (LAU Form: 3D2). 14409, (1455), sg158/1.

168. MO4 Mortarium base. Interior covered with red ochre (10R4/6) pigment. (Morgan, below). 18768, (1542), sg158/2.

169. MD4 Platter with inturned rim (LAU Form: 7D1), cf. Marsh 1978, fig.6.11, Type 24.22. 13066, (952), sg158/4.

170. GW4/7 Flange rim bowl (LAU Form: 6D1). 18917, (1515), sg160/4.

171. BB1 Everted rim jar (LAU Form: 3H2) Gillam Type 138, but with an obtuse lattice. 14590 + 14707 + 16867, (1515) + (1553), sg160/4.

172. CG1a Neckless ledge rim jar (LAU Form: 3D3), cf. Brown 1994, fig.24, 36. 14711, (1554), sg160/4.

173. WW3 Ring-neck flagon (LAU Form: 1C5). A complete flagon neck was recovered from sg161/1 (WW3, fig. 70.173), the form is of early to mid-2nd cent. AD date (Marsh and Tyers 1978, Form: I.B.5) and is thus probably residual.

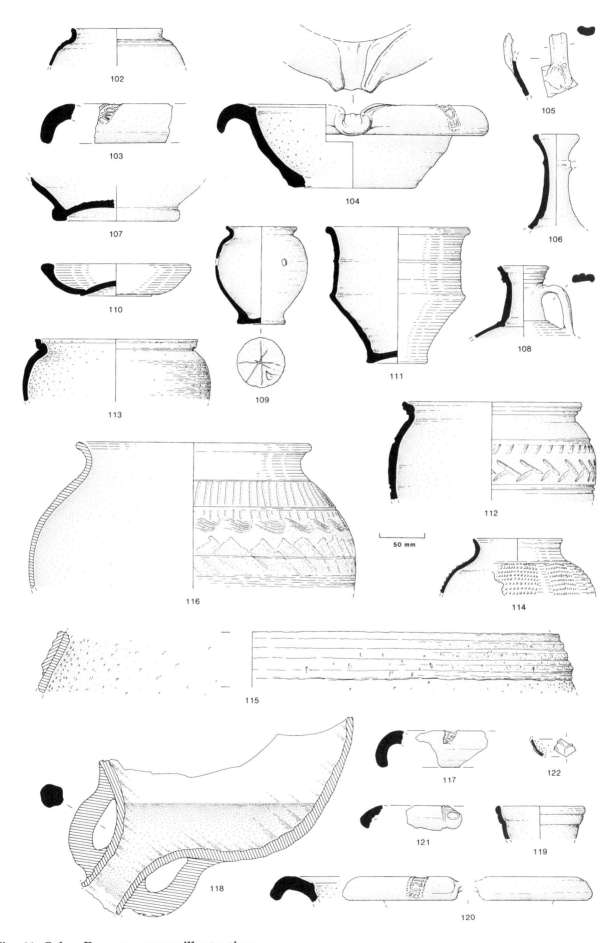

Fig. 66: *Other Roman pottery illustrations*

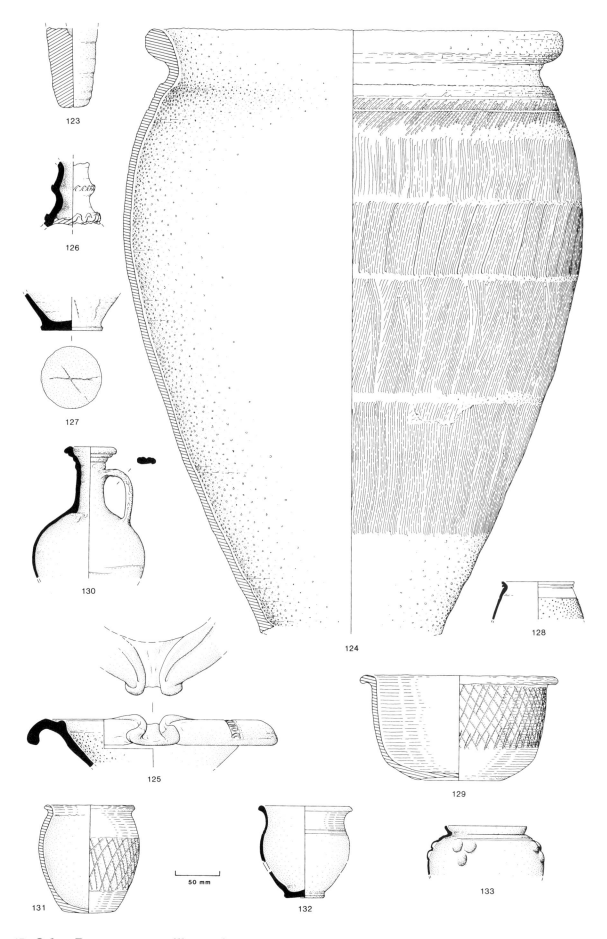

Fig. 67: *Other Roman pottery illustrations*

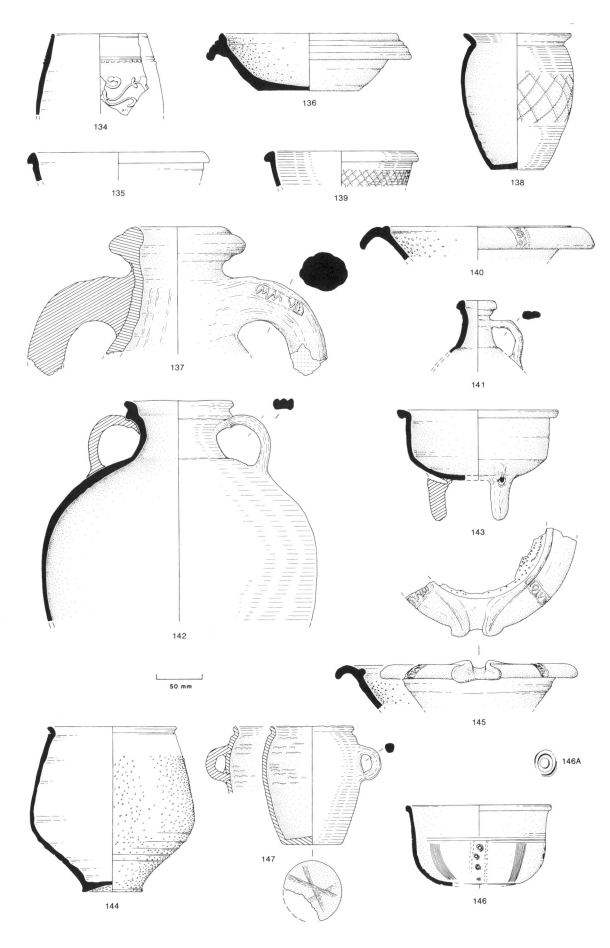

Fig. 68: *Other Roman pottery illustrations*

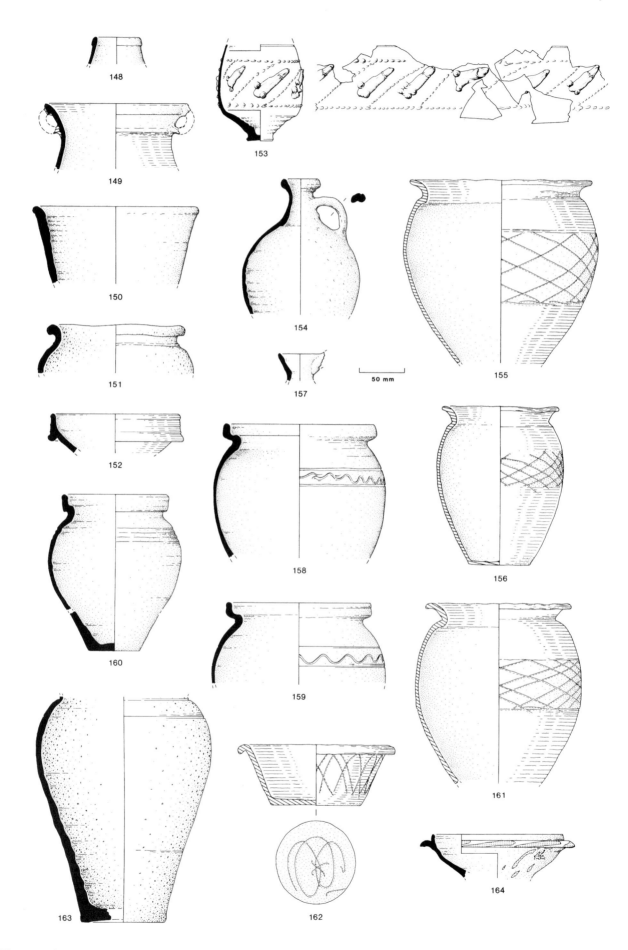

Fig. 69: *Other Roman pottery illustrations*

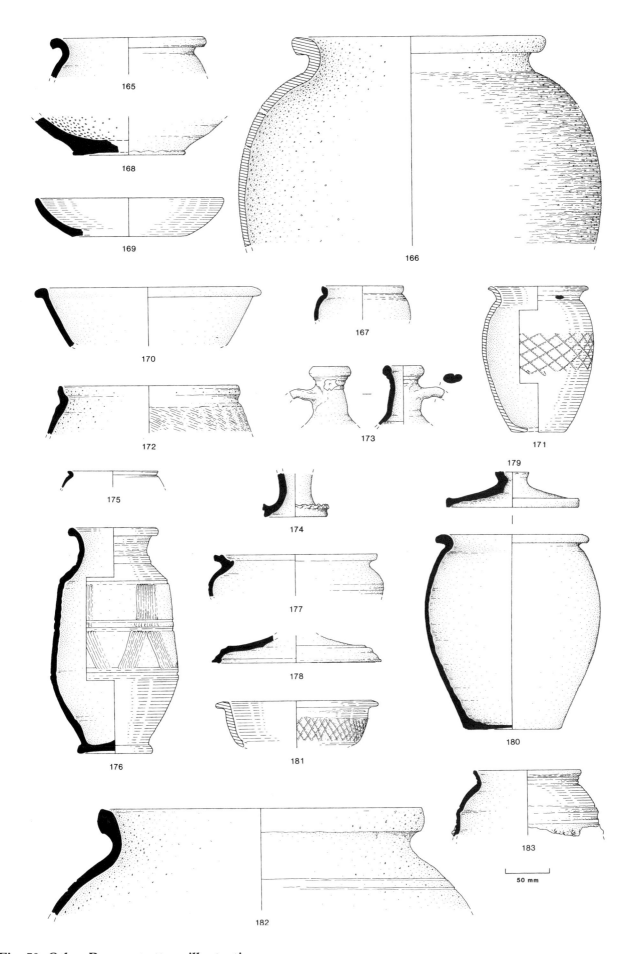

Fig. 70: *Other Roman pottery illustrations*

However, the vessel is unusual as it carries a splash of glaze adhering to the neck below the rim. The fabric is indistinguishable in the hand from WW's generally ascribed a Midland or Mancetter origin, however, no evidence of glazed vessels have been suggested at those kilns. 18918, (588), sg161/1.

Phase 5B

174. WW4 Everted flagon rim (LAU Form: 1A3) or possibly tazza base with pie-crust decoration. 13051, (948), sg162/2.

175. C3 Cornice rim beaker (LAU Form: 9D2). 12758, (848), sg162/3.

176. GW3 Necked jar (LAU Form: 3M4), dating uncertain, however, form can be paralleled among the group II (mid-2nd to mid 3rd cent. AD) assemblage at the Forum, Leicester and among unstratified material from the Norfolk Street villa, Leicester. The vessel may represent a butt beaker derived form (Pollard 1994, fig.62, 250). Comparison may also be drawn with the carinated beaker (LAU Form 9J4, ibid fig.55, 101). 18777, (848), sg162/3.

177. GW3 Wide mouthed bowl with ledge rim (LAU Form: 5C3). 12576, (792), sg162/3.

178. GW5 Carinated lid (LAU Form: 10A6). 13184, (978), sg162/3.

179. GW6 Pierced lid (LAU Form: 10A3). Found as cover to 180. 18774, (848), sg162/3.

180. GW6 Everted rim jar (LAU Form: 3G1). Vessel contained adult cremation (Wakely below p.00). 18773, (848), sg162/3.

181. BB1 Flange rim dish (LAU Form: 6D1) Gillam Type 307. 12763, (848), sg162/3.

182. CG1 Necked storage jar (LAU Form: 3M2), cf. Brown 1994, fig.22, 12. The parallel grooves around the shoulder may be a 2nd cent. AD simplification of the early rilled and combed motifs (cf. no. 124). As Pollard notes (1994, 96, fig.60, 180) the squared rim appears to replace the rounded version from the end of the 1st cent. AD. 12764, (848), sg162/3.

183. MG3 Everted rim jar (LAU Form: 3G2). Grooved shoulder with rusticated panel below. 18936, (931), sg162/7.

184. WW2 Globular beaker (LAU Form: 3F3). Fine vertical scoring. 12056, (725), sg167/1.

185. OW3 Globular beaker with everted rim (LAU Form: 9C4). 11323, (651), sg167/1.

186. BB1 Plain flange rim dish (LAU Form: 6D1) Gillam Type 218, the vessel lacks any form of burnished motif. 12012, (702), sg167/1.

Phase 5C

187. MO4 Stamped mortarium of Bonoxus. (Stamp fig. 59.M14; Hartley, above). 17704, (522), sg164/1.

188. MO4 Mortarium stamped by a Loccius Pro[..., possibly Probus or Proculus. (Stamp fig. 59.M15; Hartley, above). 17703, (498), sg164/1.

189. OW2 Flange rim dish (LAU Form: 6B3). Burnished, with grooved flange. Base may have been pierced, probably for a repair. 10594, (586), sg164/1.

190. OW2 Everted, ledge rim beaker (LAU Form: 9B1). Horizontal rilling around body. 10594, (586), sg164/1.

191. CG1b Necked jar (LAU Form: 3M2), finely rilled body, cf. Brown 1994, fig.34, 310. 10255, (266), sg166/1.

192. GW5 Deep plain rim bowl (LAU Form: 5M1) cf. Cam 306. 10557, (317), sg166/2.

193. CG3b Grooved flange rim dish (LAU Form: 6E1). Dark olive grey exterior (5Y3/2) and olive grey (5Y5/2) interior. 11083, (514), sg166/3.

194. CG1b Necked, everted rim jar (LAU Form: 3M2), cf. Brown 1994, fig.34, 244. 10982, (462), sg166/4.

195. OW5 Deep plain rim bowl (LAU Form: 5M1) cf. Cam 306. 10978 + 10263, (462) + (268), sg166/4+166/5.

196. GT3a Seria/dolia rim (LAU Form: 3Q1), see above 64, 115 (Hammerson 1988, fig.123, 1083). 10266, (268), sg166/5.

197. DS Ledge rim jar (LAU Form: 3E5), Derbyshire ware vessel Type A1 (Martin forthcoming). 16212, (315), sg168/1.

Phase 5D

198. C2 Funnel mouthed beaker (LAU Form: 9F2), indented with barbotine applied scales. 10700 + 10714, (349) + (381), sg186/1.

199. OW3 Base of deep plain rim bowl (LAU Form: 5M1) cf. Cam 306. 10703, (349), sg186/1.

200. GW3 Flask with everted rim (LAU Form: 2A2). Cordon at top of shoulder, grooved at girth. 10718, (381), sg186/1.

201. GW3 Necked jar (LAU Form: 3M2). 10704, (349), sg186/1.

202. BB1 Everted rim jar (LAU Form: 3H3), cf. Gillam Type 148. 10705, (349), sg186/1.

203. BB1 Bead and flanged dish (LAU Form: 6F1), cf. Gillam Type 228. 10705, (349), sg186/1.

Area 3

Phase 5E

204. MO12 Stamped mortarium of Icotasgus (Gillam Type 254). (Stamp fig. 59.M16; Hartley, above). 17729, (3930), sg339/4.

205. OW3 Necked jar (LAU Form: 3M2). Incised decoration as 158, 159. 15615, (3825), sg339/4.

206. GW3 Jar with short everted rim (LAU Form: 3F3). 15875, (3940), sg339/5.

207. CG1b Necked jar (LAU Form: 3M2) cf. Brown 1994, fig.37, 310. 15618, (3825), sg339/4.

208. GT6 Carinated bowl (LAU Form: 5D2). Burnished and rouletted. 15868, (3939), sg339/4.

209. C2 Plain rimmed beaker (LAU Form: 9F1). Barbotine chevrons or lattice (Howe et.al. 1980, fig.3, 34). 15900, (3954), sg360/1.

210. C13 Plain rimmed cup (LAU Form: 8B3), cf. Drag.33. (Young Type C88.1). 18833, (3954), sg360/1.

211. C17 Flanged bowl (LAU Form: 5L2), cf. Drag.38 (Howe et.al. 1980, fig.7, 83). 18082, (3954), sg360/1.

212. MO19 Hammer-head mortarium (Gillam Type 283), typologically dated to the 3rd cent. AD (Hartley 1993, in archive). 17817, (3954), sg360/1.

213. MO4 Stamped mortarium of Iunius Loccius (Gillam Type 280). (Stamp fig. 59.M17; Hartley, above). 17730, (3954), sg360/1.

214. MO4 Hammer-head mortarium (Gillam Type 279). Hartley (1993, in archive) suggests 3rd cent. AD. date. 15901, (3954), sg360/1.

215. OW9 Much Hadham flange necked flagon (LAU Form: 1D1). 15905, (3954), sg360/1.

216. OW9 Much Hadham flange necked flagon (LAU Form: 1D1). 15905, (3954), sg360/1.

217. GW3 Body of necked jar (LAU Form: 3M2). Rouletted bands at shoulder and girth with burnished line spiralling around lower body. 15906, (3954), sg360/1.

218. GW5 Rouletted and burnished jar (LAU Form: 3M2), cf. 217. 15906, (3954), sg360/1.

219. BB1 Plain rim dish (LAU Form: 6A1) cf. Holbrook & Bidwell 1991, fig.32, 59.4; Gillam Type 329. Graffito (G13) on exterior. 18272, (3954), sg360/1.

220. GT3a Necked storage jar (LAU Form: 3M2). Vessel in a grogged fabric with pink (7.5YR7/4) to reddish yellow (7.5YR6/6) surfaces and dark grey core. Comparable with Milton Keynes Fabric 2 (Marney 1989, 64-69 and fig.27, 1). 15911, (3954), sg360/1.

Phase 5F

221. C2 Plain rim beaker (LAU Form: 9F1). Unusual combination of barbotine motifs, scales above lattice. 15913, (3960), sg339/6.

222. WS2 Flanged bowl (LAU Form: 5H3), interior very worn. 15776, (3908), sg339/6.

223. AM18 Rim of rilled amphora, Cam 189 (Peacock & Williams 1986, Class 12), one handle extant. 17880, (3893), sg339/9.

224. MO19 Stamped mortarium of Loccius Vibo (Gillam Type 253). (Stamp fig. 59.M18; Hartley, above). 17727, (3908), sg339/7.

225. MO19 Fragmentary mortarium (Gillam Type 253) stamped]FE. Probably stamped CICVRFE (Stamp fig. 59.M19; Hartley, above). 17807, (3908), sg339/7.

226. MO4 Stamped mortarium of Mossius (Gillam Type 244). (Stamp fig. 59.M20; Hartley, above). 17728, (3908), sg339/7.

227. OW3 Beaker with short everted rim (LAU Form: 9D4). Roller stamped panel. 15777, (3908), sg339/7.

228. OW3 Cup and fragment of ring from triple vase (LAU Form: 11E1). Cup burnished on outer surface only. 15777, (3908), sg339/7.

229. GW5 Everted rim jar (LAU Form: 3H1). 15778, (3908), sg339/7.

230. GW6 Necked jar (LAU Form: 3M2). 15778, (3908), sg339/7.

231. GW5 Necked jar (LAU Form: 3N3). 15925, (3961), sg364/1.

232. GW5 Wide-mouthed necked jar (LAU Form: 3M2). Burnished linear design around shoulder, with burnish line spiralling around lower body. 15778, (3908), sg339/7.

233. DS Ledge rim jar (LAU Form: 3E5), Derbyshire ware vessel Type A1 (Martin forthcoming). 15783, (3908), sg339/7.

234. C2 Beaker with everted rim (LAU Form: 9E2). 15570, (3795), sg362/3.

235. C3 Globular beaker with everted rim (LAU Form: 9E2). Barbotine scale and indented body (Howe et al 1980, fig.4, 36). 15558, (3792), sg362/3.

236. MO19 Stamped mortarium of Minomelus (Gillam Type 261). (Stamp fig. 59.M21; Hartley, above). 17724, (3792), sg362/3.

237. MO4 Mortarium (Gillam Type 253) with fragmentary stamp. (Stamp fig. 59.M22; Hartley, above). 17723, (3792), sg362/3.

238. GW2 Carinated bowl (LAU Form: 5E1). 15575, (3795), sg362/3.

239. GW3 Handled beaker (LAU Form: 9Z3). Burnished exterior. 15575, (3795), sg362/3.

240. DS Ledge rim jar (LAU Form: 3E5), Derbyshire ware vessel Type A1 (Martin, forthcoming). 15579, (3795), sg362/3.

Phase 5G

241. BB1 Flange and grooved dish (LAU Form: 6E2) cf. Holbrook & Bidwell 1991, fig.31, 43.1; Gillam Type 227. Red (10R4/6) paint splashed over break (Morgan, below). 15714, (3884), sg333/1.

242. MO4 Hammer-head mortarium (Gillam Type 279). Red painted flange. Typologically dated to the to the date range AD240-350 (Hartley 1993, in archive). 15363, (3608), sg334/2.

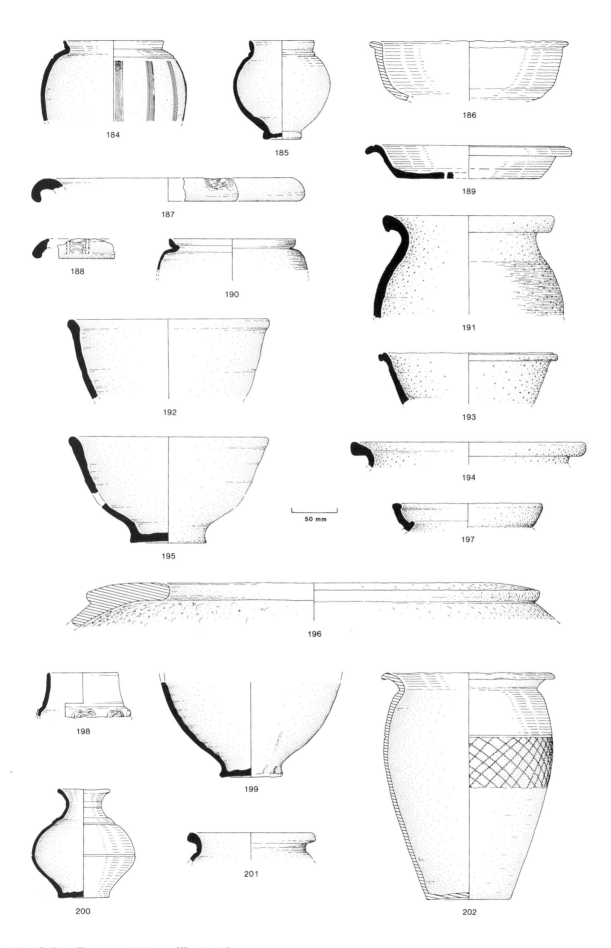

Fig. 71: *Other Roman pottery illustrations*

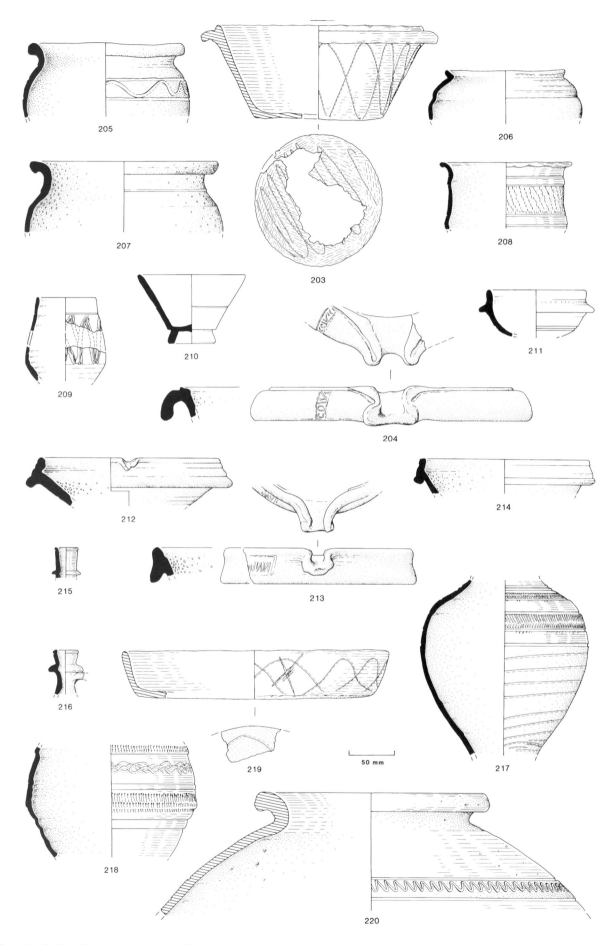

Fig. 72: *Other Roman pottery illustrations*

Fig. 73: *Other Roman pottery illustrations*

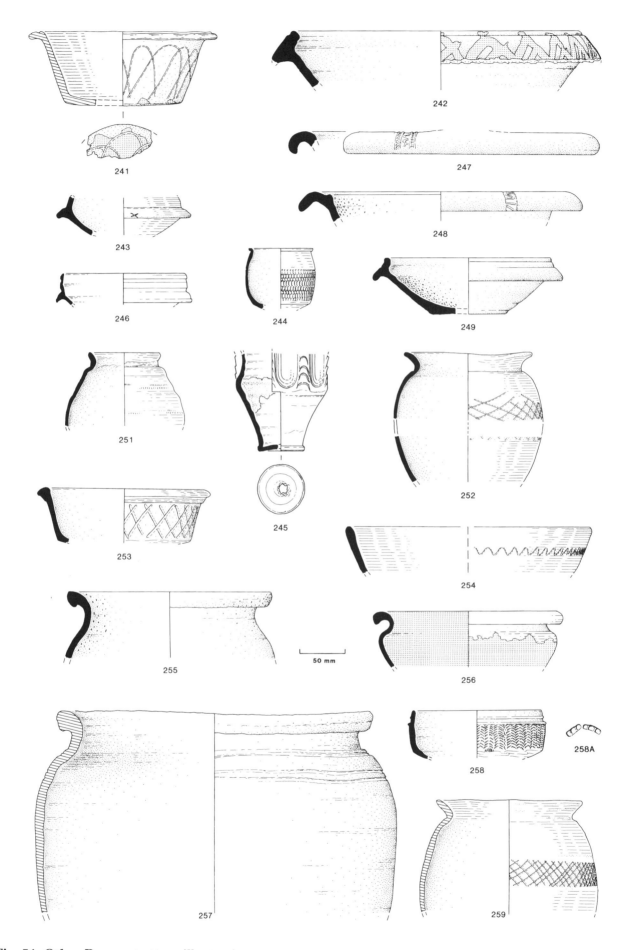

Fig. 74: *Other Roman pottery illustrations*

243. GW5 Flanged bowl (LAU Form: 5L2). Graffito at point of rim (Graffito fig. 60.G11). 15367, (3608), sg334/2.

244. OW3 Bead rim beaker (LAU Form: 9D3). Rouletted body. 15652, (3853), sg337/2.

245. C2 Base of scale and indented beaker (LAU Form: 9F2) cf. Howe *et al* 1980, fig.4, 39. Vessel appears to have been used as a paint pot with the body removed at the base of the indented zone. Traces of a red (10R4/6) pigment/paint were found on the fracture, with the interior of the 'pot' covered with a lime wash. Subsequently a hole was pierced in the base. The complete base and a fragment of the decorated zone were recovered from the same (Morgan, below). 18305, (3879), sg359/4.

246. C17 Fine flanged bowl (LAU Form: 5L1), cf. Drag 38., as 206. 18310, (3879), sg359/4.

247. MO12 Semi-literate stamped mortarium. (Stamp fig. 59.M23; Hartley, above). 17725, (3879), sg359/4.

248. MO19 Stamped mortarium (Gillam Type 242) of Iunius. (Stamp fig. 59.M24; Hartley, above). 17726, (3879), sg359/4.

249. MO4 Hammer-head mortarium (Gillam Type 282). Hartley (1993, in archive) suggests a date of the 3rd cent. AD. 15588, (3804), sg359/4.

250. OW10 Stamped and impressed vessel (LAU Class: 11). Monaghan comments (1993, in archive): fragments of a degenerate head pot, probably the back of the head. The fabric is a perfect match for the appropriate Eboracum ware (cf. Monaghan, 1993). 18325, (3879), sg359/4.

251. GW3 Necked jar (LAU Form: 3M1), rouletted bands around body, see 289. 15755, (3879), sg359/4.

252. GW3 Everted rim jar (LAU Form: 3H2). 15815, (3918), sg359/4.

253. GW5 Flange rim dish (LAU Form: 6D1), perhaps based on BB2 form cf. Gillam Type 222/3 .15755 + 15798, (3879) + (3918), sg359/4 + 338/2.

254. BB2 Plain rimmed dish (LAU Form: 6A1) cf. Gillam Type 184. 15763, (3879), sg359/4.

255. CG1b Necked jar (LAU Form: 3M2), paralleled at Harrold and dated from the late 2nd to 4th cent. AD (Brown 1994, fig.26, 92-98). 15764, (3879), sg359/4.

Phase 5H

256. GW3 Wide-mouthed bowl (LAU Form: 5C2). Red (10R4/6) paint thickly covering interior and partially exterior. Vessel appears to have been used as paint pot (Morgan, below). 18771 + 15636, (3643) + (3836), sg338/1+367/1.

257. GT5/6 Necked storage jar (LAU Form: 3M2). 15437, (3645), sg338/1.

258/258a. GW6 Carinated bowl (LAU Form: 5Q1), apparently a grey ware 'Castor box'. Repeated stamped decoration to create a rouletted appearance (258a, stamp at 1:1). A similar vessel was recovered from The Park, Lincoln and postulated to be of 4th century date (Darling 1977, fig.7, 132). Also cf. Woodfield 1982, fig.23, 96. 15666, (3866), sg338/2.

259. BB1 Everted rim jar (LAU Form: 3H2), cf. Holbrook & Bidwell 1991 fig.28, 20.1f; Gillam Type 146). 15668, (3866), sg338/2.

260. BB1 Flange and bead dish (LAU Form: 6F1), cf. Holbrook & Bidwell 1991 fig.32, 54.1; Gillam Type 228. Graffito, fig. 60, G14. 15668, (3866), sg338/2.

261. BB1 Flange and bead dish (LAU Form: 6F1), cf. Holbrook & Bidwell 1991 fig.31, 45.3b; Gillam Type 228. 15584, (3801), sg338/2.

262. C17 Plain rim beaker (LAU Form: 9F1). Barbotine linear motif. 18355, (3663), sg353/1.

263. BB1 Flange and groove dish (LAU Form: 6E2), cf. Holbrook & Bidwell 1991 fig.31, 43.1; Gillam Type 227). Graffito on exterior wall (Graffito fig. 60.G15). 15625, (3827), sg354/1.

PHASE 6

Area 3

Phase 6A

264. MO4 Mancetter/Hartshill hammer-head mortarium (Gillam Type 280) with red painted flange. Dated typologically AD 230-330 (Hartley 1993, in archive). 15097, (3521), sg336/1.

265. C17 Probable Nene Valley colour-coat grooved beaker (LAU Form: 9F1), cf. Howe et al 1980, fig.5, 44. Size and shape suggest 4th century cup form (ibid fig.5, 59). 15514, (3677), sg338/3.

266. MO4 Mancetter/Hartshill hammer-head mortarium with reeded flange (Gillam Type 282). Dated typologically AD240-320 (Hartley 1993, in archive). 15493, (3672), sg338/3.

267. MO4 Mancetter/Hartshill hammer-head mortarium (Gillam Type 282) with reeded and red painted flange. Dated typologically AD240-250 (Hartley 1993, in archive). 15405, (3618), sg338/3.

268. GW3 Jar with everted and thickened rim (LAU Form: 3G1). 15426, (3640), sg338/3.

269. CG1b Everted rim jar (LAU Form: 3M1), rilled exterior body (Brown 1994, fig.34, 244). 15521, (3677), sg338/3.

270. OW9 Much Hadham flagon or flask mouth (LAU Form: 1A2). Similar to bottle-like flask at the Barley Hill Hadham kilns. (Swan 1988, fig.XIV, 217). 15379, (3610), sg341/1.

271. WW2 Collared jar with reeded and pinched rim (LAU Form: 3Q2), (probably) residual in these contexts. 15727, (3890), sg 367/1.

272. MO4 Mancetter/Hartshill mortarium (Gillam Type 253), with red painted 'vegetal' motif on flange. Dated typologically AD 180-230 (Hartley 1993, in archive). 15632, (3836), sg367/1.

273. MO6 Lower Nene Valley mortarium, cf. Howe *et al* 1980, fig.8, 102. Dated typologically AD 250-400 (Hartley 1993, in archive). 17805, (3836), sg 367/1.

274. GW2 Neck of finely burnished flagon of flask (LAU Form: 1D1), possibly a reduced Much Hadham product. 15266, (3576), sg367/1.

275. GW3 Necked wide-mouthed bowl (LAU Form: 5C2). 15636, (3836), sg367/1.

276. GW5 Everted rimmed deep bowl (LAU Form: 5A2). 15636, (3836), sg367/1.

277. GW6 Small everted rim jar (LAU Form: 3H2), a long lived form (Darling 1977, fig.3, 63-66. 15511, (3675), sg338/3.

278. GW5 Wide-mouthed necked bowl/jar (LAU Form: 4B2). 15385, (3613), sg338/3.

279. GW3 Wide-mouthed bowl (LAU Form: 5C2). 15408, (3618), sg338/3.

280. GW5 Inturned bead and flange bowl (LAU Form: 5K1) Swanpool Type D13-23, (Webster and Booth 1947). 15550, (3790), sg338/3.

281. GW5 Deep plain rimmed bowl (LAU Form: 5M1), cf. Cam 306. 15504, (3674), sg338/3.

282. GW4/7 Necked deep bowl/jar (LAU Form: 4B2), Howe et al. 1980, fig.1, 4,10). 15554, (3790), sg338/3.

283. BB1 Plain rim dish (LAU Form: 6A1) cf. Holbrook and Bidwell 1991, fig.32, 59.4; Gillam Type 329). 15552, (3790), sg338/3.

284. BB1 Plain rimmed dish (LAU Form: 6A1) Gillam Type 329, possibly an oval 'fishdish'. 15552, (3790), sg338/3.

285. BB1 Flanged and beaded dish (LAU Form: 6F1) cf. Holbrook and Bidwell 1991, fig.32, 54.1; Gillam Type 228. Exterior surface abraded, however, no decorative motif is apparent. 15552, (3790), sg363/3.

286. GW1 Base of jar, graffito on exterior of base. The squiggle burnish is unusual on jar forms, generally confined to dishes. Graffito, fig. 60, G12. 15637, (3836), sg367/1.

Phase 6B

287. WW5 Bead rimmed beaker (LAU Form: 9D4) or possibly crucible. See 148. 15217, (3560), sg363/1.

288. GW3 Everted rim jar (LAU Form: 3N1) with rim thickened near collar. 15218, (3560), sg363/1.

289. GW3 Everted rim jar (LAU Form: 3M1) with rouletted cordons, see 251. 15218, (3560), sg363/1.

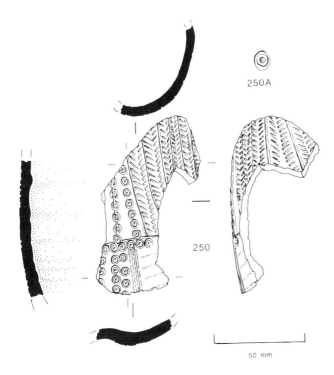

250A

250

50 mm

Fig. 75: *Other Roman pottery illustrations*

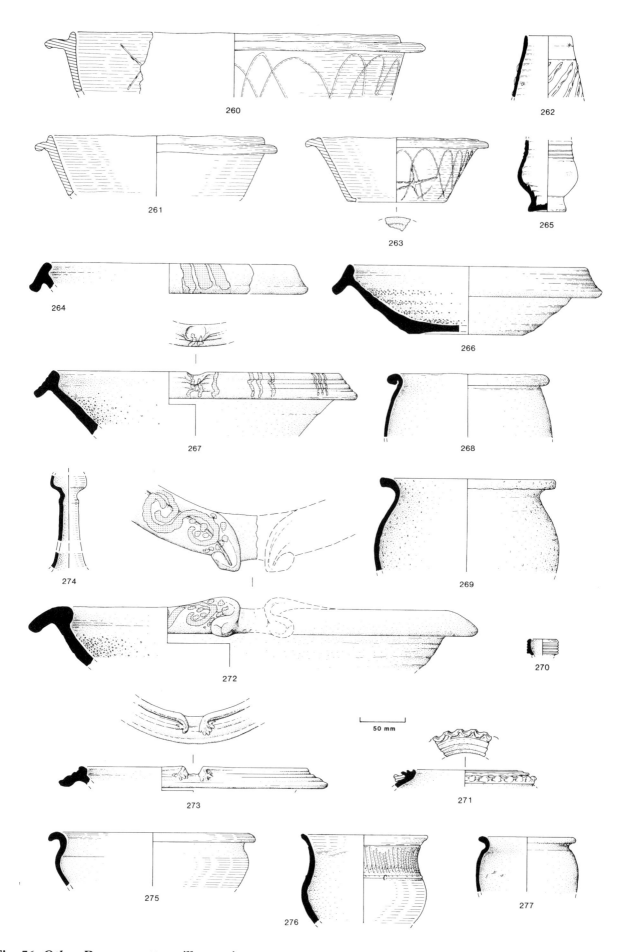

Fig. 76: *Other Roman pottery illustrations*

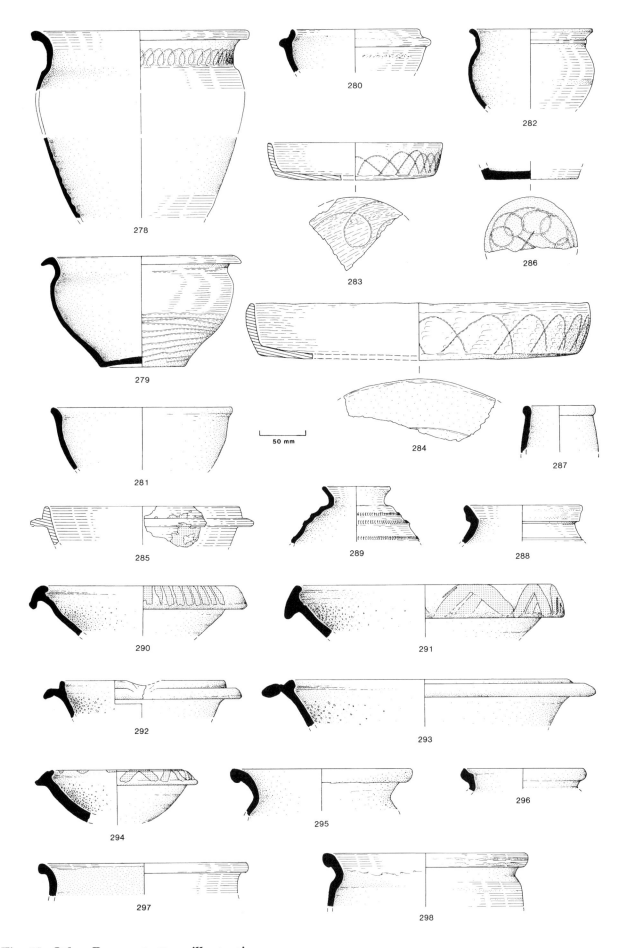

Fig. 77: *Other Roman pottery illustrations*

290. MO4 Mancetter/Hartshill hammer-head mortarium (Gillam Type 280) with red painted flange. Dated typologically to the 3rd cent. AD (Hartley 1993, in archive). 15088, (3519), sg340/1.

291. MO4 Mancetter/Hartshill hammer-head mortarium (Gillam Type 280) with red painted flange. Dated typologically to AD250-350 (Hartley 1993, in archive). 15088, (3519), sg340/1.

292. MO2 Oxfordshire white-slipped mortarium (Young 1977, Type WC5). Dated typologically AD240-300. 17854, (3519), sg340/1.

293. MO6 Lower Nene Valley mortarium (Howe et al. 1980, fig.8, 103). Dated typologically AD250-400. 17853, (3519), sg340/1.

294. MO6 Lower Nene Valley mortarium with brown painted chevrons on flange. Hartley (1993, in archive) comments, a very unusual mortarium, not certainly a Lower Nene Valley product. Parallels might be drawn among the shallow, thick walled and painted bowls from the late occupation levels at Lincoln (Darling 1977, fig.1, 15). 17853, (3519), sg340/1.

295. OW3 Everted and undercut rim jar (LAU Form: 3M2), parallels can be found among the Late Roman Shelly wares (Brown 1994, fig.26, 92-8), cf. 255. 15091, (3519), sg340/1.

296. GW3 Everted and lid-seated jar (LAU Form: 3E4), comparable with the 'double lid-seated' forms of Lincolnshire and the north-east Midlands (Darling 1977, fig.6, 113). 15092, (3519), sg340/1.

297. GW5 Wide-mouthed bowl or bowl/jar (LAU Form: 4B2). 15092, (3519), sg340/1.

298. GW3 Wide-mouthed bowl (LAU Form: 5C2). 15092, (3519), sg340/1.

299. GW3 Plain rim dish (LAU Form: 6A1). 15092, (3519), sg340/1.

300. GW5 Bead and flange dish (LAU Form: 6F1). 15092, (3519), sg340/1.

301. BB1 Small everted rim cooking jar (LAU Form: 3H3), cf. Gillam Type 148; Holbrook and Bidwell 1991, fig.28, Type 20.1c). 15093, (3519), sg340/1.

302. BB1 Bead and flange dish (LAU Form: 6F1), cf. 329 below, (Holbrook and Bidwell 1991, fig.31, Type 45.1g). 15093, (3519), sg340/1.

303. BB1 Everted rim jar (LAU Form: 3H2), cf. Gillam Type 139, well burnished upper body, and relatively fine fabric indicate the vessel may not be of Dorset manufacture. The vessel is clearly not wheel thrown. 15150, (3519), sg340/1.

304. BB2 Dish (LAU Form: 6D1) with the early down-turned flange (Gillam Type 222). 15150, (3519), sg340/1.

305. CG1b Flanged dish (LAU Form: 6F4) in the late shell tempered fabric, a rare example of the form (Brown 1991, fig.28, 134). 15094, (3519), sg340/1.

306. MO6 Possible Lower Nene Valley hammer-head mortarium. As with 294 above, Hartley (1993, in archive) regards the form as unusual. Dated typologically to the late 3rd to 4th cent. AD. See also Rollo 1994, fig.14, 58; fig.13, 40, both are dated to the late 3rd and 4th cent. AD. 17851, (3523), sg365/1.

307. MO4 Mancetter/Hartshill hammer-head mortarium (Gillam Type 280) with red painted motif. Dated typologically AD200-350 (Hartley 1993, in archive). 15071, (3515), sg366/1.

POST-ROMAN PHASES

Area 1

308. MO10 Mortarium (Gillam Type 240), stamped by the potter Albinus (AD60-90). (Stamp fig. 59.M25; Hartley, above). 17720, (1459), sg100/1, Ph.12.

309. MO12 Mortarium (Gillam Type 245), stamped by the potter Vitalis iv (AD115-145). (Stamp fig. 59.M26; Hartley, above). 17700, (200), sg100/1, Ph.12.

310. MO18 Mortarium (Gillam Type 243), stamped by the potter Similis i (AD130-160). (Stamp fig. 59.M27; Hartley above). 17701, (200), sg100/1, Ph.12.

311. MO15 Mortarium (Gillam Type 238), stamped by Mottius Bollus (AD 50-85), a potter of Gallia Belgica. (Stamp fig. 59.M28; Hartley above). 17717 + 14162 + 13508, (1101) + (1315) + (1047), sg103/1 + 145/1 + 162/7, Ph.12, + 2.17 + 3.25.

312. AM9a Rim sherd of a Haltern 70 type amphora (Peacock & Williams 1986, Class 15), cf. Pollard 1994, fig.62, 206, and with slight cut out of rim as ibid. fig.61, 183. 18011, F204, (386), sg120/6, Ph.9 .

Area 2

313. C12T Trier 'Rhenish' ware beaker (Trier form: 2), plain high-shouldered. Symonds suggests the form may have remain in production into the 4th cent. AD (Symonds 1992, 54). 10862, F615, (2327), sg255/1, Ph.9.

314. C13 Oxfordshire colour-coat bowl (Young 1977, Type C77; AD325-400+). 11781, F540, (2136), sg247/1, Ph.8.

315. MO4 Mancetter mortarium (Gillam Type 249) stamped by the potter Iunius (AD150-175). (Stamp fig.59.M29; Hartley above). 17706, F536, (2133), sg252/5, Ph.9.

316. OW2 Carinated bowl (LAU Form: 5E2), possibly derived from the Drag 29 or 30 forms. Probably a 2nd cent. AD product, cf. Pollard 1994, fig.67, 284. 11526, F558, (2256), sg261/7, Ph.9.

317. OW5 Base of rilled jar (LAU Class: 3) cf. rilled jar 327 below. 10808, (2268), sg290/1, Ph.9.

318. GW5 Ledge rim jar (LAU Form: 3E2) cf. 158-160, 205. 16154, (2178), sg259/4, Ph.11.

319. GW6 Flange rim dish (LAU Form: 6D1). 10769, F536, (2210), sg252/5, Ph.9.

320. GW5 Flange and bead rim bowl (LAU Form: 6F2), Swanpool Type D11. 11673, F615, (2658), sg258/10, Ph.9.

321. CG1c Ledged and everted rim jar (LAU Form: 3E3). The 'Dales Ware type' can be paralleled among late groups at Lincoln (Darling 1977, fig.6, 110) and has been discussed by Loughlin (1977, 85f). 11791, F521, (2140), sg249/3, Ph.8.

322. CG3b Bead rim jar (LAU Form: 3B2). 11771, F536, (2126), sg252/5, Ph.9.

Area 3

323. MO4 Mortarium (Gillam Type 254), probably stamped by the potter Maurius (AD150-175). (Stamp fig. 59.M30; Hartley above p.00). 17842, F719, (3568), sg314/2, Ph.9.

324. MO19 Mortarium (Gillam Type 253), stamped by the potter Sennius (AD150-175). (Stamp fig. 59.M31; Hartley above p.00). 15293, (3583), sg301/1, Ph.12.

325. MO5 Fragments of two Lower Nene Valley mortaria (Gillam Type 287), patchy dark brown slip, imitation of Drag 45 form. Cf. Howe et al 1980, fig.7, 84. 17849, F714, (3541), sg315/3, Ph.9.

326. AM20 Handle of Chalk Type 6 amphora (Peacock & Williams 1986, Class 50). 18731, F724, (3570), sg305/5, Ph.7.

327. OW5 Everted rim jar (LAU Form: 3M1), finely rilled body, cf. 317 above. Sooting around rim indicates use of a lid. F727, (3576), sg307/2, Ph.9.

328. GW3 Flanged and inturned bowl (LAU Form: 5K1), Swanpool Type D13-23, cf. 280 above. 15251, F726, (3574), sg310/1, Ph.9.

329. BB1 Flanged and beaded dish (LAU Form: 6F1), Gillam Type 228. 15252, F726, (3574), sg310/1, Ph.9.

330/330a. BB1 Flanged and beaded dish (LAU Form: 6F1), Gillam Type 228. Lime plaster covering both rim and fracture. 15252, F726, (3574), sg310/1, Ph.9.

Area 4

(A475.1979) Catalogue by Dr R. J. Pollard. Pottery drawn by E. MacRobert and Dr R. J. Pollard.

331. C2 Trefoil-mouthed jug (LAU Form: 1H3), virtually complete. This is a lower Nene Valley product (Howe et al 1980, fig.6, 64-5). F(90)5 + F(9)16, ((80)9) + ((80)32), sg.116/3, Ph.9.

332. MO7 Stamped mortarium of the potter Albinus (AD60-90). Die as Hartley 1972, fig.145, 6. (Stamp fig. 59.M32; Hartley above p.00). F(9)11, ((80)21), sg119/10, Ph.9.

333. MO7 Mortarium, stamped by the potter Matugenus (AD80-125). (Stamp fig. 59.M33; Hartley above p.00). F(90)2, ((800)4), sg108/1, Ph.11.

334. MO12 Mortarium, stamped by the potter Candidus ii (AD100-140). (Stamp fig. 59.M34; Hartley above p.00). F(90)6, ((80)14), UP.

335. MO19 Mortarium, stamped by the potter Iunius (AD150-175). (Stamp fig. 59.M35; Hartley above p.00). F(90)6, ((80)14), UP.

336. MO7 Mortarium with bead and stubby flange, cf. (e.g.) Verulamium 777, 1041, 1043 (Wilson 1972), dated c. AD 140-200 (Hartley 1984). F(90)1, ((800)2), sg108/1, Ph.11.

337. MO23 Mortarium (Gillam Type 272), a Rhineland import of c. AD 150-250, cf. Haupt 1984, and Taf. 183. F(90)2, ((800)4). sg108/1, Ph.11.

338. WW2 Flange-rim bowl (LAU Form: 5H3), flange painted reddish brown (Munsell 2.5 YR 5/4). F(90)9, ((80)18) , sg124/5, Ph.9.

339. WW3 Flange-rim bowl (LAU Form: 5H3), flange painted reddish brown (2.5YR 4/4-5/4). F (9)11, ((80)21), sg119/10, Ph.9.

340/340a. WW3 Closed form, body ext painted with squiggles of dusky red (2.5YR 3/2) to red). F(90)1 + (90)9 + (9)11 + (9)12, ((800)2) + ((80)18) + ((80)21) + ((80)22), sg108/1 + 124/5 + 119/10 + 115/4, Ph.11 + Ph.9.

341. OW9, Much Hadham Flagon(?), handle stump. The handle and neck had broken off in antiquity, leaving edges which had been worn smooth to give a narrow mouthed 'neckless jar'. The original vessel had a hole, to facilitate pouring, drilled to one side of the handle. F(90)2, ((80)15), UP.

342. GW3 Narrow mouthed jar (LAU Form: 3M1/2), rouletted. F(9)11, ((80)20) + ((80)21), UP.

343. GW3 Narrow mouthed storage jar (LAU Form: 3M2), burnished lattice. F(90)9, ((80)18), sg124/5, Ph.9.

344. GW5 Necked jar (LAU Form: 3M2). The form and burnished motif are typical of the innovations of the mid 2nd century, and continued in use through the 3rd. F(90)4 + (90)6, ((800)8) + ((80)14), UP.

345. GW6 Everted rim necked jar (LAU Form: 3J1), burnished lattice; cf. 2nd century BB1 types. F(90)9, ((80)23), sg117/5, Ph.9.

346. GW6 Bead rim dish (LAU Form: 6A3), burnished arcading. F(9)11, ((80)21), sg119/10, Ph.9.

347. GW8 Beaker base with turned foot. The type has a small everted rim, as demonstrated by examples from Little Lane, and appeared in the mid 2nd

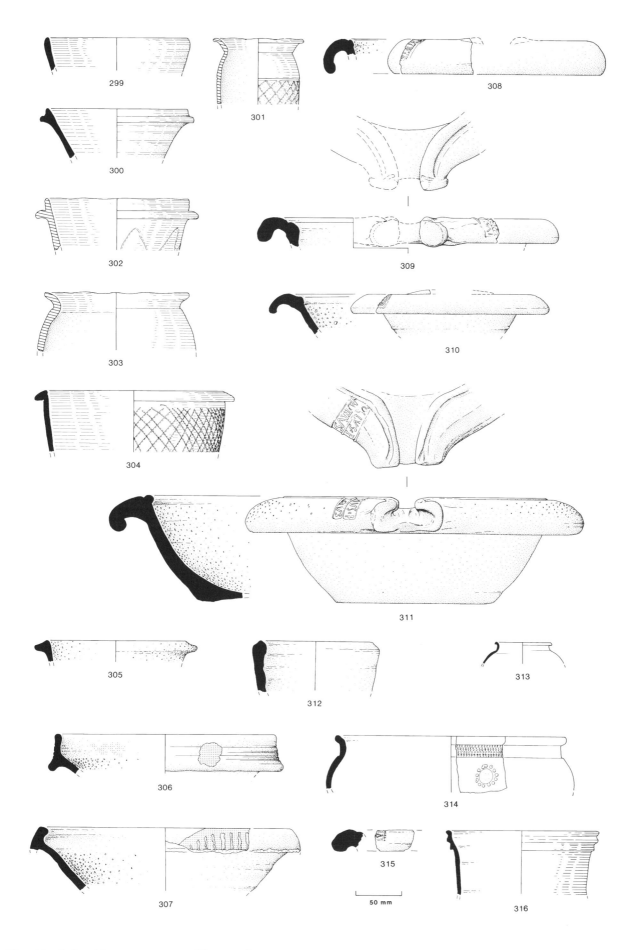

Fig. 78: *Other Roman pottery illustrations*

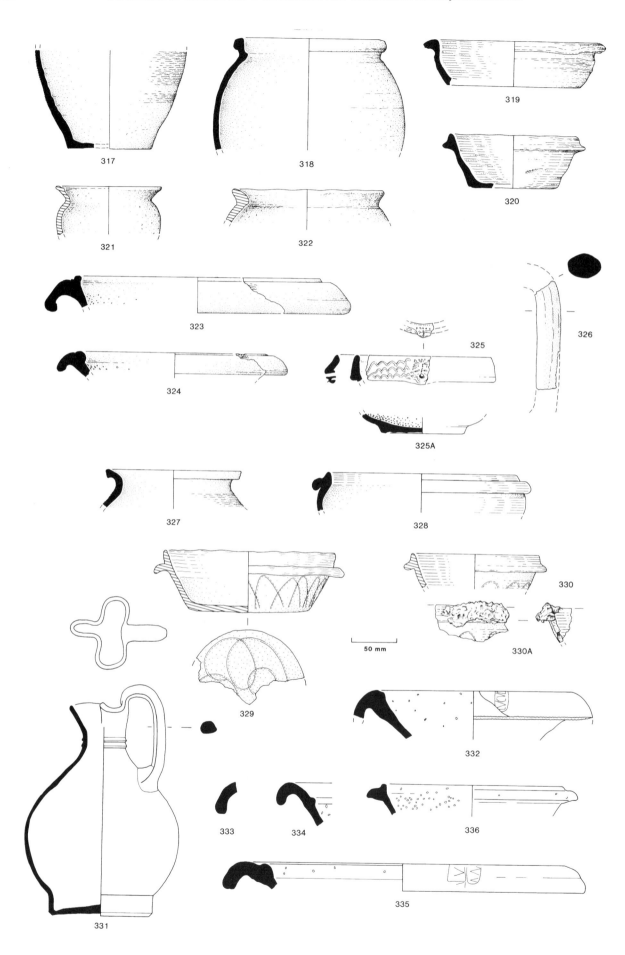

Fig. 79: *Other Roman pottery illustrations*

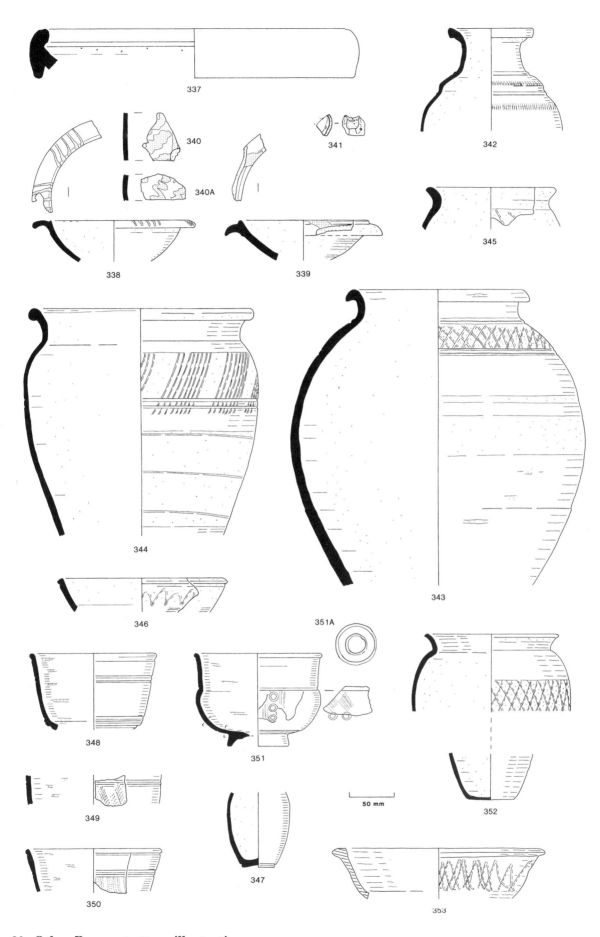

Fig. 80: *Other Roman pottery illustrations*

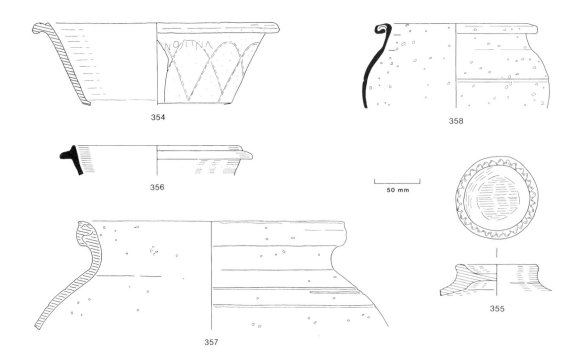

Fig. 81: *Other Roman pottery illustrations*

century. F(90)9, ((80)18), sg124/5, Ph.9.

348. GW12 Bowl (LAU Form: 5E1), cf. Pollard 1994, fig. 69, 312. F(90)9, ((80)18), sg124/5, Ph.9.

349. GW12 Bowl (LAU Form: 5E1?), fine rouletted or stabbed decoration, resembling Pollard 1994, fig. 69, 312. F(90)9, ((80)18), sg124/5, Ph.9.

350. GW12 Bowl (LAU Form: 5E1?), decorated by the same method as no. 350. F(90)9, ((80)18), sg124/5, Ph.9.

351/351a. GW12 Bowl (LAU Form: 5N1), cf. no. 146, with stamped and rouletted or stabbed motifs. F(90)9, ((80)18), sg124/5, Ph.9.

352. GW1 (LAU Form: 3H2). The vessel is probably wheel-thrown and has a very smooth burnish, covering the full interior of the rim as on BB1. The form parallels Gillam Types 138 and 143; it is more usual on BB2 jars for only the upper part of the interior rim to be burnished, but parallels for this rim are known (Farrar 1973, Pl. VB). The base may be from the same vessel. F(90)9, ((80)18), sg124/5, Ph.9.

353. BB1 Pie dish (LAU Form: 6D1), with an unusually loosely tooled lattice. F(90)9, ((80)18), sg124/5, Ph.9.

354. BB1 Incipient-flange dish, Gillam Type 227 (LAU Form: 6E2). Graffito, fig. 60.G17. F(90)5, ((800)9), sg128/5, Ph.11.

355. BB1 (LAU Form: 10A3). This vessel has been classed as BB1 in the broad sense (Pollard forthcoming e) and can be seen as in the BB1 tradition although it is probably not a Dorset product (Ray Farrar pers. comm.). The form is unusual for the BB1 range. It may be a lid knob as the ring is decorated with a burnished zigzag. However, as some BB1 dishes and bowls have burnished patterns on their bases, this possibility cannot be excluded. F(90)6, ((80)16), UP.

356. BB2 (LAU Form: 6F1). Pollard (1983) has indicated that, although not found on northern sites, the bead and flange dish is a BB2 product, mainly for a local market. The fine fabric and smooth burnishing suggests that this vessel may have been made in the south-east. Jason Monaghan (pers. comm.) confirms Pollard's identification as BB2. F(90)8, ((80)17), sg126/4, Ph.9.

357. CG1 Necked storage jar (LAU Form: 3M2), cf. Pollard 1994, fig. 60, 180. Coil built. F(90)9, ((80)18), sg124/5, Ph.9.

358. CG3b Jar (LAU Form: 3M2) cf. Bolton 1967-8, no. 9. F(9)14 + F (90)8, ((80)24) + ((80)17), Ph.8 sg126/4, Ph.9.

THE POST ROMAN POTTERY AND TILE

Siân Davies and Deborah Sawday

THE SAXON POTTERY

Paul Blinkhorn

(table 29)

Twenty eight sherds of Saxon pottery were recovered from the site. Of these, 24 were residual in later medieval or post-medieval contexts, two were intrusive in phase 6 Roman contexts and a further two were found in phase 7, which may be early post-Roman in date.

The following fabric descriptions are based on an examination of the sherds from the site, and of the material from the excavations on St. Peters and Little Lane, Leicester, in 1988 (Blinkhorn forthcoming, a) – which produced an additional 85 sherds of Saxon pottery, although these too were unfortunately all residual in later contexts. Each sherd was analysed using a binocular microscope at x10 magnification. The fabric groups have been kept deliberately broad to allow for other minerals which are sometimes present, as they may occur naturally in the clay. Three of the fabrics identified from the St. Peters and Little Lane sites were not present on Causeway Lane, and hence are not described here.

Fabric 1: WHITE QUARTZITE. Moderate to dense temper of sub-angular white quartzite (?crushed metaquartzite), mainly up to 1mm diameter with rare grains *c.* 2.5mm. Rare grains of quartzite.

Fabric 2: GREY QUARTZITE. Dense temper of iron-rich, sub-angular quartzite, dark grey to black in colour. Grain size as Fabric 1.

Fabric 4: COARSE GRANITE. Moderate to dense temper of angular lumps of ?crushed granite up to 3mm.

Fabric 5: SPARSE SANDY. Sparse temper of sub-rounded white quartzite up to 0.5mm.

Fabric 6: FINE GRANITE. As for Fabric 4, but with much more finely crushed inclusions, mainly *c.* 1mm.

Fabric 7: QUARTZ/CALCAREOUS. As Fabric 1, but with occasional angular fragments of chalk/limestone up to 2mm.

Table 29: *The Saxon fabrics.*

Fabric	F1	F2	F4	F5	F6	F7
sherds	5	3	15	1	1	3

Summary

The decorated sherd (in fabric 1) suggests that all the material is early (late 5th – 6th century) Anglo-Saxon domestic pottery.

A slightly wider range of fabrics occurred at St. Peter's Lane and Little Lane, (Blinkhorn, forthcoming, a). However, all were tempered with quartz or crushed minerals, suggesting a local source of manufacture. The fabrics appear to be typical of pottery assemblages of this period from the East Midlands. Similar material has also been recorded at Northampton (Pearson forthcoming) and Milton Keynes (Blinkhorn forthcoming, b) from early Saxon contexts. The only exception amongst these Saxon fabrics so far identified in Leicester being a fine micaceous ware, which occurred on Little Lane, and which may be Iron Age in date.

Illustration list (fig.82)

Illus. No.	Phase	Pot No.	Feat. No.	Area	Context No.	Fabric
1	11	50433	(90)1	4	(800)2	F1
2	11	20003	225	1	206	F7
3	10	50432	(90)2	4	(800)4	F4

THE MEDIEVAL AND LATER POTTERY

Siân Davies and Deborah Sawday

Introduction

A total of 14,056 sherds, (241,369g) of post-Roman pottery and tile was recovered from the site, (table 31) of which 64% by sherds numbers was included in areas targeted for specific study. Most of the pottery dated from the early or mid 11th to the mid 13th centuries.

The report covers the following:
1. Methodology
2. The pottery from Areas 1-3, phases 8-11
3. Plots A – G, Area 1
4. The pits in plot H, Areas 2 and 3
5. The timber structure and associated features in plot J, area 2
6. The possibly industrial pits in Area 2
7. The features with datable coins.

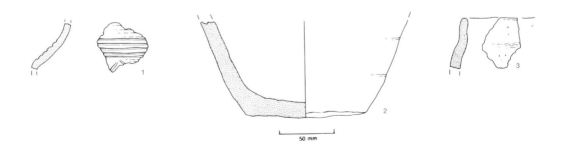

Fig. 82: *Saxon pottery illustrations*

Table 30: *Medieval and post-medieval pottery and ridge tile: the fabrics*

Code	Common Name/Source/Kiln & Fabric Equivalent where known	Approx Date Range
SX	Saxon ware (1)	
ST1	Stamford ware 1 - Stamford fabrics B/C (2)	c.1150-13th C.
ST2	Stamford ware 2 - Stamford fabrics G B/(A) (2)	c.1050-12th C.
ST3	Stamford ware 3 - Stamford fabrics E F/H A/D (2)	c.900-1050+
TO	Torksey type ware (3)-?local/Lincs	c.10th-12th C.
LI1	Lincoln/Lincolnshire ware 1 - ?Lincoln Kiln type/Lincs. Saxo Norman shelly wares (4)	c.late 9th-11th C.
LI2	Lincoln/Lincolnshire ware 2 - ?Lincs. Saxo Norman shelly (4)	c.late 9th-mid 11th C.
NH	Northampton ware - ?Northampton fabric W1 (5)	c.850-1100
SN	Saint Neots type ware - ?Northampton fabric T1 (5)	c.850-1100
PM	Potters Marston - Potters Marston - S.W. Leics (6)	c.1100-1300
LY1	Stanion Lyveden type ware 1 - ?S.E Leics? Stanion/Lyveden/Yardley Hastings - Northampton fabric T2 (7)	c.1200-1400
LY2	Stanion Lyveden type ware 2 - as above - Northampton fabric T1-2 T2 (7)	c.1100-1400
LY3	Stanion Lyveden type ware 3 - as above - Northampton fabric T1-2 T2 (7)	c.1200-1400
LY4	Stanion Lyveden type ware 4 - as above - Northampton fabric T1-2 T2 (7)	c.1100-1400
LY5	Stanion Lyveden type ware 5 - as above - Northampton fabric T2 T6 (7)	c.1200-1400
CG	Calcite gritted ware - unclassified - ?local	c.1100-1400
SP1	Splashed ware 1 - Nottingham Splashed ware (8)	c.1180-1250
SP2	Splashed ware 2 - Nottingham Splashed ware (8)	c.1075-1250
SP3	Splashed ware 3 - ?Leicester	c.1100-1250
SP4	Splashed ware 4 -?Leicester	c.1100-1250
SP	Splashed ware - unclassified	c.1100-1250
RS1	Reduced Sandy ware - ?local	c.1200-1400
RS	Reduced Sandy ware - unclassified	c.850-1400
OS1	Oxidised Sandy ware 1 - ?S.E. Leics/Northants/Beds -?Brackley fabric T68 (9)	late 12th-early 13th C.
OS2	Oxidised Sandy ware 2 - ?Northants/Beds/Oxon (10)	12th-13th C.
OS3	Oxidised Sandy ware 3 - ?local/Nottingham	12th-13th C.
CC1	Chilvers Coton ware 1 - Chilvers Coton/Warwicks fabric A/Ai (11)	c.1200-1400
CC2	Chilvers Coton ware 2 - Chilvers Coton/Warwicks fabric C (11)	c.1200-1475
CC5	Chilvers Coton ware 5 - Chilvers Coton/Warwicks fabric D (11)	c.1200-1475
NO1	Nottingham ware 1 - Nottingham (8)	c.1250-1270/1300
NO2	Nottingham ware 2 - Nottingham (8)	c.1230-1300
NO3	Nottingham ware 3 - Nottingham (8)	c.1250-1350
NO4	Nottingham ware 4 - Nottingham (8)	c.1250-1300
MS1	Medieval Sandy ware 1 - ?local/? a fine version of Chilvers Coton fabric A (11)	c.1200-1400
MS2	Medieval Sandy ware 2 - ?local/Chilvers Coton/Nottingham/Burley Hill- Allestree (12) or pos. Coventry	c.1200-1400
MS3	Medieval Sandy ware 3 - ?local/Burley Hill/Allestree/Ticknall (12)	c.1200-1400
MS	Medieval Sandy ware - unclassified	c.1200-1400
BO2	Bourne Ware - Bourne fabric A/B (13)	?13th-14th C.
BO	Bourne Ware - unclassified	?13th-17th C.
TG1	Tudor Green type ware 1 - ?Chilvers Coton/Oxford or pos. Cheam/Kingston type Surrey White ware (14)	c.1400-1600
TG2	Tudor Green type ware 2 - ?Surrey White ware (14)	c.1400-1600
TG	Tudor Green type ware - unclassified	c.1400-1600
MP2	Midland Purple - ?Ticknall/Derbyshire (12)	c.1375-1550
MP	Midland Purple - unclassified	c.1375-1550
CW2/MB	Cistercian ware/ Midland Blackware - ?Ticknall/Derbys. (15)(16)	c.1475-1750
MY	Midland Yellow ware - Ticknall/Derbys. (15)(17)	c.1500-1725
EA1	Earthenware 1 - Chilvers Coton/Ticknall/Derbys. (15)(17)	c.1500-1750
EA2	Earthenware 2 - Chilvers Coton/Ticknall/Derbys. (15)(17)	17th/18th C.
EA3	Mottled ware - ?Staffs. (15)(17)	c.1650-1770
EA4	Mottled ware - ?local (17)	c.1650-1770
EA5	'Imitation' Mottled ware - ?local (17)	c.1650-1750
EA6	Black Glazed Earthenware - (17)	16th/18th C.
EA7	Slipware (15)(17) - Staffs etc.	17th/18th C
EA8-10	Cream & Pearl wares, White Earthenware-Staffs etc.	18th/19th C.
EA11	Tin Glazed Earthenware - English	18th C.
EA	Unclassified Post Med Earthenware	post-medieval
FR	Frechen Stoneware	17th/18th c.
WE	Westerwald Stoneware	17th/18th c.
SW3/5/6/7	Misc. English Stonewares	post med-mod
SW4	White Salt Glazed Stoneware - Staffs etc.	18th c.
SW	Unclassified Stoneware	modern
PO	Porcelain - Chinese (18)	1750+

(1) Blinkhorn pp.
(2) Kilmurry 1980, Leach 1987
(3) Barley 1964, 1981
(4) Adams Gilmour 1988
(5) McCarthy 1979
(6) Haynes 1952, Sawday 1991
(7) McCarthy 1979, Brown 1993/4
(8) Coppack 1980, V. Nailor pers. comm.
(9) M. Mellor pers. comm.

(10) T. Pearson pers. comm.
(11) Mayes & Scott 1984
(12) Coppack 1980
(13) original id. of fabrics by H Healey, McCarthy & Brooks 1988
(14) Pearce, Vince *et al* 1988
(15) Gooder (2) 1984
(16) Woodland 1981
(17) Sawday 1989
(18) D. Higgins *et al* pp.

1. Methodology

The classification of the fabrics was based on the L.A.U. fabric type series. The fabric codes, sources – where known – and approximate dates are shown in the fabric list (table 30). Full details of all the fabrics, and a description of the later medieval and post-medieval fabrics, which are not discussed here, save for the post-medieval pottery from the clay pipe kiln dump (see below p.196) are contained in the site archive. The pottery and tile was quantified by fabric, sherd numbers and weight per context and summarised by phase (table 31). The forms were catalogued with reference to Kilmurry's Stamford ware rim and vessel typologies and surface treatment, (Kilmurry, 1980) and the L.A.U vessel form series. Unfortunately, the classification was made prior to the publication of *A Guide to the Classification of Medieval Ceramic Forms* in 1998 (MPRG).

The following vessel form abbreviations have been used: cp/stj – cooking pot storage jar; stj – storage jar; caul – cauldron; dri – dripping dish; fir – firecover; lam – lamp; ped – pedestal based vessel; ski – skillet; str – strainer; spo – spouted pitcher; tub – tubular pouted pitcher; uri – urinal; vtu – vessel type unknown.

A separate rim (fig. 83) and vessel form series (fig. 84) has been attempted for the major Potters Marston vessel forms, excluding the jug profiles which were too fragmentary to fully classify. Kilmurry's Stamford ware typologies and the L.A.U's form and rim series for Potters Marston are quoted in the illustration list (see below p.199ff.). The detailed analysis of the targeted pottery groups included also the recording of the rim diameter; decoration; the presence of sooting and residues; glaze and any unusual features such as wear or evidence for re-use. The illustrated vessels were selected to show the range of forms present, those important to dating and any significant features, such as evidence of re-use. The ridge tile was classified using Allin's form and crest typology, (Allin, 1981a).

The quantification of the medieval pottery from targeted groups was also undertaken using vessel rim equivalents (EVE's), (table 32). Only rims were used, as the bases of individual pots were not always a reliable indicator as to the vessel form. The drawbacks included the inadequate size of some of the assemblages, the under representation of certain forms such as dripping dishes and other identifiable vessels without surviving rims, and the bias created by the presence of more complete vessels. The presence of the latter has been noted where applicable. The variation in size between vessel forms may lead to the over representation of certain, relatively small vessels, such as lamps.

The identification of the residual material was not easy. Most of the post-Roman pottery recovered lay within the late Saxo-Norman and early medieval pottery traditions, and the early medieval wares in particular, for example Potters Marston and the Lyveden Stanion type wares, cannot be closely dated. An attempt to assess the levels of residuality was made quantifying the Roman pottery present, and by comparing the average sherd sizes between assemblages and the degree of abrasion.

The allocation of features to phases 8 and 9 was initially based on the few instances where intercutting features and other stratified deposits provided a stratigraphic sequence. Phase 9 was used as a starting point. Only those features which could be demonstrated to be stratigraphically earlier were allocated to phase 8, hence most of the features occur within phase 9. Some adjustments were made to this sequence where the pottery provided independent dating evidence, in the case of features allocated to phase 10 this was the only criterion used.

Very little pottery was recovered from the phase 11 deposits which were relatively few in number. The same is true of later post medieval deposits, the majority of which were removed by machine at the onset of the excavation. Only the pottery from phase 11 features which were near to the structure in Area 2, plot J; the small quantity of late medieval pottery from the truncation and post medieval deposits within Area 2; a feature with a datable coin in Area 3; and the post medieval pottery from the clay pipe kiln dump, phase 12 is discussed here, (see below). A few vessels from untargeted features have also been included where they merited discussion or illustration.

The pottery is first described in approximate chronological order by fabric/ware group from the plots in Area 1, and the

Table 31: *Post-Roman pottery totals by sherd count and weight*

Fabric sub-groups recorded above the column codes: st (st1, st2, st3); li2 (li1); sp (sp1, sp2, sp3, sp4); cg (ly5, ly1, ly2, ly3, ly4, ly); rs (rs1, rs2); os (os1, os2, os3); cc (cc1, cc2, cc5); no (no1, no2, no3, no4); ms (ms1, ms2, ms3); bo2 (bo); tg (tg1, tg2); mp (mp2); mb (cw2); ea1 (ea2); ea7 (ea3, ea4, ea4/5, ea5, ea6); sw (sw3, sw4, sw5, sw6, sw7); ea (ea8, ea9, ea10).

		sx	st	to	li2	sn	nh	pm	sp	cg	rs	os	cc	no	ms	bo2	tg	mp	mb	ea1	my	ea6	ea7	ea11	fr	we	sw	po	ea	Totals
PH7	sh	2								1																				3
	wt(g)	46								28																				74
PH8	sh		352	3			1			856	110	96	5	1	5	3														1432
	wt(g)		2841	78			6			17474.5	1378	1308	30	15	51	15														23196.5
PH9	sh	5	555	3	4		1			4199	478	327	18	27	225	4	7	1	1	1			1				4		5	5866
	wt(g)	82	5609.5	75	139		10			81350.5	11921	6216	185	469	3478	15	87	25	2	5			3				75		663	110410
PH10	sh	2	76							1302	78	63	228	4	100	58	5													1916
	wt(g)	31	429							19099	1844	669.5	5242	70	1324	537	108													29353.5
PH11	sh	15	130	1	3					1295	139	135	12	20	132	19	34	43	3	1			1						1	1984
	wt(g)	594	988	3	57					19622	2767	3226	127	211	1373	216	468	468	24	1			6						19	30170
PH12	sh	1	166							1053	69	100		7	204	21	17	11	26	25	30	46	419	113	1	1	149	7	392	2858
	wt(g)	16	1162.5							13890	1103	1464.5		84	2029	111	270	61.5	470	160	606	1160	15174.5	1167	5	2	1555	42	7020	40271
Totals	sh	23	1279	7	7	1	1			8705	874	721	263	59	666	102	66	43	11	30	27	30	420	113	1	1	153	7	398	14056
	wt(g)	723	11030	156	196	6	10			151426	19013	12884	5584	849	8255	879	957	468	61.5	519	172	695	1161	15177.5	1157	5	2	1631	42	8310	241369

Table 32: *EVE totals of pottery from targeted groups by form and phase*

Phase No.	Form	BOWL	CAUL.	CP/STJ	DRI	FIR	JUG	LAM	LID	OBJ.	PED.	SKI.	SPO	STJ	STR	TUB	URI	VTU	Totals
8	EVE	0.50		10.15	0.12	0.00	1.30	0.20		0.00	0.00		0.66	0.95		0.00		0.22	14.10
	EVE%	3.55		71.99	0.85	0.00	9.22	1.42		0.00	0.00		4.68	6.74		0.00		1.56	100.00
9	EVE	3.45		47.90	0.06		11.58	0.80	0.00	0.00	0.00		1.19	1.35	0.00	0.00		1.06	67.39
	EVE%	5.12		71.08	0.09		17.18	1.19	0.00	0.00	0.00		1.77	2.00	0.00	0.00		1.57	100.00
10	EVE	0.74	1.21	5.54	0.39	0.00	2.35						0.06	0.11			0.00	0.22	10.62
	EVE%	6.97	11.39	52.17	3.67	0.00	22.13						0.56	1.04			0.00	2.07	100.00
11	EVE	0.65		5.19			1.14	0.00						0.09				0.00	7.07
	EVE%	9.19		73.41			16.12	0.00						1.27				0.00	100.00
12	EVE	0.12		0.55			0.00					0.00						0.00	0.67
	EVE%	17.91		82.09			0.00					0.00						0.00	100.00
TOTAL	EVE	5.46	1.21	69.33	0.57	0.00	16.37	1.00	0.00	0.00	0.00	0.00	1.91	2.50	0.00	0.00	0.00	1.50	99.85
	EVE%	5.47	1.21	69.43	0.57	0.00	16.39	1.00	0.00	0.00	0.00	0.00	1.91	2.50	0.00	0.00	0.00	1.50	100.00

structures and other features noted above in Areas 2 and 3, followed by a summary and discussion of the material from the targeted features.

Thanks to Rosemary Woodland who undertook the original identification of the material from the 1979 excavation.

2. The pottery from Areas 1-3, phases 8-11
(tables 33-37)

THE SAXO-NORMAN WARES

Stamford ware (fig.87.1-13)

As is typical on excavations in Leicester, the Stamford wares dominated the Saxo-Norman pottery assemblages, (Woodland 1981, 1987) (Sawday 1989, 1994) and accounted for 24% of the total pottery, by sherd numbers, though much of the material was very fragmentary, and relatively few vessel forms could be positively identified. Most of the pottery was residual in phases 9-12. Much of the dating of this ware in Leicester is based on the chronology at Stamford (Kilmurry 1980; Leach 1987).

PHASE 8

Plot D: The identifiable vessel forms in ST2 comprised: two cooking pots/storage jars; a spouted pitcher, and a pedestalled vessel, with a date range lying within the late 11th to mid 12th century (Kilmurry 1980, 136 -142).

Plot J: The earliest Stamford ware was represented by four sherds of ST3, which included two cooking pot/storage jars, one with rouletting on the shoulder, which are typically 10th or 11th century in date. The ST2 assemblage included a pedestalled vessel (fig. 87.7); five everted lid seated cooking pot/storage jars dating from the 10th century, and three rim fragments from collared cooking pot/storage jars. Twenty sherds of ST1, dating from the 12th century, were also present, including part of a glazed and sooted spouted pitcher, with a slightly convex, knife trimmed base (*ibid.*).

Area 2 F540: The Stamford ware included a possibly residual ST2 spouted pitcher. Fifty percent of the Stamford ware sherds were glazed, which Kilmurry identifies as a mid 12th century characteristic at Stamford, the proportion of the glazed wares being slightly higher amongst the traded wares of the same date (*ibid.*, 134, 166-170). This dating evidence is supported by the presence of a thumbed and glazed bridge fragment (fig 87.3) from a tubular spouted pitcher dating from the mid or late 12th century (*ibid.*, 141). The high proportion of Stamford material relative to the other wares is also indicative of a 12th rather than 13th century date in Leicester.

PHASE 9

Plot A: The undiagnostic body sherds in ST3, an ST2 cooking pot (form 3-26) possibly dated to the eleventh century (*ibid.*, 136) and an ST2 spouted pitcher rim fragment, were all residual in this phase. Two handle fragments, two body sherds decorated with comb stabbing and incised horizontal lines, and the two vessel rims (fig 87.1 and 2) in ST2, probably all belong to jugs or tubular spouted pitchers dating from the mid or late twelfth century. Glazed sherds accounted for 64% of the ST2 present, again suggesting that most of this assemblage consists of the glazed table wares commonly traded toward the end of the Stamford industry.

Plot B: The early Stamford forms included two 11th century cooking pot/storage jars in ST2 with everted, lid seated rims (form 2-35), and collared cooking pot/storage jars or spouted pitchers, also dating from the 11th century. The later Stamford wares included a strainer in ST2 (fig. 87.4). This may have come from the spout of a tubular spouted pitcher for serving mulled wine, (*ibid.*, 27), or perhaps a watering bottle, and dates from the mid/late 12th century to early 13th century at Stamford (*ibid.*, 141). The fragment consists of a disc with the remains of several holes which had been pierced through from the upper side, before the vessel was glazed and fired. Typically, only one of the four fragments of ST1 was decorated with a 'developed' copper glaze, dating from the mid 12th century at Stamford (*ibid.*, 141). Examples of this type of glaze are relatively uncommon amongst the Stamford wares found in Leicester (Sawday 1989, 34), the trade in which may have been exaggerated in the past (Kilmurry 1980, 164).

Plot C: The assemblage is notable for the large number of sherds from the lower half of a very abraded copper glazed jug or tubular spouted pitcher in ST1, decorated with applied thumbed and comb streaked clay strips, and dating from the late twelfth or early thirteenth century (fig. 87.9). A crudely made but glazed, pedestal vessel in ST2, may be a cup or dish, (fig. 87.6), and is dated to between the tenth and thirteenth century at Stamford (*ibid.*, 141).

Plot D: Much of the Stamford ware is apparently residual, consisting predominantly of fabric ST2. The earliest identifiable forms in this fabric included a bowl with an inturned and rouletted rim, dated to between the tenth and later 11th century (*ibid.*, 137) and two cooking pot/storage jars of a similar date. The most common identifiable form was the collared cooking pot/storage jar or spouted pitcher dated at Stamford to the late 11th or 12th century (*ibid.*, 136). A spouted pitcher with combed curvilinear decoration on the body, dated from the late 12th century was also present. Many body sherds were decorated with incised patterns, a single sherd having a combination of incised curvilinear and horizontal lines, a style which Kilmurry identifies as a twelfth century trait, usually found on cooking pot/storage jars and jugs, forms 4 and 6 (*ibid.*, 143). Three sherds of fabric ST1 were present including a lead glazed spout from a tubular spouted pitcher (fig. 87.11), dated from the mid 12th to 13th century.

Plot F: The earliest material present was fabric ST2 which included three glazed sherds decorated with incised horizontal lines, probably from a table ware form such as a jug or pitcher. Fabric ST1 included a small rim sherd from a jug with a rich copper glaze dated from the mid 12th century. The relatively high proportion of glazed sherds present, 58% of the total in Stamford ware, also suggests a late terminal date for this group.

Plot G: The residual pottery included four cooking pot/storage jar rim fragments in ST2, three of which were early everted lid seated forms, dated to the 11th century. The one sherd on fabric ST1 with the copper glaze dated from the mid 12th century (fig. 87.10), is possibly from a jug or tubular spouted pitcher, or perhaps a bottle. Although wheel thrown, it is in an unusually crude and thick walled vessel for such a fine fabric.

Plot H: Two everted lid seated cooking pot/storage jar rims were present in ST2 and ST3. Fabric ST2 also included a collared jar/cooking pot/storage rim, a spouted pitcher rim fragment and a decorated body sherd with diagonal and horizontal combing possibly from a jug or tubular spouted pitcher and dated from the late 12th century, and a jug rim. Those with a copper glaze comprised two rims and a strap handle from jugs or tubular spouted pitchers. The handle was decorated with centrally applied and twisted clay strips similar to Kilmurry's 'surface modifier' M51 dated from the mid 12th century (*ibid.*, 143). A copper glazed, collared jug or tubular spouted pitcher lid fragment (fig. 87.12) similar to form 22-5, decorated on the exterior with incised horizontal lines, was also present.

Plot J: The Stamford pottery was very fragmentary and consisted mainly of undiagnostic body sherds. The exception was a thick walled storage jar fragment in fabric ST2 with a large applied and thumbed clay strip and lead glaze on both interior and exterior surfaces (fig. 87.5). These vessels apparently go out of production at Stamford in the mid 12th century, (*ibid.*, 142). Kilmurry identified few of these vessel forms outside Stamford, (*ibid.*, 168, 296) and this is the first identified in Leicester. Also present in the same fabric was a glazed rim fragment from a spouted pitcher dated at Stamford to the first half of the 12th century.

Area 2 F550: A lamp (fig 87.8) occurred in fabric ST2.

PHASE 10

Plot D: The residual pottery included a handle fragment in fabric ST1 with short combed decoration (Kilmurry's 'surface modifier' M33), and a body sherd decorated with thumbed and combed applied clay strips, Kilmurry's 'surface modifier' M76, both from jugs or tubular spouted pitchers.

Plot E: The residual Stamford ware included a rim and handle fragment from a jug or tubular spouted pitcher with incised curvilinear decoration on the upper body and a twisted handle, consisting of two rods, each made up of three twisted strands of clay in ST2. This method of manufacture has also been previously noted on several sites in Leicester and the county, including Humberstone Earthworks (Rahtz 1959, fig. 3.ST3) and on a tubular spouted pitcher strut from Redcross Street, Leicester (Sawday 1994, fig. 71.27), but has been rejected by Kilmurry as not being a product of the Stamford potters, (Kilmurry, pers. comm.). One lead glazed sherd in fabric ST1 was also present.

PHASE 11

Area 3: The only Stamford ware worthy of note came from, F703, a copper glazed lid fragment in ST1, (fig 87.13).

Torksey type ware (fig. 87.14 – 16)

This type ware is found in small quantities on most excavations in Leicester and the county, the range of vessels, the forms and the manufacturing techniques employed, all suggesting that the pottery lies within the Torksey tradition (Barley 1964, 1981), (Mainman 1990), dating from the 9th to the 12th centuries. Typically, as on other excavations in Leicester, where this pottery has been recovered, all the material is residual.

PHASE 8

Plot B: The only identifiable vessels present, two bowls (fig. 87.14 and 15), with flanged and inturned rims respectively, may be paralleled with material from Kiln 1 at Torksey (Barley 1964, 181, fig. 8.14), and at York (Mainman 1990, fig. 177.183) dating from the first half to the mid 11th century.

PHASE 9

Plot J: A fragment of a cooking pot/storage jar rim with rouletted decoration around the upper shoulder was residual in F503. The rim form and decoration being similar to the Torksey type wares at York, (*ibid.*, 422-440, fig.172), although the sherd was too small to illustrate.

Area 2 F632: A flanged bowl rim (fig. 87.16) may also be paralleled in material from phase 5B at Coppergate (*ibid.*, 383, fig.177), dating from the mid 11th century, and was residual in this context.

Lincoln/Lincolnshire wares (fig. 87.17)

Sherds of both Lincoln and Lincolnshire shelly wares, have been identified by J. Young from several excavations in Leicester, notably from the site of medieval tenements on what is now St. Nicholas Circle, Leicester. The LAU fabric LI1 may relate to the to the generally wheel thrown Lincoln Kiln Type Shelly wares (Adams Gilmour 1988, 83-93), or alternatively, may be a Lincolnshire product. Fabric LI2 is thought to be a Lincolnshire shelly ware and appears to be coil built and wheel finished. The pottery dates from the 9th to the 11th centuries at Lincoln and is all residual here.

PHASE 9

Plot A: The Lincoln/Lincolnshire shelly wares identified included a wheel thrown inturned bowl rim in LI1 with rouletted decoration on the rim top (fig. 87.17). A cooking pot/storage jar fragment in LI2 with an everted lid seated rim was also present.

Northampton ware

PHASE 9

Plot H: F714 produced a Northampton ware body sherd (McCarthy 1979), the only example of this ware from the site, and one of only two sherds of this fabric identified in excavations in Leicester, the other being residual in a modern context on Little Lane.

THE EARLY MEDIEVAL WARES

Potters Marston (figs. 83-84, 87-94, illus. 18-131)

The source of this pottery lies approximately 12.8 km. south west of Leicester at the now deserted medieval village of Potters Marston, where several kilns are known, and one 13th century kiln has been excavated (Haynes 1952). Petrological

Potters Marston Rim Types

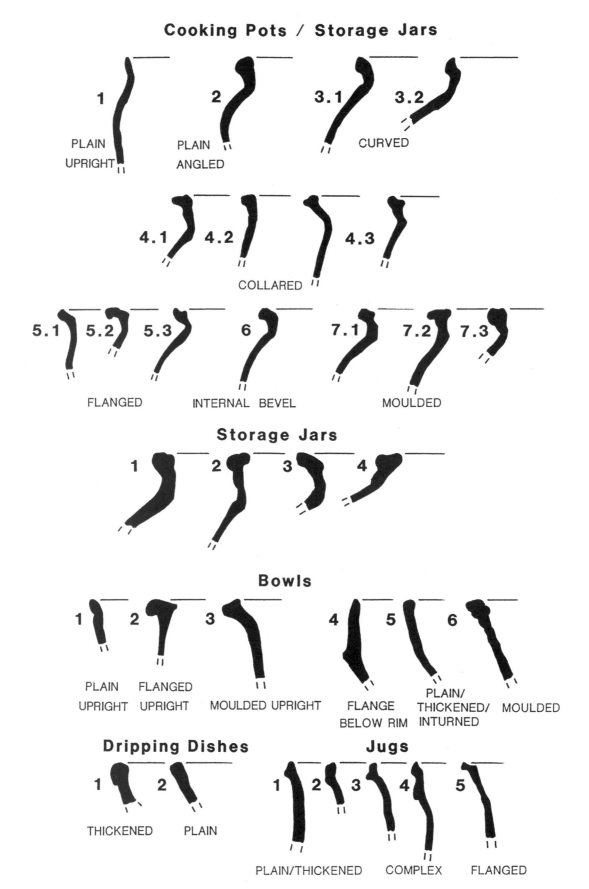

Fig. 83: *Potters Marston rim types*

Identifiable Potters Marston Vessel Forms

Cooking Pots / Storage Jars

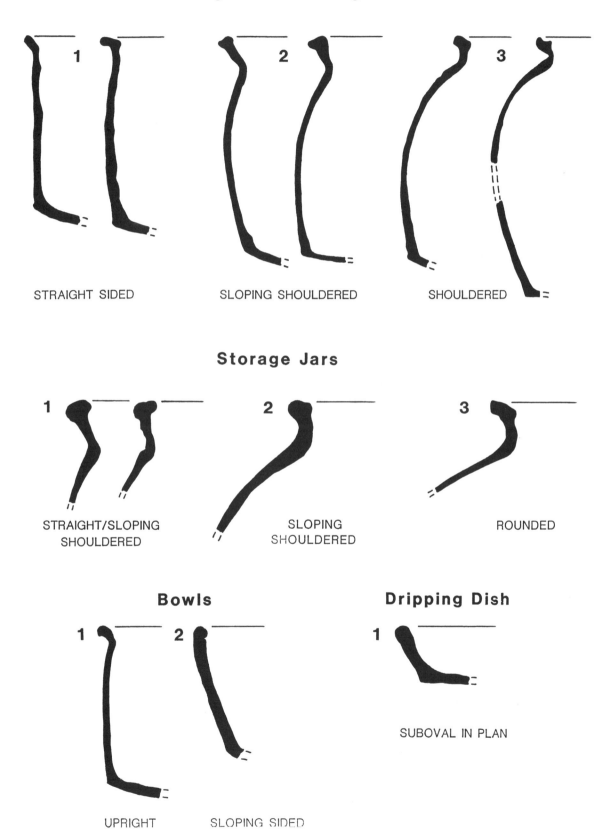

Fig. 84: *Identifiable Potters Marston vessel forms*

examination of the pottery has identified the igneous rock inclusions as syenite, a source for the rock having been pinpointed at Croft, just 1.2km from Potters Marston kilns. (Vince 1984, 38-40). Examination of the post Roman pottery from excavations in Leicester has shown that between 45 and 60% of the pottery from the late Saxon and early medieval levels is in this ware (Sawday 1991, 34). A similar picture is evident here, where Potters Marston dominates the pottery assemblages in phases 8-11 (tables 31-36).

Potters Marston generally appears to be coil built on flattened or rolled out bases, though the evidence for the join between the base and wall can only rarely be seen in section. Evidence that the bases were stood on sand or some other material during the coil building process has been noted elsewhere but is very rare. The base of only one of the vessels illustrated here has any surface impressions on the exterior, in this instance the marks left by a coarse open weave cloth, possibly hessian (fig. 89.50). Presumably this kind of evidence was usually removed during the subsequent handling of the pot once the base was formed, not only to achieve the concave base profile, typical of this ware, but also during the process of building up the coil built wall from the base, and achieving a good join between the two. The coils can only occasionally be seen in the section of some vessels, such as the storage jar (fig. 91.89) or as horizontal lines on the inner wall, usually on the necks of jugs, (fig. 93.108). More unusually, the line of a coil joining the shoulder to the neck occurs on some of the cooking pot/storage jars with curved rim styles, (fig. 88.26). Some of the cooking pot/storage jars, storage jars and jugs also show evidence of 'pulling marks' on the interior wall, where the clay has been smoothed over the coils (figs. 88.28, 91.81 and 94.119). Overall, however, subsequent smoothing of the still plastic surfaces has removed, in most cases, all surface evidence of primary manufacture.

Typologically the pottery appears to date from the late 11th or early 12th century to the mid to late 13th century and is the dominant ware in Leicester and the south west of the county during the later 12th century and early to mid/late 13th century, (Woodland 1981, table 17; Woodland 1987, 97, Sawday 1994, 118). The pottery occurs in a wide range of vessel forms (Sawday 1989, 34-37) and rim styles, many of which are present here (figs. 83 and 84). The presence of the urinal handle (fig. 94.128) confirms a previously tentative identification of this form in Potters Marston (ibid., 34). New forms are indicated by the presence of the spout (fig 94.130) and the rim (fig. 94.131), possibly representing industrial vessels, (see below p.) but the vessel profiles of these and of another rim (fig. 94.129) remain undefined.

Much of the early pottery appears to be have been fired in a clamp or bonfire kiln, the twin flued kiln at Potters Marston apparently representing a technological innovation occurring in the 13th century (ibid., 35). What proportion of the Potters Marston from this site was kiln fired is not clear, but much of the pottery had patchy areas of reduction on the exterior surfaces, suggesting that it had been in contact with organic material during firing, perhaps in a bonfire or clamp kiln. Some of the vessels are reduced throughout (fig. 88.27) and most of the pottery is imperfectly oxidised with a grey core, implying that it was fired for a relatively short time, unlike much of the pottery excavated from the kiln site, which is often completely oxidised. Other vessels, including bowls (fig. 92.90) and, most notably, the storage jars, (fig. 91.81, 84 85, 86 and 88), show evidence of being stacked perhaps upside down during firing, being reduced on the interior and often also, in patches on the top of the rim.

Few glazed sherds were recorded, the use of liquid glaze apparently representing a development towards the end of the industry, though at least one example of a spouted pitcher with a powdered lead glaze is known, (ibid., 36- 37). A wide range of plastic decoration was noted especially on the jugs (fig. 93.105-108, 112, 115, 118 and fig. 94.119, 123-127), which seems to characterise the earlier part of the industry, (ibid., 34) perhaps in response to competition provided by the highly decorated table wares imported from Stamford. For a discussion of the rim styles and vessel profiles, see below.

PHASE 8

Plot D: The most common cooking pot/storage jar rim styles were the collared and plain upright, two of the former were slashed under the rim; a generally 12th century characteristic of this ware in Leicester (Dunning 1948, 22-248). One of these rims and a storage jar rim were also thumbed (fig. 88.48, 91.88), thumbing appears to be most popular during the twelfth and early thirteenth centuries on Potters Marston vessels, but also occurs on thirteenth century kiln material (Haynes 1952). The storage jar rim (fig. 91.88) is typically crudely made, a similar rim from the same vessel form was identified in plot F, phase 9 (fig. 91.89). A sloping sided bowl fragment, with a slightly inturned rim was also present, a similar vessel in the same fabric occurred in phase 9 (fig. 92.99). No jugs were identified possibly suggesting an early to mid 12th century date for this pottery.

Plot F: The Potters Marston ware included two cooking pot/storage jars both with collared rims, one vessel had thumbing around the rim top and slashing under the rim. A storage jar had applied and thumbed clay strips on the exterior wall. Jugs were represented by a plain thumbed rim and a rouletted body sherd, both thought to be early decorative motifs on these jugs in this fabric.

Plot J: Only a few vessels were identifiable, the cooking pot/storage jar with the early collared rim (fig. 88.31, 35 and 40) the latter with a straight sided profile, being the most common. Also present was a storage jar fragment, but no jugs were recovered, possibly indicating a latest deposition date in the early to mid 12th century as with plot D above.

Area 2 F568: The cooking pot/storage jars had shouldered profiles with plain angled or curved rims (fig. 87.20, 22 and 23). Also present was a jug with a plain rim and a finely thumbed strap handle (fig. 93.108), and part of a firecover; a pierced body sherd, with internal sooting. Firecovers are regarded as an essentially 13th century form in Leicester.

F540: The cooking pot/storage jar was the dominant vessel form, with relatively early rim styles, several with slashing on the exterior neck or thumbing around the exterior rim. The main rim styles were the plain angled (fig. 87.21), the collared upright (fig. 88.32) and the collared everted (fig 88.27, 28 and 34) associated with straight sided (not illustrated) or sloping shouldered vessel profiles (fig. 88.28 and 34). Three storage jars, all with collared rims and straight sided or sloping shouldered profiles were also present. Two of the vessels were slashed on the exterior neck and decorated with thumbing on the rim, (fig. 91.84 and 85), the other had thumbed, applied clay strips running vertically from the base of the neck down the body (fig. 91.86), presumably both to strengthen the vessel and as decoration. Only one bowl, with an inturned rim, (similar to fig. 92.96 and 99) was present (not illustrated), and there were no jugs. An unusual vessel rim from the same plot, (fig. 94.131) with pronounced internal lid seating, may have been part of an industrial vessel.

F620: A dripping dish fragment with a thickened rim and heavy sooting on the exterior occurred here (fig. 93.103), the first appearance of this Potters Marston form, which is thought to date from the 13th century, on the site.

F657: A fragment of a crudely made storage jar, (fig. 91.82) with a coil clearly visible in the section, was found here.

PHASE 9

Plot A: The dominant Potters Marston form was the cooking pot/storage jar which included vessels with straight sided (fig. 89.54), sloping shouldered (fig. 88.41) and shouldered profiles (fig. 90.67). The majority of the thirty individual rims present in this form were in the collared upright or everted style (fig. 88.36, 41, 42, 45) a number of which had slashing under the rim. Flanged rims were also present (fig. 89.52 and 60). Less common were the simple upright (fig. 87.18), the bevelled, and the upright moulded rim styles (fig. 90.67 and 77). The two latter, with shouldered vessel profiles are thought to be relatively late in the Potters Marston sequence of cooking pot/storage jar vessel forms. A storage jar (fig. 91.87) and four bowls were identified, including vessels with upright profiles and a plain upright rim (fig. 92.90), and sloping sided profiles (fig. 92.96). An unidentified vessel, possibly a cooking pot/storage jar (fig. 94.129) has a plain everted rim. Very few jug fragments were identified, the exception being a neck fragment with incised curvilinear decoration (not illustrated).

Plot B: A wide range of different cooking pot/storage jar rim styles were present (fig. 88.29, 43, 49, fig 89.57, fig. 90.71 and 76) the most common being the collared upright (fig. 88.49) and the later upright moulded rim styles (fig. 90.71 and 76), the latter with shouldered vessel profiles. Two vessels had incised curvilinear decoration on the top of the rim, one of which is illustrated here (fig. 89.57). Two rims were thumbed, (not illustrated) and three showed evidence of slashing under the rim (fig. 88.29, 43 and 49). A rounded storage jar with an upright rim and thumbed applied clay strips on the body (fig. 91.83) was also present. The bowls included a sloping sided vessel with a slightly inturned rim (not illus.). Jugs were represented by decorated body sherds and base fragments some with thumbing on the basal angle. The decoration was quite simple consisting of incised horizontal lines on the upper body and neck of two vessels, comb stabbing on the lower body of another and also a fragment with decorative rilling on the upper body. Also present was the base and lower body of a large jug or possibly a cooking pot/storage jar (fig. 93.118) with random comb stabbed decoration with a fifteen pronged comb. Similar comb stabbed decoration on jugs in this ware, dated to the mid or late 12th/early 13th century, has been noted elsewhere in Leicester, notably on the site of medieval tenements on St. Nicholas Circle. The thumbing on the basal angles of the jugs noted here, is a feature also found on other vessels from this site (Plot D, phase 10, fig. 94.120 and 121) and from other sites in Leicester, including the Shires and St. Nicholas Circle, and is thought to be a 13th century trait.

Plot C: A range of cooking pot/storage jar rim styles were present, the most common being the flanged upright (fig. 89.56 and 66). Two of the vessels had incised curvilinear decoration on the rim (fig. 89.66), a feature which possibly dates from the mid or later 12th century. A cooking pot/storage jar with a plain upright rim had a band of sooting around the rim top consistent with the use of a lid during cooking. Body fragments from a storage jar with an applied thumbed clay strip and a jug decorated with rouletting was also identified. An upright bowl with a simple flanged rim was also present (fig. 92.91).

Plot D: The vessel forms present included cooking pot/storage jars, bowls and jugs with a significant number of large sherds joining together. The most common form was the cooking pot/storage jar, and early vessels with straight sided profiles and simple collared or flanged rims were present (fig. 88.38 and fig. 89.55). However, vessels with sloping shouldered or shouldered profiles and a range of rim styles (fig. 87.19 and fig. 88.33) including the later, moulded upright (fig. 90.74 and 75) predominated. The incised horizontal lines on the body of the cooking pot/storage jars (fig. 87.19) is relatively unusual in the extent of its decoration. Two of the shouldered vessels had incised or combed curvilinear decoration on the rim top (fig. 89.62 and 63). Of note was the presence of the lower body and base of a storage jar (fig. 91.81) with vertical applied and thumbed clay strips on the exterior body, the largest vessel of its kind so far recorded from Leicester in Potters Marston. Three small bowl rim fragments were present, all with the plain thickened style. Three jugs with the plain rims, two of which are illustrated here, (fig. 93.113 and 114) were present, together with a number of decorated body fragments which may also have come from jugs.

Plot F: The vessel forms included a dripping dish as well as the more common cooking pot/storage jars, jugs, and bowls. The cooking pot/storage jar rim styles comprised; the early collared upright with slashing under the rim (fig. 88.46); flanged rims (fig. 89.59), some with an incised curvilinear line on the rim top, a common feature on this rim style (not illustrated); and the later moulded rims (fig. 90.73). The storage jar fragments present included a vessel with a separate coil of clay used to make the rim, clearly visible in section (fig. 91.89), and decorated with applied and notched clay strips on the exterior body. Two other thick walled fragments with applied and thumbed clay strips have also been identified as storage jars. Three fragments from bowls were present, all with upright profiles and plain or flanged rims (fig. 92.92). A number of jug rims in the plain style were present (fig. 93.105, 106, 107 and 112) together with both plain (not illustrated) and decorated strap handles (fig. 93.107, 112 and fig. 94.124). A range of decorative techniques were also present on the body fragments from several other jugs including rouletting, comb stabbing, combed horizontal and curvilinear patterns, and incised horizontal lines, these techniques often appearing in combination. One dripping dish fragment was also present (not illus.). The interior of the vessel had a blackened residue which derived from animal fat (see Evershed, below).

Plot G: Amongst the Potters Marston assemblage twenty three individual cooking pot/storage jar rims were present representing a wide range of different styles (fig. 88.30, 37, 39, 47 and fig. 90.70). Two of the rims in the early collared, everted or upright rim style were slashed on the collar, (fig. 88.30 and 39). A number of thick walled body fragments with applied clay strips on the exterior indicated the presence of storage jars. One of the sherds (not illus.) also had incised curvilinear decoration marked on the body before the application of the strips. Seven bowls with plain/thickened rim styles were identified, of the three with identifiable vessel profiles, two had sloping sides (fig. 92.97 and 98), the former being sooted externally, and the other was upright (not illus.). Another, also not illustrated, was decorated with an incised curvilinear pattern on the rim top. Fragments from jugs included two strap handles and a plain style rim and possibly a number of body sherds, which were decorated with incised and combed horizontal lines, rilling and rouletting.

Plot H: The identifiable vessels included mainly cooking pot/storage jars, some of the vessels having the typologically early rim styles, one, a plain upright rim with thumbing on the rim exterior, collared or flanged, the latter with a shouldered profile (fig. 89.53). Interestingly, F726, produced one of the two complete vessels, both cooking pot/storage jars from the site, (fig. 89.65) dating typologically to the 12th rather than the 13th century, with a straight sided profile, and a flanged rim with slashing on the exterior neck. Whilst the material from this cess pit was recorded as one context (3574), the complete vessel was found within the lower fills of the feature. Later forms included the upright moulded cooking pot/storage jar rim styles similar to those identified in assemblages from the rear pits in Plot D, and dated to the 13th century.

A storage jar body fragment with an applied and thumbed clay strip was also identified together with two bowls. Both of the latter had sloping sided profiles, one with a plain upright rim with thumbing on the rim interior and the other with a plain, slightly inturned rim. A number of decorated jug body fragments were noted, the decoration included comb stabbing, incised and combed lines, rouletting and rilling. Jug rims with plain (fig. 93.109) and complex (fig. 93.116) rim styles, and thumbed jug strap handles were also present.

Plot J: The cooking pot/storage jar was the dominant form but bowls, and jugs were also represented, and two, possibly industrial vessels. The cooking pot/storage jar rims included a wide range of styles, the most common being the flanged upright (fig. 89.50, 51 and 58), but the later bevelled rim style was also present (fig. 90.68). Both straight sided (fig. 88.44 and 89.50) and shouldered (fig. 89.25 and fig. 90.68) vessel profiles were present with later sloping shouldered and shouldered profiles being predominant. One of the latter, (not illus.) had thumb nail impressions around the rim exterior. Some of the sloping shouldered and shouldered vessels had incised horizontal or curvilinear decoration on the upper body (not illus.).

Bowls with both upright and sloping sided profiles were present, (fig. 92.93) and (fig. 92.95, 99 and 100) respectively. All the vessels had plain rims save one vessel, (fig. 92.93) which had a flanged rim, and another (fig. 92.95), which had a carination below the rim. The latter is one of only two examples known in Potters Marston, the other being found during excavations at a Norman undercroft on Guildhall Lane, Leicester. Interestingly a bowl with a similar rim style occurs in the local Splashed ware, SP3 (fig. 95.137) from phase 8 in Plot D, and this vessel may be residual here. Similar vessels were identified at Northampton in St. Neots type ware, dating to the pre or post conquest, in fabric T1-2 (McCarthy 1979, 156, fig. 93.448) and in the medieval fabric, T2 (*ibid.*, fig.99.590 and fig. 90.334) in contexts dating from 11th to the 14th or 15th centuries.

The jugs included a number of rims, chiefly variations of the plain style (fig. 93.111) though a complex rim was also present (fig. 93.115). The decorative techniques noted on some of these vessels consisted mainly of incised curvilinear patterns, (fig. 93.115). The many other 'undiagnostic' decorated body sherds present, could either have come from cooking pot/storage jars or jugs. A number of undecorated strap handles were also present, these most probably belonging to jugs.

Three unusual vessels were noted here, one, a rim, was possibly residual in F510, as it joined with another rim sherd from Area 2 F540 in phase 8, (fig. 94.131). The vessel is possibly part of an industrial base or cucurbit. In the same feature was a spout (fig. 94.130) which may also be part of an industrial vessel, possibly an alembic, or a fish smoker. The lower part of an externally sooted vessel, probably a cooking pot/storage jar, was recovered from F509 (fig. 90.80), with a hole bored through the lower wall. These vessels are discussed below in relation to the industrial features in Area 2.

Area 3 F704: The only vessel of interest was a jug with a plain rim, worn smooth by secondary use, (fig. 93.110).

F719: A sloping sided bowl with a .typologically 'late' moulded rim with incised decoration (fig 92.101) occurred here.

PHASE 10

Plot D: The cooking pot/storage jars were the most common form, none were decorated. The moulded rim style (fig. 90.72, 78 and 79) appears in significant numbers for the first time in this phase, together with the earlier curved (fig. 87.24 and 88.26), flanged (fig. 89.64), the latter with combed decoration on the top of the rim, and collared rim styles.

Storage jars with thumbed applied clay strips were identified from a number of thick walled vessels. Bowls were better represented than in earlier phases, ten vessels being identified here. The most common profile was the sloping sided form, but also present were two bowls with upright profiles and relatively uncommon curved out turned rims (fig. 92.94).

A large number of jug fragments were recovered with complex (fig. 93.117) and flanged rims (fig. 94.119), the latter with a sloping shouldered profile. One small jug rim fragment had thumbing around the rim exterior (not illus.). Two jug bases (fig. 94.120 and 121) had thumbing around the basal angle and were heavily sooted to one side, thought to be associated with the heating of liquids. Another jug base (fig. 94.122) was notched at the basal angle. Six body fragments were decorated with incised lines. Ten strap handle fragments were recovered, four were decorated with thumbing or stabbing (fig. 94.126 and 127). A large, necked vessel, apparently a jug, was decorated with fine applied, notched and interlaced clay strips on the body, overlying incised horizontal lines (fig. 94.123). This complex decoration has not been previously recorded in this ware, but is reminiscent of the highly decorated Stamford table wares.

The dripping dish fragments included a vessel with a band of burning on the interior and sooting on the exterior of the upper body (fig. 93.104). One urinal was present, represented by a fragment of a horizontal handle, slightly curved to one side (fig. 94.128), the first such form to be definitely identified in this fabric. A number of urinals were recovered from the Austin Friars excavations in Leicester (Woodland 1981) where the form was particularly well represented, mainly in later medieval wares. A firecover (fig. 93.102) was also identified. The vessel was sooted on the interior and the top was pierced from the outside before firing. Firecovers generally seem to date from the 13th century, though it has been suggested that the form may have first appeared during the 12th century (Hurst and Hurst 1964, 94-142). Five sherds of Potters Marston had been reworked as discs or counters.

Plot E: A wide range of forms were identified, very similar to those found in phase 10 in plot D, including cooking pot/storage jars, a storage jar, bowls, jugs and dripping dishes. The cooking pot/storage jar was the most popular form and a range of rim styles present included the early and probably residual collared type. The flanged rim style was well represented, and two were decorated, one with a combed curvilinear design rather than the more commonly incised pattern shown here (fig. 89.61). A thick walled fragment from a storage jar with an applied and thumbed clay strip, and a bowl fragment with incised decoration on the rim top, were also present. A number of jug fragments were recorded including parts of two thumbed bases similar to those from plot D (fig. 94.120 and 121); a rim and four strap handle fragments, one thumbed (fig. 94.125). Two sherds were also identified from one or more dripping dishes.

The Leicester Splashed Wares
(figs. 94 & 95, illus. 132-141)

These quartz and iron tempered fabrics, SP3 and SP4, derive their common name from the method of glazing which entailed the sprinkling of powdered lead onto the still wet surface of the pottery. On firing, the lead produced a small crater surrounded by a ring of glaze, giving a splashed effect. The name is not totally satisfactory however, as glazing seems to be confined to the jugs and tripod pitchers in SP3 and SP4 respectively. The only known examples of tubular spouted pitchers in SP3, which were found here in phase 9, plot D (fig. 95.140) and from phase 9, plot F (not illustrated) are also glazed. However, the spots of glaze occasionally found on many of the other vessel forms in this fabric, including fire covers, pipkins, and as here, cooking pot/storage jars (fig. 94.132) suggests that they were made by the same potters or at least fired in the same kiln as the glazed vessels.

The fabrics are generally coarser than the Coventry or Nottingham Splashed wares, and unlike many of their Nottingham counterparts, the Leicester vessels generally appear to be hand or coil built, though wheel thrown pots in SP3 are known (Woodland 1987, figs.36.23 and 41.105). The vessel forms, handles and rim styles and decoration also appear quite different from the Nottingham Splashed wares, especially in the case of jugs and pitchers, the Splashed ware 3 vessels employing a distinctive range of shapes and decorative motifs, many of which are evident here, but also include applied horizontal, vertical or patterned clay strips, notching, and rouletting. One externally glazed sherd in SP3 was found in Freeschool Lane, Leicester, decorated with applied clay strips thought to be in the form of a dog (Clarke 1957, 60). Re-examination of this sherd suggests it may represent a fox. This and another sherd with zoomorphic decoration from Cumberland Street, Leicester (Sawday 1998, fig. 5) represent the only examples of zoomorphic decoration found in this fabric on excavations to date.

The coils of the hand built vessels, formed on rolled or flattened out bases, are rarely visible in section or on the exterior surface, but can be seen on the inner neck of some of the jugs and on the inner wall of some of the cooking pot/storage jars. The spout (fig. 95.140) may have been formed by wrapping clay around a stick. The pots generally have a smooth exterior, finishing with a template or former is occasionally evident on the rims of both cooking pot/storage jars and jugs (fig. 95.138 and 139). The rod handles of the jugs are generally doweled into the neck of the vessel at the top. The base of some of these handles may also have been doweled into the body of the pot, or the handle base was pushed into a hole in the body wall, which was subsequently plugged from the interior, the evidence is not clear. Most of the vessels are imperfectly oxidised with a grey core, though the firing conditions seem to have been quite well controlled. Some of the cooking pot/storage jars have reduced surfaces, but most of the pots, especially the jugs have oxidised surfaces with little of the patchy discolouration evident on the surfaces of much of the earlier clamp or bonfire fired Potters Marston ware, suggesting that these Splashed wares were fired in a kiln.

Interestingly in terms of forms, fabric SP3 shows some similarities with the other local ware, Potters Marston, the two bowls with the cordon below the rim, (figs. 92.95 and 95.137) being a case in point. However, unlike Potters Marston, these local Splashed wares only form a relatively small part of any early medieval assemblage in the town. The dating is thought to be broadly contemporary with that of the Nottingham Splashed wares, that is, from the 12th to the mid 13th century.

A source, possibly limited to one or two workshops, is suggested in the north eastern quarter of the medieval town in South Bond Street or Freeschool Lane, where several clay pits were found in 1956. A complete tripod pitcher, the base of another in SP4, and the decorated sherd in SP3 mentioned above were also found at the same time (Clarke 1957, 60).

PHASE 8

Plot D: The Splashed ware fabric SP3 included a bowl with a carination below the rim (fig. 95.137) which is paralleled at Northampton in fabrics T1-2 and T2, where it is dated from the 11th to the 14th or 15th centuries (McCarthy 1979), and here in Potters Marston (fig. 92.95).

PHASE 9

Plot A: The three cooking pot/storage jars in fabric SP3 included a sloping shouldered vessel with a simple curved and thumbed rim (fig. 94.132) with a band of reduction on the rim interior. The two other vessels had plain curved and plain everted rims. Two jugs, one with a sloping shoulder and the other with a more rounded profile (fig. 95.138 and 139) were also present. Both were coil built and evidently finished on a turntable, being decorated with cordons on the neck and shoulder and glaze on the upper bodies. The top of the rod handle of the latter vessel was doweled into the neck and thumbed at each side. The top of the handle was decorated with an incised chevron pattern on the upper surface. The cordons, the decorated rod handle, and the dowel are all characteristic features of the jugs in SP3. The latter is the most complete vessel known in this fabric in Leicester, though fragments of similarly decorated vessels have been found on most medieval excavations in the town.

Plot B: Fabric SP3 included two cooking pot/storage jar rim fragments one of which is illustrated here (fig. 94.133) and a rod handle, the latter being identical in style to that found in plot A from the same phase (fig. 95.139). There were also a number of glazed jug body fragments decorated with cordons and incised horizontal lines, the latter being another characteristic of the Leicester Splashed ware jugs in this fabric.

Plot C: The assemblage in SP3 included fragments from a cooking pot/storage jar and a storage jar.

Plot D: Jugs, or possibly pitchers, were the most common vessel form present judging from the number of glazed sherds in SP3. A hitherto unrecorded form in this fabric was the remains of a spout from a tubular spouted pitcher decorated with applied and thumbed clay strips (fig. 95.140). The broken end of the spout had subsequently been smoothed or worn down by further use. This form appears in Nottingham by the early 13th century (Coppack 1980, fig. 71.145), and a similar date may be assumed for this local Splashed ware vessel.

Plot F: The SP3 assemblage included a multi-cordoned, complex jug rim, which was possibly a second, as the glaze runs over a break in the fragment. A strap handle and an incised decorated body fragment may also have come from a jug or pitcher. A small spout from a tubular spouted pitcher was also present.

Plot G: The SP3 forms identified included two cooking pot/storage jar rims, the larger of the two with a flanged rim and rounded vessel profile (fig. 94.134). A single glazed sherd probably from a jug was also present.

Plot J: The SP3 forms included cooking pot/storage jars, jugs and a lamp. The two cooking pot/storage jars (fig. 94.135 and 95.136) had shouldered profiles and flanged or moulded rims, the latter with incised curvilinear decoration on the upper body. The pedestal lamp fragment (fig. 95.141) had a band of sooting around the rim interior and was the only vessel in this form and fabric recovered from the site.

PHASE 10

Plot D: The SP3 assemblage included two feet and base fragments from a cauldron. The presence of this vessel here is significant. The form was previously though to have been produced towards the end of the SP3 industry, and it appears in this phase and plot in association with the medieval sandy ware fabric N03, dating from towards the end of the 13th century. The only other cauldron fragment recorded in SP3 was from the site of medieval tenements in Leicester, where the vessel was residual in a late medieval context. SP3 jugs and/or pitchers, were represented by a plain jug rim and by externally glazed body sherds.

Plot E: A flanged rim fragment from a cooking pot/storage jar in SP3 was present, and also a number of glazed body sherds indicating the presence of jugs or pitchers.

The Nottingham Splashed Wares (fig. 95, illus. 142-148)

A small but not insignificant amount of Nottingham Splashed ware occurs in the early medieval pottery assemblages in Leicester. The fabrics are dated generally as late 11th/early 12th century to mid 13th century, the finer fabric, SP2 corresponding to the early Splashed wares dated *c*.1075-*c*.1180 at Nottingham, the coarser fabric SP1 dating to *c*.1180/90-*c*.1250 (V. Nailor, pers. comm); (Coppack 1980, 169, 218-221, table 7). The Nottingham Splashed wares found in Leicester are generally represented by glazed jug fragments, but increasingly, as here, cooking pot/storage jars are also being recognised in this ware.

PHASE 9

Plot A: The only identifiable vessels in SP2 were two wheel thrown jugs, a decorated shoulder (fig. 95,147) and a base fragment (fig. 95.145). The combed decoration on the former was noted on Splashed ware jugs in Nottingham dating from the early 12th century (*ibid.*, fig. 63.31). The latter had been inscribed with graffiti on the underneath of the base before firing. A strap handle with heavily incised decoration (fig. 95.146) was also identified as a possible Nottingham product in SP2.

Plot B: The SP2 assemblage included a jug with a complex rim and a strap handle, (fig. 95.144) dating from the mid 12th century at Nottingham, (*ibid.*, fig. 63.41).

Plot D: The pottery in SP1 included a rim and strap handle from a jug. The complex rim is angular and inturned, a characteristic feature of Nottingham splashed ware jugs of the late 12th and early 13th century (*ibid.*, figs 63-65, fig. 67.72). A decorated body sherd with incised and applied clay strips may also have come from a jug, perhaps dating from the mid 13th century (*ibid.*, figs. 70,71).

Plot F: The pottery in SP2 included part of a jug rim, the accumulation of glaze on the upper surface of the rim indicative of stacking upside down in the kiln. Interestingly, the Splashed wares from the St. Anne's Street kiln or waster pit in Nottingham were found stacked in an inverted position (*ibid.*, 175).

Plot G: Two SP2 curved cooking pot/storage jar rim fragments were present, one of which is illustrated here (fig. 95.142), both are probably residual, a similar vessel being found in contexts dating to the early 12th century at Nottingham. (*ibid.*, fig.62.19).

Plot H: A wheel thrown cooking pot/storage jar with a curved rim was found here in SP2 (fig. 95.143). Similar Splashed ware rims, identified as belonging to bowls, were recorded in contexts dated to the first quarter of the 13th century at Nottingham (*ibid.*, fig.66.70 and 71).

Plot J: Fabrics SP1 and SP2 produced only glazed body sherds from jugs and or pitchers.

Area 3 The only Nottingham Splashed ware of note was a wheel thrown SP1 jug rim and neck, rouletted and glazed on the exterior (fig. 95.148), a similar rim, decorated with combing, being dated to the early 12th century at Nottingham (*ibid.*, fig. 63.31).

PHASE 10

Plot D: A residual fragment of a SP1 jug was present, the complex inturned rim is dated to the early 12th century at Nottingham (*ibid.*, fig.63.31).

Stanion/Lyveden type wares (figs. 95 & 96, illus. 149-167)

The kiln sources for this calcite gritted pottery are based in north-east Northamptonshire at Lyveden and Stanion, (Steane 1967, Byrant and Steane 1969; 1971) (Webster 1975) (Steane and Byrant 1975) (McCarthy 1979), and possibly, Yardley Hastings, (Brown 1993/94) though outlier kilns on the borders of south-east Leicestershire are also a possibility. Like the Nottingham and Leicester Splashed wares, the most common fabrics, LY4, (McCarthy 1979 fabrics T1-2, T2) and the often glazed oolitic fabric LY1 (*ibid.*, fabric T2) form a small but not insignificant proportion of the early medieval pottery assemblages in Leicester. Fabric LY2 (*ibid.*, fabric T2) is uncommon in Leicester; it is more sandy than LY4, and is possibly early in the fabric sequence (T. Pearson pers. comm.). Fabrics LY3 and LY5 (*ibid.*, fabric T6) both have sparse iron ore inclusions and are comparatively rare in Leicester. Fabric LY3 was the most common fabric identified on excavations at the deserted medieval village of Nether Hambleton in Rutland (R. Woodland, pers. comm.). Fabrics LY2 and LY4 are thought to date from the 12th century and fabrics LY1, LY3 and LY5 from the 13th century.

PHASE 8

Plot F: LY4 was well represented by numerous fragments from a cooking pot/storage jar with a flanged rim (fig. 95.151) paralleled at Northampton in fabric T2, and dated to the 13th century. The rounded vessel profile and upright rim are characteristic of the later vessels in this fabric, (McCarthy 1979, 156-157, fig.97.525).

Plot J: A cooking pot/storage jar with a collared upright rim (fig. 96.167) was present in an unclassified coarse calcite gritted fabric (LY). A sherd of LY2 and undiagnostic fragments in LY4 were also present, the only other identifiable vessel was another cooking pot/storage jar with a plain rim and shouldered profile in LY4 (fig. 95.150), perhaps corresponding to the simple curved rims at Northampton, which occur throughout the period of production of fabric T2 (*ibid.*, 156).

PHASE 9

Plot A: Fabrics LY3 and LY4 were present, represented by undiagnostic body sherds. The LY4 fragment showed evidence of bonfire or clamp firing, having a reduced patch on the exterior of the base.

Plot B: The LY4 assemblage included a near residual but almost complete pedestal lamp (fig. 96.164). A similar vessel in fabric T2 occurs in contexts dated *c*.1100-1250 at Northampton, (*ibid.*, fig.99.581, p.209). A cooking pot/storage jar (fig. 96.152), with a sloping shouldered profile and plain flanged rim is characteristic of the upright rim styles found at Northampton and dated from the 13th century (*ibid.*, 156-7), was present in the same fabric, as well as sherds of LY1 also dating from the 13th century.

Plot C: Only two identifiable forms were present, both cooking pot/storage jars in LY4. The wheel thrown vessel (fig. 96.153), has a sloping shouldered profile with a simple everted rim. Similar cooking pot/storage jar forms are also found at

Northampton in the comparable T2 fabric, (*ibid.*, fig. 68.255), possibly dating from the 13th century.

Plot D: The LY4 assemblage included a cooking pot storage jar (fig 96.154), the upright form suggesting a 13th century date, and a bowl with a plain rim (fig. 96.161), also found at Northampton (*ibid.*, fig. 90.326) and probably of a similar date.

Plot E: The pottery included a residual Saxo-Norman wheel thrown cooking pot/storage jar with a curved rim (fig 95.149), originally classified as LY4, but now thought to be a Saint Neots type ware, corresponding to fabric T1, at Northampton, with which it is paralleled (*ibid.*, 156, fig. 96.485). Two sherds of LY5 were identified, including a rim fragment from a cooking pot/storage jar.

Plot G: The LY4 forms included a bowl with a plain thickened rim (fig. 96.160), and a residual cooking pot/storage jar (fig. 96.156), the plain rim suggesting that this may belong to a vessel with the early cylindrical profile found in fabrics T1-2, T2 at Northampton (*ibid.*, fig. 84.130). A plain bowl rim (fig. 96.166) with a sloping sided profile was also present in LY5.

Plot H: Two vessels, a cooking pot/storage jar with a simple curved rim and a bowl with a plain upright rim were present in LY4.

Plot J: The neck and body of a sloping sided jug (fig. 96.162), was present in LY4, the body profile and apparent lack of decoration perhaps suggesting a late 12th or early 13th century date. Also present in the same fabric, was a decorated storage jar rim (fig. 96.159), with elaborate thumbing around the interior and exterior of the rim. Heavy thumbing is a common feature of the storage jar rims found at Lyveden (Steane 1967, fig. 6) where they are dated to the 13th and 14th centuries. This particular vessel is notable for the quality of its manufacture. Undiagnostic body fragments of LY1 were also present.

Area 2 F632: A cooking pot/storage jar (fig. 96.157) with the upright rim characteristic of these fabrics at Northampton in the 13th century was recovered in LY4.

PHASE 10

Plot D: The cooking pot/storage jars in LY4 included a vessel with an upright rim (fig. 96.155) dating from the 13th century, as well as the curved, and typologically earlier, everted rims. A sloping sided bowl with a plain rim was also present.

PHASE 11

Plot J: A cooking pot/storage jar (fig. 96.158) with a moulded upright rim and sloping shouldered profile occurred in LY4. An unusual vessel with spots of glaze on the exterior wall (fig. 96.165) was also present in LY1. The form may suggest an industrial use, though there was no evidence of any residues or sooting, and little of the vessel survived.

Area 3: F703: A slashed jug handle (fig. 96.163) was recovered in LY4. Jug handles with similar decoration were noted in fabric T2 at Northampton, (McCarthy 1979, 157).

The Reduced Sandy wares
(figs. 96 & 97, illus. 169 & 170)

The fabrics have all been grouped together under RS in the tables, and may also include undiagnostic body sherds in Torksey type ware. This is a coarsely tempered, hand built, sandy ware, generally reduced grey throughout, but occasionally with red or grey margins. The ware occurs in small numbers on many excavations in Leicester and possibly dates from the 12th to the 14th centuries. Few vessel forms have been identified, but several rims, in RS1 and RS2, notably from the site of medieval tenements in Leicester, suggested the presence of cauldrons in both fabrics, which is now confirmed for RS1 by the two vessels found here in plot D phase 10.

PHASE 10

Plot D: The pottery in fabric RS1 consisted of two hand made cauldrons, which were apparently slab built and coil built respectively (fig. 96.168 and 169), with applied feet and handles. The slab built vessel was almost complete, whilst the latter appeared to have been fired at a lower temperature and was much more fragmented and abraded. Sherds from this vessel were also recovered from a phase 10 pit in the neighbouring plot E (F218). Similar vessels have been dated from *circa* 1270 to 1340 in London (Pearce, Vince and Jenner 1985, fig. 69, 43). A residue was noted on the interior of one vessel (fig. 96.169).

The Oxidized Sandy wares (fig. 97.170)

A minor ware group, primarily sand tempered and generally oxidised, with a grey core. Fabric OS1, is thought to be coil built. Fabric OS2 generally appears to be wheel thrown as does fabric OS3 which is characterised by well made and finished vessels. Fragments of cooking pots, bowl and jugs have been recovered in this ware from various excavations in Leicester, which appear to date typologically to the early medieval period. Various sources are suggested for OS1: Bedfordshire (M. Mellor pers. comm.); the south-east of the county; Northamptonshire and Oxfordshire. Similar sources are also suggested for OS2. The fabric of OS3 has some affinities with the Splashed wares, especially SP1 and SP2 and may originate in Nottingham, though a similar fabric was also identified at Lyddington in Rutland (R. Woodland, pers. comm.).

PHASE 9

Plot A: Only undiagnostic body sherds of fabrics OS2 and OS3 were present.

Plot F: An Oxidised Sandy ware rim fragment in an unclassified fabric (fig. 97.170) from a hand made cooking pot/storage jar with a simple rim was present.

PHASE 10

Plot E: A plain upright bowl fragment in fabric OS1 was present in F218.

THE MEDIEVAL WARES
The Chilvers Coton wares (fig. 97.172-175)

The two fabrics CC1 and CC2 approximate to the Chilvers Coton fabrics A and Ai, and C respectively, (Mayes and Scott 1984, 41). The pottery is not discussed in detail here as the material from excavations at the kiln site has been extensively catalogued and described by the excavators. Thermo-luminescence dates gave readings of *circa* 1340 and *circa* 1375 for two of the kilns at Chilvers Coton, but some time in the 13th century is suggested for the beginnings of the pottery industry here (*ibid.*, 23, table 1). Documentary sources suggest a possibly earlier starting date for the industry to the west of Nuneaton and Chilvers Coton (Gooder 1984 a, 8). Fabrics A and Ai are predominant on the kiln site in the 13th century, fabric C becoming more common in the 14th century (Mayes and Scott 1984, 41, table 2). In Leicester, fabrics CC1 and CC2 are frequently the most common wheel thrown sandy wares found in quantity on excavations on the medieval levels in the town, typically as here, glazed jugs dominate the vessel form assemblage.

Plot F: The two externally glazed body sherds in fabric CC1, probably represent jugs dated to the 13th century.

PHASE 9

Plot B: A number of glazed and highly decorated body fragments from jugs in fabric CC1 with applied and notched clay strips were present. This type of decoration is regarded as an early feature of the Chilvers Coton industry, and was found on Site 12, kiln 30 and Site 16, kiln 36a-b, two of the earliest kilns in the sequence at Chilvers Coton, dating to the 13th century (*ibid.*, table 1, fig.103.164 and fig. 110.271).

Plot D: Fabric CC1 was the latest pottery present in this plot. The two fragments both coming from jugs, one, a green glazed and thumbed jug base (fig. 97.171), once again with early parallels in the Chilvers Coton sequence, from Site 12, Kiln 30 (*ibid.*, table 1, fig.46.330, 331).

Plot F: The pottery in CC1 consisted mostly of undiagnostic body sherds, but a number of early decorated sherds from jugs were also present (fig. 97.174). The decoration consisted of applied and notched clay strips, similar to those from Plot B in the same phase (*ibid.*, table 1, fig.103.164 and fig. 110.271). Two small glazed body sherds of CC2 were also present, probably from jugs dating from the 13th or possibly, the 14th centuries (*ibid.*, 41).

Plot G: CC1 consisted mainly of externally glazed body sherds from jugs. Three body sherds were decorated, one had a combination of horizontal and curvilinear combing, another an applied, thumbed and incised clay strip the third, an applied and notched clay strip. All the sherds were patchily fired and appeared to be examples of the early and highly decorated jugs from Chilvers Coton, as with the pottery from Plots B and C above. Three sherds of fabric CC2 were also present.

Plot H: F513 produced a CC1 fragment from an early 13th century highly decorated jug with applied clay strips similar to those from Plots B, C, and G. Fabrics CC1 and CC2 were also present in F714.

Plot J: The glazed body sherds, which made up the bulk of the assemblage in fabric CC1, were assumed to be from jugs. A large number of fragments from a sloping shouldered jug with a plain rim and rilled neck and decorated strap handle (fig. 97.172) were recovered from several contexts within F507, and from F508. The vessel was oxidised pink throughout, but the surface colouration was very variable, ranging from pink to grey. The glaze colour also varied between yellow and orange, and was speckled with flecks of green copper, which was not properly fluxed into the glaze. A jug with a similar profile was recorded from the early Kiln 30, Site 12, (*ibid.*, fig. 103.160) but unlike the latter, which had a coil built neck luted on to a wheel thrown body, all of the vessels from Causeway Lane had been wheel thrown. Fabric CC2 was also found here but only as undiagnostic body sherds, dating from the 13th or possibly the 14th centuries.

PHASE 10

Plot D: The pottery in CC1 included a jug rim (fig. 97.173), similar to a 13th century rim from site 1 F4 (*ibid.*, fig.65.2) at Chilvers Coton, and a jug base fragment (fig 97.175). The latter, with a flat unthumbed base first occurring on site 13, kiln 32a-b, dated towards the end of the 13th century at Chilvers Coton (*ibid.*, table 1, fig. 105.217). Two sherds had applied and notched clay strips characteristic of the early part of the industry, and are presumed residual here. The remaining sherds were lead glazed body fragments probably from jugs.

Plot E: An unglazed fragment decorated with incised horizontal lines and a fragment of a pouring lip, both from jugs in CC1 was found in F218.

The Nottingham wares (fig. 97.176)

The medieval Nottingham green glazed wares, fabrics NO1, NO2, NO3 and NO4, as with the Nottingham Splashed wares, generally constitute a small but consistent part of the pottery assemblages from excavations in Leicester. From sites along the lines of the medieval town defences for instance, the pottery never comprised more that 3% of the total, by maximum vessel numbers (Woodland 1987, 98). Most of the traded vessel forms appear to be jugs, though an aquamanile in NO4 was recovered from the site of medieval tenements in Leicester (Coppack 1980, 223). Fabric NO2 is dated from circa 1230 and fabrics NO1, NO3 and NO4, from *circa* 1250.

PHASE 9

Plot B: Two glazed body sherds from jugs were present in NO3, with varying degrees of reduction on the interior body, a characteristic which has been dated as occurring from the mid 13th to the early 14th century at Nottingham (V. Nailor, pers. comm.).

Plot F: The four body sherds present, in NO3, one of which was glazed, probably all represented jugs dating from the mid 13th century.

Plot H: Glazed jug fragments in NO3, dating from the mid thirteenth century were present.

Plot J: Fabric NO3 was represented by two body sherds, one of which had a rich copper glaze and was probably from a jug, perhaps dating from the late 13th or early 14th century.

PHASE 10

Plot D: A jug rim fragment in NO2 was present. All the fragments in NO3 appeared to be from jugs with a rich copper glaze. A large proportion of the pottery, 33 sherds in total, came from one vessel, a base with extensive sooting around the exterior and a slight residue on the interior (fig. 97.176). Jugs with similarly flat, waisted and slightly splayed bases occur in Nottingham from the late 13th century (*ibid.*, fig.196.149). Sherds decorated with applied clay strips were also present.

Plot E: Fabrics NO3 and NO4 were all represented by jugs and all had a rich copper glaze on the exterior. Seven of the NO3 sherds came from the base of a jug which had evidence of kiln stacking in the form of a glaze ring on the underside of the base, a feature noted on a Nottingham cream sandy ware jug at Derby (*ibid.*, 248, fig.98.133). A sherd in NO4 had incised curvilinear decoration on the upper body a common style of decoration on late 13th century Nottingham jugs (*ibid.*, fig.72.149, fig.150, fig.197.151).

PHASE 11

Area 3: F703 produced a large assemblage of mainly residual early medieval pottery in what may be a later 13th or 14th century deposit, based on the presence of the later medieval fabrics, Medieval Sandy ware 3 (MS3) and Bourne ware 2 (BO2). The pottery was associated with a silver coin dated 1180-1247 (Rutland, below p.238).

LATER MEDIEVAL AND POST MEDIEVAL POTTERY
PHASE 9

Plot HJ: Intrusive post medieval pottery was recovered from F503.

3.   The pottery from plots A – G, Area 1
(fig.85, table 33)

The proportions of the early medieval Potters Marston ware relative to the Saxo-Norman Stamford ware, and the presence or absence of the medieval sandy wares from Chilvers Coton and Nottingham, has been the primary method used to date the pottery groups. Unfortunately, the pottery evidence from

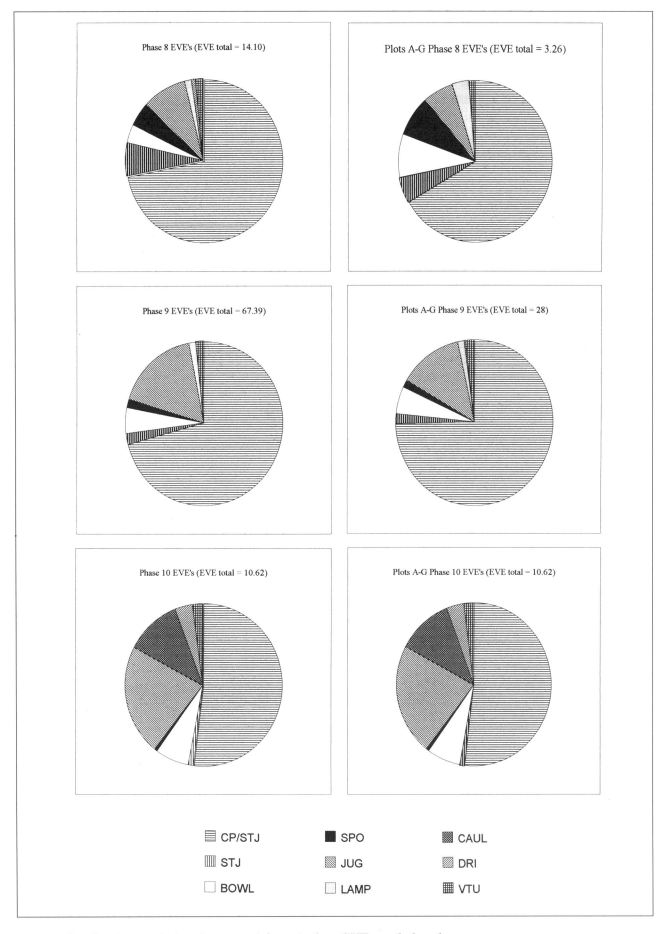

Fig. 85: *EVE's site totals by phase, and Area 1 plots EVE totals by phase*

Table 33: Medieval pottery from targeted features in Area 1, plots A-G by sherd numbers and weight (g)

sx	st3	st2	st1	to	li1	li2	pm	sp3	sp2	sp1	sp4	ly2	ly4	rs1	rs	os1	os2	os3	os	ly1	ly3	ly5	cc1	cc2	no2	no3	Totals	Roman
PLOT A																												
PH8 frags		2					2		1																		5	108
PH8 frag%		40					40		20																			
PH8 wt(g)		15					50		20																		85	1796
PH8 wt%		17.65					58.82		23.53																			
PH8 Av Sh		7.5					25		20																			
PH9 frags		2	50			1	3	255	118	2	1			6	10		8		7			1					464	637
PH9 frag%		0.43	10.78			0.22	0.65	54.96	25.43	0.43	0.22			1.29	2.16		1.72		1.51			0.22						
PH9 wt(g)		29	653			36	91	5166	3217	62	20			61	89		109		202			9					9744	10055
PH9 wt%		0.3	6.7			0.37	0.93	53.02	33.02	0.64	0.21			0.63	0.91		1.12		2.07			0.09						
PH9 Av Sh		14.5	13.06			36	30.33	20.26	27.26	31	20			10.17	8.9		13.63		28.86			9						
PLOT B																												
PH8 frags			4					5	1					2		2											14	19
PH8 frag%			28.57					35.71	7.14					14.29		14.29												
PH8 wt(g)			50					182	19					4		46											301	194
PH8 wt%			16.61					60.47	6.31					1.33		15.28												
PH8 Av Sh			12.5					36.4	19					2		23												
PH9 frags			40	4	2			251	48	12	1			28	2						2			10		2	402	1091
PH9 frag%			9.95	1	0.5			62.44	11.94	2.99	0.25			6.97	0.5						0.5			2.49		0.5		
PH9 wt(g)			268	24	40			5597	1125	310	15			525	41						4			130		60	8139	22296
PH9 wt%			3.29	0.29	0.49			68.77	13.82	3.81	0.18			6.45	0.5						0.05			1.6		0.74		
PH9 Av Sh			6.7	6	20			22.3	23.44	25.83	15			18.75	20.5						2			13		30		
PLOT C																												
PH9 frags	1	8		48				123	15						26												221	186
PH9 frag%	0.45	3.62		21.72				55.66	6.79						11.76													
PH9 wt(g)	3	123		1271				2322	417						886												5022	2048
PH9 wt%	0.06	2.45		25.31				46.24	8.3						17.64													
PH9 Av Sh	3	15.38		26.48				18.88	27.8						34.08													
PLOT D																												
PH8 frags		50						147	16				1	16													230	92
PH8 frag%		21.74						63.91	6.96				0.43	6.96														
PH8 wt(g)		318						1764	213				19	49													2363	1191
PH8 wt%		13.46						74.65	9.01				0.8	2.07														
PH8 Av Sh		6.36						12	13.31				19	3.06														

Group		sx	st3	st2	st1	to	li1	li2	pm	sp3	sp2	sp1	sp4	ly2	ly4	rs1	rs	os1	os2	os3	os	ly1	ly3	ly5	cc1	cc2	no2	no3	Totals	Roman
PH9	frags				82	3			913	47	4	7		1	27			1								2			1087	294
	frag%				7.54	0.28			83.99	4.32	0.37	0.64		0.09	2.48			0.09								0.18				
	wt(g)				514	25			18320	789	26	184		6	209			5								60			20138	4333
	wt%				2.55	0.12			90.97	3.92	0.13	0.91		0.03	1.04			0.02								0.3				
	Av Sh				6.27	8.33			20.07	16.79	6.5	26.29		6	7.74			5								30				
PH10	frags				67	8			787	23	7	3			37		215	1				1			52	1	1	58	1261	436
	frag%				5.31	0.63			62.41	1.82	0.56	0.24			2.93		17.05	0.08				0.08			4.12	0.08	0.08	4.6		
	wt(g)				220	40			11753	761	90	105			326		4730	22				20			515	3	15	703	19303	4676
	wt%				1.14	0.21			60.89	3.94	0.47	0.54			1.69		24.5	0.11				0.1			2.67	0.02	0.08	3.64		
	Av Sh				3.28	5			14.93	33.09	12.86	35			8.81		22	22				20			9.9	3	3	12.12		
PLOT E																														
PH9	frags								1							3									2				6	21
	frag%								16.67							50									33.33					
	wt(g)								11							41									26				78	166
	wt%								14.1							52.56									33.33					
	Av Sh								11							13.67									13					
PH10	frags		2							261	8	7			10		27		1						10	2	9		347	84
	frag%		0.57							75	2.3	2.01			2.87		7.76		0.29						2.87	0.57	2.59			
	wt(g)		13							3070	142	136			64		404		10						102	8	78		4129	497
	wt%		0.31							74.14	3.43	3.28			1.55		9.76		0.24						2.46	0.19	1.88			
	Av Sh		6.5							11.76	17.75	19.43			6.4		14.96		10						10.2	4	8.67			
PLOT F																														
PH8	frags				10					75	2				23										2				112	121
	frag%				8.93					66.96	1.79				20.54										1.79					
	wt(g)				30					933	36				721										31				1751	2732
	wt%				1.71					53.28	2.06				41.18										1.77					
	Av Sh				3					12.44	18				31.35										15.5					
PH9	frags				58	2				372	18		1		23						2				30	3	4		513	445
	frag%				11.31	0.39				72.51	3.51		0.19		4.48						0.39				5.85	0.58	0.78			
	wt(g)				236	15				4816	151		2		223						50				196	10	46		5745	4256
	wt%				4.11	0.26				83.83	2.63		0.03		3.88						0.87				3.41	0.17	0.8			
	Av Sh				4.07	7.5				12.95	8.39		2		9.7						25				6.53	3.33	11.5			
PLOT G																														
PH9	frags				20	1				335	11	5				28									2	17	1		420	148
	frag%				4.76	0.24				79.76	2.62	1.19				6.67									0.48	4.05	0.24			
	wt(c)				188	45				5460	190	116				347									75	138	5		6564	2473
	wt%				2.86	0.69				83.18	2.89	1.77				5.29									1.14	2.1	0.08			
	Av Sh				9.4	45				16.3	17.27	23.2				12.39									37.5	8.12	5			

the plots is distorted by residuality in all periods, demonstrated most clearly by the presence of Roman in all the assemblages. The truncation of the area by later medieval garden activity in the early 14th century also distorts the pottery record in the later phases (see below p.192).

Any comparison of the pottery assemblages recovered from the plots was also limited by the small size of many of the assemblages, notably in plots A and B in phase 8, and plot E in phase 9. The pottery record for phase 10 may also be biased by the truncation episode noted above. The assemblages mainly lay within phases 8 and 9, dated from the 11th to the 13th centuries.

A number of links between sherds were identified from various contexts in phase 9 plot A: F908 and F911; F903 and F911. The pottery from two pits in phase 9, plot A F903 and F908 also linked with that from phase 9 plot B, F909, and with the garden soil, phase 11, F901 evidence of the disturbance noted above. Links were noted in plot F between features in both phases 8 and 9, suggesting that these features were in fact contemporary (see below). The links between sherds from features in the rear of plot D and plot E in phase 10, may suggest that the boundaries between these two plots changed during this phase.

PLOT A:

Phase 8: F914 (Roman 108 sherds, post Roman 5 sherds, 85g)

Phase 9: F491, F903, F908, F911 (Roman 637 sherds, post Roman 464 sherds, 9,744g)

The high proportion of residual Roman pottery in both phases 8 and 9, is accompanied by residual Saxo Norman pottery from Stamford, Lincoln and Lincolnshire dating from the 11th century in phase 9. Analysis of the major forms in Potters Marston, the cooking pot/storage jars showed that in phase 9 the straight sided, sloping shouldered and shouldered profiles were present. The collared rim styles dominated this form in F903 but in F908 the flanged upright was more common. The later upright moulded rims were also present with shouldered profiles. Storage jars, four upright bowls, and one jug were also identified in Potters Marston. The assemblage contained an unusually large concentration of the local Splashed ware, fabric SP3, accounting for 25% of the total by sherd numbers in phase 9, when compared to the other plots. This figure is partly explained by the presence of a near complete jug in this fabric.

The presence of the Stamford ware jugs and tubular spouted pitchers, and the fact that 64% of the fabric ST2 sherds were glazed in phase 9, confirms that, even allowing for residuality, a significant proportion of the Stamford ware here represents the table wares, exported during the latter part of the Stamford industry. The jug in Potters Marston and the highly decorated Splashed ware jugs from Nottingham in fabric SP2 also indicates a terminal date for the assemblage in the late 12th or the early/mid 13th century. This corresponds with the date of truncation for the area, noted in the material from the 1980 excavations.

PLOT B:

Phase 8: F245, F269 (Roman 19 sherds, post Roman 14 sherds, 301g)

Phase 9: F203, F204, F217, F228, F235, F238, F292, F349, F384, F909, F913 (Roman 1,091 sherds, post Roman 402 sherds, 8,139g)

The Saxo Norman pottery in phase 8 included two Torksey type ware bowls, dated from the first half of the 11th century at York. The pottery from phase 9 made up the bulk of the assemblage even though several features, F292, F349, F384 and F913 had been truncated by later activity. The identifiable forms included the Stamford ware strainer fragment from a tubular spouted pitcher or perhaps a watering bottle, the Potters Marston cooking pot/storage jars with collared upright and upright moulded rims, storage jars, a bowl with sloping sides and jugs with thumbed bases. A near complete lamp in LY4 was also present. A sherd of LY1 dated from *circa* 1200, and the early, highly decorated Chilvers Coton, fabric CC1 and Nottingham wares, fabric NO3, suggesting a terminal date from the mid to late thirteenth century. Typically the wares from Chilvers Coton and Nottingham made up less than 3% of the total by sherd numbers in phase 9.

PLOT C:

Phase 9: F207, F276, F444 (Roman 186 sherds, post Roman 221 sherds, 5,022g)

Plot C produced the smallest assemblage of all the plots with a correspondingly limited range of fabrics. It seems that activity in the plot was on a small scale in phase 9 and restricted to a relatively short period in the late 12th or early 13th century, although F444 was a truncated feature, so the pottery record is incomplete. The presence of the lower half of a copper glazed Stamford vessel in fabric ST1 in the secondary deposits from the pit, F207, also indicates limited post depositional disturbance. The Stamford ware figures in table 33 are above average in terms of the relative proportions of sherd numbers present in this plot due to this vessel. The Stamford wares also included a cup/dish in fabric ST2. The Potters Marston included cooking pots/storage jars with incised curvilinear decoration, a storage jar, an upright bowl and a jug with rouletting. A wheel thrown cooking pot/storage jar in LY4 is paralleled at Northampton, where the form is dated from the 13th century.

PLOT D:

Phase 8: F247, F248 (Roman 92 sherds, post Roman 230 sherds, 2,363g)

Phase 9: F214, F216, F231, F242 (Roman 294 sherds, post Roman 1,087 sherds, 20,138g)

Phase 10: F205, F206 (Roman 436 sherds, post Roman 1,261 sherds, 19,303g)

Plot D produced a larger and a much wider range of fabric groups and forms than noted from the other plots. The dating for phase 8 appears to be late 11th to mid/late 12th century, based on the presence of the Stamford wares, of which 44% were glazed, and the Potters Marston vessel forms. The collared and plain upright rims associated with Potters Marston cooking pot/storage jars being the most common rim style, whilst there was a notable lack of jugs in this ware. A crudely made and thumbed storage jar and a sloping sided bowl with inturned rim were also present in this fabric. The Splashed ware fabric, SP3, included the bowl with the carination below the rim.

Phase 9 produced much residual Stamford ware including a tubular spouted pitcher dated from the mid 12th century. The sherds in Potters Marston accounted for 83% of the assemblage. The range of forms in this fabric included cooking pot/storage jars with sloping shouldered or shouldered profiles predominating, an unusually large storage jar base, bowls, and jugs – except in F216 which is unusual as it produced the largest group (469 sherds) in this phase. Glazed jug or pitcher sherds in fabric SP3 predominated and included a spout from a tubular spouted vessel, similar forms being dated from the early 13th century at Nottingham. An upright LY4 cooking pot/storage jar was dated from the 13th century at Northampton. Two sherds of CC1, including a thumbed jug base dating from 13th century contexts at Chilvers Coton were also present.

In phase 10, later Potters Marston forms included cooking pot/storage jars with moulded rims, which appear in this phase in significant numbers for the first time. Bowls were also more common, generally with a sloping sided profile. Jugs with complex rims and thumbed jug bases were present and also a highly decorated jug neck and body, reminiscent of the Stamford table wares. Other Potters Marston vessel forms – fire covers, a dripping dish and an urinal found here – all suggest a date from the 13th century. (Sawday 1989). Highly decorated jug sherds in CC1, and fragments of the possibly later fabric CC2, and NO3 were also present as well as two cauldrons in RS1, perhaps dating to the late 13th/early 14th centuries. The two latter vessels accounting for the unusually high proportion of RS1 in this assemblage, 17% by sherd numbers. Another cauldron was also present in SP3.

PLOT E:

Phase 9: F279 (Roman 21 sherds, post Roman 6 sherds, 78g)

Phase 10: F218 (Roman 84 sherds, post Roman 348 sherds, 4,141g)

F279 in phase 9 was a truncated feature and, not surprisingly perhaps, most of the pottery recovered from Plot E came from F218 Phase 10, which produced pottery linking it with material in the same phase from the adjacent Plot D, in F206 and F205. The assemblages from both plots are very similar, though that from plot E is somewhat more restricted in terms of the forms present especially amongst the Potters Marston ware. The dating for F218 appears be late 13th or early 14th century as for Plot D above, the area probably being truncated or falling into disuse soon after this phase.

PLOT F:

Phase 8: F443, F482 (Roman 121 sherds, post Roman 112 sherds, 1751g)

Phase 9: F213, F243, F389 (Roman 445 sherds, post Roman 513 sherds, 5,745g)

The plot as a whole produced pottery dating from the Saxo-Norman period to the 13th century, based on the presence of the Chilvers Coton and the Nottingham wares, in both phases 8 and 9, suggesting that the material from both phases may, in fact, be contemporary. Links were noted between the pottery in fabric SP2 from phase 8, F482 and phase 9, F213. A possibly early 14th century terminal date for phase 9 may be suggested by the presence of fabric CC2, but this evidence is limited to only two sherds in this fabric, which also occurs in the 13th century at Chilvers Coton. A date from the 13th century may be suggested by the presence of the Potters Marston, the dripping dish and the high proportion of jugs in phase 9. Uniquely on the site, jugs in Potters Marston, some of which were highly decorated, were the dominant form in this plot in phase 9.

PLOT G:

Phase 9: F257, F263, F264, F265, F438 (Roman 148 sherds, post Roman 420 sherds, 6,564g)

The presence of sherds in fabrics LY5, CC1 and CC2 in phase 9, gives a terminal date in the 13th, or possibly early 14th century for this group. The presence of early Potters Marston cooking pot/storage jar vessel forms, as well as bowls, storage jars and highly decorated jugs in the same fabric, together with twenty sherds of the Stamford ware fabric ST2 and one sherd of ST1, suggest that at least some of this pottery may be residual in this context.

Summary

The pottery from plots A, B, and F suggested limited activity in phase 8, that from plot F suggesting a terminal date in the 13th rather than the 12th century. Plots C and G produced no pottery in phase 8 but, together with plots A, B and F, contained later pottery from phase 9 only. Plot E produced little pottery overall, but provided some evidence of activity in phases 9 and 10. Only plot D showed evidence of activity during phases 8 to 10, the great bulk of material occurring in phases 9 and 10. It is possible that all the pottery from plot F may be contemporary based on the links between the two phases and the late date of the phase 8 assemblage.

The front and rear pits in plot D also produced very different pottery assemblages. Whilst direct links were noted between the pottery from the features in the rear of plot D, F205 and F206, with the pottery from the rear of Plot E, F218 in phase 10, which was dated to the later 13th or possibly early 14th century. The material from both plots showed little abrasion, and the assemblages from the three pits, were very similar in terms of the fabric groups and the vessel forms present, especially amongst the Potters Marston ware. This suggest that all three pits may have been in contemporary use, and the land in question, under common ownership.

The vessel forms present in the three pits also suggest that they could have been associated with an establishment concerned with the consumption of food and drink in quantity, perhaps a tavern or inn. Alternatively the range of pottery may simply reflect a change in the eating and drinking habits in the later 13th century. Interestingly, the five sherds reworked as discs or counters possibly for use as gaming pieces, were also found here. The small quantities of the possibly later Chilvers Coton ware, CC2, and the lack of the late medieval wares such as Medieval Sandy ware 3 and the Midland Purples suggests that the site was truncated or abandoned during the early 14th century.

4. The pottery from the features in plot H, Areas 2 and 3 (table 34)

A number of features were identified within Areas 2 and 3 that appeared to form a linear alignment adjacent to East Bond Street (Torchmere). These features were thought to represent either a long plot extending from Causeway Lane, plot H, or possibly individual features from plots extending away from buildings fronting on to East Bond Street in Areas 2 and 3. All the features in Area 3 were incompletely excavated due to lack of time.

PHASE 8

Area 2 F604 and F609 (Roman 4 sherds, post Roman 21 sherds, 147g)

The two features contained little pottery, they produced a typical range of fabrics dating from the 12th century, but there was little diagnostic material present in terms of form.

PHASE 9

Area 2: F587 (Roman 22 sherds, post Roman 106 sherds, 881g) Although in phase 9, this feature appeared to have an early assemblage, the range of fabrics being confined to the Saxo-Norman and early medieval period in date. The pit contained higher than average proportions of Stamford pottery when compared to the other pits in this plot and typologically early Potters Marston cooking pot/storage jars with either collared or flanged rims. The absence of jug fragments in this fabric perhaps suggesting a terminal date in the early to mid 12th century for this pit fill.

Table 34: Medieval pottery totals for targeted features in Areas 2 and 3 (plots H, HjJ)

Plot J		sx	st3	st2	st1	to	nh	pm	sp3	sp2	sp1	sp4	ly2	ly4	rs	os3	os	ly1	ly	cc1	cc2	no3	no4	ms	bo2	ms3	mp	my	ea2	Tots	RB
PH8																															
F504	frags			4				3																						7	11
	frag%			57.14				42.86																							
	wt			44				66																						110	208
	wt%			40				60																							
	Av Sh			11				22																							
F521	frags		1		46	20		86	8	1				1	13					1										177	138
	frag%		0.56		25.99	11.3		48.59	4.52	0.56				0.56	7.34					0.56											
	wt		10		323	255		996	21	2				23	194					20										1844	2242
	wt%		0.54		17.52	13.83		54.01	1.14	0.11				1.25	10.52					1.08											
	Av Sh		10		7.02	12.75		11.58	2.63	2				23	14.92					20											
F579	frags		3	36					5						4															48	50
	frag%		6.25	75					10.42						8.33																
	wt		19	137					20						6															182	263
	wt%		10.44	75.27					10.99						3.3																
	Av Sh		6.33	3.81					4						1.5																
F592	frags			48				70	18						5	1														142	99
	frag%			33.8				49.3	12.68						3.52	0.7															
	wt			216				520	171						19	5														931	724
	wt%			23.2				55.85	18.37						2.04	0.54															
	Av Sh			4.5				7.43	9.5						3.8	5															
F606	frags			3																										3	4
	frag%			100																											
	wt			20																										20	17
	wt%			100																											
	Av Sh			20																											
F657	frags			6			1	12	3						5			1												21	19
	frag%			28.57			3.33	57.14	14.28						16.67			3.33													
	wt			39			16	196	35						15			1												270	748
	wt%			14.44			10.96	72.59	12.96						10.27			0.68													
	Av Sh			6.5			16	16.33	11.66						3			1													
PH9																															
F503	frags						1		1	1		1			5		1	1											1	30	131
	frag%						3.33		3.33	3.33		4.55			16.67		3.33	3.33		54.55									3.33		
	wt						16		1	1		22			15			1												146	1520
	wt%						10.96		0.68	0.68		3.17			10.27			0.68													
	Av Sh						16		1	1		22			3			1											5		
F507	frags							9												12										22	5
	frag%							40.91					4.55							54.55											
	wt							152					22							521										695	75
	wt%							21.87					3.17							74.96											
	Av Sh							16.89					22							43.42											

Feature	Stat	sx	st3	st2	st1	to	nh	pm	sp3	sp2	sp1	sp4	ly2	ly4	rs	os3	os	ly1	ly	cc1	cc2	no3	no4	ms	bo2	ms3	mp	my	ea2	Tots	RB
F508	frags				2			21							8					4										35	1
	frag%				5.71			60							22.86					11.43											
	wt				11			473							145					60										689	22
	wt%				1.6			68.65							21.04					8.71											
	Av Sh				5.5			22.52							18.13					15											
F509	frags				1			104	4						4			1												114	12
	frag%				0.88			91.23	3.51						3.51			0.88													
	wt				5			4136	330						502			24												4997	275
	wt%				0.1			82.77	6.6						10.05			0.48													
	Av Sh				5			39.77	82.5						125.5			24													
F510	frags				7			205	4		2				5	1		1	1	7	1									234	53
	frag%				2.99			87.61	1.71		0.85				2.14	0.43		0.43	0.43	2.99	0.43										
	wt				80			3699	74		26				26	2		6	15	81	4									4013	569
	wt%				1.99			92.18	1.84		0.65				0.65	0.05		0.15	0.37	2.02	0.1										
	Av Sh				11.43			18.04	18.5		13				5.2	2		6	15	11.57	4										
F511	frags				5	1		19	6			2			2					1										36	25
	frag%				13.89	2.78		52.78	16.67			5.56			5.56					2.78											
	wt				36	18		564	324			35			22					19										1018	655
	wt%				3.54	1.77		55.4	31.83			3.44			2.16					1.87											
	Av Sh				7.2	18		29.68	54			17.5			11					19											
F536	frags							13	1						1					1	1	1	2							20	187
	frag%							65	5						5					5	5	5	10								
	wt							99	3						4					5	6	6	8							131	2072
	wt%							75.57	2.29						3.05					3.82	4.58	4.58	6.11								
	AvSh							7.62	3						4					5	6	6	4								
F553	frags		1	7				3	1																					12	13
	frag%		8.33	58.33				25	8.33																						
	wt		6	89				65	4																					164	95
	wt%		3.66	54.27				39.63	2.44																						
	Av Sh		6	12.71				21.67	4																						

Table 34: Medieval pottery totals for targeted features in Areas 2 and 3 (plots H, HjJ) continued

	sx	st3	st2	st1	to	nh	pm	sp3	sp2	sp1	sp4	ly2	ly4	rs	os3	os	ly1	ly	cc1	cc2	no3	no4	ms	bo2	ms3	mp	my	ea2	Tots	RB
F573 frags							5																	1					6	3
frag%							83.33																	16.67						
wt							97																	10					107	18
wt%							90.65																	9.35						
Av Sh							19.4																	10						
F603 frags							1																						1	1
frag%							100																							
wt							15																						15	3
wt%							100																							
Av Sh							15																							
PH11																														
F564 frags	1			5	1			51	5	1				2				1	4	1	3	2				1	1	1	79	24
frag%	1.27			6.33	1.27			64.56	6.33	1.27				2.53				1.27	5.06	1.27	3.8	2.53				1.27	1.27	1.27		
wt	35			31	10			626	75	9				66				25	62	6	17	11				6	6	6	985	206
wt%	3.55			3.15	1.02			63.55	7.61	0.91				6.7				2.54	6.29	0.61	1.73	1.12				0.61	0.61	0.61		
Av Sh	35			6.2	10			12.27	15	9				33				25	15.5	6	5.67	5.5				6	6	6		
PH12																														
F538 frags							11							1															12	8
frag%							91.67							8.33																
wt							179							30															209	113
wt%							85.65							14.35																
Av Sh							16.27							30																
PLOT H																														
PH8																														
F604 frags							11		1																				12	3
frag%							91.67		8.33																					
wt							105		2																				107	47
wt%							98.13		1.87																					
Av Sh							9.55		2																					
F609 frags			3				4		1				1																9	1
frag%			33.33				44.44		11.11				11.11																	
wt			9				27		2				2																40	4
wt%			22.5				67.5		5				5																	
Av Sh			3				6.75		2				2																	

	sx	st3	st2	st1	to	nh	pm	sp3	sp2	sp1	sp4	ly2	ly4	rs	os3	os	ly1	ly	cc1	cc2	no3	no4	ms	bo2	ms3	mp	my	ea2	Tots	RB
PH9																														
F513 frags				2	1		98		3					1				1	1										107	9
frac%				1.87	0.93		91.59		2.8					0.93				0.93	0.93											43
wt				3	1		2925		24					2				4	3										2962	
wt%				0.1	0.03		98.75		0.81					0.07				0.14	0.1											
Av Sh				1.5	1		29.85		8					2				4	3											
F587 frags			20				58		15					12	1														106	22
frac%			18.87				54.72		14.15					11.32	0.94															100
wt			72				594		174					38	3														881	
wt%			8.17				67.42		19.75					4.31	0.34															
Av Sh			3.6				10.24		11.6					3.17	3															
F714 frags			6	32	4		1	263	27		1			34	1		1			12	2	4			1		1		390	257
frac%			1.54	8.21	1.03		0.26	67.44	6.92		0.26			8.72	0.26		0.26			3.08	0.51	1.03			0.26		0.26			4708
wt			60	153	80		9	3116	406		70			384	10		16			50	26	15			5		10		4410	
wt%			1.36	3.47	1.81		0.2	70.66	9.21		1.59			8.71	0.23		0.36			1.13	0.59	0.34			0.11		0.23			
Av Sh			10	4.78	20		9	11.85	15.04		70			11.29	10		16			4.17	13	3.75			5		10			
F726 frags				14	2		106		3								1							1					127	311
frac%				11.02	1.57		83.46		2.36								0.79							0.79						6340
wt				56	10		3193		37								20							5					3321	
wt%				1.69	0.3		96.15		1.11								0.6							0.15						
Av Sh				4	5		30.12		12.33								20							5						
F727 frags			15				22		1																				38	239
frag%			39.47				57.89		2.63																					3951
wt			91				245		6																				342	
wt%			26.61				71.64		1.75																					
Av Sh			6.07				11.14		6																					

Area 2: F513 (Roman 9 sherds, post Roman 107 sherds, 2962g) Potters Marston dominated this assemblage, producing 91% of the pottery by sherd numbers, the fabric also had an above average sherd size (29g) indicating limited post depositional disturbance. The cooking pot/storage jars in Potters Marston included an almost complete vessel with a later, shouldered profile and a flanged rim (fig. 89.53). A shouldered jug (fig. 93.109), and another with a 'late', complex rim (fig. 93.116) were also present in this fabric. The presence of fabric LY1 and a highly decorated jug fragment with applied clay strips in CC1 suggests a terminal date in the 13th century for this group.

Area 3: F714 (Roman 257 sherds, post Roman 390 sherds, 4410g) This feature contained a noticeably different assemblage to the others in this plot, having a much broader range of fabrics. This feature produced the only fragment of the Saxo-Norman fabric, Northampton ware, from the site, one of only two sherds in this fabric recognised so far in Leicester, as well as one of the two Stamford ware jug or tubular spouted pitcher lids from the site (fig. 87.12). There was also an above average proportion of late cooking pot/storage jar vessel forms in Potters Marston, and of bowls and jugs in the same fabric. The presence of fabrics CC1, CC2 and NO3 indicating a terminal date during the mid to late 13th century for the assemblage. The two sherds of early post-medieval pottery in Midland Yellow ware, fabric MY, and earthenware, fabric EA2, which were also present are regarded as intrusive.

F726, F727 (Roman 550 sherds, post Roman 165 sherds, 3,663g) The pottery from the fills of these two pits appeared to be contemporary, both contained Stamford table wares and jugs in Potters Marston or Splashed ware 3. A complete cooking pot/storage jar in Potters Marston was recovered from F726, (fig. 89.65). The presence of a sherd in unclassified medieval sandy ware (MS) in F726, and Potters Marston cooking pots/storage jars with upright moulded rims and an oxidised sandy ware tile fragment (see below p.197), suggest a terminal date, possibly in early 13th century for these two features.

Summary

The assemblages from this group of features were varied in term of the fabrics, and vessel forms, their dates ranging from the early/mid 12th century to the mid/late 13th century. Spatially, the association of the pits F604 and 609, in phase 8, with the linear alignment was particularly tenuous. If the features do relate to plots, it seems more likely that these ran at right angles off East Bond Street rather than from Causeway Lane.

5. The pottery from the timber structure and associated features in Area 2, plot J

(table 34)

The timber structure produced a series of stratified deposits/floor layers. A number of possibly associated features were also identified. Not surprisingly, all the features containing medieval pottery also produced residual Roman material.

PHASE 8

F504, F521, F579, F592, F606, F657: pits (Roman 322 sherds, post Roman 398 sherds, 3,357g) The pottery from these pits date from the 12th century. Twenty sherds of the fabric ST1 were present in F521, including the base of a glazed and sooted vessel, possibly a spouted pitcher, though collared jars are also occasionally glazed (Kilmurry 1980, 14) and a fragment of a 'rare' pedestal base (fig. 87.7) from a cup or dish,

dated at Stamford from the 12th or early 13th century (*ibid.*, 141). The Potters Marston in F521 and F592 produced cooking pot/storage jars with the early straight sided profiles and collared rims (fig. 88.31, 35 and 40) and a storage jar fragment. Cooking pot/storage jars in the Stanion Lyveden type ware LY4 (fig. 95.150) and an unclassified fabric, LY, (fig. 96.167); a sherd of the early fabric LY2 and of the early Nottingham Splashed ware fabric, SP2, were also present in F521.

PHASE 9

F503: cess pit (Roman 131 sherds, post Roman 30 sherds, 146g)

The cess pit, contained a small group of pottery, dating from the 11th or 12th centuries. An intrusive sherd of post medieval earthenware, fabric EA2, was also present.

F573 (253l7): floor, F507, F508, F509, F510, F511: pits, F536, F553, F603 : robber trenches (Roman 300 sherds, post Roman 480 sherds, 11,829g)

Much of the pottery consisted of domestic assemblages very similar to those from the plots A – G in area 1. However, the only pits with assemblages of a significant size were features F509 and F510 with 114 and 234 sherds of post Roman pottery respectively. F509 in particular contained a notably high proportion of Potters Marston, 91% of the total number of post Roman sherds from this feature. F511 produced late cooking pot/storage forms in Potters Marston with shouldered profiles and upright bevelled rims (fig. 90.68), but flanged upright rims (fig. 89.50, 51, and 58) were also present in F508, F510 and F511, with straight sided (fig. 88.44 and fig. 89.50) vessel profiles. F511 also contained two cooking pot/storage jars in SP3 (fig 94.135 and 95.136), and a fragment of a jug or pitcher in the same fabric. Both upright (fig. 92.93), and sloping sided bowls (fig. 92.95, 99, 100) were present in Potters Marston in features F509 and F510. Jugs in this fabric were present in F510 and F509 with plain (fig. 93.111) and complex (fig 93.115) rims. F509 contained the neck and body of a jug in LY4 (fig 96.162) and a sherd of the fabric LY1, whilst F510 also produced a sherd of LY1 and eight sherds of fabrics CC1, and CC2, all dating from the 13th century. Joining sherds from a jug thought to be an early product of the Chilvers Coton industry (Mayes and Scott 1984, fig. 103.160) in fabric CC1 (fig. 97.172) were recovered from features F507 and F508.

These features also contained some unusual pottery. A body sherd from F510 in fabric ST2, with a lead glaze on both interior and exterior surfaces and a thumbed applied clay strip has been identified as part of a storage jar (fig. 87.5). The large size of these vessels seems to have meant that they were not part of the usual repertoire of traded Stamford ware vessels, and they are rarely found outside Stamford. Production of this vessel form is thought to have ceased at Stamford in the mid 12th century (Kilmurry 1980, 142). The presence of this vessel suggests that the contents had been transported here either by a trader, or by an individual moving his household goods, (*ibid.,* 18-20, 168-170). Storage jars were also present in Potters Marston in F510. A rim from a large, finely made, storage jar in fabric LY4 (fig. 96.159) was also found in F509; the elaborate thumbing being a common features on these vessels at Lyveden, where they are dated from the 13th and 14th centuries (Steane, 1967, fig.6).

Feature F511 contained a lamp in SP3 (fig. 95.141), which is not a common vessel form, though it usually occurs in small numbers, as here, on most excavations in the town. A Potters Marston bowl (fig. 92.93) with a sooted interior from F510 may in fact have been part of a firecover. Both vessel forms share the same sloping sided profile, the firecovers generally being modified by the additions of a handle and pierced holes on the inverted base. However, the evidence from the excavations on medieval tenements in Leicester, suggested that at least some of the firecovers were purpose made from the start, incorporating distinctive manufacturing techniques and a rim style not evident here. Feature F509 also produced the vessel with a flange below the rim, a new rim style in Potters Marston (fig. 92.95), but one which was also found on an SP3 bowl in plot D.

The pits, F507, F508 and F509 were all thought to be related to some kind of industrial activity. Only F508 and F509 contained pottery sherds with any significant surface deposits, but similar fragments were also noted in F510, (see below p.190 for further discussion of this and the pottery vessels). The two pits, F509 and F510 also contained an interesting group of vessels (fig. 90.80, fig 94.130 and 131) in Potters Marston, perhaps relating to some kind of industrial usage. The latter vessel (fig. 94.131) joined with a sherd from an untargeted feature, a well F540 in area 2, just to the north of the structure. Similarly, another well, F564 to the west of F508, from phase 11, also contained a vessel rim in LY1, (fig. 96.165) which may also have had an industrial function.

F536, F553, F603: robber trenches (Roman 201 sherds, post Roman 33 sherds, 311g)

The trenches F553 and F603 produced only thirteen sherds of post Roman pottery, fabrics ST2 and ST3 predominating with a total of eight sherds, the rest of the group being made up of four sherds of Potters Marston and one of the local Splashed ware, SP3. It is possible that the fill of these two robber trenches dates no later than the 12th century, but the evidence is limited by the small quantity of material found here.

The robber trench F536 also produced a very small group of post Roman pottery, of the twenty sherds recovered, one sherd was in the Stamford fabric ST2, and fifteen were in the early medieval wares, Potters Marston, Splashed ware 3 and Stanion Lyveden type ware, fabric LY4. The identifiable forms in Potters Marston included jugs, possibly dating from the late 12th or early 13th century. Also in the trench were single glazed sherds of the Chilvers Coton fabrics CC1, and CC2 dating from the 13th century, if not slightly later. The only fragments of the Nottingham green glazed ware from targeted features in this plot in phase 9, were also found here, represented by two sherds of fabric NO3, dating from the second half of the 13th century.

F573 (253l7): mend in floor of the structure (Roman 3 sherds, post Roman 6 sherds, 107g)

Five sherds of Potters Marston and a fragment in an unclassified Medieval Sandy ware, probably dating from the 13th century, were recovered from this feature.

PHASE 11

F564: well (Roman 24 sherds, post Roman 79 sherds 985g)

The well contained pottery dating from the Saxon to the early post-medieval period, most of the material occurring in Potters Marston ware. Fabrics dating from the 13th century LY1, CC1, CC2, NO3 and NO4 were also present, represented by less than five sherds in all cases, together with single sherds of the late medieval Midland Purple ware and the post medieval Midland Yellow ware. The latter fabric is dated from the 16th or 17th centuries, (table 30). Identifiable vessels included a cooking pot/storage jar in LY4 (fig. 96.158) with a 'late' upright moulded rim, and a possibly industrial vessel in LY1 (fig. 96.165). The bulk of the assemblage is presumed residual in this phase.

PHASE 12:

F538: pit (Roman 8 sherds, post Roman 12 sherds, 209g)

This small assemblage consisted of 11 sherds of Potters Marston and one sherd of the Stanion Lyveden type ware fabric, LY4, presumably all residual in this phase.

Summary

The high proportion of Roman pottery in the majority of the features indicates the likelihood of some residuality within the post Roman material. This is born out by the Saxo-Norman pottery. A comparison between the total numbers of glazed to unglazed sherds of Stamford ware in phase 8 and 9, revealed a similar proportion for both phases. Twenty per cent of the Stamford ware in phase 8 was glazed, the corresponding figure for phase 9 being 19%.

However, phase 8 produced a far more fragmentary assemblage with fewer fabrics and forms represented than in phase 9. All but one of the features, F536, in phase 9, produced an above average sherd weight in Potters Marston, 18g or more. This seems to suggest relatively less post depositional disturbance than in the preceding phase. However, even in phase 9, the presence of earlier clearly residual pottery, the fragmentary nature of the vessels recovered and the lack of joining sherds – the only link between the targeted features occurring in F507 and F508 – suggests that none of the rubbish in the pits represented primary deposits.

The assemblages appear to indicate two main phases of activity. The pits F504, F521, F579 and F592 in phase 8 contained pottery dating from the 12th century. The pits in phase 9 containing pottery dating from the 13th century. Residual material being present in all these features, notably in the cess pit F503. The robber trenches F553 and F603 contained small groups of material dating from the 12th century, that from the robber trench F536 containing slightly later pottery dating from the 13th century. Phases 11 and 12 appear to represent truncation episodes in this area of the site.

A number of interesting and unusual pottery forms were recovered, as well as domestic vessels in a typical range of fabrics and forms. Of the latter, the cooking pot/storage jar was the most common form in both phases 8 and 9, interestingly, bowls and jugs were only present from phase 9 onwards. The presence of the large Stamford ware storage jar is particularly noteworthy in that it apparently represents the movement of goods rather than of traded pottery, and may have been bought and kept on the site for the storage of materials related to the specialist activities noted here.

The presence of lime residue on some of the pottery and the unusual vessel forms present, suggest some sort of industrial activity during phase 9. The links noted between the pottery from plot J and area 2 also suggest that this activity was not limited to the one plot.

6. The pottery from the possible industrial features in Area 2, phase 9.

(table 35)

Six pits were identified during the excavation of Area 2 which contained concentrations of a lime deposit thought to be industrial in origin; F507, F508, F509, F516, F537 and F570. A study of the vessel proportions for these features represented by EVES showed that, typically, the cooking pot/storage jar was the most common form. However, unlike the pottery from the plots in Area 1, (fig. 85) bowls and storage jars were much more common here.

An examination of the pottery from the features showed that only F508, and F509 from plot J phase 9, contained pottery with a lime deposit other than the usual lime scale coating found on the interior of many vessels. When tested with hydrochloric acid the sherds noted below reacted positively. Two other features in Area 2 produced pottery with lime deposits, F510 also phase 9, and the well, F540 phase 8. These sherds

Table 35: *Post-Roman pottery from features containing lime deposits*

		st3	st2	pm	sp3	sp4	ly4	ly1	ly5	cc1	ea9	totals	Roman
F507	frags			9		1				12		22	5
	frag%			40.91		4.55				54.55			
	wt			152		22				521		695	75
	wt%			21.87		3.17				74.96			
	Av Sh			16.89		22				43.42			
F508	frags		2	21			8			4		35	1
	frag%		5.71	60			22.86			11.43			
	wt		11	473			145			60		689	22
	wt%		1.6	68.65			21.04			8.71			
	Av Sh		5.5	22.52			18.13			15			
F509	frags		1	104	4		4	1				114	12
	frag%		0.88	91.2281	3.51		3.51	0.88					
	wt		5	4136	330		502	24				4997	275
	wt%		0.1	82.77	6.60		10.05	0.48					
	Av Sh		5	39.77	82.5		125.5	24					
F516	frags		1	7	1						1	10	3
	frag%		10	70	10						10		
	wt		3	60	3						1	67	19
	wt%		4.48	89.55	4.48						1.49		
	Av Sh		3	8.57	3						1		
F537	frags		2	20	7				1	5		35	11
	frag%		5.71	57.14	20				2.86	14.29			
	wt		12	314	326				32	78		762	124
	wt%		1.57	41.21	42.78				4.2	10.24			
	Av Sh		6	15.7	46.57				32	15.6			
F570	frags	1	4	18	2		1					26	3
	frag%	3.8462	15.3846	69.2308	7.69		3.85						
	wt	20	10	223	6		11					270	10
	wt%	7.4074	3.70	82.5926	2.22		4.07						
	Av Sh	20	2.5	12.39	3		11						

may have been used during industrial processes but the deposits may equally have resulted from intensive domestic use.

F508 produced 35 sherds of post Roman pottery, and lime was noted on two of the Stamford sherds which was clearly post-depositional as it covered the broken edges of the sherd. Of the 114 sherds of post Roman pottery in F509, five had a lime residue on the interior, all came from one context (2023). Four of the sherds came from the base and lower body of one vessel, which has been identified as a cooking pot/storage jar in Potters Marston (fig. 90.80). The pot had a number of interesting features. Firstly, a thin lime residue covered the interior of the base and lower body. Secondly there was intense sooting on the base which stopped at the basal angle, indicating that charcoal had been used as a fuel source, possibly for the heating of artisan's material (Moorhouse 1983, 184). Thirdly, the vessel appeared to have been reused as a single hole had been ?drilled into the wall of the lower body 55mm up from the basal angle. The hole had been made by piercing the wall from the interior outward, and the resulting scar on the interior was also covered with lime residue. The hole may have been an attempt to create a small bung hole as its location is similar to that found on cisterns in the later medieval period. Residue analysis of sooted sherds associated with this vessel, (sample 20681), failed to reveal any significant deposits.

Lime residue was also noted on the interior of one body sherd from F510, context 2029, from an unidentified vessel in Potters Marston ware. The residue was quite thick and respected the fractured edges of the sherd, evidently having been deposited on the pot before the vessel was broken and discarded. The pit fill also contained the fragmentary remains of number of other interesting vessels, all in Potters Marston.

A rather puzzling find was part of a spout with a thumbed rim (fig. 94.130), which had evidently been applied at an angle to a relatively straight sided vessel. One side of the exterior wall of the spout had been diagonally slashed and had also been pierced right through at an angle of approximately 45°. The spout had also been pierced through the two opposing walls at an angle of 90°. Both holes had been made before the vessel was fired. The fragment was unsooted and showed no evidence of any other deposits or of wear. The spout may possibly be part of a fish smoker (White 1984, 29-35) or perhaps a distilling vessel or alembic (Moorhouse 1972, fig.31.1-5).

Another unusual vessel (fig. 94.131) was represented by an

upright moulded rim, thumbed internally and externally, and with pronounced internal lid seating. This may be a base or cucurbit, the lower part of a set of distilling equipment, the closest parallel with similar lid seating, being from the Lyveden kilns in Northamptonshire (*ibid.*, fig. 32.11), though pottery bases are also known at Chilvers Coton, Nuneaton (*ibid.*, fig.31.8). Not surprisingly perhaps, residue analysis of the rim revealed no distinctive deposits. The rim joined another sherd found in the well, F540 (context 2143) adjacent to the structure in Area 2.

Interestingly the pottery assemblage from F540 also contained two body sherds from a sloping shouldered cooking pot/storage jar in Potters Marston (fig. 88.34) (2143). The vessel had a thick, pre-depositional, burnt lime residue on the interior.

A vessel in the Stanion Lyveden fabric, LY1, with a possibly industrial function was recovered from another feature, F564 associated with the structure in plot J, (fig. 96.165), close to the pits F507-F510. This well contained possibly intrusive early post medieval as well as earlier medieval pottery, but was allocated to phase 11 on the basis of the later pottery. The vessel was hand made with traces of glaze on the exterior wall. There was no evidence of any residues or sooting, but again, little of the vessel survived. A glazed vessel with a similar rim, though slightly narrow in form has been identified as an industrial base or cucurbit (Bellamy and Nicholson 1972, fig. 28.4). This latter vessel however, in an oxidised ware darkened through use, survived as a complete profile, with a projecting ledge on the exterior wall to support the alembic above.

The date when pottery distilling equipment first began to be used is not clear, but distilling bases seem to have been introduced by the late 13th century, though there is little evidence of pottery alembics at such an early date (Moorhouse 1972, 105). F540 which contained a fragment on the internally lid seated rim noted above, was allocated to phase 8, but dated to the late 12th or early 13th century, by the presence of a Stamford ware tubular spouted pitcher in fabric ST2 (fig. 87.3). All the other targeted industrial features were allocated to phase 9 by the presence of fabrics CC1, LY1 and LY5, and all date from the 13th, or possibly the 14th century.

7. The pottery from the features with datable coins (table 36)

Two features, a well, F568 and a pit, F703, neither of which fell into any of the other targeted categories, contained medieval silver pennies. The well produced a coin dated to reign of Richard 1 (1189-1199) and the pit, a coin dated to 1180-1247. The latter had been cut in half for use as a half penny, of the short cross issue (1180-1247) (see p.238).

PHASE 8

Area 2 F568: well (Roman 94 sherds, post Roman 99 sherds, 4134g)

The coin was recovered from a slump layer below deposits containing much of the pottery which was recovered from the secondary fills of a truncated feature which was not fully excavated. Despite this and the high levels of residual Roman pottery present, a reasonably sized pottery assemblage was recovered with a relatively high average sherd weight, some of the vessels surviving with complete profiles. The major fabric was Potters Marston which produced a range of forms including cooking pot/storage jars with sloping shouldered and shouldered profiles (fig. 87.20, 22 and 23) with plain angled or curved rim styles, including a complete vessel (fig. 87.22) with a pouring lip. A jug with a plain rim, shouldered profile and finely thumbed strap handle (fig. 93.108), bowls, and a firecover were also present, the latter (not illustrated) fitting in well with the coin evidence as firecovers are generally dated from the 13th century or later in Leicester although they are also known from 12th century contexts elsewhere (Hurst 1961, 265).

PHASE 11

Area 3 F703: pit (Roman 205 sherds, post Roman 586 sherds, 9345g.)

The pottery assemblage contained residual Stamford ware, as well as a large group of Potters Marston and Stanion Lyveden type ware fabric LY4, dating from the 12th and 13th centuries, and fragments of the Nottingham Splashed wares, the latter fabric SP1, being dated to *circa* 1180/90 to 1250 at Nottingham (V. Nailor, pers. comm). The Chilvers Coton fabrics CC1 and CC2, dating from the 13th century were also present, together with a significant group of the Bourne ware fabric, BO2. This fabric corresponds to fabrics A/B at Bourne, where the kilns were dated typologically to *circa* 1300, though fabric A is thought to date from the 13th century, (McCarthy and Brooks 1988, 259). The coin, which was found in the uppermost truncation slump deposits (3507), may be residual in this context, unfortunately the dating evidence is not clear.

Table 36: *Medieval pottery totals from features containing medieval coins*

		st2	st1	pm	sp3	sp2	sp1	ly4	rs	cc1	cc2	bo2	ms3	Totals	Roman
PH8															
F568	frags	3		89	3	1		3						99	94
	frag%	3.03		89.9	3.03	1.01		3.03							
	wt	23		3993	78	5		35						4134	1164
	wt%	0.56		96.59	1.89	0.12		0.85							
	Av Sh	7.67		44.87	26	5		11.67							
PH9															
F703	frags	30	5	384	34	6	3	58	2	20	1	42	1	586	205
	frag%	5.12	0.85	65.53	5.8	1.02	0.51	9.9	0.34	3.41	0.17	7.17	0.17		
	wt	197	60	6504	1054	134	45	776	13	86	2	466	8	9345	3309
	wt%	2.11	0.64	69.6	11.28	1.43	0.48	8.3	0.14	0.92	0.02	4.99	0.09		
	Av Sh	6.57	12	16.94	31	22.33	15	13.38	6.5	4.3	2	11.1	8		

8. The pottery from the medieval and post medieval truncation deposits in Areas 1 and 2

Area 1

The plot A assemblage included pottery recovered from the 1980 and 1991 excavations at Causeway Lane. The 1980 material was recovered from a series of intercutting pits and overlying garden soil. Links were identified between the pit material and pottery recovered from the overlying garden soil by R. Woodland, providing a date for the truncation of this area to around the early 13th century. This ties in well with the presence of the highly decorated local Splashed ware, SP3, and the Stamford table ware jugs and tubular spouted pitchers, which suggest a terminal date for the pottery from stratified deposits within this assemblage from the late 12th or early 13th century.

Area 2

During the excavation a number of deposits from Area 2 were identified as possible truncation layers and were carefully excavated by hand in order to gather dating evidence. The context groups identified were as follows:- G290 G291 G292. Detailed analysis of the pottery assemblages from these groups was undertaken, but many of the assemblages were small and abraded.

G290 consisted of garden soil and related features. The pottery present indicated a deposition date during the 13th century. Residuality was evident from the presence of an early Stamford cooking pot/storage jar with an everted, lid seated rim dated to the 10th and 11th centuries. Potters Marston dominated the assemblage but produced few identifiable forms, the exception being some cooking pot/storage jar rim fragments of the collared upright style. The latest material identified was in the Chilvers Coton and Nottingham fabrics, CC1 and NO3, dating from the 13th or early 14th centuries.

G291 produced a very different assemblage from G290. A range of post-medieval fabrics, mainly earthenwares, was present dating from the early post-medieval period. They included Midland Yellow Ware, fabric MY and Midland Blackwares, MB, and also the Pearlwares, EA9, suggesting a terminal date in the 17th or possibly the 18th century for this group.

G292 produced the smallest assemblage which was also very fragmented and abraded. The latest material identified was Midland Purple, MP, and Midland Blackware, MB, the latter dated from the late 16th or 17th centuries. Of interest was the handle fragment from a skillet, in a Medieval Sandy ware, fabric MS3, the only recorded example of this late medieval form from the site.

Summary

The pottery assemblages from the post medieval truncation deposits were very small and fragmentary making dating difficult. Group 290 produced material of late 13th/early 14th century date, the other two groups (291 & 292) produced material dating to the early post-medieval period suggesting the possibility that there were at least two episodes when garden soil was deposited and truncation may have taken place, the first in the 14th century and a second in the 17th or possibly 18th century.

9. The pottery forms

The pottery from area 1 was quantified using EVES (fig. 86) to enable comparison of the assemblages from the different plots. The totals for the whole area provide an interesting summary of the range of domestic vessels in use here from the Saxo-

Norman to the early medieval/medieval period. Not surprisingly, given the amount of residual Roman and later Saxo-Norman pottery present, the cooking pot/storage jar was the most common form followed by jugs, other forms accounting for a very small proportion of the EVE's recorded. This contrasts with the pottery from the earliest post Roman phases 1 to 2D at the Austin Friars, Leicester, which were dated up to the late 13th or early 14th century, where the essentially medieval form, the jug, dominated the pottery assemblages (Woodland 1981, table 18).

The forms present in area 1 but not represented by EVE's included the Stamford ware pedestalled vessels, tubular spouted pitchers and the spout strainer; the firecovers and the urinal in Potters Marston, and vessels of unidentifiable form.

Looking at the pottery from the site as a whole, the Stamford ware vessel forms and rim types have already been described at their kiln source by Kilmurry (1980). Of the remaining wares, only the local Potters Marston occurred in sufficient quantity to merit discussion of the rim styles (fig. 83) and vessel profiles (fig. 84).

The Potters Marston cooking pot/storage jars occurred in a range of rim styles. The collared rim (fig. 83. 4.1-4.3) occurred predominantly on straight sided and on sloping shouldered vessels in phase 8 (fig 88.28 and 34) where it accounted for over 40% of the total EVE's recorded across the site. This style appears to be influenced by the Stamford collared forms (Kilmurry 1980 form 4/5) produced from the mid to late 11th century, but unlike the finely made, wheel thrown, Stamford wares, the local coil built pots are often, though not always, crudely made and finished with slashing under the rim on the exterior collar.

Flanged rims (fig. 83. 5.1-5.3) became more common in phases 9 and 10, but this rim style was also particularly common in Area 2, F540, phase 8, which was dated later than most features in this group to the mid/late 12th or early 13th century. Numerous variations in this rim style were present, but all had the basic characteristic of a short neck and a flanged rim top. The vessels generally had sloping shouldered (fig. 89.56) or shouldered profiles (fig. 89.60) which, typologically, appear to be later than the straight sided form, though flanged rims also occur with this profile (fig. 89.54 and 55).

Upright moulded rims (fig. 83 7.1-7.3) appear in phase 9 but seem to become more common in phase 10. One of the more significant finds from the study of the cooking pot/storage jar rim styles was the occurrence of this rim in the 13th century features in plots D and E phase 10, (fig. 90.72, 78 and 79), at the expense of the flanged upright style. Generally, this rim style occurs with the shouldered vessel profile (fig. 90.78), though sloping shouldered vessels are also present (fig. 90.73).

The plain upright rim (fig. 83.1) (fig 87.18-19) and the rim with an internal bevel (fig. 83.6) (fig. 90.67 and 68) are uncommon and only occur sporadically on the site. The plain angled or thickened rim (fig. 83.2) with the sloping shouldered profile (fig. 87.20, 21) appears early in the sequence, as does the curved rim (fig. 83. 3.1 and 3.2) (fig. 88.22-25 and 88.26). Both were found in the well F568 in phase 8, with the coin dated *circa* 1189-1199 (see above) where the latter was the most common rim style present. The curved rim was associated with both sloping shouldered and shouldered vessel profiles, one of the latter was a small vessel with a pouring lip (fig. 87.22).

Several storage jar rim styles were identified (fig. 83.1-4) (fig. 91.82-89). One, (fig. 83. 2) (fig. 91.84-86) is clearly related to the collared cooking pot/storage jars and appears with straight sided or sloping shouldered profiles. Storage jars with sloping shouldered and rounded profiles also occur in a variety of other rim styles (fig. 83.1, 3 and 4) (fig. 91.83, 87-89). How-

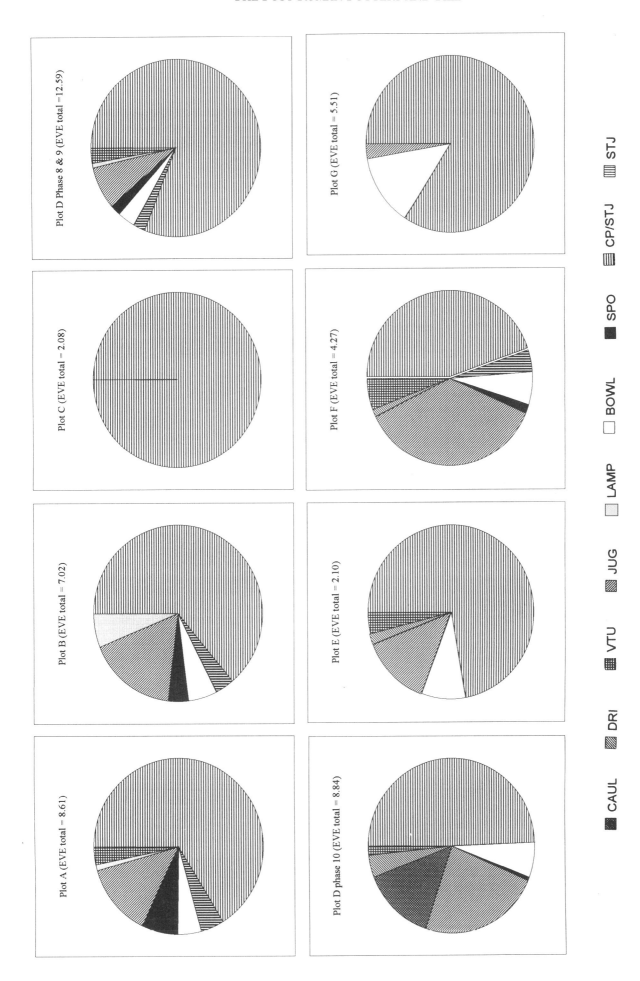

Fig. 86: *Area 1 EVE's totals by plot*

ever, these were too few in number and too fragmentary to allow any conclusions to be drawn concerning the relationship between the vessel profile and the rim style. Indeed, most of the vessels, which first appear in phase 8, were identified by the occurrence of thick walled body sherds with applied and thumbed clay strips. The base, (fig. 91.81) represents an unusually large pot, perhaps made to order.

Bowls were present from the earliest phases but become far more common in phase 10. There appeared to be two main profiles, the upright form (fig. 83. 1-3) with plain, flanged or occasionally moulded rims (fig. 92.90-94) and a sloping sided, wide mouthed form, (fig. 92.95-101). The upright profile (fig. 92.91) has similarities with the Potters Marston cooking pot/storage jars, and many of these vessels were also sooted externally. However the bowls are characterised by having a base diameter greater than their height and a rim diameter greater than the base diameter.

The sloping sided bowl with the flange below the rim from phase 9 (fig. 83. 4) (fig. 92.95), also occurred in phase 8 in Splashed ware 3, (fig. 95.137), suggesting that this profile appears early in the sequence amongst the local wares. However the profile seems to become more popular in the later phases and made up a significant proportion of the phase 10 assemblages, where it occurs with plain, thickened or slightly inturned rims, (fig. 83. 5). Similar vessels were identified in the same fabric from the later medieval phases of the Austin Friars (Woodland 1981, 124, fig. 30.61), whilst the moulded rim from phase 9 (fig. 83 6) (fig. 92.101) is reminiscent of the more complex rims found in the medieval sandy wares in 13th century contexts at Chilvers Coton (Mayes and Scott 1984, 62, fig. 83.632-625).

Two firecovers were identified, one, which was too fragmentary to illustrate, was found in F568, dated by a coin to the late 12th or early 13th century. The other occurred in phase 10 (fig. 93.102), but only part of the upper half of the vessel was recovered. Enough of the latter survived, however, to show that this pot, in. common with others found in this ware in the town, was circular in plan for use over a central hearth, with a handle smeared on to the upper surface, and holes pierced through the upper wall.

The Potters Marston dripping dishes are thought to date generally from the 13th century. Too few vessel were present to comment on the dating of the rim styles (figs. 83 and 84) (fig. 93.103 and 104), but comparative material from other excavations in Leicester confirms that the vessels are generally sub oval in plan with two opposed pouring lips and a centrally placed handle at one side.

The majority of the jugs had plain rims (fig. 83.1-2; fig. 93 fig. 93.105-114). One vessel (illus. 108) occurring with the coin dated *circa* 1189-1199 (see p.238). The jugs with complex rims (fig. 83.3-4) (fig. 93.115-117) are apparently later in the sequence. Although too few profiles survived to enable a classification of the vessel forms, jugs with flanged rims (fig. 83.5) and thumbed bases, (fig. 94.119 and 120) also appear to be later in the sequence, only occurring here in phase 10. A profile of a jug with a similar flanged rim and thumbed base was found on the site of medieval tenements in Leicester. Strap handles, either plain or thumbed, are the most common handle form, though as with the jug bodies, other forms of decoration are also found on the handles.

The most convincing evidence to date for a urinal in this fabric, part of a horizontal handle (fig. 94.128) also occurs here. Urinals with similar handles were found in the medieval sandy ware fabrics at the Austin Friars (Woodland 1981). Fragments of two, possibly industrial, vessels, also occurred in Potters Marston (fig. 94.130 and 131). These have already been described in detail (see above), and were probably 'one offs' made to order, for a specific function, their fragmentary nature

meaning that, unfortunately, their vessel form remains undefined.

10. Evidence of wear and use

Pottery was an inexpensive commodity and its length of use is uncertain. Some pottery forms such as storage jars, dripping dishes and firecovers may have had a longer life than the cooking pots and bowls which were subject to heavier usage.

Many of the cooking pot/storage jars and bowls from Causeway Lane were sooted externally, the pattern of the sooting was generally consistent with the vessels having been used several times at least on, or next to, a wood or coal fire. Straight sided or sloping shouldered cooking pot/storage jars were often sooted over the whole exterior surface including the rim. Conversely the shouldered vessels often displayed a lack of sooting above the shoulder, where the vessel was not in the path of the flame (Moorhouse 1986, 108). Many of the pots also had patches of burning on the interior, where the contents had over heated and burnt on to the wall. The streaked sooting, noted on the exterior body of some of the Potters Marston and the Stanion Lyveden type ware cooking pot/storage jars, was indicative of the liquid contents of the vessel having boiled over and run down the exterior walls during heating over a fire. Several Potters Marston vessels classified by their relative size as storage jars, also had evidence of external sooting (fig. 91.84 and 85). Sooting was also noted on the exterior surfaces of both the cauldrons in RS1. The presence of fatty residues on the interior of one cauldron analysed by Dr. Evershed, (fig. 96.169) suggested that it had been used for the cooking of meat, whilst residue analysis of externally sooted cooking pot/storage jars in Potters Marston, failed to reveal any significant fatty deposits.

The firecovers in Potters Marston are usually lightly sooted on the interior (fig. 93.102), bowls in the same fabric are also occasionally sooted on the interior (fig. 92.93), suggesting that too may have been used as a makeshift fire cover.

A number of distinctive sooting patterns were also identified. The patterns are often difficult to interpret however, as in many instances only a fraction of the vessel survives and hence the full extent of the sooting is not clear. A number of the more complete Potters Marston cooking pot/storage jars, showed evidence of sooting on one side of the vessel but not the base, consistent with the vessel being placed next to the fire rather than on it, and perhaps indicative of the vessel having been used only once. Interestingly many medieval cookery, craft and medical recipes call for a new earthenware pot to be used, (Moorhouse 1983, 173,176,183).

The localised sooting on some Potters Marston jugs (fig. 94.120 and 121) is believed to have resulted from the sides of these vessels being placed near a fire, perhaps to heat mulled wine (*ibid.*, 183). One of these vessels (fig. 94.121) was examined for any traces of residue, but unfortunately there is at present no reliable test for the presence of water based liquids such as wine or beer (see below). Similar vessels in the same fabric from elsewhere in the town show that the sooting is usually present on the lower body and exterior base opposite the handle, and suggests that jugs with thumbed bases were consistently used for this purpose. The sooting on the Potters Marston dripping dishes demonstrates a similar pattern. One of the fragmentary vessels had evidence of sooting on the outer wall (fig. 93.104). An examination of the more complete vessels in this ware shows that the sooting consistently occurs on the longitudinal side of the vessel opposite the handle, evidence that the vessel was placed next to the fire to collect the juices from the meat roasting on the spit above. Residue analysis of four of the dripping dishes from Causeway Lane, of which two are illustrated here (fig. 93.103 and 104), confirmed the function of these vessels, as appreciable quantities of fatty residues were present (see below p.00).

The distinct band of sooting present on the interior of the upper body of the Splashed ware 3 pedestalled lamp (fig. 95.141), indicates the level of the fuel used in the lamp. Residue analysis of this vessel, and of vessels in Stanion Lyveden type ware (fig. 96.164) and Stamford ware (fig. 87.8), confirmed the presence of the fatty deposits left by the fuel used to light these lamps (see below).

Concentrations of sooting were noted on some cooking pot/storage jar and jug fragments, that did not extend above the basal angle. This was most evident, on a cooking pot/storage jar base fragment in Potters Marston (fig. 90.80). This feature is believed to be the result of the use of charcoal as a fuel source but, the evidence from the site as a whole suggests that charcoal was rarely used as a source of heat, in spite of its superiority over wood and coal (*ibid.*, 184).

A thin lime scale residue was noted on the interior of a number of vessels, mainly Potters Marston cooking pot/storage jars and jugs. The residue is very similar in appearance to that found locally on later medieval cisterns in Medieval Sandy ware 3 and Midland Purple and appears on unsooted vessels to be the result of long term liquid storage, or is perhaps indicative of the vessel having been placed within another over the fire (*ibid.*, 176, 183). The deposit on externally sooted vessels may also be the result of the frequent boiling of liquids over the fire.

A few sherds from Area 2 had a much thicker residue that resembled a heavy lime scale deposit, which reacted positively to hydrochloric acid. The nature of this deposit is uncertain but was found on sherds in features thought to relate to some sort of industrial activity, (see above).

Pre-depositional wear marks were only noted on three vessels from the site, two tubular spouted pitcher spout fragments in the Stamford ware fabric ST1 (fig. 87.11) and the Leicester Splashed ware fabric SP3, (fig. 95.140) were worn smooth at one end. A Potters Marston jug was also worn smooth at an acute angle on the rim (fig. 93.110). How these wear marks were caused is not clear but all apparently occurred once the vessels had been broken. Five sherds in Potters Marston from area 1, plot D phase 10, had been re-worked as counters.

Two complete Potters Marston cooking pot/storage jars were recovered from the site, including a small vessel with a pouring lip (fig. 87.22) and a straight sided pot (fig. 89.65) from a well and a cess pit in Areas 2 and 3 respectively. The find spots suggested that both pots had been accidentally discarded rather than being placed *in situ* for some specific use (Moorhouse 1986, 115-117).

11. Conclusions

The targeted features provided a useful series of assemblages dating from the 12th to the 13th or possibly early 14th centuries. A typical range of domestic vessels were present, save for those associated with the timber structure and 'industrial' features in Areas 2 and 3. The cooking pot/storage jar was the most common pottery vessel in use during the late 11th and 12th centuries. Jugs and bowls became more common in the pottery groups dating from the 13th century, notably in area 1, plots D and E.

Turning to the fabrics, the range of pottery found here confirms that even the more distantly traded vessels from Stamford, Nottingham and elsewhere had a wide distribution amongst the local population in the town, even though some of the fabrics only occur in relatively small numbers. Typically, the Torksey type wares only appear, as on many sites in Leicester, in small quantities in early medieval contexts.

Another minor group, the Lincoln/Lincolnshire shelly wares are also increasingly being recognised in Leicester, usually as here, in residual contexts. However, the Stamford wares were the most common Saxo-Norman pottery present, and represented the bulk of the glazed pottery in Area 1, phase 8, plot D and phase 9, plot C, the proportion of the ware declining in the later groups from plots A and B in phase 9.

Potters Marston is the most common pottery in use in Leicester from the early 12th century to the late 13th century, (Sawday 1991, 34). Excluding plots A and B in phase 8, the ware dominated all the pottery assemblages in Area 1, ranging from 54% of the total, by sherd numbers, in phase 9 plot A and 55% in phase 9 plot C, to 83% in phase 9 plot D, the percentages only dropping to 75% and 62% in phase 10 plots E and D respectively. The relatively low proportion of Potters Marston in phase 9 plot A may be explained by the unusually high proportion of Splashed ware 3 present, 25%, whilst in the early assemblage in phase 9 plot C, Stamford wares were also present in relatively high proportions, representing 24% of the total number of sherds. The other local ware, Splashed ware 3, was also present in all the assemblages, excluding that from phase 9 plot E.

Of the imported wares, the early Stanion Lyveden types ware, LY4, was present in all groups in Area 1 excluding that from phase 8 plot A, whilst the other early fabric LY2 was only found in plot D phase 8. The later fabrics LY1, LY3 and LY5, dating from the 13th century, only occurring sporadically in Area 1, phase 9 plots A, B and E, whilst one or both of the imported Nottingham Splashed wares, SP1 and SP2 occur in all the plots from phase 9 onwards. The later Nottingham medieval sandy wares, NO2, NO3 and NO4 and the Chilvers Coton fabrics CC1 and CC2 also occur in small quantities in phases 9 and 10, the pottery in fabric CC1 in Area 1, plot F, phase 8, implying that this group is of 13th century date. Typically the wares from Chilvers Coton and Nottingham made up less than 5% of the total by sherd numbers in phases 9 and 10.

The Oxidised and the Reduced sandy wares occur in small quantities in all the pottery groups except those from plots C and G in area 1. The assemblage in RS in plot D phase 10, is an unusually large group in terms of sherd numbers, and represents the two near complete cauldrons in RS1.

The range of fabrics present provides an indication as to the network of trade that existed between Leicester and elsewhere during the late Saxon and early medieval period. Typically here, as on other sites in Leicester, Stamford provided most of the pottery during the Saxo-Norman period, the pottery from Lincoln and Lincolnshire and the Torksey type wares accounting for only a very small part of the assemblages. Potters Marston was the most common ware in the early medieval period, producing 61% of the total of the pottery recovered from the site by sherd numbers. The Leicester and Nottingham Splashed wares and Stanion Lyveden type wares from Northamptonshire accounting for 6% and 5% of the total number of sherds respectively. The pottery from Chilvers Coton, Warwickshire, made up the bulk of the medieval wares from the site, but the Nottingham medieval sandy wares also produced a sizeable proportion of the glazed medieval pottery present.

All these major pottery sources lie approximately within a 55 km (35 miles) radius of Leicester. Evidently the pottery would have arrived in the town, especially during the late Saxon and early medieval period, along established trade routes to east of the country from Lincolnshire. The focus of trade switched during the 12th century chiefly to Potters Marston, approximately 13km to the south-west of Leicester, but also diversified to some extent, embracing not only the Splashed wares from Nottingham to the north, but also the

Stanion Lyveden type wares from the south-east. The local Splashed ware industry also providing some of the pottery used in Leicester at this time.

During the 13th century, the focus of trade began to change again, Warwickshire becoming an increasingly important source of glazed wares, and the trade with Nottingham now included the high quality glazed table wares from the town, as well as some unglazed kitchen wares. Glazed and unglazed pottery from the Stanion Lyveden industries also continued as a minor element of the pottery imported into the town.

The sources of the other minor wares found on the site during the early medieval and medieval periods remain uncertain. The Reduced Sandy wares appear to be local, whilst the sources for the Oxidised sandy wares may be local and also include Bedfordshire and Oxfordshire. The glazed Medieval Sandy wares (MS1-3) may originate from Chilvers Coton or Derbyshire. All these wares appear to be traded as they occur regularly, albeit sometimes in very small quantities, on excavations in Leicester.

12. The pottery from the clay pipe kiln dump (table 37)

David Higgins of the University of Liverpool, Miranda Goodby of Newcastle under Lyme Museum, David Barker of Stoke City Museum and Eleanor Thomas of Leicestershire Museums, Arts & Records Services, kindly commented on the dating of the post medieval wares.

PHASE 12

Area 2: F581 (290 sherds, 9,755g)

The residual material included Saxo Norman and medieval wares. The residual post medieval pottery dating from the 16th to the 18th centuries comprised: Midland Yellow (MY); Midland Blackware (MB); the post medieval earthenware (EA1); a fine sandy black glazed earthenware (EA6) and the slipware (EA7), the latter including a fragment of a press

moulded dish. The mottled wares, (EA3)(EA4), probably date to the pre 1770s.

The continental stonewares comprised two fragments, one possibly Frechen (FR) and the other Westerwald (WE), dating to the 17th or 18th centuries. The Chinese hard paste porcelain (PO) was represented by fragments of a tea bowl and a saucer which were made for export and date from the second half of the 18th century.

The residual material apart, the majority of the group consists of later 18th and early 19th century wares, including the English tin glazed earthenware (EA11), the brown salt glazed Nottingham and Derby type stonewares (SW5) and unclassified earthenwares (EA) – which included sherds of yellow glazed kitchen ware, flower pots and unglazed earthenwares. The English white salt glazed stonewares (SW4) dating from circa 1720-1780, creamwares (EA8) and pearl-wares (EA9) and the white earthenwares (EA10) account for the bulk of the finds.

The creamwares cover the standard forms including a substantially complete bowl with a green rim and brown sponged decoration on the body dating from *circa* 1790. The majority of the transfer printed designs in pearlware and the white earthenware appear to date from *circa* 1820-40. The pearlwares included fragments of two teapots and a bowl. The most complete teapot, is decorated with a Chinese scene in a brown transfer print. The pot (fig. 97.177) appears to be a second as it has not been coloured with enamels and refired as would have been originally intended. The white earthenware included the transfer printed fragments of a hand basin from a washing set (plate 15). Overall a date for the group around 1820 would accommodate the later decorated types, though this means that the salt glazed wares were about 40 or 50 years old at the time of deposition.

However the best dating evidence for the group comes from the clay pipes, the makers' marks giving a date of deposition of *circa* 1820, (see below p.00.). The pipes thus provide a *terminus ante quem* for the deposit which was sealed beneath the floor of

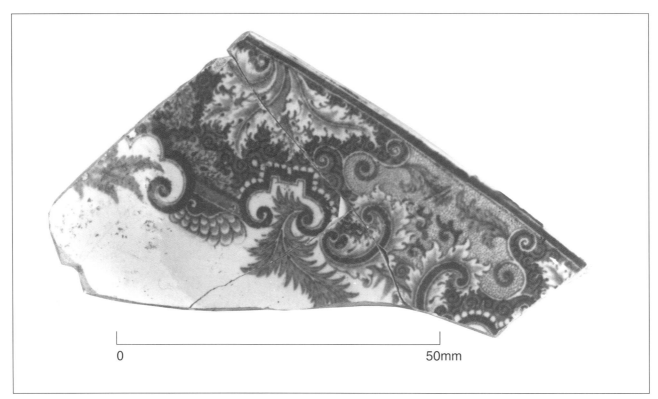

0   50mm

Plate 15: *Detail of a transfer printed design on a hand basin dated c. 1820*

an early to mid 19th century cellar. The wheel thrown pancheon or wide mouthed bowls and shallow bowls or pans (fig. 97.178-182) in the dark glazed earthenware EA2 thus represent an unusually well dated group, in a ware which is generally only broadly dated from the post-medieval to the modern period, and hence only those vessels which are substantially complete are illustrated to avoid problems of residuality. All the vessels are coated with a dark slip, enhancing the dark brown/black appearance to the glaze. The well fired fabrics are a pink or a light reddish colour, or often a streaky mix of white and pink firing clays. White or pale buff lumps of clay or marl are also present in the body, suggesting Chilvers Coton in Warwickshire (Gooder 1984b, 210) or Ticknall in Derbyshire as possible source for these pots.

13. The medieval and post medieval tile

Siân Davies

A total of 45 fragments of tile, weighing 3,624g, was recovered from the site. The assemblage consisted predominantly of medieval sandy ware roof tile (24 fragments 638g) and unprovenanced earthenware floor tile (19 fragments 2,961g). Most of the material was residual in post medieval contexts. The roof tile included fragments of nibbed and ridge tiles, many of which were small and abraded. The only material of interest was part of a serpentine style ridge crest (Allin 1981a, 64) in the Chilvers Coton fabric, CC1, recovered from the truncation deposits in Area 2. This crest type is more commonly found in fabrics dating towards the end of the medieval period in Leicester and was recorded at the Austin Friars (*ibid.*, fig 16.6, 16.7 & 17.14) and at Bonners Lane (Finn, forthcoming). An Oxidised Sandy ware tile fragment was also recovered in F726, plot H, Area 2 in phase 9. A glazed floor tile fragment was found in the 13th/14th century 'garden soils' G290 in Area 2.

14. Analysis of the organic residues

Richard P. Evershed

Aims

The aim of the investigation was to determine the presence (or absence) of organic residues, particularly lipids (i.e. the fat and wax components of plants and animals), in pottery from the Causeway Lane excavation. A specific goal of the investigation was a comparative study of residues present in two vessel types, namely lamps and oval shaped dishes (also referred to as 'dripping dish' or 'fish dishes'), which, based on our previous experience, were highly likely to contain lipids.

Samples

Samples were received from Leicestershire Archaeological Unit packaged in zip lock plastic bags and stored in the dark until required for analysis. The samples included sherds from lamps, cauldrons, dripping dishes, jugs a possible industrial base and sooted sherds, vessel type unknown, but possibly from cooking pot/storage jars or bowls (table 38).

Table 38: *Concentration of lipid in pot sherds.*

Phase	area/ plot	context	Sample number	Feature	Vessel type	Lipid content μg g-1	Fabric	Illus. type
9	1/B	377	20802	235	lamp	829	LY4	164
9	2/J	2024	21619	511	lamp	518	SP3	141
9	1	2478	23006	550	lamp	2568	ST2	8
10	1/D	757	21828	206	cauldron	305	RS1	169
10	1/D	233	20582	206	dripping dish	241	PM	-
8	2	2740	21449	620	dripping dish	237	PM	103
10	1/D	1605	21823	206	dripping dish	533	PM	-
10	1/D	1606	21826	206	dripping dish	552	PM	104
8	2/J	2019	20643	510	vtu	14	PM	-
10	1/D	232	20577	206	jug	56	PM	121
9	2/J	2023	20681	509	vtu	57	PM	-
10	1/D	232	20579	206	jug	52	NO3	176
8	2	2143	21539	540	?ind base	82	PM	131
8	2	2132	20674	540	vtu	19	PM	-

(vtu – vessel type unknown)

Analytical approach

Apart from sooting, none of the sherds displayed appreciable surface residues, hence, analyses focused upon organic residues absorbed within the ceramic fabric. The sherds were submitted to our standard analytical protocol (Evershed *et al*, 1990; Charters *et al*, 1993) in which the surfaces of the sherds to be sampled are cleaned with a modelling drill fitted with an abrasive bit to remove contamination from the burial matrix or that which might have been introduced during handling by excavators. Portions of the cleaned sherd were then taken and crushed to a fine powder in a pestle and mortar. Two gram samples were then extracted with a mixture of chloroform and methanol to yield a total lipid extract. Portions of the extract were then trimethylsilylated and submitted directly to gas chromatography (GC) and combined gas chromatography/mass spectrometry (GC/MS). GC was used to screen for the presence of lipids and determine their concentrations in pot sherds. GC/MS employing the conventional full scan mode of operation was used to identify the major compounds. Additional GC/MS was performed after carrying out a methylthiolation reaction to determine the position of double bonds in remnant mono-unsaturated fatty acids (Evershed 1992).

Results and discussion

Quantitative analyses – GC analyses were performed on the total lipid extract of all the potsherds listed in table 38. The lipid content of each sherd was calculated by comparing the peak areas in each chromatogram with the peak area of an internal standard (n-tetratriacontane) that was added in known amounts at the extraction stage. As expected the lamps, 'dripping dishes' and cauldron contained much higher concentrations of lipid than the jugs, and the other vessels (table 38). The lipid concentrations of the lamps and 'dripping dishes' varied in the range ca. 200 μg g-1 to >2 mg g-1, values which are, in our experience, typical of vessels of these types. The low concentrations of lipid seen in the jugs are also typical of the results we have seen in our previous studies of medieval pottery (Charters *et al*, 1993).

Table 37: *Post-Roman pottery totals from clay pipe kiln dump F581*

F581 Fabric	Med	MY	MB	EA1	EA2	EA3	EA4	EA6	EA7	EA8	EA9	EA10	EA11	EA	PO	FR	WE	SW4	SW5	Totals
frags	16	1	1	1	111	11	2	4	2	47	17	17	8	6	4	1	1	26	14	290
frag%	5.52	0.34	0.34	0.34	38.28	3.79	0.69	1.38	0.69	16.21	5.86	5.86	2.76	2.07	1.38	0.34	0.34	8.97	4.83	
wt(g)	183	10	16	12	7519	74	18	42	31	652	212	370	46	127	16	5	2	200	220	9755
wt%	1.88	0.10	0.16	0.12	77.08	0.76	0.18	0.43	0.32	6.68	2.17	3.79	0.47	1.30	0.16	0.05	0.02	2.05	2.26	
Av Sh	11.4	10	16	12	67.77	6.72	9	10.5	15.5	13.87	12.47	21.76	5.75	21.16	4	5	2	7.69	15.71	

Qualitative analyses The total lipid extracts of those vessels that exhibited appreciable lipid residues were shown by GC/MS to be composed largely of free fatty acids with smaller amounts of triacylglycerols, and some instances diacylglycerols. The free fatty acids comprised mainly hexadecanoic ($C_{16:0}$), octadecanoic ($C_{18:0}$) and octadecenoic ($C_{18:1}$) acids, as indicated in figures 14 and 15.

The total lipid extracts can be separated into two distinct groups according to their fatty acid compositions. This is illustrated by comparing the compositional data listed for the lipid extracts in table 39. The relative proportions of the major fatty acids, namely: hexadecanoic ($C_{16:0}$) and octadecanoic ($C_{18:0}$) acid components, is similar for all the lamps (≤ 0.5). In contrast, the ratio for the 'dripping dishes' lies in the range 2.4-3.3. The cauldron has an intermediate value of 0.9. The conclusion is that the fatty residues from the different vessel types have different origins.

Table 39: *Ratios of 16:0/18:0 and 18:0/18:1 free fatty acrboxylic acids in lipid extracts of sherds.*

Sample number	Vessel type	%16:0	%18:0	%18:1	Ratio 16:0/18:0	Ratio 18:0/18:1
20802	lamp	18.8	35.9	13.0	0.5	2.8
21619	lamp	18.8	34.3	7.8	0.5	4.4
23006	lamp	16.5	52.7	7.3	0.3	7.2
21828	cauldron	27.7	31.0	10.4	0.9	3.0
20582	dripping dish	39.3	17.4	16.8	2.3	1.0
21449	dripping dish	49.1	14.8	21.2	3.3	0.7
21823	dripping dish	37.9	16.7	20.2	2.3	0.8
21826	dripping dish	36.0	14.5	11.7	2.5	1.2

The obvious next step in defining the origins of these animal fat residues would appear to be to compare the relative abundances of the individual fatty acids in the pot sherd extracts to those values given in current literature for fresh animal fats. The data obtained suggest two different sources for the fat residues in the vessels studied. The high saturated fatty acid content, notably $C_{16:0}$ and $C_{18:0}$ components, indicates an animal source for both residues. If only the most commonly occurring domesticated animals are considered then the saturated fatty acid 'fingerprints' suggest that the lamp residues may derive from a ruminant source, i.e. beef or mutton, while the residues in the 'dripping dishes' more closely resembles pig fat (Mills and White 1994).

We always approach the use of the fatty acids as indicators of the origins of fats with great caution and would stress that these assignments should be regarded as highly tentative. Other properties of animal fats that may be of value in interpreting the origins of fat residues in archaeological ceramics include: (i) the distribution of isomers of mono-unsaturated components; (ii) the presence of mixtures of branched chain fatty acids, and (iii) the composition of the saturated fatty acids in intact triacylglycerols (Enser 1991). The use of all these parameters would have meant us breaking considerable new ground in the study of archaeological fats. Such an approach to the classification of fats of archaeological origin has not been attempted previously, and an application for funding from this group, to develop and test such a protocol is currently under consideration by NERC's Science Based Archaeology Committee.

Practical considerations and time restrictions precluded the use of all three parameters discussed above and further investigations of these residues were restricted to an assessment of the compositions of the mono-unsaturated fatty acid components. This was achieved by performing a methylthiolation reaction and then submitting the dimethyl disulphide derivatives obtained to GC/MS analysis, employing electron ionisation. The double-bond positions can be

determined directly from the spectra and the proportions of Z- and E-isomers deduced directly from the GC elution orders. The distribution of the isomers of the mono-unsaturated eighteen carbon number fatty acid components for the lamps and the 'dripping dishes' was examined.

The results are summarised in table 39. This is the first time that classification of a group of archaeological animal fats has been attempted by this approach. It is immediately obvious that very different mixtures of mono-unsaturated fatty acids exist in the extracts derived from the different vessel groups. The lamp extracts were found to contain a complex mixture of positionally isomeric mono-unsaturated fatty acids, which is entirely compatible with their originating from ruminant animals (Enser, 1991). The complex mixtures of mono-unsaturated fatty acids present in fresh ruminant subcutaneous fats arises through the biohydrogenation of dietary fats in rumin. Such mixtures of mono-unsaturated fatty acids are not observed in the fats of monogastric animals. Hence, the presence of only oleic acid (Z-9-octadecenoic acid) in the lipid extract of the 'dripping dishes' indicates an origin in a monogastric species, such as pig or boar. The conclusions drawn from the assessment of the mono-unsaturated fatty acid composition agree with our tentative suggestions of origin based on the saturated fatty acid compositions already discussed above.

In drawing conclusions from studies of the mono-unsaturated fatty acid composition, it should be borne in mind that mixtures of positional and geometric isomers can be generated diagenetically in certain situations. For example, we have evidence for the formation of a mixture of positional isomers of mono-unsaturated fatty acids in a bog body adipocere (Evershed 1992). However, the formation of a mixture in this instance is almost certainly due to the activities of enzymes and micro-organisms, normally associated with a body in life, becoming involved in the complex taphonomic processes involved in the decay of a cadaver.

Evidence for the mono-unsaturated fatty acids being those present in the sherds at the time of discard comes from a consideration of their burial contexts. As seen in table 40 all the sherds were recovered from soil-filled pits, either with or without cess present. It is clear that different vessel types from related burial contexts display markedly different fatty acid compositions, thus confirming that the differences seen in fatty acid composition, including the mono-unsaturated fatty acid components, are unambiguously related to the original source of the fat in antiquity and are not a diagenetic anomaly.

Table 40: *Distributions of mono-unsaturated fatty carboxylic acid isomers in lipid extracts of sherds.*

Sample number	context type	Vessel type	Positional isomers present.
20802	Rubbish fill in shallow sequence. Cess present	lamp	$\Delta^{9,11,13,14,15,16}$
21619	Rubbish fill in pit. No cess present	lamp	$\Delta^{9,11,13,14,15,16}$
23006	Rubbish fill in pit. No cess present	lamp	$\Delta^{9,11,13,14,15,16}$
20582	Fills of deep pit. No cess present	dripping dish	Δ^{9}
21823	Pit with cess present	dripping dish	Δ^{9}

Conclusion

In this study we have assessed the lipid composition of a small assemblage of sherds from lamps, dripping pans, jugs, an industrial base (?) and sherds of unknown vessel type – but possibly cooking pots/storage jars or bowls – and a cauldron. Clear distinctions can be drawn between the different vessel types on the basis of the absolute yield of lipid (table 38). As expected, the lamps, 'dripping dishes' and cauldron contained appreciable amounts of lipid, whereas only low concentrations were seen in the other vessels including the jugs. This is consistent with the latter vessels having been used in connection with the transport and/or serving of aqueous substances, e.g. water, ale, wine, etc. There is currently no reliable test for the presence of residues of aqueous beverages such as wine or beer.

The finding of appreciable quantities of fat residues in the sherds is entirely consistent with their anticipated functions: lamp residue remaining from fuel; 'dripping dish' residues remaining from fat collected during spit roasting; and cauldron residues remaining from the cooking of meat products or perhaps fat rendering. It is clear from the results obtained that the fats in the different vessels, particularly in the lamps and 'dripping dishes', originated from different species of animals. Using a new criterion based on the composition of mono-unsaturated fatty acids it is concluded that the lamp residues originate from ruminant animals and the 'dripping dish' residues from monogastric animals, such as pig or boar.

Acknowledgements

In presenting this report I should like to thank Mr. Greg Lawrence for assistance with the analyses.

15. The Illustrations

Siân Davies and David Hopkins

List of illustrations (figs. 87-97)

Illus. No.	Ph	Pot No.	Feat. No.	Area/ Plot	Context No.	Fab.	Vessel Plot	Vessel Form	rim type	Comments
Fig. 87										
1	9	21923	491	1 /A	1301	ST2	jug/spo	6/24		no evidence for glaze on surviving fragment
2	9	127	903	1 /A	8025	ST2	jug/spo	6/24		no glaze as above
3	8	21524	540	2	2153 8007	ST2	tub	24		strut glazed & thumbed on upper surfaces
4	9	21626	217	1 /B	264	ST2	tub	?24		?strainer for spout glazed upper surface holes pushed through from top
5	9	20657	510	2 /J	2029	ST2	stj	21		glazed ext surfaces & on thumbed applied clay strip
6	9	21556	207	1 /C	410 [127]	ST2	Cup/dish	10/23		glazed ext [127]
7	8	20949	521	2 /J	2267	ST2	cup/dish	10/23		glazed ext
8	9	23006	550	2	2478	ST2	lamp	10		
9	9	20558	207	1 /C	238	ST1	jug/tub	6/24		applied thumbed & comb streaked clay strips & copper glaze on ext very abraded
10	9	21072	257	1 /G	503	ST1	?jug/tub	?6/24/18		dark green copper glaze on ext pos a bottle?
11	9	21974	216	1 /D	366	ST1	tub	24		spout one edge worn through secondary use glazed ext
12	9	21710	714	3 /H	3541	ST1	lid jug/	22		copper glaze upper surfaces ext
13	11	21942	703	3	3556	ST1	asabove	22		copper glaze as above
14	8	23112	245	1 /B	400 [139]	TO	bowl			
15	8	21051	245	1 /B	400	TO	bowl			
16	9	21472	632	2	2763	TO	bowl			
17	9	347	911	1 /A	8021	LI1	bowl			rouletted & sooted ext rim
18	9	209	903	1 /A	8007	PM	cp/stj	1	1	sooted ext & rim top int
19	9	20623	275	1 /D	216	PM	cp/stj	2	1	incised horizontal line
	9		216	1 /D	297					dec sooted ext & rim top
	9	9		216	1 /D	350				int
20	8	21335	568	2	2569	PM	cp/stj	2	2	patchy sooting ext patch of burning int
21	8	20674	540	2	2132	PM	cp/stj		2	sooted ext below shoulder
22	8	21909	568	2	2554	PM	cp/stj	3	3.1	with pouring lip lightly sooted ext below shoulder
23	8	21335	568	2	2569	PM	cp/stj	3	3.1	patchy sooting ext
24	10	20577	206	1 /D	232	PM	cp/stj	3	3.1	finely made pot
25	9	20681	509	2 /J	2023	PM	cp/stj	3	3.2	'pulled' int wall sooted ext below shoulder
Fig. 88										
26	10	21840	206	1 /D	760	PM	cp/stj	3	3.2	coil clearly visible on int wall at neck base
27	8	21539	540	2	2143	PM	cp/stj	2	4.1	reduced grey throughout sooted ext slashed under rim
28	8	21540	540	2	2143 2144	PM	cp/stj	2	4.1	'pulled int wall' residue int & rim top sooted ext thumbed ext rim slashed ext neck
29	9	20835	235	1 /B	383	PM	cp/stj	2	4.1	sooted int below neck patchy sooting ext slashed ext neck
30	9	21084	263	1 /G	516	PM	cp/stj		4.1	slashed ext neck
31	8	21311	592	2 /J	2527	PM	cp/stj		4.2	sooted/burnt int & ext
32	8	21539	540	2	2143	PM	cp/stj	2	4.2	sooted/burnt patches ext & rim top slashed ext neck
33	9	20760	216	1 /D	350	PM	cp/stj	3	4.2	sooted ext below shoulder
34	8	21539	540	2	2143	PM	cp/stj	2	4.3	slashed ext neck sooted ext burnt int
35	8	21311	592	2 /J	2527	PM	cp/stj		4.3	slashed ext neck sooted ext sooted/burnt int
36	9	210	903	1 /A	8007	PM	cp/stj	1	4.3	slashed ext neck patchy sooting rim/neck ext & rim top
37	9	21087	265	1 /G	518	PM	cp/stj	1	4.3	roughly made heavily sooted ext & part of rim & neck int

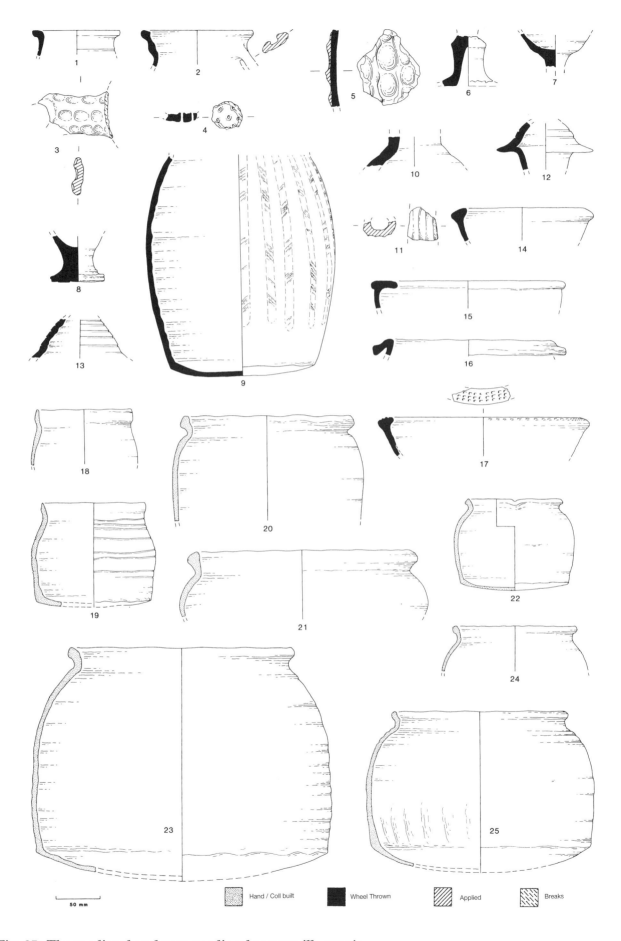

Fig. 87: *The medieval and post-medieval pottery illustrations*

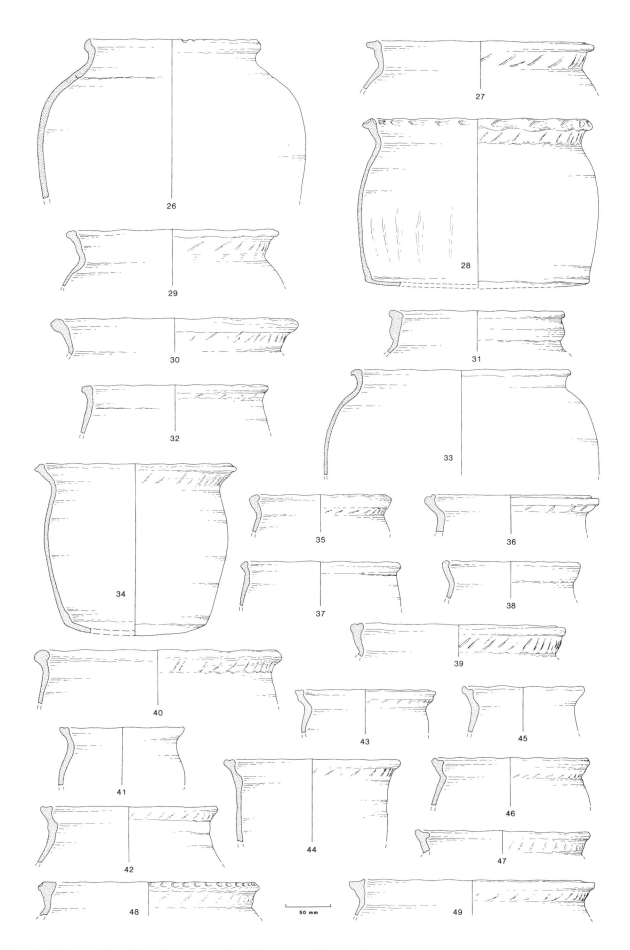

Fig. 88: *The medieval and post-medieval pottery illustrations*

Illus. No.	Ph	Pot No.	Feat. No.	Area/ Plot	Context No.	Fab.	Vessel Plot	Vessel Form	rim type	Comments
38	9	20760	216	1 /D	350	PM	cp/stj		4.3	sooted ext burnt patches int
39	9	21771	438	1 /G	1380	PM	cp/stj		4.3	slashed ext neck sooted ext rim
40	8	20915	521	2 /J	2261	PM	cp/stj	1	4.3	slashed ext neck sooted ext & patchy burning int
41	9	211	903	1 /A	8007	PM	cp/stj	2	4.3	roughly made patchy sooting ext rim & neck int
42	9	211	903	1 /A	8007	PM	cp/stj	2	4.3	slashed ext neck roughly made & finished ext
43	9	20604	217	1 /B	264	PM	cp/stj	1	4.3	roughly made & finished slashed ext neck sooted ext & rim top
44	9	21562	510	2 /J	2030	PM	cp/stj	1	4.3	slashed ext neck sooted ext
45	9	256	903	1 /A	8025	PM	cp/stj	1	4.3	roughly made & finished sooted int neck
46	9	20791	213	1 /F	306	PM	cp/stj	2	4.3	slashed ext neck sooted ext below rim sooted/burnt int rim/neck
47	9	21621	263	1 /G	637	PM	cp/stj		4.3	slashed ext neck sooted ext
48	8	23289	248	1 /D	465	PM	cp/stj		4.3	rim ext thumbed neck ext slashed sooted ext
49	9	20604	217	1 /B	264	PM	cp/stj		4.3	slashed ext neck patchy sooting ext & rim top

Fig. 89

Illus. No.	Ph	Pot No.	Feat. No.	Area/ Plot	Context No.	Fab.	Vessel Plot	Vessel Form	rim type	Comments
50	9	20916	508	2 /J	2213	PM	cp/stj	1	5.1	patchy sooting on rim cloth impression under base ext
51	9	20664	511	2 /J	2024	PM	cp/stj	1	5.1	sooted ext
52	9	222	908	1 /A	8017	PM	cp/stj	2	5.1	
53	9	20676	513	2 /H	2088	PM	cp/stj	3	5.1	fine walled
54	9	227	908	1 /A	8017 [8]	PM	cp/stj	1	5.2	sooted ext burnt int
55	9	20623	216	1 /D	275	PM	cp/stj	1	5.2	patchy sooting ext wall & rim heavy sooting under base
56	9	20600	207 20869	1 /C	257 417	PM	cp/stj	2	5.2	sooted ext below shoulder
57	9	244	909	1 /B	8018	PM	cp/stj	2	5.2	incised dec on rim top patchy sooting under rim ext & ext body
58	9	20643	510	2 /J	2019	PM	cp/stj		5.2	patchy sooting ext
59	9	20796	213	1 /F	343	PM	cp/stj	2	5.2	faint sooting ext rim
60	9	225	908	1 /A	8017	PM	cp/stj	3	5.2	incised dec on rim top int patchy sooting ext neck & body
61	10	20778	218	1 /E	305	PM	cp/stj		5.2	incised dec on rim top faint sooting below ext neck
62	9	20760	216	1 /D	350	PM	cp/stj	?3	5.2	incised dec on rim top
63	9	20619	216	1 /D	297 350	PM	cp/stj	?3	5.2	combed dec on rim top
64	10	21894	205	1 /D	986 350	PM	cp/stj	2	5.2	combed dec on rim top
65	9	21886	726	3 /H	3574	PM	cp/stj	1	5.3	slashed ext neck
66	9	20602	207	1 /C	257	PM	cp/stj	3	5.3	incised dec on rim top sooted ext below shoulder

Fig. 90

Illus. No.	Ph	Pot No.	Feat. No.	Area/ Plot	Context No.	Fab.	Vessel Plot	Vessel Form	rim type	Comments
67	9	226	908	1 /A	8017	PM	cp/stj	3	6	sooted ext below shoulder
68	9	20664	511	2 /J	2024	PM	cp/stj	3	6	
69	9	20564	214	1 /D	229	PM	cp/stj	3	7.1	sooted below shoulder & base ext
70	9	21771	438	1 /G	1380	PM	cp/stj	3	7.1	
71	9	20604	217	1 /B	264	PM	cp/stj	3	7.1	finely made
72	10	20584	206	1 /D	234	PM	cp/stj	3	7.1	
73	9	20612	213	1 /F	273	PM	cp/stj	2	7.2	
74	9	20760	216	1 /D	350	PM	cp/stj		7.2	patchy reduction on rim top
75	9	20767	231	1 /D	396	PM	cp/stj	3	7.2	
76	9	20604	217	1 /B	264	PM	cp/stj	3	7.2	patchy sooting ext rim
77	9	222	908	1 /A	8017	PM	cp/stj	3	7.3	patchy sooting ext burnt int neck
78	10	20584	206	1 /D	234	PM	cp/stj	3	7.3	
79	10	20582	206	1 /D	233	PM	cp/stj	2	7.3	
80	9	20681	509	2 /J	2023	PM	cp/stj?			base ext sooted by charcoal evidence of secondary use hole bored into lower wall from ext

Fig. 91

Illus. No.	Ph	Pot No.	Feat. No.	Area/ Plot	Context No.	Fab.	Vessel Plot	Vessel Form	rim type	Comments
81	9	20755	216	1 /D	366	PM	?stj/jug			reduced interior patchy reduction under base ext pulling marks int wall thumbed applied clay strips ext body
82	8	21479	657	2	2847	PM	stj		1	coils visible in section very crudely made
83	9	20758	238	1 /B	345	PM	stj	2	1	oxidised surfaces thumbed applied clay strips ext body
84	8	21539	540	2	2143	PM	stj	1	2	reduced int & rim top sooted ext slashed neck ext & thumbed int & ext rim
85	8	20660	540	2	2167	PM	stj	1	2	reduced int & rim top slashed ext neck thumbed and sooted ext rim

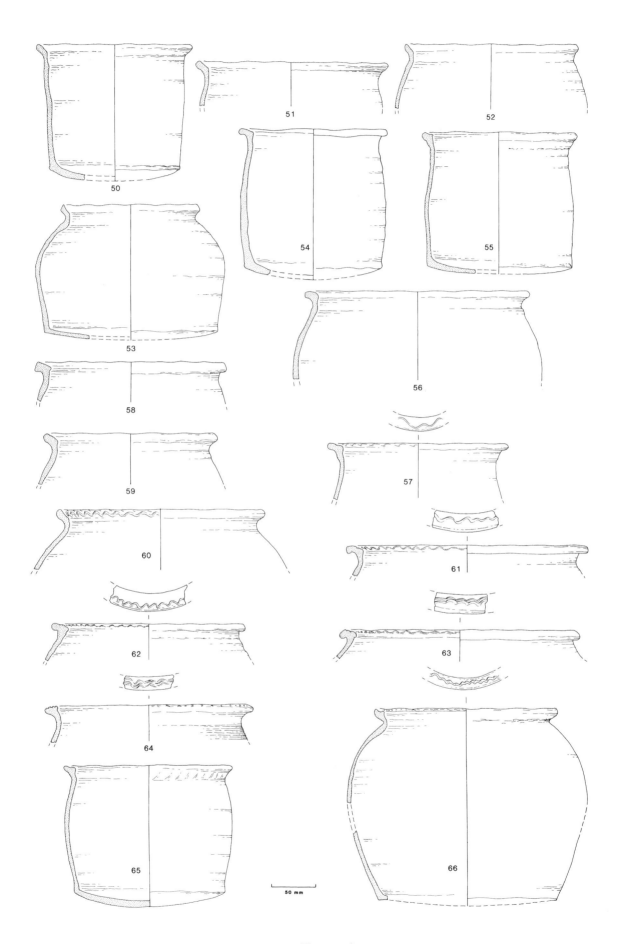

Fig. 89: *The medieval and post-medieval pottery illustrations*

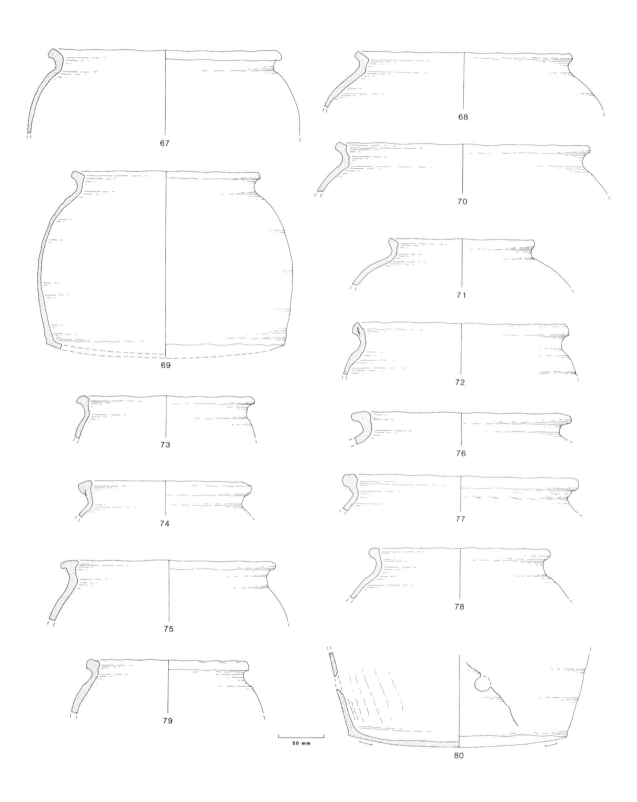

Fig. 90: *The medieval and post-medieval pottery illustrations*

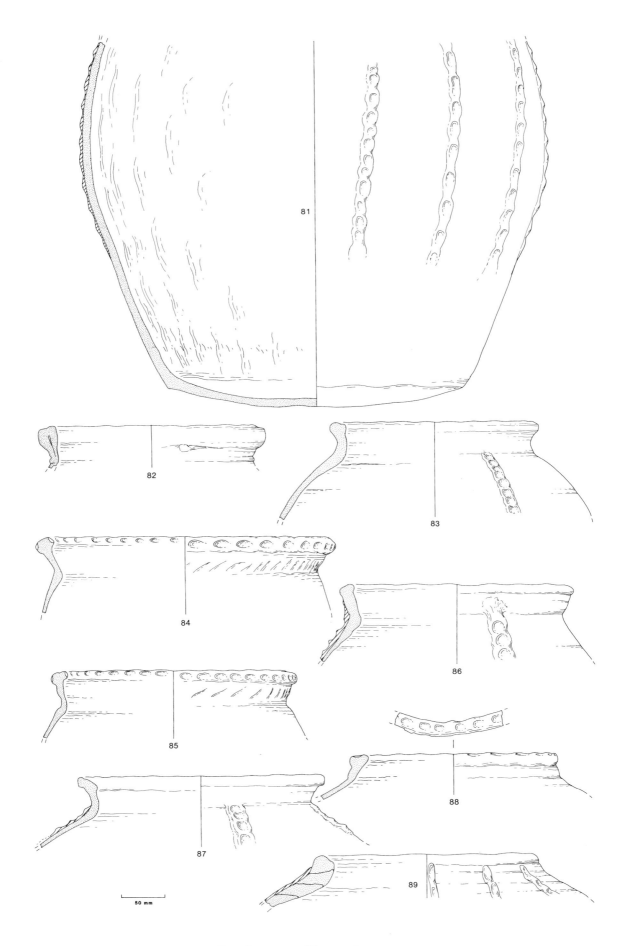

Fig. 91: *The medieval and post-medieval pottery illustrations*

Illus. No.	Ph	Pot No.	Feat. No.	Area/ Plot	Context No.	Fab.	Vessel Plot	Vessel Form	rim type	Comments
86	8	21573	540	2	2144	PM	stj	1	2	reduced int & rim top thumbed applied clay strip on ext body
87	9	231	908	1 /A	8017	PM	stj	3	3	thumbed applied clay strips ext body
88	8	20875	248	1 /D	466	PM	stj	3	4	patches of reduction rim top reduced int thumbed rim top
89	9	21394	389	1 /F	894	PM	stj	3	4	roughly finished coils visible thumbed applied clay strips ext

Fig. 92

Illus. No.	Ph	Pot No.	Feat. No.	Area/ Plot	Context No.	Fab.	Vessel Plot	Vessel Form	rim type	Comments
90	9	248	911	1 /A	8021	PM	bowl	1	1	reduced int slashed ext rim
91	9	20587	207	1 /C	236	PM	bowl	1	2	sooted ext
92	9	20796	213	1 /F	343	PM	bowl	1	2	faint sooting ext rim & body
93	9	20643	510	2 /J	2019	PM	bowl?	1	2	sooted int (pos a fire cover)
94	10	20584	206	1 /D	1606 234	PM	bowl	1	3	sooted ext body & rim
95	9	20681	509	2 /J	2023	PM	bowl	2	4	sooted ext below carination
96	9	230	908	1 /A	8017	PM	bowl	2	5	
97	9	21084	263	1 /G	516	PM	bowl	2	5	sooted ext rim & body
98	9	21621	263	1 /G	637	PM	bowl	2	5	sooted ext
99	9	20681	509	2 /J	2023	PM	bowl	2	5	sooted ext
100	9	20681	509	2 /J	2023	PM	bowl	2	5	sooted ext
101	9	21729	719	3	3568	PM	bowl	2	6	incised wavy line dec rim int sooted ext

Fig. 93

Illus. No.	Ph	Pot No.	Feat. No.	Area/ Plot	Context No.	Fab.	Vessel Plot	Vessel Form	rim type	Comments
102	10	21822	205	1 /D	1617	PM	fire cover			hole pushed through from cover ext evidence for handle light sooting int
103	8	21449	620	2	2740	PM	drip		1	sooted ext dish
104	10	21826	206	1 /D	1606	PM	drip		2	sooted ext burnt int dish
105	9	20831	213	1 /F	341	PM	jug		1	with pouring lip incised dec on rim and comb stabbed dec on ext neck
106	9	20796	213	1 /F	343	PM	jug		1	incised dec neck ext no ev for/against pouring lip
107	9	20859	243	1 /F	404	PM	jug		1	no ev for/against pouring lip circular stabbing on strap handle
108	8	21358	568	2	2610	PM	jug		1	coils and 'pulling' marks visible int wall thumbed strap handle pouring lip
109	9	20655	513	2 /H	2034	PM	jug		1	coils visible on neck int with pouring lip
110	9	26191	704	3	3514	PM	jug		1	no ev for/against pouring lip rim top worn smooth by secondary use
111	9	20681	509	2 /J	2023	PM	jug		1	coils visible on neck int with pouring lip
112	9	21424	389	1 /F	976	PM	jug		1	no ev for/against pouring lip thumbed strap handle
113	9	20767	231	1 /D	396	PM	jug		2	no ev for/against pouring lip
114	9	20767	231	1 /D	396	PM	jug		2	no ev for/against pouring lip
115	9	20643	510	2 /J	2019	PM	jug		3	no ev for/against pouring lip coils visible neck int combed curvilinear dec ext shoulder
116	9	20655	513	2 /H	2034	PM	jug		4	no ev for/against pouring lip
117	10	21826	206	1 /D	1606	PM	jug		4	no ev for/against pouring lip
118	9	20801	235	1 /B	377	PM	jug/cp?			rouletted ext wall patchy sooting ext base

Fig. 94

Illus. No.	Ph	Pot No.	Feat. No.	Area/ Plot	Context No.	Fab.	Vessel Plot	Vessel Form	rim type	Comments
119	10	21826	206	1 /D	1606	PM	jug		5	no ev for/against pouring lip combed curvilinear dec ext shoulder thumbed strap handle
120	10	21823 20584	206 206	1 /D	1605 234	PM	jug			ext basal angle thumbed pos same pot as illus 119 above heavily sooted ext wall to one side
121	10	20577	206	1 /D	232	PM	jug			ext basal angle thumbed sooted as above
122	10	21826	206	1 /D	1606	PM	jug			ext basal angle notched
123	10	21822 20584	206 206	1 /D	234 1617 1606	PM	jug			incised line dec & applied notched clay strips
124	9	20796	213	1 /F	343	PM	jug			incised dec on handle
125	10	20778	218	1 /E	305	PM	jug			thumbed strap handle
126	10	20577	206	1 /D	232	PM	jug/stj			thumbed strap handle
127	10	20558	205	1 /D	224	PM	jug			ridged & stabbed strap handle
128	10	20584	206	1 /D	234	PM	urinal			horizontal handle
129	9	232	908	1 /A	8017	PM	vtu			very light patchy sooting ext rim
130	9	20643	510	2 /J	2019	PM	ind?			spout pierced thumbed ext rim slashed and pierced ext wall if an alembic spout would be pointing downwards
131	8 9	21501 21539	540 510	2 2 /J	2143 2136	PM	ind base?			thumbed rim top & rim int
132	9	343	903	1 /A	8025	SP3	cp/stj			spots of lead glaze thumbed ext rim lightly sooted ext

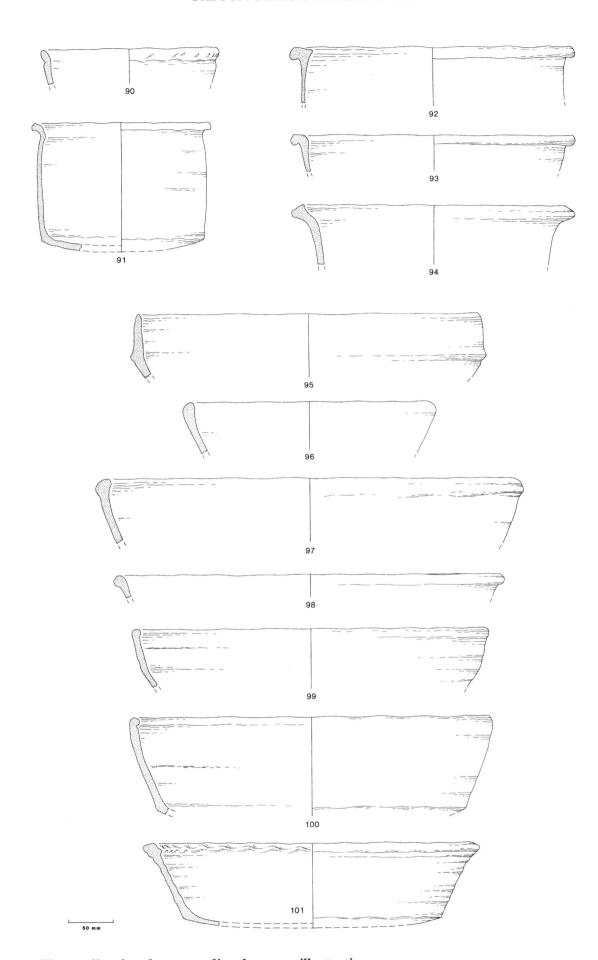

Fig. 92: *The medieval and post-medieval pottery illustrations*

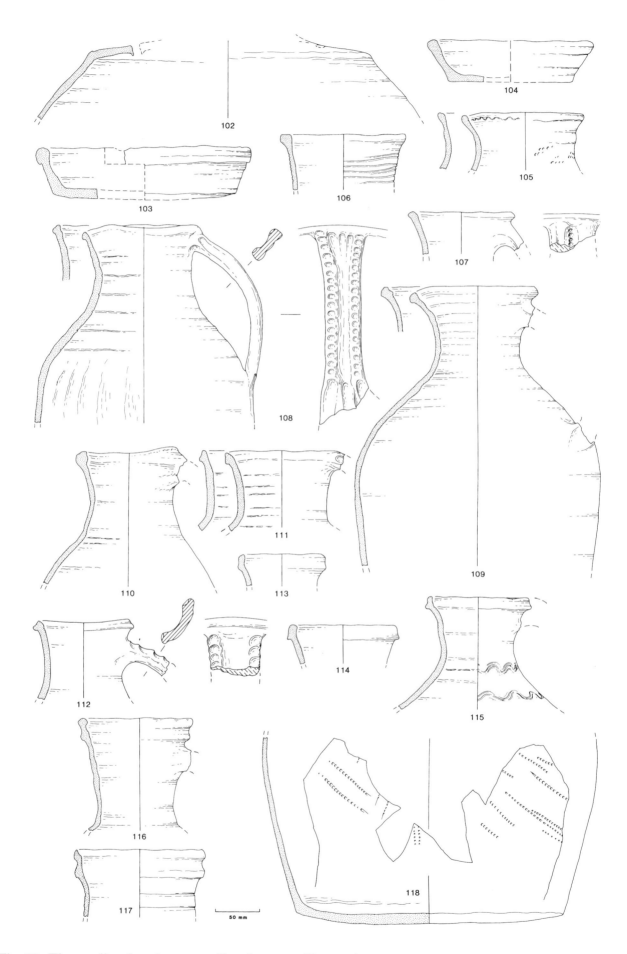

Fig. 93: *The medieval and post-medieval pottery illustrations*

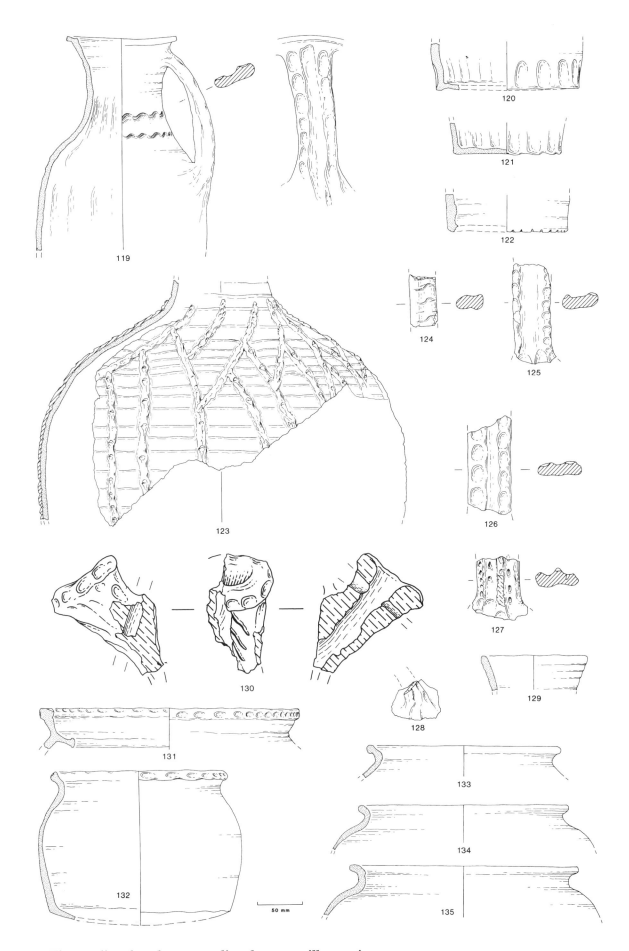

Fig. 94: *The medieval and post-medieval pottery illustrations*

Illus. No.	Ph	Pot No.	Feat. No.	Area/Plot	Context No.	Fab.	Vessel Plot	Vessel Form	rim type	Comments
133	9	20633	204	1 /B	239	SP3	cp/stj			patches of sooting ext rim & body
134	9	20896	257	1 /G	490	SP3	cp/stj			patches of sooting ext rim & body
135	9	21737	511	2 /J	2842	SP3	cp/stj			finely made
Fig. 95										
136	9	21619	511	2 /J	2024	SP3	cp/stj			inscribed curvilinear dec shoulder ext sooted ext
137	8	20901	247	1 /D	494	SP3	bowl			similar rim to illus. 95 above
138	9	341	903	1 /A	8007	SP3	jug			cordons on neck ext patchy orange glaze ext
139	9	342	903	1 /A	8017 8007 8025 8023	SP3	jug			cordons on neck ext glaze ext incised dec on rod handle which is dowelled into neck no ev for against pouring lip
140	9	21054	216	1 /D	469	SP3	tub			spout traces of green/ orange glaze upper surfaces applied thumbed strips broken end worn smooth by 'secondary use'
141	9	21619	511	2 /J	2024	SP3	lamp			sooted int
142	9	21768	265	1 /G	518	SP2	cp/stj			glaze spots ext
143	9	23004	550	2 /H	2478	SP2	cp/stj			lightly sooted ext
144	9	21976	238	1 /B	345	SP2	jug			with pouring lip thin traces of glaze ext
145	9	319	903	1 /A	8012	SP2	jug			finely incised lines under base ext patchy green/ brown glaze ext wall
146	9	320	911	1 /A	8021	SP2	jug			strap handle olive green glaze & incised dec upper surfaces
147	9	315	908 903	1 /A	8017 8007	SP2?	jug			combed curvilinear dec & thick green glaze ext
148	9	20910		3	2286	SP1	jug			rouletting & glossy glaze neck ext
149	9	21102	279	1 /E	556	SN	cp/stj			classified as LY4 in tables now thought to be Saxo Norman
150	8	20948	521	2 /J	2267	LY4	cp/stj			
151	8	21639	482	1 /F	1278	LY4	cp/stj			sooted ext
Fig. 96										
152	9	20606	217	1 /B	264	LY4	cp/stj			
153	9	20602	207	1 /C	257	LY4	cp/stj			finely made & finished sooted ext
154	9	20598	216	1 /D	256	LY4	cp/stj			?rim formed with template
155	10	20573	206	1 /D	225	LY4	cp/stj			?rim formed with template
156	9	21086	263	1 /G	516	LY4	cp/stj			sooted ext rim top int burnt
157	9	21469	632	2	2763	LY4	cp/stj			sooted ext rim & below shoulder base int burnt
158	11	21299	564	2 /J	2519	LY4	cp/stj			
159	9	20667	509	2 /J	2031	LY4	stj			thumbed rim top int applied thumbed clay strip at neck
160	9	21086	263	1 /G	516	LY4	bowl			
161	9	20763	216	1 /D	350	LY4	bowl			patchy sooting ext
162	9	20680	509	2 /J	2023	LY4	jug			
163	11	20764	703	3	3556	LY4	jug			slashed strap handle
164	9	20802	235	1 /B	377	LY4	lamp			
165	11	21303	564	2 /J	2519	LY1	vtu			glaze spots ext ?/ind
166	9	21070	257	1 /G	503	LY5	bowl			
167	8	23169	521	2 /J	2085	LY	cp/stj			sooted ext
168	10	21828	206	1 /D	757	RS1	cauldron			sooted ext slab built
169	10	21828	206	1 /D	757	RS1	cauldron			slab built sooted ext
Fig. 97										
170	9	21416	213	1 /F	343	OS	cp/stj			patchy sooting ext
171	9	21169	231	1 /D	396 [82]	CC1	jug			thumbed ext basal angle green glaze ext wall
172	9	2110 20991	507 507 508	2 /J 2 /J 2 /J	2409 2322 2213	CC1	jug			oxidised pale pink body surfaces pink/grey glaze orange/yellow with green copper glaze spots
173	10	21854	206	1 /D	1610	CC1	jug			with pouring lip yellow glaze ext
174	9	21418	389	1 /F	976	CC1	jug			pink body glaze firing yellow over body & brown over iron rich applied & notched clay strips
175	10	21047	206	1 /D	234	CC1	jug			green glaze ext wall spots under base
176	10	20579	206	1 /D	232	NO3	jug			green glaze ext wall sooted ext
177	12	22243	581	2	2358	EA9	teapot			dec with a brown transfer print only a second
178	12	22134	581	2	2358	EA2	bowl			glaze int & ext over iron rich slip
179	12	22134	581	2	2358	EA2	bowl			glaze int over iron rich slip
180	12	22134	581	2	2358	EA2	bowl			glaze int over iron rich slip
181	12	22134	581	2	2358	EA2	bowl			glaze int over iron rich slip
182	12	22134	581	2	2358	EA2	bowl			glaze int over iron rich slip

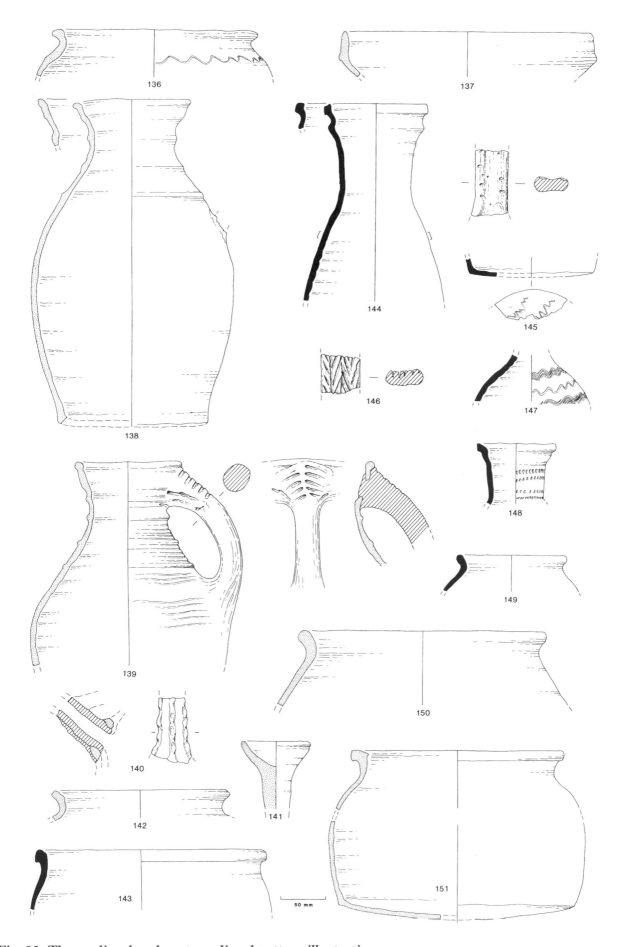

Fig. 95: *The medieval and post-medieval pottery illustrations*

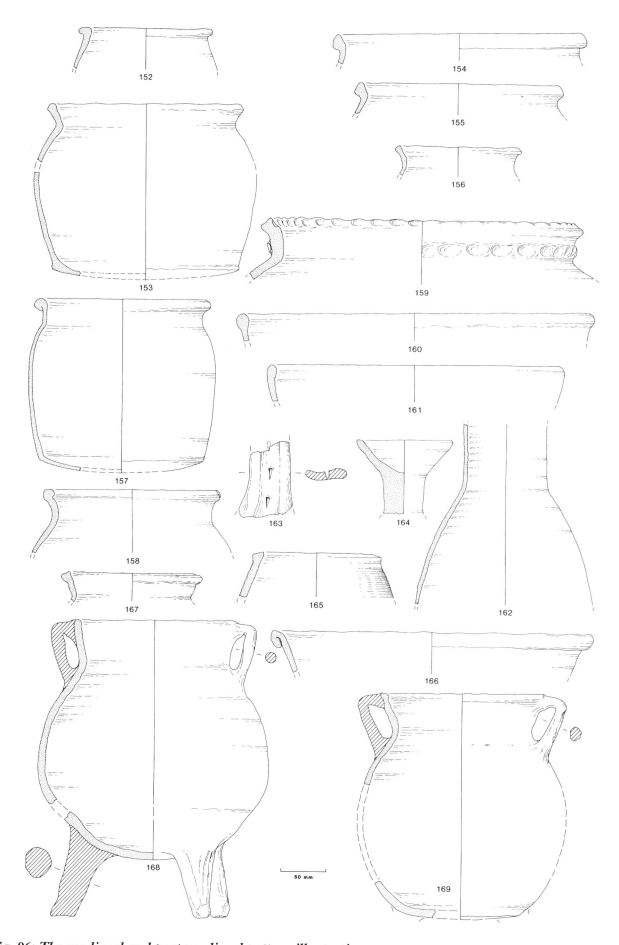

Fig. 96: *The medieval and post-medieval pottery illustrations*

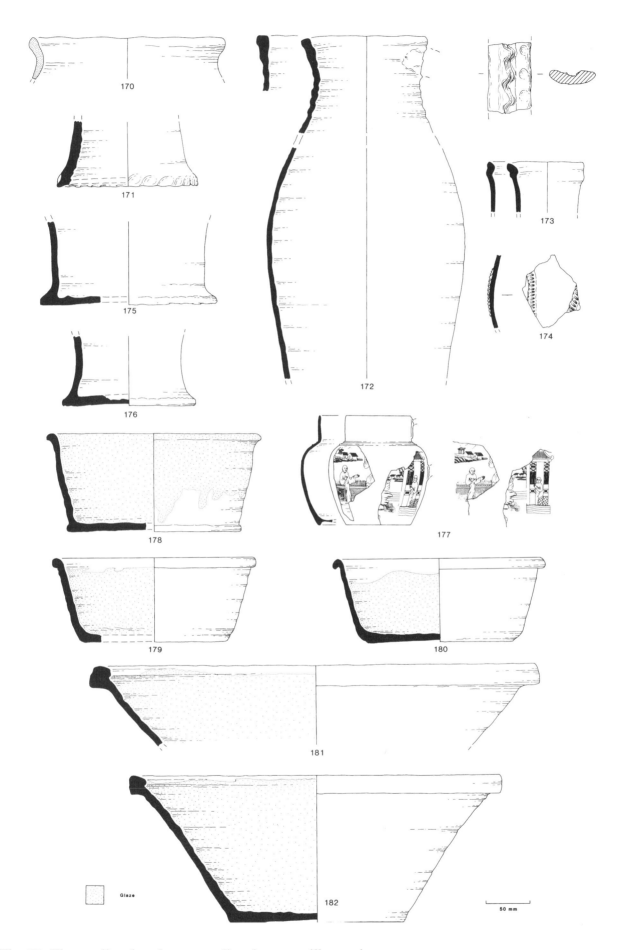

Fig. 97: *The medieval and post-medieval pottery illustrations*

THE CLAY TOBACCO PIPES

D. A. Higgins

with contributions from *P. J. Hammond, A. A. Peacey and J. Mirdamadi*

Introduction

The 1991 excavations produced 6,328 fragments of pipe (770 bowl, 5,246 stem and 312 mouthpiece fragments) from fifty-two different contexts. The number of pipes recovered is disproportionately large in relation to the number of excavated contexts because two of the contexts contained dumps of kiln waste, one of which was particularly large. These dumps not only produced significant numbers of pipes but also important evidence for the nature and form of the kilns in which they were fired (Peacey, below). These kiln groups are the first to have been excavated from the county and provide a wealth of new information about the styles of pipe which were being made and the technology that was employed to produce them. These groups were clearly of more than local interest and warranted detailed study. For this reason the report is divided into sections; the first deals with the contexts which contained purely domestic groups of pipe. This section also deals with residual or intrusive pieces from the kiln groups. The two groups of pipes from the kiln dumps are then presented followed by a detailed analysis and discussion of the kiln waste. Documentary information regarding the site and pipemakers is presented by P. J. Hammond below.

All of the pipe fragments have been examined, catalogued and context summaries produced using the recording system developed at the University of Liverpool. Copies of these detailed lists have been deposited in the site archive. This report presents a more general synthesis and discussion of the finds.

The domestic pipes

Apart from the two kiln groups, 277 fragments of pipe were recovered from 50 contexts, an average of 5.5 fragments per context. There were 40 bowl, 232 stem and 5 mouthpiece fragments ranging from the 17th to the 19th century in date. Only eight of the groups contained ten or more pieces of pipe and the largest group contained just 36 fragments. Although these pipes provide some dating evidence for the post-medieval deposits the small size of the groups limits their reliability. The small number of diagnostic pieces in any context also limits the information which can be derived regarding the currency and evolution of local pipe styles.

The pipes recovered fit within the broad pattern which has been established for the city (Higgins 1985) with the addition of some interesting new forms and detail (figs. 98.1-15). The earliest closely datable pieces date from the 1640's, some sixty or seventy years after the introduction of smoking to this country. By the mid-17th century a 'Midlands spur type' (Higgins 1985, 291) had become established and this continued to be the principal form used in Leicester until the end of the seventeenth century. The evolution of this type is represented by a number of examples from the excavation (figs. 98.1-8).

The spur bowls are generally of good form and neatly finished. Despite this, one of them has a very uneven and 'lumpy' surface formed by irregularities in the surface of the mould. These are most unusual and appear as a rash of small raised bumps on both sides of the bowl (fig. 98.1). This example is fully milled unlike the other examples which tend to be only half-milled on the side facing the smoker. The latest example, dating from *c*.1680-1710 (fig. 98.8), is not milled at all. A second example, from the same context and made in the same mould, has a quarter-milled rim facing the smoker. The

spur pipes from the excavation reflect a decline in the use of milling from the first half of the 17th century, when pipes were generally fully milled, to the end of the century, when milling was abandoned altogether.

Two spur pipes, figs. 98.3 & 4, were recovered from context 2301. This is one of the 'larger' groups containing ten fragments and which appears to date from *c*.1660-80. The occurrence of these bowls in the same context provides an indication of contemporary styles. The same applies to figs.98.7 and 8 which are two of the bowls recovered from a group of 36 pieces in context 374; a group which appears to have been deposited *c*.1680-1710. Both of these later bowls have been internally knife trimmed, to give a finer edge to the bowl, and then bottered to give a smooth finish. This has caused a slight internal lip to form inside the bowl rim. This finishing technique appears to be characteristic of late 17th to early 18th century pipes.

As noted above, two bowls from the same mould were recovered from context 374, one of which was milled and one of which was not (fig. 98.8). Another difference between these bowls is that the illustrated example has a stem bore of $^6/_{64}$" while the other example has a bore of $^7/_{64}$". A piece of stem also fits the unillustrated example and this has an uneven bulge in it, suggesting that the stem became damaged and was repaired during the manufacturing process. These features demonstrate that differences in workshop practice occurred and show how they could affect the appearance and attributes of the finished product.

During the late 17th and early 18th century radical changes in fashion took place. The Midlands spur type fell from favour to be replaced by a new range of heel forms, an unusual example of which is a Broseley style of pipe, dating from *c*.1680-1730 (fig. 98.9). Broseley, in Shropshire, became a major pipe manufacturing centre which generated distinctive styles of its own (Higgins 1987). The 'Type 5' form (Atkinson 1975), with its large, tailed, heel is perhaps the most distinctive product of this centre. The example from Causeway Lane has an incuse stamped initial mark on the base, which, on the basis of a more complete example from elsewhere in Leicester, is likely to have read IW or LW (Green 1984, fig. 24). There is another example of either a Broseley type 3 or type 5 bowl from Stanhopes Field, High Cross near Lutterworth (Jewry Wall Museum; fieldwalking collections) which is certainly marked IW. Although the Causeway Lane example is in a Broseley style the lack of a burnished surface, the use of an incuse initial mark, which was not used at Broseley, and the occurrence of other examples from Leicestershire all point to its being a local copy.

During the eighteenth century more upright, thin-walled bowls were in fashion. The bowls of these pipes are much more fragile than the thick 17th century styles and they survive poorly in the archaeological record. A good example was, however, recovered from context 2755. This has a well proportioned bowl with a simple cut rim and an internal bowl cross (fig. 98.10). Two fitting pieces of stem give a surviving stem length of 14cm. This is all plain, almost certainly indicating that the pipe was not marked or decorated. The stem bore is surprisingly small, being only $^4/_{64}$" in diameter. There is a similar damaged bowl from context 2162 which has a stem bore of just over $^4/_{64}$". This example does not have an internal bowl cross.

There are three stems, dating from c.1760-90, with Midlands style stem borders on them (figs. 98.11-13). This particular pattern of decoration was used by makers from as far apart as Chesterfield and Cambridge (Walker & Wells 1979, 9). Two of the Causeway Lane examples also have maker's stamps, showing them to have been made by John Ward of Derby. It is interesting that Ward should have found a market in Leicester since pipes usually do not move far from their place of manufacture. Similar decorated stems were produced in Nottingham and a few of these have also been found in Leicester (for example, Green 1991, fig. 4). It seems highly probable that the Leicester makers would also have used this type of decorative stem border although most of the borders found in the city do not have names on them and none of those that do has yet been linked to a known Leicester maker.

At the same time that decorated stems were being produced moulded bowl decoration became popular. One of the earliest common motifs to be used consisted of scalloped decoration, one example of which was found amongst the domestic material (fig. 98.14). This piece is particularly interesting since it also has a moulded eagle facing the smoker and the maker's name and LEICESTER moulded in relief around the rim. Unfortunately the maker's name is not clear, although it possibly reads FLUDE with a small fleur-de-lys at the end. A John Flude, son of John Flude of Leicester, labourer, was apprenticed to the pipemaker Henry Headley in 1738 and took his freedom in 1754 (Hartopp 1927, 310 & 435). He is known to have worked in Leicester until 1768 (Gault 1979, 373). Another excavated example of this bowl is known from the garden of Castle House in Leicester, but with a damaged rim so the name is missing (Leicester Museum, A17.1986 U/S). There is also a bowl in the Jewry Wall Museum with fluted decoration and .....E / LEISTER (sic) moulded around the rim (Acc. No. A185.1966.12). The spur of this pipe is marked IF. The last letter of the surname together with the initials strongly suggest this can also be attributed to John Flude. The use of moulded rim lettering is characteristic of pipes produced in Lincolnshire and Nottinghamshire where the style is likely to have evolved during the 1760's or 70's (Walker & Wells, 1979). These pieces clearly show that the style was also being used in Leicester at an early date. It also means that Leicester can be added as a new production centre at the southwesterly limit of the core production area (Walker & Wells 1979, fig. 9).

The other mould decorated fragments are of 19th century date and consist of a small rim sherd with leaf decorated seams from context 542, a spur pipe fragment with leaf decorated seams from context 1293 (fig. 98.15) and four decorated pieces from context 2000, all of which can be mould matched with examples from the kiln waste (1 example of fig. 100.28; 3 examples of fig. 100.29). From the kiln waste there is also one decorated piece which is clearly intrusive. This consists of a bowl fragment with traces of a standing figure above a scroll containing lettering (fig. 100.30). The lettering appears to read SHERR.. / ..AIN. This almost certainly represents a pipe made by Edward Sherry of Gainsborough who is recorded working from 1792-1820 and who died in 1822 (Wells 1979, 138).

Even including the Sherry pipe and one of the John Ward pipes, both of which came from one of the kiln groups, a total of only five marked pipes were recovered from amongst the domestic material. These were pipes made by IW, Flude of Leicester, Sherry of Gainsborough and two by Ward of Derby. Of these, three are certainly imports to the city in addition to which the IW pipe may well be, leaving only the Flude pipe as a local product. This underlines the low level of marking amongst the Leicester pipemakers and emphasizes the importance of good pit groups or kiln groups from which the local typology can be established and refined. There were also very few decorated pieces recovered. This is principally due to

the lack of more recent domestic contexts which are likely to have contained this type of material. Although the excavation produced a relatively small quantity of domestic material it has still provided some important new information about the local industry, in particular by establishing Leicester as a production centre for pipes with moulded rim lettering.

The first kiln group
(Context 2358; figs 98.13 and 99.16-100.32)

The largest, and most significant, group of kiln waste was recovered from context 2358, the bedding layer for a brick cellar floor. This provided a well sealed context with little risk of contamination from either the layers through which the cellar had been cut or from later disturbance. The deposit included large quantities of kiln debris from a muffle kiln (Peacey, below) as well as numerous pipes, many of which showed clear signs of being wasters. A significant proportion of the bowls were intact which, together with the survival of long stem fragments, suggested that this was a 'fresh' deposit of waste rather than a redeposited one. A total of 5,839 fragments of pipe were recovered, consisting of 654 bowl, 4,886 stem and 299 mouthpiece fragments. This does not include pipe fragments still embedded within kiln waste.

Despite the clear and well sealed evidence for a pipe kiln in the area both the origin and dating of the material has proved to be a problem. Initially it was hoped that the pipe kiln might have actually been on the site and that the date of the deposit could be determined from maps and deeds relating to the construction of the cellar. Documentary research, however, did not produce any evidence for either a pipemaker or kiln on the site (Hammond, below). It also failed to locate any building which could be related to the excavated cellar. The first detailed map of the site is the 1st Edition 25" O.S. map of 1887 which shows the site of the cellar occupied by a building fronting onto Countess Street. The cellar, however, does not appear to be related to this building, the building plans for which suggests that it was constructed in about 1866 as Countess Street was being laid out. The style of the pipes clearly indicated an early 19th century date for the deposit and so an earlier building had to be searched for.

Combe's map of 1802 only depicts the buildings of Leicester as general blocks. One such block is depicted at the junction of Causeway Lane but fronting onto East Bond Street. This is fairly well to the east of the cellar and on a different alignment so it seems unlikely that these buildings relate to the cellar. In this case the map provides a *terminus post quem* of 1802 for the deposit. By 1828 Fowler depicts a row of housing along the north side of Causeway Lane with strip gardens running back behind them. These are on the same orientation as the cellar which seems likely to have been in one of these, presumably beneath some sort of outbuilding. If the outbuilding were contemporary with the development of the north side of Causeway Lane then this would give *terminus ante quem* of 1828 for the waste.

On archaeological grounds there are a number of factors which support and help refine these suggested dates. The group contains a number of pipes, including wasters, which are marked RK. These can be attributed to the Leicester maker Richard King, who was pipemaking by 1805 and who died in 1828 (Hammond, below). This confirms the *terminus ante quem* of 1828, suggested by the cartographic evidence. In addition there is a single marked piece which can be attributed to Edward Sherry of Gainsborough who is recorded working from 1792-1820 and who died in 1822 (Wells 1979, 138). Since pipes had a very short life expectancy this suggests that the terminal date of the deposit can be pushed back to c.1822. On stylistic grounds the use of foliage sprigs on the stems of some of the pipes indicates a date in the second decade of the

19th century or later. The pottery includes pearlwares and transfer-printed earthenwares of a similar date. Taken together this evidence strongly suggests a date of *c.*1810-20 for this material, with the preferred date of deposition being around 1820. This close dating together with the sealed nature of the deposit is important in that it provides a chronological bench mark against which other groups of pipes and pottery from the region can be measured.

In determining the origin of the pipe and kiln debris, the key pieces are the waste pipes marked RK which must have originated in King's workshop. These pipes only constitute a small proportion of the pipes recovered but it seems unlikely that a single sealed foundation deposit would have been made up of waste from more than one different production site. As a result this group must be seen as waste from King's workshop, representing a sample of his production range from the second decade of the nineteenth century. By this time King was working at the western end of Belgrave Gate where he stayed until his death in 1828 (Hammond, below). This workshop lay about a quarter of a mile to the southeast of the excavated site.

Treatment of the material

The material was badly affected by iron staining, making it difficult to examine and compare the pieces and impossible to attempt reconstruction. An effective method of removing this staining was found to be an EDTA (ethylenediaminetetra-acetic acid solution). A description of the process used is given by J. Mirdamadi on p.233 below.

The nature of the assemblage was such that it seemed highly likely that complete pipes could be reconstructed. The pieces were systematically sorted and an attempt to reconstruct them made using the methodology described elsewhere (Higgins 1982). It was the junctions between bowls and stems which were principally checked since these are the easiest to find and provide the key to whether sufficient joins are present to allow complete pipes to be reassembled. There were a total of 419 fragments of bowls with stem junctions and 292 stems which were opening out into bowls. Of these only twenty stem to bowl joins were found; a success rate of only 6.8%. This was a disappointingly low rate and suggested that a lot of material was missing from the assemblage. Given that there were about 5,000 pieces of stem and mouthpiece for the 419 bowl junctions each stem must have been broken into about 12 pieces. With a potential success rate of only 6.8% for each successive join it was most unlikely that any complete pipes could be reassembled and so the attempt was abandoned.

The material was then sorted into different bowl forms and

an attempt made to identify the number of different mould types represented. This was relatively easy with the decorated bowls but much more difficult with the plain bowls which had to be matched by reference to small mould flaws. These occur most frequently around the spur or heel of the pipe. With the exception of about twenty very fragmentary pieces all of the bowl stem junctions were mould sorted, but the majority of the plain bowl fragments could not be attributed. This was in contrast to the decorated fragments which could easily be recognised. For this reason the minimum number of each type represented was also recorded. For the two largest groups the minimum number was based on the number of bowl/stem junctions so that the two figures are comparable. For features such as stem bore and finishing techniques only a sample of the two large groups were examined.

A total of seventeen different mould types were identified; a summary of the attributes of each type is given in Table 61, followed by a more detailed description of each type. This is followed by a discussion of the workshop practices represented.

The mould types represented

Almost all of the bowl/stem junctions and all of the decorated fragments could be sorted into individual mould types. A total of seventeen different moulds were identified and these are described below using the figure number for identification.

Fig. 99.16 Plain spur form. The mould is identified by a fine scratch running the full length of the right hand side of the spur and by a series of scratches on the left hand side of the bowl. Several of the examples have evidence of an internal bowl cross, which appears to be tilted slightly to the right. Composite bowl drawing from three of the fragments.

Fig. 99.17 Plain spur form. The mould is identified by a small, oval irregularity and a small scratch on the right hand side of the spur. There are also flaws on the bowl sides but these are less regularly evident. This pipe is also characterised by a distinctive internal bowl mark consisting of a double cross. Almost all of the rims show evidence of having been wiped to smooth them. The wiping is often very light and it can be intermittent.

Fig. 99.18 Plain spur form. This type appears to have a finer spur than the previous examples. It has an internal bowl cross and is particularly distinctive in that there are four pronounced ribs, caused by grooves in the stopper, which occur inside the bowl on the left hand side, away from the smoker. The stem bores of these pipes were both just over $4/64$" but both are

Table 41: *Summary of bowl forms from context 2358*

Fig. No	No. of frags	Min No. of pipes	No. Smoked	Bowl rims wiped?	Trimmed or flattened heels or spurs	Stem bore range (inches)	No. of wasters
16	6	6	1	Yes	Flattened	$5/64$th	0
17	169	168	8	Yes	Trimmed	$5/64$th	8
18	2	2	0	Yes?	-	$5/64$th	2
19	1	1	0	-	-	$4/64$th	1
20	1	1	0	No	No	$4/64$th	0
21	7	7	0	Yes	No	$5/64$th	2
22	10	10	2	Yes	No	$4/64$-$5/64$th	0
23	12	12	1	Yes	No	$4/64$-$5/64$th	0
24	1	1	-	-	No	$4/64$th	0
25	6	6	1	Some	No	$4/64$th	0
26	1	1	0	-	No	$4/64$th	0
27	2	1	0	-	-	-	2
28	27	13	2	No	Flattened	$4/64$th	?1
29	283	234	5	No	No	$4/64$th-$5/64$th	3
30	1	1	0	-	No	$5/64$th	0
31	1	1	?	-	-	$5/64$th	0
32	1	1	?	-	-	$4/64$th	0

vitrified, which would have resulted in additional shrinkage, so they have been recorded above as $^5/_{64}$".

Fig. 99.19 Plain spur fragment. This has a forward pointing spur and an internal bowl cross where the rib on the long axis of the pipe is much more pronounced than the lateral one. This pipe had a bore of $^4/_{64}$" but was vitrified and could originally have been as much as $^5/_{64}$".

Fig. 99.20 Plain spur form. The spur has a square section to it and there is no internal bowl cross.

Fig. 99.21 Plain heel pipe. The initials are quite neatly executed but with a tail to the leg of the K, which also has a small flaw to the right of it.

Fig. 99.22 Plain heel pipe. The initials are very similar to 21 but without the flaws around the K. The tail of the R tends to be surrounded by a small hollow. Bowl form has flaws on it and is clearly different to 21. Nine of the examples have wiped rims but one may not have been wiped.

Fig. 99.23 Plain heel pipe. The initials are rather poor , the K typically being poorly defined and with the R at an odd angle.

Fig. 99.24 Fragment from a heel bowl with fluted decoration. This may be from the same mould as one from the Austin Friars, Leicester (A389.1973 U/S; SF 1312). This has simple flutes on the bowl but no other decoration or lettering.

Fig. 100.25 Decorated heel pipe. There is a star mark on the heel and a faint foliage frieze above the fluting.

Fig. 100.26 Heel fragment. This is very similar to 25 above but seems to be of a slightly heavier build and without decoration.

Fig. 100.27 Decorated spur pipe, one fragment from the front and one from the back of the bowl. These have been mould matched with a more complete example from Elbow Lane, Leicester (Higgins 1985, fig 90).

Fig. 100.28 Decorated spur pipe. The clay in one of the bowls has been poorly mixed causing it to laminate, particularly at the bowl/stem junction. This may have been the cause of the pipe having been wasted.

Fig. 100.29 Decorated spur pipe. This is a particularly crudely designed mould with poorly designed flutes and a large mould flaw on the right hand side away from the smoker. Small, off centre, internal bowl cross.

Fig. 100.30 Single fragment of a decorated spur pipe having the relief moulded lettering SHERR.. / ...AIN in a scroll with traces of a standing figure above. This can be attributed to Edward Sherry of Gainsborough who is recorded working from 1792-1820 and who died in 1822 (Wells 1979, 138).

Fig. 100.31 Single fragment from a pipe with moulded leaf decoration on the seams. This consists of leaves with small spikes between.

Fig. 100.32 Single fragment from a pipe with moulded leaf decoration on the seams.

Although these seventeen different bowl forms were found together with the kiln waste at least one of them, the Sherry piece, is clearly intrusive to the group. This raises the question as to whether any of the other material is intrusive. Six or seven of the other forms include wasters (types 17, 18, 19, 21, 27, 28 and 29) and these can certainly be seen as part of the kiln group. The other pieces are less certain. Many of them only occur as single examples from which it is almost impossible to draw any firm conclusions. Even with large groups, like the type 29 bowls, it is very rare that kiln wasters as such can be identified. Out of the whole sample of 531 bowls listed above only 19 fragments could clearly seen to be wasters because they were deformed or vitrified; just 3.6%. The main indication that these pipes represented kiln rather than domestic waste comes not so much from their physical shape or condition but

from secondary attributes such as whether they have been smoked or not. The majority of the pipes, 96.2%, did not show any sign of having been smoked while only about 20 examples, 3.8%, did so. The fact that such a high proportion of the pipes had never been used provides perhaps the clearest indication that this is a kiln group.

Where only a few examples of a particular mould type occur neither traces of having been smoked nor evidence for being a waster can be used as a reliable indicator. The number of examples present does not provide a reliable indicator either, since types 18, 19 and 21 were only represented by 1 or 2 fragments each and yet all were clearly kiln wasters. Types 31 and 32 occurred as single examples which may have been smoked. If this is the case it is more likely that they are intrusive. All that can really be said of this group is that six or seven of the types clearly represent production waste, very few of the pipes appear to have been smoked and that only one of the contemporary bowls is clearly intrusive. The group did also contain some earlier residual material, such as six 17th century fragments, including a bowl (fig. 98.6), and a piece of 18th century decorated stem (fig. 98.13). These pieces, however, only constitute a very small percentage, 0.1%, of the total and suggest that the risk of contamination to the deposit is very low.

Evidence for workshop practice

One of the most important things about any group of kiln waste is the evidence which it can provide for workshop practice at a given point in time. From the study of such groups it is possible to refine the dating and interpretation of pipes and manufacturing techniques observed elsewhere.

This assemblage is dominated by pipes from two moulds, types 17 and 29. These two types represent 402 of the minimum number of 466 pipes, or 86% of the total. This suggests that not all of the moulds were in use at any one time but that batches of particular patterns were produced to build up stock. Since the press had to be re-set each time the mould was changed it would have made sense to produce a run of pipes before changing to a different mould. It would also make handling easier since the product would be more uniform and there would be less sorting of different types as the kiln was unloaded.

Amongst the mould groups differences were observed which seem to have been pattern specific. The wiping of rims to smooth them after they have been cut with a knife is a case in point. Types 16, 17, 21, 22, 23 and possibly 18 all had consistently wiped rims while types 20, 28 and 29 did not. Only in type 25 did there appear to be a difference with three rims appearing to have been wiped and two showing no sign of wiping. Likewise the finishing of the heel or spur differs from pattern to pattern. In types 16 and 28 the base of the spur has consistently been flattened during the trimming stage. In type 17 it appears to have been properly trimmed with a knife cut. None of the other bowls had been so treated. The bases of the heel types are particularly poor, often exhibiting very rough and irregular mould seams in this area. These finishing differences may reflect the quality or status of the pipes.

Type 29, although decorated, has neither wiped rim nor trimmed spur. This is in contrast to the other common type, 17, which, although plain, has both a wiped rim and a trimmed spur. This plain pipe with its elegant lines and neat finishing would have taken longer to prepare than the crudely decorated and roughly finished type 29 and is likely to have retailed at a higher price. This suggests that the traditional plain pipe may have retained its place at the top end of the market while the crudely produced mould decorated forms were catering for the everyday market. Such a difference in status is likely to have been reflected in stem length.

The longest surviving stems attached to bowls occur on the

type 17 pipes. These do not appear to be straight which suggests curved stems had become established in Leicester by the 1810's. Some of the type 17 pipes have a reverse curve on the stem and partially deformed bowls. These pieces are overfired and have started to collapse in the kiln. The manner in which they have done so confirms the normal stacking arrangement for a muffle kiln at this period with the bowls leaning up at an angle and resting on the edge of the bowl farthest from the smoker (see Peacey, below).

The stem bores of the pipes are generally consistent to mould type although not invariably so. Types 22 and 23 have a mixture of $^4/_{64}$" and $^5/_{64}$" bores while type 29 had mainly $^4/_{64}$" bores with a few $^5/_{64}$" ones. These differences suggest that specific moulding and trimming wires were not always kept with each pipe, a pattern which has been noted from other sites but which contrasts with the evidence from the second kiln group (see below). It may be that the specific association of a mould and moulding wire was only occasionally adopted, or that it only emerged with the introduction of shorter moulds around the middle of the 19th century.

A few of the pipes exhibited signs of having been repaired during the manufacturing process. Two of the type 17 and one of the type 28 pipes have spurs which have been 'stuck on' or completely remodelled by hand. Presumably they became detached as the pipes were being taken from the mould and so, rather than waste the pipe, it was pushed back on again by the pipemaker. Evidence for this kind of repair has been noted from the 17th century onwards.

Four of the pieces had a red wax coating from the mouthpiece surviving. Documentary sources suggest that the mouthpieces of pipes were treated with a variety of finishes to prevent the porous clay from sticking to the smokers' lips but only glazed tips tend to survive in the archaeological record. These wax coated pieces not only provide a date by which this medium was being used in Leicester but also indicate that slightly damaged pipes were considered saleable since one of the pieces has the wax coating extending across a broken end. No doubt only a short section was missing but it provides another indication of the slight variability that could be expected from a mould produced product and the fact that, wherever possible, the pipemaker would try to salvage rather than scrap a pipe.

Internal bowl crosses were present in five of the types; 16-19 and 29. These are all spur types, crosses did not occur with any of the heel types.

Discussion of the first kiln group

The bowl forms from King's workshop provide an indication of the range of products which were being produced in Leicester during the 1810's. All of these pipes are likely to have been of the long stemmed type which were typical of the period. There are likely to have been different lengths produced according to the quality and status of the pipe but it has not been possible to gather any information about this aspect. A range of bowl forms was clearly being produced with both spur (16-20, 27-29) and heel forms (21-26) available. Both were produced in plain or decorated styles. The decoration appears to have been confined to a range of fairly simple scalloped or fluted designs, each of which is different in detail.

A group of early 19th century pipes from a site at Elbow Lane, Leicester produced more than one mould type with the same type of decoration. It was postulated that these might represent the products of different makers who were competing by copying one another's designs (Higgins 1985, 300). This suggestion is supported by the kiln group since two of these patterns, 25 and 28, can now be attributed to Richard King. Both of these types were found at Elbow Lane together with similar copies which are not present in the kiln group.

This suggests that the matching pairs are the products of another maker competing with King.

The kiln group also shows that King did not mark all of his products. He only appears to have marked the heel pipes, four of which have his initials on while the remaining two have symbol marks consisting of a star. None of the spur pipes are marked. This suggests that marking may have been as much a subject of fashion as anything else. It appears to have been important to have a mark on the sides of a heel pipe, even if this were only a symbol, while such marking was not part of the expected design for a spur pipe.

While this group provides an important sample of King's production range, it is clearly not definitive. A different large plain heel type with the moulded initials RK was found at the Austin Friars site (Higgins 1985, fig. 30), and another version was found at Elbow Lane (Higgins 1985, fig. 122). The Elbow Lane site also produced an RK bowl with leaf decorated seams (Higgins 1985, fig. 123) while from the Austin Friars is a fluted bowl with the initials RK on the spur and LESTER moulded around the right hand side of the rim (Leicester Museum A389.1973, SF 1093). Unfortunately the left hand side of this bowl, which would have had the maker's name on it, is missing. It seems almost certain, however, that this design was produced by King. It provides another example of this style from Leicester, showing that it continued to be used into the 19th century.

The absence of these other known varieties of King's pipes from the kiln group does not necessarily mean that they were not being made at the time. Apart from the two dominant types most of the varieties in the group were only represented by a few, or single, examples. Erratic numbers of types, often with a few forms dominating, have been noted from other kiln groups. This can be explained by the nature of the material. On a production site waste would have accumulated quite rapidly. Some of this would become deposited around the site but the majority, particularly in urban areas, would have to be disposed of on a regular basis. Construction sites requiring hardcore would have been an ideal place where this material could be utilised. The material deposited, however, would only be likely to represent a brief period of rubbish accumulation at the kiln site. The numbers of different patterns contained in the kiln waste and the quantities present will, therefore, have been dependent on the production and handling activities of a short period during which particular types may have been broken in large numbers, or not at all. For this reason the Causeway Lane group can only be regarded as a sample, showing some of the types which were certainly being produced at this time. A series of such deposits will be required before a comprehensive picture of the dating and development of individual styles within the workshop can be arrived at.

The second kiln group (Context 3501; figs. 100.33-101.46)

This group of material was recovered from a general cleaning layer. The comparatively late date and general nature of this context meant that the pipes could easily have been dismissed as being of little consequence. In fact, they provide one of the few good groups of 19th century pipes known from Leicester-shire and are particularly important since they represent production debris from another of the city's workshops.

This material can be regarded as a discrete deposit of production waste for several reasons. First, the fragments are generally well preserved, occurring as quite large, un-abraded pieces and with a large number of whole bowls present. There are also a number of cross joins between the fragments. Secondly, a small amount of production waste and kiln debris was recovered with the pipes. This strongly suggests that the pipes come from a kiln site, although waste pipes are notoriously difficult to identify since they rarely show any physical differences from purely domestic waste. Thirdly, the majority of the pipes show no signs of having been smoked and, in a few cases, the bowls are slightly deformed or otherwise defective. These features, including the presence of a few smoked examples (probably used and discarded by workers at the kiln), are typical of pipes recovered from production sites. Finally, although quite a sizable group there are only twelve basic patterns of pipe represented. Domestic waste usually contains a diversity of forms with little duplication and a high percentage of smoked examples.

The group as a whole consists of 212 pieces of pipe; 76 bowl, 128 stem and 8 mouthpiece fragments. Five of the stem fragments date from the 17th century and are residual but all of the remaining stems appear to date from the 19th century. These have all been considered to form part of the kiln group although where single examples occur, particularly if they have been smoked, it may be that they are stray pieces which should be treated with caution (see below).

All of the 19th century bowls were sorted and an attempt made to reconstruct complete examples of the pipes using the methodology described elsewhere (Higgins 1982). Some bowl/stem junction joins and one mouthpiece/stem join were found but this could not be joined to any other stems. There were no other mouthpiece/stem joins and so no pipes could be completed. The low recovery rate of stem and mouthpiece fragments from this context clearly limited the chances of reconstructing complete pipes.

The bowls were then sorted into types. A careful search for mould flaws was carried out in an attempt to identify the number of individual mould types present. This was possible for the decorated pipes but few distinctive flaws could be found amongst the plain types and so they could only be sorted into general groups.

Twelve basic bowl forms were present within the context and these were lettered A-L. A summary of the information about the twelve bowl types is given in table 42 followed by a more detailed description of each type.

Table 42: *Summary of bowl forms from context 3501*

Bowl type	Fig. No.	No. of frags	Min No. of pipes	No. Smoked	Internally Cut or trimmed?	Size of Bore (inches)	Stem length	Wasters?
A	33	2	2	1	Yes	$^5/_{64}$th	Long	No
B	34	18	18	5	No	$^5/_{64}$th	Long	No
C	36	8	8	2	Yes	$^4/_{64}$th	Long	No
D	38	1	1	0	No	$^4/_{64}$th	Long	No
E	39	3	2	0	No	$^5/_{64}$th	Short	No
F	40	1	1	0	No	$^4/_{64}$th	Short	No
G	41	1	1	1	No	$^4/_{64}$th	Long	No
H	42	1	1	1	No	$^5/_{64}$th	Long	No
I	43	14	14	2	No	$^5/_{64}$th	Long	No
J	44	4	4	0	No	$^5/_{64}$th	Long	Yes
K	45	3	2	0	No	$^5/_{64}$th	Short	Yes
L	46	3	3	0	No	$^4/_{64}$th	Short	Yes

The mould types represented:

The bowl types present were sorted into twelve groups. Insufficient distinguishing marks could be found for all of these to be mould specific. The types are described below together with a note as to whether or not they are mould specific.

Type A (fig. 100.33); These pipes could not be mould matched from identifiable flaws although the close similarity of form suggests that they are almost certainly from the same mould. Both examples have been internally knife trimmed at the rim but not wiped. This particular bowl form is characteristic of the long-stemmed 'churchwarden' pipe and is likely to have been the most expensive type produced. The form can be closely paralleled amongst the products of the Broseley industry (Higgins 1987, fig. 22.9h), which was famed for its long-

stemmed pipes, although the products from there often had wiped rims.

Type B (fig. 100.34); Although these could not be mould matched through flaws the bowls are all very similar in form. One of the smoked examples, with a damaged bowl, may be slightly different but the others are all likely to come from the same mould. All of these pipes have simple cut rims without any evidence of internal trimming or wiping. Just one of these bowls is marked with an incuse, sans serif mark reading CHENNERY LESTER (fig. 100.35). This is the only known example of this maker's mark.

Type C (fig. 101.36); This group can be sub-divided into those with plain spurs (fig. 101.36) and one example which has a small mould mark on the right hand side (fig. 101.37). No other mould flaws have been identified within this group and so it is impossible to be sure whether this mark represents a different mould or simply the same mould which was later damaged or had this dot added intentionally. All 8 bowls are of very similar form with a more slender, elegant bowl than type C and a thinner stem. The stems of this type are about 6.5mm wide and 8mm deep just behind the bowl as opposed to 8mm wide and 9mm deep in type C. The bowls also differ from type C in that they all have stem bores of $^4/_{64}$" and internally trimmed rims. The example with the dot also appears to have had the rim wiped, lending weight to the argument that it represents a different mould.

Type D (fig. 101.38); Single example of a small bowl with a tiny spur and thin stem. Simple cut rim.

Type E (fig. 101.39); One of the two examples is damaged and the bowls cannot be positively mould matched. The one surviving rim has simply been cut. These would probably have been short-stemmed 'cutty' pipes.

Type F (fig. 101.40); The angle of the surviving stem bore suggests that the stem was quite sharply angled (see dotted reconstruction). It would probably have been a short stemmed 'cutty' style of pipe. Cut rim

Type G (fig. 101.41); Moulded seam decoration consisting of leaves with acorns between. The decoration is simply executed and the rim is cut. The spur is chipped but enough of the right hand side survives to show that it was marked with a small circle, moulded in relief. Stylistically this bowl appears to be a little earlier than the rest of the group. This may be residual, unconnected with the kiln waste.

Type H (fig. 101.42); Moulded seam decoration consisting of simply executed leaves without ribs. The rim is cut. As an isolated, smoked example, this piece may well be intrusive to the kiln group.

Type I (fig. 101.43); There is a two-handled cup on either side of the bowl, leaf decoration on the seams and a symbol mark on the spur. The length of surviving stem (85mm) suggests that this was quite a long-stemmed pattern of pipe. All of these examples can be mould matched by flaws, in particular a vertical scratch from the right hand handle of the cup on the left hand side of the bowl.

Type J (fig. 101.44); This pattern is very similar to type I although the bowl is a little shorter. There is a glass on either side of the bowl, leaf decoration on the seams and a symbol mark on the spur. All of these examples can be mould matched. One of the bowls has been slightly squashed in from the end and may have been regarded as a waster because of this. There are two joining fragments which may represent a fifth example of this type but the leaf decoration on the seam is too poorly preserved to be sure of this.

Type K (fig. 101.45); Two pipes from the same mould. Both are likely to be wasters since both have spalled surfaces and the illustrated example has a copper coloured encrustation on the stem. The rims have been cut and the one surviving stem bore is 5/64". This pipe is likely to have been a short-stemmed cutty type, although long-stemmed versions of this pattern are known.

Type L (fig. 101.46); Three examples, all from the same mould. The bowl has been shaped as a boot and has a cut rim. Along both sides of the stem the words EASY FIT are moulded, incuse, within a relief moulded beaded border. The mouthpiece is of a nipple type but the surviving example has been very poorly moulded. There was not quite enough clay in the mould so the uneven rolling marks are still visible. It also appears that it should have had a lozenge-shaped section near the mouthpiece but that, because of the lack of clay, this has not been properly taken up. The heel of one of the boots appears to have spalled off. The poorly moulded mouthpiece and the missing heel both suggest that these pipes were wasters. Examples of both this type and of a different boot pattern have been recorded from Leicester (Green 1991, 41).

Most of the twelve types described match at least one of the criteria listed above for kiln groups. The types which can most confidently be seen as production waste are B, C, I, J, K and L. These all occur as multiple examples or with clear evidence of being wasters. In contrast, types G and H occurred as single examples which had been smoked. These pieces could be stray bowls which had become mixed with the kiln debris and so should be treated with suspicion. The other four types (A, D, E and F) occurred in small numbers but had generally not been smoked. Stylistically they fit well with the other production waste and are seen as being likely to form part of it.

The 10 forms which are most likely to represent kiln waste were represented by 57 examples of which 12 (21%) showed signs of having been smoked. The presence of smoked pipes has been noted amongst other kiln groups and seems likely to represent pipes smoked by the workers at the manufactory.

Although no complete pipes could be re-assembled it was still possible to reconstruct the form of one of the pipes by overlapping the marked fragments (fig. 101.46). This showed the boot pattern to be a short stemmed or 'cutty' pipe with an advertising slogan, EASY FIT, along the stem. Short stemmed pipes were only introduced in the mid-19th century and, as in this example, usually has a nipple type of mouthpiece. Of the eight mouthpiece fragments recovered this was the only nipple type, all of the others having simple cut ends, a form usually associated with longer stemmed pipes. This suggests that the majority of patterns represented in this kiln group had long stems. This is born out by the bowl types which were often related to stem length too. Table 42 shows the likely length of each form based on an assessment of the bowl type. Eight of the types, represented by 49 (83%) of the fragments, are likely to have been longer stemmed pipes while four of the types, represented by 10 (17%) of the fragments, are likely to have been 'cutty' pipes.

Evidence for workshop practice

Evidence of variation in stem length for the longer stemmed pipes is provided by one of the waste fragments recovered. These pipes would have been made in metal moulds where the stem terminated with a rounded end beyond which was a guide groove for the wire which formed the bore. The maximum length for a pipe was, therefore, determined by this rounded end. In practice it was difficult to achieve a good mouthpiece on a long-stemmed pipe by moulding alone and so the pipemaker usually trimmed the stem with a knife to form a neat mouthpiece. Examination of 17th century kiln waste from Rainford has shown that this led to a variations in the length of pipes, even when they were produced in the same mould

(Higgins, 1982, 200). One of the fragments from context 3501 consists of the accidentally fired waste trimmed from the end of a pipe. The rounded mould terminal is visible at the left hand of the illustration while at the other end is the knife cut where the stem was trimmed by the pipemaker (fig 101.47). This surplus length has then been ripped off the moulding wire leaving a ragged slot along one edge of the fragment. The original stem bore is likely to have been 4/64" and the length of the fragment is 31mm. This provides a minimum variable for the length of this pipe as a result of trimming the mouthpiece.

The stem bores are all either 4/64" or 5/64" in diameter; the size range that would be expected for a 19th century group. Each pattern of pipe was associated with a particular size of stem bore (table 41). This suggests that each mould is likely to have had its own specific moulding wire. This is in contrast with the 17th century evidence from the Vergulde Draeck, a Dutch East Indiaman lost off the western coast of Australia in 1656. At this site analysis of the stem bores from a box of unused pipes clearly showed that two wires giving different stem bores had been used to mould the pipes (Green 1977, 162). The Leicester stem bores also show that there does not appear to be any relationship between stem length and bore size, the narrower and wider bores being used for both long and short patterns of pipe.

All of the pipes had simple cut rims, formed by a horizontal knife cut through a slot at the top of the mould. In addition, some of the bowls have internal knife trimming. This is where a sliver of clay has been removed from around the inside lip of the bowl rim to give a narrower or more refined finish. This seems likely to have been reserved for the better qualities of pipe. It was only found on two of the bowl forms, types A and C, but it occurred consistently on all of them. Type A is likely to have been a very long-stemmed 'churchwarden' type. Type C has a much more slender form and stem but appears to be essentially a smaller version of type A. It would be interesting to know whether this type also had a particularly long stem.

Fired pipeclay is very porous and so tends to stick to the smoker's lips as it draws moisture from them. This is the reason why mouthpieces were often sealed with wax, glaze or other substances, many of which do not survive archaeologically. Although no treated mouthpieces were identified, two stem fragments from near the mouthpiece and with traces of a finish were recovered. These both have areas of a thin, pale bluish-grey coating on them. These stems are clearly from a long, thin-stemmed pipe and both have stem bores of 4/64". Only bowl forms C, D and G match these requirements and type G is a rather chunky pipe which may not form part of the kiln group anyway. It seems most likely, therefore, that this type of coating is associated with form C or D. Type C might be the more likely if it represents a long stemmed pipe of higher quality.

Discussion of the second kiln group

The bowl designs represented in this group are fairly typical of those found in Leicester and Nottingham during the second half of the 19th century (Green 1984; Green 1991; Hammond 1982). There are, however, other common forms, such as acorn, thorn or fluted designs, which might have been expected but which are absent. Most of these designs had a wide currency and versions of them can be found all over the country. One pattern which seems to have been more narrowly confined to the East Midlands is the handled cup design (fig. 101.43) which has already been recorded from Leicester (Green 1991). Variations of this design have also been found at Nottingham (Hammond 1982, fig. 22.141) and are known to have been made at Boston (Wells 1970) and at Market Rasen in Lincolnshire (Hammond 1982, fig. 30.219). These examples have been variously dated to the period *c.*1870-1890 and provide an indication of the likely date for the Leicester group. This is supported by the Chennery bowl stamp since John and Martha Chennery were pipemakers in Leicester from *c.*1855-86. It seems likely that from *c.*1855 until shortly after 1861 they were working in Canning Street, about a quarter of a mile to the north of the excavated site, and that by 1864 and until about 1886 they were working in Sycamore Lane, about a quarter of a mile to the west of the excavation (Hammond, below p.00).

The single marked pipe consists of a fragmentary bowl which cannot be positively mould matched with the other type B bowls. It is not certain, therefore, whether the whole kiln group can be attributed to the Chennerys' workshop or whether the marked piece should be regarded as a stray fragment which has become mixed with it. The Chennerys' workshops were not far from the site, but even closer was the Salisbury's workshop which lay less than 200yds away at 12 East Bond Street. This operated until 1864 and provides another potential source for the material. Given the evidence for an apparently unsmoked Chennery pipe amongst this group and the fact that the material has clearly been imported to the site from elsewhere the balance of probability must fall, however, in favour of the Chennerys'.

Documentary research has shown that there was wholesale redevelopment of the larger part of the excavated area in about 1865. At this date blocks of land were sold off by the Countess of Devonshire's Charity and Countess Street was laid out (Hammond, below; and Courtney, above). This development would have required large quantities of building materials and provided an ideal opportunity for kiln waste to be used as hardcore, a function which it often served. The documented development provides a plausible event with which to link the archaeological evidence and the date falls firmly within the working life of the Chennerys' workshop. For these reasons it is considered that the kiln waste be seen as a well dated group of material, providing an important fixed point for typological studies and an example of the range of forms being produced by Leicester makers in the mid-1860's.

General discussion

In 1979 Gault was able to list over two hundred known pipemakers from Leicestershire, most of them working in Leicester itself (Gault & Alvey, 1979). Despite this, very few of their products could be identified with any certainty (Higgins 1985), mainly due to the fact that hardly any of them appear to have marked their pipes. The material from this excavation has filled some of the gaps in our knowledge of the Leicester industry, particularly through the kiln groups which have provided a wealth of information about two of the 19th century workshops.

Both groups of kiln waste were found dumped away from their place of manufacture where at least one of them had been used as bedding for a floor. A small group of kiln waste from Flannagan's Frog Island works has been recorded from under the floor of a terrace in Sylvan Street, Leicester while a number of similar bedding deposits have been recorded from Nottingham (Hammond 1982, 27-33). The 1864 specification for laying out Countess Street includes the use of 'hard rubbish' for foundations and it seems clear that pipe kiln waste was widely used as hardcore in urban areas. Such deposits form a valuable source of information, particularly if the buildings under which they are sealed can be accurately dated.

The waste from King's workshop of *c.*1820 has shown that a range of marked and decorated heel and spur pipes were in production. The marks consisted of his initials or symbols moulded onto the heels of the pipes. No bowl marks were recovered from this group although it is known that he employed moulded lettering around the rim of some of his

designs. The decoration consists of a variety of fluted or scalloped designs, sometimes used in conjunction with leaf moulded seams and other foliage motifs. This range of marking and decoration is very similar to that found in Nottingham during the early 19th century (Hammond 1982). There are a few examples of similar designs in Derby Museum, but insufficient work has been carried out to draw any firm conclusions about the industry there at this period. At Lincoln similar designs are also found although there they tend to be accompanied by a wider range of other decorative motifs (Mann 1977). To the south and west in Northamptonshire and Coventry these designs do not appear to form a significant part of the local assemblages (Moore 1980; Muldoon 1979).

It appears that Leicester lay towards the south-western edge of an area over which fluted and scalloped designs were common. The evidence from the decorative stem borders and moulded bowl lettering supports this view and suggests that a 'stylistic region' developed during the later 18th and early 19th centuries over which common styles developed and spread. Despite the common links over this area there are not as many specific points of similarity between the pipes produced at each centre as there are differences between them. For example, slave and indian motifs occur in Lincolnshire but not at Nottingham while royal coats of arms occur at Nottingham but not in Leicester. Conversely, different makers in Leicester appear to have been making virtually identical, and specific, patterns of fluted pipe which are not found in Nottingham. These differences may be due to the influence of the elusive mould makers who, although working within a common tradition, may have influenced local markets by the range of designs with which they were familiar and which they could produce.

Whatever the mechanisms for style and change it is clear that by the 1860's the patterns represented in the second kiln group were distinctly different from the first. Although plain and decorated forms were still being produced they were by then all of spur rather than heel types. The best quality pipes were probably still plain, being represented by a neatly finished 'churchwarden' type (fig. 100.33). Fluted decoration had disappeared to be replaced by other decorative elements such as the boot, cup and glass motifs. The biggest change had come with the introduction of short stemmed 'cutty' pipes, which represented about 17% of the later group.

Summary

The pipes from this excavation have established that Leicester lay on the south-western limits of a 'stylistic region' extending east and north into Lincolnshire, Nottinghamshire and, probably, Derbyshire during the later 18th and early 19th centuries. It was also a production centre for pipes with moulded lettering around the rim of the bowl. The most significant groups recovered consisted of two dumps of kiln waste which had apparently been used as hardcore for building work.

The first group dates from *c.*1820 and contains 16 different patterns of pipe which can be attributed to Richard King. He was producing a range of plain and decorated long-stemmed pipes with red wax being used to coat the tips. The pipes had curved stems and the best quality ones appear to have had plain bowls. Other makers appear to have been making the same range of designs as King which suggests a competitive industry producing a fairly limited range of designs.

The second kiln group can be dated to *c.*1865 and illustrates ten or twelve forms of pipe which were being produced in Leicester, probably in the Chennerys' workshop. About half of the pipes were plain and over 80% of them were long-stemmed varieties, which is interesting for a period when cutty pipes were rapidly gaining a foothold in the market. It has been shown that stem length could vary by at least 31mm as a result of finishing methods and that specific workshop practices, such as internal bowl trimming, stem bore and mouthpiece coatings, can be associated with particular patterns of pipe.

Acknowledgements

Many people have been involved with the finds work and data collection which has made this report possible. Particular thanks must go to Professor Elizabeth Slater and Jennifer Mirdamadi at the University of Liverpool for their advice and help with the chemical cleaning of the pipes; to Helen Godwin and Andrea Scott for their patience and perseverance in the cleaning, sorting and laying out the main kiln group; to Dr. Paul Courtney and Peter Hammond for their documentary research into the background of the site; to David Barker, Dr. Peter Davey, Miranda Goodby and Eleanor Thomas for their comments on the pottery; to Dr. Allan Peacey for his report on the kiln material and last, but by no means least, to the Leicestershire Archaeological Unit who, by collecting and processing this material, have made this advance in our understanding of the Leicester pipe industry possible.

Illustrations

fig. 98 *The domestic pipes*

1. Spur bowl, fully milled, quite a good overall form to the bowl but with rough nodules or lumps on the surface of both sides, c.1660-80, stem bore $^8/_{64}$". A1.1991 2147.

2. Spur bowl, half milled, internally trimmed rim, c.1660-80, stem bore $^8/_{64}$". A1.1991 2062.

3. Spur bowl, three-quarters milled, internally trimmed rim, stem bore $^7/_{64}$", c.1660-80. A1.1991 2301.

4. Spur bowl, three-quarters milled, stem bore $^7/_{64}$", c.1660-80. A1.1991 2301.

5. Spur bowl, half-milled rim, stem bore $^6/_{64}$", c.1670-90. A1.1991 363.

6. Spur bowl, half-milled rim, stem bore $^7/_{64}$", c.1670-90. A1.1991 2358.

7. Spur bowl, half-milled and internally trimmed rim, stem bore $^7/_{64}$", c.1680-1710. A1.1991 374.

8. Spur bowl, not milled, internally trimmed rim, stem bore $^6/_{64}$", c.16801710. A1.1991 374.

9. Broseley style heel bowl with traces of an incuse maker's mark, which probably read IW. Not burnished, stem bore $^7/_{64}$", c.1680-1730. A1.1991 971.

10. Heel bowl, with a cut rim and an internal bowl cross, stem bore $^4/_{64}$", c.1730-70. A1.1991 2755.

11. Stem fragment with part of an incuse Midlands style stem border, c.1760-90, stem bore $^5/_{64}$". A1.1991 2358.

12. Stem fragment with an incuse Midlands style stem border and a stamp reading IOHN WARD DARBY, c.1760-90. Stem bore $^5/_{64}$". A1.1991 3505.

13. Stem fragment with part of an incuse Midlands style stem border and a stamp reading IOHN WARD DARBY, c.1760-90. Stem bore $^5/_{64}$". A1.1991 2358.

14. Spur bowl with relief moulded decoration and maker's mark. The bowl has a cut rim, below which is moulded ??FLUDE / LEICESTER. There are almost completely illegible initials moulded on the spur, the second of which may be a B or an R. Stem bore $^4/_{64}$". Probably made by John Flude, of Leicester who was apprenticed in 1738 and working until at least 1768. A1.1991 3505

15. Fragment of a spur bowl with simple leaf decoration on the seams, stem bore $^4/_{64}$", c.1800-1840. A1.1991 1293.

fig. 99 (16-24) and **100** (25-32) Kiln Group I (A1.1991 2358); attributed to the workshop of Richard King of Belgrave Gate and with likely deposition date of c.1820.

16. Plain spur bowl, with an internal bowl cross. Composite drawing from three fragments.

17. Plain spur bowl, with a double internal bowl cross.

18. Plain spur bowl, with an internal bowl cross.

19. Plain spur bowl, with an internal bowl cross.

20. Plain spur bowl, without an internal bowl cross.

21. Plain heel bowl, with relief moulded initials RK. Composite drawing from more than one fragment.

22. Plain heel bowl, with relief moulded initials RK.

23. Plain heel bowl, with relief moulded initials RK.

24. Decorated heel bowl, with relief moulded initials RK.

25. Decorated heel bowl, with relief moulded star mark.

26. Heel bowl fragment, with relief moulded star mark.

27. Decorated spur bowl. Drawing of a bowl in the author's possession but from the same mould as two fragments from this context, the outlines of which are indicated with dashed lines.

28. Decorated spur bowl.

29. Decorated spur bowl.

30. Decorated spur bowl, with the moulded lettering SHERR.. / ..AIN for Edward Sherry of Gainsborough, recorded working 1792-1820; died 1822.

31. Decorated bowl fragment.

32. Decorated bowl fragment.

fig. 100 (33-35) and **101** (36-47) Kiln Group II (A1.1991 3501); attributed to the workshop of John and Martha Chennery of Sycamore Lane and with likely deposition date of c.1865. A full description of these bowls can be found in the text.

33. Plain spur bowl, from a 'churchwarden' type of pipe.

34. Plain spur bowl.

35. Plain bowl fragment, similar design to 34 but with an incuse bowl stamp reading CHENNERY / LESTER. Made by John and Martha Chennery of Sycamore Lane.

36. Plain spur bowl.

37. Plain spur bowl, similar to 36 but with a small dot on the right hand side of the spur.

38. Plain spur bowl.

39. Plain spurless bowl.

40. Plain spurless bowl, the likely angle of the stem based on the stem bore is indicated by a dotted line.

41. Decorated spur bowl, with a moulded symbol mark consisting of a circle on the spur.

42. Decorated spur bowl.

43. Decorated spur bowl, with a moulded symbol mark on the spur.

44. Decorated spur bowl, with a moulded symbol mark on the spur.

45. Spurless bowl, with ribbed seams. There is a metallic encrustation on the stem and the bowl has spalled, suggesting that it is a waster.

46. Promotional pipe with the bowl moulded in the form of a boot and the incuse, sans-serif lettering 'EASY FIT' moulded on both sides of the stem with in a relief moulded beaded border. The complete form has been reconstructed from two overlapping fragments. The mouthpiece fragment has been

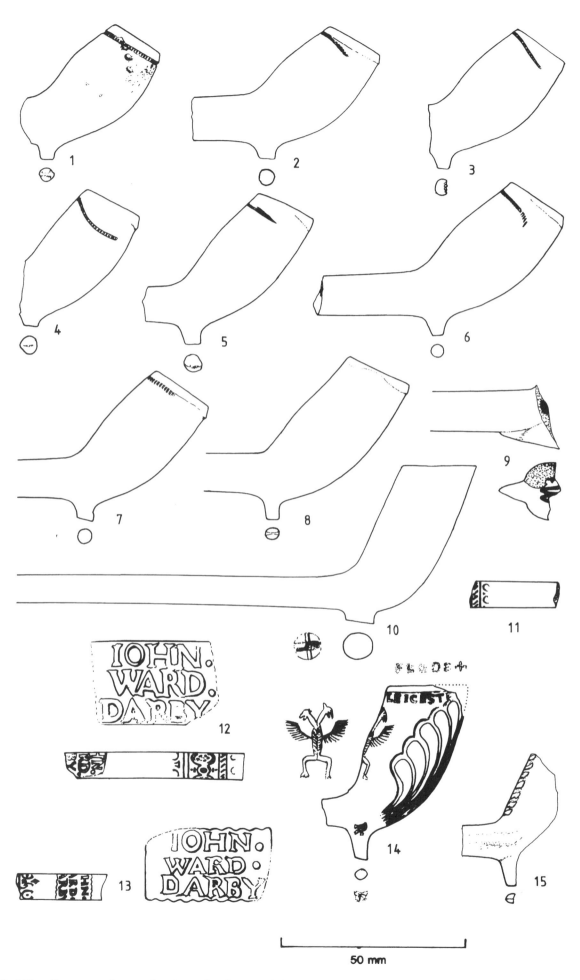

Fig. 98: *Miscellaneous domestic pipes. Scale 1:1 with stamp details at 2:1.*

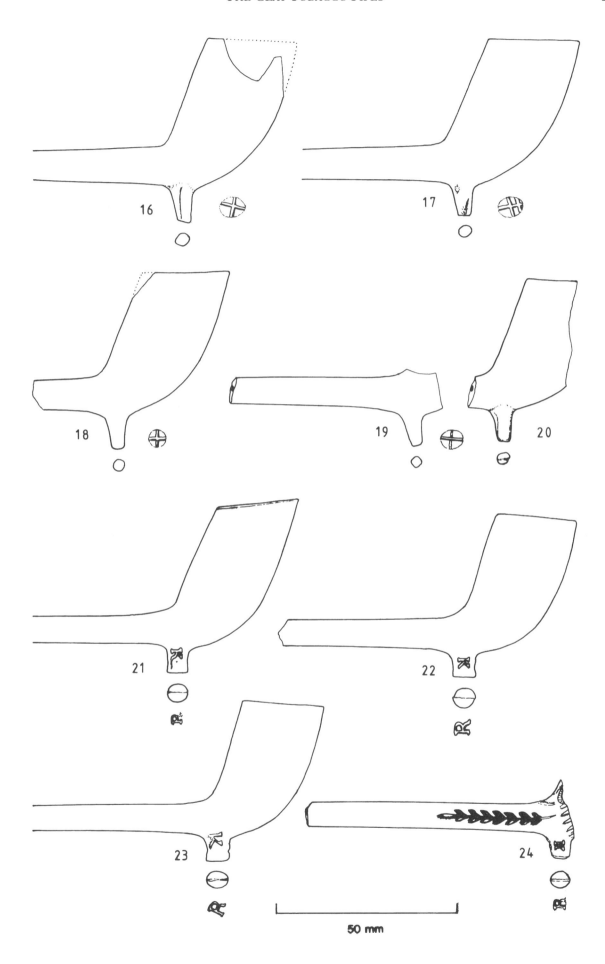

Fig. 99: *Kiln Group 1, c.1820, attributed to Richard King. Scale 1:1.*

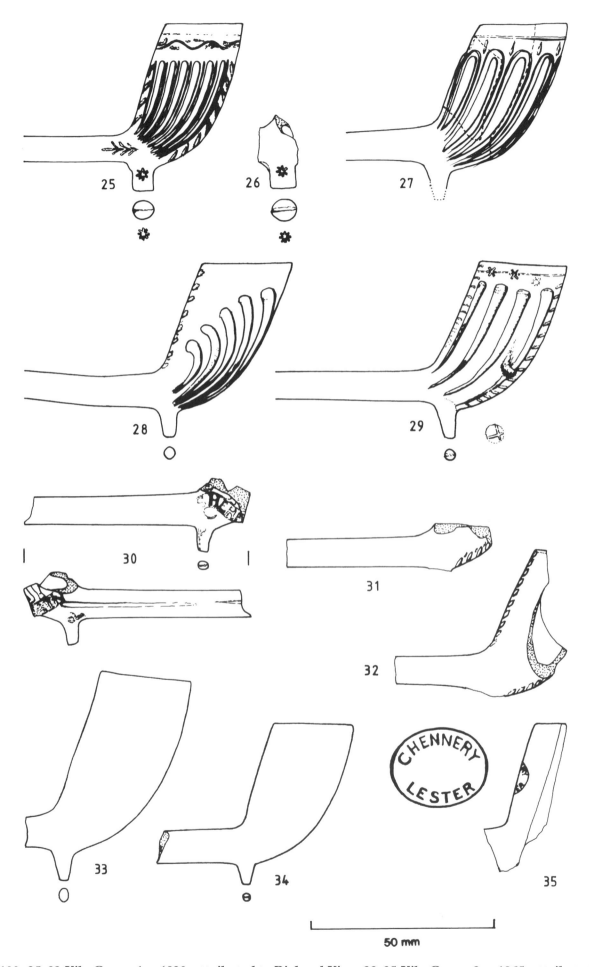

Fig. 100: *25-32 Kiln Group 1, c.1820, attributed to Richard King; 33-35 Kiln Group 2, c.1865, attributed to John and Martha Chennery. Scale 1:1 with stamp detail at 2:1.*

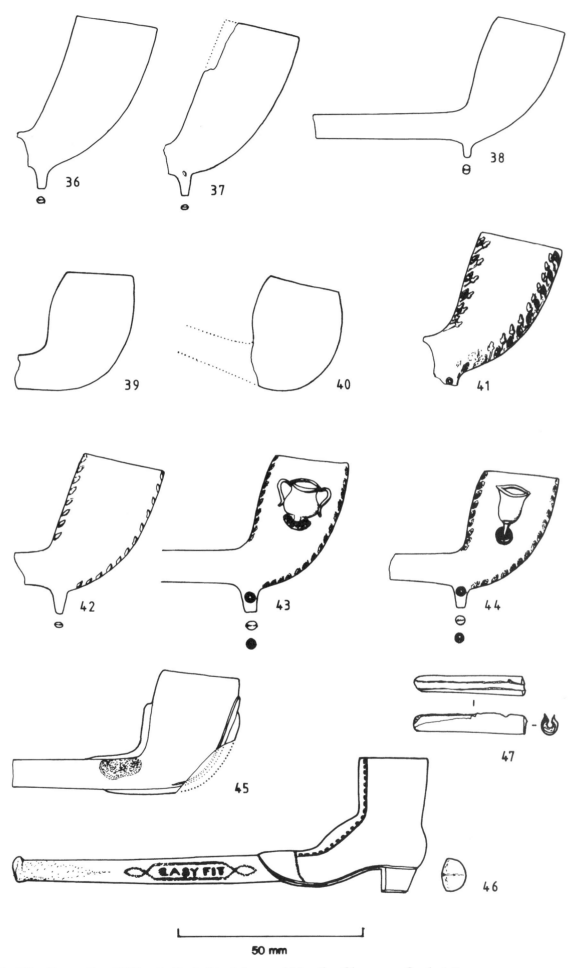

Fig. 101: *Kiln Group 2, c.1865, attributed to John and Martha Chennery. Scale 1:1.*

incompletely moulded but would have been of a nipple form with a diamond shape terminal to the stem. Stem bore 4/64".

47. A waste trimming, 31mm long, from the mouthpiece end of a long-stemmed pipe which has been accidentally fired in the kiln. One end is rounded where it has taken up the 'mouthpiece' end of the stem from the mould, the other is knife cut where it has been trimmed off. The whole piece has then been ripped off the moulding wire leaving an irregular slot along one site. The original stem bore is now rather distorted but is likely to have been 4/64".

Pipemakers in the vicinity of East Bond Street
P. J. Hammond

This is a summary of the documentary evidence collected about buildings and pipemakers in the vicinity of East Bond Street. A complete version is available in the site archive.

Detailed examination of the inhabitants and occupations of the East Bond Street/Causeway Lane area of Leicester has revealed only one clay pipe manufactory in this vicinity during the 19th century.

The manufactory in question was located at what became 12 East Bond Street and was owned and run by the Salisbury family, viz George and his son Thomas. George Salisbury was born and married in Derby and appears to have moved to Leicester *c.*1790. George appears to have retired by *c.*1840 when he was in his mid 70's in favour of his son Thomas. The latter advertised in Trade Directories as a 'Pipe Manufacturer and China, glass and Staffordshire dealer' (Green 1984, 9) and took sole responsibility for the business following his father's death in 1847. Thomas died in 1855, aged 59, after which both his wife Matilda and his daughter Emma continued to run the workshop until *c.*1864 – after which they are no longer listed.

Other clay pipe making workshops appear to have been some distance away from East Bond Street. One of these was in Sycamore Lane where John Chennery was working by March 1864 (Leicestershire Record Office; 7D67/576). The 1861 census records that he was at Canning Street. Both Canning Street and Sycamore Lane are some distance from East Bond Street and, unless Chennery worked elsewhere in the meantime, it would appear that his kiln waste, possibly like that of Richard King (below), was being transported some distance for use as hardcore.

Richard King (1775-1828); grocer, tallow chandler and tobacco pipe maker

Richard King was baptised in 1775, the son of William King, framework knitter, and his wife Mary. At the age of 14, Richard was described as a poor child of the parish of St. Mary when he was apprenticed to Thomas Veasey, a framesmith. Sometime after 1796 Richard must have decided that being a framesmith was not for him – possibly he changed his occupation during the period when he met his wife to be Mary Hichman. On 3 December 1803 they were married at Leicester St. Margaret.

The earliest entry indicating that Richard was a pipe maker occurs on 31 May 1805 when he advertised in the *Leicester Journal* for an apprentice.

A further advertisement appeared less than two years later on 26 July 1807:-

> Wanted – A stout lad, about 13 or 14 years of age, as an apprentice to a pipe maker. Enquire of R. KING, chandler and pipe maker, West Bridge, Leicester.

These advertisements not only confirm that Richard was actively involved in manufacturing pipes by this time, but also that he worked at West Bridge prior to his move to Belgrave Gate. West Bridge was situated on the River Soar at the west of Leicester, quite some distance from both Bond Street and Belgrave Gate.

Although King is recorded at West Bridge in 1807 the first directory to refer to him was in 1811 when he was listed as being a grocer of Belgrave Gate. Subsequent directories, such as *Fowler's Directory* of 1815, describe him as a grocer, tallow chandler and pipe maker of the same address. A detailed search of the Rate Books and comparison with directories and the 1841 census has demonstrated that King's house was situated at the western end of Belgrave Gate close to the Haymarket and was next door to the 'Star' public house on the east side of Belgrave Gate. It would appear that King actually occupied the property which subsequently became either 11 Haymarket or 1 Belgrave Gate.

Confirmation of the move was made in the *Leicester Journal* by an advertisement dated 25 March 1808, as follows:-

> RICHARD KING
> Grocer, chandler, and tobacco pipe maker
>
> Returns grateful acknowledgements to his numerous friends and the public, for the liberal patronage expended in his late situation, and respectfully informs them, he is removed to more desirable premises at the tope of Belgrave Gate, where he hopes to meet a continuance of the favour and support.
> N.B. A stout active lad of good morals and disposition wanted as an apprentice. Leicester Mar 24 1808.

Following his move from West Bridge, Richard King remained at Belgrave Gate, where he was listed in the trade directories. King clearly established a flourishing business since the apprenticeship registers show that he took on at least eight apprentices between 1804 and 1820: George Hall 1804; Thomas Banford 1805; Henry Kirkby 1808; Robert Bennett 1810 (free 1820); John Gamble 1814; Robert Wilson 1817 (free 1826); Joseph King, his son, 1818 (free 1826) and Benjamin Bull Dexter 1820. This means that, in addition to his full time staff, King usually had three or four apprentices at any one time. In the apprenticeship registers King is variously described as a grocer, tallow chandler and pipe maker and it seems likely that most of these apprentices would have worked for at least some of the time in the pipe shop. Two of them, Bennett and Wilson, later became master pipe makers in their own right (Green 1984; Gault & Alvey 1979). King died on 16 February 1828 and was buried four days later at Harvey Lane Baptist Chapel burial ground, being described in the register as 'Richard, husband of Mary King, aged 53 years, of St. Margaret's parish'.

Neither Richard King nor his widow left a will, but it would appear that none of his children continued with the pipe making side of the business.

Tobacco pipe kiln material.
A.A. Peacey

Three groups of tobacco pipe kiln material have been recovered from this site, a single fragment of stem slag laminate which was excavated in 1980 (8052, F911) and two 19th century assemblages excavated in 1991. The first of these (2358) was sealed in about 1820 beneath a brick cellar floor and has been attributed to the workshop of Richard King (Higgins, above) The second (3501), consists of material from a general cleaning layer. This dates from about 1865 and may derive from the kiln of John and Martha Chennery (Higgins, above). This report deals primarily with the first group which by virtue of both stratigraphy and size assumes most importance.

Material from the kiln structure and furnishings is divided according to composition of fabric. In the catalogue thirteen divisions are listed, ten of these are distinctly different fabrics whilst three cannot be fully assessed due to vitrification, discoloration and slagging. Fabric type numbers, allocated on a first encountered basis, are as follows:

Fabric

1. Red brick earth with well rounded mineral inclusions up to 3mm.
3. White fabric with visible quartz, other mineral inclusions and organic voiding. Opaque quartz chips up to 8mm and occasional stem trimmings.
4. White fabric with visible quartz, other mineral inclusions and organic voiding. The mineral inclusions are fine rounded grains up to 1mm with similarly fine organic voiding.
5. White fabric consisting of compacted pipe trimmings.
6. Finest white fabric, used predominantly for the manufacture of the pipes themselves. Inclusion free to the naked eye.
7. Pinky buff fabric with quartz and other mineral inclusions upto 3mm with occasional pipe trimmings.
8. White fabric with visible quartz, other mineral inclusions and organic voiding. The inclusions, upto 3mm in size, include iron bearing material which bleeds into the surrounding matrix.
9. White clay with added organic matter indicated by voiding. Of relatively low density.
10. Light coloured clay, content obscured by vitrification.
11. Fine red fabric. Inclusion free to the naked eye.
12. Light coloured firebrick fabric with self coloured grog.
13. White clay, vitrified, content obscured by vitrification.
14. White clay with organic inclusions, exact composition obscured by vitrification.

The mineral inclusions may occur in the parent clay. The crushed pipe and organic material are clearly additions.

Pipe kilns are known in two basic forms: muffle kilns and open flame kilns. The former has a sealed inner chamber or muffle to contain the ware whilst in the latter saggars fulfil this function. A muffle kiln depends upon internal load bearing features and furniture to support and separate, whilst in an open flame kiln the saggars satisfy these requirements also. Both kiln groups from this site are from muffle kilns, and the first group includes muffle material, furniture, furniture supplements together with sub-structure and shell fragments.

The muffle material is distinguished by a number of well established criteria common to the majority of muffle assemblages previously examined. These are:-

1. Fabric liberally reinforced with prefired pipe stems.
2. External [convex] surface slagged/glazed/or discoloured by direct contact with fire.
3. Internal [concave] surface covered with layer or layers of clean white clay lute.
4. Step or cornice type peripheral shelving projecting inwards from the internal surface.
5. Prop or bar type buttresses projecting outwards from the external surface.

All of these criteria are present in the first kiln group (2358). Sixty eight muffle fragments are formed from Fabric 3, one muffle fragment is formed from Fabric 4 and a further 16 muffle fragments, being vitrified, have not been allocated to a fabric group.

The muffle represented by this assemblage was of the developed type known from early nineteenth century encyclopaedias (Good et al 1813 ; Rees 1819, 3, 31). The type example from the archaeological record comes from Waverly Street, Bristol (Peacey 1982, 10-13; fig.102 inset). The Causeway Lane muffle was of cylindrical form with external bar type buttresses and internal peripheral shelves of cornice type (fig. 102b). The flue space around the muffle varied between 30 and 60mm. Thirteen fragments from the muffle rim were recovered. The stem reinforcing in the muffle walls is predominantly horizontal with diagonal stems at the buttress interface with the muffle wall. An assemblage of this size cannot be considered fully representative. The absence of step type shelf or side opening fragments must not be overstated since these features almost certainly existed in the complete muffle. One idiosyncrasy in the method of construction is worthy of note. The buttressing, of bar type without any pipe stem reinforcement, is formed from rolls placed one upon another as the building progressed (fig.102a). This suggests either a muffle constructed inside an existing shell or coincidental building of muffle and shell. As other muffle builders dealt with the problem in other ways, the use of rolls seems more likely to stem from a personal idiosyncrasy rather than to have been dictated by conditions imposed by the structure. This idiosyncrasy appears to manifest itself again in a series of unparalleled furniture supplements from this site.

Material which occupied a position outside the muffle is generally contaminated by the fire either by slag build up, flash glazing or discoloration. Material which occupied a position inside the muffle is by contrast clean, slag free, often displaying evidence of lute wash. Such objects or fragments derive from furniture and furniture supplements. The former are prefabricated reusable objects whilst the latter, formed from unfired clay whilst the packing was in progress, were discarded after each firing.

This assemblage includes 4 fragments of furniture from 3 separate objects. One Type P4a (Peacey 1996, 43) hollow waisted cylinder 65mm high and two Type 2a props, hollow cylinders 59mm and 75mm high (fig. 103). Fabric 7 is used solely for this object whilst Fabric 8 is also used for repairs and alterations to the muffle. Amongst these are muffle lining (distinguished by its luted inner surface and unstained contact outer surface), lute wash, and a fragment representing alteration of a shelf height.

Furniture supplements are represented by 203 fragments in 3 Fabrics. These are:-

Rolls – Idiosyncratic irregular serpentine rolls apparently formed by combinations of rolling twisting and squeezing a very wet fabric in a cloth covering (figs. 104a-g).

Roll Type 5 – Short roll with ends spread or flattened to form a strut (figs. 105h-j).

Strap Type 1 – Straight or near straight strap formed from a roll by flattening into a strip or strap (fig. 105k).

Wad Type 1 – Straight or near straight wad with near parallel contact surfaces; formed from a roll by pressing between other objects (fig. 106n).

Wad Type 4 – Shaped as if pressed into a joint between bricks and smoothed over the vertical surface to form a T section (fig. 106p).

Wad Type 5 – Circular wad or fragment from such; with near parallel contact surfaces; formed from a roll looped into a ring (fig. 106o & q-s).

Applied strip Type 1 – Of D section formed from a roll by pressing against another surface; having a single contact surface (fig. 105l).

Applied strip Type 2 – Of triangular section; having a single contact surface (fig. 107u).

Thin sheet Type 1 – A flat thin sheet up to 3mm thick having near parallel surfaces (figs. 107t & v).

The study of furniture supplements is in its infancy. These classifications are based on cross-section and contact deformation, neither of which are necessarily consistent throughout. There is no reason why fragments displaying the characteristics of rolls, wads, applied strips and straps, should not all come from one object. An example of this is shown (fig. 106m) which illustrates a roll with one end deformed into a wad. Although there are examples of furniture supplements found complete (Type 5 wad and Type 5 roll for example), the greater body of evidence, encountered as fragments, reflects less formalised objects.

With the exception of roll Type 5 the supplements from Causeway Lane are all closely parallelled from many other sites (Peacey 1996, Chapter 6). It is usual for them to be made either from clean white clay or white clay with voiding from organic additions. Whilst 31 of the fragments in the Causeway Lane assemblage fall into this pattern, the remaining 272 fragments are in Fabric 4. It may be that this fabric represents the residue of some part of the refining process used to obtain inclusion free clay for pipe making. Sieving or settling would both produce concentrations of such material, either in the sieve or as stratified deposits left in the bottom of settlement tanks after fine clay in suspension had been drawn off. The absence of similar material from other sites may indicate use of a different clay source, alternatively different methods of preparation. The former appears the more likely. Evidence from a number of documentary sources confirms that very little that could be used, was wasted. Material too coarse for the manufacture of tobacco pipes could be used to fabricate the muffle, for structural work or even clamming for the wicket and cracks in the ever moving brickwork of the kiln shell. From Tweedmouth there is a record of material swept from the cobbles being used for this last purpose (Roberts 1988, 94).

The purpose of the roll formed struts (Type 5) is unclear. They clearly occupied positions in the angle formed between objects. The angles vary between 65° and 90°. Although furniture supplements are recorded from another 90 sites, they include no similar objects. The rolls from the Causeway Lane assemblage also differ from the consensus form. They are generally of larger diameter, less well formed by a combination of rolling and squeezing, with a surface texture indicative of sticky wet handling characteristics. Longitudinal undulations in the roll surface suggest formation in cloth. Vestigial patches of texture suggest either palm prints or contact with a twill woven cloth. Although the group is substantial, 146 fragments, there are few stem and no bowl impressions. Of the stem impressions that are apparent 24 are concentric mouthpiece end impressions (fig. 104d & e) whilst only 4 reflect the more usual transverse stem contacts. The only indicators of function are occasional pinches (fig. 104c) or finger wipes (fig. 104f) which may indicate location to some other object, but no firm conclusion can be drawn from them. Approximately one third of the fragments have one existing unbroken end. These ends are carelessly formed, of no particular shape. Six examples have been overlapped and crudely squeezed together. The crude form and surface texture of these rolls probably result from the course nature of the fabric which would demand a greater quantity of moisture for it to remain plastic. The predominance of stem end impressions suggest a position above the charge possibly providing support for some other covering material. As none of the rolls display any significant fire damage it is unlikely that they represent the entire crowning structure.

Evidence from other sites (Peacey forthcoming, Chapter 7), together with contemporary descriptions (Good 1813; Rees 1819, 3, 31), show that in general practice the muffle was supported on pillars above the firebox. This part of the kiln was subject to heavy slagging. The massive structural fragments listed in the catalogue, all heavily slagged, probably come from this part of the structure. Debris falling down the flues around the muffle each time the cover and wicket were broken open would end up in the fire box. Some loosely bound heavily slagged material recovered is consistent with such debris rather than structure.

The assemblage includes a number of brick fragments which might derive from the outer shell or base of the kiln. These include fragments of commercial fire brick. Both Good and Rees record the use of fire brick for kiln linings in the first two decades of the 19th century (ibid).

Small, often overlooked, fragments of fired white clay were retained. Some of these illustrate details of the manufacturing process. Three items in particular have been identified:

'Dottle'- clay built up on the leading end of the piercing wire as it passes through the stem blank to form the bore; sometimes seen still attached inside the pipe bowl on pipes of lesser quality pellets of clay, up to 3mm across, built up in layers, having one concave surface and one convex surface.

'Stem Trimmings' – Extruded fragments of shallow triangular section, up to 4mm across, having a smooth basal surface and rippled upper surfaces formed against the surface of a tool as it was drawn along the stem to remove the seam. Similar fragments have been reproduced in the workshop.

Stem end trimmings – Short blunt rounded stem ends cut with a twisting movement of knife round a wire in place in the stem bore. Helical forms which if flattened would form a thin slice through a pipe stem. These latter probably reflect a second finer cut.

As this type of material represents the interface between pipe and mould its collection and study could cast additional light upon the form and development of these crucial objects. Archaeological data is already massing concerning mould design at the bowl mouth (Peacey 1996, Chapter 6). To date this supports the use of a knife slot design. Unfired clay trimmings, or 'spew' as it was sometimes known (Walker 1977 137), seems to have been used in a number of cases to form crude bricks or other objects for use in the kiln. Fabric 5 from this assemblage falls into this category. Of the 11 fragments recovered only one displays any significant form. One surface is formed as if in a round bottomed dish, all others being breaks. As the material has been fired it clearly passed through the kiln. It may be that it represents spalls and other debris collected in the base of the muffle bound together by lute spillage from the washes applied to the interior of the muffle between firings. Its nature is extremely friable.

The second kiln group (3501), contains one fragment from a category of material not included above. This fragment consists of a layer of pipe stems, laid parallel, sandwiched between a thin clay sheet and a layer of slag (fig. 107w). The clay sheet is formed from white clay with voiding from included organic matter. Similar material hase been recorded from 27 other sites in the British Isles. Clearly this material represents a common process. The slagged surface opposed to a surface free from fire damage indicates a position between the muffle contents and the flue. This position is largely filled by the muffle itself. Slag laminates are, therefore, likely to come from the temporary closures of the openings in the side and top or the muffle. Combined documentary and archaeological evidence suggests that it was common practice to cover the loaded muffle with sheets of clayed paper followed by a framework of prefired pipe stems rendered over with fusible material (Peacey forthcoming Chapter 6).

A Catalogue of the finds is kept in the site archive.

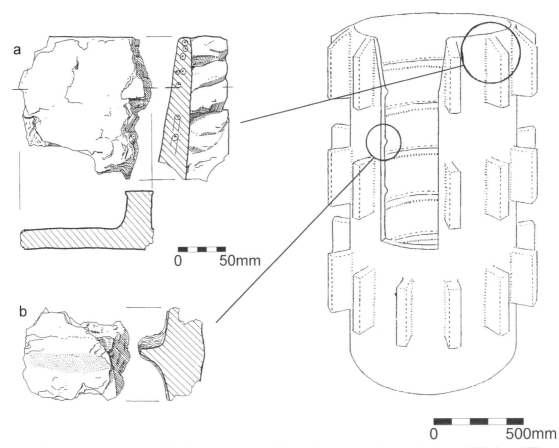

0   50mm

0   500mm

Fig. 102: *Muffle fragments from Kiln Group 1, c. 1820 attributed to the workshop of Richard King*

Fig. 102 *Kiln Group 1, c.1820: Muffle fragments*

a) Rim fragment from the muffle wall with external buttress formed from short rolls. The elevation shows the inner surface. To the right is a vertical section through the stem reinforced wall with side elevation of a buttress. Below is a horizontal section. Scale 1:2

b) Muffle wall fragment with cornice type peripheral shelf. The elevation shows the inner surface. To the right is a vertical section showing lute accumulation on the inner surface and shelf. Scale 1:2

Inset A developed muffle typical of the period based on a contemporary section illustrated by Rees (1819) modified in compliance with archaeological evidence. Scale 1:20

Fig. 103 *Kiln Group 1, c.1820: Props*

a) Type 4a prop liberally coated with white clay lute. Formed from Fabric 8.

b) Type 2a prop with traces of white clay lute. Formed from Fabric 7.

c) Type 2a prop with traces of white clay lute. Formed from fabric 7.

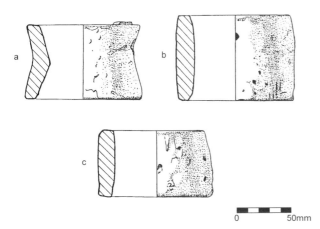

0   50mm

Fig. 103: *(a) Type 4a b) Type 2a c) Type 2a*

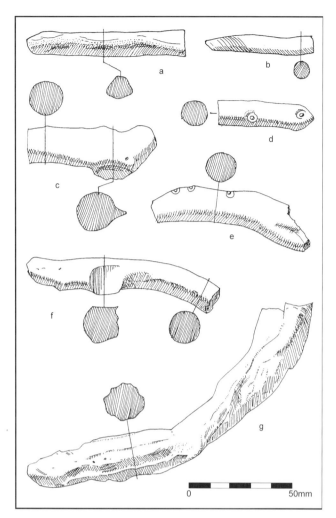

Fig. 104: *Roll fragments*

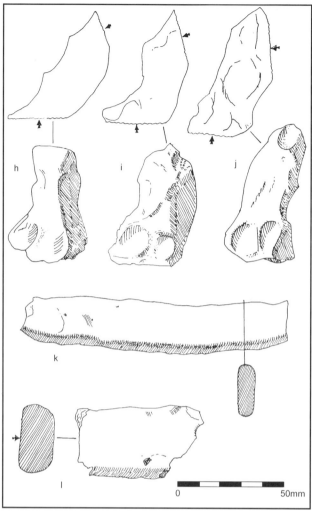

Fig. 105: *Roll, strap and strip fragments*

Fig. 104 *Kiln Group 1, c.1820: Furniture supplements.*

a) Straight roll fragment with one unbroken end.

b) Straight roll fragment with one unbroken end.

c) Roll fragment with one unbroken end and pinch.

d) Straight roll fragment with one unbroken end and two stem end impressions.

e) Curved roll fragment with three stem end impressions.

f) Curved roll fragment with one unbroken end and finger wipe.

g) Curved roll fragment with one unbroken end. The regular ridges and furrows suggest formation in cloth.

Fig. 105 *Kiln Group 1, c.1820: Furniture supplements*

h-j) Type 5 rolls. The angled contact surfaces arrowed, and the finger press marks indicate use as struts.

k) Type 1 strap fragment formed by flattening a roll. The absence of contact impressions indicates that this was done prior to use distinguishing it from an applied strip.

l) Type 1 applied strip fragment with contact surface arrowed.

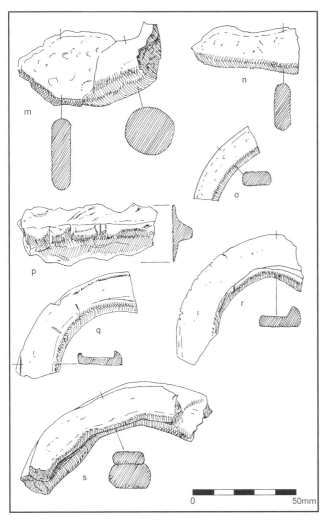

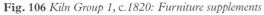

Fig. 106: *Roll and wad fragments*

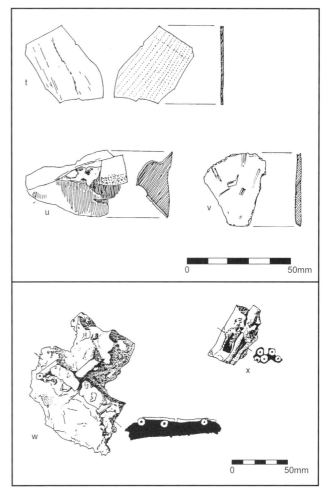

Fig. 107: *Sheet fragments, strip fragments, stem slag laminates*

Fig. 106 *Kiln Group 1, c.1820: Furniture supplements*

m) Roll fragment with one unbroken end deformed by pressure between parallel surfaces to form a wad.

n) Type 1 wad fragment with two opposed parallel contact surfaces.

o) Type 5 wad fragment.

p) Type 4 wad fragment.

q) Type 5 wad fragment.

r) Type 5 wad fragment.

s) Doubled up Type 5 wad fragment.

Fig. 107 *Kiln Group 1,* c.*1820: (t-v): Kiln Group 2,* c.*1865(w); 1980 stray find (x)*

t) Thin sheet fragment with one side scraped, the other with paper contact impression. Formed from Fabric 6.

u) Type 2 applied strip fragment, of triangular section, coated on two surfaces with white clay lute. Formed from Fabric 4.

v) Thin sheet fragment with one side scraped, the other with paper contact impression. Formed from Fabric 9.

w) Thin sheet, stem, slag laminate. The thin sheet is formed from Fabric 9.

v) Stem slag laminate.

Method used for the removal of iron staining from the pipes   *J. Mirdamadi*

The following method used was found to be very effective for the removal of iron staining from the pipes and may be of use in dealing with other groups of iron stained ceramics. The method employed was to soak the fragments in a 0.1M solution of ethylenediaminetetra-acetic acid (EDTA). The disodium salt ($EDTA Na_2$) was used, as the free acid is practically insoluble in water.

The solution was made up in tap water by dissolving 37.2g of the salt in each litre of water. Great accuracy is not necessary. The clay tobacco pipe fragments were put into large deep trays and sufficient solution was added to cover them. It was found that 10 litres of solution was sufficient to submerge 6kg of fragments. The tray was covered to reduce evaporation and left for several days.

Each day the fragments were brushed with a soft tooth brush, and any clean fragments were transferred to clean water. After about one week the solution was very dark in colour, and the remaining fragments with stubborn stains were transferred to a smaller volume of fresh solution. This routine was repeated until the only fragments remaining were those resistant to further cleaning.

Meanwhile the rinsing routine was to place the fragments in running water for about one hour and then to soak each batch in a large volume of water in a bucket, the water being changed each day to remove the EDTA which had been absorbed by the fragments. The final soak on the fifth day was in deionised water.

It was found that most iron stain could be removed by this method, except where there was very heavy encrustation, a rough surface or cracks in the clay. Unfortunately the site code markings, presumably in india ink, were also largely removed since the majority of them had been applied over iron staining. Where the markings had been applied to a clean clay surface they were not affected by the EDTA.

There is no particular hazard from the chemical if used as above, but rubber or disposable gloves should be worn when brushing the fragments and care should be taken not to breathe in the dust when weighing out large quantities of the dry chemical.

THE COINS

THE ROMAN COINS
John A. Davies

A total of 100 Roman coins was found during excavations at Causeway Lane. Of these, 86 are closely identifiable. A feature of this assemblage is that the coins are evenly distributed chronologically and also include the earliest and latest issues used in Roman Britain. A summary of the assemblage is shown in table 43.

Table 43: *Chronological breakdown of the Roman coins*

Issue	Period	Total	%
i	To AD 41	1	1
iia	41-54		
iib	54-68	1	1
iii	69-96	6	7
iv	96-117	5	6
v	117-38	1	1
vi	138-61	4	5
viia	161-80	4	5
viib	180-92		
viii	193-222	6	7
ixa	222-38	3	4
ixb	238-59		
x	259-75	15	17
xi	275-96	11	13
xii	296-317		
xiiia	317-30	2	2
xiiib	330-48	16	19
xiv	348-64	4	5
xva	364-78	4	5
xvb	378-88		
xvi	388-402	3	4
Totals		86	
1st-2nd century		2	
1st-3rd century		1	
3rd-4th century		11	
Total		100	

A substantial proportion, accounting for 36% of these coins, belong to the coinage system established by Augustus, which operated just into the second half of the third century AD. These coins have been summarised in table 44, separated into their denominations. The *denarius*, the only silver denomination, accounts for a surprisingly high proportion of site finds. In addition to the 19 listed there, which represents 61% of the Augustan types, there are also two other illegible *denarius* fragments which are not closely datable. The second most common denomination is the *as*, with six which are restricted to the years 54-117. The larger *sestercii* (each worth four asses) number 5 and all belong to the period 96-180. These replace the asses in the coin list at the end of the first century, perhaps reflecting inflation, taking over as the most common bronze denomination. The *denarii* span the years in question but almost half belong to the 1st four decades of the third century.

The earliest coin from the site is a legionary *denarius* of Marc Antony, struck in 32-31BC and brought into Britain during the early post-Invasion years. Among the *denarii* are two base examples (catalogue numbers 24, 28) and there is an additional illegible *denarius* core, listed among the undated

finds (number 92). Other than the *denarii*, there is only one other silver coin from the site, which is a fragmentary *antoninianus* of the years 215-60 (cat.No. 95). The remainder of the site finds are all aes denominations which are commonly found on Romano-British sites.

Among the more common coin types are a substantial number of irregular issues. Most of these are irregular *antoniniani*, or barbarous radiates, which were struck between 270-84 and represent most of the coinage in circulation between 275 and 287. There are only three irregular mid-Constantinian folles of the early 340's but irregular 'falling horseman' issues account for all of the coinage of the period 348-64.

Table 44: *Coins of the Augustan system by denomination*

Issue	Period	DENARIUS	SESTERTIUS	DUPONDIUS	AS
i	To AD 41	1			
iia	41-54				
iib	54-68				1
iii	69-96	2			4
iv	96-117	1	2	1	1
v	117-38	1			
vi	138-61	2	2		
viia	161-80	3	1		
viib	180-92				
viii	193-222	6			
ixa	222-38	3			
Totals		19	5	1	6

The strong presence of early coins is a characteristic of major Romano-British towns. The peak recorded for the Flavian period (69-96) was similarly recorded at the Leicester Jewry Wall site, as well as at other towns. Another feature typical of towns is the strong late third century coin loss (259-96) which is similar in percentage terms to that of the later fourth century coinage (330-402). The major episodes of coin loss are recorded in fig. 108, in terms of four phases, alongside the values from other Leicester sites. The Causeway Lane group is seen to closely resemble the Jewry Wall and Forum groups in this respect. Figure 108 also serves to show the steady evenly spread coin loss at this site. It should be noted that loss from phase C (296-330) is low on all Romano-British sites.

The mints of origin of the fourth century coins have been summarised in table 45. A restricted range of mints is indicated, with coinage from only Lyons, Trier and Arles represented. These were the major sources of coin for Britain during the fourth century, after the closure of the London mint.

The latest Roman coins recovered from Causeway Lane are Theodosian bronzes.

Table 45: *Allocation of legible 4th century coins to mints*

Issue	Period	Lyons	Trier	Arles	Irregular
xiiia	317-30		1		
xiiib	330-48		9	1	3
xiv	348-64				4
xva	364-78	1		2	
xvb	378-88				
xvi	388-402		1		

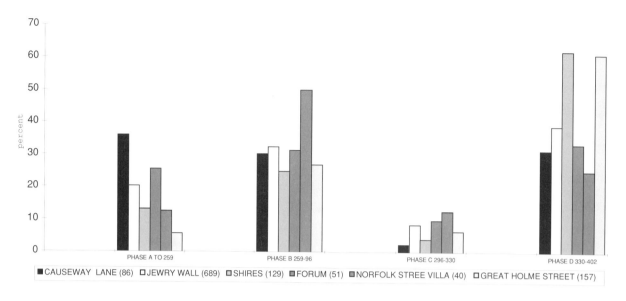

Fig. 108: *Relative percentages of Roman coins from Leicester sites*

Table 46: *Catalogue of identifiable Roman coins*

Phase	Small find	Subgroup	Emperor/type	Denom.	Mint	Rel.	Date
Phase 2							
2K	sf2205	203/1	Nero	*As*	Lyons	RIC I (rev): 543	*c.* AD 66
2K	sf2343	144/1	Vespasian	*As*	-		AD 69-79
2K	sf2002	201/2	Vespasian	*As*	-		AD 69-79
Phase 3							
3B	sf2170	157/5	Trajan	*Sestertius*	-		AD 98-117
3B	sf2187	154/1	Trajan	As	-		AD 98-117
3B	sf2101	154/3	Illegible	*Denarius*	-		1st C.-AD 235
3D	sf2047	186/1	Vespasian	*Denarius*	Rome	RIC II: 15	AD 69-79
3D	sf2100	187/1	Septimius Severus	Base *denarius*	-		AD 193-211
Phase 4							
4A	sf2143	174/2	Antoninus Pius	*Sestertius*	Rome		AD 140-144
Phase 5							
5A	sf2105	160/5	Trajan	*Sestertius*	-		AD 98-117
5B	sf2180	162/1	Domitian	*As*	-		AD 81-96
5C	sf5004	166/4	Vespasian	*Denarius*	-		AD 69-79
5C	sf5003	166/4	Antoninus Pius	*Denarius*	Rome	RIC III: 64	AD 140-143
5C	sf2013	163/7	Claudius II	*Antoninianus*	-		AD 268-270
5E	sf5046	360/1	Caracalla	Base *denarius*	-		AD 206-217
5F	sf2400	339/9	Lucius Verus	*Denarius*	Rome	RIC III: 491	AD 162-163
5F	sf2363	339/9	Caracalla	*Denarius*	Rome	RIC IV: 546	AD 201
5F	sf2382	339/7	Septimius Severus	*Denarius*	-		AD 202-210
5G	sf2302	334/2	House of Theodosius	*AE4*	-		AD 388-395
5H	sf2385	338/2	Maximinus I	*Denarius*	Rome	RIC IV: 12	AD 235-236
5H	sf2330	350/1	Constantius II	Irregular	as Lyons	as RIC VIII: 189	AD 354-364
Phase 6							
6A	sf2342	338/3	Marc Antony	*Denarius*	Rome	Crawford: 544	32-31 BC
6A	sf2334	336/1	Antoninus Pius	*Sestertius*	-		AD 138-161
6A	sf2332	341/1	Antoninus Pius	Base *denarius*	-		AD 138-161
6A	sf2344	348/1	Severus Alexander	*Denarius*	Rome	RIC IV: 200	AD 228-231
6B	sf2306	340/1	Gallienus	*Antoninianus*	Rome		AD 260-268
6B	sf2305	340/1	Gallienus	*Antoninianus*	Rome		AD 260-268
6B	sf2307	340/1	Tetricus I	*Antoninianus*	Cologne	Elmer: 770	AD 270-274
6B	sf2294	340/1	Barbarous Radiate				AD 270-284
6B	sf2293	340/1	Barbarous Radiate				AD 270-284
6B	sf2295	340/1	Carausius	*Antoninianus*	-	as RIC V: 983	AD 287-293
6B	sf2298	340/1	Helena	*Follis*	Trier	RIC VIII: 78	AD 337-340
6B	sf2339	363/1	Valens	*AE3*	Arles	RIC IX: 19a	AD 375-378
6B	sf2236	338/3	Illegible	*Denarius*	-		1st C.-AD 235

Phase	Small find	Subgroup	Emperor/type	Denom.	Mint	Rel.	Date
Phase 8							
	sf2154	253/1	Domitian	*As*	Rome	RIC II: 335	AD 86
	sf2161	253/3	Lucius Verus	*Denarius*	Rome	RIC III: 578	AD 167-168
	sf2138	254/9	Gallienus	*Antoninianus*	Rome	as RIC V: 208	AD 260-268
	sf2029	247/1	Claudius II	*Antoninianus*	Rome	as RIC V: 109	AD 268-270
	sf2224	254/9	Tetricus I	*Antoninianus*	Trier	Elmer: 786/7	AD 270-274
	sf2128	255/1	Tetricus II	*Antoninianus*	Cologne	Elmer: 769/770	AD 270-274
	sf2127	255/1	Tetricus I	*Antoninianus*	Trier	Elmer: 789	AD 270-274
	sf2228	254/9	Tetricus II	*Antoninianus*	Trier	Elmer: 791	AD 270-274
	sf2132	254/4	Tetricus II	*Antoninianus*	-		AD 270-274
	sf2090	253/9	Barbarous Radiate				AD 270-284
	sf2093	247/1	Barbarous Radiate				AD 275-284
	sf2140	254/9	Illegible	*Antoninianus*	-		AD 260-296
	sf2153	253/1	Illegible	*Antoninianus*	-		AD 260-296
	sf2070	253/3	Constantine I	*Follis*	Trier	RIC VII: 554	AD 333-334
	sf2023	252/5	Constantine I	*Follis*	Trier	RIC VII: 561	AD 333-334
	sf2133	252/5	House of Constantine	*Follis*	Trier	RIC VII: 586	AD 335-340
	sf5012	254/1	Constantius II	*Follis*	Trier	RIC VIII: 50	AD 337-340
	sf2167	253/6	Constantine I	*Follis*	Arles	RIC VII: 375	AD 333-334
	sf2094	249/1	House of Constantine	Irreg. *Follis*	-		AD 341-346
Phase 9							
	sf5013	261/7	Trajan	*Denarius*	Rome	RIC II: 165	AD 103-104
	sf2174	119/3	Marcus Aurelius	*Denarius*	-		AD 161-180
	sf2060	257/3	Tetricus I	*Antoninianus*	-		AD 270-274
	sf2375	119/3	Barbarous Radiate				AD 270-284
	sf2173	119/3	Carausius	*Antoninianus*	-		AD 297-293
	sf2011	260/1	Illegible	*Antoninianus*	-		AD 260-296
	sf2012	118/2	Constantine I/II	*Follis*	-		AD 324-325
	sf2055	290/1	Constantine I	Irreg. *Follis*	-as Lyons	as RIC VII: 241	AD 341-346
	sf2237	315/1	House of Constantine	Irregular	-		AD 354-364
	sf2416	307/1	House of Constantine	Irregular	-		AD 354-364
	sf2279	307/1	Arcadius	*AE4*	Trier	RIC IX: 107b	AD 392-395
Phase 12							
	sf2068	102/1	Trajan	*Dupondius*	Rome	RIC II: 502	AD 103-111
	sf2009	100/1	Hadrian	*Denarius*	Rome	RIC II: 11	AD 117
	sf2032	104/1	Marcus Aurelius	*Sestertius*	Rome		AD 161-180
	sf2272	301/1	Caracalla	*Denarius*	-		AD 196-217
	sf2044	291/2	Septimius Severus	*Denarius*	-		AD 193-211
	sf2255	302/2	Severus Alexander	*Denarius*	Rome	RIC IV: 45	AD 225
	sf2204	291/2	Gallienus	*Antoninianus*	-		AD 260-268
	sf2065	296/1	Gallienus	*Antoninianus*	-		AD 260-268
	sf2288	302/1	Barbarous Radiate				AD 270-284
	sf2239	301/1	Barbarous Radiate				AD 270-284
	sf2019	296/1	Barbarous Radiate				AD 275-284
	sf2232	302/1	Illegible	*Antoninianus*			AD 260-296
	sf2244	290/2	Constantine II	*Follis*	Trier	RIC VII: 520	AD 330-331
	sf2234	302/1	Constantius II	*Follis*	Trier	RIC VIII: 102	AD 340
	sf2236	301/1	Constans	*Follis*	Trier	RIC VIII: 186	AD 347-348
	sf2240	301/1	House of Constantine	*Follis*	-		AD 335-340
	sf2235	301/1	House of Constantine	*Follis*	-		AD 335-340
	sf2243	301/1	House of Constantine	Irregular	-		AD 354-364
	sf2233	301/1	Gratian	*AE3*	Lyons	RIC IX: 20c	AD 367-375
	sf2285	301/1	Valentinian I	*AE3*	-		AD 364-375
	sf2084	296/1	House of Theodosius	*AE4*	-		AD 388-395
Unphased							
	sf9063	-	Tetricus I	*Antoninianus*	Cologne		AD 270-274
	sf2303	-	Barbarous Radiate				AD 270-284
	sf2313	US	Illegible	*Antoninianus*			AD 260-296
	sf9053	-	Crispus	*Follis*	Trier	as RIC VII: 308	AD 321
	sf9067	-	Helena	*Follis*	Trier	RIC VIII: 47	AD 337-340
	sf9009	-	House of Constantine	*Follis*	-		AD 335-340
	sf9005	-	Constantine I	Irreg. *Follis*	-		AD 341-346
	sf2229	US	Gratian	*AE3*	Arles	RIC IX: 15	AD 367-375

Hoard of siliquae

On July 3rd 1906 a Roman coin hoard, contained in an urn, was discovered in Causeway Lane at a depth of eleven feet during sewering operations. There were 'about 60' coins of which 'the bulk' was purchased (by Mr. Noel Spurway) after having been distributed amongst the finders *(Transactions Leicestershire Archaeol. and Hist. Soc* **10**, 59). The hoard was purchased by Leicester Museum in 1962 as part of the Spurway Collection. Whether the urn was purchased by Spurway is uncertain, and its present whereabouts remains unknown. The coins occupied three drawers of Spurway's coin cabinet, each of which was headed by him 'Roman. Found

corner of Friars Causeway and Bond St. 11 feet deep July 3rd 1906 in Jar'. This locates the find spot to the corner of Causeway Lane and East Bond Street.

The earliest coin in the hoard is a siliqua of Constans from the Trier mint, of 347-8 AD. The latest are issues of Theodosius and Magnus Maximus, of 383-88. With regard to the mints represented, coins of Trier dominate, with those from Arles and Lyons the next most prolific.

The latest emperors are well represented and the hoard finishes strongly. I would suggest a deposition date of mid to late 380's to have been most likely.

Table 47: *Emperors and mints of coins from the hoard*

	TRIER	LYONS	ARLES	ROME	AQUILEIA	ANTIOCH	OTHER	TOTAL
Constans	1							1
Julian Augustus	1	6	10			1		18
Constantius II		3	1					4
Jovian						1		1
Valentinian I	3			1			2	6
Valens	4		1				2	7
Gratian	6				2		1	9
Valentinian II					1			1
Theodosius	2						2	4
Magnus Maximus	9							9
	26	9	12	1	3	2	7	60

THE MEDIEVAL COINS   *R.A. Rutland*

Both coins are silver pennies, one cut in half for use as a halfpenny, of the short cross issue (1180-1247).

1. SF 5009 F568 247/2 Phase 8

Silver penny.

Obverse: HENRICVSR[EX] Facing bust holding sceptre.

Reverse: R REINALDONCA (indistinct). Short cross.

Condition: worn, with some holes.

Reinald minted at Canterbury for classes 2 - 4a. All of these classes fall within the reign of Richard I (1189-1199) and are differentiated mainly by details of the bust. This coin cannot be assigned to a specific class because of its worn condition.

2. SF 5023 F703 308/1 Phase 9

Silver penny cut along vertical line of reverse cross. Because obverse and reverse dies are not always exactly aligned, the obverse is cut diagonally from one to seven o'clock.

Obverse: HENR[ICVSR]EX

Reverse: R • T • ON • NOR (O and R ligatured). Also half of initial cross.

The reverse legend indicates Roberd T of Northampton (to distinguish from another Roberd). He minted only class 5b (1205-1210), i.e. reign of John.

THE SMALL FINDS

Nicholas J. Cooper

with contributions by *Donald Mackreth and Peter Liddle*
Illustrations by David Hopkins   Conservation by *A.R.Read and K. Hall*

Introduction

This report considers objects of copper alloy, iron, lead, bone and stone from the excavations as well as those of glass and fired clay not included in the reports on vessels. The assemblage from Causeway Lane, comprising 2268 finds records (in excess of 6000 objects including bulk accessioning of iron nails), represents the largest excavated so far from the Roman and medieval levels of Leicester, and alongside the similarly-sized groups from St. Peter's Lane and Little Lane (The Shires development, Cooper forthcoming a), the assemblage makes a significant contribution to the corpus of finds types from the town. For this reason, the traditional object-oriented report layout in catalogue form has been considered justified to illustrate the range of material present. The catalogue comprises a selection of 226 objects categorised by function and considered to represent the best preserved examples of recognized types, worthy of detailed study for their contribution to the functional interpretation of the site, or their intrinsic or stratigraphic value.

The division of objects into functional categories is considered to be particularly appropriate for large assemblages of small finds, and has been used to good effect by Crummy (1983) in her treatment of the Roman small finds from excavations in Colchester. The category names and order devised by Crummy have been followed, and despite the lack of objects belonging to certain categories the numbers have also been retained (with the exception of Category 17) to avoid confusion when consulting comparable reports.

Category

1: Objects of Personal Adornment or Dress
2: Toilet, Surgical or Pharmaceutical Instruments
3: Objects Used in the Manufacture or Working of Textiles
4: Household Utensils and Furniture
5: Objects Used for Recreational Purposes
8: Objects Associated with Transport
10: Tools
11: Fasteners and Fittings
13: Military Equipment
14: Objects Associated with Religious Beliefs and Practices
16: Objects and Waste Material Associated with Bone and Antler Working
17: Objects and Waste Material Associated with Flint Knapping.
18: Objects of unknown function

Materials relating to two further functional categories defined by Crummy (1983) are discussed in separate reports, namely Objects and Waste Material Associated with Metal Working, and Buildings and Services.

Alongside the catalogue, it is considered that the assemblage size might support a more synthetic discussion that could usefully incorporate information on small finds assemblages excavated elsewhere in the town. Few published reports have so far attempted to go beyond the traditional catalogue to analyse small find function data numerically. Such analysis might help contribute to an understanding of the activities that produced the assemblage and consequently to the overall interpretation of the site and its economic and social context. The catalogue is therefore preceded by a consideration of the Causeway Lane assemblage and three others from the town

integrating a discussion of the problems and potential of interpreting small finds assemblages generally.

It is considered that the numerical analysis of functional categories could provide profiles of assemblages for particular site types in the same way as Richard Reece has developed the concept of the 'British background' for coins and deviations from the 'typical' (which might not be immediately apparent from a catalogue) could therefore be highlighted. This method of analysis has been used to good effect by Wilmott in assessing the assemblages from sites along the Middle Walbrook Valley in Roman London (Wilmott 1991), while Clarke (1994) has undertaken quantitative analysis of a range of finds categories from the Roman fort at Newstead. Most recently Cool, Lloyd-Morgan, and Hooley (1995, 1626) have used correspondence analysis to demonstrate similarities and differences between assemblages from the Roman legionary fortresses at York and Caerleon, in an attempt to determine the functions of the buildings to which they relate.

In the Walbrook report, comparison of bankside and stream bed assemblages (Wilmott 1991, 170, figs. 116 and 117), successfully demonstrated the marked similarity between the groups while highlighting and explaining the anomalies in terms of specific industrial activity and dispelling the supposed importance of votive offerings in this part of the valley. The Walbrook analyses highlighted a consistent pattern of urban rubbish disposal which (allowing for the changes in retrieval methods in modern excavation), might be usefully compared with any other Roman urban (or rural?) assemblage in the country or indeed those of medieval date.

The analysis of small finds from Causeway Lane and other Leicester sites

The numerical breakdown of the identifiable portion of the small finds assemblage by functional category is illustrated in fig. 109. Iron fasteners and fittings, which were predominantly nails, have been excluded from the analysis due first to the distorting effect of their large numbers and second to the need to highlight variations in the portable material culture rather than the structural element of which they formed a part. Their exclusion also helps to even out discrepencies when looking at other assemblages where such items did not occur, or were not retrieved, in such profusion. In terms of categorised finds, there is a marked bias of the assemblage towards the Roman period (89%). This can be contrasted with the assemblage from the Shires development as a whole which is more evenly split (figs. 113-114), but which is itself internally divided between a predominantly Roman (Little Lane) and a predominantly medieval assemblage (St. Peter's Lane).

Stratigraphic profile

The stratigraphic distribution of the small finds assemblage as a whole (fig. 110) opens up some useful areas of discussion relating to the scale of activity in the town over time, which are to an extent confirmed by looking at the distribution of a single datable artefact type such as the Roman bone hair pin (fig. 111).

Within the Roman period, Period 3 dated 120-200 represents the time of greatest small find deposition yielding 27% of the assemblage, and it is no coincidence that this corresponds to a period of accelerating activity in the town

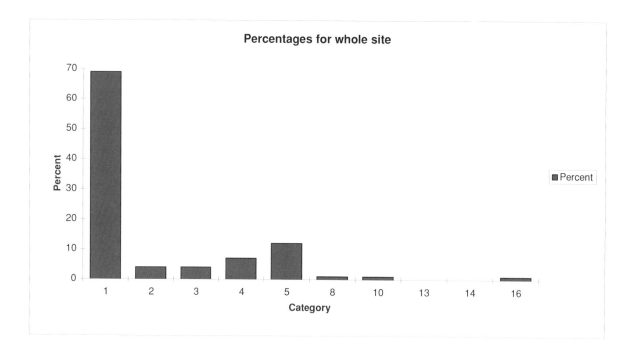

Category	1	2	3	4	5	8	10	13	14	16	
Total	248	15	14	26	43	4	5	1	1	5	362

Category	1	2	3	4	5	8	10	13	14	16	
Percent	69	4	4	7	12	1	1	0	0	1	100

Fig 109: *Numerical breakdown by functional category*

generally. Increased activity will generate more rubbish (and accidental loss) and indeed more rubbish may be imported to provide make-up levels for structures and so the high figure is to be expected. By AD 200 then, 41% of the phased assemblage has been deposited with only a further 22% being deposited in the succeeding 200 years to the end of the Roman period. This would tend to promote the idea of a decline in activity in the area as a whole during the later Roman period.

The low figure for the later Roman period may be due to poor preservation of such levels due to later disturbance, but unless these levels are physically removed (the effect of quarrying is not relevant to the later Roman levels), then the finds contained therein should simply move up and be redeposited in medieval layers, as demonstrated by the occurrence of large numbers of finds in Period 9 (involving the robbing of Roman stone buildings). The analysis of bone hair pin types would tend to indicate that a later Roman decline in activity is genuine. The assemblage contains a much higher proportion of early types (Crummy's Types 1 and 2) dated up to 200, than later types (Types 3-6) dated to the third and fourth century. The deposition pattern follows that for the finds assemblage as a whole with 22 (43%) of the 51 phased early pins having been deposited by AD 200 and 72 % of all phased pins having been deposited by the end of the Roman period (early types outnumbering late types by 36:9). In post Roman levels early types still outnumber late types by 15:7.

Study of the pottery from the site tends to support this contention on all areas of the site except Area 3, which is peculiar in having a substantial late third-fourth century assemblage. It would appear that it is part of a deliberate policy of (?imported) rubbish disposal during levelling up and is associated with other 'hardcore' materials such as wallplaster rather that normal domestic rubbish that might incorporate small finds.

The prevalence of early pin types (particularly Type 2) is mirrored in other assemblages from the town, particularly Great Holme St (Boothroyd, forthcoming), and to a lesser extent the Shires, and this is in marked contrast to the assemblage from Colchester (Crummy 1983) which shows such a marked prevalence of the later Type 3. It may therefore be possible to use this artefact type as an index of residential/social activity across the town to detect areas of decline, and as many result from accidental loss they may act as a relatively reliable guide to where people are spending their time.

Functional profile

Due to the low number of identifiable medieval finds the figures given are those for combined Roman and medieval. The analysis does not contain figures for buildings and services, fasteners and fittings, waste material associated with metal working or prehistoric flint, or objects of unknown function.

The creation of a functional profile for sites based on finds data is fraught with danger, but unless attempts are made on many assemblages then the potential for detecting patterning

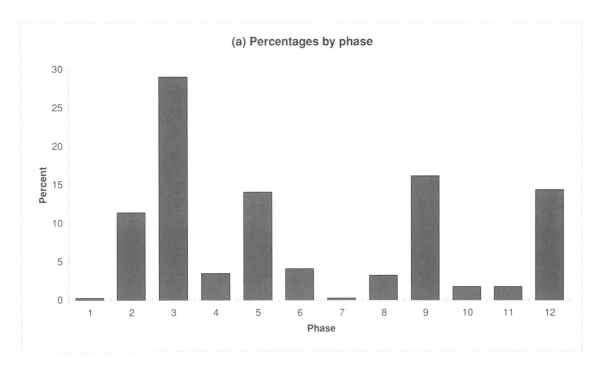

Fig 110: *Numerical breakdown by phase and functional category*

(a) Percentages by phase

(b) Category totals for whole site by phase

Category	1	2	3	4	5	8	10	13	14	16	Period Totals
Phase 1	0	0	0	0	0	0	1	0	0	0	1
Phase 2	28	1	0	5	3	1	1	0	0	0	39
Phase 3	66	7	2	10	10	1	2	1	0	0	99
Phase 4	8	0	0	1	1	1	0	0	1	0	12
Phase 5	32	3	2	2	5	0	0	0	0	4	48
Phase 6	9	0	0	1	3	0	1	0	0	0	14
Phase 7	1	0	0	0	0	0	0	0	0	0	1
Phase 8	8	0	2	0	1	0	0	0	0	0	11
Phase 9	33	2	4	5	10	1	0	0	0	0	55
Phase 10	3	0	1	1	1	0	0	0	0	0	6
Phase 11	6	0	0	0	0	0	0	0	0	0	6
Phase 12	40	1	2	1	5	0	0	0	0	0	49
Total	234	14	13	26	39	4	5	1	1	4	341

will never be assessed. In relation to the stratigraphic profile above, there are clearly problems in relating the assemblage to the site itself, and thus doubts concerning the level of inference that can be drawn from the analysis, especially if material is imported from outside the immediate vicinity for make-up levels. Even if the level of disturbance is small, doubts might be cast on whether the owners of the objects actually lived in the area occupied by the site. Accidental loss probably accounts for many of the losses of personal items such as brooches and hairpins, and while some may have fallen between the floorboards of local residences and reflect the predilections of those living in the immediate vicinity, others may have dropped as people passed through the site along the road to somewhere else!

Overall, and in common with most asssemblages, objects of Category One (personal adornment and dress) are by far the most common items of portable material culture present. However it is important to bear in mind those factors which might exaggerate their contribution. The most significant of these is that nearly all such items probably entered the

archaeological record as accidental losses, a factor exacerbated by their small size, and dictating that many escaped recycling or transference to the next generation. The high number of complete or near-complete objects of personal adornment certainly supports the prevalence of accidental loss rather than deliberate disposal, although its significance in the Walbrook assemblages has been questioned by Wilmott (1991, 172), who points to the ready availability of replacement items in Early Roman London as reason enough to throw away damaged items rather than repairing them. While this idea might have some validity in profligate Early Roman London, most items surely had some modest scrap value that was worth recouping, and so accidental loss must be considered an overriding factor in penny-pinching areas of the province at least. A secondary factor promoting Category One figures is that such finds are perhaps intrinsically more identifiable due, not only to their often higher degree of completeness, but to the ability to identify them from small fragments due to typological complexity.

At the intra-site level, although arbitrary in size the four

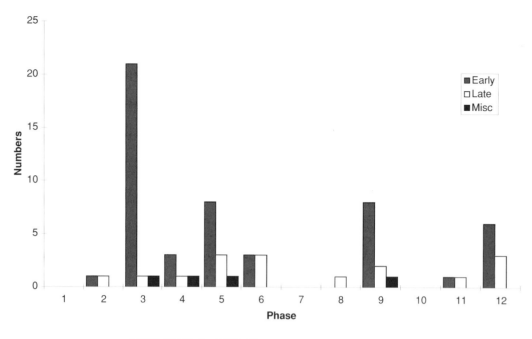

		Numbers of Finds		
		Early	Late	Misc
Phase	1	0	0	0
Phase	2	1	1	0
Phase	3	21	1	1
Phase	4	3	1	1
Phase	5	8	3	1
Phase	6	3	3	0
Phase	7	0	0	0
Phase	8	0	1	0
Phase	9	8	2	1
Phase	10	0	0	0
Phase	11	1	1	0
Phase	12	6	3	0
Total		51	16	4

Fig. 111: *Category 1 pins, numbers of finds*

areas of the site do form archaeologically useful divisions as they fill three of the four quadrants created by the Roman crossroads (with Area 4 away to the west), and the pattern of activity from the stratigraphic evidence does appear to be different in each. However, to what extent is this apparent difference reflected in the small finds? Fig. 112 shows profiles for the four internal areas of the site which show a remarkable similarity given the variation in sample size. The contribution of the largest category (personal adornment and dress) varies from 64-69% if the Area 4 figure (87%) is ignored due to small sample size, and this is in line with the level of similarity remarked upon at the Middle Walbrook sites (Wilmott 1991). All areas might then be said to be producing a fairly consistent pattern of rubbish disposal and/or accidental loss which is not greatly affected by changing activity. This may indicate either that the bulk of the material was derived from outside the area, or that the predominant finds generating activity in the area as a whole (largely residential) remained the same.

Area 1 (north west of the road junction) yielded 57% of located finds which is broadly in line with its greater size, and the range of finds types represented is correspondingly wider. In all areas though, the vast majority of finds fall into the first five categories (95% overall), which may be indicative of a

largely residential rubbish component. The notable exception to this is the occurrence of bone working evidence, confined to Area 3, north east of the crossroads. Even allowing for the lack of quantified data for metalworking evidence which is in any case small, the range is distinctly narrower than that of the Walbrook groups, with a complete lack of finds relating to written communication and market activities and very low numbers relating to military and religious activities for example. Although figures for iron knife blade fragments are not included (if included the tool contribution rises to 14%), the small number that could be classified probably derive from domestic contexts; no specialist workshop tools have otherwise been identified and activity of this type would appear to have been negligible in this area. This is clearly not a factor of sample size, and the group might therefore be said to have a smaller industrial element and a generally more provincial feel than its London counterparts. By contrast, the contribution relating to personal adornment and dress is remarkably higher at 68% than the Walbrook groups which vary between 20% and 30%. The narrower range of finds may partly explain this on top of the greater proportion of industrial objects in the latter groups.

How similar is the Causeway Lane group to others from

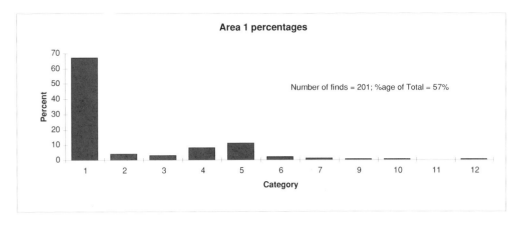

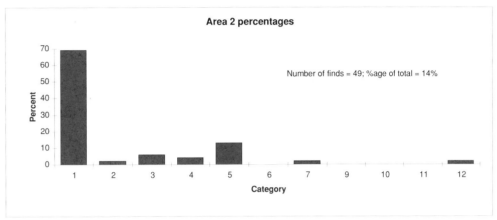

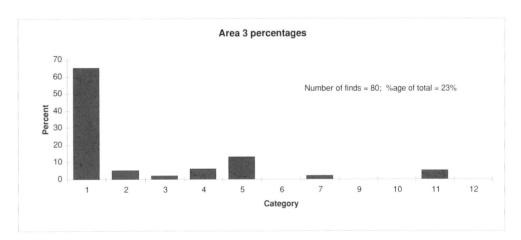

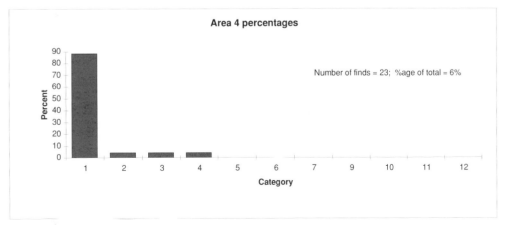

Fig. 112: *Functional analysis by Area*

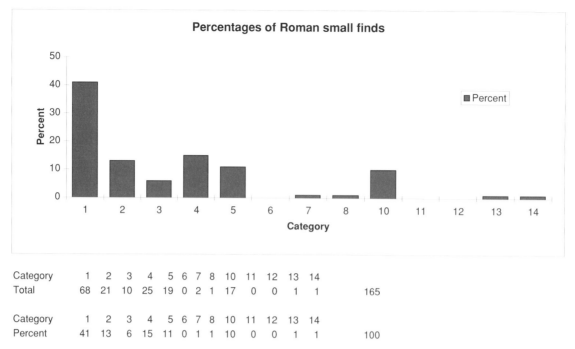

Category	1	2	3	4	5	6	7	8	10	11	12	13	14	
Total	68	21	10	25	19	0	2	1	17	0	0	1	1	165

Category	1	2	3	4	5	6	7	8	10	11	12	13	14	
Percent	41	13	6	15	11	0	1	1	10	0	0	1	1	100

Fig 113: *Roman small finds from The Shires*

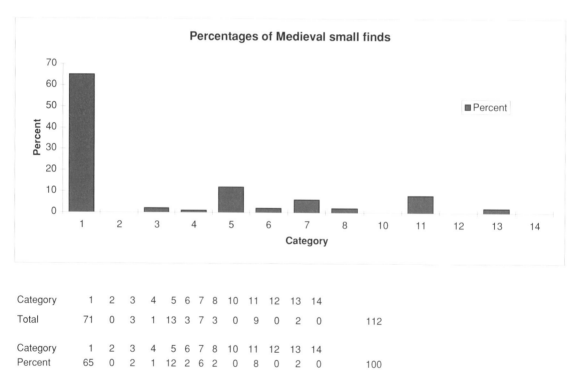

Category	1	2	3	4	5	6	7	8	10	11	12	13	14	
Total	71	0	3	1	13	3	7	3	0	9	0	2	0	112

Category	1	2	3	4	5	6	7	8	10	11	12	13	14	
Percent	65	0	2	1	12	2	6	2	0	8	0	2	0	100

Fig 114: *Medieval small finds from The Shires*

Leicester? Functional profiles have been drawn up for three other assemblages; the Shires (Little Lane and St. Peter's Lane, Cooper forthcoming a) and Blue Boar Lane (Lentowicz forthcoming) within the walls, and the extramural site of Great Holme St. (Boothroyd forthcoming), lying close to the south-western exit from the town in the direction of the Norfolk St. villa (Lucas 1980).

The Shires is the largest of the three, with 274 Roman and medieval finds identifiable to category (figs.113-114 and table 48). However, only 165 are of Roman date, making it the third largest after Causeway Lane and Great Holme St. The bulk of both the Roman and medieval material falls into the first five categories (85% for Roman only, 86% for combined). The Category 1 figure is 41% (51% overall) somewhat lower than for Causeway Lane, but when toilet implements are also considered the figures even out. One notable difference is the presence of objects relating to written communication such as seal boxes for the Roman period and pens and parchment prickers for the medieval period, totally absent from Causeway Lane.

Table 48: *Functional analysis of Roman and medieval small finds from The Shires (A39.1988lA40.1988)*

Category	Roman	%	Medieval	%	All	%
1 person	68	41	71	65	139	51
2 toilet	21	13	–	–	21	8
3 text.	10	6	3	2	13	5
4 house	25	15	1	1	26	9
5 recre	19	11	13	12	32	12
6 weigh	–	–	3	2	3	1
7 writcom	2	1	7	6	9	3
8 transp.	1	1	3	2	4	1
10 tools	17	10	-	-	17	6
11 fastfit	–	—	9	8	9	3
12 agric.	–	–	–	–	–	–
13 military	1	1	2	2	3	1
14 relig.	1	1	–	–	1	<1
Total	165	100	109	100	274	100

The assemblage from Blue Boar Lane (table 49 and fig. 115) comprises only 87 categorised finds and the Category 1 figure falls to 34% which would appear to be due to the very low number of bone pins.

Table 49: *Functional analysis of Roman small finds from Blue Boar Lane, Leicester 1958.*

Category	No.items	%
1 person	30	34
2 toilet	4	5
3 text.	6	7
4 house	14	16
5 recre	7	8
6 weigh	-	-
7 writcom	-	-
8 transp.	-	-
10 tools	3	3
11 fastfit	23	27
12 agric.	-	-
13 military	-	-
14 relig.	-	-
Total	87	100

The profile for the extramural site of Great Holme St., the second largest Roman assemblage from the town (table 50 and fig. 116), appears remarkably similar to that from Causeway Lane and it is in some ways more diverse with the presence of military lead seals and a group of pipeclay figurines. Boothroyd is right to recognise that much of it probably comprises rubbish from within the walls, but it also has a distinct agricultural processing element not present in intra-mural assemblages and which might relate to the nearby villa at Norfolk St. (woolcombs are included in Category 12 rather than Category 3).

Table 50: *Functional analysis of Roman small finds from Great Holme St. (A77.1975lA78.1977)*

Category	No.items	%
1 person	152	57
2 toilet	15	6
3 text.	22	8
4 house	10	4
5 recre	35	13
6 weigh	-	-
7 writcom	–	-
8 transp.	-	-
10 tools	4	1
11 fastfit	16	6
12 agric.	3	1
13 military	6	2
14 relig.	6	2
Total	269	100

Access and wealth profile

Calculating the ratios of 'high-value'(eg metal, jet/shale) to 'low-value' (eg bone) examples within an object category such as hairpins might help to create a profile of relative wealth or access amongst a population, since their proportions should broadly reflect the life assemblage and access to replacements. However, a number of biasing factors come into play. Accidental loss will be directly influenced by the care taken in curating an object as well as how muddy the roads were and the high proportion of objects in 'lower status' materials such as bone will reflect not only a genuine predominance in the life assemblage, but also the lack of effort put into searching for examples accidentally dropped into a muddy roadside ditch, in the same way as the proportion of low denomination coinage is exaggerated. In addition, the recycling of metal examples not passed on to the next generation might also

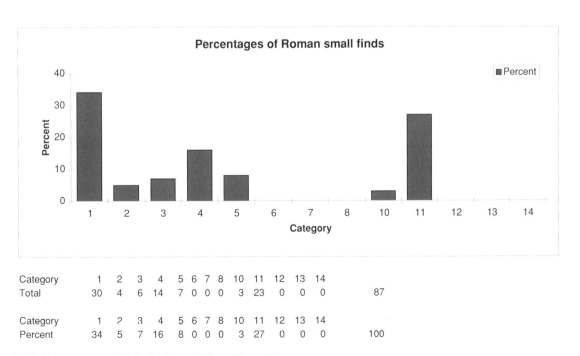

Category	1	2	3	4	5	6	7	8	10	11	12	13	14	
Total	30	4	6	14	7	0	0	0	3	23	0	0	0	87

Category	1	2	3	4	5	6	7	8	10	11	12	13	14	
Percent	34	5	7	16	8	0	0	0	3	27	0	0	0	100

Fig. 115: *Roman small finds from Blue Boar Lane*

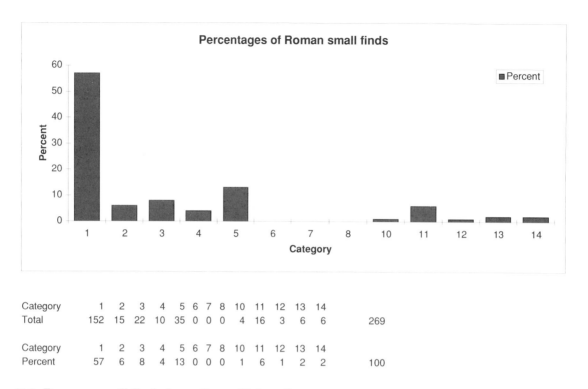

Category	1	2	3	4	5	6	7	8	10	11	12	13	14	
Total	152	15	22	10	35	0	0	0	4	16	3	6	6	269

Category	1	2	3	4	5	6	7	8	10	11	12	13	14	
Percent	57	6	8	4	13	0	0	0	1	6	1	2	2	100

Fig. 116: *Roman small finds from Great Holme Street*

enhance this anomaly, but such factors are likely to play a part in any assemblage.

Can the profiles of the other Leicester sites contribute anything to an assessment of relative wealth and access across the town or across the Province? Comparing ratios of copper alloy to bone pins (table 51) illustrates wide variation but from Causeway Lane and Great Holme St. a typical ratio appears to be about 1:10, although at Colchester (Crummy 1983) the combination of jet and copper alloy brings this down to nearly 1:5 which may suggest greater access to exotic materials. The equal ratio at Blue Boar Lane is unexplained unless bone examples were unrecognised during excavation, and may be due to sample size. The consideration of data from a greater range of sites would help to establish more coherent patterns.

Table 51: *Numbers of Roman pins in different materials.*

	Cu Alloy	Bone	Jet	Total
Causeway Lane	10	105	–	115
Shires	–	37	–	37
Blue Boar Lane 1958	3	3	–	6
Great Holme St	10	101	–	111
Colchester 1971-79	49	342	15	406

Conclusion

The small finds assemblage from Causeway Lane is predominantly Roman in character and amongst the Roman finds that are closely datable, the vast majority belong to the first and second century, with Period 3 appearing to represent the most active phase of deposition. This corresponds to the most intense period of construction of both public and private buildings across the town and also the time when the population were most eager to adopt newly available fashion accessories. The brooch assemblage indicates that this fashion consciousness extends further back into the immediately pre-Conquest period and this is of particularly significant given the site's location away from the supposed core of the late Iron Age settlement in the St. Nicholas area. The high proportion

of finds belonging to Categories 1 and 2 especially, suggests a predominantly residential population, an idea supported by a lack of finds relating to written communication, market and workshop activities.

Notwithstanding the biasing factors discussed above, there is scope for intra and inter site comparison in the future, particularly in Roman Leicester during the first two centuries AD when deposits are relatively undisturbed and activity appears intense. Analyses would also lead to the identification of town-wide trends in rubbish disposal that can be internally refined as more assemblages are studied and externally compared as analysis extends in other urban areas.

THE CATALOGUE

Editorial Notes

i) Each catalogue entry description is preceded by the stratigraphic information relating to it, and comprises the small find number, the context number, the feature number, the phase, and the feature type. This order is also followed by the archive small finds catalogue.

ii) Due to the editing out of a small number of less important objects during the later stages of writing the report there are occasional gaps in the numbering sequence.

Category 1: Objects of personal adornment or dress *(figs. 117-126)*

***Brooches of Iron Age and Roman Date** (figs. 117-120)*
Donald Mackreth

One feature of the present collection calls for comment: the high proportion of brooches with integral four-coil-internal-chord springs. Not counting fragments into the total number of brooches from the site, just over 28% belong to this group. Elsewhere in Leicester, and in the first instance only counting those from excavations carried out since Miss Kenyon's at Jewry Wall, the percentage is 7.4, while there are 4.8% from that site and in the museum collections as they were in 1969.

The division between pre and post Jewry Wall is made because of the possibility that, as brooches belonging to this group tend to be unattractive, there would have been a greater tendency to discount them when building up collections, either private or in the museum. The total number of brooches from Leicester recorded by the writer, apart from those in this report, is 233 and, in brooch terms, that rates as a large and therefore representative group for such a site.

What the bare statistics of just over 28% may mean is difficult to tell. The writer discussed a similar phenomenon when dealing with brooches at Chichester (Mackreth 1989b, 182-184 fig.26.3). The conclusion there was that an overall figure of about 40% could well represent the predilection of the brooch wearing public in immediately pre-Roman times, and the other sites chosen for comparison, Winchester and Canterbury, could be said to belong to the same broad cultural province when it comes to brooches. There is a shift in the preferred type in the twenty to thirty years after the conquest the further one moves away from this area. The shift is different depending on which direction is taken, but there is a shift.

However, in Leicestershire and the lands to the north and east, there is no major pre-Roman brooch type to provide a guide. The whole of the Fosse 'frontier' outside the south-west tends to be peripheral, brooch wearing only becoming common once the area is taken within the developing Province. The other sites excavated since the Jewry Wall site provide a more acceptable percentage both in comparison with the possibly skewed figures from the museum and with other sites especially within the East Midlands. Therefore, when a site produces an imbalance directly comparable with Winchester and Canterbury (ibid., fig.26.3), there should be a reason. Unfortunately, the elucidation of that does not lie easily with the brooches themselves: the easiest course is to suggest an immigrant population from the deep south-east. But there must be other evidence before this is seriously considered, and that can surely only be in the other material recovered from the site.

Colchester

1) Sf2273 (1398) 175/4 Ph.3C. The hook is moderately long and has its end formed into a thin circular disc bearing stamped annulus in relief. Each wing is moulded, the better preserved one has a flute and a convex moulding seperated by a thin ridge. The upper bow has a thick almost square section with chamfered corners. The lower bow is very thin in the front view. The catch-plate may have been pierced.

The behaviour of the lower part of the bow when viewed from the front shows that this is not a typical Colchester. The profile lacks the continuous arch typical of British Colchesters, but the decorated wings and hook are known elsewhere. The only considerable body of brooches representing Late La Tène times in Britain comes from the King Harry Lane Cemetery at St.Albans (Stead and Rigby 1989) and the distribution of similar profiles (P), wings (W) and hooks (H) in the phases there is: Phase 1, G202 3W2H★, G206 W★, G312 W★, G410 W★, G397 WP?, G410 2W, G424 W★; Phase 2, G53 W, G231 WH, G259 W, G361 W, G420 WHP?, G433 W; Phase 3, G205 W, G230 WH. The evidence is clear: Phase 1 has most graves, eight, with these features, Phase 2 comes next with five while Phase 3 only has two. Those marked ★ have fat octagonal sections directly comparable with that of the present example, but none has a directly similar profile and those with P? are straighter than the usual British style without necessarily merely reflecting the Continental original. The Leicester brooch is unlikely to be a late specimen, but its proper *floruit* depends on the dating of the King Harry Lane Cemetery.

The published dating of the phases is not entirely secure. While the earliest likely date for the cemetery is admitted to be 15 BC (ibid., 83), the authors preferred a more conservative scheme: Phase 1, AD1-40; Phase 2, 30-55; Phase 3, 40-60; Phase 4, 60+ (ibid., 84). Over half the burials should therefore be statistically later than the Roman conquest. However, the samian report (ibid., 113) comments that it is surprising that there should be only six vessels: three earlier than 25, none dating to 25-50, two dating 45-65 and one being much later. Looking at the published dating, it is equally surprising that there should only be one Colchester Derivative (G136,4) and no fully formed Hod Hill, both types well represented in Verulamium scarcely 500 metres away. If the dating is, however, taken back to 15 BC most of the problem is removed and the following ranges can be suggested without doing undue damage to the evidence: Phase 1, 15 BC–AD30; Phase 2 20-40; Phase 3 35-50/55; Phase 4, 45+. Most of the burials would then become pre-conquest.

The end date of 50/55 for phase 3 was arrived at by using general evidence for the dating of Colchesters and is relevant here as it would be subject to the same rules of residuality which governs all material not melted down or otherwise removed from a normal site assemblage. In the case of such a specialised collection like that from King Harry Lane, the writer would be happier with a terminal date for Phase 3 of 40/45. This should mean an adjustment in the phases before then, but no suggestions are made here. The Leicester brooch may not have survived in use as late as 40/45.

Colchester derivatives

2) Sf2119 (818) F337 158/5 Ph.5A. An axis bar through the coils of the spring is held in the lower of two holes in a plate projecting behind the head of the bow, the chord passes through the upper. Each wing is plain and curved to seat the spring. The plate is carried over the head to form a skeuomorph of the Colchester's hook. The bow has a concave face on each side of the centre which bears a line of rocker-arm ornament. The catch-plate has a pin-groove.

This is the immediate successor of the Colchester in the lands of the Catuvellauni and Trinovantes. The pin-groove is typical and the brooch is too small for any decorative piercings in the catch-plate. A recent review of the dating evidence for this type (Mackreth in Jackson and Potter, forthcoming a) has shown that the floruit for it and its varieties is from c.40-75/80.

3) Sf2003 (2977) 201/2 Ph.2K. The spring is held in the Polden Hill manner: an axis bar through the coils is mounted in pierced plates at the ends of the wings and the chord is held by a rearward-facing hook behind the head of the bow. Each wing is very thin and had its end bent back to form the pierced plate. On the front are three sunken bead-rows. The bow has a very thin section and tapers to a pointed foot. There is a marked step at the top, and a short, plain, sunken ridge down the upper part of the bow. The catch-plate has a large piercing.

A good example of a distinctive type at home in the lower Severn Valley, although the distribution has an extension up to Derby (Mackreth 1985b, 281-3, fig.123,2). It is, however, poorly dated and a review of the general development of which it is part has recently been carried out (Mackreth forthcoming b) and the conclusion was that this variety should be earlier than 60/70.

4) Sf2357 (1589) 143/1 Ph.2D. The spring is mounted like that in the last brooch. Each wing has a pair of ridges joined by a broad flute at its end. The bow has a cross-cut ridge down the middle and a short sunken ridge running away on each side from the top. One of these ridges has a trace of punched dots along its side. The catch-plate return has a single sunken cross-ridge at the top, bottom and middle.

This brooch, unfortunately, does not belong to a well

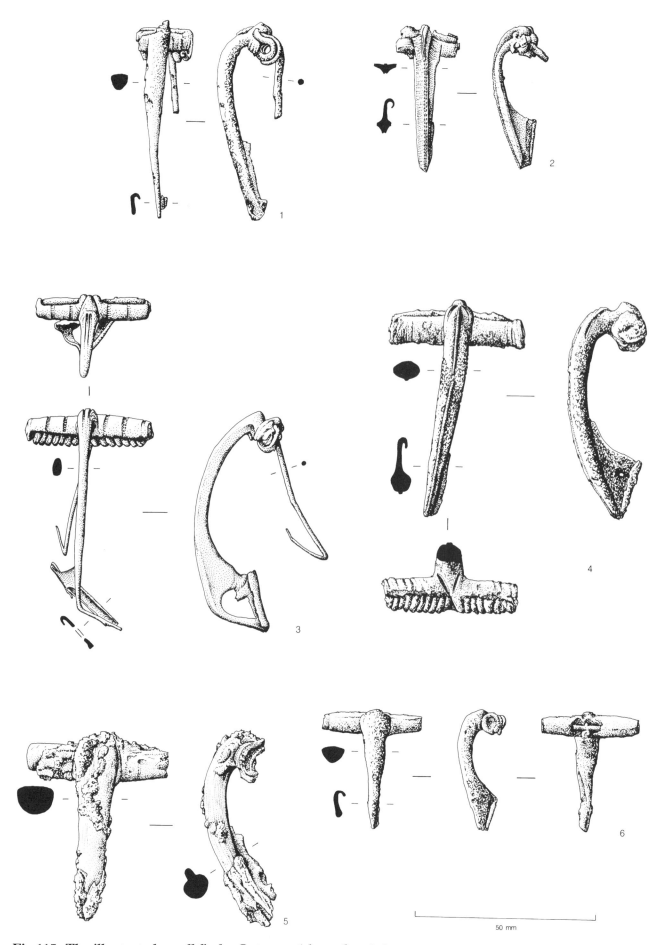

Fig 117: *The illustrated small finds: Category 1 brooches 1-6*

known group. The mouldings at the ends of the wings are, perhaps, more typical of the first century than of the second and this is supported by the decoration on the head and on the return of the catch-plate.

The next three Colchester Derivatives have or had hinged pins.

5) Sf2201 (1072) F417 151/1 Ph.3B. The notch in the top at the back shows that the pin had been hinged. Its axis bar had probably been mounted in a tube placed in the mould before casting. Although there are considerable corrosion accretions, the wings and bow had obviously been plain.

6) Sf2120 US. The axis bar for the pin was inserted into a slot in the back of the wings which were then closed round it. The brooch is completely plain.

Utterly plain brooches are difficult to date. The technique indicated for holding the axis bar of a hinged pin on brooch 5 is first-century and not the last quarter at that. As for brooch 6, it may not be earlier than 75, but wil not be later than *c*.150.

7) Sf2118 (832) F343 141/1 Ph.3A. The axis bar for the pin was inserted into the wings like that of the last brooch. Each wing has a flat front face with a groove at the end. The bow has a flat front face with a series of narrow projections on each side, nine on the left and eight on the right. There is a groove on each margin and, between at the top, is a rectangular recess with a hole in its middle, probably to secure a seperately-made dog, although these are usually slotted into the recess from the top, the overhanging sides of the slot keeping it in place. Beneath the recess is a line of reserved lozenges between two rows of triangular recesses for enamel, now missing. At the foot of the bow is a forward-facing oval boss with a flute between two ridges on its face.

The enamelled bow and the projections on each side, coupled with the forward-facing foot, mark the group to which this brooch belongs. The ornament on the head can be replaced by a cast-on crest or stud. The dating is: Wall, Staffs., with Neronian rubbish (Gould 1967, 15, fig.7,2); Kinvaston, with Neronian samian (Webster 1957, 102, fig.2,8); The Lunt, Baginton, four examples from pit 86, before 75 (Hobley 1973, 66, fig.19,1,4,6 and not illustrated); Crundale, Kent, before *c*.75 (Hume 1863, 64 and fig); Harlow, before 80 (France and Gobel 1985, 79, fig.41,69); Newstead, after 80 (Curle 1911, 323, pl.86,23); Carlisle, late first-105-115 (Mackreth 1990, 107, fig.100,3); Verulamium, 105-115 (Frere 1972, 116, fig.30,12), 105-130 (*ibid.*, 116, fig.29,11); Marshfield, Avon, fourth century (Mackreth 1985a, 142-143, fig.45,20); Derby, late fourth century (Mackreth 1985b, 287-289, fig.126,21). These dates show two things: most date to before 75, there is a clutch dating to the late first and early second century, and the two which are fourth century must have been residual in their contexts. The impression is that manufacture ended before 75, but some examples continued in use into the second century, although the two from Verulamium may have been residual from Boudican destruction.

8) Sf2099 (667) F318 153/1 Ph.3B. The head is lost, all that survives is the flat-fronted lower bow which has a groove down each side and what appears to be a foot-knob with three cross-mouldings. The catch-plate has a large irregular piercing.

Without the head, all that can be suggested is that the open catch-plate is better suited to the first century than the second.

Trumpets

Of these, the first has a hinged pin, the others, save for 13, having a bilateral spring mounted on a loop behind the head

of the bow. Brooch 13 has its spring mounted between a pair of pierced lugs. None of the knops runs all the way round the bow.

9) Sf2053 (200) 100/1 Ph.12. The axis bar of the hinged pin is housed in a half-cylindrical projection across the base of the trumpet head. On the top of this are the remains of a cast-on loop on a pedestal. The head itself is plain apart from a groove around its upper edge. The petalled knop is separated from the rest of the brooch by a pair of cross-mouldings above and below. The lower bow has a groove down each side, an arris down the middle and ends in a crudely petalled foot-knob.

10) Sf2323 (1510) 145/1 Ph.2F. The trumpet head is flattened across the top and is plain apart from a bordering groove. The knop consists of three widely splayed cross-mouldings with triple cross-mouldings above and below. The lower bow is almost completely lost and nothing can be seen on the stump.

11) Sf2164 (893) 162/5 Ph.5B. The trumpet head has been reduced to an oval disc from which issues a straight-side upper bow with a marked central arris. The knop consists of a prominent moulding, with a slight step above and below, which has a trace of a sunken diagonal ridge probably one of a series forming a chevron. There is a single cross-moulding above and below the knop. The lower bow is missing. Not illustrated.

12) Sf2095 (736) 104/1 Ph.12. The upper bow rises from a disc and still retains some trumpet expansion. The knop is like that of the last, only crudely beaded in the middle. The mouldings above and below dip in the centre towards the knop. What is left of the lower bow has a step down each side and a median ridge.

13) Sf2148 (1060) 154/1 Ph.3B. There is a cast-on loop and pedestal, the latter having a groove across its top. The oval head-plate is elongated and the upper bow, with only a very slight trumpet splay, rises from a stepped platform. There is a cross-moulding half-way down the upper bow. The knop is petalled and is separated from the rest of the brooch by a single cross-moulding above and below. The lower bow is lost.

Of these, only brooch 9 is close to a standard Trumpet, the hinged pin should show that the brooch had been made in the southern Pennines where there was a tendency to replace springs with hinges. As for 10, there is a hint that the tendency for the head to be extended on each side, and for the knop to have plain mouldings, is at home in the East Midlands and up the eastern side of the Pennines into Yorkshire. 11 and 12 are southern brooches, the distinctive mouldings above and below the knop of 12 are typical, the simple knops and thin heads unite the two and both should come from the south-west and the southern marches. As for brooch 13, the mouldings half way down the elongated head are the hallmark of the group to which this example belongs. Its distribution is the same as that for brooches 11 and 12. The dating of all Trumpets has recently been reviewed (Mackreth forthcoming c) and, while the full range is from before 75 to mainly 150/175, none of the present pieces is likely to be earlier than the latest first century.

Late La Tène

14) Sf2080 (687) F317 163/1 Ph.5B. The hinged pin is mounted between two pierced lugs behind the top of the disc and fantail plate. A hole in the middle of the disc was presumably for a decorative stud, and there is a poorly formed flute slightly off-centre on the foot. There is no sign of anything having been applied to the front of the disc.

A Rosette sadly devolved from the brooch typical of Augustan-Tiberian times. One like this occurs in a Phase 3 burial of the King Harry Lane Cemetery (Stead and Rigby

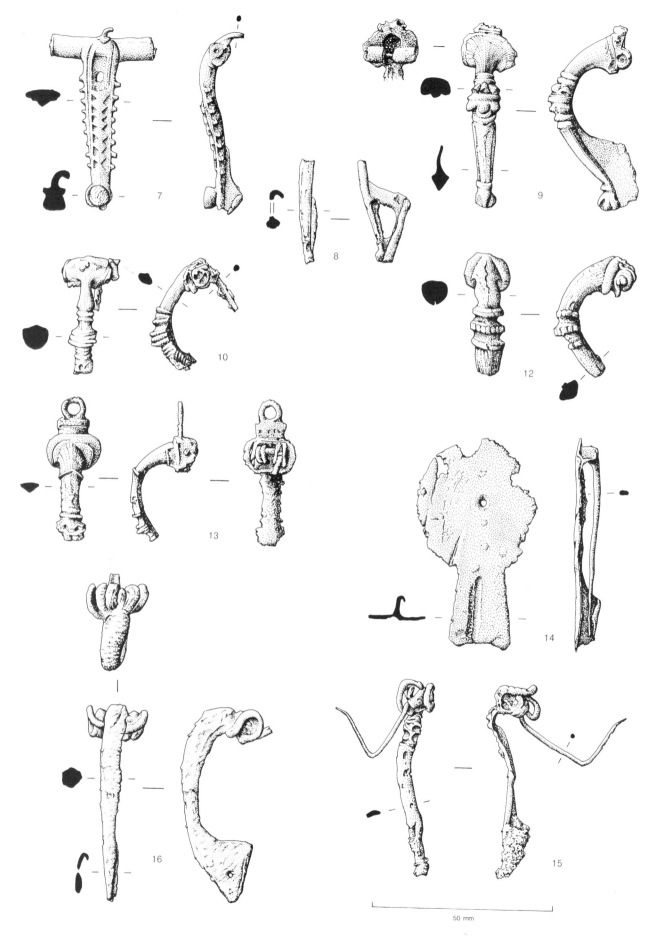

Fig. 118: *The illustrated small finds: Category 1 brooches 7-10, 12-16*

1989, G203), and there is only one of the earlier stage with a spring-case, from a Phase 2 grave (*ibid.*, G67). For comments on the dating of the cemetery, see after Brooch 1. The rest of the British dating for those like Brooch 14 is: Hod Hill, before 50, two examples (Brailsford 1962, 8, fig.7.C27,C28: Richmond 1968, 117-119); Kelvedon, mid-late first century (Rodwell 1988, 57, fig.44,23); Silchester, mid-late first century (Cotton 1947, 144, fig.7,6). Manufacture possibly began 30/40, but the small numbers suggest that it was a final effort and hardly any probably remained in use as late as 60/70.

The remaining brooches in this category all have or had four-coil internal chord springs integral with the bow, except for Brooch 24 which has six coils.

15) Sf2116 (766) F343 141/3 Ph.3B. The bow is broad and has only a slight taper to what had been a squared-off foot. The profile has a marked arch at the top with a recurve to an almost straight lower bow. The shape of the catch-plate, as far as that can be guaranteed in its corroded state, suggests that the profile is that intended by its maker. At the top of the bow is a series of cross-mouldings whose complete form is obscured by deep corrosion pits. However, at the top and in the middle appear to be paired diagonal elements.

The exaggerated profile is reminiscent of the Rosettes and some Langton Downs, and is shown on the brooch depicted on the coins of Criciru (Allen 1972), but the absence of either an open-framed, simply divided (eg Feugère 1985, pl.65,908) or highly fretted catch-plate shows that the brooch should not be as early as the mid-first century BC. The relationship of the profile to the bulk of the Augustan-Tiberian Rosettes and Langton Downs with a recurve is almost certainly a better guide. The combination of the spring system with the profile is distinctly uncommon and there are very few British examples to offer help. An iron brooch from Kingsholm (Mackreth forthcoming c) has an almost identical profile, the same style of broad bow and a concentration of ornament on the head. On this site, it should be no earlier than about 50/55. If the profile is ignored, a brooch from near Northampton may be related, although the style of the upper bow recalls a particular group of East Anglian Aesica brooches (Hattatt 1987, 29, fig.11,748). A brooch from St.Nicholas Circle, Leicester (Mackreth 1994, 141 fig.73,10) came from a context dated to the early-mid first century AD. The bow has a pointed foot and its profile is slack in comparison with the present piece, nevertheless, the concentration of the decoration in a panel on the flat upper bow may be a link. On balance, had the profile of the present piece been like the last, a similar date might be proposed, but its very individuality suggests that it is better related to the date of the same general style on the Rosette: the very end of the first century BC and the first two or three decades of the present era.

16) Sf1461 (714) F335 187/1 Ph.3D Iron. The rectangular section runs from front to back. The profile is simple and there is no sign of there having been any decoration.

17) Sf2147 (1059) F405 147/1 Ph.2E. A repeat of the last, half the spring is missing.

18) Sf1526 (2342) F572 203/1 Ph.2K Iron. The spring appears to have been repaired by winding a wire pin round a bar inserted into the original spring thus giving the appearance of having six coils. The bow has a square section and appears to be plain.

19) Sf9037 (8021) F911 119/10 Ph.9. The bow has a thin circular section hardly wider than the spring.

20) Sf6112 (2972) F686 201/2 Ph.2K Iron. Only the very top of the bow and this has a thin rectangular section.

None of these is distinguished by any feature which helps provide a date within the overall possible range. The sections of the bows are various and only that of Brooch 19 is sufficiently rod-like for it to be likely that its ancestor was the *Drahtfibel*: the others have a tendency towards rectangular sections, none is broad and flat enough to be called a Nauheim Derivative. The catch-plates are uniformly solid, where they survive, and the profiles generally slack: first century AD but possibly not the last decade.

21) Sf2263 (1218) 148/2 Ph.2E. The spring is missing. The section of the bow is oval and the bow tapers to a pointed foot. The profile has a recurve in it.

22) Sf2136 (888) F373 129/1 Ph.9. An almost exact repeat of the last brooch, the foot is damaged and the spring is missing.

The difference between these and the previous group is that the section of the bow is more consistently the same and both have the same recurve in the profile, but not so marked as that in Brooch 15. Dating is not useful as there are too few with dates and the style is not consistent enough for useful boundaries to be defined. These two brooches should fall into the same date-range as the previous group.

23) Sf2086 (630) 164/1 Ph.5C. Only the beginning of the spring is present. The bow has a thin circular section and the profile reveals an almost right-angled bend with the distinct trace of a recurve at the bottom.

The unusual profile, with what is practically a right-angle, is rare in this country: the only other one in several hundred plain brooches with this spring system recorded by the writer comes from Baldock where it was dated 120-150 (Stead and Rigby 1986, 109, fig.41,40). They are commoner in parts of the continent, Böhme recognising their *Drahtfibel* origin and groups them all together as the 'so-called Soldiers' Brooch' and subdivides them into two basic types. The first has a short arc between the two straight parts of the bow and the second a definite right-angle (Böhme 1972, 13-14, Tafln.3-4, 49-308). The presen piece is clearly a member of her *Variant A*, amongst which she has chosen to group a few which, on the criteria adopted here, would have been grouped with either Brooches 16-20 or 21-22 (*ibid.*, Taf.3, 91, 116, 126, 131-142; Taf.155, 161, 189,224) and there are two which should have been given to other groups (*ibid.*, Taf.4, 256, 292). Nevertheless, there is a basic unity. While the type is known in Germany before Domitianic times, Böhme runs it on into Hadrianic times (*ibid.*,14) which may suit the German Limes, but runs counter to all the dating in this country for four-spring-internal-chord brooches, none of which, saving pure accidents of survival, should have been worn after 100. A view of the dating available at Augst for the same type, Riha's 1.6.1, shows that none need date before 70/75 (Riha 1979, 60, Taf. 3,92-106) and where there is a very high residual factor, this is worthy of note. Their rarity in Britain is matched by their virtual absence from the mouth of the Rhine (Haalebos 1986, fig.43,113). The question arises concerning the date which should be given to the present example. As it falls outside any British type, and is rare here, it should perhaps be given the range indicated by Böhme, in which case the specimen from Baldock is partly just within its correct *floruit*.

24) Sf2337 (1552) 144/1 Ph.2D. The spring has six coils instead of the more usual four. The bow has a square section and a simple profile.

Brooches with internal chords and integral springs having more than four coils are uncommon. Those with dates recorded by the writer are: Werrington Cambs., 50/60-100 (Mackreth 1988, 91 fig.20,2); Derby, *c*.55-80/85 (Mackreth 1985b, 294, fig.128,34); Fishbourne, before *c*.75 (Cunliffe 1971, 100, fig.37,15); Old Winteringham, before *c*.75 (Stead and Rigby 1986, 198, fig.100,21); Weekley, Northants., mid-late first century (Jackson and Dix 1987, M78, fig.24,21);

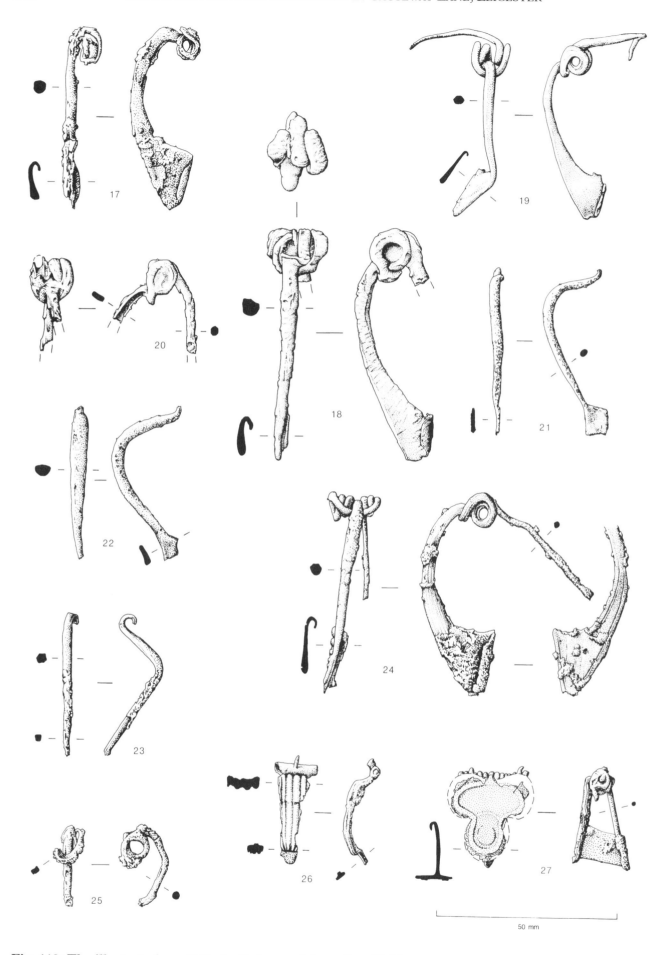

Fig. 119: *The illustrated small finds: Category 1 brooches 17-27*

Chichester. late first – mid/late second century (Mackreth 1989b, 256-257, fig.10.1,12). More than half of those recorded are dated and, apart from one, come from sites published since 1981 which suggests that many more have been found in excavations, but have either gone unrecognised or have been passed over. The dating is probably before the last decades of the first century, but more evidence is needed.

25) Sf2404 (3943) F756 359/4 Ph.5G. Part of the pin with half the spring from a four-coil-internal chord system.

Without the bow, only the overall likely date-range can be proposed: first century AD but possibly not the last decade.

Hod Hill

26) Sf2165 (893) 162/5 Ph.5B. The axis bar of the hinged pin was housed in the rolled-over head of the bow. Only the upper bow survives. There is a ridge on each border separated from three central mouldings by a flute. The middle of the three ridges is beaded.

No Hod Hill has been published from a convincingly pre-conquest context: one from Baldock dated to the first quarter of the first century AD must be wrongly assigned (Stead and Rigby 1986, 120, fig.47,112) as it would then predate its parent. Another from Skeleton Green was not securely sealed under the flood which means that, while it *could* have been earlier than the conquest, this cannot be guaranteed (Mackreth 1981, 141-142, fig.72,53). This was the only Hod Hill from that excavation and is a sign of how soon after the conquest the whole sequence must close down: hardly later than 45. The general date-range for the whole of the main Hod Hill family to which this example belongs is given by its distribution in Britain. Few come from sites north-west of the Fosse Way, and the bulk of those that do have occupation dating to before 60. As the type is largely absent from the northern lands taken into the province in the earliest 70's, it was passing out of use between 60 and 70 and by the latter date most had entered the ground. There is no need to seek dating on the continent as it is the British evidence *par excellence* which dates the whole, except for the very few patterns which carry on to give rise to enamelled versions in the late first century and the early second.

Unclassified

27) Sf2008 (200) 100/1 Ph.12. The long bilateral spring is mounted in a single pierced lug between two of the three conjoined lobes making up the plate. There are traces of solder for some form of appliqué decoration on the front, probably in the form of repoussé metal. The catch-plate is excessively long in comparison with those found on Roman brooches.

The length of both the spring and the catch-plate show that this brooch was made in Free Germany and, indeed, this brooch is a member of Almgren's *Typ* 227. Springs mounted on single lugs are a feature of British Plate brooches, but none has either an original spring or a catch-plate to match those here.

The distribution of the Type 227 is described by Almgren as mainly in the Elbe region of North Germany, stretching from Schleswig Holstein, through Hannover, Mecklenburg, and Saxony to Bohemia, with only a few examples further east. The dating is uncertain, with Almgren ascribing the general form to *der jungeren romischen Periode* (the Early Roman Period) (Adrian Olivier pers. comm.).

Plate

28) Sf2391 (3786) F760 354/1 Ph.5H. The original lugs for a hinged pin have been largely removed to allow a pierced plate for a bilateral spring, now missing, to be riveted through the circular plate. There had been eight projecting circular lugs,

each with a recess for enamel, now a dirty green, but one was lost when the new pin was fitted. The main plate has an annular recess around the border still carrying traces of two enamels, now an opalescent turquoise alternating with a dirty green. The rest of the plate around a reserved area from which rises a stud is recessed for enamel and has in it eight reserved annuli each filled with a turquoise enamel, the field having extensive traces of a dirty green. The stud is riveted through the plate and has an annular recess, again filled with a dirty green enamel, around a spot of glassy mid-blue frit.

The brooch itself is continental and is basically second century in date. The replacement of the original pin, if Roman, was done in Britain, possibly as late as the early third century. However, there is the possibility that the spring had been long and the repair carried out in post-Roman times.

Penannulars

29) Sf2169 (1025) 154/1 Ph.3B. The ring has a circular section. Each terminal consists of a flat boss with knurling around its edge. The pin has a marked hump.

The design of the terminal of brooch 29 is a standard one whose dating is: Exeter, late first century (Mackreth 1991, 240, fig.103,35); Chichester, late first-early second century, or second century (Down and Rule 1971, 81, fig.5.14,302e); Prestatyn, *c.*90-135/40 (Mackreth 1989a, 98, fig.40,24); Newstead, 80-*c.*200, two examples (Curle 1911, pl.88,12,16: Hartley 1972, 54); Leicester, *c.*130-225 (Clay and Mellor 1985, 69, fig.38,7); Mumrills, *c.*140-163 (MacDonald and Curle 1929, 555, fig.115,7); Cappuck, *c.*140-200 (Stevenson and Miller 1912, fig.11,2: Hartley 1972, 41); Derby, mid-second century?(Brassington 1980, 18, fig.8,c); Carlisle, 150s-180s (Mackreth 1990, 113, MF.2.21, fig.103,26) late second-early third century (*ibid.*, 113, MF.2.21, fig.103,24); Leicester, early third century (Kenyon 1948, 252, fig.82,3); Old Winteringham, third or fourth century (Stead 1976, 198, fig.100,120); Carlisle, late third-mid-late fourth century (Mackreth 1990, 113, MF.2.21, fig.103,25), late third-early fourth century (*ibid.*, 113, MF.2.21, fig.103,23); Old Winteringham, after 320 (Stead 1976, 201, fig.102,33). The dating runs in a fairly consistent manner from the late first century to the early third, later brooches were almost certainly residual in their contexts. The humped pin on 29 would, in the south of England, be a sign of a pre-conquest date, but in the north of Britain in the Roman period it is the normal form: Leicester is more or less on the borderline between south and north.

Brooch of early Anglo-Saxon date (fig. 120)
Peter Liddle

30) Sf2010 (200) 100/1 Ph.12. Fragment of a silver-gilt brooch (A.R.Read pers.comm.). Decoration is cast, but probably finished with a fine punch. The fragment has been deliberately cut from the original brooch, presumably as part of a melting-down process. The profile of the breaks suggests that a chisel has been used and the piece then snapped (A.R.Read pers.comm.). The piece has been distorted in the process, but it is clear that it is part of the bow and foot of a brooch. The bow has two standing arches and the start of a third; above is a frame containing part of a scroll. On the foot is a tendril and a larger part of a scroll. The border line is decorated with fine punch marks.

Although the fragment is not large enough to make an entirely conclusive identification, it seems very likely that it is from an equal-arm brooch. These are commonly produced in silver-gilt and the motifs present here can be readily paralleled from other such brooches. Particularly close is an example from Little Wilbrahim, Cambs., although the angle between the bow and foot is less sharp in the present example and

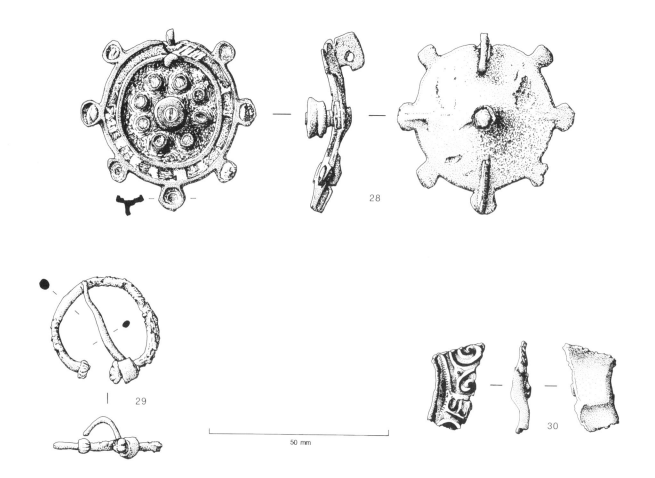

50 mm

Fig. 120: *The illustrated small finds: Category 1 brooches 28-30*

there is no sign of ornamentation in the border (not enough survives to preclude this). We may tentatively identify this as a Dosemoor type of which Evison (1977) was able to list six examples from England, including fragments of the one found near the plough-shattered Grave 4 at the Empingham I Anglo-Saxon Cemetery, Rutland (Middleton and Liddle, forthcoming). The type is dated to the fifth Century AD.

Bone hairpins (figs. 121 and 122)

One hundred and five complete or fragmentary bone pins were retrieved and classified into types according to Crummy (1983). Only Types 1 to 3 were represented in addition to a small number of miscellaneous examples. Nineteen examples belonged to Type 1, 32 to Type 2, ten to Type 3, and four were of Miscellaneous Type. 40 unclassified fragments were identified as belonging to the shaft or tips of broken examples, of which nine are tapering, suggesting Types 1 or 2, and four are swollen suggesting Types 3 to 6. Four fragments possess green staining in imitation their more valuable copper alloy equivalents.

Type 1

Of the 19 catalogued examples, four are complete in their original form, and three more have had broken tips resharpened. The complete examples range from 103mm to 129mm in length, while the resharpened examples are 53mm, 67mm and 84mm. The width of head across all examples ranges from 4-7mm, the upper limit being consistent with examples from Colchester (Crummy 1983, 20). The heads are, in general, crudely conical or completely flat, in line with

Crummy 113, seven examples exhibiting some facetting of the head into a cone, with twelve flat or nearly flat.

The earliest stratified examples of Type 1 come from Period 3 phase 5A, dated 120-200, with shaft fragments of Types 1 or 2 coming from Period 2 (50-120), the six other examples coming from Period 4 (200-250). Crummy has placed the date of pins with tapering stems (Types 1 and 2) from Colchester between *c.* 50 and 200 AD, and the Leicester evidence tends to corroborate this.

31) Sf44 (446) F255 174/2 Ph.4A, pit. Complete pin with flat head. Length 108mm, max. width 5mm.

32) Sf62 (444) F255 174/3 Ph.4A, pit. Complete pin with flat head. Length 129mm, max. width 5mm.

33) Sf84 (1409)161/1 Ph.5A. Complete pin with flat head. Length 111mm, max. width 6mm.

34) Sf9074 (8039) F918 unphased. Pit. Complete pin with highly polished shaft. Length 103mm, max. width 5mm.

35) Sf121 (3953) F757 334/1 Ph.5G pit. Resharpened. Length 67mm, max. width 5mm.

36) Sf123 US. Resharpened pin with flat head. Length 84mm, max. width 4mm.

37) Sf135 (3954) F798 360/1 Ph.5E. Resharpened. Length 53mm, max.width 4mm. Not illustrated.

Type 2

This is the most common bone pin type from the site, a feature also of the much smaller assemblage from Little Lane (Cooper, forthcoming a). Of the 32 catalogued examples, seven are complete and four are resharpened. The complete examples vary in length from 74mm to 99mm, while the resharpened examples vary from 63 to 79mm in length. The maximum width at the base of the head varies from 2 – 5mm, with the majority lying between 3 and 4mm. In general they are more slender than those of Type 1 and so more typically exhibit a bend in the shaft.

The range of forms appears very conservative in comparison to the assemblage from Colchester (Crummy 1983), with the majority conforming to Crummy's 197 and 198 with two transverse grooves beneath a long conical head, or 194 with a more stunted head, and this appears generally true of other Leicester assemblages such as that from Little Lane (Cooper forthcoming a) and Great Holme St. (Boothroyd forthcoming). 23 examples have two grooves, three have a single groove, with six others being incomplete but being certainly of Type 2. Green staining is apparent on four examples, the copper alloy equivalent being the generally more ornate Cool Group 5 (1990, 157 especially fig.4 no.11).

The majority of examples come from Phase 3 deposits dated 120-200 AD with only five coming from third century contexts, and this reinforces the view gained from those at Colchester (Crummy 1983, 21), and their metal equivalents generally (Cool 1990, 157), that this is a predominantly second century type.

38) Sf9 (271) F212 187/1 Ph.3D, pit. Resharpened. Length 67mm, width 2.5mm.

39) Sf10 (304) F212 187/1 Ph.3D, pit. Complete. Length 97mm, width 2.5mm.

40) Sf11 (200) 100/1 Ph.12. Complete. Length 80mm, width 4mm

41) Sf58 (1038) F376 152/1 Ph.3B, pit. Complete. Length 94mm, width 3mm.

42) Sf82 (3673) F763 338/3 Ph.6A, gravel quarry. Complete. Length 85mm, width 4mm.

43) Sf9046 (8029) F903 120/9 Ph.9. Complete. Length 99mm, width 3mm.

Type 3
All ten catalogued examples have swollen stems and more or less spherical heads. Only two examples (45 and 47 are complete of 81mm and 82mm in length, rather shorter than their early Roman counterparts of Types 1 and 2. Three others (44, 48 and 49) have clearly continued in use despite being broken, the obliquely broken tips appearing to have become polished through wear, rather than being actually resharpened (as with 46), with lengths of 79mm, 58mm, and 62mm respectively. The longest of these (44) was probably over a 100mm long when complete. The width of the head varies from 4mm to 10mm, and no examples exhibit deliberate staining which is perhaps of interest given the widespread occurrence of this form in copper alloy (Cool 1990, Group 1).

The earliest stratified example (sf 63) comes from phase 2G dated 50-120, with the three other examples from Roman deposits deriving from Phase 4 and 5 dated 200-300 AD. While the start date is rather earlier than at Colchester where no members of a 137-strong assemblage occurred before 150 AD, the evidence supports Crummy's basic assertion (1983, 22) that the type does not become popular until *c*.AD 200 eclipsing Types 1 and 2. Type 3 pins and their metal equivalents appear widespread in the south of Britain particularly in the later Roman period and it is by far the most common form from Colchester (Crummy 1983, 22). Here it is the least abundant of the three main types, and this tends to reflect the lower intensity of activity in this part of the town in

the later Roman period, supported by the absence of Crummy's other late Roman bone pin types and generally apparent in other finds categories.

Seven examples have spherical heads which relate closely to Crummy's Head Types A and B.

44) Sf59 (3501) 301/1 Ph.12. Broken but reused. As Crummy 1983, 22, fig. 19.252. Length 79mm, width 8mm.

45) Sf77 (3618) F763 338/3 Ph.6A. Gravel quarry. Complete. As Crummy 1983, 22, fig. 19.275. Length 81mm, width 5mm.

46) Sf9011 (8004) F902 108/1 Ph.11. Resharpened. As 45 above, but heavier in appearance with larger head. Length 67mm, width 8mm.

47) Sf26 (2658) F615 254/10 Ph.9. Structure? Complete. As Crummy 1983, fig.19.268. Length 82mm, width 6mm.

One example is of Head Type C (lenticular)

48) Sf81 (3662) F757 334/2 Ph.5G, pit. Broken but reused. Length 58mm, width 6mm.

The two remaining examples have spherical heads which are flattened on opposing faces, so as to be no wider than the stem. One is illustrated.

49) Sf107 (3790) F763 338/3 Ph.6A, gravel quarry. Broken but reused. Length 62mm, width 5mm.

Miscellaneous Types
Four bone pins fall into none of Crummy's first six types and have thus been classified as miscellaneous.

50) Sf40 (444) F255 174/3 Ph.4A, pit. Complete pin. Length 114mm. Max. head width 6.5mm. The form basically belongs to Type 1 with a tapering shaft, but differs because of the head decoration which comprises a band of incised hatching between transverse grooves. The top of the head is flattened, and the surfaces are highly polished.

The present context dates this example to 200-250, although it is most likely to belong to the first or second century in line with Type 1 pins. Two parallels come from Brancaster, Norfolk (Green and Hinchliffe 1985, 56 and fig.37.116 and 117) both of which are unfortunately unstratified.

51) Sf46 (969) F343 141/4 Ph.3B, ditch. Incomplete. Well made and imitating metal pins of Cool's Group 8 (1990, 160 fig.6) and Crummy Type 2, (1983, fig.27 469 and 470). The head comprises a spool and single groove surmounted by a spherical head with flattened section. Tip broken. Surviving length 57mm. Max. width of head 8mm.

At Colchester no equivalent bone examples occurred. This example comes from a context dated AD 120-200, which would be in agreement with evidence from Colchester where the metal type appears to have been introduced in the early second century with a terminus in the third century (Crummy 1983, 28). It is interesting to note that it appears that no closely comparable metal example has been published from Leicester, the variant published by Cool (1990 Group 8 fig. 6.8) being distinctly different and closer to the metal examples described below.

52) Sf114 (3825) F764 339/4 Ph.5E, pit? Incomplete. Top of the head and lower portion of the tapering shaft missing. While it is based on Type 2, it is clear that an extra motif surmounted the conical head, and this may have comprised a further, but smaller, reel and cone as exhibited by Crummy 441 and 442 (1983, fig.23). Wear on the shaft break indicates continued use. Surviving length 58mm. Max. width 5mm.

The present phasing of 120-200 AD, and the tapering shaft would tend to support the idea that this is a variant of Type 2.

53) Sf9027 (8019) 122/1 Ph.9. Complete. A single reel supports a thistle-like head surmounted by a rough cone.

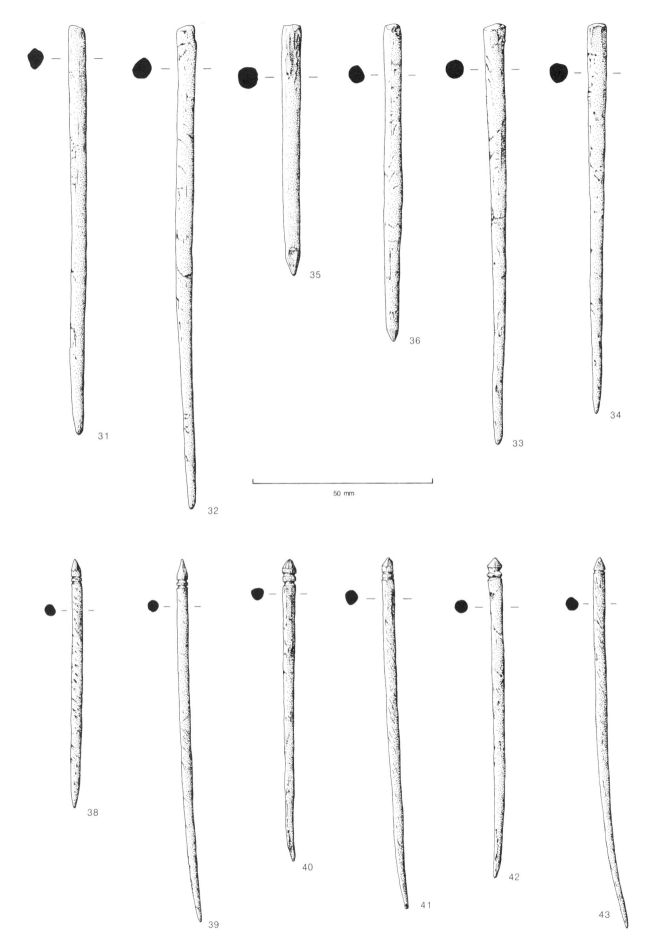

50 mm

Fig 121: *The illustrated small finds: Category 1 bone hairpins 31-36, 38-43*

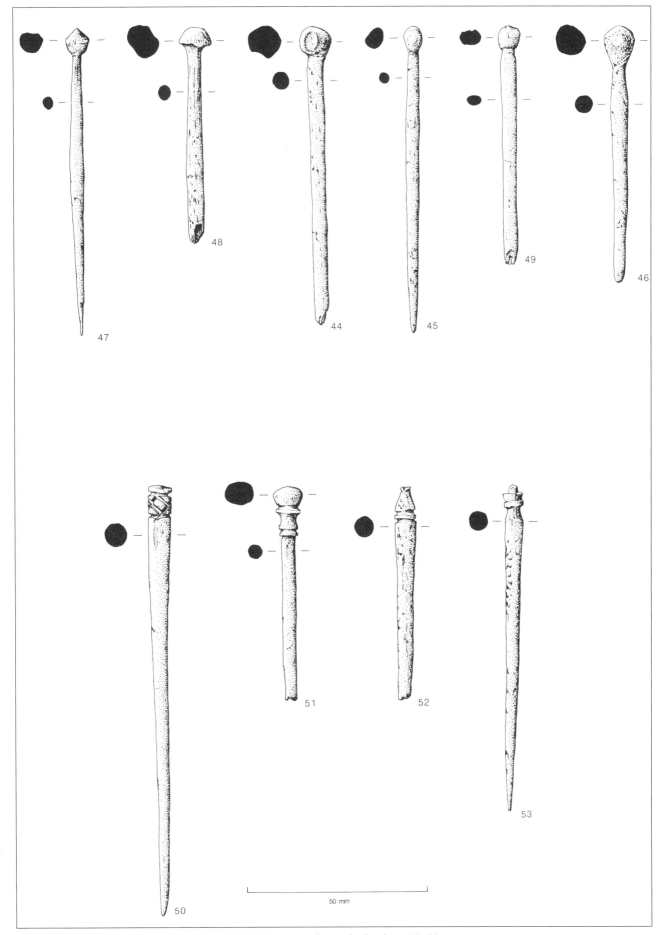

Fig 122: *The illustrated small finds: Category 1 bone hairpins 44-53*

Highly polished surface. Length 87mm, max.width 6mm.

While the single reel arrangement is similar to Type 5 (Crummy 1983, fig.21), apart from the constriction beneath the reel, the shaft tapers and the head is flush with it which indicates a greater affinity with the early Roman Type 2. The pin was residual in a medieval context and no parallels have been traced.

Metal hairpins

Ten complete or near complete hairpins were retrieved, all of which are of cast in copper alloy. They are classified according to Cool (1990). Two belong to Group 3B, five to Group 8, and the remaining two to Group 27, the last being of particular interest since they appear to have a military connection. In line with those in bone, the types present are predominantly first and second century in date, and their generally long length (over 80mm) and highly decorated heads during this period, has been connected with the popularity of very elaborate hairstyles involving the piling of hair on top of the head (Cool 1990, 174).

Group 3B

Cool's Group 3 comprises a wide range of head types and the two examples here both fall into subgroup B, the members of which are widespread and made throughout much of the period at a number of centres (1990, 154). However, the 'flask and stopper' head does appear distinctive and further sub-division of the group may be possible. The two are particularly close to Cool's 1990 fig.2. 12, and four further Leicester examples are known, two from Great Holme St. (Boothroyd

forthcoming, nos.33-34), one from the Norfolk St. villa to the west of the town (A287 1975.105) and one most recently from excavations in Newarke St. in 1993 with two basal rings. A further close parallel away from Leicester comes from the Romano-British roadside settlement of Billingford in Central Norfolk (Cooper forthcoming b, no.11). The tapering shaft and flush head is in line with the earlier Roman bone types and the later third century context of no. 54 may therefore be misleading.

54) Sf2025 (385) 164/1 Ph.5C. Complete, bent. The motifs comprise from bottom to top, reel/bead/ constriction/ reel and small conical head. The form of the head is best described as 'flask and stopper'. Shaft tapers and is of circular section. Length 120mm. Max. diameter of head 4mm.

55) Sf2016 (270) F212 187/1 Ph.3D, pit. Near complete. Similar to, but more slender than 54 above, with tip of shaft broken. The very ornate head comprises a knurled disc and reel surmounted by an elongated bead terminated by a second, smaller reel, above which sits a small conical head. Tapering shaft of circular section. Length 108mm, max. diameter of head 3mm.

Group 8 (Crummy Type 2)

All five examples belonging to this Type are of a very similar design which incorporates discs or cordons with milled edges. While none of the examples sit comfortably with the general run of Cool's Group 8 (1990, 160, fig.6.1-4) or Crummy's Type 2, they are somewhat similar to Cool's variant represented by three examples from Leicester (1990 fig.6.8) where the hemispheres are less well defined. Other Leicester

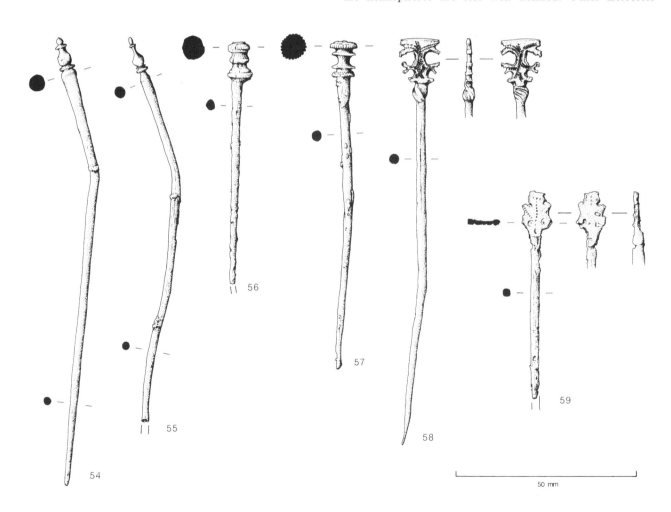

Fig 123: *The illustrated small finds: Category 1 copper alloy hairpins 54-59*

examples with milled discs include one from the Jewry Wall excavations (Kenyon 1948, 262, fig. 89.3) and this distinctive feature may define them as a separate Group. The later first or early second century origin for Group 8 indicated by the Colchester evidence (Cool, 1990, 160) is supported here as three examples come from Period 2 contexts dated 50-120 AD with another from Period 3 dated 120-200 AD.

The three examples not catalogued were too corroded to be illustrated (sf.2355, 2114, and 2203).

56) Sf2356 (1614) 144/1 Ph.2D. The head comprises two flattened spheres separated by a reel. The head does not appear to have been centrally placed. The shaft tapers and the tip is broken. Length 64mm. Diameter of head 6mm.

57) Sf2296 US. A complete pin, the head of which comprises two discs with milled edges, the upper one being larger, separated by a sharply defined spool. The shaft is tapering and of circular section. Length 87mm. Max. diameter of head 7.5mm.

Group 27
Two examples appear to belong to Cool's Military Standard Head Group (1990, 172, fig.13.1-3), sharing the flat head of rectangular section and the use of punched decoration. Their similarity to depictions of military standards on Trajan's column, the use of punched decoration, and their occurrence in military deposits at sites such as Wroxeter, Cirencester, and Richborough confirms them as a mid-late first century type with military connections or influence (Cool, 1990, 172). The complete example, 58, would support their function as hairpins, but the only well stratified one (59) comes from Period 3.

58) Sf2345 (3541) F714 315/3 Ph.9, Pit. Complete. The tapering shaft is surmounted by a bead with spiral incisions, surmounted by a flat T-shaped plate with branches. Both faces of the plate are decorated with punch marks forming a pattern of intertwining ropes. Length 112mm, head width 11mm.

While differing in design from those illustrated by Cool, the branched appearance and 'ropes' are reminiscent of the top parts of the standards with drapery depicted on Trajan's column (Lepper and Frere 1988, pl.XXXIII).

59) Sf2162 (852) F230 155/1 Ph.3B Well. Incomplete. Shaft tip broken and head damaged. Similar to 2345 above with the head formed from a flat plate, both faces of which are punch-decorated with lines of dots. Surviving length 55mm.

Beads (fig 124)
A total of 25 complete or fragmentary beads were recovered during excavation with further possible fragments retrieved during the wet sieving of soil samples.

Glass Beads
Melon Beads
All examples are melon beads, manufactured from turquoise glass frit. Seven fragments were retrieved, belonging to five examples, none of which was complete. However, four complete profiles in a range of sizes were represented. Such beads tend to be found in first and second century contexts (Guido 1978, 100), and the examples here, all from Periods 2 and 3, would support this idea. It has been suggested that the smaller examples may be early in date (Crummy 1983, 30), but this small group does not offer much support for this.

60) Sf3015 (725) F307 167/1 Ph.5B Pit. Frit has weathered to a light blue-green. Length 13mm, estimated diameter 15mm.

61) Sf3012 (1177) F417 151/1 Ph.5B Cobble spread. Turquoise frit with white patina at one end. Length 14mm, estimated diameter 17mm. Not illustrated.

62) Sf3011 (1632) 138/2 Ph.2B. Length 15mm, diameter 17mm.

63) Sf3008 (1511) 144/1 Ph.2D. Length 16mm, diameter 20mm. Not illustrated.

Annular Beads with Marvered Decoration
64) Sf3002 (917) F387 182/1 Ph.2J Dumping. Bead in translucent cobalt blue glass, punctuated by rings or eyes of opaque white glass, marvered flush with the surface of the bead. Length 17mm, diameter 26mm.

This bead belongs within Guido's Decorated Classes of the Iron Age, falling into Class 3: South Harting type (1978, 49 fig. 8 and plates I.3 and IIIa). The eyes tend to be equidistant, and this suggests that in common with most examples this bead also had three eyes, although only two survive. Such beads are of continental origin or inspiration, and are not Roman, and although the date of the majority tends to fall within the early Romano-British period, as this example from Phase 2 illustrates, it is unlikely that many were in use in the third century (Guido 1978, 49).

Plain Annular Beads
The remains of six annular beads of Guido's (1978) Group 6 were recorded, three of which were in blue translucent glass, and three in green translucent glass. All three blue examples are very similar, conforming to Guido's subGroup 6*iva* medium annular blue, translucent or opaque glass, and only one is illustrated. Such beads were imported from the sixth century BC, and Guido notes that when they occur on Roman sites, 'a native British element is apparent in the culture' (Guido 1978, 67). The pre- or early post-conquest phasing in Period 1 for 65 and 66 would concur with this, and it is likely that both beads came from the same string. 68 in green glass conforms to Guido's subGroup 6*iia* medium annular natural greenish translucent glass which run right through the Roman period (Guido 1978, 66) and so this example from Period 2 would appear to be an early one. 70 possibly belongs to Guido's subGroup 6*viii*.

65) Sf3004 (2962) 201/2 Ph.2K. Mid-blue translucent glass. Length 7mm, diameter 17mm. Not illustrated.

66) Sf3005 (2962) 201/2 Ph.2K. Light blue translucent glass. Length 5mm, diameter 15mm.

67) Sf3013 (688) F315 165/1 Ph.5B Pit. Light blue translucent glass. Length 6mm, diameter 15mm. Not illustrated.

68) Sf3009 (1218) 148/2 Ph.2G. Light green glass. Length 6mm, diameter 17mm. Not illustrated

70) Sf3024, Unstratified. Very dark green/blue glass. Length 4mm, diameter 15mm.

Short Beads
71) Sf3019 (2559) F568 247/2 Ph.8, Pit/well. Bead in opaque pinky-white glass, made by spinning around a metal rod. The external surface is decorated with faint spirals in relief, and yellow gilt. Length 5mm, diameter 5mm.

This would appear to be an example of a gold-in-glass bead, which has lost its outer cover of glass (Hilary Cool pers.comm.). Such beads are rare finds in Roman Britain and it is similar to an example from Caerleon (Boon 1977, 198, fig.1.1 and pl.XVI, 2) dated from the Antonine to the Severan period.

Short Oblate
72) Sf3021 (1664) F1005 134/1 Ph.2A, Dump. Fragment of short oblate bead in deep blue glass. Length 4mm, diameter 10mm

73) Sf3007 (3503) F701 302/1 Ph.12 Quarry. Bead in opaque mid-blue glass. Length 8mm, diameter 9mm.

Short Cylinder or Barrel Beads

74) Sf3010 (1552) 144/1 Ph.2D. Bead in opaque light blue glass, weathered white surface. Length 4mm, diameter 5mm.

Standard Spherical Beads

75) Sf3016 (725) F307 167/1 Ph.5B Pit. Bead in opaque blue glass, weathered white. Ends flattened, possibly through wear. Length 5mm, diameter 5mm.

Cylinder Beads

76) Sf3017 (667) F318 153/1 Ph.3B, Well. Turquoise translucent glass with internal surface of perforation yellow in colour. Heptagonal section. Length 8mm, diameter 6mm.

This is a rare form with examples coming from Denver, Norfolk (Gurney 1986, 110 no.24 fig.70) and Whitton, S.Glamorgan (Jarret and Wrathmell 1981, 161 no.16, pl.XVIII) (Hilary Cool pers.comm.)

77) Sf3006 (1027) F255 174/2 Ph.4A Pit. Translucent amber-coloured with circular section. Length 4mm, diameter 2mm.

Segmented Beads

78) Sf3018 (2294) F568 247/2 Ph.8. Pit/well. Opaque dark brown glass with white patina. Circular section. Length 7mm, diameter 4mm.

Jet Beads

Note: the identification as jet is based on visual examination only.

79) Sf4570 (2468) 253/3 Ph.9. Short, broken length of a long cylinder bead with transverse grooves. Only two grooves remain, 1.5-2.0mm apart. One end of the bead is scooped out, perhaps to accommodate a spacer on a necklace. Similar to more complete examples from Colchester (Crummy 1983 nos. 1183-4) and South Shields (Allason-Jones and Miket 1984, 302, 7.9-7.16). Surviving length 4mm, diameter 5mm.

80) Sf5044 (3600) F757 334/2 Ph.5G Pit. Long cylinder with square section, each face of which is decorated with longitudinal parallel grooves. One end damaged. Length 35mm, width 7mm.

Bone Bead

81) Sf134 (349) F240 186/1 Ph.5D linear feature. A short cylinder bead in bone with faint transverse grooving. Length 2.5mm, diameter 5.5mm.

Stone Bead

82) Sf4578 (2937) 207/5 Ph.12. Manufactured from an opaque, smooth, waterworn grey brown pebble of oval shape. Perforation not centrally placed. Length 3mm, diameter 8mm.

Shell Bead

83) Sf5040 (1197) 174/2 F255 Ph.4A. Crudely shaped oval or disc of oyster shell with a circular perforation of 2mm diameter which is not centrally placed. Length 1mm, diameter 15mm. Not illustrated.

Copper Alloy ?Bead

84) Sf2198 (832) F343 141/1 Ph.3A Ditch. Disc bead of copper alloy with concentric groove filled with red and green enamel. Length 3mm, diameter 13mm.

No parallels have been traced for this object and its

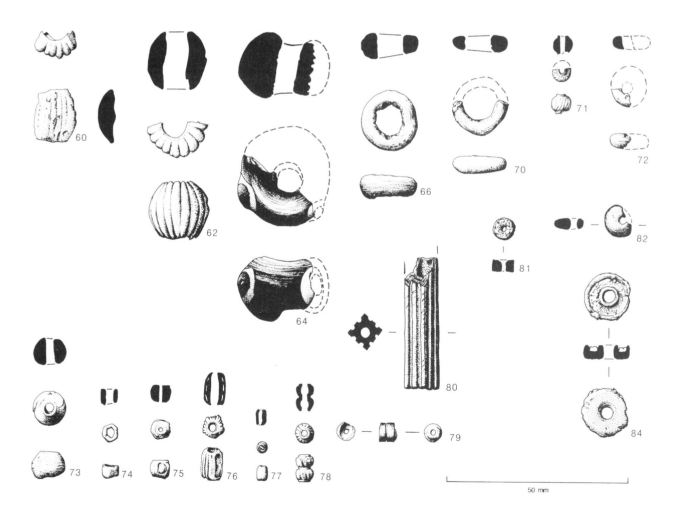

50 mm

Fig 124: *The illustrated small finds: Category 1 beads 60, 62, 64, 66, 70-82, 84*

identification as a bead is based largely on the presence of a central perforation.

Armlets (fig. 125)

Armlets of jet and shale
Note: the distinction between jet and shale is based on visual examination only

Eleven examples belong to this group (six are catalogued), of which two are of jet (85 and 86) and nine are of shale. One example in each material is decorated (85 and 87), the remainder are plain. The earliest dated example (Sf 5005) comes from phase 3B dated 120-200 AD and represents the earliest occurrence of this material on the site. Generally they occur in later Roman contexts.

The armlets vary in internal diameter from 44mm to 68mm, with varying band thicknesses. Crummy (1983, 36) has demonstrated how the internal diameters of armlets accompanying corpses from the later Butt Road cemetery at Colchester increase with the estimated age of the associated skeleton. By comparison, the smaller examples here (under *c.*50mm) were probably worn by children and the larger examples by adolescents and adults.

85) Sf4571 (3501) 301/1 Ph.12. Jet. Decorated armlet or rectangular section with carved outer edge to give the appearance of segmented beading. Very finely made. Internal diameter 60mm.

Two examples from South Shields have similar rectangular profiles (Allason-Jones and Miket 1984, 313, 7.111 and 112) with the decoration on the latter being similar.

86) Sf4557 (311) F220 169/2 Ph.5C Pit. Jet. Fragment of an undecorated armlet. Internal diameter 48mm. The diameter and slender appearance suggest it was worn by a child.

87) Sf5026 (3519) 340/1 Ph.6B. Shale with cable decoration presumably derived from the much thinner copper alloy examples. Internal diameter 60mm.

Similar examples come from South Shields (Allason-Jones and Miket 1984, 313, 7.116-9), Colchester dated to AD 275-*c.*400, (Crummy 1983, 36 fig.38.1556) and Blake St., York (Cool *et al.* 1995, 1540 fig.719 no.5816).

The sections of plain shale armlets are generally sub-circular or polygonal with the internal surface being particularly angled. Three are illustrated to show the range.

88) Sf5019 (446) F255 174/2 Ph.4A Pit. Shale. Plano-convex section. Internal diameter 68mm. A second fragment (Sf5020) from a different band came from the same context.

89) Sf5022 (3505) F702 302/2 Ph.12, quarry. Shale. Circular section with internal facet. Internal diameter 52mm.

90) Sf5031 (3576) F727 307/2 Ph.9 Pit. Shale. Thin, of circular section. Internal diameter 62mm.

Armlets of Copper Alloy
Wire

91) Sf2409 (3954) F798 360/1 Ph.5E Pit. Complete but straightened-out, made from a single piece of wire of circular section incorporating simple hook and eye arrangement. Length of wire 185mm, giving approximate diameter of 60mm. Width of wire 1.5mm.

Cable

92) Sf2261 (3501) 301/1 Ph.12. Fragment of cable armlet made from two strands of twisted wire of circular section, one of which emerges to form a hook. Surviving length 80mm, width 2.5mm. Similar in appearance to Crummy 1983 no. 1628 which is made of three strands.

93) Sf2045 (2026) F512 259/3 Ph.11 Pit. Fragment of cable armlet made from three strands of twisted wire of circular section. Surviving length 30mm, width 2mm. Not illustrated.

94) Sf2199 (1038) F376 152/1 Ph.3B Pit. Fragment of ?segmented armlet with hollow centre infilled with black material. Internal diameter 48mm, width 2.5mm.

This is an unusual type which is similar to an example from a fourth century burial group from Rochester, Kent (Harrison 1981, 128 and 130 no.15, fig.10). (Hilary Cool pers.comm.)

Notched, Toothed or Crenellated Armlets.

95) Sf2194 (832) F343 141/1 Ph.3A Ditch. Fragment of small ?armlet with longitudinal grooves, the central of the three appearing to be further decorated with circular punch marks. Estimated internal diameter 32mm. This is rather too rigid to be an armlet, and if so would only be suitable for a child.

c) Crenellated with toothing between the crenellations.

96) Sf2254 (3501) 301/1 Ph.12. Fragment of armlet with rectangular section, the outer edge of which is punctuated with evenly-spaced bands of transverse notches, up to six or seven in number. Estimated internal diameter 46mm.

This is one of the commonest armlet types during the fourth century and is identical to an example from Colchester (Crummy 1983, 40 and fig.43.1659), and another from Rochester (Harrison 1981, 128 no.11 and fig.10.14. (Hilary Cool pers.comm.)

Transverse grooves

97) Sf2316 (3580) F722 307/2 Ph.9. Incomplete. Two joining fragments. Decorated with zone of oblique transverse grooves between margins. No terminals preserved. Length of fragment 105mm.

This possibly indigenous type of fourth century armlet is again common, although it is rare to find exact parallels. It is similar to an example from Colchester (Crummy 1983, fig.44.1679) from a Period 2 Grave deposit, and another from Caister-on-Sea, Norfolk (Darling 1993, 83-4, fig.50 no.187) (Hilary Cool pers.comm.).

98) Sf2231 F246 Ph.5C. Complete penannular armlet in thick wire with ovoid section. Surface decorated with incised crosshatching. Internal diameter 40mm

Armlets of this type tend to be late third to fourth century in date, and there is no standardization in the decorative schemes employed (Hilary Cool pers.comm).

Finger rings (fig 126)

Iron

99) Sf1469, (859) unphased. Complete but distorted, with setting lost. Plain hoop of circular section with ovoid bezel set longitudinally. Estimated internal diameter 18mm.

Rings of this general form are usually of later Roman date, but by this time they are rarely made in iron (Hilary Cool pers.comm.).

Copper-Alloy
Plain

100) Sf2251 (200) 100/1 Ph.12. Complete. Penannular hoop. One terminal damaged, the other tapers. Internal diameter 17mm.

101) Sf2221 (884) F343 141/1 Ph.3A. Complete. In form of coiled strip. One terminal tapers, the other possibly damaged. Possibly cut down from an armlet? Internal diameter 13mm.

Two similar examples come from South Shields (Allason-Jones and Miket 1984, 125, 3.199 and 3.202).

102) Sf2389 (3541) F714 315/3 Ph.9. Complete. Plain hoop with polygonal section. Internal diameter 17mm. Possibly not a finger ring.

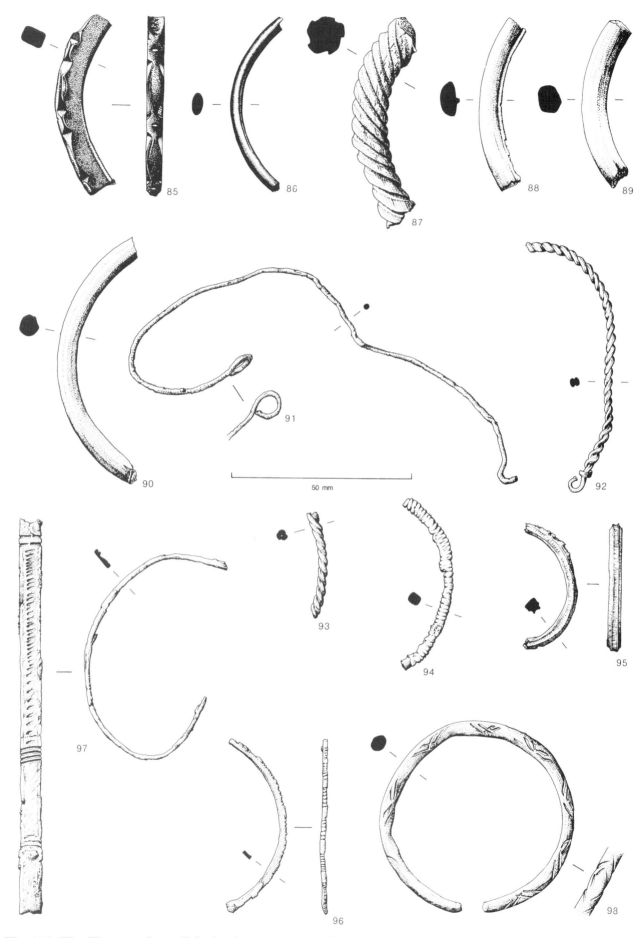

50 mm

Fig. 125: *The illustrated small finds: Category 1 armlets 85-98*

103) Sf2247 (3501) 301/1 Ph.12. Complete. Small decorated band with grooved margins. Internal diameter 12mm.

Possibly a ferrule rather than a ring.

With Setting

104) Sf2028 (2154) F545 252/6 Ph.9. Complete. Cast. The hoop thickens to form a bezel with a longitudinal oval setting. Slightly flattened and heavily corroded. Internal diameter 18mm.

Intaglio

105) Sf3003 (1219) F417 150/1 Ph.3B Cobble spread. Complete. Plano-convex oval moulded in blue glass, chipped around the base. Depiction is of a standing figure facing to its right with left arm flexed and right arm extended and possibly holding an object vertically. Length 10mm, width 8mm, Height 3mm.

This is a representation of Mercury, usually depicted holding a caduceus and money bag, a range of examples of which are known (Henig 1974, Pl.II 38-45). The moulding of the present example is too crude to identify the objects held, and in terms of quality and dimensions, it is best paralleled by an example from Wanborough, Wilts (Pl.II.45) of second or third century date, although no glass examples are cited by Henig. This example comes from a Period 3 context dated 120-200 AD, and it may be an early example of the glass imitation gems that become popular in the third century (Henig 1974, 42).

Belt fittings (fig. 126)

Belt buckles

The examples do not represent as wide a range of medieval examples as from the Little Lane and St Peters Lane groups (Cooper forthcoming a), but including two unusual examples, one of which (106) may be Roman.

106) Sf 2034 (396) Ph.9 Complete oval frame with pin rest and grooved decoration, pin missing. Plate incomplete. Recesses for pin and frame on outside edge. Two centrally positioned rivets. Upper and lower edges have scalloped cutouts. Inner edge, damaged but also has cutout decoration. Outer face decorated with two incised crosses and punched dots between the arms. Frame length 15mm, width 42mm. Plate length 32mm, width 28mm.

Although the context indicates a 12th or early 13th century date, it is possible that this is residual from a Roman context. No close medieval examples have been traced and it bears a similarity to late Roman examples belonging to groups I and III (Simpson 1976, 193-4, fig 1 no.1 and 196-7, fig.3 nos. 1 and 2), although the exaggerated cutouts are not closely matched.

107) Sf2117 (2607) F568 247/2 Ph.8 pit/well. Complete oval frame with offset bar and pin rest on inside of an exagerated internal lip. Pin missing. Length 15mm, width 24mm.

Oval frames with ornate outer edges are widely paralleled from London and the wide variety of forms comprised a long lasting fashion from the late 12th to the late 14th century (Egan and Pritchard 1991, 76). However, no direct parallels for the internal lip are apparent. This example comes from Phase 8 dating to 12th/13th century and so would represent and early form. An additional plain example of oval frame without the internal lip also came from the excavations.

Decorated buckle plates

108) Sf2146 (234) F206 119/3 Ph.10 well. Incomplete outer face of plate with single central rivet hole (second one may have been close to outer edge), rectangular frame cutouts and circular pin hole now damaged. Outer edge missing. Upper and lower margins decorated with incised zig-zags.

The use of incised zig-zag decoration is common on medieval examples, the earliest dated examples coming from London belong to ceramic phase 7 and 9 dating to *c.*1200-1230 and 1270-1350 respectively (Egan and Pritchard 1991 fig.46.313 and fig.49.330). This example comes from Phase 10, dating to late 13th-early 14th century.

109) Sf2172 (234) F206 119/3 Ph.10 well. Incomplete plain plate of trapezoidal form, with single single rivet hole close to outer edge and circular pin hole.

From same context as 108 above.

Footwear

Over 500 hobnails of Roman date were recorded (Manning 1985, Type 10), some occurring in incomplete fragments of shoe soles not diagnostic enough to warrant illustration. The material is discussed in more detail under Category 11 fastenings and fittings.

Category 2: Toilet, surgical or pharmaceutical instruments (fig. 127)

Nail cleaner

110) Sf2207 (764) F343 141/3 Ph.3B Ditch. Incomplete composite nail cleaner, the blade tip of which is missing. The top of the shaft is of circular section and is decorated with incised lattice, and is surmounted by a biconical disc of bone, stained green. The lower part of the shaft flattens, and broadens to form the forked blade. Surviving length 42mm. Width of head 7mm.

This is an unusual type, but three identical examples were excavated from the Shrine of Apollo at Nettleton, Wilts (Wedlake 1982, fig.94.7,8, and 11) with bone heads, and were excavated from third to fourth century levels. The current example comes from Phase 3 dated 120-200 AD, suggesting that the Nettleton examples may be residual, and this is supported by an example from Cirencester (Viner 1982, 103, fig.30.71) from a later first century context.

Tweezers

111) Sf9015 (8015) F932 Unphased Layer. Complete pair of tweezers made from a single sheet of copper alloy, beaten out and folded in order to incorporate a suspension loop at the top. The blade width flares. The external surfaces of both blades are decorated with two parallel lines of opposed, crescentic punch marks. Length 32mm, blade width at tips 5mm.

Toilet spoons

With the exception of 74 below, all examples are cast in copper alloy.

a) With small, round, flat or cupped scoop.

114) Sf2026 (367) F230 164/1 Ph.5C Well. Complete. A double-ended instrument, both ends of which are formed into flattened ovoid spoon shapes, with no attempt to form a bowl. Rather crude and heavy in appearance. The shaft is of rectangular section and tapers and flattens at either end. Length 75mm, width of shaft 5mm.

115) Sf2079 (687) F317 163/1 Ph.5B Post hole. Incomplete. A presumably single-ended toilet spoon. Shaft tip missing. The flat spoon in the form of a droplet is angled at 30 degrees. Shaft of circular section is bent. Surviving length 90mm, shaft diameter 2mm.

Similar to an examples from Little Lane (Shires), Leicester (Cooper, forthcoming a, no.117), and Colchester (Crummy 1983, 60, fig. 64.1907).

116) Sf2300 (1153) F412 186/4 Ph.3C Pit. Incomplete single-ended toilet spoon with ovoid, flattened spoon, one

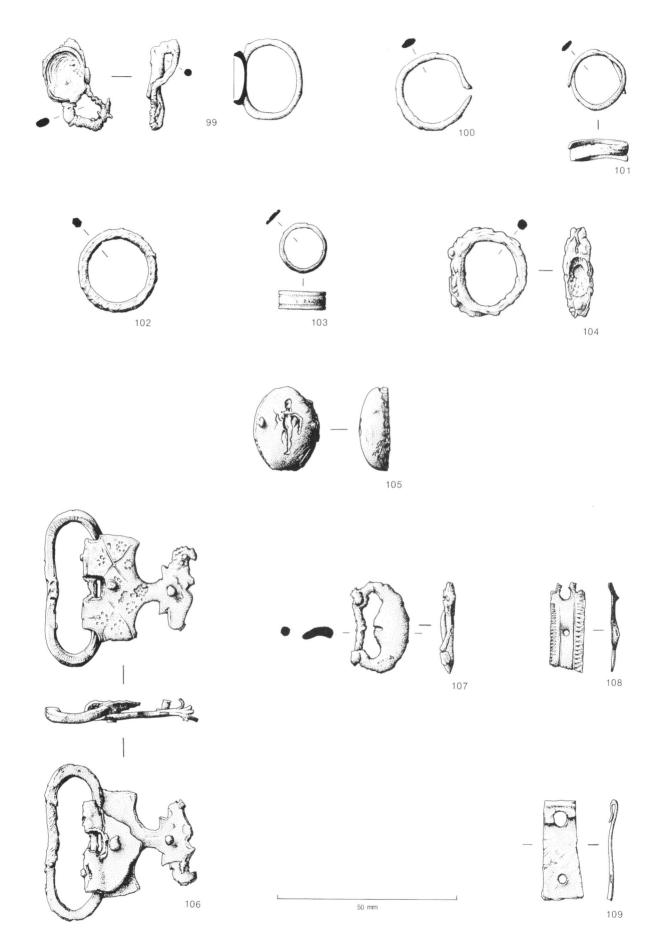

Fig 126: *The illustrated small finds: Category 1 finger rings and belt fittings*

edge damaged. Rather corroded. Shaft of circular section and tapering. Length 125mm, max. shaft diameter 1.5mm.

Noticibly more slender than 115 above.

b) With long, cupped scoop.

117) Sf74 (3549) F711 332/1 Ph.2L. Incomplete Bone example. Midshaft fragment of circular section with part of tapering scoop cut into it. Length 70mm Width 7mm.

Bone is rarely used for such instruments, although a complete example comes from Blue Boar Lane, Leicester (Lentowicz forthcoming, no.34)

118) Sf2083 (631) 162/5 Ph.5B. The most complete example of this type. Tip of spoon bowl broken. Shaft is a 'barley-sugar' twist which tapers to a small knob-like terminal, the tip of which may be missing. The junction between shaft and bowl is flattened and moulded, with both faces incised with opposed crescents, giving the appearance of eyes. Length 91mm, width of shaft 3mm.

A similar, but also incomplete, example comes from Colchester (Crummy 1983, 60, fig.64.1917) from Period 5, whilst an identical example with the same 'zoomorphic' junction decoration comes from Little Lane (Cooper, forthcoming a no.125) and indicates that both the above examples are probably incomplete spoon probes. The present example comes from a third century context.

119) Sf2144 (2703) F615 254/9 Ph.9, Structure? Fragment incorporating part of the scoop and a length of plain shaft. Length 39mm, width of shaft 1.5mm.

Spoon probe

Only one complete example of this double-ended type of instrument was retrieved. The incomplete spoon, 118 above is probably also a spoon probe.

120) Sf2152 (969) F343 141/4 Ph.3B Ditch. Complete example with unusually long spoon bowl at one end, and a relatively slim probe at the other. Junction between probe and shaft is demarcated by transverse grooving. Shaft swells at this point and is of polygonal section. The junction between shaft and bowl comprises two bands of transverse decorative moulding, providing the weak point at which it is bent. Length 160mm, max. diameter of shaft 3mm, max. diameter of probe 4mm, width of bowl 7mm.

From a second century context (Phase 3)

Spatula

Only one fragment of this Roman instrument type has been recorded from the assemblage.

121) Sf2037 (200) 100/1 Ph.12. Incomplete. Droplet-shaped spatula head with convex surfaces. Length 44mm, width 7mm.

Toilet set elements

122) Sf2176 (991) 157/5 Ph.3B. Incomplete. Probably a (?long-cupped) spoon, the bowl of which has broken. Made from a single length of wire, looped over in the fashion of a modern hair grip to enable suspension, the loop being secured by winding one end of the wire five times around the shaft. The other end of the wire forms the shaft which has been hammered flat and flares to form the bowl. Length 57mm.

The presence of the suspension loop suggests that it formed one element of a toilet set of a type similar to that from Colchester (Crummy 1983, 62, fig.67. 1943) of late 3rd to 4th century date, disturbed from the late cemetery, the elements of which were suspended from a bar and loop handle.

The present example however, comes from a second century context of Phase 3.

123) Sf2387 (3866) F763 338/2 Ph.5H Gravel quarry. Toilet instrument in the form of a pin with a swollen shaft of circular section, the head of which is bent over to form a suspension loop. The tip appears to be pointed to act as a pick, but may have been broken. Length 77mm, shaft diameter 1mm.

This probably forms one element of a toilet set similar to one from Colchester (Crummy 1983, 62, fig.67.1945), which did not conclusively contain a pick, and is probably of late third to fourth century date. The phasing of the present example in the second half of the third century concurs with this.

124) Sf2408 (3908) F784 339/7 Ph.5F. Suspension device comprising two similar and linked elements each of which is made from a single piece of flattened wire of rectangular section, narrowing at the loop heads. Both ends of each element are bent back on themselves to form suspension loops with one end wrapped around the other, towards the centre of the shaft. The two elements are of different lengths, and have a makeshift appearance. Length of longest element 77mm. width of shaft 2mm.

Could conceivably have been used to suspend a variety of small items, but toilet instruments appear most likely.

Category 3: Objects used in the manufacture or working of textiles (fig. 128)

Needles

A total of 14 sewing needles of Roman date were identified and classified according to Crummy's three fold typology (1983, 65). Eleven were of bone, of which only two were complete (125 and 126), and two more had complete heads. The remainder comprised shaft fragments with the base of an eye groove at one end, demonstrating breakage at the weakest point. Of these fragments, five appear to have circular eyes and two rectangular ones. Three needles of copper alloy were identified, only one of which was complete.

Type 1 Needles with pointed heads

Both examples are of bone.

125) Sf45 (1075) F411 186/2 Ph.3C recut of pit. Complete. Plain conical head and circular perforation. Length 105mm, width of head 3.5mm.

126) Sf116 (3936) F784 339/7 Ph.5F pit. Complete. Strictly not of Type 1 as head, though facetted, is squared off. However, head is of circular section unlike Type 2. Figure-of-eight eye. Length 115mm, width of head 4.5mm.

Type 2 Needles with a flat spatulate head

The single example of this type is of bone, although it also occurs in copper alloy at Colchester (Crummy 1983, 65, fig.70.1976 and 1977), and elsewhere in Leicester (Kenyon 1948 fig.89.19).

127) Sf9032 (8015) F932 Unphased Layer. Incomplete. Flat, flaring head and long rectangular eye. Length 74mm, width of head 6mm.

Type 3 Needles with a groove above and below the eye

The three identified needles of copper alloy all belong to this Type, although 2022 is a variant.

128) Sf2074 (687) F317 163/1 Ph.5B Post hole. Needle with long thin eye and narrow tapering groove on both faces. Shaft of circular section, becoming rectangular towards the eye. Length 120mm, diameter 2.5mm.

129) Sf2317 (3583) 301/1 Ph.12. Head and upper shaft of incomplete needle. Eye longer and narrower than 128 above, and shaft is of rectangular section. Surviving length 48mm, width 2mm.

130) Sf2022 (305) F218 119/4 Ph.2E. Incomplete with tip broken. A variant of Type 3, perhaps designed for use with

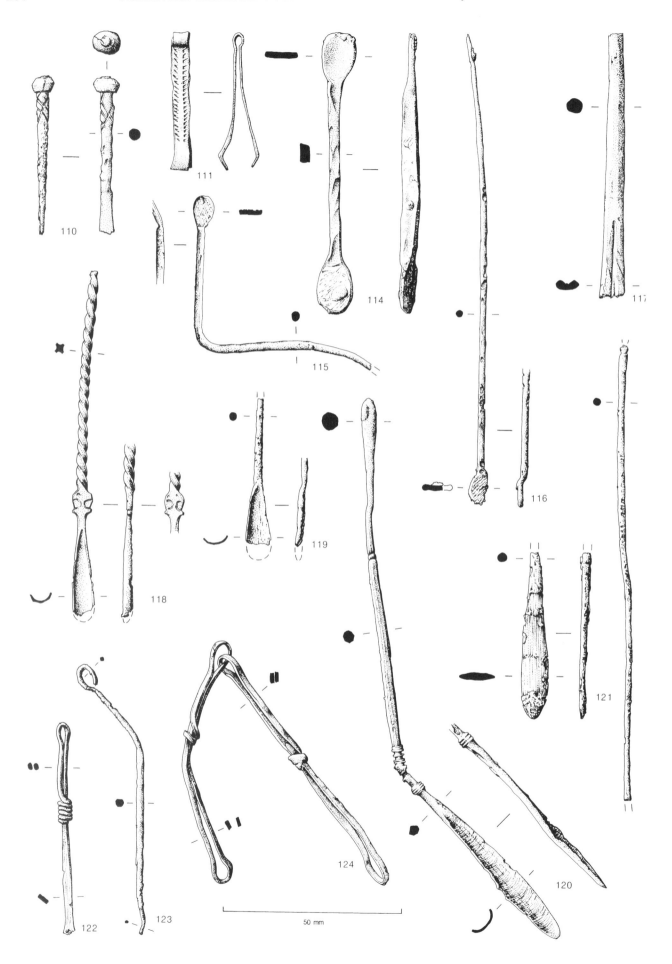

Fig. 127: *The illustrated small finds: Category 2 toilet instruments 110, 111, 114-124*

thicker threads. The eye is long and swollen, the groove does not extend far above and below and is only present on one side. The shaft is flattened around the eye. Surviving length 70mm, width 6mm.

Similar examples came from excavations at the Jewry Wall, one of which was from Phase VII, and it was suggested that they were probably netting needles (Kenyon 1948, 262, fig.89.18). It is worth noting the similarity of the eye with those of Anglo-Scandinavian iron examples from York of 9th-11th century date, where the Y-eyed design involves splitting the needle head and rewelding (Ottaway 1992, 544, fig.215.2535).

Pinbeater

A single incomplete example was recovered. These tools were used to press down the threads of the weft during the weaving process and often show signs of wear and polish at either tapered ends. They are often found alongside other weaving tools in early Anglo-Saxon contexts from site such as West Stow (West 1985, fig.55.5).

131) Sf9010,(8004) F902 Incomplete, one tip broken, other end highly polished. Length 100mm, width 10mm.

Spindlewhorls

Only four spindlewhorls have been recorded, three manufactured from pottery sherds (133 and 134), and the other from shale (132).

132) Sf5007 (516) F263 120/5 Ph.9 Pit. Complete. Shale, with flat surfaces and curved sides. One of original surfaces has been lost. The perforation has a slight hourglass profile. Diameter 41mm, thickness 9mm, diameter of perforation 10mm.

133) Sf4529 (514) F246 166/3 Ph.5C well. Incomplete, broken across the perforation. Manufactured from a sherd of South Gaulish decorated samian ware of later first century date. The perforation has an hourglass profile having been drilled from both sides. Diameter 47mm, thickness 6mm, diameter of perforation 7mm.

134) Sf4506 (1264) 143/2 Ph.2D. Complete. Manufactured from a complete pedestal base sherd in a fine greyware fabric (?GW4). The hourglass perforation is slightly off-centre. Diameter 47mm, thickness 10mm, diameter of perforation 9mm.

Textile fragments

Five examples of surviving textiles have been recorded, under small finds numbers 5002, 5030, 5036, 5037, and 5038. 5002 comprises over 60 individual fragments, while the others are single mineralised pieces, none of which have an area exceeding 1 sq.cm. All have been identified as linen and all come from medieval pit deposits belonging to Phase 8, (12th/13th century) and Phase 10 (late 13th-early 14th century).

Category 4: Household utensils and furniture (fig. 129)

Spoons

The remains of six spoons of Roman date have been identified, only one of which is complete (9030), and all of which belong to either Crummy's Class 1 or 2 (Crummy 1983, 69), with round or pear-shaped bowls respectively. With the exception of the bone example of Type 1 (91), all are cast in copper alloy.

Type 1

This type dates from the second half of the first and the second century AD (Wilson 1968, 101). The present group is confined to phase 1-3 contexts dating before 200 AD. 136 is of interest coming from a pre- or early post-conquest context in phase 1

135) Sf91 (1511) 144/1 Ph.2D. Bone. Incomplete. Round bowl with part of handle of circular section. Diameter of bowl 21mm.

136) Sf2208 (2948) 201/2 Ph.2K. Incomplete. Round bowl of copper alloy with silver or white metal plating. Part of handle remains. Diameter of bowl 20mm.

137) Sf2027,(349) F240 186/1 Ph.5D linear feature. Incomplete. Round bowl of copper alloy with silver or white metal plating. Base of handle remains. Diameter of bowl 25mm

138) Sf2188 (1072) F417 151/1 Ph.3B Cobble spread. Incomplete. Tapered handle in copper alloy of circular section, widening and flattening to form base of ?circular spoon bowl. The tapered end is bent over and does not appear to be pointed. Length 85mm. Not illustrated.

Type 2

This type appears to have been in production by the first half of the second century (Waugh and Goodburn 1972, 124).

139) Sf9030 (8018) F909 124/5 Ph.9 Pit. Complete copper alloy spoon, bowl torn and flattened, handle bent. Handle offset, and tapers to a point. Length 120mm, width of bowl 25mm.

Similar to an example from Colchester (Crummy 1983, 69, fig 73.2014).

140) Sf2277 (3503) F701 302/1 Ph.12 Quarry. Handle, detached from bowl at its junction. Handle of square section decorated with moulded reels of square section. Remaining part tapers with circular section. Length 95mm.

Shale bowls

Fragments from five separate vessels were identified, all of which derive from Area 1. The forms represented appear to be shallow bowls with curving sides, and plain tapered rims. The earliest dated examples come from third century phase 5A contexts.

141) Sf5024 (1003) F246 166/4 Ph.5C Well. Vessel with upright, tapered rim and curving sides. Diameter 140mm, body thickness 4mm.

142) Sf5010 (654) 161/1 Ph.5A. Vessel with footring base and shallow curving sides. Diameter of base 60mm, diameter of fragment 130mm, suggesting vessel diameter of c.150mm. Body thickness 6mm.

143) Sf5011 (654) 161/1 Ph.5A. Two joining fragments from side of curve-sided bowl. Vessel diameter greater than 160mm. Body thickness 4mm.

142 and 143 from the same context may represent parts of the same vessel.

144) Sf5001 (223) F205 126/2 Ph.10 Well. Fragment of ?shallow bowl deriving from lower part of vessel side. Vessel diameter greater than 85mm. Body thickness 4mm. Not illustrated.

145) Sf5032 (1540) 161/3 Ph.5A. Two joining fragments with tapering profile which, judging by the degree of curvature, appear to come from a vessel with a very large diameter (c.250mm). Body thickness 3-8mm.

Lighting: candleholders

146) Sf2200 (1116) F409 156/1 Ph.3B Shallow pit. Incomplete. Sheet disc of copper alloy surmounted by sheet cylinder which is damaged. The underside of the disc has a suspension loop to which a circular link chain is attached.

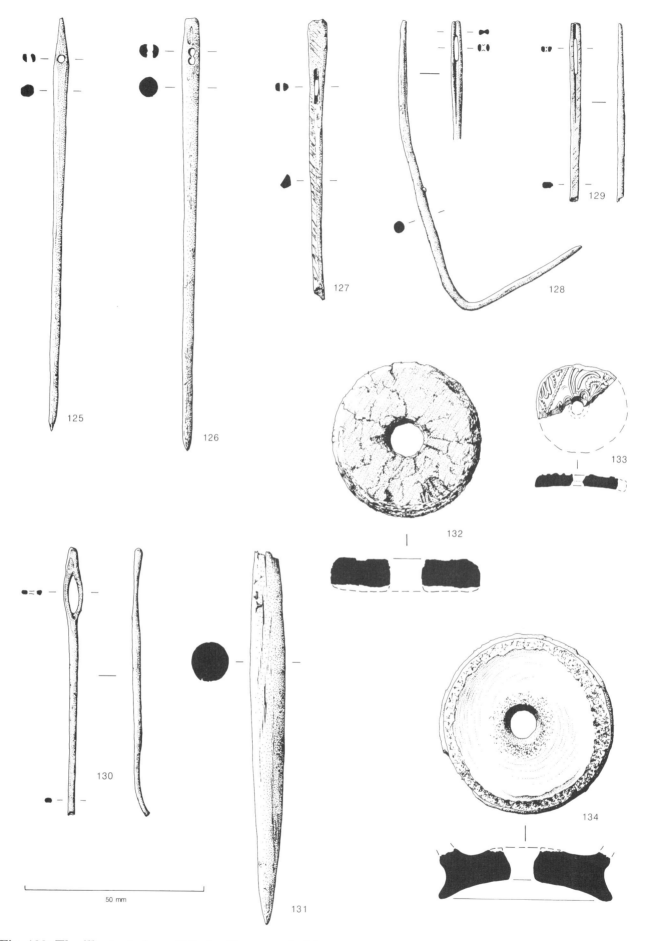

50 mm

Fig. 128: *The illustrated small finds: Category 3 objects used in the manufacture or working of textiles 125-134*

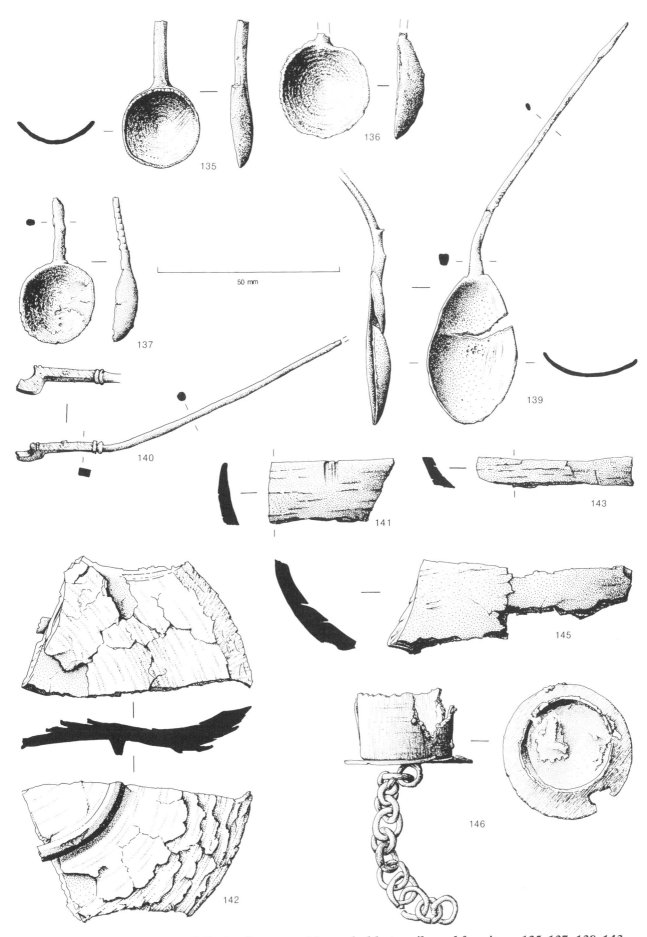

Fig. 129: *The illustrated small finds: Category 4 household utensils and furniture 135-137, 139-143, 145-146*

Furniture fragments or fittings

Bone inlay

149) Sf88 (3618) F763 338/3 Ph.6A Gravel quarry. Bow-tie shaped inlay fragment cut from a longbone, thus giving a slightly curved profile and remains of cancellous bone on the internal, concave surface. External surface is decorated with two ring and dot motifs placed centrally in each triangle. Length 44mm, width 28mm, thickness 8mm.

150) Sf 7 (358) F216 120/2 Ph.9 well. Incomplete inlay fragment. Flat sheet, with upper surface decorated with incised ring and dot motifs. The motifs comprise three concentric circles around a central dot, and are arranged into two rows, and some overlap along the centre line. The sheet is pierced by a single circular perforation of 1mm diameter for attachment.

Similar pieces incorporating the same motif come from other Leicester sites including Jewry Wall (Kenyon 1948, 269, fig.92.2), and Blue Boar Lane (Lentowicz, forthcoming no.50)

Bone furniture handle or box hinge

151) Sf97 (3884) F781 333/1 Ph.5G Pit. Cylindrical fitting made from the shaft of a longbone, the centre of which has been hollowed presumably to accommodate a ?metal insert. Transverse decoration moulded (lathe-turned) and incised. The ends are recessed possibly through wear due to revolving on insert. Length 45mm, diameter 22mm.

The exact function of this object is uncertain. Shorter cylinders of similar diameter and decoration from Colchester are thought to be hinge spacers (Crummy 1983, 121, fig.131.4097), and objects of a similar size with perforations through the side, appear to be hinges, the functioning of which is explained in detail (Waugh and Goodburn 1972, 149 and fig.54.186-92). If this is not a handle, then it is most likely to be a long hinge spacer. Examples of bone hinges from London are known to have wooden rather than metal inserts (Jones 1984, 19-22)

Box fittings

152) Sf2241 (516) F263 120/5 Ph.9 Pit. A square sheet with cut off corners and repoussée (in relief) decoration, punched from the inside, comprising five bosses, each surrounded by ten smaller bosses. The border is defined by a line of similarly sized bosses, overlapping with those of the rings. Length of sheet 26mm, thickness 0.5mm.

Appears to be a plate for attachment to an ?organic surface, but there is no evidence for tacking, riveting, or soldering. Context suggests a medieval date.

153) Sf2209 (1140) F395 141/5 Ph.3B Spread. Corner fitting, diamond shaped with lobed terminal which are perforated for attachment. Length 72mm, width 23mm, thickness 0.5mm.

154) Sf2340 (1192) F412 186/4 Ph.3C Pit. Corner fitting. Triangular with lobed terminal and two perforations. Length 55mm, width 22mm, thickness 0.5mm .

The context of 153 and 154 suggests a Roman date.

155) Sf2017 (264) F217 126/3 Ph.9 Gravel? Pit. Base of octagonal box of copper alloy sheet with straight-sided walls. Each angle has a rounded pillar-moulding.
Width 37mm, height 9mm.

The context suggests a medieval date before 1400

Querns

The remains of seven quernstones were recovered, only one of which (4588 or 4592) is complete enough to illustrate. Two stone types are represented, a coarse sandstone, and lava from the Rhineland represented by only two small fragments.

155A) Sf4592 (801) F343 Ph.3B Quarter section of upper stone with central perforation and groove for insertion of rod or attachment to allow rotation. Made from coarse sandstone.

Category 5: Objects associated with recreation (figs. 131-132)

Gaming counters or roundels

A total of 45 objects belonging to this category were recorded, one of glass, 13 of bone, 17 ceramic, 12 of slate, and two of other stone.

The question of function, especially for counters manufactured from pottery sherds, has been discussed at length (Crummy 1983, 93, Cooper, forthcoming). While the small, well-made roundels clearly appear to be counters for board games, debate surrounds the larger and often rougher examples (?>50mm diameter) usually made from large thick pot sherds or in some cases readily available stone fragments, such as slate tile used in Leicester, and micaceous sandstone wall-facing as at Catterick, Yorks. (Cooper, forthcoming c). Use as lids is a possibility, but they would only be suitable for very narrow-necked vessels such as flagons. It is most likely that they were used for ground-based games and were perhaps manufactured on the spot for immediate use during the 'lunch break'.

Glass and bone counters would have involved some form of workshop facility, although the latter would presumably have been the easiest to produce at the household level with access to a lathe. Some work has been done to elucidate their chronological development. Data has been collected together from the legionary fortress of Caerleon (Greep, 1986) and fortress/ colonia sites of Colchester (Crummy 1983 and York (Cool et al. 1995, table 125) in an attempt to place the York material in context. The evidence from Causeway Lane is therefore presented to build on this foundation and draw comparisons.

Table 52: *Chronological distribution of bone and glass counters from Causeway Lane.*

Period	Bone Type 1	Bone Type 2	Glass	Total
2 (AD50-120)	2	-	-	2
3 (AD120-200)	1	2	-	3
4 (AD200-250)	-	1	-	1
5 (AD250-300)	1	2	1	4
6 (Post 300)	1	-	-	1
Unpha/Resid.	1	2	-	3
Totals	6	7	1	14

The evidence from Caerleon suggests ths glass counters are most common in the late first and early second century and this might account for the single occurrence here which is probably in a residual context. Bone counters of Type 1 are also most common in the early deposit from the fortress baths (AD 75-110) coinciding with earliest bone examples from Causeway Lane. Those of Type 2 are commoner in the later drain deposit (late second/early third cent.), which is consistent with the Causeway Lane evidence where they do not occur before AD 120 and are spread between deposits of phases 3 to 5. The absence of Type 3 counters is unusual judging from their contribution of *c.*25% to the other sites throughout the Roman Period, but the small sample size may be responsible for this anomaly.

Glass

156) Sf3014 (1515) F463 160/4 Ph.5A Pit. Plano-convex glass counter of ovoid shape, manufactured in dark glass which has a white patinated surface. The base is scratched perhaps through wear. Maximum diameter 13mm, height 5mm.

The size makes it comparable to the smaller examples from Colchester (Crummy 1983, 92, fig.95.2286 and 2287).

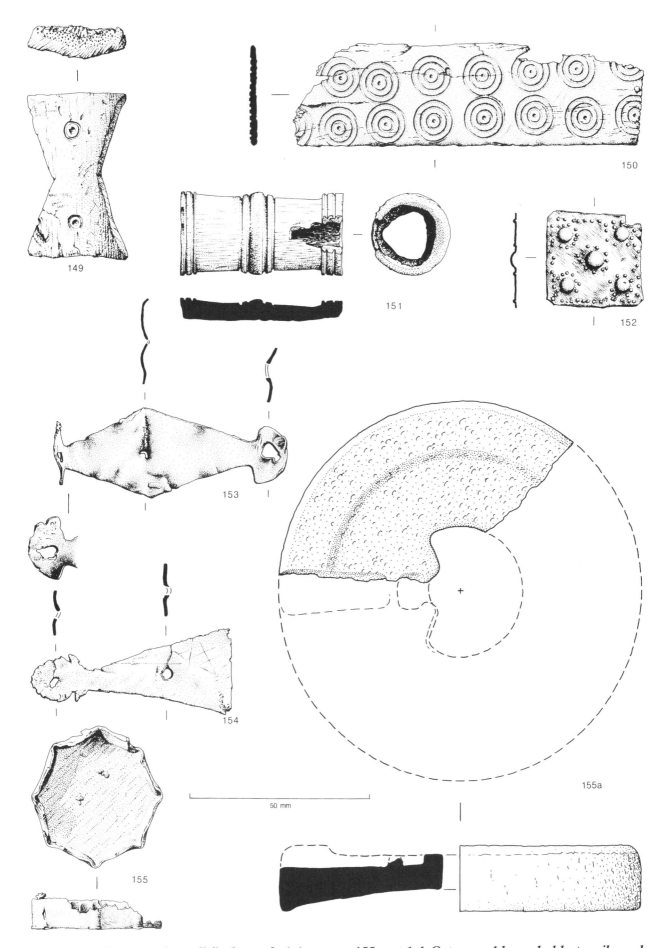

Fig. 130: *The illustrated small finds: scale 1:1, except 155a, at 1:4. Category 4 household utensils and furniture 149-155a*

Bone

Of the 13 examples, six are of Crummy's Type 1 (1983, 91) equivalent to Kenyon's Type A (1948, 266) and are plain, while the other seven belong to Type 2 (Kenyon's Type B), and are decorated. No convex counters (Crummy Type 3) were recorded. All appear to have been manufactured by face-plate turning on a lathe, which leaves the characteristic central indentation on the obverse (except 159 and 160). A further characteristic is the occurrence of worn or bevelled areas on opposed edges on the reverse of a number of examples, which is due, not to wear, but to the use of a longbone, the curved edges of which dictate that a flat surface cannot be achieved across the whole face of the counter (MacGregor 1985, 4). In a similar fashion to bone hairpins, these counters occur with a wide variety of shapes and concentric decoration and this probably reflects a relatively local production in small workshops or possibly within the household.

Both types of counter appear to have been in use from the beginning of the Roman period on the site, with only one of each occurring later than AD 200 in a Roman context.

Type 1

157) Sf30 (893) 162/5 Ph.5B. Small counter with flat surfaces, highly polished and discoloured. Carinated profile. Diameter 14mm, thickness 3mm.

158) Sf56 (1219) F417 150/1 Ph.3B Cobble Spread. Similar to 157 above with flat faces, but larger. Diameter 20mm, thickness 3mm.

159) Sf89 (1580) 144/1 Ph.2D. Small counter, no central lathe mark. Flat surfaces and rounded edges. Diameter 14mm, thickness 2.5mm.

160) Sf90 (1511) 144/1 Ph.2D. Small counter, almost identical to 159 above with no lathe mark. One surface highly polished. Carinated profile. Diameter 15mm, thickness 2mm.

161) Sf95 (3836) F766 367/1 Ph.6A. Large counter with flat reverse and obverse countersunk. Bevelled patches. Diameter 25mm, thickness 3mm.

162) Sf128 (3892) F762 332/3 Unphased ?Pit. As 95, reverse flat and obverse countersunk. Diameter 19mm, thickness 2.5mm.

Type 2

163) Sf19 (687) F317 163/1 Ph.5B Post hole. A small, straight-sided counter, the obverse decorated with two evenly spaced concentric grooves. Diameter 14mm, thickness 3mm.

164) Sf20 (578) 161/1 Ph.5A. Obverse decorated with six concentric grooves, the outermost being the deepest. Diameter 22mm, thickness 3mm.

165) Sf49 (200) 100/1 Ph.12. Half counter with very deep central lathe mark which almost penetrates right through, surrounded by two concentric grooves. Diameter 24mm.

166) Sf57 (1137) F412 186/4 Ph.3C Pit. Highly polished through wear. Obverse is decorated with four concentric grooves. The reverse is incised with a faint graffito.

167) Sf64 (1023) F255 174/2 Ph.4A Pit. Fragment of a counter or possibly inlay. Obverse decorated with three concentric rings.

168) Sf117 (671) F334 187/1 Ph.3D Pit. Obverse decorated with four concentric rings. Diameter 17mm, thickness 2mm.

169) Sf127 (3880) F762 332/3 Unphased. Quarter fragment of counter. Obverse decorated with five concentric rings. Diameter 20mm, thickness 2mm.

Slate

The use of Swithland slate from the nearby Charnwood area for roofing in Roman Leicestershire provided a ready-flattened scrap material suitable for easy conversion into roundels. The effort put into the production of the majority was minimal, with little attempt to round off the unevenly pecked edges. The twelve examples in the assemblage range from 20mm in diameter (4590) to 75mm with most falling either between 30 and 40mm or 60 to 70mm. Four are catalogued here to demonstrate the range.

170) Sf4572 (3501) 301/1 Ph.12. Small example possibly with an 'X' scratched faintly on one face denoting a value of ten. Diameter 30mm, thickness 2mm.

171) Sf4582 (3879) F756 359/4 Ph.5G Cut. Large and well-made with ground edges for 70% of the circumference, rest damaged. Diameter 75mm, thickness 7mm.

172) Sf4591 (3954) 360/1 F798 Ph.5E Pit. Very similar to 171 above, with highly polished faces which are faintly striated. Highly polished on same spot as if held between finger and thumb. Diameter 58mm, thickness 5mm.

173) Sf 4593 US. Edges bevelled with smooth but not polished surfaces probably not made from a tile fragment. The upper (narrower) face incised with XXXX to denote forty. Diameter 40mm, thickness 3.5mm.

Other stone

In two instances, naturally worn pebbles rather than slate have been employed. Both come from medieval contexts, and their size is comparable to the smallest of the ceramic, bone or glass examples.

174) Sf4558 (394) F204 114/5 Ph.9 gravel pit. Small counter with ovoid or plano-convex section. Probably a naturally rounded pebble. Surface pitted. Diameter 18mm, thickness 5mm.

175) Sf4562 (2703) F615 254/9 Ph.9 Structure? Soft, fine-grained rock. Plano-convex section, with underside recessed. Upper surface polished. Diameter 16mm, thickness 2.5mm

Ceramic

Twelve counters made from Roman potsherds and a further five in medieval fabrics have been recorded, and it is quite possible that further examples remain unrecognised within the pottery assemblage since this is the most readily available and easily manipulated raw material for counters. Four Roman examples have been illustrated to show the range of size. The sherds of thin bodied vessels in samian, greyware and white ware are most suitable for counters between 15mm and c.30mm, whilst the sherds of thicker storage jars in calcite-gritted and grog-tempered fabrics, or amphorae and tile have been used for those between 40mm and 70mm in diameter.

The medieval examples all derive from contexts, dating before 1400 AD.

176) Sf4511 (1052) 154/1 Ph.3B. Small counter in whiteware, with straight sides. Diameter 18mm, thickness 2.5mm.

177) (261) F210 187/1 Ph.3D. Small counter in whiteware. Diameter 15mm, thickness 3.5mm.

178) (827) 164/1 Ph.5C. Large counter made from sherd of Dressel 20 amphora (fabric AM9A) with ground straight edges. Diameter 60mm, thickness 10mm.

179) (3574) F726 310/1 Ph.9. Counter made from sherd of plain samian ware, with ground edges. Diameter 22mm, thickness 7mm.

Spherical stones and sling shots

180) Sf4559 (2000) 296/1 Ph.12. Two small spherical stones, one is a naturally spherical flint or marble pebble, the other is a fine sandstone which appears to have been ground into a perfect sphere. Diameter of both 15mm. Not illustrated.

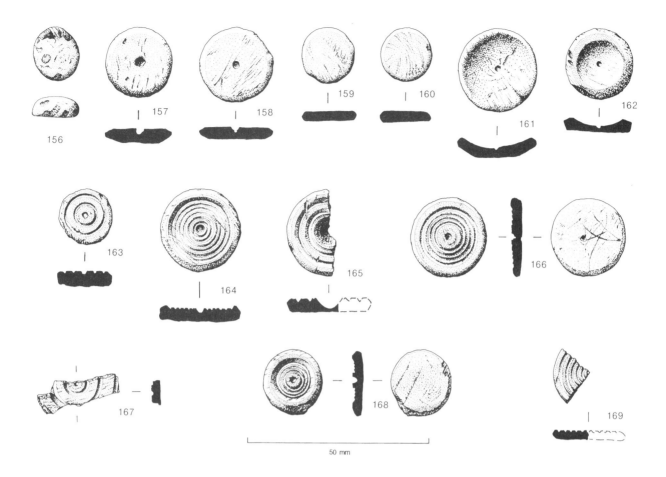

50 mm

Fig. 131: *The illustrated small finds: Category 5 bone counters 156-159*

Possibly used for gaming. Similar examples come from sites of Roman date at Empingham, Rutland, (Fraser forthcoming no.60) and Mallows Cotton, Northants. (Cooper, unpublished archive report for C.A.S.), but their dating is uncertain and a medieval or post-medieval provenance cannot be ruled out.

Four examples of larger, naturally spherical flint pebbles ranging in diameter from 35-75mm have been recorded. One example comes from a Roman context, the others are medieval and later. Such stones may have been specifically selected as slingshots.

Bone dice

Two single examples were recovered and are of uncertain date.

181) Sf37 (223) F205 126/2 Ph.10 Well. Small cuboid with sides of 6mm. Motifs made from single ring and dot and rather irregularly arranged. Opposing faces do not add up to seven, with 1 and 5 needing to be interchanged, probably due to a manufacturing error.

182) Sf9023 (8000) Unphased. Die made from a length of long bone of square section which is less than the width giving four faces of rectangular section. The numbers are represented by double ring and dot motifs. Two faces represent 'two', one of which appears to have originally been a 'four' but the opposing corners were filed down to try and remove the two extra motifs. Trials show that the die most commonly falls on to the square sides representing 'two' and 'three'. Dimensions 11mm x 10mm x 8mm.

Category 8: Objects associated with transport (fig. 133)

Harness fittings

183) Sf1714 (410) Ph.9 Complete. Iron D-shaped two-piece buckle frame of rectangular section, with remains of pin attached to bar. Length 34mm, width of bar 41mm.

Heavy appearance indicates use as a harness buckle, a close parallel coming from Southampton (Harvey 1975, 277, Fig.250.1973), of 11th-12th century date.

Spurs

Two spurs have been recorded, one in copper alloy of Roman date and one of iron from a medieval context. Roman spurs are relatively unusual finds and their occurrence at sites such as Corbridge have been taken to indicate the presence of auxiliary units from east of the Rhine (Allason- Jones 1988, fig.84.153 and 154). Evidence for Roman spurs in Britain has been discussed by Shortt (1959, 61-76), and Manning (1985, 69-70).

184) Sf2362 (1678) F1012 149/3 Ph.2H Post hole. Copper alloy. Complete single spur with straight arms and terminals comprising transverse bar and external grooves. The point is a simple conical prick soldered onto the thickened part of the arm. Not set centrally. Length 60mm, width 80mm.

The simple prick appears most commonly on the so-called hook spur (Manning 1985, fig.18.1) which appears to be rare in Britain, next to the commoner loop and rivet types (Manning 1985, fig.18.2 and 3), and the method of attachment displayed by this example is not paralleled by any of the examples cited by Shortt or Manning.

The form is however also similar to one of Viking date, Type

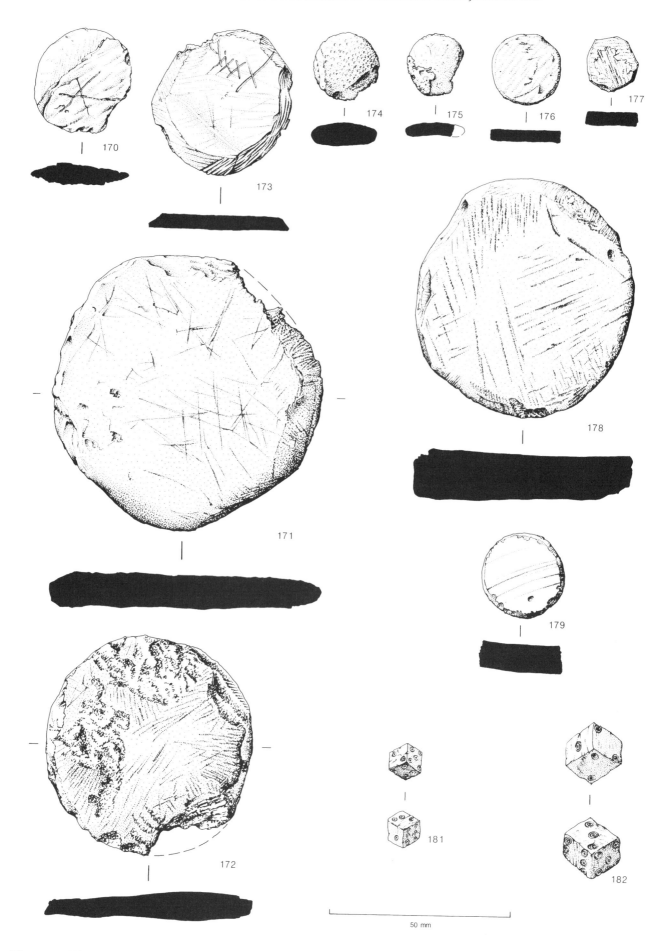

Fig. 132: *The illustrated small finds: Category 5 stone counters and bone dice 170-179, 181, 182*

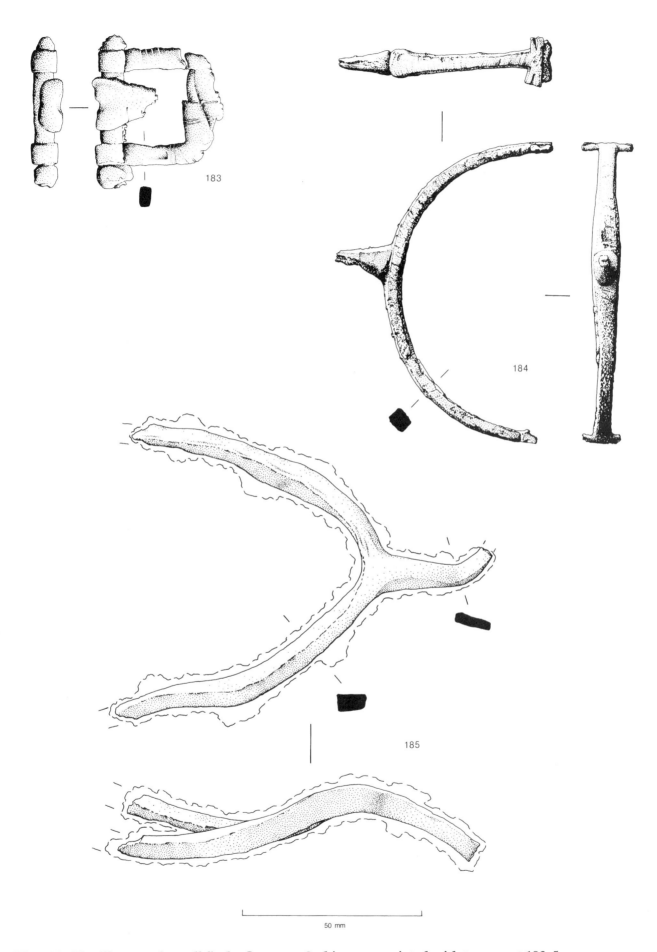

50 mm

Fig. 133: *The illustrated small finds: Category 8 objects associated with transport 183-5*

1 (HMSO 1954, 95, fig.28), the simple conical point dating from the 11th century onwards to the mid-12th when the transition to curved arms took place. However, the early Roman context makes this attribution highly unlikely.

185) Sf1028 (275) F216 120/3 Ph.9 Well. Incomplete iron spur in three pieces (drawn from x-ray). Length 110mm, width 80mm.

The curving arms would suggest a date from the later 12th century onwards (HMSO 1954, 95, fig.28).

Category 10: Tools (fig. 134)

Tool handle pommel

188) Sf2282 (3533) F711 332/1 Ph.2L pit/well. Complete. A mount of splayed triangles was presumably attached to a wooden handle, and is surmounted by a suspension loop decorated with three knob-like projections. Length 37mm, width 33mm.

No close parallels have been traced for this pommel which appears to be of later first or early second century date.

Knives/cleavers

A total of 59 iron knife blade fragments have been identified, 36 of which derive from Roman contexts, 20 from medieval contexts and three from the post-medieval. All except 189 below are too incomplete to allow any further conclusive classification by Manning's (1985) typology or Cowgill's typology of medieval material from London (Cowgill *et al.* 1987). Many of the Roman examples probably belong to Manning's Types 13-15 representing general purpose knives in use throughout the Roman period, the shapes becoming much distorted by frequent whetting (Manning 1985, 114).

189) Sf6128 (3804) F756 359/4 Ph.5G Incomplete Fe knife blade probably of Manning's (1985) Type 14 with arched back. The tip and tang are missing. A small rectangular stamp inlaid with copper contains the name PALM. Length 68mm, width 21mm, thickness 1.5mm.

Examples of knives stamped by their makers are rare. Only eight have been recorded in Britain, with five from London, and one each from Colchester, Catterick and Chesterholm (Collingwood and Wright, 1991, 58, RIB 2428). That from Catterick is considered to be an import, and the concentration in London (with two makers, Basilius and Martialis) is taken to indicate a restricted market with other areas provided for by local makers not using stamps (Collingwood and Wright, 1991, 58). This find is therefore significant in indicating the possible existence of recognised workshop in Leicester dating to the first half of the third century or earlier.

Hones

Nine complete or fragmentary hones of Roman date were recovered, six of which are in a light grey, slightly calcareous sandstone possibly originating from the Spilsby sandstones of Lincolnshire. These are made in short lengths (80-90mm) of rectangular section (up to *c.*25mm), and wear produces a 'dog bone' appearance of ovoid section. Three other stone types are also represented. 4566 is of a finer grey sandstone of square section, 4568 is of brown sandstone of plano-convex section and 4573 is in a micaceous red sandstone and also of plano-convex section.

All eight stratified examples come from first or second century contexts. Three are catalogued to show the range.

190) Sf4556 (260) F210 187/1 Ph.3D. ?Spilsby sandstone Heavily worn 84mm x 24mm x 16mm.

191) Sf4566 (859) F343 141/4 Ph.3B Ditch. In a very fine grey sandstone. Square section with partial ware 36mm x 12mm x 12mm

192) Sf4573 (2928) F671 208/1 Ph.1C. In a micaceous red sandstone. Slightly bowed. Plano-convex section. 79mm x 21mm x 13mm.

Smoothing implement

193) Sf4512 (3912) F763 338/3 Ph.6A Gravel quarry. Made from the body sherd of an amphora (fabric AM12), ground into a leaf shape. The areas of wear are confined to the edges of the concave surface, particularly at the pointed end.

A similar object also made from an amphora sherd came from excavations at Billingsgate Buildings, London (Green 1980, 86 and fig.49.424). Exact function uncertain.

Category 11: Fasteners and fittings (fig. 135)

Loop headed pin

194) Sf2192 (1052) 154/1 Ph.3B. Complete copper alloy pin with a looped head. The shaft is slightly swollen and is of circular section. Length 160mm, width of shaft 4mm.

Uncertain function. Too long and head too wide to be suitable as a sewing needle.

Nails

Copper alloy nails

A selection of the more complete examples has been catalogued to illustrated the range.

With Bun-shaped Head

195) Sf9052 (8005) F931 Unphased. Diameter of head 5mm, shaft length 17mm.

A Roman type probably used for furniture upholstery (Crummy 1983, 115).

With Flat Head

196) Sf9049 (8032) 116/3 F916 Ph.9 Shaft of circular section. Diameter 20mm, shaft length 30mm.

197) Sf9007 (8001) 100/1 Ph.12. Upper surface of head stamped with EP. Shaft of square section. Diameter 8mm, length 38mm. L. Victorian roofing nail.

Iron nails

3955 complete or fragmentary iron nails were recorded, of which 2158 (55%) were complete enough to allow classification by Manning's British Museum typology for Roman examples (1985, 134, fig. 32). While the larger proportion come from Roman contexts and many more must be residual Roman examples in later deposits, their similarity dictates than an unquantifiable amount must be of medieval or later date. Of those classified, the majority 1647 (76%) were of Type 1B with flat heads and square sectioned tapering stems. Only four examples of the usually much rarer Type 2 were recorded, and the remainder (507 or 24%) were of Type 10 hobnails.

Only 40 examples of Type 1B were considered complete enough to allow accurate measurement, and while they ranged from 46mm to 140mm in length (with none falling into the 1A category over 150mm), the majority fell between 45mm and 75mm, with 55mm appearing as a common standard length. This pattern is clearly reflected by the numerous less complete examples and corresponds with the high percentage (87.3%) of Type E (40mm-70mm, equivalent to Type 1B) in the Inchtuthil Hoard (Manning 1985, 134). This size range is the most suitable for use in timber construction as clearly reflected in the timber fortress hoard and where quantified studies from other non-military sites have been undertaken it is clear that the pattern is repeated. For example, work by Rhodes (1991, 132-38) on the Bucklersbury House hoard from the Middle Walbrook Valley

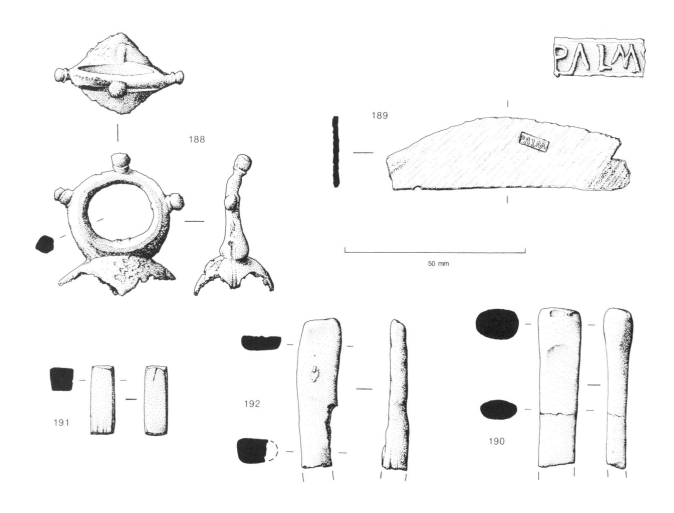

Fig. 134: *The illustrated small finds: Category 10 tools 188-192*

in London demonstrates the predominance of Type 1B nails of between 50-60mm as well as a general similarity to the assemblages from Inchtuthil, Brading Villa and Angel Court, London.

The very low number of Type 2, is perhaps of significance, but given the generally poor condition of many of the nails (most identifications being undertaken from x-rays), and the difficulty of conclusive identification when the head is damaged by use, dictates that some may have been unclassified. The lengths recorded were 26mm and 61mm which are relatively small. The lack of Manning's Types 3-9 in such a large assemblage may also be due to the difficulties outlined above. The 1797 unclassified examples comprised many where head identification was inconclusive, though it may be assumed that the bulk probably belonged to Type 1, the remainder being shaft fragments.

In contrast, the proportion of Type 10 hobnails appears quite high, although the lack of comparitive data other than from cemeteries such as Lankhills and Poundbury, besides the possible confusion with shorter examples of Manning's Type 8, makes any assessment difficult. Many occurred in clumps representing parts of decayed shoe soles, and when it is considered that each shoe sole requires up to fifty hobnails (Mills 1993,99), this only amounts to the discard of five pairs across the whole site throughout the Roman period, which places the figure in context.

Studs

Six studs of Roman date were recorded, five of which had flat heads often with down curved edges and in one case a concentric moulding to improve attachment. The remaining example had a domed head. In all cases the shaft was integral and tapering. Silver gilding on the upper surface was recorded on two examples.

With flat heads

198) Sf2168 (989) F392 163/8 Ph.5C Post hole. With concentric moulding. Diameter 18mm, shaft length 8mm.

199) Sf2171 (2722) 253/1 Ph.9. Damaged. Diameter 34mm, shaft length 16mm.

200) Sf2309 (3519) 340/1 Ph.6B. Downturned edges. Traces of silver gilding. Diameter 12mm, shaft length 9mm.

With domed head

201) Sf2061 (522) 164/1 Ph.5C. Damaged. Diameter 13mm, shaft length 7mm.

Mounts

202) Sf9006 (8001) 100/1 Ph.12. Complete copper alloy bar mount of medieval date made from folded sheet with two perforations for attachment by copper wire rivets, one of which is *in situ*. Length 34mm, width 6mm.

Bar mounts were worn vertically across leather belts and a

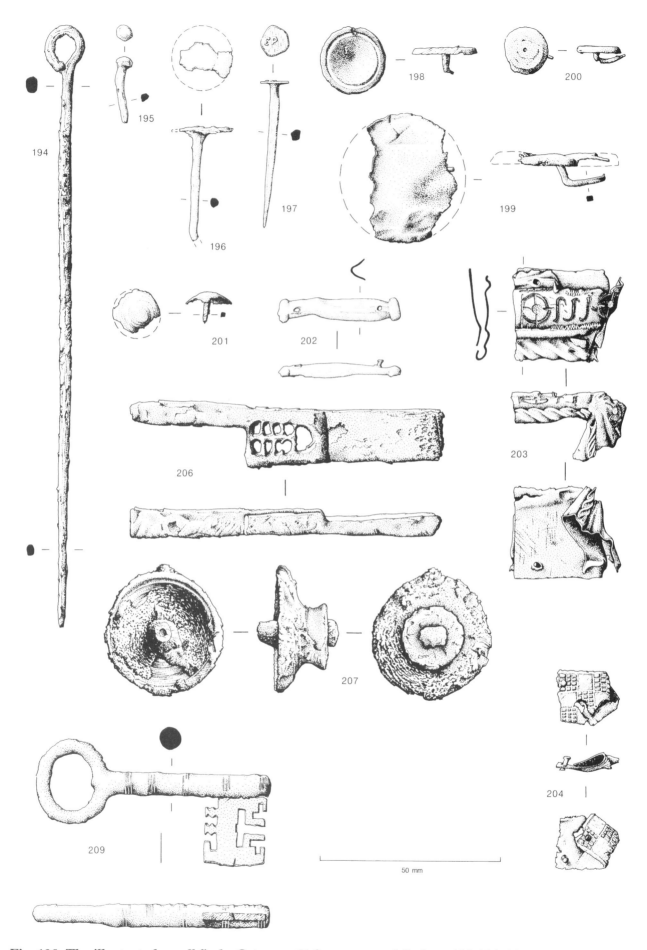

Fig. 135: *The illustrated small finds: Category 11 fasteners and fittings 194-204, 206, 207, 209*

number of parallel examples come from London (Egan and Pritchard 1991, 209 and fig. 134. 1150 and 1151) deriving from Ceramic Phase 9 dated *c*.1270-*c*.1350.

Decorated sheet fittings

203) Sf2048 (2252) F587 260/3 Ph.9 Rectangle of copper alloy sheet folded in half and decorated on the external face. The fold line is deorated with a moulded candy twist. The central panel is decorated with punched circles and incised crosses flanking an interlocking S pattern. Lower edge of the sheet is perforated for attachment. length along fold 30mm.The context suggests a 12th century date.

204) Unprov. Square fragment of sheet folded irregularly. External face decorated with an incised chequer board pattern. Upper and lower edges perforated. Length unfolded 25mm.

205) Sf5014 (2255) F558 261/7 Ph.9 Copper alloy strip of rectangular section, one end curved and sheared off. Upper surface decorated with central groove and incised herring bone pattern. Terminal decorated with incised cross. Not illustrated.

Locks and keys

206) Sf4011 (631) 162/5 Ph.5B. Complete lock bolt cast in copper alloy with a single semicircular cutout and eight small rectangular cutouts. Length 85mm. This has a similar arrangement to an example from Colchester (Crummy 1983, fig. 136.4136).

207) Sf1001 (220) 101/1 Ph.12. Head of a lock pin, the shaft of which has broken to leave a stump of rectangular section. Head is recessed around a central cone. Length 23mm, diameter of head 32mm.

A number of examples are known and have been alternatively identified as bell-shaped studs (e.g. South Shields, Allason-Jones and Miket 1984, 240), and discussed more fully by Allason-Jones 1985. This one is close to an example from Colchester (Crummy 1983, fig.137.4143).

208) Unprov. Incomplete. Fragment of iron barrel lock.

Similar to examples from the medieval village site of Goltho (I. H. Goodall 1990, 185, fig.158.101 and 102). Such locks appear to have been in use before the Norman Conquest, with the Goltho examples dated 1000-1080.

209) Unprov. Complete Fe key. Shaft incised with bands of three rings. Length 66mm, length of cut out 20mm

Category 13: Military equipment (fig. 136)

Finds of military equipment from the town are rare, the most notable being the cavalry cheek piece from Bath Lane (Clay and Mellor 1985, 64 fig.38.2), to which may be added a strap mount from St Peter's Lane (Cooper, forthcoming a, no.226), both of which probably derive from first century military occupation. The scabbard fitting (210) below, however, belongs to a period post-dating any military occupation in Leicester and must represent a casual loss perhaps from personnel passing through the town on the way to the Military North.

Scabbard fitting

210) Sf2341 (1409) 161/1 Ph.5A. Incomplete cast copper-alloy scabbard runner with a ring terminal or suspension loop, chamfered edges, and a single spike for attachment. Length 56mm, width 15mm.

A very similar example comes from the Roman fort at South Shields (Allason-Jones and Miket 1984, 197, no. 3.646). Bishop and Coulston illustrate a range of examples (none with ring terminals), and state that the use of runners or slides for suspension probably came into Roman use through contact with Steppe peoples of the Danubian Zone (1993,112 and fig.80), and their development belongs to the Antonine Period. This present example comes from a phase 5 context dated as third century.

Category 14: Objects associated with religious practices or beliefs (fig. 136)

Figurine

211) Sf4502 (1027) 174/2 Ph.4A. Fragment from the torso of a pipeclay, hollow-cast figurine representing Venus. Length 50mm, width 29mm.

Venus figurines, along with others such as those of 'Dea Nutrix' were mass-produced in Central Gaulish workshops during the first and second centuries, and were particularly popular in the Trajanic to Antonine Period (Jenkins 1986, 205). They formed a cheap alternative to *ex votos* presented to the gods at temples and are associated with women during childbirth (Green 1978 pl.40). There is too little of this example remaining to draw any close stylistic parallels, but examples are widespread in the Military North at South Shields, Carlisle (Green 1978 pl.40 and pl.36), and Catterick (Cooper, forthcoming d, no.1). In civilian areas (Green 1976, 23, fig.13 and pl.14) distribution is fairly even across the Lowland Zone with a concentration in London (Jenkins 1986, 206, 5.1 – 5.6) and the South East and other notable peaks in Colchester and Wroxeter. At least eight examples are now known from Leicester including one from Little Lane (Cooper, forthcoming a, no.229), and a notable concentration of four from the extramural sites of Great Holme Street and the Austin Friars which also included two examples of *dea nutrix* (Boothroyd 1994, nos.101-103).

Category 16: Objects and waste material associated with bone and antler working (fig. 136)

Bone working offcuts

Six pieces of waste material were recovered, three of the illustrated pieces coming from Phase 5 and 6 in Area 3. The extensive Roman quarrying and deliberate backfilling probably indicates that the material is rubbish derived from activity outside the immediate area. The offcut shapes and dimensions are similar to those derived from the Balkerne Lane area of Colchester (Crummy 1983, 150 and fig.185).

212) Sf122 (3795) F768 362/3 Ph.5F Pit? Parallel sided offcut from longbone. Length 75mm, width 8mm.

213) Sf126 (3825) 764 339/4 Ph.5E Pit? Parallel sided offcut from longbone. Length 51mm, width 7mm.

214) Sf124 (3879) F756 359/4 Ph.5G Cut. Tapering offcut from longbone. Length 120mm, width 9mm.

215) Sf9091 (8000) Unphased. Plano-convex fragment from outer edge of a large longbone, sawn on three sides. Waste from production of straight edged lengths. Not illustrated.

Antler

216) Sf112 (3879) F756 359/4 Ph.5G Curving antler tine sawn transversely. Length 110mm, diameter 25mm. Probably intended for production of a knife handle.

Category 17: Objects and waste materials associated with flint knapping (fig. 136)

Thirty nine pieces of worked flint, presumably all of prehistoric date, were recovered as residual finds in all phases of activity on the site. The greater proportion (33) are struck flakes (including blade-like flakes), without retouch, the remainder comprise an end-scraper and a blade-like flake with retouch (catalogued below), a possible core and three other pieces with retouch.

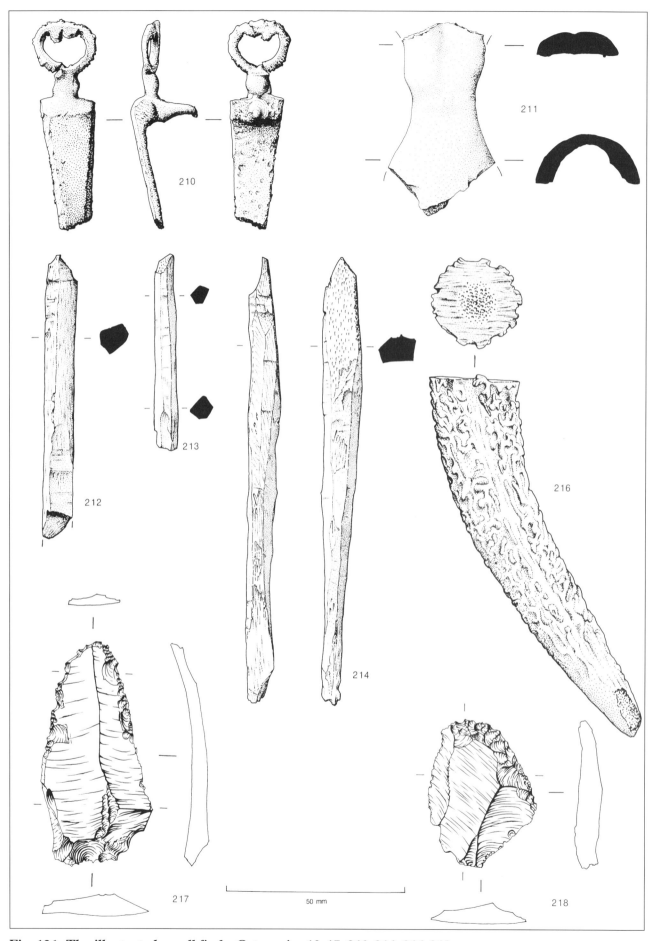

Fig. 136: *The illustrated small finds: Categories 13-17, 210-214, 216-218*

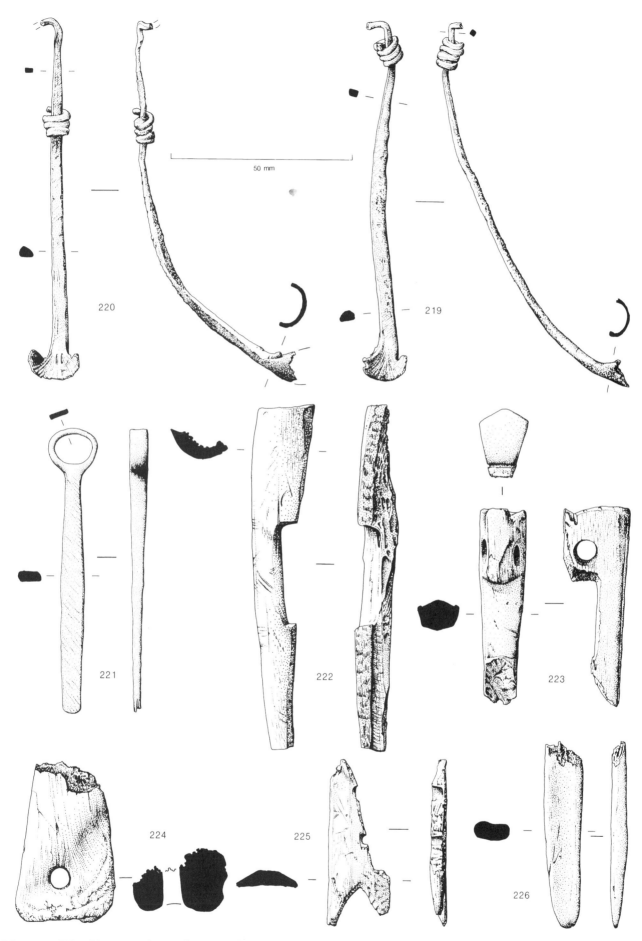

Fig. 137: *The illustrated small finds: Category 18 objects of uncertain function 219-226*

217) Sf7002 (1377) 130/5 Ph.1B. Complete end-scraper of Neolithic date.

218) Sf 7022 (2937) 207/5 Ph.3G. Blade-like flake with retouched end.

Category 18: Objects of uncertain function (fig. 137)

Copper alloy

219) Sf2149 (952) 158/4 Ph.5A.

and 220) Sf2182 (1060) 154/1 Ph.3B.

These two objects are described together as they appear to form identical elements of a single, composite object, of uncertain function. Both are formed from a single (?cast) piece of copper alloy, of plano-convex section, smoothly curving so that the flat surface is internal. One end opens into a spoon-like bowl, which in neither example is complete; the other end tapers and is bent into a right-angle as if to form a spiral, which in both cases has been clipped. In both cases a separate length of wire has been wound three times around the upper part of the shaft and clipped. (2149) Length 110mm, width of bowl 17mm.

The pair would appear to represent the suspension arms of a so-called 'arm purse' a complete example of which came from a Roman quarry at Barcombe, south of Housesteads on Hadrian's Wall in 1835, lost during construction of the wall. Such purses were probably suspended from belts (de la Bedoyere 1989, 128 and fig.76a).

221) Sf1792 (1495) F318 Ph.3B. Loop-headed implement with shaft of rectangular section tapering to a flattened terminal. Length 76mm, width of shaft 6mm.

Looped head suggests suspension. Rather heavy appearance to have a toiletry function.

Bone

222) Sf52 (1017) F343 141/2 Ph.3B ditch. Length of worked bone from a hollowed, possibly tapering, cylinder with part of a rectangular cut out half way along the length. Length 91mm, width 16mm.

Two more complete examples of hollow cylinders with rectangular cutouts on one side come from Colchester (Crummy 1983, 168, fig. 209.4747 and 4748) and are possibly toggles.

223) Sf72 (3519) 340/1 Ph.6B. Incomplete object comprising a length of bone of polygonal section, incorporating a rectangular cut out, with a circular perforation above. Length 52mm, width 14mm.

224) Sf73 (3501) 301/1 Ph.12. Head of a longbone, with a circular perforation. No other signs of working. Length 42mm, width 26mm.

225) Sf93 (3836) F766 367/1 Ph.6A pit. Incomplete, flat object with plano-convex section. Appears to taper, with V-shaped cut out at the widest end, and evidence for two small perforations set longitudinally above it probably for attachment. Length 44mm, width 18mm.

The object is comparable to two possible pieces of inlay of Roman date from Colchester with plano-convex section which also have peg holes along their length (Crummy 1983, 84, fig. 88.2161 and 2162).

226) Unprov. Incomplete length of woked bone broken at one end. Profile worn with shaft tapering to a rounded terminal. Length 50mm, width 10mm. Possibly a form of smoothing implement.

THE ROMAN GLASS

Siân Davies

Introduction

The excavations at Causeway Lane produced a total of 1,241 fragments of Roman glass; 538 fragments of window glass and 677 from vessels. A further 26 unidentifiable fragments were recovered from samples. A minimum of 43 vessels was identified and these offer a useful contribution to our knowledge on the range and use of glass vessels within Leicester from the mid first to fourth century AD. The minimum number of vessels in use at a particular time may be summarised as follows: Pre-Flavian and Flavian...10, late first to mid second century...14, first and second century containers...7, late second and third centuries...13, fourth century...2. Since the majority of the glass may be dated to between the late first and the late second century, with apparently little residual material present within the Roman phases of Area 1, discussion of the material in relation to the site will concentrate on this area. Numbers in parentheses refer to the catalogue.

The condition of the glass was very good, iridescence was slight and there was very little post depositional wear on robust fragments such as bases, rims and handles. The range of forms present are those quite commonly found on Romano-British sites, although the opaque blue fragment (4) is quite uncommon and the decorated hemispherical cup (29) is distinctive in its quality of glass and decoration. The proportions of glass by colour may be summarised as follows:- Blue/green 63%, Colourless 24%, Polychrome/monochrome 5%, Yellow & Green Colourless 7%, Bubbly Green >1%

Table 53: *Fragment totals including phased and unphased material from the site.*

Area	1	2	3	Totals
Vessel	450	90	137	677
Window	505	9	24	538
Unclass	19	4	3	26
Total	974	103	164	1241

Table 54: *Fragment totals from Roman phases.*

Area	1	2	3	Totals
Vessel	386	30	117	533
Window	414	1	20	435
Totals	800	31	137	968

The pre-Flavian and Flavian vessels

A minimum of ten vessels were identified as having their main period of use during the pre-Flavian or Flavian period. Glass in use during much of the first century is characterised by use of strongly coloured monochrome and polychrome glass, including deep blue, dark yellow brown, emerald green, amber etc. Many of these colours continued to be produced into the Flavian period.

A total of 11 fragments from pillar moulded bowls (Isings 1957, form 3; Cool & Price 1995 nos.1-184) were identified representing a minimum of three vessels.

The method of manufacture for these vessels is debated (Cool & Price 1993, 2) but the more widely accepted method is that of flat casting and then shaping over a bowl shaped former. It is possible that fragments (2) and (3) came from shallow segmental bowls as the rim diameters are quite wide.

The rims of these vessels are fairly thick and wheel polished internally and externally. The body exterior is fire polished and the interior wheel polished making even small body fragments from these vessels quite diagnostic.

(1) is a fragment from a polychrome bowl of deep blue glass with opaque white and yellow marbling. This colour combination is frequently found but it is difficult to assess how common it was as the opaque yellow often only appears in patches and not all fragments may indicate that they originated from a three coloured bowl (Cool & Price forthcoming b). Blue, yellow and white colour combination bowls have been recorded from a number of sites including Wroxeter (*ibid.*, no 4-6), Caersws (Cool & Price 1989, no.1), Richborough (Bushe-Fox 1932, plxv, 59) and Camulodunum (Harden 1947, no.13).

A polychrome pillar moulded bowl of emerald green glass with opaque yellow and red marbling was recorded from the Blue Boar Lane site in Leicester (Cool & Price forthcoming b no.1). Polychrome pillar moulded bowls were in use primarily during the first half of the first century (Berger 1960, 10), however, sites occupied later do produce a small proportion of these vessels. The bowls were also produced in strongly coloured monochrome glass but the most common colour found is blue/green of which two vessels were represented by the rim fragment nos. 2 and 3. Blue/green bowls continued in production into the Flavian period (Cool & Price forthcoming a).

(4) is a very small fragment of opaque violet blue glass. One surface remains and this shows evidence for it being from a cast and ground vessel. Opaque cast vessels are quite uncommon on Romano-British sites (Cool & Price forthcoming a). Their use is believed to have ended around the time of the conquest although fragments do appear in contexts dated to the Claudian or early Neronian period (Cool & Price 1989, 32). The Claudio-Neronian site of Sheepen in Colchester has produced the largest number of opaque vessel fragments from a Romano-British site (Charlesworth 1985b mf3, f6, no.33).

(18) and (47) are rim fragments from Hofheim cups (Isings form 12) (Cool & Price 1995 nos. 279-331) so called due to the large quantities of these cups found at the Claudian fort of Hofheim (Harden & Price 1971, 321). They are extremely common on sites occupied during the pre-Flavian period (Cool & Price forthcoming a). (18) is a green/ yellow colourless vessel and (47) blue/green. These vessels were produced in a variety of colours but blue/green is most commonly found. The cups are distinctive with cracked off, ground and slightly inturned rims, a wheel cut groove just below the rim and a concave base. The body is frequently decorated with horizontal abraded bands and the overall shape of the cups may vary from cylindrical to hemispherical. The base fragment (59) in blue/green glass may have come from this type of vessel.

Numerous Hofheim cups are often recorded from sites with sizeable first century assemblages such as Colchester and Wroxeter, while an emerald green Hofheim cup was recovered from the Blue Boar Lane in Leicester (Cool & Price forthcoming b no.32, 5 & 6). These vessels are dated predominately to the Claudian and Neronian period and become less common after the early Flavian period (Cool & Price 1995).

One of the most common tableware forms in use from the late first century was the tubular rimmed bowl (Isings form 44 & 45), (Cool & Price 1995 nos. 6, 30-92). The rim fragments are distinctive with the rim edge rolled outward and down creating a hollow tube. The bowls were produced in a shallow segmental (Isings form 44) and a deep cylindrical form (Isings form 45) and usually had applied pad bases or applied true base rings.

Four tubular rim fragments were identified representing a minimum of four vessels, (13), (20), (49), (50) and one possible base fragment (58). The average rim diameter from these fragments was 180mm.

(13) is a fragment from a deep cylindrical bowl in yellow/green colourless glass, (20) of light green glass and nos. (49, 50) and the applied true base ring fragment (58) were blue/green. Although these vessels were produced in a wide range of colours blue/green was by far the most common and rims from these bowls are extremely common finds on Romano-British sites of this period.

Fragments of yellow/green bowls have been found at Caersws (Cool & Price 1989 no.32) and Greyhound Yard, Dorchester (Cool & Price 1993 no. 35) and fragments of light green bowls at Wroxeter (Cool & Price 1993, 160 no.24 fig 84), Richborough (Bushe-Fox 1949, no. 372) in a context dated AD 60-80 and also at Colchester (Cool & Price 1995 no. 649).

The bowls are believed to have been in popular use by the Flavian period and their use appears to have continued until the second half of the second century as two vessels were recovered from an Antonine pit at Felmongers, Harlow dated AD 160-170 (Price 1985a, 202, no. 4 & 5).

(12) is a fragment of emerald green glass decorated with a horizontal abraded band and may have come from a cup or beaker. Emerald green glass was used for a wide variety of cast and blown vessel forms during the pre-Flavian period but largely went out of use during the Flavian period.

Facet cut beakers (Isings form 21; Cool & Price 1995 no. 395-410) were the first drinking vessels to be produced in truly colourless glass. Their main period of manufacture was during the late first century but this may have continued into the second. (38) is a decorated body fragment from such a vessel with hexagonal intercutting facets.

The beakers had truncated conical bodies and were produced in a tall and squat form. The facet decoration, which gives the form its name, occurs on the centre of the body, consisting of a series of intercutting oval or hexagonal facets set in quincunx. The tall form tends to have elongated hexagonal facets such as those found on (38).

The exterior of the vessels were totally wheel polished giving them a cast appearance but the interior is smooth and clear indicating it was free blown (Harden & Price 1971, 339). The area above and below the faceted zone was either left plain or contained a wheel cut ridge. Oliver (1984) undertook a study of these vessels and divided them into two groups; those without ridges (Group 1) and those with (Group 2). Examples of Oliver's group 2 have already been recorded in Leicester from the Jewry Wall excavations (Jewry Wall Museum LP123.9) and Blue Boar Lane (Cool & Price forthcoming b no. 14). Both groups are believed to have been in use at the same time but group 2 is possibly more common on British sites (Cool & Price 1995). They are quite common vessels and have been found all over the western provinces and beyond (Welker 1974, 59).

Late first – mid second century vessels

The late first to second centuries saw a gradual decline in the use of strongly coloured glass, it being replaced by colourless and yellow and green colourless in use along side blue/green. A minimum of 14 vessels have been identified as being in use during this period.

(6) and (8) are rim fragments from collared jars (Isings form 67c; Cool & Price 1995 nos. 732-64); a very common Flavian form. These vessels have an out turned tubular collared rim which often has a concave profile. They may be globular or ovoid in form and have a concave, open pushed in base ring, very similar to those found on Isings form 52 and 55 jugs.

The globular jars are frequently decorated on the body with vertical tooled up ribs as found on (6) in deep blue glass. Ribbed globular jars have been found on Romano-British sites from the Neronian period into the second century (Cool & Price 1995) but deep blue glass such as (6) appears to go out of use during the Flavian period. A blue/green ribbed globular jar was recorded at Verulamium (Charlesworth 1972 fig.76.25) from a context dated AD 60-75 and ribbed fragments in deep blue glass have been found on many sites although it is difficult to distinguish whether they came from collared jars or globular jugs. (8) is from a dark yellow brown collared jar, paralleled at Colchester (Cool & Price 1995 nos.733-6) and Fishbourne (Harden & Price 1971 356.79). Glass of this colour begins to disappear during the Flavian period.

The only identifiable cast vessel from the assemblage was a colourless cast and ground bowl with an angular overhanging rim, (5). These bowls are quite common finds on sites of this period, but first appear in Britain during the Flavian period (H.E.M. Cool pers. comm.). Fragments of these vessels have previously been recorded from two sites in Leicester, Bath Lane (Clay and Mellor 1985 fig. 40.29) and Blue Boar Lane (Cool & Price forthcoming b no. 4). Other sites include New Market Hall, Gloucester (Hassal & Rhodes 1974), Fishbourne (Harden & Price 1971 no. 26), Lullingstone (Cool & Price 1987, no. 325, 326) and Wroxeter (Cool & Price forthcoming a no.30).

The bowls were mainly produced in colourless glass but vessels produced in different colours are also known such as the peacock blue bowl from Pentre Farm, Flint (Price, 1989a, no. 1), and the opaque red bowl from Ditchely, Oxon (Harden 1936, 64, fig. 12.3). Coloured bowls are quite rare but they are believed to have been in use alongside colourless during the first century AD.

(39) is a colourless body fragment with five abraded bands. Abraded bands are an extremely common form of simple decoration used on a wide variety of forms.

Fragments (7), (9), (10), (11), (14), (17), (21), (22) & (51)-(55) have all been identified as belonging to either conical or globular jugs of Isings form 52 and 55. These are a common form of jug found on Romano-British sites occupied during the late first and early second centuries. They represent a minimum of seven vessels: two conical jugs, three globular and two unidentified. The jugs were produced in a wide range of colours but strongly coloured glass like deep blue (7), dark yellow brown (9) & (10) and amber (17) tend to go out of use during the Flavian period while yellow/green (14), light green (21) & (22) and blue/green (51)-(55) continue in production into the early second century.

Both forms share a number of common features which can make identification of individual forms difficult. Both have simple folded rims, cylindrical necks frequently constricted at the base, angular ribbon handles and concave or open pushed in base rings. Handle and body fragments allow the best evidence for identification. Plain, single ribbed and double ribbed handles may be found on both forms, but multi-ribbed handles are generally associated with globular jugs and pinched lower extension trails with conical jugs. (7) and (52) are pinched extension trails from two conical jugs, in deep blue and blue/green glass, while (9) and (51) are multi ribbed handles from two globular jugs in dark yellow brown and blue/green glass.

Both jug forms may be decorated, commonly with optic blown, tooled and/or trailed ribbing. Fragments (7), (11) and

(55) show evidence for ribbing, (7) and (11) have optic blown ribs and (55) trailed and tooled ribs. Ribbed blue/green jugs have been found at Inchtuthil (Price 1985c, no.3) and Richborough (Bushe-Fox 1949, 368) in a context dated AD 75-90. Deep blue ribbed body fragments are quite commonly found on first century sites but may come from jugs or collared jars. A plain deep blue conical jug was found at Kingsholm, Gloucester (Price & Cool 1985 fig. 18.27).

Both forms were in use alongside each other and the earliest recorded fragments in Britain come from the site of Sheepen in Colchester (Harden 1947, 305 no. 94) and from the Lunt, Warwickshire occupied between AD 60/4 – 75 (Charlesworth 1971/3, 79). Conical jugs may have continued in use into the mid second century as fragments of yellowish green and yellowish brown jugs have been found at Park St. Towcester (Price 1980, 66 nos. 7-9 fig. 15) and a yellowish green ribbed jug from an Antonine deposit at Felmongers, Harlow (Price, 1985a, 204, no. 20.3).

Conical and Globular jugs are believed to have been produced in the glasshouses of the lower Rhineland and northern Gaul from the mid first century to the early/mid second century (Price 1980, 66).

(16) a yellow/green colourless fragment is possibly from an Isings form 16 flask. The globular body is decorated with a horizontal abraded band on the shoulder. Flasks are a common form and variations of it are found throughout the Roman period. The vessel is smaller than the Isings form 16 and has abraded rather than wheel cut lines on the shoulder. The glass is bubbly but of good quality and very thin.

(19), (25) and (56) are ribbed body fragments that come from either collared jars or globular jugs, too little of the vessels remain to provide further identification.

(48) is the out-turned fire rounded rim fragment from a large bowl, too little of the fragment remains to allow identification but the large rim diameter indicates that this was an open vessel.

(57) is a blue/green tubular pushed in base ring probably from a cup or beaker. This type of base has been found on a number of vessels of mid to late Flavian date such as indented and arcaded beakers. Examples have been found at Wroxeter (Cool & Price forthcoming a, no.105 & 107) on a light green wheel cut beaker, at King Harry Lane, Verulamium (Price 1989b, no. 290) and at Fishbourne on a colourless vessel dated to the late first to early second century (Harden & Price 1971, no.76).

(60)-(64) are all base fragments that have not retained enough of their form to be identified closely. They have been grouped together here but may have been in use any time between the first to third centuries.

(60) is a fragment from a kicked base possibly from a small flask. It was produced in poor quality bubbly blue/green glass and is similar to one described from Corbridge (Allen 1988, no. 22) identified as a small flask or unguent bottle and given a general date range of late first to second century.

(61-64) are all fragments of blue/green tubular base rings. The base diameters range between 40-80mm and may well have came from either cups or bowls. A general date range of late first to third century may be suggested for these vessels.

Late second to early third century vessels

A minimum of ten vessels were identified as belonging to this period, five being examples of cylindrical cups of Isings form 85 and its variant (Cool & Price 1995, nos. 465-540).

Cylindrical cups with a double base ring and fire rounded rim were the most common type of drinking vessel to be produced during the Roman period. They are found in large quantities on many Romano-British sites. The cup has two forms, decorated and undecorated, both being produced predominantly in colourless glass but also in blue/green.

(31)-(36) and (46) are base and rim fragments from four undecorated cups. (31)-(36) are colourless fragments and (46) is of blue/green. A complete example of an undecorated colourless cup is known from Airlie, Angus (Charlesworth 1959, 44, pl.1.4).

(37) is the lower body and base fragment from the trailed variant. These cups were decorated with horizontal trails on the upper and lower body. The double base ring in this example consists of two thin trailed circles of glass instead of the more common tubular outer and trailed inner ring. The trailed variants are not as common as the undecorated cups but an example has already been noted from the Blue Boar Lane site in Leicester (Cool & Price forthcoming b, no.24). Other trailed examples are known from Colchester (Cool & Price 1995), Baldock, Herts, (Westell 1931, 276, no.4828, fig. 6), Pentre Farm, Flint (Price 1989a, fig. 48.6) and Gloucester Defences, (Price & Cool 1986, fig. 48.6).

Both forms were in use alongside each other, the earliest recorded example of an undecorated cup coming from an Antonine deposit at Harlow, Essex (Price 1985a, no. 19) and both varieties were found in a late Antonine drain at Housesteads (Charlesworth 1971, fig. 1,2,4 & 5 and 1975, 24). There appears to be no evidence to assume that these vessels were in use prior to the mid second century, their main period of use being the late second to early third. Some cups appear to have continued in use until the middle of the third century, as examples have been found in a dated deposit AD 235-250/60 at Chesterholm (Price 1985b, 206-214). The large quantities of these vessels do appear to indicate a major increase in the supply and use of colourless drinking cups in the late second

Table 55: *Fragment totals of vessel glass by phase and type from Area 1.*

	Vessel Type											
DATE/SUBPHASE	*1*	*2*	*3*	*4*	*5*	*6*	*7*	*8*	*9*	*10*	*11*	*12*
Late 1st / 1A, 1B			1							1	1	
Late 1st-Early 2nd / 2A, 2B, 2D		1	1	1		4				17	13	
Late 1st-Early 2nd / 2F, 2G, 2J	3	8	1	1				3		2	28	
Early 2nd / 2H, 2I, 3A	3					1		1	1	4	13	
Mid 2nd-Mid 3rd / 3B, 3C, 3D		4	1		2	13	5		47	30	39	246
Late 2nd / 5A, 5B	2	1				2	1		5	11	30	63
Mid-late 3rd / 5C, 4A		4				2		1	20	14	49	97
Late 3rd-Early 4th / 5D									4		1	8

1 = pillar moulded bowls , 2 = dark blue , 3 = dark yellow brown, 4 = emerald green, 5 = light yellow brown, 6 = yellow green, 7 = green yellow, 8 = light green, 9 = colourless, 10 = 1st/2nd century containers, 11 = blue/green, 12 = window glass

century, a popularity not to be seen at any other time during the Roman period (Cool & Price 1995).

(41)-(45) are fragments from unidentifiable small jugs or flasks that probably had their main period of use during the first to third centuries. They have been grouped here as all were recovered from late second and early third contexts but some may be residual. All were produced in blue/green glass and represent a minimum of five vessels.

(41), a small rim and neck fragment, may have come from an unguentium or small flask. There is no evidence for a handle and the rim has had its edge fire rounded and rolled inward. It is difficult to closely identify or date this vessel as little remains but it appears to be a common type of flask rim of the late first to second century based on examples found at Caerleon (Allen 1986, no. 25, 25) and King Harry Lane, Verulamium (Price 1989b, no. 316).

(42) and **(43)** are funnel-mouthed blue/green rim fragments. Funnel-mouthed vessels appear to be general utilitarian containers, they usually have short necks and globular bodies. Vessels with large rim diameters are generally described as jars and smaller vessels, flasks or jugs. **(42)** is a funnel mouthed jug which retains part of the handle while **(43)** is probably from a flask as it has quite a small diameter of 40mm. Funnel mouthed vessels are common from many Romano-British sites and have been tentatively dated to the first half of the second century (Cool & Price 1989, 34).

(44) and **(45)** are spouted rim fragments from blue/green jugs of Isings form 88. The spouts have been produced by drawing out the rim. **(44)** has a fire-rounded rim and **(45)** has its rim edge rolled in. Spouted jugs generally have funnelled mouths, globular or discoid bodies, concave bases and curved ribbon handles with a thumb rest. The spouts may either be drawn out or pinched. A colourless spout fragment with a rolled in rim was found at Gloucester (Price & Cool 1986, no.18). A discoid jug with a drawn out rim was found at Colchester (Thorpe 1935, pl.viiia) and a blue/green jug is recorded from The Park in Lincoln (H.E.M. Cool pers. comm.). Most jugs were plain although the common form of decoration was trailed spirals as found on a jug from Verulamium dated to AD 175-275 (Charlesworth 1972, no 76.24). The jugs are not uncommon finds on sites occupied during the second and third centuries.

Third century vessels

A minimum of three vessels were identified from this period.

(29) and **(30)** are rim fragments from hemispherical cups a very common third century drinking vessel. **(29)** has an out-turned, cracked off rim and the body is decorated with alternating rows of pinched up ribs and knobs. Cracked off rims are not common on this style of cup which usually have fire rounded rims. The distinctive decoration has been produced by applied and pinched blobs of glass to form alternate relief decoration. Both the glass and the decoration is of very good quality. A similarly decorated cup was recovered from a grave deposit in Brougham, Cumbria dated AD. 220/30 – 270/80 (Cool 1990b, fig 1.2). The Brougham example differed in that it had rows of two pinched knobs rather than three and had a fire rounded rather than a cracked off rim. H.E.M. Cool in a study of third century drinking vessels (1990b), suggests that hemispherical cups with cracked off and ground rims were produced during the later third century and cups with fire rounded rims were possibly in use during the middle of the century.

Pinched up decoration noted on another fragment **(40)** has been dated from contextual information to the late third/early fourth century. Fragments with pinched decoration have been recorded from a number of sites across the country at Chesterholm (Price 1985b, 208.15), Chilgrove villa, Sussex (Down 1979, 163, fig. 56.6) and Colchester (Cool & Price 1995) and appears to be a third century phenomenon in Britain (Cool 1990b)

(24) is a concave base fragment with a pontil scar indicating a fire-rounded rim. The green tinged colourless glass and contextual information indicates a possible third century date for this piece. It is possible that this may be a similar vessel to the hemispherical drinking cups with fire rounded rim that H.E.M. Cool identified as mid third century drinking vessels (Cool 1990). The grave deposit at Brougham, Cumbria produced a number of hemispherical cups with fire rounded rims in both colourless and greenish colourless glass that have been dated to around this period (Cool 1990b, figs. 1-8).

Fourth century vessels

Vessels produced during the fourth century are quite diagnostic as the colour of the glass used changed from blue/green and colourless to bubbly greenish and yellow/greenish colourless glass. Four fragments of bubbly fourth century glass and one fragment of yellow/green colourless were identified, all were recovered from medieval layers. From these a minimum of two vessels were identified, both were truncated conical beakers a common drinking vessel of the fourth century.

(23) a green tinged body fragment, retains trailed decoration in the form of a loop or teardrop. Trailed decoration was used throughout the Roman period on a wide range of vessel forms including jugs, flasks, bowls and beakers (Price & Cool 1986, 47).

(15) is a yellowish/green colourless fragment from an indented truncated conical beaker a variant of the Isings form 106 dated to the second half of the fourth century (H.E.M. Cool pers. comm.). A trailed and indented beaker similar to this was recorded from the Lankhills cemetery, Winchester in a deposit dated AD 370-90 (Harden 1979, fig. 27.51).

(26) is a rim fragment from a plain truncated conical beaker (Isings form 106c). These are very common vessels from fourth century Romano-British sites generally having fire-rounded slightly out-turned rims, truncated conical bodies and a simple concave base. A complete beaker with trailed decoration was recovered from a grave at Gallowtree gate, Leicester during the 1920s (Dare 1927, pl. 11.1.2). Beakers with fire rounded rims are believed to have been in use by the mid fourth century and examples are known from Towcester (Price & Cool 1983, no. 40-44), also Burgh Castle (Harden 1983, no. 85) also Milton Keynes (Price 1987, nos. 234-238) and Colchester (Cool & Price 1995, nos. 618-629). These beakers are seen as the precursors to the pointed cone beakers, common drinking vessels in use during the fifth and sixth centuries (Harden 1983, 86).

(28) is a simple concave base fragment in bubbly green glass that may have come from a number of vessels. The absence of a pontil scar indicates that the rim may well have been cracked off and ground down. Beakers with these rims are common in the fourth century and were probably in use alongside those with fire rounded rims or slightly earlier. Examples are known from Frocester Court (Price 1979, fig. 16 9-11) also Lankhills cemetery, Winchester (Harden 1979, nos. 382,391,530 and 634) and Barnsley Park, Gloucester (Price 1982, fig. 59 10-13).

A decorated fragment in bubbly green glass was also recovered, **(27)** which has two trailed ribs of different widths. Trailed decoration is commonly found on many popular fourth century forms.

First and second century containers

Prismatic and cylindrical bottles (Isings form 50 & 51; Cool & Price 1995, nos. 1834-2239) are extremely common finds on Romano-British sites and are one of the most abundant forms in use during the first and second century. 'Prismatic' is a term used to describe a straight sided container that cannot be securely identified as either square or hexagonal.

136 fragments from containers were identified and these accounted for 20% of the total vessel glass recovered. A minimum of one square, one hexagonal, three prismatic and two cylindrical bottles were present. As the rims, necks and handles of containers are similar on all the forms, identification can usually only be made from body and base fragments.

(65)-(69) are all simple folded rim fragments a number of which show the characteristic triangular profile created when the rim is folded outward then in. A number of the rims retained fragments of the upper attachments of the handles which were attached underneath the rim.

(70)-(76) are handle fragments, (70), (72) and (73) are fragments of multi-reeded angular handles commonly found on all three forms, while the remaining plain ribbon handles came from smaller vessels. The lower attachments of these handles frequently retain fragments of the shoulder and from this identification of form is sometimes possible. (74) and (75) are the lower attachments from cylindrical bottles.

(77)-(81) are base fragments from one square, one hexagonal and three prismatic bottles. Only the prismatic bottles have the moulded base designs as represented by (77)-(80) which are commonly found on Romano-British sites.

(77) has a moulded design of four concentric circles, the most common style of base design which is frequently accompanied by a central dot or moulded design in the centre and angular corner mouldings.

(78) is a moulded base from a square bottle which has three concentric circles and the remains of corner mouldings. A similar base design was found at Inchtuthill (Price 1985c, fig. 94.12) and is a common base design for square bottles (Charlesworth, 1966, fig. 3).

(79) has a central cross moulding within what appears to be an inner circle. This is a common base design and examples have been found at Gestingthorpe, Essex (Charlesworth 1985a, fig. 30.308) and at Verulamium (referred to in Charlesworth 1966, fig. 12). A study of square bottles has suggested that base designs were possibly individual trademarks of particular glass works (Charlesworth 1966, 34).

(80) is a fragment of a moulded design of which only two intersecting arcs remain, which may have come from a wide variety of base designs.

(83) is the lower body and base edge fragment from a small hexagonal bottle. The base of which appears to be plain with no moulding. Hexagonal bottles are less common than cylindrical and square containers but they appear consistently in assemblages on Romano-British sites from the Claudio-Neronian period and are believed to continue into the mid second century. Larger examples have been recorded at Alcester (cited in Cool & Price 1995) and Caerleon (Allen 1986, fig. 41.29).

Wear marks were noted on a number of container fragments, (68) showed horizontal scratch marks around the neck caused by cord or similar material which would have been used to secure a lid or stopper. Vertical scratch marks on the body of cylindrical bottles are commonly found and would have been caused by the continuous removal of the vessel in and out of some form of protective casing, possibly of wicker. These utilitarian containers were used for the transport and storage of liquid and semi-liquid products. The range of sizes produced varied, and many of the larger containers had later secondary use such as cremation urns in burials. The bottles were produced throughout the Empire and show many regional variations. The prismatic bottles would have been produced either by a free blown cylinder which had the sides flattened or more commonly by mould blowing, while the cylindrical bottles were always free blown.

The bottles had their main period of use during the later first and second centuries(Cool & Price 1995). Cylindrical and square bottles were probably produced in equal proportions during the Flavian period but cylindrical bottles appear to go out of use in the early second century while square bottles continued in production until the later second or even into the third century.

Window glass

A total of 538 fragments of cast window glass was recovered from the site, 414 fragments from phased groups. Cast window glass was primarily in use during the first to third centuries but may well have continued into the fourth. The quality of the window glass as a whole was very good with few impurities and bubbles and very little post depositional wear. No complete panes could be reconstructed despite the presence of numerous edge fragments. Five of these edge fragments retained traces of mortar indicating the method by which they were fixed. A total of 51 fragments showed evidence for the reworking of one or more edges, possibly the result of cutting a pane to size or for some other purpose. The area of the window glass was measured and covered approximately 0.33m^2.

The vast majority of the material recovered came from Area 1 and was concentrated in phase 3B onwards. This is an unusually large assemblage of window glass from a site that does not contain a baths building. Window panes were usually removed for reuse before a building was abandoned, and the relatively large quantity of glass recovered on Causeway Lane may possibly result from the destruction or upgrading of nearby structures.

Acknowledgements

I would like to thank Hilary Cool for all her help and advice during the writing of this report and allowing access to the Colchester report ahead of publication.

CATALOGUE

Abbreviations

PH Present Height, RD Rim Diameter, BD Base Diameter, WT Wall Thickness, RT Rim Thickness
Dm. Dimensions of fragment (millimetres)

Pillar Moulded Bowls (Isings Form 3)

Polychrome

1) (1218) Phase 2G 1 lower body fragment. Deep blue glass with opaque white and yellow marbling. Part of 1 prominent rib. Dm. 31 x 25, WT 2.5 *Not illustrated*

Blue/green

2) (792) Phase 5B: Rim fragment. Part of 1 prominent rib from a deep bowl. PH 44, RD 140-180, RT 4, WT 4.

3) (1218) Phase 2G: Rim fragment. Part of prominent rib from bowl.

Cast

Opaque

4) (2978) phase 2K. 1 small body fragment of opaque violet blue glass. One surface remaining which is ground. Slight iridescence. Dm. 10 x 9. *Not illustrated*

Colourless

5) (220) Phase 12. Rim fragment of bowl. Cast and ground angular, overhanging rim fragment, ground on interior and exterior. Iridescent surfaces. PH 18, RD 160, RT 3, WT 2.

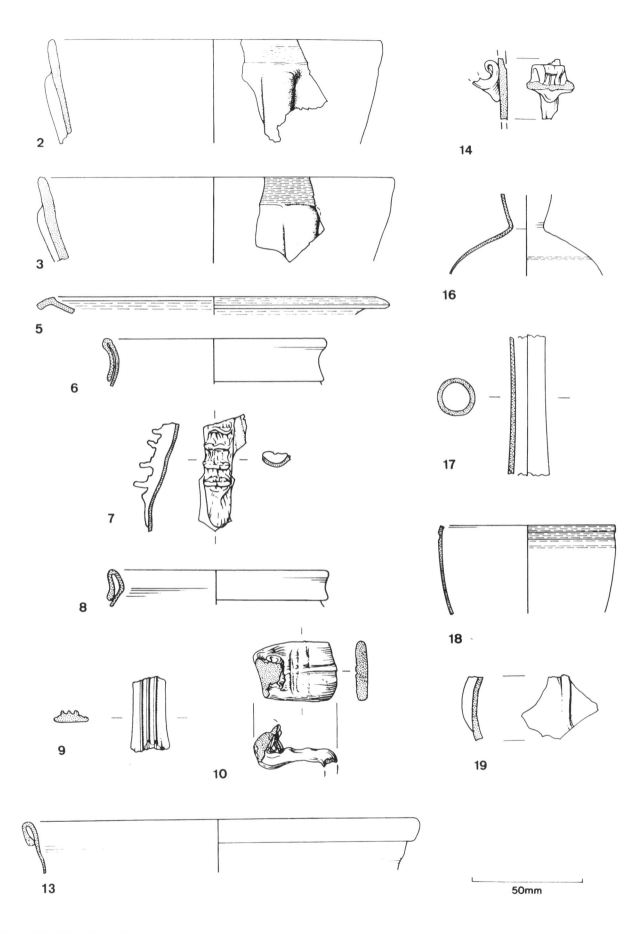

Fig. 138: *The glass illustrations*

Blown

Deep Blue

6) (1218) Phase 2G. 1 rim and 6 associated lower body fragments of collared and ribbed globular jar. Rim folded outward and down to create collar with concave profile. 2 body fragments retain part of 1 tooled vertical rib. Occasional small bubbles and flaking iridescence. PH 20, RD 100, RT 4, WT 1.

7) (3551) Phase 2L. Lower handle attachment and body fragment of ribbed conical jug. Vertical pinched extension trail with 4 tooled up ribs. Body fragment retains part of 1 optic blown rib in very low relief. Dm. 49 x 21, WT 1.

Dark Yellow/Brown

8) (1552) Phase 2D. Rim fragment of tubular collared jar. Collar rim folded outward and down forming a hollow tube with a concave profile. Horizontal wear marks present on the rim interior. PH 15, RD 100, RT 6.5, WT 1.

9) (1316) Phase 2F. Handle fragment of globular jug. Angular ribbon handle with 3 prominent vertical ribs. Good quality glass. Dm. 33 x 17, WT 3.5.

10) (3908) Phase 5F. Handle and neck fragment of jug. Folded upper attachment of a ribbon handle which retains part of the cylindrical neck. Tooling marks. Dm. 38 x 26, WT 6.

11) (2608) Phase 8. Lower body and base edge of globular jug or ?jar. Lower body has 3 optic blown ribs in very low relief radiating from the base ring. Flaking iridescence. Dm. 45 x 41, WT 2. *Not illustrated*

Emerald Green

12) (1757) Phase 2A. 1 small body fragment with part of 5 thin horizontal abraded bands, slight iridescence. Dm. 20 x 7, WT 0.5. *Not illustrated*

Yellow Green

13) (761) Phase 12. Rim fragment of tubular rimmed bowl. Rim folded outward and down forming a hollow tube. Diagonal scratch marks present of the rim exterior. Straight sided upper body. Slight iridescence. PH 23, RD 180, RT 6.5, WT 1.

14) (859) Phase 3B. Handle and neck fragment of jug. Upper folded attachment of a ribbon handle, sharp tooling marks present on the underside of the handle. Dm. 26 x 22, WT 3.

15) (2457) Phase 8. Body fragment of indented, truncated, conical beaker. Yellow tinged glass, straight sided fragment with convex curved end and horizontal abraded band. Dm. 31 x 15. WT 1. *Not illustrated*

16) (756) Phase 3B. 7 upper body and neck fragments of globular flask. Convex curved upper body with a horizontal abraded band on the shoulder. Occasional bubbles, slight iridescence. Dm. 50 x 40, WT 1, Neck diameter 17.

Light Yellow/Brown (Amber)

17) (1112) Phase 3B. Neck fragment of jug or flask. Cylindrical tube/neck fragment in fairly thick glass. Occasional vertical scratch marks, slight iridescence. Dm. 60 x 18, WT 3.

Green Yellow

18) (1786) Phase 1C. Rim fragment of cylindrical cup. Slightly inturned rim cracked off and ground down. 1 horizontal wheel cut lines on the upper body, 1 directly below the rim and 1 on the upper carination. Broad abraded band also present below the rim. Occasional small bubbles. PH 38, RD 80, rt 2, wt 1.

19) (1264) Phase 2D. Body fragment from cup, bowl or jug. Convex curved body fragment with 1 applied and tooled vertical rib in high relief. Impurities present, clouded iridescent surfaces. Dm. 29 x 36, WT 3.

Light Green

20) (2942) Phase 2K. Rim fragment of tubular rimmed bowl. Rim folded outward and down forming a hollow tube. Convex curved upper body. A large proportion of the rim remains. Occasional bubbles. PH 44, RD 180, RT 9, WT 2.

21) (1194) Phase 3A. Rim fragment of jar or flask. Fire rounded rim, rolled in and flattened. Occasional bubbles, slight iridescence. PH 12, RD 39, RT 6, WT 3.

22) (606), (681) Phase 5C. 3 handle fragments of jug. Ribbon handle with slight vertical ribbing/corrugations in very low relief. Occasional impurities and elongated bubbles. Dm. 22 x 26, WT 6.5. *Not illustrated*

Pale Green Tinged Colourless

23) (2147) F505 Phase 11. Body fragment of cup, bowl or jar. Trailed loop decoration in the form of a teardrop. Tooling marks visible. Dm. 26 x 15, WT 1.5.

24) (3520) Phase 6B. Base fragment of hemispherical cup. Thickened concave base with remains of pontil scar. Convex curved lower body. Flaking iridescence. PH 10, BD c.30, WT 1.5.

25) (2936) Phase 3G. Body fragment of cup or bowl. Convex curved body fragment with 1 pinched up vertical rib in high relief. Slight surface abrasion. Dm. 28 x 32, WT 2.

Bubbly Fourth Century

26) (3576) Phase 9. Rim fragment of cup or beaker. Fire rounded, slightly out turned rim. Convex curved upper body. Very bubbly glass with slight iridescence. PH 17, RD 60, RT 3, WT 1.

27) (3576) Phase 9. Body fragment with 2 tooled vertical ribs of different thickness. Convex curved body fragment. Clouded iridescent surfaces. Occasional small bubbles. Dm. 15 x 11, WT 1. *Not illustrated*

28) (2087) Phase 8. Base fragment of cup or beaker. Pushed in concave fragment with wear marks on outer edge. Occasional small bubbles. Dm. 33 x 3. WT 1.

Colourless

29) (3866) Phase 5H. Rim and body fragment of hemispherical cup. Out-turned rim cracked off and ground down. Body decorated with a vertical row of 3 pinched up projections separated by a vertical pinched up rib. 1 pinched up projection and 1 other rib remains of an alternating row. Abraded band present on the exterior of the upper body and on the rim interior. Occasional bubbles, good quality glass. PH 50, RD 60-80, RT 1.5, WT 2.5-3.

30) (3825) Phase 5E. Rim fragment of cylindrical cup. Vertical rim, cracked off and ground down, slightly irregular. Horizontal abraded band present below the rim, on the exterior. PH 31, RD 80, RT 2, WT 1.

31) (3908) Phase 5F. Rim fragment of cylindrical cup. Fire rounded rim, quite thick, with slight convex upper body. Wheel polished externally. Clouded iridescent surfaces. PH 14, RD 100, RT 4, WT 2. *Not illustrated*

32) (3879) Phase 5G. 2 rim fragments of cylindrical cup. Fire rounded vertical rim with 2 abraded bands on the upper body. Wear mark on the rim exterior. Occasional bubbles. PH 28, RD 90, RT 4, WT 1.

33) (3790) Phase 6A. Rim fragment of cylindrical cup. Fire rounded rim, clouded iridescent surfaces. PH 22, RD 100, RT 4, WT 1.8.

34) (3790) & (3640) Phase 6A. Adjoining base fragments of a cylindrical cup. Double base ring. Tubular outer ring and trailed inner ring. Occasional bubbles. BD 60 (outer ring), WT 1.

35) (984) Phase 3B. 2 base fragments. Inner trailed circular base ring with remains of pontil scar. Clouded iridescent surfaces. BD 50, WT 3.

36) (3507) Phase 9. Base fragment. Applied solid base ring with fragment of a possible inner trail. Slight iridescence. BD 40, WT 1. *Not illustrated*

37) (1016) Phase 3B. 11 base and lower body fragments of cylindrical cup. Base consists of two thinly trailed concentric rings, creating an inner and outer base ring. Outer ring slightly uneven. Carinated lower body with the remains of a horizontal trail on carination. Very fractured glass. BD 40 (outer ring), WT 2.

38) (756) Phase 3B. Body fragment of facet-cut beaker. Straight sided facet-cut fragment with ground and wheel polished exterior. Part of 4 facets in 3 rows set in quincunx forming hexagons. Dm. 28 x 22, WT 3.

39) (444) Phase 4A. Body fragment of bowl or cup. Convex curved body fragment with 5 horizontal abraded bands. The lower band is quite broad (1mm) with the upper 4 bands reasonably thin. Occasional bubbles. Dm. 31 x 15, WT 1.

40) (348) Phase 5D. 3 associated convex curved body fragments, 1 with remains of small pinched projection. *Not illustrated.*

Blue/Green

41) (702) Phase 5B. Rim and neck fragment of a small flask or unguentium. Fire rounded rim, edge rolled inward. Cylindrical neck with elongated bubbles and many impurities. PH 29, RD 27, RT 3, WT 1.5.

42) (3804) Phase 5G & (3910) unphased Roman. 2 adjoining fragments of funnel mouthed jug. Out turned fire rounded rim with edge rolled inward. Remains of upper folded attachment of handle on the rim. Uneven rim thickness, occasional bubbles. PH 20, RD 48, RT 4-6, WT 2.

43) (3879) Phase 5G. Rim fragment of funnel mouthed jar or flask. Fire rounded, out turned rim. Occasional bubbles, clouded iridescent surfaces. PH 13, RD 40, RT 3, WT 2. *Not illustrated*

44) (3836) Phase 6A. Rim fragment of spouted jug. Out turned fire rounded rim edge rolled inward, pulling outward to form spout. Varying rim thickness. Slight iridescence. PH 22, RT 2-5, WT 2. *Not illustrated.*

45) (588) Phase 5A. Rim fragment of spouted jug. Fire rounded spout rim. Vertical side curving inward. Bubbly glass with slight iridescent surfaces. PH 34, RT 3, WT 1.5. *Not illustrated*

46) (3619) Phase 5G. Rim fragment of cylindrical cup. Fire rounded rim quite thick, upper body curving inward. Occasional elongated bubbles and impurities. Slight iridescence. PH 14, RD c.65, RT 3, WT 1.

47) (1632) Phase 2B. Rim fragment of cylindrical cup. Slightly inturned cracked off and ground rim. Thin horizontal abraded band below the rim on the exterior. Clouded iridescent surfaces, occasional small bubbles. PH 18, RD 65, RT 1, WT 1. *Not illustrated*

48) (229) Phase 9. Rim fragment of straight sided bowl or beaker. Fire rounded slightly out turned rim. Slight wear mark on top of rim. Occasional bubbles, clouded iridescent surfaces, many impurities. PH 25, RD 120, RT 2.5, WT 1.

49) (1024) Phase 2J. Rim fragment of tubular flat rimmed jar or bowl. Rim folded outward then inward to form a flattened hollow tube. PH 4, RD 180, RT 4, WT 1.

50) (462) Phase 5C. Rim fragment of tubular rimmed bowl. Rim folded outward, over and down forming a hollow tube which has been flattened slightly. RD 160, RT 5, Dm. 27 x 13. *Not illustrated*

51) (1218) Phase 2G. Handle fragment of jug. Ribbon handle with three tooled vertical ribs in high relief. Slight iridescence. Dm. 19 x 16, WT 6.5.

52) (3879) Phase 5G. Handle fragment of jug. Ribbon handle fragment with a pronounced central groove and tooling marks on outer surface. Elongated bubbles, impurities. Dm. 25 x 23, WT 4.5.

53) (3879) Phase 5G. Handle fragment of conical jug. Extension trail of a lower attachment with 4 pinched up ridges. Retains fragment of body. Occasional bubbles, slight iridescence. Dm. 22 x 9, WT 6.

54) (270) Phase 3D. Handle fragment of jug. Upper angular section of a ribbon handle, distinct tooling marks on underside of handle. Slight iridescence. Dm. 38 x 29, WT 6. *Not illustrated*

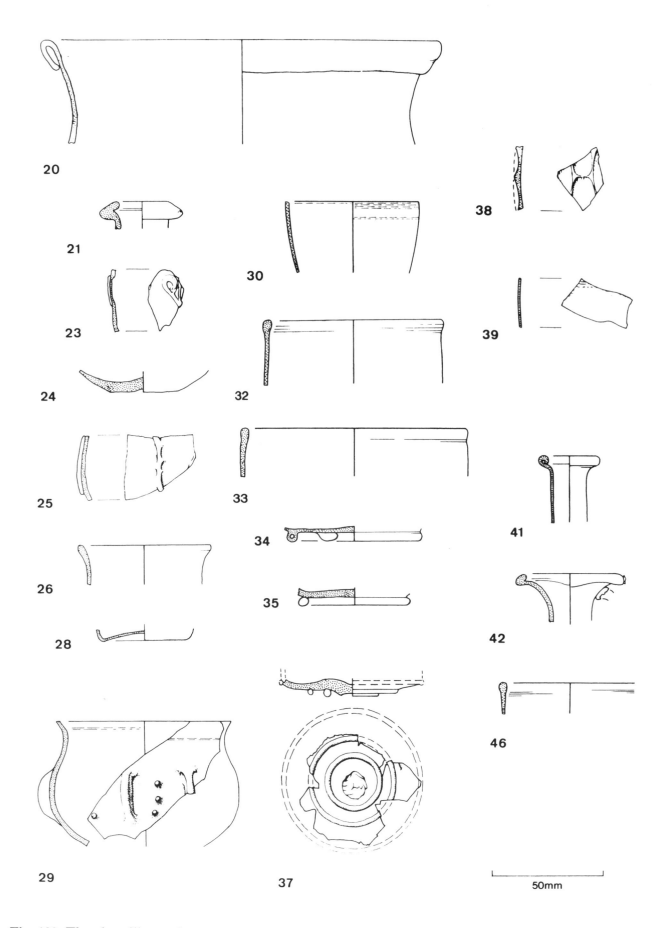

Fig. 139: *The glass illustrations*

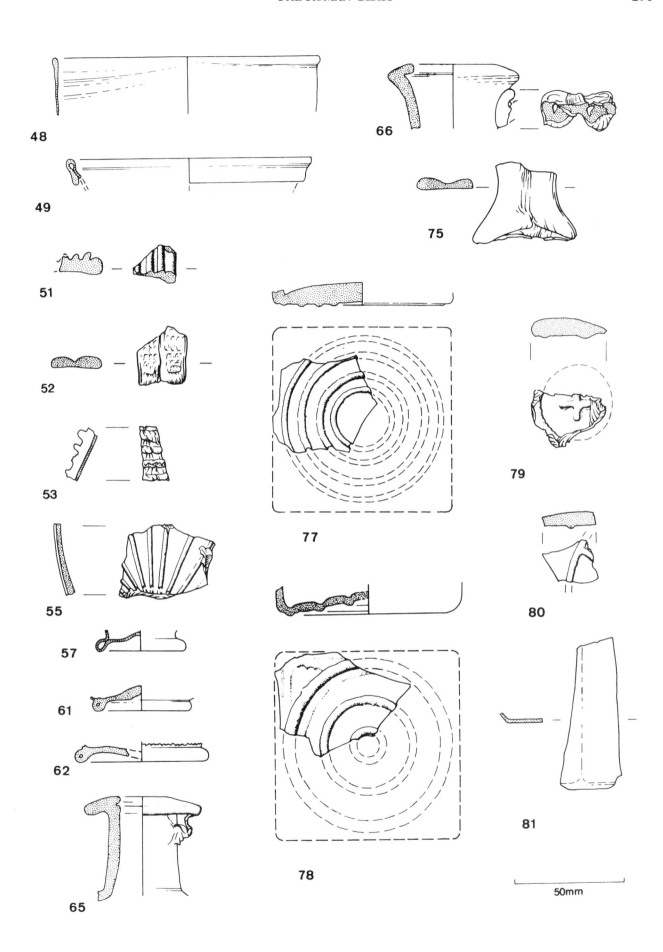

Fig. 140: *The glass illustrations*

55) (2934) Phase 2K. Lower body fragment of ribbed globular jug. Convex curved body fragment broken at the base retaining part of the handle lower attachment. Part of 8 vertical trailed and tooled ribs in high relief, converging towards the base, occasional bubbles. Dm. 30 x 13, WT 1.

56) (1055) & (667) Phase 3B. 2 lower body fragments of ribbed hug, bowl or jar. Each fragment has 1 rib in high relief dying out toward the base. Occasional bubbles, slight iridescence. Dm. 52 x 62, WT 1-2. *Not illustrated*

57) (2140) Phase 8. Base fragment of cup or beaker. Convex lower body curving in toward base. Tubular pushed in base ring, splayed outward, concave base. Clouded iridescent surfaces. PH 9, BD 40, WT 1.

58) (1052) Phase 3B. Base fragment. Applied true base ring, slightly pushed in base with remains of pontil scar. PH 8, BD 70. *Not illustrated*

59) (699) Phase 3B. Base fragment of cup or bowl. Simple concave base with wear marks around the outer edge. Convex curved lower body. Slight iridescence. PH 13.5, BD c.60, WT 1. *Not illustrated*

60) (3574) Phase 9. Base fragment. Internal base fragment with the remains of high central kick and pontil scar. Very bubbly glass. Dm. 42 x 22. *Not illustrated*

61) (3836) Phase 6A. Base fragment. Tubular out base ring, pushed in concave base with remains of pontil scar. Slight iridescence. PH 12, BD 40, WT 0.5.

62) (405) Phase 9. Base fragment of bowl or cup. Tubular out splayed base ring with wear marks. Lower body ground down to base. Occasional bubbles, slight iridescence. PH 8, BD 50, Thickness 3-5.

63) (444) Phase 4A. Base fragment. Pushed in base with outer tubular base ring. PH 8, BD 60. *Not illustrated*

64) (3879) Phase 5G. Base fragment. Outsplayed tubular base ring. Slight iridescence. PH 2, BD 80, WT 1. *Not illustrated*

Containers

Blue Green

65) (848) Phase 5B. Rim and neck fragment of bottle. Rim bent outward and in creating a triangular profile. Part of handle upper attachment trail present on and below the rim. Neck broken off at the shoulder. Occasional impurities and elongated bubbles. Clouded iridescent surfaces. PH 44, RD 48, RT 6, WT 5, Inner RD 21.

66) (1552) Phase 2D. Rim and neck fragment of bottle. Rim bent outward and in creating a triangular profile. Pronounced inner lip of rim edge. Part of handle upper attachment remains. Occasional small bubbles. PH 16, RD 44, Inner RD 10.

67) (3676) Phase 6A. Rim and neck fragment of bottle. Rim folded outward then in and flattened. Tooling marks around narrow mouth. Retains part of handle upper attachment. Occasional bubbles. PH 16, RD 44, Inner RD 10. *Not illustrated*

68) (1264) Phase 2D. Rim and neck fragment of bottle. Rim folded outward and in creating a triangular profile. Horizontal wear marks on the neck below the rim. PH 32.5, RD c.50. *Not illustrated*

69) (200) clearance. 3 rim and 1 neck fragments of bottle. Rim folded outward then in and flattened. Remains of handle upper attachment on rim. *Not illustrated*

70) (982) Phase 3B. 5 handle fragments of prismatic bottle. Multi reeded lower attachment retaining part of shoulder. Very fractured glass with occasional bubbles and impurities. Dm. 67 x 60, Wt 5. *Not illustrated*

71) (200) clearance. Handle fragment of prismatic bottle. Lower attachment of angular ribbon handle, retaining part of shoulder. Handle applied as 3 blobs of glass drawn upwards forming 3 ridges. Occasional impurities and bubbles. Dm. 53 x 48, WT 5. *Not illustrated*

72) US. Handle and neck fragment of bottle. Folded upper attachment of a multi reeded angular handle, retaining part of neck. Occasional bubbles and impurities. Dm. 45 x 55, WT 6. *Not illustrated*

73) (3792) Phase 5F. Handle fragment of bottle. Simple lower attachment of a multi reeded handle. Occasional bubbles and impurities. Dm. 25 x 37, WT 3. *Not illustrated*

74) (2942) Phase 2K. Handle fragment possibly from a cylindrical bottle. Remains of lower attachment with fragment of shoulder. Occasional bubbles. Dm. 25 x 19 WT 5.

75) (3890) Phase 6A. Handle fragment possibly of cylindrical bottle. Simple lower attachment applied in 2 blobs of glass, drawn upward to form a ribbon handle with a central groove. Retains a fragment of the shoulder. Dm. 36 x 47, WT 4.5. *Not illustrated*

76) (3825) Phase 5E. Handle fragment of bottle. Folded upper attachment of angular ribbon handle. Iridescent surfaces, occasional bubbles and impurities. Dm. 45 x 36, WT 5. *Not illustrated*

77) (674) Phase 3D. Base fragment of prismatic bottle. Base design has 4 concentric circular mouldings in relief. Dm. 44 x 42, Diameter of outer circle c.80, WT 2.5-8.

78) (1219) Phase 3B. Base fragment of square bottle. Base design has 3 concentric circular mouldings and angular corner mouldings in relief. Concave base with extensive wear marks on the corner angular mouldings. Base interior has corresponding circular grooves. Good quality glass of even thickness, occasional small bubbles. Dm. 59 x 45, Diameter of outer circle c.60, WT 2-3.

79) (2280) F 560 Phase 11. Base fragment of prismatic bottle. Base design has remains of a circular and central cross-moulding. Thick glass with occasional bubbles and impurities. Dm. 34 x 24, WT 5.5.

80) (2469) Phase 8. Base fragment of prismatic bottle. Base design has the remains of what appears to be 2 intersecting/joining arcs. Very bubbly glass. Dm. 20 x 18, WT 5.

81) (1027) Phase 4A. Lower body and base fragment of a hexagonal bottle. Corner body and base fragment, 2 sides present with angle of 120°. Slightly concave base and base corner has extensive wear marks. Bubbly glass. PH 66, WT 1.5.

ROMAN PAINTED WALL PLASTER

Susan Ripper

INTRODUCTION

Wall paintings, which were totally unknown in Celtic society, were extensively used throughout the Roman Empire and were quick to appear as one of the marks of the Romanisation of Britain. All types of buildings were decorated with paintings and the quality and design of the work is thought to be a measure of the wealth of the commissioning patron, the importance of a building and sometimes even a reflection of the function of a room. It is this universal availability of painted plaster from archaeological sites that 'give Roman wall painting its unique appeal and its exceptional social interest' (Ling 1985).

No *in situ* wall paintings were found during the excavations at Causeway Lane but some 6,962 fragments of painted plaster (total area of 12.5 square metres) were recovered from the site. Much of the material was well preserved, with little abrasion to the painted surfaces and occasionally surviving to its full thickness. It was therefore considered that detailed analysis of the collection had the potential to contribute not only to the corpus of material recovered elsewhere in Leicester, but also to national studies of painted wall plaster in terms of changing styles of decoration, painting and plastering techniques, dating, and the organisation of the industry

This report is a synopsis, based on the full catalogue which is part of the site archive. The results of the analysis will be presented in the following way:

i)   The collection of material recovered from Area 1.
ii)   The collection of material recovered from Area 2.
iii)   The collection of material recovered from Area 3 (schemes 1 – 6, other unusual groups)
iv)   General discussion of painting and plastering techniques.

Glossary of terms

buon (or true) *fresco*	*technique of painting without an organic medium on damp plaster*
dado	*the lowest part of a wall, and especially the clearly-differentiated base-zone in a tripartite scheme of wall.*
intonaco	*the top coat of plaster.*
tempera or fresco secco	*technique of painting with organic medium to bind pigments to the surface.*

AREA 1

The wall plaster recovered from Area 1 was a relatively small collection (87 fragments). These came from 34 different contexts, ranging from periods 2, 3, 4, 5 (Roman), to 8, 9 (early medieval) to 12 (post-medieval). All pieces were small with no joins and no groups of designs were identified. Individual fragments retained remnants of patterns (a selection of the more unusual designs are illustrated in fig. 141), but even these were too fragmentary to discern the intended design. The largest group was found in the backfill of a medieval well/cess pit from plot D but even this group weighed only 95 grams, barely a handful!

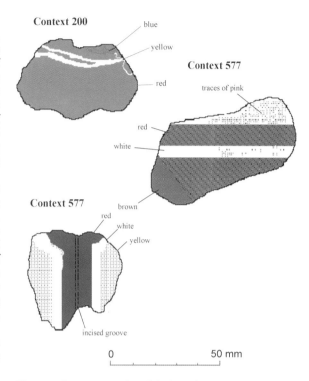

Fig. 141: *Some examples of designs from area 1*

AREA 2

As with Area 1, the wall plaster recovered from Area 2 was also a relatively small collection (271 fragments). These were from 69 different contexts ranging from periods 3 (Roman) to 8 and 9 (early medieval) to 12 (post-medieval). Although some fragments included the vestiges of designs (fig. 142) no groups bearing the same designs were identified. It is possible that some decorated fragments were parts of schemes identified in Area 3, but no collection was large enough to be conclusive and even where pigments and colour combinations appeared similar, differences in the mortar suggest they were not from the same source.

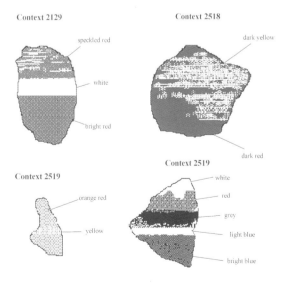

Fig. 142: *Some examples of designs from area 2*

AREA 3

An overwhelming majority of the painted wall plaster was found in Area 3 of the excavations. The bulk of this came from the backfill of a large gravel quarrying pit together with a quantity of building demolition material (Group 359.004 has 172,832g of Roman tile, 51,404g of slate, 7,320g of mortar, 490g of *opus signinum* and 75g of tesserae). The mixed nature of this debris suggests that the wall plaster derived from the demolition of a nearby building, rather than from refurbishment. However, the presence of a number of fragments of Roman pottery with residues of pigments were also found within this pit which may suggest refurbishment. The debris then seems to have been deliberately deposited as backfill to the quarry, sometime in the early fourth century AD, presumably to consolidate unstable ground.

The original location of the plaster is not known but there is no substantial evidence to suggest that it originated from any of the buildings excavated on the Causeway Lane site. Some characteristics of the collection itself also suggest that the wall plaster had been brought-in from elsewhere:-

- Many of the fragments were relatively large (up to 500 sq. cm.) but less than 5% of the fragments were found to have joins with other pieces.

- Some of the plaster was heavily eroded.
- Over 100 'elements' (groups of fragments with vestiges of the same design) were identified from Area 3. (i.e. the diverse character of the collection might suggest that the wall paintings came from more than one wall, perhaps from more than one building).

Retrieval and analysis procedures

Much of the plaster recovered from Area 3 was found face down, obscuring the nature of the painting, but the quantity of plaster observed suggested a potential for considerable reconstruction. To preserve this potential the plaster was not only lifted stratigraphically, but was also located to a superimposed grid of 1m squares identified by letters (A – O, site plan 155/535/10). All the fragments were then carefully placed in trays and removed to the Unit headquarters.

An initial sort of the wall plaster fragments then began, separating painted from plain plaster and weighing each context. Analysis of the assemblage used the same methodology as that developed for material from the Norfolk Street Roman villa, Leicester (Buckley, forthcoming). All painted fragments from the larger contexts were colour coded,

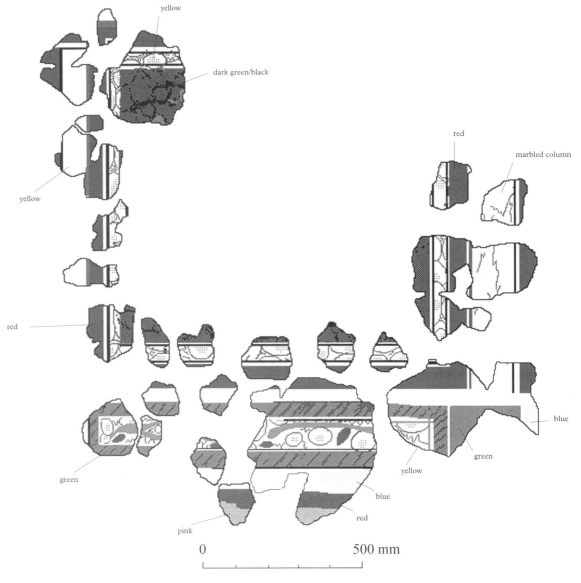

Fig. 143: *A conjectural reconstruction of scheme 1*

with a dab of coloured poster paint on the reverse of each piece as a way of identifying each context (e.g. green = context 3501, yellow = 3804 etc.). The painted plaster was then grouped according to colour/design and each group of fragments bearing the same design was described as an 'element'. Information on each element identified was recorded on a relational database on a *pro forma* customised for this collection.

Groups of elements bearing links were then collated and reconstructions were attempted. The more successful groupings have tentatively been described as 'schemes'. The fragmented remains of six schemes have been suggested from Area 3, which will be described in this report. A full catalogue of each element group and a detailed account of the methods of recording, conservation and reconstruction are held in the site archive.

Scheme 1

The illustration above (fig. 143) shows one interpretation of how some of the larger fragments from Scheme 1 may have related to each other. The lower half of this scheme has been securely reconstructed (the area with the highest frequency of joins has been mounted), but many fragments placed in the upper half of this scheme are 'floating' and therefore this arrangement is only tentative.

Summary of the design

Scheme 1 consists of a dark green and black imitation marble veneer panel surrounded by a frame of yellow based imitation marbling. This frame has been decorated with veins of red in circles and semi-circles, which can best be described as 'fried eggs'. The 'yolks' of these eggs are dark yellow and between the eggs are zig-zag scribbles of red.

A second, outer frame of plain red surrounds the yellow. To one side of this frame lies an impressionistic column, in the form of a vertical band of white 150mm wide but of unknown height, edged with narrow black 'tram lines' (8mm wide). This fascia or column has then been decorated with broad washes of pale blue and pink and finally ornamented with a thin trailing vein of red (perhaps representing a vine-scroll, or just another form of marbling). To another side of the red frame lies a band of yellow, edged with a stripe of rust.

Below the main panel lies a smaller horizontal panel. This panel has a pale yellow base coat which has been decorated with: a) more red scribbled 'fried eggs' b) solid ovals of red,

highlighted with white and vaguely reminiscent of fruit and c) a sinuous line of solid grey, perhaps representing a vine. The lower panel has been framed in green and then cross-hatched in diagonal stripes of dark green. Below this lies a band of coarse pink rough plaster applied to a surface of slightly rougher plaster. This paint may be indicative of the base of the design, the coarser material functioning as a skirting board.

There was no definitive indication of which way up this painting originally lay (no scenes with a 'correct' orientation or positive drip marks), and in fact the reverse of what is illustrated (with the fried egg/foliate design running either across the top or up the side like a garden trestle) is equally feasible.

Similar, but slightly differing versions of elements of this scheme were also observed (e.g. fragments of a column, as seen to the right of the illustration, but surrounded with a cross-hatched green panel or green and black marbling, as seen in the central panel, but further decorated with splashes of pale green). This suggests that the wall may have been decorated with a series of repeating panels, divided by vertical spaces.

A number of fragments bearing parts of the Scheme 1 design are also angled in relief (fig.144). These presumably represent parts of window or door frames.

The fragmentary survival of this scheme has precluded any attempts to even estimate its original dimensions. However, similarities with the north-west room added to the fortress *principia* at York should be noted. In York the dimensions of the wall painting measure some 5m wide by approximately 3.5m high. Here the 'fried egg' marbling forms one part of a dado, made up of a series of panels with varying designs. The upper section of the wall also contains illusionistic columns separating panels. This has been dated to the early fourth century.

The general effect of Scheme 1 is of a dense amount of colour and a collision of 'busy' marble effects, separated by a range of differing plain but colourful stripes. The quantity of colour used in this scheme would seem to indicate a degree of wealth in its patron.

The whole scheme was painted on white *intonaco*. The thickest surviving examples of the backing layers showed that the mortar consisted of two layers of buff sandy plaster (12 and 14mm thick), on lighter sandy plaster (16mm), on sandy plaster (13mm) on a shaped layer (wood impressions ?, 18mm). The application and survival of so many backing coats of plaster is rarely seen in this country (see 'Plaster Analysis' later in this report).

Scheme 2
Summary of the design

Some 182 fragments of plaster (from 8 element groups, covering an area of 4,965 sq. cm) seem to have formed part of a scheme which included fluted columns and Corinthian capitals separating zones of varying colours. The columns were created by a series of finely painted pink and red vertical lines over pale pink or white *intonaco*. Each line was about 10mm wide but of unknown length. At least five alternating dark and light lines made up each column (up to 70mm wide), with darker lines to the sides of the columns perhaps intending to create an illusion of depth or fluting. The remnants of this group of plaster are too fragmentary to suggest the full height of the columns, but the partial remains of two Corinthian-style capitals were found. These capitals took the form of trailing dark red acanthus type leaves, fountaining out of a small base (fig. 146).

Each of these columns separated areas of white, blue, yellow or green, but the position of, and relationship between, the panels is not clear. Some panels appeared to be framed with

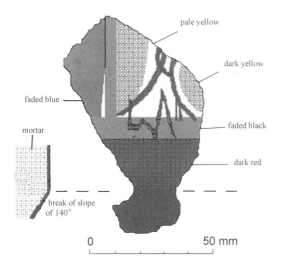

pale yellow

dark yellow

faded blue

faded black

mortar

dark red

break of slope
of 140°

0   50 mm

Fig. 144: *Element 101*

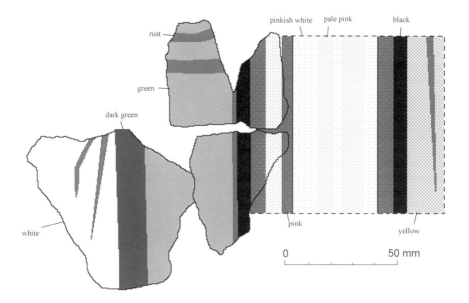

Fig.145: *Scheme 2, element 73: section of column*

another colour (e.g. the white panel is framed with green) and these are sometimes highlighted with 'tramlines'. There is also one example of a panel containing a trailing line decoration (fig. 145).

There are also a few fragments which suggest that an angled frame, or 'frame in perspective', emerges out from a column. Only two fragments represent this frame but they show the vertical pink and white column with a red and yellow frame emerging at 60° from the column. The yellow band is 20mm wide, followed by a thin stripe of maroon and finally a band of bright red, of unknown width. The frame appears to enclose an area of green. Three dimensional effects of this kind have also been observed at the painted house at Dover *circa* AD 200 (Philp, 1989).

Scheme 2 was painted in true *fresco* on a sandy plaster, 28mm thick with some mud daub still present.

Scheme 3
Summary of the design

15 element groups have been tentatively assigned to Scheme 3, totalling some 1,113 fragments of wall plaster. All fragments were small and often eroded with only 4% being found to have joins. The fragments were all decorated in true *fresco* with a white or grey *intonaco* and then painted with a rich, vibrant combination of blues, greens and reds (fig. 147). The pigments used in this scheme include generous applications of cinnabar and coarse chunks of Egyptian blue as well as the more usual ochres, earth pigments, lime and carbon. The thickness and purity of the Egyptian blue pigment and the expense of the raw material may indicate an early date for this scheme (second-third C. – Graham Morgan, pers. comm.). The effects of the rarer pigments was to produce vivid, slightly sparkling colours. The smallness of the fragments and the scarcity of joins, however, make it difficult to even guess at the original form of the design. Some fragments have vestiges of what may have been intricate detail. Brushmarks are clearly visible on numerous pieces, often intentionally used to produce wispy lines and the painting seems to have been applied freehand (no guidelines or compass marks were seen) depicting a swirling, curving scene. Perhaps these fragments were part of a free-style foliate design (some solid ovals of red and green, highlighted with yellow are vaguely reminiscent of fruit) or perhaps this scheme represents the remains of a portrait (the swirling lines representing folds of cloth).

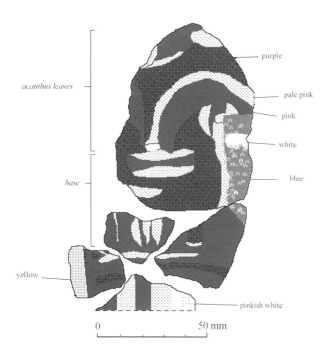

Fig.146: *Scheme 2, element 72: example of a capital*

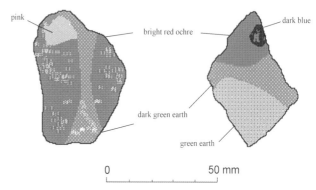

Fig. 147: *Scheme 3, element 10*

The coarse, sandy backing mortar to this scheme was generally between 15 – 40mm thick, applied in two layers and with some mud daub present.

Scheme 4
Summary of the design

800 small, eroded fragments of plaster from 11 elements groups were assigned to scheme 4. All were decorated with various combinations of Egyptian blue and green earth colours, but not with the coarse chunks seen in Scheme 3. This blue/green ground colour may have been the plain background to a panel or scene. Many fragments were further decorated with either a cream to rust-red design or a dark green motif. The design appeared to be a free-style painting (possibly foliate) but as only 17 joins were found (2%), the overall design was not clear. Much of the dark green decoration appeared as thin waving lines, reminiscent of grass stalks or leaves (fig. 148). Brush marks were visible on many pieces and all pigments were applied in true *fresco.*

The backing mortar was relatively thin (approx. 18mm thick), and was made up of only two layers, with some mud daub present.

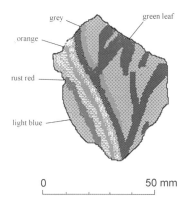

Fig.148: *Scheme 4, element 67*

Scheme 5
Summary of the design

58 fragments of painted plaster were assigned to Scheme 5. All were painted with a coarse, dull yellow ochre ground colour and then crossed by a thick band of purple/brown (charcoal and red ochre), up to 80mm wide. These fragments would seem to represent the remains of a relatively plain design (plain yellow with a broad brown frame) and contrast with the vibrancy of schemes 1 – 4.

To one side of the brown line some fragments have then had another layer of plain white plaster crudely applied. This may indicate a phase of re-decoration or repair, or may show that these fragments came from the edge of a wall, a 'skirting board' zone, subject to wear or from a discrete area not central to the aesthetic of the design.

Scheme 6
Summary of the design

8 elements were assigned to Scheme 6, which combined consist of some 156 relatively large fragments of plaster covering a total area of 8,855 sq. cm. Each of the 8 elements are linked by a dark yellow ochre base colour, but the applied decoration shows a variety of differing design elements. These include:-

i) Plain yellow crossed by a white stripe (40mm wide).

ii) Plain black crossed by a white stripe (40mm wide).To either side of this line patches of red in the shape of elongated ovals, with a darker shade of red along the central line. The largest oval was 80mm long by 20mm wide. On one fragment the surface is convex, sloping down on one side as though forming the beginning of a door or window frame.

Two fragments in this collection have curving incised guidelines scratched into the surface, perhaps with a compass (fig. 149).

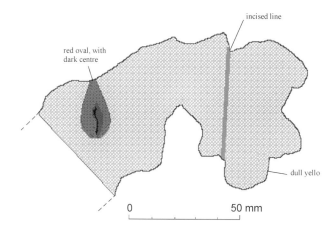

Fig. 149: *Scheme 6, element 56*

Another fragment has the feint traces of a curving thin red line (5mm wide with a ?300mm diameter).

iii) On some fragments red, black and white has been splashed onto the yellow.

iv) Surrounding the yellow panel was a line of white (12mm wide) which gradually merged into a line of dark reddish purple (12mm wide) and was finally edged by a band of dark red (unknown width).

v) Some fragments are decorated with a basic dark yellow background, onto which a swag, or garland has been painted. This consists of alternate red and green leaves suspended from an incised guideline, or compass mark (fig.150). These swags appear to be 'tied' at either end by what look like triangles, but may have been intended to represent bows. The tied ends of the swags seem to emerge, possibly, from the corner of a panel (a white rectangle infilled with black and purple can be seen on two fragments).

The whole scheme has been painted on a white *intonaco* which lay on four layers of sandy plaster totalling 52mm; 8mm, 13mm, 18mm and 13mm thick, the lower two layers possibly being combined.

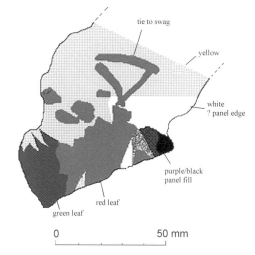

Fig. 150: *Scheme 6, element 79*

Other designs or unusual groups from Area 3

Roundels

Ten different groups of roundel design were also identified from the Area 3 wall plaster collection. Some of the designs may have been different parts of the same scheme, or perhaps part of the schemes already identified but no direct links could be made. The roundel groups identified include:-

i) Roundels with a 100 – 160mm diameter (central circle). These were all painted with a white *intonaco*, covering mortar which was only 20mm thick. The circles varied in colour (red, green, yellow and white) and were surrounded by up to four outer circles (fig. 151). Some circles had four petalled rosettes at the centre applied in *tempera*. At the centre of some circles a central point had also been pecked out. This may represent the damage inflicted by the use of a compass to aid the drawing of regular circles.

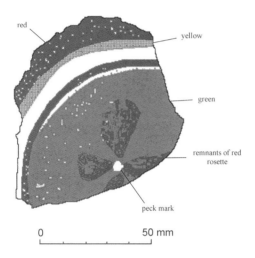

Fig. 151: *Element 22, an example of a roundel*

Some roundels also had the remnants of a band of red filling the space between two circles. This suggests that the roundels constituted a repetitive design perhaps intended to imitate moulded stucco work (Ling, 1985).

Other fragments bear the remains of the tail end of a faded black motif (fig. 152), but the remains are too fragmentary to distinguish the original design. Running perpendicular to the curving lines, and through the black motif are the remains of a straight incised line. This may have served as a guideline to aid the alignment of a series of roundels.

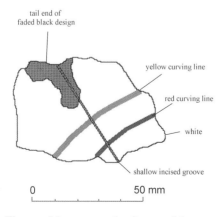

Fig. 152: *Element 26, an example of a roundel*

ii) Other roundels include:

(a) A yellow ground with two thin black circles drawn on. The inner black ring has a diameter of 560mm. At the centre of the circle the edge of a trailing black motif can be seen, but its survival is too fragmentary to discern the original design.

(b) Finally, the vestiges of a very different, vividly coloured roundel design were also noted. This included a dark red semi-circle, edged with white and lying within a pink border. This pink band was separated from an area of swirling reds and pinks by a thin line of white. The mortar backing to this design was at least 30mm thick, with some clay daub present, suggesting it was from a wall rather than a ceiling.

Swags or garlands

Apart from the swag seen in Scheme 6, fragments of two other swags or garlands were also observed. Both consisted of fronds, of alternating coloured leaves, hanging from a curving line. In one instance the leaves are red and green (fig. 153), while in the other example the leaves are green and black. The designs, however, are otherwise identical, so it would seem probable that both came from the same wall perhaps as a repeating design within Scheme 6. In both instances the curving line, perhaps representing a vine, has been scored into the surface of the plaster with a sharp object.

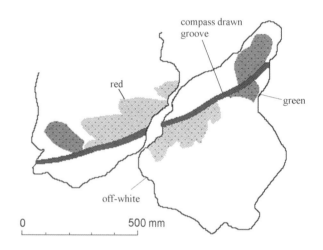

Fig. 153: *Element 49, a swag*

Other panel designs

Apart from the panels identified in the schemes, exceedingly fragmentary remains of other panels were also recognised. These included:-

i) A white background with a narrow red frame. The corner of the frame has been embellished with circles or pellets of red (fig. 154). This design has been seen in the wall plaster collection from the painted house at Dover (Period VII, circa AD 160 – 180, Group 4 – Philp 1989)

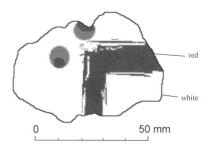

Fig. 154: *Element 16, corner of a panel with pellets*

ii) A white background decorated with a narrow red stripe and a broader green stripe. This area of plaster has also been re-plastered and re-painted white.

iii) A white background edged with a red frame highlighted with a narrow strip of green. On some fragments there is an additional set of green 'tramlines' within the white panel, perhaps intended to add an element of perspective.

Graffiti

Two fragments of plain white wall plaster from Area 3 contained the vestiges of some graffiti (fig. 155):-

(i) Context: 3918

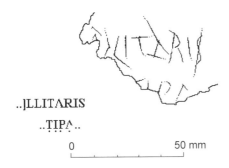

..]LLITARIS

..TIPA..

0   50 mm

Fig. 155: *Graffiti*

Mr M. W. C. Hassall (Institute of Archaeology, London) analysed this fragment of plaster and suggests that the inscription may represent either an adjective like militaris or the second person passive of a first conjugation verb ending in -lito. If so, 34 possible endings exist (Gradenwitz). Hassall, on further study of the piece, felt the reading should be ..]llitaris, including a second 'l' at the beginning of the fragment. Bearing in mind the nature of graffiti, it is then conceivable that these words represent an obscene phrase such as fe]llitaris, from fellito (see J.N.Adams (1982), *The Latin Sexual Vocabulary*). Other fragments of obscene graffiti on wall paintings have also been identified in Leicester, from Blue Boar Lane (Wright 1962 and Wright 1963).

(ii) Context: 3879.

A possible cursive graffito too abraded to translate.

PLASTERING AND PAINTING TECHNIQUES

Plaster composition and application

Some ten samples of plaster were examined microscopically and analysed by chemical removal of the lime by dilute hydrochloric acid. The natural aggregates were composed of river sand and gravel, being mainly; quartz, flint, quartzite, ferruginous and plain sandstones, some with mica, some fine micaceous schist and fossil material, probably derived from the lime. The aggregate gradings show that they were probably all derived from the same source. Samples were taken of the natural gravels of all three areas of site. They were all of similar composition being river pebbles and round to angular sand. Most of the plaster samples show a sand grading centred around 0.25mm which is the same for the 'natural' sands from Areas 1 and 3. The gravel analyses are not so comparable as the mortar sample sizes were too small, but similarities can be inferred.

Vitruvius, in his 'Ten Books on Architecture' suggests that for durability, the plaster layers should be composed of a rough cast layer containing a coarse filler, followed by at least three coats of a fairly coarse lime and sand mixture. These were covered by finer layers of lime and marble powder. He states that 'When the walls have been made solid with three coats of sand and also of marble, they will not be subject to cracks or any other faults' (i.e. six layers of backing plaster). These instructions, however, are rarely adhered to in Roman Britain and most plaster grounds are composed of only two or three layers. The presence of five layers (seen in Scheme 1) is therefore unusual and of some note, perhaps suggesting the maintenance of cultural links with Rome.

Also from Scheme 1, the lowest layer of plaster contained some traces of a shaped surface, possible wood impressions, from a lath-clad wall.

Plaster from context 3501 (painted plain white) had reed impressions and a high lime content, perhaps suggesting ceiling rather than wall plaster.

No roller marks were observed, so it must be assumed that either the lowest coats were generally lost or that most plaster was applied with a trowel.

A full report on the wall plaster mortar analysis with graphs showing the varying proportions of inclusions is lodged with the site archive.

Pigment analysis and painting techniques

The pigments used in Roman wall paintings were obtained from mineral, vegetable and animal sources. The samples analysed from Causeway Lane were all 'natural' with the exception of Egyptian blue which was manufactured and quite common. The mineral pigments included earth colours such as the ochres: red ochre (haematite, composed mostly of oxides of iron), yellow ochre (limonite, a different form of iron oxides) and green earth (glauconite). White was achieved by using slaked lime and black was made from ground carbon mixed with size. The cinnabar or vermilion, seen in Scheme 2, was mercuric sulphide, usually imported from Spain and considered to be very expensive. It was originally thought to be rare in Roman Britain, but it has since been identified on at least a dozen British sites (Morgan *in* Philp 1989). According to Vitruvius. cinnabar was prepared by heating and washing cinnabar ore to remove waste and to make it friable and then it was ground to a fine powder for use. The Egyptian blue or blue frit was prepared by combining copper, silica and calcium. The different components fused together to form a crystalline compound which is bright blue in colour and slightly sparkling.

Each pigment would have been ground to a fine powder and mixed with water on a palette before being applied to a wall. 36 fragments of Roman pottery recovered from the site had pigment and/or plaster residues still adhering to them which probably represent the remnants of such palettes. The majority of these pot sherds were found in a probable fourth century backfill in Area 3 but they include a range of fabrics and forms. The nature of the residue deposits fall broadly into seven categories reflecting different stages in the preparation of wall painting:-

i) Pieces with traces of pure pigments (red ochre and green earth). These include two fragments of mortaria and one sherd of grey ware and probably represent the grinding stage of the paint preparation.

ii) Vessels used to mix pure lime, presumably for an *intonaco*. (one fragment of black burnished ware and one fragment of colour-coat).

iii) Five sherds with residues of red ochre mixed with lime (perhaps blended to form a pink *intonaco* undercoat or as a pink paint). These included four grey ware fragments and one piece of colour-coat.

iv) Two sherds of grey ware with traces of red ochre lying on top of traces of lime. This perhaps suggests the re-use of a palette, first in the preparation of an *intonaco* and then as a paint jar.

v) One sherd of grey ware with red ochre lying beneath a residue of lime (as above but in reverse).

There were also nine sherds of colour-coat with residues of lime on the inside and red ochre traces on the broken edge.

vi) One fragment of black burnished ware with traces of red ochre and lime splashed over the broken section of the pot. This obviously implies that the broken pot fragment was utilised as a palette rather than the whole pot being deliberately created for this function.

vii) Finally, there was one fragment of a black burnished ware rim sherd with lime attached on the outer part of the rim. This may be from waste lime which has become stuck to the sherd. The presence of a hard translucent calcite film around the edge of the deposit suggests that the sherd had fallen into some lime or more likely that some lime had fallen onto the sherd.

The pigments were then applied to fresh, damp plaster. As water from the plaster dried, it evaporated bringing lime from the plaster to the surface. The lime, reacting with air then formed a layer of transparent calcium carbonate. This effectively sealed the pigments under a transparent film and created a durable surface over the wall painting. The presence of an *intonaco* (top coat) layer and plentiful examples of visible brushmarks suggests that this true or *buon fresco* technique was used in almost every instance at Causeway Lane. Guidelines, such as those seen in the painting of the swags, were scored into the fresh plaster to direct the free-hand artist.

Detail was also added to the ground colour by using the paints in *tempera*. This technique involved mixing a pigment with an organic medium such as size which produced paint which adhere to a dry surface. The rosettes seen at the centre of some of the roundels may have been painted this way as the colour seemed to flake off away from the ground paint.

Designs

Although the plaster recovered from Causeway Lane was generally too fragmented to allow a complete understanding of decorative schemes it was possible to identify the use of a number of different design types. These included both plain and florid, geometric and free-style designs, perhaps reflecting the relative importance or function of the room it decorated. The different styles observed include:-

i) At least 20 examples of two-dimensional panels, mostly involving a simple frame contrasted against a white or yellow background. In some instances multiple frames were used, the frames were highlighted with 'tramlines' or the corners of the frame embellished with pellets to produce an element of perspective (see 'Other panel designs').

ii) Some panel schemes were further embellished with architectural features such as the columns seen in Scheme 1 and 2.

iii) Imitation marbling was also used, both as an infill to panels and in the frame (Scheme 1). Fragments of splashed decoration were also noted (e.g. white splashes on a pink background, dark blue splashes on a pale blue ground) which may have also been intended to imitate marbling.

iv) The use of repeating designs (as seen in the roundels) may represent attempts at imitating moulded stucco work.

v) Vegetal or floral designs were also used (as seen in the swags).

vi) Free style designs may also have been present in schemes 3 and 4, although the fragmentary survival of these paintings prohibits a precise understanding of the design.

CONCLUSION

Wall paintings were a characteristic amenity to buildings of even moderate pretension in Roman Britain. Even modest buildings were whitewashed or painted in plain colours, so the abundance of vivid, sometimes imported, colours and elaborate polychrome murals found at Causeway Lane may therefore be indicative of the collection originating from a building with at least some fine rooms. The survival of five backing layers of mortar from the Scheme 1 can be seen as an almost 'textbook' example of the construction of a plaster wall, in the method advocated by Vitruvius. This reflects a degree of exemplary craftsmanship rarely seen in Roman Britain and could suggest a degree of cultural influence still emanating from Rome. Stylistic links with Catterick, York (for the Scheme 1 'fried-egg' pattern) supports the concept of wall painters perhaps being mobile specialists rather than local artists. The presence of cinnabar (imported from Spain) in Scheme 2 confirms the existence of long distance trade links, and shows that patrons were not constrained by materials that could be produced locally.

On the assumption that these wall paintings originated in a building near, if not actually from the site, it may be reasonable to suppose that the economic status of this zone of the city was one of comparative wealth. However, although six schemes have been suggested the fragmentary survival of particular designs and the fact that all the wall plaster had been re-deposited has precluded any attempt to ascribe paintings to buildings or rooms with a particular function.

The date of the painted plaster collection has also proved problematic. The 'fried-egg' design of Scheme 1 can tentatively be dated to the fourth century from comparable designs at Catterick, although the pottery from the backfill of the quarry suggests an early fourth century date for the destruction of the paintings. This could suggest that the painting was relatively short lived. The presence of large chunks of Egyptian blue in Scheme 2, however, may imply an early date (second-third century, Morgan, pers. comm.), as it has been suggested that the crystals of blue were progressively more refined through the Roman period. Assuming these schemes came from different walls, if not different buildings, they may reflect a longevity in the relative wealth of that quarter of the city.

The abundance of material recovered from the Causeway Lane excavations has contributed to the corpus of material found in Leicester. Leicester has not only produced the unparalleled Norfolk Street wall paintings (a remarkably well preserved series of paintings from the cellar of a fourth century suburban villa, Buckley, forthcoming) but there are also fine examples of paintings from the walls of a house of second century date within the town (Blue Boar Lane, Cooper, forthcoming).

ACKNOWLEDGEMENTS:

I would like to thank Dr. Graham Morgan for his contributions to the pigment, mortar and residue analysis, and Richard Clark for his identifications of the Roman pottery.

THE BUILDING MATERIALS
AND INDUSTRIAL RESIDUES

THE ROMAN TILE
T. S. Martin

Introduction

A policy of total recovery of ceramic building material resulted in the collection of 1,556.26 kg (12,724 fragments) of tile, 70% of which was from stratified Roman levels, but none was recovered *in situ*. On the whole, the tile was fragmentary and lacking in diagnostic elements and much of it was from dumped contexts rather than deposits of any structural significance.

Methodology

The analysis of the ceramic building materials comprised:

(a) initial quantification by weight (kg) and fragment count of all tile, by type,

(b) a rapid examination of features containing over 10 kg of tile to identify material for more detailed analysis,

(c) detailed analysis of selected material.

The detailed analysis comprised an examination of fabric and form, accidental markings, (footprints and fingerprints), deliberate marks (graffiti, finger signatures and decoration), condition and evidence of reuse. Only limited fabric analysis was undertaken with the aim of providing a guide to the range of fabrics present and hence some indication of the variety of kiln sources represented.

Classification.

The identified tile types, based on primary function, comprised roof tile – tegulae and imbrices; flue tile – box, voussoir and armchair (half box); and wall tile. Tiles with insufficient evidence to classify to type are listed as unclassified.

Summary of the tile by type

Roofing tile – *tegula and imbrex*

These made up over 50% by weight of the tile. The tegulae, large flat flanged tiles, can be described as being very typical Leicester examples. Few had holes for nails, suggesting that they were laid on a shallow pitched roof, where additional adhesion was either only occasionally considered necessary or confined to the eaves. Some of the tegulae had finger impressed patterns on their upper faces, which are usually interpreted as tiler's marks and are known as finger signatures. The bulk, as is generally the case in Leicester, had simple curved or semi-circular motifs. The tegulae exhibited a variety of accidental and deliberate marks. Of particular interest was a fragment from F763 (3790) phase 5H (Area 3) which had hoof marks overlain by impressions of other tiles suggesting stacking while still soft. The imbrices were simply classified on the basis of thickness, with type A, less than 20mm thick, and type B, in excess of 20mm, reflecting the presence of both finely made and crude, heavy examples. The imbrices otherwise had no distinguishing features.

Table 56: *Roman tile by area*

	TYPE	ROMAN PHASES weight (kg)	fragments	POST ROMAN PHASES weight (kg)	fragments
AREA 1	imbrex	45.48	310	15.58	155
	tegula	192.56	1,149	47.54	312
	wall tile	165.23	600	40.67	139
	flue tile	17.54	51	5.91	57
	unclassified	36.90	1,182	18.68	747
Area Total		457.70	3,292	128.37	1,410
AREA 2	imbrex	2.63	24	10.26	131
	tegula	8.22	63	36.91	293
	wall tile	24.80	83	30.00	99
	flue tile	0.96	6	16.18	177
	unclassified	4.12	135	11.18	1045
Area Total		40.71	311	100.50	1,745
AREA 3	imbrex	97.27	706	22.23	240
	tegula	232.00	1,084	37.45	296
	wall tile	155.65	454	34.50	115
	flue tile	27.20	218	14.42	127
	unclassified	24.94	935	10.10	363
Area Total		537.04	3,397	118.67	1,141
AREA 4	imbrex	3.31	26	12.30	105
	tegula	7.73	39	24.16	135
	wall tile	6.04	21	51.01	162
	flue tile	1.10	10	4.97	43
	unclassified	9.14	119	49.39	768
Area Total		27.32	215	141.83	1213
SITE TOTAL	imbrex	148.68	1,066	60.37	629
	tegula	440.51	2,335	146.06	1,036
	wall tile	351.72	1,158	156.13	515
	flue tile	46.79	295	41.18	404
	unclassified	75.09	2,371	89.35	2,923
Total		1,062.79	7,225	493.39	5,507

Wall tile – *lydion*

These large, flat, rectangular tiles formed the largest category after roof tile. They represent the closest equivalent to the modern day brick, but were only used to form occasional brick courses in stone walls. They varied in thickness, between 35mm and 80mm and two fragments had measurable widths of 163mm and 208mm. No other significant measurements were obtained. Wall tiles are occasionally marked with finger signatures that are comparable in form to those found on tegulae, suggesting that manufacturers were producing both types.

Tile from hypocaust systems

The box flue tiles (*tubulus*), that is the square sectioned hollow pipes used to conduct the heat through hypocaust systems, usually had two rectangular side vents, which were provided to increase the circulation of hot air. The voussoir tiles (*tubulus cuneatus*) had a similar function to box flue tiles, but were tapered to construct flue systems in vaulted roofs. These are difficult to distinguish from box tile and hence may be quantitatively under represented. Overall only a small quantity of abraded fragments of flue tile was recovered and of these only six were voussoirs. None appear to be directly derived from demolition deposits. Their outer surfaces were usually keyed by combing, but two fragments were roller stamped with an unidentified die. Several tiles in a grey coloured shell tempered fabric were probably produced in Northamptonshire and Bedfordshire (Zeepvat 1987, 119) and indicate a small scale long distance trade in ceramic tiles.

The armchair tiles are very similar to wall tile but with cut outs that enable them to be used as an alternative method of constructing hypocaust systems in vaulted roofs. The presence of combing on their outer surface is taken as a diagnostic feature for their identification here. As with the other central heating tiles, their small number suggests residuality.

Unclassified

This category comprised 42% of all fragments, but 10% by weight, and consisted of small featureless fragments.

Reworked and reused tile

1) Well F246, (268), phase 5C: a small fragment, whose thickness suggests it is a wall tile, was worked into the shape that closely resembles a miniature loaf of bread (fig. 156.1).

2) (1218), phase 2G: both faces of a possible wall tile have scored intersecting lines that form a possible chequerboard pattern and may possibly be part of a gaming board.

3) F726 (3574), phase 9: half of a circular flat disc which could be a counter, or possibly a weight (fig. 156.2).

4) F726, (3574), phase 9: a small triangular fragment, with polished breaks on two sides, could be part of a tegula that was reworked for a secondary use as a weight.

5) F756, (3879), phase 5G: a wedge shaped fragment of a probable tegula, which has been reworked for reuse as a roofing slate (fig. 156.3).

6) F756, (3879) & (3804), phase 5G: two linking fragments of a tegula, with a deeply scored lattice work motif on the underside, that was perhaps part of a gaming board.

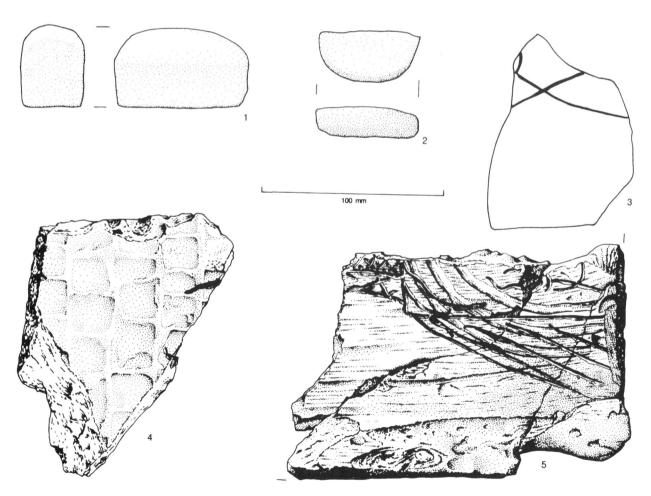

100 mm

Fig. 156: *The Roman tile and non-ceramic building materials illustrations, 1-5*

Table 57: *The targeted tile groups – features with 10 kg or more Roman tile.*

Phase	Feature	Subgroup	Roof tile in kg (frags) tegula/imbrex	Other tile in kg (frags) wall tile/flue tile/unclassified
AREA 1				
2I	F433(343) Ditch	141/2	0.92 (5) / 0.25 (3)	0.15 (1)/ 0.15 (1)/0.77 (9)
2I		141/3	1.83 (15)/-	0.19 (2)/ 0.02 (1)/ 0.36 (9)
3A		141/1	7.57 (38)/-	2.86 (11)/-/ 1.09 (20)
3B		141/4	6.14 (52)/ 0.90 (15)	5.34 (21)/ 0.14 (1)/ 0.92 (35)
3B	F421 Constr. Layers	150/1	8.69 (34)/0.06 (1)	0.54 (4)/-/1.13 (6)
3B	F417 Cobble Spread	150/1	2.25 (9)/0.70 (4)	6.95 (24)/-/ 1.93 (24)
3B		151/1	5.18 (32)/1.05 (8)	3.82 (18)/-/ 0.85 (25)
3B	F376 Pit	152/1	11.28 (78)/ 2.16(22)	6.95 (26)/ 0.43 (4)/ 0.95 (28)
3D	F212 Pit	186/1	4.78 (36)/0.36 (1)	7.35 (29)/0.73 (2)/1.00 (35)
3D	F412 Pit	186/4	3.99 (24)/1.13 (8)	6.72 (23)/ 0.55 (3)/ 0.74 (42)
3D	F334 Pit	187/1	4.61 (25)/0.40 (3)	5.67 (25)/-/ 0.62 (11)
4A	F255 Pit	174/1	6.05 (21)/1.51 (8)	0.50 (2)/-/ 0.27 (16)
4A		174/2	7.25 (31)/3.28 (18)	0.65 (1)/ 0.10 (1)/2.18 (33)
4A		174/3	5.65 (52)/1.77 (13)	2.65 (6)/-/1.04 (20)
5C	F246 Well	166/1	-/ 0.06 (1)	0.25 (1)/-/ 0.03 (10)
5C		166/2	1.95 (13)/1.10 (11)	-/-/ 0.68 (19)
5C		166/3	4.03 (19)/0.93 (10)	0.78 (3)/ 0.27 (3)/ 0.45 (22)
5C		166/4	8.07 (56)/2.03 (20)	3.74 (21)/ 0.10 (1)/ 1.32 (47)
5C		166/5	6.48 (28)/2.45 (19)	3.38 (11)/ 0.55 (3)/ 1.70 (20)
5C		166/6		-/-/ 0.01 (2)
AREA 3				
5E	F798 Quarry Pit	360/1	7.59 (47)/-	8.76 (27)/ 0.53 (3)/ 0.73 (15)
5F	F784 Pit	339/7	12.78 (64)/6.68 (41)	13.62 (41)/ 0.14 (1)/1.53 (52)
5F	F768 Pit?	362/3	6.22 (37)/2.48 (19)	5.04 (18)/ 0.62 (6)/1.35 (25)
5G	F756 Make up	359/4	83.03 (312) /28.94 (167)	55.56 (146)/2.16 (18)/3.18 (63)
5G	F757 Pit	334/1	1.47 (12)/3.56 (24)	1.55 (4)/ 0.05 (1)/ 0.18 (6)
5G		334/2	6.08 (21)/3.02 (21)	5.12 (11)/ 0.71 (4)/1.10 (24)
5H	F763 Gravel Quarry	338/2	2.21 (9)/1.10 (5)	0.65 (2)/-/-
6A		338/3	40.41 (195)/15.44 (128)	19.84 (54)/4.24(26)/5.20 (144)
6A	F737 make-up	336/1	9.60 (46)/3.95 (32)	5.38 (19)/3.03 (21)/1.23 (25)
6A	F766 Pit	367/1	20.59 (128)/ 12.21 (103)	5.58 (26)/4.35 (43)/3.13 (377)

Marked tile

Graffiti

7) Context (3501), phase 12: three linking tegulae fragments with a drawing etched on the upper surface at the bottom end of the tile, carried out prior to firing. The drawing may tentatively be interpreted as showing part of the hull of a merchant ship of the Ponto type. If this interpretation is correct then the fragments illustrate the balcony jutting over the stern and part of the hull. Crude crosses represent the cross braces of the vessel's rails and the planking of the hull is also clearly marked. This may have been drawn whilst the tiles were laid out to dry and the rest of the ship could have been drawn on an adjacent tile. The relatively small size of the surviving drawing makes alternative interpretations a possibility (fig. 156).

8) (3519), phase 6B: a wall tile fragment with what resembles the letter 'N' on the underside.

10) F765 (3677), phase 6A: on the upper face of a probable tegula fragment is possibly the letter 'h', but it may be part of a pattern.

11) F756, (3879), phase 5G: a fragment of imbrex with a possible slip trailed or barbotine decoration. A very speculative identification of the motif suggests that it could be a Chi-Rho monogram (fig. 156.4). It could very easily represent an accidental dripping of very wet clay onto the tile.

Tile with unusual impressions

12) F756, (3879), phase 5G: a fairly thick tegula fragment with what seems to be the imprint of a tessellated pavement on the underside (fig. 156.5). To have made this impression some

pressure would have had to be applied and this may have been a deliberate attempt to create the impression, unless the pressure was created by the stacking of tiles. The proximity of tile manufacture to tessellated pavements is interesting. There is a similar example from Piddington, Northants (A. D. McWhirr pers. comm.)

The targeted tile groups

A total of 17 features contained over 10 kg of tile and these accounted for 58% of the tile by weight from Roman deposits and 40% of all tile recovered.

A total of nineteen contexts were sampled to define the range of fabrics present. These represented 20% of the tile from each context. Only large fragments were sampled as these were considered to represent material that was less likely to exhibit a high residuality.

Comments on the targeted groups by area

Area 1

There is evidence for timber structures here in the late second and early third centuries, but much of the tile is derived from pits and wells and a direct link cannot therefore be made. By and large, the tile was very abraded and fragmentary. There are two features in which the presence of tile may have some functional reason. Tile from a construction layer, F421, could be indicating the presence of building rubble, and tile in a cobble spread could be indicative of tile used as hardcore.

Area 2

Little tile came from this area, and although there is a stone structure, subsequent activity has displaced any associated tile. This is emphasised by the sum weight of the tegulae recovered representing the equivalent of a single tile.

Area 3

This area provided eight features with 10 kg and over, and five with more than 30 kg. Compared with Area 1, these groups were generally larger and less fragmentary (table 57). Much of the area consisted of large pits or quarries which may have been used as dumps for material derived from demolition. Two features, F756 and F763 produced large quantities of tile commensurate with the demolition of a substantial structure with a tiled roof. Overall, F756 produced the largest group, which consisted of some fairly substantial unabraded fragments, but even here, the sum weight of the tegulae, for example, represents no more than 8-10 complete tiles, which compares with 23-25 tiles for Area 3 as a whole. The bulk of the tegulae and wall tile consisted of largely featureless fragments.

The other large groups in the area include the gravel quarry F763 and the pit F766, but the condition of the material was much poorer compared with F756. As with F343 and F255 in Area 1, the mass of the tile from F763 was derived from the upper fills (sg338/3), while the primary fills (sg338/2) produced a very small and highly abraded assemblage.

Area 4

None of the targeted groups were from this area where only 16% of the Roman tile was actually from Roman levels. Although predominantly residual there was a large quantity of wall tile, but its significance, given the great destruction of Roman levels in this area, cannot be determined.

Discussion

The quantity of tile recovered can be regarded as an average amount for a site of this size, where there were some large rubbish deposits but no significantly large constructional or demolition deposits directly associated with a specific building.

The wide range of fabrics identified in the sampled groups indicates that a variety of sources supplied the town, but as no definite local kilns have been identified, it can only be suggested that the tile did not travel far, particularly as there were plentiful local supplies of clay and fuel. A quite small element came from further afield, as is indicated by the shell tempered fabrics. This variety of fabrics and the abraded, fragmentary nature of the deposits also suggests that this material was derived from more than a single building. There is very little direct evidence of primary use or reuse of this tile. The mix of tile and painted wallplaster in Area 3 does suggest that at least some of the material derived from a comparatively high status building.

Hence beyond saying much of this material is very residual, much of it may have been reused, possibly as hardcore, and that the large groups from Area 3 may derive from demolition sites somewhere in the town, the assemblage provides little scope for any in depth analysis of the tile and its functions.

Though many of the targeted groups were of limited value regarding the information they provided about the usage of tile in this quarter of Roman Leicester, they do nevertheless confirm that it was apparently widely used from the town's earliest phases, first appearing in any quantity in phase 2B in Area 1 and phase 5E in Area 3, emphasising the importance of the primary use of tile as a common roofing material, and to a lesser extent as bonding courses in masonry walls.

NON-CERAMIC BUILDING MATERIALS   *A.G. Gnanaratnam*

SLATE

The site collection policy was to retain only perforated slates and those complete enough to suggest a form. Weights and number counts therefore represent only a sample of the total amount of slate from the site. When slate was present but discarded it was recorded in the site notes.

The site produced 326 complete and incomplete slates, the bulk of which came from Area 3, occurring in decreasing amounts from Roman to post-medieval. Much of the slate from medieval and later contexts is residual Roman, deriving from disturbance to earlier levels. The largest assemblage came from quarry fills in phase 5G, sg359/4, which also produced large amounts of plaster, mortar and other building materials, suggesting a single dump of building material. No slate came from any defined structure.

The slates were examined for shape, dimensions, material, nail or peg-holes and the presence of mortar (torching).

Table 58: *Slate: summary of the assemblage*

113 Diamond shaped slates	60 from Roman contexts, 43 measurable
15 Triangular slates	14 from Roman contexts
1 Inverted triangle	1 from Roman context
11 Rectangular	7 from Roman contexts
3 Rectangular	3 from Post-Medieval contexts
10 Medieval Long slates	3 from Medieval contexts
1 Medieval Elongated Diamond	1 from Post-Medieval context
7 Discs	5 from Roman contexts
165 indeterminate fragments	

Apart from the slate discs, all were roofing slates, the bulk of them Roman.

Roman slates

Diamond-shaped

These are a variant on the hexagonal and near hexagonal forms found in Leicestershire (McWhirr 1988, 2-3) and elsewhere in the country e.g. Marshfield, Vindolanda or Housesteads (Blockley 1985; Bidwell 1985, 60; Bosanquet 1904, 193-300) and the pear-shaped slate (Davey 1961, 149). The diamonds, with one exception, had a perforation in one end, the head, by which they were hung. The diamonds generally fall between 190mm from head to base x 90mm maximum width to 360mm x 300mm. The small size of the sample means that any statistical analysis is unwarranted, however in spite of a fairly even distribution of sizes visual inspection suggests that there may be four loose size categories represented. These are:

Small tile -	up to 230mm x 190mm -	weighing about 1000g
Mid tile -	tending toward 280mm x 230mm -	weighing about 1500g
Mid tile -	tending toward 300mm x 230mm -	weighing about 1500g
Large tile -	up to 360mm x 300mm -	weighing about 2 – 3000g

As all the slate was to one degree or another residual (Roskams 1992) there is no reason to assume that the slate all derives from the same building. Hitherto, the largest Roman Swithland slate noted comes from a site at Narborough, measuring 293mm by 230mm, whilst the smallest is from Haceby, Lincs, and measured 175mm by 165mm (McWhirr 1988, 2).

Triangular

Fifteen triangular slates were found, 14 deriving from Roman contexts. These appear to fall into two categories, one a large head-nailed triangle with the long side horizontal and the second a smaller head or side nailed triangle with the long side probably vertical.

The larger type is around 230mm-250mm x 200mm and is likely to be an eaves slate the height being just over half that of the largest diamonds which were likely the last course by the eaves. The smaller type is around 250mm x 150mm and may have been used for infilling at the gable end and appear to be re-used diamonds. The smaller type, being single nailed, could also be pivoted for use on a sloping gable (hipped roof).

Inverted triangle

This is classified as inverted on the assumption that slates were head nailed and suspended. It is possible that the slate was base nailed and if used at the eaves, the pressure of the overlying slates would keep it in place. The alternative is that the slate was hung and head nailed, in which case the slate would probably have been used at the ridge of the roof. In this location the large surface area of the slate, 240mm x 200mm, may have made it vulnerable to lifting in heavy winds unless covered, perhaps by ridge tiles.

Rectangular

Seven possible rectangular or sub-rectangular slates were found in Roman contexts. They vary in size from 140mm x 75mm to 120mm x 215mm and have nail-holes suggesting that they were roofing slate. If this is the case, it is unclear where on the roof they might have been used. It is possible that they were used for infilling between diamonds on a gable end although it is equally possible that they were used on the ridge.

Two unperforated slates, measuring 65 x 195mm and 230 x 125mm were also found but there is no indication of function, being unperforated they would have been difficult to use as roofing slates and so may have fulfilled a different, possibly structural purpose.

Medieval slates

Two complete medieval slates were found. The first was a standard long sub-rectangular slate 95mm x 280mm with a bored perforation in the head. The second was an elongated diamond 88mm x 240mm with two notches in the shoulders which may have been for pegs. The other fragments were classified as medieval on the basis of occurring in medieval contexts and possessing a bored rather than pecked hole, the former not occurring in the Roman slates, implying that these fragments were not residual.

Post-medieval slates

Three rectangular post-medieval slates were found. These were of blue-grey Welsh slate and typical of the form of roofing slate in use from the Victorian period onward.

Discs

Seven slate discs were recovered, five of them from Roman contexts. This suggests that the discs may possibly be residual when occurring in medieval contexts. They are between 60mm and 105mm in diameter and around 10mm thick. The function of these pieces is unknown, they may be pot lids or gaming counters.

Technological details

With the exception of the three post-medieval Welsh slates, the rest of the assemblage was composed of Swithland slate or more accurately slate from the Charnwood area. Typically this slate is fairly coarse and poorly laminated in comparison with Welsh slate and so both medieval and Roman craftsmen followed roughly the same methods in working the slate. Although the Swithland slate was, until recently, quarried from deep deposits, it is likely that in Roman times it was exposed at the surface (Evans 1976,50).

The slate provides few clues as to the methods of retrieval and initial working. Some of the Roman slates have a flat worn edge, which may be the weathered surface of the original block from which it was split. If so this may imply the working of exposed surface slate. Alternately it may represent the surface of a weathered quarried block, it being common practice to leave a block exposed for a winter to allow the laminae to separate.

Once a block was selected the slate was split off, although again there are no surviving marks to allow identification of the tools used. As Swithland slate is fairly coarse the blanks were usually about 20mm-30mm thick as opposed to the 5-10mm attainable with Welsh slate. The medieval and Roman blanks were brought to shape by flaking, in much the same way as flint. In the case of Roman slates they were generally flaked from one side only giving the slate a plano-convex section. The medieval slates tend to be flaked from both sides. The softness of the stone means that flaking is very rapid.

The main difference between medieval and Roman slateworking methods lies in the method of perforating the slate. The Roman method was to use a sharp point or chisel to create a depression in the surface, frequently on the convex surface, down to a depth of about half the thickness of the slate. At this point a sharp blow with a pointed tool will perforate the slate, removing a flake from the reverse. This flake scar can be observed on all Roman slates from the assemblage. In the manufacture of modern slates the holes are perforated with a short handled sharp pick known as a 'holing bill' (Bowden 1992, 64) and a similar tool may have been used. The holes in the slates are typically 3.5mm-5mm square and occasionally contain nail fragments which together with their small size suggest that the slates were nailed into position rather than pegged. The process is fairly rapid and reasonably reliable, and could feasibly be carried out on the building site itself, the quarry supplying roughed out blanks. This would allow a more accurate fitting of the slate than if they were supplied as completed varying sized irregular slates.

The holes in the medieval slates were bored and the hole was frequently around 10mm wide, and probably hung on a peg rather than a nail. The boring usually leaves a bevel about 2mm wide around the hole and normally the hole was bored from both sides.

There is little evidence to suggest how a Roman slate roof was constructed. Barry (1989) suggests that a slate roof requires a steeper pitch than tile roofs, and so the pitch may have been steeper than that reconstructed by de la Bedoyere (1991, 23). The diamond slates present variations in size although there is no reason to assume that they are from a single structure. The variations in size may represent different roofs or more likely represent the grading in size of slate found in medieval and modern roofs (Osbourn 1989, 376). If this is the case it is probable that the smaller diamond slates would be used toward the top of the roof by the ridge, the mid size for the main area and the larger slates used toward the eaves. The inverted triangles would be used by the ridge and the ridge itself possibly covered with imbrices. The smaller triangular slates would be attached to the gable, filling in between the diamonds. The larger triangular slates would be head-nailed at the eaves, filling in between the largest diamonds.

Visually the roof would have a fish scale effect. The term *pavonacea* used by Pliny (XXXVI, 44,159) refers to the peacock feather effect probably achieved using pear shaped slates. It is of note that both Pliny and Vitruvius refer to the use of stone roof tiles as a provincial curiosity (Pliny XXXVI,44,139; Vitruvius II, i, 4) and is contrasted with the standard Roman use of ceramic tiles.

Summary

The slate from Causeway Lane was dominated by Roman roofing slate. This was entirely residual to one level or another (Roskams 1992) and was thus considered as one assemblage. The forms of Roman roofing slate are fairly standard diamonds and triangular slates together with less frequent sub-rectangular slates. The whole Roman assemblage if considered together was sufficient to cover approximately 5-6 m^2.

The medieval and modern slates are again fairly standard although poorly represented. The lack of medieval slates may relate to the general lack of settlement in the north-east quarter of Leicester during the medieval period. Certainly the production of roofing slate is known from at least 1260 (Evans 1976, 50).

The small slate discs are unusual and are not roofing slates. They are probably some sort of pot lid or gaming counter, and first occur in Roman contexts and may be residual in medieval contexts.

THE TESSERAE

The assemblage as a whole was examined for size and a smaller sample was examined for material. The sample consisted of the tesserae deriving from the Roman contexts on Area 3 of the excavation. None of the tesserae were mortared together, although all displayed a white lime bonding material.

Tesserae were divided into one of three categories, these being small, medium and large. Small were those less than 15mm, medium those between 15-25mm and large were those greater than 25mm. These sizes are based on the most frequently found sizes in surviving mosaics, (Cookson 1984, 8-9). The small tesserae are those usually used for mosaic work rather than plain paving. The medium tesserae are used for either borders to mosaic work, or used together with large tesserae for plain tessellated paving.

The stone was identified visually with the use of dilute hydrochloric acid to test for carbonates. Further identifications were carried out by J. Martin of the Geology Section of the Leicestershire Museums Service. The stones identified were the standard types used in Leicester for tesserae. These are a grey, light brown, yellow and dark grey limestone, together with another dark grey stone which was probably a quartzite.

Table 59: *Summary of the tesserae results*

Complete Assemblage

Stone Tesserae	Small	Medium	Large	Total
Number of tess	50	910	43	1003
% of stone tess	5%	90.7%	4.3%	100%
Ceramic Tesserae				
Number of tess	5	150	20	175
% of ceramic tess	2.9%	86%	11%	100%

Table 60: *Summary of sampled rock types*

	Small	Medium	Large
Grey Limestone	0	132	5
Pale Yellow/Brown Limestone	5	135	2
Red Sandstone	0	1	0
Yellow Sandstone	0	1	0
Dark Grey Limestone	0	2	0
Dark Grey Quartzite	0	1	0
Reddish Limestone	0	3	0
Black Limestone	1	0	0

The following were identified by J. Martin;

Yellow sandstone – Sandstone with calcareous cement and iron oxides. Origins unknown, could be Permian (Nottinghamshire) or Jurassic.

Pale Brown/Yellow Limestone – Lower Jurassic (Liassic) Limestone – the local outcrop is the Vale of Belvoir, Barrow upon Soar, South Wigston and beyond.

Black Limestone – Black fine-grained limestone; not local,

possibly Carboniferous Limestone from e.g. Ashbourne Derbyshire.

Conclusion

The paucity of smaller tesserae may be due to problems in recovery rather than an absence of small tesserae as such. It is of note, however, that very few small tesserae were recovered from environmental samples in comparison with medium and large, which suggests that the lack of fine tesserae may reflect their general absence from the site. The bulk of both the stone and the ceramic tesserae were medium sized. The stone tesserae were predominately either grey limestone or pale yellow/brown, and are around six times as numerous as ceramic tesserae. The ceramic tesserae were almost entirely composed of broken tile; two tegula, one imbrex and one box flue tile fragments were recognised. One potsherd was used as a medium tessera, this was identified by R. Clark as a Whiteware sherd probably dating to between AD 80 – 200.

One tessera was found embedded in *opus signinum* from context 667. This was a medium grey limestone tessera, embedded singly in a large, otherwise plain mortar fragment, laid flush with the surface. This was not a mosaic fragment but may have been part of a decorative scheme picked out with single tesserae in a plain *opus signinum* floor, as occurs for example at Watling Court London (Roskams and Perring 1991, 92) (fig. 156.4).

Overall the entire assemblage is residual and so cannot be ascribed to a single floor. Tesserae are small and could easily be carted considerable distances in building waste. However the large number of tesserae found in Area 3, came largely from quarry fills which contained building debris, including dumps of quite large fragments of wall plaster. This been taken to imply that the plaster and thus the debris came from a building near to the site. If this is the case then the sizes of tesserae present do not suggest the presence of mosaic floors but rather may derive from plain tessellated flooring.

THE WORKED STONE

Two worked stone blocks were recovered from the excavations. These were Sf4551 and 4585. Full drawn records at 1:1 are stored in the archive. The blocks were recovered from a pit and a well respectively, both of which were medieval features. The stone for both blocks was identified by J. Martin as a Triassic Sandstone, possibly from middle Triassic 'waterstones', but considering the location is most likely an upper Triassic (Mercia mudstone Group) skerry sandstone, especially Dane Hills Sandstone.

Sf 4551 – F207 (287) sg120/7 ph 9 – Rectangular block 480mm l x 225mm w x 95mm th. The long front face is chamfered. The faces have been worked with a drove or bolster although the tooling has been left visible. The upper and lower surfaces (beds) have been coarsely chiselled. The block may be part of a plinth or a string course.

Sf 4585 – F238 (340) sg120/1 ph 9 – Damaged ashlar block 3.40mm l x 340mm w x 225mm h. The block is not square in plan the faces/joints are slightly angled. The block has rebates 55mm deep. The faces/joints display drove/bolster marks and the surfaces have been worked to around 2mm deviation from flat. The beds are roughly chiselled. The block is probably part of a door jamb, although its exact orientation within a wall is unclear.

THE MORTAR AND *OPUS SIGNINUM*

The mortar was examined primarily with a view to selecting samples for comparative analysis. In the coarse of the selection a few interesting pieces were noted. The bulk of the mortar consisted of a lime and silty sand and gravel or a lime and clean clear quartz sand mix, typical of Roman mortar. It is likely that almost all the mortar from the site was residual Roman, only one piece of probable mediaeval mortar was found. The *opus signinum* was briefly scanned for any unusual fragments. Again all the *opus signinum* was residual. A list of the mortar samples submitted to Dr G.C. Morgan of the School of Archaeological Studies at Leicester University for comparative analysis is kept in archive.

Mortar

The more interesting fragments of mortar analysed were as follows;

F206 (1530) sg 119/2 ph 10 – a mix of lime and fibrous organic material. Probably a lime and dung plaster, more typical of medieval than Roman technique.

(3501) sg 301/1 ph 12 – two fragments of a white mortar with a cleaned, clear quartz aggregate, with reed impressions on the reverse. One piece has three layers of mortar and a final lime coat, the other two mortar layers and an intonaco and white lime paint layer. This is consistent with Vitruvius' method of using washed river sand applied to reed bundles, for plastering ceilings (Vitruvius VII,iii,2 Faventinus 21). These are probably residual Roman.

F732 (3594) sg 308/3 ph 9 – two fragments of light grey mortar with clean clear quartz sand aggregate, one has reed impressions on the reverse. The fragment has at least three layers of mortar, the surface is abraded and shows no trace of an *intonaco* layer. May be ceiling plaster and probably residual Roman.

(3609) sg 349/1 ph 5H – light brown sandy mortar, tapering cylinder, with no surface finish, base damaged but bears two linear impressions. Mortar used for bonding imbrex to tegulae, bearing cast of inside of imbrex and top of tegulae flanges.

(3836) sg 367/1 ph 5G – as (3609) cast of inside of imbrex and top of tegulae flanges. However the flanges are uneven.

(3897) sg 367/1 ph 5G – light brown sandy mortar fragment containing part of a base of a jar. This was identified by R. Clark as a greyware jar, with spiral burnished decoration, the form and fabric is probably mid second to late fourth century. The jar fragment is embedded within the mortar and so does not seem to fulfil any function but is merely fortuitous.

The *opus signinum*

The *opus signinum* was less common than the mortar but again is residual Roman. A number of fragments preserved a worn upper surface which was undoubtedly the original floor surface. The following pieces were also noted;

(667) sg 153/1 ph 3B – fragment of *op.sig.* floor with grey medium tessera embedded in the surface. Possibly part of decoration picked out in single tesserae (c.f. Perring and Roskams 1991,92).

(1020) sg 152/1 ph 3B – *op. sig.* fragment with curved surface springing from a flatter face. The surface has been covered with a white lime coat possibly in preparation for painting. The fragment is probably part of a skirting board, similar to that found at Whittington Avenue, London (Spence and Grew 1990).

(3522) sg 336/1 ph 6A – two fragments of a white limey *op. sig.* with sharply angled surface. A lime wash has been applied but there is no trace of painting. The *op. sig.* seems to contain less tile and silt than other *op. sig.* frags. The fragments probably are part of a sloping window sill or embrasure, possibly op. sig. was used to exclude damp, (c.f. Vitruvius VII, iv, 1 – 3 Faventinus ch. 24).

(3522) sg 336/1 ph 6A – flat *op. sig.* fragment with right-angled edge, flat upper surface and concave lower surface. May be jointing from wall between tile and stone. Use of *op. sig.* in bonding lower courses in walls is consistent with Vitruvius' writings (Vitr. VII, iv, 1 – 3).

THE BURNT CLAY AND DAUB

The clay and daub breaks down as follows:

Undiagnostic fragments were found in nine Roman, three medieval and one post-medieval context.

(1589) sg 143/1 ph 6A – five fragments of possibly dried rather than fired clay, one frag of which had a flat base and a curved side. It is not clear what this is although it may be part of a mould.

F540 (2294) sg 247/2 ph 8 – a daub fragment with wattle impressions on the reverse. This shows a sail greater than 25mm in diameter, with two rods greater than 10 and 15mm in diameter. Presumably the piece derives from some sort of structure but there is no evidence of what.

INDUSTRIAL RESIDUES G.C.Morgan

These were examined by microscopy and microchemical analysis.

The crucibles mainly show copper alloy casting, in particular brass. There are also several samples which may show glass working residues, although intensive fuel ash slagging can also produce glass-like coatings. The presence of copper/silver alloy residues also shows casting of that material. The cupellation type residues, being rich in copper lead and tin, suggest that silver may have been extracted from base silver coins, as has been seen in several sites around the country (Silchester being a notable example). The hearth bottom slags and hearth lining fragments are mainly from iron working with the possibility of some iron smelting being carried out somewhere in the vicinity. The considerable quantities of calcareous concretions and kiln residues points to lime burning but there is little charcoal present in the samples. If the burning process was particularly efficient it is possible that all the wood was burnt, leaving just fuel ash slag and lime behind. This has subsequently become slaked and set to form the concretions found. The fuel ash slag here was rich in silica, alumina, calcium carbonate and traces of phosphates. This is fairly typical for wood fuel ash but the lime and phosphates may point to bone being burnt as well. It would be tempting to suggest that bone ash was being made for incorporation into cupels for cupellation although the evidence is somewhat slight.

Table 61: *Roman crucibles*.

Group	Context	Description.
Phase 2		
201/2	(2979)	Crucible fragment
Phase 3		
154/1	(1052)	Lead frags.
Phase 5		
354/1	(3786)	Crucible fragment repeated use Copper and Zinc.
354/1	(3786)	Crucible fragment repeated use Copper and Zinc.
353/1	(3664)	Crucible fragment glassy slagging Copper and Zinc.
354/1	(3827)	Crucible fragment p.green glassy.
334/2	(3600)	Copper Crucible rim fragment black/brown ?
	(3954)	Copper Galena 90g Lead ore.
Phase 6		
367/1	(3836)	Glass furnace part White/Green.

Table 62: *Roman slag*

Group	Feature/ Context	Description
Phase 2		
148/2	(1218)	Iron bloom or billet
145/6	(1316)	Vitrified clay
144/1	(1511)	Vitrified brick or tile from ?furnace or hearth
145/3	(1546)	Hearth bottom slag
Phase 3		
141/4	F343	Crucible fragment or flat cupel part
151/1	F417	Fayalite slag in vitrified clay ?hearth lining and residue
101/1	(1409)	
Phase 4		
174/3	F255	Vitrified clay lining
Phase 5		
351/1	(3617)	Hearth bottom slag. Vitrified clay
Phase 6		
350/1	F736	Vitrified clay hearth or furnace lining
367/1	F766	Rusty Iron object and concretions and vitrified clay
367/1	F766	Iron concretions and corroded object

Table 63: *Medieval slag*

Group	Feature/Context	Description
Phase 8		
124/2	F245	Cupellation residues Copper Tin and Lead ?from extraction of Silver from bronze coins?
118/3	F247	Vitrified Clay, lining and hearth bottom X2 and Vesicular fayalite.
253/9	F549	Dense fayalite possible tap slag.
114/3	F482	Hearth bottom slag.
247/2	F568	Calcareous concretions.
253/3	(2377)	Dense fayalite and charcoal, hearth bottom or possible tap slag.
Phase 9		
127/1	F203	Hearth bottom slag.
120/6	F204	Calcareous concretions.
119/1	F205	Furnace slag.
120/8	F207	Fuel ash, hearth residues and calcareous concretions.
120/3	F216	Vitrified clay, hearth bottom slag fayalite ?tap slag.
126/3	F217	Vitrified clay lining hearth bottom slag.
116/1	F235	Hearth bottom slag hammer scale and spheroids.
127/1	F238	Vesicular fayalite furnace slag.
120/1	F238	Hearth bottom slag.
121/1	F292	Hearth bottom slag.
256/3	F508	Calcareous concretions and kiln residues.
260/4	F513	Calcareous concretions and fuel ash slag.
247/2	F516	Calcareous concretions.
256/1	F570	Calcareous concretions fuel ash slag and kiln residues.
312/1	F712	Vitrified clay with glassy coating and some slagging.
Phase 10		
119/3	F206	Furnace slag, haematite, possible tap slag, vitrified clay, fayalite slag and hearth bottom slag.
Phase 12		
101/1	F226	Hearth bottom.
294/3	F581	Vitrified sandy clay 30mm thick and glassy coating, lead droplets possible cupel or crucible, Probable smithing and metal working residues and waste, rust concretions Charcoal and Copper alloy traces. Copper alloy sheet, Copper and Zinc and Silver traces, probable brass sheet. Also tap slag with Iron scintered white clay ?crucible fragments.
301/1	(3501)	Coal, stone and tar. Vitrified clay hearth and furnace lining, hearth residue, vesicular fayalite furnace slag.

THE ENVIRONMENTAL EVIDENCE
edited by *Angela Monckton*

ENVIRONMENTAL SAMPLING

Angela Monckton

In addition to the animal bones and oyster shells recovered by hand during excavation 15 tonnes of soil samples were taken to wet sieve for smaller remains. These included the small animal bones, fish bones and scales, shell and insect remains together with charred cereal grains and seeds which would not be found otherwise. Small samples were also taken to examine for other microscopic remains such as pollen. These plant and animal remains recovered from the environmental samples provide evidence of the diet of the people as well as evidence of the environment and economy in the past.

Extensive sampling had been carried out for the first time in Leicester on the Shires excavation at Little Lane and St. Peter's Lane recovering a range of remains including large and small animal bones, fish remains and plant remains. A very little waterlogged material which included pollen was recovered from the bottoms of the deeper wells, evidence for gut parasites was also found. Sampling on the Shires had the objective of surveying the range of remains in a large number of contexts, and preliminary results available at the start of this excavation showed plant remains were often present at a low concentration. More selective bulk sampling was therefore necessary to produce larger assemblages of material for analysis in order to extend the information already obtained from the Shires and other sites in the area (Monckton 1995). However it was still considered necessary to sample as extensively as possible in order to recover more of the range of plants and animals present.

Preservation

Most of the sediments were free draining and bone was generally well preserved on the site, including small bones and fish remains recovered from sieved samples. Charred plant remains do not decay and are preserved in most types of soils. They generally represent plant products such as cereals, which come into contact with fire during their processing, use or disposal; they can provide information about plant materials used or consumed on the site. Plants such as legumes, which do not require parching in their processing, and vegetables, which may not be allowed to seed or the remains of which may be composted are not often preserved, so more extensive sampling is required to increase the chance of their recovery. Other remains included eggshell, charcoal and oyster shell. Such remains are often found in rubbish pits and can give evidence about life on the site.

Preservation by mineralisation of some remains was found, this occurs in such conditions as are found in cesspits where sewage or latrine waste was dumped. In such conditions the organic remains become impregnated with calcium salts which preserve the form of the plant and animal remains in a semi-fossilised state. Mineralised plant remains from cesspits tend to represent food remains such as fruit stones and pips these, together with chewed fishbones which having passed through the gut, were deposited in the pit in sewage. These pits also preserved microscopic eggs of gut parasites confirming their use as cesspits with occasional finds of coprolites (mineralised or dried faeces) adding to this evidence. Mineralised remains of flies, other insects and woodlice were also preserved which give evidence about the putrid conditions in the pits.

Little waterlogged material was found on this site, as at the Shires the waterlogged preservation was poor, insects and plant remains not surviving in these conditions, although there was some pollen present in these deposits. Pollen was analysed from some of the wells because it can provide evidence about material brought to the site for use, plants growing on the site or pollen from the surrounding region.

Sampling

Environmental samples were taken from contexts which were well defined, potentially datable and productive (Greig 1989 22) while attempting to cover the main periods of the site. Usual sample size was about 20 litres, although smaller samples were taken where material was limited and a number of contexts with good potential for remains, particularly bone, were selected and larger samples taken. Hence a range of samples of 5 to 35 litres were taken for the recovery of plant remains and small bones, a further number of selected contexts had larger samples taken for the consistent recovery of the smaller bones of the larger animals (Payne 1989). Auger samples were taken with a Dutch auger (8cm diameter) from the wells and deeper pits in order to recover any waterlogged remains as well as to establish the depth of the features and water table.

Processing

Samples were wet-sieved in a sieving tank obtained from York Archaeological Trust using a 1mm mesh with flotation into a 0.5mm mesh sieve. Samples were processed in units up to 35 litres with additional units for selected contexts this amounted to 778 sample units (from 698 contexts) totalling 12,184 litres (15.1 tonnes), (table 64). The residues were air dried and then separated on a 4mm riddle and the coarse fractions over 4mm were all sorted for bone and finds. The remaining residue was separated again on a 2mm sieve and the fine fraction of 2-4mm was sorted, this was done for the first sample unit only, amounting to 698 samples. Residues of 1-2mm were not sorted as they were found to have low potential for remains.

Table 64: *Distribution of samples by group and phase*

Phase	Total Subgroups	Subgroups sampled	Samples Taken	Samples Sieved	Volume Sieved (Litres)
1	17	11	48	42	573
2	68	38	124	114	1556
3	95	55	202	180	2722
4	4	4	30	29	465
5	88	32	68	57	916
6	14	5	18	15	174
7	12	1	1	1	10
8	44	25	111	104	1620
9	151	76	228	173	2925
10	9	9	30	26	586
11	17	8	12	11	179
12	41	13	32	26	458
Totals	**560**	**277**	**904**	**778**	**12184**

The flotation fractions (flots) from all sample units were air dried and assessed for the presence of plant remains. As the flots also contained small bones, fish and insect remains all the flots were sorted and the remains added to those from the other residues for identification and analysis. The archaeological integrity of the samples was considered in evaluating all the remains for analysis and samples with high percentages of residual pottery were not analysed.

Sub-samples were retained from all the sieved samples and some of these, together with some spot samples were tested for parasite remains, and some together with auger samples analysed for pollen. Samples were also taken for sediment analysis. All sample records are held in the archive.

Results

The presence of remains was recorded by subgroup (tables 2 and 3). These include the weight of animal bone and oyster shell, and the presence of fish bone, fish scales and eggshell. For the plant remains only samples with over 20 grains or seeds or with any mineralised fruit stones were recorded, and samples with abundant charcoal were recorded. For the parasites only positive results were recorded for the three types of material tested; cesspit fill, coprolites or soil sub-samples. The presence of flies and woodlice was also recorded.

The reports follow in the order of evidence from animal remains for foods and environmental conditions followed by the evidence from the plant remains and finally the human bone.

THE ANIMAL BONES   *Louisa Gidney*

The animal bones from the Roman phases

Introduction

The animal bones from the Roman deposits are discussed in two groups: Phase 1-3, Earlier Roman AD 50-200 and phases 4-6, Later Roman AD 200-400.

This report is a synopsis based on the archive report held in the Jewry Wall Museum, Leicester.

Methods of recording

To maximise the useful information to be obtained from the Roman animal bone assemblage from Causeway Lane, two levels of recording fragments were used. The full catalogue recorded only fragments of cattle, sheep/goat and pig with a diagnostic 'zone'

All fragments of any other species present were catalogued. The zones used are those defined by Rackham (unpubl.). Other contexts were scanned, that is the number of fragments per species was counted using the same criteria as the full record. Metrical and ageing data were also recorded. Details of this recording system have been described more fully in Gidney (1991, 2).

Results

The overwhelming majority of the identified animal bones from Phases 1-3 derive from cattle, sheep/goat and pig, table 66. These are the domestic farm animals that have been, and still are, exploited as the main source of meat for human consumption. Table 65 suggests some chronological and spatial variation in the deposition of bones of the domesticates. In Area 1 there are proportionally more sheep/goat than cattle bones present in phases 1 and 2. In phase 3, cattle bones outnumber those of sheep/goat, with a particularly high proportion of cattle bones recovered from the north-south

ditch, F343 G141. Areas 2 and 3 produced only small assemblages from phases 2 and 3, cattle bones outnumber those of sheep/goat but this could be partly a product of small sample size. The later Roman assemblage from phases 4-6 continues to be dominated by cattle bones, tables 65 and 66. However, in Area 3, phase 6 there is an increase in the proportion of pig rather than sheep bones relative to those of cattle.

Table 65: *Relative proportions of the domestic species in Roman contexts by fragment counts*

	Phase 1 Area 1	Phase 2 Area 1	Area 2	Area 3
Cattle & Lg.Ungulate	19 33%	510 35%	92 50%	30 47%
Sheep/Goat & Sm.Ungulate	30 53%	665 46%	75 41%	24 38%
Pig	8 14%	282 19%	16 9%	10 15%
Totals	57	1457	183	64

	Phase 3 Area 1		Area 2	
	Ditch	Non-Ditch	ALL	
Cattle & Lg.Ungulate	630 72%	1098 50%	1728 56%	43 64%
Sheep/Goat & Sm.Ungulate	171 19%	765 34%	952 30%	16 24%
Pig	76 9%	349 16%	425 14%	8 12%
Totals	877	2212	3105	67

	Phase 4 Area 1	Phase 5 Area 1	Area 3	Phase 6 Area 3
Cattle & Lg.Ungulate	82 47%	380 58%	492 49%	268 42%
Sheep/Goat & Sm.Ungulate	59 34%	196 30%	319 38%	191 30%
Pig	33 19%	81 12%	194 19%	176 28%
Totals	174	657	1005	635

Cattle

The pattern of skeletal representation for cattle bones in phases 1 and 2, fig. 157, suggests that whole carcases were used and that the more robust elements have survived better. In contrast fig. 158 for the cattle remains from Area 1, phase 3 shows strong selectivity with high proportions of horn core, lower jaw and metapodial fragments. This pattern is particularly marked in the ditch, F343 G141. Such a pattern suggests the deposition of a large component of industrial waste from horn working and/or tanning with only a small proportion of household waste. The horns and feet may have been attached to hides and later removed for the horn to be utilised and perhaps for neats foot oil to be extracted from the metapodials (Serjeantson 1989, 139-141). The abundance of extremities suggests that the industrial processing in this area was supplied from more carcases than were consumed in the immediate vicinity.

Considerable variation in the morphology of the horn cores was apparent, with a range similar to that illustrated for Roman Sheepen (Luff 1982, plate 3). Two shapes occur commonly, the classic 'Celtic Shorthorn' (plate 16) which is pre-eminent in Northern England, for example at Carlisle (Stallibrass 1991, plate 13) but becomes a less dominant form further south at York (O'Connor 1988, 95 and plate V) and a short horned form (plate 17) with a less markedly oval basal cross section. Despite the visual variation, plotting of the basal diameters produced a normal distribution for the minimum diameter and a bimodal distribution for the maximum diameter, fig. 159. The latter is interpreted as sexual dimorphism rather than two 'breed' types. The fact that visual morphs do not separate metrically suggests

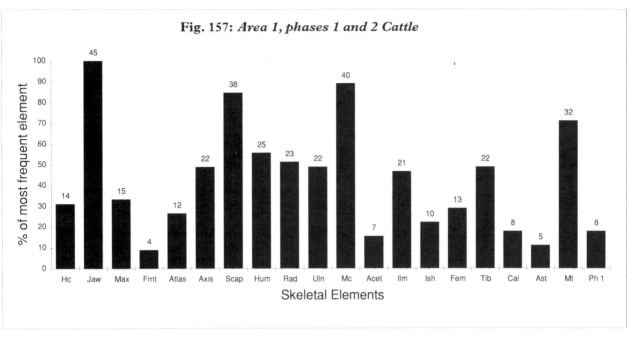

Fig. 157: *Area 1, phases 1 and 2 Cattle*

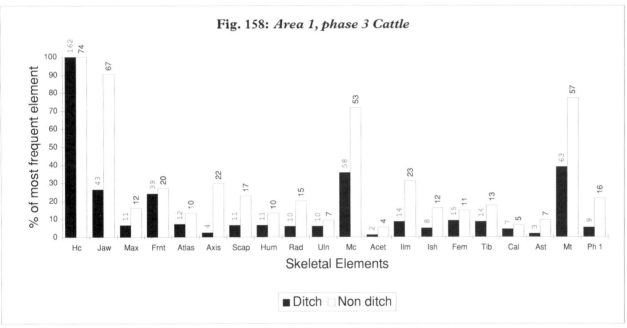

Fig. 158: *Area 1, phase 3 Cattle*

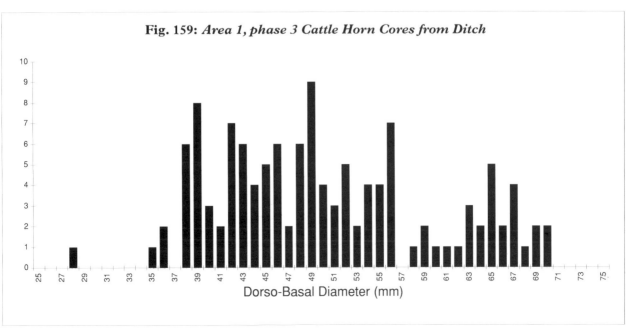

Fig. 159: *Area 1, phase 3 Cattle Horn Cores from Ditch*

Table 66: *Fragment counts for the species present in Roman phases.*

Phase	1B	2A	2B	2C	2D	2E	2F	2G	2H	2K	2L	3A	3B	3B	3C	3D	3E	3F	3G	1-3 Totals	4A	5A	5B	5C	5D	5E	5F	5G	5H	6A	4-6 Totals
Area	1	1	1	1	1	1	1	1	1	2	3	1d	1d	1	1	1	2	2	2	Totals	1	1	1	1	1	3	3	3	3	3	Totals
Cattle	15	29	65	5	73	3	78	190	7	82	21	323	269	644	25	110	2	5	37	**1983**	69	75	156	260	91	57	121	186	52	224	**1291**
Sheep/Goat	30	25	121	-	98	2	90	284	6	67	21	55	108	464	10	80	-	5	9	**1475**	53	67	110	177	8	47	87	118	25	153	**845**
Sheep	-	-	3	4	-	-	-	2	-	6	1	-	1	6	-	3	-	-	-	**26**	1	-	-	1	-	4	4	4	-	3	**17**
Pig	8	18	50	3	52	2	37	113	7	16	10	28	48	209	5	61	-	3	5	**675**	33	33	41	78	3	31	56	77	30	176	**558**
Horse	4	-	7	-	1	-	1	7	3	4	-	7	1	8	-	1	-	-	1	**45**	4	4	31	53	6	2	2	3	1	4	**110**
Dog	-	-	-	-	-	*1	-	3	-	3	-	*5	4	19	-	9	-	-	-	**38**	6	6	-	17	28	2	3	6	3	11	**82**
Cat	-	-	-	-	-	-	-	-	-	-	-	-	-	2	-	-	-	-	-	**2**	-	-	1	1	-	-	-	-	-	1	**3**
Red Deer	-	-	-	-	-	-	-	1	-	-	-	-	-	-	-	-	-	-	-	**1**	2	-	-	3	-	-	5	4	1	1	**16**
Roe Deer	-	-	-	-	-	-	-	1	-	-	-	-	2	-	-	1	-	-	-	**4**	-	1	3	3	-	-	1	4	-	3	**15**
Hare	-	-	-	-	-	-	1	1	-	-	-	-	5	5	-	1	-	-	-	**8**	1	-	1	2	-	-	1	2	1	17	**25**
L. Ungulate	4	8	12	-	5	1	8	24	2	8	9	12	26	44	1	20	-	-	1	**185**	13	11	12	25	4	15	15	40	6	44	**185**
S. Ungulate	-	2	5	-	8	2	6	6	1	2	2	-	7	16	2	15	-	1	1	**76**	5	2	6	5	5	3	9	12	5	35	**87**
Fowl	1	1	6	-	4	2	4	10	-	5	2	2	6	36	-	40	-	1	2	**122**	8	15	8	21	1	10	18	17	20	121	**239**
Duck	-	-	-	-	3	-	1	1	-	-	-	-	1	1	1	1	-	-	-	**8**	-	1	-	-	1	-	-	1	-	23	**26**
Goose	-	-	2	-	-	-	-	-	-	-	-	-	1	1	1	1	-	-	-	**4**	1	1	2	2	-	1	1	5	2	11	**26**
Pigeon	-	-	-	-	-	-	1	-	-	-	-	-	-	-	-	-	-	-	-	**1**	-	-	1	-	-	-	-	-	-	-	**1**
Woodcock	-	-	-	-	-	-	1	-	-	1	1	-	1	4	-	-	-	-	-	**8**	-	-	-	2	-	1	3	-	1	3	**10**
Teal	-	-	-	-	-	-	-	-	-	-	-	-	-	-	-	-	-	-	-	**0**	1	-	-	-	-	-	-	-	-	-	**1**
Golden Plover	-	-	-	-	-	-	-	-	-	-	-	-	-	-	-	-	-	-	-	**0**	-	-	-	-	-	-	-	-	2	2	**4**
Raven	-	-	-	-	-	-	-	-	-	-	-	-	-	-	-	-	-	-	-	**7**	-	-	-	-	-	-	-	-	-	-	**0**
Rook/Crow	-	-	-	-	-	-	-	-	-	-	-	-	-	3	-	-	-	-	-	**3**	1	-	-	-	-	-	-	-	-	-	**1**
Lapwing	-	-	-	-	-	-	-	-	-	-	-	-	-	-	-	-	-	-	-	**0**	1	-	-	-	-	-	-	-	-	-	**1**
Frog/Toad	-	-	-	-	-	-	-	-	-	-	-	-	-	2	-	-	-	-	-	**2**	-	-	-	-	-	-	-	-	-	-	**0**
Totals	62	83	271	12	244	13	228	643	26	194	67	427	472	1473	43	343	2	15	56	**4673**	199	216	372	650	147	173	327	479	149	832	**3543**

* number includes partial skeleton counted as one bone   d = ditch contexts.

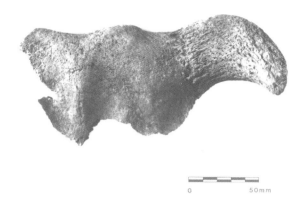

Plate 16: *Typical example of 'Celtic Shorthorn' cattle horn core.*

Plate 17: *Another common form of cattle horn core with less markedly oval cross section*

that this is the range of type within one population.

No naturally polled frontals were seen, though one example from F240 186/1 phase 5D had had the horn core deliberately or accidentally removed. A few horn cores of unusual shape were seen. In these cases the base of the horn core where it attaches to the frontal is unusually broad and deep and mirrors the angle of the frontal-parietal suture. The body of the horn core is lightly built compared to the size of the base (plate 18). Possible explanations of this condition include: nutritional problems, castration, tethering or yoking by the horns when the horns were actively growing.

The representation of skeletal elements from phases 4-6 suggests largely undifferentiated use of the post-cranial beef carcase for food. Horn cores were infrequent compared to phase 3, suggesting either a spatial or temporal distribution of waste from hornworking centred on Area 1.

Mandibles with intact molar rows had Mandible Wear Scores (MWS) calculated after Grant (1982). Figure 160 indicates three groupings of MWS. Firstly a single jaw at MWS 7 with the first molar coming into wear, from an animal aged about 6 months at death. Secondly, 12 jaws at MWS 15-23 with the second molar erupting. These compare with the tooth wear on modern Dexters killed from 15-27 months old (Gidney, personal reference collection). Thirdly, 29 jaws from MWS 31-55 with the third molar erupting and wearing down. These will span animals killed from about three years old onwards, a modern Dexter had MWS 35 when killed at exactly 3 years old. Some very aged animals are indicated. Five modern Dexter cows aged 11-17 years had MWS 45-8. There are 8 Roman jaws with MWS 49-55, suggesting that a fifth of the slaughter population represented by jaws had survived into or beyond their late teens. The epiphysial fusion evidence also indicates few remains from infant animals, a cull of immature animals but most bones from animals with all epiphyses fused.

The MWS for phases 4-6 in fig. 160 show only two jaws from immature animals, with the remaining jaws ranging from young adults with the third molar erupting to aged animals with severe tooth wear. One such jaw had extreme wear on molar 3 such that only a stump of the first cusp was left, this jaw could not be included for MWS as the wear stage was beyond the scale. It is extremely interesting that the younger age group represented in phases 1-3 is virtually absent from phases 4-6. This suggests either a chronological change in the supply of meat or a change in patterns of consumption and waste disposal by the local residents. The epiphysial evidence also suggests that the first preferential cull was of animals three years old or over, with the majority of bones from animals that were skeletally mature.

The Roman cattle appear to have been relatively small beasts. Withers heights were estimated from intact metapodials using the factors given by Zalkin (1960, 126) where the sex of the animal is unknown. For phases 1-3 this results in a mean height of 1.09m with a range from 1-1.21m, fig. 162. This is comparable with the variation between the sexes seen in modern non-dwarf Dexter cattle. Fewer complete bones were found in phases 4-6. These fall within the range established for the earlier Roman cattle. The mean height is slightly greater at 1.14m, but this may only be a product of the small sample size.

The metapodials are sexually dimorphic. The distal breadths of the metacarpals are plotted in fig. 161, which shows bimodal distributions for both earlier and later Roman examples. If the smaller bones are interpreted as female and the larger bones as male, this would indicate a cull of two thirds female to one third male animals for phases 1-3 and threequarters female to one quarter male for phases 4-6. Such a pattern, together with the evidence for elderly animals, suggests that the live animals were valued for breeding, milk and traction rather than being kept primarily for meat production.

Sheep/Goat

No evidence for the presence of goat was found in phases 1-3. In phases 4-6 a single metacarpal of goat was found in phase 5F. In all the Roman phases, the sheep were a type with both horned and polled animals present. The sheep bones found in all phases come from all parts of the body but fragments of lower jaws and tibia are particularly abundant. This suggests a bias towards the preservation of the more robust skeletal elements. Since the burial environment has been benign, such bias was caused before burial by such agents as consumption by canids. Horn cores and metapodials are infrequent compared to those of cattle in phase 3, indicating that commercial processing of sheep hides and/or horns was not a local activity.

Many more complete tooth rows of sheep were found than of cattle. The MWS in fig. 164 indicate that in phase 1-3 the majority of jaws are from young animals. Meat would appear to have been a primary product of the flock. Two peaks of culling are indicated in fig. 164. Lambs from about three months old with the first molar erupting are indicated by the jaws at MWS 6-11. These are followed by a cull of weaned sheep with the second molar erupting aged from about nine months. Threequarters of the lower jaws come from sheep aged less than two years at slaughter. Such a pattern indicates sheep management designed to produce prime young meat for the urban consumer. The remaining quarter of the jaws

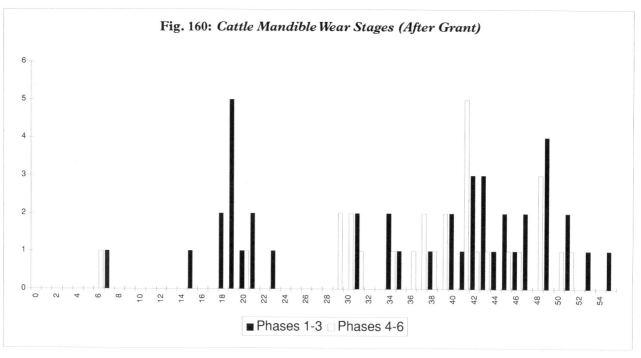

Fig. 160: *Cattle Mandible Wear Stages (After Grant)*

■ Phases 1-3 □ Phases 4-6

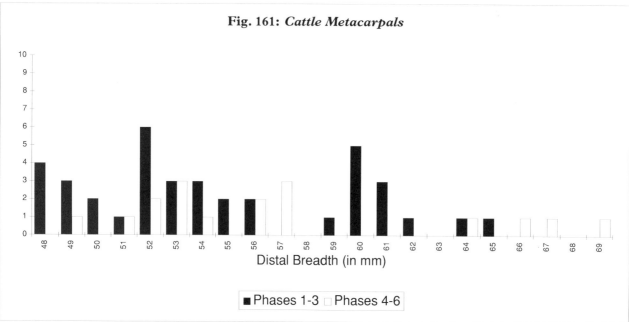

Fig. 161: *Cattle Metacarpals*

Distal Breadth (in mm)

■ Phases 1-3 □ Phases 4-6

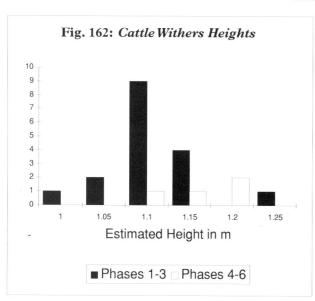

Fig. 162: *Cattle Withers Heights*

Estimated Height in m

■ Phases 1-3 □ Phases 4-6

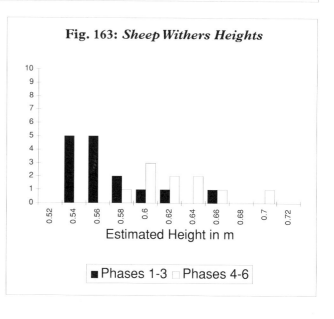

Fig. 163: *Sheep Withers Heights*

Estimated Height in m

■ Phases 1-3 □ Phases 4-6

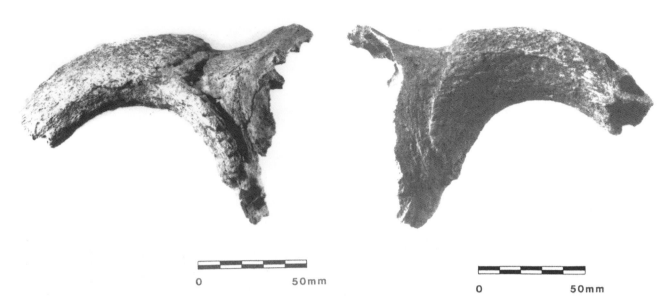

0   50mm

0   50mm

Plate 18 (i) and (ii). *Cattle horn core showing distorted basal shape*

from older animals include roughly half with molar 3 erupting, at MWS 26-35, aged about two years from prime mutton animals. Those jaws at MWS 36-44 have all permanent teeth present and in wear and are from sheep aged upwards of two years at slaughter. These probably represent culls from the breeding flock. The high cull of juvenile sheep suggests efficient sheep production with few young stock needed to maintain the breeding population. Wool production appears to have been of less importance than meat, as a large proportion of the slaughter population were too young to have been shorn first.

In phases 4-6 the same cull pattern is apparent in fig. 164. Young lambs at MWS 6-12 still contribute over a third of the jaws present but there is a change of emphasis with less than a quarter of the jaws at MWS 18-23 and proportionally more at MWS 29-44. This may reflect a change in consumer taste or grazing management with a higher proportion of animals over wintered to produce a larger carcase of prime young mutton.

Much of the epiphysial evidence for the younger sheep appears to have been destroyed by canid gnawing. For subsequent age groups the epiphysial evidence confirms the trends observed from the teeth.

The Roman sheep appear to have been quite small, gracile animals with a mean withers height of 0.56m in phases 1-3 and 0.62m in phases 4-6. The withers heights have been estimated from the factors given by Teichert (*in* von den Driesch & Boessneck 1974). It can be seen from fig. 163 that there is a skewed distribution of heights for phases 1-3 and a more normal distribution for phases 4-6. If the smaller animals are the females, then males and castrates are under represented in phases 1-3 while females are under represented in phases 4-6. Such a chronological change in the sex ratio of the slaughter population complements the suggestion from the MWS for a change in sheep management practices.

Pig

The pigs appear to have been a small, long snouted type. All parts of the body are present but there is a bias towards the more robust parts of the skeleton. Like the sheep bones, this indicates factors, such as canid gnawing, affecting the assemblage of bones entering the burial environment.

It is more difficult to obtain an impression of the Roman pig as the majority of the bones are from immature animals. The MWS in fig. 166 show no differences between the earlier and later Roman periods. Sucking pigs, with milk teeth only, and weaned piglets with molar 1 erupting, aged from about four months, are represented. However most jaws, between MWS 15-21, have molar 2 erupting indicating a preferred slaughter of animals over 7 months old. There are a few jaws with molar 3 erupting at MWS 26-31 from animals over 18 months old, which may have been used for breeding. No jaws with excessively worn teeth associated with advanced age were found. Pig management appears to have been even more streamlined than that of sheep for the production of prime young meat. The epiphysial evidence supports that from the teeth for predominantly juvenile animals. Since the majority of pigs were killed before many epiphyses had fused, there were no intact bones from which withers heights could be estimated.

Horse

Horse bones were generally infrequent in all phases. Most fragments were found singly and may be seen as 'background' debris incorporated into, for example, make-up deposits. Only two bones, from phases 1-3, were complete for an estimate of withers heights and fell within the modern range for ponies at 1.31m and 1.39m, approximating to 13 and 14 hands. In phase 5B an unusual concentration of horse bones was found in 162/2 F211. This was a shallow pit containing the greater part of four feet from one animal. These feet had been severely butchered and further use, rather than butchery, appears to have been made of two sets of toe bones (plates 19 and 20). The anterior aspect of the third phalanges appears to have been rubbed or worn away and this wear extends onto the second phalanges. The first phalanges would have made a convenient grip for using the foot as a tool. The function these feet were employed for is obscure but must have involved a rubbing or scraping action.

In the later Roman phases, a concentration of horse bones was found in a well of phase 5C, G166 F246. None of these bones were articulated but only one animal appears to be represented. The corpse had been attacked by scavenging dogs and the disintegrating carcase then became incorporated in the collapse of the feature.

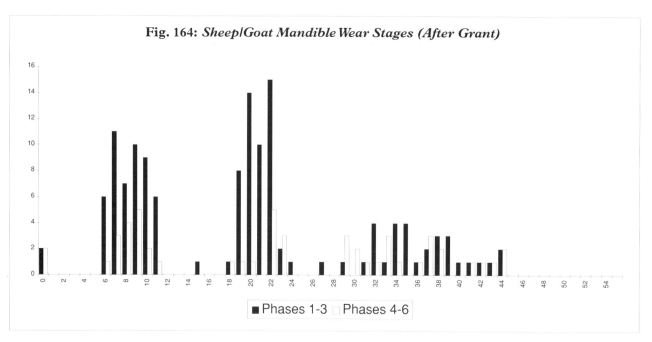

Fig. 164: *Sheep/Goat Mandible Wear Stages (After Grant)*

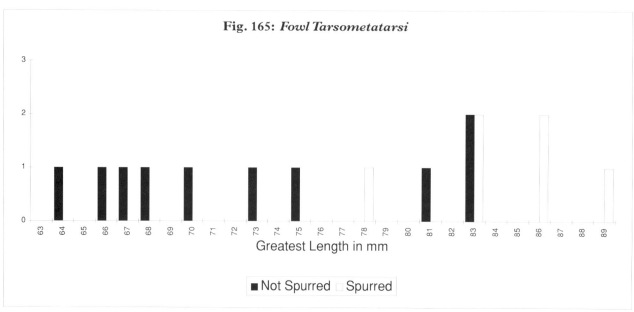

Fig. 165: *Fowl Tarsometatarsi*

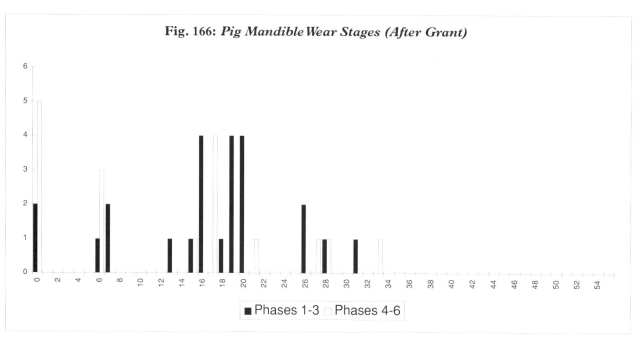

Fig. 166: *Pig Mandible Wear Stages (After Grant)*

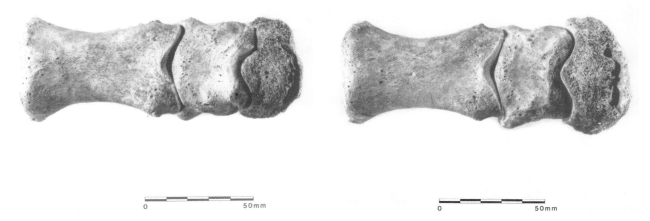

Plates 19 & 20: *Two sets of horse phalanges with unusual wear from rubbing or scraping action*

Dog

Dog bones were also uncommon in all phases. In phases 1-3 these include in phase 2E part of a puppy skeleton from a well, G147 F405. The fill of ditch G141 F343 produced part of the skeleton of an elderly dog in phase 3A. The non ditch deposits in phase 3B produced a puppy skeleton from a well, G153 F318, and parts of adult dog bodies from three other features. This pattern suggests that puppies were disposed of as intact corpses while the adult animals were probably buried elsewhere initially and subsequently redeposited in earth used to backfill features. In phases 4-6 the dog bones all appear to be redeposited, rather than primary burials, and include some notable for their diminutive size (plate 21). Two types of miniature are represented: one with stocky bowed or bandy legs and one with gracile straight legs, with an estimated height of 22cm. Two of these bones have clear cut marks, unrelated to skinning, though the purpose of dismemberment is unclear.

Cat

Cat remains are extremely infrequent with only three bones recovered from phase 3 and one from phase 6. These Roman cat bones may derive from wild animals hunted for fur, rather than domestic pets.

Red Deer

Only one red deer bone was found in phase 1-3. This was a toe bone from phase 2G. Red deer remains were scarce, but more consistently present, in phases 4-6 and comprised four pieces of antler to seven bone fragments. With one exception the bones were all from the extremities and could have been brought onto the site attached to a skin. Minimal use of red deer seems to have been made, either as a source of meat or raw material for craft work.

Roe Deer

Remains of this deer were slightly more common than those of red deer in the earlier Roman collection but of similar frequency in the later phases. Most fragments comprised lower leg and jaw bones which could be waste from skins rather than the dressed carcase.

Hare

The hare bones occurred as isolated finds in phases 1-3 with most from phase 3. Over half the fragments were from the pelvis, the saddle in culinary terms. The hare bones represent meat rather than skins. In phases 4-6, hare bones are most common in phase 6A, 338/3 F763 and 337/1 F766. A hare was often used as an attribute of Winter in Roman art and these hare bones may be the result of some winter hunting.

Birds

The most numerous bird bones in phases 1-3 are from domestic fowl. Fowl bones are the only bird remains to be consistently present in nearly every phase, which may suggest that fowl is the only domestic bird present. The duck bones were all comparable in size to the modern mallard apart from two bones which were both of similar size to modern wigeon. The goose bones were generally of similar size to the modern greylag apart from one bone from a larger bird comparable to a modern domestic specimen. A few woodcock bones were also present which, with the probably wild duck and goose bones, indicate some opportunistic winter wildfowling. The pigeon, rook/crow and raven bones are more likely to represent birds attracted to the urban environment. The pigeon is more likely to have been eaten than the corvids. The raven bones derive from one bird, which could have been a tame bird.

In the later Roman phases, fowl bones are particularly abundant in phase 6A, where they were concentrated in three

Plate 21: *Examples of bones from diminutive dogs*

features: 336/1 F737, 338/3 F763 and 367/1 F766. This suggests very discrete deposition of refuse containing poultry bones in quantity. These deposits may indicate refuse from one household, celebratory dining or the season of the year. Too few measurable fowl bones were found to contrast the earlier and later phases. All the tarsometatarsi have been included in fig. 165. It can be seen that the spurred bones, from cocks, form a discrete group but three unspurred examples fall within the same range. These could be from large hens or young cocks where the spur has not yet fused to the shaft. Duck bones were also numerous in phase 6A with concentrations in 383/3 F763 and 367/1 F766. Half the duck bones were comparable to mallard, the remainder were from smaller wild ducks, including teal in phase 4. The goose bones were generally comparable with the greylag but two bones were from larger, possibly domestic, birds and two were from smaller, wild birds. Like the hare bones, the wild ducks and geese are probably indicative of winter hunting. Three birds of the wader group are represented. One lapwing bone was found in phase 4. Woodcock bones were present in small numbers in phases 5 and 6 and plover bones were present in phases 5H and 6A. These are more likely to derive from golden than grey plover as the latter is today a winter migrant confined to coastal areas. These waders are very palatable and would have found suitable habitats locally. The bones are small and may be easily missed during hand excavation. Ducks and geese appear to have been more popular quarry for the sportsman than the waders. A single bone from a rook or crow was found in phase 4. This is the only bird in the later phase that may not represent food debris.

Amphibian

Only two frog/toad bones were recovered by hand excavation, both from the upper fills of the ditch, G141 F343 phase3.

Samples

For phases 1-3, the coarse fraction of the sieved residue, over 4mm, from G141 F343 phase 3 confirmed the abundance of cattle remains in this ditch. Sheep/goat also predominated in the samples from Area 1, phase 2. Otherwise the fragments from the coarse fractions suggest some under-recovery of sheep/goat compared to cattle bones in the hand recovered collection, while pig bones occur in similar proportions. The fine fractions, 2mm to 4mm, produced frog/toad bones from features other than F343 and more small mammal bones than the coarse fractions. Mice, voles and shrews are represented but are not abundant.

The coarse fractions from the later phases suggest that pig bones may be under-represented in the hand recovered assemblage compared to cattle bones. Bird bones were abundant and indicate that fowl and goose are over represented in the hand recovered material at the expense of duck and woodcock. Woodcock bones in particular are more numerous in phase 5H than the hand recovered assemblage indicates. Small mammal, including mouse and vole, and frog/toad bones were present in the fine fractions but were infrequent, suggesting that the human activity in Area 3 particularly did not provide an attractive habitat for these animals. The flots also produced golden plover bones from phase 6A.

Summary of the animal bones from Roman phases

The Roman deposits from Causeway Lane have produced a large assemblage of animal bone spanning the first to fourth centuries. Throughout this period cattle bones predominate. The cattle were horned and in phase 3 the ditch, F343, was used to dump horners' and probably skinners' or tanners'

waste. Large numbers of horn cores and metapodials were found and this rubbish dumping pervades the assemblage from Area 1, phase 3. The slaughter pattern for cattle suggests a cull of second year animals for meat in the earlier phases but in all phases the majority of cattle appear to have lived to maturity. This suggests the value of the live animals as breeding, milking or draft stock, or even as wealth on the hoof, outweighed any advantage in producing beef as a primary product rather than as the last use of an animal after a productive life.

Only one goat bone was found, from phase 5. The sheep were a variety that included both horned and polled animals. Sheep bones were particularly common in phases 1 and 2. Sheep may therefore have been more important than cattle in local husbandry, before the Romanised demand for cattle and their products influenced stock management. While output may have declined, there appears to have been continuity in sheep production throughout the Roman periods with an emphasis on first and second year animals in the slaughter population and very few elderly culls. The later Roman sheep bones give a greater mean height than those from the earlier phases. This is thought to indicate a higher proportion of wethers rather than a change in the type of sheep.

The pigs were almost all immature animals at slaughter. The proportion of pig bones is consistently lower than that of cattle and sheep with the exception of phase 6, where there is an increase in pig bones relative to those of cattle.

Other domestic animals present were horse and dog. The horse bones were from pony-sized animals. Phase 3 produced an unusual group of feet bones which appear to have been used as rubbing implements. A variety of dogs were represented including, in the later phases, some particularly small animals.

Wild, hunted, animals are indicated by bones of cat, red deer, roe deer and hare. None of these are abundant, suggesting that wild animals were only intermittently utilised for meat and skins or antler for craft working.

Amongst the birds present, only domestic fowl bones were consistently represented, with particularly high numbers of bones in phase 6A.. The goose and duck bones resemble the wild ancestors, greylag and mallard, and smaller wild ducks were also present. Other edible species present were pigeon, lapwing, woodcock and golden plover. Rook/crow and raven bones may indicate urban scavengers or, in the case of the raven, a tame bird.

The samples produced bones from small mammals, including mice, voles and shrews, and frog or toad. Bones from none of these species were abundant.

The animal bones from the medieval and post-medieval phases

Introduction

This discussion is a synopsis based on the archive reports.

The medieval features encountered in Area 1 are thought to fall within seven property boundaries, referred to as Plots A-G. The amount of archaeological deposit surviving varied considerably between the Plots, though the feature types encountered on each Plot were similar. Bone refuse was very localised within each property. A number of substantial features attracted virtually no faunal material within their infills, while other equally large features contained only one or two contexts that included any quantity of animal bones. This may reflect the function of some features, such as wells, that, even in desuetude, were not considered appropriate disposal sites for refuse including bones. There were few instances where individual features attracted bones through several layers of infill. Some features produced a quantity of bones from only one context, which may suggest that these bones had accumulated in some other container before being dumped. All the medieval faunal remains from Area 1 fall into the earlier medieval phases, 8-10.

The majority of the bones recovered from Area 2 are from the earlier medieval phases 8-10 but there is also a small group from the early post medieval phase 11. No more than three features within each phase attracted the deposition of bone debris in quantity, suggesting differing depositional functions for individual pits.

The medieval deposits in Area 3 were dug in haste because of external time constraints on the excavation. For this reason only four pits from Area 3 were selected for study of the animal bone. Three of these pits contained only one context rich in animal bone. There are similar numbers of fragments from phases 8-10 and phase 11.

The later post-medieval deposits in all Areas, phase 12, were also removed with despatch. No features were rich in animal bone, even though large quarry pits were encountered of a type which produced abundant faunal remains at Little Lane (Gidney 1992). Documentary evidence, such as maps, indicates orchards but no housing in this part of the city. Freshly deposited household refuse was therefore less likely to be encountered and much of the faunal debris that found its way into these features appeared to have been weathered, rolled and redeposited. Bones in good condition were conspicuous and in a minority. It is not suggested that degradation occurred after burial

Methods of recording

The excavations at the nearby site of the Shires produced large numbers of animal bones from the medieval phases which were analysed in detail (Gidney 1991 a & b). A different approach has been adopted for the medieval deposits at Causeway Lane. The Shires provided the opportunity to examine contemporary material from features that were often heavily intercut. Discrete features were more in evidence at Causeway Lane giving the chance to examine which features attracted the disposal of faunal waste.

All the animal bones from the medieval and post-medieval phases have been scanned only. The information recorded has been, firstly, the numbers of identifiable fragments present for each species. For cattle, sheep/goat and pig only fragments with 'zones' were counted, following the method described for the Roman deposits. Information on the age structure of the domesticates from teeth and epiphyses was recorded. Measurements were also taken where appropriate. No data were recorded for skeletal element representation, gnawing or butchery.

Results

Table 68 clearly demonstrates that the bones most commonly disposed of derive from domestic stock. For the common domestic species, table 67 gives the relative proportions of cattle: sheep/goat: pig. These show that, for Area 1 as a whole, in phases 8-10 over half the fragments were of sheep/goat, over a third of cattle and an eighth of pig. However in Area 2 cattle

and sheep/goat remains were found in similar proportions and in Area 3 cattle remains predominate at over a half, with sheep/goat at less than a third. For phase 11, the small groups from Areas 2 and 3 were amalgamated for table 67, which shows an increase in the proportion of sheep/goat to cattle fragments compared to the earlier medieval phase in these Areas. Phase 12, table 67, shows a very even division between cattle and sheep/goat remains, similar to that observed for Area 2, phases 8-10. Spatial and chronological differences in the disposal of faunal waste are therefore indicated between the Areas.

Within Area 1 some preferential trends were observed, for example there was a high proportion of cattle bones in Plot A compared to a high proportion of sheep/goat bones in Plot D. In both Plots this distinction was apparent in several features besides the total for the Plot. Given the time span of the deposits, the species proportions were remarkably consistent in the features in Plot D. Plot B had, overall, a higher proportion of cattle to sheep/goat bones but within this Plot there was considerable variation between the two features producing most bones. F909 had similar species proportions to F903 in Plot A, with cattle outnumbering sheep/goat by a margin of 10-15%. F217 had better representation of sheep/goat rather than cattle bones, in the order of 12%, comparable with F207 in Plot C. Plot C produced a small collection of bones, which may not necessarily be representative of the whole Plot. However, cattle and sheep/goat bones had equal representation. Cattle jaws and teeth were concentrated in Plots A, B and G while sheep teeth and jaws were predominant in Plots C, D, E and F. Pig bones were far less numerous and fluctuated less in frequency than the two herbivores. Plot A had the lowest proportion of pig bones and Plot C the highest. Most pig bones found were from juvenile animals, which do not stand the rigours of the archaeological record as well as adult cattle bones. However preservation of juvenile cattle and sheep was excellent at Causeway Lane so there should be no undue bias against pig bones. Much cattle and sheep meat was probably procured fresh on the bone whereas pig meat may have been cured into bacon and boned out as part of the processing. The bones may therefore not be deposited where the meat was consumed. Cattle, and to a lesser extent sheep, bones can have the marrow utilised and be used as the raw material for artifacts. Pig bones are not so useful in this respect which may affect the circumstances of their disposal.

Ratios of sheep/goat: cattle fragments were calculated for phases within Areas as a whole and compared with results from the Shires. It was hoped to establish a trend for Leicester, comparable with that established by O'Connor (1989,18) for York and Lincoln, showing a general chronological increase in sheep remains at the expense of cattle. No such result was produced. Instead wide variations were found between the individual Shires sites and the Causeway Lane Areas, further reinforcing the evidence for spatial variation in the deposition of faunal waste in contemporary deposits. Combining data from the Shires and Causeway Lane gave ratios that remained almost constant from the 11th to 15th centuries. This ratio of 1.1 sheep/goat: 1 cattle fragments is comparable with

Table 67: *Relative proportions of domestic species by fragment counts phases 8 – 12*

| | Phases 8-10 | | | Phase 11 | Phase 12 | | |
	Area 1	Area 2	Area 3	Areas 2 & 3	Area 1	Area 2	Area 3
Cattle & Lg.Ungulate	1298 35%	657 45%	247 55%	175 37%	87 46%	165 44%	44 46%
Sheep/Goat & Sm.Ungulate	1917 52%	632 44%	132 30%	226 47%	85 45%	153 41%	40 42%
Pig	458 12%	163 11%	66 15%	74 16%	16 9%	53 14%	11 12%
Totals	3673	1452	445	475	188	374	95

Table 68: Fragment counts for species present in phases 7-12

Note: Columns A–G are the Area 1 Plots.

	Phases 8-10											Phase 11			Phase 12			
	A	B	C	D	E	F	G	Area 1	Area 2	Area 3	Total Phase 8-10	Area 2	Area 3	Total Phase 11	Area 1	Area 2	Area 3	Total Phase 12
Cattle	308	250	43	400	18	75	65	1159	594	222	**1975**	35	121	**156**	83	147	43	**273**
Sheep/Goat	138	183	39	989	43	129	58	1579	545	109	**2233**	51	136	**187**	79	145	40	**264**
Sheep	7	7	3	71	3	2	2	95	44	3	**142**	3	8	**11**	3	3	-	**6**
Goat	-	-	-	1	-	-	-	1	2	-	**3**	-	-	**0**	1	1	-	**2**
Pig	54	81	23	231	12	32	25	458	163	66	**687**	8	66	**74**	16	53	11	**80**
Horse	31	13	1	6	1	3	4	59	30	5	**94**	1	2	**3**	5	5	1	**11**
Red Deer	1	1	-	-	-	1	-	3	2	1	**6**	-	-	**0**	1	4	-	**5**
Roe Deer	-	-	-	-	-	-	-	-	1	-	**1**	-	-	**0**	-	-	-	**0**
Fallow Deer	-	-	-	-	-	-	-	-	-	-	**0**	-	-	**0**	-	1	-	**1**
Dog	5	18	-	19	2	4	6	54	35	1	**90**	2	1	**3**	-	11	3	**14**
Cat	5	8	15	431	1	25	4	489	31	5	**525**	1	3	**4**	3	24	1	**28**
Hare	-	1	-	7	1	1	-	10	4	1	**15**	-	-	**0**	-	-	-	**0**
Rabbit	-	-	-	-	-	-	-	-	-	-	**0**	-	-	**0**	1	-	-	**1**
Rat	-	-	1	-	-	-	-	1	-	-	**1**	-	-	**0**	-	-	-	**0**
Lg. Ungulate	24	21	7	65	3	9	10	139	63	25	**227**	4	15	**19**	4	18	1	**23**
Sm. Ungulate	9	18	7	182	4	14	8	242	41	20	**303**	2	26	**28**	2	4	-	**6**
Frog/Toad	-	-	-	1	-	-	-	2	3	-	**5**	-	-	**0**	-	-	-	**0**
Fowl	16	31	30	334	18	28	20	477	130	22	**629**	5	42	**47**	5	14	6	**25**
Goose	13	14	4	178	15	10	13	247	33	10	**290**	4	42	**46**	3	4	2	**9**
Duck	-	-	-	21	2	-	-	23	8	1	**32**	-	-	**0**	-	2	2	**4**
Teal	-	-	-	-	-	-	-	-	2	-	**2**	-	-	**0**	-	-	-	**0**
Woodcock	-	2	-	2	-	-	-	4	-	1	**5**	-	1	**1**	-	1	1	**2**
Golden Plover	-	-	-	-	-	-	-	-	2	1	**3**	-	-	**0**	-	-	-	**0**
Wader sp.	-	-	5	3	-	-	-	8	3	-	**11**	-	1	**1**	-	-	-	**0**
Raven	-	1	-	-	-	-	-	1	1	-	**2**	-	-	**0**	-	-	-	**0**
cf Owl	-	-	-	1	-	-	-	1	-	-	**1**	-	-	**0**	-	-	-	**0**
Thrush sp.	-	-	1	-	-	-	-	1	-	-	**1**	-	-	**0**	-	-	-	**0**
Lapwing	-	-	-	-	-	-	-	-	-	-	**0**	-	-	**0**	-	-	-	**0**
Red Kite	-	-	-	-	-	-	-	-	-	-	**0**	-	1	**1**	1	-	-	**1**
Totals	611	650	179	2942	123	333	215	5053	1723	493	**7269**	116	465	**581**	207	437	111	**755**

O'Connor's 17th century ratio for Lincoln and mid 14th century ratio for York. This may suggest that, compared to York and Lincoln, sheep farming in the environs of Leicester was well established at a much earlier date and able to cope with demand until the 16th century.

Cattle

O'Connor (1989, 15) has argued that the red meat supplied to the medieval urban market reflects the surplus from the farming economy, rather than consumer demand. If true, it is therefore unlikely that any differences in the age structure of the cattle bones from each Area will be observable, given the small numbers of cattle jaws with complete tooth rows, or bones with epiphysial ends, recovered from each Area. For this reason data from phases 8-11 in all three Areas have been combined for the following analyses.

The Mandible Wear Stages (MWS) in fig. 167 illustrate the paucity of jaws with complete molar rows, which may relate to breakage for culinary purposes.

In the medieval phases 8-11, those jaws with intact tooth rows indicate only one from an infant calf with only deciduous teeth present at MWS 0. There are three jaws at MWS 7 with the first molar coming into wear, probably from animals aged about six months old. Four jaws at MWS 19-23 have the second molar coming into wear and so are probably from animals aged about eighteen months. The remaining jaws include three at MWS 34-37 from animals with the third molar present, aged about three years. The remaining jaws span MWS 39-52 and indicate mature to elderly animals aged from over three years into at least their teens.

The evidence from the jaws suggests that about 40% are from animals about or less than three years old, with a fairly even division between first, second and third year animals. The remaining 60% of the jaws show increasing wear associated with age, with some cattle surviving into their second decade. This pattern is similar to that seen for the Roman deposits and suggests limited culling of younger animals for meat. Most jaws would appear to derive from animals that had come to the end of a useful, productive working life, whether as breeding, milking or draught animals.

Only three jaws with intact tooth rows were found in phase 12. These show comparable wear to the medieval examples with two falling in the range MWS 18-23, probably from second year animals, and the remaining jaw at MWS 45 from a mature animal with advanced tooth wear. No jaws from veal calves were found in phase 12, which is a striking contrast with the post-medieval deposits at the Shires where these were abundant (Gidney 1991c & 1992)

Unfused epiphyses in the youngest age category were found to complement the jaw at MWS 0 in fig. 167. Some veal or baby beef would appear to have been utilised but possibly in an opportunistic manner, for example making use of casualties. In Area 1, F247 in Plot D contained four bones from a foetal calf in one context. Unfortunately none of the bones could be measured to estimate the stage of gestation. They were considerably smaller than a modern still born Dexter calf. Ryder (1983, 732-3) notes that in the Middle Ages the best parchment, known as virgin parchment, was made from the skin of unborn calves. The skin of a foetus which had not developed hair was preferred. The preservation of these fragile foetal bones is exceptional and the utilisation of such carcases is therefore severely under represented in the archaeological record. Area 2 also produced bones with unfused epiphyses from neonatal and older calves. These could include natural deaths as well as deliberate culling of veal calves, perhaps to liberate the dams for milking. The cows may have been owned by the local inhabitants as there is documentary evidence that burgesses within the town owned cattle and grazed them daily

on the Cow Hay, a pasture to the south of Leicester granted to the burgesses in 1239 by Simon de Montfort (Thompson 1879, 42-3). The epiphysial evidence from phase 12 indicates the presence of young calves, from unfused distal humeri, which were lacking from the tooth data.

The proportions of unfused epiphysial ends from bones that fuse after the first year suggest limited culling of second year animals, corresponding roughly with the jaws at MWS19-23, but a much higher cull of third to fourth year animals than the jaws at MWS 34-39 would suggest. Only about a quarter of the vertebral epiphyses were fused, indicating animals past full skeletal maturity, compared to the peak of jaws at MWS 41-52. This may suggest different sources for the jaws and post-cranial bones. For phase 12 there were almost equal numbers of fused and unfused epiphysial ends among those that fuse between roughly two and four years of age, indicating a substantial cull in this age bracket. Fused vertebrae, from skeletally mature animals, were infrequent.

Only 26 intact metapodials were found from all the medieval phases and none from phase 12. These were measured for withers heights to be estimated using the coefficients given by Zalkin (1960) where the sex of the animal is not known and are plotted in fig. 168. A mean height of 1.11m was obtained with a range of 0.99-1.26m (N=26). This shows an increase of 2cm in the mean height compared to the Roman examples, but the range is still comparable. Fourteen of the medieval metapodials were found in Area 2 and twelve of these were from F503, phase 9, including the example giving an estimated height of 1.26m. This bone is exceptional and derives from the tallest medieval animal so far encountered from the Shires and Causeway Lane. One possible explanation for this unusual animal is that it was castrated, whether deliberately or accidentally, as a calf rather than at about two or three years old. Castrates, whether cattle or sheep, grow taller than entire males if the operation is carried out before the male hormones can act as natural inhibitors of further growth.

The distal breadth measurements of the metacarpals are plotted in fig. 169. Two bones stand out as being exceptionally broad, but there is not the clear bimodality, suggestive of two sexes, that was seen for the Roman examples. The frequencies of the distal breadth measurements as accumulative frequencies were plotted on arithmetic probability paper to ascertain whether one or two distributions were represented in the main body of measurements. This method also failed to produce any clear separation. The bulk of the metacarpals therefore appear to derive from one sex and are presumed to be female. The three examples from phase 12 fall within the lower half of the medieval range.

Horn cores and frontals in the medieval and post-medieval phases were not abundant compared to the Roman deposits of phase 3, but indicate that the cattle were horned, with no evidence for polled animals. The distinctive 'Celtic Shorthorn' form seen in the Roman deposits was absent from the medieval deposits. The medieval horn cores probably indicate domestic horn working. The plot of the greatest basal diameters in fig. 170 indicates that the smaller horns, interpreted as females and possibly castrates, predominate. There is a small increase in the average size of the medieval horn cores, with a mean basal diameter of 51.1 mm, relative to the Roman examples, with a mean diameter of 49.7mm.

The small sample of six horn cores from phase 12 has been amalgamated with the five from contemporary deposits at St Peter's Lane (Gidney 1991c). These all fall within the range established for phases 8-11 in fig. 170 but show two clear groups within the medieval spread of proposed female or castrate sizes. One interpretation of this pattern is equal numbers of females and castrates and one entire male. There is a decrease in the average size of the horn cores compared

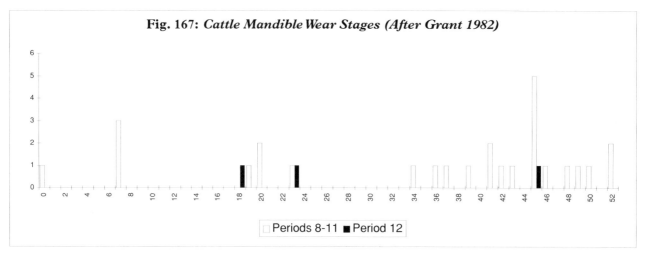

Fig. 167: *Cattle Mandible Wear Stages (After Grant 1982)*

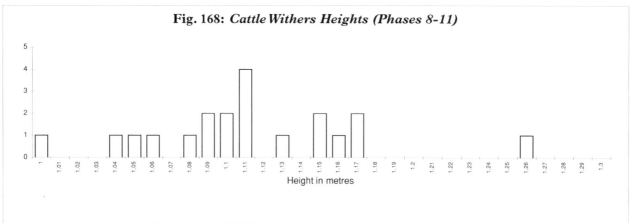

Fig. 168: *Cattle Withers Heights (Phases 8-11)*

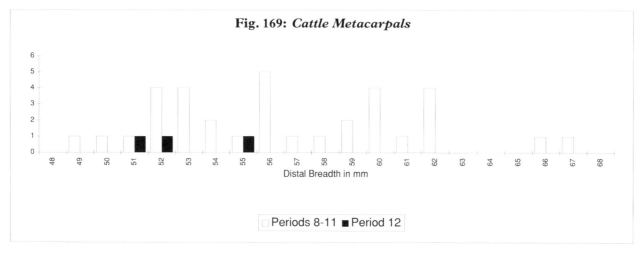

Fig. 169: *Cattle Metacarpals*

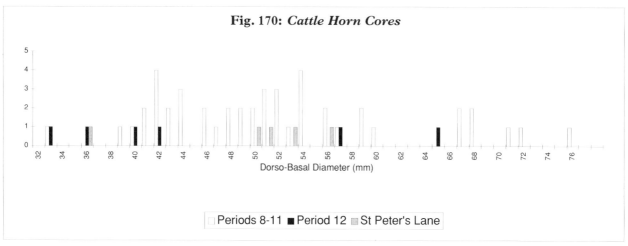

Fig. 170: *Cattle Horn Cores*

to all the earlier phases, with a mean basal diameter of 46.8mm

The medieval cattle show a slight shift in size and conformation from the Roman animals but in life would probably still have appeared visually similar. The post medieval cattle would appear indistinguishable from the smaller medieval animals.

Few congenital or pathological abnormalities were seen on the cattle bones, these were mostly arthropathies associated with age.

Sheep and Goat

Goat bones were very infrequent in Phases 8-11, with one identified from Area 1 and two from Area 2. The example from Area 1 is a metacarpal from an infant kid which, as discussed below, may represent a kid skin. The two bones from Area 2 were horn cores from male animals. No metapodials or other post cranial elements from Area 2 exhibited the characteristics of goat. This suggests that the horn cores were detached from the skull and traded with the horn sheath attached. Phase 12 produced one goat metacarpal and one male goat horn core. All other fragments in the sheep/goat category in all phases were considered to be from sheep.

Fragments of sheep skull were encountered regularly in phases 8-11. In general the sheep heads had been split sagittally, to facilitate removal of the brain, tongue and other head meat, and the horn cores, where present, had been chopped off. Fragments of detached horn core were infrequent on Areas 1 and 3 but were as common as skull fragments on Area 2, suggesting small scale, domestic, working of sheep and goat horn only by the occupants of Area 2.

Table 69: *Sheep skulls*

Sheep skulls	Area 1	Area 2	Area 3
Horned, male	16	4	2
Horned, female (or castrate)	62	17	7
Polled, female (or castrate)	9	5	-

The polled skull fragments all appeared to be from females or castrates, as none exhibited the thickening of the frontal bone associated with entire males. Skulls of polled sheep were present only in Areas 1 and 2, where they were outnumbered by the horned female/castrate skull fragments alone. This suggests that the local sheep population was a variety where both sexes are horned but a minority of polled females occur. Polled is a trait which can be actively selected for or against by breeding from or slaughtering such animals. For example modern female Soays have been selected for horns on mainland Britain, whereas half the females in the original population on St Kilda are polled (Jewell *et al* 1974). Polled sheep may not have been desirable if sheep horn was a marketable commodity. A single example of a multi-horned skull was found in Area 2. This appeared to be from a female or castrate. The four horned trait occurs sporadically in medieval archaeological assemblages, for example at Lincoln (O'Connor 1982, 31) and Exeter (Maltby 1979, 51). This trait is associated with modern primitive sheep breeds, such as the Manx Loghtan, which exhibit the range of two horned, multi horned and polled types and in which polled females carry the multi horned character. Phase 12 produced only five sheep skull fragments and no loose horn cores. All the skulls appeared to be from females or castrates: three were horned, one had vestigial horn cores and one was polled. Sheep jaws with complete tooth rows were abundant in phases 8-11 compared to those of cattle. In fig. 172, three culls of young sheep are indicated: neonatal mortalities; lambs with molar 1 erupting aged about five months; yearlings with molar 2 coming into wear. Thereafter is a continuing spread from second year animals with molar 3 erupting, through to aged animals with

well worn teeth. The seven jaws from phase 12 fall within the pattern described for phases 8-11. Over half the jaws with MWS were from the first three peaks, that is animals less than two years old with molar 3 unerupted. This cull pattern suggests that meat was a primary product of the local flocks.

In phases 8-11 unfused epiphysial ends from bones in the youngest age category, less than one year, were scarce. This may in part represent pre-burial skeletal selectivity, destruction during cooking or consumption of these particular elements by dogs. Post depositional loss is less likely, as other elements of infant lambs have been well preserved in the burial environment at Causeway Lane. Suckling lambs are only available for a short season each year, so recovery of such bones partly depends on an excavated feature having been used for rubbish disposal in the spring. Such baby lambs have also been considered an expensive delicacy (Spry 1956, 553), which the general populace may not have been able to afford.

In the second age category, less than two years, Area 1 has about 40% of the epiphyses either unfused or just fusing. An explanation may lie in the metapodials, 32 of the 69 unfused metapodials were noted as being from infant lambs. These were all recovered from Plot D, Features 247 and 216. There was a noteworthy absence in these features of other skeletal elements from animals of comparable age. These bones may therefore represent waste from skins rather than meat. Lambskins were an integral part of medieval costume (Veale 1966, 5). Domestic production was augmented by imports, known by the generic name of Budge (Veale 1966 216-7). Native lambskins were generally worn by working people while the imported skins were available to richer citizens. Further terms for lambskins include Shanks, which refers to furs made of skins from legs of budge, and Tavelon which indicates a bundle of four skins of legs of black budge. This suggests that lambskin legs were available detached from the rest of the skin. Pieces of black budge shanks were often used in preference to ermine tails, and these were called powderyngs (Veale 1966, 221). It is therefore possible that these very juvenile lamb metapodials, and the single kid metacarpal, represent either complete lambskins, or the leg skin used for trimming garments.

In the third age category, two-three years, approximately threequarters of the epiphysial ends were unfused or fusing. Such animals would be prime young mutton. The vertebrae indicate that only some 15% of the sheep population achieved full skeletal maturity before slaughter.

The cull pattern indicated by the epiphyses is in agreement with that suggested from the MWS for preferential slaughter of animals less than three years old. It would appear that meat and probably skins were the main products of the local flocks sent to Leicester. The low proportion of adult to aged animals may suggest that wool or milk production from the flock was of secondary importance. However bones from elderly animals may not have found their way to this part of the town. The infant lamb bones, even if procured as skins or trimmed from skins, indicate that someone, somewhere was milking the ewes.

Phase 12 produced low overall numbers of unfused epiphysial ends which may reflect, for example, preferential dog gnawing obliterating the evidence. The bones of infant lambs present were well preserved and concentrated in F701, Area 3. The epiphyses suggest most sheep survived beyond one year but were culled steadily thereafter, with few surviving to skeletal maturity.

From all three Areas, only ten complete sheep bones in phases 8-11 and four in phase 12 were found that could be measured for an estimate of withers height. The coefficients given by Teichert (*in* von den Driesch & Boessneck 1974) were used. For phases 8-11 a mean height of 0.58m was obtained with a range of 0.52-0.70m while for phase 12 the mean height

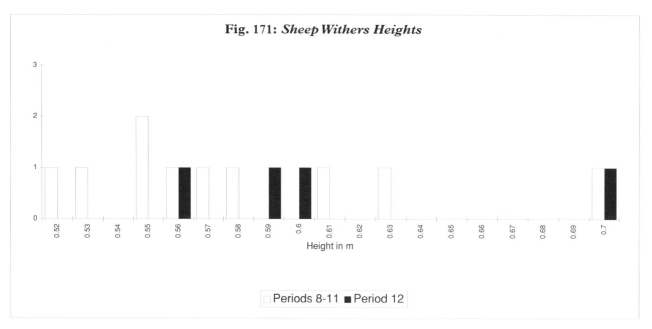

Fig. 171: *Sheep Withers Heights*

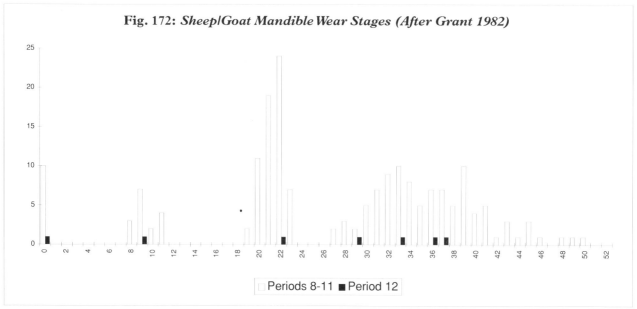

Fig. 172: *Sheep/Goat Mandible Wear Stages (After Grant 1982)*

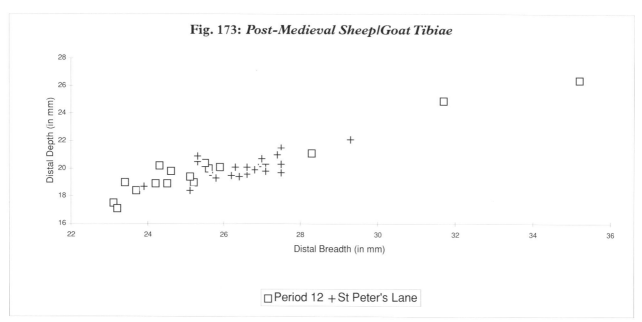

Fig. 173: *Post-Medieval Sheep/Goat Tibiae*

was 0.61m with a range of 0.56-0.70m. Figure 171 illustrates how the phase 12 examples fall within the medieval range and that the difference in mean height is a product of small sample size.

Phase 12 did produce five sheep bones which stood out as being exceptionally large compared to the other sheep bones encountered. All appeared in fresh condition, not redeposited. Two distal tibiae were measurable and are plotted in fig. 173 where they appear particularly robust against the others from phase 12 and those from contemporary deposits at St Peter's Lane. These unusually large sheep bones may be archaeological evidence for the New Leicester sheep, bred by Robert Bakewell from the mid-18th century. Given the exorbitant costs of hiring such a ram (Hall & Clutton-Brock 1989, 151), it is not surprising that such animals were slow to percolate to the dining table and rubbish pits of the lower classes. While these sheep bones appear distinctively large compared to the general archaeological finds from Leicester, they do not approach the size of modern Lincoln and Leicester Longwool rams (Gidney, personal reference collection), breeds which are descended from Bakewell's New Leicester sheep.

Pig

The pig bones from phases 8-11 appear to derive from an indigenous long snouted type, similar to the Roman animals. Most of the pig bones found were from juvenile animals. Area 3 produced a unique find of part of an adult pig skeleton, dispersed in the fills of F727. The canine teeth indicate this was a sow. She may have been a particularly prolific animal to have been kept to a relatively advanced age, probably in excess of five years. Two complete, fused, bones were measured for an estimated withers height of 0.79m. This appears to be an appropriate size relative to the contemporary cattle and sheep, though it is unclear how representative this animal is.

Several partial skeletons of younger animals were found in Area 2. F549 produced unfused bones from an animal larger than a neonatal piglet, this could represent the remains of half a roast sucking pig. F513 produced a practically complete skeleton of a similar sized piglet. This could be the remnant of a whole roast sucking pig or a natural mortality. F592 produced a partial skeleton of a neonatal piglet and a further infant piglet is represented by one bone in F542. There is documentary evidence for the keeping of pigs within the town (Thompson 1879, 66), so natural infant mortalities are to be expected. To avoid distorting the cull pattern, the teeth and epiphysial data from the partial skeletons have not been included in the calculations.

Phase 12 produced a pig frontal with a dished profile. This is the first example from either the Shires or Causeway Lane for a variety of pig other than the standard primitive long snouted type. This skull fragment does not have the excessively foreshortened face associated with, for example, the modern Vietnamese Pot-Bellied pig. It probably represents experimental breeding between pigs of Asian origin and indigenous pigs. Such cross breeding was extensive during the 19th century, to the extent that no modern pig breed is without such lineage (Hall & Clutton-Brock 1989, 203-6). F581 contained bones from at least two perinatal piglets. Urban free range sows with piglets were still sufficiently common in the 18th century to be depicted in Hogarth's 'Chairing the Members' print, first published in 1758, where the sow and litter show the dished face influence of Asian blood.

The MWS for the pig jaws in fig. 174 show an absence of the infant piglets that are represented by partial skeletons in Area 2 and phase 12. There is a peak of jaws at MWS 6-9, indicating molar 1 coming into wear at about six months. These could have been killed for pork. The next cull is represented by the spread of jaws at MWS 14-20, from animals

with molar 2 erupting and aged about one year. The larger carcases from these animals could have been cured for bacon and ham. The jaws at MWS 31-36 have the molar 3 erupting and in wear, aged from about 18 months. Animals of this age could have been bred from as there are no other aged, presumably breeding, stock comparable to those seen for the cattle and sheep. The jaw at MWS 36, from Area 1, has tooth wear comparable with that from the mature sow seen in Area 3. These older animals may have ended up as pie meat.

The epiphysial evidence also indicates that pigs were slaughtered as immature animals. The fused epiphyses suggest that only a minority were killed at more than two years, with only two bones from animals that had survived beyond two and a half years old. This pattern of a high cull of juvenile pigs is commonplace and reflects the large litter size of the pig and lack of uses for the live animal compared to cattle and sheep.

Horse

Horse remains were generally sporadic finds of single teeth or bones dispersed throughout the Areas and representing the general 'background' debris which became incorporated in the fills of features. One exception is Area 1, Plot A, where F911 produced an interesting concentration of horse fragments. These were all of tibia, radius or metapodials and had been chopped longitudinally and/or transversely. These bones do not appear to represent butchery for the consumption of the meat, as they appear very distinctive compared to the butchered cattle bones. They may have been comminuted to extract the marrow or to make stock. Alternatively they may be offcuts from bone working. Whichever explanation is valid, a great deal of force was expended in chopping up these bones. Utilisation of horse bones, rather than incidental incorporation, appears to be confined to Plot A. Plot G produced part of a bone skate made from a horse metapodial from F263.

In Area 2, the articulating bones of the hind leg of a horse were found in F550.

Red, Roe and Fallow Deer

Red deer remains were very sparse in phases 8-10: two bones and a piece of antler from Area 1; one bone and a piece of antler from Area 2 and one bone from Area 3. One roe deer bone was found in Area 2. Deer fragments were absent from phase 11. Phase 12 produced four fragments of antler and one bone of red deer, also one bone of fallow deer. These pieces probably represent incidental inclusions, rather than utilisation of deer by the occupants of Areas 1-3.

Dog

Dog bones were not numerous. Like the occasional finds of horse bones, many of the individual occurrences of dog bones may represent unintentional incorporation of bones present within the soil used for backfilling these features.

In Area 1 a deliberate burial is probably indicated by the partial skeleton of a neonatal puppy which was found in Plot B, F492. This may well have been disposed of by the household as an unwanted birth or a natural demise. The life expectancy of the dogs does not appear to have been great, as there were more unfused than fused epiphyses. It is possible that these bones do not merely represent household animals which died untimely. Dispersed debris from corpses, whether or not killed deliberately, whose skins had been utilised may be indicated.

Area 2 produced the largely complete skeleton of an adult male dog, with an estimated height of 50-51cm, from F569. A different type of animal is indicated by a small bowed tibia from F536. The skeleton of an infant, but not neonatal, puppy was found in F503, also a further skeleton of an adult animal. Part of another animal was found in F616. The radius and ulna had been broken in life and healed out of alignment, with

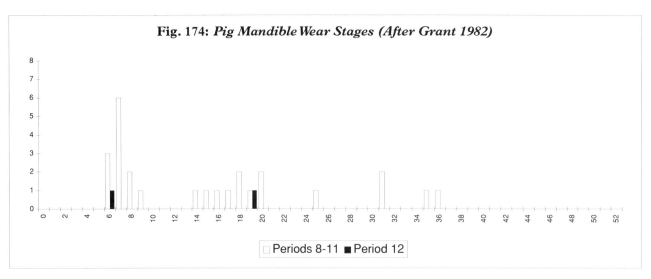

Fig. 174: *Pig Mandible Wear Stages (After Grant 1982)*

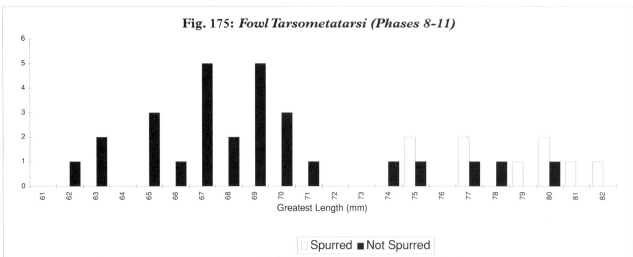

Fig. 175: *Fowl Tarsometatarsi (Phases 8-11)*

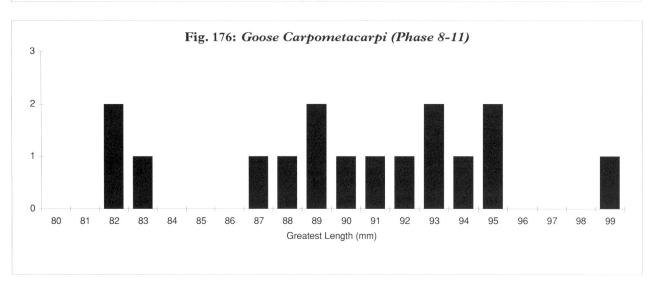

Fig. 176: *Goose Carpometacarpi (Phase 8-11)*

much additional bone growth. The extent of healing indicates the animal survived for some time after the accident but it would have had a permanently foreshortened and swollen leg. Although its leg was not set, this animal presumably received some care and attention when recovering from this injury, until it eventually died. The dogs kept by the occupants of Area 2 appear to have been medium sized, straight legged animals. They may have been household animals, which probably died naturally and were interred on the property. Some of these bodies were subsequently disturbed and redeposited over time.

Cat

Cat remains were much more abundant than those of dog in Areas 1 and 3 but occurred in similar numbers to dog bones in Area 2.

In Area 1, Plot D has an overwhelming number of cat bones, about 18% of the identified bones. Only sheep/goat bones outnumber those of cat. The cat bones in Plot D are concentrated in F216. The most reasonable explanation for this abundance of cat bones is that they represent carcases which were the waste from skins. Indeed, eight jaws bore fine knife marks which may be consistent with skinning. No comparable marks were seen on the facial area of the skulls.

Silver (1969) does not give ages of fusion for cat bones. Sisson & Grossman (1975, 1544 & 1546) state that both the dog and the cat have all permanent teeth present by 5-6 months. Given this similarity in tooth eruption, the epiphysial fusion order for dog has been used for cat to gain an impression of the proportion of juveniles present. Some two thirds of the cat bones were unfused, indicating animals less than eighteen months old at death. A proportion of these are from kittens less than 6 months old as several jaws were seen with deciduous dentition only, including one with fine knife marks, probably from skinning. It is suggested that the medieval occupants of Plot D specialised at one time in procuring cat skins. The presence of cat bones in adjoining Plots may either indicate dispersal and reworking of debris from Plot D, or smaller scale emulation of the activities in Plot D on the other Plots. Alternatively, cat bone rich deposits may have existed on the other Plots but did not fall within the area of excavation. Plot D would not be so striking if F216 had not been available for excavation.

Cats could have been bred by the occupants of the Plots more for their fur than for their rodent control and companion animal functions. More expensive furs may have been beyond the means and social status (Veale 1966, 3-5) of the local inhabitants.

The somewhat lowly status of catskins emerges from a story told about the Saxon Wulfstan, the 11th century Bishop of Worcester, whose admirers pointed out to him that even if he did not wear sable, beaver, or fox as he ought to do, he might at least wear catskins rather than lambskins. 'Believe me,' retorted the Bishop, 'men sing oftener of the Lamb of God than of the cat of God.' (Veale 1966, 4). Cat skins, both of wild and domestic animals, could also have been brought into the town. An element of opportunism in the acquisition of cat skins is suggested: 'I haue as moche pite of pore men as pedlere hath of cattes, That wolde kille hem, if he cacche hem mygte, for coueitise of here skynnes' (Skeat 1867, Piers the Plowman, Text Bv, lines 257-8)

Several contexts in F216 appeared to have more jaws than postcranial elements to match, which may suggest some pelts were brought onto this site with the head and possibly paws still attached. By the 13th century there is documentary evidence for trade in skins, including cat skins, within Britain and between Britain and Europe (Veale 1966, 59-66).

Concentrations of bones from immature cats have also been found at King's Lynn (Noddle 1977) and Exeter (Maltby 1979) and interpreted as waste from skinning (Serjeantson 1989, 131).

In Area 2, four features produced parts of cat skeletons. One adult cat, two immature animals and one kitten are represented. These appear to have more in common with the bodies of dogs found in this Area, suggesting these are more likely to be the remains of household animals. All the cat bones from Area 3 were from juvenile or immature animals, suggesting a generally low life expectancy for the local cat population.

Cat remains were more numerous than those of dog in phase 12, with immature and adult animals represented.

Hare and Rabbit

Hare bones were very infrequent with ten from Area 1, four from Area 2 and one from Area 3 in phases 8-10 only. This paucity of hare bones suggests the animal was either not highly regarded as food or could not be afforded by the local inhabitants.

There is no evidence to suggest that hare skins were processed here either, though documentary evidence (Veale 1966, 58) indicates that hare skins were traded from manors. Like the meat, the skins may have been generally beyond the means of the local residents and their customers.

No hare bones and only a single rabbit bone were found in phase 12.

Rat

Only one rat bone was found among the hand recovered bones, from Area 1 Plot C. This will be black rat on historical grounds (Taylor, Fenn & Macdonald 1991, 250).

Birds

In phases 8-11, the most commonly found bird bones in all Areas were of domestic fowl and goose. Fowl bones were overall the most numerous but, given the larger size of the goose, the quantity of meat provided by both species would probably have been similar. In phase 12 bird bones were generally sparse, with those of domestic fowl being most commonly found. A decline in the proportion of goose to fowl bones was noted for post 16th century deposits at the Shires (Gidney 1993, 13) and similarly few goose bones, compared to those of fowl, were found in phase 12.

The fowl tarso-metatarsi length measurements fall into a bimodal distribution in fig. 175. The spurred bones are from mature cocks. The unspurred examples that fall within the spurred range may be young cocks where the spur has not yet fused to the shaft (Sadler 1991, 41). This would give a sex ratio of fourteen male to twenty three female birds. The fowl present at Causeway Lane are comparable in size to those from contemporary deposits at the Shires (Gidney 1993), Exeter (Maltby 1979, 210) and Lincoln (O'Connor 1982, Appendix II). These birds were very small compared to modern barnyard fowl. The longest spurred medieval tarsometatarsal is comparable in size with a modern silkie cross bantam cock. The medieval fowl appear to have had shorter legs, mean TMT length 70.8mm (N=37), compared to the Roman birds with a mean TMT length of 76.7mm (N=16).

Juvenile fowl bones were present in Area 1, Plots C, D, E and F and Area 2. The proportion of juvenile fowl bones varies: 6-7% of the fowl bones from Plots E and F and Area 2; up to 28% in Plot D and a peak of 47% from Plot C. It is of interest that the Plots producing the highest proportions of juvenile fowl bones also produced eggshell (tables 3 and 71). This may reflect seasonal availability of eggs and young poultry as much as a genuine preference for young birds or the social standing of the occupants. In comparison the later medieval deposits from the Shires only produced a peak of 19% juvenile fowl bones (Gidney 1993, 8), as did a deposit of 1520 from Baynard's Castle (Carey 1982, 266).

The goose bones are thought to derive from domestic birds, though the bones were of comparable size to modern greylag, the ancestor of domestic geese. The carpometacarpal was the most commonly found measurable goose bone. The distribution of length measurements in fig. 176 falls within the range established at the Shires (Gidney 1993).

Duck bones comparable with mallard were found in all three Areas in phases 8-10, were absent from phase 11 but present in phase 12 deposits. The small numbers of duck bones compared to those of fowl and goose may suggest these are not domestic birds. Teal bones were present in Area 2 only. Woodcock bones were found on Areas 1 and 3 only. There are only six bones in total, suggesting either that woodcock were generally beyond the means of the occupants or that these features were not receiving rubbish when woodcock were in season. The unidentified wader bones include fragments of bill which could also derive from woodcock. Two golden plover bones were found on Area 2.

Woodcock and lapwing were also present in phase 12.

The greater part of a raven skeleton was found in Area 1, Plot B. Since the corpse appears to have been deposited intact this may have been a tame bird rather than a natural mortality of an urban scavenger. A further raven bone was found in Area 2.

An owl species is represented in Area 1, Plot C by the phalanx of a talon, which does not appear comparable with the other raptors.

A single red kite bone was found in Area 3, phase 11.

One of the thrush family is represented by a single bone from Area 1, Plot D. This bird could have been eaten or may have died naturally.

The wild bird species were generally represented by finds of single bones, whether a game or commensal species. Natural mortalities of wild birds appear rare in the archaeological record. The level of consumption of wild birds equates with that for the game animals, noted above, as representing a very scarce resource for the local inhabitants.

Amphibian

Single bones of frog or toad were only found in Area 1, Plots B and D. Such small bones are not easily retrieved by hand excavation.

Samples

The sampling procedure followed that previously described for the Roman deposits. No samples were taken from Area 1, Plot A.

Coarse Fraction

The coarse fractions produced both the greatest quantity of bones and the widest range of species. The relative proportions of the three common domesticates suggest better representation of sheep/goat compared to cattle bones than was seen in the hand recovered bones. The proportion of pig bones remains at a similar level in both the coarse fractions and hand recovered bones.

An increase in the presence of smaller species such as fowl, woodcock, golden plover, thrush family, pigeon, cat dog, amphibian and small mammal bones was seen. The coarse fractions from Area 2 retrieved the only buzzard bone from the medieval deposits. However low numbers of bones from these smaller species were found for the volume of deposits sampled. This suggests both that the edible species were rarely exploited during the timescale of this occupation and that the human occupation was not attractive to commensal species.

Fine fraction and flots

Larger animals are virtually absent from the fine fractions, only elements of cat and sheep/goat teeth were found. More evidence was recovered for the presence of small mammals, birds and amphibians. The teeth and jaws indicate that mice, voles and shrews are represented.

The number of identifiable fragments from these small species is very low in relation to the volume of earth processed, suggesting that the human environment was not attractive to small birds, small mammals or amphibians.

Summary of animal bones from post-Roman phases

A large assemblage of earlier medieval bones, from phases 8-10, was examined and smaller groups of bones from the post-medieval phases 11 and 12.

The proposed properties within Area 1 and the faunal remains from Areas 2 and 3 provided evidence of spatial variation in the disposal of bone waste in the earlier medieval material. These may indicate household preferences in food-stuffs in the case of cattle and sheep/goat bones. A small concentration of sheep and goat horn cores in Area 2 may result from domestic horn working. Seasonality may be the explanation for very high proportions of juvenile domestic fowl bones in Plots C and D, associated with finds of eggshell. Refuse from a specialist skinner or tanner was found on Plot D, indicated by large numbers of cat bones from F216 phase 9. These included jaws with knife marks, presumed to be incurred in skinning. There were also metapodials only from infant lamb bones and one kid, thought to represent either complete lambskins or the leg skin used for trimming garments. One find of foetal calf bones may indicate a skin for first quality parchment.

The cattle and sheep bones fell within the size ranges established for the Roman animals. The cattle horn cores suggest a change of type from the Roman examples with the absence of the 'Celtic Shorthorn' and a higher mean size for the maximum basal diameter. The sheep show less change from the Roman predecessors, with horned and polled present and similar estimated height range. Five exceptionally large sheep bones were found in phase 12. These are the first sheep bones to show noticeable divergence from the general type and are thought to represent the improved livestock of the 18th century.

The slaughter patterns for the medieval and post-medieval assemblages are remarkably similar to the Roman patterns, with predominantly mature cattle and immature sheep. This is suggestive of very stable livestock management systems, which did not need to respond to changing demands from consumers.

The pig bones were mostly from juvenile animals, including neonatal examples. Bones from an adult sow were an unusual find in Area 3. Phase 12 produced a pig frontal with a dished profile. Like the large sheep, this is the first instance of a new phenotype, which may derive from an 18th century infusion of Asiatic stock.

Most horse bones were sporadic finds but Plot A produced a group of chopped and split fragments. These may be debris from craft work rather than butchery. Dog bones were not numerous either but included disturbed burials.

Finds of wild mammals include red, roe and fallow deer besides hare and rabbit. None of these were common so wild faunal resources cannot have supplied a significant source of either food or raw materials.

There was a single rat bone and three frog or toad bones from the hand recovered assemblage. Such small bones are not easily retrieved during hand excavation.

The bird bones were mostly of domestic fowl with goose bones also frequent. Other culinary birds present include mallard size duck, teal, woodcock, golden plover, lapwing and unspecified wader. None of these can have provided more than an occasional delicacy. The thrush family bird could have been eaten or have been an urban resident. Red kite and raven were probably carrion eaters, while the owl may have roosted in the town.

The samples, not surprisingly, showed an increase in the presence of smaller species, such as sheep, relative to cattle, also fowl, woodcock, golden plover, thrush family, cat, dog, and amphibian. Bones of pigeon, buzzard, mice, voles and shrews were also found in the samples, species not seen in the hand recovered assemblage. However, the numbers of fragments from these small species is low in relation to the volume of earth processed.

THE EGGSHELL   *Peter Boyer*

Introduction

Small fragments assumed to be eggshell were recovered from sieved samples, the quantity ranging from one to hundreds of pieces per sample totalling over 2,200 in all. It was decided to investigate the possible methods of identifying it to ascertain whether eggs from just domestic fowl or from a wider range of species were used.

It was confirmed that most of the material was eggshell of which 67.7% came from Roman contexts, 31.8% medieval and 0.5% post medieval. The thickness was measured as an aid to identification but as this could not confirm the species present, a sample was selected for detailed examination by scanning electron microscopy. It was necessary to compare the sample with modern reference eggshell and to evaluate the methods available. Previous work has been carried out for example by Jones (1975), Murphy (1978, 1991) and Keepax (1977, 1981) and it was decided to use some of the methods of the latter.

The fine structure of eggshell is complex (Romanoff and Romanoff 1949). On the inside are two membranes which do not survive in archaeological material. The innermost layer of the shell is the mammillary layer (plate 22) which consists of many rounded knobs (mammillae) which are partly embedded in the outer membrane but which extend into the shell and join together forming tightly packed columns towards the centre of the section. Outside the mammillary layer is the palisade layer, which in many species is the thickest element and is traversed by many minute canals, visible as tiny perforations in section. Towards the exterior the palisade layer becomes more compact and can appear to be a distinct element in section. A very thin surface layer sometimes occurs on top of this, which is pitted and consists of numerous polygons. On the exterior is a very thin cuticle which did not survive in archaeological material. Between the mammillae on the inside of the shell there are pores which mostly run right through the shell and can be seen on the outer surface. The criteria used for identification were size, number and height of mammillae, number and size of pores, and characteristics of the layers and outer surface.

Methods

The material was examined and presence of eggshell was recorded by subgroup (tables 2 and 3). The thickness was measured for all but the smallest fragments with the eyepiece graticule of a microscope at a magnification of x100. Because there were many fine variations in thickness, the measurements were combined into 25 micron size ranges and all of the samples from phases grouped together in order to produce a bar chart of thickness ranges (fig. 174). These could then be compared with ranges from prepared reference specimens and

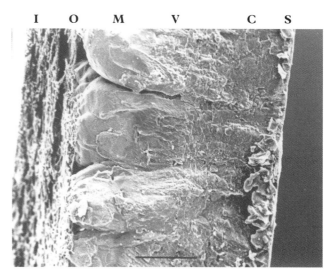

I   O   M   V   C   S

Plate 22: *Reference domestic fowl eggshell cross-section (x150)*

Key to Plate 26:
I = Inner membrane
O = Outer membrane
M = Mammilla
V = Vesicular layer
C = Compact layer
S = Surface crystalline layer

Key to Plates 26-31
Black Bar = 100 microns

Plate 23: *Archaeological domestic fowl eggshell cross-section (sample 194) (x150)*

from published data (Keepax 1981) (table 70). Some observations of colour were made.

Archaeological samples were selected for scanning electron microscopy from the three areas of the site, eleven from Roman contexts, eleven medieval and two post-medieval. Scanning electron microscopy was carried out by George McTurk at the University of Leicester, Department of Anatomy. Micrographs (SEMs) of each fragment were produced, showing inner and outer surfaces and cross sections at a number of magnifications. The eggshells of selected domesticated and wild bird species from the collection of Leicestershire Museums were prepared as reference material (table 70) by removal of the membranes so that the inner surface was visible for comparison.

The SEMs were then examined for criteria for identification.

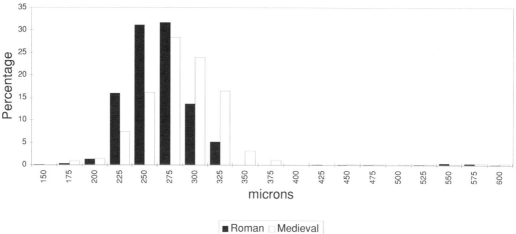

Fig 177: *Thickness ranges of eggshell*

Diameter measurements for a range of individual mammillae were taken from SEMs of the inner surfaces and sections. The concentration of mammillae within a given area was measured as number per square millimetre. The mammillae were found to be very variable in shape, size and concentration within each species and so the ranges were recorded. When compared with the samples most fitted in with the ranges of a number of possible species so using this alone was unsuitable to determine species. The height of the mammillae was measured from the exposed tip of the mammilla to the point where it joins its neighbours. The measurements were taken at magnifications of $c.100$-$1000x$ and the ranges of heights for each of the reference species recorded. The species could be broadly divided into those with a height greater than 60 microns, namely duck, domestic fowl and goose (and herring gull), and all of the other reference species. There was a degree of overlap within each of the groups but this criterion was found to be a far more valuable guide to species type. Differences were found between these measurements for domestic fowl and duck and those quoted by Keepax (1981) which suggested that mammillae height could be somewhat less than that found in the reference material used here.

It has been shown that the mammillary layer and the two divisions of the spongy or palisade layer (compact and vesicular) varied in proportions according to species; those where the mammillary layer was the thickest and those where it was not (Keepax 1981). These were measured in the reference material from the section micrographs and the proportions calculated (table 72). A similar pattern was found here with the difference that Keepax found that both domestic fowl and pheasant ($c.50\%$) had thick mammillary layers, whereas here only domestic fowl (and lapwing) showed this with pheasant only $c.36\%$. Thus with the samples it was felt that where the mammillary layer was thicker it was more likely to represent domestic fowl than pheasant and using this criterion alone it was possible to divide domestic fowl from other species. This character in conjunction with other criteria and the data of Keepax could also be used for the identification of pheasant.

Attempts were made to measure the dimensions and concentration of pores per unit area but this was abandoned due to partial or total concealment of the pores by surface material. Finally other external characteristics were then compared with the samples as there is considerable variation in the external morphology of the eggshell and Becking (1975)

used it as an aid in identification. Some species have relatively smooth shell outer surfaces such as guinea fowl, partridge and domestic fowl, and others have polygonal plate-like structures such as goose (plate 27), duck and herring gull. It was possible to see surface characteristics on some of the archaeological eggshell and although this feature may be of limited value because post depositional changes may occur (Keepax 1981) observations were recorded. All of the SEMs produced were catalogued and form part of the archive together with data from the reference material and samples and a full discussion of SEM criteria.

Table 70: *Reference eggshell*

		Thickness in microns
Domestic Fowl	*(Gallus sp.)* ★	220-480 (K)
Domestic Goose	*(Anser sp.)* ★	400-700 (K)
Quail	*(Coturnix coturnix)* ★	180-200
Guinea Fowl	*(Numida meleagris)* ★	400-710 (K)
Turkey	*(Meleagris gallopava)* ★	280-450 (K)
Duck	*(ANATIDAE)* ★	250-550 (K)
Razorbill	*(Alca torda L.)*	330-350
Pheasant	*(Phasianus colchicus L.)* ★	200-400 (K)
Moorhen	*(Gallinula chloropus (L.))*	210-220
Partridge	*(Perdix perdix (L.))* ★	180-210
Rook	*(Corvus frugilegus L.)*	160-190
Wood Pigeon	*(Columba palumbus L.)* ★	140-160
Lapwing	*(Vanellus vanellus (L.))* ★	120-140
Herring Gull	*(Larus argenatus* Pontoppidan)★	250-260

★ = SEMs used in detailed study. (K)= data from Keepax (1981)

Results

The thickness measurements (fig. 177) showed that there were two broad groups into which the shell fitted. Most of the shell belonged to the thinner group of between $c.200$ and $c.350$ microns within the thickness ranges of pheasant, domestic fowl, turkey and duck. Whilst other types such as razorbill, herring gull and moorhen also came into this range, these were thought unlikely. Rook, quail and partridge were considered where very thin shell was found. There was a second small group of thick shell in the range of $c.500$-600 microns with occasional fragments as thin as 400 microns, which fitted the ranges of goose and guinea fowl, and just within the range of the thicker duck eggshell. Throughout the Roman and medieval material, especially in phases where there was a large number and therefore a more representative sample, a sizeable

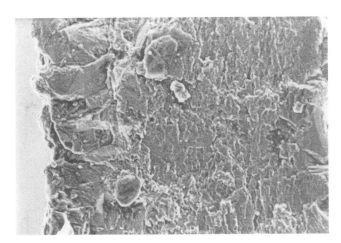

Plate 24: *Reference Pheasant eggshell cross-section (x325)*

Plate 26: *Archaeological domestic fowl/duck eggshell inner surface showing mammillae (sample 530) (x80)*

Plate 25: *Archaeological Pheasant eggshell cross-section (sample 822) (x250)*

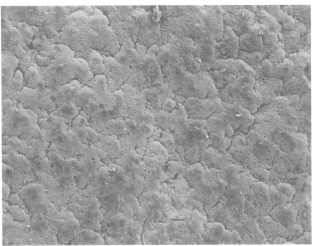

Plate 27: *Reference goose eggshell outer surface showing polygonal structure (x40)*

majority of the shell fitted within the 250-300 micron thickness range, well within the suggested ranges for pheasant, domestic fowl and duck, though not so much, turkey. Turkey would be very unlikely as it was not introduced into Britain until the 16th century (Zeuner 1963). This thinner shell was thus almost certain to be from eggs of the former three bird types with the exception of the very thin shell. Similarly with the thicker group, the possibility of the material being guinea fowl eggshell could also be virtually discounted, as this species was not introduced until the 15th or 16th century. On the basis of this the thicker group could be assumed to be goose eggshell, with the slightly thinner pieces possibly being duck.

The colour observations concurred with those of Keepax (1981), most being of a white or cream colour. Keepax discussed one fragment of darker grey shell assumed to have been charred. In this material there were many darker pieces for example from 208/2 F672 phase 1C, 174/2 F255 phase 4A, G166 F246 phase 5C, and F554 phase 12 ranging from light grey to dark brown also thought to have been charred, some on one side only. The writer has observed the baking of eggs which was done by making a small hole in the pointed end of the egg and placing it blunt end down in the embers of a bonfire. The outer surface was found to be coloured in a similar way to some of this material and the possibility of egg baking is suggested. The shell charred on both sides is assumed to have been burnt as rubbish.

The thickness (table 83) was then considered in conjunction

with criteria from SEMs (table 84). Roman samples 580a and 813 and medieval sample 5b all fitted into the thick eggshell group, with 580a and 5b being thick enough to discount duck as a possibility. This left goose or guinea fowl, and the height of mammillae suggested that this was goose. All of the other samples were of much thinner shell and fitted a broad range of species. Sample 822 (plate 29), from medieval F703 phase 9, differed slightly from the rest. It had quite a thin shell which put it in the range of pheasant, duck, domestic fowl (and herring gull). Mammillae size suggested the possibility of pheasant, duck and domestic fowl, and while the mammillae number suggested domestic fowl and pheasant, the mammillae height fell in the range of pheasant only. This along with the fact that pheasant was a closer fit for all of the other criteria gave a strong suggestion that this sample was of pheasant (plate 28). Roman samples 815a, 815c and 580b, medieval samples 3, 5, 5c, 194, 361, 766a, 766b, and post medieval sample 190 were all specimens which the combined criteria suggested were domestic fowl eggshell (plate 27 of sample 194). In each case the thickness suggested a number of possible species, but as each criterion was tested so the number of alternatives was reduced. Layer proportions was the key factor, as each fragment showed a thick mammillary layer and with pheasant being discounted by mammillae height measurements.

With the remaining samples the possible identifications were less clear. Roman samples 554 and 566c. were not studied for all criteria as the sections did not show up clearly

Table 71: *Eggshell determinations*

SAMPLE	FEATURE GROUP	CONTEXT	PHASE	THICKNESS	DETERMINATION
Roman				microns	
554	671 208/1	2928	1C	276-293	Duck/Domestic Fowl/Pheasant
566c	672 208/2	2930	1C	285-309	Duck/Domestic Fowl/Pheasant
775.1	405 147/1	1753	2E	275-310	Domestic Fowl (Duck)
580	255 174/2	446	4A	207-247	cf Domestic Fowl (Duck)
580a	255 174/2	446	4A	567-578	Goose
580b	255 174/2	446	4A	275-309	Domestic Fowl7
815a	798 360/1	3954	5E	265-287	Domestic Fowl
815b	798 360/1	3954	5E	274-304	Domestic Fowl (Duck)
815c	798 360/1	3954	5E	280-300	Domestic Fowl
786	786 339/8	3921	5F	195-226	cf Domestic Fowl (Duck/Pheasant)
813	757 334/2	3600	5G	536-562	Goose
Medieval					
361	568 247/2	2607	8	228-266	Domestic fowl
3	204 120/6	227	9	288-300	Domestic Fowl
5	509 256/4	2023	9	234-260	Domestic Fowl
5a	509 256/4	2023	9	330-334	Domestic Fowl (Duck/Pheasant)
5b	509 256/4	2023	9	565-595	Goose
5c	509 256/4	2023	9	293-318	Domestic Fowl
24	207 120/7	236	9	272-295	cf Domestic Fowl (Duck)
194	508 256/3	2213	9	281-301	Domestic Fowl
822	703 307/1	3556	9	230-254	Pheasant
766a	206 119/2	1238	10	270-302	Domestic Fowl
766b	206 119/2	1238	10	294-315	Domestic Fowl
Post medieval					
133a	554 294/2	2192	12	299-316	Domestic Fowl (Duck)
190	563 291/2	2232	12	275-295	Domestic Fowl

c.f. species = all readings not possible so identification cannot be certain. Types separated by / then both types are possible. Types in brackets are likely, but less so than those not in brackets.

enough in each for layer proportions and mammillae height to be measured, so three species were possible. Using measurable criteria alone it could be suggested that Roman sample 786 and medieval sample 5a were of domestic fowl eggshell. However, examination of the outer surface of each showed polygonal plates were faintly visible, suggesting the possibility of duck or pheasant. Sample 786 appeared burnt and was thus too far damaged for any reliable deduction to be made. Finally, Roman samples 580 (plate 30), 775.1 and 815b, medieval sample 24 and post medieval sample 133, could all be reduced to the possibility of either hen or duck. In each case layer proportions showed a thick mammillary layer and therefore pointed to domestic fowl. However the mammillae height contradicted this suggesting duck to be the only possibility (with the possible addition of turkey in post-medieval sample 133). For this reason both domestic fowl and duck were considered as possible.

Discussion

The majority of the samples were identified as domestic fowl although some of the thinner specimens may have been duck or pheasant. Three specimens of goose were identified and a thinner sample was identified as pheasant. Based on the SEM evidence there were no clear patterns of species change between periods. Goose, domestic fowl and possibly duck and pheasant were present in the Roman and medieval samples, and all but goose were present in the few post-medieval samples. A slight difference was found between the Roman and medieval assemblages in the thickness ranges of the thinner shell groups, which accounted for almost 99% of the total in each case. Comparing the Roman thickness data with the medieval (fig. 178) a clear variation could be seen. Both showed that more shell fitted into the thickness range of 275-300 microns than any other but while the Roman data showed the vast majority falling into the 250-300 micron ranges with

little thicker than this, the medieval showed a far greater proportion occurring in the thicker ranges from 300-400 microns. Given the number of fragments measured (1514 Roman and 711 medieval) this is unlikely to have been a chance bias and so a real change was represented. It may have been that eggshell, most probably of domestic fowl, did become slightly thicker on average between the Roman and medieval periods, which could have been due to any of a number of factors such as increasing size of birds or seasonality, or it may have resulted from longer periods of burial.

Conclusions

The thickness measurements carried out on all of the eggshell showed that it fitted into two broad groups. The first thinner group covered a similar size range to pheasant, duck, domestic fowl and turkey, and the second thicker group a similar size range to goose and guinea fowl. The latter in each group could probably be discounted in most cases as they were recent introductions. Colour was only useful in determining baked or charred material. Scanning electron microscopy methods meant it was possible to confirm the identification of some fragments of shell as domestic fowl, goose and pheasant, which is not possible from thickness measurements alone. It was found necessary to use a number of SEM criteria together and the methods were evaluated and discussed. The suggested identifications infer that the eggs of at least domestic fowl and goose were used in the Roman period with the addition of pheasant in the medieval period. The majority of the shell in all phases was probably domestic fowl which was identified in the majority of the samples examined in detail. There was very little goose egg despite its thickness which may have been due either because there were originally few of them or less resistant to decay than some thinner types. Thickness ranges varied slightly between phases but not enough to warrant different conclusions of species presence being made,

Table 72: *SEM data for eggshell*

SPECIES	Diam Ma	Mammillae measurements (microns)		Layer proportions		
		Ma/sq mm	Ht. Ma	ML%	Ve%	Co%
Turkey	40-125	65-625	45-65	39	47	14
G. Fowl	50-100	100-400	49-58	32	57	12
Goose	60-180	30-280	112-140	32	53	15
Duck	60-100	100-280	60-100	40	49	11
Quail	25-60	270-1600	40-50	40	47	12
Partridge	30-100	100-1100	35-45	42	44	14
Pheasant	40-70	200-625	40-50	36	48	17
H. Gull	80-150	45-155	80-90	44	41	15
Hen	50-150	40-400	85-120	51	36	13
W. Pigeon	70-160	40-210	31-50	35	55	10
Lapwing	60-120	60-280	55-60	47	32	21
SAMPLE						
3	50-140	51-400	80-120	51	36	13
5	80-142	50-156	80-100	54	32	15
5a	56-111	81-319	85-105	45	42	14
5b	55-145	48-330	15-145	34	38	27
5c	65-92	119-231	75-105	45	36	19
24	75-132	57-178	50-65	49	38	13
133a	63-117	73-252	60-70	46	39	15
190	64-113	78-244	80-90	55	34	12
194	54-84	141-343	85-100	47	38	16
361	64-138	52-244	80-90	49	37	14
554	63-100	100-252	–	–	–	–
566c	49-98	104-416	–	–	–	–
580	50-143	49-400	5-80	60	40	0
580a	72-117	73-192	120-130	33	55	12
580b	66-116	74-230	80-90	44	40	15
766a	47-109	84-453	80-110	55	35	11
766b	85-108	85-138	60-100	49	38	14
775.1	63-103	94-252	65-85	50	35	16
786	43-78	164-540	65-75	60	32	9
813	73-102	96-188	90-150	38	49	13
815a	75-108	85-178	65-80	53	35	12
815b	57-83	145-308	65-80	55	33	12
815c	54-105	90-343	50-85	54	32	14
822	39-74	182-657	30-60	42	43	15

Key:
Ma = Mammillae ML = Mammillary layer
Ve = Vesicular layer Co = Compact layer (divisions of palisade layer)

especially given low total numbers in some phases. However, subtle variations in the thickness ranges of the thinner types from Roman and medieval assemblages were noted.

FISH REMAINS
Rebecca Nicholson

Introduction

Nearly 3000 fish bones and scales were identified, providing the opportunity to refine the discussion of fish exploitation given by the analysis of fish remains from the Shires, Leicester (Nicholson 1992). With the exception of one bone from Area 4, all the fish remains were recovered from Areas 1, 2 and 3, with the greatest number from Area 1. While the time-span of occupation was similar to the Shires, a greater amount of Roman material was sampled here, particularly from Areas 1 and 3, so providing the means to enhance our understanding of fish exploitation in Roman Leicester.

By contrast, only a small amount of post medieval material was found. Fish bones were present in 85/157 (54%) of the sampled features in Area 1; 58/71 (72%) in Area 2; and 16/23 (70%) in Area 3. These figures are of similar magnitudes to those for the concentration of fish remains from Little Lane and St. Peter's Lane, the Shires, and as there, most were from medieval contexts.

Identification and recording methods

All bones and scales were identified where possible to skeletal element and family, genus or species, but large numbers of small bone and scale fragments, as well as branchial bones, ribs, rays and spines remained unidentified. These fragments were counted when twenty or less, but otherwise the number of fragments was estimated by counting a proportion. Identifications were made by reference to the author's own comparative collection and that of the Environmental Archaeology Unit, University of York. Terminology for the skeletal elements follows Wheeler and Jones (1989). Most of the medieval contexts included in the analysis contained less than 30% residual Roman pottery, often none. Very few measurements were taken, owing to the small size of the great majority of bones. Where they were taken, measurements follow Morales and Rosenlund (1977), Wheeler and Jones (1979) and Jones (unpublished). More usually, fish size was estimated by visual comparison with bones from fish of known length and weight. All data have been stored as an archive using the computer package D-base III Plus, and include details of identification, bone condition, butchery, and fish size estimates, as well as notes on crushed or chewed specimens.

Quantities and distribution of fish bone

In total, 2664 bones and 87 scales were identified (tables 73 and 74). Most of these were from Area 1 (1396 bones and 32 scales), and all but 28 bones were recovered from the sieved residues and flots. A similar number of bone fragments and over 600 scale fragments were too small for identification; even complete scales may be difficult to identify to species.

As at the Shires, most of the bones were recovered from features of medieval date (82%), with relatively small numbers of fragments deriving from deposits of Roman date, despite the sieving of large volumes of earth. This discrepancy may in part be accounted for by differences in the types of feature represented in the various periods. While the great majority of sampled medieval deposits were pit or well fills, a much greater range of feature types was represented in the Roman period, including gulleys, ditches, post holes, structures and gravel quarries as well as pits and wells. While pits were probably used either primarily or secondarily for the disposal of rubbish and/or sewage, no such function is likely for smaller holes such as post holes, and gulleys and larger holes such as quarries. Wells may have been used to dump rubbish at the end of their useful life. These differences are also reflected in the fish bone condition; in general the bone from the medieval deposits was in a better state of preservation than that from deposits of earlier date, although the recovery of scales from deposits of all ages demonstrates that in all periods some features contained very well preserved material. As at the Shires, very few samples comprised waterlogged material, and the recovery of tiny bones and scales was not confined to these deposits. The consistent recovery of small bones and scales from free-draining deposits in Leicester would seem to be due to the implementation of an extensive sieving programme, rather than as a result of exceptional preservational circumstances. Of the sampled features, the fills of well F206 (phase 10) and pit F207 (phase 9) both in Area 1 proved to be particularly rich in fish bone, although large quantities of earth (over 250 litres) were sieved in each case. Undisturbed features of post-medieval date were far fewer in number than those of medieval date, and consequently few fish bones were recovered.

Species abundance

Although a range of taxa was represented, the majority of bones (62% of the identified sieved bones) were from herring *Clupea harengus* or herring family (*Clupeidae*) and eel *Anguilla anguilla* (30%). The increase of abundance of the former relative to the latter characterised the assemblages from the medieval compared with the Roman period in all three excavation areas. The other major difference in taxon distribution through time was that the representation of fish of the cod family (*Gadidae*), including cod *Gadus morhua*, saithe *Pollachius virens*, haddock *Melanogrammus aeglefinus* and ling *Molva* cf.*molva*, was almost exclusively restricted to the medieval and post medieval periods. Freshwater species including perch *Perca fluviatilis*, pike *Esox lucius*, trout *Salmo trutta*, tench *Tinca tinca*, gudgeon *Gobio gobio*, chub *Leuciscus cephalus* and other members of the *Cyprinidae* (carp family) were relatively more abundant in the phases dating to the Roman occupation, although they were represented, albeit in low frequencies, throughout all later phases. This pattern was also true for mackerel *Scomber scombrus*, salmon *Salmo salar* and flatfish (mainly of the family *Pleuronectidae*). With the exception of the anadromous salmon, and the flounder *Platichthys flesus* which tolerates brackish conditions and is often found in estuaries, all of these occasional species are exclusively marine. Occasional taxa found only in medieval and post-medieval deposits included the elasmobranchs (only one species, the thornback ray or roker *Raja clavata* was identified) and possibly the stickleback *Gasterosteus aculeatus*, while the grey gurnard *Eutrigla gurnardus* was found only in the Roman period in Area 3.

The relative distribution of taxa was similar for each of the excavated areas, although the great differences in the volumes of earth processed from each phase and area preclude very detailed statistical comparisons. While in general relatively few bones and scales were recovered from Roman features, there does appear to be a tendency towards a higher proportion of freshwater species represented in Area 3 than from Areas 1 and

2, and herring, though never common in the Roman deposits, was particularly rare in Area 3. The similarity both in species and in the relative abundance of the various taxa recovered from this site and the Shires in the Roman, medieval and post-medieval periods is striking, and indicates a genuine change from the consumption of mainly small freshwater fish and the euryhaline eel in the Roman period, to a piscivorous diet comprising mainly marine species, in particular herring and gadids, supplemented by a small amount of freshwater fish, eel and salmon from about AD 1100 onwards (fig. 178, and Nicholson 1992). Interestingly, the range and relative abundance of species from the medieval deposits here and the Shires is very similar to that recorded from Alms Lane in medieval Norwich (Jones and Scott 1985), which suggests the establishment of a fishing tradition over a fairly wide geographical area in eastern England.

Of the recovered scales, almost all were from freshwater fish, perch, possibly grayling *Thymallus thymallus*, pike and members of the *Cyprinidae*. These scales are all relatively large and robust, in contrast to the scales of many marine species (Nicholson 1992). Although most of the freshwater fish bones were from fish of small size (about 150-300 mm or sometimes smaller), the presence of a few large scales from perch in Roman deposits from Area 1 and cyprinid bones and scales from medieval deposits on Area 1 indicated the occasional consumption of fish of 350-450 mm, and salmon of 700-900 mm in length are indicated by the size of vertebrae recovered from Roman deposits on Areas 1 and 3. Surprisingly, as pike grow to over 1 m, all of the pike bones and scales were from small fish of under 300 mm. Of the gadid bones, almost all were from fish of over 600 mm long, although a single bone from cod or whiting *Merluccius merluccius* indicates the occasional consumption of smaller gadids. Of the flatfish, most seem to have been in the size range 300-500 mm, and there was no evidence for large fish such as halibut or turbot. The size of the eel and herring bones indicated that a wide age range of fish were exploited, although few bones appeared to come from fish at the upper end of the range (over 600 mm for eel and 400 mm for herring).

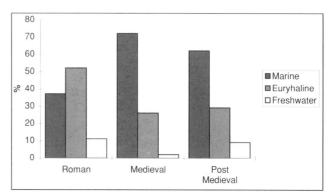

Fig. 178: *Proportions of marine, euryhaline, and freshwater fish bones*

The medieval plots A–G, Area 1

Examination of the fish bone assemblages from plots A-G, indicated some differences in taxon abundances, not all of which seemed to be related to the volumes of sieved earth (table 73). Deposits from plot C contained the greatest concentration of identified fish bone, with approximately 2 bones for every litre of earth sieved; the equivalent figure for plot D was 1 bone per litre of earth. All the other plots yielded much lower concentrations of bones, making it unrealistic to look closely at variations in species composition between the groups. In terms of taxon abundance, plot C produced a much higher ratio of eel to clupeid (herring family) bones than did plot D (a ratio of 1:1.4 compared with 1:10.57). Gadid bones also seemed to be relatively more common in plot D than C in phase 9, and these two characteristics would suggest that the refuse from plot D is more typically 'medieval', as described by the whole assemblages from this site and the Shires, than is that from Plot C. Similar proportions of freshwater species were associated with both Plots. As both Plots appear to have been occupied in the earlier medieval phases differences in fish species composition cannot be readily explained in temporal terms. As both herring and eel were considered cheap and commonly available fish in the medieval period (see below) it is possible that the occupants of Plot C in general were simply more fond of eel than the occupants of Plot D. There is no good evidence to suggest a difference in status between the two households, and as herring and eel bones commonly occur together, are of similar size and are likely to have undergone the same pre- and post-depositional modifications, the variations in bone ratio are unlikely to be explicable in taphonomic terms alone.

Fish preparation and economic significance

Only two bones exhibited cut marks, but as relatively few large bones were recovered no significance can be placed on this fact. One ling abdominal vertebra from F206, Area 1 phase 10 exhibited a possible cut of the lateral aspect, probably as a consequence of filleting. A gadid vertebral centrum had been cut along the dorso-ventral plane, probably when the fish was split into sides (Wilkinson 1979, 75). Obviously, fish sold already in fillets will leave little trace archaeologically at the site of consumption, so the absence of large fish bones does not prove that flesh from large fish was not eaten. During the preparation of stockfish (dried fish), usually fish of the cod family, fish were beheaded and part of the spine removed; this butchery usually took place at sea or at port during the medieval period. Traces of this butchery method may be seen on vertebrae and bones at the back of the head; the cleithrum, supracleithrum and post-temporal may all be cut, and portions will remain with the flesh sold at market. Unfortunately the very low numbers of gadid bones precludes the drawing of more than very tentative conclusions, especially as the majority of bones were vertebrae (as would be expected given their numerical dominance in the skeleton). Although rare, bones from the head included a haddock premaxilla, cod parasphenoid and cod ceratohyals, indicating that at least some large fish were marketed with the heads on. Large fish bones may also be under represented if table waste were disposed of separately from kitchen waste, with the former being more usually thrown into local rubbish pits than the latter. The recovery of large amounts of domestic mammal bone would tend to indicate that quantities of kitchen waste were present in the excavated deposits however, so again the paucity of large fish bones cannot be so easily explained.

Of the other species, thornback ray was clearly imported with the skin on, as testified by the discovery of the distinctive dermal denticles or bucklers. While it is not currently possible to identify salted, pickled or smoked fish from the bones recovered archaeologically, herring and mackerel were almost certainly preserved by one of these methods, as oily fish spoil rapidly and until the late medieval period it is extremely unlikely that they could be transported to Leicester in a fresh state. Smoked herring (kippers) were not available prior to the 13th century (Wilson 1973, 33). White fish, by contrast, could have been transported fresh if wrapped in wet cloths or seaweed; however salt or dried fish of the cod family (stockfish or hardfish) were commonly available in the medieval period and formed a standard poor man's fare (Bond 1988, 73). When fresh marine fish became available in inland areas from about the mid-15th century it commanded a high price, and

was therefore the food of wealthy householders (Dyer 1988, 30). Freshwater fish was generally the only fresh fish available to the common person, and consequently prices were relatively high (Cutting 1962). Larger freshwater fish were again generally too expensive for all but the wealthy householder to purchase (Dyer 1988), but records show that small and even tiny freshwater fish were eaten (Cutting 1962), and these were within the reach of the less well-off. The dominance of bones from herring and eel, as well as the predominance of small and tiny freshwater fish over larger specimens, provides reasonably good evidence that the households concerned were, if not poor, at least not very wealthy in the medieval period. In 1461 records from south Staffordshire give the median relative prices for individual freshwater fish as follows (Dyer 1988, 31): pike 12d., tench 6d., chub 4 $^1/_2$d., perch 2d., small roach and dace $^1/_4$d., eel 1$^1/_2$d. Of the marine fish, salt fish cost 8d., stockfish 3d., plaice/flounder $^1/_2$d., and herring $^1/_4$d.

Table 73: *Area 1. Distribution of identified medieval fish bones by plot*

Plot Area 1	A	B	C	D	E	F	G
No. of features	6	20	5	9	2	8	5
Vol. sieved (L.)	0	89	250	543	184	227	28
Elasmobranch	-	-	1	1	-	-	-
Ray indet.	-	-	1	-	-	-	-
Eel	-	11	176	35	9	17	4
Clupeid indet.	-	4	11	94	19	5	-
Herring	-	15	254	370	59	32	17
Salmonid indet.	-	-	1	-	-	-	-
Trout	-	-	2	-	-	-	-
?Pike	-	-	1	2	-	-	-
?Cyprinid	-	-	1	1	-	-	-
Cyprinid indet.	-	-	1	4	1	-	-
?Gadid	-	-	-	-	-	1	-
Gadid indet.	-	-	2	7	1	-	-
Cod/Saithe/Pollack	-	-	-	3	2	1	2
Cod/Saithe	-	-	-	5	-	-	-
Cod	-	-	2	4	1	-	-
Saithe	-	-	-	1	-	-	-
?Haddock	-	-	-	-	1	-	-
Haddock	-	-	1	-	-	-	-
Ling	-	-	-	-	-	-	-
?Perch	-	-	-	-	-	-	-
Perch	-	-	3	4	-	-	-
Mackerel	-	-	-	1	1	-	-
?Flatfish	-	-	-	1	-	-	-
Flatfish indet.	-	-	1	-	-	-	-
Right-sided flatfish indet.	-	-	-	3	1	-	-
Plaice/Flounder	-	-	1	-	-	-	-
Total	0	30	470	544	96	57	23

Chewed and corroded bones

A considerable number of bones, particularly from eel and herring, appeared to have been digested. Typically these bones appeared crushed, corroded and/or covered in a calcareous deposit (for further discussion of fish bones after consumption by humans and other mammals see Jones 1984, Wheeler and Jones 1989, 69-76, and Nicholson 1993). That many of these bones were recovered from pits strongly suggests that they had been deposited in human faeces, and the lack of bones from taxa with more robust bones supports this view; dogs and pigs seem to be less discriminatory about which bones they are prepared to swallow, while rodents leave very little trace of consumed bones in their droppings (Wheeler and Jones 1989, 70). One salmon bone did appear to have been chewed, however, from a fish of 700-900 mm in length (Area 3, phase 5H), which may indicate scavenging by dogs or pigs, though humans may also chew (but are unlikely to swallow) large bones. Chewed and corroded bones were present in deposits from all phases, but were more common in medieval samples. The fill of pit F207 was particularly rich in chewed bones (Area 1, phase 9), as was pit or well F540 and pit F620 (phase 8, Area 2), and pit fills in F503, F513, F570 and F587 (phase 9, Area 2). Occasional charred and completely burnt bones were recovered, often from the same pits as the chewed bones, which may indicate that the pit fills included not only faeces but also general table waste and ashes thrown from the fire.

The fishing industry

As evidence for fishing in the Roman and medieval periods accumulates with the implementation of comprehensive sieving strategies in British towns, it is clear that the increasing abundance of fish remains in the medieval compared with the Roman period is a common trend, rather than a local phenomenon at this site caused by unequal amounts of sieving and different context types. A similar pattern has been seen not only at the Shires (Nicholson 1992), but also, for example, in Worcester (Nicholson and Scott, forthcoming), Exeter (Wilkinson 1979), Ipswich (Jones and Locker n.d.), and York (O'Connor 1988, 115-6). The emergence of the herring industry is well documented, and appears to have taken place from late Anglo-Saxon times (Muus and Dahlstrøm 1985, 210). Likewise the proliferation of gadids in the medieval period reflects the burgeoning trade in white fish, which resulted in vessels sailing as far as Newfoundland to fish for

cod from the 16th century (*ibid.*, 212). By contrast, fishing seems to have been predominantly local in the Roman period, and eel and salmonids are usually the most frequent taxa. Small-scale industries based on the use of hook and line, weirs and traps in rivers and estuaries, and hook and line, inshore traps and surface nets in the sea seem to have been the usual source of fish for Roman townsfolk, with riverine fish being more easily available to the populace of inland settlements.

Conclusions

The assemblage of fish bones and scales recovered bears a striking similarity to that from excavations at the Shires, and displays trends that have also been observed in fish assemblages from other towns where an extensive sieving policy has been practised. Fish exploitation appears to have been fairly small-scale and local during the Roman period, concentrating on freshwater and euryhaline species such as eel, salmonids and cyprinids. Herring seems to have been available, almost certainly in a preserved form, but became much more abundant in the medieval period when its remains dominated the fish bone assemblage. Large gadids were seen only from the medieval period, reflecting the development of mid and deep water sea fishing as an organised industry, more akin to that practiced today.

Judging by the types and sizes of fish represented in the medieval deposits, the populace of Causeway Lane were not particularly wealthy. Comparisons with the admittedly small,

Table 74: *Summary of fish remains in Roman phases 1-6 and post Roman phases 8-12*

	Area 1					Area 2			Area 3			Area 1				Area 2				Area 3	
Phase	1	2	3	4	5	1	2	3	2	5	6	8	9	10	12	8	9	11	12	9	11
FRESHWATER																					
Trout	-	1	-	-	-	-	-	-	-	-	-	-	2	-	-	-	-	-	-	-	-
?Pike	-	-	2	-	-	-	-	1	-	-	-	1	2	-	-	-	-	-	-	1	-
Pike	-	1	-	-	1	-	-	-	1	-	-	-	-	-	-	-	1	-	-	-	-
?Grayling	-	-	-	-	-	-	-	-	-	-	-	-	-	-	-	1	-	-	-	-	-
?Cyprinid	1	5	12	1	-	-	-	4	-	2	6	-	1	5	-	4	5	-	3	-	6
Cyprinid indet.	-	1	5	1	1	-	1	-	-	4	6	2	1	2	-	4	1	-	3	2	6
?Roach/Rudd	-	-	-	1	-	-	-	-	-	-	-	-	-	-	-	1	-	-	-	-	-
Gudgeon	-	-	2	-	-	-	-	-	-	-	-	-	-	-	-	-	-	-	-	-	-
Chub	-	-	-	-	1	-	-	-	-	-	-	-	-	-	-	-	-	-	-	-	-
?Chub/Dace	-	-	-	-	-	-	-	-	-	-	1	-	-	-	-	-	-	-	-	-	-
?Tench	-	-	1	1	-	-	-	-	-	-	-	-	-	-	-	-	-	-	-	-	-
Stickleback	-	-	-	-	-	-	-	-	-	-	-	-	-	-	-	2	-	-	-	-	-
Perch	-	-	1	-	5	-	1	-	-	3	2	6	6	1	-	6	5	-	4	-	1
?Perch	-	2	4	-	-	-	-	-	1	2	2	-	-	-	-	-	1	-	1	-	1
EURYHALINE																					
?Eel	-	-	2	-	-	2	-	2	-	1	-	-	-	-	-	2	2	-	-	-	-
Eel	-	13	78	9	15	3	79	2	1	7	10	13	215	30	3	196	46	3	11	5	56
Salmonid indet.	-	-	-	-	-	-	-	-	-	1	-	-	1	-	-	-	-	-	-	-	-
Salmon	-	-	-	2	-	-	-	-	-	1	2	-	-	-	-	-	-	-	-	-	-
MARINE																					
Elasmobranch	-	-	-	-	-	-	-	-	-	-	-	-	1	1	-	-	-	-	-	-	1
Ray indet.	-	-	-	-	-	-	-	-	-	-	-	-	1	-	-	-	-	-	-	-	-
Thornback ray	-	-	-	-	-	-	-	-	-	-	-	-	-	-	-	-	-	-	-	-	13
Conger eel	-	-	-	-	-	-	-	-	-	-	-	-	-	-	1	-	-	-	-	-	-
Clupeid indet.	1	1	25	2	6	-	1	-	-	-	1	2	47	90	2	26	8	-	3	-	-
?Herring	-	-	-	-	-	-	-	-	-	-	-	-	2	1	-	-	-	-	2	-	-
Herring	-	1	20	8	10	-	34	2	-	1	-	48	559	152	4	326	137	3	21	40	113
?Gadid	-	-	-	-	-	-	-	-	-	-	-	-	1	-	-	1	1	-	-	-	-
Gadid indet.	-	-	-	-	-	-	-	-	-	-	1	-	9	1	-	-	3	-	-	1	3
Saithe	-	-	-	-	-	-	-	-	-	-	-	-	1	-	-	-	-	-	-	-	-
Cod/Saithe/Pollack	-	-	-	-	-	-	-	-	-	-	-	-	3	5	-	-	1	-	-	-	2
Cod/Saithe	-	-	-	-	-	-	-	-	-	-	-	-	3	2	-	-	-	-	-	-	-
Cod	-	-	-	-	-	-	-	-	-	-	-	-	3	4	-	-	2	-	-	-	3
Cod/Whiting	-	-	-	-	-	-	-	-	-	-	-	-	-	-	-	-	1	-	-	-	-
?Haddock	-	-	-	-	-	-	-	-	-	-	-	-	-	1	-	-	-	-	-	-	-
Haddock	-	-	-	-	-	-	-	-	-	-	-	-	2	-	-	1	1	-	-	2	6
?Gurnard indet.	-	-	-	-	-	-	-	-	-	1	1	-	-	-	-	-	-	-	-	-	-
Grey Gurnard	-	-	-	-	-	-	-	-	-	-	-	-	-	-	-	-	-	-	-	-	-
?Smelt	-	-	1	-	-	-	-	-	-	-	-	-	-	-	-	-	-	-	-	-	-
Mackerel	-	-	2	-	1	-	-	2	-	1	3	1	-	1	-	-	-	-	-	-	-
?Flatfish	-	-	-	-	-	-	-	-	-	1	2	-	1	-	-	-	-	-	-	-	-
Flatfish indet.	-	-	-	-	-	-	-	-	-	2	5	-	-	-	-	-	-	-	-	-	-
Right sided flatfish indet.	-	-	6	-	-	-	-	-	1	3	6	-	1	4	-	-	2	-	-	-	-
Ling	-	-	-	-	-	-	-	-	-	-	-	-	-	3	-	-	-	-	-	-	-
Plaice/Flounder	-	-	4	-	-	-	-	-	-	1	9	-	1	-	-	-	1	-	-	-	-
Flounder	-	-	1	-	-	-	-	-	-	-	-	-	-	-	-	-	-	-	-	-	-
Unidentified	4	70	201	30	72	6	122	17	0	145	54	72	1001	339	12	291	269	7	45	35	403
Total Identified	2	25	166	23	42	5	119	12	2	32	57	73	863	303	10	570	218	6	49	50	210

hand-picked fishbone assemblage from the Austin Friars in Leicester (Thawley 1981) show the friars to have eaten a wider range of fish, including large flatfish and sturgeon, demonstrating that these fish were available to those who could afford them. By contrast, the inhabitants of Causeway Lane appear to have selected in the main the cheapest fish: herring, eel, small freshwater fish and probably salted or dried whitefish of the cod family.

Table 75: *Hand-collected fish bones. All areas*.

Area	A1	A1	A1	A2	A3	A4	A4	A4	
Phase	U/S	9	11	1	U/S	2	9	11	Total
Conger eel	-	-	1	-	-	-	-	-	1
Gadid indet.	-	8	-	-	-	-	1	-	9
Cod	-	4	-	-	-	-	1	-	5
Cod/Saithe	-	6	-	-	-	-	-	-	6
Saithe	-	1	-	-	-	-	-	-	1
Haddock	-	-	-	-	-	-	1	-	1
Ling	-	3	-	-	-	-	-	1	4
Plaice/Flounder	-	-	-	-	-	1	-	-	1
Unidentified	1	60	-	2	12	2	2	-	79
Total identified	0	22	1	0	0	1	3	1	28

OYSTERS

Angela Monckton

Introduction

Comparison of size and infestation of oyster shells has been used by Winder (1992) to study the sources and exploitation of oysters in the past and her methods were used here. Shells of oyster (*Ostrea edulis*) from Roman and medieval context groups were analysed by measuring size and recording the infestation and other shell characters for comparison on an intrasite and intersite level, particularly with those from the Shires Excavation (Monckton 1994). The objective was to find evidence for the source of the oysters and to detect any changes in their exploitation during the phases of the site.

Methods

After excavation the shells were allowed to dry and then packed, labelled and weighed, the weight was recorded by subgroup on the finds tables 2 and 3. During examination they were carefully washed under gently running water with a soft-bristled brush and air dried. The oyster shells were considered by context or contexts grouped by phases into sufficient numbers for the analysis (table 76). The shells were sorted into left and right valves and length and width measured. They were also examined for infestation by marine worms, sponges, barnacles and other organisms and for the attachment of young oysters. The condition and any unusual characters of the shells were also recorded together with the presence of notches or cut marks (after Winder 1992).

Analysis was carried out in consultation with Jessica Winder. The percentage of all measured shells with each infestation or character was calculated (table 76). The most useful dimension for comparison is the largest diameter, either width or length, of the left, cupped valve. This gives the maximum size of the live oyster as the flat, right valve lies inside it. This measurement (left valve maximum diameter, LVMD) is used for the survey of modern oyster populations. For each group the mean of the maximum left valve diameter and standard deviation were calculated and the data used in t-tests to compare the groups (table 78). Histograms of the percentages of shells in successive 5mm size classes were plotted (figs. 179-81). A second statistical test which does not rely on a normal distribution, the Kolmogorov-Smirnov test (Shennan 1988) was used to compare the size frequency distribution of the groups of shells. The results were compared with each other

and the Roman groups were compared with those from other selected sites of the same dates (table 78).

The general shape of the oysters was quantified simply by dividing the width by the length so that those with a ratio of more than one were classified as broad, those less than one as long. The proportion of long shells was calculated. The relationship of width to length was examined by calculating the regression line for representative groups. The numbers of shells measured for each group of contexts, the minimum number (the largest number of either left or right valves totalled for the group including broken shells), and the percentage of broken unmeasurable shells were also recorded (table 76). Records of all the shell by context are in the site archive.

Results

Size

On analysis of size the shells from the five context groups examined formed two different groups of oysters. The first group consisted of the shell from Roman phase 6; these were the best preserved, and they showed a normal distribution of sizes (fig. 179) indicating that they were from a single source and had the largest mean diameter from the site. When compared with shell from the Shires, Leicester, (table 78) no significant difference was found between these shells and those from the main deposit from the late second century cellar (F186.1264 Little Lane). The same results were found when the shell from 338/3 F763 phase 6A was considered alone.

The second oyster group consisted of the those from phase 5C-H and those from phases 1 to 5B, (the phase 1 to 5B oysters were considered together because those of phase 5A and 5B were thought to be from redeposited earlier material). These two context groups were found to have no significant difference from each other, but were significantly different from those from phase 6 (table 78). The shell from both these context groups had a size distribution with more than one mode indicating that they were from more than one source (figs. 180-81), and they had a smaller average diameter than those from phase 6. On comparison with shell from the Shires, no significant difference was found between these shells and the rest of the Roman shell from the Shires.

The medieval context group consisted of all the measurable shells from medieval contexts with low residuality of Romano-British pottery. Only 26 left valves were measurable and when compared with those from the Roman groups were found to have no significant difference from the shell of phase 5C-H and phases 1-5B (table 87). Comparison was also made with the medieval shell from the Shires sites and found to give significantly different results on the Kolmogorov-Smirnov test and the t-test (t = 4.7). Hence, although there are too few shells to allow definite conclusions, it does appear to consist mainly of residual Roman shell. The post medieval oysters were similarly grouped but were too few to consider further. The size distribution of the medieval shells is not normal and compares with those of phases 5C-H and phases 1-5B. The mean size of these shells (right valve maximum width 61.58mm) does not compare with other medieval shells at the Shires (right valve maximum width 53.91mm), giving further evidence that this is residual Roman shell. The shell from these medieval contexts is however only slightly larger than that from other medieval sites for example Salisbury (Winder in prep.) and Reading Abbey Wharf (Winder 1994), right valve maximum widths 57.65mm and 57.46 mm respectively.

Infestation

When the infestation of the three Roman context groups was considered (table 76) the two different oyster groups showed similarities in the organisms present, however, the significant

Table 76: *Oyster infestations and observations.*

	Phase 6 with F763	Phase 6A F763 only	Phase 5C-H	Phase 1-5B	Medieval
INFESTATION	%	%	%	%	%
Polydora ciliata	61.3	49.0	40.7	24.5	31.1
Polydora hoplura	0.0	0.0	0.0	0.0	0.0
Cliona celata	4.3	5.3	3.2	2.5	2.2
Calc tubes	0.0	0.0	0.0	0.4	0.0
Barnacles	13.0	14.5	5.2	5.4	6.7
Polyzoa	9.0	8.3	7.5	3.3	0.0
Bore holes	1.0	0.5	2.4	0.8	0.0
Sand tubes	11.0	6.8	7.9	1.7	0.0
SHELL CHARACTERS					
Thin	1.7	2.4	0.4	1.3	2.2
Thick	8.3	11.7	4.2	1.7	2.2
Heavy	1.7	2.4	1.2	1.7	2.2
Chambered	27.7	27.7	17.8	11.6	6.7
Chalky deposit	12.7	3.4	25.7	26.6	42.2
Worn	41.3	37.9	83.0	36.1	86.7
Flakey	45.0	41.8	79.1	50.6	55.6
Colour/Stain	1.3	0.5	0.4	0.8	0.0
Oysters attached	7.7	8.3	6.3	6.6	0.0
Irregular shape	33.0	36.9	27.3	29.0	26.7
Notches/Cuts	4.7	5.8	2.4	6.6	4.4
Ligament	0.0	0.0	0.0	0.0	0.0
TOTALS					
Measured Left	167	123	140	128	26
Measured Right	133	83	113	113	19
Total Measured	300	206	253	241	45
Broken Left	69	24	65	67	12
Broken Right	33	15	40	41	10
Total Number	402	245	358	349	67
% Broken	25.4	15.9	29.3	30.9	32.8
Minimum Number	256	161	236	251	53
Long: Broad	1:15	1:11	1:11	1:9	1:6
% Long	6.6	8.9	9.3	11.7	15.0
Left Valve Mean Diameter (mm)	79.47	80.21	72.45	71.82	68.42
Standard Deviation	10.33	10.42	10.77	10.55	11.70

difference in size shows that the two groups are distinct. Some quantitative differences in infestation were found; the shell from phases 1-5B differs not only in having a high percentage of broken and flaking shells but also in a much lower incidence of the encrusting organism, Polyzoa, and a lower incidence of chambered shells which have hollow spaces below the inner lining. Polyzoa can be lost in poorly preserved shells but the two differences taken together indicate a different and probably mixed source for these oysters.

The shell from the Shires showed major differences between the infestation of the Roman and medieval shells. The Shires Roman shell had two to three times more incidence of the burrowing worm *Polydora ciliata* (16-19%), four to five times more barnacles (5-6%) and a higher incidence of sand tubes (5-8%) than the medieval, with Polyzoa only present in the Roman shells (3-14%). Compared with the ranges quoted above for the Shires Roman shell the Causeway Lane Roman shell had even higher levels of *Polydora ciliata* (25-61%) and barnacles (5-15%) with similar levels of sand tubes and Polyzoa. It is known that higher levels of infestation develop in warmer shallow water as indicated for the Shires Roman oysters compared with the medieval, and this is also indicated for the Causeway Lane shell by the even higher rates of infestation.

Other characters

Considering other characters, the Roman shells from this site, like those from the Shires, have a high incidence of chambering which may indicate changes in salinity, and also

have a high incidence of attached young oysters and many irregular shaped shells. The attachment of young oysters arises in natural populations which are not disturbed or deliberately spread out to grow so that more irregular shells are produced as a consequence of crowding. The shape was considered by plotting width against length of the left valve and calculating the regression line (table 77). The phase 6 shell was compared with the Shires cellar context 1264 and the regression lines showed some difference in shape although the difference was much less marked than that between the Shires Roman and medieval shell. Similarities were found between phase 5C-H and phase 6 shells. The phase 1-5B shells showed similarities to the shells from Pudding Lane context 3218.

Table 77: *Regression of width against length of left valves*

	Intercept	Slope	Angle	Coefficient
Shires F186.1264	33.6078	0.6157	31.62	0.68779
Phase 6	27.2085	0.7395	36.50	0.80284
Phase 5C-H	26.1606	0.7228	35.90	0.73076
Phase 1 to 5B	24.1778	0.7406	36.52	0.47640
Pudding Lane 3218	28.1868	0.7011	35.03	0.61270
Shires Medieval	11.0253	0.9226	42.69	0.85705

When the numbers of long to broad shells are considered (table 76) the Roman groups have around 7% to 12% from this site while those from the Shires had around 20% long shells in the Roman groups with the post Roman having only around 5%. This shape difference reflects the oysters' response to the type of sediment (Winder 1992b), longer shells being an adaptation to softer sediments while broader shells originate on firmer substrates in deeper water. This may indicate that the

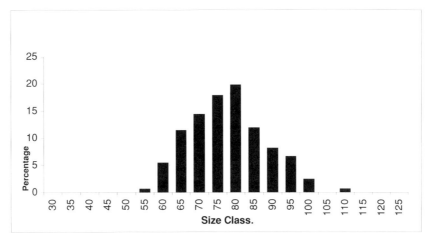

Fig. 179: *All phase 6 oysters*

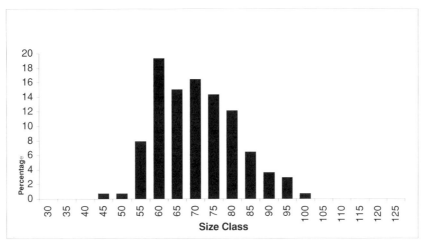

Fig. 180: *Phase 5C-H oysters*

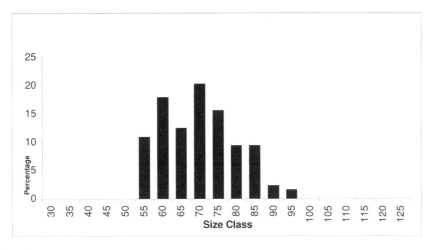

Fig. 181: *Phase 1-5B oysters*

oysters from this site were from firmer sediments than those from Shires Roman phases.

Discussion

Comparison with oysters from the Shires Excavation

The two different groups of shell were found to be comparable in size and size distribution with the shell from the Shires. Firstly, both sites have a group with normal distribution and no significant difference from each other or from shells from North Shoebury, leading to the conclusion that they share a similar origin. These shells were from the Shires, Roman cellar context 1264 (late second century) and from phase 6 of this site mainly from 338/3 F763 (post 300 AD). They also share the same range of infestations and other characters but with some differences in proportions indicating that they may be from different seabed types within the same area. The shells from the Shires are from a closely dated second century rubbish deposit but those from this site are from phase 6 surface make-up deposits. This shell does, however, form a coherent group and it is suggested that it originates from the same period as the residual pottery from the deposits (late second to early third century). This residual pottery comprises 25 to 30% of the Roman pottery in 338/3 F763 which contains most of the shell from this phase. This is consistent with the similarities the shell shows to the late second century group from the Shires, although the possibility that the shell dates from the time of the later material in the deposit cannot be excluded.

The second oyster group consisted of shell from phases 1-5B (late first to late second century AD) and phase 5C-H (late second to mid fourth century AD) from this site, which was comparable with that from the rest of the Shires Roman contexts (c.60 AD to fourth century AD) and the similar shell from Shires F186 contexts 992-1263 (late second century). None of these context groups has shell with a normal distribution of sizes and there are variations in proportions of some of the infestations and recorded characters suggesting mixed groups of oysters as may be expected from grouped contexts. No similarities were found between this shell from the Shires or from phase 5C-H here with shell from the other sites available for comparison though they were most similar to the shell from Pudding Lane, London context 3218 (Winder 1984). However the shell from phases 1-5B was found to give no significant difference on both tests to this group from Pudding Lane. This also compares with the Pudding Lane shells on the slope of the regression of width against length (Winder 1984) indicating that the oysters are a similar shape; also comparison of the infestation showed similarities, worm infestation was similar (*Polydora ciliata* 29.8% of the total at Pudding Lane and 24.5% here), although less barnacle infestation was found at Pudding Lane (0.04%) than here (5.4%). Because this context group from Leicester does not have a normal distribution and may be of mixed origin as it is a small number of shells from a group of contexts there is insufficient evidence to draw conclusions about its origin. The similarities found would be worth further investigation should a large group of well stratified shell be found in the future.

Source of Roman oysters

The three context groups of Roman oysters from the site were

compared with archive data from groups from the sites listed below (table 78).

The better preserved group from phase 6, like those from the Shires cellar context 1264, was found to be similar in both size and size frequency to the four groups of shells from North Shoebury, Essex (Murphy 1995). No similarity was found between any of the Causeway Lane or the Shires Roman shell with Newport Roman villa, Isle of Wight (Winder 1989) or with context 1714 Pudding Lane, London (Winder 1984), however Causeway Lane phase 1-5B shell showed similarities with Pudding Lane context 3218 but this cannot be confirmed from this small disparate group.

Comparing infestation of this shell with North Shoebury material, neither have any infestation by *Polydora hoplura*, a burrowing worm with a known modern Southern distribution (Hancock 1974), nor do they have any calcareous tube worms. The occurence of the boring sponge, *Cliona celata*, is comparably low and levels of barnacles and Polyzoa compare. The North Shoebury oysters have rates of infestation with the burrowing worm *Polydora ciliata* ranging from 45-90%, a range of 25-61% was found at Causeway Lane while those from the Shires had lower rates of 16-19%. Like the Shires, the Causeway Lane shell had a higher incidence of worms forming sand tubes than those from North Shoebury. From the size and size distribution and the absence of *Polydora hoplura*, an East coast origin for the oysters from phase 6 and the Shires cellar context 1264 is strongly indicated, possibly the Essex creeks from a similar but not identical source as the North Shoebury oysters.

Transport of oysters

It is known that oysters can survive up to ten days out of water (Winder 1985) if kept moist and cool. Barrels, jars or other containers may have been used to keep the oysters moist during the journey inland but it has been suggested that oysters transported along the coast could have been kept in baskets on the boat deck or in the water allowing a longer time for transportation. Oyster beds are known in Britain at Richborough, the Thames estuary and the Essex coast. The route taken in Roman times is unknown but could have involved coastal barges and then transport inland along the rivers or roads. There is no evidence at present for the location of natural oyster beds in the past other than on the south coast and around East Anglia (Winder 1992) but they have been suggested further north in the Humber estuary (O'Connor 1989) so may possibly have

Table 78: *Comparison of left valves of oysters*

	Phase 6		Phase 5C-H		Phase 1-5B		LVMD mean	Total shells	SD
	t	k	t	k	t	k			
Phase 5C-H	5.8	+					72.5	140	10.8
Phase 1-5B	6.4	+	0.5	-			71.8	128	10.1
Medieval	2.3	+	1.6	+	1.4	-	68.4	26	11.7
Shires F186.1264	0.4	-	6.1	+	6.8	+	79.1	301	10.3
Shires 992-1263	4.7	+	1.8	-	2.3	+	74.5	233	11.0
Shires Rest Roman	6.0	+	0.3	-	0.8	-	72.8	134	9.0
Shires Medieval	19.6	+	12.6	+	12.2	+	56.9	144	10.0
N.Shoebury s299	1.2	-	5.9	+	6.4	+	81.1	98	11.3
N.Shoebury s422	0.2	-	5.5	+	6.1	+	79.7	156	11.7
N.Shoebury s446	0.2	-	2.5	+	5.6	+	79.7	143	13.1
N.Shoebury s917b	1.6	-	6.1	+	6.6	+	81.8	93	11.8
Newport Villa 37	3.4	+	13.2	+	14.1	+	85.6	700	10.7
Pudding Lane 3218	4.2	+	0.2	+	0.5	-	72.2	739	8.2
Pudding Lane 1714	5.5	+	9.9	+	5.2	+	86.5	106	11.2

Key to Table

    t, values greater than 2 are significantly different results of t-test at 0.05 level of probability

    k, Kolmogorov-Smirnov cumulative frequency test (+) = significant difference. (-) = no significant difference at 0.01 level of probability.

    LVMD, mean left valve maximum diameter (mm); SD, standard deviation.

Data from: Newport Roman Villa (Winder 1989), Pudding Lane, London (Winder 1984,1985)

North Shoebury, Essex (Murphy 1995) and The Shires, Leicester (Monckton 1994).

existed at other locations along the east coast. Containers used to transport the oysters to Leicester may have been barrels which do not survive or large wide necked jars. At Richborough a wide necked jar or olla was coated with bitumen inside and out as described by Apicius for the storage of oysters (Edwards 1984) but no evidence of this was found here.

Consumption of oysters

Recipes for sauces to be served with oysters recorded in Apicius (Edwards 1984) include wine, olive oil and fish sauce. Pottery from the site includes amphorae of types associated with these commodities.

Notches of triangular shape were found on some of the oyster shells probably made with a pointed knife. Around 86% from this site phase 6 and 60% at the Shires cellar context 1264 were directly opposite the hinge indicating a fairly uniform opening technique. It should be noted that the evidence was only found in a small percentage of the shells. It was found that 25% of the left cupped valves were absent from this group from the Shires so, as the oyster is usually served in this valve, they appear to have been consumed elsewhere. In contrast, at Causeway Lane an excess of left valves was found. A few shells from phase 5C-H and phases 1-5B were found with rounded notches suggesting opening some of the shells with a different type of implement. The majority of recorded notches of these groups were at various positions about half way between the hinge and the opposite edge of the shell showing a difference from phase 6.

Other shellfish

Mussels (*Mytilus edulis*) were found in small numbers or as fragments only from sieved samples from Roman and medieval contexts providing evidence that they were consumed in Leicester but were possibly less common than oysters. However, mussels may be under represented in comparison to oysters as the shells are less robust so do not survive so well. A very small number of whelks (*Buccinium undatum*) large enough for consumption were found together with a few small cockles (*Cerastoderma edule*) probably brought to the site with the oyster shell, both were found occasionally in Roman and medieval contexts.

Conclusions

The shell from medieval deposits appears to be residual Roman shell and the post medieval shells were too few to analyse. Two distinct groups of oyster shell were found on the site which were found to be directly comparable with the two Roman oyster groups from the Shires excavation. The Roman shells could be from shallow waters which is indicated by higher levels of infestation, possibly from an estuary or where freshwater enters the sea which may be indicated by chambering of the shells, and possibly from somewhat firmer sediments than the Shires Roman oysters, as is indicated by the presence of a smaller proportion of longer shells. The irregular shape and attachment of young oysters indicate a natural unmanaged population. The shells from phase 6 and those from the Shires cellar context 1264 were found to be closely similar to shells from North Shoebury, Essex, and the Essex coast is suggested as their origin.

Acknowledgements

I am most grateful to Jessica Winder for advice given during this project and to the following authors and organisations for their consent to use their archived data for comparison:-
Jessica Winder (1989) for Isle of Wight County Archaeological Committee (Newport Roman villa, Isle of Wight) and (1984) for The Department of Urban Archaeology, Museum of London (Pudding Lane, London). Also Peter Murphy (1995), for East Anglian Archaeology (North Shoebury, Essex).

THE MINERALISED FLIES *Peter Skidmore*

Introduction

The material upon which this report is based was from 778 sieved samples, 89 of which contained about 1200 specimens. The condition throughout was extremely poor, almost all of the specimens having been mineralised to the point of fossilization. This meant that the inevitable problems of identification were greatly exacerbated. Many specimens were in the form of casts, the organic parts having dissolved so that vital cuticular features such as microsculpture had been erased. Notwithstanding the condition however, the material proved interesting in many respects, spanning over a thousand years of human presence on a single site. The mineralised state of the material raises the question of its origin in this non-calcareous site and the suggestion is made that it may have resulted from attempts at primitive methods of hygiene by the human inhabitants of the site.

Methods

The material was received dry by the writer and the condition precluded the normal techniques of examination in spirit and identification by means of microslide preparations. Gross features only were available for study and there was no recourse to dissection of unemerged adults to check specific identity. Submersion of specimens in spirit failed to reveal useful characters so the material was mostly examined dry. As usual (Skidmore, in press) specimens were tentatively referred to taxonomic groups in an initial examination of all of the samples. Then these groups were re-examined and identified to the lowest hierarchical level (usually genus).

Results

The species found in this study in Roman and medieval samples are listed in table 79.

Initial interpretation was based on whether the species in each sample indicated putrid or uncontaminated conditions. The criterion used in this separation was the presence or absence of species indicative of cess (see discussion). In table 82 the number of samples in which these cess indicators occurred is shown. A full list of all specimens identified is available in the site archive. Contaminated features and groups are summarised by phase, area and sample in table 80, whilst table 81 shows the relative percentages of cess-indicators throughout the sequence.

Discussion

This study has differed in many respects from any other of this nature in which the writer has been involved. The state of the material was incomparably the poorest but the period represented was by far the longest. In interpreting insect assemblages, the absent taxa are often as revealing as those present; and this was certainly the case here.

The species list is notable in the total absence of several characteristic synanthropic flies, especially such calliphorids (blowflies) as *Lucilia* (greenbottles) and *Calliphora* (bluebottles), piophilids and the muscids *Musca domestica* (common house-fly), *Stomoxys calcitrans* (stable-fly) and *Muscina stabulans* (room-fly). The absence of these suggests that the environment in which the others were breeding was in total darkness, and probably in a thermal regime inadequate for *Musca* and *Stomoxys*. These two require temperatures elevated by bacterial activity resulting from continuous addition of decomposing matter (Skidmore 1985) and their absence would infer breaks in that continuity. It is perhaps worth noting here that this

Table 79: *Taxonomic list of insects*

Family	Insects	Roman Phase 2-6	Medieval Phase 8	Medieval Phase 9-10	Late Med Phase 11
DIPTERA	FLIES				
Scatopsidae	Scatopse notata (L.)	+	+	+	–
Cecidomidae	Mayetiola sp	–	–	+	–
Stratiomyidae	?Oxycera sp	+	–	–	–
	Chloromya formosa (Scop.)	–	+	–	–
Phoridae	Megaselia sp	+	+	–	–
Syrphidae	Eristalis tenax (L.)	+	+	–	–
Sepsidae	spp	+	?	+	+
Helomyzidae	Tephrochlamys rufiventris (Mg.)	–	+	–	–
Sphaeroceridae	Ischiolepta sp	–	–	+	+
	Thoracochaeta zosterae (Hal.)	+	+	+	+
	?Telomerina flavipes (Meigen)	+	+	+	+
	?Trachyopella sp	–	+	–	–
Drosophilidae	?Drosophila sp	+	+	–	–
Ephydridae	?Hydrellia sp	+	–	–	–
	?Scatella sp	+	+	+	–
Agromyzidae	spp	+	+	+	–
?Chloropidae	spp	+	+	–	–
Anthomyiidae	?Botanophila sp	–	+	–	–
	indet sp (modern)	–	–	+	–
Fanniidae	Fannia ?scalaris (L.)	+	+	+	–
	Fannia sp	+	–	–	–
Muscidae	Hydrotaea dentipes (F.)	+	?	–	–
	?Spilogona	–	+	–	–
COLEOPTERA	BEETLES				
	Elaterid larvae	+	–	–	–
	Aglenus brunneus (Gyll.)	–	–	+	–
	Blaps sp	–	–	+	–
DIPLOPODA	MILLIPEDES				
	Julid millipedes	+	+	+	–
	Polydesmid millipedes	+	+	+	–

accounts for these two flies not breeding in cow-pats in pastures in Britain, although they regularly breed in cow-manure heaps (Skidmore 1991).

Summer kill of flies

The poor state of the material seems not to have resulted purely from edaphic conditions on site. Two factors point to this belief. Firstly it is not situated in a calcareous area, although marls are present and some limestone could have been incorporated into the buildings. But more significantly, it is clear from the dipterous material that sudden lethal conditions periodically recurred. The bulk of the specimens were virtually fossilized and most of them died before the adults had emerged. The writer has found that under normal conditions up to 10 percent of the individuals in a fly population may fail to emerge from the puparia (Skidmore 1993). When the majority have failed to emerge, highly abnormal conditions are indicated. In fact it is particularly evident from the specimens of *Eristalis tenax* that death was very sudden. Some specimens were at the point in the pre-pupal stage when the larva has contracted and the pupal respiratory horns have appeared as vague protuberances on the dorsal surface of the first abdominal segment before they are extruded to form the familiar shape. This was found particularly in F405 Phase 2E and F579 Phase 8. The entire prepupal stage lasts only a matter of hours so that death in these specimens must have been almost instantaneous. Also, death occurred during the summer (July-early September), since the overwintering adults oviposit in spring

to produce the next generation of adults during this period of summer.

The presence of large numbers of *Eristalis tenax* (drone-fly), *Thoracochaeta zosterae* (lesser dung-fly), and *Fannia scalaris* (latrine-fly) strongly infer extremely foul liquid or semi-liquid conditions such as would prevail in cesspits. The stench particularly in high summer could have been such that the human inhabitants were driven to periodic remedial action. The fossilized state of the dipterous material, together with the evidence of their sudden demise, point to the possibility of applications of lime. If this interpretation is correct, it should be noted that the practice was in regular use on this site from Roman to medieval times.

Table 80: *Features exhibiting contaminated (putrid) conditions.*

Roman	Area	Features and Groups
Phase 2E	1:	F405 147/1.
Phase 3B	1:	F376 152/1, F230 155/2,155/3.
Phase 5H	3:	(3664) 353/1 (?).
Phase 6A	3:	F763 338/3, F766 367/1 (?).

Medieval

Phase 8	2:	F521 249/3, F579 249/2, F540 247/1, 246/1, F568 247/2 (?), F604 247/3.
Phase 9	1:	F207 120/7, 120/8 (Plot C).
Phase 9	2:	F509 256/4 (?), F513 260/4, F537 257/3, F587 260/3.
Phase 10	1:	F206 113/2 (Plot D).
Phase 11	3:	F703 307/1.
Phase 12	1:	F234 102/1.

Cesspit flies

Of the taxa represented, eight belong to the cess-pit fauna, and it was upon the presence of one or more of these that samples were designated 'putrid'. The 'cesspit' species recovered in this study were; *Scatopse notata, Eristalis tenax, Heleomyza serrata, Tephrochlamys rufiventris, Telomerina flavipes, Fannia scalaris* and *Hydrotaea dentipes*. *Thoracochaeta zosterae* also once belonged to this community, having been ubiquitous throughout Britain until late medieval times. Today however it occurs only on the coast, amongst decaying seaweed, and very rare captures in inland localities have always been regarded as representing stray specimens (Pitkin 1988, 1c). The remarkable change of habit which has clearly taken place over a few hundred years in this fly remains unexplained but it is undoubtedly related to improved standards of hygiene. A very similar range of habitats is shared by the now rare Urinal fly *Teichomyza fusca* (Smith 1986), although records of this insect from archaeological excavations in Britain have proved to refer to *T. zosterae* (Belshaw 1989, Skidmore 1993). British specimens of the fly formerly known as *Heleomyza serrata* have proved to belong to the recently described but extremely similar *H. capitosa* and it is likely that this is the case here.

Telomerina flavipes is said to favour dark situations in which to breed and it has a preference for animal protein, either in the form of carrion or in the dung of carnivores or omnivores (including man) (Rohacek 1982-5). Having entered the system this fly could probably have bred continuously in total darkness. This would not have been possible however for such heliophilous flies as *Fannia* and *Eristalis*, so there was clearly easy access into the system from outside.

There appears to be a distinct faunal change on the site through the period represented which could result from sampling bias. However, as comparable numbers of samples were taken from Roman and medieval contexts, and all pits were sampled, a peak of human activity during the earlier medieval period is indicated. The apparent faunal change however is best seen by considering the relative frequency of uncontaminated and putrid environments through the phases concerned. In table 81 below, the samples indicating putrid conditions are represented as a percentage of the number of samples with insect remains for that period. This suggests that the cess-pit element increased from 38% in the Roman period to 59% in Phase 8 and 53% in Phases 9 and 10, or when the total number of samples taken is considered from around 2% of the Roman samples to 12% of the earlier medieval samples. Little evidence came from a few samples from phase 11 from pit F703 of the late medieval period. If correct this could infer a peak in human activity during early medieval times.

Table 81: *The occurrence of putrid conditions according to incidence of Dipterous cess-indicators.*

Phase	Total samples taken	Samples with Insects	Putrid Samples	% samples with cess insects
Roman				
Phases 2-6	437	24	9	38%
E. Medieval				
Phase 8	105	27	16	59%
Phases 9 and 10	205	34	18	53%
Late/Post-med				
Phases 11 and 12	31	4	3	75%

In table 82 the eight cess species are listed according to the numbers of samples in which each was found in this study, under the broad chronological divisions used throughout this report. The percentage frequency of each taxon within each period is shown, and the peak of this fauna during the early medieval phases 8, 9 and 10 can be seen. It will be noted that

by far the commonest species in the phase 8 was *F. scalaris*, but *T. zosterae* was equally frequent in the Roman period and marginally most frequent in phases 9 and 10. *T. flavipes* was the third commonest throughout the sequence. The heleomyzids were remarkably scarce, whilst *Eristalis tenax* was not recovered from phases 9 and 10. Whether these apparent changes were real is not certain, but fluctuations in frequency could be expected without necessarily inferring marked changes in the type of materials deposited.

Table 82: *Number of samples in which each species occurs by phase.*

Cess Insects	Roman Phase 2-6		Medieval Phase 8		Medieval Phase 9-10	
	Number	%	Number	%	Number	%
Scatopse notata	1	5%	1	4%	3	9%
Eristalis tenax	2	11%	2	8%	-	-
Tephrochlamys rufiventris	1	5%	1	4%	1	3%
Heleomyza serrata	-	-	-	-	1	3%
Thoracochaeta zosterae	6	33%	1	4%	13	37%
Telomerina flavipes	2	11%	5	19%	5	14%
Fannia scalaris	6	33%	14	54%	12	34%
Hydrotaea dentipes	-	-	2	8%	-	-
Total	18		26		35	

Conclusions

Despite the poor condition of the dipterous material examined from this site it appears to testify to an extremely foul environment persisting over a period of more than 1000 years of human inhabitation. The fly assemblage suggests accumulations of cess in total darkness though with easy access for a range of coprophagous and saprophagous species. There is some evidence that odours may have become so obnoxious during summer that lime was regularly applied throughout the period of human occupation of the site. The uncontaminated environments range from deep soil to patches of open water with moss, algae and waterside grasses.

Acknowledgements

My thanks are due to Dr. P. C. Buckland of the Department of Archaeology and Prehistory at Sheffield University for his help and support in many details of this work which is to be submitted to his Department as one of many site-studies towards a Doctorate.

THE MINERALISED WOODLICE

Jon Dawes

Introduction

Mineralised woodlice fragments were found in 41 of the sieved samples. Some of this material dated from Roman times (phases 2 and 3) but the bulk of the woodlice specimens came from the early medieval period.

Woodlice are crustacea related to crabs and lobsters, they have 7 pairs of legs and their bodies are made up of segments consisting of rigid plates. The body is divided into 3 groups of segments: the head, with the eyes and antenna, followed by 7 segments called the pereion or thorax and finally 5 segments called the pleon or abdomen, attached to which are the uropods and telson or tail.

Although large fragments of woodlice bodies were present, the most useful pieces for their identification, their antenna and telson (tail) were, for the former, completely absent and for the latter, very few in number. Despite this handicap, identification was attempted for all except the most minute fragments. Where identification was uncertain (due to the small size of the fragments) they are recorded as woodlouse sp.

The maximum number of specimens found in each sample was counted (table 83).

Discussion

Altogether four species of woodlice were identified, these were: *Armadillidium vulgare* (common pill woodlouse), *Oniscus asellus* (common smooth woodlouse), *Porcellio dilatatus* and *Porcellio scaber* (common rough woodlouse). Today (1993) three of these species are common and widespread in Leicestershire, being found in a variety of habitats, but the fourth species *P.dilatatus* is usually associated with dairy farms and stables.

A. vulgare is easily recognised due to its smooth rounded body plates called pereonites; amongst the material there were several almost complete specimens of this species which can roll into a ball when disturbed. There were also several heads showing the characteristic triangular shaped forehead as well as a few telsons which do not protrude beyond the end of the last body segments (pleonites). This species is often found in fairly dry open areas in both natural and synanthropic habitats and it can even be found wandering around in full sunlight.

O. asellus was identified from a number of heads and a single telson as well as from pieces of body plates (pereonites) which unlike those of *P. scaber* are not roughly tubercled. *O. asellus* is a ubiquitous species favouring damp conditions. It is often found in the company of *P. scaber*.

P. dilatatus was identified from a single telson which shows characteristically rounded tip. In the same sample there were 2 pieces of a pereonite which has a characteristic smooth patterned surface which on comparison with a recently collected specimen shows them to be consistent with *P. dilatatus*. A further sample also contained some pieces of this species pereonites. Hence this species was present in samples from F521 249/3 and F604 247/3 both from Area 2 phase 8. Today this species is usually found on dairy farms and in stables, where it is often found in association with mortared walls close to straw and dung. *P. dilatatus* has recently been recorded in Leicester from the Abbey Grounds around the dung/rubbish heap adjacent to Pet's Corner and from Abbey Park, associated with a rubbish heap. This species may have been more common in the past when horses were an important mode of transport and more animals were kept around dwellings. The present day distribution of *P. dilatatus* is of a scattering of records throughout Britain, but the lack of records is mainly due to the fact that looking through dung heaps is not every naturalist's idea of fun.

P. scaber was identified from the many heads and several telsons as well as the roughly tubercled surface of the pereonites. This is an extremely common species usually found in slightly drier micro-sites than the equally ubiquitous *O. asellus*. *P. scaber* is found in most types of habitats from woodland to seashore and is the commonest species met with inside houses today.

Conclusion

The largest group of woodlice was found on Area 2 from phase 8 including *Porcellio dilatatus*, a species now found associated with mortared walls near to straw and dung. This study has provided early records of woodlice species to compare with Leicestershire today where 17 species have been recorded. The three main sources for woodlice records are Michael Evans's early 1980's survey which concentrated on churchyards around the county, Adrian Rundle's survey in the late 1980's which concentrated on sites within Leicester city boundary and my own ongoing county wide survey. Woodlice species are little recorded from archaeological sites and it is hoped that future sites in the county may provide more of this material for comparison with modern studies to give a better understanding of conditions in Leicester in the past.

Table 83: *Mineralised woodlice, number of individuals of each species.*

	A. vulgare	*O. asellus*	*P. dilatatus*	*P. scaber*	WL sp.	Number of Samples
Roman	-	1	-	3	1	4
Phase 8 Area 2	18	29	2	71	1	17
Phase 9	11	5	-	13	1	15
Phase 10	8	2	-	24	4	5

Key: *Armadillidium vulgare, Oniscus asellus, Porcellio dilatatus, Porcellio scaber* WL sp. Woodlouse indeterminate species

THE PARASITES   *Peter Boyer*

Introduction

Recent work on archaeological deposits within the city of Leicester has shown that the ova of intestinal parasites can be preserved in some conditions, and the presence and relative concentrations of these has been used to identify layers of human waste and therefore the functions of certain features, as well as giving indications of levels of health and hygiene. It was decided to examine a number of samples from the site for this type of evidence.

The two types of ova most commonly encountered in archaeological deposits are *Trichuris* (whip worm) and *Ascaris* (maw or round worm) species. Normally it is the species which parasitise humans, namely *T. trichiura* and *A. lumbricoides* which are found, and it is only these types which have so far been found from Leicester (Boyer, 1990 and forthcoming a,b; Mackie, 1989), though writers elsewhere have also reported other species (de Rouffignac, 1985, 1987; Jones, 1990, Jones *et al*, 1988, Pike and Biddle, 1966). It has been shown (Boyer, forthcoming a,b) that parasite ova could be recovered from a number of types of contexts and when analysis was carried out on sub-samples of deposits some yielded small numbers of ova. However material described as 'cess' (possible mineralised sewage) was recovered from some sieved samples and some of this also produced parasite ova, often in greater concentrations. Some sieved samples yielded coprolites (mineralised faeces) which have also been subjected to analysis, in some cases giving positive results. A small number of hand collected coprolites have also been recovered from excavations. Bearing this in mind sub-samples of various materials were selected from contexts across all three areas of the site. Sub-samples were taken of: soil from bulk samples, soil from small spot samples, 'cess' material and coprolites recovered from sieved samples, suspected 'industrial residues', one hand-collected coprolite; and the residue from around an excavated piece of textile (thought to be the medieval equivalent of toilet paper). A total of 247 samples were subjected to analysis from 115 different Roman and medieval contexts, mainly from pit fills, though a few also came from general layers.

Method

20ml of dilute hydrochloric acid was added to 6g of the sample and left overnight to break down the material then 64ml of water was added to make a total of 90ml. The solution was then passed through a 0.3mm sieve to remove any coarse material and 0.15 ml of solution was taken, on a microscope slide for scanning. Any ova present were counted and measured and the total multiplied by 100 to give an equivalent concentration of ova per gram of material.

Results and discussion

A number of samples yielded some parasite ova and the positive results are recorded by subgroup on the finds summary tables for Roman (table 2) and medieval (table 3)

phases. These record only the presence of parasite ova for the three types of material tested; cess, coprolites and subsamples of background material. The levels of contamination of the samples are discussed below. Full details of all tests are held in the archive.

The actual number of *Trichuris* sp. and *Ascaris* sp. ova were recorded, with the former divided into complete, incomplete and other examples and the latter divided into fertilized, unfertilized and other examples. Average dimensions were calculated.

The suspected industrial residues (F570 and F509 from area 2 phase 9) and the textile (2102 from F 537 area 2 phase 9) gave negative results.

Conclusions about the contamination of samples from concentration of ova have been made (Jones 1985, 112 and pers comm.). Jones, working on waterlogged archaeological material, divided concentrations into four groups: 100-200 ova per gram show insignificant or background level of contamination, 200-500 ova per gram are difficult to interpret, 500-20000 ova per gram show abundant faecal material present and 20000+ ova per gram = excrement! Given that waterlogged material showed far better preservation than the mineralised material from Leicester, it can be assumed that presence of parasite ova in these deposits does show at least some background level of contamination.

The parasites

The ova of whip worm and round worms are passed out with the faeces before they are ultimately re-ingested thus perpetuating the animals' life cycle (Chandler and Read 1961). It would therefore be safe to assume some level of faecal content where the eggs were recovered. The majority of ova present were of whip worm, *Trichuris*, of which there are a number of species which parasitise various animals. All of these ova have a distinctive barrel shape, and when complete, 'polar plugs' over the openings at each end. The clearest way of identifying the different species is by size. These range from the large ova of *T. vulpis* which is parasitic in dogs, to the small *T. trichiura* which parasitises humans, though each type of ova may be found in the faeces of an intermediate host, as Mackie (1989) found, for example. The results were compared with published size ranges (length and breadth) for the complete ova of the different *Trichuris* species (eg. Burrows, 1965, Thienpont *et al*, 1986). The ova found were too small for most of the suggested ranges for species which are parasitic in dogs, sheep and mice, however, all of the ova, with a couple of exceptions, fitted into the suggested size ranges for *T. trichiura* (human) or *T. suis* (pig).

The situation regarding round worm, *Ascaris* species, ova is less clear because of the varying degrees of preservation in which these were found. When complete they have a coarse outer shell but examples with varying degrees of decortification were found, and these may become confused with other microscopic organisms. This may have occurred with the identification of some of the *Ascaris* ova here and so their presence was not always as certain as that of *Trichuris* ova. Again the *Ascaris* ova were of species parasitic in humans or pigs, i.e. *A. lumbricoides* or *A. suum*.

Two coprolite samples yielded the ova of *Fasciola hepatica*, the sheep liver fluke (Spencer and Monroe 1975), the first time this has been found in archaeological samples from Leicester.

Roman

Eight features and one layer of Roman date yielded parasite ova. Seven of the features were in Area 1, the remainder were from Area 2. There was no evidence of Roman parasite ova in

Area 3. All of the material came from earlier phases of occupation, up to about 200 AD.

In Area 1, two early Roman features produced ova though one of these F494 130/7 phase 1B just yielded an isolated *Trichuris* ova which could be interpreted as no more than background contamination. The second feature F405 147/1 phase 2E, yielded more evidence, albeit from one context. Here there were small numbers of ova (500-700 per gram) from cess like material and quite a high concentration from a coprolite (2900 per gram), its presence alone suggesting some sewage deposition and the other findings supporting this. The remaining Area 1 features containing ova were as follows; F240 186/1 phase 5D and F376 152/1 phase 3B yielded small quantities of ova from single contexts suggestive of moderate contamination, the other features F230 G155 phase 3B, F390 182/2 phase 3C and F463 160/4 phase 5A produced evidence from more than one context with abundant faecal material suggested in F230 and F390. Only two Area 2 Roman contexts produced evidence of parasite ova, both of phase 2K. A coprolite from 202/3 F656 contained a single ova of what appeared to be the sheep liver fluke, *Fasciola hepatica* and whilst this was not substantial evidence of sewage deposition, there may have been some possible level of fascioliasis contraction amongst local human or animal populations (Faust & Russell 1964). The second Area 2 Roman context (2924) 201/1 contained a high concentration of parasite ova (6100 per gram) suggesting a concentration of faecal material. The nature of the deposit implying an area of manuring or a heavily truncated pit. The three Roman features showing the heaviest concentrations of parasite ova were from Area 1; G147 F405 phase 2E, G155 F230 phase 3B and G182 F390 phase 3C, all produced far more *Trichuris* than *Ascaris* ova. A high concentration was also found in Area 2 context (2924) G201 phase 2K where numbers these two species were almost equal.

Medieval

A total of 51 contexts from 18 medieval features contained parasite ova. Of these, there were 18 contexts from five features on Area 1, 31 contexts from 11 features on Area 2 and two contexts from two features on Area 3.

All of the Area 1 material came from earlier medieval contexts in phases 9 and 10. Two of the features in this area F213 and F292 only produced very small numbers of ova from single contexts which can only be interpreted as background contamination. The other three features contained far more abundant material, mainly from the upper fills. F235 produced sufficient ova from 'cess' and a coprolite to suggest faecal contamination and F206 and F207 yielded evidence from four and ten contexts respectively. Results from F206 113/2 (757) a secondary fill and 119/2 (1238) an upper fill suggested high levels of faecal material. Moderate levels of such material were suggested throughout F207.

Eight of the 11 features containing such evidence from Area 2 were from phase 8, and of these, only two F542 and F620 produced evidence from few contexts to suggest just a background contamination. The remainder F540, F568, F604, F579, F521 and F609 all yielded sufficient evidence from multiple contexts to suggest the presence of moderate to high levels of faecal material, though the evidence from F609 is enhanced by findings from a coprolite which may have distorted the overall pattern for that feature. F540 was the first of medieval date to produce evidence of *Fasciola hepatica* ova. Unlike the isolated Roman example, also from Area 2, there were a number in the medieval material and the same feature also yielded evidence of *Trichuris* and *Ascaris* ova, suggesting that contaminated meat or vegetation had been consumed. The remaining features on Area 2 were from phase 9. Of these, only F503 produced a moderate amount of parasite evidence with no more than background contamination being suggested. Again the majority of samples yielding ova from features in Area 2 produced far more *Trichuris* than *Ascaris* eggs, a pattern often seen in archaeological material.

Area 3 produced little evidence of parasite ova. Two features gave positive results, F703, in phase 11, only produced evidence suggestive of background contamination whereas that from F726, in phase 9, was slightly more substantial, but not sufficient to suggest high levels of faecal material.

Discussion

Analysis of samples of Roman and medieval date from across all areas of the site has shown the presence of parasite ova. Most of these were of *Trichuris* and *Ascaris* species which measurement has suggested were of the types infecting humans or pigs, most probably the species *T. trichiura* and *A. lumbricoides* which parasitise humans. Two contexts also yielded the ova of *Fasciola hepatica*, the sheep liver fluke, which, given the nature of deposits and surrounding materials were probably evidence of human populations consuming contaminated food products. Because ova of all three species are deposited in the faeces, it is strongly suggested that where they were recovered, there existed some level of faecal contamination. The material recovered and referred to as 'cess' often contained parasite ova and so it can be concluded that the description of this material was fair as faecal contamination was present. The numbers of ova recovered varied considerably between contexts with quantities only sufficient to suggest that there was a background level of faecal contamination. Other samples, however, yielded heavy concentrations of ova, and, particularly where this was repeated within features, strongly suggested the deliberate deposition of human faecal waste and thus the utilisation of certain features as cesspits.

The evidence for the Roman period was far less abundant than that for the medieval. Only eight features and one layer produced ova, with five of the features with background contamination. The remaining three features G147 F405, G155 F230 and G182 F390 did produce more ova, suggesting a moderate level of faecal deposition though not on the same scale as was evident from the medieval material. These Roman features were all from Area 1 from the earlier Roman phases. However, the general layer in Area 2 G201 which produced by far the largest concentration of ova from any Roman layer showed that faecal material was deposited here also, possibly spread as manure in phase 2K.

The medieval parasite evidence was more substantial with a number of contexts yielding sufficient material to suggest concentrated faecal deposition, with all evidence coming from within cut features. On Area 2, five pits of the earlier medieval period F540, F568, F604, F579 and F521 produced sufficient evidence to suggest they were utilised, at least in part, as cess pits, with evidence from woodlice (Dawes above) suggesting that F568 and F604 may also have contained animal dung. The medieval evidence from Area 1 showed three pits F235, F207 and F206 with sufficient evidence to infer concentrated faecal deposition. These three were situated in the proposed plot divisions in Area 1, with one each in plots B, C and D respectively.

The results suggest that successive populations, particularly in the medieval period, were experiencing some level of of parasitic worm infestation although the level of of infection cannot be accurately assessed. A mild infection with either *Trichuris* or *Ascaris* may go unnoticed but may have more serious symptoms in the young and infirm. However, if infection is greater the symptoms may include loss of apetite, nausea, diarrhoea, weakness, weight loss, anaemia, abdominal discomfort and sometimes fever (Chandler and Read 1961). Infection with *Ascaris* is generally more serious than *Trichuris* infection and can lead to infestation of the lungs with larvae which may cause pneumonia which may be fatal. There is also the added danger that in heavy infections of *Ascaris* the worms may form a tangled mass in the intestines causing blockages which can be fatal in some cases.

Conclusions

Three Roman and eight medieval cesspits are suggested for the site, with a great deal of background faecal contamination throughout many other features. These conclusions rely entirely upon positive evidence of parasite ova presence so faecal remains could only be inferred. It may therefore be possible that other, uninfected faecal material was present, but undetected by these methods. The positive evidence does however provide a clear indication of the nature of sewage deposition across the site, showing that parasitic infection in the Roman and medieval periods was widespread, especially considered along with evidence from the Shires and Guildhall Lane (Boyer forthcoming). Furthermore, this work has shown that not only was there infection of the population by intestinal worms but possibly also from liver fluke, the latter may have been from the droppings of infected sheep but may have been from people infected by consumption of contaminated meat or vegetation.

THE PLANT REMAINS   *Angela Monckton*

Introduction

Charred cereal grains, some cereal chaff and seeds were recovered from the environmental samples as well as mineralised fruit stones, fruit pips and seeds from the cesspits. The identification and analysis of the remains showed the cereal crops consumed on the site and the changes in the crops from the Roman to medieval period including some evidence of the arable weeds which grew in the fields. Evidence for other food plants including fruit, nuts and legumes and some evidence for vegetables was found. The presence of mineralised fruit remains contributed to the identification of the cesspits. Other evidence included some possible garden plants, some imported foods, and evidence for hay probably for animal fodder, mainly from the Roman period. The evidence was compared with that from the Shires (Moffett 1993).

Methods

Of the 778 flotation fractions (flots) collected in a 0.5mm mesh sieve from wet sieved samples a total of 139 were large or of good potential and were assessed by Lisa Moffett of the Department of Archaeology, Birmingham University, and 50 were selected for analysis. The rest of the flots were scanned for plant remains during sorting for small bones, fish and insect remains and the additional plants noted, these are referred to in the text as scanned samples.

The analysis of the plant remains was carried out in consultation with Lisa Moffett. All the selected flots were 100% sorted and the plant remains were identified, counted and recorded on the site database, tables were then produced using a spreadsheet. Counts are of seeds in the broad sense except where specified, and plant remains from the other residues of the analysed samples are included. Identification was carried out as far as possible within the limits of time available and the condition of the material. Sub-groups with more abundant plant remains were noted on finds tables 2 and 3. The Roman plant remains were considered by phase and sub-group and medieval by phase and feature in plot or area in line with the project design for the site.

Plants were listed in order with reference to Stace (1991), they were grouped in types and habitats but as many plants can occur in a variety of habitats and these may not have been the same in the past, this should only be considered as a guide to interpretation (tables 84 and 85).

In order to compare the plant remains from the Roman samples the proportions of cereal grains, chaff, seeds of wild plants, useful plants (legumes, cultivated plants and collected fruit and nut shell), other items (stem nodes, buds, fungus and other fragments) and indetermined seeds were calculated (fig. 182). This was done because the proportions of types of remains in a sample can assist in interpretation and indicate activities such as crop processing (Hillman 1981).

Roman plant remains

Results, the plants and contexts sampled

Cereals

The cereals found were wheat (*Triticum* spp) and barley (*Hordeum vulgare*); oat (*Avena* sp) was present though possibly not a cultivated species as the grains were small but the species could not be confirmed in the absence of chaff, there were also a few possible rye grains (*cf Secale cereale*).

The most common wheat identified was spelt (*Triticum spelta*) with emmer (*Triticum dicoccum*) and a free-threshing wheat in smaller quantities. The latter is most probably bread wheat (*Triticum aestivum s.l.*) which is the only species of free-threshing wheat identified in Roman Britain. The better preserved barley grains were identified as the hulled form and the twisted grains indicate that this is possibly 6-row hulled barley. Oat was probably a weed of the other cereals and there were a few possible rye grains from phases 2A and 5G but this could not be confirmed. Wheat and barley were about equally represented in terms of numbers of identified grains in phases 2 and 4, although phase 2 produced the most wheat chaff, barley was most numerous in samples from phases 3, 5 and 6 and was most abundant in phase 5. Many grains could only be identified as cereal indeterminate because of distortion during charring, so the proportions of the cereals are only an estimate.

Cultivated or collected plants

Edible legumes were represented by bean (*Vicia faba*) and pea (*Pisum sativum*). The identified peas from phases 2 and 6 were small (*c.*4mm) but identified from the form of the hilum. There were also incomplete legumes of a similar size, only identifiable as *Vicia/Pisum/Lathyrus*, these may be poorly preserved peas. Lentil (*Lens culinaris*) was found in the sample from 174/2 F255 phase 4A, possibly as an imported foodstuff although cultivation in Britain is possible. Other cultivated plants are opium poppy (*Papaver somniferum*), fig (*Ficus carica*), both of which were mineralised, flax (*Linum usitatissimum*) and coriander (*Coriandrum sativum*). Fig and coriander may be imports or garden plants and columbine (*Aquilegia vulgaris*) was found possibly cultivated as a garden flower. A seed of beet (*Beta vulgaris*) was found from a scanned sample as evidence of cultivated vegetables. Apple or pear (*Malus/Pyrus*) and bullace (*Prunus domestica*) may have been from orchard trees or gathered from the wild and other gathered foodstuffs may be represented by hazel nut shell (*Corylus avellana*) and sloe (*Prunus spinosa*).

Other plants

Many plants classed as arable weeds are not characteristic of particular types of soils or conditions but some, such as nettles (*Urtica* sp), persicaria (*Persicaria maculosa/lapathifolium*) and henbane (*Hyoscyamus niger*) are found on nutrient rich soils

such as farmyards and manure heaps. Stinking mayweed (*Anthemis cotula*) is a weed of heavy soils (Jones 1981) and may indicate that the cereals were grown on such soils as found in Leicestershire. Cleavers (*Galium aparine*), when found associated with cereals suggests that they may have been autumn sown (Jones 1981). An additional species of arable weed was wild radish (*Raphanus raphanistrum*). A group of plants now found on grassland, including some which are characteristic of hay meadow such as yellow rattle (*Rhinanthus* sp), ox-eye daisy (*Leucanthemum vulgare*) and crested dog's-tail (*Cynosurus cristatus*), were found in some of the samples particularly in phase 4A.

A number of damp ground plants such as rushes (*Juncus* sp) were represented possibly from ditches at crop field margins or being brought into the town for use as flooring or bedding. Hedgerow plants were represented possibly by elder (*Sambucus nigra*) which is also common on waste ground, the berries of which may have been gathered for use, and white bryony (*Bryonia dioica*), a climber of hedgerows is of note here as a group of seeds were found in phase 3. The remaining seeds were unclassified either because they have no common habitat or because they could not be identified further. The latter include the sedges (*Carex* spp), many of which are plants of damp ground and the small leguminous seeds (Fabaceae) of clover type such as *Lotus*, *Trifolium*, *Melilotus* and *Medicago*, which include many grassland plants.

Early Roman

Phase 2 (50 – 150AD)

Area 1: Sample 726 was from a hearth 134/1 phase 2A or deposit derived from a hearth on surface 1. The sample was dominated by cereal grains with only two chaff fragments found. Free-threshing wheat and some barley grains were present with beans, peas and hazelnut shell indicating domestic rubbish. Sample 775 F405 147/1 phase 2E was from a well which contained parasite eggs and mineralised insect remains indicating putrid deposits. Mineralised plant remains included fig, cherry or sloe and apple or pear representing remains of fruit consumed. A few mineralised weed seeds and carbonised cereal remains were found. The remains were all in poor condition which made identification difficult, however the mineralised fruit remains add to the evidence of secondary use of this well as a cesspit (table 84).

Area 2: Samples 522, 572 and 538 from G201 layers phase 2K, are similar in being dominated by weed seeds with goosefoot, brome grass (*Bromus hordeaceus/secalinus*), with other grasses and sedges most numerous. There were few cereal grains including wheat and barley but sample 538 F686 201/2 has the largest percentage of chaff found on the site (17% see fig. 182) represented mainly by spelt glumes which are also present in sample 572 201/2. These remains may be the waste chaff and weed seeds from cleaning of the grain by fine sieving although residual material may also be present.

Phase 3 (120 – 200AD)

Area 1: Of the six samples, five were dominated by weed seeds particularly the two most productive. These are sample 379 from ditch F343 141/4 phase 3B and sample 569 from rectangular pit F412 186/4 phase 3C. The former had a small amount of cereal evidence including a spelt glume; flax and coriander were found and the most numerous weeds were goosefoots. The grassland plants ribwort plantain (*Plantago lanceolata*) and crested dog's-tail (*Cynosurus cristatus*) were most numerous and yellow rattle and ox-eye daisy were present suggesting the possible presence of hay. A few wet ground plants; lesser spearwort (*Ranunculus flammula*), marsh stitchwort (*Stellaria palustris*) and ragged robin (*Lychnis flos-*

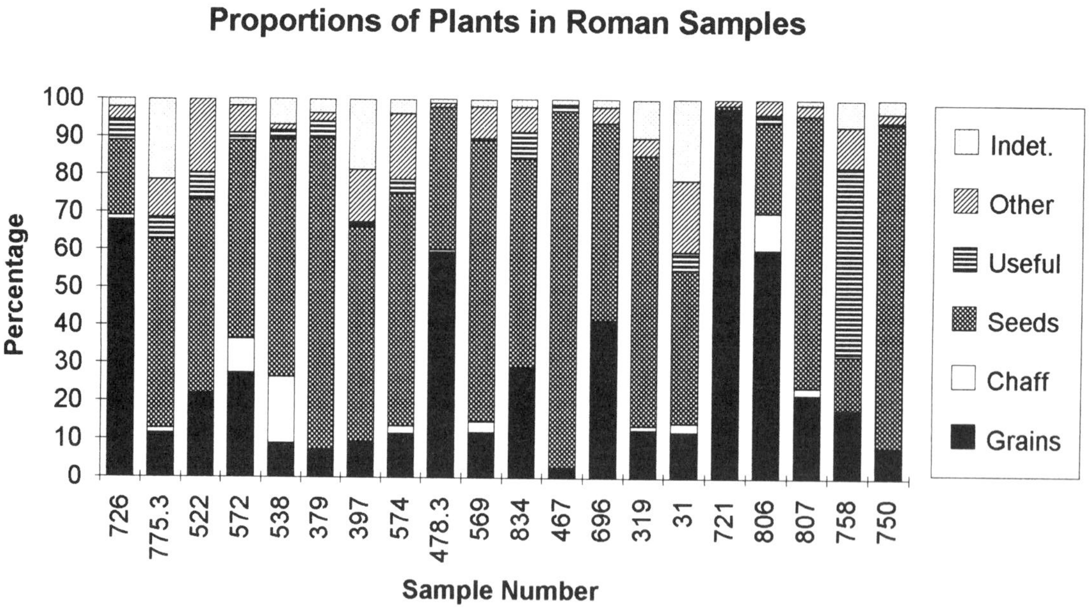

Proportions of Plants in Roman Samples

Legend: Indet., Other, Useful, Seeds, Chaff, Grains

Y-axis: Percentage (0–100)

X-axis: Sample Number — 726, 775.3, 522, 572, 538, 379, 397, 574, 478.3, 569, 834, 467, 696, 319, 31, 721, 806, 807, 758, 750

Fig. 182: *Percentages of types of plant remains in Roman samples*

cuculi) were found. An unusual find was of a group of white bryony seeds suggesting perhaps a hedgerow. This is one of the plants suggested as being part of the urban flora (Hall 1988), as are fat-hen, knotgrass, docks, chickweed and henbane which all occur here, however these and the other weeds could have been brought to the site mixed with plant material for another purpose such as with cereals, fodder or animal bedding. These remains may represent a mixture of redeposited domestic rubbish from food plants, possible fodder or disposal of weeds growing on the site. An additional arable weed found from a scanned sample from F343 141/4 phase 3B was wild radish. Sample 569 F412 186/4 phase 3C was similar in cereal composition and in the most common weed species. Sample 834 from 187/1 phase 3D was less productive and less diverse although similar in cereals it has coriander present. F230 G155 phase 3B, a well with evidence of a timber lining, was re-used as a cesspit confirmed by the insect evidence. There is little evidence of this from the plant remains as only a mineralised seed of opium poppy was found in one of the samples with weed seeds, of which grasses and small leguminous seeds are most numerous.

Sample 478 from a burnt area 154/1 phase 3B on surface 4 differed in having cereal grains as the most numerous items present with barley as the most numerous grain, it had the grassland species in small numbers with small leguminous seeds, sedges and grasses. This sample compares with the hearth derived deposit from phase 2A, sample 726 134/1, both being dominated by cereal grains with weed seeds present, possibly representing domestic waste from cereal consumption.

Later Roman

Phase 4A. 200 – 250 AD.

Area 1: Sample 467 from rubbish pit F255 174/2 was the most productive sample by far. While containing some cereal and food plant remains it was dominated by wild plant seeds (94%), the majority being very small seeded types (*c.* 1mm) notably a large number of small grasses and small leguminous seeds.

The sample included a range of species which are characteristic of tall grassland including yellow rattle (*Rhinanthus* sp), knapweed (*Centaurea nigra*), crested dog's-tail (*Cynosurus cristatus*), fairy flax (*Linum catharticum*), possible cowslip (*Primula cf veris*), ribwort plantain and ox-eye daisy (*Leucanthemum vulgare*), which were found together with a large number of small grass seeds, some of which could be identified as timothy (*Phleum* sp). Many charred grass stem fragments which were too small to be from cereals were also found. In addition eye-bright or bartsia (*Euphrasia/Odontites*), self-heal (*Prunella vulgaris*) and heath grass (*Danthonia decumbens*) also belong to this grassland group (Greig 1988) giving a total of 11 grassland taxa. A pod of bird's-foot (*Ornithopus perpusillus*) identified by James Greig, was found which is a grassland plant of bare, sandy, gravelly ground (Stace 1991) and such conditions are found in and near the town. Some of the small leguminous seeds which cannot be identified further from charred seeds at present, are possibly *Lotus*, *Trifolium* and *Medicago* species, many of which are plants of grassland. This is also true of a number of *Potentilla* species and the seeds here were of *P. erecta* type, common tormentil. The presence of the taller plants such as yellow rattle and ox-eye daisy suggests an origin from hay meadow rather than short grassland (Greig 1988). The group of plants found is similar to those of a traditional grazed hay meadow although the species present may be under represented, possibly because of loss during charring. Hay meadow is a type of grassland maintained by mowing and limited grazing which returns nutrients to the soil as dung (Greig 1991). The hay remains were burnt, possibly during clearing stables or animal housing or possibly as reuse of old fodder as fuel or kindling, or burnt accidentally.

Considering the composition of the sample the grassland plants form 46% of the sample if the *Lotus/Trifolium*, which form 26% of the total, and *Danthonia decumbens* are included with the grassland species (table 84) The seeds of unclassified small grasses form a further 20% of the seeds in the sample. Unclassified plants which may also be from grassland include *Medicago/Trifolium* and Buttercups (*Ranunculus acris/ repens/bulbosus*) and sedges (*Carex* sp) which form a further

Table 84: *Plant remains in Roman phases 1-6 and post-Roman phase 7*

Taxon	Common																							
Area		1	1	2	2	2	1	1	1	1	1	1	1	1	1	1	3	3	3	3	3	3	3
Phase		2A	2E	2K	2K	2K	3B	3B	3B	3B	3C	3D	4A	5A	5B	5C	5G	5G	5G	6A	6A	6A	7.31
Group		134/1	147/1	201/1	201/2	201/2	141/4	154/1	155/1	155/1	186/4	187/1	174/2	158/3	167/1	168/1	333/1	334/2	337/2	338/3	338/3	367/1	305/1
Feature		1005	405			686	343	-	230	230	412	334	255	477	307	221	781	757	765	763	763	766	705
Sample		726	775	522	572	538	379	478	397	574	569	834	467	696	319	31	721	806	807	797	758	750	597
CEREAL GRAINS																							
Triticum dicoccum/spelta	Emmer/Spelt												3						5				
Triticum cf aestivum	Bread Wheat type		1										3										
Triticum free-threshing	Free-threshing Wheat	2											6						4				
Triticum sp(p)	Wheat	13		2	2	1	2	6	2		3	1	23	5	1	2	33	3	21		1	1	11
Triticum sp tail grain	Wheat tail-grain												1										
Triticum (germd)	Wheat germinated												1										
cf Triticum sp (m)	Wheat	1	1																				
cf Secale cereale L.	cf Rye	1																					1
Hordeum vulgare L.	Barley	3		3	4		7	9	3		3	3	15	53			57	2	31		8		18
Hordeum vulgare L. (germd)	Barley												1										
Hordeum vulgare L. (hu)	Barley	1		1	4	2	4	10			1		19	21			9	4	12			6	5
Hordeum vulgare L. (tw)	Barley	1				1								2					3				1
Hordeum vulgare L. (hu.tw)	Barley																		1				
Avena sp	Oat	15										3											
Avena/Poaceae	Oat/Grass																11						
Cereal indet	Cereal	77	4	5	17	11	17	76	3	6	19	6	63	99	6	3	176	21	73		4	5	86
Cereal indet (germd)	Cereal germinated	3	1																1				1
Cereal indet (m)	Cereal		1																				
CEREAL CHAFF																							
Triticum dicoccum Schubl. (gl)	Emmer										1												
Triticum spelta L. (gl)	Spelt				4	7	1				2		3		1	1		2	3				
Triticum spelta L. (sf)	Spelt					1				1													
Triticum spelta L. (ra)	Spelt												2										
Triticum cf spelta L. (gl)	cf Spelt												3										
Triticum dicoccum/spelta (gl)	Emmer/Spelt	1	1	5	27						5		13					3	1				
Triticum dicoccum/spelta (sf)	Emmer/Spelt	1				1																	
Triticum spelta/aestivum (ra)	Spelt/Bread Wheat												4										
Triticum free-threshing (ra)	Wheat												1										
Triticum cf free-threshing (gl)	cf Free-threshing Wheat												2										
Triticum cf free-threshing (sf)	cf Free-threshing Wheat																						
Triticum sp (ra)	Wheat												1						1				
Hordeum vulgare L. (ra)	Barley													1				1					
cf Hordeum vulgare L. (ra)	cf Barley	1																					
Rachis fragment	Rachis fragment						1	1		1													
Culm node large	Cereal stem	2			4						6			9		1							
Cereal culm base	Cereal culm base						1			1													
Cereal sprout	Cereal sprout						1																
LEGUMES																							
Vicia faba L.	Bean	2																1					
Pisum sativum L.	Pea	1																			1		
Lens culinaris Medikus	Lentil	1											1										
Vicia/Pisum	Bean/Pea	1				3																	
Vicia/Lathyrus/Pisum	Bean/Peas	1									2									5	8		
CULTIVATED																							
Papaver somniferum L. (m)	Opium poppy									1													
Ficus carica L. (m)	Fig		1																				

Table 84: Plant remains in Roman phases 1-6 and post-Roman phase 7 continued

Area	1	1	2	2	2	1	1	1	1	1	1	1	1	1	1	1	3	3	3	3	3	3	3	
Phase	2A	2E	2K	2K	2K	3B	3B	3B	3B	3B	3C	3D	4A	5A	5B	5C	5G	5G	5G	6A	6A	6A	7.31	
Group	134/1	147/1	201/1	201/2	201/2	141/4	155/1	154/1	155/1	155/1	186/4	187/1	174/2	158/3	167/1	168/1	333/1	334/2	337/2	338/3	338/3	367/1	305/1	
Aquilegia vulgaris L.	-	-	-	-	-	-	-	-	-	-	-	-	1	-	-	-	-	-	-	-	-	-	-	Columbine
Beta vulgaris L.	-	-	-	-	-	-	-	-	-	-	-	-	-	-	-	-	-	-	-	-	-	+	-	Beet
Linum usitatissimum L.	-	-	-	-	-	12	-	-	-	-	-	-	85	-	-	-	-	-	-	-	-	-	-	Flax
Linum usitatissimum L.(m)	-	-	-	-	-	-	-	-	-	-	-	-	-	-	-	-	-	-	1	-	-	-	-	Flax
Linum usitatissimum capsule	-	-	-	-	-	-	-	-	-	-	-	-	1	-	-	-	-	-	-	-	-	-	-	Flax
Coriandrum sativum L.	-	-	1	-	-	3	-	-	-	-	-	2	2	-	-	-	-	-	-	-	-	-	-	Coriander
COLLECTED / CULTIVATED																								
Corylus avellana L.	4	-	2	2	2	1	-	-	1	-	-	1	3	-	-	-	-	-	-	-	-	1	-	Hazel nutshell
Prunus spinosa L. (m)	-	-	-	-	-	-	-	-	-	-	-	-	-	-	-	2	-	-	-	-	-	-	-	Blackthorn, Sloe
Prunus domestica L. bullace	-	-	-	-	-	-	-	-	-	-	-	-	1	-	-	-	-	-	-	-	-	-	-	Bullace
Prunus sp sloe/cherry(m)	-	1	-	-	-	-	-	-	-	-	-	-	-	-	-	-	-	-	-	-	-	-	-	Sloe/Cherry
Malus/Pyrus (m)	1	2	-	-	-	-	-	-	-	-	-	-	-	-	-	-	-	-	-	-	-	-	-	Apple/Pear
ARABLE OR DISTURBED																								
Urtica urens L.	2	-	-	-	-	8	-	-	-	-	-	-	3	-	-	-	-	-	2	-	-	1	-	Small Nettle
Chenopodium sp	2	-	-	-	5	36	1	-	2	-	-	-	42	3	1	-	-	-	24	-	-	-	-	Goosefoots
Chenopodium sp (m)	-	-	-	-	-	2	-	-	-	-	-	-	-	-	-	-	-	-	-	-	-	-	-	Goosefoots
C. bonus-henricus L.	-	-	-	-	-	-	-	-	-	-	-	-	4	-	-	-	-	-	-	-	-	-	-	Good-King-Henry
Chenopodium murale L.	-	-	-	-	1	9	-	1	-	-	-	-	6	-	-	-	-	-	3	-	-	-	-	Nettle-leaved Goosefoot
Chenopodium album type	8	-	1	-	6	14	-	1	-	-	-	-	61	3	2	-	-	-	9	-	-	-	-	Fat-hen
Stellaria media type	-	-	-	-	-	-	-	-	-	-	-	-	122	-	3	-	-	-	-	-	-	-	-	Chickweed
Persicaria maculosa/lapathifolia	-	-	-	2	5	6	-	-	2	-	-	-	18	-	-	-	-	-	5	-	-	-	-	Redshank/Pale Persicaria
Polygonum aviculare L.	-	-	-	-	1	-	-	-	1	-	-	-	20	-	-	-	-	-	-	-	-	-	1	Knotgrass
Fallopia convolvulus (L)	-	-	-	1	-	-	-	-	2	-	-	-	1	-	-	-	-	-	-	-	-	-	-	Black-bindweed
Rumex sp	2	-	-	-	-	5	1	-	-	-	7	2	19	15	-	1	2	-	20	-	-	2	-	Docks
Rumex acetosella L.	-	-	-	-	-	2	-	-	-	-	1	-	10	-	-	1	-	-	-	-	-	-	-	Sheep's Sorrel
Malva sylvestris L.	-	-	-	-	-	2	-	-	-	-	-	-	11	-	-	-	-	-	-	-	-	-	-	Common Mallow
Thlaspi arvense L.	-	-	-	-	-	-	-	-	-	-	-	-	3	-	-	-	-	-	-	-	-	-	-	Field Penny-cress
Brassica/Sinapis	-	-	-	-	3	3	-	2	-	-	-	-	2	-	-	-	-	-	-	-	-	-	-	Cabbages/Mustards
Brassica rapa/nigra	-	-	-	-	-	-	-	-	-	-	-	-	-	-	-	1	-	-	-	-	-	-	-	Wild Turnip/Black Mustard
Vicia tetrasperma/sativa	-	-	-	-	5	-	-	-	-	-	-	-	2	-	-	-	-	-	-	-	-	-	-	Smooth Tare/ Vetch
Hyoscyamus niger L.	-	-	-	-	-	5	-	-	-	-	-	-	-	-	-	-	-	-	-	-	-	-	-	Henbane
Lithospermum arvense L.	-	1	-	-	-	-	-	-	1	-	-	-	-	-	-	-	-	-	-	-	-	-	-	Field Gromwell
Plantago major L.	-	-	-	-	-	-	-	-	-	-	-	-	1	1	-	-	-	-	-	-	-	-	-	Greater Plantain
Veronica polita/agrestis	-	-	-	-	-	-	-	-	-	-	-	-	2	-	-	-	-	-	-	-	-	-	-	Field-speedwell
Galium aparine L.	-	6	-	-	-	-	1	-	-	-	-	-	10	-	2	-	-	-	-	-	-	-	-	Cleavers
Anthemis cotula L.	-	-	-	-	-	1	-	-	-	-	-	-	9	-	-	-	-	-	1	1	-	-	-	Stinking Mayweed
Poa annua L.	-	-	-	-	-	-	-	-	-	-	-	-	1	-	-	-	-	-	1	-	-	-	-	Annual Meadow-grass
Bromus hordeaceus/secalinus	3	-	3	12	11	1	4	-	2	-	3	4	68	5	7	-	-	-	20	-	-	-	-	Lop-grass/Rye-brome
GRASSLAND																								
Primula cf veris	-	-	-	-	-	-	-	-	-	-	-	-	1	-	-	-	-	-	-	-	-	-	-	Cowslip
Potentilla sp	-	4	-	-	-	1	-	-	-	-	-	-	85	1	-	-	-	-	-	-	-	5	-	Cinquefoil
Potentilla sp (m)	-	-	-	-	-	-	-	-	3	-	-	-	-	-	-	-	-	-	-	-	-	-	-	Cinquefoil
Lotus/Trifolium	5	-	3	4	3	95	-	9	10	-	33	5	1484	42	2	-	-	6	143	2	-	35	-	Bird's-foot-trefoil/Clover
Lotus/Trifolium (germd)	-	-	-	-	-	-	-	-	-	-	-	-	-	1	-	-	-	-	-	-	-	-	-	Bird's-foot-trefoil/Clover
Lotus sp pod	-	-	-	-	-	-	-	-	-	-	-	-	1	-	-	-	-	-	-	-	-	-	-	Bird's-foot-trefoil type
Lotus/Trifolium (m)	-	1	-	-	-	-	-	-	-	-	-	-	-	-	-	-	-	-	-	-	-	-	-	Bird's-foot-trefoil/Clover
Trifolium small. germinated.	-	1	-	-	-	-	-	-	-	-	-	-	1	-	-	-	-	-	-	-	-	-	-	Clover
Ornithopus perpusillus L. pod	-	-	-	-	-	-	-	-	-	-	-	-	1	-	-	-	-	-	-	-	-	-	-	Bird's-foot
Linum catharticum L.	-	-	-	-	-	-	-	-	-	-	-	-	1	-	-	-	-	-	1	-	-	1	-	Fairy Flax

Table 84: Plant remains in Roman phases 1-6 and post-Roman phase 7 continued

Taxon	Common name	Area																					
	Phase	2A	2E	2K	2K	2K	3B	3B	3B	3B	3C	3D	4A	5A	5B	5C	5G	5G	5G	6A	6A	6A	7.31
	Group	134/1	147/1	201/1	201/2	201/2	141/4	154/1	155/1	155/1	186/4	187/1	174/2	158/3	167/1	168/1	333/1	334/2	337/2	338/3	338/3	367/1	305/1
Plantago lanceolata L.	Ribwort Plantain	-	-	3	-	-	7	2	1	1	11	2	105	-	-	2	-	-	18	-	-	5	-
Rhinanthus cf minor L.	Yellow Rattle	-	-	-	-	-	-	-	-	-	-	-	4	-	-	-	-	-	-	-	-	-	-
Rhinanthus sp	Yellow Rattle	1	-	-	-	-	1	-	-	-	-	-	130	1	-	-	-	-	-	-	-	8	-
Euphrasia sp	Eyebright	-	-	-	-	-	-	-	-	-	-	-	1	-	-	-	-	-	1	-	-	-	-
Euphrasia/Odontites	Eyebright/Bartsia	-	-	1	-	1	6	-	2	-	5	-	191	3	-	-	-	-	12	-	-	7	-
Centaurea nigra L.	Common Knapweed	-	1	-	-	-	-	-	-	-	-	-	8	-	-	-	-	1	-	-	-	-	-
Leucanthemum vulgare Lam.	Ox-eye Daisy	-	1	-	-	-	1	-	-	-	-	-	8	-	-	-	-	-	1	-	-	-	-
Cynosurus cristatus L.	Crested Dog's-tail	-	1	4	4	-	13	2	2	-	25	1	193	41	-	-	-	1	34	-	-	20	-
Arrhenatherum elatius (L.) (tu)	Onion Couch Grass	-	-	-	-	-	-	-	1	-	-	-	-	-	-	-	-	-	-	-	-	-	-
Phleum type	Cat's-tails type	-	-	-	-	-	-	-	-	-	-	-	449	-	1	-	-	-	2	-	-	-	-
cf Phleum sp	cf Cat's-tails	-	-	-	-	-	-	-	-	-	-	-	66	-	-	-	-	-	-	-	-	-	-
Danthonia decumbens (L.) DC	Heath Grass	-	-	-	1	-	-	1	-	-	1	-	92	-	2	-	-	-	10	-	-	32	-
Danthonia sp flower	Heath Grass	-	-	-	-	-	-	-	1	-	-	-	-	-	-	-	-	-	-	-	-	-	-
DAMP OR WET GROUND																							
Ranunculus lingua L.	Greater Spearwort	-	-	-	-	-	-	-	-	-	-	-	1	-	-	-	-	-	-	-	-	-	-
Ranunculus flammula L.	Lesser Spearwort	-	1	-	-	-	1	-	1	-	-	-	11	-	-	-	-	-	-	-	-	-	-
Montia fontana ssp minor Hayw.	Blinks	-	1	-	-	-	-	-	-	-	-	-	-	-	-	-	-	-	-	-	-	-	-
Montia sp (m)	Blinks	-	1	-	-	-	-	-	-	-	-	-	-	-	-	-	-	-	-	-	-	-	-
Stellaria palustris Retz.	Marsh Stitchwort	-	-	-	2	-	3	-	1	-	1	-	48	3	-	-	-	-	1	-	-	-	-
Lychnis flos-cuculi L.	Ragged-Robin	-	-	-	-	-	1	-	-	-	-	-	5	-	-	-	-	-	-	-	-	-	-
Berula erecta (Hudson) Cov.	Lesser Water-parsnip	-	-	-	1	-	-	-	-	-	-	-	-	-	-	-	-	-	-	-	-	-	-
Galium palustre L.	Common Marsh-bedstraw	-	-	-	-	-	-	-	1	-	1	-	6	-	-	-	-	-	-	-	-	-	-
Juncus sp capsule	Rush	-	-	-	-	-	-	-	-	-	-	-	1	-	-	-	-	-	-	-	-	-	-
cf Juncus sp capsule	cf Rush	-	-	-	-	-	-	-	1	-	-	-	-	-	-	-	-	-	-	-	-	-	-
Luzula sp	Wood-rush	-	-	-	-	-	-	-	-	-	-	1	6	-	-	-	-	-	-	-	-	1	-
Eleocharis palustris/uniglumis	Spike-rush	-	1	1	5	-	6	-	1	-	6	1	24	3	2	-	-	-	5	-	-	-	-
Eleocharis sp (m)	Spike-rush	-	1	-	7	-	-	-	-	-	-	-	-	-	-	-	-	-	-	-	-	-	-
cf Schenoplectus	Club-rushes	-	-	-	-	-	-	-	2	-	1	-	1	-	-	-	-	-	-	-	-	-	-
HEDGE OR WOODLAND																							
Bryonia dioica Jacq.	White Bryony	-	-	-	-	-	11	-	-	-	-	-	-	-	-	-	-	-	-	-	-	-	-
Sorbus cf aria	Common Whitebeam	-	-	-	-	-	-	-	-	-	-	-	1	-	-	-	-	-	-	-	-	-	-
Sambucus nigra L.	Elder	-	1	1	-	-	-	-	-	-	-	-	7	-	-	-	-	1	5	-	-	1	-
Sambucus nigra L. (u)	Elder	-	-	-	-	-	-	-	-	-	-	-	7	-	-	-	-	-	-	-	-	1	-
UNCLASSIFIED																							
Ranunculus sp	Buttercup	-	-	-	-	-	-	-	-	-	1	-	1	-	-	-	-	-	-	-	-	-	-
R. acris/repens/bulbosus	Buttercup	-	-	-	2	-	12	-	2	-	7	-	279	-	-	-	-	-	7	-	-	11	-
Atriplex sp	Oraches	-	-	1	1	-	1	-	-	-	-	-	-	-	-	-	-	-	2	-	-	-	-
Atriplex sp (m)	Oraches	-	1	-	4	-	-	-	-	-	-	-	-	-	-	-	-	-	-	-	-	-	-
Caryophyllaceae	Pink family	-	-	-	-	-	-	-	-	-	-	-	177	-	-	-	-	-	-	-	-	-	-
Cerastium/Stellaria	Mouse-ear/Stitchwort	-	-	-	1	-	-	-	1	-	-	-	29	-	-	-	-	-	4	-	-	-	-
Polygonum sp	Knotweed	1	-	-	1	-	-	-	2	-	-	-	-	-	-	-	-	1	11	-	-	5	-
Malva sp	Mallow	-	-	-	-	-	-	-	-	-	-	-	-	-	-	-	-	1	-	-	-	-	-
Cruciferae small	Cabbage family	1	-	1	1	-	4	-	1	-	-	-	2	2	-	-	-	-	-	-	-	3	-
Calluna vulgaris L. flower	Heather flower	-	-	-	-	-	-	-	1	-	-	-	-	-	1	-	-	-	-	-	-	-	-
Vicia cf hirsuta	cf Hairy Tare	-	-	-	1	-	-	-	-	-	-	-	-	-	-	-	-	-	-	-	-	-	-
Vicia hirsuta/tetrasperma	Hairy Tare/Smooth Tare	-	-	-	1	-	1	-	-	-	-	-	-	-	1	-	-	-	-	-	-	-	-
Vicia/Lathyrus	Tare/Vetch/Vetchling	4	-	7	7	-	10	-	7	-	5	-	137	8	4	-	-	-	12	-	-	5	1
Medicago/Melilotus/Trifolium	Medick/Melilot/Clover	-	-	-	-	-	11	-	-	-	10	-	33	-	-	-	-	-	-	-	-	-	-
cf Medicago sp	cf Medick	-	-	-	-	-	-	-	-	-	-	-	-	-	-	-	-	-	-	-	-	-	-

Table 84: *Plant Remains in Roman Phases 1-6 and Post Roman Phase 7 continued*

Taxon	1 2A 134/1	1 2E 147/1	2 2K 201/1	2 2K 201/2	2 2K 201/2	1 3B 141/4	1 3B 154/1	1 3B 155/1	1 3B 155/1	1 3C 186/4	1 3D 187/1	1 4A 174/2	1 5A 158/3	1 5B 167/1	1 5C 168/1	3 5G 333/1	3 5G 334/2	3 5G 337/2	3 6A 338/1	3 6A 338/3	3 6A 367/1	3 7.31 305/1	Common name
Medicago cf lupulina	-	-	-	-	-	-	-	-	-	-	-	-	-	-	-	-	-	1	-	-	-	-	cf Black Medick
Apiaceae fruit (m)	-	1	-	-	-	-	-	-	-	-	-	-	-	-	-	-	-	-	-	-	-	-	Carrot family
Apiaceae	-	-	-	-	-	-	-	-	-	-	-	1	-	-	-	-	-	-	-	-	-	-	Carrot family
Galeopsis sp	-	-	-	-	1	-	-	-	-	-	-	-	-	-	-	-	-	-	-	-	-	-	Hemp-nettle
Prunella vulgaris L.	-	1	-	-	-	-	-	2	-	-	-	1	-	-	-	-	-	11	-	-	11	-	Self-heal
Plantago sp capsule	-	-	-	-	-	-	-	-	-	-	-	-	-	-	-	-	-	-	-	-	-	-	Plantain
Plantago sp.	1	-	-	-	-	-	-	-	-	8	1	2	-	-	-	-	-	-	-	-	-	-	cf Plantain
Galium sp	-	-	-	-	-	-	-	-	-	-	-	-	-	-	-	-	-	-	-	-	-	-	Bedstraws
Valerianella sp	-	-	-	1	-	-	-	-	-	-	-	-	-	-	-	-	-	-	-	-	-	-	Cornsalad
Asteraceae	-	-	-	-	-	21	4	-	-	-	-	3	-	-	-	-	-	4	-	-	-	-	Daisy family
Asteraceae capsule	-	-	-	-	-	-	-	-	-	-	-	7	3	-	-	-	-	-	-	-	-	-	Daisy family capsule
Asteraceae (m)	-	1	-	-	-	-	-	-	-	-	-	2	-	-	-	-	-	-	-	-	-	-	Daisy family
Carduus/Cirsium	1	1	2	-	-	1	1	-	-	-	-	18	1	-	-	-	-	2	-	-	2	-	Thistles
Centaurea sp	-	-	-	-	-	-	-	-	-	1	-	-	-	-	-	-	-	-	-	-	-	-	Knapweeds
Leontodon sp	-	-	-	-	-	-	-	-	-	-	-	-	-	-	-	-	-	1	-	-	-	-	Hawkbits
Carex spp (2-sided)	-	-	1	1	20	12	3	1	-	21	-	224	11	4	1	-	-	9	-	-	7	-	Sedges
Carex spp (3-sided)	-	1	2	2	18	3	4	3	-	31	-	164	5	2	1	-	1	1	-	-	3	-	Sedges
Carex sp (m)	-	1	-	-	-	-	-	-	-	-	-	-	-	-	-	-	-	-	-	-	-	-	Sedges
Poaceae (small)	1	-	4	3	11	26	7	9	6	12	7	1266	60	11	4	-	-	36	-	1	15	-	Grasses
Poaceae (small) germinated	-	-	-	-	-	-	-	-	-	-	-	-	-	-	-	-	-	-	-	-	-	-	Grasses
Poaceae (small) flower	-	-	-	-	-	-	-	-	-	-	-	-	-	-	-	1	-	-	-	-	-	-	Grasses
Poaceae (medium)	-	3	-	-	-	3	4	5	-	8	-	3	9	1	2	-	-	26	-	-	15	-	Grasses medium
Poaceae (medium) (u)	-	-	-	-	-	-	-	-	-	-	-	72	-	2	-	-	-	-	-	-	-	-	Grasses medium
Poaceae (large)	4	-	-	9	8	9	5	-	-	9	-	55	15	5	1	-	-	37	-	-	11	-	Grasses large
Poaceae embryo	-	-	-	-	-	-	-	-	-	-	-	1	-	-	-	-	-	-	-	-	-	-	Grass embryo
Indeterminate seeds	4	5	2	-	14	16	2	16	2	6	1	90	10	6	8	-	2	11	-	2	9	-	Indeterminate seeds
Indeterminate seeds (u)	-	10	-	-	-	-	-	-	-	-	-	-	-	3	1	-	-	-	-	-	-	-	Indeterminate seeds
Pod fragment	-	-	-	-	-	1	-	-	-	-	-	1	-	-	-	-	-	-	-	-	-	-	Pod fragment
Culm node small	-	-	-	-	-	-	-	-	-	9	-	5	1	-	-	-	-	13	-	-	-	-	Grass stem
Culm fragment (small)	-	-	-	-	-	1	-	3	1	3	-	3	3	-	-	-	-	2	-	-	1	-	Grass stem fragments
Other fragments	3	6	2	2	2	67	2	10	9	6	3	14	6	3	6	5	2	4	2	1	5	2	Other fragments
Totals	171	70	41	99	204	431	170	87	53	288	45	6202	457	88	42	294	50	674	9	19	245	125	Total
Vol Sieved (L)	30	28	31	7.5	9	26.5	17.5	30	24	26	17	21	6	24	41	10	8	8	10	12.5	16	10	Volume sample, litres
Items/litre	5.7	2.5	1.3	13.2	22.7	16.3	9.7	2.9	2.2	11.1	2.6	295.1	76	3.7	1.01	29.4	6.3	84	0.9	1.6	15.3	12.5	items per litre
Flot vol (mls)	240	34	31	95	140	22	15	28	28	95	100	44	20	54	50	190	50	200	205	75	110	12	Flot volume (mls)

Key: (gl) = glume base, (sf) = spikelet fork, (hu) = hulled, (tw) = twisted, (tu) = tuber, (m) = mineralised, (u) = uncharred, + = present in subgroup. Remains are seeds in the broad sense unless stated.

12% of the sample although some of these may be from damp areas of cultivated fields (Monckton 1996). This sample may therefore consist mainly of fodder remains possibly mixed with domestic and other rubbish.

The flax may be an element of domestic rubbish showing the use of this crop in the town while the presence of a columbine seed suggests that garden waste may also be an element of this sample. The cereal remains probably originated as domestic waste and included grains, chaff and arable weed seeds; it is possible that the heath grass was an arable weed brought in with the cereals rather than a grassland plant, as it has been suggested that it is associated with ard cultivation (Hillman 1982). Other food plant remains include lentil and coriander as possible imports, and hazel nut shell and a bullace or small plum stone as remains of collected or cultivated foods.

Phase 5. 250 -300 AD.

Area 1: Material from phases 5A and 5B may derive from phase 3 although re-deposited in phase 5; these are respectively sample 696 from a gully F477 158/3 in make-up layer for surface 5 and sample 319 of backfills of F307 167/1. These samples from Area 1 were all weed dominated and had low amounts of chaff although sample 696 had a number of cereal grains with barley being in the majority. The weeds were docks (*Rumex* sp), a few damp ground species including sedges and grassland plants including small leguminous seeds, crested dog's-tail and small grasses. This was similar to the phase 3B sample 379 of Area 1 but also to the phase 5G sample 807 337/2 of Area 3. Area 1 sample 319 167/1 phase 5B and sample 31 168/1 phase 5C were similar to each other and less productive with few cereal grains, spelt glumes and a higher percentage of weeds.

Area 3: Phase 5G sample 721 F781 333/1 and sample 806 F757 334/2 also of phase 5G were dominated by cereal grains, the former from a fire pit which compares with other hearth type deposits being dominated by cereals, a further sample 807 F765 337/2 is dominated by weeds. Spelt was present in samples 806 and 807 although barley was the most numerous grain. Sample 807 was the most productive with goosefoot, docks and brome grass the most numerous weeds; also found were the grassland plants ribwort plantain, crested dog's-tail and fairy flax with small leguminous seeds and grasses and some damp ground species.

Phase 6A. Post 300 AD.

Area 3: Two samples from F763 338/2 make-up and floor levels over an earlier quarry, samples 797 and 758, have very few items so were considered together as they were selected for the presence of legumes of Roman date, pea *(Pisum sativum)* was identified. Other remains were few although abundant charcoal was in the samples. This material may be redeposited from earlier Roman phases.

Sample 750 from F766 367/1, rubbish fills of a quarry, was more productive and dominated by weeds although wheat and barley were present. Grassland species were found with crested dog's-tail and heath grass numerous, fairy flax and yellow rattle present, suggesting hay rather than short grassland. A scanned sample from this feature of the same sub-group sample 708 produced the additional find of a seed of beet (*Beta vulgaris*) recorded as present on table 84.

Discussion

Most of the 393 Roman contexts sampled (6406 litres) produced a few charred cereal grains which were present in 73% of the total although only 7% of the samples had over 20 cereal grains and only 16% contained chaff (mainly glumes). Very few additional species were found during scanning all the samples. The analysed samples were generally dominated either by grains or weed seeds with the exception of samples from F763 338/2 phase 6A which were selected for the presence of legumes in a small number of items.

The sample with the most chaff is from F686 202/1 phase 2K Area 2 and the cereal remains in this sample may represent the final preparation of the glume wheat for use. The glume wheats (spelt and emmer) require two main stages of processing, an initial stage of threshing to break the ears into spikelets where the grain is held tightly in the glumes, followed by winnowing and coarse sieving to remove the larger contaminants. The spikelets can then be stored or transported and processed in small quantities as required. The final stage of preparation involves parching and pounding to free the grains from the chaff and then fine sieving to remove the chaff and weed seeds (Hillman 1981). It may be waste from fine sieving which is found here because the glumes outnumber the wheat grains in sample 538, in contrast to the wheat ear where there is one glume to each grain. In the second sample from this subgroup the numbers were about equal and this type of waste could originate from accidental burning of wheat stored as spikelets, however this small amount is likely to be from domestic activity and cereal consumption in both cases. Other samples contained cereal grains, a little chaff and weed seeds which probably represent final cleaning of the cereals for consumption as even after dehusking and fine sieving some contaminants remain to be removed by hand during food preparation, then were probably disposed of by burning as domestic rubbish. The consistent presence of glumes even in low numbers shows the consumption of glume wheat, mainly spelt, throughout the Roman phases, glumes are present in phases 1 to 5 although less evidence for cereals was found in phase 6, but this is inconclusive as less samples were taken from this area.

There is no evidence to suggest threshing of grain produced nearby, but this evidence is rare even on rural sites as the straw is a useful comodity and would have been used rather than burnt. On an urban site, however, it is likely that grain would have been brought to the town after threshing elsewhere to reduce the bulk for transport, even if the landowners lived in the town. There is too little chaff to suggest that this waste was being used as fuel as found at some sites such as Tiddington (Moffett 1986) and Norfolk St. villa, Leicester (Jones 1982). Little chaff was found here so it is likely that even if wheat was supplied to the town as spikelets it was dehusked elsewhere, perhaps on the outskirts of the town, although this may have been carried out near the sites where the grain was grown. Large amounts of chaff are more often found on rural settlements although there is little evidence for this in Leicestershire at present. The evidence from both the Shires (Moffett 1993) and this site indicates only the consumption of cereals in the town.

Legumes used for food are thought to be under represented in charred material as their preparation does not involve exposure to fire. Peas and beans were found; they may have been garden crops or foodstuff brought into the town. Cultivation of other vegetables was suggested by the find of a beet seed as has been found on a few other Roman sites such as at Alcester (Moffett 1988) and probably of the type grown as a leaf rather than a root vegetable.

Lentil was also represented which is cultivated in the Mediterranean region and may therefore represent an import. Cultivation in Britain is not impossible although it is only known to have been grown as a fodder crop in the post medieval period. Similarly fig is a Mediterranean plant although it will produce seed in this country in good conditions so may be either an import or garden plant. These plants may represent foodstuff imported into the town.

The flax seeds may represent a crop grown for oil or for fibre and a large group of seeds was found in 174/2 phase 4A, the seeds are also edible so may represent food remains. Phases 3 and 4 both have flax present. Coriander is recorded as being used in Roman recipes (Edwards 1984) and was found in phases 2, 3 and 4, it is now naturalised in this country so this may represent a garden crop. Opium poppy was found mineralised as was the fig, they were not thought to be intrusive from medieval levels. They may be garden plants and opium poppy has been found charred in a garden context at Fishbourne palace (Carruthers 1991). The charred columbine seed from 174/2 phase 4A may also represent a garden plant adding to evidence from other Roman sites (Moffett 1988). Apple or pear and bullace may represent garden fruit trees or wild gathering. Other gathered foods may be sloe and hazelnut and possibly elder.

The sample from phase 4A 174/2 contained a large number of seeds of grasses and seeds of at least 11 grassland taxa including plants typical of hay meadow such as yellow rattle, fairy flax and crested dog's-taii. There is some overlap between the plants found on wet grassland, meadows and pastures but the plants present here suggest a hay meadow (Greig 1988). This sample contains material which is similar to that found in a first-second century well at Tiddington (Greig 1988c) where 18 grassland taxa including the above species were found in a waterlogged deposit interpreted as including hay or dung. The sample here although less diverse, perhaps because of the lack of waterlogged remains and being charred, was interpreted as containing burnt hay. Both deposits also contained domestic rubbish and other material with which the remains of the hay was mixed. This suggests the presence of hay meadows nearby to supply fodder for animals kept in the town.

Conclusions

The samples from Area 2 202/1 of phase 2 appear to consist of a small amount of charred cereal cleaning waste including glumes and arable weeds as evidence of the preparation of glume wheat, mainly spelt, for consumption. The waste included weeds of heavy soils which suggests that the cereals may have been grown on the clay land in the area although such soils are common in the region. Samples representing waste from food preparation attested to the domestic activity and consumption of glume wheat throughout phases 1 to 5 although little evidence was recovered from phase 6 Area 3.

A sample interpreted as including hay was found on Area 1 174/2 phase 4A suggesting the presence of hay meadows used to supply fodder for animals kept in the town. Hay may also be present in phase 3B ditch G141 Area 1 and phase 6A quarry G367 Area 3 amongst other rubbish. Seeds of flax were found in phases 3 and 4 showing the cultivation of this crop although there was no evidence of whether this was for oil or fibre.

The main cereals in use were spelt and barley, probably 6 row hulled barley. Peas and beans were part of the diet with lentil and fig possibly imported. Opium poppy and coriander may have been cultivated in gardens for food flavourings with perhaps fruit trees represented by apple or pear and bullace or plum, ornamental plants are suggested by the presence of columbine and vegetables by beet. Gathered foodstuffs and possible hedgerows are suggested by the hazel nut shell, sloe and elder.

Medieval Plant Remains

Introduction

Charred plant remains were found together with more mineralised remains than from the Roman samples. Mineralisation occurs in such conditions as those which occur in cesspits where organic material is replaced by calcium phosphates and carbonates from the high concentrations of these minerals which occur in sewage and latrine waste. They often take the form of casts of the internal parts of the seed coat, impressions of the outside of the seed on other material or seeds of normal appearance which are petrified. A further type of preservation found here, as at the Shires (Moffett 1993), is described as uncharred where the seeds are not mineralised as above although the seed coat survives. Some of those from the Shires have been shown to be archaeological by accelerator dating (Moffett 1993), and are considered so here where they occur in well-sealed deposits.

The plant remains were listed by area and period (table 85).

Results, the plants and contexts sampled

Cereals

Charred grains of wheat and barley with smaller quantities of oats and rye were found, chaff which is more diagnostic for identification was also present in small quantities. The wheat included bread wheat (*Triticum aestivum* sl) and rivet or macaroni wheat (*Triticum turgidum/durum*). This is most probably rivet wheat (*T. turgidum*) which has been found in recent years on an increasing number of medieval sites in England (Moffett 1991). It is known from descriptions in post medieval documents such as Fitzherbert's Book of Husbandry of 1534 (Skeat 1882) and will be referred to as rivet wheat here, although it cannot be distinguished from macaroni wheat from the rachis (chaff) fragments found. Bread wheat and rivet wheat are both free-threshing and have similar grains but can be distinguished from each other by their rachis fragments. Wheat was the most numerous cereal present. No glumes were found in the samples analysed so unlike in the Roman period, there was no evidence for the use of the glume wheats (spelt and emmer). Oats were identified from the grains only and were probably cultivated oat as the grains were large, rye was identified from grains and rachis fragments but was present only in small amounts.

Cultivated or collected plants

Legumes included beans (*Vicia faba*), of a small type known as celtic bean, and peas (*Pisum sativum*) from all three areas. Opium poppy (*Papaver somniferum*) was present in highest numbers on Plot D Area 1 and also found on Area 2 in mineralised condition as was fig (*Ficus carica*) found in small numbers in Area 2 phases 8 and 9. The only evidence for vegetable crops was a leek seed (*Allium porrum*) from Plot C Area 1 adding to the evidence for this crop found from the Shires earlier medieval phase (Moffett 1993). The leaves of edible plants such as cornsalad (*Valerianella dentata*) may have been consumed and some of the Brassicaceae, cabbage family, may have been gathered for food or may represent cultivated plants, although this could not be confirmed from the seeds found.

More mineralised material was found from this site than at the Shires and fruit stones included sloe, damson and primitive plums as the most numerous, stones of which are much smaller than those of the sweet plums known today. A grape pip (*Vitis vinifera*) was found in phase 9, Area 2 which may have been cultivated locally or imported. Possible cultivated fruits included apple and pear with blackberry (*Rubus fruticosus*) and elder (*Sambucus nigra*) probably representing gathered fruits. Nuts represented by charred hazelnut shell were present in many of the samples.

Arable weeds.

Corn cockle (*Agrostemma githago*) and cornflower (*Centaurea cyanus*) were found and these weeds are often found associated with free-threshing cereals (Jones 1988). Stinking mayweed (*Anthemis cotula*) was also present, as in the Roman period possibly indicating the cultivation of heavy, damp land. Field gromwell (*Lithospermum arvense*) was more common and cleavers *(Galium aparine)* less common than in the Roman phases.

Early post-Roman
Phase 7

Little evidence was found from this phase on the site and only one sample from Area 3 had sufficient remains to analyse. Sample 597 from F705, a shallow pit, was dominated by cereal grains. Wheat which could not be identified further was found with barley, probably 6-row hulled barley, more numerous than the wheat. A possible rye grain was present and a single seed of knotweed (*Polygonum aviculare*). The remains were in an abraded condition and similar to the Roman material and were therefore thought to be possibly redeposited from Roman contexts (table 84).

Earlier medieval 11th to mid 13th century

Phases 8, 9 and 10: Most of the plant remains were found from pits of these phases. The remains are considered by area in line with the other medieval evidence from the site. On archaeological evidence Area 1 was divided into plots, possibly representing property boundaries. The plots B-F all date from the earlier medieval period of the site and are discussed in phase and plot order below (table 85).

AREA 1
Phase 8

Plot F samples from F482 a deep square pit include sample 586 from 120/4, a well-sealed fill, which was reasonably productive but had few cereals, however, rivet and bread wheat rachis fragments were found with a few free-threshing wheat grains, oat was the only other cereal. Arable weeds included goosefoots as most numerous with stinking mayweed and tares (*Vicia hirsuta* and *V. tetrasperma*). Other weeds included vetches or vetchling (*Vicia/Lathyrus*), sedges and small grasses most numerous with cornsalad present. Also in this sample was a large charred flower receptacle of a member of the daisy family (Asteraceae) which was similar to an ox-eye daisy (*Leucanthemum* sp) and large enough to be a cultivated form. It is known from documentary records that medieval gardeners selected flowers for size (Mabey 1987) and ox-eye daisy is known from descriptions and early plant lists such as Westminster Abbey in the 14th century (Harvey 1992). This could, therefore, be the remains of a garden flower, however there is too little evidence to conclude that this was from a garden on the site. A second sample 588 from F482 127/3 represented disuse of the feature and was less productive (28 items from a 24 litre sample) so was not tabulated. It contained a few cereal grains including free-threshing wheat and barley and a few seeds including uncharred greater celandine (*Chelidonium majus*). On archaeological evidence this sample may represent material from the garden soil and probably includes reworked pit fills.

Phase 9

Plot B remains were from two samples from two square pits. F235 116/1, a shallow square rubbish pit with evidence of parasite ova, had additional evidence of latrine waste from mineralised sloe stones. Seeds included henbane, a few charred wheat grains and hazelnut shell. F238 120/1, a deep square well re-used as a rubbish pit, had few mineralised remains but

more charred cereal grains and weed seeds particularly grasses and sedges. Both pits had wheat, including free-threshing wheat, as the only identified cereal, and both included mineralised seeds of field gromwell and elder with the charred seeds of docks (*Rumex* sp), grasses and sedges.

Plot C remains came from 120/7 F207, a deep square pit with parasite ova throughout and with fly puparia in 120/7. The mineralised plant remains consisted of a large group of fruit stones including sloe and primitive plums of different types ranging from bullace to damson and small plum adding to the evidence that this was a cesspit. Other fruit included pear and possibly apple. A few mineralised weed seeds were found which may represent plants growing nearby or originate from rubbish deposited in the pit. Charred remains included a seed of leek suggesting the use of this vegetable. Other charred remains include cereal grains of wheat mainly free-threshing wheat, and a little barley ith possibly rye and oat in small quantities. Charred arable weed seeds include cornflower, stinking mayweed and cleavers and a few grassland and damp ground plants with undiagnostic weeds such as grasses and sedges most numerous. Cornsalad, sometimes considered as edible, and field gromwell were found. This cesspit also contains domestic rubbish, and seeds of grass and sedges may represent the remains of fodder, thatch or bedding material rather than weeds of the cereals.

Phase 10

Plot D remains consist of those from samples from F206 a deep circular well with evidence of re-use as a cesspit. Evidence from a primary context sample 747 113/2 showed faecal contamination, as fly puparia of putrid deposits were found together with mineralised remains. This suggested seepage from layers above unless the feature was used as a cesspit originally. Plant remains include mineralised apple pips, a few mineralised seeds, charred cereal grains and nutshell in small quantities. Two further samples from this feature from 119/2 samples 761 and 766, also from putrid contexts, were richer in mineralised remains particularly the latter which had apple pips with opium poppy and blackberry in larger numbers. There was a range of mineralised seeds including goosefoots, knotgrass, henbane and elder which may have been growing near the pit. A few charred cereal grains and evidence of legumes suggests other domestic rubbish. The remaining sample from this feature sample 740 119/3 had more cereal grains present including wheat, possible rye and oat with mainly charred weed seeds and a few mineralised seeds including hemlock and duckweed (*Lemna* sp). Duckweed only sets seed in standing water and so may have been brought to the site with water or material from wet areas as suggested at the Shires (Moffett 1993), too few seeds were found to suggest that it grew in this pit.

Plot E had evidence from two samples from 119/4 F218 which from the backfill of a deep circular pit interpreted as the secondary use of a well. This did not have evidence from parasites or insects of putrid deposits. Cereal evidence was not abundant but included rachis fragments of both rivet and bread wheat. Rye, barley and oat grains and rachis were found. Arable weeds included cleavers, cornflower and stinking mayweed, other seeds included cornsalad and uncharred hemlock (*Conium maculatum*); grasses and sedges were not numerous. The food plants broad bean and pea were found together with hazelnut fragments. This appears to represent domestic rubbish.

AREA 2
Phase 8

This phase is represented by five samples including two from F540 247/1 samples 98 and 100 which are from a circular well with secondary use as a cesspit confirmed by parasite ova and insects of putrid deposits. Sample 98 is one of the most productive medieval samples but has little mineralised material. Uncharred elder seeds, which are probably archaeological although not mineralised, were found. Cereal grains include free-threshing wheat and a little barley. The arable weeds include cleavers and stinking mayweed with goosefoots and chickweed (*Stellaria media*). A few grassland or wetland plants were found and the most numerous seeds were grasses. Sample 100 was less productive but similar and contained black nightshade (*Solanum nigrum*) which is also a weed of arable or disturbed ground.

F568 also a well with secondary use as a cesspit contained parasite eggs in sample 361 247/2 and the plant remains include mineralised opium poppy and fig with mineralised weed seeds and casts or impressions of seeds in organic material. A few charred cereal grains occured and mineralised straw, small grass stem fragments and concretions of cereal chaff, probably from coprolites, were found. Mineralised seeds include the distinctive impressions of corn cockle and henbane together with seeds of the latter. The range of mineralised seeds present is similar to those found charred in other samples suggesting disposal of similar rubbish in a cesspit rather than by burning. This probably represents seeds of arable weeds and cereals together with the weeds growing nearby and mixed with latrine waste in the cesspit.

The sample 118 was from 249/3 F521, a rectangular pit with evidence of latrine waste from parasites and insects. The plant remains were mainly mineralised and included fruit stones of sloe or cherry and bullace. Mineralised seeds were also found together with concretions of cereal chaff. Scanned samples from this feature produced groups of mineralised fruit stones from three other contexts in 249/3 showing that this feature was rich in material from latrine waste. A scanned sample from F579 249/2 also had a group of fruit stones showing that this pit also contained latrine waste.

Sample 388 was from 253/4, the floors and make-up layers with burnt areas in a timber building, this was reasonably productive with more charred cereal remains including free-threshing wheat, probable rye with rather small grains, and a little barley. Beans were present and the arable weeds included stinking mayweed as the most numerous weed with few other seeds present except grasses. This appears to follow the pattern of hearth deposits seen in the Roman phases where the assemblage is also much less diverse and dominated by cereal grains. The association of stinking mayweed with the cereal is particularly marked in this sample.

Phase 9

Two samples from 256/1 F570, samples 248 and 280, are from a deposit of lime and wood ash in a pit. They are similar having charred cereals present including free-threshing wheat with a few arable weeds including spreading hedge-parsley (*Torilis arvensis*) in the former, a plant which is rare today. Legume fragments were also present. A holly seed (*Ilex aquifolium*) was found in sample 280 and groups of seeds of dwarf elder (*Sambucus ebulus*) in both samples. The latter only occur in this context group which suggests that the plant remains were from a different source from the rest of the material on the site and were possibly brought mixed with the lime.

Samples from pit F537 which contained lime and general rubbish were analysed, samples 129, 130 and 207 from 257/3, the general rubbish fill. Sample 129 had a few cereal grains present mainly free-threshing wheat with disturbed ground plants including sheep's sorrel (*Rumex acetosella*) and black nightshade. Food plants included bean, hazelnut, apple or crab apple and a charred grape pip. Grape pips may originate from garden plants or imported raisins which were brought in in large quantities at this time (Dyer 1989). The most numerous weeds from this sample are vetches (*Vicia* sp) and common vetch (*Vicia sativa* ssp *nigra*) was identified among these seeds. Sample 130 had more mineralised material and concretions with chaff in them as found in the samples from F521 and F568 phase 8 Area 2. The remains here appeared to be more intensely mineralised than those found on Area 1. Sample 130 also had mineralised sloe, bullace or damson and a number of apple pips which can only be identified as crab or garden apple as the seeds are not distinctive.

A further sample 207 also from F537 257/3 had more cereal evidence including rachis segments of bread wheat and free-threshing grains. Rye and oat grains were found and barley chaff with a number of nodes from cereal straw and grass stems. The arable weeds, cornflower and stinking mayweed, a few damp ground species and possible ground-elder or pignut (*Aegopodium/Conopodium*) were found with grasses most numerous. The sample may represent waste straw being burnt and suggests the association of the free-threshing cereals with cornflower and stinking mayweed.

The remaining two samples from Phase 9 are from G260 possible cesspit fills in several pits. F587 sample 261 had insect remains of putrid deposits but this was not reflected in the plant remains which were mainly charred. Free-threshing wheat was present in small numbers and stinking mayweed was the most numerous weed seed followed by large grasses. Legumes were present and peas (*Pisum sativum*) identified. Vetches were most numerous amongst the few weeds. F513 sample 93 also of this group was less productive but has free-threshing wheat and cornflower and few weeds. Elder was most numerous and vetches present. Food plants in mineralised condition are only represented by one or two apple pips. These features seem to represent mixed rubbish pits with some layers containing latrine waste.

AREA 3

Phase 9

Two samples were analysed, sample 612 from F704 314/1 and sample 632 F719 315/2. F704 is a moderately deep square pit and the sample was dominated by cereal grains including free-threshing wheat and barley with large grasses as the most numerous weeds. F719 315/2 represents the slumping fills of a deep square pit in disuse, sample 632 was dominated by cereal grains including free-threshing wheat, barley and oat. This sample also had legume fragments and nutshell and a range of arable or disturbed ground weeds including small nettle (*Urtica urens*), goosefoots, docks and brome grass. A larger range of weeds was present than in sample 612 and this may represent redeposited materials from the garden soil layer as may sample 588 F482 Area 1 Phase 8.

Late medieval and post medieval

Late medieval. Phase 11. c.1500-1700 AD

This period was represented by only two samples from Area 3 samples 619 and 822 both from 307/1 F703 (plot H), a deep circular pit with insect evidence of putrid conditions and parasite eggs found in other contexts of the feature. The plant remains are mainly charred and are dominated by cereals including free-threshing wheat with hulled barley in smaller quantities with bean and legume fragments. A seed of possibly cultivated vetch (*Vicia sativa* cf ssp *sativa*) was found, suggested by the large size of the seed, but this could not be confirmed from a single find. Hazelnut shell was also present as an element of this probably domestic rubbish. The most numerous weed seeds were large grasses which with cornflower and stinking mayweed probably brought in with the cereals as arable weeds. Uncharred elder seeds were numerous and as these were present in many samples they probably represent plants growing on the site.

Post medieval. Phase 12 c.1600-1900 AD

The most productive sample of this period, sample 61 F226 101/1, was found to be re-deposited material in a Victorian foundation trench so was not analysed although it contained a number of charred cherry stones. The following samples were the most productive of the phase. Sample 190 from 291/2 F563, a shallow pit had a few cereal grains including free-threshing wheat and oat with goosefoots and a few weed seeds. Sample 607 from 294/3 F581, a pit with clay pipe kiln waste (see Higgins and Peacey above) was unusual as it had no cereals present. The weeds goosefoots, knotweed, black bind-weed (*Fallopia convolvulus*) and sun spurge (*Euphorbia helioscopia*) with abundant elder were found. These with a few uncharred or mineralised seeds of blackberry, dead-nettles (*Lamium* sp) and cinquefoil (*Potentilla* sp), possibly remains of the more robust seeds, these may represent plants growing on the site. These are all plants of disturbed or waste ground and a number of them are suggested as plants of the urban flora (Hall 1988).

Discussion

Of the 286 medieval contexts sampled (5778 litres) 86% had cereal grains present with only 12% having over 20 cereal grains, and only 4% with chaff, mainly rachis, present. This compares with the Roman samples except that chaff is much less common from the free threshing cereals in the medieval period, only two medieval contexts had glumes present which were probably residual. Scanning all the samples produced very few additional plants.

Bread wheat and rivet wheat were found, both are free-threshing wheats and show a change from the Roman period when mainly glume wheat was grown. Rivet wheat was identified from phases 8 and 10 of 11th to mid 13th century date, it was also found from earlier medieval phases at the Shires (Moffett 1993) where unlike here it was also found in late medieval phases. This may be explained by there being less domestic activity on this site in the later medieval phases than on the Shires sites. Very little wheat rachis was found here probably because the free-threshing wheats are supplied as threshed grain which is largely free from chaff, unlike the glume wheats of the Roman period. However if whole grains are used for some purposes, as must be the case here rather than as milled flour alone, sorting the grain for weed seeds and impurities is necessary before using the grain in the medieval staple food of pottage. Rivet wheat is a productive wheat but not favoured for bread making so possibly used more in pottages. Cereals were often used and even grown in mixtures (Greig 1988b) and the barley, oats and rye found here show that these cereals were in use but the small quantities found make further conclusions difficult. The consistent small numbers of grains found in the samples may reflect the way cereals were supplied to the town. Bread was usually purchased from bakers (Dyer 1989) and if whole grain was purchased ready threshed for other uses there should be little waste unless it was burnt accidentally or because it was spoiled.

Rivet wheat has now been identified from a number of medieval sites south of a curve from Chester, through Stafford and West Cotton (Northamptonshire) to Ipswich (Moffett 1991). The finds of rivet wheat from this site and the Shires extend the distribution of finds of this cereal to the north-east of the present area. The finds from Leicester are of the 11th century which is the earliest date that finds elsewhere have been made, such as Ipswich (11th century) and Stafford (12th century) (Moffett 1991). This shows that this cereal was in use in Leicester soon after it appeared in this country according to the present knowledge of this crop. Further work, however, may add to the distribution and date range of cultivation of this cereal. Rivet wheat is a productive, tall cereal, resistant to disease and bird attack (Moffett 1991), the long straw being used as bedding or roofing material.

The consistent presence of stinking mayweed with the cereals suggests that they were grown on heavy soils, possibly on clay soils locally although such soils exist throughout the region. Cornflower is also present as a weed of the free-threshing cereals. Although seeds of cleavers are less common in the medieval samples both types of free-threshing wheat are known from documentary evidence to have been sown in the autumn.

The late medieval period has some domestic evidence and has the addition of possibly cultivated vetch which was a crop mainly grown for animal fodder and as an element in crop rotation, but this cannot be confirmed here as the identification is insecure. The post medieval samples may have evidence of plants of waste ground growing on the site from a feature with trade waste rather than domestic rubbish.

Considering the areas of the site the earlier medieval material includes mineralised remains from cesspits and charred plant remains from rubbish pits often a mixture of the two. Area 1 cesspit F207 preserves the greater amount of fruit remains while Area 2 cesspits had most fruit stones from F521 and a larger range of smaller mineralised seeds and remains. The only wheat identified is free-threshing wheat both rivet wheat and and bread wheat being found on Area 1 and bread wheat alone identified on Area 2 although this is inconclusive as only a small amount of rachis material was found. The cereals occur many times with stinking mayweed and cornflower also the brome grasses, lop-grass or rye-brome. The lime filled pit F570 differs from other material and seems to contain plant remains from elsewhere probably brought with the lime. From the evidence of the plant remains the pits sampled on Area 3 appear to be rubbish pits rather than cesspits but the presence of parasite ova in F703 plot H in phase 11 suggest the presence of latrine waste as well as domestic rubbish.

A comparison of the plots shows Plot C F207 phase 9 was most productive having the largest group of fruit stones preserved by mineralisation. A leek seed gave evidence for the use of vegetables, and cereals were not numerous but free threshing wheat was much more abundant than barley. Plot D was next most productive represented by F206 phase 10, less fruit stones were found but more mineralised seeds perhaps representing the use of opium poppy as a garden plant or medicine. Plots B, E and F were less productive although the most chaff was found on Plots E and F showing the free threshing wheats bread and rivet wheats in use in phases 8 and 10. Rye was found on Plot E phase 10 in small numbers and was possibly present on Plots C and D. Wheat is the most numerous cereal throughout and only free-threshing wheats were found.

Conclusions

There was little evidence for the early post Roman period, the sample examined from F705 probably containing redeposited Roman material. The bulk of the evidence found was from the earlier medieval period 11th to mid 13th century reflecting the peak of pit digging and back yard activity on the site. This material seems mainly domestic in nature consisting of food and other plant material from cesspits and rubbish pits, the latrine waste and rubbish often mixed. It is difficult to tell if differences are real or caused by the chance of preservation in

Table 85: *Plant remains in medieval and post-medieval phases (8-12)*

Taxon	F482	F235	F238	F207	F207	F206	F206	F206	F218	F540	F568	F521	—	F570	F537	F537	F587	F513	F704	F719	F703	F563	F581	Common
Area Plot	1F	1B	1B	1C	1C	1D	1D	1D	1E	2	2	2	2	2	2	2	2	2	3	3	3	2	2	
Phase	8	9	9	9	10	10	10	10	10	8	8	8	8	9	9	9	9	9	9	9	11	12	12	
Group	120/4	116/1	120/1	120/7	120/7	113/2	119/2	119/3	119/4	247/1	247/2	249/3	253/4	256/1	257/3	257/3	260/3	260/4	314/1	315/2	307/1	291/2	294/3	
Samples	586	850	94	32	53	747	761/766	740	68	98/100	361	118	388	248/280	129/130	207	261	93	612	632	619/822	190	607	
CEREAL GRAINS																								
Triticum free-threshing	2	2	8	4	10	-	-	3	6	6/-	2	5	12	17/3	5/1	2	14	9	2	2	6/2	2	-	Free-threshing Wheat
Triticum sp(p)	4	2	35	4	17	1	2/1	4	9	12/2	-	-	6	12/4	2	2	9	-	7	18	15/3	3	-	Wheat
Triticum sp tail grain	-	-	1	-	-	-	-	-	-	-	-	-	-	-	-	-	-	-	-	-	-	-	-	Wheat tail-grain
Triticum sp (m)	-	-	-	-	-	-	1/-	-	-	-	-	-	-	-	-	-	-	-	-	-	-	-	-	Wheat
Secale cereale L.	-	-	-	-	-	-	-	-	4	-	2	-	-	-	1	-	-	2	-	-	-	-	-	Rye
cf Secale cereale L.	-	-	-	1	-	2	-	2	1	-	-	-	-	-	-	1	-	-	-	-	1/-	-	-	cf Rye
Hordeum vulgare L.	-	-	-	-	5	-	-	-	-	-	-	-	-	-	-	-	-	-	5	-	-	-	-	Barley
Hordeum vulgare L. (hu)	-	-	-	1	5	-	-	1	1	2/1	-	-	2	-	-	-	-	-	2	6	3/-	-	-	Barley
Hordeum vulgare L. (hu,tw)	-	-	-	-	-	-	-	-	-	3/2	-	-	-	-	-	-	-	-	1	-	4/6	-	-	Barley
cf Hordeum vulgare (m)	-	-	-	-	1	1	-	-	1	1/-	-	-	-	-	-	-	-	-	-	-	-	-	-	Barley
Avena sp	-	-	-	-	-	-	-	-	4	-	-	-	-	-	-	2	-	-	-	5	-	1	-	Oat
Avena sp (m)	1	-	-	-	-	-	-	-	-	-	-	-	-	1/-	-	-	-	-	-	-	-	-	-	Oat
Avena/Poaceae	-	-	-	5	-	-	-	2	-	-	-	-	-	-	-	-	-	2	-	-	-	-	-	Oat/Grass
Avena/Poaceae (m)	-	-	18	19	-	10	7/-	-	10	-	6	6	-	-	-	3	3	-	-	-	-	3	-	Oat/Grass
Cereal indet	4	4	-	4	59	2	2/-	22	39	49/19	4	2	51	-	5/-	8	55	14	50	66	44/40	5	-	Cereal
Cereal indet (m)	-	-	-	-	4	-	-	-	-	-	-	12	-	-/3	-	-	-	-	-	-	-	-	-	Cereal
CEREAL CHAFF																								
Triticum turgidum/durum (ra)	1	-	-	-	-	-	-	-	1	-	-	-	-	-	-	-	-	-	-	-	-	-	-	Rivet wheat
T. cf turgidum/durum (ra)	1	-	-	-	-	-	-	-	-	-	-	-	-	-	-	-	-	-	-	-	-	-	-	cf Rivet wheat
Triticum spelta/aestivum (ra)	-	-	-	-	-	-	-	-	1	-	-	-	-	-	-	6	-	-	-	-	-	-	-	Spelt/Bread Wheat
Triticum aestivum s l (ra)	2	-	-	-	-	-	-	-	1	-	-	-	-	-	-	-	-	-	-	-	-	-	-	Bread wheat
Triticum cf aestivum (ra)	-	-	-	-	-	-	-	-	1	-	-	-	-	-	-	-	-	-	-	-	-	-	-	Bread wheat type
Triticum free-threshing (ra)	3	-	-	-	-	-	-/1	-	-	-	-	-	-	-/1	-	-	-	-	-	-	-	-	-	Wheat
Triticum sp (ra)	-	-	1	-	1	1	-	-	2	-	-	-	-	1/-	-	-	-	-	-	-	-	-	-	Wheat
Secale cereale L. (ra)	-	-	-	-	1	-	-	2	6	-	-	-	-	-	-	-	-	-	-	-	-	-	-	Rye
cf Secale cereale L. (ra)	-	-	-	-	-	-	-	-	1	-	-	-	-	-	-	-	-	-	-	-	-	-	-	cf Rye
Hordeum vulgare L. (ra)	-	-	-	-	-	-	-	-	1	-	-	-	-	-	-	-	-	-	-	-	-	-	-	Barley
Hordeum vulgare L. awn	-	-	-	-	-	-	-	-	-	-	-	-	-	-	-	1	-	-	-	-	-	-	-	Barley awn
Rachis fragment	-	-	-	1	1	-	-	-	-	1/-	-	-	-	1/1	-	-	-	-	-	-	-	-	-	Rachis fragment
Culm node large	-	-	-	-	-	-	-	-	-	-	-	-	-	-	-	11	-	-	-	-	-	-	-	Cereal stem
Cereal sprout	1	-	-	1	1	-	-	-	-	-	-	-	-	-	-	-	1	-	-	-	-	-	-	Cereal sprout
LEGUMES																								
Vicia sativa cf ssp sativa	-	-	-	-	-	-	-	-	-	-	-	-	-	-	-	-	-	-	-	-	1/-	-	-	Vetch cf cultivated
Vicia faba L.	-	-	-	-	-	-	-	-	1	-	2	1	-	1/-	1/-	-	-	-	-	-	-/2	-	-	Bean
Vicia faba L. hilum	-	-	-	-	-	-	1/-	-	-	-	-	-	-	-	-	-	-	-	-	-	-	-	-	Bean
Vicia/Lathyrus/Pisum	-	-	-	-	-	-	-	-	-	-	-	-	-	-	-	-	-	-	-	2	-	-	2	Bean/Peas
Vicia/Pisum	2	-	-	-	-	2	-	2	-	2/-	-	-	-	-	3/1	-	-	-	-	-	1/-	-	-/2	Bean/Pea
Vicia/Pisum (m)	-	-	-	-	-	-	-	-	3	-/2	-	-	3	-/2	-	-	-	-	-	-	-/2	-	-	Bean/Pea
Pisum sativum L.	-	-	-	-	-	-	-	-	1	-	-	-	-	-	-	-	1	-	-	-	-	-	-	Pea
CULTIVATED																								
Papaver somniferum L. (m)	-	-	-	-	-	-	-/45	-	-	-	10	-	-	-	-	-	-	-	-	-	-	-	-	Opium poppy
Ficus carica L. (m)	-	-	-	-	-	-	-	-	-	-	1	-	-	1/1	-	-	-	-	-	-	-	-	-	Fig
Vitis vinifera L.	-	-	-	-	-	-	-	-	-	-	-	-	-	1/-	-	-	-	-	-	-	-	-	-	Grape-vine
Linum usitatissimum L.	-	-	-	1	-	-	-	-	-	-	-	-	-	-	-	-	-	-	-	-	-	-	-	Flax
Allium porrum L.	-	-	-	-	1	-	-	-	-	-	-	-	-	-	-	-	-	-	-	-	-	-	-	Leek

Table 85: Plant remains in medieval and post-medieval phases (8–12) continued

Area Plot	1F	1B	1B	1C	1C	1D	1D	1D	1E	2	2	2	2	2	2	2	2	2	3	3	3	2	2	Area
Phase	8	9	9	9	9	10	10	10	10	8	8	8	8	9	9	9	9	9	9	9	11	12	12	Phase
Group	120/4	116/1	120/1	120/7	120/7	113/2	119/2	119/3	119/4	247/1	247/2	249/3	253/4	256/1	257/3	257/3	260/3	260/4	314/1	315/2	307/1	291/2	294/3	Group
FRUIT AND NUTS																								
Corylus avellana L.	-	1	-	7	2	1	-	6	10	1/-	-	-	-	1/-	1/1	-	-	-	-	5	2/3	-	-	Hazel nutshell
Rubus fruticosus L. agg (m)	-	-	-	-	-	-	1/50	-	-	-	-	-	-	1/-	-/1	-/1	-	-	-	-	-	-	4	Brambles
Prunus spinosa L. (m)	-	3	-	2	8	-	-	-	-	-	-	-	-	-	-/1	-	-	-	-	-	-	-	-	Blackthorn, Sloe
P. domestica L. bullace (m)	-	-	-	23	29	-	-/9	-	-	-	-	-	-	-	-/1	-	-	-	-	-	-	-	-	Bullace
P. domestica L. damson (m)	-	-	-	9	16	-	-	-	-	-	-	1	-	-	-	-	-	-	-	-	-	-	-	Damson
Prunus sp sloe/cherry (m)	-	-	-	16	19	-	5/-	-	-	-	-	1	-	-	1/5	-	-	-	-	-	-	-	-	Sloe/Cherry
Prunus sp fragments (m)	-	-	-	18	19	-	-	-	-	-	-	2	-	-	-	-	-	-	-	-	-	-	-	Bullace/Damson
Pyrus sp (m)	-	-	-	-	1	-	-	-	-	-	-	-	-	-	-	-	-	-	-	-	-	-	-	Pear
Malus sylvestris s.l. (m)	-	-	-	-	-	3	2/2	-	-	-	-	-	-	-	2/4	-	-	1	-	-	-	-	-	Crab Apple/Apple
Malus/Pyrus (m)	-	-	-	-	-	5	3/1	-	-	-	-	-	-	-	1/3	-	-	1	-	-	-	-	-	Apple/Pear
ARABLE / DISTURBED																								
Papaver rhoeas/dubium (m)	-	-	-	-	-	-	1/1	-	-	-	-	-	-	-	-	-	-	-	-	-	-	-	-	Poppy
Urtica urens L.	-	-	-	1	-	-	-	-	-	1/-	-	-	-	-	-	-	-	-	-	5	-	-	-	Small Nettle
Urtica urens L. (m)	-	-	-	-	-	-	-	1	4	4/-	-	-	-	-	-	-	-	-	-	-	-	-	-	Small Nettle
Chenopodium sp (m)	5	-	-	-	-	-	-/12	-	4	-	1	-	-	-	-	-	-	-	-	1	-	2	4	Goosefoots
Chenopodium sp	-	-	-	1	1	-	-	-	-	-	1	1	-	-	-	-	-	-	-	1	-	-	3	Goosefoots
C. bonus-henricus L.	3	-	-	-	-	-	-	-	-	-	-	-	-	-	-	-	-	-	-	1	-	-	-	Good-King-Henry
C. bonus-henricus L. (m)	-	-	-	-	-	-	-/5	-	-	-	1	-	-	-	-	-	-	-	-	1	-	-	-	Good-King-Henry
Chenopodium album type	9	-	-	1	-	-	-/6	-	-	1/-	-	-	-	-	2/-	-	-	-	-	2	-/1	2	6	Fat-hen
C. album type (m)	1	-	-	-	-	-	-/1	-	-	-	-	-	-	-	-	-	-	-	-	-	-	-	-	Fat-hen
Chenopodiaceae (m)	1	-	-	1	1	-	-	-	-	-	-	-	-	-	-	-	-	1	-	-	-	-	-	Goosefoot family
Chenopodiaceae	1	-	1	1	1	-	-/1	-	-	7/-	-	-	-	-	1/-	-	-	-	-	-	1/-	1/-	-	Goosefoot family
Stellaria media type	1	-	-	1	1	-	-	-	-	-	-	-	-	-	-	-	-	-	-	-	-	-	-	Chickweed
Agrostemma githago L.	1	-	-	1	1	-	-	-	-	-	-	-	-	-	-	-	-	-	-	-	-	-	-	Corn Cockle
Agrostemma githago L. (m)	-	1	-	-	-	-	-	-	-	1/-	-	1	1	-	-	-	-	-	-	-	-	-	-	Corn Cockle
Persicaria maculosa type	-	-	-	-	-	-	-	-	1	-	-	1	-	-	1/-	-	-	-	-	-	-	-	-	Redshank/Persicaria
Polygonum aviculare L.	2	1	-	1	-	-	-	-	1	-	-	-	-	-	-	-	-	-	-	-	-	-	1	Knotgrass
Polygonum aviculare L. (m)	-	-	1	1	-	-	-/4	-	-	-	-	-	-	1/-	-	-	-	-	-	-	-	-	-	Knotgrass
Fallopia convolvulus (L)	-	1	-	1	-	-	-	-	-	-	-	-	-	-	-	-	-	1	-	1	-	-	6	Black-bindweed
Rumex sp	2	1	2	7	5	1	-	3	2	3/-	-	-	-	2/-	3/1	-	2	-	-	3	-/2	-	-	Docks
Rumex sp capsule (m)	-	-	-	-	-	-	-	-	-	-	1	-	-	-	1/-	-	2	-	-	-	-/2	-/2	-	Docks
Rumex acetosella L.	-	-	-	-	-	-	-	-	-	-	-	1	-	1/-	-	-	-	-	-	-	-/2	-	-	Sheep's Sorrel
Thlaspi arvense L. (m)	-	-	-	-	-	-	-/4	-	-	-	-	-	-	-	-	-	-	-	-	-	-	-	-	Field Penny-cress
Brassica/Sinapis	-	1	1	1	-	-	-	-	-	-	1	-	-	1/-	-	-	-	-	-	-	-	-	-	Cabbages/Mustards
Brassica rapa/nigra	-	-	-	3	3	-	-	-	1	-	-	-	-	-	-	-	-	-	-	-	-	-	1	Wild Turnip/Mustard
Brassica nigra	1	-	-	-	-	-	-	-	-	-	-	-	-	-	-	-	-	-	-	-	-	-	-	Black Mustard
Vicia tetrasperma (L.)	1	-	-	-	-	-	-	-	-	-	-	-	-	-	-	-	-	-	-	-	-	-	-	Smooth Tare
Vicia sativa ssp nigra (L) Ehrh	-	-	1	-	-	-	-	-	-	-	-	-	-	1/1	1/1	-	-	1	-	-	-	-	1	Common Vetch
Euphorbia helioscopia L.	-	1	-	-	-	-	-	-	-	-	-	-	-	-	-	-	-	-	-	-	-	-	-	Sun Spurge
Aethusa cynapium L.	-	-	-	-	-	-	-	-	-	-	-	1	-	1/-	-	-	-	-	-	-	-	-	-	Fool's Parsley
Torilis arvensis (Hudson) Link	-	-	-	-	-	-	-	-	-	-	-	1	-	-	-	-	-	-	-	-	-	-	-	Spreading Hedge-parsley
Hyoscyamus niger L. (m)	-	3	-	-	-	-	-/3	-	-	-	7	-	-	-	1/-	-	-	-	-	-	1/-	1/-	-	Henbane
Solanum nigrum L.	-	-	-	-	-	-	-	7	3	-/1	-	-	-	-/1	-	-	-	-	-	-	-	-	-	Black nightshade
Lithospermum arvense L.	-	2	-	1	-	-	-	-	-	-	-	-	-	-	-	-	-	-	-	-	1/-	-	-	Field Gromwell
Lithospermum arvense L. (m)	-	3	-	-	-	-	-	-	-	-	-	-	-	-	1/-	-	-	-	-	-	-	1/-	-	Field Gromwell
Galium aparine L.	-	-	-	1	-	-	-	-	3	1/1	-	-	-	-	-	-	-	-	-	-	-/1	-	-	Cleavers

Table 85: Plant remains in medieval and post-medieval phases (8–12) continued

Area Plot	1F	1B	1B	1C	1C	1C	1D	1D	1D	1E	2	2	2	2	2	2	2	2	2	3	3	3	2	2	
Phase	8	9	9	9	9	9	10	10	10	10	8	8	8	8	9	9	9	9	9	9	9	11	12	12	
Group	120/4	116/1	120/1	120/7	120/7	120/7	113/2	119/2	119/3	119/4	247/1	247/2	249/3	253/4	256/1	257/3	257/3	260/3	260/4	314/1	315/2	307/1	291/2	294/3	
Centaurea cyanus L.	-	-	-	2	-	-	-	-	-	-	-	-	-	-	-	-	-	-	-	-	-	1/-	-	-	Cornflower
Centaurea cyanus L. (m)	-	-	-	-	-	-	-	-	-	-	-	-	-	-	-	-/2	-	-	1	-	-	-	-	-	Cornflower
Anthemis cotula L.	2	-	-	5	7	-	-	-	-	3	14/2	-	-	22	-	1	-	8	1	1	-	2/-	-	-	Stinking Mayweed
Chrysanthemum segetum L.	-	-	-	-	-	-	-	-	-	-	-	-	-	-	-	-	-	-	1m	-	-	-	-	-	Corn Marigold
Vicia hirsuta (L.)	1	-	-	-	-	-	-	-	-	-	-	-	-	-	-	1/-	-	-	-	-	-	-	-	-	Hairy Tare
Bromus hordeaceus/secalinus	-	-	-	4	-	-	-	-	-	-	1	-	-	1	1/-	-	4	4	4	3	3	4/3	-	-	Lop-grass/Rye-brome
GRASSLAND																									
Potentilla sp	-	-	-	1	-	-	-	-	-	-	-/2	-	-	-	-	-	-	-	-	-	-	-	-	-	Cinquefoil
Potentilla sp (m)	-	-	-	-	-	-	-	-	-	-	-	-	-	-	-	-	-	-	-	-	4	-	2	-	Cinquefoil
Lotus/Trifolium	7	7	-	2	5	-	1	-	-	2	12/2	-	-	-	-/8	-	1	1	-	-	-	4/-	-	1	Bird's-foot-trefoil/Clover
Plantago lanceolata L.	-	-	-	1	1	-	-	-	-	-	-	-	-	-	-	-	-	-	-	-	4	-/1	-	-	Ribwort Plantain
Plantago lanceolata L. (m)	-	-	-	2	-	-	-	-	-	-	-	-	-	-	-	-	-	-	-	-	-	-	-	-	Ribwort Plantain
Rhinanthus sp	-	-	-	1	-	-	-	-	-	-	-	-	-	-	-	-	-	-	-	-	-	-	-	-	Yellow Rattle
Euphrasia/Odontites	-	-	-	1	-	-	-	-	-	-	1/-	-	-	-	-	1/-	-	-	-	-	-	-	-	-	Eyebright/Bartsia
Euphrasia/Odontites (m)	1	1	-	-	-	-	-	-	-	-	-	1	-	-	-	-	-	-	-	-	-	-	-	-	Eyebright/Bartsia
Cynosurus cristatus L.	-	-	-	-	-	-	-	-	-	-	3/-	1	-	-	-	-	-	-	-	-	-	-	-	-	Crested Dog's-tail
cf Phleum (m)	-	-	-	-	-	-	-	-	-	-	-	1	-	-	-	-	-	-	-	-	-	-	-	-	cf Cat's-tails
Danthonia decumbens (L.) DC	-	-	-	1	-	-	-	-	-	-	-	-	-	-	-/1	-	-	-	-	-	-	1/-	-	-	Heath Grass
DAMP OR WET GROUND																									
Sparganium sp	-	-	-	1	-	-	-	-	-	-	-	-	-	-	-	-	-	-	-	-	-	-	-	-	Bur-reed
Ranunculus flammula L.	-	-	-	1	-	1	-	-	-	-	-	-	-	-	-	1	-	-	1	-	-	-	-	-	Lesser Spearwort
Juncus sp capsule	-	-	-	1	-	-	-	-	-	-	-	2	-	2	-	5	-	-	-	-	-	-	-	-	Rush
Juncus sp stem (m)	-	-	-	-	-	-	-	-	-	-	-	1	-	1	-	-	-	-	-	-	-	-	-	-	Rush
Juncus sp capsule (m)	-	-	-	-	-	-	-	-	-	-	-	-	-	-	-	-	-	-	-	-	-	-	-	-	Rush
Eleocharis palustris/uniglumis	2	-	1	-	3	-	-	1/-	1	1	1/-	-	-	-	-	1/-	1	1	-	-	-	1/-	-	-	Spike-rush
Lemna sp (m)	-	-	-	-	-	-	-	1/-	1	-	-	-	-	-	-	-	-	-	-	-	-	-	-	-	Duck-weed
HEDGE OR WOODLAND																									
Bryonia dioica Jacq.	-	-	-	-	-	-	-	1	-	-	-	-	-	-	-	-	-	-	-	-	-	-	-	-	White Bryony
Ilex aquifolium L.	-	-	-	-	-	-	-	-	-	-	-	-	-	1	-/1	-	-	-	-	-	-	-	-	-	Holly
Sambucus nigra L.	11	-	-	1	1	-	-	3/10	4	-	16/1	-	-	-	-	-	-	-	-	-	-	-	-	-	Elder
Sambucus nigra L. (u)	3	8	14	1	12	-	-	-	4	5	137/5	4	-	-	2/3	1	1	1	20	3	-	15/-	1	-	Elder
UNCLASSIFIED																									
Chelidonium majus L. (u)	-	-	-	-	-	-	-	-	-	4	4/-	-	-	-	-	-	-	-	-	-	-	-	-	-	Greater Celandine
Ranunculus sp	-	-	-	-	-	-	-	-	-	-	1/-	-	-	-	-	-	-	-	-	-	-	-	-	-	Buttercup
Ranunculus sp (m)	-	-	-	-	-	-	-	-	-	-	-	-	-	-	-	-	-	-	-	-	-	-	-	2	Buttercup
R. acris/repens/bulbosus	2	-	-	2	-	-	-	-/1	1	-	-	1	-	-	1/-	-	-	1	-	-	-	-	-	-	Buttercup
Fumaria sp (u)	1	-	-	-	-	-	-	-/1	1	-	1/-	-	-	-	-	-	-	-	-	-	-	-	-	-	Fumitory
Urtica dioica L.	-	1	-	-	-	-	-	-	-	-	1/-	-	1	-	-	1	-	1	-	-	-	-	-	-	Common Nettle
Urtica dioica L.(m)	1	1	-	-	-	-	-	1	-	-	-	-	-	-	-	-	-	-	-	-	-	-	-	-	Common Nettle
Atriplex sp	1	-	-	-	-	-	-	-/2	-	-	2/-	-	-	-	-	1/-	-	-	-	-	3	-	1	-	Oraches
Atriplex sp (m)	-	-	-	-	-	-	-	-/1	1	-	-	3	1	-	-	-	-	-	-	-	-	-	-	-	Oraches
Caryophyllaceae (m)	-	-	-	-	-	-	-	-	-	-	11/-	1	-	-	-	-	-	-	-	-	-	-	-	-	Pink family
Cerastium/Stellaria	-	-	-	-	1	1	-	-	-	-	-	-	-	1	-	1/-	-	-	1	1	1	-	-	-	Mouse-ear/Stitchwort
Polygonum sp	6	-	-	-	1	-	-	-/9	-	-	2/-	-	1	-	-	-	-	-	-	1	1	-	-	-	Knotweed
Polygonum sp (m)	-	-	-	-	1	-	-	-/1	-	-	-	-	-	-	-	-	-	-	-	-	-	1/-	-	-	Knotweed
Malva sp (m)	-	-	-	-	-	-	-	-	-	-	3/-	-	-	-	-	1/-	-	-	-	-	1	-	-	-	Mallow
Malva sp	-	-	-	1	-	-	-	-	-	-	-	-	-	3/-	-	1/-	-	-	-	1	-	1/-	-	-	Mallow
Brassicaceae	-	-	-	7	1	-	1	-	-	-	2/-	2	-	1	4/1	-	-	-	-	-	-	1/-	1	1	Cabbage family
Brassicaceae (m)	-	-	-	-	1	-	1	-	-	-	1	-	1	1	-	-	-	-	-	-	-	1/-	-	1	Cabbage family

Table 85: Plant remains in medieval and post-medieval phases (8-12) continued

Taxon	1F 8 120/4	1B 9 116/1	1B 9 120/1	1C 9 120/7	1C 9 120/7	1C 10 113/2	1D 10 119/2	1D 10 119/3	1E 10 119/4	2 8 247/1	2 8 247/2	2 8 249/3	2 8 253/4	2 9 256/1	2 9 257/3	2 9 257/3	2 9 260/3	2 9 260/4	3 9 314/1	3 9 315/2	3 11 307/1	2 12 291/2	2 12 294/3	Group
Vicia sp	-	-	-	-	-	-	-	-	-	3/-	-	-	-	3/-	14/-	-	5	1	-	-	1/-	-	-	Vetch
Vicia/Lathyrus	10	-	-	4	-	-	-	-	6	4/-	-	-	-	5/-	-	-	4	1	1	3	1/-	1	-	Tare/Vetch/Vetchling
Vicia/Lathyrus (m)	-	-	-	-	-	1/-	-	-	-	-	-	-	-	-	-	-	-	-	-	-	2/-	1	1	Tare/Vetch/Vetchling
Medicago/Melilotus/Trifolium	14	3	1	7	1	-	-	-	6	9/-	-	3	1	1/4	12/-	2	1	2	1	3	2/1	1	1	Medick/Melilot/Clover
Medicago type (m)	-	-	-	1	1	-	-	-	-	-	-	-	-	-	-	-	-	-	-	-	-	-	-	Medick/Melilot/Clover
Apiaceae	1	-	1	-	-	-	-	-	1	-	-	-	-	-	-	-	-	-	-	-	-	-	-	Carrot family
Apiaceae (m)	-	-	-	-	-	-	-	-	2	-	-	-	-	-	-	1	-	-	-	-	-	1	-	Carrot family
Aegopodium/Conopodium	-	-	-	1	-	-	-	-	2	-	-	-	-	-	-	1	-	-	-	-	-	-	-	Ground-elder/Pignut
Conium maculatum L. (u)	-	-	-	-	-	-	-	-	2	-	-	-	-	-	-	-	-	-	-	-	-	-	-	Hemlock
Lamiaceae (m)	-	-	-	-	-	2/-	-	-	-	2/-	1	-	-	-	-	6	-	-	-	-	-	-	-	Deadnettle family
Lamium sp (m)	-	-	-	-	-	-	-	-	-	-	-	-	-	-	-	-	-	-	-	-	-	-	8	Dead-nettles
Prunella vulgaris L.	-	1	1	-	-	-	-	-	-	3/-	-	-	-	2/1	-	2	-	-	-	-	-	-	-	Self-heal
Prunella vulgaris L. (m)	-	-	-	-	-	-/1	-	-	-	-	-	-	-	-/3	-	-	-	-	-	-	-	-	-	Self-heal
Galium sp	-	-	-	-	2	-	-	3	-	-	-	-	-	-	-	-	-	-	-	-	-	-	-	Bedstraws
Galium sp (m)	-	-	-	-	-	-	-	-	-	-	-	-	-	-	-	-	-	1	-	-	-	-	-	Bedstraws
Sambucus ebulus L. (m)	1	-	-	3	6	-	-	-	-	-	-	-	-	13/13	-	-	-	-	-	-	-	-	-	Dwarf Elder
Valerianella dentata (L.) Poll.	-	-	1	2	-	-	-	-	2	-	-	-	-	-	-/1	-/1	-	-	-	-	-	-	-	Cornsalad
Asteraceae	-	-	-	-	-	-	-	-	-	-/1	-	-	-	-/1	-	-	-	-	-	2	-/2	-	-	Daisy family
Asteraceae flower	-	-	-	-	-	-	-	-	-	-	-	-	-	5/4	-	-	1	-	1	-	-	-	-	Daisy family
Asteraceae (m)	2	1	1	-	-	-	-	-	2	-	2	-	-	-/1	-	-/1	-	-	-	-	-	-	-	Daisy family
Carduus/Cirsium (m)	-	-	-	-	-	-	-	-	-	-	4	-	-	-	-	-	-	-	-	-	-	-	-	Thistles
Carex spp (2-sided)	2	1	1	7	3	-	-	-	2	-	2	-	-	4/-	-	-	1	-	-	-	-	-	-	Sedges
Carex spp (3-sided)	25	7	7	16	1	-	-	-	2	5/1	2	-	2	4/-	-	-	-	2	-	1	1/3	-	-	Sedges
Carex sp (m)	-	-	-	-	-	-	-	-	-	-	-	2	2	-	-	-	-	-	-	-	-	-	-	Sedges
Carex/Rumex (m)	-	1	3	-	-	3/-	-	-	1	-	2	-	-	4/-	-	-	-	-	-	-	1/-	-	-	Sedges/Docks
Poaceae (small)	9	4	6	6	1	-	-	1	3	10/4	-	-	1	-	1/-	-	-	-	-	-	1/1	-	-	Grasses
Poaceae (small) flower	-	-	-	-	-	-	-	-	-	-	-	-	-	-	-	-	-	3	-	-	-	-	-	Grasses
Poaceae small (m)	-	-	-	-	-/3	-	-	-/3	-	-/4	-	-	1	-	1/-	-	-	-	-	-	-	-	-	Grasses
Poaceae rachis	-	-	-	-	-	-	-	-	-	1	1	-	1	-	-	-	-	-	-	-	-	-	-	Grasses
Poaceae (large)	15	1	-	27	-	-	-	-	8	8/-	-	6	7	4/2	15	-	5	7	5	7	15/6	1	-	Grasses large
Poaceae (large) (m)	-	-	-	-	-	6/-	-	-	7	-/1	2	-	-	3/-	3/-	-	-	-	-	-	-/1	-	-	Grasses
Indeterminate seeds	8	1	5	4	-	4	7	7	7	25/11	-	2	5	15	2	3	3	1	-	1	2/-	-	-	Indeterminate seeds
Indeterminate seeds (m)	1	1	-	3	-	1/5	2	1	2	1/-	14	1	14	1/1	-/3	1	1	-	7	7	-/3	7	2	Indeterminate seeds
Chaff concretions	-	-	-	-	-	-	-	-	-	-/4	1	1	-	-/2	-/2	-	-	-	-	-	-	-	-	Chaff concretions
Cereal concretions	-	-	-	-	-	-	-	-	-	-	-	1	-	-/2	-/2	-	-	-	-	-	-	-	-	Cereal concretions
Culm node small	-	2	1	-	-	-	-	-	4	-	-	-	-	-	10	-	-	-	-	-	-/1	-	-	Grass stem
Other fragments	7	14	18	34	13	17/7	-	10	32	18/54	7	10	7	8/5	7/15	17	3	8	3	7	12/9	4	5	Other fragments
Total	180	42	128	229	362	46	62/185	93	212	363/60	77	79	130	95/108	91/55	110	135	69	85	155	150/92	37	151	Total
Volume sampled (L)	22	28	15	31	37	26	20/20	22.5	53.5	25/11	15	25	5	40/21	10/8	14	30	20	17	35	34/29	32	10	Volume sampled (L)
Items/L	8.2	1.5	8.5	6.6	9.8	1.8	3.1/3.4	4.1	3.9	14.5/5.3	5.3	3.2	26.6	2.4/5.1	9.1/6.9	8.6	4.5	3.5	5	4.4	4.4/3.2	1.2	15.1	items/litre
Flot Vol (mls)	145	46	155	400	645	46	3/45	95	148	40/5	35	35	14	32/48	150/90	980	220	10	19	100	160/12	32	490	Flot volume (mls)

Key: (ra) = rachis segment, (Hu) = hulled, (tw) = twisted, (germd) = germinated, (m) = mineralised, (u) = uncharred.
Results, for example 1/1 = number of items in first context/ number of items in second context of group. Remains are seeds in the broad sense unless stated.

different conditions but F207 from plot C on Area 1 shows the widest range of fruit and food remains perhaps indicating higher status or the season of deposition. Cesspits on the other Area 1 plots and from Area 2 provide additional evidence of the variety of foods available.

The cereals included free-threshing wheat, both bread wheat and rivet wheat were found, with barley and smaller quantities of oats and rye, fruits included damson, primitive plums, apple and pear all possibly cultivated, and sloes, blackberry and hazel nuts probably gathered. Legumes including peas and beans were consumed with evidence for leeks as vegetable crop, leaves of other edible plants may also have been used. Figs and grapes may have been imported, possibly as dried fruit. Weeds of the crops and surroundings were also found including the unusual occurrence of dwarf elder. A little domestic evidence was found from late medieval samples but that from the small amount of post medieval material is insufficient to suggest domestic activity.

Acknowledgements

I am very grateful to Lisa Moffett of Birmingham University for advice and help with the identification of the plant remains and to Lucy Wheeler and Stefan Gula for their efficient processing of the samples. I am also grateful to Alan Clapham for his useful comments on this report and to James Greig for his help and for reading the draft report and making helpful suggestions.

I am also grateful to James Greig for reading all the reports in the environmental section and offering helpful editorial advice.

THE POLLEN   *James Greig*

Summary

Pollen was preserved in some samples, but not in others, a few uncharred seeds were also preserved. The Roman samples that contained pollen produced generally similar pollen spectra with grass pollen and other indications of an open grassy landscape with may represent local vegetation and a relatively clean environment. The medieval samples, on the other hand contained large amounts of grass, cereal and cornfield weed pollen including cornflower, probably from pollen contained in remains of hay and straw, or of herbivore and human excrement. The environment was dirty.

Methods

The samples were collected during the excavations. They were stored at ca. 5°C until prepared. The coarse sievings >100 μm were examined. The samples were prepared with Hydrofluoric acid and acetolysis treatment, stained in safranin and mounted in glycerin jelly. Counting was done with a Leitz Dialux microscope at a magnification of 500x, and critical identifications were made using comparative reference material viewed with a Leitz SM Lux. The counts are regarded as qualitative and are therefore smaller than quantitative ones. After each count the rest of the slide was scanned under low power and any extra pollen taxa recorded on a presence or absence basis. Samples from 15 features and one layer were examined. Pollen was only preserved in some samples, not in others. Pollen was not preserved in the samples from Roman features F376 and F711 and medieval pit F205. This patchy preservation may be the result of fluctuating water tables in the gravelly soil, and also due to the generally neutral to basic geology.

Results

Roman samples

Area 1: The well fill F405 phase 2E, contained little organic matter and produced an undistinguished pollen flora, such

floras contain only the more robust pollen which has survived, and are therefore not truly representative (table 86). The ditch fill F343 phase 3B produced a pollen flora which included a number of grassland plants in addition to Cichorioidae (dandelion group) and grasses. Although grasses grow in almost every habitat, knapweed (*Centaurea nigra*) is a meadow plant which is unlikely to have been part of the urban flora, and may represent hay. The only taxon indicative of damp conditions in any way is meadowsweet (*Filipendula*). The well fill of F230 phase 3B contained possible grassy material, the pollen was well preserved although rather crumpled and shrunken. The flora was mainly a rather unspecific grassland one, together with records of goosefoot family (Chenopodiaceae) and chickweed family (Caryophyllaceae) which seem likely to represent weeds, and the umbellifers (Apiaceae) might also do so. Weeds normally give a rather poor pollen record, but in this case it may be the local vegetation of grassland and weeds that is represented. This sample also contained pollen of Brassicaceae or Scrophulariaceae which could not be identified further partly because of the general state of the pollen. Area 3: Of phase 5G the primary quarry fill of F757 produced a pollen spectrum dominated by grasses, Cichorioidae, knapweed and ribwort plantain (*Plantago lanceolata*) and other probable grassland taxa. There was a single cereal pollen grain and virtually no woody or wetland plants represented. This spectrum may represent the open occupied landscape, and some hay as well; the pollen spectrum from context 3664 was also of open grassland.

Medieval and later samples

The fill of pit F203, phase 9 Area 1, and most of the other medieval samples differed from the Roman samples in containing large amounts of cereal pollen, substantial amounts of cornflower (*Centaurea cyanus*) and Asteraceae of *Anthemis*-type, stinking mayweed (table 86). This represents a 'dirtier' kind of deposit, which is known from better preserved examples at other sites from which there is also waterlogged macrofossil evidence to represent material such as straw, hay and animal dung.

Also of phase 9; on Area 1, F207 has a similar pollen flora with the addition of parasite ova which suggests that the pit had contained sewage. A possible grain of columbine (*Aquilegia*) could represent gardening. Pollen of restharrow (*Ononis*) is an unexpected find in a town; the commoner species grow in rough grassy places, especially well-drained ones (Stace 1991), a habitat which could possibly have occurred in a town. F218 contained pollen of cereals, cornflower, grass and grassland plants. On Area 2 phase 9 the pits F513 and F537 were similar in containing cereal pollen and weeds. The pits F719 of phase 9 on Area 3 in common with F206 of phase 10 on area 1, contained pollen of Brassicaceae or Scrophulariaceae in addition to cereal and weed pollen. The post medieval pit F576 on Area 2 was exceptional in containing no cereal or cornflower pollen but very large amounts of Brassicaceae or Scrophulariacea pollen type.

Discussion

The floras recovered from this material are rather small and uninformative, the taxa mainly represented being those producing abundant, robust and distinctive pollen. Similarly, the uncharred macrofossil floras seem to consist largely of taxa producing abundant robust seeds.

Some of the Roman samples produced pollen spectra dominated by grasses (Poaceae), Cichorioidae, common knapweed (*Centaurea nigra)* and ribwort plantain (*Plantago lanceolata)*, together with some other pollen such as clovers (*Trifolium* species). The last three pollen taxa clearly represent grassland plants, while Poaceae and Cichorioidae include many grassland taxa. Such a pollen spectrum has previously

Table 86: *Pollen list*

Area	1	1	1	3	3	1	1	1	2	2	3	1	2
Phase	2E	3B	3B	5G	5G	9	9	9	9	9	9	10	12
Group	147/1	141	155/3	334/1	358/1	127/1	120/7	113/3	260/4	257/3	313/2	113/2	291/8
Feature/Layer	F405	F343	F230	F757	3664	F203	F207	F218	F513	F537	F719	F206	F576
Pteridium, bracken	-	-	1	+	2	-	-	-	-	-	1	-	-
POLYPODIACEAE													
Polypodium, fern	-	-	-	+	-	-	-	-	-	-	-	-	-
Pinus, pine	-	-	1	-	-	-	1	-	-	-	-	-	-
RANUNCULACEAE													
Ranunculus acris-type, buttercup	2	-	+	1	-	-	1	1	+	-	-	2	+
R. subg *Batrachium*-type, water-crowfoot	-	-	-	-	-	-	-	1	-	-	1	-	-
cf. *Aquilegia*, columbine	-	-	-	-	-	-	+	-	-	-	-	-	-
URTICACEAE													
Urtica, nettle	-	-	-	-	-	-	1	2	-	1	-	+	-
FAGACEAE													
Quercus, oak	-	-	+	-	-	2	-	4	1	-	3	+	1
BETULACEAE													
Betula, birch	-	-	-	-	2	-	-	-	-	-	-	-	-
Alnus, alder	5	5	-	-	2	1	1	-	4	-	-	+	1
Corylus, hazel	-	-	1	1	-	2	1	1	7	-	-	-	1
CHENOPODIACEAE, Goosefoot family	-	-	8	1	-	1	1	1	1	1	1	17	2
CARYOPHYLLACEAE, Pink family	-	-	2	-	-	-	-	-	-	-	-	-	-
POLYGONACEAE													
Persicaria bistorta, bistort	-	-	-	-	-	-	-	-	-	-	-	-	+
Persicaria maculosa, persicaria	-	-	-	-	-	-	-	-	-	-	+	-	-
MALVACEAE													
Malva, mallow	-	-	-	-	-	1	-	-	-	-	-	-	-
SALICACEAE													
Salix, willow	-	-	-	-	-	-	-	-	-	-	1	-	-
BRASSICACEAE, Cabbage family	10	-	4	-	-	1	5	4	-	-	15	1	5
ROSACEAE													
Filipendula, meadowsweet	-	3	-	+	-	2	-	-	-	-	-	-	1
Crataegus, hawthorn	-	-	-	-	-	-	-	-	-	-	1	-	-
FABACEAE				+	1	-	1	-	-	-	-	-	-	+
Lotus, bird's-foot trefoil	-	-	-	-	-	1	1	-	-	-	-	-	-
Ononis, restharrow	-	-	-	-	-	2	-	-	-	-	-	-	-
Trifolium pratense-type, red clover	-	+	-	+	-	-	-	-	-	-	-	-	-
T. repens-type, white clover	-	5	-	-	3	-	2	1	-	-	13	1	-
Vicia faba, bean	-	-	-	-	-	-	-	-	-	-	1	-	-
RHAMNACEAE													
cf. *Frangula alnus*, alder buckthorn	-	-	-	-	-	1	-	-	-	-	-	-	-
ACERACEAE													
cf. *Acer*, field maple	-	-	-	-	-	-	-	-	-	1	-	-	-
APIACEAE, Carrot family	-	-	9	-	-	4	1	3	2	1	6	+	2
LAMIACEAE													
cf. *Lamium*-type, deadnettle	-	-	-	-	-	1	-	-	-	1	-	-	-
PLANTAGINACEAE													
Plantago major, greater plantain	-	3	-	-	-	1	-	-	-	-	-	-	-
P. lanceolata, ribwort plantain	-	3	1	5	2	1	1	2	-	2	1	+	1
SCROPHULARIACEAE													
Scrophulariaceae/Brassicaceae figwort or cabbage family	63	3	49	1	-	11	3	-	3	1	-	23	69
RUBIACEAE													
Galium-type, bedstraw	-	3	+	1	2	1	-	-	-	-	-	2	+
CAPRIFOLIACEAE													
Sambucus nigra, elder	-	-	-	-	-	-	-	1	-	-	-	-	-
ASTERACEAE													
Cichorioidae, dandelion group	7	43	9	51	65	17	2	11	1	13	19	7	5
Aster-type, aster group	-	-	-	-	-	2	-	-	5	4	1	-	1
Artemisia, mugwort	-	-	-	-	-	1	1	-	-	-	-	-	-
Anthemis-type, mayweed	-	-	-	1	-	-	2	5	4	7	3	4	-
Centaurea cyanus, cornflower	-	-	-	-	-	5	14	3	1	4	17	5	-
C. nigra, common knapweed	-	5	3	4	2	2	1	2	-	-	2	4	1
Cirsium-type, thistles	-	-	-	-	-	1	1	-	-	-	-	-	+
DIPSACACEAE, scabious/teasel	-	-	-	-	-	-	-	-	-	-	-	+	-
CYPERACEAE, Sedge family	-	-	+	+	-	1	1	-	-	-	-	1	-
POACEAE <40μm, Grasses	12	27	12	30	21	21	12	50	18	11	13	14	9
Cerealia >40μm, Cereals	-	-	+	+	-	26	42	9	51	52	5	19	2
pollen sum	41	37	222	221	58	123	162	191	110	75	190	254	325
total parasite ova													
Ascaris	-	-	-	-	-	-	7	-	-	-	-	-	-

The pollen types are given in taxonomic order (Stace 1991). The numbers represent the percentages of pollen grains, and the total pollen sums are given excluding parasite ova.

been obtained from ditch and well sediments, usually from Roman sites. The presence of common knapweed which is a tall, hay meadow plant, shows that some of the grassy material could have come from hay and dung in hay brought in to Leicester, as in the case of the macrofossil flora in the charred sample from F255, G174 phase 4A. Otherwise, some grass pollen could represent local vegetation including weed communities growing on the spot; this kind of spectrum has often been found in urban material (Greig 1982).

The main distinctive feature is that cornflower (*Centaurea cyanus*) is present in seven out of the eight medieval samples, but in none of the Roman ones. The appearance or increase in abundance of cornflower among plant remains in the medieval period has been remarked upon and charred remains were also found in some of the medieval samples (table 85). Almost all the samples with cornflower pollen also contain *Anthemis*-type pollen, which may also have come from cornfield weeds such as stinking mayweed (*Anthemis cotula*) and corn marigold (*Chrysanthemum segetum*), which are also commonly found in medieval material. The third feature of most of the medieval features is the abundance of cereal pollen in them, which includes a few pollen grains further identified as rye (*Secale cereale*). A single grain of bean pollen (*Vicia faba*) was found. Such pollen spectra with high cereal pollen are normally recovered from medieval pits, and are interpreted as the residues from various kinds of rubbish such as animal dung, household waste and human faeces. Further evidence comes from parasite ova such as roundworm (*Ascaris*) which were seen in the pollen preparation and latrine fly remains (see above), from these pits. Medieval and post medieval pollen spectra have been studied at the Shires sites in Leicester (Greig 1993), and some of these deposits produced similar results to those outlined above.

CHARCOAL
G. C. Morgan

Charcoal from 167 sieved samples was identified. Samples were selected as the most productive for charcoal from each phase. The identified fragments of each species were counted by sample and the diameter, number of rings, estimate of age, fast or slow growth rate and other features recorded in the site archive. The data was tabulated as number of fragments by feature and phase with totals and percentages for the broad period divisions of the site (table 75). The percentage of analysed samples in which each species occurred is also shown. The fragment counts and occurrence in samples are only a guide to the relative amounts of each species as charcoal is difficult to quantify and only selected samples were analysed.

Table 87: *Species list*

Charcoal	Botanical name	Comments
Oak	*Quercus* spp.	
Ash	*Fraxinus excelsior* L.	
Hazel	*Corylus avellana* L.	or alder *Alnus* spp.
Poplar	*Populus* spp.	or willow *Salix* spp.
Hawthorn	*Crataegus* spp.	hawthorn type
Blackthorn	*Prunus spinosa* L.	
Field maple	*Acer campestre* L.	
Rowan	*Sorbus* spp.	rowan type
Elder	*Sambucus* sp.	
Gorse	*Ulex* sp.	
Pine	*Pinus* sp.	confirmed by resin ducts

Conclusions

Oak is the most common charcoal by far, being present in around 90% of samples in all phases. The other species are in about equal proportions but pine, gorse and elder are single

Table 88: *Identified charcoal fragments*

Phase	Area	Feature	Group	Oak	Ash	Black-thorn	Poplar	Haw-thorn	Hazel	Field maple	Gorse	Rowan	Elder	Pine
E. Roman														
1A	1	F467	177/1	2	-	-	-	-	-	-	-	-	-	-
1B	1	F462	130/8	4	1	-	-	-	-	-	-	-	-	-
2A	1	F451	133/7	1	1	1	1	1	-	-	-	-	-	-
2F	1	1439	145/3	-	1	1	-	-	-	-	-	-	-	-
2F	1	F481	146/1	6	-	-	2	2	2	1	-	-	-	-
3A	1	F343	141/3	16	3	3	2	2	-	1	-	-	-	-
3B	1	F343	141/4	10	2	1	1	4	2	1	1	-	-	-
3D	1	F335	187/1	13	-	-	1	1	1	-	-	-	-	-
L. Roman														
4A	1	F255	174/2	21	-	1	2	-	7	5	-	1	1	-
5G	3	F757	334/2	6	-	-	1	1	1	1	-	1	-	-
5G	3	F765	337/2	1	-	-	-	1	-	-	-	-	-	-
5G	3	F781	333/1	2	1	-	-	-	1	-	-	-	-	1
6A	3	F766	367/1	9	-	1	2	2	3	2	-	2	-	-
Medieval														
8	2	F568	247/2	19	-	-	1	1	3	-	-	-	-	-
9	1	F286	181/1	14	-	-	-	2	-	-	-	-	-	-
9	2	F513	260/4	16	3	1	1	-	2	2	-	-	-	-
9	2	F537	257/4	12	-	-	1	2	4	-	-	-	-	-
9	2	F570	256/1	11	1	-	1	1	4	-	-	2	-	-
9	1	F207	120/7	23	1	1	2	1	16	-	-	-	-	-
10	1	F206	119/3	25	-	-	-	3	1	1	-	-	-	-
Late/Post-medieval														
11	3	F703	307/1	7	-	-	-	1	2	-	-	-	-	-
12	2	F581	294/3	5	-	-	3	-	3	-	-	-	-	-

TOTALS Phases	Frags.	Frags.	Oak	Ash	Black-thorn	Poplar	Haw-thorn	Hazel	Field maple	Gorse	Rowan	Elder	Pine
1-3	102	%	61	8	6	7	10	5	3	1	0	0	0
4-6	77	%	51	1	3	7	5	16	10	0	5	1	1
8-10	172	%	67	3	1	3	6	17	2	0	1	0	0
11-12	21	%	57	0	0	14	5	24	0	0	0	0	0

Phases	Samples	Samples	Oak	Ash	Black-thorn	Poplar	Haw-thorn	Hazel	Field maple	Gorse	Rowan	Elder	Pine
1-3	56	%	86	9	14	13	18	9	5	2	0	0	0
4-6	30	%	90	7	7	17	14	40	23	0	14	3	3
8-10	75	%	95	7	3	5	12	23	5	0	4	0	0
11-12	6	%	100	0	0	16	16	50	0	0	0	0	0

Number of identified charcoal fragments by feature, percentage of each type of charcoal of total fragments from each phase group, and percentage of samples with each type of charcoal from samples analysed for each phase group.

fragments from Roman samples only. The find of pine in F781 331/1 phase 5G area 3 is unusual before the medieval period. A plum type stone from (1027) and a sloe stone from (1099) were found in F255 G174 phase 4A. The charcoal generally represents woodland trees but the pine and gorse would be more likely associated with open heathland, both are from the Roman phases. The range of growth rates for oak suggests a variety of sites for the trees, some being more suitable for quick growth, with ample moisture, than others.

The large proportion of oak may also point to deliberate selection, perhaps for structural timber, which is borne out by the presence of wood chippings suggesting the use of off cuts and waste as a fuel source. Wood chippings were found in F343 phase 3, F207, F513, and F537 phase 9 showing this to have occurred in both Roman and medieval periods. Selection in size for charcoal making for industrial use may also be indicated in F581 294/3 phase 12 where various species are represented in similar sizes. This is roundwood charcoal and is particuarly hard and probably represents the remains of manufactured charcoal rather than firewood residues. The presence of coal in many samples does point to its deliberate use as a fuel, and this was found in F343 phase 3, F255 phase 4, F568 phase 8, F218 and F207 phase 9 suggesting the use of coal throughout the occupation of the site.

THE HUMAN BONE   *J. Wakely*

No actual cemetery was found, the human remains that were recovered appeared as incidental discoveries in various, features of the site. Most were fragmentary, and probably represented earlier burials disturbed in later activities on the site, such as the digging of pits or ditches. All, except one, of the remains were found in Roman phases.

Occasionally where bone ends were present it was possible to assign a rough estimate of age to an incomplete bone, i.e. juvenile, adult or elderly on the basis of epiphysial fusion and/or degenerative changes in joints (Brothwell, 1981). Likewise the presence of bone ends sometimes enabled a diagnosis of sex from measurement of their diameter (Bass, 1983). However, in most cases where only midshaft fragments were present no meaningful anthropological information was obtainable. Beyond mild osteoarthritic changes associated with old age in two cases F246 (462) 166/4 phase 5C and F786 (3925) 339/7 phase 6B no disease was identified.

One almost complete skull F208 (241) 187/1, phase 3, was found alone. Sufficient dentition survived to estimate age on the basis of the eruption and wear of the permanent teeth as 25-45 years. The surviving teeth were in good condition. Next to the pelvis the skull is the most useful part of a skeleton for the diagnosis of sex. The skulls of adult females are usually rounded in form, with poorly developed brow ridges and

muscle attachments. The jaw is usually small with a round or oval chin. By contrast the skull of a man is generally square in form, with well marked brow ridges, muscle markings and mastoid processes, and a heavy jaw with a square chin. Skull F208 approximated most closely to the 'male' type and so was classified as a male. The other incomplete skull (3908) 339/7, phase 5F, was identified as a probable female.

The other substantial collection of human bone is a cremated body found in an urn of Roman date (1233) 162/3 phase 5B. Burial of the dead inside the city walls was illegal in the Roman Empire (Merrifield, 1987) so this burial probably represents either an illicit disposal or a ritual deposit. Potentially, cremated bone can be analysed in the same way as an inhumation. However the extent of such an analysis is limited by the small amount of anatomically recognisable material among the crushed fragments, pyre debris and animal bone (from grave offerings) that may accompany the human remains in a cremation urn. Few such identifiable fragments were found in this cremation. There was sufficient only to identify the bones as those of an adult, i.e. more than 20 years old, but not to assign sex with certainty. The small size of the limb bones and smooth skull fragments suggest a possible female. It is unlikely that more than one individual was represented in the urn, as matched left and right arm and foot fragments could be identified among other large pieces that could only be generally identified as 'long bone' or 'rib' without being able to identify the exact bone or side of the body from which it came.

Table 89: *Human bone from the site*

Phase	Group	Feature context	Context	Type of Human bone
Phase 3D	G187	F212 (270)	Pit fill	Fragment of left femur
Phase 3	G141	F343 (903)	Ditch fill	Midshaft fragment of adult left tibia
Phase 3	G141	F343 (874)	Ditch fill	Shaft of adult left femur, gnawed by dog.
Phase 3		F208 (241)	Pit fill	Fragmented but almost complete skull.
Phase 4A	183/1	F311 (682)	Pit fill	Left femoral shaft with trauma of large adult
Phase 5G	359/4	F756 (3879)	Pit fill	Right humerus of newborn infant
Phase 5C	166/4	F246 (462)	Well fill	Head and greater trochnter of male adult.
Phase 5F	339/8	F786 (3925)	Quarry fill	First lumbar vertebra of elderly adult.
Phase 5		(3908)	Quarry fill	Two skull fragments of adult, possibly female
Phase 5B	162/3	(1233)	Urn	Cremation
Phase 6A	338/3	F763 (3640)	Make up	A fragment of right femur shaft of adult
Phase 6		(3613)	Make up	Head and lesser trochanter of femur of adult ?male
Phase 9	120/7	F207 (257)	Pit	Part of left femur of large adult, probably male.

BIBLIOGRAPHY

Adams, J.N., 1982 *The Latin Sexual Vocabulary.* London: Duckworth.

Adams Gilmour, L., *et al* 1988 *Early Medieval Pottery from Flaxengate,* Archaeol. of Lincoln Vol. **17/2** London: Trust for Lincolnshire Archaeol.

Allason-Jones, L., 1985 'Bell-shaped studs?' *in* M.C. Bishop, *The Production and Distribution of Roman Military Equipment* Oxford: Brit. Archaeol. Reports S275.

Allason-Jones, L., 1988 'The small finds' *in* M.C. Bishop and J.N. Dore 1985.

Allason-Jones, L., 1989 *Women in Roman Britain.* London: British Museum Publications.

Allason-Jones, L. and Miket, R., 1984 *The Catalogue of Small Finds from South Shields Roman Fort.* Newcastle-upon-Tyne: The Soc. of Antiquaries of Newcastle-upon-Tyne.

Allen, D., 1986 'The glass vessels' *in* J.D. Zienkiewicz 1986, 98-116

Allen, D., 1988 'Roman glass from Corbridge' *in* M.C. Bishop and J.N. Dore 1988.

Allen, D.F., 1972 'The fibula of Criciru', *Germania* **50**, 122-132.

Allin, C.E., 1981a 'The ridge tile' *in* J. E. Mellor and T. Pearce 1981, 52-70.

Allin, C.E., 1981b *The Medieval Leather Industry in Leicester.* Leicester: Leicestershire Museums, Art Galleries and Records Service Archaeol. Report No.3.

Almgren, O., 1923 *Studien uber Nordeuropaische Fibelformen der ersten nachchristlichen Jahrhunderte mit Beruchsichtigung der provinzialromishcen und sudrussischen Formen.* Leipzig.

Anderson, A.C., 1980 *A Guide to Roman Fine Wares.* Highworth Wilts: VORDA.

Anderson, A.C., and Anderson, A.S., (eds) 1981 *Roman Pottery Research in Britain and North-West Europe.* Oxford: Brit. Archaeol. Rep. (Int. Ser.) **123**.

Anderson, A.C., Fulford, M.G., Hatcher, H. and Pollard, A.M., 1982 'Chemical analysis of hunt cups and allied wares from Britain', *Britannia* **13**, 229-38.

Arthur, P.A., 1986 'Roman amphorae from Canterbury', *Britannia* **17**, 239-58.

Arthur, P.A. and Marsh, G., (eds) 1978 *Early Fine Wares in Roman Britain.* Oxford: Brit. Archaeol. Rep. (Brit. Ser.) **57**.

Arthur, P.A., and Williams, D.F., 1992 'Campanian wine, Roman Britain and the third century AD', *Journ. Roman Archaeol.* **5**, 250-60.

Atkinson 1975, *Tobacco Pipes of Broseley Shropshire.* Privately published.

Atkinson, D., 1914 'A hoard of samian ware from Pompeii', *Journ. Roman Stud.* **4**, 26-64.

Atkinson, D., 1942 *Report on Excavations at Wroxeter 1923-1927.* Oxford: Birmingham Archaeol. Soc.

Ayers, B., 1994 *Norwich.* London: English Heritage, Batsford.

Bailey, M., 1991 'Per impetum maris: Natural disaster and economic decline in eastern England 1275-1350' *in* Bruce M.S Campbell, *Before the Black Death, Studies in the 'Crisis' of the Early 14th Century.* Manchester and New York: Manchester University Press.

Barley, M.W., 1964 'Medieval borough of Torksey: Excavations 1960-2', *Antiq. Journ.* **44**, 175-187.

Barley, M.W., 1981 'Medieval borough of Torksey; Excavations 1963-8', *Antiq. Journ.*.**61** (pt 2), 264-291.

Barry, D., 1989 *Construction,* **1**. London: Mitchell.

Bass, W.M., 1983 *Human Osteology, a Laboratory and Field Manual.* (3rd Edition). Columbia:Missouri Archaeol. Soc.

Bateson, M., 1899 *Records of the Borough of Leicester 1103-1327.* Cambridge: Cambridge University Press.

Baudoux, J., 1990 *Les Amphores d'Alsace et de Lorraine: contribution a l'histoire de l'economie provincialessous l'Empire Romain.* Ph.D. Thesis, University of Strasbourg.

Becking, J.H., 1975 'The ultrastructure of the Avian eggshell', *Ibis* **4**, 390-395.

Bellamy, C.V. and Nicholson, W.E., 1972 'Distilling groups from Pontefract and Selbourne Priories', *in* S. Moorhouse 1972, 89-98.

Belshaw, R., 1989 'A note on the recovery of *Thoracochaeta zosterae* (Haliday) (Diptera: Sphaeroceridae) from archaeological deposits', *Circaea* **6**(1), 39-41.

Beltran, M., 1970 *Las anforas romanas en Espana.* Zaragosa.

Berger, L., 1960 *Romische Glas aus Vindonissa.* Basel.

Bidwell P., 1985 *The Roman Fort at Vindolanda.* London: Historic Buildings and Monuments Commission Archaeol. Rep. **1**.

Bidwell, P.T., 1979 *The Legionary Bath-house and Basilica and Forum at Exeter.* Exeter: Exeter City Counc. and University of Exeter. Exeter Archaeol. Rep. **1**.

Billson, C.J., 1920 *Mediaeval Leicester.* Leicester: Edgar Backus.

Bird, J., 1977 'African Red Slip ware in Roman Britain', *in* J. Dore and K. Greene, (eds) 1977, 269-77.

Birss, R.S., 1986 'Coarse pottery' *in* H.M.Wheeler 1986, 'North-west sector excavations 1979-80', *Derbyshire Archaeol. Journ.* **105**, 38-154 (90-124).

Bishop, C. and Dore, J.N., 1988 *Corbridge. Excavations of the Roman fort and town, 1947-80.* London: Historic Buildings and Monuments Commission Archaeol. Report no. **8**.

Bishop, M.C. and Coulston, J.C.N., 1993 *Roman Military Equipment: from the Punic Wars to the Fall of Rome.* London: Batsford.

BL British Library.

Blinkhorn, P., forthcoming a *The Saxon pottery from St. Peters and Little Lane, Leicester.*

Blinkhorn, P., forthcoming b *The Saxon pottery from Milton Keynes.*

Blockley, K.,1985 *Marshfield; Ironmongers Piece Excavations 1982-3. An Iron Age and Romano-British Settlement in the South Cotswolds.* Oxford: Brit. Archaeol. Rep. (Brit. Ser.) **141**.

Blockley, K., 1989 *Prestatyn 1984-5, An Iron Age Farmstead and Romano-British Industrial Settlement in North Wales.* Oxford: Brit. Archaeol. Rep.(Brit. Ser.) **210**.

Blurton, T.R. 1977 'Excavations at Angel Court, Walbrook, 1974', *Trans. London & Middlesex Archaeol. Soc.* **28**, 14-100.

Bodl. Bodleian Library, Oxford.

Bohme A., 1972 *Die Fibeln der Kastelle Saalburg und Zugmantel.* Saalburg Jahrbuch, Bericht des Saalburg Museums **29**.

Brodribb G., 1979 *Roman Brick and Tile.* Oxford: Alan Sutton.

Bolton E.G., 1967-8 'A Romano-British pottery kiln at Greetham, Rutland', *Trans. Leicestershire Archaeol. and Hist. Soc.* **43**, 1-3.

Bond, C.J., 1988 'Monastic fishponds', *in*: M. Aston (ed.) *Medieval Fish, Fisheries and Fishponds in England,* 69-122. Oxford: Brit. Archaeol. Rep. (Brit. Ser.), **182 (i)**.

Boon, G.C., 1977 'Gold-in-glass beads', *Britannia* **7**, 193-207.

Booth, P.M. and Green, S., 1989 'The nature and distribution of certain pink, grog tempered vessels', *Journ. Roman Pottery Stud.* **2**, 77-84.

Boothroyd, N., forthcoming *Small Finds from Two Extramural sites of Roman and Medieval Leicester: Great Holme St. and the Austin Friars).* Unpub. MA thesis, University of Leicester 1994.

Bosanquet, R., 1904 'The Roman camp at Housesteads', *Archaeologia Aeliana* **2**, 25.

Bowden I., 1992 *Roman Slate and Tile from Narborough.* Unpub. M.A thesis, University of Leicester.

Boyer, P., 1989 *A Pottery Typology of Romano-British Grey Wares From Kilns at Ravenstone, Leicestershire.* Archive Report, Jewry Wall Museum, Leicester.

Boyer, P., 1990 *The Analysis of Environmental Samples from a Medieval Cesspit from Little Lane, Leicester.* Unpub. MA thesis, University of Leicester.

Boyer, P., 1991 *The Parasite Ova from the Shires Excavations.* Archive Report, Jewry Wall Museum, Leicester.

Boyer, P. 1992 *The Parasite Ova from a Medieval Undercroft in Guildhall Lane, Leicester.* Archive Report, Jewry Wall Museum, Leicester.

Brailsford, J.W., 1962 *Hod Hill, volume one, Antiquities from Hod Hill in the Durden Collection.* London.

Brassington, M., 1980 'Derby Racecourse kiln excavations 1972-3', *Antiquaries Journ.* **60**, 8-47.

Brothwell, D.R., 1981 *Digging Up Bones.* British Museum/Oxford University Press.

Brown, A.E.,1994 'A Romano-British shell-tempered pottery and tile manufacturing site at Harrold, Bedfordshire', *Bedfordshire Archaeol. Journ.* **21**, 19-107.

Brown, K., 1993-4 'A medieval pottery kiln at Yardley Hastings, Northampton', *Northants Archaeol.* **25**, 159-175.

Buckley, R.J., 1979-80 'An excavation in Causeway Lane, Leicester', *Trans. Leicestershire Archaeol. and Hist. Soc.,* **55**, 83-4.

Buckley, R.J., 1987 'A watching-brief at Soar Lane, Leicester', *Trans. Leicestershire Archaeol. and Hist. Soc.* **61**, 92.

Buckley, R.J., forthcoming 'The painted wall plaster from Norfolk Street Roman Villa, Leicester'.

Buckley R.J. and Lucas, J.N., 1987 *Leicester Town Defences.* Leicester: Leicestershire Museums Art Galleries and Records Service.

Burrows, R.B., 1965 *Microscopic Diagnosis Of The Parasites Of Man.* Yale.

Bushe-Fox, J.P., 1932 *Third Report on the Excavations of the Roman Fort at Richborough, Kent.* London: Rep. Res. Comm. Soc. Antiq. London. **10**.

Bushe-Fox, J P., 1949 *Fourth Report on the Excavation of the Roman Fort at Richborough, Kent.* London: Rep. Res. Comm. Soc. Antiq. London. **16**.

Byrant, G.F. and Steane, J.M., 1969 'Excavations at the deserted medieval village at Lyveden', *Journ. Northampton Museums*, **5**.

Byrant, G.F. and Steane, J.M., 1971 'Excavations at the deserted medieval village at Lyveden', *Journ. Northampton Museums*, **9**.

Callender, M.H., 1965 *Roman Amphorae*. Oxford.

Cam. Hawkes and Hull 1947.

Carey, G., 1982. 'Ageing and sexing domestic bird bones from some late medieval deposits at Baynard's Castle, City of London'. *in* B. Wilson, C. Grigson, and S. Payne (eds) 1982.

Carreras, C. and Williams, D.F., 1993 *Roman Amphorae from Leicester*. Unpub. archive report, Jewry Wall Museum, Leicester.

Carreras, C. and Williams, D.F., 1995 'Spanish olive-oil trade in late Roman Britain', *Journ. Roman Pottery Studies*, **7**.

Carruthers, W., 1991. *Fishbourne Roman Palace, West Sussex: Carbonised Plant Remains from Garden Features*. London: English Heritage Ancient Monuments Laboratory Report **130/91**.

Carver, M., 1987, *Underneath English Towns*. London: Batsford.

Castle, S.A., 1978 'Amphorae from Brockley Hill 1975', *Britannia*, **9**, 383-392.

Chandler, A.C. and Read, C.P., 1961 *Introduction to Parasitology*. New York: John Wiley.

Charlesworth, D., 1959 'Roman glass from Northern Britain', *Archaeologia Aeliana* 4, **XXXVII**, 33-58.

Charlesworth, D., 1966 'Roman square bottles', *Journ. of Glass Studies*, **VIII**, 26-40.

Charlesworth, D., 1971 'A group of vessels from the Commandant's House, Housesteads', *Journ. of Glass Studies*, **13**, 34-7.

Charlesworth, D., 1971/3 'Glass found in 1970', *in* B. Hobley, 'Excavations at 'The Lunt' Roman military site, Baginton, Warwickshire 1968-1971 second interim report', *Trans. Birmingham and Warwickshire Archaeol. Soc.* **85**, 7-92.

Charlesworth, D., 1972 'The glass', *in* S.S. Frere 1972.

Charlesworth, D., 1975 'The Commandants House, Housesteads', *Archaeologia Aeliana*, 5, **III**, 17-42.

Charlesworth, D., 1985a 'The glass', *in* J. Draper *Excavations by Mr H.P. Cooper on the Roman site at Hill Farm, Gestingthorpe, Essex*, 64-66. East Anglian Archaeol. Report **25**.

Charlesworth, D., 1985b 'The glass', MF 1: A6-A9, 3: F1-11 *in* R. Niblett, *Sheepen : an early Roman industrial site at Camulodunum*. London: Counc. Brit. Archaeol. Res. Rep. **57**.

Charters, S., Evershed, R.P., Goad, L.J., Blinkhorn, P.W. and Denham, V., 1993 'Quantification and distribution of lipid in archaeological ceramics: implications for sampling pot sherds for organic residue analysis', *Archaeometry* 35, 211-223.

Clamp, H., 1985 'The Late Iron Age and Romano-British pottery', *in* P. Clay and J.E. Mellor 1985, 41-59.

Clarke, S., 1994 'A quantitative analysis of the finds from the Roman fort of Newstead – some preliminary findings', *in* S. Cottam, D. Dungworth, S. Scott, and J. Taylor (eds) *Theoretical Roman Archaeology, Proceedings of the Fourth Conference 1994*, 72-82. Oxford: Oxbow.

Clarke, T.D., 1957 'Archaeology in Leicestershire 1956-7', *Trans. Leicestershire Archaeol. and Hist. Soc.* **33**, 59-65.

Clay, P.N., and Mellor, J.E., 1985 *Excavations in Bath Lane, Leicester*. Leicester: Leicestershire Museums Archaeol. Report **10**.

Clay, P.N., and Pollard, R.J., 1994 *Iron Age and Roman Occupation in the West Bridge Area, Leicester. Excavations 1962-1971*. Leicester: Leicestershire Museums, Arts and Records Service.

Collingwood, R.G. and Wright, R.P., 1991 *Roman Inscriptions in Britain*, Vol. **II** fasc.3, *Instrumentum Domesticum*, ed. S.S. Frere and R.S.O. Tomlin.

Connor, A.A., 1990 *Shorts Gardens Excavation*. Unpub. Greater London Archaeol. Unit Archive Rep.

Cookson N., 1984 *Romano-British Mosaics*. Oxford: Brit. Archaeol. Rep. (Brit. Ser.) **135**.

Cool, H.E.M., 1990a 'Roman metal hair pins from Southern Britain', *Archaeol. Journ.* **147**, 148-182.

Cool, H.E.M. 1990b 'The problem of third century drinking vessels in Britain', *Annales du 11e congres de l'association internationale pour l'histoire du verre*, 167-175. Amsterdam.

Cool, H.E.M., Lloyd-Morgan, G. and Hooley, A.D., 1995 *Finds from the Fortress*. York: The Archaeology of York: The Small Finds 17/10.

Cool, H.E.M. & Price, J., 1987 'The glass', *in* G.W. Meates 1987, 110-42.

Cool H.E.M., & Price J., 1989 'The glass vessels', *in* J. Britnell, *Caersws Vicus, Powys: Excavations at the Old Primary School*. Oxford: Brit. Archaeol. Rep. (Brit. Ser.) **205**, 31-43.

Cool H.E.M., & Price J., 1993 'Roman glass' *in* P.J. Woodward, S.N. Davies and A.H. Graham 1993, *Excavations at the Old Methodist Chapel and Greyhound yard, Dorchester 1981-1984*, 150-167. Dorset

Nat. Hist. and Archaeol. Soc. Monograph Ser. **12**.

Cool, H.E.M. & Price, J., 1995 *The Roman Vessel Glass From Excavations In Colchester 1971-85*. Colchester: Colchester Archaeol. Rep. **8**.

Cool, H.E.M. & Price, J., forthcoming a 'The Roman glass from Wroxeter'

Cool, H.E.M. & Price, J., forthcoming b 'The Roman Glass from Blue Boar Lane, Leicester' in N. Cooper, forthcoming 'Excavations in Blue Boar Lane, Leicester 1958'.

Cool, H.E.M. & Price, J., forthcoming c 'The glass from the park, Lincoln'.

Cooper, L., unpub., *Excavations in Bath Lane, Leicester*. Unpub. Archive Rep. Jewry Wall Museum, Leicester.

Cooper, L., 1993 'An evaluation and excavation at the Cameo Cinema, 45-50 High Street, Leicester', *Trans. Leicestershire Archaeol. and Hist. Soc.* 67, 88-93.

Cooper, L., 1994 'Newarke Street, Leicester', *Trans. Leicestershire Archaeol. and Hist. Soc.*, 68, 170-1.

Cooper, L., 1996 'A Roman cemetery in Newarke Street Leicester', *Trans. Leicestershire. Archaeol. and Hist. Soc.*, 70, 1-91.

Cooper, N.J., 1989 'A study of Roman pottery from the Lower Nene Valley kiln site at Park Farm, Stanground, near Peterborough, Cambs.', *Journ. Roman Pottery Stud.* 2, 59-65.

Cooper, N.J., 1998 'The supply of pottery to Roman Cirencester' in N. Holbrook, *Cirencester:the Roman Town Defences, Public Buildings and Shops*, 324-350., Cirencester: Cotswold Archaeological Trust, Cirencester Excavations **5**.

Cooper, N.J., forthcoming a 'Small finds from excavations at Little Lane and St. Peter's Lane, Leicester', *in* J.N. Lucas and R.J. Buckley forthcoming.

Cooper, N.J., forthcoming b 'Metal objects' in H. Wallis forthcoming, *Excavations at Billingford, Norfolk*. East Anglian Archaeology.

Cooper, N.J., forthcoming c 'Ceramic and stone counters from the excavations of J.S. Wacher at Catterick 1958-9' *in* P.R. Wilson forthcoming, *Excavations at Catterick*.

Cooper, N.J., forthcoming d 'Ceramic figurines from the excavations of J.S. Wacher at Catterick 1958-9' *in* P.R. Wilson forthcoming, *Excavations at Catterick*.

Coppack, G., 1980. *The Medieval Pottery of Lincoln, Nottingham & Derby*. Unpub. PhD thesis, University of Nottingham.

Corder, P., 1961 *The Roman Town and Villa at Great Casterton, Rutland. Third Report*. University of Nottingham.

Cotton, M. Aylwin, 1947 'Excavations at Silchester 1938-9', *Archaeologia* 92, 121-167.

Courtney, P., 1994 *Medieval and Later Usk*. Cardiff.

Courtney, P., 1996 'The origins of Leicester's market place', *Leicestershire Historian* 4, no 4, 5-15.

Courtney, P., 1998 'Saxon and medieval Leicester: the making of an urban landscape', *Trans. Leicestershire Archaeol. and Hist. Soc.* 72, 110-45.

Courtney, P., forthcoming 'The historical background', *in* J.N. Lucas and R.J. Buckley, forthcoming.

Cowgill, J., de Neergaard, M. and Griffiths, N., 1987 *Knives and Scabbards Medieval: Finds from Excavations in London:* 1 HMSO.

Coy, J., 1989 'The provision of fowl and fish for towns', *in* D. Serjeantson and T. Waldron, 1989.

Crummy N., 1983 *The Roman Small Finds from Excavations in Colchester 1971-9*. Colchester: Colchester Archaeol. Rep. **2**.

Cummings, K., 1980 *The Technique of Glass Forming*. London.

Cunliffe, B.W., (ed) 1968 *Fifth Report on the Excavations of the Roman Fort at Richborough, Kent*. Oxford: Rep. Res. Comm. Soc. Antiq. London **23**.

Cunliffe, B.W., 1971 *Excavations at Fishbourne 1961-1969*, Vol. **II** : the *Finds*. Leeds: Rep. Res. Comm. Soc. Antiq. London **27**.

Curle, J., 1911 *A Roman Frontier Post and its People, The Fort of Newstead in the Parish of Melrose*. Glasgow.

Cutting, C.L., 1962 'Historical aspects of fish', *in* G. Borgstrcm (ed.) *Fish as Food*, vol.2. London and New York: Academic Press.

D. = Dechelette 1904

Dannell, G.B., 1971 'The samian pottery', *in* B.W. Cunliffe 1971, 230-316.

Dannell, G.B., 1973 'The potter Indixivixus', *in* A.P. Detsicas (ed) *Current Research in Romano-British Coarse Pottery*, 139-42. London: Counc. Brit. Archaeol. Res. Rep. **10**.

Dannell, G.B., 1985 'The Arretine and Samian Pottery', *in* P. Clay and J.E. Mellor 1985, 59-61.

Dannell, G.B., 1994 *Leicester Causeway Lane Decorated Samian Report*. Archive Report, Jewry Wall Museum, Leicester.

Dare, M.P., 1927 'Cemeteries of Leicester', *Trans. Leicestershire Archaeol. Soc.* 40, part 1, 39.

Darling, M.J., 1977a *A group of Late Roman Pottery from Lincoln*. Lincs.

Archaeol. Trust Monograph Ser., **16-1**.

Darling, M.J., 1977b 'Pottery from early military sites in western Britain' *in* J. Dore and K. Greene (eds) 1977, 57-100.

Darling, M.J., 1984 *Roman Pottery from the Upper Defences*. The Archaeology of Lincoln, **16/2**. London: Trust Lincolnshire Archaeol. and Counc. Brit. Archaeol.

Darling, M.J., 1993 'Caister-on-Sea excavations by Charles Green, 1951-55', *East Anglian Archaeol.* **60**.

Darling, M.J. and Jones, M.J., 1988 'Early settlement at Lincoln', *Britannia* **19**, 1-57.

Davey N., 1961 *A History of Building Materials*. London: Phoenix House.

Davey N. and Ling, R., 1982 *Wall-Painting in Roman Britain*. *Britannia* Monograph Ser. **3**.

Davey, P.J. (ed), 1979 *The Archaeology of the Clay Tobacco Pipe*, Vol **I**. Oxford: Brit. Archaeol. Reports (Brit. Ser.) **63**.

Davey, P.J. (ed), 1982 *The Archaeology of the Clay Tobacco Pipe*, Vol **VII**. Oxford: Brit. Archaeol. Rep. (Brit. Ser.) **100**.

Dechelette, J., 1904 *Les Vases céramiques ornés de la Gaule romaine*. Paris.

de la Bedoyere, G., 1989 *The Finds of Roman Britain*. London: Batsford.

de la Bedoyere, G., 1991 *The Buildings of Roman Britain*. London: Batsford.

De Rouffignac, C., 1985 'Parasite egg survival and identification from Hibernia Wharf, Southwark', *The London Archaeologist* 5, no. **4**, 103-105.

De Rouffignac, C., 1987 'Mediaeval man and his worms', *Biologist* 34, 187- 190.

Detsicas, A.P. (ed), 1973 *Romano-British Coarse Pottery*. London: Counc. Brit. Archaeol. Res. Rep. **10**.

Dickinson, B.M., 1984 'The samian ware' *in* S.S. Frere 1984, 175-97.

Dickinson, B.M., 1986 'Potters' stamps and signatures on the samian', *in* T. Dyson (ed) *The Roman Quay at St. Magnus House, London*, 186-98. London: London and Middlesex Archaeol. Soc. Special. Paper **8**.

Dickinson, B.M. and Hartley, B.R., 1987 'The samian', *in* R.J. Buckley and J.N. Lucas 1987, 75-8.

Dickinson, B.M. and Hartley, B.R., 1993 'Illustrated samian', *in* J. Monaghan 1993, 745-69.

Dixon, P., 1992 'The cities are not populated as once they were', *in* J. Rich (ed) *The City in Late Antiquity*, 145-160. Leicester and Nottingham Studies in Ancient Society 3. London: Routledge.

Dool J., Wheeler, H., *et al.* 1985 'Roman Derby: Excavations – 1968-1983', *Derbyshire Archaeol. Journ.* **105**.

Dore, J. and Greene, K.T., (eds) 1977 *Roman Pottery Studies in Britain and Beyond*. Oxford: Brit. Archaeol. Rep. (Supp. Ser.) 30.

Down, A., 1979 *The Roman Villa at Chilgrove and Upmarden*. Chichester: Chichester Excavations 4.

Down, A., 1981 *Chichester Excavations V.* Chichester.

Down, A., 1989 *Chichester Excavations VI.* Chichester.

Down, A. and Rule, M., 1971 *Chichester Excavations I.* Chichester.

Dressel, H., 1899 *Corpus Inscriptionum Latinarum*, XV, Pars **1**, Berlin.

Driesch, A. von den and Boessneck, J., 1974. 'Kritische Anmerkungen zur Widerristhöhenberechnung aus Langenmassen vor- und frühgeschichtlicher Tierknochen', *Säugetierkundliche Mitteilungen* 22, 325-48.

Dunning, G.C., 1948 'The medieval pottery', *in* K.M. Kenyon 1948, 222-248.

du Plat Taylor, J. and Cleere, H., (eds) 1978 *Roman shipping and trade: Britain and the Rhine provinces*. London: Counc. Brit. Archaeol. Res. Rep. 24.

Durand-Lefebvre, M., 1963 *Marques de Potiers gallo-romains trouvée à Paris*. Paris.

Dyer, C.C., 1988 'The consumption of fresh-water fish in medieval England', *in* M. Aston (ed.) *Medieval Fish, Fisheries and Fishponds in England*, 27-38. Oxford: Brit. Archaeol. Rep.(Brit. Ser.), **182 (i)**.

Dyer, C., 1989 *Standards of Living in the Later Middle Ages*. Cambridge: Cambridge University Press.

Edwards, J., 1984. *The Roman Cookery of Apicius Translated and adapted for the modern kitchen*. London: Rider.

Egan, G. and Pritchard, F., 1991 *Dress Accessories c.1150 -c.1450*. Medieval Finds from London 3. London: HMSO.

Ellis, C.D.B. 1976 *History in Leicester*. Leicester: Leicester City Council

Empereur, J-Y. and Tuna, N., 1989 'Hieroteles, potier Rhodien de la Peree', *Bull. Corres. Hellenique* 113, 277-299.

Enser, M., 1991 'Animal carcass fats and fish oils' *in* J.L.R. Pritchard and J.B. Rossell (eds.) *Analysis of Oilseeds, Fats and Fatty Foods*, 329-394. London: Elsevier.

Evans, J., 1995 'Discussion of the pottery in the context of Roman Alcester', in S. Cracknell and C. Mahany *Roman Alcester: Southern Extramural Areas*, 144-9. London: Counc. Brit. Archaeol. Res. Rep. **97**.

Evans, I., 1976 *Charnwood's Heritage*. Leicester: Leicestershire County Council.

Evershed, R.P., 1992 'Chemical composition of a bog body adipocere', *Archaeometry* 34, 253-265.

Evershed, R.P., Heron C. and Goad, L.J., 1990 'Analysis of organic residues of archaeological origin by high temperature gas chromatography/mass spectrometry', *Analyst* 115, 1339-1342.

Evison, V.I., 1977 'Supporting Arm Brooches and Equal-Arm Brooches in England', in *Studien Zur Sachsenforschung*, 127-147.

Farrah, R.A.H. 1973 'The techniques and sources of Romano-British black-burnished ware', *in* A.P. Detsicas (ed) 1973, 67-103.

Farrah, R.A.H. 1981 'The first Darfield Hoard and the dating of black-burnished ware', *in* A.C. Anderson and A.S. Anderson 1981, 417-30.

Faulkner, N., unpub. 'The decline of Roman Leicester', unpub. paper; Jewry wall Museum, Leicester.

Faventinus, M. *in* H. Plommer 1973.

Feugere, M., 1985 *Les Fibules en Gaule Meridionale de la conquete a la fin du Ve siecle apres J.C.* Paris: Revue Archeologique de Narbonnaise Supplement **12**.

Fiches, J-L., 1978 'Les coupes Drag. 29 en Languedoc-Roussillon' *Figlina* 3, 43-70.

Fiches, J-L., Guy, M. and Poncin, L., 1978 'Un lot de vases sigillees de premieres annees du regne de Neron dans l'un des Ports de Narbonne', *Archaeonautica* **2**.

Fielding-Johnson, Mrs. T., 1891 *Glimpses of Ancient Leicester in Six Periods*. Leicester.

Finn, N., 1993 'An archaeological evaluation at 71-95 Sanvey Gate, Leicester', *Trans. Leicestershire Archaeol. and Hist. Soc.* **67**, 93-4.

Finn., N.J., 1994 'Bonners Lane, Leicester', *Trans. Leicestershire Archaeol. and Hist. Soc.* **68**, 165-70.

Finn, N.J, forthcoming *Excavations in Bonner's Lane, Leicester*.

Forbes, R.J., 1956, 'Hydraulic engineering and sanitation' *in* C. Singer, et al 1956, 663-695.

Foster, P.J., 1976 'Romano-British finds at Kettering', *Northamptonshire Archaeol.* **11**, 170-7.

France, N.E. and Gobel, B.M., 1985 *The Romano-British Temple at Harlow*. Gloucester.

Fraser, S.M., forthcoming 'The small finds', *in* N.J. Cooper forthcoming *The Archaeology of Rutland Water: Excavations in the Gwash Valley, Rutland 1967-73 and 1990*.

Freed, J., 1989 'Late stamped Dressel 2-4 amphorae from a deposit dated post A.D. 200 at villa site 10 on the Via Gabina', in *Amphores romaines et historoire economique: dix ans de recherche, Coll. de L'Ecole Francaise de Rome*, **114**, 564-567.

Frere, S.S., 1972 *Verulamium Excavations*, Vol. I. Oxford: Rep. Res. Comm. Soc. Antiq. London **28**.

Frere, S.S., 1984 *Verulamium Excavations*, Vol. III Oxford: Oxford Univ. Comm. Archaeol. Monograph **1**.

Fulford, M.G. 1975 *New Forest Roman Pottery*. Oxford: Brit. Archaeol. Rep. (Brit. Ser.) **17**.

Fulford, M.G., 1977 'The location of Romano-British pottery kilns: institutional trade and the market' *in* J. Dore and K.T. Greene 1977, 301-316.

Fulford, M.G. and Bird, J., 1975 'Imported pottery from Germany in Late Roman Britain', *Britannia* **6**, 171-81.

Fulford, M.G. and Peacock, D.P.S., 1984 *Excavations at Carthage: the British Mission. The Avenue du President Habib Bourguiba, Salammbo: the pottery and other ceramic objects from the site*, Vol. 1, 2. Sheffield

Gault W.R. and Alvey R.C., 1979, 'County lists of clay tobacco pipe makers', *in* P.J.Davey (ed) 1979, 363-411.

Gidney, L.J., 1991. *Leicester, The Shires 1988 Excavations. The Animal Bones from the Roman Deposits*. London: English Heritage Ancient Monuments Laboratory Report **56/91**.

Gidney, L.J., 1991a. *Leicester, The Shires 1988 Excavations: The Animal Bones from the Medieval Deposits at Little Lane*. . London: English Heritage Ancient Monuments Laboratory Report **57/91**.

Gidney, L.J., 1991b. *Leicester, The Shires 1988 Excavations: The Animal Bones from the Medieval Deposits at St Peter's Lane*. London: English Heritage Ancient Monuments Laboratory Report **116/91**.

Gidney, L.J., 1991c. *Leicester, The Shires 1988 Excavations. The Animal Bones from the Post-Medieval Deposits at St Peter's Lane*. London: English Heritage Ancient Monuments Laboratory Report **131/91**.

Gidney, L.J., 1992. *Leicester, The Shires 1988 Excavations. The Animal Bones from the Post-Medieval Deposits at Little Lane*. London: English Heritage Ancient Monuments Laboratory Report **24/92**.

Gidney, L.J., 1993. *Leicester, The Shires 1988 Excavations: Further Identifications of Small Mammal and Bird Bones*. London: English Heritage Ancient Monuments Laboratory Report **92/93**.

Gidney, L.J., Unpublished *Animal Bone from Causeway Lane, Leicester* (A1.1991). Archive Report, Jewry Wall Museum, Leicester.

Gillam = Gillam 1970

Gillam, J.P., 1970 *Types of Roman Coarse Pottery Vessels in northern Britain* 3rd edition. Newcastle upon Tyne: Oriel Press.

Gillam, J.P., 1976 'Coarse fumed ware in North Britain and beyond', *Glasgow Archaeol. Journ.* **4**, 57-80.

Gillam, J.P. and Mann, J.C., 1970 'The northern British frontier from Antoninus Pius to Caracalla', *Archaeol. Aeliana* ser 4, **48**, 1-44.

Glasbergen, W., 1948 'Terra Sigillata uit de Thermenopgraving te Heerlen-Coriovallum', *L'Antiquite Classique* **17**, 237-62.

Going, C.J., 1987 *The Mansio And Other Sites In The South-Eastern Sector Of Caesaromagus: The Roman Pottery.* London: Counc. Brit. Archaeol. Res. Rep. **62**.

Going, C.J., 1992 'Economic "Longwaves" in the Roman Period? A reconnaissance of the Romano-British ceramic evidence', *Oxford Journ. Archaeol.* **11.1**, 93-117.

Good J., Gregory O. and Bosworth N., 1813 *Pantalogia a New Cyclopaedia*, Vol **IX**. London.

Goodall, I.H., 1987 'Objects of iron' *in* G. Beresford 1987 *Goltho: Development of an Early Medieval Manor 850-1150*, 177-187. London: Historic Buildings Monuments Commission Archaeol. Rep. **4**.

Gooder, E., 1984a 'Clayworking in the Nuneaton area, part 1' *in* P. Mayes and K. Scott 1984, 3-18.

Gooder, E., 1984b 'The finds from the cellar of the Old Hall, Temple Balsall, Warwickshire', *Post Medieval Archaeol.*, **18**, 149-249.

Gould, J., 1967 'Excavations at Wall, Staffs, 1964-6, on the site of the Roman forts', *Transactions Lichfield and South Staffordshire Archaeol. and Hist. Soc.* **8**, 1-40.

Gose, E., 1950 *Gefasstypen der Romischen Keramik im Rheinland.* Beheifter der Bonner Jahrbucher, Band 1, Bonn) reprinted 1976, 1984.

Gossip, J., 1998 'York Road/Oxford Street (SK 585 039)', *Trans. Leicestershire Archaeol. and Hist. Soc.* **72**, 159-60.

Grant, A., 1982. 'The use of tooth wear as a guide to the age of domestic ungulates', *in* B. Wilson, C. Grigson and S. Payne 1982, 91-108.

Green J.N., 1977 *The Loss of the Verenigde Oostindische Compagnie Jacht Vergulde Draeck, Western Australia 1656.* Oxford: Brit. Archaeol. Rep., (Supp. Ser.) **36**.

Green M.J., 1984, *Clay Tobacco Pipes and Pipe Makers of Leicester.* Privately published.

Green M.J, 1991, 'Clay tobacco pipes and pipemakers of Leicester, part 2', *in Clay Pipe Research*, **2**, 37-57. The Soc. for Clay Pipe Research.

Green, C. and Hinchliffe, J., 1985 *Excavations at Brancaster 1974 and 1977.* East Anglian Archaeol. Report **23**.

Green, C.J.S., 1977 *Excavations in the Roman Kiln Field at Brampton, 1973-4*, 31-95. Gressenhall: Norfolk Archaeol Unit. East Anglian Archaeol Rep. **5**.

Green, C.M., 1980 'Ceramic objects' *in* D.M. Jones *Excavations at Billingsgate Buildings 'Triangle', Lower Thames St 1974* London: London and Middlesex Archaeol. Soc. Special Paper **4**.

Green, C.M., 1986 'The waterfront group: amphorae and analogous vessels', *in* T.Dyson (ed) *The Roman Quay at St Magnus House*, London, 100-06. London: London and Middlesex Archaeol. Soc. Special Paper **8**.

Green, C.M., 1980 'Roman pottery' *in* D. Jones and M. Rhodes, *Excavations at Billingsgate Buildings ('Triangle') Lower Thames Street, 1974*, 39-79. London: London and Middlesex Archaeol. Soc. Special Paper **4**.

Green, M.J., 1976 *A Corpus of Religious Material from Civilian Areas of Roman Britain.* Oxford: Brit. Archaeol. Rep. **24**.

Green, M.J., 1978 *Small Cult Objects from the Military Areas of Roman Britain.* Oxford: Brit. Archaeol. Rep. **52**.

Greene, K.T., 1978 'Imported fine wares in Britain to AD 250: a guide to identification' *in* P.A. Arthur and G. Marsh (eds) 1978, 15-30.

Greene, K.T., 1979 *The Pre-Flavian Fine Wares, Report On The Excavations At Usk, 1965-1976.* Cardiff: University of Wales Press.

Greene, K.T. and Hartley, B.R., 1974 'The Roman pottery' *in* 'Excavations outside the north-east gate of Segontium, 1971', *Archaeol. Cambrensis* **123**, 62-6.

Greep, S.J., 1986 'The objects of worked bone' *in* J.D. Zienkiewicz 1986, 197-212.

Greig J.R.A., 1982 'The interpretation of pollen spectra from urban archaeological deposits', *in* A.R. Hall and H. Kenward (eds) *Environmental Archaeology in the urban context*, 47-65. London: Counc. Brit. Archaeol. Res. Rep. **43**.

Greig J., 1988. 'Some evidence of the development of grassland plant communities', *in* M. Jones (ed) *Archaeology and the Flora of the British Isles*, 39-54. Oxford: Oxford University Committee for Archaeol.

Greig J., 1988b '*Plant Resources*' in G. Astill. and A. Grant (eds) *The Countryside of Medieval England*, 108-127. Blackwell.

Greig J., 1988c 'The interpretation of some Roman well fills from the midlands of England' *in* H. Küster (ed.) *Der Pähistorische Mensch und Seine Umwelt*, 367-377. Konrad Theiss Verlag Stuttgart.

Greig J.,1989 *Handbooks for Archaeologists*,4, *Archaeobotany.* European Science Foundation.

Greig J.R.A., 1991 'The British Isles', *in* W. Van Zeist, K. Wasilikowa and K.E. Behra (eds) *Progress in Old World Palaeoethnobotany*, 299-334. Rotterdam: A.A. Balkema.

Greig J., unpublished *Report On Pollen And Some Seeds From The Shires, High Street, Leicester.* Archive Report, Jewry Wall Museum, Leicester.

Grimes, W.F., 1930 'Holt, Denbighshire: the works depot of the twentieth legion at Castle Lyons', *Y Cymmrodor* **41**, 1-235

Guido, M., 1978 *Prehistoric and Roman Glass beads in Britain and Ireland.* Oxford: Rep. Res. Comm. Soc. Antiq. London **33**.

Gurney, D., 1986 *Settlement, Religion and Industry on the Fen-edge: three Romano-British Sites in Norfolk.* East Anglian Archaeol. Report **31**.

H. = figure type in Hermet 1934

Hagar, J., unpublished *Excavations in St. Nicholas Circle, Leicester: The Medieval Levels.* Archive Report, Jewry Wall Museum, Leicester.

Hagar, J., and Buckley R., 1990 'A twelfth century undercroft in Guildhall Lane, Leicester', *Trans. Leicestershire Archaeol. and Hist. Soc.* **64**, 99-101.

Hall A.R., 1988 'The problem of reconstructing past urban floras and vegetation', *in* M.Jones (ed) *Archaeology and the Flora of the British Isles*, 93-95. Oxford: Oxford University Committee for Archaeol.

Hall, S J.G. and Clutton-Brock, J., 1989 *Two Hundred Years of British Farm Livestock.* London: British Museum (Natural History).

Hammerson, M., 1988 'The Roman pottery' *in* P. Hinton (ed) *Excavations in Southwark 1973-1976 and Lambeth 1973-79*, 193-294 London: London and Middlesex Archaeol. Soc. and Surrey Archaeol. Soc. Rep. **3**.

Hammond P.J., 1982, 'Pipemaking in Nottingham after 1800', *in* P.J. Davey (ed) 1982, 19-89.

Hancock D.A., 1974. *Oyster Pests and their Control.* Laboratory Leaflet No **19** (New Ser.) Fisheries Laboratory Burnham on Crouch, Essex. Revised 1974.

Harden, D.B. & Price, J., 1971 'The glass' *in* B. Cunliffe, *Excavations at Fishbourne, 1961-1969 Volume II : The Finds*, 317-68. London: Res. Rep. Comm. Soc. Antiqs. London **27**.

Harden, D.B., 1936 'The glass' *in* C.A. Ralegh Radford 1936, 'The Roman Villa at Ditchley, Oxon', *Oxon.* **1**, 24-69.

Harden, D.B., 1947 'The glass' *in* C.F.C. Hawkes, and M.R. Hull *Camulodunum, First Report on the Excavations at Colchester 1930-1939*, 287-307. Oxford: Rep. Res. Comm. Soc. Antiqs. London **XIV**.

Harden, D.B., 1979 'Glass vessels' *in* G. Clarke 1979, *The Roman Cemetary at Lankhills, Winchester, Studies 3, Pre-Roman and Roman Winchester, part 11*, 209-20. Oxford.

Harden, D.B., 1983 'The glass hoard' *in* S. Johnson 1983 *Burgh Castle, Excavations by Charles Green 1958-61.* East Anglian Archaeol. Report **20**.

Harden, D.B., Painter, K.S., Pinder-Wilson, R.H. and Tait, H., 1968 *Masterpieces of Glass.*

Harding, A., 1993, *England in the Thirteenth Century.* Cambridge: Cambridge University Press.

Harrison, A.C., 1981 'Rochester 1974-5', *Archaeologia Cantiana* **97**, 95-136.

Hartley, B.R., 1960-1 'The samian ware', *in* K.A. Steer, 1960-1 'Excavations at Mumrills Roman fort, 1958-60', *Proc. Soc. Ant. Scot.* **94**, 100-110.

Hartley, B.R., 1972a 'The samian ware', *in* S.S. Frere 1972, 216-62

Hartley, B.R., 1972b 'The Roman occupations of Scotland: the evidence of samian ware', *Britannia* **3**, 1-55.

Hartley, B.R. and Dickinson, B.M., 1981 'The samian stamps', *in* C. Partridge, 1981, 266-8.

Hartley, K.F., 1972 'The mortarium stamps', *in* S.S Frere 1972, 371-81.

Hartley, K.F., 1973 'The marketing and distribution of mortaria', *in* A.P. Detsicas (ed) 1973, 39-51.

Hartley, K.F., 1977 'Two major potteries producing mortaria in the first century AD', *in* J. Dore, and K.T. Greene (eds) 1977, 5-17.

Hartley, K.F., 1984 'The mortarium stamps', *in* S. S. Frere 1984, 280-92.

Hartley, K.F., 1986 *Mortarium Stamps from Leicester.* Archive report, Jewry Wall Museum, Leicester.

Hartley, K.F., 1987 'The mortarium stamps', *in* R.J. Buckley and J.N. Lucas 1987, 79.

Hartley, K.F., 1993 *Mortaria from Causeway Lane, Leicester.* Archive report, Jewry Wall Museum Leicester.

Hartley K.F., 1994 'Stamped mortaria', *in* P.Clay and R.J. Pollard 1994, 66-7.

Hartopp H., (ed), 1927 *Records of the Borough of Leicester*, Vol **I**. Leicester: Corporation of the City of Leicester.

Harvey J.H., 1992 'Westminster Abbey: The Infirmarers Garden', *Garden History* 20(2), 97-115.

Harvey, B.F., 1991, 'The crisis of the early 14th Century', *in* Bruce M.S. Campbell 1991, *Before the Black Death, Studies in the 'Crisis' of the Early 14th Century*. Manchester and New York: Manchester University Press.

Harvey, Y., 1975 'Small finds', *in* C. Platt, and R. Coleman-Smith 1975, *Excavations in Medieval Southampton 1953-1969*, Vol.2, 254-293. Leicester: Leicester University Press.

Hassal, M. and Rhodes, J., 1974 'Excavations at New Market Hall, Gloucester', *Trans. Bristol and Gloucester Archaeol. Soc.* **93**, 15-100.

Hassall, M.W.C. and Tomlin, R.S.O., 1986 'Roman Britain in 1985: II Inscriptions', *Britannia* 17, 428-54.

Hassall, M.W.C. and Tomlin, R.S.O., 1989 'Roman Britain in 1988: II Inscriptions', *Britannia* 20, 327-45.

Hassall, M.W.C. and Tomlin, R.S.O., 1982 'Roman Britain in 1981: II. Inscriptions', *Britannia* 13, 396-422.

Hassall, M.W.C. and Tomlin, R.S.O., 1994 'Roman Britain in 1993: II. Inscriptions', *Britannia* 25, 293-314.

Hattatt, R., 1987 *Brooches of Antiquity, a third selection of brooches from the author's collection*. Oxford.

Haupt, D., 1984 'Römischer Topfereibezirk bei Soller, Kreis Duren Beitrage zur Archaologie des Romischen', *Rheinlands* 4, 391-476. Rheinische Ausgrabungen, Band 23.

Hawkes, C.F.C. and Hull, M.R., 1947 *Camulodunum*. Oxford: Rep. Res. Comm. Soc. Antiq. London, 14.

Haynes, J., 1952 'A thirteenth century kiln site at Potters Marston', *Trans. Leicestershire Archaeol. Soc.* **28**, 55-62.

Hebditch, M. and Mellor, J.E., 1973 'The forum and basilica of Roman Leicester', *Britannia* **4**, 1-83.

Henig, M., 1974 *A Corpus of Roman Engraved Gemstones from British Sites*. Oxford: Brit. Archaeol. Rep. **8**.

Hermet, F., 1934 *La Graufesenque*. Paris: Condatomago.

Higgins D.A., 1982 'Reconstruction and interpretation of the pipes', *in* P.J.Davey *et al.* 1982 'The Rainford clay pipe industry: some archaeological evidence' *in* P.J. Davey (ed) 1982, 197-207.

Higgins D.A., 1985, 'Leicester clay tobacco pipes', *in* P.J. Davey (ed) *The Archaeology of the Clay Tobacco Pipe*, Vol **IX**, 291- 307. Oxford: Brit. Archaeol. Rep. (Brit. Ser.) **146.**

Higgins D.A., 1987 *The Interpretation and Regional Study of Clay Tobacco Pipes: A Case Study of the Broseley District*, Ph.D. Thesis submitted at the University of Liverpool.

Hill, J.W.F., 1965 *Medieval Lincoln*. Cambridge.

Hillman G., 1981 'Reconstructing crop husbandry practices from charred remains of crops' *in* R. Mercer 1981 *Farming Practice in British Prehistory*, 123-162. Edinburgh: Edinburgh University Press.

Hillman, G., 1982 'Crop husbandry at the medieval farmstead at Cefn Graenog', *Bull. of the Board of Celtic Studies* 4, 859-908 (901-906).

Hird, L., 1977 *Report on the Pottery Found in the Pre-Hadrianic Levels at Vindolanda*. Vindolanda 5.

Hird, L., 1992 'Coarse pottery', *in* I.D. Caruana 1992 'Carlisle: excavation of a section of the annexe ditch of the first Flavian Fort, 1990', *Britannia* 23, 45-110 (58-62).

HMSO, 1954 *London Museum Medieval Catalogue*.

Hobley, B., 1973 'Excavations at "The Lunt" Roman military site, Baginton, Warwickshire, 1968-71, Second Interim Report', *Trans. Birmingham and Warwickshire Archaeol. Soc.* 85, 7-92.

Holbrook, N. and Bidwell, P.T., 1991 *Roman Finds from Exeter*. Exeter: Exeter City Council & University of Exeter; Exeter Archaeol. Rep. **4.**

Holt, R., 1990, 'Gloucester in the century after the Black Death' *in* R. Holt and G. Rosser 1990 *The Medieval Town 1200-1540*. London: Longman.

Howe, M.D., Perrin, J.R. and Mackreth, D.F., 1980 *Roman Pottery from the Nene Valley: a Guide*. Peterborough: Peterborough City Museums Occasional Paper 2.

Hull, M.R., 1958 *Roman Colchester*. Oxford: Rep. Res. Comm. Soc. Antiq. London 20.

Hull, M.R., 1963 *The Roman Potters' Kilns at Colchester*. Oxford: Rep. Res. Comm. Soc. Antiq. London 21.

Hume, A., 1863 *Ancient Meols; or, some account of the antiquities found near Dove Point, on the sea-coast of Cheshire*. London.

Hurst, J.G., 1961 'The kitchen area of Northolt Manor, Middlesex', *Medieval Archaeol* 5, 211-299.

Hurst, J.G. and Hurst, D.G., 1964 'Excavations at the deserted medieval village of Hangleton Part II', *Sussex Archaeol. Collect.* 102 94-142.

Ijzereef, F. Gerard, 1989 'Social differentiation from animal bone studies' *in* D.Serjeantson. and T.Waldron. (eds.) 1989.

Isings, C., 1957 *Roman Glass fron Dated Finds*. Groningen, Djakarta.

Jackson, D. and Dix, B., 1987 'Late Iron Age and Roman settlement at

Weekley, Northants.', *Northamptonshire Archaeology* 21, 41-93.

Jarrett, M.G. and Wrathmell, S., 1981 *Whitton: an Iron Age and Roman Farmstead in South Glamorgan*. Cardiff.

Jenkins, F., 1986 'The ceramic figurines' *in* L. Miller, J. Schofield and M. Rhodes, *The Roman Quay at St Magnus House; Excavations at New Fresh Wharf, Lower Thames St* , London 1974-8, 205-208. London: London and Middlesex Archaeol. Soc. special paper **8**.

Jenkins, J.G., 1978 *Traditional Country Craftsmen*. London: Routledge and Kegan Paul.

Jewell, P.A., Milner, C. and Boyd, J. M. (eds) 1974. *Island Survivors: The Ecology of the Soay Sheep of St Kilda*. London: Athlone Press.

Jewry Wall Types Kenyon 1948

Johnson, S., 1980 'The mosaics of Roman Leicester', *Trans. Leicestershire Archaeol. and Hist. Soc.* **55**, 1-10.

Jones, A.K.G., 1984 'Some effects of the mammalian digestive system on fish bones', *in:* J. Desse and N. Desse-Berset (ed.) *2èmes Rencontres d'Archéo- ichthyologie.* C.N.R.S. Centre de Recherches Archéologiques. Notes et Monographies Techniques **16**, 61-66. Valbonne: Sophia Antipolis.

Jones, A.K.G., 1985 'Trichurid ova in archaeological deposits: their value as indicators of ancient faeces.' *in* N.R.J. Fieller, D.D. Gilbertson, and N.G.A. Ralph, (eds.) *Palaeobiological Investigations. Research Design, Methods and Data Analysis*, 105-116. Oxford: Brit. Archaeol. Rep. (International Ser.) **266**.

Jones, A.K.G., 1990 'Coprolites and faecal concretions' *in* M. Bell 1990, *Brean Down Excavations 1983-1987*, 242-245. London: English Heritage.

Jones, A.K.G. and Scott, S.A., 1985 'The fish bones', *in* M. Atkin, A. Carter and D.H. Evans: *Excavations in Norwich 1971-1978*, Part **II**, 223-228. East Anglian Archaeol. Report **26**.

Jones, A.K.G., Hutchinson, A.R. and Nicholson, C., 1988 'The worms of Roman horses and other intestinal parasite eggs from unpromising deposits', *Antiquity* 62, no. 235, 275-276.

Jones, C., 1984 'Romano-British bone hinges from London', *Trans. London and Middlesex Archaeol. Soc.* 35, 19-22.

Jones, G., 1982 *The Plant Remains from the Roman Villa at Norfolk Street Leicester*. London: English Heritage Ancient Monuments Laboratory Report No. **4973**.

Jones, M., 1988 'The arable field: a botanical battlefield', *in* M. Jones *Archaeology and the Flora of the British Isles*. Oxford: Oxford Univ. Committee for Archaeol.

Jones, M., 1981. 'The development of crop husbandry' *in* M. Jones and G. Dimbleby *The Environment of Man*, 95-127. Oxford: Brit. Archaeol. Rep. (Brit. Ser.) **87**.

Jones, M.U., 1972 'Potters' graffiti from Mucking, Essex', *Antiq. Journ.* 52, 335-8.

Jones, R.T., 1975 *Identification of Eggshells, Wicken Bonhunt*. London: English Heritage Ancient Monuments Laboratory Report No. **1889.**

Karnitsch, P., 1959 *Die Reliefsigillata von Ovilava*. Linz

Karnitsch, P., 1970 *Sigillata von Iuvavum (Die reliefverzierte Sigllata im Salzburger Museum Carolino Augusteum)*, Salzburg Museum Jahresschrift 1970, Salzburg 1971.

Keepax, C.A., 1977 *Identification of Avian Egg Shell from Archaeological Sites and the Potential Use of the Scanning Electron Microscope.* London: English Heritage Ancient Monuments Laboratory Report No. **2415.**

Keepax, C.A. 1981 'Avian egg-shell from archaeological sites', *Journ. of Archaeol. Science* 8, 315-36.

Kenyon, K.M., 1948 *Excavations at the Jewry Wall Site, Leicester*. Oxford: Rep. Res. Comm. Soc Antiq. London **15.**

Kilmurry, K., 1980 *The Pottery Industry of Stamford, Lincolnshire, AD 850-1250*. Oxford: Brit.Archaeol.Rep. (Brit. Ser.), **84**.

King, A. 1978 'A comparative survey of bone assemblages from Roman sites in Britain', *Bull. Instit. Archaeol London* 15, 207-232.

King, A., 1991, 'Food production and consumption – meat' *in* R.F.J. Jones (ed.) *Roman Britain: Recent Trends*. Sheffield: J.R. Collis Publications, University of Sheffield.

Knorr, R., 1905 *Die verzierten Terra-sigillata-Gefasse von Cannstatt und Kongen-Grinario*. Stuttgart.

Knorr R., 1907 *Die verzierten Terra-sigillata-Gefässe von Rottweil*. Stuttgart.

Knorr, R., 1912 *Sudgallische Terra-sigillata-Gefase von Rottweil*. Stuttgart.

Knorr, R., 1919 *Topfer und Fabriken verzierter Terra-sigillata des ersten Jahrhunderts*. Stuttgart.

Knorr, R., 1921 *Cannstatt zur Römerzeit*. Vol. 1. Stuttgart.

Knorr, R., 1952 *Terra-sigillata-Gefase des ersten Jahrhunderts mit Topfernamen*. Stuttgart.

Laubenheimer, F., 1979 'La collection de céramiques sigillées gallo-romaines estampillées du Musée de Rabat', *Antiquités Africaines* 13, 99-225.

Laubenheimer, F., 1985 *La Production Des Amphores En Gaul Narbonnaise*. Paris.

LCSAP Leicester City Sanitary Authority Plans (LRO): see chronological indexes for full ordering details.

Leach, H., 1987 'Stamford Ware fabrics', *Medieval Ceramics* **11**, 69-74.

Lentowicz I, forthcoming 'The Small Finds' *in* Cooper, N J, forthcoming, *Excavations at Blue Boar Lane, Leicester*.

Lepper, F.A. and Frere, S.S., 1988 *Trajan's Column*. Alan Sutton.

Lethbridge, T.C., 1956 'Shipbuilding' *in* C. Singer *et al* 1956, 563-589.

Ling R., 1985 *Romano-British Wall Painting*. Shire Publications Ltd.

Locker, A. and Jones, A., undated *Ipswich: The Fish Remains*. Manuscript.

Loeschcke, S., 1909 'Keramische funde in Haltern', *Mitteilungen der Altertumskommission fur Westfalen* **V**, 103-322.

Loughlin, N., 1977 'Dales Ware: a contribution to the study of Roman coarse pottery', *in* D. P. S. Peacock (ed), 1977a, 85-146.

LRO Leicestershire Record Office.

Lucas, J.N., 1976-7 'Excavations at Great Holme Street, Leicester', *Trans. Leicestershire Archaeol. and Hist. Soc.* **52**, .86-7.

Lucas, J.N., 1978-9 'The town walls of Leicester; the evidence for a west wall', *Trans. Leicestershire Archaeol. and Hist. Soc.*, **54**, 61-6.

Lucas, J.N., 1980-81a 'The debris of history: an archaeological topographic survey of Leicester', *Trans. Leicestershire Archaeol. and Hist. Soc.*, **56**, 1-9.

Lucas, J.N., 1980-81b 'Norfolk St. Roman Villa, Leicester', *Trans. Leicestershire Archaeol. and Hist. Soc.*, **56**, 103-4.

Lucas, J.N., *et al* 1989. 'An excavation in the north-east quarter of Leicester: Elbow Lane, 1977', *Trans. Leicestershire Archaeol. and Hist. Soc.* **63**, 18-47.

Lucas, J.N., forthcoming a *Excavations on a Roman Extra-Mural site at Great Holme Street, Leicester, 1975-76*.

Lucas, J.N., forthcoming b *The Roman Tile from the Norfolk Street Villa*.

Lucas, J.N. and Buckley, R.J., 1989 'The Shires excavation – an interim report', *Trans. Leicestershire Archaeol. and Hist. Soc.* **63**, 105-106.

Lucas, J.N. and Buckley, R.J., forthcoming, *Excavations at St. Peters Lane and Little Lane (The Shires), Leicester*.

Ludowici, W., 1927 *Stempel-Namen und Bilder römischer Töpfer, Legions-Ziegel-Stempel, Formen von Sigillata- und anderen Gefüssen aus meinen Ausgrabungen in Rheinzabern 1901-1914.*

Luff, R.M., 1982. *A Zooarchaeological Study of the Roman North-Western Provinces*. Oxford: Brit. Archaeol. Rep. (International Ser.) **137**.

Lyne, M.A.B. and Jefferies, R.S., 1979 *The Alice Holt/Farnham Road Pottery Industry*. London: Counc. Brit. Archaeol. Res. Rep. **30**.

Mabey R., 1987 *The Gardener's Labyrinth by Thomas Hill*. Oxford University Press.

McCarthy, M., 1979 'The pottery', *in* J.H. Williams 1979, 151-240.

McCarthy, M.R., 1990 *A Roman, Anglian and Medieval Site at Blackfriars Street, Carlisle. Excavations 1977-9*. Kendal: Cumberland and Westmorland Antiquarian and Archaeol. Soc., Res. Ser. **4**.

McCarthy, M.R., and Brooks, C.M., 1988. *Medieval Pottery in Britain AD 900-1600*. Leicester: Leicester University Press.

MacDonald, G. and Curle, A.O., 1929 'The Roman fort at Mumrills, near Falkirk', *Proc. Soc. Antiqs. Scotland* **63**, 396-575.

MacGregor, A., 1985 *Bone, Antler, Ivory and Horn*. Croom Helm.

Mackie, D.J.A., 1989 *The Analysis of Faecal Material from the Excavation on St. Nicholas Circle, Leicester*. Leicester University. Unpublished Report.

McKinley, J., 1989 'Cremations: expectations, methodologies and realities', *in*: C.A Roberts, F.Lee and J.Bintligffe (eds.) *Burial Archaeology; Current Research, Methods and Developments*, 65-76. Oxford: Brit. Archaeol.Rep. (Brit. Ser.) **211**.

Mackreth, D.F., 1981 'The brooches' *in* C. Partridge 1981, 130-151.

Mackreth, D.F., 1985a, 'Brooches' *in* K. Blockley 1985, 136-150.

Mackreth, D.F., 1985b 'Brooches from Roman Derby', *in* J. Dool *et al* 1985, 281-299.

Mackreth, D. F., 1988 'Excavations of an Iron Age and Roman Enclosure at Werrington, Cambridgeshire', *Britannia* **19**, 59-151.

Mackreth, D.F., 1989a 'Brooches', *in* K. Blockley 1989, 87-99.

Mackreth, D.F., 1989b 'The Roman Brooches from Chichester', *in* A. Down 1989, 182-194.

Mackreth, D.F., 1990 'Brooches', *in* M. McCarthy 1990, 105-113.

Mackreth, D.F., 1991 'Brooches', *in* N. Holbrook and P. Bidwell 1991, 232-241.

Mackreth, D.F. and Butcher, S.A., 1981 'The Roman brooches', *in* A. Down 1981, 254-261.

MacRobert, E.H., 1985 'The ceramic evidence', *in* S. Taylor and B. Dix 1985, 'Iron Age and Roman settlement at Ashley, Northants', *Northamptonshire Archaeol.* **20**, 87-111 (100-10).

MacRobert, E.H., 1987 'The Roman pottery (excluding samian)', *in* R.J. Buckley and J.N. Lucas 1987, 65-75.

MacRobert, E.H., 1988 'The pottery', *in* B. Dix and S. Taylor 1988, 'Excavations at Bannaventa Whilton Lodge, Northants, 1970-71', *Britannia* **19**, 299-339 (316-34).

MacRobert, E.H., 1988-9 'Advice on the pottery', *in* D.J. Smith, L. Hird, and B. Dix, 1988-9 'The Roman villa at Great Weldon, Northamptonshire', *Northamptonshire Archaeol.* **22**, 1988-9 (1990), 23-67 (31-2, 35, 42, 45, 53, 58).

McWhirr, A., 1988 'The Roman Swithland slate industry', *Trans. Leicestershire Archaeol. and Hist. Soc.* **62**, 1-8.

Mainman, A.J., 1990 *Anglo-Scandinavian Pottery from Coppergate, The Archaeology of York* **16/5**: *The Pottery*. London: Counc. Brit. Archaeol.

Maltby, M., 1979. *The Animal Bones from Exeter 1971-75*. Exeter Archaeol. Reports vol **2**.

Maltby, M., 1989, 'Urban-rural variations in the butchering of cattle in Romano-British Hampshire', *in* D. Serjeantson and T. Waldron (eds) 1989.

Mann J.E., 1977, *Clay Tobacco Pipes from Excavations in Lincoln 1970-74*. Lincolnshire Archaeol. Trust Monograph Ser., Volume **XV-1**

Manning, W.H., 1972 'The iron objects' *in* S.S. Frere 1972, 163-195

Manning, W.H., 1985 *Catalogue of the Romano-British Iron Tools, Fittings and Weapons in the British Museum*.

Marney, P.T., 1989 *Roman and Belgic Pottery from excavations in Milton Keynes 1972-82*. Aylesbury: Buckinghamshire Archaeol. Soc. Monograph **2**.

Marsden, P., forthcoming 'Roman pottery from Bonners Lane, Leicester'.

Marsh, G., 1978 'Early second century fine wares in the London area', *in* P.A. Arthur and G. Marsh (eds.), 1978.

Marsh, G., 1981 'London's samian supply and its relationship to the development of the Gallic samian industry' *in* A.C. Anderson, and A.S. Anderson 1981, 173-238.

Marsh G. and Tyers, P., 1978 'The Roman pottery from Southwark', *in* J. Bird, A.H. Graham, H.L. Sheldon & P. Townsend 1978, *Southwark Excavations 1972-74*, 533-582. London: London & Middlesex Archaeol. Soc. & Surrey Archaeol. Soc., **1**.

Martin, E.A., 1988 *Burgh: The Iron Age and Roman Enclosure*. Ipswich: East Anglian Archaeol. Rep. **40**; Suffolk County Planning Dept.

Martin, G., 1991 *Causeway Lane 1991 Evaluation*. Unpublished Archive Report, Jewry Wall Museum, Leicester.

Martin, J., 1990 'St Michael's church and parish, Leicester', *Trans. Leicestershire Archaeol. and Hist. Soc.* **64**, 21-5.

Martin, T.S., forthcoming 'Derbyshire Ware'.

Martin-Kilcher, S., 1983 'Les amphores romaines a huile de Betique (Dressel 20 et 23) d'Augst (Colonia Augusta Rauricorum) et Kaiseraugst (Cstrum Rauracense). Un rapport preliminaire', *in* J.M. Blaquez and J. Remesal (eds) 1983 *Produccion y Comercio del Aceite en la Antiguedad. II Congreso (Madrid)*, 337-42.

Mary, G.T., 1967 *Novaesium I. Die sudgallischen Terra Sigillata aus Neuss. Limesforschungen* **6**.

Mayes, P. and Scott, K., 1984. *Pottery kilns at Chilvers Coton, Nuneaton*. Soc. Medieval Archaeol. Mon. Ser. **10**.

Meates, G.W., 1987, *Lullingstone Roman Villa*. Vol. **2** *The Wall paintings and Finds*. Maidstone: Kent Archaeol. Soc. Monograph **3**.

Mellor, J.E., 1968-9 'Excavations in Leicester 1965-1968', *Trans. Leicestershire Archaeol. and Hist. Soc.* **44**, 1-10.

Mellor, J.E., 1969-70 'St. Nicholas Circle', *Trans. Leicestershire Archaeol. and Hist. Soc.* **45**, 74-5.

Mellor, J.E., 1971-2 'St. Nicholas Circle', *in* A. McWhirr (ed) 1971-2 'Archaeology in Leicestershire and Rutland 1970-1972' *Trans. Leicestershire Archaeol. and Hist. Soc.* **47**, 62-75 (64).

Mellor, J.E., 1976 'Roman Leicester' *in* C.D.B. Ellis 1976, *History in Leicester*. Leicester: Leicester City Council.

Mellor J.E., and Pearce, T., 1981 *The Austin Friars, Leicester*. London: Counc.Brit. Archaeol. Res. Rep. **35**.

Merrifield, R., 1987 *The Archaeology of Ritual and Magic*. London: Guild Publishing.

Middleton, S.J. and Liddle, P., forthcoming 'The Empingham I Anglo-Saxon cemetery' *in* N.J. Cooper *The Archaeology of Rutland Water: Excavations in the Gwash Valley, Rutland 1967-73 and 1990.*

Miller S.N., 1922 *The Roman Fort at Balmuildy*. Glasgow.

Millett, M., 1990, *The Romanization of Britain*. Cambridge: Cambridge University Press.

Mills, J.M., 1993 'Hobnails', *in* D.E. Farwell and T.I. Molleson *Poundbury Volume 2: the Cemeteries*, 99. Dorset Natural History and Archaeol. Soc. Monograph **11**.

Mills, J.S., and White, R., 1994 *The Organic Chemistry of Museum Objects*, 33. Oxford: Butterworth-Heinemann.

Milne, G. (ed.), 1985 *The Port of Roman London*. London: Batsford.

Mocsy, A., 1983 *Nomenclator.* Budapest: Dissertationes Pannonicae Series III, Vol **1.**

Moffett L.C., 1986. *Crops and Crop Processing in a Romano-British Village at Tiddington: the evidence from charred plant remains.* London: English Heritage Ancient Monuments Laboratory Report **123/91.**

Moffett L.C., 1988 'Gardening in Roman Alcester', *Circaea,* 5 (2), 73-78.

Moffett L.C., 1991 'The archaeobotanical evidence for free-threshing tetraploid wheat in Britain', in *Palaeoethnobotany and Archaeology.* International workgroup for Palaeoethnobotany 8th Symposium 1989 Acta Interdisciplinaria Archaeologica 7, 233-243. Nitra: Slovac Academy of Sciences

Moffett L.C., 1993 *Macrofossil Plant Remains from the Shires, Leicester.* London: English Heritage Ancient Monuments Laboratory Report **31/93.**

Monaghan, J., 1993 *Roman Pottery from the Fortress: 9 Blake Street.* York: The Archaeology of York, **16/7,** York Archaeol. Trust and Counc. Brit. Archaeol.

Monaghan, J., 1994 'Ceramic disributions and the history of Roman York', paper given at the 23rd Annual Meeting of the Study Group for Roman Pottery, Durham, 9 April 1994.

Monckton A., 1994 *Oysters from the Shires Excavation, Leicester.* Archive Report, Jewry Wall Museum, Leicester.

Monckton A., 1995 'Environmental evidence in Leicestershire', *Trans. Leicestershire Archaeol. and Hist. Soc.* **69,** 32-41.

Monckton A., 1996 'Evidence for food and fodder from plant remains', *Circaea* 12 92, 252-258.

Monckton A., forthcoming 'Environmental evidence from the Shires Excavations, Leicester'.

Moore W.R.G., 1980, *Northamptonshire Clay Tobacco-Pipes and Pipemakers.* Northampton: Northampton Museums and Art Gallery

Moorhouse, S., 1972 'Pottery distilling apparatus of glass and pottery', *Medieval. Archaeol.* **16,** 79-121.

Moorhouse, S., 1983. 'The medieval pottery' *in* P. Mayes and L.A.S. Butler 1983, *Sandal Castle Excavations 1964-1973,* 83-212. West Yorkshire: Wakefield Historical Publications.

Moorhouse, S., 1986. 'Non dating uses of medieval pottery', *Medieval Ceramics* 10, 85-123.

Morales, A. and Rosenlund, K., 1977 *A Guide to the Measurement of Fish Bones.* Copenhagen: Steenstrupia.

Morgan G.C., 1992 *Romano-British Mortar and Plaster.* Unpublished doctoral thesis, University of Leicester.

Morgan M.H., 1960 *Vitruvius; The Ten Books On Architecture.* New York: Dover.

MPRG 1998 *A Guide to the Classification of Medieval Ceramic Forms.* Medieval Pottery Research Group Occasional Paper **1.**

Muldoon S., 1979 'Marked clay pipes from Coventry' *in* P.J. Davey (ed.) 1979, 255-278.

Murphy P., 1995 'Marine molluscs', *in* J. Wymer and N. Brown (eds) *Excavations at North Shoebury,* 142. East Anglian Archaeol. **75.**

Murphy, P., 1978 *Norwich: Avian Eggshell.* London: English Heritage Ancient Monuments Laboratory Report **2673.**

Murphy, P., 1991 *Stansted Airport, Essex: Molluscs and Avian Eggshell.* London: English Heritage Ancient Monuments Laboratory Report **37/91.**

Muus, B.J. and Dahlstrøm, P., 1985 *Collins Guide to the Sea Fishes of Britain and North-Western Europe.* London: Collins.

Mynard, D.C., (ed.) 1987 *Roman Milton Keynes, Excavations and Fieldwork 1971-82.* Aylesbury: Buckinghamshire Archaeol. Soc. Monograph Ser. **1**

NV 'types' c.f. Howe et al 1980

Niblett, R., 1990, 'Verulamium', *Current Archaeol.* **120**

Nichols, J., 1795 *The History and Antiquities of the County of Leicester,* . vol. **Ii.** Leicester

Nichols, J., 1798 *The History and Antiquities of the County of Leicester,* . vol. **Iii.** Leicester.

Nicholson, R.A., 1992 *Fish Remains from excavations at The Shires: Little Lane (A39) and St. Peter's Lane (A40), Leicester.* London: English Heritage Ancient Monuments Laboratory Report **56/92.**

Nicholson, R.A., 1993 'An investigation into the effects on fish bone of passage through the human gut: some experiments and comparisons with archaeological material', *Circaea* **10** (1), 38-50.

Nicholson, R.A. and Scott, S.A., forthcoming *The Animal Bones from Deansway, Worcester.*

Nieto Prieto, J., *et al* 1989   *Excavations arqueologiques subaquatiques a Cala Culip 1.* Girona.

Noddle, B., 1977. 'Mammal bone' *in* H. Clarke and A. Carter (eds) *Excavations in King's Lynn 1963-70,* 378-398. Soc. for Medieval Archaeol. Monograph **7.**

O. = figure-type in Oswald 1937a

O'Connor, T., 1982. *Animal Bones from Flaxengate, Lincoln c.870-1500.* Lincoln: The Archaeology of Lincoln, Vol. **XVIII-1.**

O'Connor, T., 1989. 'What shall we have for dinner? Food remains from urban sites', *in* D. Serjeantson and T. Waldron (eds.) 1989, 13-23.

O'Connor, T. P., 1988. *Bones from the General Accident Site, Tanner Row,* 114-116. Counc. Brit. Archaeol. and York Archaeol. Trust, The Archaeology of York, Vol. **15,** Fasicule **2.**

Oliver, A., 1984 'Early Roman faceted glass', *Journ. of Glass Studies* **26.**

Orton, C.R., 1975 'Quantative pottery studies: some progress, problems and prospects', *Science in Archaeology* **16,** 30-35.

Orton, C.R., 1977 'Intoduction to the pottery reports', *in* T.R. Blurton 1977, 28-30.

Orton, C.R., 1980 *Mathematics in Archaeology.* London: Collins.

Orton, C.R., 1985 'Two useful parameters for pottery vessel research', *in* E. Webb (ed) 1985, 114-120.

Osbourn D., 1989 *Components.* London: Mitchell's Building Series, Mitchell Publishing.

Oswald, F., 1937a *Index of Figure-types on Terra Sigillata ('Samian ware').* Liverpool: Gregg Press Reprint 1964.

Oswald, F, 1937b 'Carinated bowls (Form 29) from Lezoux', *Journ. Roman Stud.* **27,** pt. 2, 210-4.

Oswald, F. and Pryce, T.D., 1920 *An introduction to the study of terra sigillata.* London: Gregg Press reprint, 1965.

Ottaway, P., 1992 *Anglo-Scandinavian Ironwork from 16-22 Coppergate.* The Archaeology of York **17/6.**

Ottaway, P., 1992 *Archaeology in British Towns from the Emperor Claudius to the Black Death.* London and New York: Routledge.

Panella, C., 1972 'Annotazioni in margine alle stratigrafie delle terme Ostiensi del nuaotore', *Collection de l'Ecole Française de Rome* **10,** 69-106.

Partridge, C.R., 1981 *Skeleton Green.* London: *Britannia* Monograph Ser. **2,** Soc. Promotion Roman Stud.

Payne S., 1988. *Some notes on Sampling and Sieving for Animal Bones.* London: English Heritage Ancient Monuments Laboratory Report **55/92.**

Peacey A.A., 1982 'The structural development of clay tobacco pipe kilns in England; a preliminary study' *in* P.J. Davey (ed.) 1982, 3-17.

Peacey A.A., 1996 'The development of the clay tobacco pipe kiln in the British Isles', *in* P.Davey (ed.) *The Archaeology of the Clay Tobacco Pipe* XIV. Oxford: Brit. Archaeol. Rep (Brit. Ser.) 246; Tempvs Reparatvm:

Peacock, D.P.S., 1974 'Amphorae and the Baetican fish industry', *Antiq. Journ.* **54,** 232-43.

Peacock, D.P.S., (ed.), 1977a *Pottery and Early Commerce, Characterisation and Trade in Roman and Later Ceramics.* London: Academic Press.

Peacock, D.P.S., 1977b 'Pompeian Red Ware', *in* D.P.S. Peacock (ed.) 1977a, 147-62.

Peacock, D.P.S., 1977c 'Roman amphorae: typology, fabric, origins', *Collection de l'Ecole Francaise de Rome* **32,** 261-78. Rome.

Peacock, D.P.S., 1977d 'Late Roman amphorae from Chalk, near Gravesend, Kent', *in* J. Dore and K. Greene (eds.) 1977, 295-300.

Peacock, D.P.S., 1978 'The Rhine and the problem of Gaulish wine in Roman Britain' *in* J. du Plat Taylor and H. Cleere (eds.) 1978, 49-51.

Peacock, D.P.S. and Williams, D.F., 1986 *Amphorae and the Roman economy: an introductory guide.* London: Longman.

Pearce, J.E., Vince, A.G. and Jenner, M.A., 1985 *London Type Ware.* London: London and Middlesex Archaeol. Soc. Special Paper **6**

Pearce, J.E., Vince, A.G., *et al* 1988 *A Dated Type Series of London Medieval Pottery Part 4: Surrey Whitewares.* Museum of London and London and Middlesex Archaeol. Soc.

Pearson, J., forthcoming *The Saxon Pottery from Northampton.*

Percival More, A., 1907-8 'The metropolitan visitations of Archbishop Laud', *Association of Archit. Socs. Reports and Papers* **29,** 479-534

Perrin, J.R., 1981 *Roman Pottery from the Colonia: Skeldergate & Bishophill.* York Archaeol. Trust & Counc. Brit. Archaeol., The Archaeology of York, **16/2**

Perrin, J.R., 1990 *Roman Pottery from the Colonia 2: General Accident & Rougier Street.* York Archaeol. Trust & Counc. Brit. Archaeol., The Archaeology of York, **16/4**

Perrin, J.R. and Webster, G., 1990 'Roman Pottery from excavations in Normangate Field, Castor, Peterborough, 1962-3', *Journ. Roman Pottery Stud.* **3,** 35-62

Perring, D., 1991(a) 'The buildings', *in* D. Perring, S. Roskams and P. Allen 1991, 67-106.

Perring, D., 1991(b) 'Watling Court', *in* D. Perring, S. Roskams, and P. Allen 1991, 26-44

Perring, D., Roskams, S. and Allen, P., 1991 *The Archaeology of Roman London. Vol 2: Early Development of Roman London West of the Walbrook.* London: Counc. Brit. Archaeol. Res. Rep. **70**

PH Property Holdings Deeds, St. Catherine's House, London.

Philp, B., 1989 *The Roman House with Bacchic Murals at Dover*. Kent Archaeol. Unit.

Pike, A.W. and Biddle, M., 1966 'Parasite eggs in medieval Winchester', *Antiquity* 40, no. 160, 293-296.

Pitkin, B.R. 1988 *Lesser Dung Flies (Diptera, Sphaeroceridae)*. Handbook for Identification of British Insects. 10(5e)

Pliny *Natural History*. London: Loeb

Plommer, H., 1973 *Vitruvius and Later Roman Building Manuals*. Oxford

Pollard, R.J., 1987 'The other Roman pottery', *in* G.W. Meates 1987

Pollard, R.J., 1992 'Pot spot: keen eyes and kilns- a Roman pottery kiln site on the High Street, Leicester', *Down to Earth: Leicestershire Archaeol. News* 5, 2-3

Pollard, R.J., 1983 'The coarse pottery, including the kiln products' *in* P.D. Catterall 1983, 'A Romano-British pottery manufacturing site at Oakley farm, Higham, Kent', *Britannia* 14, 121-138 (103-41)

Pollard, R.J., 1994 'The Late Iron Age and Roman pottery', *in* P. Clay and R.J. Pollard 1994, 51-114

Pollard, R.J., forthcoming a 'The Roman pottery', *in* J.E. Mellor, forthcoming *Excavations in St. Nicholas Circle, Leicester 1. The Roman Forum*.

Pollard, R.J., forthcoming b 'The Roman pottery', *in* J.N. Lucas, forthcoming a

Pollard, R.J., forthcoming c 'The Roman pottery from Excavations on Silver Street, Leicester'.

Pollard, R.J., forthcoming d 'The Roman pottery from Excavations at the Norfolk Street Villa, Leicester

Pollard, R.J., forthcoming e 'The Roman pottery', *in* J.N. Lucas and R.J. Buckley, forthcoming.

Price, J., 1987 'The glass' *in* D.C. Maynard 1987, *Roman Milton Keynes, Excavations and Fieldwork 1971-1982*, 147-57. Buckinghamshire Archaeol. Soc. Monograph Ser. 1.

Price, J., 1979 'The glass', *in* 'Frocester Court, Roman Villa', *Trans. Bristol and Gloucestershire Archaeol. Soc.* 97, 37-45

Price, J., 1980 'The Roman glass' *in* G. Lambrick, 'Excavations at Park Street, Towcester', *Northamptonshire Archaeol.* 15, 35-118 (63-8)

Price, J., 1982 'The glass' *in* G.Webster and L. Smith 'The excavation of a Romano-British rural settlement at Barnsley Park : Part 2', *Trans. Bristol and Gloucestershire Archaeol. Soc.* 100, 174-184

Price, J., 1985a 'Glass from Felmongers, Harlow in Essex. A dated deposit of vessel glass found in an Antonine pit', *Annales du 10e congres l`association internationale pour l`histoire du verre*. Amsterdam

Price, J., 1985b 'The glass' *in* P.T. Bidwell 1985, *The Roman fort of Vindolanda at Chesterholm, Northumberland*. London.

Price, J., 1985c 'The Roman glass', *in* L.F. Pitts and J.K. St. Joseph 1985, *Inchtuthil, the Roman Legionary Fortress Excavations 1952-65*, 305-12. London: Soc. for Promotion of Roman Studies, *Britannia* Monograph 6

Price, J., 1989a 'The glass' *in* T.J. O'Leary 1989, *Pentre Farm Flint 1976-81 An official building in the Roman Lead mining district*, 77-86. Oxford: Brit. Archaeol. Rep.(Brit. Ser.) 207

Price, J., 1989b 'The glass' *in* I.M. Stead and V. Rigby 1989, 108-9

Price, J. and Cool, H.E.M., 1983 'Glass from the excavations of 1974-76', *in* A.E. Brown and C. Woodfield 'Excavations at Towcester, Northamptonshire: The Alcester Road Suburb', *Northamptonshire Archaeol.* 18, 43- 140. (115-24)

Price, J. and Cool, H.E.M., 1985 'The glass', *in* H.R. Hurst 1985 *Excavations at Kingsholm, Gloucester*. Gloucester Archaeol. Reports Vol. 1.

Price, J. and Cool, H.E.M., 1986 'The Roman glass' *in* H.R. Hurst 1986 *Gloucester, The Roman and Later Defences*. Gloucester Archaeol. Reports Vol. 2.

PRO Public Record Office.

Pye, N., 1972 *Leicester and its Region*. Leicester University Press

Rackham, D.J., unpub. *The use of diagnostic zones for considerations of quantification, preservation, level of fragmentation, skeletal selection and butchery*.

Rahtz, P.A., 1959 'Humberstone earthworks', *Trans. Leicestershire Archaeol. and Hist. Soc.* 35, 1-32

RBL *Records of the Borough of Leicester*, vols 1-7, edited by M. Bateson, R.B. Stocks and A. Chinnery. Leicester 1901-74.

Rebuffat, R. and Marion, J., 1977 *Thamusida: fouilles due Service des Antiquités du Maroc*. Ecole française de Rome. Mélange d'Arcéologie et d'Histoire Suppl.3, Rome.

Rees A., 1819, 'Manufacturing industry; furnace – tobacco pipe' 3, 31. *Pipe – Tobacc.*, 4, 141, London.

Remesal, J., 1986 *La Annona Militaris y la Exportacion de Aceite Betico a Germania*. Madrid.

Reynolds, S., 1977 *An Introduction to the History of English Medieval Towns*. Oxford: Oxford University Press.

Richmond, I., 1968 *Hod Hill, volume two, Excavations carried out between 1951 and 1958 for the Trustees of the British Museum*. London.

Richardson, B., 1986 'Pottery' *in* L. Miller, J. Scofield & M. Rhodes *The Roman Quay at St. Magnus House, London*, 96-138. London: London and Middlesex Archaeol. Soc. Special Paper 8.

Ricken, H. and Ludowici, W., 1948 *Die Bilderschusseln der Romischen Topfer von Rheinzabern*. Katalog VI, Speyer.

Ricken, H. and Fischer, C., 1963 *Bilderschusseln der Romischen Topfer von Rheinzabern: Textband mit Typernbildern zu Katalog VI der Ausgrabungen von Wilhelm Ludowici in Rheinabern 1901-1914*. Matrialien zur Romischgermanischen Keramik, 7, Habelt, Bonn.

Riha, E., 1979 'Die Romischen Fibeln aus Augst und Kaiseraugst', Forschungen in Augst, Band 3, Augst.

Riley, J.A., 1979 'The coarse pottery from Benghazi', *in* J.A. Lloyd (ed)1979 *Sidi Khrebish Excavations, Benghazi (Berenice),Vol II*, 91-497. Tripoli.

Rivet, A.L.F., 1964 *Town and Country in Roman Britain*. London: Hutchinson.

Roberts J.E., 1988 'Tennant's pipe factory, Tweedmouth', *History of Berwickshire Naturalists Field Club*, 44, Pt 2, 87-102.

Rodwell, K.A., 1988 *The prehistoric and Roman settlement at Kelvedon, Essex*. London: Counc. Brit. Archaeol.Res. Rep. 63; Chelmsford Archaeol. Trust Rep.6.

Rodwell, W.J., 1978 'Stamp-decorated pottery of the early Roman period in Eastern England' *in* P.A. Arthur and G. Marsh (eds) 1978, 225-92.

Rogers = Rogers 1974

Rogers, G., 1974 *Poteries sigillees de la Gaule Centrale*. Paris.

Rogerson, A., 1977 *Excavations at Scole, 1973*, 97-224. Gressenhall: Norfolk Archaeol. Unit, East Anglian Archaeol. Rep. 5.

Rohacek, J., 1982-5 *A Monograph and reclassification of the previous genus Limosina Macquart (Diptera, Sphaeroceridae) of Europe Beitrage zur Entomologie* Pt.1 (1982) 32(1): 195-282; Pt.2.(1983) 33(1): 3-195; Pt.3 (1984) 33(2): 203-255; Pt.4 (1985) 35(1): 101-179.

Rollo, L., 1994 *Iron Age and Roman Piddington: The Mortaria 1979-1993*. Northampton: Upper Nene Archaeol. Soc.

Romanoff, A.L. and Romanoff, A.J., 1949 *The Avian Egg*. New York: Wiley.

Roskams, S., 1992 'Finds context and deposit status', *in* K. Steane (ed.) 1992, 27-30.

Rot. Hugh. *Rotuli Hugonis de Welles*, 1, ed. W.P.W. Phillimore. Lincoln 1912.

Ryder, M., 1983. *Sheep and Man*. London: Duckworth.

S & S i. = Stanfield and Simpson 1958

S & S ii = Stanfield and Simpson 1990

Sadler, P., 1991 'The use of tarsometatarsi in sexing and ageing domestic fowl (*Gallus gallus* L.), and recognising five toed breeds in archaeological material', *Circaea* 8, No. 1, 41-48.

Sawday, D., 1989 'The post Roman pottery' *in* J.Lucas 1989, 28-41.

Sawday, D., 1991. 'Potters Marston Ware', *Trans. Leicestershire Archaeol. and Hist. Soc.* 65, 34-37.

Sawday, D., 1994 'The post Roman pottery' *in* P.Clay, and R. Pollard 1994, 115-129.

Sawday, D., 1998 'The post Roman pottery', *in* L. Cooper 'New evidence for the northern defences of Roman Leicester: An archaeological excavation at Cumberland Street', *Trans. Leicestershire Archaeol. and Hist. Soc.* 72, 100-102 (92-109).

Saxl, H., 1956 'A note on parchment' *in* C. Singer *et al* 1956, 187-190

Schleiermacher, W., 1953 'Cambodunumforschungen I: Terra Sigillata', *Materialien zur Bayerischen Vorgeschichte* 9, 82-93.

Schofield, J. and Vince, A., 1994, *Medieval Towns*. London: Leicester University Press.

Sealey, P.R., 1985 *Amphoras from the 1970 Excavations at Colchester Sheepen*. Oxford: Brit. Archaeol. Rep. (Brit. Ser.) 142.

Serjeantson, D., 1989 'Animal remains and the tanning trade' *in* D. Serjeantson and T. Waldron (eds.) 1989, 129-146.

Serjeantson, D. and Waldron. T., (eds.) 1989 *Diet and Crafts in Towns*. Oxford: Brit. Archaeol. Rep. (Brit. Ser.) 199.

Shackley, M., 1975 *Archaeological Sediments*. London.

Shaw, M., 1987 'Early post-medieval tanning in Northampton', *England in Archaeol*. 40.2.

Shennan S., 1988 *Quantifying archaeology*. Edinburgh University Press.

Shortt, H. de S., 1959 'A provincial Roman spur from Longstock, Hants., and other spurs from Roman Britain', *Antiq. Journ.* 39, 61-76.

Silver, I. A., 1969. 'The ageing of domestic animals' *in* D. Brothwell and E. Higgs (eds.) *Science in Archaeology*, 283-302.

Simon, H-G., 1977 'Die Funde aus dem Bereich der Sumpfbrucke bei Bickenbach (Kreiss Darmstadt)', *Saalburg Jahrbuch* 34, 52-77.

Simon, H-G., 1978 'Fundkatalog C: Terra Sigillata', *in* H.

Schönberger, 1978 'Kastell Oberstimm. Die Grabungen von 1968 bis 1971', *Limesforschungen* **18**, 227-58.

Simpson, C.J., 1976 'Belt buckles and strap-ends of the later Roman empire: a preliminary survey of several new groups', *Britannia* 7, 192-223.

Simpson, G, 1968 'The decorated samian pottery', *in* B.W. Cunliffe 1968, 148-62.

Simpson, G., 1987 'The decorated and plain samian pottery', *in* G.W. Meates 1987, 153-63.

Singer, C., Holmyard, E.J., and Hall, A.R., (eds.) 1954-57 *A History of Technology.* Vol I (1954), II (1956), III (1957). Oxford.

Sisson, S. and Grossman, J. D., 1975 *The Anatomy of the Domestic Animals.* (5th ed.). London: W. B. Saunders.

Skeat, W.W., 1882 *The book of Husbandry by Master Fitzherbert,* Reprinted from the edition of 1534 for the English Dialect Soc. Trubner and Co. Ludgate Hill London 1882.

Skeat, W.W. (ed.), 1867 (edition of 1954) *Piers the Plowman.* Oxford University Press.

Skidmore P., 1993 'Notes on the taxonomy of the puparia of British Sphaeroceridae', *Dipterists Digest* **13**, 6-22.

Skidmore, P., (in press) *The Diptera of Buiston Crannog.* AOC (Scotland) Ltd.

Skidmore, P., 1985 'The biology of the *Muscidae* of the world series', *Ent.* **29**; 550p.

Skidmore, P., 1991 *Insects of the British Cow-dung Community.* AIDGAP Series Occasional Publication No.21; Field Studies Council.

Smith, K.G.V., 1986 *A Manual of Forensic Entomology.* London: British Museum (Natural History).

Spence, C. and Grew, F., (eds.) 1990 '1-7 Whittington Avenue', *in* Museum of London Dept. of Archaeol., *The Annual Review 1989,* 28-29.

Spencer, F.M. and Monroe, L.S., 1975 *The Color Atlas of Intestinal Parasites.* Springfield, Illinois: Charles C. Thomas.

Spry, C., 1956. *The Constance Spry Cookery Book.* London: J. M. Dent

Stace, C., 1991. *New Flora of the British Isles.* Cambridge University Press.

Stallibrass, S., 1991. *Animal Bones from Excavations at Annetwell Street, Carlisle, 1982-4. Period 3: The Earlier Timber Fort.* London: English Heritage Ancient Monuments Laboratory Report **132/91**.

Stanfield, J.A., 1937 'Romano-Gaulish decorated jugs and the work of the potter Sabinus', *Journ. Roman Stud.* **27.2**.

Stanfield, J.A., and Simpson, G., 1958 *Central Gaulish Potters.* Oxford Univ. Press.

Stanfield, J.A. and Simpson, G., 1990 *Les Potiers de la Gaule Centrale.* Recherches sur les ateliers de potiers de la Gaule Centrale V, Gonfaron.

Stanfield, J.A., 1929 'Unusual forms of Terra Sigillata', *Archaeol. Journ.* **86**, 113-50.

Stead, I.M., 1976 *Excavations at Winterton Roman Villa, and other Roman sites in north Lincolnshire, 1958-1969.* London: Dept. of the Environment Archaeol. Rep. 9, London.

Stead, I.M. and Rigby, V., 1986 *Baldock. The Excavation of a Roman and pre-Roman Settlement. 1968-72.* London: Soc. Promotion Roman Stud., *Britannia* Monograph Ser. 7.

Stead, I.M., and Rigby, V., 1989 *Verulamium: the King Harry Lane Site.* London: English Heritage Archaeol. Rep.12.

Steane, K., 1992 *The Interpretaion of Stratigraphy: A Review of the Art.* Lincoln: City of Lincoln Archaeol. Unit Rep. **31**.

Steane, J.M., 1967 'Excavations at Lyveden, 1965-1967', *Northampton County Borough Museums and Art Gallery Journ.* 2.

Steane, J.M. and Byrant, G.F., 1975 'Excavations at the deserted medieval settlement at Lyveden fourth report', *Northampton County Borough Museums and Art Gallery Journ.* **12**, 60-95.

Steer, K., 1960-1 'Excavations at Mumrills Roman Fort 1958-60', *Proc. Soc. Antiq. Scot.* **94**, (1963 for 1960-1), 86-132.

Stevenson, G.H. and Miller, S.N., 1912 'Report on the excavation of the Roman fort of Cappuck, Roxbrughshire', *Proc. Soc. Antiquaries of Scotland* **46**, 446-483.

Swan, V.G., 1988 *Pottery in Roman Britain,* 4th Edition. Aylesbury: Princes Risborough, Shire Archaeol. **3**.

Symonds, R.P., 1990 'The problems of Roughcast Beakers, and related Colour-Coated wares', *Journ. Roman Pottery Stud.* 3, 1-17.

Symonds, R.P., 1992 *Rhenish Wares. Fine Dark Coloured Pottery from Gaul and Germany.* Oxford: Oxford Univ. Comm. Archaeol. Monograph **23**.

Symonds, R.P., and Tomber, R.S., 1991 'Late Roman London: an assessment of the ceramic evidence from the City of London', *Trans. London Middlesex Archaeol. Soc.* 42, 1991 (1994), 59-99.

Taylor, F. Sherwood and Singer, C., 1956 (1979) 'Pre-scientific industrial chemistry' *in* C. Singer *et al* 1954-57.

Taylor, K.D., Fenn, M.G. and MacDonald, D.W., 1991. 'Genus *Rattus* (Rats)', *in* G.B. Corbet and S. Harris (eds), *The Handbook of British Mammals.* Oxford: Blackwell Scientific Publications.

Tchernia, A. and Zevi, F., 1972 'Amphores vinaires de Campanie et de Tarraconaise a Ostia', *Collection de l'Ecole Française de Rome* **10**, 35-67.

Terrisse, J-R., 1968 *Les Ceramiques Sigillees Gallo Romaine des Martres-de-Veyre.* Paris.

Thawley, C.R., 1981. 'The mammal, bird and fish bones' *in* J.E. Mellor and T. Pearce 1981, 173-4.

Thienpont, D., Rochette, F. and Vanparijs, O.F.J., 1986 *Diagnosing Helminthiasis by Coprological Examination.* Janssen Research foundation.

Thomas, C., 1981 *A Provisional List of Imported Pottery in Post-Roman Western Britain and Ireland.* Redruth.

Thompson, A. Hamilton, 1933 A *Calendar of Charters and Other Documents belonging to the Hospital of William Wyggeston at Leicester.* Leicester.

Thompson, J., 1879 *The History of Leicester.* Leicester: F. Hewitt.

Thompson, R., 1981 'Leather manufacture in the post-medieval period, with special reference to Northamptonshire', *Post-Medieval Archaeol.* **15**, 161-175.

Thorpe, W.A., 1935 *English Glass.*

Timby, J.R., 1985 'TF 10, Amphorae', *in* H.R. Hurst, *Kingsholm,* 72-6. Cambridge: Gloucester Archaeol. Rep. **1**.

Todd, M., 1968 'The commoner coarse wares of the East Midlands', *Antiquaries Journ.* **48**, 192-209.

Todd, M., 1973 'Coarse pottery', *in* M. Hebditch and J.E. Mellor 1973, 71-81.

Tomlin, R.S.O., 1991 'Roman Britain in 1990: II Inscriptions', *Britannia* **22**, 293-311.

Tomlin, R.S.O., 1992 'The Roman carrot amphora and its Egyptian provenance', *Journ. Egyptian Archaeol.* **78,** 307-312.

Tyers P., 1978 'The poppy-head beakers of Britain and their relationship to the barbotine decorated vessels of the Rhineland and Switzerland' *in* P.A. Arthur and G. Marsh (eds.) 1978, 61-108.

Tyers, P., 1984 'An assemblage of Roman ceramics from London', *London Archaeol.* **4**, No. 14, 367-75.

Ulbert, G., 1959 *Die römischen Donau-Kastelle Aislingen und Berghöfe.* Berlin: Limesforschungen **1**.

Vanderhoeven, M., 1974-8 *Funde aus Asciburgium.* Duisburg.

Vanderhoeven, M., 1975 *De Terra Sigillata te Tongeren.* Tongeren.

Vanderhoeven, M., 1976 'Terra Sigillata aus Sudgallien: Die reliefverzierten Gefasse II', *Funde aus Asciburgium.* Duisburg.

VCH Victoria County History of Leicestershire, vol. 4 1958..

Veale, E.M., 1966. *The English Fur Trade in the Later Middle Ages.* Oxford: Clarendon Press.

Vince, A.G. and Jenner, M.A., 1991. 'Aspects of Saxon and Norman London: the Saxon and early medieval pottery of London', *London and Middlesex Archaeol. Soc. Special Paper* **12**, 19-119.

Vince, A.G., 1984 'The use of petrology in the study of medieval ceramics: case studies from southern England', *Medieval Ceramics* 8, 31-45.

Vince A.G., *et al* 1988 *Surrey Whiteware.*

Viner, L., 1982 'The objects of bone, shale, clay, stone and lead', *in* J.S. Wacher and A.D. McWhirr, *Early Roman Occupation at Cirencester,* 103-5. Cirencester Excavations **I**.

Vitruvius M.P., *On Architecture.* Books 2 and 7. London: Loeb.

von den Driesch, A. and Boessneck, J., 1974. 'Kritische Anmerkungen zur Widerristhohenberechnung aus Langenmassen vor-und fruhgeschichtlicher Tierknochen', *Saugetierkundliche Mitteilungen* 22, 325-48.

Wacher, J.S., 1969 *Excavations at Brough-on-Humber, 1958-61.* Leeds: Rep. Res. Comm. Soc. Antiq. London **10**.

Wacher, J.S., 1974, *The Towns of Roman Britain.* London: Book Club Associates.

Waddington, R.G., 1931 *Leicester: the Making of a Modern City.* Leicester.

Wakely, J., Manchester, K. and Roberts, C., 1985 'Scanning electron microscope study of normal vertebrae and ribs from early medieval human skeletons', *Journ. Archaeol. Sci.* **16**, 627-642.

Walke, N., 1965 'Das römische Donaukastell Straubing-Sorviodurum', *Limesforschungen* 3, Berlin.

Walker, I.C., and Wells P.K., 1979, 'Regional varieties of clay tobacco pipe markings in eastern England', *in* P.J. Davey (ed) 1979, 3-66.

Walker I.C., 1977, *Clay Tobacco Pipes with Particular Reference to the Bristol Industry, National Historic Parks and Sites, Canada,* 4 Vols.

Wallace, C. and Webster, P.V., 1989 'Jugs and lids in Black-Burnished Ware', *Journ. of Roman Pot. Stud.* 2, 88-91.

Waterer, J.W., 1956 'Leather' *in* C. Singer *et. al.* 1956, 147-187.

Waugh, H. and Goodburn, R., 1972 'The non-ferrous objects' *in* S.S. Frere 1972, 114-62.

Webb, E., (ed.), 1985 *Computer Applications in Archaeology*. London.

Webster, G., 1957 'Further excavations at the Roman fort, Kinvaston, Staffordshire', *Trans. Birmingham Archaeol. Soc.* **73**, 100-108.

Webster, G., 1989 'Deities and religious scenes on Romano-British pottery', *Journ. of Roman Pot. Stud.* **2**, 1-28.

Webster, G. and Booth, N., 1947 'A Romano-British pottery kiln at Swanpool, near Lincoln', *Antiq. Journ.* **27**, 61-79.

Webster, P.A.., 1975 'Pottery report' *in* J.M. Steane and G.F. Byrant 1975, 60-95.

Webster, P.V., 1987 *Roman Samian Ware Background Notes*. 3rd edition. Cardiff: University College.

Webster, P.V., 1976 'Severn Valley Ware: a preliminary study', *Trans. Bristol and Gloucestershire Archaeol. Soc.* **94**, 18-46.

Webster, P.V., 1993 *Roman Samian Pottery in Britain*. Cardiff: Counc. Brit. Archaeol. practical handbook draft.

Webster 1993b 'The post-fortress coarse wares', *in* W.H. Manning (ed) *Report on the Excavations at Usk 1965-1976*, 227-361. Cardiff: University of Wales Press.

Webster, P.V., 1996 *Roman Samian Pottery in Britain*. York: Counc.Brit. Archaeol. Practical Handbook **13**.

Wedlake, W.J., 1982 *The Excavation of the Shrine of Apollo at Nettleton, Wilts. 1956-71*. London: Res. Rep. Soc. Antiq, **40**.

Welker, E., 1974 'Die Romischen Glaser Von Nida-Heddernheim', *Schriften des Frankfurter Museums fur Vorund Fruhgeschicte* **VIII**. Bonn.

Wells, P.K., 1970, 'The excavation of a 19th century clay tobacco pipe kiln in Boston, Lincolnshire', *Lincolnshire History and Archaeol.*, **1**, No **5**.

Wells, P.K., 1979, 'The pipemakers of Lincolnshire', *in* P.J.Davey (ed.) 1979, 123-169.

West, S., 1985 'West Stow: The Anglo-Saxon village', *East Anglian Archaeol.* **24**.

Westell, W.P., 1931 'A Romano-British cemetery at Baldock, Herts', *Archaeol. Journ.* **88**, 247-301.

Wheeler, A. and Jones, A.K.G., 1989. *Fishes*. Cambridge: Cambridge University Press.

Wheeler, R.E.M., 1924 'Segontium, and the Roman occupation of Wales', *Y Cymmrodor* **33**. London.

Wheeler, R.E.M., 1926 'The Roman fort near Brecon', *Y Cymmrodor* **37**. London.

White, A.J., 1984 'Medieval fisheries in the Witham and its tributaries', *Lincolnshire Hist. Archaeol. Soc.* **19**, 29-35.

Wilkinson, M., 1979. 'The fish remains', *in*: M. Maltby *The animal bones from Exeter 1971-1975*, 74-82. Exeter Archaeol. Reports **2**, Sheffield: Dept. of Prehistory and Archaeol., University of Sheffield.

Williams, D.F., 1990 'Amphorae from York', *in* J.R. Perrin *Roman Pottery from the Colonia 2: General Accident and Rougier Street*. The Archaeol. of York, **16/4**, 342-62. London:York Archaeol. Trust and Counc. Brit. Archaeol.

Williams, D F, 1993a 'The amphorae', archive report, A1.1991. Jewry Wall Museum, Leicester.

Williams, D.F., 1993b 'The amphorae', *in* A.G. Kinsley 1993, *Broughton Lodge*, 15. . Nottingham: Nottingham Archaeol. Monograph **4**.

Williams, D.F., 1994a 'Campanian amphorae', *in* P.Bidwell and S. Speak 1994, *Excavations at South Shields Roman Fort* Volume **1**, 217-19. Newcastle-upon-Tyne: Soc. Antiq. Newcastle-upon-Tyne Monograph **4**.

Williams, D.F., 1994b 'A note on the petrology of examples of amphora type Fishbourne 148.3 from Leicester,' *in* P. Clay and R.J. Pollard 1994, 66.

Williams, D.F. and Carreras, C., 1995 'North African amphorae in Roman Britain: a re-appraisal', *Britannia* **26**, 231-252.

Williams, D.F. and Peacock, D.P.S., 1983 'The importation of olive-oil into Roman Britain', *in* J. Blazquez and J. Remesal (eds.), *Produccion Y Comercio de Aceite en la Antiguedad. II Congresso*, 263- 280. Madrid.

Williams, J.H., 1979 *St.Peters Street, Northampton. Excavations 1973-76*. Northampton: Northampton Development Corporation Archaeol. Monograph No.2.

Wilmott, T., 1991 *Excavations in The Middle Walbrook Valley 1927-1960*. London and Middlesex Archaeol. Soc. Special Paper no. **13**.

Wilson, C.A., 1973. *Food and Drink in England*. London: Constable.

Wilson, M.G., 1968 'Other objects' *in* B.W.Cunliffe 1968, 93-109.

Wilson, M.G., 1972 'The other pottery', *in* S.S. Frere 1972.

Wilson, M.G., 1984 'The other pottery' *in* S.S. Frere 1984, 200-76.

Wilson, B., Grigson, C. and Payne, S., (eds.) *Ageing and Sexing Animal Bones from Archaeological Sites*. Oxford: Brit. Archaeol. Rep. (Brit. Ser.) **109**.

Winder, J.M., 1984 *Oyster shells from excavations at Pudding Lane*. Report for the Dept. of Urban Archaeol. Museum of London. Unpublished report.

Winder, J.M., 1985. 'Oyster culture', *in* G. Milne. (ed.) 1985, 91-95

Winder J.M., 1989 *Oyster Shell From Newport Roman Villa: An Interim Report*. Isle of Wight County Archaeol. Committee.

Winder, J.M., 1992. *A study in the variation in oyster shells from archaeological sites and a discussion of oyster exploitation*. Thesis for the degree of Doctor of Philosophy, University of Southampton.

Winder, J.M., 1992b 'The Oysters', *in* I.P Horsey (ed.), *Excavations in Poole 1973-83*. Dorset Natural History and Archaeol. Soc. Monograph Series No **10** 194-200.

Winder, J.M., 1994 'Oyster and other shells from Reading Abbey Wharf,' *in* J.W. Hawkes and P.F Fasham.(eds), *Excavations on the Reading waterfront sites 1979-1988*. Berkshire Archaeol. Trust Monograph Series No **1**.

Winder, J.M., in prep. 'Oyster and other marine shells from 39, Brown St. Salisbury', *in* J.W. Hawkes forthcoming, *Archaeological excavation, evaluation and observation in Salisbury 1984-1989*. Monograph of Trust for Wessex Archaeol.

Woodfield, C., 1983 'The remainder of the Roman pottery', *in* A.E. Brown and C. Woodfield 1983, 'Excavations at Towcester, Northamptonshire,: The Alchester Road Suburb', *Northants. Archaeol.* **18**, 74-100.

Woodfield, C.C.S., 1992 'The defences of Towcester, Northants', *Northamptonshire Archaeol.*, **24**, 13-66.

Woodland, R.R., 1981 'The pottery', *in* J.E. Mellor and T. Pearce 1981, 81-129.

Woodland, R.R., 1987 'The post Roman pottery' *in* R. Buckley and J. Lucas 1987, 80-99.

Woods, P.J., 1972 *Brixworth Excavations Vol 1,The Romano-British Villa 1965-70, The Roman Coarse Pottery and Decorated Samian Ware*, Northampton. Reprinted from *Journ. Northampton Mus.* **8** (1970), 3-102.

Wright, R.P., 1962 'Inscriptions and graffiti from Roman Britain: Leicester', *Journ. of Roman Studies*, **52**, 196-7.

Young, C.J., 1977 *Oxfordshire Roman Pottery*. Oxford: Brit. Archaeol. Reports. (Brit. Ser.) **43**.

Young Types c.f. Young 1977

Yule, B., 1982 'A third century well group, and the later Roman settlement in Southwark', *London Archaeol.* **4**, 243-50.

Zalkin, V.I., 1960. 'Metapodial variation and its significance for the study of ancient horned cattle', *Bull. D. Mosk. Ges. D. Nat.Forscher. Abt. Biol.* **65**, 109-126. (Russian with English summary).

Zeepvat, R.J., 1987 'Tiles' *in* D.C. Mynard (ed.). *Roman Milton Keynes*, 118-125.

Zeuner, F.E., 1963 *A History of Domesticated Animals*. London: Hutchinson.

Zienkiwiczcz, J.D., 1986 *The Legionary Fortress Baths at Caerleon*. Vol.**1**: *The Buildings*. Cardiff.

Table 2: Summary of finds in Roman phases (1-6)

SUBPHASE	SUBGROUP	Description	RBpot	PRpot	Wall plaster	Tile	Slate	Mortar	Opsig	Tesserae	Animal bone	Oyster	Slag	Coins	Glass	Small Finds (Bone)	CA	Ceramic	Glass	Iron	Lead	Other	Sampled?	Cess	Coprolite	Parasites	Fish scales	Fish bones	Egg shell	Flies	Woodlice	Fruit stones	Grains	Seeds	Charcoal
1A	177/1	Ambiguous features F467, F474, F1017, F1014	629	20		135					274										x	x	x												x
1B	180/1	Layers (disturbed)	946			745																													
	130/1	Quarry and fills F1027, F1037, F1045, F1046	494								60												x												x
	130/2	Quarry? F1031, F1036 and fills	712			910					450												x												x
	130/3	Quarry? F1024 and fills	992								1080																								x
	130/4	Quarry fills?	3675			200					1230																								x
	130/5	Quarry fills? F435, F497, F498, F499	340			20															x		x												x
	130/6	Quarry fills? F472, F476, F1011, F1020, F1038	952			500					619	20			2		x					x	x												x
	130/7	Gravel pits & back fills F448, F496, F1026	16		12						12											x	x	x											x
	130/8	Gravel pits & back fills F369, F462,					35				51											x	x									x			x
	131/1	Pits & backfills F299, F1034	292																			x	x												x
	131/2	Pits & backfills F1000, F1001, F1021, F1040	400			100					501												x												x
1C	200/1	Layers																																	
	200/2	Layer Roman soil	4532			2200		19			1125	6						x			x		x												x
	208/1	Ditch F671 and fills (pre structure A)	107			1225		246			10				2			x		x	x	x	x			x			x						x
	208/2	Pit F672 and fills (pre structure A)																					x												
	208/3	Posthole F679 (pre structure A)																					x												
2A	132/1	Surface 1.	1954								1025	10			1							x						x							x
	133/1	Stakeholes.	686								40																								
	133/2	Postholes F1006, F1022.	412								60																								
	133/3	Line of 12 stakeholes F1047.																																	
	133/4	Pair of stakeholes F1018, F1019																																	
	133/5	Line of 9 stakeholes F1030.																																	
	133/6	Line of 11 stakeholes F1007.																																	
	133/7	East/West gully F451 & backfills.	3939			1220					1911	40						x			x		x	x					x						x
	133/8	North/South F1028 gully & backfills.	72								35												x												x
	134/1	F1005 burnt layers;hearth/hearth derived.	808			25					809		84					x		x	x		x			x		x							x
	134/2	Burnt layer.	1696			1200					205												x												x
	135/1	Pit F1023 & backfills	1283								410	10	20		2					x	x		x												x
	136/1	F1032, F1035, assoc. with surface 5?	20								110												x												x
	137/1	Cut feature F1039.	540								11																								
2B	138/1	Makeup for surface 2.	8023	6		1050					3633	5			1		x	x		x	x	x	x	x	x	x	x		x	x				x	x
	138/2	Makeup for surface 2.	13717			10580					7915	225	11		14		x	x		x	x	x	x	x	x	x			x	x			x	x	x
	138/3	Surface 2.	920			1398					585	5						x					x												x
	139/1	Pit F1025 & backfills	188								12												x												x
2C	140/1	Ditch F433 & primary fills.	875			590					545	30					x	x		x	x	x	x	x					x					x	x
2D	143/1	Part of gravel surface 2A	358			485					233	55	16		2								x												x
	143/2	Part of gravel surface 2A.	8003			8365					3894	125	2305		14		x	x		x	x	x	x	x	x			x	x	x			x	x	x
2E	144/1	Interleaving layers of burning.	12120			9895	5	886			8453	255		1			x	x		x	x	x	x	x	x	x	x		x	x			x	x	x
2F	147/1	Circular well F405 & backkfills.	2881			220				5	588	5			4			x		x	x	x	x	x	x	x			x	x			x	x	x
	145/1	Makeup layers for surface 3.	3473			960		151			1286	330						x					x												x
	145/2	Makeup layers for surface 3.																																	
	145/3	Makeup layers for surface 3?	3546			5820					3190	420	220				x	x		x	x	x	x	x					x						x
	145/4	Makeup layers for surface 3?	83			2130					10												x												x
	145/5	Staining of layers from hearth F481																																	
	145/6	Compacted gravel surface 3.	4680	6		6430		5			3900	460	50		4		x	x		x	x	x	x	x					x					x	x
	146/1	Amphora lined hearth F481	23964			4150					592	65	10		7		x	x		x	x	x	x	x					x					x	x
	146/2	Hearth/fireplace? F449	15								5												x												x
2G	148/1	Homogenous layers.	128	86	805	200		270		300	105	80	260		24		x	x		x	x	x	x	x				x	x				x	x	x
	148/2	Homogenous layers.	52639			23645					21929	425					x	x		x	x	x	x	x				x	x				x	x	x
	148/3	Hearth F1004and floor/occupation layer.	1975			100					585				2			x			x	x	x	x				x	x				x	x	x
2H	149/1	Floor layers in structure C	1890			2400					902				1		x	x		x	x	x	x	x											x
	149/2	Postholes F1008/ 9, 12/13 part of structure C.	161			1070					50	20			1			x			x	x	x	x					x					x	x
	149/3	Marl & sand layers F483 in structure C.	332			55	5				388		1								x	x	x	x								x		x	x
	149/4	Posthole F410 in structure C	397			35		25			503				1							x	x												x
	149/5	Features F358, F495 in slump of ditch F433.	24			10					115												x												x
2I	142/1	Ditches? F453, F465, F447, & fills.	84			470					226												x												x
2J	172/1	Ditch F333/415 & fills.	2013								35							x			x	x	x	x					x	x				x	x
	172/2	Ditch F484/5/6 & fills.	118								15							x												x					x
	172/3	Irreg. cuts F386, F487,																																	

377

Table 2: *Summary of finds in Roman phases (1-6) continued*

SUBPHASE	SUBGROUP	Description	RBpot	PRpot	Wall plaster	Tile	Slate	Mortar	Opsig	Tesserae	Animal bone	Oyster	Slag	Coins	Glass	Bone	CA	Ceramic	Glass	Iron	Lead	Other	Sampled?	Cess	Coprolite	Parasites	Fish scales	Fish bones	Egg shell	Flies	Woodlice	Fruit stones	Grains	Seeds	Charcoal
	173/2	Irreg. shaped cuts F1016, F1015, F469, F1010	65																				X												
	176/1	Shallow pits F445, F452, F457.	275																				X												X
	178/1	Layers	537			40					220																								
	179/1	Layers	308	9		505					130												X												X
	181/1	Ambig. feats F285-6, F249, F277, F250-1, F280	582		5	430		55			612						X			X		X							X						X
	182/1	Dumping (makeup?)				100					1460		20									X													X
	183/2	Miscellaneous feature F471																				X													
	183/4	Shallow pit F1029	124								370																								
	183/5	Miscellaneous feature F375	2152			970		10			2355				1			X			X		X		X				X						X
	184/1	Shallow pits F388, F407, F418-19, F493-95	200			305					720			1				X			X		X		X				X						X
2K	186/3	Pits (rectangular) + fills F414, F459	3616		5	3635		552			4780	16	11	1	9	X	X			X	X	X	X	X			X	X		X					X
	201/1	Layers	1680			225		5			2475				4	X	X			X	X	X	X	X			X	X							X
	201/2	Layers	1681								250				1					X			X												X
	201/3	Gully? F683	7294		53	8675		1864			4938		4		4	X	X			X	X		X			X	X	X	X						X
	202/1	Ditch F678 and fills	85			355					130																								
	202/2	Ditch F681 and fills	1615					5			535	20		1		X				X	X	X	X	X											X
	202/3	Ditch F656 and fills	289	13							70	35				X					X		X							X					X
	202/4	Upper fills of ditch F600	1359			200					505	105				X				X	X		X					X							X
	203/1	N-S ditch F572 and fills	168	20	16	990		15		15	70					X				X	X	X	X				X	X							X
	203/2	F669, re-cut of ditch F572	200	25		35					410					X	X				X		X	X				X					X		X
	204/1	Truncated features F680, F682, F684																																	
	204/2	Layers (lower fills of a ditch?)																																	
	205/1	Pit F658 and fills																																	
	212/1	Ditch F561 and fills (roadside??)																																	
	212/2	Ditch F645 and fills (Roadside??)																																	
	212/3	Posthole F654																																	
2L	332/1	Pit/well F711 and fills	7535			3430		55			2665				7	X	X			X	X	X	X	X			X			X					X
3A	141/1	F343 recut of/slumping into F433.	28710	7		11510		65			40921	54	17		12	X	X			X	X	X	X	X	X		X	X	X	X		X	X	X	X
	142/2	Pit F377 & backfills.	2564			1560		25			9782				1	X	X			X	X	X	X	X	X		X	X	X	X		X	X	X	X
	142/3	Posthole? F354	16			10					20																								
3B	141/2	(F343) slumped surface 4 into F433.	2559			2230		10			3545	5		1	5	X	X			X	X	X	X	X			X			X		X		X	X
	141/3	(F343) slump into ditch F433.	3311		184	2241					6135					X	X				X	X	X	X			X	X		X				X	X
	141/4	(F343) slump & consolid. into ditch F433.	26057			13451		46	5		26271	167	336	1	46	X	X			X	X	X	X	X	X		X	X	X	X		X		X	X
	141/5	F395 consolidatiaon & slumps into ditch F433.	7													X	X				X		X	X											
	150/1	Makeup for surface 4.	21207			23030					8405	35			7		X			X	X	X	X	X				X		X					X
	150/2	Makeup for surface 4.	2602	30		610					1105				1																				
	151/1	Compacted gravel - surface 4.	18174			13270					7355	166	205		7	X	X			X	X	X	X	X			X	X							X
	152/1	Pit F376 & backfills.	19820		539	21750					9387	10	385		25	X	X			X	X	X	X	X	X		X	X	X						X
	153/1	Slumped fills/levelling layers in well F318	16168			9245	1070	60	180		4270	210				X	X			X	X	X	X	X	X		X	X	X	X					X
	153/2	Secondary rubbish deposits in Well F318	1025			255					1175	109				X	X			X	X	X	X	X			X		X						X
	153/3	Primary fills of circular well F318.	730			25					810			1		X	X			X	X	X	X	X	X		X					X			X
	154/1	Clay & marl layers over surface 4.	7335		36	10135		90			4261	295		1	8	X	X			X	X	X	X	X			X	X		X		X	X	X	X
	154/2	Layers overlying surface 4.	11277			1870		5		5	3450	295			22	X	X				X	X	X	X	X		X	X				X		X	X
	154/3	Layers overlying surface 4.	5768		5	5590		230	5		2000	5		1	35	X	X			X	X	X	X	X			X	X		X					X
	154/4	Layers overlying surface 4.																																	
	154/5	Layers over surface 4.	6089	65		4885		140	715	50	3921	40			36	X	X			X	X	X	X	X	X		X	X		X		X	X	X	X
	154/6	Layers over surface 4.				315																													
3C	155/1	Slump fill/levelling layers in Well F230.	7042	19		6225					4835		25		15	X	X			X	X	X	X	X	X		X	X		X		X	X	X	X
	155/2	Cess layers in well F230	921			1090					975				1	X	X			X	X	X	X	X	X	X	X	X	X	X		X	X	X	X
	155/3	Primary fills in well F230.	345			105					84					X	X				X		X	X	X	X	X	X		X		X		X	X
	156/1	Features F409, F413. F416 assoc. surface 4.	2180			2515		54			1115				4	X	X			X	X	X	X	X			X			X					X
	157/1	Posthole F361 & fills.	62			10					10																								
	157/2	Postholes F326-7, F341, F346, F352 & fills.	749			1250					485				8	X	X			X	X		X	X			X			X					X
	157/3	Hearth F357	223								74				6		X			X	X	X	X	X			X			X		X	X	X	X
	157/4	Beam slot? F364	1152			560					270	1			6	X	X			X	X	X	X	X			X	X				X	X	X	X
	157/5	Pit F374 & fills.	7591			9610			285	60	2910	85		1	9	X	X			X	X	X	X	X			X	X		X		X	X	X	X
	170/1	F398, F400 ambiguous features																																	
	171/1	F261, F304, F305 ambiguous features	921			1195		20		5	990		11		1	X						X	X		X				X				X	X	X	X
	171/2	Cut + fills of shallow trench F450.	64			75					25						X						X											X	
	175/1	Postholes F222, F232-33, F431, 37, F475,.79	330		41	895		30			568	10			1	X	X			X	X	X	X	X											X

Stratigraphic Information			Bulk Finds quantities present by weight in grams										No			Small Finds materials present							Environmental materials present												
SUBPHASE	SUBGROUP	Description	RBpot	PRBpot	Wall plaster	Tile	Slate	Mortar	Opsig	Tesserae	Animal bone	Oyster	Slag	Coins	Glass	Bone	CA	Ceramic	Glass	Iron	Lead	Other	Sampled?	Cess	Coprolite	Parasites	Fish scales	Fish bones	Egg shell	Flies	Woodlice	Fruit stones	Grains	Seeds	Charcoal
	175/3	Postholes F223-4, F227, F236.	74		45	115		20			627	10			1								X	X											X
	175/4	Spreads and layers (makeup?)	2157	10		2150		50			1290	57				X	X			X			X	X		X	X			X				X	X
	186/2	Pits (rectangular) F390,95,96, F403,411 + fills	2982			4240		117	638	55	1979	32	91		8	X	X			X			X	X	X	X	X	X		X	X			X	X
3D	183/3	Pit(rectangular) F412 + fills	10243	1	30	13080		6	4203		7168	4			103					X			no			X									
	187/1	Miscellaneous feature F422, F430	14015	161	2	32450		35	979	20	8208	50	5	1	14	X	X			X	X	X	X	X	X	X	X	X	X	X	X			X	X
3E	209/1	Pits (intercutting) F208,210,212,215, F334-5	7			300		110	160	15	265		5		32	X	X			X			X	X	X	X	X	X	X	X				X	X
	209/2	Posthole F610, structure E				105					30																								
	209/3	Pit or gully F661, structure E	13																																
	209/4	Postholes F663, F666-67, structure E				2045					225	15			15																				
	209/5	Beamslot F668, structure E																																	
	209/6	Beamslot F617, structure E																					X		X										X
3F	210/1	Beamslot F546, structure E	1246		20	510		115			809	330			1	X				X			X	X		X									X
	210/2	Wall footings F543, structure F	59		20	1045		90			115	25											X	X		X									X
	210/3	Wall footings F547, structure F	13			10					20															X									
	210/4	Wall footings F633, structure F													1								X		X		X								X
	211/1	Wall footings F635, structure F	36			100		400			10				1					X			X	X		X									X
3G	211/2	Wall footings F660, structure G								20													X	X											X
	206/1	Metalled surface F629, structure G	42	39		155		80			100	48			1	X				X			X	X	X	X	X			X	X				X
	206/2	Metalled surface F634	46			175		370			20									X			X	X		X									X
	206/3	Metalled surfaces F625	130		54	40		191			100				1					X			X	X	X	X		X							X
	207/1	Pit F673 and fills	970		495	4295		2825			1660				1					X			X	X		X									X
	207/2	Pit F676 and fills	12			85					145	140			2								X	X	X	X		X		X					X
	207/3	Pit F677 and fills	612		281	1940		4540			290	5			2	X	X			X			X	X		X		X		X			X		X
	207/4	Pit F664 and fills	3314	3	10	8750		130		41	1759	550	1	1	8	X	X	X	X	X			X	X		X	X	X	X	X			X	X	X
4A	174/1	Makeup layers and surfacing	10398		5	13460		376			3625	30			45	X	X			X			X	X		X	X		X	X			X	X	X
	174/2	Makeup layers and surfaces	9033	80	5	11035		228	60	20	3920	2	390		26		X		X	X			X	X	X	X	X								X
	174/3	Rubbish fills of pit F255.	2948		2	551					2640	140			3					X			X	X		X									X
	183/1	Pit F255 (circular) + fills	3890			11360			225		735	105			15	X			X	X			X	X	X	X	X		X	X			X		X
5A	158/1	Pit F255 (circular) + fills	496			2375		5			709									X			X	X		X									X
	158/2	Misc.feats F239,260, F311,31,36,78,98-9	130			185					158		7							X			X	X		X									X
	158/3	Makeup for surface 5	1575			2110			245		320									X			X	X	X	X	X								X
	158/4	Makeup for surface 5	1968			5370		4			1560	85	10	1		X				X			X	X		X	X	X							X
	158/5	Makeup for surface 5	386	35		10			120	65	240	105	7		5		X			X		X	X	X		X									X
	159/1	Surface 5	490			365		25	5	5	1120				1	X				X			X	X	X	X	X								X
	160/1	Features F383, F385 assoc. with structure H?					75	22			1520	85			3					X			X	X		X									X
	160/2	Postholes F432, F464, F468, F480 & fills.	1409		10	4530				20	106																								
	160/3	Walls F439, F440, F496, - structure H?	279				50			40	5		5		6								X	X	X		X	X							X
	160/4	Part of slate floor? F460	95	1		9430	405		15		4610	505	25			X	X	X		X			X	X		X	X	X	X						X
	160/5	F463, F470, drain and sump within structure H.	4760			100		20	120		95	10				X				X			X	X	X	X	X		X						X
	160/6	F301 hearth base/post pad/floor?	204			1240					325	15				X				X			X	X		X		X							X
	161/1	Postholes F294, F295, F351 - structure H?	464		32	5030		60			682	20		1	4					X			X	X	X	X				X					X
	161/2	Layers - structure H?	2401			3350					2175				4	X	X			X			X	X		X	X		X						X
	161/3	Layers - structure H?	2908	14		3485					1670				5		X			X			X	X		X	X	X					X		X
5B	162/1	Layers slumped into fills of F376.	5793			355		25		20	200	35			2	X	X		X	X			X	X		X	X								X
	162/2	Layers over cobbled surface 4.	474	26		11391			15	40	4014	120	10		40	X	X			X			X	X	X	X		X	X	X			X	X	X
	162/3	Layers over surf. 2 slump. in F318.	15011			80					180	10					X			X			X	X											X
	162/4	Spreads & layers over cob. surf. 4.	483			895			120		785	15			8		X		X	X			X	X		X	X	X	X				X	X	X
	162/5	Spreads over cobbled surface 4.	3773			1554			145	10	145	2				X				X			X	X		X			X						X
	162/6	Spreads over cobbled surface 4.	2722																																
	162/7	Postholes F308-9, F317, F332 - structure I.															X			X			X	X											
	163/1	Postholes F344, F350 - structure I.																		X			X	X		X									
	163/2	Shallow pit F300.	65			5		25			40		5		1	X				X			X	X		X							X	X	X
	163/3	Postholes? F287, F289, F293, F296	14			125		30			90	15			2	X				X			X	X		X									X
	163/4	Postholes F282, F312, F314	704			1280			200		580				4	X	X		X	X			X	X		X	X			X			X		X
	163/5	F315 sub-rectangular ash filled cut, structure J	39			2315					125	15	5		1	X				X			X	X		X				X					X
	165/1	F259, F325, - part of structure J															X			X			X	X		X									X
	165/2	Square pit F307 & backfills.	9370			3530		4			10610	15	15		13	X	X		X	X			X	X		X	X	X	X		X			X	X

Table 2: Summary of finds in Roman phases (1-6) continued

Column groups: *Stratigraphic Information* (SUBPHASE, SUBGROUP, Description); *Bulk Finds quantities present by weight in grams* (RBPot, PRPot, Wall plaster, Tile, Slate, Mortar, Opsig, Tesserae, Animal bone, Oyster); *No* (Slag, Coins, Glass); *Small Finds materials present* (Bone, CA, Ceramic, Glass, Iron, Lead, Other); *Environmental materials present* (Sampled?, Cess, Coprolite, Parasites, Fish scales, Fish bones, Egg shell, Flies, Woodlice, Fruit stones, Grains, Seeds, Charcoal)

SUBPHASE	SUBGROUP	Description	RBPot	PRPot	Wall plaster	Tile	Slate	Mortar	Opsig	Tesserae	Animal bone	Oyster	Slag	Coins	Glass	Bone	CA	Ceramic	Glass	Iron	Lead	Other	Sampled?	Cess	Coprolite	Parasites	Fish scales	Fish bones	Egg shell	Flies	Woodlice	Fruit stones	Grains	Seeds	Charcoal
5C	167/2	Square pit F211 & backfills.	80			210		20			950												x													x
	163/6	Postholes F302, F303, F313 - structure I.	28			675		40			57																									x
	163/7	Postholes, slots F209,25,53,68 - structure I	767			360	135				840	5											x													x
	163/8	Postholes F275, F392- structure I.	222		1	1760		5			145	5		1	1		x			x								x							x
	163/9	Small pit F252- structure I.	47			25		10			410			1	1		x			x			x												x
	163/10	Posthole F436- structure I.	8			15					40				3					x			x												x
	164/1	Spits & cleaning layers.	15921	37	20	12210		40	280	40	8060	212	15	1	69	x	x			x		x	x				x	x	x				x	x	x
	164/2	Contexts grouped - section drawing.																																		
	165/3	Stakeholes F272, F273- structure J	296			320		16			290												x												x
	165/4	Ambiguous features F360, F391 - structure J	389			130		195			225	15	15							x			x					x							x
	165/5	Postholes F345, F355, F366 - structure J	1240	43	15	9500		165			523	130	15		10					x			x					x							x
	166/1	Features F290, F316, F340 - structure J.	433			335					1466												x												x
	166/2	Fill of stone lined Well F246.	2953	17		3725	300	10		25	2010	15	2		2	x		x	x			x				x	x	x				x	x	x
	166/3	Silting around collapsed lining of Well F246	2941			6445	1700				5710	675	1	1	1							x				x	x	x				x	x	x
	166/4	Silting around collapsed lining of Well F246	11886	3		15255	1470	40	155	65	6995	524		2	15	x	x		x	x		x				x	x	x				x	x	x
	166/5	Collapsed clay lining in Well F246.	5066	206		13460	1470		2435		6020	181			6	x			x		x	x				x	x	x				x	x	x
	166/6	Collapsed clay & rubble lining in Well F246	3			10					15				1				x																x
	166/7	Collapsed stone lining in Well F246.	134																				x												x
	166/8	Orig. cut & in situ stone lining of Well F246.																					x												
	168/1	Slumped fills of earlier features F221 & F380.	718		125	745	115			50	1040		42	1	1		x	x	x	x		x				x	x	x				x	x	x
	169/1	Pit F281 & backfills.	9			995			5		5												x												x
	169/2	Pit F220 & backfills.	949			2100	90	20			1185		5							x			x				x	x							x
	169/3	Pit F229 & backfills.	214			205		20			480		15							x			x				x	x							x
5D	186/1	Pit (rectangular) F240 + fills	5947	594	30	4090	740	545	105	10	13145	85		1	36	x				x	x	x	x			x	x	x	x	x		x	x	x	x
5E	339/1	Primary fills of quarry pit F791																					x												x
	339/2	Primary fills of a quarry pit F769																																	x
	339/3	Primary fills of quarry pits F764, F776, F788																					x												x
	339/4	Primary fills of quarry pits F764, F776, F788	2718		1250	8605		6			1674	45				x				x			x												x
	339/5	Sealing fills of quarry pits F764, F776, F788	1235		580	575					375												x												x
	360/1	Primary fills of quarry pit F802	13797			17601	8085	30		45	6130	470		1	5	x				x			x	x			x	x						x	x
	361/1	Primary fills of Quarry pits F798-801	85								20																								x
		Layer (3881) cut by quarries G360	1208								525												x												x
5F	339/6	Primary fills of quarry pits F796, F797	18350		705	34735					6155	970		1	21	x				x			x	x		x	x	x	x					x	x
	339/7	Primary fills of quarry pit F784	823			935					514	20		1									x				x	x							x
	339/8	Primary & secondary fills of quarry F786	3957		12	920		1049		10	2354	415		2		x	x			x			x	x		x	x	x	x				x	x	x
	339/9	Secondary fills of quarry pits F764, F776, F788				4440	950																x												x
	362/1	Primary fills of quarry pit F795																																	x
	362/2	Primary fill of quarry pit F794																																	x
5G	362/3	Primary & secondary fills of quarry F768	10475	20	10	15690	1685	135	265	110	5940	105	62		6	x	x		x	x		x	x	x		x	x	x	x				x	x	x
	364/1	Quarry fills excavated by machine	4100	2	1348	8470	2745	40	70	51	2155	270				x	x	x	x	x		x	x			x	x	x	x				x	x	x
	333/1	Square pit F781 and fills	1708		235	1345	45				741					x	x			x			x												x
	334/1	Primary slumped quarry fills F757	4485			8325	2520		15	270	1371	260	62			x	x			x			x	x		x	x	x						x	x
	334/2	Deliberate makeup in quarry F757	4849		455	16025		15		130	7473	75		1		x	x			x			x	x		x	x	x	x					x	x
	337/1	Ditch/quarry pit F735 and fill	701		400	7030		95			1425	10				x	x			x			x	x			x	x							x
	337/2	Pit/quarry? F765 and fills	1897			1110					675	85			1								x												x
	337/3	Pit F787 and fill	283		270	1075					436	30			2	x	x			x			x												x
	355/1	Shallow cut F758	5				8855																												
	356/1	Stakehole F767																																	
	356/2	Stakehole F771																																	
	356/3	Stakehole F770																																	
	356/4	Stakehole F772																																	
	356/5	Stakehole F773																																	
	356/6	Stakehole F774																																	
	356/7	Stakehole F748																																	
	356/8	Stakehole F749																																	
	356/9	Stakehole F750																																	
	356/10	Stakehole F751																																	
	356/11	Stakehole F747																																	
	356/12	Stakehole F745										2																							
	356/13	Stakehole F746																																	
	356/14	Stakehole F744																																	

SUBPHASE	SUBGROUP	Description	RBpot	PRpot	Wall plaster	Tile	Slate	Mortar	Opsig	Tesserae	Animal bone	Oyster	Slag	Coins	Glass	Bone	CA	Ceramic	Glass	Iron	Lead	Other	Sampled?	Cess	Coprolite	Parasites	Fish scales	Fish bones	Egg shell	Flies	Woodlice	Fruit stones	Grains	Seeds	Charcoal
	356/15	Stakehole F742									5																								
	356/16	Stakehole F754																																	
	356/17	Stakehole F755																																	
	356/18	Stakehole F710	57			140	670	240			160																								
	356/19	Stakehole F780																																	
	356/20	Stakehole F783																																	
	357/1	Stakehole F777																																	
	357/2	Stakehole F778	261			195					75																								
	357/3	Stakehole F779	149			135									1																				
	357/4	Stakehole F775																																	
	358/1	Surface (compacted gravel)	310			45					255							x			x			x											
	359/1	Makeup layer	572		380	275					95																								
	359/2	Makeup layer	260		7453	4025					107							x			x														
	359/3	Pit F790 and fill	855			425	750				130	133									x			x											
5H	359/4	Makeup and surfaces F756	31103	80	639744	172832	51404	7320	490	75	16402	7524			10	x	x	x		x		x	x												
	338/1	Pit F761 and fills (makeup layers)	1151		180	310				30	10	120		1		x	x			x								x	x	x					
	338/2	Makeup layers and surfacing F763	4531		2294	3960		5			2658	750		1			x			x															
	343/2	Makeup layer	67			300					45																								
	345/1	Gully? F759 and fill	26			470				10	35	65																							
	346/1	Posthole F743 and fill																																	
	347/1	Posthole F730 and fill			150																														
	347/2	Posthole F731 and fill																																	
	349/1	Gully F739	72			40					20																								
	350/1	Post pit F736 and fill	130		80			580		70	230		30				x			x															
	351/1	Makeup layer	111		50	1150		150		50	310		5	1			x			x			x												
	352/1	Cultivation marks ?	996		440	1650		20		35	930			1																					
	353/1	Makeup layers	2075		170	3045		150		75	1925	295		1		x	x			x			x							x					
	354/1	Pit F760 and fills	2431		350	4660	125	11	125	435	2560	660				x	x	x		x	x		x				x	x	x	x				x	x
6A	336/1	Arbitrary splits	6732	75	2020	23185	635	1715		835	3145	1295		1			x																		
	338/3	Makeup and floor layers over quarry F763	23616	325	3773	90585	2580	2274	1280	75	17516	7283		2		x	x	x		x	x		x				x	x	x	x				x	x
	341/1	Pits F738, F740 and fills	761			3225	1664				505			1		x	x	x		x										x					
	342/1	Pit/post pit F729 and fill	141			50					150	15		1			x																		
	342/2	Pit F733 and fill	295			4000	225	65		35	150																								
	343/1	Makeup layer	56			55				215	150	90					x			x															
	344/1	Truncated shallow depression F728	201		45	1110				360	610						x			x										x					
	348/1	Makeup layer	625	21	245	955					715	15		1			x			x										x					
	367/1	Rubbish fills in quarry pit F766	24575	75	9224	45845	389	2483	35	850	13987	660	555	1	20	x	x	x	x	x	x	x	x				x		x	x				x	x
6B	335/1	Shallow depression F716	15								475				1	x	x							x				x							x	
	340/1	Cultivation layers & demolition	7498	562	4330	31240	14365	1170	70	620	11993	575	10	7	1	x	x	x		x	x	x	x				x			x				x	x
	363/1	Possible postholes F708, F720	2339		825	11815	500	610	380	205	4280	145		1	5		x	x		x	x	x	x							x			x		
	365/1	Makeup layers	393		695	2150			305	305	221						x	x					x							x					
	366/1	Makeup layer (3515) -wallplaster	223	15	2675	1475		855		265	215									x															

Table 3: *Summary of finds in post-Roman phases (7-12)*

Stratigraphic information				Finds quantities present by weight (g)												No.
Feature	Subgroups	Description	Plot	RBpot	PRpot	Plaster	Tile	Slate	Mortar	Opsig	Tess	Glass	Bone	Oyster	Slag	Coins
PHASE 7																
F705	sg305/1	Shallow pit cut and fills		332	-	121	650	-	-	-	-	-	531	10	1	-
F706	sg305/2	Shallow pit cut and fills		79	-	-	45	-	-	-	-	-	735	40	-	-
F707	sg305/4	Shallow pit cut and fills		262	28	-	4170	32310	-	150	115	-	565	-	-	-
F709	sg305/3	Shallow pit cut and fills		1954	46	35	5260	2370	27	-	20	-	2625	165	-	-
F713	sg304/1	Posthole cut and fill		-	-	-	660	-	-	-	30	-	240	10	-	-
F717	sg304/2	Beam slot? cut and fill		-	-	-	-	-	-	-	-	-	-	-	-	-
F721	sg304/3	Beam slot? cut and fill		152	-	5	565	-	-	-	20	-	440	-	-	-
F722	sg304/4	Post hole cut and fill		-	-	-	260	-	-	-	-	-	105	-	-	-
F723	sg304/5	Post hole cut and fill		-	-	-	35	-	-	-	-	-	50	-	-	-
F724	sg305/5	Shallow pit cut and fills		245	-	-	780	-	-	-	85	-	10	-	-	-
F725	sg304/6	Post hole cut and fill		86	-	-	540	-	-	-	-	-	200	10	-	-
F929	sg128/4	Post-hole		7	-	-	-	-	-	-	-	-	-	-	-	-
		PHASE 7 TOTALS		3117	74	161	12965	34680	27	150	270	0	5501	235	1	0
PHASE 8																
F245	sg111/2, 117/2, 124/2	mod deep circular pit	B	178	65	-	1320	-	295	-	-	-	230	-	347	-
F247	sg112/5, 118/3	mod deep square pit	D	945	2096	-	4110	-	125	-	115	-	8280	45	1265	-
F248	sg109/1, 115/1	Fill & Cut of shallow circular pit	D	246	246	-	205	-	-	50	-	2	540	-	15	-
F269	sg112/1, 125/1	moderately deep square pit	B	16	262	-	35	-	-	-	30	-	905	-	-	-
F363	sg111/4, 117/3, 124/3	Cut of mod deep circular pit	C	506	6	-	-	-	-	-	-	-	1330	-	-	-
F442	sg121/2	Backfills in truncated feature	F	-	-	-	-	-	-	-	-	-	-	-	-	-
F443	sg113/6, 119/7, 119/8	Fills and cut of deep circular pit	F	1137	336	-	1335	-	-	-	30	2	318	-	-	-
F482	sg114/3, 120/4, 127/3	Fills and cut of deep square pit	F	1595	1430	5	2240	-	153	250	-	1	3640	15	207	-
F504	sg244/1	Subcircular truncated pit	HJ	208	115	-	60	-	-	-	-	4	100	-	-	-
F521	sg249/3	Pit (rectangular) + secondary fills	HJ	2241	2236	127	3525	-	3360	1250	230	13	6955	-	22	1
F539	sg251/5	Pit and secondary fills		13	193	-	2170	45	-	-	30	-	686	-	-	-
F540	sg246/1, 247/1	Well? and fills		752	6361	145	8705	70	595	-	105	21	5305	10	20	2
F542	sg251/4	Pit (rectangular) + secondary fills		258	107	-	2845	-	340	-	60	-	1815	-	-	-
F568	sg246/2	Well? and primary fills		1164	4317	847	4045	1300	110	-	10	-	3190	55	20	1
F569	sg250/2	Pit (rectangular) + primary fills		204	1518	45	2335	200	70	-	270	-	3856	30	12	-
F579	sg248/2, 249/2	Pit (rectangular) primary + slump		263	233	15	315	-	90	1650	55	2	1085	-	5	-
F592	sg265/1	Pit (rectangular)		724	952	326	5577	60	580	1450	80	-	3774	150	15	-
F604	sg247/3	Well? and secondary fills		47	105	-	1275	-	75	-	-	-	140	-	-	-
F606	sg250/3	Pit (rectangular) + primary fills		17	15	65	766	-	-	-	25	-	400	-	-	-
F607	sg245/1	Post hole		-	-	-	-	-	-	-	-	-	-	-	-	-
F609	sg250/1, 251/1	Pit (rectangular) + primary fills		4	43	1	15	-	-	-	5	2	985	-	1	-
F616	sg251/3	Pit (rectangular) + secondary fills		548	1585	-	3020	-	-	-	25	-	3700	80	50	-
F620	sg251/2	Pit (rectangular) + secondary fills		5	275	-	1285	-	-	-	-	-	370	-	-	-
F657	sg244/2	Subcircular truncated pit		748	266	395	845	80	202	-	5	-	855	-	-	-
F907	sg111/5, 124/4	Fill & Cut of mod deep circular pit	AB	1099	140	-	-	-	-	-	-	-	-	-	-	-
F914	sg109/5, 115/5	Cut of shallow circular pit	A	1796	90	-	-	-	-	-	-	-	-	-	-	-
F915	sg109/3, 115/3	shallow circular pit	B	508	-	-	-	-	-	-	-	-	-	-	-	-
		PHASE 8 TOTALS		15222	22992	1971	46028	1755	5995	4650	1075	47	48459	385	1979	4
PHASE 9																
Medieval Timber Building (MTB)																
F647	sg253/1	Structure 1 - Make-up + postholes		671	30	720	2392	-	825	2350	30	-	585	440	-	2
F626	sg253/2	Structure 1 - Posthole		-	-	-	-	-	-	-	-	-	-	-	-	-
	sg253/3	Structure 1 - Floor	HJ	245	554	325	2331	390	840	150	50	-	410	25	295	2
	sg253/4	Structure 1 - Burnt layers (hearth)	HJ	20	342	-	10	-	95	-	-	-	5	-	10	-
F611	sg253/5	Structure 1 - Postholes		26	7	-	10	-	720	-	-	1	10	-	5	-
	sg253/6	Structure 1 - Floor? Layers	HJ	31	362	-	480	-	-	1350	-	-	290	-	-	1
F573	sg253/7	Structure 1 - mend in floor?	HJ	18	110	-	160	-	115	-	-	-	35	-	-	-
F583	sg253/8	Structure 1-Posthole assoc. F588?		6	9	-	-	-	7	-	-	-	5	-	-	-
F549	sg253/9	Pit and fills		161	892	140	1270	750	19	-	-	-	4163	15	252	1
F653	sg254/1	Structure 2 - Floor? Layers		118	-	-	135	-	345	-	-	-	75	-	-	-
	sg254/2	Structure 2 - Make-up layers		113	-	-	-	970	536	-	-	-	85	-	-	-
F653	sg254/3	Structure 2 - Floor? Layers		202	-	-	-	-	80	-	-	-	-	-	-	-

Stratigraphic information		Small Finds materials present							Environmental materials present												
Feature	Subgroups	Bone	CA	Ceramic	Glass	Iron	Lead	Other	Sampled?	Cess	Coprolite	Parasites	Fishscales	Fishbones	Egg shell	Flies	Woodlice	Fruitstones	Grains	Seeds	Charcoal
PHASE 7																					
F705	sg305/1	-	-	-	-	x	x	-	x	-	-	-	-	-	-	-	-	-	x	-	x
F706	sg305/2	-	-	-	-	x	-	-	-	-	-	-	-	-	-	-	-	-	-	-	-
F707	sg305/4	-	-	-	-	-	-	-	-	-	-	-	-	-	-	-	-	-	-	-	-
F709	sg305/3	-	-	-	-	x	-	-	-	-	-	-	-	-	-	-	-	-	-	-	-
F713	sg304/1	-	x	-	-	x	-	-	-	-	-	-	-	-	-	-	-	-	-	-	-
F717	sg304/2	-	-	-	-	x	-	-	-	-	-	-	-	-	-	-	-	-	-	-	-
F721	sg304/3	-	-	-	-	x	-	-	-	-	-	-	-	-	-	-	-	-	-	-	-
F722	sg304/4	-	x	-	-	-	-	-	-	-	-	-	-	-	-	-	-	-	-	-	-
F723	sg304/5	-	-	-	-	-	-	-	-	-	-	-	-	-	-	-	-	-	-	-	-
F724	sg305/5	-	x	-	-	x	-	-	-	-	-	-	-	-	-	-	-	-	-	-	-
F725	sg304/6	-	x	-	-	x	-	-	-	-	-	-	-	-	-	-	-	-	-	-	-
F929	sg128/4	-	-	-	-	-	-	-	-	-	-	-	-	-	-	-	-	-	-	-	-
PHASE 8																					
F245	sg111/2, 117/2, 124/2	-	-	-	-	x	-	-	x	-	-	-	-	-	-	x	-	-	x	x	x
F247	sg112/5, 118/3	-	-	-	-	x	x	-	x	-	-	-	x	x	-	-	-	-	x	x	x
F248	sg109/1, 115/1	-	-	-	-	x	x	-	x	-	-	-	-	-	-	-	-	-	-	-	x
F269	sg112/1, 125/1	-	-	-	-	-	-	-	-	-	-	-	-	-	-	-	-	-	-	-	-
F363	sg111/4, 117/3, 124/3	-	-	-	-	x	-	-	x	-	-	-	-	-	-	-	-	-	-	-	x
F442	sg121/2	-	-	-	-	-	-	-	-	-	-	-	-	-	-	-	-	-	-	-	-
F443	sg113/6, 119/7, 119/8	-	-	-	-	x	-	-	x	-	-	-	-	-	-	-	-	-	-	-	x
F482	sg114/3, 120/4, 127/3	-	-	-	-	x	-	-	x	x	x	-	-	x	-	x	-	-	x	x	x
F504	sg244/1	-	-	-	-	x	-	-	-	-	-	-	-	-	-	-	-	-	-	-	-
F521	sg249/3	-	x	-	-	x	-	-	x	x	-	x	x	x	x	x	x	x	x	-	x
F539	sg251/5	-	-	-	-	x	-	x	x	-	-	-	-	-	-	-	-	-	-	-	x
F540	sg246/1, 247/1	-	x	-	-	x	-	-	x	x	x	x	x	x	-	x	x	-	x	x	x
F542	sg251/4	-	-	-	-	-	x	x	x	x	x	x	-	-	-	-	-	x	-	-	x
F568	sg246/2	x	x	-	x	x	-	x	x	x	x	x	x	x	x	-	x	-	-	x	x
F569	sg250/2	x	x	-	-	x	-	-	x	-	-	-	x	x	x	-	-	-	-	-	x
F579	sg248/2, 249/2	-	-	-	-	x	x	-	x	x	x	x	x	x	x	x	x	x	x	-	x
F592	sg265/1	-	-	-	-	x	-	x	x	-	-	-	-	-	x	-	-	-	-	-	x
F604	sg247/3	-	-	-	-	x	-	-	x	x	-	-	x	x	x	x	x	-	-	-	x
F606	sg250/3	-	-	-	-	-	-	x	-	-	-	-	-	-	-	-	-	-	-	-	-
F607	sg245/1	-	-	-	-	-	-	x	-	-	-	-	-	-	-	-	-	-	-	-	-
F609	sg250/1, 251/1	-	x	-	-	x	-	-	x	x	x	x	x	-	x	-	x	-	-	-	x
F616	sg251/3	-	-	-	-	x	-	x	-	-	-	-	-	-	-	-	-	-	-	-	-
F620	sg251/2	-	-	-	-	x	-	x	x	x	-	x	-	x	x	-	-	-	-	-	x
F657	sg244/2	-	-	-	-	x	-	-	x	-	-	-	-	-	-	-	-	-	-	-	x
F907	sg111/5, 124/4	-	-	-	-	-	-	-	-	-	-	-	-	-	-	-	-	-	-	-	-
F914	sg109/5, 115/5	-	-	-	-	-	-	-	-	-	-	-	-	-	-	-	-	-	-	-	-
F915	sg109/3, 115/3	-	-	-	-	-	-	-	-	-	-	-	-	-	-	-	-	-	-	-	-
PHASE 9																					
Medieval Timber Building (MTB)																					
F647	sg253/1	-	x	-	-	x	-	-	x	-	-	-	x	-	x	-	-	-	x	x	x
F626	sg253/2	-	-	-	-	-	-	-	-	-	-	-	-	-	-	-	-	-	-	-	-
	sg253/3	-	x	-	-	x	x	x	x	-	-	-	-	x	-	-	-	-	-	-	x
	sg253/4	-	-	-	-	x	-	-	x	-	-	-	-	-	x	-	-	-	-	x	x
F611	sg253/5	-	-	-	-	-	-	-	x	-	-	-	-	-	-	-	-	-	-	-	x
	sg253/6	-	x	-	-	-	-	-	x	-	-	-	x	x	-	-	-	-	-	x	x
F573	sg253/7	-	-	-	-	x	-	-	x	-	-	-	-	-	-	-	-	-	-	x	x
F583	sg253/8	-	-	-	-	-	-	-	x	-	-	-	-	-	x	-	-	-	-	-	x
F549	sg253/9	-	x	-	-	x	-	-	x	-	-	-	x	x	-	-	-	-	-	-	x
F653	sg254/1	-	-	-	-	x	-	-	x	-	-	-	-	-	-	-	-	-	-	-	x
	sg254/2	-	-	-	-	x	-	-	x	-	-	-	-	-	x	-	-	-	-	-	x
F653	sg254/3	-	-	-	-	-	-	-	-	-	-	-	-	-	-	-	-	-	-	-	-

Stratigraphic information				Finds quantities present by weight (g)												No.	Small Finds materials present							Environmental materials present												
Feature	Subgroups	Description	Plot	RBpot	PRpot	Plaster	Tile	Slate	Mortar	Opsig	Tess	Glass	Bone	Oyster	Slag	Coins	Bone	CA	Ceramic	Glass	Iron	Lead	Other	Sampled?	Cess	Coprolite	Parasites	Fishscales	Fishbones	Egg shell	Flies	Woodlice	Fruitstones	Grains	Seeds	Charcoal
F653	sg254/4	Structure 2 - Slag + Burnt layers		186	-	210	5	-	570	-	-	-	50	-	-	1	-	x	-	-	x	-	-	x	-	-	-	-	-	-	-	-	-	-	-	x
F665	sg254/5	Structure 2 - Postholes		-	-	-	-	-	-	-	-	-	-	-	-	-	-	-	-	-	-	-	-	-	-	-	-	-	-	-	-	-	-	-	-	-
F662	sg254/6	Structure 2 - Posthole		-	-	-	-	-	-	-	-	-	-	-	-	-	-	-	-	-	-	-	-	-	-	-	-	-	-	-	-	-	-	-	-	-
F670	sg254/7	Structure 2 - Posthole		-	-	-	-	-	-	-	-	-	-	-	-	-	-	-	-	-	-	-	-	-	-	-	-	-	-	-	-	-	-	-	-	-
	sg254/8	Structure 2 - Make-up Layers	HJ	31	-	226	220	-	551	-	-	-	30	-	-	-	-	-	-	-	x	-	-	x	-	-	-	-	x	x	-	-	-	-	-	x
F615	sg254/9	Structure 2 - Floor? Layers	HJ	701	3	1901	725	-	1365	-	50	-	520	150	1	4	-	x	-	-	x	-	x	x	-	-	-	-	-	x	-	-	-	-	-	x
F615	sg254/10	Structure 2 - Demolition? Layers	HJ	563	143	665	670	290	3615	-	233	-	595	40	6	1	x	-	-	-	x	-	x	x	-	-	-	-	-	x	x	-	-	-	-	x
F670	sg254/11	Postholes		-	-	-	-	-	-	-	-	-	-	-	-	-	-	-	-	-	-	-	-	x	-	-	-	-	-	-	-	-	-	-	-	-
F615	sg255/1	Garden soil? layers	HJ	1370	254	565	2280	995	4920	200	30	-	1400	25	10	2	-	x	-	-	x	-	-	x	-	-	-	-	-	-	-	-	-	-	-	x
F688	sg255/2	Posthole? Not believable		-	-	-	-	-	-	-	-	-	-	-	-	-	-	-	-	-	-	-	-	-	-	-	-	-	-	-	-	-	-	-	-	-
F522	sg258/1	Beam Slot?		50	1906	-	1585	-	-	-	-	-	975	20	-	-	-	-	-	-	-	-	-	-	-	-	-	-	-	-	-	-	-	-	-	-
F526	sg258/2	Postholes		-	-	-	-	-	-	-	-	-	-	-	-	-	-	-	-	-	-	-	-	-	-	-	-	-	-	-	-	-	-	-	-	-
F636	sg262/1	Postholes		10	-	-	35	-	-	-	-	-	35	-	-	-	-	-	-	-	-	-	-	-	-	-	-	-	-	-	-	-	-	-	-	-
F594	sg263/1	Postholes + beam slot?		5	21	7	300	-	-	-	-	-	142	-	-	-	-	-	-	-	x	-	-	-	-	-	-	-	-	-	-	-	-	-	-	-
Robber Trenches																																				
F630	sg252/1	Robber trench + fills		8	-	35	-	-	-	-	-	6	50	-	-	-	-	x	-	-	x	-	-	x	-	-	-	-	-	x	-	-	-	-	-	x
F553	sg252/2	Robber trench and fills		95	183	-	1085	-	625	-	95	-	1035	-	-	-	-	x	-	-	-	-	-	x	-	-	-	-	-	-	-	-	-	-	-	-
F556	sg252/3	Robber trench and fills		60	50	-	1120	-	20	-	65	-	195	20	-	-	-	-	-	-	x	-	-	x	-	-	-	-	-	-	-	-	-	-	-	x
F659	sg252/4	Robber trench and fills		-	-	-	-	-	-	-	-	-	-	-	-	-	-	-	-	-	-	-	-	-	-	-	-	-	-	-	-	-	-	-	-	-
F646	sg252/5	Robber trench and fills		2197	583	97	5175	325	815	-	110	-	2965	395	-	2	-	x	-	-	x	-	-	x	-	-	-	-	-	-	-	-	-	-	-	x
F545	sg252/6	Robber Trench and fills		130	-	125	790	-	645	-	-	-	380	30	-	-	-	x	-	-	x	-	-	x	-	-	-	-	-	-	-	-	-	-	-	x
Garden Soil																																				
	sg290/1	Garden soil		1506	878	180	1660	-	1295	-	150	2	1595	30	-	1	-	x	-	-	x	-	-	x	-	-	-	-	-	-	-	-	-	-	-	-
Pits																																				
F203	sg114/2	Fills and cut of deep square pit	B	-	-	-	-	-	-	-	40	-	-	-	-	-	-	-	-	-	-	-	-	-	-	-	-	-	-	-	-	-	-	-	-	-
F204	sg114/5, 120/6,127/5	Fills and cut of deep square pit	B	3225	383	-	3020	-	151	-	41	-	3546	-	10	-	-	-	x	-	x	x	x	x	-	-	-	x	x	x	-	-	-	-	-	x
F207	sg114/4, 120/7-8, 127/4	Fills and cut of deep square pit	C	1555	5562	1465	9407	815	4145	-	350	-	5836	100	123	-	-	x	-	-	x	x	x	x	x	-	x	x	x	x	x	x	x	x	x	x
F213	sg112/3, 118/1	Fills & cut of mod deep square pit	F	984	1780	-	5040	-	55	200	-	-	4174	-	95	-	-	x	-	-	x	-	-	x	x	-	x	x	x	-	x	-	-	-	x	x
F214	sg112/4	Cut of mod deep square pit	D	-	-	-	-	-	-	-	-	-	-	-	-	-	-	-	-	-	-	-	-	-	-	-	-	-	-	-	-	-	-	-	-	-
F216	sg114/1, 120/2-3, 127/2	Deep square pit	D	1309	17428	121	9235	250	20	1400	110	-	30521	75	1025	-	x	x	x	-	x	x	x	x	-	x	-	x	x	x	-	-	x	-	-	x
F217	sg113/7, 119/6, 126/3	Deep Circular pit		1267	3132	-	6765	60	200	500	20	-	4116	-	1860	-																				
F231	sg118/2	Backfills in mod deep square pit	D	3024	5881	-	2656	20	55	1850	125	-	11335	49	50	1	-	x	x	-	x	-	-	x	x	-	-	x	x	-	x	x	-	-	-	x
F235	sg110/1, 116/1	Cut of shallow square pit	B	162	1504	-	15	-	-	-	-	-	570	80	1683	-	-	-	-	-	x	-	-	x	x	x	-	x	x	x	x	x	x	-	x	x
F238	sg120/1, 127/1	Backfills in deep square pit	B	249	2423	12	3860	-	1075	-	45	-	1960	-	625	-	-	x	-	-	x	-	x	x	-	-	-	x	x	-	-	-	-	x	x	x
F242	sg112/2, 125/2	Cut of moderately deep square pit	D	-	201	-	-	-	-	-	-	-	345	-	-	-	-	-	-	-	-	-	-	-	-	-	-	-	-	-	-	-	-	-	-	-
F243	sg111/3, 117/4	Fill & Cut of mod deep circular pit	F	1689	750	5	1035	-	5	-	5	-	1189	34	15	-	-	-	-	-	x	-	-	x	-	-	-	x	x	-	-	-	-	-	x	x
F244	sg121/6	Backfills in truncated feature	D	-	-	-	-	-	-	-	-	-	-	-	-	-	-	-	-	-	-	-	-	-	-	-	-	-	-	-	-	-	-	-	-	-
F257	sg113/4, 119/5, 126/6	Fill and cut of deep circular pit	G	1539	1725	-	4215	50	12	-	55	-	1898	45	7	-	-	-	-	-	x	-	-	x	-	-	-	x	x	x	x	-	-	-	-	x
F262	sg121.012	Pit and Fills	B	7	-	-	30	-	5	-	-	-	40	-	-	-	-	-	-	-	-	-	-	-	-	-	-	-	-	-	-	-	-	-	-	-
F263	sg114/7	Fills and cut of deep square pit	G	893	4033	125	4430	220	-	1400	-	4	5370	-	37	-	-	x	-	-	x	x	x	x	-	-	-	x	-	-	-	-	-	-	-	x
F265	sg110/2	shallow square pit	G	397	219	-	715	-	-	-	-	-	155	-	-	-	-	-	-	-	x	-	-	x	-	-	-	x	-	-	-	-	-	-	-	x
F276	sg110/3, 123/2	shallow square pit	C	452	33	-	685	-	-	-	-	-	440	20	105	-	-	-	-	-	x	-	-	x	-	-	-	-	-	-	-	-	-	-	-	x
F279	sg121/5	Backfills in truncated feature	E	166	82	-	60	-	25	-	-	-	395	5	-	-	-	-	-	-	x	-	-	x	-	-	-	-	-	-	-	-	-	-	-	x
F292	sg121/1	Backfills in truncated feature	B	50	98	-	277	-	10	-	-	-	230	-	385	-	-	-	-	-	x	-	-	x	-	-	x	-	-	-	-	-	-	-	-	x
F297	sg121/7	Backfills in truncated feature	F	21	-	-	70	-	185	-	20	-	25	-	-	-	-	-	-	-	x	-	-	x	-	-	-	-	-	-	-	-	-	-	-	x
F298	sg121/8	Backfills in truncated feature	F	-	-	-	-	-	-	-	-	-	-	-	-	-	-	-	-	-	-	-	-	-	-	-	-	-	-	-	-	-	-	-	-	-
F349	sg121/4	Backfills in truncated feature	B	-	16	-	-	-	-	-	-	-	6	-	-	-	-	-	-	-	-	-	-	x	-	-	-	-	-	-	-	-	-	-	-	x
F353	sg121/9	Backfills in truncated feature		-	6	-	-	-	50	-	-	-	5	-	5	-	-	-	-	-	x	-	-	x	-	-	-	-	-	-	-	-	-	-	-	-
F384	sg121/3	Backfills in truncated feature	B	73	40	-	-	-	-	-	-	-	275	-	-	-	-	-	-	-	-	-	-	x	-	-	-	-	-	-	-	-	-	-	-	-
F389	sg113/5, 126/5	Cut of deep circular pit	F	1583	4696	-	2545	-	53	140	64	-	2935	6	15	-	x	x	-	-	x	-	x	x	-	-	-	-	-	-	-	-	-	-	-	-
F438	sg112/6, 118/4	Cut of mod deep square pit	G	367	1108	-	1950	-	-	-	10	-	1240	-	-	-	-	-	-	-	x	x	-	x	-	-	-	-	-	-	-	-	-	-	-	-
F444	sg121/10	Backfills in truncated feature	C	41	10	-	-	-	-	-	-	-	10	-	-	-	-	-	-	-	-	-	-	-	-	-	-	-	-	-	-	-	-	-	-	-
F491	sg111/1, 117/1, 124/1	Fill & Cut of mod deep circular pit	A	50	191	-	2630	-	5	-	25	-	930	-	-	1	-	x	-	-	-	-	-	-	-	-	-	-	-	-	-	-	-	-	-	-
F492	sg109/2, 115/2	Cut of shallow circular pit	B	106	-	-	360	210	5	-	10	-	497	-	-	-	-	-	-	-	-	-	-	x	-	-	-	-	-	-	-	-	-	-	-	x
F503	sg260/1	Pit + cess like fills		1494	179	167	6205	855	655	-	225	4	11525	45	-	1	x	x	-	-	x	-	x	x	x	-	-	-	x	x	x	-	x	x	x	x
F507	sg256/6	Pit; circular, filled with "lime"		75	736	160	2235	-	100	-	-	-	305	-	-	-	-	-	-	-	-	-	-	-	-	-	-	-	-	-	-	-	-	-	-	-
F508	sg256/3	Pit; circular. Fills; "lime"		22	697	-	640	-	215	-	-	-	267	-	-	-	-	-	-	-	-	-	-	x	-	-	-	x	x	x	-	-	-	-	-	x
F509	sg256/4	Pit; circular		275	5208	80	2195	-	-	-	-	-	3255	20	5	-	-	-	-	-	-	-	-	x	-	-	-	x	-	x	x	-	-	-	-	x

Table 3: Summary of finds in post-Roman phases (7–12) continued

Feature	Subgroups	Description	Plot	RBpot	PRpot	Plaster	Tile	Slate	Mortar	Opsig	Tess	Glass	Bone	Oyster	Slag	Coins
F510	sg248/1,249/1	Pit (rectangular) + primary fills		579	4065	220	4334	795	760		230		3984	10	10	1
F511	sg261/1	Pit + secondary rubbish fills		655	1026		3550		1070		35		3950	45	35	
F513	sg260/4	Pit + cess like fills		43	3102	5	665		35			3	3165		37	
F516	sg256/2	Pit; circular. Fills; "lime"		19	67		300		20				165			
F537	sg256/5, 257/3/4/5	Pit; circular, fills, lime		124	1609	60	830	85	95		30		1405	50	495	1
F550	sg260/2	Pit + secondary cess like fills		178	1824	10	1830				150		4920			
F570	sg256/1	Pit; circular, fills; lime		10	305		60				25		323			
F587	sg260/3	Pit + cess like fills		100	1046		1145	100	141		30		3428	75	5	1
F605	sg261/2	Pit + secondary rubbish fills		329	1588		2940		285		35		2285		5	
F613	sg261/3	Pit + secondary rubbish fills														
F614	sg261/4	Pit + secondary rubbish fills		179	346		862				100		785			
F616	sg261/6	Pit + secondary rubbish fills														
F619	sg261/7	Pit + secondary rubbish fills		923	529	85	655				30		1095	5		
F627	sg290/2	Garden soil & assoc. features		552	318	625	1470	15	7080		140		1815	15		1
F632	sg261/5	Pit + secondary rubbish fills		1484	1145		925						1075	15		
F704	sg313/1, 314/1, 315/1	Cut of moderately deep square pit	A	1361	5585	540	4725		695	3600	180	2	4320	135	10	1
F712	sg311/1, 312/1	Moderately deep circular pit	A	651	1300	2695	8680		3335		305		9445		155	
F714	sg313/3, 315/3	Cut of moderately deep square pit	B	4708	4595	290	12745	3475	710	3600	1600	2	6587	456	5	
F719	sg313/2, 314/2, 315/2	Cut of moderately deep square pit	B	1491	1840	165	4125	360	305	450	555		3595	10		
F726	sg309/1, 310/1	Cut of deep square pit	A	6340	3322	1195	13950	12845	1045	1200	2250	2	12295	2691		
F727	sg306/2, 307/2, 308/2	Deep square pit cut	B	3951	571	2651	13230	6990	1970	1200	670	2	12431	1355	5	
F732	sg306/3, 308/3	Deep circular pit cut	A	1207	233	326	7160	250	1240	450	110	1	1580	595	5	
F903	sg114/6, 120/9, 127/6	Fills and cut of deep square pit	A	1179	5032											
F908	sg113/8, 119/9, 126/4	Cut of deep circular pit	A	3641	4034											
F909	sg111/6, 117/5, 124/5	Fill & Cut of mod deep circular pit	B	17215	608											
F910	sg109/4, 115/4, 122/1	Cut of shallow circular pit	B	3052	1247											
F911	sg113/9, 119/10, 126/7	Cut of deep circular pit	A	5185	39											
F913	sg121.011	Backfills in truncated feature	B	43	31											
F916	sg110/4, 116/3	Cut of shallow square pit		3556												
F925	sg109/6, 122/2	Cut of shallow circular pit	A	98												
		PHASE 9 TOTALS		88451	109855	16198	176894	31115	43815	15240	8433	27	187673	7126	7381	26
PHASE 10																
F205	sg113/1, 119/1, 126/2	Cut of deep circular pit	D	1629	5001		3250	60	105	1350	75		1869	15	67	3
F206	sg113/2, 119/2-3, 126/1	Fills and cut of deep circular pit	D	3047	20125	12	6915		40	100	117		10404	55	576	3
F218	sg113/3, 119/4	Fill and cut of deep circular pit	E	497	4228	12	2155	60	35	1450	192		3332	20	20	
		PHASE 10 TOTALS		5173	29354	12	12320	60	180	1450	192	0	15605	90	663	3
PHASE 11																
F108	sg108/1	Garden Soil		11541	8985											
F505	sg292/1	Pit and fills		119	324		195		105		140		490	20	10	
F506	sg291/6	Pit and fills		23	100		80						315			
F512	sg259/9	Pit + fills (shallow + truncated)		394	543		3215	95			20		2075	75		
F520	sg259/2	Pit + fills (shallow + truncated)		20	76		40						285			
F538	sg291/1	Pit and fills		113	220		85		80				100			
F544	sg259/1	Pit + fills (shallow + truncated)		167	102								95			
F551	sg259/1	Pit + fills (shallow + truncated)		120	34								200	10	5	
F552	sg259/4	Pit + fills (shallow + truncated)		581	378								150			
F559	sg291/11	Ditch? and fills		99	311		1080						740		5	
F560	sg291/4	Pit and fills		1293	1677	212	1165		65		75	2	420	15	10	3
F563	sg291/2	Pit and fills														
F564	sg264/1	Well + demolition fills		206	1103	395	3670		44		15		1245			
F565	sg291/3	Ditch? and fills														
F574	sg291/9	Well and fills														
F576	sg291/8	Pit and fills		2401	601		3265		20	600			2545	105		1
F578	sg291/10	Pit and fills		77	78								440			
F586	sg259/6	Pit + fills (shallow + truncated)		283	43		180		40				130	5	5	
F591	sg264/2	Pit + fills		78	68		65						120			
F612	sg291/5	Pit and fills		10	149							2	205			
F631	sg292/2	Pit and fills		33	75	20	1245						577	60		

			Finds quantities present by weight (g)												No.	Small Finds materials present							Environmental materials present												
Feature	**Subgroups**	**Description**	RBpot	PRpot	Plaster	Tile	Slate	Mortar	Opsig	Tess	Glass	Bone	Oyster	Slag	Coins	Bone	CA	Ceramic	Glass	Iron	Lead	Other	Sampled?	Cess	Coprolite	Parasites	Fishscales	Fishbones	Egg shell	Flies	Woodlice	Fruitstones	Grains	Seeds	Charcoal
F652	sg291/7	Pit and fills	620	18				877	3650	1405		15469	165	17	3	×	×					×	×	×	×		×	×	×	×	×		×	×	×
F703	sg306/1, 307/1, 308/1	Deep circular pit cut	3309	19533	2982	9590	697								7		×	×		×	×	×	×							×			×	×	×
F905	sg128/5	Linear gully	841														×		×	×	×	×						×	×		×					×
		PHASE 10 TOTALS	22378	34418	3609	23875	792	1126	4250	1655	4	26816	455	47																					
PHASE 12																																		
F0000	sg100/1	Unstratified layers	22488	4929	105	15440	240	71	600	75	57	10695	101	20	1	×	×	×	×	×	×	×													
	sg103/1	Pit cuts and backfills	3769	2492	415	6535		575		64	8	6749	35	167			×			×	×	×	×												
	sg104/1	Clearance layers	35	106	40	360						40		100	1		×			×	×		×												
	sg296/1	General cleaning & overburden	2836	4930	160	2540	5425	580	1200	135	24	1476	235	20	3	×	×			×	×	×	×				×	×							×
	sg301/1	Cleaning layers/garden soil	9578	2631	14140	33430	765	1740	8300	4670	31	1627	1150	300	8	×	×			×	×	×	×				×	×							×
F201	sg101/1	Victorian foundation trenches	2623	2312	30	4968		1395	1750	25		3380	50	715	1	×	×			×	×	×	×				×	×		×			×	×	×
F234	sg102/1	Quarry cuts and backfills	4149	1955		25540		80		30		3847		25			×			×	×	×	×												×
F458	sg106/1	Miscellaneous Features	106					5				205																							
F461	sg105/1	Post holes												2220			×			×	×	×	×				×	×							×
F50C	sg293/1	Quarry and fills	1371	5122	150	5520	340	150		85		4691	342				×	×		×	×	×	×				×	×					×	×	×
F502	sg295/1	Quarry and fills	43	19	100	625	840	830				455	90					×		×	×	×	×				×	×			×		×		×
F517	sg293/7	Pits assoc. with quarries	11	144		15		120			7	80	50																						
F518	sg293/5	Quarry and fills	189	388	15	65				25	6	375	30	15						×	×	×	×				×	×							×
F548	sg294/5	Well? and fills	190	700	335	1460		60		85		1120	37	20			×			×	×	×	×				×	×	×						×
F554	sg294/2	Well and fills	125	456	110	930		465			26	185	5										×												
F562	sg294/4	Pit and fills	168	446		885	50	130			26	800					×			×	×	×	×												
F566	sg294/1	Pit and fills																																	
F567	sg293/4	Quarry and fills		83		520					2	50	25																						
F581	sg294/3	Pit and fills	335	9367	25	6345	1445	425	250	25	70	1207	160	320	1	×	×			×	×	×	×				×	×					×	×	×
F582	sg293/2	Quarry and fills	614	433	42	455				20	8	310	10			×	×			×	×	×	×				×	×							×
F584	sg293/6	Quarry and fills	363	189		2090		110		10	1	550	5							×	×														
F589	sg294/7	Pit and Fills	209	428		5120					4	455	5							×	×	×	×				×	×							×
F59C	sg294/8	Pit and fills	58	2744		3415		15		15		65																							
F593	sg294/3	Quarry and fills	592	129	35	515						295																							
F675	sg294/6	Pit and fills																																	
F70C	sg300/1	19th Century Countess St.															×			×	×	×													
F701	sg302/1	Quarry	5690	1490	1375	15855	1180	845	1100	555		6355	425		4	×	×			×	×	×	×				×	×							×
F702	sg302/2	Quarry	1237	252	315	2070		235		165		565	75		1																				
		Phase 12 totals	56779	41745	17392	134698	10285	7831	13200	5984	270	45577	2830	3922	20																				
UNPHASED																																		
	sg180/1	Layers disturbed natural?						2100															×												
F278	sg128/1	Post-hole	10									12											×												
F283	sg128/2	Post-hole	77	6		95						65					×	×	×	×	×														
F284	sg128/3	Post-hole	5									20											×												
		Unphased totals	92	6	0	95	0	2100	0	0	0	97	0	0	0																				